FINANCIAL ACCOUNTING
Tools for Business Decision-Making

Second Canadian Edition

Paul D. Kimmel PhD, CPA
University of Wisconsin—Milwaukee

Jerry J. Weygandt PhD, CPA
Arthur Andersen Alumni Professor of Accounting
University of Wisconsin—Madison

Donald E. Kieso PhD, CPA
KPMG Emeritus Professor of Accountancy
Northern Illinois University

Barbara Trenholm MBA, FCA
University of New Brunswick

John Wiley & Sons Canada, Ltd.

Dedicated to our students.

Canadian Cataloguing in Publication Data

Financial accounting: tools for business decision making

2nd Canadian ed.
Includes index.
ISBN 0-470-83338-6

1. Accounting. I. Trenholm, Barbara

Production Credits

Publisher: John Horne
Editorial Manager: Karen Staudinger
Publishing Services Director: Karen Bryan
Developmental Editor: Zoë Craig
New Media Editor: Elsa Passera
Editorial Assistant: Gail Brown
Senior Marketing Manager: Janine Daoust
Business & On-line Marketing Manager: Carolyn J. Wells
Cover Design: Interrobang Graphic Design Inc.
Design and Typesetting: Appleby Color Lab
CD Design & Programming: Ian Koo/Tia Siefert
Printing and Binding: Tri-Graphic Printing Limited

Printed and bound in Canada
10 9 8 7 6 5 4 3 2 1

John Wiley & Sons Canada, Ltd.
22 Worcester Road
Etobicoke, Ontario
M9W 1L1
Visit our website at: www.wiley.com/canada

CANADIAN EDITION

Barbara Trenholm, MBA, FCA, is a professor of accounting at the University of New Brunswick. Her teaching and educational leadership is renowned. She is a recipient of the National Post/Pricewaterhouse Coopers Leaders in Management Education Award, the Global Teaching Excellence Award, and the University of New Brunswick's Merit Award and Dr. Allan P. Stuart Award for Excellence in Teaching. A recent edition of the *Maclean's Guide to Canadian Universities and Colleges* named her as one of the University of New Brunswick's most popular professors. In 2003, she was named a Teaching Fellow of the University of New Brunswick.

Her experience and involvement in professional accounting education is widely recognized throughout Canada. She is a past-president of the New Brunswick Institute of Chartered Accountants. She has served as chair of the Canadian Institute of Chartered Accountants Academic Research Committee, Interprovincial Education Committee, and Canadian Institute of Chartered Accountants/Canadian Academic Accounting Association Liaison Committee. She has served as a member of the Canadian Institute of Chartered Accountants Qualification Committee, International Qualifications Appraisal Board, Education Reeingineering Task Force, and the American Accounting Association's Globalization Initiatives Task Force. She has chaired and been a member of numerous other education committees at both the national and provincial levels of the profession.

Professor Trenholm is a member of the boards of many organizations, including Atomic Energy of Canada and the Canadian Institute of Chartered Accountants. She is co-chair of the University of New Brunswick Pension Board of Trustees. She has also served as a member of the Atlantic School of Chartered Accountancy Board of Governors.

In addition to her involvement with her profession, she has an extensive record of service in leadership roles in the university and community. She has served as acting dean of the Faculty of Administration and as a member of the University Senate, in addition to chairing and serving on many university and faculty committees.

She has published widely in the field of accounting standard-setting and explored various director and auditor liability issues in journals including *Accounting Horizons, International Journal of Production Economics, CAmagazine, CGA Magazine,* and *CMA Magazine.* She is on the editorial board of the *Journal of Academy of Business Administration* and on the board of reviewers for the *Journal of Business Education.* She is also the Canadian author of the Weygandt, Kieso, Kimmel, Trenholm, *Accounting Principles,* published by John Wiley & Sons Canada, Ltd.

Paul D. Kimmel, PhD, CPA, received his bachelor's degree from the University of Minnesota and his doctorate in accounting from the University of Wisconsin. He is an Associate Professor at the University of Wisconsin—Milwaukee, and has public accounting experience with Deloitte & Touche (Minneapolis). He was the recipient of the UWM School of Business Advisory Council Teaching Award and the Reggie Taite Excellence in Teaching Award, and is a three-time winner of the Outstanding Teaching Assistant Award at the University of Wisconsin. He is also a recipient of the Elijah Watts Sells Award for Honorary Distinction for his results on the CPA exam. He is a member of the American Accounting Association and has published articles in *Accounting Review, Accounting Horizons, Advances in Management Accounting, Managerial Finance, Issues in Accounting Education,* and *Journal of Accounting Education,* as well as other journals. His research interests include accounting for financial instruments and innovation in accounting education. He has published papers and given numerous talks on incorporating critical thinking into accounting education, and helped prepare a catalogue of critical thinking resources for the Federated Schools of Accountancy.

Jerry J. Weygandt, PhD, CPA, is the Arthur Andersen Alumni Professor of Accounting at the University of Wisconsin—Madison. He holds a PhD in accounting from the University of Illinois. Articles by Professor Weygandt have appeared in *Accounting Review, Journal of Accounting Research, Accounting Horizons, Journal of Accountancy,* and other academic and professional journals. These articles have examined such financial reporting issues as accounting for price-level adjustments, pensions, convertible securities, stock option contracts, and interim reports. Professor Weygandt is the author of other accounting and financial reporting books and is a member of the American Accounting Association, the American Institute of Certified Public Accountants, and the Wisconsin Society of Certified Public Accountants. He has served on numerous committees of the American Accounting Association and as a member of the editorial board of *Accounting Review*; he also has served as President and Secretary-Treasurer of the American Accounting Association. In addition, he has been actively involved with the American Institute of Certified Public Accountants and has been a member of the Accounting Standards Executive Committee (AcSEC) of that organization. He has served on the FASB task force that examined the reporting issues related to accounting for income taxes and is presently a trustee of the Financial Accounting Foundation. Professor Weygandt has received the Chancellor's Award for Excellence in Teaching and the Beta Gamma Sigma Dean's Teaching Award. He is on the board of directors of M&I Bank of Southern Wisconsin and the Dean Foundation. He is the recipient of the Wisconsin Institute of CPA's Outstanding Educator's Award and the Lifetime Achievement Award. In 2001 he received the American Accounting Association's Outstanding Accounting Educator Award.

Donald E. Kieso, PhD, CPA, received his bachelor's degree from Aurora University and his doctorate in accounting from the University of Illinois. He has served as chairman of the Department of Accountancy and is currently the KPMG Emeritus Professor of Accounting at Northern Illinois University. He has public accounting experience with Price Waterhouse & Co. (San Francisco and Chicago) and Arthur Andersen & Co. (Chicago) and research experience with the Research Division of the American Institute of Certified Public Accountants (New York). He has done post-doctoral work as a Visiting Scholar at the University of California at Berkeley and is a recipient of NIU's Teaching Excellence Award and four Golden Apple Teaching Awards. Professor Kieso is the author of other accounting and business books and is a member of the American Accounting Association, the American Institute of Certified Public Accountants, and the Illinois CPA Society. He has served as a member of the Board of Directors of the Illinois CPA Society, the AACSB's Accounting Accreditation Committees, the State of Illinois Comptroller's Commission, as Secretary-Treasurer of the Federation of Schools of Accountancy, and as Secretary-Treasurer of the American Accounting Association. Professor Kieso is currently serving on the Board of Trustees and Executive Committee of Aurora University, as a member of the Board of Directors of Castle Banc-Group Inc., and as Treasurer and Director of Valley West Community Hospital. He served as a charter member of the national Accounting Education Change Commission. He is the recipient of the Outstanding Accounting Educator Award from the Illinois CPA Society, the FSA's Joseph A. Silvoso Award of Merit, the NIU Foundation's Humanitarian Award for Service to Higher Education, the Distinguished Service Award from the Illinois CPA Society, and the Community Citizen of the Year Award from Rotary International.

Our efforts to continually improve this text are driven by a few key beliefs:

"It really matters."

The recent economic turbulence caused in part by the lack of credible financial information demonstrates the importance of accounting to a smoothly-running economic system. Our Business Insight—Ethics Perspective boxes, ethics cases, and a number of our feature stories and research cases are designed to reveal accounting's critical role. In short, it has never been more evident that accounting really matters.

"Less is more."

Our instructional objective is to provide students with an understanding of those concepts that are fundamental to the use of accounting. Most students will forget procedural details within a short period of time. On the other hand, concepts, if well taught, should be remembered for a lifetime. Concepts are especially important in a world where the details are constantly changing.

"Don't just sit there—do something."

Students learn best when they are actively engaged. The overriding pedagogical objective of this book is to provide students with continual opportunities for active learning. One of the best tools for active learning is strategically placed questions. Our discussions are framed by questions, often beginning with rhetorical questions and ending with review questions. Even our selection of analytical devices, called Decision Tools, is referenced using key questions to emphasize the purpose of each device.

"I'll believe it when I see it."

Students are most willing to commit time and energy to a topic when they believe that it is relevant to their future career. There is no better way to demonstrate relevance than to ground discussion in the real world as we do with our feature stories and Business Insight boxes. In addition, by using high-profile companies such as Air Canada, Bombardier, Canadian Tire, Loblaw, Molson, Quebecor, and Sears to frame our discussion of accounting issues, we demonstrate the relevance of accounting while teaching students about companies with which they have daily contact. As they become acquainted with the financial successes and failures of these companies, many students will begin to follow business news more closely, making their learning a dynamic, ongoing process. We also discuss smaller companies to highlight the challenges they face as they try to grow.

"You need to make a decision."

All business people must make decisions. Decision-making involves critical evaluation and analysis of the information at hand, and this takes practice. We have integrated important analytical tools throughout the book. After each new decision tool is presented, we summarize the key features of that tool in a Decision Toolkit. At the end of each chapter we provide a comprehensive demonstration of an analysis of a real company using the decision tools presented in the chapter. The presentation of these tools throughout the book is cumulative, sequenced to take full advantage of the tools presented in earlier chapters.

"It's a small world."

Rapid improvements to both information technology and transportation have resulted in a single global economy. Few business decisions can be made without consideration of international factors. In fact, a significant number of Canadian companies operate globally and have key U.S. or non–North American competitors. To heighten student awareness of international issues, we reference non-Canadian companies and discuss how to compare financial statements of companies in other countries.

KEY FEATURES OF EACH CHAPTER

Chapter 1: Introduction to Financial Statements

- Identifies the users and uses of financial accounting information.
- Explains the content and purpose of each of the financial statements.
- Uses the financial statements of a hypothetical company (to keep it simple), followed by those for a real company, Loblaw Companies Limited (to make it relevant).
- Presents accounting assumptions and selected principles.
- Using the Decision Toolkit compares Sobeys' financial statements to Loblaw's.

Chapter 2: A Further Look at Financial Statements

- Describes the objective of financial reporting.
- Presents the classified balance sheet.
- Applies ratio analysis to Sears and Hudson's Bay (working capital, current ratio, debt to total assets, earnings per share, price-earnings ratio, cash current debt coverage, and cash total debt coverage).
- Using the Decision Toolkit analyses Canadian Tire, and compares it to Sears and Hudson's Bay.

Chapter 3: The Accounting Information System

- Covers transaction analysis—emphasizes fundamentals while avoiding unnecessary detail.
- Explains the first steps in accounting cycle, from journalizing through the preparation of a trial balance.
- Using the Decision Toolkit prepares a trial balance for Prairie Grain Growers.

Chapter 4: Accrual Accounting Concepts

- Explains the revenue recognition and matching principles.
- Emphasizes the difference between cash and accrual accounting.
- Completes the accounting cycle, from adjusting entries to the closing process.
- Discusses how some companies manage earnings through accrual practices.
- Using the Decision Toolkit prepares financial statements for FPI Limited.

Chapter 5: Merchandising Operations

- Introduces merchandising concepts using the perpetual inventory system (periodic inventory system presented in an appendix).
- Presents the multiple-step statement of earnings.
- Applies ratio analysis to Leon's Furniture and Sears (gross profit margin and profit margin).
- Using the Decision Toolkit compares Wal-Mart's and Costco's profitability.

Chapter 6: Reporting and Analysing Inventory

- Covers cost flow assumptions and implications for financial reporting. For simplification, emphasizes the periodic inventory system (perpetual inventory system covered in an appendix).
- Discusses the effects of inventory errors on financial statements.
- Explains the lower of cost and market basis of valuing inventory.
- Applies ratio analysis to Office Depot (inventory turnover and days in inventory).
- Using the Decision Toolkit reviews IPSCO inventory performance.

Chapter 7: Internal Control and Cash

- Covers internal control concepts and implications of control failures.
- Presents the bank reconciliation as a control device.
- Discusses cash management, including cash budgeting.
- Using the Decision Toolkit reviews cash adequacy for a toy manufacturer.

Chapter 8: Reporting and Analysing Receivables

- Presents the basics of accounts and notes receivable and bad debt estimation.
- Discusses receivables management, including methods used to accelerate cash receipts.

- Applies ratio analysis to Wyeth (receivables turnover and average collection period).
- Using the Decision Toolkit compares Aventis' receivables management and liquidity to Wyeth's.

Chapter 9: Reporting and Analysing Long-Lived Assets

- Covers the basics of tangible and intangible assets.
- Reviews buy or lease decisions.
- Discusses the implications of alternative amortization methods (details the calculation of declining-balance and units-of-activity amortization methods in an appendix).
- Applies ratio analysis to Air Canada and WestJet Airlines (return on assets and asset turnover).
- Using the Decision Toolkit analyses Krispy Kreme Doughnuts' accounting for its long-lived assets.

Chapter 10: Reporting and Analysing Liabilities

- Covers current and long-term liabilities.
- Presents the straight-line and effective-interest methods of amortization in appendices.
- Applies ratio analysis to Quebecor (current ratio, acid-test ratio, debt to total assets, and times interest earned).
- Discusses other analysis issues, including contingencies and off–balance sheet financing.
- Using the Decision Toolkit compares CanWest Global Communications' liquidity and solvency to Quebecor's.

Chapter 11: Reporting and Analysing Shareholders' Equity

- Discusses the corporate form of organization.
- Covers issues related to common and preferred shares, including reasons why companies repurchase their own shares.
- Explains cash dividends, stock dividends, stock splits, and their implications for analysis.
- Discusses debt versus equity choice.
- Applies ratio analysis to Nike (payout ratio and return on common shareholders' equity).
- Using the Decision Toolkit compares Reebok's dividend record and earnings performance to Nike's.

Chapter 12: Reporting and Analysing Investments

- Explains why companies purchase debt and equity investments.
- Describes the accounting for short- and long-term debt investments.
- Describes the accounting for equity investments, including the cost and equity methods.
- Presents consolidation accounting for financial reporting purposes at a conceptual level.
- Discusses the potential for earnings management with the valuation and reporting of investments.
- Using the Decision Toolkit reviews Exxon Mobil's accounting for its investments.

Chapter 13: Cash Flow Statement

- Explains the purpose and usefulness of the cash flow statement.
- Splits chapter into two parts, allowing instructor to use either the indirect approach of preparing the operating activities section or the direct approach, or both.
- Applies ratio analysis to Microsoft and Corel (free cash flow).
- Using the Decision Toolkit compares cash-based measures for Rogers Communications and Shaw Communications.

Chapter 14: Performance Measurement

- Discusses sustainable earnings, and the implications of discontinued operations, extraordinary items, and changes in accounting principles.
- Demonstrates horizontal and vertical analysis for Molson.
- Summarizes ratios introduced in previous chapters.
- Discusses factors that affect the quality of earnings.
- A comprehensive analysis of Molson compared to Interbrew is included in an appendix, to reinforce analytical tools and demonstrate how the tools relate to each other.

NEW IN THIS EDITION

The first edition was a tremendous success. Faculty and students alike have praised the format and presentation of the material and the use of real-world examples. While we did not want to tamper with the distinguishing features of this text, in the spirit of continuous improvement we did feel some changes would be beneficial to the book's users. Some of the more significant changes include the following:

- To enhance the pedagogical usefulness of the text, we incorporated a Navigator learning system to guide students through the text material. This system, accompanied by the Toolkit student CD, empowers students by teaching them how to study, what to study, and why they study.
- Our "focus companies" are unchanged with Loblaw and Sobeys. They were chosen because they have high name recognition with students, they operate primarily in a single industry, and they have relatively simple financial statements. We updated to the December 28, 2002, annual report for Loblaw and the May 3, 2003, annual report for Sobeys.
- This edition was subject to comprehensive updating to ensure that it continues to be relevant and fresh. Updating involved replacing numerous feature stories, Business Insight boxes, and real-world examples cited in the text. In addition, we have enhanced relevance by adding many new references to real companies.
- We added a new type of Business Insight—the Ethics Perspective—to inform students about the consequences of various actions on reporting situations. This supplements the existing Business Insight perspectives of Management, Investors, and International Users.
- In addition to the Ethics Perspective insights throughout the text, we added a section about ethics in Chapter 1.
- To enhance students' conceptual understanding of the impact of transactions on the financial position of the company, we have added an accounting equation analysis box in the margin next to each journal entry.
- We have expanded the use of the cash flow statement as an analytical tool in two ways: (1) the effect of a transaction on cash flows is shown throughout the text as part of the accounting equation analysis presented in the margin next to each journal entry; and (2) cash flow analysis has been integrated within certain chapters, such as the chapters on long-lived assets, debt, and equity.
- We clarified and expanded explanations of difficult topics. We also condensed or deleted concepts and procedures that are little used or are better suited to advanced courses. For example, in Chapter 4 the appendix describing the use of a work sheet and in Chapter 7 the appendix describing the use of a petty cash system have been deleted.
- The presentation of journal entries for periodic inventory systems was moved from Chapter 6 to an appendix to Chapter 5 to even out coverage and difficulty.
- We expanded the discussion in Chapter 6 on the periodic inventory method to make a better bridge between Chapters 5 and 6. In addition, the chapter now incorporates material directly into the text on inventory errors. This material was previously presented as an appendix to Chapter 6.
- In Chapter 8, the primary focus in the section on estimating bad debts is now on the aging method, concurrent with its predominance in practice. We also added a section to this chapter on debit card sales, to supplement the section on credit card sales.
- Chapter 9 was updated for changes to the *CICA Handbook* sections on tangible and intangible assets. In addition, the section on impairment losses was moved and clarified.
- Chapter 10 was revised for greater flexibility of use. The discussion of current liabilities was expanded to include operating lines of credit and property taxes. The section on bonds payable was simplified, and the section on procedures for amortizing bond discounts or premiums was moved to an appendix. The long-term notes payable section was moved from an appendix into the body of the chapter.
- In Chapter 11, we simplified the section on share capital and removed coverage of stated value and par value shares. New sections on stock compensation plans and making the debt/equity decision were added.
- Chapter 14 discusses sustainable earnings, and the implications of discontinued operations and extraordinary items. A new section on the quality of earnings was added, including a discussion of pro forma earnings and improper recognition of revenue and expense. There is a new summary discussion of ratio analysis, with a comprehensive analysis comparing Molson and Interbrew included as an appendix to the chapter.
- We have changed the sequence and reduced the quantity of ratios to enhance usefulness for analysis.
- The end-of-chapter material now includes a selection of Interactive Homework exercises. These exercises derived from Exercises in the end-of-chapter section of the text, provide students with immediate feedback on their work. Many of the exercises contain an algorithmic function that allows students to work through the same exercise with different data every time the exercise file is

opened. Students can keep practising until they reach the level of success they desire.

- To ensure complete coverage of concepts, we have added more than 225 new questions, brief exercises, exercises, problems, and cases to the end-of-chapter material. The remaining material was updated and revised, as required.

PROVEN PEDAGOGICAL FRAMEWORK

In this book we have used many proven pedagogical tools to help students learn accounting concepts and apply them to decision-making in the business world. This pedagogical framework emphasizes the processes students undergo as they learn.

Learning How to Use the Text

- A Student Owner's Manual begins the text to help students understand the value of the pedagogical framework and how to use it.
- Chapter 1 contains notes (printed in red) that explain each pedagogical element the first time it appears.
- **The Navigator** pulls all the learning aids together into a learning system. It is designed to guide students through each chapter and help them succeed in learning the material. The Navigator consists of (1) a checklist at the beginning of the chapter, which outlines text features and study aids students will need in order to master the topics, and (2) a series of check boxes that prompt students to use the learning aids and set priorities as they study. At the end of the chapter, students are reminded to return to the Navigator to check off their completed work.

Understanding the Context

- **Study Objectives**, listed at the beginning of each chapter, form a learning framework throughout the text, with each objective repeated in the margin at the appropriate place in the main body of the chapter and again in the **Summary of Study Objectives**. Also, end-of-chapter assignment materials are linked to the Study Objectives.
- A chapter-opening **Feature Story** presents a scenario that relates an actual business situation of a well-known company to the topic of the chapter. It also serves as a recurring example throughout the chapter. The feature stories include company Internet addresses to encourage students to go on-line to get more information about these companies.
- A chapter **Preview** links the feature story to the major topics of the chapter. First, an introductory paragraph explains how the story relates to the topics to be discussed; then a graphic outline of the chapter provides a "road map," useful for seeing the big picture as well as the connections between subtopics.

Learning the Material

- This book emphasizes the accounting experiences of **real companies and business situations** throughout, from chapter-opening feature stories to the chapter's last item of assignment material. In addition, every chapter uses financial statements from real companies. These specimen financial statements are easily identified by the company logo or related photo that appears near the statement heading.
- Continuing the real-world flavour of the book, **Business Insight** boxes in each chapter give students glimpses into how real companies make decisions using accounting information. The boxes, highlighted with striking photographs, focus on four different accounting perspectives—those of investors, managers, international business, and ethics.
- Colour **illustrations** support and reinforce the concepts of the text. **Infographics** are a special type of illustration that helps students visualize and apply accounting concepts to the real world. The infographics often portray important concepts in entertaining and memorable ways.
- **Before You Go On** sections occur at the end of each key topic and consist of two parts: **Review It** serves as a learning check within the chapter by asking students to stop and answer knowledge and comprehension questions about the material just covered. **Review It** questions marked with the Loblaw symbol **Loblaws** send students to find information in Loblaw's 2002 financial statements, which are printed in Appendix A at the back of the book. These exercises help cement students' understanding of how topics covered in the chapter are reported in real-world financial statements. Answers appear at the end of the chapter. **Do It** is a brief demonstration problem that gives immediate practice using the material just covered. An **Action Plan** lists the steps necessary to complete the task, and a **Solution** is provided to help students understand the reasoning involved in reaching an answer.
- **Accounting equation analyses** have been inserted in the margin next to key journal entries. This feature reinforces students' understanding of the impact of an accounting transaction on the financial position and cash flows of a company.
- **Helpful Hints** in the margins expand upon or help clarify concepts under discussion in the nearby

text. This feature actually makes the book an Annotated Student Edition.

- **Alternative Terminology** notes in the margins present synonymous terms that students may come across in later accounting courses and in business.
- Marginal **International Notes** provide a helpful and convenient way for instructors to begin to expose students to international issues in accounting, reporting, and decision-making.
- Each chapter presents **Decision Tools** that are useful for analysing the financial statement components discussed in that chapter. At the end of the text discussion relating to the decision tool, a **Decision Toolkit** summarizes the key features of that decision tool and reinforces its purpose.
- A **Using the Decision Toolkit** exercise, which follows the final Before You Go On section in the chapter, asks students to use the decision tools presented in that chapter. Students evaluate the financial situation of a real-world company, often using ratio analysis to do so. In many cases the company used in this analysis is a competitor of the example company in the chapter. Intercompany, intracompany, and industry comparisons expand and enrich the analysis and help focus student attention on comparative situations that flavour real-world decision-making.

Putting It Together

- At the end of each chapter, between the body of the text and the assignment materials, are several useful features for review and reference: a **Summary of Study Objectives** lists the main points of the chapter; the **Decision Toolkit—A Summary** presents in one place the decision tools used throughout the chapter; and a **Glossary** of important terms gives definitions with page references to the text. A CD icon refers students to the Toolkit student CD for a comprehensive Decision Toolkit Summary and searchable glossary.
- Next, a **Demonstration Problem** gives students another opportunity to refer to a detailed solution to a representative problem before they do any of the end-of-chapter assignments. An **Action Plan** presented in the margin lists strategies to assist students in understanding the solution and establishing a logic for approaching similar problems. A CD icon tells students that additional demonstration problems are available on the Toolkit CD.

Developing Skills through Practice

Throughout the assignment material, certain questions, exercises, and problems make use of the decision tools presented in the chapter. These are marked with the icon. The financial results

of real companies are included in many exercises and problems. These are indicated by the company name shown in red in the end-of-chapter material.

- **Self-Study Questions** comprise a practice test to enable students to check their understanding of important concepts. Answers to these questions appear at the end of the chapter. A CD icon directs students to the text's CD, where they will find another multiple choice quiz to help them master the material.
- **Questions** provide a full review of chapter content and help students prepare for class discussions and testing situations.
- **Brief Exercises** build students' confidence and test their basic skills. Each brief exercise normally focuses on a single Study Objective.
- Each of the **Exercises** focuses on one or more of the Study Objectives. These tend to take a little longer to complete, and they present more of a challenge to students than Brief Exercises. The Exercises help instructors and students make a manageable transition to more challenging problems. Certain exercises, marked with an **Interactive Homework icon**, indicate that students can complete these in an interactive format on the text's website.
- **Problems** stress the applications of the concepts presented in the chapter, and are paired in **Sets A** and **B**. Each set provides corresponding problems keyed to the same Study Objectives, thus giving greater flexibility in assigning problems.
- Each Self-Study Question, Question, Brief Exercise, Exercise, and Problem has a description of the concept covered and is keyed to the Study Objectives. Certain end-of-chapter materials, marked with the icon, help build business writing skills.

Expanding and Applying Knowledge

Broadening Your Perspective is a unique section at the end of each chapter that offers a wealth of resources to help instructors and students pull together the learning for the chapter. This section offers problems and projects for those instructors who want to broaden the learning experience by bringing in more real-world decision-making and critical-thinking activities.

- **Financial Reporting and Analysis** problems use financial statements of real-world companies for further practice in understanding and interpreting financial reporting. A *Financial Reporting Problem* in each chapter directs students to study various aspects of the financial statements of Loblaw Companies Limited, which are printed in Chapter 1 (in simplified form) and in Appendix A (in full). A *Comparative Analysis Problem* offers the opportunity to compare and contrast the financial reporting of Loblaw Companies Limited with a competitor, Sobeys Inc. Since the ability to read and understand business publications is an asset over the span of one's career, *Research Cases* direct students to articles published in popular business news sources and periodicals for further study and analysis of key topics. The *Interpreting Financial Statements* cases ask students to read parts of financial statements of actual companies and use the decision tools presented in the chapter to interpret this information. A *Global Focus* problem asks students to apply concepts presented in the chapter to specific situations faced by international companies. *Financial Analysis on the Web* guides students to web sites from which they can mine and analyse information related to the chapter topic.

• **Critical Thinking** problems offer additional opportunities and activities. The *Collaborative Learning Activities* help students build decision-making skills by analysing accounting information in a less structured situation. These cases require teams of students to evaluate a manager's decision or lead to a decision among alternative courses of action. They also give practice in building business communication skills. *Communication Activities* provide practice in written communication—a skill much in demand among employers. *Ethics Cases* describe typical ethical dilemmas and ask students to analyse the situation, identify the ethical issues involved, and decide on an appropriate course of action.

ACTIVE STUDENT LEARNING SUPPLEMENTARY MATERIAL

Financial Accounting: Tools for Business Decision-Making features a full line of learning resources. Driven by the same basic beliefs as the textbook, these supplements provide a consistent and well-integrated active learning system. This hands-on, real-world package creates an interactive learning environment that encourages you, the student, to take an active role and prepares you for decision-making in a real-world context.

Kimmel Website *(www.wiley.com/canada/kimmel)*

The Kimmel website serves as a launching pad to numerous activities, resources, and related sites. On the website you will find interactive quizzing, PowerPoint presentations, Interactive Homework exercises, profiles of real-life accountants, additional demonstration problems with solutions, company links, a checklist of key figures, links to the web cases in the Broadening Your Perspective section, and much more. Visit the site often for updates and new material.

eGrade

If your instructor has adopted eGrade, you will be able to complete your assignments on-line and receive feedback right away. Hundreds of end-of-chapter questions will be available to help you develop your conceptual understanding of the class material and increase your ability to solve problems. These assignments will be graded automatically so you benefit by receiving immediate feedback on your work, allowing you to determine right away how well you understand the course material. The majority are generated algorithmically so that each time you access a problem the variables will be different, thus providing unlimited opportunities for practice. Also, a Personal Gradebook will allow you to view your results from past assignments at any time.

The Toolkit CD

 An innovative multimedia supplement that accompanies this textbook is the interactive Toolkit CD. The CD includes tools to help you practice your analysis skills and improve your study skills, animated tutorials and videos, and many more learning aids designed to strengthen your understanding of financial accounting.

Study Guide to Accompany *Financial Accounting: Tools for Business Decision-Making*

The study guide is a comprehensive review of financial accounting that is a powerful tool when used in the classroom and in preparation for exams. The study guide takes you through chapter content while focusing on study objectives and the decision-making process.

Each chapter includes an overview of the chapter, a review of study objectives, and a summary of key points. You can test your knowledge and skills through completion statements, matching exercises, multiple-choice questions, and problems—each linked to specific study objectives. You can also apply the decision toolkit against two competitor companies—Domtar Inc. and Cascades Inc.—in each chapter. Detailed solutions are then presented in order to effectively provide immediate feedback.

ACKNOWLEDGEMENTS

During the course of development of the second Canadian edition of *Financial Accounting: Tools for Business Decision-Making*, the author benefitted greatly from the input of manuscript reviewers, ancillary authors, contributors, and proofers. The constructive suggestions and innovative ideas of the reviewers and the creativity and accuracy of the ancillary authors, contributors, and proofers are greatly appreciated.

REVIEWERS

Paul Berry, *Mount Allison University*
Gerry Dupont, *Carleton University*
Larry Goldsman, *McGill University*
Lori Kopp, *University of Lethbridge*
Shari Mann, *University of Waterloo*
John Rawle, *University of Toronto*
Robert Schenk, *Bishop's University*

Peggy Ann Coady, *Memorial University of Newfoundland*
Lawrence Elkow, *University of Winnipeg*
Melissa Harty, *University of Western Ontario*
Valerie Leonard, *Laurentian University*
Debbie Musil, *Kwantlen University College*
Sandra M. Robinson, *Concordia University*

ANCILLARY AUTHORS, CONTRIBUTORS, AND PROOFERS

Tashia Batstone, *Memorial University of Newfoundland*—Solutions Manual author and Toolkit CD contributor
Hilary Becker, *Carleton University*—Toolkit CD contributor
Paul Berry, *Mount Allison University*—Toolkit CD contributor
Peggy Ann Coady, *Memorial University of Newfoundland*—PowerPoint presentation author
Susan Cohlmeyer, *Memorial University of Newfoundland*—Computerized Test Bank author and Toolkit CD contributor
Suzanne Coombs, *Kwantlen University College*—Toolkit CD contributor
Elizabeth d'Anjou—CD Toolkit contributor
Gerry Dupont, *Carleton University*—Study Guide author
Lawrence Elkow, *University of Winnipeg*—Website contributor
Ian Farmer—Solutions Manual Checker
Françoise Giovannangeli—Feature Story author
Ruth Heathcote—Toolkit CD Contributor
Joanne Hinton, *University of New Brunswick*—Problem Material contributor and Solutions Manual checker
Ian Hutchinson, *Acadia University*—Website contributor
James Hughes, *British Columbia Institute of Technology*—Toolkit CD contributor
Zofia Laubitz—proofreader
Robert Maher, *University of New Brunswick*—Website contributor and Toolkit CD contributor
Debbie Musil, *Kwantlen University College*—Instructor's Manual author
David Schwinghamer—copyeditor and Toolkit contributor
Enola Stoyle, *University of Toronto*—Solutions Manual checker
Sabra Surkis—Toolkit CD contributor
Deborah Wybou—Toolkit CD contributor

This Canadian edition is based on the U.S. edition of *Financial Accounting: Tools for Business Decision-Making*, authored by Paul Kimmel, Jerry Weygandt, and Don Kieso. I would like to express my appreciation to Paul, Jerry, and Don for their willingness to share their extensive teaching and writing experiences with me.

I appreciate the exemplary support and professional commitment given me by the talented team in the Wiley Canada higher education division. I especially wish to thank Wiley's dedicated sales representatives who work tirelessly to service your needs.

I thank Loblaw and Sobeys for permitting the use of their financial statements. I would also like to acknowledge the co-operation of many Canadian and international companies that allowed me to include extracts from their financial statements in the text and end-of-chapter material.

It would not have been possible to write this text without the understanding of my employer, colleagues, students, friends, and family. Together, they provided a creative and supportive environment for my work.

Suggestions and comments from users are encouraged and appreciated.

Barbara Trenholm
trenholm@unb.ca
Fredericton, New Brunswick
November 2003

CHAPTER 2

A Further Look at Financial Statements

Study Objectives at the beginning of each chapter provide you with a framework for learning the specific concepts covered in the chapter. Each Study Objective then reappears at the point within the chapter where the concept is discussed and all the objectives are also summarized at the end of the chapter.

The Navigator is a learning system designed to guide you through each chapter and help you succeed in learning the material. It consists of (1) a checklist at the beginning of the chapter, which outlines text features and study aids you will need, and (2) a series of check boxes that prompt you to use the learning aids in the chapter and set priorities as you study.

Just Fooling Around?

Few people could have predicted how dramatically the Internet would change the investment world. One of the most interesting results is how it has changed the way ordinary people invest their savings. More and more people are spurning investment professionals and instead are choosing to strike out on their own, making personal investment decisions using the Internet.

Two early pioneers in providing investment information to the masses were Tom and David Gardner, brothers who created an on-line investor service called The Motley Fool. The name comes from Shakespeare's *As You Like It*. The brothers note that the fool in Shakespeare's plays was the only one who could speak unpleasant

truths to kings and queens without being killed. Tom and David view themselves as twentieth-century "fools," revealing the "truth" of the stock markets to the small investor, who they feel insiders have taken advantage of. Their on-line bulletin board enables investors to exchange information and insights about companies.

Critics of these bulletin boards contend that they are nothing more than high-tech rumour mills that are largely responsible for building a speculative house of cards. They suggest that, because of the fervour created by the bulletin board chatter, share prices get bid up to unreasonable levels and people often pay prices that are far higher than the underlying worth of the company. One potentially troubling aspect of bulletin boards is that participants on the board rarely give their real identities—instead using aliases. Consequently, there is little to stop peo-

50

The **Feature Story** helps you picture how the topics of the chapter relate to the real world of accounting and business. References to the Feature Story throughout the chapter will help you put new ideas in context, organize them, and remember them. Each one ends with the Internet addresses of the companies cited in the story.

The **Preview** links the Feature Story with the major topics of the chapter. It then gives a graphic outline of major topics and subtopics that will be discussed. This narrative and visual preview helps you organize the information you are learning.

SECTION 1
OBJECTIVE OF FINANCIAL REPORTING

Financial reporting is the term used to describe all of the financial information presented by a company—both in its financial statements and in additional disclosures provided in the annual report. For example, if you are deciding whether to invest in Sears shares, you need financial information to help make your decision. Such information should help you understand Sears' past financial performance and current financial picture, and it should give you some idea of its future prospects. Although information found on electronic bulletin boards, like The Motley Fool, is useful, it is no substitute for careful study of financial reports.

Characteristics of Useful Information

STUDY OBJECTIVE
1

Describe the basic objective of financial reporting and the qualitative characteristics of accounting information.

How does a company like Sears decide on the amount and type of financial information to disclose? What format should it use? How should assets, liabilities, revenues, and expenses be measured? The answers to these questions are found in accounting rules that have substantial authoritative support and are recognized as a general guide for financial reporting purposes. These rules are referred to as generally accepted accounting principles (GAAP).

The accounting standard-setting body in Canada is the Canadian Institute of Chartered Accountants (CICA). All federal and provincial incorporating acts

52

PREPARING CLOSING ENTRIES

At the end of the accounting period, the temporary account balances are transferred to the permanent shareholders' equity account—Retained Earnings through the preparation of closing entries. Closing entries transfer net earnings (or net loss) and dividends to Retained Earnings, so that the balance in the Retained Earnings account agrees with the balance reported in the statement of retained earnings. For example, notice that in Illustration 4-14, Retained Earnings has an adjusted balance of zero. Prior to the closing entries, the balance in Retained Earnings will be its beginning-of-the-period balance. For Sierra, this is zero because it is Sierra's first year of operations.

In addition to updating Retained Earnings to its ending balance, closing entries produce a **zero balance in each temporary account**. As a result, these accounts are ready to accumulate data about revenues, expenses, and dividends in the next accounting period separate from the data in the prior periods. Permanent accounts are not closed.

When closing entries are prepared, each statement of earnings account could be closed directly to Retained Earnings. However, to do so would result in excessive detail in the Retained Earnings account. Accordingly, the revenue and expense accounts are first closed to another temporary account, Income Summary. Only the resulting net earnings or net loss is transferred from this account to Retained Earnings. Illustration 4-18 shows the closing process.

Helpful Hint Income Summary is a very descriptive title. Total revenues are closed to Income Summary, total expenses are closed to Income Summary, and the balance in the Income Summary is the net earnings or net loss.

Illustration 4-18
Closing process

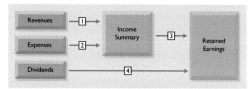

To prepare closing entries:

1. To close revenue accounts: Debit each individual revenue account for its balance, and credit Income Summary for total revenues.
2. To close expense accounts: Debit Income Summary for total ⌐, credit each individual expense account for its balance.
3. To close Income Summary: Debit Income Summary for the bala⌐ count (or credit if a net loss), and credit (debit) Retained Earni⌐
4. To close Dividends: Debit Retained Earnings, and credit Div⌐ balance.

The closing entries for Sierra Corporation are shown in Illustrat⌐

Key Terms that represent essential concepts are printed in blue where they are first explained in the text. They are listed and defined again in the end-of-chapter Glossary.

Helpful Hints in the margins are like having an instructor with you as you read. They help clarify concepts being discussed.

Colour illustrations, such as this infographic, help you visualize and apply the information as you study. They reinforce important concepts.

Statement of Earnings Presentation

Two forms of the statement of earnings are widely used by companies. One is the **single-step statement of earnings**. The statement is called this because only one step—subtracting total expenses from total revenues—is required in determining net earnings (or net loss). In a single-step statement, all data are classified into two categories: (1) **revenues**, which include both operating revenues and non-operating revenues (for example, interest revenue and a gain on sale of equipment); and (2) **expenses**, which include cost of goods sold, operating expenses, and non-operating expenses (for example, interest expense and a loss on the sale of equipment). Sometimes income tax expense is listed with the expenses, but more often it is disclosed separately. A condensed single-step statement for Leon's Furniture is shown in Illustration 5-5.

STUDY OBJECTIVE
4
Distinguish between a single-step and a multiple-step statement of earnings.

Illustration 5-5
Single-step statement of earnings

Leon's

Alternative Terminology Note that Leon's *statement of earnings* is entitled *Statement of Income*.

LEON'S FURNITURE	
Statement of Income	
Year Ended December 31, 2002	
(in thousands)	
Revenues	
Sales	$449,693
Interest income	2,650
Other income	10,727
Total revenues	463,070
Expenses	
Cost of sales	201,265
Salaries and commissions	66,610
Advertising	27,306
Other operating expenses	25,807
Amortization	8,552
Rent and property taxes	7,316
Employee profit-sharing plan	2,483
Total expenses	399,339
Income before income taxes	63,731
Income tax expense	25,211
Net income	$ 38,520

The single-step statement of earnings is the form we have used in the text so far. There are two main reasons for using the single-step form: (1) a company does not realize any type of profit or earnings until total revenues exceed total expenses, so it makes sense to divide the statement into these two categories; and (2) the single-step form is simple and easy to read.

A second form of the statement of earnings is the **multiple-step statement of earnings**. The multiple-step statement is often considered more useful because it highlights the components of net earnings. Leon's statement of earnings in Illustration 5-6 is an example.

Study Objectives reappear in the margins at the point where the topic is discussed. End-of-chapter exercises and problems are keyed to the Study Objectives.

Financial statements appear regularly throughout the book. Those from real companies are identified by a logo or photo. Often, numbers or categories are highlighted in red type to draw your attention to key information.

Alternative Terminology notes present synonymous terms that you may come across in practice.

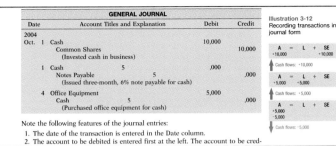

GENERAL JOURNAL			
Date	Account Titles and Explanation	Debit	Credit
2004			
Oct. 1	Cash	10,000	
	Common Shares		10,000
	(Invested cash in business)		
1	Cash 5	,000	
	Notes Payable 5		,000
	(Issued three-month, 6% note payable for cash)		
4	Office Equipment	5,000	
	Cash 5		,000
	(Purchased office equipment for cash)		

Illustration 3-12
Recording transactions in journal form

Note the following features of the journal entries:
1. The date of the transaction is entered in the Date column.
2. The account to be debited is entered first at the left. The account to be cred-

Accounting equation analyses appear in the margin next to key journal entries. They will help you understand the impact of an accounting transaction on the financial position and cash flows.

International Notes introduce international issues and similarities and differences in accounting between Canada and other countries.

Business Insight examples give glimpses into how real companies make decisions using accounting information. These high-interest boxes are classified by four different points of view—*investor perspectives*, *management perspectives*, *international perspectives*, and *ethics perspectives*.

🌐 **International Note**

Almost every country in the world applies the LCM rule; however, the definition of **market** can vary. The International Accounting Standards Committee defines market as net realizable value, as do the UK, France, and Germany. The U.S., Italy, and Japan define it as replacement cost.

is written down to its market value. This is done by valuing the inventory at the lower of cost and market (LCM) in the period in which the decline in value occurs. LCM is an example of the accounting concept of **conservatism**, which holds that the best choice among accounting alternatives is the method that is least likely to overstate assets and net earnings.

LCM is applied to the inventory after specific identification or one of the cost flow assumptions (FIFO, average, or LIFO) has been used to determine cost.

The term *market* in the phrase *lower of cost and market* is not specifically defined in Canada. It can mean replacement cost or net realizable value, among other things. The majority of Canadian companies use net realizable value to define market for LCM purposes. For a merchandising company, net realizable value is the selling price, less any costs required to make the goods ready for sale.

BUSINESS INSIGHT

INVESTOR PERSPECTIVE

In its 2002 third quarter financial statements, Falconbridge Limited wrote down the value of its metal inventory by $11 million, after taxes. Falconbridge's president and chief executive officer, Aaron Regent, commented that global economic conditions were uncertain and business confidence low. He said that this had a negative impact on demand for metals, particularly copper and zinc. On receiving the news, analysts immediately cut share price targets by 12% for Falconbridge.

A **CD icon** directs you to the Toolkit CD, where additional learning resources are available.

OTHER ELEMENTS OF AN ANNUAL REPORT

Annual Report Walkthrough

Publicly traded companies must provide their shareholders with an annual report each year. The annual report is a document that includes useful nonfinancial information about the company, as well as financial information. Nonfinancial information may include the company's mission, goals and objectives, products, and people. Financial information may include a management discussion and analysis, a statement of management responsibility for the financial statements, an auditors' report, the comparative financial statements introduced in this chapter, notes to the financial statements, and a historical summary of key financial ratios and

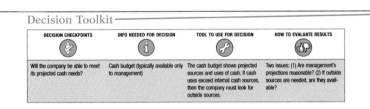

Decision Toolkit			
DECISION CHECKPOINTS	**INFO NEEDED FOR DECISION**	**TOOL TO USE FOR DECISION**	**HOW TO EVALUATE RESULTS**
Will the company be able to meet its projected cash needs?	Cash budget (typically available only to management)	The cash budget shows projected sources and uses of cash. If cash uses exceed internal cash sources, then the company must look for outside sources.	Two issues: (1) Are management's projections reasonable? (2) If outside sources are needed, are they available?

Each chapter presents **decision tools** that help business makers use financial statements. At the end of the text discussion, a **Decision Toolkit** summarizes the key features of a decision tool and reviews why and how you would use it.

BEFORE YOU GO ON ...

● **REVIEW IT**
1. What are the five principal elements of cash management?
2. What are the three sections of the cash budget?
3. What was Loblaw's balance in cash and cash equivalents as at December 28, 2002? How did Loblaw define cash equivalents (see Note 1)? The answers to these questions are provided at the end of this chapter.

● **DO IT**
The management of Staudinger Ltd. wants to maintain a minimum monthly cash balance of $5,000. At the beginning of March, the cash balance is $13,500; expected cash receipts for March are $210,000; and cash disbursements are expected to be $220,000. How much cash, if any, must be borrowed to maintain the desired minimum monthly balance?

Action Plan
• Insert the dollar data into the basic form of the cash budget.

Solution

Beginning cash balance	$ 13,500
Add: Cash receipts	210,000
Total available cash	223,500
Less: Cash disbursements	220,000
Excess of available cash over cash disbursements	3,500
Financing	1,500
Ending cash balance	$ 5,000

To maintain the desired minimum cash balance of $5,000, Staudinger needs to borrow $1,500.

Before You Go On sections follow each key topic. *Review It* questions prompt you to stop and review the key points you have just studied. Review It questions marked with the Loblaw logo direct you to find information in Loblaw's financial statements, printed in Appendix A. Answers appear at the end of the chapter. If you cannot answer these questions, you should go back and read the section again.

Brief *Do It* exercises ask you to put newly acquired knowledge to work in some form of financial statement preparation. They outline an *Action Plan* necessary to complete the exercise and show a *Solution*.

Loblaws
A passion for food... and a lot more!

Using the Decision Toolkit

French-based Aventis is one of Wyeth's top competitors. Selected financial information taken from Aventis' December 31, 2002, financial statements follows:

AVENTIS Selected Financial Information December 31, 2002 (in € millions)		
	2002	2001
Sales	€20,622	€22,941
Accounts and notes receivable	2,680	3,861
Allowance for doubtful accounts	136	339
Total current assets	9,646	12,785
Total current liabilities	10,478	13,939

Instructions

Comment on Aventis' accounts receivable management and liquidity relative to that of Wyeth for 2002, by considering the current ratio, receivables turnover, and average collection period. Wyeth's current ratio was 2.1:1; the industry average, 1.4:1. Wyeth's receivables turnover and average collection period were calculated earlier in the chapter.

Solution

Current Ratio

	Aventis	Wyeth	Industry
	$\frac{€9,646}{€10,478} = 0.9{:}1$	2.1:1	1.4:1

Aventis' current ratio is significantly lower than that of Wyeth and the industry. However, a high current ratio does not always mean that a company has more liquidity. Wyeth's current ratio could be artificially high because of uncollectible receivables or slow-moving inventory. So, further investigation is warranted before we can fully compare Aventis' and Wyeth's liquidity.

Receivables Turnover and Average Collection Period

	Aventis	Wyeth	Industry
Receivables turnover	$\frac{€20,622}{(€2,680 + €3,861) \div 2} = 6.3$ times	5.4 times	6.0 times
Average collection period	$\frac{365 \text{ days}}{6.3} = 58$ days	68 days	61 days

Despite Aventis' current ratio being lower than that of Wyeth and the industry, it is collecting its receivables faster than both. Therefore, it is not uncollectible receivables that is influencing Aventis' lower current ratio. We would have to investigate Aventis' and Wyeth's inventory turnover ratios to determine whether Wyeth's current ratio is artificially high because of slow-moving inventory.

NAVIGATOR

A **Using the Decision Toolkit** exercise follows the final set of Review It questions in the chapter. It asks you to use information from financial statements to make decisions. You should think through the questions related to the decision before you study the printed *Solution.*

Summary of Study Objectives

❶ Describe the primary forms of business organization. A proprietorship is a business owned by one person. A partnership is a business owned by two or more people. A corporation is a separate legal entity whose shares provide evidence of ownership.

❷ Identify the users and uses of accounting. Internal users work for the business and need accounting information to plan, organize, and run operations. The primary external users are investors and creditors. Investors (present and future shareholders) use accounting information to help decide whether to buy, hold, or sell shares. Creditors (suppliers and bankers) use accounting information to assess the risk of granting credit or loaning money to a business.

❸ Explain the three principal types of business activity. Financing activities involve collecting the necessary funds (through debt or equity) to support the business. Investing activities involve acquiring the resources (capital assets) necessary to run the business. Operating activities involve putting the resources of the business into action to generate a profit.

❹ Describe the content and purpose of each of the financial statements. A statement of earnings presents the revenues and expenses of a company for a specific period of time. A statement of retained earnings summarizes the changes in retained earnings that have occurred for a specific period of time. Retained earnings are the cumulative earnings (less losses) over the company's life, less any dividends paid to shareholders. A balance sheet reports the assets, liabilities, and shareholders' equity of a business

at a specific date. A cash flow statement summarizes information concerning the cash inflows (receipts) and outflows (payments) for a specific period of time.

❺ Explain the meaning of assets, liabilities, and shareholders' equity, and state the basic accounting equation. Assets are resources owned by a business. Liabilities are the debts and obligations of the business. Liabilities represent creditors' claims on the assets of the business. Shareholders' equity represents the claims of shareholders on the assets of the business. It is composed of two parts: share capital and retained earnings. The basic accounting equation is: Assets = Liabilities + Shareholders' Equity.

❻ Explain the basic assumptions and principles underlying financial statements. The monetary unit assumption requires that only transaction data capable of being expressed in terms of money be included in the accounting records of the economic entity. The economic entity assumption states that economic events should be identified with a particular unit of accountability. The time period assumption states that the economic life of a business can be divided into artificial time periods and that meaningful accounting reports can be prepared for each period. The going concern assumption states that the business will continue operating long enough to carry out its existing objectives. The cost principle states that assets should be recorded at their cost. The full disclosure principle states that circumstances and events which matter to financial statement users should be disclosed.

The **Summary of Study Objectives** reviews the main points related to the Study Objectives. It provides you with another opportunity to review, as well as to see how all the key topics within the chapter are related.

At the end of each chapter, **Decision Toolkit—A Summary** reviews the contexts and useful techniques for decision-making that were covered in the chapter. A **CD icon** directs you to the Toolkit CD, where a comprehensive summary of the Decision Toolkits in each chapter is available.

The **Glossary** defines all the **key terms** and concepts introduced in the chapter. A **CD icon** directs you to the Toolkit CD, where a searchable, comprehensive glossary is available.

---

78   CHAPTER 2   A Further Look at Financial Statements

  Decision Toolkit—A Summary

DECISION CHECKPOINTS	INFO NEEDED FOR DECISION	TOOL TO USE FOR DECISION	HOW TO EVALUATE RESULTS
How does the company's earnings performance compare with previous years?	Net earnings available to common shareholders and average number of common shares	$\text{Earnings per share} = \dfrac{\text{Net earnings} - \text{Preferred dividends}}{\text{Average number of common shares}}$	A higher measure suggests improved performance, although the number is subject to manipulation. Values should not be compared across companies.
How does the market perceive the company's prospects for future earnings?	Earnings per share and market price per share	$\text{Price-earnings ratio} = \dfrac{\text{Market price per share}}{\text{Earnings per share}}$	A high ratio suggests the market has favourable expectations, although it also may suggest shares are overvalued.
Can the company meet its short-term obligations?	Current assets and current liabilities	$\text{Working capital} = \text{Current assets} - \text{Current liabilities}$	A higher amount indicates liquidity.
		$\text{Current ratio} = \dfrac{\text{Current assets}}{\text{Current liabilities}}$	A higher ratio suggests favourable liquidity.
	Current liabilities and cash provided (used) by operating activities	$\text{Cash current debt coverage} = \dfrac{\text{Cash provided (used) by operating activities}}{\text{Average current liabilities}}$	A higher ratio indicates liquidity—that the company is generating sufficient cash to meet its short-term needs.
Can the company meet its long-term obligations?	Total debt and total assets	$\text{Debt to total assets} = \dfrac{\text{Total liabilities}}{\text{Total assets}}$	A lower value suggests favourable solvency.
	Total liabilities and cash provided (used) by operating activities	$\text{Cash total debt coverage} = \dfrac{\text{Cash provided (used) by operating activities}}{\text{Average total liabilities}}$	A higher ratio indicates solvency—that the company is generating sufficient cash to meet its long-term needs.

Glossary

Cash current debt coverage A measure of liquidity that is calculated as follows: cash provided by operating activities divided by average current liabilities. (p. 73)

Cash total debt coverage A measure of solvency that is calculated as follows: cash provided by operating activities divided by average total liabilities. (p. 73)

Comparability A quality for describing accounting information that can be compared among companies in similar circumstances, because they use similar accounting principles. (p. 54)

Conservatism The approach of choosing an accounting

method that will be least likely to overstate assets and net earnings. (p. 54)

Consistency Use of the same accounting principles and methods from year to year within a company. (p. 55)

Cost-benefit The constraint that the costs of obtaining and providing information should not exceed the benefits gained. (p. 56)

Current assets Cash and other resources that it is reasonable to expect will be realized in cash, or sold, or used up by the business, within one year. (p. 58)

Current liabilities Obligations that will be paid from

---

130   CHAPTER 3   The Accounting Information System

Glossary

Account An individual accounting record of increases and decreases in specific asset, liability, and shareholders' equity items. (p. 108)

Accounting information system The system of collecting and processing transaction data and communicating financial information to interested parties. (p. 102)

Accounting transactions Events that require recording in the financial statements because they involve an exchange affecting assets, liabilities, or shareholders' equity. (p. 102)

Chart of accounts A list of a company's accounts. (p. 117)

Credit The right side of an account. (p. 109)

Debit The left side of an account. (p. 109)

Double-entry fect of each tra

General journa tions are initial

General ledger a company's a counts. (p. 116

Posting The the ledger acco

T account Th

Trial balance balances at a g

Additional Demonstration Problems

Action Plan

- Make separate journal entries for each transaction.
- Note that debit entries precede credit entries
- In journalizing, make sure debits equal credits.
- In journalizing, use specific account titles taken from the chart of accounts.
- Provide an appropriate explanation of the journal entry.
- Arrange the general ledger in statement order, beginning with the balance sheet accounts.
- Post in chronological order.
- Prepare a trial balance which lists accounts in the order in which they appear in the ledger.
- In the trial balance, list debit balances in the left column and credit balances in the right column.

Demonstration Problem

Campus Laundry Inc. opened on September 1, 2004. During the first month of operations the following transactions occurred:

Sept. 1 Shareholders invested $20,000 cash in the business.
2 Paid $1,000 cash for store rent for the month of September.
3 Purchased washers and dryers for $25,000, paying $10,000 in cash and signing a $15,000, six-month, 8% note payable.
4 Paid $1,200 for a one-year accident insurance policy.
10 Received a bill from the *Daily News* for advertising the opening of the laundromat, $200.
15 Performed services on account for $6,200.
20 Paid a $700 cash dividend to shareholders.
30 Received $5,000 from customers billed on September 15.

The chart of accounts for the company is the same as for Sierra Corporation except for the following: Laundry Equipment and Advertising Expense.

Instructions

(a) Journalize the September transactions.
(b) Open general ledger accounts and post the September transactions.
(c) Prepare a trial balance at September 30, 2004.

Solution to Demonstration Problem

(a)

GENERAL JOURNAL			
Date	Account Titles and Explanation	Debit	Credit
2004			
Sept. 1	Cash	20,000	
	Common Shares		20,000
	(Invested cash in business)		
2	Rent Expense	1,000	
	Cash	1	,000
	(Paid September rent)		

A **Demonstration Problem** is the final step before you begin homework. These sample problems provide you with an *Action Plan* in the margin that lists the strategies needed to approach and solve the problem. The *Solution* demonstrates both the form and content of complete answers. A **CD icon** directs you to the Toolkit CD, where additional demonstration problems are available.

Self-Study Questions provide a practice test that gives you an opportunity to check your knowledge of important topics. Answers appear on the last page of the chapter. **CD icons** tell you that there is a multiple choice quiz on the Toolkit CD that can further help you master the material.

Questions allow you to explain your understanding of concepts and relationships covered in the chapter. Use them to help prepare for class discussion and tests.

Self-Study Questions

Multiple Choice Quiz

Answers are at the end of the chapter.

(SO 1) 1. Generally accepted accounting principles are:
(a) a set of standards and rules that are recognized as a general guide for financial reporting.
(b) usually established by the Canada Customs and Revenue Agency.
(c) the guidelines used to resolve ethical dilemmas.
(d) fundamental truths that can be derived from the laws of nature.

(SO 1) 2. What is the primary criterion by which accounting information can be judged?
(a) Consistency
(b) Predictive value
(c) Usefulness for decision-making
(d) Comparability

(SO 1) 3. What accounting characteristic refers to the ten
...tainty in the
...and earnings?
...atism
...andability
...n:
...nge a decision.
...re usually clas-
...t, and equip-
...nts, and share

(c) current assets; long-term investments; property, plant, and equipment; and intangible assets.
(d) current assets and noncurrent assets.

6. Current assets are listed: (SO 3)
(a) by liquidity.
(b) by importance.
(c) by longevity.
(d) alphabetically.

7. Which is not an indicator of profitability? (SO 4)
(a) Current ratio
(b) Earnings per share
(c) Net earnings
(d) Price-earnings ratio

8. For 2004, Breau Corporation reported net earnings (SO 4) $24,000; common shares $400,000; average number of common shares 6,000; and a share market value of $60. Breau had no preferred shares. What was its 2004 earnings per share?
(a) $0.06   (c) $15.00
(b) $4.00   (d) $16.67

9. The balance in retained earnings is not affected by: (SO 5)
(a) net earnings.
(b) net loss.
(c) common shares.
(d) dividends.

10. Which of these measures is an evaluation of (SO 6) a company's ability to pay current liabilities?
(a) Price-earnings ratio
(b) Current ratio
(c) Debt to total assets
(d) None of the above

NAVIGATOR ✓

82   CHAPTER 2   A Further Look at Financial Statements

Questions

(SO 1) 1. (a) What are generally accepted accounting principles (GAAP)?
(b) What is the basic objective of financial reporting?
(c) Identify the qualitative characteristics of accounting information.

(SO 1) 2. Ray Aldag, the president of Raynard Corporation, is pleased. Raynard substantially increased its net earnings in 2004, while keeping its unit inventory almost the same. Chief accountant Tom Erhardt has cautioned Aldag, however. Erhardt says that since Raynard changed its method of inventory valuation, there is a consistency problem and it is difficult to determine whether Raynard is better off. Is Erhardt correct? Why or why not?

(SO 1) 3. What is the distinction between comparability and consistency?

(SO 2) 4. Describe the two constraints in the presentation of accounting information.

(SO 2) 5. The newly hired accountant of a corporation rounded all dollar figures in the annual report's financial statements to the nearest thousand dollars. "It's not important for our users to know how many pennies we spend," she said. Do you believe rounded financial figures can still provide useful information to external users for decision-making? Explain why or why not.

(SO 3) 6. Define current assets. What basis is used for ordering individual items within the current assets section?

(SO 3) 7. Distinguish between long-term investments and intangible assets.

(SO 3) 8. How do current liabilities differ from long-term liabilities?

(SO 3) 9. Identify the two parts of shareholders' equity in a corporation, and indicate the purpose of each.

(SO 4) 10. The manager of Robins Ltd is puzzled. Robins had a price-earnings ratio of 25 times in

2004. He feels that this indicates that shareholders believe that the company is doing well. Amod Phatarpekar, the company accountant, says that more information is needed to determine the company's profitability. Who is correct? Why?

11. Explain how the statement of retained earnings (SO 5) is interrelated with the statement of earnings and balance sheet.

12. [icon]
(a) Tia Kim believes that the analysis of financial statements is directed at two characteristics of a company: liquidity and profitability. Is Tia correct? Explain. (SO 4, 6)
(b) Are short-term creditors, long-term creditors, and shareholders primarily interested in the same characteristics of a company? Explain.

13. [icon] Name ratios that are useful in assessing (SO 4, 6)
(a) liquidity, (b) solvency, and (c) profitability.

14. [icon] What do these classes of ratios measure? (SO 4, 6)
(a) Liquidity ratios
(b) Profitability ratios
(c) Solvency ratios

15. [icon] Keeping all other factors constant, indi (SO 4, 6) cate whether each of the following signals generally good or bad news about a company:
(a) Increase in the earnings per share
(b) Increase in the current ratio
(c) Increase in the debt to total assets ratio
(d) Decrease in the cash current debt coverage ratio

16. [icon] In your opinion, which ratio(s) from this (SO 4, 6) chapter should be of greatest interest to:
(a) a pension fund considering investing in a corporation's 20-year bonds?
(b) a bank contemplating a short-term loan?
(c) a common shareholder?

A special icon indicates material that asks you to use the **decision tools** presented in the chapter.

Brief Exercises help you focus on one Study Objective at a time and thus help you build confidence in your basic skills and knowledge.

Brief Exercises

Identify qualitative characteristics.
(SO 1)

BE2-1   Presented below is a chart showing the qualitative characteristics of accounting information. Fill in the blanks from (a) to (f).

Qualitative Characteristics of Accounting Information

Understandability	Revelance	Reliability	Comparability
1. Accounting concepts and procedures 2. (a)	1. (b) 2. (c) 3. Timely	1. (d) 2. Faithful representation 3. Neutral 4. (e)	1. (f) 2. Consistent use of principles

...d's common shares. During the year, Dong re...dicate whether using the equity method instead ...rease (+), a decrease (−), or no effect (NE) in

Compare financial impact of cost and equity methods.
(SO 3)

Statement of Earnings

		Net
Revenues	Expenses	Earnings

...rt-term investments of Deal.com Ltd. at Decem...pectively. Prepare the adjusting entry to record ...ket value, if one is required.

Journalize LCM for short-term investment.
(SO 6)

...7, show the financial statement presentation of ...unts.

Indicate statement presentation.
(SO 6)

...gen Corporation holds equity securities costing ...mber 31, 2004, the market value of the securi...to record the securities at market value assum

Journalize LCM for long-term investment.
(SO 6)

...9, show the financial statement presentation of ...unts.

Indicate statement presentation.
(SO 6)

...wing long-term investments at November 30, ...(10% ownership), cost $108,000, market value ...80% ownership), cost $210,000, equity $250,000; ...market value $175,000. Prepare the investments

Prepare investments section of balance sheet.
(SO 6)

BE12-12   Indicate whether each of the following transactions would increase or decrease earnings:

(a) Reclassification of short-term investments with temporary declines in market value as long-term investments
(b) Sale of long-term investments with market value less than cost. The decline was not anticipated to be permanent.

Identify impact of earnings manipulation.
(SO 6) [icon]

Exercises which gradually increase in difficulty help you continue to build your confidence in your ability to use the material learned in the chapter.

An **Interactive Homework** icon tells you that you can practise certain Exercises interactively on the website.

Exercises

E12-1   Piper Corporation had these transactions pertaining to debt investments:

Jan.   1 Purchased 60 $1,000, 6% Harris Corp. bonds for $60,000 cash plus brokerage fees of $900. Interest is payable semi-annually on July 1 and January 1.
July   1 Received semi-annual interest on Harris bonds.
        1 Sold 30 Harris bonds for $32,000 less $500 of brokerage fees.
Dec. 31 Accrued interest at Piper's year-end.

Journalize debt investment transactions.
(SO 2)

Interactive Homework

Instructions
Journalize the transactions.

Certain exercises or problems marked with a pencil icon ▭▭▭▭▷ help you practise **written business communication**, a skill much in demand among employers.

E12-7 At December 31, 2004, the short-term investments for Nielson, Inc., are as follows:

Security	Cost	Market Value
A	$17,500	$16,000
B	12,500	14,000
C	23,000	19,000
Total	$53,000	$49,000

Journalize LCM for short-term investments.
(SO 6)

Instructions
(a) Prepare the adjusting entry at December 31, 2004, to report the investment portfolio at the lower of cost and market value.
(b) Show the balance sheet and statement of earnings presentation at December 31, 2004.

E12-8 Data for investments in shares classified as short-term investments are presented in E12-7. Assume instead that the investments are classified as long-term with the same cost and market value.

Journalize LCM for long-term investments, indicate statement presentation, and prepare memo.
(SO 6)
◁▭▭▭

Instructions
(a) Prepare the adjusting entry at December 31, 2004, to report the securities at the lower of cost and market value, assuming that any declines in value are permanent.
(b) Show the balance sheet and statement of earnings presentation at December 31, 2004.
(c) J. Arnet, a member of the board of directors, does not understand why a loss is recorded when nothing has been sold. Write a letter to Ms. Arnet explaining the reporting and the purposes it serves.

E12-9 Shaw Communications Inc. reports the following selected information related to investments (in thousands) in its financial statements for the year ended August 31, 2002:

Indicate statement presentation.
(SO 6)
Interactive Homework

Account	Amount	Financial Statement	Classification
Investment in Terayon Communication Systems, at cost	$ 45,872		
Investments in specialty channel networks, at equity	2,918		
Write-down of investments	330,466		
Equity loss on investees	53,487		
Cash paid for cable and MDU business acquisitions	40,454		
Cash paid for acquisition of investments	28,158		

Instructions
Indicate on which financial statement (i.e., balance sheet, statement of earnings, or cash flow statement) each of the above accounts would be reported. Also note the appropriate

---

86   CHAPTER 2 A Further Look at Financial Statements

Instructions
(a) Calculate the working capital and curren
(b) Did Wal-Mart's liquidity improve or dete
(c) Using the data in the chapter, compare Bay, and the industry.

Calculate and interpret solvency ratios.
(SO 6)

E2-8 The following data were taken from the Winter Carnival:

Current assets		
Total assets		
Current liabilities	551,540	437,946
Total liabilities	564,821	466,017
Total shareholders' equity	1,091,427	1,066,540
Cash provided by operating activities	117,716	64,501
Cash used by investing activities	107,393	33,782

Instructions
Do each of the following:
(a) Calculate the debt to total assets ratio for each year.
(b) Calculate the cash current debt coverage and the cash total debt coverage for 2002.
(c) Discuss the Carnival's solvency in 2002 versus 2001.
(d) Discuss the Carnival's ability to finance its investing activities with cash provided by operating activities, and explain how any deficiency would be met.

Problems: Set A

Comment on objective and qualitative characteristics of financial reporting.
(SO 1)

P2-1A A friend of yours, Emily Collis, recently completed an undergraduate degree in science and has just started working with a biotechnology company. Emily tells you that the owners of the business are trying to secure new sources of financing which are needed in order for the company to proceed with the development of a new health-care product. Emily said her boss told her that the company must put together a report to present to potential investors.

Emily thought that the company's package should include the detailed scientific findings related to the Phase I clinical trials for this product. She said, "I know that the biotech industry sometimes has only a 10% success rate with new products, but if we report all the scientific findings, everyone will see what a sure success this is going to be! The president was talking about the importance of following some set of accounting principles. Why do we need to look at some accounting rules? What they need to realize is that we have scientific results that are quite encouraging, some of the most talented employees around, and the start of some really great customer relationships. We haven't made any sales yet, but we will. We just need the funds to get through all the clinical testing and get government approval for our product. Then these investors will be quite happy that they bought into our company early!"

Instructions
(a) Explain to Emily what is meant by generally accepted accounting principles.
(b) What is the objective of financial reporting?
(c) Comment on how Emily's suggestions for what should be reported to prospective investors conform to the qualitative characteristics of accounting information.

Comment on the constraints of accounting.
(SO 2)

P2-2A No separate disclosure is required on the statement of earnings for the cost of goods sold (the cost of merchandise sold to customers). Because this disclosure is not specifically required, less than half of reporting companies disclose their cost of goods sold separately on their statements of earnings. Most companies include it with other expenses in their reporting of this item, similar to that reported by Sears Canada Inc. in its statement of earnings for the year ended December 28, 2002:

Each **Problem** helps you pull together and apply several concepts from the chapter. Two sets of problems—**A** and **B**—are generally keyed to the same Study Objectives and provide additional opportunities to apply or expand concepts learned in the chapter.

Receivables	339,131	Other Accounts Receivable	117,412
	38,912	Other Assets	496,702
s	1,205,333	Other Long-Term Liabilities	230,824
	152,294	Other Shareholders' Equity	
Expense	42,421	Items	199,231
perse	45,428	Prepaid Expenses and Other	
Debt	388,543	Current Assets	122,860
Debt Due		Retained Earnings	668,304
ne Year	258,870	Sales and Revenue	7,383,813
Receivables	12,105	Short-Term Borrowings	24,744
se nventories	1,551,104	Short-Term Deposits	51,418
Expenses	7,184,503	Trade Accounts Payable	436,368

Instructions
(a) Prepare a trial balance, sorting each account balance into the debit column or the credit column.
(b) Prepare a statement of earnings and a statement of retained earnings for the year ended January 31, 2003, and a classified balance sheet as at January 31, 2003, for Hudson's Bay.

The financial results of real companies are included in the end-of-chapter material. These are indicated by the company name here in red.

Problems: Set B

Analyse transactions, classify cash flows, and calculate net earnings.
(SO 1)

P3-1B On April 1, the Seall Travel Agency, Inc., started operations. These transactions were completed during the month:
1. Issued common shares to shareholders for $20,000 cash.
2. Paid $700 cash for April office rent.
3. Purchased office equipment for $2,500 cash.
4. Purchased $300 of advertising in the *Halifax Herald*, on account.
5. Paid $600 cash for office supplies.
6. Earned $9,000 for services performed: cash of $1,000 is received from customers, and the balance of $8,000 is billed to customers on account.
7. Paid $400 cash dividends.
8. Paid *Halifax Herald* amount due in transaction (4).
9. Paid employees' salaries, $1,200.
10. Received $8,000 in cash from customers who had been billed in transaction (6).
11. Paid income tax of $2,000.

The **Broadening Your Perspective** section helps you pull together various concepts covered in the chapter and apply them to real-world business decisions. A **CD icon** tells you that there are more analysis tools available on the Toolkit CD, including additional interpreting financial statement and comparative analysis problems.

In the **Financial Reporting Problem** you study various aspects of the financial statements of Loblaw Companies Limited which are printed in Chapter 1 (in simplified form) and in Appendix A (in full).

A **Comparative Analysis Problem** offers the opportunity to compare and contrast the financial reporting of Loblaw with a competitor, Sobeys Inc., whose financial statements are printed in Chapter 1 (in simplified form) and in Appendix B (in full).

Research Cases ask students to find a source of data, and then study or analyse the data and evaluate it.

BROADENING YOUR PERSPECTIVE

Financial Reporting and Analysis Analysis Tools

FINANCIAL REPORTING PROBLEM: *Loblaw Companies Limited*

BYP5-1 The financial statements for Loblaw are presented in Appendix A at the end of this book.

Instructions
Answer these questions using the consolidated statement of earnings:
(a) What was the percentage change in sales and in net earnings from 2001 to 2002?
(b) Is there sufficient information in the statement to determine Loblaw's gross profit margin? If so, calculate it for each of the two years.
(c) What was the profit margin in each of the two years presented in the annual report? Comment on the trend.
(d) Are any non-operating revenues and non-operating expenses included in Loblaw's statement of earnings? If so, identify the accounts included.

COMPARATIVE ANALYSIS PROBLEM: *Loblaw and Sobeys*

BYP5-2 The financial statements of Sobeys Inc. are presented in Appendix B following the financial statements for Loblaw in Appendix A.

Instructions
(a) Based on the information contained in these financial statements, determine the following values for each company for each of the two most recent years presented in their annual reports:
1. Percentage change in sales
2. Percentage change in operating income
3. Gross profit margin
4. Profit margin
(b) What conclusions concerning the relative profitability of the two companies can be drawn from these data?

RESEARCH CASE

BYP5-3 The article "Wal Around the World," published in the December 8, 2001, issue of *The Economist*, discusses Wal-Mart as the world's largest retailer which still thinks of itself as a small-town outfit. The article states that perception may be Wal-Mart's greatest strength.

Instructions
Read the article and answer the following questions:
(a) Lacking customers, staff, and suppliers, what did Sam Walton have to do differently from established retailers to get his business going?
(b) Wal-Mart turns its inventory over twice as fast as the industry average. How is this accomplished?
... to real-time data from Wal-Mart on how their ... y is this an advantage to both Wal-Mart and its ...
al-Mart's overseas efforts. Has Wal-Mart been ... in why or why not.

INTERPRETING FINANCIAL STATEMENTS

BYP5-4 Big Rock Brewery Ltd. is a western producer and marketer of premium quality beers. Selected information from Big Rock's statement of earnings for the past three years follows:

	2003	2002	2001
Sales	$30,463,010	$24,909,081	$23,199,678
Cost of sales	11,728,022	10,167,456	9,240,503
Operating expenses	15,694,624	12,772,839	11,951,602
Income tax expense	747,367	751,000	655,000

Instructions
(a) Calculate gross profit and net earnings for each of the three years.
(b) Calculate the percentage change in sales and net earnings from 2001 to 2003.
(c) Calculate the gross profit margin for each of the three years. Comment on any trend in this percentage.
(d) Calculate the profit margin for each of the three years. Comment on any trend in this percentage.
(e) How well has Big Rock managed operating expenses over the three-year period?

A GLOBAL FOCUS

BYP5-5 Carrefour, headquartered in Paris, is the world's second largest retailer—second only to Wal-Mart. Although Wal-Mart is still the world's #1 retailer, its international sales are far lower than Carrefour's. This is a concern for Wal-Mart, since its primary opportunity for future growth lies outside of North America.

Below are selected financial data for Carrefour (in euros) and Wal-Mart (in U.S. dollars). Even though their results are presented in different currencies, by employing ratios, we can make some basic comparisons.

	Carrefour (in billions)	Wal-Mart (in billions)
Sales	€69.5	$217.8
Cost of goods sold	53.9	171.6
Net earnings	1.3	6.7
Total assets	43.5	83.5
Average total assets	43.8	80.8
Current assets	16.9	28.2
Current liabilities	13.0	27.3
Total liabilities	32.8	48.3

Instructions
Compare the two companies by doing the following:
(a) Calculate the gross profit margin, profit margin, and return on assets ratios for each company. Discuss their relative profitability.
(b) Calculate the current ratios and the debt to total assets ratios for the two companies. Discuss their relative liquidity and solvency.
(c) What concerns might you have in relying on this comparison?

FINANCIAL ANALYSIS ON THE WEB

BYP5-6 Identify profitability ratios for Nortel Networks Corp., and compare this information to industry, sector, and market indices.

Instructions
Specific requirements for this Web case can be found on the Kimmel website.

Interpreting Financial Statements offers minicases that ask you to read parts of financial statements of real companies and use the decision tools presented in the chapter to interpret this information.

A Global Focus asks you to apply concepts presented in the chapter to specific situations faced by real international companies.

Financial Analysis on the Web exercises guide you to the Kimmel website where you can find and analyse information related to the chapter topic.

Critical Thinking offers additional opportunities and activities to build decision-making skills by analysing accounting information in a less structured situation.

Collaborative Learning Activities require teams of students to evaluate a manager's decision or lead to a decision among alternative courses of action. They also give you practice in building business communication skills.

Communication Activities ask you to engage in real-world business situations writing and speaking skills, including giving presentations.

Critical Thinking

COLLABORATIVE LEARNING ACTIVITY

BYP5-7 Three years ago, Kathy Webb and her brother-in-law, John Utley, formed the Wu Department Store Ltd. For the first two years, business was good, but the following results for 2004 were disappointing:

WU DEPARTMENT STORE LTD.
Statement of Earnings
Year Ended December 31, 2004

Net sales	$700,000
Cost of goods sold	546,000
Gross profit	154,000
Operating expenses	125,000
Earnings before income tax	29,000
Income tax expense	11,000
Net earnings	$ 18,000

Kathy believes the problem lies in the relatively low gross profit margin of 22%. John believes the problem is that operating expenses are too high. Kathy thinks the gross profit margin can be improved by making two changes: (1) Increase average selling prices by 17%. This increase is expected to lower sales volume so that total sales will increase only 6%. (2) Buy merchandise in larger quantities and take all purchase discounts. These changes are expected to increase the gross profit margin by 3%. Kathy does not expect these changes to have any effect on operating expenses.

John thinks expenses can be cut by making these two changes: (1) Cut sales salaries of $60,000 in half and give sales personnel a commission of 2% of net sales. (2) Reduce store deliveries to one day per week rather than twice a week. This change will reduce delivery expenses of $30,000 by 40%. John feels that these changes will not have any effect on net sales.

Kathy and John come to you for help in deciding the best way to improve net earnings. The income tax rate is anticipated to be 40% of earnings before income tax in 2005.

Instructions

With the class divided into groups, do the following:

(a) Prepare a projected statement of earnings for 2005 assuming (1) Kathy's changes are implemented and (2) John's ideas are adopted.
(b) What is your recommendation to Kathy and John?
(c) Prepare a projected statement of earnings for 2005 assuming both sets of proposed changes are made.
(d) Discuss the impact that other factors might have. For example, would increasing the quantity of inventory increase costs? Would a salary cut affect employee morale? Would decreased morale affect sales? Would decreased store deliveries decrease customer satisfaction? What other suggestions might be considered?

COMMUNICATION ACTIVITY

BYP5-8 Consider the following events, which are listed in chronological order:

1. Dexter Maersk decides to buy a custom-made snowboard and calls The Great Canadian Snowboard Company, Inc., to inquire about its products.
2. Dexter asks Great Canadian Snowboard to manufacture a custom board for him.
3. The company sends Dexter a purchase order to fill out, which he immediately completes, signs, and sends back with a required 25% down payment.
4. Great Canadian Snowboard receives Dexter's purchase order and down payment, and begins working on the board.
5. The Great Canadian Snowboard Company has its fiscal year end. At this time, Dexter's board is 75% completed.
6. The company completes the snowboard for Dexter and notifies him to take delivery.
7. Dexter picks up his snowboard from the company and takes it home.
8. Dexter tries the snowboard out and likes it so much that he carves his initials in it.

---

9. The Great Canadian Snowboard Compan[...]
less the 25% down payment.
10. The company receives payment of the bal[...]

Instructions

In a memo to the president of The Great Ca[...]
questions:

(a) When should The Great Canadian Snowb[...]
related to the snowboard? Refer to the r[...]
in your answer.
(b) Suppose that with his purchase order De[...]
ment. Would that change your answer to part (a)?

ETHICS CASE

BYP5-9 Rita Pelzer was just hired as the assistant treasurer of Zaz Stores Ltd., a specialty chain store company that has nine retail stores concentrated in one city. Among other things, the payment of all invoices is centralized in one of the departments Rita will manage. Her primary responsibility is to maintain the company's high credit rating by paying all bills when due and to take advantage of all cash discounts.

Jamie Caterino, the treasurer, is training Rita in her new duties. He instructs Rita that she is to continue the practice of preparing all cheques "net of discount" and dating the cheques the last day of the discount period. "But," Jamie continues, "we always hold the cheques at least four days beyond the discount period before mailing them. That way we get another four days of interest on our money. Most of our creditors need our business and don't complain. And, if they scream about our missing the discount period, we blame it on the mailroom or the post office. We've only lost one discount out of every hundred we take that way. I think everybody does it. By the way, welcome to our team!"

Instructions

(a) What are the ethical considerations in this case?
(b) What stakeholders are harmed or benefited?
(c) Should Rita continue the practice started by Jamie? Does she have any choice?

Answers to Self-Study Questions
1. b   2. d   3. c   4. b   5. b   6. d   7. c   8. b   *9. b   *10. c

Answer to Loblaw Review It Question 3
Loblaw uses a multiple-step statement of earnings and reports its non-operating interest expense separate from operating income. However, the first portion of its statement of earnings is not the same as the multiple-step statements presented in this chapter. For competitive reasons, Loblaw does not report its cost of sales or its gross profit separately.

Ethics In
Accounting

Through the **Ethics Cases** you will reflect on typical ethical dilemmas and decide on an appropriate course of action. A **CD icon** directs you to the Toolkit CD, where you will find an expanded discussion of ethical issues.

Answers to Self-Study Questions provide feedback on your understanding of concepts.

Answers to Review It questions based on Loblaw's financial statements appear here.

After you complete your assignments, it is a good idea to go back to **The Navigator** checklist at the start of the chapter to see if you have used all of the chapter's study aids.

Remember to go back to the Navigator box on the
chapter-opening page to check off your completed work.

Now that you have looked at your Student Owner's Manual, take some time to find out how you learn best. This quiz is designed to help you find out something about your preferred learning method. Research on left brain/right brain differences and also on learning and personality differences suggests that each person has preferred ways to receive and communicate information. After taking the quiz, we will help you pinpoint the study aids in this test that will help you learn the material based on your learning style.

Circle the letter of the answer that best explains your preferences. If a single answer does not match your perception, please circle two or more choices. Leave blank any question that does not apply.

1. You are about to give directions to a person. She is staying in a hotel and wants to visit your house. She has a rental car. Would you
    V) draw a map on paper?
    R) write down the directions (without a map)?
    A) tell her the directions?
    K) pick her up at the hotel in your car?

2. You are staying in a hotel and have a rental car. You would like to visit friends whose address/location you do not know. Would you like them to
    V) draw you a map on paper?
    R) write down the directions (without a map)?
    A) tell you the directions by phone?
    K) pick you up at the hotel in their car?

3. You have just received a copy of your itinerary for a world trip. This is of interest to a friend. Would you
    A) call her immediately and tell her about it?
    R) send her a copy of the printed itinerary?
    V) show her on a map of the world?
    K) share what you plan to do at each place you visit?

4. You are going to cook a dessert as a special treat for your family. Do you
    K) cook something familiar without need for instructions?
    V) thumb through the cookbook looking for ideas from the pictures?
    R) refer to a specific cookbook where there is a good recipe?
    A) ask for advice from others?

5. A group of tourists has been assigned to you to find out about national parks. Would you
    K) drive them to a national park?
    R) give them a book on national parks?
    V) show them slides and photographs?
    A) give them a talk on national parks?

6. You are about to purchase a new DVD player. Other than price, what would most influence your decision?
    A) The salesperson telling you what you want to know
    K) Listening to it
    R) Reading the details about it
    V) Its distinctive, upscale appearance

7. Recall a time in your life when you learned how to do something like playing a new board game. (Try to avoid choosing a very physical skill, e.g., riding a bike.) How did you learn best? By
    V) visual clues—pictures, diagrams, charts?
    A) listening to somebody explaining it?
    R) written instructions?
    K) doing it?

8. You have an eye problem. Would you prefer that the doctor
    A) tell you what is wrong?
    V) show you a diagram of what is wrong?
    K) use a model to show what is wrong?

9. You are about to learn to use a new program on a computer. Would you
    K) sit down at the keyboard and begin to experiment with the program's features?
    R) read the manual that comes with the program?
    A) telephone a friend and ask questions about it?

10. You are not sure whether a word should be spelled "dependent" or "dependant." Do you
    R) look it up in the dictionary or check the grammar software?
    V) see the word in your mind and choose the best way it looks?
    A) sound it out in your mind?
    K) write both versions down?

11. Apart from price, what would most influence your decision to buy a particular book?
    K) You have used a copy before
    R) Quickly reading parts of it
    A) A friend talking about it
    V) The way it looks is appealing

12. A new movie has arrived in town. What would most influence your decision to go or not to go?
    A) You heard a radio review of it.
    R) You read a review of it.
    V) You saw a preview of it.

13. Do you prefer an instructor who likes to use
    R) textbook, handouts, reading?
    V) flow diagrams, charts, graphics?
    K) field trips, labs, practical sessions?
    A) discussion, guest speakers?

Results: To determine your learning preference, add up the number of individual *V*s, *A*s, *R*s, and *K*s you have circled. Take the letter you have the greatest number of and match it to the same letter in the Learning Styles Chart. Next to each letter in the chart are suggestions that will refer you to different learning aids throughout this text.

LEARNING STYLES CHART

VISUAL

WHAT TO DO IN CLASS	WHAT TO DO WHEN STUDYING	TEXT FEATURES THAT MAY HELP YOU THE MOST	WHAT TO DO PRIOR TO EXAMS
• Pay close attention to charts, drawings, and handouts your instructor uses. • Underline and highlight. • Use different colours. • Use symbols, flow charts, graphs, different arrangements on the page, white space.	Convert your lecture notes into "page pictures." To do this: • Use the "What to do in class" strategies. • Reconstruct images in different ways. • Redraw pages from memory. • Replace words with symbols and initials. • Look at your pages.	• The Navigator • Feature Story • Preview • Infographics/Illustrations • Accounting Equation Analyses in margins • Photos • Business Insights • Decision Toolkits • Key Terms in blue • Words in bold • Demonstration Problem/Action Plan • Questions/Exercises/ Problems • Financial Reporting and Analysis	• Recall the "pictures of the pages." • Draw and use diagrams where appropriate. • Practise turning visuals back into words.

AURAL

WHAT TO DO IN CLASS	WHAT TO DO WHEN STUDYING	TEXT FEATURES THAT MAY HELP YOU THE MOST	WHAT TO DO PRIOR TO EXAMS
• Attend lectures and tutorials. • Discuss topics with students. • Explain new ideas to other people. • Use a tape recorder. • Describe overheads, pictures, and visuals to somebody who was not in class. • Leave space in your lecture notes for later recall.	You may take poor notes because you prefer to listen. Therefore: • Expand your notes. • Put summarized notes on tape and listen. • Read summarized notes out loud. • Explain notes to another "aural" person.	• Preview • Infographics/Illustrations • Business Insights • Review It/Do It/Action Plan • Summary of Study Objectives • Glossary • Demonstration Problem/Action Plan • Self-Study Questions • Questions/Exercises/ Problems • Financial Reporting and Analysis • Critical Thinking	• Talk with the instructor. • Spend time in quiet places recalling the ideas. • Say your answers out loud. • Practise writing answers to old exam questions.

R READING/WRITING

WHAT TO DO IN CLASS	WHAT TO DO WHEN STUDYING	TEXT FEATURES THAT MAY HELP YOU THE MOST	WHAT TO DO PRIOR TO EXAMS
• Use lists and headings. • Use dictionaries, glossaries and definitions. • Read handouts and textbooks. • Use lecture notes.	• Write out words again and again. • Reread notes silently. • Rewrite ideas and principles into other words. • Organize diagrams into statements.	• The Navigator • Feature Story • Study Objectives • Preview • Accounting Equation Analyses in margins • Review It/Do It/Action Plan • Using the Decision Toolkit • Summary of Study Objectives • Glossary • Self-Study Questions • Questions/Exercises/Problems • Writing Problems • Financial Reporting and Analysis • Critical Thinking	• Practise with multiple-choice questions. • Write out lists in outline form. • Write paragraphs, beginnings, and endings. • Write exam answers. • Arrange your words into hierarchies and points.

K KINESTHETIC

WHAT TO DO IN CLASS	WHAT TO DO WHEN STUDYING	TEXT FEATURES THAT MAY HELP YOU THE MOST	WHAT TO DO PRIOR TO EXAMS
• Use all your senses. • Go to labs and take field trips. • Use trial-and-error methods. • Listen to real-life examples. • Use hands-on approaches. • Pay attention to applications.	• You may take notes poorly because topics do not seem concrete or relevant. Therefore: • Put examples in note summaries. • Use pictures and photos to illustrate an idea. • Talk about notes with another "kinesthetic" person. • Use case studies and applications to help with principles and abstract concepts.	• The Navigator • Feature Story • Preview • Infographics/Illustrations • Decision Toolkits • Review It/Do It/Action Plan • Using the Decision Toolkit • Summary of Study Objectives • Demonstration Problem/Action Plan • Self-Study Questions • Questions/Exercises/Problems • Financial Reporting and Analysis • Critical Thinking	• Write practice answers. • Role-play the exam situation.

BRIEF CONTENTS

CONTENTS

CHAPTER 13

Cash Flow Statement

I've Got $40 Billion Burning a Hole in My Pocket
600

CHAPTER 14

Performance Measurement

Brewery Produces Sparkling Report 666

APPENDIX A

APPENDIX B

Introduction to Financial Statements

The Feature Story helps you picture how the chapter relates to the real world of accounting and business. You will find references to the story throughout the chapter.

NAVIGATOR

Need Milk?

Every time you pick up President's Choice chocolate-chip cookies, or buy milk at IGA, Dominion, Loblaws, Atlantic SaveEasy, Provigo, Zehrs—or one of several dozen other grocery stores—and every time you purchase food in bulk from No Frills, Valu-Mart, or SuperValu, you are shopping at Canada's #1 grocery retailer and wholesaler: Loblaw Companies Limited.

How does a company become one of the largest names in Canadian business? Largely through well-planned operating and financial strategies. For Loblaw, these have included practices such as owning its own real estate, reinvesting in the business, enhancing its stores with non-traditional depart-

ments and services, and maintaining a strong balance sheet.

But strategic acquisitions have also played an important role. In fact, Loblaw was born as a result of one such move. During the 1940s, Garfield Weston, CEO of a family business specializing in bakery goods, began acquiring shares in the leading Canadian supermarket company of the day, Toronto-based Loblaw Groceterias. In 1956, he owned enough shares to control the company and changed its name to Loblaw Companies Limited. Over the next two decades, he steadily acquired dozens of food distributors and wholesalers in both the U.S. and Canada.

When Garfield died in 1978, his son Galen set out to restructure and revitalize Loblaw, which had become an underper-

forming part of the Weston empire by then. In the 1980s, he acquired Golden Dawn Foods, Star Supermarkets, Wittington Leaseholds, and a number of Kroger stores in St. Louis, and he also expanded west to Winnipeg. In the early 1990s, Loblaw opened new Ontario stores and made inroads into New Brunswick.

In 1995 and 1996, Loblaw expanded to 50 new Canadian locations and moved into the Quebec market by buying the Montreal-based Provigo chain for $1.8 billion. It also expanded significantly in Atlantic Canada, buying over 80 stores from Agora Foods.

Careful not to spread the company too thinly, however, Weston had divested Loblaw of its U.S. holdings in the mid-1990s to focus on this

Every feature story includes the **Internet address** of the company cited in the story to help you connect with real businesses and explore them further.

The Navigator learning system encourages you to use the learning aids in the chapter and set priorities as you study.

Loblaw Companies Limited www.loblaw.com

THE NAVIGATOR

Scan *Study Objectives* ☐

Read *Feature Story* ☐

Read *Chapter Preview* ☐

Read text and answer *Before You Go On*
p. 9 ☐ p. 15 ☐ p. 23 ☐

Work *Using the Decision Toolkit* ☐

Review *Summary of Study Objectives*
and *Decision Toolkit* ☐

Work *Demonstration Problem* ☐

Answer *Self-Study Questions* ☐

Complete assignments ☐

Canadian expansion. Furthermore, part of the deal to aquire Provigo involved selling or franchising some 90 stores in Ontario.

Another aspect of Loblaw's success was innovation at the retail level. Many of its new stores were unusually large, boasting extra amenities such as a flower shop, pharmacy, photo shop, financial services pavilion, and at Toronto's enormous Queen's Quay location, even an interior market and restaurant.

The company also led the trend toward private labels in Canada, first with the launch in 1978 of the no name brand, which featured low-priced products with a simple packaging design, then with President's Choice, G-R-E-E-N, and Too Good To Be True! In 2001, the company added President's Choice Organics in response to

growing consumer demand for healthy choices.

The high profitability of private labels makes them an expanding segment of today's grocery market. For Loblaw, the program has been a huge success. Its President's Choice products are now sold in supermarkets in the United States, Barbados, Bermuda, the Cayman Islands, Colombia, Israel, Hong Kong, Trinidad, and Jamaica. In 1998, the label was extended to include a line of financial services.

Through innovations such as these, and by ensuring that its operations are always cost-effective, the company has enjoyed long-term stable growth. Today, Loblaw Companies Limited operates nearly 1,700 stores across Canada and employs more than 122,000 people, making it one of

the largest private employers in Canada. Not bad for a company that grew out of a small family bakery!

Over time, the path of a huge corporation like this one naturally involves a myriad of decisions. Should Loblaw purchase a particular distributing operation or introduce a new frozen entrée? Sell groceries online? Exit a particular market and reallocate assets elsewhere? Other decisions that affect the company are external—should investors purchase some of the shares being issued by Loblaw to finance a new acquisition? To make such financial decisions, both internal and external parties rely on their primary tool, accounting.

NAVIGATOR ✔

3

The **preview** describes the purpose of the chapter and outlines its major topics and subtopics.

How do you start a business? How do you make it grow into a widely recognized brand name like Loblaw? How do you determine whether your business is making or losing money? When you need to expand your operations, where do you get money to finance expansion—should you borrow or issue shares? How do you convince lenders to lend you money or investors to buy your shares? Success in business requires making countless decisions, and decisions require financial information.

The purpose of this chapter is to show you the role accounting plays in providing financial information. The content and organization of the chapter are as follows:

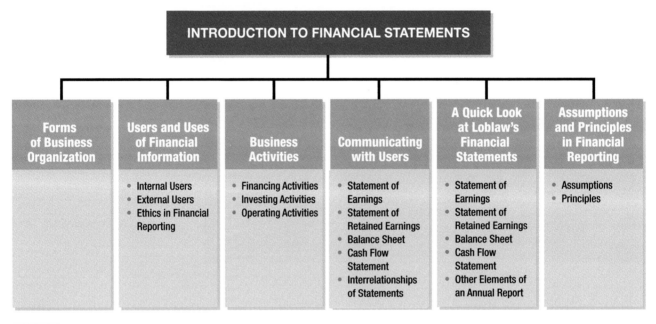

INTRODUCTION TO FINANCIAL STATEMENTS

Forms of Business Organization	Users and Uses of Financial Information	Business Activities	Communicating with Users	A Quick Look at Loblaw's Financial Statements	Assumptions and Principles in Financial Reporting
	• Internal Users • External Users • Ethics in Financial Reporting	• Financing Activities • Investing Activities • Operating Activities	• Statement of Earnings • Statement of Retained Earnings • Balance Sheet • Cash Flow Statement • Interrelationships of Statements	• Statement of Earnings • Statement of Retained Earnings • Balance Sheet • Cash Flow Statement • Other Elements of an Annual Report	• Assumptions • Principles

NAVIGATOR

Forms of Business Organization

STUDY OBJECTIVE

1

Describe the primary forms of business organization.

Essential **terms** are printed in blue when they first appear. They are defined again in the **glossary** at the end of the chapter.

Suppose you open your own marketing agency. One of your initial decisions is what organizational form your business should take. You have three choices—proprietorship, partnership, or corporation. A business owned by one person is a proprietorship. A business owned by more than one person is a partnership. A business organized as a separate legal entity owned by shareholders is a corporation.

You will probably choose the proprietorship form for your marketing agency. It is **simple to set up and gives you control** over the business. Small owner-operated businesses such as hair salons, service stations, and restaurants are often proprietorships, as are farms and small retail stores.

Another possibility is for you to join forces with other individuals to form a partnership. Partnerships are often formed because one individual does not have **enough economic resources** to initiate or expand the business, or because partners bring **unique skills or resources** to the partnership. Partnerships are used to organize retail and service-type businesses, including professional practices (lawyers, doctors, architects, engineers, and accountants).

As a third alternative, you might organize as a corporation. As an investor in a corporation, you receive shares to indicate your ownership claim. Buying shares in a corporation is often more attractive than investing in a partnership because shares are easy to sell. Selling a proprietorship or partnership interest is much more involved. Also, individuals can become shareholders by investing relatively small amounts of money. Therefore, it is **easier for corporations to raise funds.** Successful corporations often have thousands of shareholders, and their shares are traded on organized stock exchanges like the Toronto Stock Exchange. Many businesses start as proprietorships or partnerships and eventually incorporate.

Other factors to consider in deciding which organizational form to choose are **legal liability** and **income taxes.** If you choose a proprietorship or partnership, you are personally liable for all debts of the business, whereas corporate shareholders are not. Proprietors and partners pay personal income tax on their respective share of the profits, while corporations pay income taxes as separate legal entities on any corporate profits. Corporations may also receive a more favourable tax treatment than other forms of business organization. We will discuss these issues in more depth in a later chapter.

Although the combined number of proprietorships and partnerships in Canada is more than the number of corporations, the revenue produced by corporations is far greater. Most of the largest companies in Canada—for example, General Motors of Canada Ltd., BCE Inc., Nortel Networks Corporation, George Weston Limited, Bombardier Inc., and Loblaw Companies Limited—are corporations. Because the majority of Canadian business is transacted by corporations, the emphasis in this book is on the corporate form of organization.

Users and Uses of Financial Information

The purpose of financial information is to provide data for decision-making. **Accounting** is the information system that identifies, records, and communicates the economic events of an organization to interested users. Many people have an interest in knowing about the ongoing activities of a business. These people are users of accounting information. Users can be divided broadly into two groups: internal users and external users.

INTERNAL USERS

Internal users of accounting information are managers who plan, organize, and run a business. These include **marketing managers**, **production supervisors**, **finance directors**, and **company officers**. In running a business, internal users must answer many important questions, as shown in Illustration 1-1.

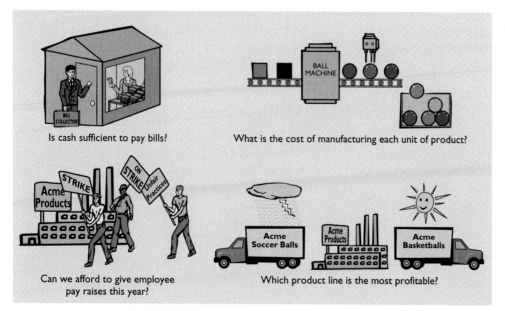

Is cash sufficient to pay bills?

What is the cost of manufacturing each unit of product?

Can we afford to give employee pay raises this year?

Which product line is the most profitable?

To answer these and other questions, users need detailed information on a timely basis. For internal users, accounting provides internal reports, such as financial comparisons of operating alternatives, projections of earnings from new sales campaigns, and forecasts of cash needs for the next year. In addition, summarized financial information is presented in financial statements.

EXTERNAL USERS

There are several types of **external users** of accounting information. **Investors** (shareholders) use accounting information to make decisions to buy, hold, or sell their shares. **Creditors**, such as suppliers and bankers, use accounting information to evaluate the risks of granting credit or lending money. Some questions that may be asked by investors and creditors about a company are shown in Illustration 1-2.

Illustration 1-2
Questions asked by external users

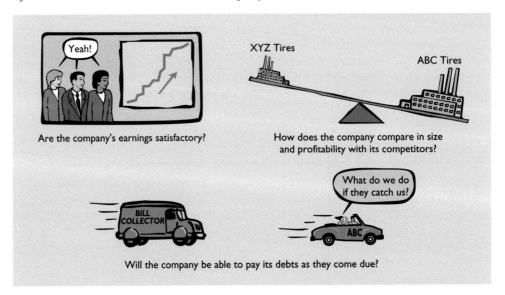

The information needs and questions of other external users vary considerably. **Taxing authorities**, such as the Canada Customs and Revenue Agency, want to know whether the company complies with the tax laws. **Regulatory agencies**, such as provincial securities commissions, want to know whether the company is operating within prescribed rules. **Customers** are interested in whether a company will continue to honour product warranties and support its product lines. **Labour unions** want to know whether the company has the ability to pay increased wages and benefits. **Economic planners** use accounting information to analyse and forecast economic activity.

ETHICS IN FINANCIAL REPORTING

Imagine trying to carry on a business or invest money if you could not depend on the financial statements being prepared honestly. Effective communication and economic activity would be impossible. Information would have no credibility. Effective financial reporting depends on sound ethical behaviour.

BUSINESS INSIGHT

ETHICS PERSPECTIVE

In 2002, the financial press was full of articles about financial scandals. It started with Enron, but then spread to Xerox, Qwest, Global Crossing, Adelphia, and WorldCom, among others. In each case, rogue executives inflated earnings or hid debt. This irrevocably tarred the integrity of all those involved—management, investment bankers, and auditors. It was "an accumulation of disasters in a world where, in the end, everything depends on trust." These articles provide the most compelling case in a generation for the importance of business ethics.

Source: "Trust Is Everything," *CAmagazine*, August 2002, 7.

Business Insights provide examples of accounting situations from various perspectives—ethics, investor, international, and management.

Ethics in Accounting

The **CD icon** informs you of additional resources available on the CD that came with your text.

Illustration 1-3
Steps used to analyse ethical dilemmas.

To sensitize you to ethical situations and to give you practice at solving ethical dilemmas, we address ethics in a number of ways in this book: (1) Several of the feature stories, as well as other parts of the text, discuss the central importance of ethical behaviour to financial reporting. (2) Business Insight boxes with an ethics perspective highlight ethics questions and issues in actual business situations. (3) In the end-of-chapter material, an ethics case asks you to put yourself in the position of a decision-maker in a particular business situation. In the process of analysing these various ethics cases and your own ethical experiences, you should apply the three steps outlined in Illustration 1-3.

Solving an Ethical Dilemma
1. **Recognize an ethical situation and the ethical issues involved.**
   Use your personal ethics or the organization's code of ethics to identify ethical situations and issues.
2. **Identify and analyse the principal elements in the situation.**
   Identify the *stakeholders*—persons or groups who may be harmed or benefited. Ask the question: What are the responsibilities and obligations of the parties involved?
3. **Identify the alternatives, and weigh the impact of each on various stakeholders.**
   Select the most ethical alternative, considering all the consequences. Sometimes there will be one right answer. Other situations involve more than one possible solution. These situations require evaluating each alternative and choosing the best one.

Business Activities

All businesses are involved in three types of activity—**financing**, **investing**, and **operating**. For example, Loblaw needed financing to purchase Provigo. To finance the acquisition, Loblaw sold common shares to investors and borrowed money from outside sources like banks. The cash obtained was then invested in the Provigo line of supermarkets. Once the acquisition was finalized, the new supermarkets helped increase Loblaw's operating activities of buying and selling food products.

The accounting information system keeps track of the results of each of the various business activities—financing, investing, and operating. Let's look at each type of business activity in more detail.

STUDY OBJECTIVE
3

Explain the three principal types of business activity.

FINANCING ACTIVITIES

It takes money to make money. The two primary ways of raising outside funds for corporations are borrowing money and issuing (selling) shares in exchange for cash.

Loblaw may borrow money in a variety of ways. It can take out a loan at a bank, borrow directly from investors by issuing debt securities called bonds, or borrow

Financing activities

money from its suppliers by purchasing goods on credit. The persons or entities to whom Loblaw owes money are its **creditors**. Amounts owed to creditors—in the form of debt and other obligations—are called liabilities.

Specific names are given to different types of liabilities, depending on their source. For instance, if Loblaw purchases produce on credit from suppliers, the obligations to pay for these supplies are called **accounts payable**. Additionally, Loblaw may have **interest payable** on the outstanding principal of a **note payable** to a bank for the money borrowed to purchase its display cabinets. It may also have **wages payable** to employees, **provincial sales taxes** and **property taxes payable** to the provincial government, and **goods and services taxes payable** to the federal government. **Income tax payable** is an example of another liability payable to the provincial and federal governments. Debt securities sold to investors that must be repaid at a particular date some years in the future are called **bonds payable**.

Alternative Terminology The word *issued* means *sold* and is commonly used when speaking of share transactions.

A corporation may also obtain funds by selling shares to investors. When Loblaw purchased Provigo for $1.8 billion, as mentioned in the feature story, Loblaw issued common shares to interested investors to help pay for this purchase. **Common shares** is the term used to describe the amount paid by investors for shares of ownership in a company. Common shares constitute just one class or type of shares that a company can issue.

The claims of creditors differ from those of shareholders. If you loan money to a company, you are one of its creditors. In loaning money, you specify a repayment schedule—for example, payment at the end of each month. In addition, interest is normally added to the amount due. As a creditor, you have a legal right to be paid at the agreed time. In the event of nonpayment, you may legally force the company to sell its property to pay its debts. The law requires that creditor claims be paid before shareholder claims.

Shareholders, then, have no claim to corporate resources until the claims of creditors are satisfied. If you buy a company's shares instead of loaning it money, you have no legal right to expect any payments until all of its creditors are paid. Also, once shares are issued, the company has no obligation to buy them back, whereas debt obligations must be repaid. Many companies pay shareholders a return on their investment on a regular basis, as long as there is sufficient cash to cover required payments to creditors. Payments to shareholders are called dividends.

INVESTING ACTIVITIES

Investing activities

After Loblaw raises money through financing activities, it then uses that money for investing activities. Investing activities involve the purchase of resources—called assets—that a company needs to operate. For example, cash, accounts receivable, office supplies, inventory, computers, delivery trucks, buildings, and land are all assets obtained from investing activities.

Different types of assets are given different names. A very important asset to Loblaw or any other business is **cash**. If Loblaw sells goods to a customer and does not receive cash immediately, then Loblaw has a right to expect payment from that customer in the future. This right to receive money in the future is called an **account receivable**. Goods available for future sales are assets called **inventory**. Longer-lived assets such as land, buildings, and other types of equipment are referred to as **property, plant, and equipment**.

OPERATING ACTIVITIES

Once a business has the assets it needs to get started, it can begin its operating activities. Loblaw is in the business of selling groceries and household products. We call the money from the sale of these products revenues. In accounting language, revenues are increases in economic resources—normally an increase in an asset but sometimes a decrease in a liability—resulting from a business's operating activities.

Revenues arise from different sources and are identified by various names, depending on the nature of the business. For instance, Loblaw's primary source of revenue is the money it earns from grocery sales to consumers. It also earns interest revenue on securities held as short-term investments. Sources of revenue common to many businesses are **sales revenue, service revenue**, and **interest revenue**.

Operating activities

Before Loblaw can sell any groceries, it must buy produce, meat, and other food items. It also incurs costs like salaries, utilities, and income taxes. All of these costs, referred to as expenses, are necessary to sell the product. In accounting language, expenses are the cost of assets consumed or services used in the process of generating revenues.

Expenses take many forms and are identified by various names, depending on the type of asset consumed or service used. For example, Loblaw keeps track of these types of expenses: **cost of sales**, **selling and administrative expenses** (such as cost of food products, wages of store employees, advertising costs, office supplies, utilities), **amortization expense** (allocation of the cost of using long-lived assets), **interest expense** (amounts of interest paid on various debts), and **income taxes** (corporate taxes paid to the provincial and federal governments).

To determine whether it earned a profit, Loblaw compares the revenues of a period with the expenses of that period. When revenues exceed expenses, net earnings result. When expenses exceed revenues, a net loss results.

Alternative Terminology *Amortization expense* is also called *depreciation expense*.

Alternative Terminology *Net earnings* are also commonly known as *net income*.

BEFORE YOU GO ON . . .

- **REVIEW IT**

1. What are the three forms of business organization and the advantages of each?
2. What are the two primary categories of users of financial information? Give examples of each.
3. Why are ethics a fundamental business concept?
4. What are the three types of business activity?

- **DO IT**

Classify each item first as a financing, investing, or operating activity and then as an asset, liability, share capital, revenue, or expense:

(a) Cost of using truck
(b) Amount earned from providing service
(c) Notes payable
(d) Issue of shares
(e) Truck purchased
(f) Amount owed to bank

Review It questions at the end of major text sections prompt you to stop and review the key points you have just studied. Sometimes Review It questions stand alone; other times they are accompanied by practice exercises, called Do It. The **Do It** exercises, like the one here, ask you to put newly acquired knowledge to work in some form of financial statement preparation. They outline the **Action Plan** to complete the exercise and show a **Solution**.

Action Plan
- Distinguish between financing, investing, and operating activities.
- Understand the distinction between assets, liabilities, share capital, revenues, and expenses.
- Classify each item based on its economic characteristics.

Solution
(a) Operating activity; expense
(b) Operating activity; revenue
(c) Financing activity; liability
(d) Financing activity; share capital
(e) Investing activity; asset
(f) Financing activity; liability

Communicating with Users

STUDY OBJECTIVE

4

Describe the content and purpose of each of the financial statements.

Assets, liabilities, equity, revenues, and expenses are of interest to users of accounting information. For reporting purposes, it is customary to arrange this information in the format of four different **financial statements** which form the backbone of financial accounting.

To present a picture of what your business owns (its assets), what it owes (its liabilities), and its net worth (its shareholders' equity) at a specific point in time, you would present a **balance sheet**. To show how successfully your business performed during a period of time, you would report its revenues and expenses in the **statement of earnings**. To indicate how much was distributed to you and the other shareholders of your business in the form of dividends, and how much was retained in the business to allow for future growth, you would present a **statement of retained earnings**. And finally, you would present a **cash flow statement** to show where your business obtained cash during a period of time and how that cash was used.

To introduce you to these statements, in the following sections we have prepared the financial statements for a fictitious marketing agency called Sierra Corporation.

STATEMENT OF EARNINGS

Alternative Terminology The *statement of earnings* is also commonly known as the *income statement.*

The statement of earnings reports the success or failure of the company's operations for a period of time. To indicate that Sierra's statement of earnings reports the results of operations for a **period of time**, the statement is dated "Month Ended October 31, 2004." The statement of earnings lists the company's revenues followed by its expenses. Expenses are deducted from revenues to determine earnings before income tax (commonly abbreviated as EBIT). Income tax expense is usually shown separately, immediately following earnings before income tax. Finally, the net earnings (or net loss) are determined by deducting income tax expense.

Why are financial statement users interested in net earnings? Investors are interested in a company's past earnings because they provide information which suggests future earnings. Investors buy and sell shares based on their beliefs about the future performance of a company. If you believe that Sierra will be even more successful in the future, and that this success will translate into a higher share price, you should buy Sierra's shares. Creditors also use the statement of earnings to predict the future. When a bank loans money to a company, it does so with the belief that it will be repaid in the future. If it didn't think it was going to be repaid, it wouldn't loan the money. Therefore, prior to making the loan, the bank loan officer must try to predict whether the company will be profitable enough to repay it.

Note that **the issue of shares and distribution of dividends do not affect net earnings.** For example, $10,000 of cash received from issuing new shares was not treated as revenue by Sierra Corporation. Dividends paid of $500 were not regarded as a business expense because they were not incurred to generate revenue. Sierra Corporation's statement of earnings is shown in Illustration 1-4.

SIERRA CORPORATION
Statement of Earnings
Month Ended October 31, 2004

Revenues		
Service revenue		$10,600
Expenses		
Salaries expense	$5,200	
Supplies expense	1,500	
Rent expense	900	
Insurance expense	50	
Interest expense	50	
Amortization expense	40	
Total expense		7,740
Earnings before income tax		2,860
Income tax expense		600
Net earnings		$ 2,260

Illustration 1-4
Statement of earnings

Helpful Hint The heading of every statement identifies the company, the type of statement, and the time period covered by the statement. Sometimes another line is added to indicate the unit of measure. When it is used, this fourth line usually indicates that the data are presented in thousands or in millions.

Every chapter presents useful information about how decision-makers use financial statements. **Decision Toolkits** summarize discussions of key decision-making contexts and techniques.

Decision Toolkit

DECISION CHECKPOINTS	INFO NEEDED FOR DECISION	TOOL TO USE FOR DECISION	HOW TO EVALUATE RESULTS
Are the company's operations profitable?	Statement of earnings	The statement of earnings indicates the success or failure of the company's operating activities by reporting its revenues and expenses.	If the company's revenue exceeds its expenses, it will report net earnings; otherwise it will report a net loss.

STATEMENT OF RETAINED EARNINGS

If Sierra is profitable, at the end of each period it must decide what portion of earnings to pay to shareholders in dividends. In theory it could pay all of its current period earnings, but few companies choose to do this. Why? Because they want to retain part of the earnings or profits in the business to allow for further expansion. High-growth companies, for example, often choose to pay no dividends. Retained earnings are the cumulative earnings that have been retained in the corporation (that is, not paid out to shareholders).

The statement of retained earnings shows the amounts and causes of changes in retained earnings during the period. The time period is the same as that covered by the statement of earnings. The beginning retained earnings amount is shown on the first line of the statement. Then net earnings are added and dividends are deducted to calculate the retained earnings at the end of the period. If a company has a net loss, it is deducted (rather than added) in the statement of retained earnings.

By monitoring the statement of retained earnings, financial statement users can evaluate dividend payment practices. Some investors seek companies that pay high dividends. Other investors seek companies that don't pay dividends and instead reinvest earnings to increase the company's growth. Lenders monitor dividend payments because any money paid in dividends reduces a company's ability to repay its debts. Illustration 1-5 presents Sierra Corporation's statement of retained earnings.

Illustration 1-5
Statement of retained
earnings

SIERRA CORPORATION	
Statement of Retained Earnings	
Month Ended October 31, 2004	
Retained earnings, October 1	$ 0
Add: Net earnings	2,260
	2,260
Less: Dividends	500
Retained earnings, October 31	$1,760

Decision Toolkit

DECISION CHECKPOINTS	INFO NEEDED FOR DECISION	TOOL TO USE FOR DECISION	HOW TO EVALUATE RESULTS
What is the company's policy concerning dividends and growth?	Statement of retained earnings	How much did the company pay out in dividends to shareholders?	A company striving for rapid growth will pay no, or a low, dividend.

BALANCE SHEET

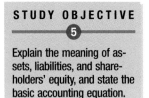

STUDY OBJECTIVE

5

Explain the meaning of assets, liabilities, and shareholders' equity, and state the basic accounting equation.

The balance sheet reports assets and claims to those assets at a specific point in time. These claims are subdivided into two categories: claims of creditors and claims of shareholders. As noted earlier, claims of creditors are called liabilities. Claims of shareholders, the owners of the company, are called shareholders' equity. This relationship is shown in equation form in Illustration 1-6. This equation is referred to as the basic accounting equation.

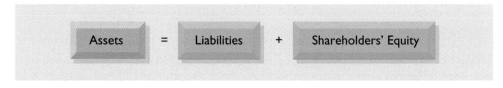

Illustration 1-6
Basic accounting
equation

This relationship is where the name *balance sheet* comes from. Assets must be in balance with the claims to the assets. The right-hand side of the equation—the liabilities and equities—shows how the assets have been financed (borrowing from creditors, investing by shareholders, or self-financing through earnings retained in the company).

As you can see from looking at Sierra's balance sheet in Illustration 1-7, assets are listed first, followed by liabilities and shareholders' equity. Shareholders' equity consists of two parts: (1) share capital and (2) retained earnings. Share capital represents the shareholders' investments and includes all the classes of shares that a company has issued. If only one class of shares is issued, it is always common shares. Retained earnings are the cumulative net earnings retained in the corporation. Sierra has common shares of $10,000 and retained earnings of $1,760, for total shareholders' equity of $11,760.

Creditors analyse a company's balance sheet to determine the likelihood that they will be repaid. They carefully evaluate the nature of the company's assets and liabilities. For example, does the company have assets that could easily be sold to repay its debts? Managers use the balance sheet to determine whether inventory is adequate to support future sales and whether cash on hand is sufficient for immediate cash needs. Managers also look at the relationship between debt and shareholders' equity to determine whether they have the best proportion of debt and equity financing. Illustration 1-7 presents Sierra Corporation's balance sheet.

SIERRA CORPORATION **Balance Sheet** **October 31, 2004**	
Assets	
Cash	$15,200
Accounts receivable	200
Advertising supplies	1,000
Prepaid insurance	550
Office equipment	4,960
Total assets	$21,910
Liabilities and Shareholders' Equity	
Liabilities	
Notes payable	$ 5,000
Accounts payable	2,500
Interest payable	50
Unearned revenue	800
Salaries payable	1,200
Income tax payable	600
Total liabilities	10,150
Shareholders' equity	
Common shares	10,000
Retained earnings	1,760
Total shareholders' equity	11,760
Total liabilities and shareholders' equity	$21,910

Helpful Hint The balance sheet is dated at a *specific point in time*. The statement of earnings, statement of retained earnings, and cash flow statement cover a *period of time*.

Decision Toolkit

DECISION CHECKPOINTS	INFO NEEDED FOR DECISION	TOOL TO USE FOR DECISION	HOW TO EVALUATE RESULTS
Does the company rely primarily on debt or equity to finance its assets?	Balance sheet	The balance sheet reports the company's resources and claims to those resources. There are two types of claims: liabilities and shareholders' equity.	Compare the amount of liabilities versus the amount of shareholders' equity to determine whether the company relies more on creditors or shareholders for its financing.

CASH FLOW STATEMENT

The primary function of a cash flow statement is to provide financial information about the cash receipts and cash payments of a business for a specific period of time. To help investors, creditors, and others in their analysis of a company's cash position, the cash flow statement reports the cash effects of a company's (1) operating activities, (2) investing activities, and (3) financing activities. In addition, the statement shows the net increase or decrease in cash during the period, and the cash amount at the end of the period.

Users are interested in the cash flow statement because they want to know what is happening to a company's most important resource. The cash flow statement provides answers to these simple but important questions:

- Where did cash come from during the period?
- How was cash used during the period?
- What was the change in the cash balance during the period?

The cash flow statement for Sierra, in Illustration 1-8, shows that cash increased by $15,200 during the month. This increase resulted because operating activities (services to clients) increased cash by $5,700, and financing activities increased cash by $14,500. Investing activities used $5,000 of cash for the purchase of office equipment.

Illustration 1-8
Cash flow statement

SIERRA CORPORATION Cash Flow Statement Month Ended October 31, 2004		
Operating activities		
Cash receipts from operating activities	$11,200	
Cash payments for operating activities	(5,500)	
Cash provided by operating activities		$ 5,700
Investing activities		
Purchase of office equipment	$(5,000)	
Cash used by investing activities		(5,000)
Financing activities		
Issue of common shares	$10,000	
Issue of note payable	5,000	
Payment of dividend	(500)	
Cash provided by financing activities		14,500
Net increase in cash		15,200
Cash, October 1		0
Cash, October 31		$15,200

Decision Toolkit

DECISION CHECKPOINTS	INFO NEEDED FOR DECISION	TOOL TO USE FOR DECISION	HOW TO EVALUATE RESULTS
Does the company generate sufficient cash from operating activities to fund its investing activities?	Cash flow statement	The cash flow statement shows the amount of cash provided or used by operating activities, investing activities, and financing activities.	Compare the amount of cash provided by operating activities with the amount of cash used by investing activities. Any deficiency in cash from operating activities must be made up with cash provided by financing activities.

INTERRELATIONSHIPS OF STATEMENTS

Because the results on some statements are used as data for other statements, the statements are said to be interrelated:

1. The statement of retained earnings is dependent on the results of the statement of earnings. Sierra reported net earnings of $2,260 for the period. This amount is added to the beginning amount of retained earnings as part of the process of determining ending retained earnings.

2. The balance sheet and statement of retained earnings are interrelated because the ending amount of $1,760 on the statement of retained earnings is reported as the retained earnings amount on the balance sheet.
3. The cash flow statement and the balance sheet are also interrelated. The cash flow statement shows how the cash account changed during the period by stating the amount of cash at the beginning of the period, the sources and uses of cash during the period, and the amount of cash at the end of the period, $15,200. The ending amount of cash shown on the cash flow statement must agree with the amount of cash on the balance sheet.

Study these interrelationships carefully. To prepare financial statements, you must understand the sequence in which these amounts are determined and how each statement affects the next. Because each financial statement depends on information contained in another, financial statements must be prepared in a certain order: (1) statement of earnings; (2) statement of retained earnings; (3) balance sheet; and (4) cash flow statement.

BEFORE YOU GO ON . . .

● REVIEW IT

1. What questions might each of the following decision-makers ask that could be answered by financial information: bank loan officer, investor, labour union, and government?
2. What are the content and purpose of each statement: statement of earnings, balance sheet, statement of retained earnings, and cash flow statement?
3. The basic accounting equation is: Assets = Liabilities + Shareholders' Equity. Replacing words with dollar amounts, what is Loblaw's accounting equation as at December 28, 2002? The answer to this question is at the end of this chapter.

Review It questions marked with this Loblaw icon require you to use Loblaw's financial statements in Appendix A at the end of this book.

● DO IT

CSU Corporation began operations on January 1, 2004. The following information is available for CSU Corporation on December 31, 2004: Service Revenue $22,200; Accounts Receivable $4,000; Accounts Payable $2,000; Building Rental Expense $9,000; Notes Payable $5,000; Common Shares $10,000; Equipment $16,000; Insurance Expense $1,000; Supplies $1,800; Supplies Expense $200; Cash $1,400; Income Tax Expense $5,200; and Dividends $600. Using this information, prepare a statement of earnings, statement of retained earnings, balance sheet, and cash flow statement for the year. Assume all transactions (other than the accounts receivable and accounts payable) were cash transactions.

Action Plan

- Classify each account as an asset, liability, shareholders' equity, revenue, or expense item.
- Report revenues and expenses for the period in the statement of earnings.
- Show the amounts and causes (net earnings and dividends) of the changes in retained earnings for the period in the statement of retained earnings.
- Present assets and claims to those assets (liabilities and shareholders' equity) at a specific point in time in the balance sheet.
- Show the changes in cash for the period, classified as an operating, investing, or financing activity in the cash flow statement.

Solution

CSU CORPORATION
Statement of Earnings
Year Ended December 31, 2004

Revenues		
Service revenue		$22,200
Expenses		
Rent expense	$9,000	
Insurance expense	1,000	
Supplies expense	200	
Total expenses		10,200
Earnings before income tax		12,000
Income tax expense		5,200
Net earnings		$ 6,800

CSU CORPORATION
Statement of Retained Earnings
Year Ended December 31, 2004

Retained earnings, January 1	$ 0
Add: Net earnings	6,800
	6,800
Less: Dividends	600
Retained earnings, December 31	$6,200

❶

CSU CORPORATION
Balance Sheet
December 31, 2004

Assets	
Cash	$ 1,400
Accounts receivable	4,000
Supplies	1,800
Equipment	16,000
Total assets	$23,200

Liabilities and Shareholders' Equity		
Liabilities		
Notes payable	$ 5,000	
Accounts payable	2,000	
Total liabilities		7,000
Shareholders' equity		
Common shares		10,000
Retained earnings		6,200
Total shareholders' equity		16,200
Total liabilities and shareholders' equity		$23,200

❷

Helpful Hint The arrows in this illustration show the inter-relationships of the four financial statements.

CSU CORPORATION
Cash Flow Statement
Year Ended December 31, 2004

Operating activities		
Cash receipts from operating activities	$ 18,200 ¹	
Cash payments for operating activities	(15,200)²	
Cash provided by operating activities		$ 3,000
Investing activities		
Purchase of equipment	$(16,000)	
Cash used by investing activities		(16,000)
Financing activities		
Issue of notes payable	$ 5,000	
Issue of common shares	10,000	
Payment of dividends	(600)	
Cash provided by financing activities		14,400
Net increase in cash		1,400
Cash, January 1		0
Cash, December 31		$ 1,400

❸

¹ $22,200 − $4,000 = $18,200
² $9,000 + $1,000 + $200 + $5,200 + $1,800 − $2,000 = $15,200

NAVIGATOR

A Quick Look at Loblaw's Financial Statements

The same relationships that you observed among the financial statements of Sierra Corporation are evident in the 2002 simplified financial statements of Loblaw Companies Limited, which are presented in Illustrations 1-9 through 1-12. Loblaw's actual financial statements are presented in Appendix A at the end of the book. We have simplified the financial statements to assist your learning—but they may look complicated to you anyway. Do not be alarmed by their seeming complexity. By the end of the book, you'll have a great deal of experience in reading and understanding financial statements such as these.

Before examining them, we need to explain three points:

1. Note that numbers are reported in millions of dollars on Loblaw's financial statements—that is, the last six zeros (000,000) are omitted. Thus, Loblaw's net earnings in 2002 are $728,000,000 not $728.
2. Loblaw, like most companies, presents its financial statements for more than one year. Financial statements that report information for more than one period are called comparative statements. Comparative statements allow users to compare the financial position of a business at the end of one accounting period to that of previous periods.
3. An accounting time period that is one year in length is referred to as a fiscal year. Loblaw's fiscal year end is the Saturday nearest the end of the calendar year. Consequently, its year end does not fall on the same date each year. For example, its fiscal year end was December 29 in 2001.

BUSINESS INSIGHT

MANAGEMENT PERSPECTIVE

About 70% of Canadian companies use December 31 for their year end. Why doesn't every company use December 31 as its accounting year end? Many companies choose to end their accounting year when the inventory or operations are at a low. This is advantageous because compiling accounting information requires much time and effort by managers. They would rather do it when they aren't too busy operating the business. Also, inventory is easier and less costly to count when it is low. Some companies whose year ends differ from December 31 are Sears (last Saturday in December), Molson's (March 31), Intrawest (June 30), and Salter Street Films (October 31). Most universities and governments use March 31 for their fiscal year end.

STATEMENT OF EARNINGS

A simplified version of Loblaw's statement of earnings is presented in Illustration 1-9. Sierra is a service company: it provides services to earn its revenue. Loblaw sells a product: its primary source of revenue is called sales. For 2002, Loblaw reports sales of $23,082 million. It then subtracts a variety of expenses related to operating the business. These operating expenses include the cost of sales, selling and administrative expenses, and amortization expense. It also deducts interest expense (payment of interest on debt) of $161 million to arrive at earnings before income taxes of $1,142 million. After subtracting income tax expense of $414 million, the company reports net earnings for the period of $728 million. Net earnings represent a 29% increase over the results of the previous year.

Illustration 1-9
Loblaw statement of
earnings

Financial statements of real
companies are accompanied
by a company logo.

LOBLAW COMPANIES LIMITED Statement of Earnings Year Ended December 28, 2002 (in millions)		
	2002	2001
Revenues		
Sales	$23,082	$21,486
Expenses		
Cost of sales, selling and administrative expenses	21,425	20,035
Amortization expense	354	315
Interest expense	161	158
Total expenses	21,940	20,508
Earnings before income taxes	1,142	978
Income tax expense	414	372
Earnings before goodwill	728	606
Goodwill charges, net of tax		43
Net earnings	$ 728	$ 563

STATEMENT OF RETAINED EARNINGS

Loblaw presents information about its retained earnings in the statement of retained earnings in Illustration 1-10. Unlike Loblaw, some companies use a single statement to present their earnings and retained earnings. Find the line "Retained earnings, beginning of year," in Illustration 1-10 and you will see that
retained earnings at the beginning of 2002 were $2,375 million. Note that this
amount agrees with the end-of-year balance for 2001. The next figure for 2002
is net earnings of $728 million. Loblaw paid $133 million in dividends to its
shareholders. The 2002 ending balance of retained earnings, after adjustment
for other items (which we will learn about in a later chapter), is $2,929 million.
Find this amount of retained earnings near the bottom of Loblaw's 2002 balance
sheet, presented in Illustration 1-11.

Illustration 1-10
Loblaw statement of
retained earnings

LOBLAW COMPANIES LIMITED Statement of Retained Earnings Year Ended December 28, 2002 (in millions)		
	2002	2001
Retained earnings, beginning of year	$2,375	$1,930
Add: Net earnings	728	563
	3,103	2,493
Less: Other adjustments	41	8
Dividends	133	110
Retained earnings, end of year	$2,929	$2,375

BALANCE SHEET

Alternative Terminology
Fixed assets is another term for
property, plant, and equipment.

As shown in Loblaw's balance sheet in Illustration 1-11, Loblaw's assets include
the types of assets mentioned in our discussion of Sierra Corporation, such as
cash, accounts receivable, inventories, and fixed assets, plus other types of assets that we will discuss in later chapters, such as goodwill and prepaid expenses.

Similarly, its liabilities include notes payable, accounts payable, and income taxes payable, as well as items not yet discussed, such as accrued liabilities. Loblaw's balance sheet shows that total assets increased from $10,025 million on December 29, 2001, to $11,110 million on December 28, 2002.

You can see that Loblaw relies more on debt financing than equity—it has nearly 70% more total liabilities than it has shareholders' equity. As you learn more about financial statements, we will discuss how to interpret the relationships and changes in financial statement items.

Illustration 1-11
Loblaw balance sheet

LOBLAW COMPANIES LIMITED **Balance Sheet** **December 28, 2002** **(in millions)**		
	2002	2001
Assets		
Cash and cash equivalents	$ 823	$ 575
Short-term investments	304	426
Accounts receivable	605	472
Inventories	1,702	1,512
Prepaid expenses and other assets	92	101
Fixed assets	5,587	4,931
Goodwill	1,599	1,599
Other assets	398	409
Total assets	$11,110	$10,025
Liabilities and Shareholders' Equity		
Liabilities		
Bank indebtedness		$ 95
Notes payable	$ 533	191
Accounts payable and accrued liabilities	2,336	2,291
Income taxes payable	179	138
Long-term debt	3,526	3,414
Other liabilities	412	327
Total liabilities	6,986	6,456
Shareholders' equity		
Common shares	1,195	1,194
Retained earnings	2,929	2,375
Total shareholders' equity	4,124	3,569
Total liabilities and shareholders' equity	$11,110	$10,025

CASH FLOW STATEMENT

Loblaw's cash and cash equivalents increased by $248 million from 2001 to 2002. The reasons for this increase can be determined by examining the cash flow statement in Illustration 1-12. This statement presents Loblaw's sources and uses of cash during the period.

Loblaw is in an expansion mode. Consequently, it spent considerable cash, $978 million, on investing activities. For example, it spent $1,079 million on new fixed assets in order to expand. Note that the cash provided by operating activities, $981 million, was sufficient to finance a significant portion of this expansion. The remainder of its expansion was financed by borrowing and issuing shares. An examination of the $245 million cash provided by financing activities shows that Loblaw received $542 million from debt financing and $2 million from equity financing.

Proceeds from this financing were used to repay some of its other debt and retire shares. In addition, Loblaw paid dividends to its shareholders. The net result of the sources and uses of cash during the year was a cash increase of $248 million.

Illustration 1-12
Loblaw cash flow statement

LOBLAW COMPANIES LIMITED Cash Flow Statement Year Ended December 28, 2002 (in millions)		
	2002	2001
Operating activities		
Cash receipts from operating activities	$22,949	$21,395
Cash payments for operating activities	(21,968)	(20,577)
Cash provided by operating activities	981	818
Investing activities		
Purchases of fixed assets	(1,079)	(1,108)
Proceeds from fixed asset sales	63	44
Purchase of investments	15	(62)
Other	23	(155)
Cash used by investing activities	(978)	(1,281)
Financing activities		
Issue of debt	542	1,040
Payment of debt	(172)	(596)
Issue of common shares	2	
Retirement of common shares	(17)	(1)
Payment of dividends	(127)	(110)
Other	17	19
Cash provided by financing activities	245	352
Increase (decrease) in cash and cash equivalents	248	(111)
Cash and cash equivalents, beginning of year	575	686
Cash and cash equivalents, end of year	$ 823	$ 575

OTHER ELEMENTS OF AN ANNUAL REPORT

Annual
Report
Walkthrough

Publicly traded companies must provide their shareholders with an annual report each year. The annual report is a document that includes useful nonfinancial information about the company, as well as financial information. Nonfinancial information may include the company's mission, goals and objectives, products, and people. Financial information may include a management discussion and analysis, a statement of management responsibility for the financial statements, an auditors' report, the comparative financial statements introduced in this chapter, notes to the financial statements, and a historical summary of key financial ratios and indicators. No analysis of a company's financial situation and prospects is complete without a review of each of these items.

The elements of Loblaw's annual report are reviewed in detail on the Toolkit CD accompanying this text.

Concern over the quality and integrity of financial reporting isn't limited to North America. Recently, the Chinese Ministry of Finance reprimanded a large accounting firm for preparing fraudulent financial reports for a number of publicly traded companies. Afterward, the state-run news agency noted that investors and analysts actually felt that the punishment of the firm was not adequate. In fact, a survey of investors in China found that less than 10% had full confidence in companies' annual reports. As a result of these concerns, the Chinese Institute of Certified Public Accountants vowed to strengthen its policing of its members.

Assumptions and Principles in Financial Reporting

The preparation of financial statements relies on some key assumptions and principles. It is helpful to look at some of these now that we have begun to see how accounting can be used to convey financial information to decision-makers. These assumptions and principles underlie all financial reporting and will be referred to throughout the book.

STUDY OBJECTIVE
6

Explain the basic assumptions and principles underlying financial statements.

ASSUMPTIONS

Monetary Unit Assumption

We begin with the assumptions. In looking at Loblaw's financial statements, you will notice that everything is stated in terms of dollars. The monetary unit assumption requires that only those things that can be expressed in money be included in the accounting records. This might seem so obvious that it doesn't bear mentioning, but it has important implications for financial reporting. Because the exchange of money is fundamental to business transactions, it makes sense that we measure a business in terms of money. However, it also means that certain important information needed by investors and creditors is not reported in the financial statements. For example, customer satisfaction is important to every business, but it is not easily quantified in dollar terms; thus it is not reported in the financial statements.

Economic Entity Assumption

The economic entity assumption states that every economic entity must be separately identified and accounted for. For example, suppose you are a shareholder in Loblaw. The amount of cash you have in your personal bank account and the balance owed on your personal car loan are not reported in Loblaw's balance sheet. The reason is that, for accounting purposes, you and Loblaw are separate accounting entities. In order to accurately assess Loblaw's performance and financial position, it is important to distinguish its activities from personal transactions, or the transactions of any other company, such as George Weston Limited.

Time Period Assumption

Next, notice that Loblaw's statement of earnings, statement of retained earnings, and cash flow statement all cover periods of one year, and that the balance sheet is prepared at the end of each year. The time period assumption states that the life of a business can be divided into artificial time periods and that useful reports covering those periods can be prepared for the business. All companies report at least annually. Publicly traded companies also report to shareholders every three months (quarterly) and prepare monthly statements for internal purposes.

Going Concern Assumption

The going concern assumption states that the business will remain in operation for the foreseeable future. Of course businesses do fail, but in general, it is reasonable to assume that the business will continue operating. The going concern assumption underlies much of what we do in accounting. To give you just one example, if going concern is not assumed, assets should be stated at their liquidation value (selling price less cost of disposal), not at their cost. Only when liquidation of the business appears likely is the going concern assumption inappropriate.

Illustration 1-13
Accounting assumptions

These four accounting assumptions are shown in Illustration 1-13.

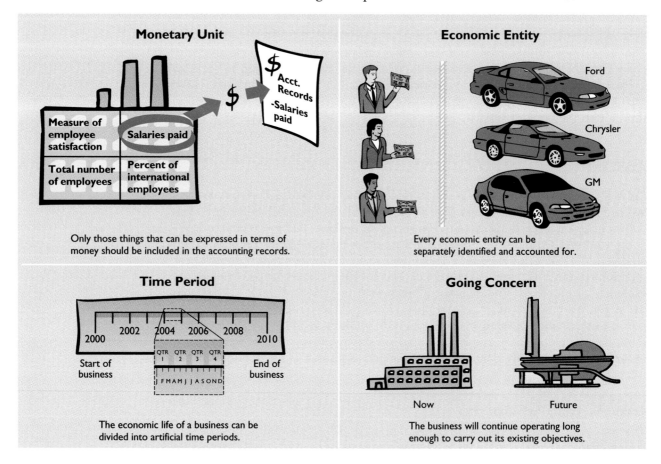

PRINCIPLES

Cost Principle

All of the assets on Loblaw's financial statements are recorded at the amount paid for them. The cost principle dictates that assets be recorded at their cost. This is true not only at the time the asset is purchased, but also over the time the asset is held. For example, if Loblaw were to purchase land for $30 million, it would initially be reported on the balance sheet at $30 million. But what would Loblaw do if by the end of the next year the land had increased in value to $40 million?

The answer is that under the cost principle the land would continue to be reported at $30 million. The land will continue to be reported at cost until either it is sold or the going concern assumption is no longer valid.

The cost principle is often criticized as being irrelevant. Critics contend that market value would be more useful to financial decision-makers. Proponents of the cost principle counter that cost is the best measure because it can be easily verified, while market value is more subjective.

Full Disclosure Principle

Some important financial information is not easily reported in the financial statements. For example, Loblaw has debt outstanding. Investors and creditors would like to know the terms of the debt: that is, when does it mature, what is its interest rate, and is it renewable? Or a customer might be suing Loblaw without investors and creditors knowing about it. The full disclosure principle requires that all circumstances and events which would make a difference to financial statement users be disclosed. If an important item cannot reasonably be reported directly in one of the four types of financial statements, then it should be discussed in the notes that accompany the statements.

Some investors who lost money in Enron and other companies complained that the lack of full disclosure regarding some of the companies' transactions caused the financial statements to be misleading. Consequently, the Canadian Institute of Chartered Accountants and professional accounting bodies in other countries are now working to improve the quality and extent of disclosure.

The cost and full disclosure principles are shown in Illustration 1-14. Other accounting principles will be introduced in later chapters.

Cost

Assets should be recorded at cost.

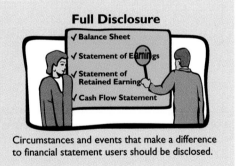
Full Disclosure

√ Balance Sheet
√ Statement of Earnings
√ Statement of Retained Earning
√ Cash Flow Statement

Circumstances and events that make a difference to financial statement users should be disclosed.

Illustration 1-14
Accounting principles

BEFORE YOU GO ON . . .

● **REVIEW IT**

1. What financial information, in addition to the financial statements, might you expect to find in an annual report?
2. Describe the monetary unit, time period, economic entity, and going concern assumptions.
3. Describe the cost and full disclosure principles.

NAVIGATOR

Using the Decision Toolkit

Sobeys Inc. is Canada's second largest grocery chain, after Loblaw. Imagine that you are considering purchasing some of Sobeys' common shares.

Instructions

Answer these questions related to your decision about whether to invest:
1. What financial statements should you request from the company?
2. What should each of these financial statements tell you?
3. Loblaw has a fiscal year end of December 28, 2002. Sobeys' fiscal year end is May 3, 2003. Is it possible to compare financial statements of these companies since they have different fiscal year ends?
4. Will the financial statements show the market value of Sobeys' assets? Explain.
5. Simplified financial statements for Sobeys Inc. are shown below. What comparisons can you make between Sobeys and Loblaw in terms of their respective financial positions and results of operations?

	2003	2002
SOBEYS INC. Statement of Earnings Year Ended May 3, 2003 (in millions)		
Revenues		
Sales	$10,414.5	$9,732.5
Expenses		
Cost of sales, selling and administrative expenses	9,964.4	9,334.9
Amortization expense	124.0	101.0
Interest expense	41.7	57.0
Other expenses		19.4
Total expenses	10,130.1	9,512.3
Earnings before income taxes	284.4	220.2
Income tax expense	105.4	88.9
Earnings before goodwill and discontinued operations	179.0	131.3
Goodwill charges, net of tax		(15.4)
Discontinued operations, net of tax		94.7
Net earnings	$ 179.0	$ 210.6

SOBEYS INC.
Statement of Retained Earnings
Year Ended May 3, 2003
(in millions)

	2003	2002
Balance, beginning of year	$382.0	$192.5
Add: Net earnings	179.0	210.6
	561.0	403.1
Less: Dividends	23.8	15.8
Other adjustments	3.8	5.3
Balance, end of year	$533.4	$382.0

SOBEYS INC.
Balance Sheet
May 3, 2003
(in millions)

	2003	2002
Assets		
Cash and cash equivalents	$ 123.1	$ 196.7
Short-term investments	191.4	77.7
Receivables	435.4	427.8
Inventories	444.0	394.6
Prepaid expenses	30.5	30.4
Property and equipment	1,243.9	1,072.1
Goodwill	555.6	553.1
Other assets	168.6	122.8
Total assets	$3,192.5	$2,875.2
Liabilities and Shareholders' Equity		
Liabilities		
Accounts payable and accrued liabilities	$ 971.9	$ 922.9
Income taxes payable	37.4	18.8
Long-term debt	585.4	523.6
Other liabilities	161.0	126.6
Total liabilities	1,775.7	1,591.9
Shareholders' equity		
Common shares	903.4	901.3
Retained earnings	533.4	382.0
Total shareholders' equity	1,436.8	1,283.3
Total liabilities and shareholders' equity	$3,192.5	$2,875.2

SOBEYS INC. Cash Flow Statement Year Ended May 3, 2003 (in millions)		
	2003	2002
Operating activities		
Cash receipts from operating activities	$10,380.1	$9,729.7
Cash payments for operating activities	(10,032.0)	(9,235.0)
Cash provided by operating activities	348.1	494.7
Investing activities		
Purchase of property and equipment	(342.3)	(424.2)
Proceeds from property and equipment sales	48.0	49.1
Sale (purchase) of investments	(9.8)	17.1
Acquisition of businesses	(2.5)	(3.6)
Other	(41.6)	(31.2)
Cash used by investing activities	(348.2)	(392.8)
Financing activities		
Issue of debt	118.6	14.1
Repayment of debt	(56.8)	(322.5)
Issue of common shares	6.7	8.6
Retirement of common shares	(5.9)	(8.4)
Payment of dividends	(23.8)	(15.8)
Other	(2.5)	(0.3)
Cash used by financing activities	36.3	(324.3)
Increase in cash from continuing operations	36.2	(222.4)
Discontinued operations	3.9	412.7
Increase in cash	40.1	190.3
Cash, beginning of year	274.4	84.1
Cash, end of year	$ 314.5	$ 274.4

Note: Cash is defined as cash and cash equivalents and short-term investments.

Solution

1. Before you invest, you should investigate the statement of earnings, statement of retained earnings, cash flow statement, balance sheet, and the accompanying notes.
2. You would probably be most interested in the statement of earnings because it shows past performance and thus gives an indication of future performance. The statement of retained earnings shows the impact current earnings and dividends have on the company's retained earnings. The cash flow statement reveals where the company is getting and spending its cash. This is especially important for a company that wants to grow. Finally, the balance sheet reveals the financial position of the company and the relationship between assets, liabilities, and shareholders' equity.
3. Both financial statements cover a one-year period, with Loblaw's fiscal year overlapping Sobeys' for eight months (May through December 2002). If there have been no substantial changes during the four-month period that Loblaw's financial results cover but Sobeys' do not, it really doesn't matter when each company's fiscal year ends. It is more important that we compare what each company was able to achieve within an equivalent period of time—whether it be one year, six months, or one quarter.

   If, however, a substantial change does occur in the intervening period, such a change would likely reduce the usefulness of a comparison of the financial statements of the two companies. Say, for example, that the Canadian economy changed dramatically during the non-overlapping period. The impact of this change would be reflected in Sobeys' current statements, but not in Loblaw's until the following fiscal year. It is important for users to be aware of relevant nonfinancial information such as this before they start their comparisons.

4. The financial statements will not show the market value of the company. The cost principle states that assets should be recorded at cost. Cost has an important advantage over other valuations: it is objective and reliable.

5. Many interesting comparisons can be made between the two companies. Sobeys is much smaller, about one third the size of Loblaw. For example, Sobeys has total assets of $3,192.5 million versus $11,110 million for Loblaw. Also, Sobeys has lower revenue—sales of $10,414.5 million versus $23,082 million. Sobeys reported net earnings for its current fiscal year of $179 million, compared to Loblaw's net earnings of $728 million.

Sobeys has a balance of $533.4 million of accumulated retained earnings, while Loblaw's retained earnings of $2,929 million are more than 5 times this amount. In 2002, Loblaw generated cash from operating activities of $981 million versus $348.1 million for Sobeys. While these comparisons are useful, these basic measures are not enough to determine whether one company will be a better investment than the other. In later chapters, you will acquire more tools to help you compare the relative profitability and financial health of these, and other, companies.

Summary of Study Objectives

1 *Describe the primary forms of business organization.* A proprietorship is a business owned by one person. A partnership is a business owned by two or more people. A corporation is a separate legal entity whose shares provide evidence of ownership.

2 *Identify the users and uses of accounting.* Internal users work for the business and need accounting information to plan, organize, and run operations. The primary external users are investors and creditors. Investors (present and future shareholders) use accounting information to help decide whether to buy, hold, or sell shares. Creditors (suppliers and bankers) use accounting information to assess the risk of granting credit or loaning money to a business.

3 *Explain the three principal types of business activity.* Financing activities involve collecting the necessary funds (through debt or equity) to support the business. Investing activities involve acquiring the resources (capital assets) necessary to run the business. Operating activities involve putting the resources of the business into action to generate a profit.

4 *Describe the content and purpose of each of the financial statements.* A statement of earnings presents the revenues and expenses of a company for a specific period of time. A statement of retained earnings summarizes the changes in retained earnings that have occurred for a specific period of time. Retained earnings are the cumulative earnings (less losses) over the company's life, less any dividends paid to shareholders. A balance sheet reports the assets, liabilities, and shareholders' equity of a business

at a specific date. A cash flow statement summarizes information concerning the cash inflows (receipts) and outflows (payments) for a specific period of time.

5 *Explain the meaning of assets, liabilities, and shareholders' equity, and state the basic accounting equation.* Assets are resources owned by a business. Liabilities are the debts and obligations of the business. Liabilities represent creditors' claims on the assets of the business. Shareholders' equity represents the claims of shareholders on the assets of the business. It is composed of two parts: share capital and retained earnings. The basic accounting equation is: Assets = Liabilities + Shareholders' Equity.

6 *Explain the basic assumptions and principles underlying financial statements.* The monetary unit assumption requires that only transaction data capable of being expressed in terms of money be included in the accounting records of the economic entity. The economic entity assumption states that economic events should be identified with a particular unit of accountability. The time period assumption states that the economic life of a business can be divided into artificial time periods and that meaningful accounting reports can be prepared for each period. The going concern assumption states that the business will continue operating long enough to carry out its existing objectives. The cost principle states that assets should be recorded at their cost. The full disclosure principle states that circumstances and events which matter to financial statement users should be disclosed.

Decision Toolkit—A Summary

Decision
Toolkit
Summary

DECISION CHECKPOINTS	INFO NEEDED FOR DECISION	TOOL TO USE FOR DECISION	HOW TO EVALUATE RESULTS
Are the company's operations profitable?	Statement of earnings	The statement of earnings indicates the success or failure of the company's operating activities by reporting its revenues and expenses.	If the company's revenue exceeds its expenses, it will report net earnings; otherwise it will report a net loss.
What is the company's policy concerning dividends and growth?	Statement of retained earnings	How much did the company pay out in dividends to shareholders?	A company striving for rapid growth will pay no, or a low, dividend.
Does the company rely primarily on debt or equity to finance its assets?	Balance sheet	The balance sheet reports the company's resources and claims to those resources. There are two types of claims: liabilities and shareholders' equity.	Compare the amount of liabilities versus the amount of shareholders' equity to determine whether the company relies more on creditors or shareholders for its financing.
Does the company generate sufficient cash from operating activities to fund its investing activities?	Cash flow statement	The cash flow statement shows the amount of cash provided or used by operating activities, investing activities, and financing activities.	Compare the amount of cash provided by operating activities with the amount of cash used by investing activities. Any deficiency in cash from operating activities must be made up with cash provided by financing activities.

Glossary

Glossary

Accounting The process of identifying, recording, and communicating the economic events of a business to interested users of the information. (p. 5)

Annual report A report, prepared by management, that presents financial and nonfinancial information about the company. (p. 20)

Assets Resources owned by a business. (p. 8)

Balance sheet A financial statement that reports the assets, liabilities, and shareholders' equity at a specific date. (p. 12)

Basic accounting equation Assets = Liabilities + Shareholders' Equity. (p. 12)

Cash flow statement A financial statement that provides information about the cash inflows (receipts) and cash outflows (payments) for a specific period of time. (p. 13)

Comparative statements A presentation of the financial statements of a company for two or more years. (p. 17)

Corporation A business organized as a separate legal entity having ownership divided into transferable shares. (p. 4)

Cost principle An accounting principle that states that assets should be recorded at their cost. (p. 22)

Dividends The distribution of retained earnings from a corporation to its shareholders in the form of cash or other assets. (p. 8)

Economic entity assumption An assumption that economic events can be identified with a particular unit of accountability. (p. 21)

Expenses The cost of assets consumed or services used in ongoing operations to generate resources. (p. 9)

Fiscal year An accounting period that is one year long. (p. 17)

Full disclosure principle An accounting principle that states that circumstances and events which matter to financial statement users should be disclosed. (p. 23)

Going concern assumption The assumption that the business will continue operating long enough to carry out its existing objectives and commitments. (p. 22)

Liabilities The debts and obligations of a business. Liabilities represent claims of creditors on the assets of a business. (p. 8)

Monetary unit assumption An assumption stating that only transaction data that can be expressed in terms of money should be included in the accounting records of the economic entity. (p. 21)

Net earnings (also known as net income) The amount by which revenues exceed expenses. (p. 9)

Net loss The amount by which expenses exceed revenues. (p. 9)

Partnership A business owned by more than one person. (p. 4)

Proprietorship A business owned by one person. (p. 4)

Retained earnings The amount of accumulated net earnings (less losses, if any), from the prior and current periods, that has been kept in the corporation for future use and not distributed to shareholders as dividends. (p. 11)

Revenues The economic resources that result from the operating activities of a business, such as the sale of a product or provision of a service. (p. 9)

Share capital Shares representing the ownership interest in a corporation. If only one class of shares exists, it is known as common shares. (p. 12)

Shareholders' equity The shareholders' claim on total assets, represented by the investments of the shareholders and undistributed earnings generated by the company. (p. 12)

Statement of earnings (also known as income statement) A financial statement that presents the revenues and expenses and resulting net earnings or net loss of a company for a specific period of time. (p. 10)

Statement of retained earnings A financial statement that summarizes the changes in retained earnings for a specific period of time. (p. 11)

Time period assumption An accounting assumption that the economic life of a business can be divided into artificial time periods. (p. 21)

Demonstration Problem

Jeff Andringa, a former university hockey player, quit his job and started Ice Camp Ltd., a hockey camp for kids from ages 8 to 18. Eventually he would like to open hockey camps nationwide. Jeff has asked you to help him prepare financial statements at the end of his first year of operations. He relates the following facts about his business activities.

In order to get the business off the ground, he decided to incorporate. He sold common shares to a few close friends and bought some of the shares himself. He initially raised $25,000 through the sale of these shares. In addition, the company borrowed $10,000 from a local bank. A used bus for transporting kids was purchased for $12,000 cash. Hockey nets and other miscellaneous equipment were purchased with $1,500 cash. The company earned camp tuition of $100,000 during the year but had collected only $80,000 of this amount. Thus, at the end of the year it was still owed $20,000. The company rents time at a local rink for $50 per hour. Total rink rental costs during the year were $8,000, insurance was $10,000, salaries were $20,000, administrative expenses totalled $9,000, and income taxes amounted to $15,000—all of which were paid in cash. The company incurred $800 in interest expense on the bank loan, which it still owed at the end of the year.

The company paid dividends during the year of $5,000 cash. The balance in the corporate bank account at December 31, 2004, was $34,500.

Instructions

Prepare a statement of earnings, statement of retained earnings, balance sheet, and cash flow statement for the year.

Additional Demonstration Problems

Demonstration Problems are a final review before you begin assignments.

Action Plan

- On the statement of earnings, show revenues and expenses for a period of time.
- On the statement of retained earnings, show the changes in retained earnings for a period of time.
- On the balance sheet, report assets, liabilities, and shareholders' equity at a specific date.
- On the cash flow statement, report sources and uses of cash provided or used by operating, investing, and financing activities for a period of time.

Action Plans that appear in the margins give you tips about how to approach the problem. The solution provided illustrates both the form and content of complete answers.

Solution to Demonstration Problem

ICE CAMP LTD.
Statement of Earnings
Year Ended December 31, 2004

Revenues		
Camp tuition revenue		$100,000
Expenses		
Salaries expense	$20,000	
Insurance expense	10,000	
Administrative expense	9,000	
Rink rental expense	8,000	
Interest expense	800	
Total expenses		47,800
Earnings before income taxes		52,200
Income tax expense		15,000
Net earnings		$ 37,200

ICE CAMP LTD.
Statement of Retained Earnings
Year Ended December 31, 2004

Retained earnings, January 1	$ 0
Add: Net earnings	37,200
	37,200
Less: Dividends	5,000
Retained earnings, December 31	$32,200

ICE CAMP LTD.
Balance Sheet
December 31, 2004

Assets	
Cash	$34,500
Accounts receivable	20,000
Bus	12,000
Equipment	1,500
Total assets	$68,000

Liabilities and Shareholders' Equity	
Liabilities	
Bank loan payable	$10,000
Interest payable	800
Total liabilities	10,800
Shareholders' equity	
Common shares	25,000
Retained earnings	32,200
Total shareholders' equity	57,200
Total liabilities and shareholders' equity	$68,000

ICE CAMP LTD.
Cash Flow Statement
Year Ended December 31, 2004

Operating activities		
Cash receipts from operating activities	$80,000	
Cash payments for operating activities[1]	(62,000)	
Cash provided by operating activities		$18,000
Investing activities		
Purchase of bus	$(12,000)	
Purchase of equipment	(1,500)	
Cash used by investing activities		(13,500)
Financing activities		
Issue of bank loan	$10,000	
Issue of common shares	25,000	
Dividends paid	(5,000)	
Cash provided by financing activities		30,000
Net increase in cash		34,500
Cash, January 1		0
Cash, December 31		$34,500

[1] $8,000 + $10,000 + $20,000 + $9,000 + $15,000 = $62,000

NAVIGATOR

This would be a good time to return to the **Student Owner's Manual** at the beginning of the book (or to look at it for the first time if you skipped it before) to read about the various types of assignment materials that appear at the end of each chapter. Knowing the purpose of the different assignments will help you appreciate what each one contributes to your accounting skills and competencies.

The tool icon means that an activity uses one of the decision tools presented in the chapter.

The pencil icon means that an activity requires you to write a detailed answer.

Multiple Choice Quiz

Self-Study Questions

Answers are at the end of the chapter.

(SO 1) 1. Which is not one of the three forms of business organization?
   (a) Proprietorship   (c) Partnership
   (b) Creditorship   (d) Corporation

(SO 1) 2. Which is an advantage of corporations compared to partnerships and proprietorships?
   (a) Harder to raise funds
   (b) Harder to transfer ownership
   (c) Harder to organize
   (d) Reduced legal liability for investors

(SO 2) 3. Which statement about users of accounting information is incorrect?
   (a) Management is an internal user.
   (b) The Canada Customs and Revenue Agency is an external user.
   (c) Creditors are external users.

   (d) Investors are internal users.

4. Ethics are the standards of conduct by which one's   (SO 2)
   actions are judged to be:
   (a) decent or indecent.
   (b) successful or unsuccessful.
   (c) profitable or unprofitable.
   (d) right or wrong.

5. Which is not one of the three primary business ac-   (SO 3)
   tivities?
   (a) Financing   (c) Planning
   (b) Operating   (d) Investing

6. Net earnings will result during a time period when: (SO 4)
   (a) assets exceed liabilities.
   (b) assets exceed revenues.
   (c) expenses exceed revenues.
   (d) revenues exceed expenses.

(SO 4) 7. ⚒ Which section of a cash flow statement indicates the cash spent on new equipment during the accounting period?
(a) The investing activities section
(b) The operating activities section
(c) The financing activities section
(d) The cash flow statement does not give this information.

(SO 4) 8. Which financial statement reports assets, liabilities, and shareholders' equity?
(a) Statement of earnings
(b) Statement of retained earnings
(c) Balance sheet
(d) Cash flow statement

(SO 5) 9. As at December 31, 2004, Stoneland Corporation has assets of $3,500 and shareholders' equity of $2,000. What are the liabilities for Stoneland Corporation as at December 31, 2004?
(a) $1,500   (c) $3,500
(b) $2,000   (d) $5,500

(SO 6) 10. The cost principle states that:
(a) the assets should be recorded at cost and adjusted when the market value changes.
(b) the activities of an entity should be kept separate and distinct from those of its shareholders.
(c) assets should be recorded at their cost.
(d) only transaction data capable of being expressed in terms of money should be included in the accounting records.

11. Valuing assets at their market value rather than at their cost is inconsistent with the: (SO 6)
(a) time period assumption.
(b) economic entity assumption.
(c) going concern assumption.
(d) All of the above

12. The full disclosure principle dictates that: (SO 6)
(a) financial statements should disclose all assets at their cost.
(b) financial statements should disclose only those events that can be measured in dollars.
(c) financial statements should disclose all events and circumstances that would matter to the statements' users.
(d) financial statements should be prepared on a timely basis in order to be useful.

Questions

(SO 1) 1. What are the three basic forms of business organizations?

(SO 1) 2. What are the advantages and disadvantages of forming a (a) proprietorship, (b) partnership, or (c) corporation?

(SO 2) 3. "Accounting is ingrained in our society and is vital to our economic system." Do you agree? Explain.

(SO 2) 4. Who are the internal users of accounting data? How does accounting provide relevant data to the internal users?

(SO 2) 5. Who are the external users of accounting data? Give examples.

(SO 2) 6. Why are ethics important to the accounting profession? To statement users?

(SO 3) 7. Name two primary kinds of financing activities for a corporation.

(SO 3) 8. ⚒ Why would a bank want to monitor the dividend payment practices of the corporation it lends funds to?

(SO 4) 9. Why do you think a balance sheet is prepared *as at a specific point in time*, while the other financial statements cover a *period of time*?

(SO 4) 10. What are retained earnings? What items increase the balance in retained earnings? What items decrease the balance in retained earnings?

(SO 4) 11. What is the purpose of the cash flow statement?

12. What are the three main categories in the cash flow statement? Why do you think these categories were chosen? (SO 4)

13. How are each of the following pairs of financial statements interrelated? (SO 4)
(a) Statement of earnings and statement of retained earnings
(b) Statement of retained earnings and balance sheet
(c) Balance sheet and cash flow statement

14. What is the basic accounting equation? (SO 5)

15. Sue Leonard is president of Better Books Dot Com. She has no accounting background. Leonard cannot understand why market value is not used as the basis for accounting measurement and reporting. Explain what basis is used and why. (SO 5)

16. (a) Define the terms *assets*, *liabilities*, and *shareholders' equity*. (SO 5)
(b) What items affect shareholders' equity?

17. Which of these items are liabilities for Kool-Jewellery Stores Inc.? (SO 5)
(a) Cash   (f) Equipment
(b) Accounts payable   (g) Salaries payable
(c) Dividends   (h) Service revenue
(d) Accounts receivable   (i) Rent expense
(e) Supplies

18. Here are some items found in the financial statements of D'Anjou, Inc. Indicate in which financial (SO 5)

statement each item would appear.

(a) Service revenue
(f) Wages payable
(b) Equipment
(g) Cash provided by operating activities
(c) Advertising expense
(d) Accounts receivable
(h) Dividends
(e) Common shares

(SO 5) 19. ⚯⚯ Loblaw's year end is not a fixed date; rather, it can vary slightly from one year to the next. What

possible problems does this pose for financial statement users?

20. What is the importance of the economic entity assumption? Give an example of its violation. (SO 6)

21. How does the going concern assumption influence the values reported on our financial statements? (SO 6)

The **financial results of real companies** are included in the end of chapter material; these are indicated by the company names being shown in red.

Brief Exercises

BE1-1 Write the correct form of business organization—proprietorship (P), partnership (PP), or corporation (C)—beside each set of characteristics.

Describe forms of business organization.
(SO 1)

(a) _____ Simple to set up; founder retains control
(b) _____ Shared control; increased skills and resources
(c) _____ Easier to transfer ownership and raise funds; no personal liability

BE1-2 Write the number of each of the following types of evaluation beside the appropriate user of accounting information in the list that follows:

Identify users of accounting information.
(SO 2)

1. Determining whether the company complied with income tax regulations
2. Determining whether the company can pay its obligations
3. Determining whether a marketing proposal will be cost-effective
4. Determining whether the company's net earnings will result in a share price increase
5. Determining whether the company should use debt or equity financing

(a) _____ Investors
(b) _____ Marketing managers
(c) _____ Creditors
(d) _____ Chief financial officer
(e) _____ Canada Customs and Revenue Agency

BE1-3 The company accountant is counting the office supplies on hand at the end of the period. She realizes there are more supplies in stock than recorded in the books and decides to take some of the extra supplies home. In her own mind, this is not stealing because it will correct a book error. In addition, she is owed by the company for all the extra unpaid work she has been doing lately anyway.

Discuss ethical issues.
(SO 2)

(a) Are the accountant's actions ethical? Explain why or why not.
(b) What might the company do to ensure that all employees adhere to appropriate ethical behaviour?

BE1-4 Indicate the section of the cash flow statement—operating activities (O), investing activities (I), or financing activities (F)—in which each of the following items would appear:

Classify items by activity.
(SO 3)

(a) _____ Cash received from customers
(b) _____ Cash dividends paid to shareholders
(c) _____ Cash received from issuing common shares
(d) _____ Cash received from borrowing money
(e) _____ Cash paid to purchase an office building

BE1-5 The Calgary Exhibition and Stampede Limited has the following selected accounts included in its financial statements. In each case, identify whether the item would appear on the balance sheet (BS) or statement of earnings (SE).

Determine on which financial statement items appear.
(SO 4)

(a) _____ Accounts receivable
(b) _____ Inventories
(c) _____ Amortization expense
(d) _____ Common shares
(e) _____ Building
(f) _____ Stampede revenue
(g) _____ Horse racing revenue
(h) _____ Accounts payable and accrued liabilities
(i) _____ Cash and short-term deposits
(j) _____ Administration, marketing, and park services expenses
(k) _____ Interest expense
(l) _____ Prepaid expenses

Determine on which financial statement items appear.
(SO 4)

BE1-6   Indicate which statement—statement of earnings (SE), balance sheet (BS), statement of retained earnings (RE), or cash flow statement (CF)—you would examine to find each of the following items:

(a) _____ Revenue during the period
(b) _____ Supplies on hand at the end of the year
(c) _____ Cash received from borrowing money during the period
(d) _____ Total debt at the end of the period

Use basic accounting equation.
(SO 5)

BE1-7   Use the basic accounting equation to determine the missing amounts below:

Assets	=	Liabilities	+	Shareholders' Equity
$90,000		$50,000		(a)
(b)		$48,000		$70,000
$94,000		(c)		$72,000

Use basic accounting equation.
(SO 5)

BE1-8   Use the basic accounting equation to answer these questions:

(a) The liabilities of Houle Corporation are $100,000 and the shareholders' equity is $240,000. What is the amount of Houle's total assets?
(b) The total assets of Pitre Limited are $170,000 and its shareholders' equity is $100,000. What is the amount of its total liabilities?
(c) The total assets of Budovitch Inc. are $700,000 and its liabilities are equal to half of its total assets. What is the amount of Budovitch's shareholders' equity?

Use basic accounting equation.
(SO 5)

BE1-9   At the beginning of the year, Lamson Ltd. had total assets of $800,000 and total liabilities of $500,000.

(a) If total assets increased by $150,000 during the year and total liabilities decreased by $80,000, what is the amount of shareholders' equity at the end of the year?
(b) If total liabilities increased by $100,000 during the year and shareholders' equity decreased by $70,000, what is the amount of total assets at the end of the year?
(c) If total assets decreased by $90,000 during the year and shareholders' equity increased by $110,000, what is the amount of total liabilities at the end of the year?

Identify assets, liabilities, and shareholders' equity.
(SO 5)

BE1-10   Indicate whether each of these items is an asset (A), a liability (L), or shareholders' equity (SE):

(a) _____ Accounts receivable   (d) _____ Office supplies
(b) _____ Salaries payable   (e) _____ Common shares
(c) _____ Equipment   (f) _____ Notes payable

Determine effect of transactions on shareholders' equity.
(SO 5)

BE1-11   Presented below are a number of transactions. Determine whether each transaction affects common shares (C), dividends (D), revenue (R), expenses (E), or has no effect on shareholders' equity (NE).

(a) _____ Cash paid to purchase equipment
(b) _____ Cash received from investors in exchange for common shares
(c) _____ Services performed
(d) _____ Costs incurred for income taxes
(e) _____ Amounts paid to employees
(f) _____ Cash dividends paid to shareholders
(g) _____ Rent received in exchange for allowing the use of a building

Exercises

Match words with descriptions.
(SO 1, 2, 3, 4)

E1-1   Here is a list of words or phrases discussed in this chapter:

1. Accounts payable   5. Corporation
2. Creditor   6. Common shares
3. Financing activities   7. Accounts receivable
4. Retained earnings   8. Ethics

Instructions

Match each word or phrase with the best description of it below:

(a) _____ Standards of conduct by which one's actions are judged as right or wrong
(b) _____ A business that raises money by issuing shares
(c) _____ Shareholders' investments
(d) _____ Amounts owed to suppliers of goods
(e) _____ Amounts due from customers
(f) _____ A party a business owes money to
(g) _____ Obtaining cash from borrowing money or issuing shares
(h) _____ Cumulative earnings that have been retained in the company

E1-2   This information relates to Kon Inc. for the year 2004:

Prepare statements of earnings and retained earnings.
(SO 4)

Retained earnings, January 1, 2004	$57,000
Advertising expense	1,800
Dividends	7,000
Rent expense	10,400
Service revenue	61,000
Utilities expense	2,400
Salaries expense	28,000
Income tax expense	6,000

Instructions

After analysing the data, prepare a statement of earnings and a statement of retained earnings for the year ending December 31, 2004.

E1-3   Kit Lucas is the bookkeeper for Aurora Ltd. Kit has been trying to get Aurora's balance sheet to balance. It finally balanced, as shown below, but now he's not sure if it's correct.

Correct incorrectly prepared balance sheet.
(SO 4)

AURORA LTD.
Balance Sheet
December 31, 2004

Assets		Liabilities and Shareholders' Equity	
Cash	$18,500	Accounts payable	$20,000
Supplies	8,000	Accounts receivable	(10,000)
Equipment	44,000	Common shares	40,000
Dividends	7,000	Retained earnings	27,500
Total assets	$77,500	Total liabilities and	
		shareholders' equity	$77,500

Instructions

Prepare a correct balance sheet.

E1-4   Sea Surf Campground, Inc. is a public camping ground in Ocean National Park. It has compiled the following financial information as at December 31, 2004:

Calculate net earnings and prepare statement of retained earnings and balance sheet.
(SO 4)

Interactive
Homework

Revenues: camping fees	$137,000	Dividends	$ 4,000
Revenues: general store	20,000	Notes payable	50,000
Accounts payable	11,000	Operating expenses	142,000
Cash	10,500	Supplies	2,500
Equipment	110,000	Common shares	40,000
Income tax expense	6,000	Retained earnings (Jan. 1, 2004)	17,000

Instructions

(a) Determine net earnings for Sea Surf Campground, Inc. for the year ended December 31, 2004.
(b) Prepare a statement of retained earnings and a balance sheet for Sea Surf Campground, Inc.

E1-5   Here is some information for Langille Professional Corporation:

Prepare statement of retained earnings.
(SO 4)

Retained earnings, January 1, 2004	$150,000
Revenues from legal services	395,000
Total expenses	205,000
Dividends	76,000

*Use financial statement rela-
tionships to determine missing amounts.*
(SO 4)

Interactive
Homework

Instructions

Prepare the statement of retained earnings for Langille Professional Corporation for the
year ended December 31, 2004.

E1-6   The summaries of data from the 2004 balance sheets and statements of earnings and
retained earnings for two corporations, Chiasson Corporation and Maxim Enterprises, Ltd.,
are presented below:

	Chiasson Corporation	Maxim Enterprises, Ltd.
Beginning of year		
Total assets	$ 90,000	$130,000
Total liabilities	80,000	(d)
Total shareholders' equity	(a)	95,000
End of year		
Total assets	(b)	180,000
Total liabilities	120,000	55,000
Total shareholders' equity	40,000	(e)
Changes during year in retained earnings		
Dividends	(c)	5,000
Total revenues	215,000	(f)
Total expenses	165,000	80,000

Instructions

Determine the missing amounts. Assume all changes in shareholders' equity are due to changes
in retained earnings.

Interpret financial facts.
(SO 4)

E1-7   Consider each of the following independent situations:

(a) The statement of retained earnings of Yu Corporation shows dividends of $68,000,
   while net earnings for the year were $75,000.
(b) The cash flow statement for Surya Corporation shows that cash provided by operating activities was $10,000, cash used by investing activities was $110,000, and cash
   provided by financing activities was $130,000.
(c) Naguib Ltd.'s balance sheet reports $150,000 of total liabilities and $250,000 of shareholders' equity.

Instructions

For each company, write a brief interpretation of these financial facts. For example, you
might discuss the company's financial health or its apparent growth philosophy.

Prepare cash flow statement.
(SO 4)

Interactive
Homework

E1-8   This information is for Van Tran Corporation for 2004:

Cash received from customers	$50,000	Cash paid for new equipment	$25,000
Cash dividends paid	6,000	Cash received from lenders	20,000
Cash paid to suppliers	30,000	Cash, January 1, 2004	10,000

Instructions

Prepare the cash flow statement for Van Tran Corporation for the year ended December 31,
2004.

Prepare cash flow statement.
(SO 4)

E1-9   The following data (in U.S. thousands) are derived from the February 2002 financial
statements of mail order and on-line direct merchant Lands' End:

Cash paid for repayment of debt	$ 771
Cash received from issue of common shares	14,520
Cash balance, January 27, 2001	75,351
Cash paid for goods and services	1,502,068
Cash paid for new buildings and equipment	40,514
Cash received from customers	1,575,573

Instructions

After analysing the data, prepare a cash flow statement for Lands' End for the year ended
February 1, 2002.

E1-10 The following items were taken from CoolBrands International Inc.'s 2002 statement of earnings and balance sheet (in thousands):

Identify financial statement components and prepare statement of earnings.
(SO 4, 5)

_____	Cash and short-term investments	$ 47,086	_____ Receivables	$ 46,793
_____	Retained earnings	42,645	_____ Income tax expense	11,890
_____	Cost of goods sold	129,246	_____ Sales	236,028
_____	Selling, general, and administrative expenses	77,558	_____ Income taxes payable	7,347
_____	Prepaid expenses	6,752	_____ Accounts payable	24,399
_____	Inventories	25,361	_____ Franchising revenues	5,187
			_____ Rental and other income	1,007
			_____ Interest expense	2,544

Instructions

(a) In each case, identify on the blank line whether the item is an asset (A), liability (L), shareholders' equity (SE), revenue (R), or expense (E) item.

(b) Prepare a statement of earnings for CoolBrands for the year ended August 31, 2002.

E1-11 The following items were taken from the January 27, 2003, balance sheet (in thousands) of The Forzani Group Ltd., Canada's biggest sporting goods retailer.

Classify items and prepare accounting equation.
(SO 5)

Instructions

(a) Classify each item ($ in thousands) as an asset (A), liability (L), or shareholders' equity (SE) item.

_____	Accounts payable and accrued liabilities	$209,873
_____	Accounts receivable	38,275
_____	Capital assets	142,236
_____	Cash	523
_____	Goodwill and other intangibles	38,684
_____	Inventory	268,519
_____	Long-term debt	35,700
_____	Other assets	7,452
_____	Other liabilities	57,516
_____	Prepaid and other expenses	11,123
_____	Retained earnings	78,857
_____	Share capital	124,866

(b) Determine Forzani's accounting equation by calculating the value of total assets, total liabilities, and total shareholders' equity.

E1-12 Presented below are the assumptions and principles discussed in this chapter:

Identify accounting assumptions and principles.
(SO 6)

1. Full disclosure principle
2. Cost principle
3. Monetary unit assumption
4. Time period assumption
5. Going concern assumption
6. Economic entity assumption

Instructions

Use the numbers from the above list to identify the accounting assumption or principle that is described below. Do not use a number more than once.

(a) _____ States the rationale for why property, plant, and equipment are not reported at liquidation value (*Note:* Do not use the cost principle.)

(b) _____ Indicates that personal and business record-keeping should be separately maintained

(c) _____ Assumes that the dollar is the measure used to report on financial performance

(d) _____ Separates financial information into time periods for reporting purposes

(e) _____ Indicates that market value changes subsequent to purchase are not recorded in the accounts

(f) _____ Dictates that all circumstances and events that make a difference to financial statement users be disclosed

E1-13 Marietta Corp. had three major business transactions during 2004:

Identify the assumption or principle violated.
(SO 6)

(a) Merchandise inventory with a cost of $208,000 was reported at its market value of $260,000.

(b) The president of Marietta, Deanna Durnford, purchased a truck for personal use and charged it to her expense account.

(c) Marietta wanted to make its 2004 net earnings look better, so it added two more weeks to the year, creating a 54-week year. Previous years were 52 weeks.

Instructions

In each situation, identify the assumption or principle that has been violated, if any, and explain what should have been done.

Problems: Set A

Determine forms of business organization.
(SO 1)

P1-1A   Presented below are five independent situations:

(a) Dawn Addington, a student looking for summer employment, opened a vegetable stand along a busy local highway. Each morning, she buys produce from local farmers, then sells it in the afternoon as people return home from work.

(b) Joseph Counsell and Sabra Surkis each own a bike shop. They have decided to combine their businesses and try to expand their operations to include skis and snowboards. They expect that in the coming year they will need significant funds to expand their operations.

(c) Three chemistry professors have formed a business which uses bacteria to clean up toxic waste sites. Each has contributed an equal amount of cash and knowledge to the venture. The use of bacteria in this situation is experimental, and legal obligations could result.

(d) Abdur Rahim has run a successful but small cooperative health and organic food store for over five years. The increased sales at his store have made him believe that the time is right to open a chain of health and organic food stores across the country. Of course, this will require a substantial investment for inventories and property, plant, and equipment, as well as for employees and other resources. Abdur has no savings or personal assets.

(e) Mary Emery and Richard Goedde recently graduated with graduate degrees in economics. They have decided to start a consulting business focused on teaching the basics of international economics to small business owners interested in international trade.

Instructions

In each case, explain what form of organization the business is likely to take: proprietorship, partnership, or corporation. Give reasons for your choice.

Identify business activities.
(SO 3)

P1-2A   All business are involved in three types of activities—financing, investing, and operating. The names and descriptions of companies in several different industries follow:

Abitibi Consolidated Inc.—manufacturer and marketer of newsprint
Students' Society of McGill University—university student union
Corel Corporation—computer software developer and retailer
Sportsco Investments—owner of the Vancouver Canucks hockey club
Grant Thornton LLP—professional accounting and business advisory firm
WestJet Airlines Ltd.—discount airline

Instructions

(a) For each of the above companies, provide examples of (1) a financing activity, (2) an investing activity, and (3) an operating activity that the company likely engages in.

(b) Which of the activities that you identified in (a) are common to most businesses? Which activities are not?

Classify accounts.
(SO 3, 4)

P1-3A   The Mill Run Golf & Country Club details the following accounts in its financial statements:

	(a)	(b)
Accounts payable and accrued liabilities	____	____
Accounts receivable	____	____
Bank overdraft	____	____
Capital assets	____	____
Food and beverage operations revenue	____	____

Golf course operations revenue	___	___
Inventory	___	___
Long-term debt	___	___
Office and general expense	___	___
Professional fees expense	___	___
Wages and benefits expense	___	___

Instructions

(a) Classify each of the above accounts as an asset (A), liability (L), shareholders' equity (SE), revenue (R), or expense (E) item.

(b) Classify each of the above accounts as a financing activity (F), investing activity (I), or operating activity (O). If you believe a particular account doesn't fit in any of these activities, explain why.

P1-4A   Financial decisions often depend on one financial statement more than the others. Consider each of the following independent hypothetical situations:

Identify users and uses of financial statements.
(SO 2, 4)

(a) An Ontario investor is considering purchasing the common shares of Total Fitness Ltd., which operates 13 fitness centres in the Toronto area. The investor plans on holding the investment for at least three years.

(b) Comeau Ltée is considering extending credit to a new customer. The terms of the credit would require the customer to pay within 45 days of receipt of the goods.

(c) The CEO of the Hilfiger Corporation is trying to determine whether the company is generating enough cash to increase the amount of dividends paid to investors in this, and future, years. He needs to ensure that there will still be enough cash to expand operations when needed.

(d) The Laurentian Bank is considering extending a loan to a small company. The company would be required to make interest payments at the end of each year for five years, and to repay the loan at the end of the fifth year.

Instructions

For each situation, state whether the individual would pay most attention to the information provided by the statement of earnings, balance sheet, or cash flow statement. Choose only one financial statement in each case, and provide a brief justification for your choice.

P1-5A   Aero Flying School Ltd. started on May 1 with cash of $45,000 and common shares of $45,000. Here are the assets and liabilities of the company on May 31, 2004, and the revenues and expenses for the month of May, its first month of operations:

Prepare statements of earnings and retained earnings and balance sheet.
(SO 4)

Cash	$ 7,800	Advertising expense	$ 900
Accounts receivable	11,200	Rent expense	1,200
Equipment	60,300	Repair expense	700
Accounts payable	2,400	Fuel expense	3,400
Notes payable	29,200	Insurance expense	400
Service revenue	9,600	Income tax expense	1,100

Additional common shares of $1,800 were issued in May, and a cash dividend of $1,000 was paid.

Instructions

Prepare a statement of earnings and a statement of retained earnings for the month of May, and a balance sheet at May 31, 2004.

P1-6A   Presented below are selected financial statement items for Frenette Corporation for June 30, 2004:

Prepare cash flow statement.
(SO 4)

Cash, July 1, 2003	$ 30,000	Cash dividends paid	$ 8,000
Inventory	55,000	Cash paid to buy equipment	15,000
Cash paid to suppliers	95,000	Equipment	40,000
Building	400,000	Revenues	200,000
Common shares	20,000	Cash received from customers	165,000
Cash paid for income tax	20,000		

Instructions

Determine which of the above items should be included in a cash flow statement, and then prepare the statement for Frenette Corporation for the year ended June 30, 2004.

Comment on proper accounting treatment and prepare corrected statement of earnings.
(SO 4)

P1-7A In January 2004, Pam Bollinger formed Kettle Corporation. At December 31, 2004, Pam prepared a statement of earnings by looking at the financial statements of other companies. She is not an accountant, but thinks she did a reasonable job. She has asked you for advice. Pam's statement of earnings appears as follows:

KETTLE CORPORATION
Statement of Earnings
December 31, 2004

Accounts receivable	$10,000
Revenue	60,000
Rent expense	15,000
Insurance expense	5,000
Vacation expense	2,000
Net earnings	$48,000

Pam has also provided you with these facts:

1. Included in the revenue account is $7,000 of revenue that the company earned and received payment for in 2003. She forgot to include it in the 2003 statement of earnings, so she put it in this year's statement.
2. Income tax expense for Kettle Corporation for the year ended December 31, 2004, was determined to be $12,000. However, the income tax payment is not due until March 31, 2005, so Pam decided not to record the income tax expense yet.
3. Pam operates her business out of the basement of her parents' home. They do not charge her anything, but she thinks that if she paid rent it would cost her about $15,000 per year. She therefore included $15,000 of rent expense in the statement.
4. To reward herself for a year of hard work, Pam went skiing for a week at Whistler. She did not use company funds to pay for the trip, but she reported it as an expense on the statement of earnings, since it was her job that made her need the vacation.

Instructions

(a) Comment on the proper accounting treatment of the four items above.
(b) Prepare a corrected statement of earnings for Kettle Corporation.

Use financial statement relationships to calculate missing amounts.
(SO 4, 5)

P1-8A Here are incomplete financial statements for Wu, Inc.:

WU, INC.
Balance Sheet
August 31, 2004

Assets		Liabilities and Shareholders' Equity	
Cash	$ (ii)	Liabilities	
Accounts receivable	20,000	Accounts payable	$15,000
Land	15,000	Shareholders' equity	
Building and equipment	40,000	Common shares	(vii)
Total assets	$ (i)	Retained earnings	(vi)
		Total liabilities and	
		shareholders' equity	$85,000

WU, INC.
Statement of Earnings
Year Ended August 31, 2004

Service revenue	$75,000
Operating expenses	(iii)
Earnings before income tax	30,000
Income tax expense	15,000
Net earnings	$ (iv)

WU, INC.
Statement of Retained Earnings
Year Ended August 31, 2004

Beginning retained earnings	$10,000
Net earnings	(v)
Dividends	5,000
Ending retained earnings	$20,000

Instructions

(a) Calculate the missing amounts (i) to (vii).

(b) Write a memo explaining (1) the sequence for preparing and presenting the financial statements, and (2) the interrelationships between the various financial statements.

P1-9A A number of accounting reporting situations are described below:

1. In preparing its financial statements, Karim Corporation tried to estimate and record the impact of the recent death of its president.
2. Topilynyckyj Ltd. does not comply with generally accepted accounting principles when it prepares its financial statements because it is a very small business.
3. The Saint John Shipbuilding Co. Ltd. takes a very long time to build ships—sometimes up to five years. It is wondering if it would be appropriate to report its financial results once every two years.
4. Paradis Inc. recently purchased a power boat. It plans on inviting clients for outings occasionally, so the boat was paid for by the company and recorded in its records. Marc Paradis's family will use the boat whenever it is not being used to entertain clients. Marc estimates that the boat will be used by the family about 75% of the time.
5. Because of a "flood sale," equipment worth $300,000 was purchased for only $200,000. The equipment was recorded at $300,000 on the Bourque Corporation's books.

Identify the assumption or principle violated.
(SO 6)

Instructions

For each of the above situations, list the assumption or principle that has been violated. Explain why the situation described violates this assumption or principle.

Problems: Set B

P1-1B Presented below are five independent situations:

(a) Three physics professors have formed a business to improve the speed of information transfer over the Internet for stock exchange transactions. Each has contributed an equal amount of cash and knowledge to the venture. While their approach looks promising, they are concerned about the legal liabilities that their business might confront.

(b) Joseph LeBlanc, a student looking for summer employment, opened a bait shop in a small shed on a local fishing dock.

(c) Robert Steven and Tom Cheng each owned a shoe manufacturing business. They have decided to combine their businesses. They expect that in the coming year, they will need significant funds to expand their operations.

(d) Darcy Becker, Ellen Sweet, and Meg Dwyer recently graduated with marketing degrees. Friends since childhood, they have decided to start a consulting business focused on marketing sporting goods over the Internet.

(e) Hervé Gaudet wants to rent CD players and CDs in airports across the country. His idea is that customers will be able to rent equipment and CDs at one airport, listen to the CDs on their flight, and return the equipment and CDs at their destination airport. Of course, this will require a substantial investment for equipment and CDs, as well as employees and locations in each airport. Hervé has no savings or personal assets. He wants to maintain control over the business.

Determine forms of business organization.
(SO 1)

Instructions

In each case, explain what form of organization the business is likely to take: proprietorship, partnership, or corporation. Give reasons for your choice.

Identify business activities.
(SO 3)

P1-2B   All businesses are involved in three types of activities—financing, investing, and operating. The names and descriptions of companies in several different industries follow:

> Indigo Books & Music—book retailer
> High Liner Foods Incorporated—processor and marketer of seafood products
> Mountain Equipment Co-op—outdoor equipment retailer
> Ganong Bros. Limited—maker of candy
> Royal Bank—banking and financial service provider
> The Gap, Inc.—casual clothing retailer

Instructions
(a) For each of the above companies, provide examples of (1) a financing activity, (2) an investing activity, and (3) an operating activity that the company likely engages in.
(b) Which of the activities that you identified in (a) are common to most businesses? Which activities are not?

Classify accounts.
(SO 3, 4)

P1-3B   The following accounts have been selected from the financial statements of Maple Leaf Foods Inc. and placed in alphabetical order:

	(a)	(b)
Accounts payable and accrued charges	____	____
Accounts receivable	____	____
Common shares	____	____
Income and other taxes payable	____	____
Interest expense	____	____
Inventories	____	____
Long-term debt	____	____
Property and equipment	____	____
Sales	____	____

Instructions
(a) Classify each of the above accounts as an asset (A), liability (L), shareholders' equity (SE), revenue (R), or expense (E) item.
(b) Classify each of the above accounts as a financing activity (F), investing activity (I), or operating activity (O). If you believe a particular account doesn't fit in any of these activities, explain why.

Identify users and uses of financial statements.
(SO 2, 4)

P1-4B   Financial decisions often depend on one financial statement more than the others. Consider each of the following independent hypothetical situations:

(a) The North Face Inc. is considering extending credit to a new customer. The terms of the credit would require the customer to pay within 30 days of receipt of goods.
(b) An investor is considering purchasing the common shares of Books Online. The investor plans on holding the investment for at least five years.
(c) Caisse d'Économie Base Montréal is thinking about extending a loan to a small company. The company would be required to make interest payments at the end of each year for five years, and to repay the loan at the end of the fifth year.
(d) The CEO of Tech Toy Limited is trying to determine whether the company is generating enough cash to increase the amount of dividends paid to investors in this, and future, years. He needs to be sure that Tech Toy will still have enough cash to buy equipment when needed.

Instructions
For each situation, state whether the individual would pay the most attention to the information provided by the statement of earnings, balance sheet, or cash flow statement. Choose only one financial statement in each case, and provide a brief justification for your choice.

Prepare statements of earnings and retained earnings and balance sheet.
(SO 4)

P1-5B   On June 1, One Planet Cosmetics Corp. was formed. Here are the assets, liabilities, and share capital of the company at June 30, and the revenues and expenses for the month of June:

Cash	$ 6,000	Service revenue	$8,000
Accounts receivable	4,000	Supplies expense	1,200
Cosmetic supplies	2,400	Gas and oil expense	900
Equipment	30,000	Advertising expense	500

Notes payable	$13,000	Utilities expense	$ 300
Accounts payable	1,300	Income tax expense	1,500
Common shares	26,200		

The company paid dividends of $1,700 during June.

Instructions

Prepare a statement of earnings and a statement of retained earnings for the month of June, and a balance sheet at June 30, 2004.

P1-6B Presented below is selected financial information for Maison Corporation at December 31, 2004:

Prepare cash flow statement.
(SO 4)

Cash, January 1, 2004	$ 50,000	Cash paid to purchase	
Inventory	25,000	equipment	$ 15,000
Cash paid to suppliers	90,000	Equipment	40,000
Building	200,000	Revenues	100,000
Common shares	50,000	Cash received from customers	120,000
Cash dividends paid	11,000		

Instructions

First determine which of the above items should be included in a cash flow statement. Then prepare the statement for Maison Corporation for the year ended December 31, 2004.

P1-7B GG Corporation was formed on January 1, 2004. At December 31, 2004, Guy Gélinas, the president and sole shareholder, decided to prepare a balance sheet, which appeared as follows:

Comment on proper account-ing treatment and prepare corrected balance sheet.
(SO 4)

GG CORPORATION
Balance Sheet
Year Ended December 31, 2004

Assets		Liabilities and Shareholders' Equity	
Cash	$20,000	Accounts payable	$ 40,000
Accounts receivable	55,000	Notes payable	15,000
Inventory	30,000	Boat loan	10,000
Boat	18,000	Shareholders' equity	55,000

Guy willingly admits that he is not an accountant by training. He is concerned that his balance sheet might not be correct. He has provided you with the following additional information:

1. The boat actually belongs to Guy Gélinas, not to GG Corporation. However, because he thinks he might take customers out on the boat occasionally, he decided to list it as an asset of the corporation. To be consistent, he also listed as a liability of the corporation his personal loan that he took out at the bank to buy the boat.
2. The inventory was originally purchased for $15,000, but due to a surge in demand Guy now thinks he could sell it for $30,000. He thought it would be best to record it at $30,000.
3. Included in the accounts receivable balance is $10,000 that Guy Gélinas loaned to his brother two years ago. Guy included this in the receivables of GG Corporation so he wouldn't forget that his brother owes him money.

Instructions

(a) Comment on the proper accounting treatment of the three items above.
(b) Provide a corrected balance sheet for GG Corporation. (*Hint*: To get the balance sheet to balance, adjust shareholders' equity.)

Use financial statement rela-
tionships to calculate missing
amounts.
(SO 4, 5)

P1-8B   Here are incomplete financial statements for Baxter, Inc.:

BAXTER, INC.
Balance Sheet
November 30, 2004

Assets		Liabilities and Shareholders' Equity	
Cash	$ 5,000	Liabilities	
Inventory	10,000	Accounts payable	$ 7,000
Building	50,000	Shareholders' equity	
Total assets	$65,000	Common shares	(i)
		Retained earnings	(ii)
		Total liabilities and	
		shareholders' equity	$65,000

BAXTER, INC.
Statement of Earnings
Year Ended November 30, 2004

Revenues	$80,000
Operating expenses	(iii)
Earnings before income tax	30,000
Income tax expense	10,000
Net earnings	$ (iv)

BAXTER, INC.
Statement of Retained Earnings
Year Ended November 30, 2004

Beginning retained earnings	$10,000
Net earnings	(v)
Dividends	5,000
Ending retained earnings	$25,000

Instructions

(a) Calculate the missing amounts (i) to (v).
(b) Write a memo explaining (1) the sequence for preparing the financial statements, and (2) the interrelationships between the statement of retained earnings, statement of earnings, and balance sheet.

Identify the assumption or
principle violated.
(SO 6)

P1-9B   A number of accounting reporting situations are described below:

(a) In preparing its financial statements, Seco Corporation omitted information about an ongoing lawsuit against it. Seco's lawyers advised the company that it could very well lose when the suit gets to court.
(b) Dot.com Corporation believes its people are its most significant assets. It estimates and records their value on its balance sheet.
(c) Barton, Inc. is carrying inventory at its current market value of $100,000. The inventory had an original cost of $75,000.
(d) Bonilla Corp. is in its fifth year of operations. It has yet to issue financial statements.
(e) Steph Wolfson, president of Classic CD Ltd., bought a computer for her personal use. She paid for the computer with company funds and debited the "Computers" account.

Instructions

For each of the above situations, list the assumption or principle that has been violated, and explain why the situation described violates this assumption or principle.

BROADENING YOUR PERSPECTIVE

Financial Reporting and Analysis

Analysis
Tools

FINANCIAL REPORTING PROBLEM: *Loblaw Companies Limited*

BYP1-1 Actual financial statements (rather than the simplified financial statements presented in the chapter) for Loblaw are presented in Appendix A at the end of this book.

Instructions

Refer to Loblaw's financial statements to answer these questions:

(a) Loblaw's current financial statements are dated December 28, 2002. What is Loblaw's fiscal year end?

(b) What were Loblaw's total assets at December 28, 2002? Total liabilities and shareholders' equity at December 28, 2002?

(c) How much cash and cash equivalents did Loblaw have on December 28, 2002?

(d) What amount of accounts payable and accrued liabilities did Loblaw report at the end of its 2002 fiscal year? Its 2001 fiscal year?

(e) What were Loblaw's sales in 2002? In 2001?

(f) What is the amount of the change in Loblaw's net earnings from 2001 to 2002?

COMPARATIVE ANALYSIS PROBLEM: *Loblaw and Sobeys*

BYP1-2 The financial statements for Sobeys are presented in Appendix B, following the financial statements for Loblaw in Appendix A.

Instructions

(a) Based on the information in these financial statements, determine the following for each company:

1. Loblaw's total assets at December 28, 2002, and Sobeys' at May 3, 2003.

2. Loblaw's accounts receivable at December 28, 2002, and Sobeys' receivables at May 3, 2003.

3. Loblaw's and Sobeys' sales for the most recent fiscal year.

4. Net earnings for Loblaws and Sobeys for the most recent fiscal year.

(b) What conclusions concerning the two companies can you draw from these data?

RESEARCH CASE

BYP1-3 The April 1, 2002, issue of *Canadian Business* includes an article by John Grey entitled "Hide and Seek" (Vol. 75, Issue 6, p. 28). The article discusses how accounting tricks make it difficult for investors to get a true picture of a company's finances.

Instructions

Read the article and answer the following questions:

(a) John Grey discusses ten red flags that investors should look for to ensure that the statement of earnings reflects the company's bottom line. Name the ten red flags.

(b) Should a shareholder read the notes to the financial statements? Explain why or why not.

(c) Name a Canadian company involved in a corporate scandal.

INTERPRETING FINANCIAL STATEMENTS

BYP1-4 In its 2002 cash flow statement, Clearly Canadian Beverage Corporation showed a U.S.$3,050 thousand decrease in cash from its operating activities and increases in cash from investing and financing activities of U.S.$1,859 thousand and U.S.$979 thousand, respectively. The largest source of cash from investing activities was from the discontinuation and sale of the company's home and office five gallon water production facility and private label bottling plant. The largest source of cash from financing activities was from bank borrowings. Overall, the cash and cash equivalents at the end of 2002 were

CLEARLY
CANADIAN.

U.S.$226 thousand less than the cash and cash equivalents at the end of 2001, and resulted in an ending cash balance of nil.

While management believes that there are sufficient financing options to fund the company's ongoing operations and repay its obligations, the auditors have indicated concerns about the financial position and future viability of the company in the notes to the financial statements.

Instructions

(a) If you were a creditor of Clearly Canadian, what reaction might you have to the above information?

(b) If you were an investor in Clearly Canadian, what reaction might you have to the above information?

(c) If you were evaluating the company as either a creditor or an investor, what other information would you be interested in seeing?

BYP1-5   With over 700 employees in two locations and sales offices worldwide, Corel Corporation is one of the world's top software developers. The Company's corporate headquarters in Ottawa, Canada, is home to its business and graphics development teams. Its Dublin, Ireland, office handles software localization, along with a portion of the Company's technical support and customer service. Recognized the world over, Corel's award-winning products ship in over 15 languages through a network of more than 160 distributors in over 60 countries.

In the assets section of its 2002 balance sheet, the following data were presented:

	2002	2001
	(in U.S. thousands)	
Current assets		
Cash and cash equivalents	$ 20,432	$ 44,291
Accounts receivable	20,208	19,961
Inventory	191	799
Prepaid expenses	2,786	1,779
Investments	65,542	87,962
Capital assets	21,768	43,123
Goodwill		37,534
Other assets		250
Total assets	$130,927	$235,699

Instructions

(a) For a software development company such as Corel, what do you think its most important economic resources (assets) would be? Where would these be recorded on the balance sheet? At what value (if any) should they be shown?

(b) Does the balance sheet tell you what Corel Corporation is worth? What information does the balance sheet give you regarding the value of the company?

(c) Why do you think a Canadian company such as Corel would prepare its financial statements in U.S. dollars?

A GLOBAL FOCUS

BYP1-6   Today, companies must compete in a global economy. For example, Canada's oldest candy company, Ganong Bros. Limited, must compete with Nestlé S.A., among others. Nestlé, a Swiss company, best known for its chocolates and confections, is also the largest food company in the world.

Comparing companies from different countries, such as Ganong's and Nestlé's, can pose some challenges. Consider the following excerpts from the notes to Nestlé's financial statements:

Good Food, Good Life

> **NESTLÉ S.A.**
> **Notes to the Financial Statements**
> **December 31, 2002**
>
> **Accounting policies**
>
> **Accounting convention and accounting standards**
>
> The Consolidated accounts comply with International Financial Reporting Standards (IFRS) issued by the International Accounting Standards Board (IASB) and with the Standing Interpretations issued by the International Financial Reporting Interpretations Committee (IFRIC) of the IASB.
>
> The accounts have been prepared on an accrual basis and under the historical cost convention ... All significant consolidated companies have a 31st December accounting year end. All disclosures required by the 4th and 7th European Union company law directives are provided.
>
> **Scope of consolidation**
>
> The Consolidated accounts comprise those of Nestlé S.A. and of its affiliated companies, including joint ventures, and associates (the Group). The list of the principal companies is provided in section "Companies of the Nestlé Group."

Instructions

Discuss the effect each of these notes might have (positive or negative) on your ability to compare Nestlé's to Ganong's.

FINANCIAL ANALYSIS ON THE WEB

BYP1-7   No financial decision-maker should ever rely solely on the financial information reported in a company's annual report to make decisions. It is important to keep abreast of financial news. This activity shows you how to search for financial news about Loblaw and Sobeys using Yahoo! Canada Finance.

Instructions

Specific requirements of this Web case can be found on the Kimmel website.

Critical Thinking

COLLABORATIVE LEARNING ACTIVITY

BYP1-8   Kelly Services (Canada), Ltd. provides personnel for temporary positions. In one of its annual reports, Kelly Services chronicled its contributions to community services. The following excerpts illustrate the variety of services provided:

1. During KellyWeek, a Saint Patrick's Day customer appreciation event, Kelly Services made donations of temporary help, in addition to stationery, office decorations, and decals containing the company's name.
2. In support of a country-wide beautification campaign, the company donated, and its employees planted, gladiolus gardens in cities across the country.
3. The company initiated a holiday draw in which thousands of customers throughout North America nominate their favourite children's charities. Winning charities in the draw receive a monetary donation from Kelly Services in the name of the customer.
4. Kelly executives regularly volunteer their time and resources to serve as role models and mentors to youth.

Instructions

With the class divided into groups, answer the following:

(a) The economic entity assumption requires that a company keep the personal expenses of its employees separate from business expenses. Which of the activities listed above were expenses of the business, and which were personal expenses of the employees? Be specific. If part of the donation is business and part is personal, note which part is which.

(b) For those items that were company expenses, state whether the expense was probably categorized as an advertising expense, employee wages expense, grounds maintenance expense, or charitable contribution expense. You may use any or all of the categories. Explain your answer.

COMMUNICATION ACTIVITY

BYP1-9   Karen Staudinger is the bookkeeper for Vermon Company, Inc., and has been trying to get the company's balance sheet to balance. She finally succeeded, but she still isn't sure that it is correct.

VERMON COMPANY, INC.
Balance Sheet
Month Ended December 31, 2004

Assets		Liabilities and Shareholders' Equity	
Equipment	$20,500	Common shares	$11,000
Cash	10,500	Accounts receivable	(3,000)
Supplies	2,000	Dividends	(2,000)
Accounts payable	(5,000)	Notes payable	12,000
Total assets	$28,000	Retained earnings	10,000
		Total liabilities and	
		shareholders' equity	$28,000

Instructions

In a memo, explain to Karen (a) the purpose of a balance sheet, (b) why her balance sheet is incorrect, and (c) what she should do to correct it.

ETHICS CASE

Ethics In
Accounting

BYP1-10 Starting in 2002, chief executive officers (CEOs) and chief financial officers (CFOs) of selected companies were required to sign a document personally attesting that their companies' most recent financial filings were accurate and complete. The certification mandate came after numerous corporate scandals as a way to hold top executives personally responsible if they knowingly file false statements.

Khan Company just hired a new management team in 2002, and its members say they're too new to the company to know whether the most recent reports are accurate or not. They refuse to sign the certification.

Instructions

(a) Who are the stakeholders in this situation?
(b) Should the CEO and CFO sign the certification? Explain why or why not.
(c) What are the CEO's and CFO's alternatives?

Answers to Self-Study Questions

1. b   2. d   3. d   4. d   5. c   6. d   7. a   8. c   9. a   10. c
11. c   12. c

Answer to Loblaw Review It Question 3

Loblaw's accounting equation as at December 28, 2002 is (in millions):

Assets	=	Liabilities	+	Shareholders' Equity
$11,110	=	$6,986	+	$4,124

Remember to go back to the Navigator box on the
chapter-opening page to check off your completed work.

A Further Look at Financial Statements

NAVIGATOR

Just Fooling Around?

Few people could have predicted how dramatically the Internet would change the investment world. One of the most interesting results is how it has changed the way ordinary people invest their savings. More and more people are spurning investment professionals and instead are choosing to strike out on their own, making personal investment decisions using the Internet.

Two early pioneers in providing investment information to the masses were Tom and David Gardner, brothers who created an on-line investor service called The Motley Fool. The name comes from Shakespeare's *As You Like It*. The brothers note that the fool in Shakespeare's plays was the only one who could speak unpleasant truths to kings and queens without being killed. Tom and David view themselves as twentieth-century "fools," revealing the "truths" of the stock markets to the small investor, who they feel insiders have taken advantage of. Their on-line bulletin board enables investors to exchange information and insights about companies.

Critics of these bulletin boards contend that they are nothing more than high-tech rumour mills that are largely responsible for building a speculative house of cards. They suggest that, because of the fervour created by the bulletin board chatter, share prices get bid up to unreasonable levels, and people often pay prices that are far higher than the underlying worth of the company. One potentially troubling aspect of bulletin boards is that participants on the board rarely give their real identi-

ties—instead using aliases. Consequently, there is little to stop people from putting misinformation on the board to influence a share's price in the direction they desire.

To show how these bulletin boards work, suppose that you were thinking about investing in Sears Canada. You scanned the Internet investment bulletin boards and found messages posted on the same topic by two different investors. Here are excerpts from actual postings on the same day in April 2001:

From: investor101, Subject: RTQ: $18.55???, April 4, 2001: "I bought at $18.75 but this is bargain of the century type pricing. This stock is an unbelievable value at its current price and I was more than happy to jump in at this price. This company has done nothing but make money over the

THE NAVIGATOR

Scan *Study Objectives* ☐

Read *Feature Story* ☐

Read *Chapter Preview* ☐

Read text and answer *Before You Go On*
p. 56 ☐ p. 62 ☐ p. 67 ☐ p. 71 ☐ p. 74 ☐

Work *Using the Decision Toolkit* ☐

Review *Summary of Study Objectives*
and *Decision Toolkit* ☐

Work *Demonstration Problem* ☐

Answer *Self-Study Questions* ☐

Complete assignments ☐

past few years and will continue to make money in the future. This stock should be a safe haven yet it's not being treated as such."

From: broker354, Subject: Investor101, bad news, April 4, 2001: "In case you haven't noticed, sales are way down, brother. If you sell tomorrow at $19.00 you can still get your share back and make 25 cents profit. Believe fairy tales if you wish but the facts speak for themselves. Sears will be trading at $15.00 before the end of the month."

One says it's the time to buy, and the other one says it isn't. Who should you believe?

If you had taken Investor 101's advice and purchased Sears shares in April 2001, you would have found that the share price did indeed rise. It reached a high

of $23.60 at the end of July.

Some observers are concerned that small investors—ironically, the very people the Gardner brothers were trying to help—will be hurt the most by misinformation and intentional scams.

One of the most notorious examples of misinformation and scams occurred with Bre-X Minerals, Ltd., a Calgary-based mining exploration company. Bre-X Minerals drew worldwide attention in the 1990s after it claimed to have discovered the largest gold find of the century in Busang, Indonesia, on the jungle island of Borneo. The share price skyrocketed in 1996 from pennies to about $280 per share based on the company's claims of massive gold deposits—claims which were never verified. It plunged to just 2.5 cents, before being delisted, after it was revealed that the Bu-

sang deposit contained only negligible amounts of gold. All told, less-than-cautious investors lost $6 billion on the Bre-X shares. With unfounded rumours and conspiracy theories abounding on the Internet, large and small buyers kept pouring money into the shares even as questions about the reliability of the find were being raised.

So, how should you decide what shares to buy? Rather than getting swept away by rumours, investors must sort the good information from the bad. There is no doubt that as information services such as The Motley Fool increase in number, gathering information will become even easier. Evaluating it will become the harder task.

If you are thinking of purchasing Sears shares on the Internet, or elsewhere, how can you decide what the shares are worth? If you own shares, how can you determine whether it is time to buy more—or time to bail out? Your decision will be influenced by a variety of considerations; one should be your careful analysis of a company's financial statements. The reason: Financial statements offer relevant and reliable information which will help you in your share purchase decisions.

In this chapter we begin by looking at the objective of financial reporting. We then take a closer look at the balance sheet and introduce some useful ways of evaluating the information provided by the statements. The content and organization of the chapter are as follows:

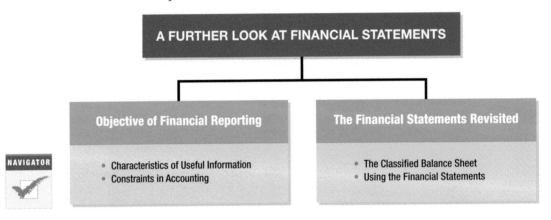

SECTION 1

OBJECTIVE OF FINANCIAL REPORTING

Financial reporting is the term used to describe all of the financial information presented by a company—both in its financial statements and in additional disclosures provided in the annual report. For example, if you are deciding whether to invest in Sears shares, you need financial information to help make your decision. Such information should help you understand Sears' past financial performance and current financial picture, and it should give you some idea of its future prospects. Although information found on electronic bulletin boards, like The Motley Fool, is useful, it is no substitute for careful study of financial reports.

Characteristics of Useful Information

STUDY OBJECTIVE

1

Describe the basic objective of financial reporting and the qualitative characteristics of accounting information.

How does a company like Sears decide on the amount and type of financial information to disclose? What format should it use? How should assets, liabilities, revenues, and expenses be measured? The answers to these questions are found in accounting rules that have substantial authoritative support and are recognized as a general guide for financial reporting purposes. These rules are referred to as generally accepted accounting principles (GAAP).

The accounting standard-setting body in Canada is the Canadian Institute of Chartered Accountants (CICA). All federal and provincial incorporating acts and provincial securities commissions recognize generally accepted accounting principles. This means that GAAP has the force of law for incorporated and publicly traded companies.

The CICA's overriding criterion is that the accounting rules should generate the most useful financial information for making business decisions. In other words, **the basic objective of financial reporting is to communicate information that is useful to investors, creditors, and other users in making investment and lending decisions and in assessing management's performance.** To be useful, information should possess these qualitative characteristics: **understandability, relevance, reliability,** and **comparability.**

UNDERSTANDABILITY

In order for information provided in financial statements to be useful, it must be understandable by all users. Users are defined primarily as investors and creditors, but can include other interested decision-makers. These users may vary in the types of decisions they must make and in their level of interest in the information. At one extreme is a sophisticated creditor who carefully scrutinizes all aspects of the financial information. At the other extreme is an unsophisticated investor who may only scan the text and not study the numbers.

It is not possible to satisfy all users' needs with one general purpose set of financial statements. It is therefore necessary to agree upon a basic level of understandability to assist both the preparer of financial information and its user. **The average user is assumed to have an understanding of accounting concepts and procedures, as well as of general business and economic conditions, to be able to study the statements intelligently.** If this level of understanding and ability does not exist, the user is expected to rely on professionals with an appropriate level of expertise. With your study of this course, you are well on your way to becoming this average user!

RELEVANCE

Accounting information has **relevance** if it will influence a business decision. For example, when Bre-X issued financial statements, the information in the statements was considered relevant because it provided a basis for forecasting Bre-X's future earnings. Accounting information is also relevant to business decisions when it confirms or corrects prior expectations. Thus, Bre-X's financial statements should have both helped **predict** future events and **provided feedback** on prior expectations about the financial health of the company. Unfortunately, premature investors did not take the time to fully analyse the company's financial statements. Not only were Bre-X's earnings not growing, it didn't have any at all, as from 1993 through 1995 the company remained in the red.

For accounting information to be relevant, it must also be **timely**; that is, it must be available to decision-makers before it loses its capacity to influence decisions. If Bre-X reported its financial information only every five years, the information would not have been very useful. Many people believe that by the time annual financial statements are issued—sometimes up to six months after year end—the information is in fact of limited usefulness for decision-making. Timely interim financial reporting is therefore essential to relevant decision-making.

RELIABILITY

Reliability of information means that the information can be depended on. To be reliable, accounting information must be **verifiable**—we must be able to prove that it is free of error. Also, the information must be a **faithful representation** of what it says it is—it must be factual. When Bre-X reported that there were over 70 million ounces of gold in the Busang deposit when there was really very little gold, the statement was not a faithful representation.

Accounting information must also be **neutral**—it cannot be selected, prepared, or presented to favour one set of interested users over another. Many accountants refer to information which is verifiable, a faithful representation, and neutral as **objective** information. That is, two or more people reviewing this information would reach the same basic conclusions about it.

In situations of uncertainty, neutrality is affected by the use of conservatism. Conservatism in accounting means that when preparing financial statements, a company should choose the accounting method that will be least likely to overstate assets and earnings. **It does not mean, however, that one should intentionally understate assets or earnings.**

Conservatism is commonly applied when valuing inventories. Inventories are normally recorded at their cost. Conservatism requires, however, that inventories be written down to their market value if market value is below cost. Conservatism also requires that when the market value of inventory is greater than the cost, the value of the inventory not be increased on the books, but instead remain at cost.

BUSINESS INSIGHT

MANAGEMENT PERSPECTIVE

Accurate reporting became a significant public policy issue following the Enron, WorldCom, and other corporate scandals. In response, the chief executive and chief financial officers of companies listed on U.S. stock exchanges—including about 220 Canadian companies—are now required to personally certify that their companies' financial statements are reliable. James Lyon, a manager of an investment firm, commented: "There's something to be said for asking the CEO and CFO to sign on the dotted line to verify that their numbers are correct. It's a sobering thing to do, [and] I think investors view this practice as being one where the officers are having their feet held to the fire."

Source: Richard Blackwell, "SEC Certification Deadline Passes with No New Scandals: U.S. Executives Sign Off on Financial Results," *The Globe and Mail*, August 15, 2002, B1.

COMPARABILITY

Let's say that you and a friend kept track of your height each year as you were growing up. If you measured your height in metres and your friend measured hers in feet, it would be difficult to compare your heights. A conversion would be necessary. In accounting, comparability results when companies with similar circumstances use the same accounting principles.

At one level, accounting standards are fairly comparable because they are based on certain basic principles and assumptions. These principles and assumptions, however, do allow for some variation in methods. For example, there are a variety of ways to report inventory. Often these different methods result in different amounts of net earnings. As we learned in Chapter 1, the **full disclosure principle** makes comparisons of companies easier, as each company must disclose the accounting methods used. From the disclosures, the external user can determine whether the financial information is comparable and can try to make adjustments. Unfortunately, converting the accounting numbers of companies that use different methods is not as easy as converting your height from metres to feet.

Users of accounting information also want to compare the same company's financial results over time. For example, to compare a company's net earnings over several years, you'd need to know that the same principles have been used from year to year; otherwise, you might be comparing apples to oranges. Consistency means that a company uses the same accounting principles and methods from year to year. Thus, if a company selects one inventory accounting method in the first year of operations, it is expected to continue to use that same method in succeeding years. When financial information has been reported on a consistent basis, the financial statements permit a meaningful analysis of trends within a company.

A company can change to a new method of accounting if management can show that the new method produces more useful financial information. In the year in which the change occurs, the change must be disclosed in the notes to the financial statements so that statement users are aware of the lack of consistency.

One factor that can affect the ability to compare two companies is their choice of accounting or fiscal year end. For example, Loblaw's current fiscal year end is December 28, 2002, and Sobeys' is May 3, 2003. This can create problems, because when you compare the companies, you are comparing neither their performance over the same period of time nor their financial position at the same point in time. You can still compare companies with different fiscal year ends, as we are doing in this text; however, you will have to be careful to identify and interpret results that may only be due to the differing time periods.

Another factor that can complicate comparisons is the use of different currencies and different accounting standards when one compares companies from different countries. For example, one of Loblaw's competitors is U.S.-based Wal-Mart. Comparing the financial statements of these two competitors can be challenging.

The characteristics that make accounting information useful are summarized in Illustration 2-1.

International Note

Accounting standards vary from country to country. Most countries have their own standard-setting body. One group, the International Accounting Standards Committee, has been working to reduce the differences in accounting practices and standards across countries.

Illustration 2-1
Characteristics of useful information

Understandability
1. Of accounting concepts and procedures
2. Of general business and economic conditions

Relevance
1. Provides a basis for forecasts
2. Confirms or corrects prior expectations
3. Is timely

Reliability
1. Is verifiable
2. Is a faithful representation
3. Is neutral
4. Is conservative

Comparability
1. Different companies use similar accounting principles
2. Company uses same accounting principles consistently year to year

Constraints in Accounting

The goal of the characteristics we have discussed is to provide users of financial statements with the most useful information. Taken to the extreme, however, the pursuit of useful financial information could be far too costly for a company. Some constraints have therefore been agreed upon to ensure that accounting rules are applied in a reasonable fashion, from the perspectives of both the company and the user. **Constraints** permit a company to apply generally accepted accounting principles without jeopardizing the usefulness of the reported information. Two constraints are cost-benefit and materiality.

STUDY OBJECTIVE

Identify the two constraints in accounting.

COST-BENEFIT

The cost-benefit constraint ensures that the value of the information exceeds the cost of providing it. Accountants could disclose every financial event that occurs and every contingency that exists. However, providing additional information increases costs, and the benefits of providing this information, in some cases, may be less than the costs.

MATERIALITY

Materiality relates to a financial statement item's impact on a company's overall financial condition and operations. An item is **material** when its size makes it likely to influence the decision of an investor or creditor. It is **not material** if it is too small to affect a user's decision. In short, if the item does not make a difference, GAAP does not have to be followed. To determine the materiality of an amount—that is, to determine its financial significance—the item is compared to such items as total assets, total liabilities, sales revenue, and net earnings.

To illustrate how the materiality constraint is applied, assume that Loblaw made a $100,000 error in recording revenue. Loblaw's total revenue exceeds $23 billion, so a $100,000 error is not material.

The two constraints are shown in Illustration 2-2.

Illustration 2-2
Accounting constraints

Materiality — For small amounts, GAAP does not have to be followed.

Cost-Benefit — Cost $\leq$ Benefit

BEFORE YOU GO ON...

● **REVIEW IT**

1. What is the basic objective of financial information?
2. What are generally accepted accounting principles?
3. What qualitative characteristics make accounting information useful?
4. What are the cost-benefit and materiality constraints?

SECTION 2

The Financial Statements Revisited

In Chapter 1, we introduced the four financial statements. In this section, we review the financial statements and present useful tools for evaluating them. We begin by introducing the classified balance sheet.

The Classified Balance Sheet

The balance sheet presents a snapshot of a company's financial position at a point in time. To improve users' understanding of a company's financial position, companies group similar assets and similar liabilities together. This is useful because it tells you that items within a group have similar economic characteristics. A classified balance sheet generally contains the standard classifications listed in Illustration 2-3.

STUDY OBJECTIVE 3

Identify the sections of a classified balance sheet.

Illustration 2-3
Standard balance sheet classifications

Assets	Liabilities and Shareholders' Equity
Current assets	Current liabilities
Long-term investments	Long-term liabilities
Property, plant, and equipment	Shareholders' equity
Intangible assets	

These groupings help readers determine such things as (1) whether the company has enough assets to pay its debts as they come due and (2) the claims of short- and long-term creditors on the company's total assets. These groupings can be seen in the balance sheet of Frenette Corporation shown in Illustration 2-4. Each of the groupings will then be explained.

Illustration 2-4
Frenette Corporation balance sheet

FRENETTE CORPORATION
Balance Sheet
October 31, 2004

Assets			
Current assets			
Cash		$ 6,600	
Short-term investments		2,000	
Accounts receivable		7,000	
Inventories		4,000	
Supplies		2,100	
Prepaid insurance		400	
Total current assets			$22,100
Long-term investments			
Investments in shares of Walters Corp.		$ 5,200	
Investment in real estate		2,000	
Total long-term investments			7,200
Property, plant, and equipment			
Land		$10,000	
Office equipment	$24,000		
Less: Accumulated amortization	5,000	19,000	
Total property, plant, and equipment			29,000
Intangible assets			
Patents			3,100
Total assets			$61,400

Liabilities and Shareholders' Equity		
Current liabilities		
Notes payable	$11,000	
Accounts payable	2,100	
Salaries payable	1,600	
Unearned revenue	900	
Interest payable	450	
Total current liabilities		$16,050
Long-term liabilities		
Mortgage payable	$10,000	
Notes payable	1,300	
Total long-term liabilities		11,300
Total liabilities		27,350
Shareholders' equity		
Common shares	$14,000	
Retained earnings	20,050	
Total shareholders' equity		34,050
Total liabilities and shareholders' equity		$61,400

CURRENT ASSETS

Current assets are assets that are expected to be converted to cash or used up by the business within a relatively short period of time. In Illustration 2-4, Frenette Corporation has current assets totalling $22,100. For most businesses the cut-off for classification as current assets is one year from the balance sheet date. For example, accounts receivable are included in current assets because they will be converted to cash through collection within one year. Supplies are a current asset because we expect that these will be used up by the business within one year.

Common types of current assets are (1) **cash**, including cash equivalents or near cash items such as treasury bills and money market funds, (2) **short-term investments**, such as debt or equity securities, (3) **receivables** such as notes receivable, accounts receivable, and interest receivable, (4) **inventories**, (5) **supplies**, and (6) **prepaid expenses** such as rent and insurance. On the balance sheet, these items are listed in the order in which they are expected to be converted into cash. This arrangement is shown in Illustration 2-5 for Canada Post.

Illustration 2-5
Current assets section

From anywhere... to anyone

CANADA POST Balance Sheet (partial) December 31, 2002 (in millions)	
Current assets	
Cash and cash equivalents	$ 450
Short-term investments	29
Accounts receivable and other receivables	517
Prepaid expenses	71
Current portion of note receivable	18
Current portion of future income taxes	47
Total current assets	1,132

A company's current assets are important in assessing its short-term debt-paying ability, as is explained later in the chapter.

LONG-TERM INVESTMENTS

Long-term investments are generally investments in debt and equity (e.g., shares) of other corporations that are normally held for many years. They also include investments in long-term assets, such as land or buildings, that are not currently being used in the company's operating activities. In Illustration 2-4, Frenette Corporation reported total long-term investments of $7,200 on its balance sheet. Imperial Tobacco's investments appear in the partial balance sheet in Illustration 2-6:

Alternative Terminology
Long-term investments are often just referred to as *investments.*

Illustration 2-6
Long-term investments section

IMPERIAL TOBACCO CANADA LIMITED Balance Sheet (partial) December 31, 2002 (in millions)	
Investments	
Securities—fixed income	$ 65
Securities—equity	43
Other	210
Investments in a company under common control	484
	802

PROPERTY, PLANT, AND EQUIPMENT

Property, plant, and equipment are assets with relatively long useful lives that are currently being used in operating the business. This category includes land, buildings, equipment, and furniture. In Illustration 2-4, Frenette Corporation reported property, plant, and equipment of $29,000.

Alternative Terminology
Property, plant, and equipment are sometimes called *capital assets* or *fixed assets.*

Although the order of property, plant, and equipment items can vary among companies, these items are normally listed in the balance sheet in order of permanency. That is, land is usually listed first as it has an indefinite life, and is followed by the asset with the next longest useful life, normally buildings, and so on.

These long-lived assets, except land, have estimated useful lives over which they are expected to generate revenues. Because property, plant, and equipment benefit future periods, their cost is matched to revenues over their estimated useful life through a process called **amortization**. This is preferable to simply expensing (recording as an expense) the full purchase price of the asset and matching the cost to revenues generated only in the year of acquisition. Land also generates revenue, but its estimated useful life is considered to be infinite as land does not usually wear out or lose its value. Consequently, the cost of land is never amortized.

Alternative Terminology
Amortization is also commonly known as *depreciation.*

Assets subject to amortization should be reported on the balance sheet at cost less accumulated amortization. Accumulated amortization shows the amount of amortization taken over the *life of the asset*. The difference between cost and accumulated amortization is referred to as **net book value**. In Illustration 2-4, Frenette Corporation reported its office equipment at a net book value of $19,000.

The Forzani Group Ltd. details its property, plant, and equipment—called capital assets—as shown in Illustration 2-7. Note that, except for land, all other capital assets are amortized. This includes leasehold improvements, which are long-lived additions or renovations made to leased property.

THE FORZANI GROUP LTD. Balance Sheet (partial) January 31, 2003 (in thousands)			
	Cost	Accumulated Amortization	Net Book Value
Capital assets			
Land	$ 638		$ 638
Building	6,280	$ 1,637	4,643
Building on leased land	3,159	1,186	1,973
Furniture, fixtures, equipment, and automotive	97,117	52,438	44,679
Leasehold improvements	145,150	54,847	90,303
Total	252,344	110,108	142,236

INTANGIBLE ASSETS

Many companies have assets that cannot be seen yet are very valuable. Intangible assets are noncurrent assets that do not have physical substance. They include goodwill, patents, copyrights, trademarks, trade names, and licences that give the company **exclusive right of use**. Similar to buildings and equipment, intangible assets with estimated useful lives are amortized. Similar to land, intangible assets with indefinite lives are not amortized. Frenette Corporation reported intangible assets of $3,100. Illustration 2-8 shows how Shaw Communications reported its intangible assets.

SHAW COMMUNICATIONS INC. Balance Sheet (partial) August 31, 2002 (in thousands)	
Intangible assets	
Broadcast licences	$4,877,256
Goodwill	145,865
	5,023,121

CURRENT LIABILITIES

In the liabilities and shareholders' equity section of the balance sheet, the first grouping is current liabilities. Current liabilities are obligations that are to be paid within the coming year. Common examples are accounts payable, wages payable, bank loans payable, interest payable, taxes payable, and current maturities of long-term obligations (payments to be made within the next year on long-term obligations). In Illustration 2-4, Frenette Corporation reported five different types of current liabilities, for a total of $16,050.

Within the current liabilities section, notes payable are usually listed first, followed by accounts payable. Other items are then listed in any order. The current liabilities section from the balance sheet of The Jean Coutu Group is shown in Illustration 2-9.

Illustration 2-9
Current liabilities section

The
Jean Coutu
Group (PJC) Inc.

THE JEAN COUTU GROUP INC. Balance Sheet (partial) May 31, 2002 (in thousands)	
Current liabilities	
Bank overdraft and bank loans	$ 46,360
Accounts payable	296,044
Income taxes payable	10,106
Current portion of long-term debt	32,618
Total current liabilities	385,128

LONG-TERM LIABILITIES

Obligations expected to be paid after one year are classified as long-term liabilities. Liabilities in this category include bonds payable, mortgages payable, long-term notes payable, lease liabilities, and pension liabilities. Many companies report long-term debt maturing after one year as a single amount in the balance sheet and show the details of the debt in notes that accompany the financial statements. Others list the various types of long-term liabilities. In Illustration 2-4, Frenette Corporation reported long-term liabilities of $11,300. Andrés Wines details its long-term obligations in Illustration 2-10.

Alternative Terminology
Long-term liabilities are also called *long-term debt.*

Illustration 2-10
Long-term liabilities section

ANDRÉS WINES LTD. Balance Sheet (partial) March 31, 2002 (in thousands)	
Long-term debt	
Term bank loan A	$16,811
Term bank loan B	7,800
Other debt	646
	25,257
Less: Current portion	3,344
	21,913

SHAREHOLDERS' EQUITY

Shareholders' equity is divided into two parts: share capital and retained earnings. Investments of assets in the business by the shareholders are recorded as either common or preferred shares. If preferred shares are issued in addition to common shares, the total of all classes of shares issued is classified as, or headed, **share capital**. Earnings retained for use in the business are recorded as **retained earnings**. These two parts are combined and reported as **shareholders' equity** on the balance sheet. In Illustration 2-4, Frenette Corporation reported Common Shares of $14,000 and Retained Earnings of $20,050.

The shareholders' equity section of Le Château's balance sheet is shown in Illustration 2-11.

Alternative Terminology *Share capital* is also commonly known as *capital stock.*

Illustration 2-11
Shareholders' equity
section

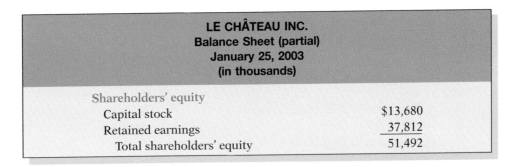

LE CHÂTEAU INC. Balance Sheet (partial) January 25, 2003 (in thousands)	
Shareholders' equity	
Capital stock	$13,680
Retained earnings	37,812
Total shareholders' equity	51,492

BEFORE YOU GO ON . . .

● REVIEW IT

1. What are the major sections in a classified balance sheet?
2. What is the primary determining factor in distinguishing current assets from long-term assets?
3. What was Loblaw's largest current asset at December 28, 2002? The answer to this question is provided at the end of the chapter.
4. Where is accumulated amortization reported on the balance sheet?

● DO IT

Hoffman Corporation recently received the following information related to its December 2004 balance sheet:

Accounts receivable	$1,100	Inventory	$ 3,400
Accumulated amortization	2,700	Prepaid expenses	2,300
Cash	800	Office equipment	10,700

Prepare the assets section of Hoffman Corporation's classified balance sheet.

Action Plan:

- Present current assets first. Current assets are cash and other resources that are reasonably expected to be consumed in one year.
- Subtract accumulated amortization from office equipment to determine the net book value.

Solution

HOFFMAN CORPORATION Balance Sheet (partial) December 31, 2004		
Assets		
Current assets		
Cash	$ 800	
Accounts receivable	1,100	
Inventory	3,400	
Prepaid expenses	2,300	
Total current assets		$ 7,600
Property, plant, and equipment		
Office equipment	$10,700	
Less: Accumulated amortization	2,700	
Total property, plant, and equipment		8,000
Total assets		$15,600

NAVIGATOR

Using the Financial Statements

In Chapter 1, we briefly discussed how the four financial statements provide information about a company's performance and financial position. In this chapter, we extend this discussion by showing you specific tools that can be used to analyse financial statements in order to make a more meaningful evaluation of a company.

RATIO ANALYSIS

Ratio analysis expresses the relationships among selected items of financial statement data. A ratio expresses the mathematical relationship between one quantity and another. The relationship is expressed as either a percentage, a rate, or a simple proportion. To illustrate, Sears Canada recently had current assets of $2,577.6 million and current liabilities of $1,451.6 million. The relationship between these amounts is determined by dividing current assets by current liabilities. The three means of expressing this ratio are:

Percentage: Current assets are 180% of current liabilities.
Rate: Current assets are 1.8 times greater than current liabilities.
Proportion: The relationship of current assets to liabilities is 1.8:1.

The ratios for analysing the primary financial statements can be classified as shown in Illustration 2-12.

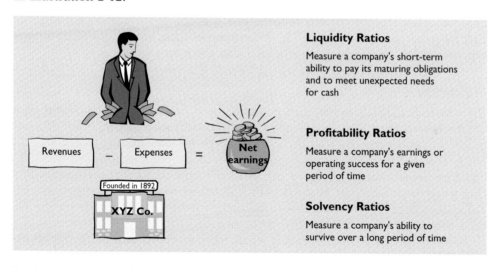

Liquidity Ratios

Measure a company's short-term ability to pay its maturing obligations and to meet unexpected needs for cash

Profitability Ratios

Measure a company's earnings or operating success for a given period of time

Solvency Ratios

Measure a company's ability to survive over a long period of time

Illustration 2-12
Financial ratio classifications

Ratios can provide clues to underlying conditions that may not be apparent when components of a paticular ratio are examined individually. Since a single ratio by itself is not very meaningful, in this and subsequent chapters, we will use:

1. **Intracompany comparisons** covering two years for the same company.
2. **Intercompany comparisons** based on comparisons with a competitor in the same industry.
3. **Industry average comparisons** based on average ratios for paticular industries.

USING THE STATEMENT OF EARNINGS

Sears generates a profit for its shareholders by selling merchandise. The statement of earnings reports how successful Sears is at generating this profit. It reports the amount earned during the period (revenues) and the costs incurred during the same period (expenses). A statement of earnings for Sears is provided in Illustration 2-13.

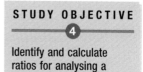

STUDY OBJECTIVE
4

Identify and calculate ratios for analysing a company's profitability.

Illustration 2-13
Sears' statement of
earnings

SEARS CANADA INC. Statement of Earnings Year Ended December 28, 2002 (in millions)		
	2002	2001
Total revenues	$6,535.9	$6,726.4
Expenses		
Cost of merchandise sold, operating, administrative, and selling expenses	6,107.9	6,320.9
Amortization	148.7	169.3
Interest	59.8	64.2
Unusual items—loss (gain)	189.1	(5.5)
Total expenses	6,505.5	6,548.9
Earnings before income taxes	30.4	177.5
Income tax expense (recovery)	(21.8)	83.4
Net earnings	$ 52.2	$ 94.1

From this statement of earnings, we can see that Sears' total revenues and net earnings both decreased during the year. Net earnings decreased from $94.1 million to $52.2 million. However, if the unusual loss of $189.1 million is excluded from the results, Sears' earnings from operations actually increased between 2001 and 2002. The majority of this unusual loss was due to the conversion of seven Eaton's stores to Sears in 2002. The integration of these stores into Sears' operations should result in operating efficiencies in the future.

Profitability

Both shareholders—existing and potential—and creditors are interested in a company's profitability. To evaluate the profitability of Sears (and later its liquidity and solvency), we will use ratio analysis for two fiscal years, 2002 and 2001. This will provide us with our **intracompany comparison**. We will then compare Sears' ratios to those of one of its primary competitors, Hudson's Bay Company, to broaden our analysis to include an **intercompany comparison**. Finally, we will compare our ratios to **industry average comparisons** for the retail department store industry.

We start with profitability ratios, which measure the income or operating success of a company for a given period of time. We will look at two examples of profitability ratios: **earnings per share** and the **price-earnings ratio**.

Earnings per Share. Earnings per share (EPS) measures the net earnings for each common share. Accordingly, earnings per share is reported only for common shareholders. It is calculated by dividing **net earnings available to the common shareholders** by the **average number of common shares** issued during the year. When a company has preferred shares in addition to common shares, earnings available to common shareholders is determined by deducting any dividends paid to preferred shareholders from net earnings.

Shareholders usually think in terms of the number of shares they own, or plan to buy or sell, so reducing net earnings to a per share amount provides a useful perspective for determining the investment return. Earnings per share amounts for Sears and its competitor, Hudson's Bay, are calculated in Illustration 2-14.

Illustration 2-14
Earnings per share

EARNINGS PER SHARE = $\dfrac{\text{NET EARNINGS} - \text{PREFERRED DIVIDENDS}}{\text{AVERAGE NUMBER OF COMMON SHARES}}$		
($ in millions except per share amounts)	2002	2001
Sears	$\dfrac{\$52.2 - \$0}{106.8} = \$0.49$	$\dfrac{\$94.1 - \$0}{106.7} = \$0.88$
Hudson's Bay	$1.40	$0.85
Industry average	n/a	n/a

B U S I N E S S   I N S I G H T

INVESTOR PERSPECTIVE

Profitability matters. Recently, when Sears missed its estimated earnings per share figure by five cents, its share price fell by 14 cents. Although it isn't unusual for a company's share price to be affected by earnings announcements, what was unusual was that the share price of other companies also fell as a result of the news. In this case, investors reacted because Sears' financial health is viewed as a good indicator of the strength of the economy as a whole. Investors were expressing their concern that difficult times for retailers were on the horizon.

Price-Earnings Ratio. Comparisons of earnings per share are not very meaningful among companies because of the wide variation in the number of shares and in the share prices. That's why there is no industry average available for earnings per share in Illustration 2-14. When industry averages are not available for the ratios we calculate in this text, "n/a" (not available) appears.

In order to compare earnings across companies, we calculate the price-earnings (P-E) ratio. The price-earnings ratio is a frequently quoted statistic that measures **the ratio of the market price of each common share to its earnings per share.** It is calculated by dividing the market price per share by earnings per share.

The price-earnings ratio reflects the investors' assessment of a company's future earnings. The ratio of price to earnings will be higher if investors think that current earnings levels will persist or increase than it will be if investors think that earnings will decline. A high price-earnings ratio might also indicate that a share is priced too high and is likely to come down.

The price-earnings ratios for Sears and its competitor, Hudson's Bay, are presented in Illustration 2-15, and use the earnings per share amounts presented above.

Illustration 2-15
Price-earnings ratio

PRICE-EARNINGS RATIO $= \dfrac{\text{MARKET PRICE PER SHARE}}{\text{EARNINGS PER SHARE}}$		
	2002	**2001**
Sears	$\dfrac{\$17.05}{\$0.49} = 34.8$ times	$\dfrac{\$18.85}{\$0.88} = 21.4$ times
Hudson's Bay	6.5 times	17.6 times
Industry average	17.3 times	18.1 times

From 2001 to 2002, Sears' earnings per share decreased. However, its price-earnings ratio increased—in contrast to the decreasing price-earnings ratios of Hudson's Bay and the industry. This increase likely reflects a belief that Sears will be able to return to its usual profitability.

As noted, earnings per share cannot be meaningfully compared across companies. Price-earnings ratios, however, can be compared. Illustration 2-16 lists four companies and their earnings per share and price-earnings ratios for 2002.

Illustration 2-16
Variability of profitability measures among companies

Company	Earnings per Share	Price-Earnings Ratio
Bank of Montreal	$2.73	14.0
Canadian Tire	2.56	12.4
Molson	1.46	23.9
Nortel Networks	(1.46)	n/a

BUSINESS INSIGHT

INVESTOR PERSPECTIVE

What company has a price-earnings ratio of 1,514 times earnings? Is it a high-tech company? No. It is Robert Half International Incorporated, a staffing services company. Although its share price is only $15.14, its earnings per share are even less at $0.01. The result? A ridiculously high price-earnings ratio.

Decision Toolkit

DECISION CHECKPOINTS	INFO NEEDED FOR DECISION	TOOL TO USE FOR DECISION	HOW TO EVALUATE RESULTS
How does the company's earnings performance compare with previous years?	Net earnings available to common shareholders and average number of common shares	$\text{Earnings per share} = \dfrac{\text{Net earnings} - \text{Preferred dividends}}{\text{Average number of common shares}}$	A higher measure suggests improved performance, although the number is subject to manipulation. Values should not be compared across companies.
How does the market perceive the company's prospects for future earnings?	Earnings per share and market price per share	$\text{Price earnings ratio} = \dfrac{\text{Market price per share}}{\text{Earnings per share}}$	A high ratio suggests the market has favourable expectations, although it also may suggest shares are overvalued.

BEFORE YOU GO ON . . .

- **REVIEW IT**

  1. Identify three types of useful comparisons in ratio analysis.
  2. What are the key features found in a statement of earnings?
  3. What are profitability ratios? Explain the earnings per share and the price-earnings ratio.

NAVIGATOR
✔

USING THE STATEMENT OF RETAINED EARNINGS

As discussed in Chapter 1, the statement of retained earnings describes the changes in retained earnings during the year. For the current period, the statement of retained earnings adds net earnings (or deducts net losses) and then subtracts dividends from the beginning retained earnings balance to arrive at ending retained earnings. The beginning balance on the statement of retained earnings represents undistributed earnings that have accumulated from prior years. Of course, at the beginning of the very first year of a company's operations, this opening balance will be zero since the company has not had time to accumulate any earnings as yet.

Dividends are distributions—normally by paying cash—of accumulated past and current period earnings (i.e., retained earnings) to shareholders. Even though dividends are included on the statement of retained earnings along with net earnings (revenues less expenses), it is important to remember that **dividends are not expenses**. They are not deducted on the statement of earnings because they are not incurred for the purpose of earning revenue. They are deducted instead on the statement of retained earnings and reduce the earnings retained in the business.

Illustration 2-17 presents the statement of retained earnings for Sears.

STUDY OBJECTIVE
5

Explain the relationship between a statement of retained earnings, a statement of earnings, and a balance sheet.

SEARS CANADA INC. Statement of Retained Earnings Year Ended December 28, 2002 (in millions)		
	2002	2001
Opening balance	$1,162.2	$1,093.7
Net earnings	52.2	94.1
	1,214.4	1,187.8
Dividends	25.6	25.6
Closing balance	$1,188.8	$1,162.2

Illustration 2-17
Sears' statement of
retained earnings

Note that the closing balance for the year ended December 29, 2001, becomes the opening balance for the subsequent year. Note also that the net earnings figures agree with the net earnings reported on Sears' statement of earnings (see Illustration 2-13). Finally, ending retained earnings is presented on Sears' balance sheet (see Illustration 2-18 in the next section of this chapter) as one of the components of shareholders' equity.

One observation that we can learn from this financial statement is that Sears has paid the same total dollar amount of dividends in each of the last two years. In fact, the 11-year summary in Sears' annual report reveals that Sears has maintained the same dividend rate ($0.24 per share) for the last 11 years. New investors would be particularly interested in this fact, as they decide whether or not to buy Sears shares from other investors, for what it suggests about future earnings potential.

USING THE CLASSIFIED BALANCE SHEET

STUDY OBJECTIVE

6

Identify and calculate ratios for analysing a company's liquidity and solvency.

Illustration 2-18
Sears' balance sheet

Alternative Terminology The *balance sheet* is sometimes called the *statement of financial position*, as with Sears.

You can learn a lot about a company's financial health by evaluating the relationships between its various assets and liabilities. A simplified balance sheet for Sears is provided in Illustration 2-18.

SEARS CANADA INC. Statement of Financial Position December 28, 2002 (in millions)		
	2002	2001
Assets		
Current assets		
Cash and short-term investments	$ 142.8	$ 329.3
Accounts receivable	1,384.2	871.9
Income taxes recoverable	4.1	
Inventories	754.0	864.5
Prepaid expenses and other assets	109.4	123.3
Current portion of future income tax assets	183.1	110.3
Total current assets	2,577.6	2,299.3
Investments and other assets	59.7	81.5
Capital assets	1,036.9	1,188.7
Other assets	387.1	310.5
Total assets	$4,061.3	$3,880.0
Liabilities and Shareholders' Equity		
Current liabilities		
Accounts payable	$ 799.0	$ 769.9
Accrued liabilities	517.3	422.1
Income and other taxes payable	99.1	127.9
Principal payments on long-term obligations due within one year	36.2	23.8
Total current liabilities	1,451.6	1,343.7
Long-term obligations	962.8	916.4
Total liabilities	2,414.4	2,260.1
Shareholders' equity		
Capital stock	458.1	457.7
Retained earnings	1,188.8	1,162.2
Total shareholders' equity	1,646.9	1,619.9
Total liabilities and shareholders' equity	$4,061.3	$3,880.0

Liquidity

Suppose you are a banker thinking of lending money to Sears, or you are a computer manufacturer interested in selling computers to Sears. You would be concerned about its liquidity—Sears' ability to pay obligations that are expected to become due within the next year. To have an idea of this, you would look closely at the relationship of its current assets to its current liabilities, using liquidity ratios. Liquidity ratios measure the short-term ability of the company to pay its maturing obligations and to meet unexpected needs for cash.

Working Capital. One measure of liquidity is working capital, which is the difference between current assets and current liabilities. When working capital is positive, there is a greater likelihood that the company will pay its liabilities. When working capital is negative, short-term creditors may not be paid, and the company may ultimately be forced into bankruptcy.

Illustration 2-19
Working capital

WORKING CAPITAL = CURRENT ASSETS − CURRENT LIABILITIES		
($ in millions)	2002	2001
Sears	$2,577.6 − $1,451.6 = $1,126.0	$2,299.3 − $1,343.7 = $955.6
Hudson's Bay	$1,147.7	$1,460.8
Industry average	n/a	n/a

Industry averages are not very meaningful for working capital, since working capital is expressed in absolute dollars rather than as a ratio.

Current Ratio. One liquidity ratio is the current ratio, which is calculated by dividing current assets by current liabilities. The current ratio is a more dependable indicator of liquidity than working capital. Two companies with the same amount of working capital may have significantly different current ratios. The 2002 and 2001 current ratios for Sears, Hudson's Bay, and the industry average are shown in Illustration 2-20.

Illustration 2-20
Current ratio

$$\text{CURRENT RATIO} = \frac{\text{CURRENT ASSETS}}{\text{CURRENT LIABILITIES}}$$		
($ in millions)	2002	2001
Sears	$\dfrac{\$2,577.6}{\$1,451.6} = 1.8{:}1$	$\dfrac{\$2,299.3}{\$1,343.7} = 1.7{:}1$
Hudson's Bay	1.9:1	2.3:1
Industry average	2.1:1	2.1:1

What does the ratio actually mean? The 2002 ratio of 1.8:1 means that for every dollar of current liabilities, Sears has $1.80 of current assets. Sears' current ratio has increased marginally in the current year. However, when compared to Hudson's Bay and the industry average, Sears' short-term liquidity falls short.

The current ratio is only one measure of liquidity. It does not take into account the **composition** of the current assets. For example, a satisfactory current ratio does not disclose the fact that a portion of the current assets may be tied up in uncollectible accounts receivable or slow-moving inventory. The composition of the assets matters because a dollar of cash is more readily available to pay the bills than is a dollar of inventory. For example, suppose a company's cash balance declined while its merchandise inventory increased substantially. If inventory increased because the company is having difficulty selling it then the current ratio might not fully reflect the reduction in the company's liquidity.

Solvency

Now suppose that instead of being a short-term creditor, you are interested in either buying Sears shares or extending the company a long-term loan. Long-term creditors and shareholders are interested in a company's long-run solvency—its ability to pay interest as it comes due and to repay the face value of the debt at maturity. Solvency ratios measure the company's ability to survive over a long period of time. The debt to total assets ratio is one source of information about debt-paying ability.

Helpful Hint Some users evaluate solvency using a ratio of debt divided by shareholders' equity. The higher this ratio, the lower a company's solvency.

Debt to Total Assets.   The debt to total assets ratio measures the percentage of assets financed by creditors rather than shareholders. Financing provided by creditors is riskier than financing provided by shareholders, because debt must be repaid at specific points in time, whether the company is performing well or not. Thus, the higher the percentage of debt financing, the riskier the company.

The debt to total assets ratio is calculated by dividing total debt (both current and long-term liabilities) by total assets. The higher the percentage of debt to total assets, the greater the risk that the company may be unable to pay its debts as they come due. The ratios of debt to total assets for Sears, Hudson's Bay, and the industry average are presented in Illustration 2-21.

Illustration 2-21
Debt to total assets

$$\text{DEBT TO TOTAL ASSETS} = \frac{\text{TOTAL LIABILITIES}}{\text{TOTAL ASSETS}}$$

($ in millions)	2002	2001
Sears	$\dfrac{\$2,414.4}{\$4,061.3} = 59.4\%$	$\dfrac{\$2,260.1}{\$3,880.0} = 58.2\%$
Hudson's Bay	44.0%	44.2%
Industry average	57.1%	44.1%

The 2002 ratio of 59.4% means that 59.4 cents of every dollar Sears invested in assets has been provided by its creditors. Sears' ratio exceeds both the Hudson's Bay debt to total assets ratio of 44.0% and the industry average of 57.1%. The higher the ratio, the lower the equity "cushion" available to creditors if the company becomes insolvent. Thus, from the creditors' point of view, a high ratio of debt to total assets is undesirable. In other words, Sears' solvency appears lower than that of both Hudson's Bay and of the average company in the industry.

The significance of this ratio is often judged in light of the company's earnings. Generally, companies with relatively stable earnings have higher debt to total assets ratios than do cyclical companies with widely fluctuating earnings.

BUSINESS INSIGHT

INVESTOR PERSPECTIVE

Debt financing differs greatly across industries and companies. Here are some debt to total assets ratios for selected companies:

Indigo Books & Music	85%
Leon's Furniture	27%
Molson	74%
Saputo	56%

Decision Toolkit

DECISION CHECKPOINTS	INFO NEEDED FOR DECISION	TOOL TO USE FOR DECISION	HOW TO EVALUATE RESULTS
Can the company meet its short-term obligations?	Current assets and current liabilities	$\text{Working capital} = \text{Current assets} - \text{Current liabilities}$	A higher amount indicates liquidity.
		$\text{Current ratio} = \dfrac{\text{Current assets}}{\text{Current liabilities}}$	A higher ratio suggests favourable liquidity.
Can the company meet its long-term obligations?	Total debt and total assets	$\text{Debt to total assets} = \dfrac{\text{Total liabilities}}{\text{Total assets}}$	A lower value suggests favourable solvency.

BEFORE YOU GO ON . . .

● **REVIEW IT**

1. Explain how a statement of retained earnings relates to a statement of earnings and balance sheet.
2. What are the major sections in a classified balance sheet?
3. What is liquidity? How can it be measured?
4. What is solvency? How can it be measured?

● **DO IT**

Selected financial data for Drummond Inc. at December 31, 2004, are as follows: cash $60,000; receivables $80,000; inventory $70,000; property, plant, and equipment $100,000. Current liabilities are $140,000 and long-term liabilities $50,000. Calculate the current ratio and debt to total assets.

Action Plan

- Use the formula for the current ratio: Current assets ÷ Current liabilities.
- Understand the composition of current assets (Cash + Receivables + Inventory).
- Use the formula for the debt to total assets ratio: Total liabilities ÷ Total assets.
- Understand how to determine total liabilities (Current liabilities + Long-term liabilities).
- Understand how to find total assets (Current assets + Property, plant, and equipment).

Solution

The current ratio is 1.5:1 [($60,000 + $80,000 + $70,000) ÷ $140,000]. The debt to total assets ratio is 61% [($140,000 + $50,000) ÷ ($60,000 + $80,000 + $70,000 + $100,000)].

USING THE CASH FLOW STATEMENT

As you learned in Chapter 1, the cash flow statement provides financial information about the sources and uses of a company's cash. Investors, creditors, and others want to know what is happening to a company's most liquid resource—its cash. In fact, it is often said that "cash is king," since a company which can't generate cash won't survive. To aid in the analysis of cash, the cash flow statement reports the cash effects of a company's (1) **operating activities**, (2) **investing activities**, and (3) **financing activities**.

Sources of cash matter. For example, you would feel much better about a company's health if you knew that its cash was generated from the operating activities of the business rather than from borrowing. A cash flow statement provides this information. Similarly, net earnings do not tell you how much cash the firm generated from operating activities. The cash flow statement, however, can tell you that. In summary, neither the statement of earnings nor the balance sheet can directly answer most of the important questions about cash, but the cash flow statement does. A simplified cash flow statement for Sears is provided in Illustration 2-22.

Illustration 2-22
Sears' cash flow statement

Alternative Terminology The *cash flow statement* is sometimes called the *statement of changes in financial position*, as with Sears.

	SEARS CANADA INC. Statement of Changes in Financial Position Year Ended December 28, 2002 (in millions)		
		2002	**2001**
Operating activities			
Cash receipts from operating activities		$6,023.6	$6,796.5
Cash payments for operating activities		(5,537.6)	(6,554.8)
Cash provided by operating activities		486.0	241.7
Investing activities			
Purchases of capital assets		(183.6)	(143.4)
Proceeds from sale of capital assets		11.5	17.7
Acquisition of Eaton's			(23.5)
Charge account receivables		(492.1)	42.7
Investments and other assets		21.8	(7.3)
Cash used by investing activities		(642.4)	(113.8)
Financing activities			
Issue of long-term obligations			200.0
Repayment of long-term obligations		(4.9)	(110.6)
Net proceeds from issue of capital stock		0.4	2.1
Dividends paid		(25.6)	(25.6)
Cash provided (used) by financing activities		(30.1)	65.9
Increase (decrease) in cash and short-term investments at end of year		(186.5)	193.8
Cash and short-term investments at beginning of year		329.3	135.5
Cash and short-term investments at end of year		$ 142.8	$ 329.3

Different users have different reasons for being interested in the cash flow statement. If you were a creditor of Sears (either short-term or long-term), you would be interested in knowing the source of its cash in recent years. This information would give you some indication of where it might get cash to pay you. If you had a long-term interest in Sears as a shareholder, you would look to the cash flow statement for information about the company's ability to generate cash over the long run to meet its cash needs for growth.

Companies get cash from two sources: operating activities and financing activities. In the early years of a company's life, it typically won't generate enough cash from operating activities to meet its investing needs, and so it will have to issue shares or borrow money. An established company, however, will often be able to meet most of its cash needs with cash from operating activities.

Sears' cash provided by operating activities increased to $486 million in 2002, primarily due to improved inventory management. Sears used $642.4 million of cash for investing activities, the most significant of which was due to renovating and opening new stores. In 2002, Sears had no significant financing activities, as it was able to reduce financing requirements because of improved cash generated from operating activities.

Earlier we introduced you to measures of liquidity and solvency. The cash flow statement can be used to calculate additional measures of liquidity and solvency. The cash current debt coverage ratio is a measure of liquidity that is calculated as follows: cash provided by operating activities divided by average current liabilities. It indicates the company's ability to generate sufficient cash to meet its short-term needs. In general, a value below 0.40 times is cause for additional investigation of a company's liquidity.

The cash total debt coverage ratio is also a measure of solvency and it is calculated in this manner: cash provided by operating activities divided by average total liabilities. The cash total debt coverage ratio indicates the company's ability to generate sufficient cash to meet its long-term needs. A general rule of thumb is that a ratio below 0.20 times is considered cause for additional investigation.

Illustration 2-23 presents the cash current and total debt coverage ratios for Sears and Hudson's Bay. Industry measures are not available for these ratios.

Illustration 2-23
Cash current debt coverage and cash total debt coverage

CASH CURRENT DEBT COVERAGE	=	$\dfrac{\text{CASH PROVIDED BY OPERATING ACTIVITIES}}{\text{AVERAGE CURRENT LIABILITIES}}$

($ in millions)	2002	2001
Sears*	$\dfrac{\$486.0}{(\$1,451.6 + \$1,343.7) \div 2} = 0.3 \text{ times}$	$\dfrac{\$241.7}{(\$1,343.7 + \$1,730.0) \div 2} = 0.2 \text{ times}$
Hudson's Bay	0.2 times	0.1 times
Industry average	n/a	n/a

CASH TOTAL DEBT COVERAGE	=	$\dfrac{\text{CASH PROVIDED BY OPERATING ACTIVITIES}}{\text{AVERAGE TOTAL LIABILITIES}}$

($ in millions)	2002	2001
Sears*	$\dfrac{\$486.0}{(\$2,414.4 + \$2,260.1) \div 2} = 0.2 \text{ times}$	$\dfrac{\$241.7}{(\$2,260.1 + \$2,405.7) \div 2} = 0.1 \text{ times}$
Hudson's Bay	0.1 times	0.1 times
Industry average	n/a	n/a

* Amounts to calculate average current liabilities and average total liabilities are taken from Sears' balance sheet (Illustration 2-18). Current liabilities in 2000 were $1,730.0 million and total liabilities in 2000 were $2,405.7 million.

Using these measures of solvency and liquidity for 2002 and 2001, Sears appears to be more liquid and solvent than its larger rival, Hudson's Bay. Hudson's Bay had less cash provided by operating activities than Sears in 2002.

Decision Toolkit

DECISION CHECKPOINTS	INFO NEEDED FOR DECISION	TOOL TO USE FOR DECISION	HOW TO EVALUATE RESULTS
Can the company meet its short-term obligations?	Current liabilities and cash provided (used) by operating activities	$$\text{Cash current debt coverage} = \frac{\text{Cash provided (used) by operating activities}}{\text{Average current liabilities}}$$	A higher ratio indicates liquidity—that the company is generating sufficient cash to meet its short-term needs.
Can the company meet its long-term obligations?	Total liabilities and cash provided (used) by operating activities	$$\text{Cash total debt coverage} = \frac{\text{Cash provided (used) by operating activities}}{\text{Average total liabilities}}$$	A higher ratio indicates solvency—that the company is generating sufficient cash to meet its long-term needs.

BEFORE YOU GO ON . . .

- **REVIEW IT**

  1. What information does the cash flow statement provide that is not available in the statement of earnings or balance sheet?
  2. What does the cash current debt coverage ratio measure? What does the cash total debt coverage ratio measure?

Using the Decision Toolkit

It may surprise you to learn that Canadian Tire Corporation, Limited, is one of Sears' top competitors. Don't be fooled by the modest name; it sells a wide array of products, including casual clothing, home, car, sports, and leisure products.

CANADIAN TIRE CORPORATION, LIMITED
Balance Sheet
December 28, 2002
(in millions)

	2002	2001
Assets		
Current assets		
Cash and cash equivalents	$ 628.2	$ 578.8
Accounts receivable	584.1	433.9
Credit charge receivables	579.8	525.3
Merchandise inventories	503.0	440.9
Prepaid expenses and deposits	19.1	14.3
Total current assets	2,314.2	1,993.2
Long-term receivables and other assets	126.7	125.8
Goodwill	32.8	8.6
Intangible assets	52.0	
Property and equipment	2,349.7	2,243.6
Total assets	$4,875.4	$4,371.2
Liabilities		
Current liabilities		
Accounts payable and other	$1,294.7	$1,009.7
Income taxes payable	80.7	70.4
Current portion of long-term debt	208.2	30.0
Total current liabilities	1,583.6	1,110.1
Long-term debt	1,125.2	1,310.0
Other long-term liabilities	359.7	347.4
Total liabilities	3,068.5	2,767.5
Shareholders' Equity		
Share capital	661.0	622.1
Other	7.9	8.5
Retained earnings	1,138.0	973.1
Total shareholders' equity	1,806.9	1,603.7
Total liabilities and shareholders' equity	$4,875.4	$4,371.2

CANADIAN TIRE CORPORATION, LIMITED
Statement of Earnings
Year Ended December 28, 2002
(in millions)

	2002	2001
Gross operating revenue	$5,944.5	$5,374.7
Operating expenses		
Cost of merchandise sold and operating expenses	5,369.5	4,854.8
Interest	83.0	88.0
Amortization	158.5	136.3
Other	27.3	19.2
Total operating expenses	5,638.3	5,098.3
Earnings before income taxes	306.2	276.4
Income taxes	103.8	99.7
Net earnings	$ 202.4	$ 176.7

Additional information: Canadian Tire's net cash provided by operating activities was $444.3 million. The average number of shares in fiscal 2002 was 79.1 million; in fiscal 2001, 78.7 million. The share price was $32.45 on December 28, 2002, and $41.99 on December 29, 2001. Canadian Tire has no preferred shares.

Instructions

Using the above statements, do the following:

1. Calculate Canadian Tire's current ratio for 2002 and 2001. Next calculate its cash current debt coverage for 2002, and finally, discuss its liquidity position.
2. Calculate Canadian Tire's debt to total assets for 2002 and 2001. Next calculate its cash total debt coverage for 2002, and finally discuss its solvency position.
3. Calculate the earnings per share and price-earnings ratio for 2002 and 2001, and discuss the change in profitability.

Solution

1. Current ratio:

   2002: $2,314.2 ÷ $1,583.6 = 1.5:1
   2001: $1,993.2 ÷ $1,110.1 = 1.8:1

   Canadian Tire's liquidity declined in 2002. Still, the current ratio is above 1:1, and Canadian Tire had 1.5 times the current assets as its current liabilities. Nonetheless, Canadian Tire's current ratio is still not as good as Sears' current ratio of 1.8:1. It is also below that of its industry competitors at 2.1:1.

   Cash current debt coverage:

   $$2002: \ \frac{\$444.3}{(\$1,583.6 + \$1,110.1) \div 2} = 0.3 \text{ times}$$

   A value above 0.40 times for this ratio is generally considered acceptable. While low, this ratio is comparable to that of Sears.

2. Debt to total assets:

   2002: $3,068.5 ÷ $4,875.4 = 62.9%
   2001: $2,767.5 ÷ $4,371.2 = 63.3%

   Based on the change in its ratio of debt to total assets, Canadian Tire's reliance on debt decreased from 2001 to 2002. Its reliance on debt is higher than that of Sears (59.4%) and the industry (57.1%). It is notable that while Canadian Tire experienced a slight improvement in its debt to total assets ratio in 2002, Sears and the industry experienced a deterioration in their debt to total assets ratios.

   Cash total debt coverage:

   $$2002: \ \frac{\$444.3}{(\$3,068.5 + \$2,767.5) \div 2} = 0.2 \text{ times}$$

   Canadian Tire's value of 0.2 times is comparable to the generally acceptable level of 0.20 times and that of Sears.

3. Earnings per share:

   2002: $202.4 ÷ 79.1 = $2.56
   2001: $176.7 ÷ 78.7 = $2.25

   Price-earnings ratio:

   2002: $32.45 ÷ $2.56 = 12.7 times
   2001: $41.99 ÷ $2.25 = 18.7 times

   Canadian Tire's earnings per share increased in 2002. However, its price-earnings ratio declined, from 18.7 times to 12.7 times. This ratio is substantially below that of Sears, at 34.8 times, and that of the industry, at 17.3 times. Investors are obviously concerned about the future prospects of the company.

Summary of Study Objectives

❶ Describe the basic objective of financial reporting and the qualitative characteristics of accounting information. The basic objective of financial reporting is to provide information that is useful for decision-making. To be judged useful, information should possess these qualitative characteristics: understandability, relevance, reliability, and comparability.

❷ Identify the two constraints in accounting. The two major constraints are cost-benefit and materiality.

❸ Identify the sections of a classified balance sheet. In a classified balance sheet, assets are classified as current assets; investments; property, plant, and equipment; and intangible assets. Liabilities are classified as either current or long-term. There is also a shareholders' equity section, which shows share capital and retained earnings.

❹ Identify and calculate ratios for analysing a company's profitability. Profitability ratios, such as earnings per share and the price-earnings ratio, measure a company's operating success for a given period of time.

❺ Explain the relationship between a statement of retained earnings, a statement of earnings, and a balance sheet. The statement of retained earnings presents the factors that changed the retained earnings balance during the period. These include the net earnings (or loss), reported in more detail on the statement of earnings, and any dividends paid to shareholders during the period. The ending balance of retained earnings is reported in the shareholders' equity section of the balance sheet.

❻ Identify and calculate ratios for analysing a company's liquidity and solvency. Liquidity ratios, such as working capital, the current ratio, and the cash current debt coverage ratio, measure a company's short-term ability to pay its maturing obligations and meet unexpected needs for cash. Solvency ratios, such as the debt to total assets ratio and cash total debt coverage ratio, measure a company's ability to survive over a long period.

Decision Toolkit—A Summary

Decision Toolkit Summary

DECISION CHECKPOINTS	INFO NEEDED FOR DECISION	TOOL TO USE FOR DECISION	HOW TO EVALUATE RESULTS
How does the company's earnings performance compare with previous years?	Net earnings available to common shareholders and average number of common shares	$\text{Earnings per share} = \dfrac{\text{Net earnings} - \text{Preferred dividends}}{\text{Average number of common shares}}$	A higher measure suggests improved performance, although the number is subject to manipulation. Values should not be compared across companies.
How does the market perceive the company's prospects for future earnings?	Earnings per share and market price per share	$\text{Price-earnings ratio} = \dfrac{\text{Market price per share}}{\text{Earnings per share}}$	A high ratio suggests the market has favourable expectations, although it also may suggest shares are overvalued.
Can the company meet its short-term obligations?	Current assets and current liabilities	$\text{Working capital} = \text{Current assets} - \text{Current liabilities}$	A higher amount indicates liquidity.
		$\text{Current ratio} = \dfrac{\text{Current assets}}{\text{Current liabilitites}}$	A higher ratio suggests favourable liquidity.
	Current liabilities and cash provided (used) by operating activities	$\text{Cash current debt coverage} = \dfrac{\text{Cash provided (used) by operating activities}}{\text{Average current liabilities}}$	A higher ratio indicates liquidity—that the company is generating sufficient cash to meet its short-term needs.
Can the company meet its long-term obligations?	Total debt and total assets	$\text{Debt to total assets} = \dfrac{\text{Total liabilities}}{\text{Total assets}}$	A lower value suggests favourable solvency.
	Total liabilities and cash provided (used) by operating activities	$\text{Cash total debt coverage} = \dfrac{\text{Cash provided (used) by operating activities}}{\text{Average total liabilities}}$	A higher ratio indicates solvency—that the company is generating sufficient cash to meet its long-term needs.

NAVIGATOR

Glossary

Glossary

Cash current debt coverage A measure of liquidity that is calculated as follows: cash provided by operating activities divided by average current liabilities. (p. 73)

Cash total debt coverage A measure of solvency that is calculated as follows: cash provided by operating activities divided by average total liabilities. (p. 73)

Comparability A quality for describing accounting information that can be compared among companies in similar circumstances, because they use similar accounting principles. (p. 54)

Conservatism The approach of choosing an accounting

method that will be least likely to overstate assets and net earnings. (p. 54)

Consistency Use of the same accounting principles and methods from year to year within a company. (p. 55)

Cost-benefit The constraint that the costs of obtaining and providing information should not exceed the benefits gained. (p. 56)

Current assets Cash and other resources that it is reasonable to expect will be realized in cash, or sold, or used up by the business, within one year. (p. 58)

Current liabilities Obligations that will be paid from

existing current assets or through the creation of other current liabilities, within the next year. (p. 60)

Current ratio A measure used to evaluate a company's liquidity and short-term debt-paying ability. It is calculated by dividing current assets by current liabilities. (p. 69)

Debt to total assets A measure showing the percentage of total financing provided by creditors. It is calculated by dividing total liabilities by total assets. (p. 70)

Earnings per share (EPS) A measure of the net earnings earned by each common share. It is calculated by dividing net earnings minus preferred dividends by the average number of common shares during the year. (p. 64)

Generally accepted accounting principles (GAAP) A set of rules and practices, having substantial authoritative support, that are recognized as a general guide for financial reporting purposes. (p. 52)

Intangible assets Assets of a long-lived nature that do not have physical substance. (p. 60)

Interim financial reporting Financial reports issued periodically within the fiscal year. Interim reports are usually issued every quarter, but may be of other time durations. (p. 53)

Liquidity The ability of a company to pay obligations that are expected to become due in the next year. (p. 68)

Liquidity ratios Measures of a company's short-term ability to pay its maturing obligations and to meet unexpected needs for cash. (p. 68)

Long-term investments Investments in debt and equity of other companies that are normally held for many years. Also includes long-term assets, such as land and buildings, not currently being used in the company's operations. (p. 59)

Long-term liabilities Obligations not expected to be paid within one year. (p. 61)

Materiality The constraint of determining whether an item is large enough to influence the decision of an investor or creditor. (p. 56)

Price-earnings (P-E) ratio A measure of the ratio of the market price of each common share to the earnings per share. It reflects the stock market's belief about a company's future earnings potential. (p. 65)

Profitability The ability of a company to generate earnings over a period of time. (p. 64)

Profitability ratios Measures of a company's earnings or operating success for a given period of time. (p. 64)

Property, plant, and equipment Assets of a long-lived nature that are being used in the business and are not intended for resale. (p. 59)

Ratio An expression of the mathematical relationship between one quantity and another. It may be expressed as a percentage, a rate, or a proportion. (p. 63)

Ratio analysis A technique for evaluating financial statements that expresses the relationships among selected financial statement data. (p. 63)

Relevance A quality for describing information that makes a difference in a decision. (p. 53)

Reliability A quality for describing information that is free of error and bias. (p. 53)

Solvency The ability of a company to pay interest as it comes due and to repay the face value of debt at maturity. (p. 69)

Solvency ratios Measures of a company's ability to survive over a long period of time. (p. 70)

Understandability A quality for describing information provided in the financial statements that is understandable for users and therefore useful. (p. 53)

Working capital The excess of current assets over current liabilities. (p. 68)

Demonstration Problem

Listed here are items taken from the statement of earnings and balance sheet of Hudson's Bay Company for the year ended January 31, 2003. Certain items have been combined for simplification and all numbers are reported in thousands.

Additional
Demonstration
Problems

Accounts payable and		Operating expenses	$7,184,503
accrued expenses	$ 977,967	Other long-term assets	496,702
Cash	7,308	Other long-term liabilities	230,824
Dividends	38,912	Prepaid expenses and	
Fixed assets	1,205,333	other current assets	122,860
Goodwill	152,294	Receivables	676,563
Income tax expense	42,421	Retained earnings,	
Interest expense	45,428	February 1, 2002	668,304
Long-term debt	388,543	Sales and revenue	7,383,813
Long-term debt due within		Share capital	1,653,886
one year	258,870	Short-term borrowings	24,744
Long-term receivables	12,105	Short-term deposits	51,418
Merchandise inventories	1,551,104		

Instructions

Prepare a statement of earnings and a classified balance sheet using the items listed.

Action Plan

- The statement of earnings is prepared first.
- The statement of earnings covers a period of time; the balance sheet is prepared at a specific point in time.
- In preparing the statement of earnings, list revenues, then expenses. Report income tax expense separately.
- In preparing a classified balance sheet, list items in order of liquidity in the current classifications and in order of longevity in the noncurrent classifications.

Solution to Demonstration Problem

HUDSON'S BAY COMPANY
Statement of Earnings
Year Ended January 31, 2003
(in thousands)

Sales and revenue	$7,383,813
Expenses	
Operating expenses	7,184,503
Interest expense	45,428
Total expenses	7,229,931
Earnings before income taxes	153,882
Income tax expense	42,421
Net earnings	$ 111,461

HUDSON'S BAY COMPANY
Balance Sheet
January 31, 2003
(in thousands)

Assets

Current assets	
Cash	$ 7,308
Short-term deposits	51,418
Receivables	676,563
Merchandise inventories	1,551,104
Prepaid expenses and other current assets	122,860
Total current assets	2,409,253
Long-term receivables	12,105
Fixed assets	1,205,333
Goodwill	152,294
Other long-term assets	496,702
Total assets	$4,275,687

Liabilities and Shareholders' Equity

Current liabilities	
Short-term borrowings	$ 24,744
Accounts payable and accrued expenses	977,967
Long-term debt due within one year	258,870
Total current liabilities	1,261,581
Long-term liabilities	
Long-term debt	388,543
Other long-term liabilities	230,824
Total long-term liabilities	619,367
Total liabilities	1,880,948
Shareholders' equity	
Share capital	1,653,886
Retained earnings	740,853*
Total shareholders' equity	2,394,739
Total liabilities and shareholders' equity	$4,275,687

* Note that ending retained earnings = beginning retained earnings + net earnings − dividends ($668,304 + $111,461 − $38,912).

Self-Study Questions

Multiple
Choice
Quiz

Answers are at the end of the chapter.

(SO 1) 1. Generally accepted accounting principles are:
(a) a set of standards and rules that are recognized as a general guide for financial reporting.
(b) usually established by the Canada Customs and Revenue Agency.
(c) the guidelines used to resolve ethical dilemmas.
(d) fundamental truths that can be derived from the laws of nature.

(SO 1) 2. What is the primary criterion by which accounting information can be judged?
(a) Consistency
(b) Predictive value
(c) Usefulness for decision-making
(d) Comparability

(SO 1) 3. What accounting characteristic refers to the tendency of accountants to resolve uncertainty in the way least likely to overstate assets and earnings?
(a) Comparability   (c) Conservatism
(b) Materiality   (d) Understandability

(SO 2) 4. An item is considered material when:
(a) it is more than $1,000.
(b) it occurs infrequently.
(c) its omission would influence or change a decision.
(d) it affects net earnings.

(SO 3) 5. In a classified balance sheet, assets are usually classified as:
(a) current assets and property, plant, and equipment.
(b) current assets, long-term investments, and share capital.

(c) current assets; long-term investments; property, plant, and equipment; and intangible assets.
(d) current assets and noncurrent assets.

6. Current assets are listed: (SO 3)
(a) by liquidity.
(b) by importance.
(c) by longevity.
(d) alphabetically.

7. Which is not an indicator of profitability?   (SO 4)
(a) Current ratio
(b) Earnings per share
(c) Net earnings
(d) Price-earnings ratio

8. For 2004, Breau Corporation reported net earnings   (SO 4)
$24,000; common shares $400,000; average number of common shares 6,000; and a share market value of $60. Breau had no preferred shares. What was its 2004 earnings per share?
(a) $0.06   (c) $15.00
(b) $4.00   (d) $16.67

9. The balance in retained earnings is not affected by: (SO 5)
(a) net earnings.
(b) net loss.
(c) common shares.
(d) dividends.

10. Which of these measures is an evaluation of   (SO 6)
a company's ability to pay current liabilities?
(a) Price-earnings ratio
(b) Current ratio
(c) Debt to total assets
(d) None of the above

Questions

(SO 1) 1. (a) What are generally accepted accounting principles (GAAP)?
(b) What is the basic objective of financial reporting?
(c) Identify the qualitative characteristics of accounting information.

(SO 1) 2. Ray Aldag, the president of Raynard Corporation, is pleased. Raynard substantially increased its net earnings in 2004, while keeping its unit inventory almost the same. Chief accountant Tom Erhardt has cautioned Aldag, however. Erhardt says that since Raynard changed its method of inventory valuation, there is a consistency problem and it is difficult to determine whether Raynard is better off. Is Erhardt correct? Why or why not?

(SO 1) 3. What is the distinction between comparability and consistency?

(SO 2) 4. Describe the two constraints in the presentation of accounting information.

(SO 2) 5. The newly hired accountant of a corporation rounded all dollar figures in the annual report's financial statements to the nearest thousand dollars. "It's not important for our users to know how many pennies we spend," she said. Do you believe rounded financial figures can still provide useful information to external users for decision-making? Explain why or why not.

(SO 3) 6. Define current assets. What basis is used for ordering individual items within the current assets section?

(SO 3) 7. Distinguish between long-term investments and intangible assets.

(SO 3) 8. How do current liabilities differ from long-term liabilities?

(SO 3) 9. Identify the two parts of shareholders' equity in a corporation, and indicate the purpose of each.

(SO 4) 10. ⚲ The manager of Robins Ltd is puzzled. Robins had a price-earnings ratio of 25 times in 2004. He feels that this indicates that shareholders believe that the company is doing well. Amod Phatarpekar, the company accountant, says that more information is needed to determine the company's profitability. Who is correct? Why?

11. Explain how the statement of retained earnings (SO 5) is interrelated with the statement of earnings and balance sheet.

12. ⚲ (SO 4, 6)
(a) Tia Kim believes that the analysis of financial statements is directed at two characteristics of a company: liquidity and profitability. Is Tia correct? Explain.
(b) Are short-term creditors, long-term creditors, and shareholders primarily interested in the same characteristics of a company? Explain.

13. ⚲ Name ratios that are useful in assessing (SO 4, 6) (a) liquidity, (b) solvency, and (c) profitability.

14. ⚲ What do these classes of ratios measure? (SO 4, 6)
(a) Liquidity ratios
(b) Profitability ratios
(c) Solvency ratios

15. ⚲ Keeping all other factors constant, indi- (SO 4, 6) cate whether each of the following signals generally good or bad news about a company:
(a) Increase in the earnings per share
(b) Increase in the current ratio
(c) Increase in the debt to total assets ratio
(d) Decrease in the cash current debt coverage ratio

16. ⚲ In your opinion, which ratio(s) from this (SO 4, 6) chapter should be of greatest interest to:
(a) a pension fund considering investing in a corporation's 20-year bonds?
(b) a bank contemplating a short-term loan?
(c) a common shareholder?

Brief Exercises

Identify qualitative characteristics.
(SO 1)

BE2-1 Presented below is a chart showing the qualitative characteristics of accounting information. Fill in the blanks from (a) to (f).

Qualitative Characteristics of Accounting Information

Understandability	Revelance	Reliability	Comparability
1. Accounting concepts and procedures 2. (a)	1. (b) 2. (c) 3. Timely	1. (d) 2. Faithful representation 3. Neutral 4. (e)	1. (f) 2. Consistent use of principles

BE2-2 Here are some qualitative characteristics of accounting information:

1. Predictive value
2. Neutral
3. Verifiable
4. Timely

Identify qualitative character-istics.
(SO 1)

Match each qualitative characteristic to one of the following statements:

(a) _____ Accounting information should help users make predictions about the outcome of past, present, and future events.

(b) _____ Accounting information cannot be selected, prepared, or presented to favour one set of interested users over another.

(c) _____ Accounting information must be proved free of error and bias.

(d) _____ Accounting information must be available to decision-makers before it loses its capacity to influence their decisions.

BE2-3 Levesque Inc. uses these accounting practices:

Identify constraints that have been violated.
(SO 2)

(a) Levesque currently records its accounting transactions and prepares its financial reports manually. The cost of implementing a new computerized accounting system to do these tasks is estimated to be $25,000. Annual savings are anticipated to be $10,000.

(b) Small tools are recorded as equipment and amortized.

(c) The statement of earnings shows paper clips expense of $5.

Indicate the accounting constraint, if any, that has been violated by each practice.

BE2-4 The following are the major balance sheet classifications:

Classify accounts on balance sheet.
(SO 3)

Current assets (CA)
Long-term investments (LTI)
Property, plant, and equipment (PPE)
Intangible assets (IA)

Current liabilities (CL)
Long-term liabilities (LTL)
Share capital (SC)
Retained earnings (RE)

Match each of the following accounts to its proper balance sheet classification:

_____ Accounts payable
_____ Accounts receivable
_____ Accumulated amortization
_____ Building
_____ Cash
_____ Goodwill

_____ Income tax payable
_____ Investment in long-term bonds
_____ Land
_____ Merchandise inventory
_____ Patent
_____ Supplies

BE2-5 A list of financial statement items for Swann Limited includes the following: accounts receivable $16,500; prepaid insurance $3,600; cash $18,400; supplies $5,200; and short-term investments $8,200. Prepare the current assets section of the balance sheet listing the items in the proper sequence.

Prepare current assets section of balance sheet.
(SO 3)

BE2-6 The following information is available for Leon's Furniture Limited for the year ended December 31 (in thousands except for share price):

Calculate earnings per share and price-earnings ratio.
(SO 4)

	2002	2001
Net earnings	$38,520	$36,323
Average number of common shares	19,956	19,926
Share price	$30.88	$23.00

Leon's has no preferred shares.

(a) Calculate earnings per share and the price-earnings ratio for each year.

(b) Indicate whether profitability improved or deteriorated in 2002.

BE2-7 For each of the following events affecting the shareholders' equity of Wu Corporation, indicate whether the event would increase retained earnings (+), decrease retained earnings (−), increase share capital (+), or decrease share capital (−). Insert "NE" if there is no effect.

Identify items affecting shareholders' equity.
(SO 5)

	Share Capital	Retained Earnings
(a) Issued common shares	_____	_____
(b) Paid a cash dividend	_____	_____
(c) Reported net earnings	_____	_____
(d) Paid cash to creditors	_____	_____
(e) Issued preferred shares	_____	_____

*Calculate liquidity and sol-
vency ratios.*

(SO 6)

BE2-8   Indigo Books & Music Inc. reported the following selected information at March 30 (in thousands):

	2002	2001
Total current assets	$252,787	$236,265
Total assets	439,832	388,810
Total current liabilities	293,625	240,819
Total liabilities	376,002	297,701
Cash used by operating activities	(2,574)	(505)

Calculate the (a) current ratio, (b) debt to total assets, and (c) cash current debt coverage for March 30, 2002.

Exercises

*Classify accounts on balance
sheet.*

(SO 3)

Interactive
Homework

E2-1   The following are the major balance sheet classifications:

Current assets (CA)	Current liabilities (CL)
Long-term investments (LTI)	Long-term liabilities (LTL)
Property, plant, and equipment (PPE)	Share capital (SC)
Intangible assets (IA)	Retained earnings (RE)

Instructions

Classify each of the following accounts taken from TELUS Corporation's balance sheet:

_____ Accounts payable and accrued liabilities	_____ Inventories
	_____ Investments
_____ Accounts receivable	_____ Land
_____ Accumulated amortization	_____ Long-term debt
_____ Buildings	_____ Materials and supplies
_____ Cash and temporary investments	_____ Office equipment and furniture
_____ Dividends payable	_____ Preferred shares
_____ Goodwill	_____ Prepaid expenses and other
_____ Income taxes receivable	

*Prepare assets section of clas-
sified balance sheet.*

(SO 3)

E2-2   The assets shown below were taken from the February 28, 2003, balance sheet for Jumbo Entertainment Inc.:

Accounts and current notes receivable	$ 415,373	DVD and video rental library	$ 166,994
		Inventory	1,231,307
Accumulated amortization—capital assets	429,241	Prepaid expenses	47,396
		Trademarks, franchise licences, and goodwill	3,789,744
Capital assets	1,001,640		
Cash and short-term investments	878,012		

Instructions

Prepare the assets section of the classified balance sheet.

*Prepare classified balance
sheet.*

(SO 3)

E2-3   These items are taken from the financial statements of Summit's Bowling Alley Ltd. at December 31, 2004:

Building	$105,800	Retained earnings, January 1	$40,000
Accounts receivable	14,520	Accumulated amortization—building	45,600
Prepaid insurance	4,680		
Cash	20,840	Accounts payable	12,480
Equipment	82,400	Mortgage payable	93,600
Land	61,200	Accumulated amortization—equipment	18,720
Insurance expense	780		
Amortization expense	5,360	Interest payable	3,600
Interest expense	2,600	Bowling revenues	18,180
Common shares	66,000		

Instructions

(a) Calculate net earnings and the ending balance of retained earnings at December 31, 2004.
(b) Prepare a classified balance sheet. Assume that $13,600 of the mortgage payable will be paid in 2005.

E2-4 The following items were taken from the May 31, 2002, balance sheet of The Jean Coutu Group (PJC) Inc. (in thousands):

Accounts receivable	$231,142	Inventories	$515,483
Accounts payable	296,044	Investments	236,679
Accumulated amortization—		Long-term debt	324,083
intangible assets	60,479	Other assets	25,726
Accumulated amortization—		Other current assets	23,323
property, plant, and equipment	157,217	Other long-term debt	6,335
Bank overdraft and bank loans	46,360	Other shareholders' equity	20,711
Capital stock	203,763	Prepaid expenses	8,493
Current portion of long-term debt	32,618	Property, plant,	
Income taxes payable	10,106	and equipment	572,712
Intangible assets	265,743	Retained earnings	721,585

Prepare classified balance sheet.
(SO 3)

Instructions

Prepare a classified balance sheet.

E2-5 These financial statement items are for Batra Corporation at year end, July 31, 2004:

Salaries expense	$48,700	Dividends	$ 4,000
Utilities expense	4,900	Amortization expense	3,975
Equipment	19,875	Retained earnings,	
Accounts payable	6,220	August 1, 2003	25,200
Commission revenue	73,100	Rent expense	10,800
Rent revenue	18,300	Income tax expense	8,000
Common shares	20,000	Supplies	1,500
Cash	12,795	Short-term investments	20,000
Accounts receivable	18,780	Long-term note payable	2,555
Accumulated amortization	7,950		

Prepare financial statements.
(SO 3, 5)

 Interactive Homework

Instructions

(a) Prepare a statement of earnings and a statement of retained earnings for the year.
(b) Prepare a classified balance sheet.

E2-6 The following information is available for the Iron Golf Co. Ltd. for the fiscal years 2003 and 2004:

Calculate profitability ratios.
(SO 4)

	2004	2003
Net earnings	$58,500	$81,000
Preferred dividends	2,000	2,000
Average number of common shares	67,000	69,000
Share price	$10	$9

Instructions

(a) Calculate the earnings per share for each year.
(b) Calculate the price-earnings ratio for each year.
(c) Based on your calculations above, how did the company's profitability change from 2003 to 2004?
(d) Would your answer in (c) above change if you were assessing profitability on behalf of a potential investor, rather than an existing shareholder?

E2-7 Wal-Mart Stores, Inc. is the primary competitor of Sears and The Bay. Wal-Mart reported the following information at January 31 (in U.S. millions):

Calculate and interpret liquidity ratios.
(SO 6)

	2003	2002
Current assets	$30,483	$27,878
Current liabilities	32,617	27,282

Instructions

(a) Calculate the working capital and current ratio for each fiscal year.
(b) Did Wal-Mart's liquidity improve or deteriorate during the year?
(c) Using the data in the chapter, compare Wal-Mart's liquidity with that of Sears, The Bay, and the industry.

Calculate and interpret solvency ratios.
(SO 6)

E2-8 The following data were taken from the April 30 financial statements of the Québec Winter Carnival:

	2002	2001
Current assets	$1,508,277	$1,405,809
Total assets	1,656,248	1,532,557
Current liabilities	551,540	437,946
Total liabilities	564,821	466,017
Total shareholders' equity	1,091,427	1,066,540
Cash provided by operating activities	117,716	64,501
Cash used by investing activities	107,393	33,782

Instructions

Do each of the following:

(a) Calculate the debt to total assets ratio for each year.
(b) Calculate the cash current debt coverage and the cash total debt coverage for 2002.
(c) Discuss the Carnival's solvency in 2002 versus 2001.
(d) Discuss the Carnival's ability to finance its investing activities with cash provided by operating activities, and explain how any deficiency would be met.

Problems: Set A

Comment on objective and qualitative characteristics of financial reporting.
(SO 1)

P2-1A A friend of yours, Emily Collis, recently completed an undergraduate degree in science and has just started working with a biotechnology company. Emily tells you that the owners of the business are trying to secure new sources of financing which are needed in order for the company to proceed with the development of a new health-care product. Emily said her boss told her that the company must put together a report to present to potential investors.

Emily thought that the company's package should include the detailed scientific findings related to the Phase I clinical trials for this product. She said, "I know that the biotech industry sometimes has only a 10% success rate with new products, but if we report all the scientific findings, everyone will see what a sure success this is going to be! The president was talking about the importance of following some set of accounting principles. Why do we need to look at some accounting rules? What they need to realize is that we have scientific results that are quite encouraging, some of the most talented employees around, and the start of some really great customer relationships. We haven't made any sales yet, but we will. We just need the funds to get through all the clinical testing and get government approval for our product. Then these investors will be quite happy that they bought into our company early!"

Instructions

(a) Explain to Emily what is meant by generally accepted accounting principles.
(b) What is the objective of financial reporting?
(c) Comment on how Emily's suggestions for what should be reported to prospective investors conform to the qualitative characteristics of accounting information.

Comment on the constraints of accounting.
(SO 2)

P2-2A No separate disclosure is required on the statement of earnings for the cost of goods sold (the cost of merchandise sold to customers). Because this disclosure is not specifically required, less than half of reporting companies disclose their cost of goods sold separately on their statements of earnings. Most companies include it with other expenses in their reporting of this item, similar to that reported by Sears Canada Inc. in its statement of earnings for the year ended December 28, 2002:

Cost of merchandise sold, operating, administrative and selling expenses	$6,107.9 million

Instructions

(a) Why do you think Sears does not report its cost of merchandise sold on its statement of earnings separately? Comment on how this lack of separate disclosure meets or does not meet the objective of financial reporting.

(b) What are the two constraints in accounting? Do either of these constraints likely have an impact on Sears' reporting policy for cost of merchandise sold? Give an example of how each constraint might affect Sears' reporting of its cost of merchandise sold.

P2-3A You are provided with the following alphabetical list of accounts:

Classify accounts.
(SO 3)

Accounts payable	Income tax expense
Accounts receivable	Income taxes payable
Accumulated amortization, building	Interest expense
Accumulated amortization, equipment	Inventories
Amortization expense	Land
Building	Long-term debt
Cash	Prepaid expenses
Common shares	Retained earnings, beginning of year
Cost of goods sold	Sales
Current portion of long-term debt	Selling expenses
Dividends	Short-term investments
Equipment	Wages payable

Instructions

Identify the financial statement and category for classifying each account. For example, Accounts Payable should be classified as a current liability on the balance sheet.

P2-4A The following items are taken from Intrawest Corporation's June 30, 2002 balance sheet (in U.S. thousands):

Prepare classified balance sheet.
(SO 3)

Capital stock	$466,899	Bank and other indebtedness,	
Amounts payable	195,254	current portion	$282,047
Other noncurrent assets	159,066	Other current liabilities	99,484
Other current assets	495,170	Retained earnings	210,370
Amounts receivable	109,948	Cash and cash equivalents	76,689
Investment properties	468,218	Long-term liabilities	138,991
Goodwill	15,985	Ski and resort operations	1,125,603
Bank and other indebtedness,		Accumulated amortization—	
noncurrent portion	773,872	ski and resort operations	283,762

Instructions

Prepare a classified balance sheet for Intrawest as at June 30, 2002.

P2-5A These items are taken from the 2004 financial statements of Beaulieu Limited:

Prepare financial statements.
(SO 3, 5)

Cash	$ 8,200	Retained earnings, January 1	$14,000
Accounts receivable	7,500	Dividends	2,200
Prepaid insurance	1,800	Service revenue	82,000
Equipment	32,000	Repair expense	3,200
Accumulated amortization	10,500	Amortization expense	7,000
Accounts payable	12,000	Insurance expense	1,200
Salaries payable	3,000	Salaries expense	36,000
Common shares	20,000	Utilities expense	3,700
Income tax expense	6,500	Rent expense	18,000
Temporary investments	15,400	Income tax payable	1,200

Instructions

(a) Prepare a statement of earnings and a statement of retained earnings for the year ended December 31, 2004.

(b) Prepare a classified balance sheet as at December 31, 2004.

Prepare financial statements and discuss relationships.
(SO 3, 5)

P2-6A You are provided with the following information for Commerce Crusaders Inc., effective as of its April 30, 2004, year end.

Accounts payable	$ 8,340	Income tax expense	$ 1,350
Accounts receivable	8,100	Income taxes payable	1,350
Accumulated amortization		Interest expense	4,000
—building	1,500	Inventories	9,670
—equipment	5,000	Land	14,000
Amortization expense	4,000	Note payable, due	
Building	15,370	April 30, 2008	35,000
Cash	5,700	Operating expenses	4,400
Common shares	9,000	Prepaid expenses	120
Cost of goods sold	9,900	Retained earnings, May 1, 2003	10,150
Current portion of long		Sales	34,000
-term debt	4,500	Short-term investments	12,000
Dividends	3,250	Wages expense	7,000
Equipment	12,200	Wages payable	2,220

Instructions

(a) Prepare a statement of earnings and a statement of retained earnings for Commerce Crusaders for the year ended April 30, 2004.
(b) Prepare a classified balance sheet for Commerce Crusaders as at April 30, 2004.
(c) Explain how each financial statement is related to the others.

Calculate ratios and comment on profitability, liquidity, and solvency.
(SO 4, 6)

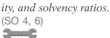

P2-7A Comparative statement data for Belliveau Corp. and Shields Corp., two competitors, are presented here. All balance sheet data are as at December 31.

	Belliveau Corp.		Shields Corp.	
	2004	2003	2004	2003
Current assets	$130,000	$110,000	$700,000	$650,000
Property, plant, and equipment	305,000	270,000	800,000	750,000
Current liabilities	60,000	52,000	250,000	275,000
Long-term liabilities	50,000	68,000	200,000	150,000
Average number of common shares	200,000		400,000	
Share price	2.50		7.00	
Cash provided by operating activities	20,000		185,000	
Net earnings	36,000		173,000	

Instructions

(a) Calculate earnings per share and the price-earnings ratio of each company for fiscal 2004. Comment on their relative profitability.
(b) Calculate the current ratio and the cash current debt coverage for each company for fiscal 2004. Comment on their relative liquidity.
(c) Calculate debt to total assets and the cash total debt coverage for each company for fiscal 2004. Comment on their relative solvency.

Calculate profitability, liquidity, and solvency ratios.
(SO 4, 6)

P2-8A The comparative statements of the Fast Corporation are presented here:

FAST CORPORATION
Statement of Earnings
Year Ended December 31

	2004	2003
Sales	$690,000	$574,000
Expenses		
Cost of goods sold	420,000	335,600
Selling and administrative	143,880	149,760
Interest	7,920	7,200
Total expenses	571,800	492,560
Earnings before income taxes	118,200	81,440
Income tax expense	35,300	24,000
Net earnings	$ 82,900	$ 57,440

FAST CORPORATION
Balance Sheet
December 31

	2004	2003
Assets		
Current assets		
Cash	$ 23,100	$ 21,600
Short-term investments	34,800	33,000
Accounts receivable	106,200	93,800
Inventory	82,400	64,000
Total current assets	246,500	212,400
Property, plant, and equipment	565,300	459,600
Total assets	$811,800	$672,000
Liabilities and Shareholders' Equity		
Current liabilities		
Accounts payable	$134,200	$132,000
Income taxes payable	25,300	24,000
Total current liabilities	159,500	156,000
Bonds payable	132,000	120,000
Total liabilities	291,500	276,000
Shareholders' equity		
Common shares	191,400	150,000
Retained earnings	328,900	246,000
Total shareholders' equity	520,300	396,000
Total liabilities and shareholders' equity	$811,800	$672,000

Additional information:
1. Cash provided by operating activities was $55,600 for 2004.
2. The average number of common shares in 2004 was 7,000.
3. The share price at December 31, 2004, was $34.

Instructions
Calculate these ratios for 2004:
(a) Current ratio
(b) Cash current debt coverage
(c) Debt to total assets
(d) Cash total debt coverage
(e) Earnings per share
(f) Price-earnings ratio

P2-9A   Condensed balance sheet and statement of earnings data for Giasson Corporation are presented below:

Calculate profitability, liquidity, and solvency ratios and discuss results.
(SO 4, 6)

GIASSON CORPORATION
Balance Sheet
December 31

	2004	2003	2002
Assets			
Cash	$ 50,000	$ 24,000	$ 20,000
Receivables	90,000	65,000	32,000
Other current assets	80,000	75,000	62,000
Investments	90,000	70,000	50,000
Property, plant, and equipment	550,000	420,000	310,000
Total assets	$860,000	$654,000	$474,000
Liabilities and Shareholders' Equity			
Current liabilities	$ 98,000	$ 75,000	$ 70,000
Long-term liabilities	105,000	75,000	65,000
Common shares	409,000	302,000	300,000
Retained earnings	248,000	202,000	39,000
Total liabilities and shareholders' equity	$860,000	$654,000	$474,000

GIASSON CORPORATION
Statement of Earnings
Year Ended December 31

	2004	2003
Sales	$660,000	$800,000
Cost of goods sold	420,000	400,000
Operating expenses (including income taxes)	194,000	237,000
Net earnings	$ 46,000	$163,000

Additional information:

1. The average number of common shares was 76,000 in 2004 and 50,000 in 2003.
2. The share price at December 31, 2004, was $4; it was $6 at the end of 2003.

Instructions

(a) Calculate these values and ratios for 2004 and 2003:
   1. Earnings per share
   2. Price-earnings ratio
   3. Working capital
   4. Current ratio
   5. Debt to total assets
(b) Based on the ratios calculated, briefly discuss Giasson's changes in financial position and operating results.

Calculate profitability, liquidity, and solvency ratios and discuss results.
(SO 4, 6)

P2-10A Selected financial data (in millions except for share price) from a recent year of two forest products companies, Abitibi-Consolidated Inc. and Tembec Inc., are presented here:

	Abitibi	Tembec
Cash provided by operating activities	$ 1,037	$ 173.6
Net earnings	289	77.9
Current assets	1,640	1,273.5
Total assets	11,707	4,138.8
Current liabilities	1,415	504.1
Total liabilities	8,442	2,771.2
Average total liabilities	8,301	2,303.8
Average number of common shares	440	82
Share price	11.63	10.10

Instructions

(a) For each company, calculate these values and ratios. Where available, industry averages have been included in parentheses.
   1. Working capital (n/a)
   2. Current ratio (1.23:1)
   3. Debt to total assets (n/a)
   4. Cash total debt coverage (n/a)
   5. Earnings per share ($0.58)
   6. Price-earnings ratio (37.72 times)
(b) Compare the liquidity, profitability, and solvency of the two companies and their industry.

Problems: Set B

Comment on the objective and qualitative characteristics of accounting information.
(SO 1)

P2-1B Net Nanny Software International Inc. specializes in Internet safety and computer security products. Its balance sheet, as at March 31, 2002, reported a deficit (negative retained earnings) of U.S.$15.9 million. It has reported only net losses since inception, June 30, 1996. In spite of these losses, Net Nanny's common shares have traded anywhere from a high of $3.70 to a low of $0.02 on the TSX Venture Exchange.

Until 1998, Net Nanny's financial statements were prepared in Canadian dollars. As of June 30, 1998, the company adopted the U.S. dollar as its reporting currency. In November 2002, Washington-based Bionet Systems, purchased Net Nanny.

Instructions

(a) What is the objective of financial reporting? How does this objective meet or not meet Net Nanny's investors' needs?

(b) Why would investors want to buy Net Nanny's shares, and Bionet Systems buy Net Nanny, if the company has consistently reported losses over the last few years? Include in your answer an assessment of the relevance and reliability of the information reported on Net Nanny's financial statements.

(c) Comment on how the change in reporting information from Canadian dollars to U.S. dollars likely affected the readers of Net Nanny's financial statements. Include in your answer an assessment of the comparability of the information.

P2-2B A friend of yours, Ryan Konotopsky, has come to you looking for some answers about financial statements. Ryan tells you that he is thinking about opening a movie theatre in his home town, Corner Brook, Newfoundland. Before doing so, he wants to find out how much in sales he could expect to make from food concessions as opposed to ticket sales. He wants to know what portion of ticket sales he could expect from children, youth, and seniors versus adults who pay the highest admission rate. He also wants to know how much profit he would make on ticket sales versus sales at the concession stands, and the average wage per employee.

Comment on the constraints of accounting.
(SO 2)

Ryan knows that Empire Theatres operates in Atlantic Canada so he downloaded the financial statements of Empire Company Limited from the Internet. He noticed that the company's statement of earnings reported revenues for the year ended April 30, 2002, of $9,926.5 million and cost of sales, selling, and administrative expenses of $9,409.4 million. He read through Empire Company Limited's annual report and learned that Empire Theatres is just one part of the Investments and Theatre Operations division of the company. There are food distribution and real estate divisions as well. Ryan discovers from reading the annual report of Empire Company Limited that the company reports segmented information. It uses the term "other operations" to describe the results of Empire Theatres and reports the following for 2002:

Revenue: $56.2 million
Operating income: $9.0 million
Identifiable assets: $80.7 million

Ryan is disillusioned because he cannot find many details about Empire Theatres in the annual report. He has come to you looking for explanations.

Instructions

What are two constraints in accounting? What impact have these constraints had on the financial reporting by Empire Company Limited?

P2-3B You are provided with the following alphabetical list of balance sheet accounts for Leon's Furniture Limited:

Classify accounts.
(SO 3)

Accounts payable and accrued liabilities
Accounts receivable
Buildings
Cash and cash equivalents
Common shares
Customers' deposits
Dividends payable
Future income tax liabilities

Income taxes recoverable
Inventory
Land
Leasehold improvements
Long-term liabilities
Marketable securities
Retained earnings
Vehicles

Instructions

Identify the balance sheet category for classifying each account. For example, Accounts Payable and Accrued Liabilities should be classified as a current liability on the balance sheet.

Prepare classified balance sheet.
(SO 3)

P2-4B   The following items are taken from the December 31, 2002, balance sheet of Yahoo! Inc. (in U.S. thousands):

Common stock	$2,270,845	Intangible assets, net	$ 96,252
Property and equipment, net	371,272	Prepaid expenses and other	
Accounts payable	18,738	current assets	82,216
Other assets	174,020	Short-term investments	463,204
Long-term investments	763,408	Deficit	(7,493)
Accounts receivable	113,612	Cash and cash equivalents	310,972
Deferred revenue—current	135,501	Accrued expenses and other	
Other shareholders' equity	(1,082)	current liabilities	257,575
Other liabilities	116,097	Goodwill	415,225

Instructions

Prepare a classified balance sheet for Yahoo! Inc. as at December 31, 2002.

Prepare financial statements.
(SO 3, 5)

P2-5B   These items are taken from the financial statements of Mbong Corporation for 2004:

Retained earnings, January 1	$16,000	Amortization expense	$ 2,600
Utilities expense	1,700	Accounts receivable	13,500
Equipment	13,000	Insurance expense	2,200
Accounts payable	13,300	Salaries expense	35,000
Cash	13,600	Accumulated amortization	5,600
Salaries payable	3,000	Income tax expense	3,000
Common shares	20,000	Rent expense	12,000
Dividends	2,000	Supplies	1,000
Service revenue	65,000	Supplies expense	700
Prepaid insurance	3,500	Note payable, due 2009	5,000
Repair expense	1,800	Investments	22,300

Instructions

(a) Prepare a statement of earnings and a statement of retained earnings for the year ended December 31, 2004.

(b) Prepare a classified balance sheet as at December 31, 2004.

Prepare financial statements and discuss relationships.
(SO 3, 5)

P2-6B   You are provided with the following information for Cheung Corporation for its April 30, 2004, year end:

Accounts payable	$ 5,972	Income taxes payable	$ 1,125
Accounts receivable	7,840	Interest expense	342
Accumulated amortization	9,220	Interest payable	28
Amortization expense	4,610	Notes payable, due 2009	5,700
Cash	20,263	Prepaid rent	500
Common shares	20,000	Rent expense	6,000
Dividends	3,650	Retained earnings, May 1, 2003	13,960
Equipment	23,050	Salaries expense	6,840
Fees earned	32,590	Short-term investments	11,000
Income tax expense	4,500		

Instructions

(a) Prepare a statement of earnings and a statement of retained earnings for Cheung Corporation for the year ended April 30, 2004.

(b) Prepare a classified balance sheet for Cheung as at April 30, 2004.

(c) Explain how each financial statement is related to the others.

Calculate ratios and comment on profitability, liquidity, and solvency.
(SO 4, 6)

P2-7B   Financial statement data for Chen Corporation and Caissie Corporation, two competitors, appear below. All balance sheet data are as at December 31.

	Chen		Cassie	
	2004	2003	2004	2003
Cash provided by operating activities	$162,594		$ 24,211	
Net earnings	311,630		113,040	
Preferred dividends	0		13,000	
Average number of common shares	100,000		50,000	
Share price	25		14	

Current assets	425,975	$412,410	190,336	$160,467
Property, plant, and equipment	521,310	500,000	139,728	125,812
Current liabilities	66,325	75,815	35,458	30,281
Long-term liabilities	108,500	90,000	29,620	25,000

Instructions

(a) Calculate earnings per share and the price-earnings ratio of each company for fiscal 2004. Comment on the relative profitability of the two companies.

(b) Calculate the working capital, current ratio, and cash current debt coverage ratio for each company for fiscal 2004. Comment on the companies' relative liquidity.

(c) Calculate the debt to total assets ratio and the cash total debt coverage ratio for each company for fiscal 2004. Comment on the companies' relative solvency.

P2-8B   Here are the comparative statements of Johannsen Inc.:

Calculate profitability, liquidity, and solvency ratios.
(SO 4, 6)

JOHANNSEN INC.
Statement of Earnings
Year Ended December 31

	2004	2003
Sales	$2,218,500	$2,100,500
Expenses		
Cost of goods sold	1,005,500	996,000
Selling and administrative	906,000	879,000
Interest	98,000	79,000
Total expenses	2,009,500	1,954,000
Earnings before income taxes	209,000	146,500
Income tax expense	86,700	77,000
Net earnings	$ 122,300	$ 69,500

JOHANNSEN INC.
Balance Sheet
December 31

	2004	2003
Assets		
Current assets		
Cash and cash equivalents	$ 144,100	$114,200
Accounts receivable	177,800	102,800
Inventory	123,000	115,500
Total current assets	444,900	332,500
Property, plant, and equipment	625,300	440,300
Total assets	$1,070,200	$772,800
Liabilities and Shareholders' Equity		
Current liabilities		
Accounts payable	$ 97,500	$ 65,400
Income taxes payable	45,000	42,000
Total current liabilities	142,500	107,400
Bonds payable	310,000	200,000
Total liabilities	452,500	307,400
Shareholders' equity		
Common shares	330,000	300,000
Retained earnings	287,700	165,400
Total shareholders' equity	617,700	465,400
Total liabilities and shareholders' equity	$1,070,200	$772,800

Additional information:

1. The cash provided by operating activities for 2004 was $74,900.
2. The average number of shares during 2004 was 50,000.
3. The share price at December 31 was $7.

Instructions

Calculate these values and ratios for 2004:

(a) Working capital

(b) Current ratio

(c) Cash current debt coverage

(d) Debt to total assets

(e) Cash total debt coverage

(f) Earnings per share

(g) Price-earnings ratio

Calculate profitability, liquidity, and solvency ratios and discuss results.
(SO 4, 6)

P2-9B Condensed balance sheet and statement of earnings data for Pitka Corporation are presented here:

PITKA CORPORATION
Balance Sheet
December 31

	2004	2003	2002
Assets			
Cash	$ 25,000	$ 20,000	$ 18,000
Receivables	70,000	65,000	48,000
Other current assets	90,000	70,000	64,000
Investments	75,000	60,000	45,000
Property, plant, and equipment	500,000	470,000	358,000
Total assets	$760,000	$685,000	$533,000
Liabilities and Shareholders' Equity			
Current liabilities	$ 75,000	$ 80,000	$ 70,000
Long-term liabilities	86,000	110,000	50,000
Common shares	340,000	330,000	300,000
Retained earnings	259,000	165,000	113,000
Total liabilities and shareholders' equity	$760,000	$685,000	$533,000

PITKA CORPORATION
Statement of Earnings
Year Ended December 31

	2004	2003
Fees earned	$750,000	$670,000
Operating expenses (including income taxes)	656,000	618,000
Net earnings	$ 94,000	$ 52,000

Additional information:

1. The average number of common shares was 82,000 in 2004 and 80,000 in 2003.

2. The share price at December 31, 2004, was $66; it was $44 at the end of 2003.

Instructions

(a) Calculate these values and ratios for 2004 and 2003:

   1. Earnings per share

   2. Price-earnings ratio

   3. Working capital

   4. Current ratio

   5. Debt to total assets

(b) Based on the ratios calculated, briefly discuss Pitka Corporation's change in financial position and operating results.

Calculate profitability, liquidity, and solvency ratios and discuss results.
(SO 4, 6)

P2-10B Selected financial data (in thousands) from a recent year of two competitors, Big Rock Brewery Ltd. and Sleeman Breweries Ltd., are presented here:

	Big Rock	Sleeman
Cash provided by operating activities	$ 2,580.5	$ 18,984.0
Net earnings	1,217.8	9,765.0
Current assets	6,492.3	44,511.0
Total assets	33,060.7	197,642.0
Current liabilities	5,357.9	46,315.0
Average current liabilities	4,916.8	43,044.5
Total liabilities	11,276.6	124,554.0
Average total liabilities	11,792.3	122,089.5
Average number of common shares	5,167.7	15,223.0
Share price	5.50	9.73

Instructions

(a) For each company, calculate these values and ratios. Where available, industry averages are included in parentheses.
  1. Working capital (n/a)
  2. Current ratio (1.18:1)
  3. Cash current debt coverage (n/a)
  4. Debt to total assets (n/a)
  5. Cash total debt coverage (n/a)
  6. Earnings per share ($0.21)
  7. Price-earnings ratio (127.14 times)
(b) Compare the liquidity, profitability, and solvency of the two companies and their industry.

BROADENING YOUR PERSPECTIVE

Financial Reporting and Analysis

Analysis Tools

FINANCIAL REPORTING PROBLEM: *Loblaw Companies Limited*

BYP2-1   The financial statements of Loblaw Companies Limited are presented in Appendix A at the end of this book.

Instructions

Answer the following questions:
(a) What were Loblaw's total current assets at December 28, 2002, and December 29, 2001?
(b) Are the assets in current assets listed in the proper order? Explain.
(c) How are Loblaw's assets classified?
(d) What were Loblaw's total current liabilities at December 28, 2002, and December 29, 2001?

COMPARATIVE ANALYSIS PROBLEM: *Loblaw and Sobeys*

BYP2-2   The financial statements of Sobeys Inc. are presented in Appendix B after the financial statements for Loblaw.

Instructions

(a) For each company, calculate or locate the following values for the most recent fiscal year.
  1. Working capital
  2. Current ratio
  3. Debt to total assets
  4. Earnings per share
  5. Price-earnings ratio
(b) Based on your findings above, discuss the relative profitability, liquidity, and solvency of the two companies.

RESEARCH CASE

BYP2-3 Several commonly available indices help individuals find articles from business publications and periodicals. Articles can generally be searched for by company name or by subject matter. Two common indices are ArticleFirst and CBCA (Canadian Business and Current Affairs) Fulltext Business.

Instructions

Use one of these resources, or others, to find a list of articles about Loblaw or Sobeys. Choose an article that you believe would be of interest to an investor in, or creditor of, your chosen company. Read the article and answer the following questions (*Note:* Your library may have either print or electronic versions of these indices.)

(a) What is the article about?
(b) What information about the company is included in the article?
(c) Is the article related to anything you read in this chapter?
(d) Identify any accounting-related issues discussed in the article.

INTERPRETING FINANCIAL STATEMENTS

BYP2-4 The following information was reported by The Gap, Inc. in its 2002 annual report:

	2002	2001	2000	1999	1998
Total assets (U.S. millions)	$9,902	$7,683	$7,013	$5,189	$3,964
Working capital (U.S. millions)	$3,013	$1,023	$(151)	$445	$319
Current ratio	2.11:1	1.48:1	0.95:1	1.25:1	1.21:1
Debt to total assets	63.1%	60.8%	58.2%	57.0%	60.3%
Earnings per share	$0.55	$(0.01)	$1.03	$1.32	$0.95

Instructions

(a) Determine the overall percentage increase in The Gap's total assets from 1998 to 2002. What was the average increase per year?
(b) Comment on the change in The Gap's liquidity. Does working capital or the current ratio appear to provide a better indication of The Gap's liquidity? What might explain the change in The Gap's liquidity during this period?
(c) Comment on the change in The Gap's solvency during this period.
(d) Comment on the change in The Gap's profitability during this period. What was the average earnings per share from 1998 to 2002? How might this affect your prediction about The Gap's future profitability?

A GLOBAL FOCUS

BYP2-5 Doman Industries Ltd. is an integrated Canadian forest products company located in British Columbia. Doman's products are sold in 30 countries, mostly in the U.S.

One of the challenges global companies face is to make themselves attractive to investors from other countries. This is difficult to do when different accounting principles in other countries can blur the real impact of earnings. For example, in its statement of earnings for the year ended December 31, 2002—which is what most investors examine—Doman reported a loss of $164 million, using Canadian accounting principles. Had it reported under U.S. accounting principles, its loss would have been $210-million.

Instructions

(a) Many companies that want to be more easily compared with U.S. and other global competitors have switched to U.S. accounting principles. Identify any advantages and disadvantages that companies should consider when switching to U.S. reporting standards.
(b) Suppose you wish to compare Doman Industries to a U.S.-based competitor, such as Weyerhaeuser. Do you believe the use of both countries' accounting principles would hinder your comparison? If so, explain how.
(c) Suppose you wish to compare Doman Industries to a Canadian-based competitor, such as Nexfor. If they chose to use different generally acceptable Canadian accounting principles, how could this affect your comparison of their financial results?
(d) Do you see any significant distinction between comparing statements prepared in different countries and comparing statements prepared using different accounting principles within the same country?

FINANCIAL ANALYSIS ON THE WEB

BYP2-6 This activity shows you how to identify summary information about companies. This information includes a basic description of various industries and companies in Canada.

Instructions

Specific requirements of this Web case can be found on the Kimmel website.

Critical Thinking

COLLABORATIVE LEARNING ACTIVITY

BYP2-7 As the accountant for Soukup Manufacturing Inc., you have been asked to develop some key ratios from the comparative financial statements. This information will be used to convince creditors that Soukup is liquid, solvent, and profitable, and therefore deserves their continued support. Lenders are particularly concerned about the company's ability to continue as a going concern.

Here are the data and calculations you developed from the financial statements:

	2004	2003
Current ratio	3.1:1	2.1:1
Working capital	Up 22%	Down 7%
Debt to total assets	60%	70%
Net earnings	Up 32%	Down 8%
Earnings per share	$2.40	$1.15
Price-earnings ratio	26.2 times	19 times

Instructions

You have been asked to prepare brief comments which explain how each of these items supports the argument that Soukup's financial health is improving. The company wishes to use these comments in a presentation to its creditors. Prepare the comments as requested, giving the implications and the limitations of each item separately, and then state what conclusions may be drawn from them as a whole about Soukup's financial well-being.

COMMUNICATION ACTIVITY

BYP2-8 S. B. Barrett is the chief executive officer of Tomorrow's Products Ltd. Barrett is an expert engineer but a novice in accounting.

Instructions

Write a letter to S. B. Barrett that explains (a) the three main types of ratios, (b) examples of each, how they are calculated, and what they mean, and (c) the bases for comparison in analysing the financial statements of Tomorrow's Products.

ETHICS CASE

BYP2-9 When new accounting principles are issued, the required implementation date is usually 12 months or more after the date of issuance, but early implementation is encouraged.

Kathy Johnston, accountant at Redondo Corporation, discusses with Redondo's vice-president the need for early implementation of a recently issued recommendation. She says it will result in a much fairer presentation of the company's financial condition and earnings. When the vice-president determines that early implementation would adversely affect reported net earnings for the year, he strongly discourages Kathy from implementating the recommendation until it is required.

**Ethics In
Accounting**

Instructions

(a) Who are the stakeholders in this situation?
(b) What, if any, are the ethical considerations in this situation?
(c) What could Kathy gain by supporting early implementation? Who might be affected by the decision against early implementation?

Answers to Self-Study Questions
1. a   2. c   3. c   4. c   5. c   6. a   7. a   8. b   9. c   10. b

Answer to Loblaw Review It Question 3
Loblaw's largest current asset at December 28, 2002, is Inventories.

Remember to go back to the Navigator box on the chapter-opening page to check off your completed work.

CHAPTER 3

The Accounting Information System

STUDY OBJECTIVES

After studying this chapter, you should be able to:

1 Analyse the effect of business transactions on the basic accounting equation.

2 Explain what an account is and how it helps in the recording process.

3 Define debits and credits and explain how they are used to record business transactions.

4 Identify the basic steps in the recording process.

5 Explain what a journal is and how it helps in the recording process.

6 Explain what a ledger is and how it helps in the recording process.

7 Explain what posting is and how it helps in the recording process.

8 Explain the purposes of a trial balance.

Accidents Happen

How organized are you financially? Take a short quiz:

- Is your wallet so stuffed with ATM receipts, Interac transaction records, and Canadian Tire money that you've been declared a walking fire hazard?
- Do you often come across credit card bills for restaurants and gas stations from towns you barely remember visiting?
- Is your wallet such a mess that rather than dig around in it for cash you sometimes fish for loonies in the crack of your car seat?
- Was Wayne Gretzky still playing hockey the last time you balanced your cheque book?
- Are you tempted to burn down your house every spring to

avoid looking for all the forms, receipts, and records that you need to fill out your tax return?

If you think it's hard to keep track of the many transactions that make up your life, imagine what it's like for huge corporations such as Fidelity Investments, Qwest Communications, or Inter-Tan. Needless to say, corporations can ill afford to be disorganized about tracking money.

Fidelity Investments is one of the world's largest financial services firms, managing mutual fund assets for over 18 million investors.

If your life savings were part of the $25 billion of assets that Fidelity manages in this country, you would no doubt be a little distressed if when you called to check your balance the representative said, "You know, I kind of remember someone with a name

like yours sending us some money—now what did we do with that?"

To ensure the accuracy of its clients' balances and the security of their funds, Fidelity, like many other companies large and small, relies on a sophisticated computerized accounting information system. But that's not to say that Fidelity—or anybody else—is error-free.

In fact, if you've ever really messed up your cheque book, you may take some comfort in learning about a mistake once made at Fidelity Investments. An accountant failed to include a minus sign while doing a calculation, making what was actually a $1.9-billion loss look like a $1.9-billion gain. Yes, billion! Fortunately, like most accounting errors, this one was detected before any real harm was done.

Fidelity Investments www.fidelity.ca

THE NAVIGATOR

Scan *Study Objectives* ☐

Read *Feature Story* ☐

Read *Chapter Preview* ☐

Read text and answer *Before You Go On*
p. 113 ☐ p. 116 ☐ p. 124 ☐ p. 126 ☐

Work *Using the Decision Toolkit* ☐

Review *Summary of Study Objectives*
and *Decision Toolkit* ☐

Work *Demonstration Problem* ☐

Answer *Self-Study Questions* ☐

Complete assignments ☐

Unfortunately, not all mistakes get caught when they should. Consider the case of Denver-based Qwest Communications, the leading telephone company in 14 U.S. states. Qwest made headlines in July 2002 when it revealed U.S.$1.16 billion in improperly recorded revenue over the previous three years. The errors resulted in inflated figures for expected revenue and earnings, key indicators used by investors in making their investment decisions.

Here in Canada, Toronto-based InterTan, owner of electronics retailer RadioShack, was forced to restate its earnings for 2002 after misreporting U.S.$1.2 million in expenses. Somehow, the errors—alleged to have been made by a former employee—had escaped notice during the company's independent year-end re-

view. They were only discovered by the company's CFO three weeks after the audit was finished! Following the release of its new figures, InterTan saw its share price fall 17%.

To promote more diligent reporting, the U.S. Securities Exchange Commission (SEC) introduced a new rule requiring CEOs and CFOs of public companies to personally certify that the financial statements their companies file are both accurate and complete. The new rule, one of many changes sweeping U.S. securities regulations, came into effect in August 2002.

For now, no such requirement exists in Canada—other than for about 220 Canadian companies listed on U.S. stock exchanges.

Securities regulators in Canada are studying a new framework for securities reform, al-

though to date there is little agreement about how best to proceed. Responsibility for securities regulation is divided among the 13 provinces and territories. The debate has once again focused attention on the fact that Canada does not have a national regulator, as the U.S. does. Consequently, making sweeping changes to securities legislation requires the agreement of 13 different jurisdictions—something that is understandably hard to achieve.

One thing that is agreed upon by everyone: increasing differences between U.S. and Canada securities standards will only hinder trading. Because of this, there are many who are calling not only for harmonized securities regulations within Canada, but also between the two countries.

NAVIGATOR ✓

As indicated in the feature story, a reliable information system is a necessity for any company. The purpose of this chapter is to explain and illustrate the features of an accounting information system. The content and organization of the chapter are as follows:

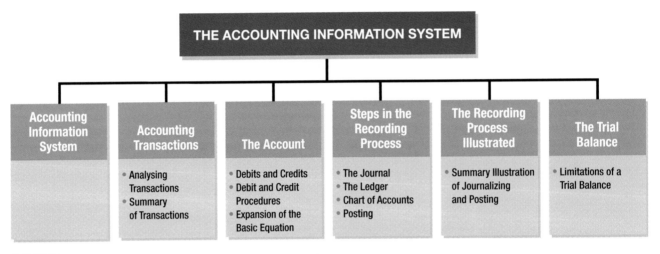

THE ACCOUNTING INFORMATION SYSTEM

Accounting Information System	Accounting Transactions	The Account	Steps in the Recording Process	The Recording Process Illustrated	The Trial Balance
	• Analysing Transactions • Summary of Transactions	• Debits and Credits • Debit and Credit Procedures • Expansion of the Basic Equation	• The Journal • The Ledger • Chart of Accounts • Posting	• Summary Illustration of Journalizing and Posting	• Limitations of a Trial Balance

Accounting Information System

The system of collecting and processing transaction data and communicating financial information to decision-makers is known as the accounting information system. Accounting information systems vary widely. Factors that shape these systems are the nature of the business and its transactions, the size of the company, the volume of data, and the information demands of management and others.

Most businesses, whatever their size, use computerized accounting systems. These systems handle all the steps in the recording process, from initial data entry to preparation of the financial statements. In order to remain competitive, companies must ensure that their accounting systems provide accurate and timely data for decision-making. For example, in one of its annual reports, Sobeys notes, under the caption "Working smarter every day," that "harnessing new technology has long been a key part of our approach."

In this chapter, we focus on a manual accounting system, because the accounting concepts and principles are the same for all accounting systems, computerized or manual.

Accounting Transactions

To use the accounting information system, you need to know what economic events to recognize (record). Not all events are recorded and reported in the financial statements. For example, suppose Bombardier hires a new employee or purchases a new computer. Are these events entered in its accounting records? The first event would not be recorded, but the second event would. We call economic events that require recording in the financial statements accounting transactions.

An accounting transaction occurs when assets, liabilities, or shareholders' equity items change as a result of some economic event. The purchase of a computer by Bombardier, the payment of salaries by Tim Hortons, and the sale of advertising space by Sierra are examples of events that change a company's assets, liabilities, or shareholders' equity. Illustration 3-1 summarizes the process used to decide whether or not to record economic events.

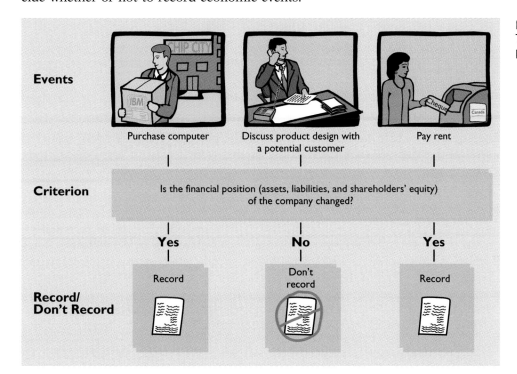

Illustration 3-1
Transaction identification process

ANALYSING TRANSACTIONS

In Chapter 1, you learned the basic accounting equation:

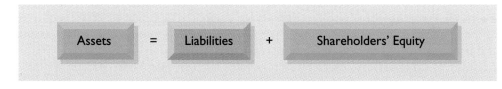

STUDY OBJECTIVE

1

Analyse the effect of business transactions on the basic accounting equation.

In this chapter, you will learn how to analyse transactions in terms of their effect on assets, liabilities, and shareholders' equity. **Transaction analysis** is the process of identifying the specific effects of economic events on the accounting equation.

The accounting equation must always balance. Each transaction has a dual (double-sided) effect on the equation. For example, if an individual asset is increased, there must be a corresponding decrease in another asset, *or* increase in a specific liability, *or* increase in shareholders' equity.

It is quite possible that two or more items could be affected when an asset is increased. For example, if a company purchases a computer for $7,500 by paying $3,500 in cash and signing a note for $4,000, one asset (Computer) increases by $7,500, another asset (Cash) decreases by $3,500, and a liability (Notes Payable) increases by $4,000. The result is that the accounting equation remains in balance—assets increased by a net $4,000 and liabilities also increased by $4,000.

Chapter 1 presented the financial statements for Sierra Corporation for its first month. To illustrate the effect of economic events on the accounting equation, we will now examine the events affecting Sierra Corporation during its first month.

Event (1). Investment of Cash by Shareholders. On October 1, cash of $10,000 was invested in the business in exchange for $10,000 of common shares. This event is an accounting transaction because it results in an increase in both assets and shareholders' equity. There is an increase of $10,000 in the asset Cash and an increase of $10,000 in Common Shares on Sierra Corporation's books. The effect of this transaction on the basic equation is:

	Assets	=	Liabilities	+	Shareholders' Equity
					Common
	Cash	=			Shares
(1)	+$10,000	=			+$10,000 Issued shares

The equation is in balance. The source of the change in shareholders' equity is noted to the right of each transaction: in this case it was an issue of common shares. Keeping track of the source of each change in shareholders' equity is essential for later accounting activities.

Event (2). Note Issued in Exchange for Cash. On October 1, Sierra issued a three-month, 6%, $5,000 note payable to CIBC. This transaction results in an equal increase in assets and liabilities: Cash (an asset) increases by $5,000 and Notes Payable (a liability) increases by $5,000. The specific effect of this transaction and the cumulative effect of the first two transactions are:

	Assets	=	Liabilities	+	Shareholders' Equity
			Notes		Common
	Cash	=	Payable	+	Shares
Beginning Balance	$10,000				$10,000
(2)	+5,000		+$5,000		
Ending Balance	$15,000	=	$5,000	+	$10,000
				$15,000	

Total assets are now $15,000 and shareholders' equity plus the new liability also total $15,000.

Event (3). Purchase of Office Equipment for Cash. On October 4, Sierra acquired office equipment by paying $5,000 cash to Superior Equipment Corp. This event is a transaction because there is an increase and decrease in Sierra's assets: Office Equipment (an asset) increases by $5,000 and Cash (an asset) decreases by $5,000, as shown.

	Assets			=	Liabilities	+	Shareholders' Equity
			Office		Notes		Common
	Cash	+	Equipment	=	Payable	+	Shares
Beginning Balance	$15,000				$5,000		$10,000
(3)	−5,000		+$5,000				
Ending Balance	$10,000	+	$5,000	=	$5,000	+	$10,000
	$15,000				$15,000		

The total assets are now $15,000. Liabilities plus shareholders' equity also total $15,000.

Event (4). Receipt of Cash in Advance from Customer. On October 4, Sierra received a $1,200 cash advance from R. Knox, a client. This event is a transaction because cash (an asset) was received for advertising services that are expected to be completed by Sierra by December 31.

Revenue should not be recorded until the work has been performed. For example, in the magazine and airline industries, customers pay for their magazine subscriptions or flight tickets in advance. These companies have a liability to the customer until the magazines are delivered or the flight provided. As soon as the product is delivered or the service provided, revenue can be recorded.

Since the cash was received prior to performing the service, Sierra has a liability for the work due. Cash increases by $1,200 and a liability, Unearned Service Revenue (abbreviated as Unearned Revenue), increases by an equal amount:

	Assets		=	Liabilities		+	Shareholders' Equity
		Office		Notes	Unearned		Common
	Cash	+ Equipment	=	Payable	+ Revenue	+	Shares
Beginning Balance	$10,000	$5,000		$5,000			$10,000
(4)	+1,200				+$1,200		
Ending Balance	$11,200 +	$5,000	=	$5,000 +	$1,200	+	$10,000
		$16,200			$16,200		

Event (5). Services Performed for Cash. On October 5, Sierra received $10,000 in cash from Copa Ltd. for advertising services performed. This event is a transaction because Sierra received an asset, cash, in exchange for services.

Advertising service is Sierra's principal revenue-producing activity. As **revenue increases shareholders' equity**, both assets and shareholders' equity are increased by this transaction. Cash is increased by $10,000, and Retained Earnings is increased by $10,000. The new balances in the equation are:

	Assets		=	Liabilities		+	Shareholders' Equity		
		Office		Notes	Unearned		Common	Retained	
	Cash	+ Equipment	=	Payable	+ Revenue	+	Shares	+ Earnings	
Beg. Balance	$11,200	$5,000		$5,000	$1,200		$10,000		
(5)	+10,000							+$10,000	Service revenue
End. Balance	$21,200 +	$5,000	=	$5,000 +	$1,200	+	$10,000 +	$10,000	
		$26,200			$26,200				

Often companies provide services "on account." That is, they provide a service that they only get paid for at a later date. Revenue, however, is earned when services are performed. Therefore, shareholders' equity increases when services are performed, even though cash has not been received. Instead of receiving cash, the company receives a different type of asset, an **account receivable.** Accounts receivable represent the right to receive payment at a later date. Suppose that Sierra had provided the services in Event (5) on account rather than for cash. This event would be reported using the accounting equation as follows:

Assets	=	Liabilities	+	Shareholders' Equity	
Accounts				Retained	
Receivable				Earnings	
+$10,000				+$10,000	Service revenue

Later, when the $10,000 is collected from the customer, Accounts Receivable would decline by $10,000, and Cash would increase by $10,000:

Assets		=	Liabilities	+	Shareholders' Equity
	Accounts				
Cash	Receivable				
+$10,000	-$10,000				

Note that in this case, shareholders' equity is not affected by the collection of cash. Instead, we record an exchange of one asset (Accounts Receivable) for a different asset (Cash).

Event (6). Payment of Rent. On October 5, Sierra Corporation paid its office rent for the month of October in cash, $900. This rent payment is a transaction because it results in a decrease in cash. Rent is an expense incurred by Sierra Corporation in its effort to generate revenues. **Expenses decrease shareholders' equity.** The rent payment is recorded by decreasing cash and decreasing shareholders' equity (specifically, Retained Earnings) to keep the accounting equation balanced. To record this transaction, Cash is decreased by $900 and Retained Earnings is decreased by $900. The effect of these payments on the accounting equation is:

	Assets		=	Liabilities		+	Shareholders' Equity		
	Cash	Office Equipment	=	Notes Payable	Unearned Revenue	+	Common Shares	Retained Earnings	
Beg. Balance	$21,200	$5,000		$5,000	$1,200		$10,000	$10,000	
(6)	−900							−900	Rent expense
End. Balance	$20,300 +	$5,000	=	$5,000 +	$1,200	+	$10,000 +	$ 9,100	
	$25,300					$25,300			

Event (7). Purchase of Insurance Policy for Cash. On October 5, Sierra paid $600 for a one-year insurance policy that will expire next year on September 30. This event is a transaction because one asset was exchanged for another. The asset Cash is decreased by $600. The asset Prepaid Insurance is increased by $600 because the payment extends to more than the current month. Payments of expenses that will benefit more than one accounting period are identified as prepaid expenses or prepayments. As shown, the balance in total assets did not change; one asset account decreased by the same amount by which another increased:

	Assets			=	Liabilities		+	Shareholders' Equity	
	Cash	Prepaid Insurance	Office Equipment	=	Notes Payable	Unearned Revenue	+	Common Shares	Retained Earnings
Beg. Balance	$20,300		$5,000		$5,000	$1,200		$10,000	$9,100
(7)	−600	+$600							
End. Balance	$19,700 +	$600 +	$5,000	=	$5,000 +	$1,200	+	$10,000 +	$9,100
	$25,300					$25,300			

Event (8). Purchase of Supplies on Credit. On October 6, Sierra purchased a three-month supply of advertising materials on account from Aero Supply Corp. for $2,500. Assets are increased by this transaction because supplies represent a resource that will be used in the process of providing services to customers. Liabilities are increased by the amount due to Aero Supply. The asset Supplies is increased by $2,500, and the liability Accounts Payable is increased by the same amount. The effect on the equation is:

	Assets				=	Liabilities			+	Shareholders' Equity	
	Cash	Supplies	Prepaid Insurance	Office Equipment	=	Notes Payable	Accounts Payable	Unearned Revenue	Common Shares	Retained Earnings	
Beg. Balance	$19,700		$600	$5,000		$5,000		$1,200	$10,000	$9,100	
(8)		+$2,500					+$2,500				
End. Balance	$19,700 +	$2,500 +	$600	+ $5,000	=	$5,000 +	$2,500 +	$1,200	+ $10,000 +	$9,100	
	$27,800						$27,800				

Event (9). Hiring of New Employees. On October 6, Sierra hired four new employees to begin work on October 8. Each employee will receive a weekly salary of $500 for a five-day (Monday–Friday) work week, payable every two weeks. Employees will receive their first paycheques on October 22. There is no effect on the accounting equation because the assets, liabilities, and shareholders' equity of the company have not changed. An accounting transaction has not occurred. At this point, there is only an agreement that the employees will begin work on October 8. [See Event (11) for the first payment.]

Event (10). Payment of Cash Dividend. On October 20, Sierra paid a $500 dividend. **Dividends** are a distribution of retained earnings and not an expense. Dividends are not incurred for the purpose of generating revenue. A cash dividend transaction affects assets and shareholders' equity: Cash and Retained Earnings are each decreased by $500.

			Assets		=		Liabilities		+	Shareholders' Equity		
	Cash	+ Supplies	+ Prepaid Insurance	+ Office Equipment	=	Notes Payable	+ Accounts Payable	+ Unearned Revenue	+	Common Shares	+ Retained Earnings	
Beg. Balance	$19,700	$2,500	$600	$5,000		$5,000	$2,500	$1,200		$10,000	$9,100	
(10)	-500										-500	Dividends
End. Balance	$19,200 +	$2,500 +	$600 +	$5,000	=	$5,000 +	$2,500 +	$1,200 +		$10,000 +	$8,600	
		$27,300						$27,300				

Event (11). Payment of Cash for Employee Salaries. Employees worked two weeks, earning $4,000 in salaries, and were paid on October 22. Salaries are an expense similar to rent because they are a cost of generating revenues. This event involving employees is a transaction because assets and shareholders' equity are affected, each by an equal amount. Thus, Cash and Retained Earnings are each decreased by $4,000.

			Assets		=		Liabilities		+	Shareholders' Equity		
	Cash	+ Supplies	+ Prepaid Insurance	+ Office Equipment	=	Notes Payable	+ Accounts Payable	+ Unearned Revenue	+	Common Shares	+ Retained Earnings	
Beg. Balance	$19,200	$2,500	$600	$5,000		$5,000	$2,500	$1,200		$10,000	$8,600	
(11)	-4,000										-4,000	Salaries
End. Balance	$15,200 +	$2,500 +	$600 +	$5,000	=	$5,000 +	$2,500 +	$1,200 +		$10,000 +	$4,600	
		$23,300						$23,300				

BUSINESS INSIGHT

MANAGEMENT PERSPECTIVE

Many companies are finding that teaching their factory workers basic accounting skills can be a useful motivational tool. For example, Rhino Foods uses a financial reporting game to motivate its production line employees. Employees are taught the costs of each element of the production process, from raw materials to machinery malfunctions, so that they will make decisions that will benefit the company. The employees' bonus cheques (for managers as well as factory workers) are based on the results of the game. The owner, a former hockey coach, believes that his workers will work harder, and enjoy their work more, if they know what the score is.

SUMMARY OF TRANSACTIONS

The transactions of Sierra Corporation are summarized in Illustration 3-2 to show their cumulative effect on the basic accounting equation. The transaction number, the specific effects of the transaction, and the balances after each transaction are indicated. Remember that Event (9) did not result in a transaction, so no entry is included for that event. The illustration demonstrates three facts:

Illustration 3-2
Summary of transactions

1. Each transaction is analysed in terms of its effect on assets, liabilities, and shareholders' equity.
2. The two sides of the equation must always be equal.
3. The cause of each change in shareholders' equity must be indicated.

	Assets				=	Liabilities			+	Shareholders' Equity		
	Cash	+ Supplies	+ Prepaid Insurance	+ Office Equipment	=	Notes Payable	+ Accounts Payable	+ Unearned Revenue	+	Common Shares	+ Retained Earnings	
(1)	+$10,000				=					+$10,000		Issued shares
(2)	+5,000				=	+$5,000						
(3)	−5,000			+$5,000	=							
(4)	+1,200				=			+$1,200				
(5)	+10,000				=						+$10,000	Service revenue
(6)	−900				=						−900	Rent expense
(7)	−600		+$600		=							
(8)		+$2,500			=		+$2,500					
(10)	−500										−500	Dividends
(11)	−4,000										−4,000	Salaries
	$15,200	+ $2,500	+ $600	+ $5,000	=	$5,000	+ $2,500	+ $1,200	+	$10,000	+ $ 4,600	
		$23,300						$23,300				

Decision Toolkit

DECISION CHECKPOINTS	INFO NEEDED FOR DECISION	TOOL TO USE FOR DECISION	HOW TO EVALUATE RESULTS
Has an accounting transaction occurred?	Details of the event	Accounting equation	Determine the effect, if any, on assets, liabilities, and shareholders' equity.

The Account

Rather than use a tabular summary like the one in Illustration 3-2 for Sierra Corporation, an accounting information system uses accounts. An account is an individual accounting record of increases and decreases in a specific asset, liability, or shareholders' equity item. For example, Sierra Corporation has separate accounts for Cash, Accounts Receivable, Accounts Payable, Service Revenue, Salaries Expense, and so on. (Note that whenever we refer to a specific account, we capitalize the name.)

In its simplest form, an account consists of three parts: (1) the title of the account, (2) a left or debit side, and (3) a right or credit side. Because the alignment of these parts of an account resembles the letter T, it is referred to as a T account. The basic form of an account is shown in Illustration 3-3.

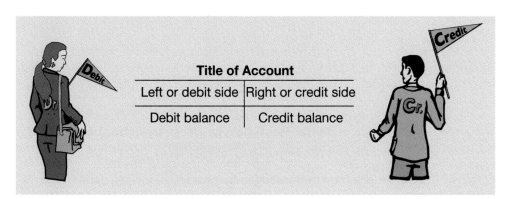

Illustration 3-3
Basic form of account

This form of account is used throughout this book to explain basic accounting relationships.

DEBITS AND CREDITS

The terms "debit" and "credit" mean "left" and "right," respectively. They are commonly abbreviated as **Dr.** for debit and **Cr.** for credit. These terms are merely directional signals. They do not mean "increase" or "decrease." The terms "debit" and "credit" are used repeatedly in the recording process to describe where entries are made in accounts. For example, the act of entering an amount on the left side of an account is called **debiting** the account, and making an entry on the right side is **crediting** the account. When the totals of the two sides are compared, an account will have a **debit balance** if the total of the debit amounts exceeds the credits. Conversely, an account will have a **credit balance** if the credit amounts exceed the debits.

The procedure of recording debits and credits in an account is shown in Illustration 3-4 for the transactions affecting the Cash account of Sierra Corporation. The data are taken from the Cash column of the tabular summary in Illustration 3-2.

Tabular Summary		T-Account Form	
Cash		**Cash**	
$10,000		10,000	5,000
5,000		5,000	900
−5,000		1,200	600
1,200		10,000	500
10,000			4,000
−900		Balance 15,200	
−600			
−500			
−4,000			
$15,200			

Illustration 3-4
Tabular summary and account form for Sierra Corporation's Cash account

Every positive item in the tabular summary represents a receipt of cash; every negative amount represents a payment of cash. Notice that in the account form, the increases in cash are recorded as debits, and the decreases in cash are recorded as credits. Having increases on one side and decreases on the other reduces recording errors and helps in determining the totals of each side of the account as well as the balance in the account. The account balance, a debit of $15,200, indicates that Sierra Corporation had $15,200 more increases than decreases in cash. Since it started with a balance of zero, it now has $15,200 in its Cash account.

DEBIT AND CREDIT PROCEDURES

Each transaction must affect two or more accounts to keep the basic accounting equation in balance. In other words, for each transaction, debits must equal credits. The equality of debits and credits provides the basis for the double-entry accounting system.

Under the double-entry system, the dual (two-sided) effect of each transaction is recorded in appropriate accounts. This system provides a logical method for recording transactions. As was the case with discovering Fidelity's accounting error in the feature story, the double-entry system also offers a means of ensuring the accuracy of the recorded amounts. If every transaction is recorded with equal debits and credits, then the sum of all the debits to the accounts must equal the sum of all the credits. The double-entry system for determining the equality of the accounting equation is much more efficient than the plus/minus procedure used earlier. There, it was necessary after each transaction to compare total assets with total liabilities and shareholders' equity to determine the equality of the two sides of the accounting equation.

Dr./Cr. Procedures for Assets and Liabilities

In Illustration 3-4 for Sierra Corporation, increases in Cash—an asset—were entered on the left side, and decreases in Cash were entered on the right side of the T account. We know that both sides of the basic equation (Assets = Liabilities + Shareholders' Equity) must be equal. It therefore follows that increases and decreases in liabilities have to be recorded *opposite from* increases and decreases in assets. Thus, increases in liabilities must be entered on the right or credit side, and decreases in liabilities must be entered on the left or debit side.

Asset accounts normally show debit balances. That is, debits to a specific asset account should exceed credits to that account. Likewise, **liability accounts normally show credit balances.** That is, credits to a liability account should exceed debits to that account. The effects that debits and credits have on assets and liabilities, and the normal balance of each account, are diagrammed in Illustration 3-5.

Helpful Hint The normal balance of an account is always on its increase side.

Illustration 3-5
Debit and credit effects—assets and liabilities

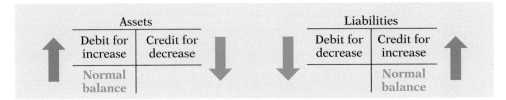

Assets		Liabilities	
Debit for increase	Credit for decrease	Debit for decrease	Credit for increase
Normal balance			Normal balance

Knowing which is the normal balance in an account may help when you are trying to identify errors. For example, a credit balance in an asset account such as Land or a debit balance in a liability account such as Wages Payable would indicate errors in recording. Occasionally, however, an abnormal balance may be correct. The Cash account, for example, will have a credit balance when a company has overdrawn its bank balance.

BUSINESS INSIGHT

MANAGEMENT PERSPECTIVE

In automated accounting systems, the computer is programmed to flag violations of the normal account balances and to print out error or exception reports. In manual systems, careful visual inspection of the accounts is required to detect normal balance problems.

Dr./Cr. Procedures for Shareholders' Equity

The five subdivisions of shareholders' equity are common shares, retained earnings, dividends, revenues, and expenses. In a double-entry system, accounts are kept for each of these subdivisions.

Common Shares. Common shares are issued in exchange for the shareholders' investments. The Common Shares account is increased by credits and decreased by debits. For example, when cash is invested in the business, Cash is debited and Common Shares is credited.

The normal balance in the Common Shares account, and the effects that debits and credits have on this account, are shown in Illustration 3-6.

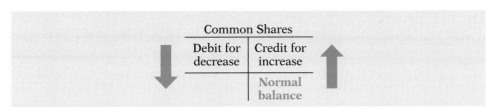

Illustration 3-6
Debit and credit effects—
Common Shares

The Preferred Shares account follows the same debit and credit rules illustrated here for the Common Shares account.

Retained Earnings. Retained Earnings is net earnings that are retained in the business. It represents the portion of shareholders' equity that has been accumulated through the profitable operation of the company. Retained Earnings is increased by credits (for example, net earnings) and decreased by debits (for example, net losses).

The normal balance for Retained Earnings, and the effects that debits and credits have on this account, are shown in Illustration 3-7.

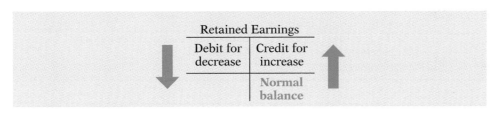

Illustration 3-7
Debit and credit effects—
Retained Earnings

Dividends. A dividend is an amount a corporation distributes to its shareholders in proportion to each investor's percentage ownership. The most common form of distribution is a cash dividend. Dividends result in a reduction of the shareholders' claims on retained earnings. Because dividends reduce shareholders' equity, increases in the Dividends account are recorded with debits. Credits to the Dividends account are unusual, but might be used to correct a dividend recorded in error, for example. As shown in Illustration 3-8, the Dividends account normally has a debit balance.

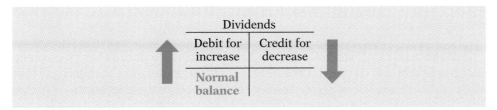

Illustration 3-8
Debit and credit effects—
Dividends

Revenues and Expenses. When revenues are earned, shareholders' equity is increased. Accordingly, **the effect of debits and credits on revenue accounts is identical to their effect on shareholders' equity.** Revenue accounts are increased by credits and decreased by debits.

On the other hand, **expenses decrease shareholders' equity**. As a result, expenses are recorded by debits. Since expenses are the negative factor in the calculation of earnings, and revenues are the positive factor, it is logical that the increase and decrease sides of expense accounts should be the reverse of revenue accounts. Thus, expense accounts are increased by debits and decreased by credits.

Credits to revenue accounts should exceed debits, and debits to expense accounts should exceed credits. Thus, **revenue accounts normally show credit balances**, and **expense accounts normally show debit balances**. The effects that debits and credits have on revenues and expenses, and the normal balance of each account, are shown in Illustration 3-9:

Illustration 3-9
Debit and credit effects—
revenues and expenses

Revenues	
Debit for decrease	Credit for increase
	Normal balance

Expenses	
Debit for increase	Credit for decrease
Normal balance	

BUSINESS INSIGHT

MANAGEMENT PERSPECTIVE

The Blue Jays baseball organization has the following major revenue and expense accounts:

Revenues	Expenses
Home admissions	Players' salaries
Radio, over-the-air television, and pay television	Team travel, lodging and meals
Concessions and publications	Team uniforms
Licensing royalties	Stadium rental
Stadium advertising	Game and other club promotions
Souvenir operations	Administration

EXPANSION OF THE BASIC EQUATION

We learned earlier in this chapter that debits (left) must equal credits (right). If we apply the debit and credit effects described in the preceding sections of this chapter to the basic accounting equation, we can see that increases in the left side of the accounting equation (asset accounts) are recorded by **debits**, while increases in the right side of the accounting equation (liability and shareholders' equity accounts) are recorded by **credits**. Of course, the converse is also true. Decreases in asset accounts are recorded by credits. Decreases in liability and shareholders' equity accounts are recorded by debits.

Illustration 3-10 expands the basic accounting equation to show the types of accounts that make up shareholders' equity. Shareholders' equity consists of common shares and retained earnings. Because shareholders' equity (on the right hand side of the accounting equation) is increased by credits, both of these accounts—common shares and retained earnings—are also increased by credits.

Retained earnings can be further divided into three components: revenues and expenses, which determine net earnings, and dividends. Since revenues increase shareholders' equity, increases in revenue accounts are recorded by credits. Expenses and dividends decrease retained earnings, and thus shareholders' equity. Decreases in shareholders' equity are recorded by debits. Because expenses and dividends decrease shareholders' equity, increases in each of these accounts are recorded by debits.

The debit/credit rules and effects on each type of account are summarized in Illustration 3-10. Study this diagram carefully. It will help you understand the fundamentals of the double-entry system. Like the basic equation, the expanded basic equation must be in balance: total debits must equal total credits.

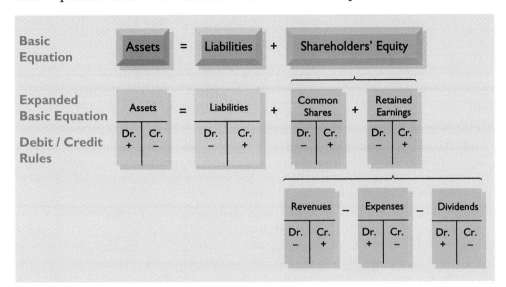

Illustration 3-10
Expansion of the basic accounting equation

 BEFORE YOU GO ON . . .

● **REVIEW IT**

1. What do the terms "debit" and "credit" mean?
2. What are the debit and credit effects on assets, liabilities, and shareholders' equity?
3. What are the debit and credit effects on revenues, expenses, and dividends?
4. What are the normal balances for Loblaw's Accounts Receivable, Long-Term Debt, Sales, and Interest Expense accounts? The answer to this question is provided at the end of the chapter.

● **DO IT**

Kate Browne, president of Hair It Is, Inc., has just rented space in a shopping mall to open and operate a beauty salon. Long before opening day and before purchasing equipment, hiring assistants, and remodelling the space, Kate is strongly advised to set up a double-entry set of accounting records in which to record all of her business transactions.

Identify the balance sheet accounts that Hair It Is, Inc., will likely need to record the transactions necessary to open for business. Also, indicate whether the normal balance of each account is a debit or a credit.

Action Plan

● Determine the types of accounts needed. First, identify asset accounts for each different type of asset invested in the business.
● Identify liability accounts for debts incurred by the business.
● Remember that Hair It Is., Inc., will need only one shareholders' equity account for common shares when it begins the business. The other shareholders' equity account (retained earnings) will be needed only after business has begun.

Solution

Hair It Is, Inc., would likely need the following accounts in which to record the transactions that ready the beauty salon for opening day: Cash (debit balance); Equipment (debit balance); Supplies (debit balance); Accounts Payable (credit balance); Notes Payable (credit balance) if the business borrows money; and Common Shares (credit balance).

Steps in the Recording Process

STUDY OBJECTIVE

④

Identify the basic steps in the recording process.

Although it is possible to enter transaction information directly into the accounts, few businesses do so. Practically every business uses these basic steps in the recording process:

1. Analyse each transaction in terms of its effect on the accounts.
2. Enter the transaction information in a general journal.
3. Transfer the journal information to the appropriate accounts in the general ledger (book of accounts).

The actual sequence of events begins with the transaction. Evidence of the transaction comes in the form of a **source document**, such as a sales slip, a cheque, a bill, or a cash register tape. This evidence is analysed to determine the effect of the transaction on specific accounts. The transaction is then entered in the general journal. Finally, the journal entry is transferred to the designated accounts in the general ledger. The sequence of events in the recording process is shown in Illustration 3-11.

Illustration 3-11
The recording process

The Recording Process

Analyse each transaction | Enter transaction in a general journal | Transfer journal information to general ledger accounts

Accounting
Cycle Tutorial

The basic steps in the recording process occur repeatedly in every business enterprise. While the analysis of transactions has already been illustrated, more examples of this step are given in this and later chapters. The other steps in the recording process are explained in the next sections.

THE JOURNAL

STUDY OBJECTIVE

⑤

Explain what a journal is and how it helps in the recording process.

Transactions are initially recorded in chronological order in a **journal** before they are transferred to the accounts. For each transaction, the journal shows the debit and credit effects on specific accounts. Companies may use various kinds of journals, but every company has the most basic form of journal, a general journal. The journal makes three contributions to the recording process:

1. It discloses the complete effect of a transaction in one place.

2. It provides a chronological record of transactions.
3. It helps to prevent or locate errors, because the debit and credit amounts for each entry can be readily compared.

Entering transaction data in the general journal is known as journalizing. To illustrate the technique of journalizing, let's look at the first three transactions of Sierra Corporation. These transactions were (1) October 1, common shares were issued in exchange for $10,000 cash; (2) October 1, $5,000 was borrowed by signing a note; and (3) October 4, office equipment was purchased for $5,000. In equation form, these transactions appeared in our earlier discussion as follows:

	Assets		=	Liabilities	+	Shareholders' Equity
	Cash	Office Equipment		Notes Payable		Common Shares
(1)	+$10,000					+$10,000 Issued shares
(2)	+5,000			+$5,000		
(3)	-5,000	+$5,000				

Separate journal entries are made for each transaction. A complete entry consists of: (1) the date of the transaction, (2) the accounts and amounts to be debited and credited, and (3) a brief explanation of the transaction. These transactions would be recorded in the journal as in Illustration 3-12.

GENERAL JOURNAL			
Date	Account Titles and Explanation	Debit	Credit
2004 Oct. 1	Cash	10,000	
	Common Shares		10,000
	(Invested cash in business)		
1	Cash	5,000	
	Notes Payable		5,000
	(Issued three-month, 6% note payable for cash)		
4	Office Equipment	5,000	
	Cash		5,000
	(Purchased office equipment for cash)		

Illustration 3-12
Recording transactions in journal form

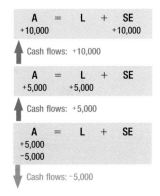

In the margins next to key journal entries are **equation analyses** that summarize the effect of the transaction on the accounting equation and cash flows.

Note the following features of the journal entries:
1. The date of the transaction is entered in the Date column.
2. The account to be debited is entered first at the left. The account to be credited is then entered on the next line, indented under the line above. The indentation differentiates debits from credits and decreases the possibility of switching the debit and credit amounts.
3. The amounts for the debits are recorded in the Debit (left) column, and the amounts for the credits are recorded in the Credit (right) column.
4. A brief explanation of the transaction is given.

It is important to use correct and specific account titles in journalizing. Since most accounts appear later in the financial statements, inaccurate account titles lead to incorrect financial statements. Some flexibility exists when first selecting account titles. The main criterion is that each title appropriately describes the content of the account. For example, a company could use any of these account titles for recording the cost of delivery trucks: Delivery Equipment, Delivery Trucks, or Trucks. Once the company chooses the specific title to use, however, all subsequent transactions involving the account should be recorded under that account title.

BEFORE YOU GO ON . . .

● **REVIEW IT**

1. What is the correct sequence of steps in the recording process?
2. What contribution does the journal make to the recording process?
3. What are the standard form and content of a journal entry made in the general journal?

● **DO IT**

The following events occurred during the first week of business of Hair It Is, Inc., Kate Browne's beauty salon:

May 1 Issued common shares to shareholders in exchange for $20,000 cash.
May 3 Purchased $4,800 of equipment on account (to be paid in 30 days).
May 5 Interviewed three people for the position of hair stylist.

(a) In what document (type of record) should the company record these three activities?
(b) Prepare the entries to record the transactions.

Action Plan

- Understand which transactions (the ones with economic effects) should be recorded.
- Determine each transaction's effect on the assets, liabilities, and shareholders' equity of the business.
- Record the transactions in the general journal, which provides a chronological record of the transactions.

Solution:

(a) Each transaction that is recorded is entered in the general journal.
(b)

May	1	Cash	20,000	
		Common Shares		20,000
		(Invested cash in the business)		
	3	Equipment	4,800	
		Accounts Payable		4,800
		(Purchased equipment on account)		
	5	No entry because no transaction occurred		

THE LEDGER

STUDY OBJECTIVE
6
Explain what a ledger is and how it helps in the recording process.

The entire group of accounts maintained by a company is referred to as the **ledger.** The ledger keeps all the information about changes in specific account balances in one place.

Companies may use various kinds of ledgers, but every company has a general ledger. A general ledger contains all the assets, liabilities, and shareholders' equity accounts, as shown in Illustration 3-13. A business can use a looseleaf binder or card file for the ledger, with each account kept on a separate sheet or card. Most businesses today, however, use a computerized accounting system.

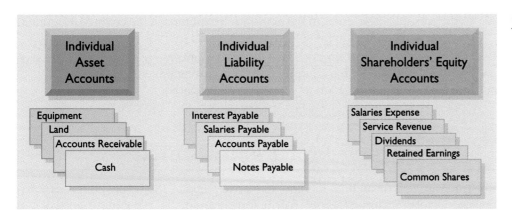

Illustration 3-13
The general ledger

CHART OF ACCOUNTS

The number and type of general ledger accounts used differ for each company, depending on the size, complexity, and type of business. For example, the number of accounts depends on the amount of detail desired by management. The management of one company may want one single account for all types of utility expense. Another may keep separate expense accounts for each type of utility expenditure, such as gas, electricity, and water. Similarly, a small corporation like Sierra will not have many accounts compared with a corporate giant like Magna International Inc. Sierra may be able to manage and report its activities in 20 to 30 accounts, whereas Magna requires thousands of accounts to keep track of its worldwide activities.

Most companies list the accounts in a chart of accounts. The chart of accounts for Sierra Corporation is shown in Illustration 3-14. Accounts shown in red are used in this chapter; accounts shown in black are explained in later chapters. New accounts may be created as needed during the life of the business.

Illustration 3-14
Chart of accounts for
Sierra Corporation

SIERRA CORPORATION—CHART OF ACCOUNTS				
Assets	Liabilities	Shareholders' Equity	Revenues	Expenses
Cash	Notes Payable	Common Shares	Service Revenue	Salaries Expense
Accounts Receivable	Accounts Payable	Retained Earnings		Advertising Supplies
Advertising Supplies	Interest Payable	Dividends		Expense
Prepaid Insurance	Unearned			Rent Expense
Office Equipment	Service Revenue			Insurance Expense
Accumulated Amortization—	Salaries Payable			Interest Expense
Office Equipment				Amortization Expense

A master chart of accounts for a sample company is included in the Study Tools section of the CD that accompanies this text.

Study Tools

POSTING

The procedure of transferring journal entries to ledger accounts is called posting. **This phase of the recording process accumulates the effects of journalized transactions in the individual accounts.** Posting involves these steps:

1. In the general ledger, enter in the appropriate columns of the debited account(s) the date and debit amount shown in the general journal.

STUDY OBJECTIVE
7

Explain what posting is and how it helps in the recording process.

2. In the general ledger, enter in the appropriate columns of the credited account(s) the date and credit amount shown in the general journal.

Posting should be done a timely basis—at least monthly—to ensure that the general ledger is up to date. In a computerized accounting system, posting usually occurs simultaneously after each journal entry is prepared.

The Recording Process Illustrated

Illustrations 3-15 through 3-25 show the basic steps in the recording process using the October transactions of Sierra Corporation. Its accounting period is a month. A basic analysis and a debit-credit analysis precede the journalizing and posting of each transaction. Study these transaction analyses carefully. **The purpose of transaction analysis is first to identify the type of account involved and then to determine whether a debit or a credit to the account is required.** You should always perform this type of analysis before preparing a journal entry. Doing so will help you understand the journal entries discussed in this chapter as well as more complex journal entries described in later chapters.

Illustration 3-15
Investment of cash by shareholders

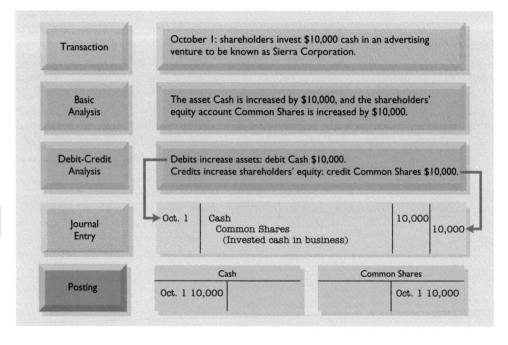

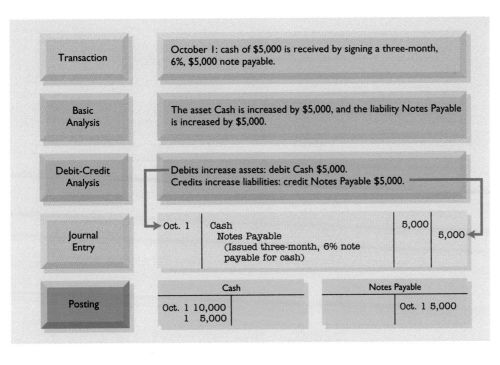

Illustration 3-16
Issue of note payable

Transaction	October 1: cash of $5,000 is received by signing a three-month, 6%, $5,000 note payable.
Basic Analysis	The asset Cash is increased by $5,000, and the liability Notes Payable is increased by $5,000.
Debit-Credit Analysis	Debits increase assets: debit Cash $5,000. Credits increase liabilities: credit Notes Payable $5,000.

Journal Entry

Oct. 1	Cash	5,000	
	Notes Payable		5,000
	(Issued three-month, 6% note payable for cash)		

A = L + SE
+5,000   +5,000

Cash flows: +5,000

Posting

Cash		Notes Payable	
Oct. 1 10,000			Oct. 1 5,000
1 5,000			

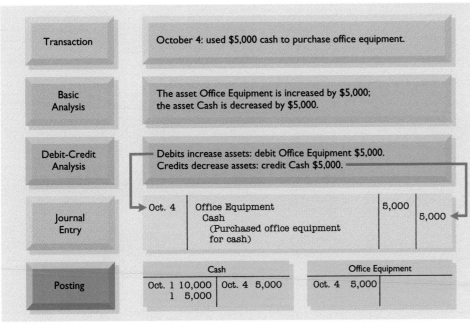

Illustration 3-17
Purchase of office equipment

Transaction	October 4: used $5,000 cash to purchase office equipment.
Basic Analysis	The asset Office Equipment is increased by $5,000; the asset Cash is decreased by $5,000.
Debit-Credit Analysis	Debits increase assets: debit Office Equipment $5,000. Credits decrease assets: credit Cash $5,000.

Journal Entry

Oct. 4	Office Equipment	5,000	
	Cash		5,000
	(Purchased office equipment for cash)		

A = L + SE
+5,000
−5,000

Cash flows: −5,000

Posting

Cash		Office Equipment	
Oct. 1 10,000	Oct. 4 5,000	Oct. 4 5,000	
1 5,000			

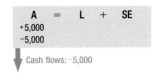

Illustration 3-18
Receipt of cash in
advance from customer

A = L + SE
+1,200   +1,200

Cash flows: +1,200

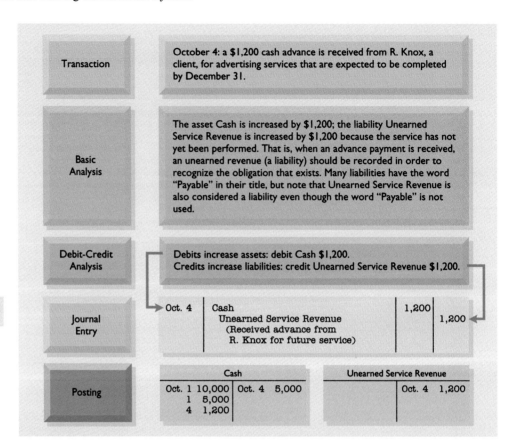

Transaction
October 4: a $1,200 cash advance is received from R. Knox, a client, for advertising services that are expected to be completed by December 31.

Basic Analysis
The asset Cash is increased by $1,200; the liability Unearned Service Revenue is increased by $1,200 because the service has not yet been performed. That is, when an advance payment is received, an unearned revenue (a liability) should be recorded in order to recognize the obligation that exists. Many liabilities have the word "Payable" in their title, but note that Unearned Service Revenue is also considered a liability even though the word "Payable" is not used.

Debit-Credit Analysis
Debits increase assets: debit Cash $1,200.
Credits increase liabilities: credit Unearned Service Revenue $1,200.

Journal Entry

Oct. 4	Cash	1,200	
	Unearned Service Revenue		1,200
	(Received advance from R. Knox for future service)		

Posting

Cash				Unearned Service Revenue	
Oct. 1	10,000	Oct. 4	5,000		Oct. 4	1,200
1	5,000				
4	1,200				

Illustration 3-19
Services performed for
cash

A = L + SE
+10,000   +10,000

Cash flows: +10,000

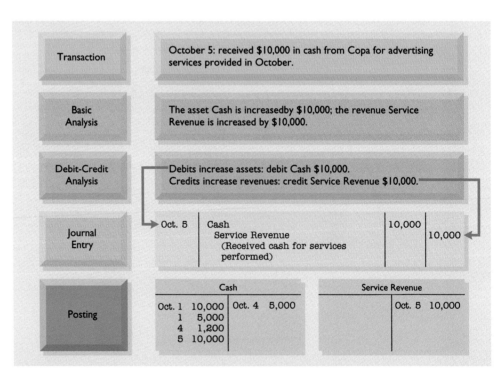

Transaction
October 5: received $10,000 in cash from Copa for advertising services provided in October.

Basic Analysis
The asset Cash is increased by $10,000; the revenue Service Revenue is increased by $10,000.

Debit-Credit Analysis
Debits increase assets: debit Cash $10,000.
Credits increase revenues: credit Service Revenue $10,000.

Journal Entry

Oct. 5	Cash	10,000	
	Service Revenue		10,000
	(Received cash for services performed)		

Posting

Cash				Service Revenue	
Oct. 1	10,000	Oct. 4	5,000		Oct. 5	10,000
1	5,000				
4	1,200				
5	10,000				

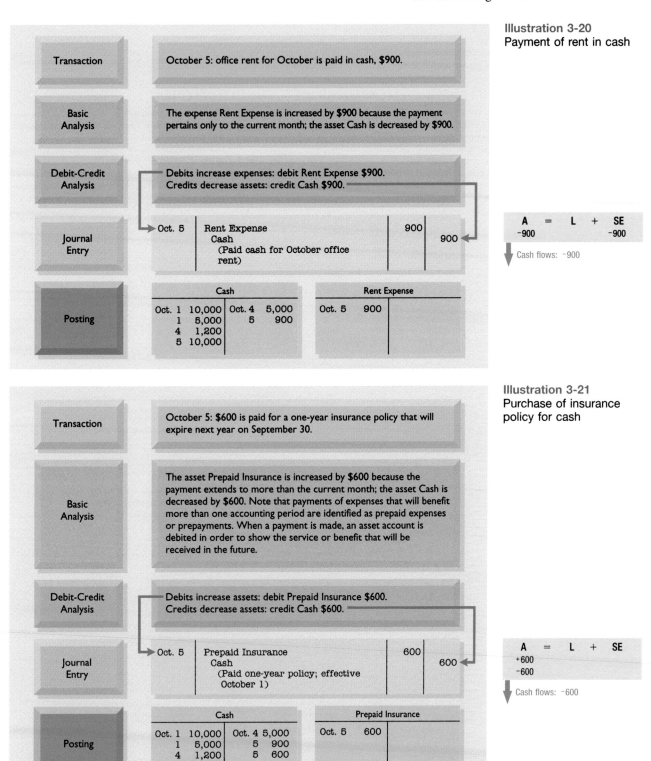

Illustration 3-20
Payment of rent in cash

| Transaction | October 5: office rent for October is paid in cash, $900. |

| Basic Analysis | The expense Rent Expense is increased by $900 because the payment pertains only to the current month; the asset Cash is decreased by $900. |

| Debit-Credit Analysis | Debits increase expenses: debit Rent Expense $900. Credits decrease assets: credit Cash $900. |

| Journal Entry | Oct. 5   Rent Expense   900
                Cash   900
                    (Paid cash for October office
                    rent) |

A = L + SE
-900   -900
Cash flows: -900

| Posting |

Cash
Oct. 1 10,000 | Oct. 4 5,000
    1   5,000 | 5   900
    4   1,200 |
    5 10,000 |

Rent Expense
Oct. 5   900

Illustration 3-21
Purchase of insurance policy for cash

| Transaction | October 5: $600 is paid for a one-year insurance policy that will expire next year on September 30. |

| Basic Analysis | The asset Prepaid Insurance is increased by $600 because the payment extends to more than the current month; the asset Cash is decreased by $600. Note that payments of expenses that will benefit more than one accounting period are identified as prepaid expenses or prepayments. When a payment is made, an asset account is debited in order to show the service or benefit that will be received in the future. |

| Debit-Credit Analysis | Debits increase assets: debit Prepaid Insurance $600. Credits decrease assets: credit Cash $600. |

| Journal Entry | Oct. 5   Prepaid Insurance   600
                Cash   600
                    (Paid one-year policy; effective
                    October 1) |

A = L + SE
+600
-600
Cash flows: -600

| Posting |

Cash
Oct. 1 10,000 | Oct. 4 5,000
    1   5,000 | 5   900
    4   1,200 | 5   600
    5 10,000 |

Prepaid Insurance
Oct. 5   600

Illustration 3-22
Purchase of supplies on credit

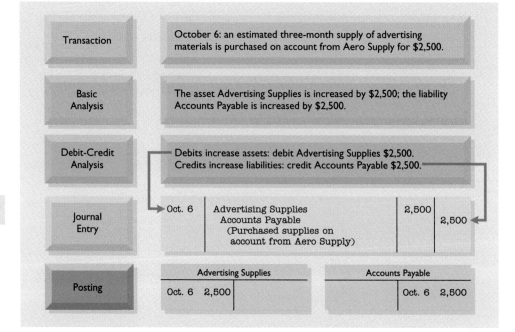

Transaction	October 6: an estimated three-month supply of advertising materials is purchased on account from Aero Supply for $2,500.
Basic Analysis	The asset Advertising Supplies is increased by $2,500; the liability Accounts Payable is increased by $2,500.
Debit-Credit Analysis	Debits increase assets: debit Advertising Supplies $2,500. Credits increase liabilities: credit Accounts Payable $2,500.

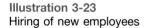

A = L + SE
+2,500 +2,500

Cash flows: no effect

| Journal Entry | Oct. 6 | Advertising Supplies
  Accounts Payable
    (Purchased supplies on
     account from Aero Supply) | 2,500 | 2,500 |

Posting

Advertising Supplies		Accounts Payable	
Oct. 6 2,500			Oct. 6 2,500

Illustration 3-23
Hiring of new employees

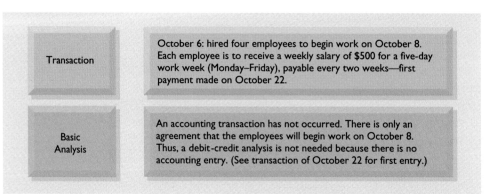

Transaction	October 6: hired four employees to begin work on October 8. Each employee is to receive a weekly salary of $500 for a five-day work week (Monday–Friday), payable every two weeks—first payment made on October 22.
Basic Analysis	An accounting transaction has not occurred. There is only an agreement that the employees will begin work on October 8. Thus, a debit-credit analysis is not needed because there is no accounting entry. (See transaction of October 22 for first entry.)

Illustration 3-24
Payment of dividend

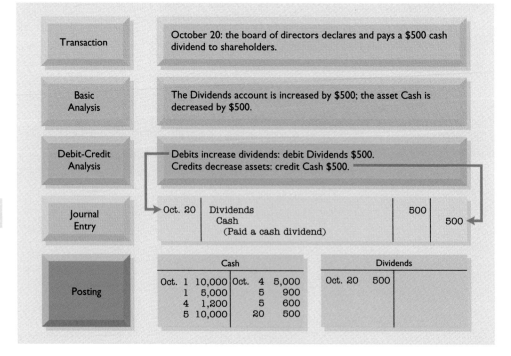

Transaction	October 20: the board of directors declares and pays a $500 cash dividend to shareholders.
Basic Analysis	The Dividends account is increased by $500; the asset Cash is decreased by $500.
Debit-Credit Analysis	Debits increase dividends: debit Dividends $500. Credits decrease assets: credit Cash $500.

A = L + SE
-500 -500

Cash flows: -500

| Journal Entry | Oct. 20 | Dividends
  Cash
    (Paid a cash dividend) | 500 | 500 |

Posting

Cash			Dividends	
Oct. 1 10,000	Oct. 4 5,000		Oct. 20 500	
1 5,000	5 900			
4 1,200	5 600			
5 10,000	20 500			

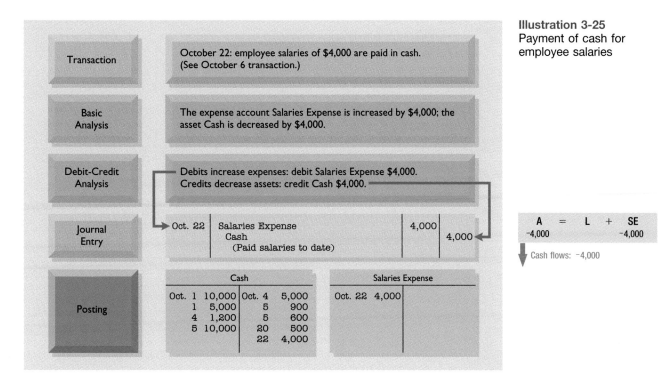

Illustration 3-25
Payment of cash for
employee salaries

SUMMARY ILLUSTRATION OF JOURNALIZING AND POSTING

The journal for Sierra Corporation for the month of October is summarized in Illustration 3-26. The ledger is shown in Illustration 3-27 with all balances highlighted in red.

Illustration 3-26
Sierra Corporation general
journal

	GENERAL JOURNAL		
Date	Account Titles and Explanations	Debit	Credit
2004			
Oct. 1	Cash	10,000	
	Common Shares		10,000
	(Invested cash in business)		
1	Cash	5,000	
	Notes Payable		5,000
	(Issued three-month, 6% note payable for cash)		
4	Office Equipment	5,000	
	Cash		5,000
	(Purchased office equipment for cash)		
4	Cash	1,200	
	Unearned Service Revenue		1,200
	(Received advance from R. Knox for future service)		
5	Cash	10,000	
	Service Revenue		10,000
	(Received cash for services performed)		
5	Rent Expense	900	
	Cash		900
	(Paid cash for October office rent)		

5	Prepaid Insurance		600	
	Cash			600
	(Paid one-year policy; effective October 1)			
6	Advertising Supplies		2,500	
	Accounts Payable			2,500
	(Purchased supplies on account from Aero Supply)			
20	Dividends		500	
	Cash			500
	(Paid a cash dividend)			
22	Salaries Expense		4,000	
	Cash			4,000
	(Paid salaries to date)			

Illustration 3-27
Sierra Corporation general ledger

GENERAL LEDGER

Cash

Oct.	1	10,000	Oct.	4	5,000
	1	5,000		5	900
		1,200		5	600
	5	10,000		20	500
				22	4,000
Bal.		15,200			

Unearned Service Revenue

			Oct.	4	1,200
			Bal.		1,200

Advertising Supplies

Oct.	6	2,500		
Bal.		2,500		

Common Shares

			Oct.	1	10,000
			Bal.		10,000

Prepaid Insurance

Oct.	5	600		
Bal.		600		

Dividends

Oct.	20	500		
Bal.		500		

Office Equipment

Oct.	4	5,000		
Bal.		5,000		

Service Revenue

			Oct.	5	10,000
			Bal.		10,000

Notes Payable

			Oct.	1	5,000
			Bal.		5,000

Salaries Expense

Oct.	22	4,000		
Bal.		4,000		

Accounts Payable

			Oct.	6	2,500
			Bal.		2,500

Rent Expense

Oct.	5	900		
Bal.		900		

BEFORE YOU GO ON . . .

● **REVIEW IT**

1. How does journalizing differ from posting?
2. What is the purpose of (a) the general ledger and (b) a chart of accounts?

● **DO IT**

Selected transactions from the general journal of Faital Inc. during its first month of operations are presented below:

Date		Account Titles	Debit	Credit
July	1	Cash	30,000	
		Common Shares		30,000
	9	Accounts Receivable	6,000	
		Service Revenue		6,000
	23	Cash	4,000	
		Accounts Receivable		4,000

Post these transactions to T accounts.

Action Plan

- Journalize transactions to keep track of financial activities (receipts, payments, receivables, payables, etc.).
- To make entries useful, classify and summarize them by posting the entries to specific ledger accounts.

Solution

Cash				Accounts Receivable				
July 1	30,000			July 9	6,000	July 23	4,000
23	4,000			Bal.	2,000		
Bal.	34,000						

Common Shares			Service Revenue		
	July 1	30,000		July 9	6,000

The Trial Balance

A trial balance is a list of general ledger accounts and their balances at a given time. It is usually prepared at the end of an accounting period. The accounts are listed in the order in which they appear in the ledger, with debit balances listed in the left column and credit balances in the right column. The totals of the two columns must be equal.

The primary purpose of a trial balance is to prove the mathematical equality of debits and credits after posting. Under the double-entry system this equality will occur when the sum of the debit account balances equals the sum of the credit account balances. **A trial balance also uncovers errors in journalizing and posting.** For example, a trial balance may well have facilitated detection of the error at Fidelity Investments discussed in the feature story. **In addition, a trial balance is useful in the preparation of financial statements,** as explained in the next chapter. The procedure for preparing a trial balance follows:

1. List the account titles and their balances.
2. Total the debit column and the credit column.
3. Verify the equality of the two columns.

The trial balance prepared from the ledger of Sierra Corporation is presented in Illustration 3-28. Note that the total debits, $28,700, equal the total credits, $28,700.

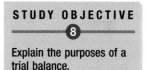

STUDY OBJECTIVE

8

Explain the purposes of a trial balance.

Ethics Note Auditors differentiate errors from irregularities when evaluating the accounting system. An error is the result of an unintentional mistake. As such, it is neither ethical nor unethical. An irregularity, on the other hand, is an intentional misstatement, which is generally viewed as unethical.

Illustration 3-28
Sierra Corporation trial balance

SIERRA CORPORATION Trial Balance October 31, 2004		
	Debit	Credit
Cash	$15,200	
Advertising supplies	2,500	
Prepaid insurance	600	
Office equipment	5,000	
Notes payable		$ 5,000
Accounts payable		2,500
Unearned service revenue		1,200
Common shares		10,000
Dividends	500	
Service revenue		10,000
Salaries expense	4,000	
Rent expense	900	
	$28,700	$28,700

LIMITATIONS OF A TRIAL BALANCE

A trial balance does not prove that all transactions have been recorded or that the ledger is correct. Numerous errors may exist even though the trial balance columns agree. For example, the trial balance may balance even when (1) a transaction is not journalized, (2) a correct journal entry is not posted, (3) a journal entry is posted twice, (4) incorrect accounts are used in journalizing or posting, or (5) off-setting errors are made in recording the amount of a transaction. In other words, as long as equal debits and credits are posted, even to the wrong account or in the wrong amount, the total debits will equal the total credits. Nevertheless, despite its limitations, the trial balance is a useful screen for finding errors and is frequently used in practice.

BEFORE YOU GO ON ...

● **REVIEW IT**

1. What is a trial balance and how is it prepared?
2. What is the primary purpose of a trial balance?
3. What are the limitations of a trial balance?

Decision Toolkit

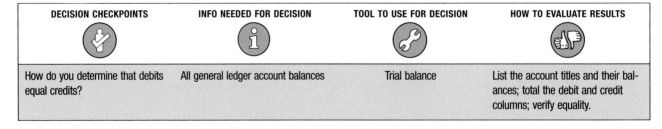

DECISION CHECKPOINTS	INFO NEEDED FOR DECISION	TOOL TO USE FOR DECISION	HOW TO EVALUATE RESULTS
How do you determine that debits equal credits?	All general ledger account balances	Trial balance	List the account titles and their balances; total the debit and credit columns; verify equality.

Using the Decision Toolkit

Prairie Grain Growers Limited is an agri-business company. Prairie Grain Growers' trial balance (which should balance but doesn't) follows. Accounts are listed in alphabetical order and have normal balances.

PRAIRIE GRAIN GROWERS LIMITED Trial Balance Year Ended July 31, 2004	Debit	Credit
Accounts payable		$ 37,000
Accounts receivable	$ 712,000	
Accumulated amortization		147,000
Advertising and promotion payable		141,000
Buildings	365,000	
Cash	32,000	
Cost of goods sold	2,384,000	
Current portion of long-term debt	12,000	
Income tax expense	353,000	
Inventories	1,291,000	
Land	110,000	
Long-term debt		873,000
Machinery and equipment	357,000	
Notes payable		495,000
Retained earnings		822,000
Sales revenue		3,741,000
Salaries and wages payable		62,000
Selling and administrative expenses	651,000	
	$6,255,000	$6,330,000

After checking with various people responsible for entering accounting data, you discover the following:
1. The purchase of a forklift, costing $7,000 and paid for with cash, was not recorded.
2. A data entry clerk accidentally deleted the account name for an account with a credit balance of $472,000, so the amount was added to the Long-Term Debt account in the trial balance.
3. July cash sales revenue of $75,000 was credited to the Sales account, but the other half of the entry was not made.
4. Selling and administrative expenses of $50,000 were mistakenly charged to Income Tax Expense.

Instructions

(a) Which mistake or mistakes have caused the trial balance to be out of balance?
(b) Should all of the items be corrected? Explain.
(c) What is the likely name of the account the data entry clerk deleted?
(d) Make the necessary corrections and balance the trial balance.
(e) On your trial balance, write "B" beside the accounts that should be shown on the balance sheet, "E" beside those that should be shown on the statement of earnings, and "RE" beside those that should be shown on the statement of retained earnings.

Solution

(a) Only mistake 3 has caused the trial balance to be out of balance.

(b) All of the items should be corrected. The misclassification error (mistake 4) on the Income Tax Expense would not affect bottom-line net earnings, but it does affect the amounts reported in the two expense accounts.

(c) There is no Common Shares account, so that must be the account that was deleted by the data entry clerk.

(d) and (e):

PRAIRIE GRAIN GROWERS LIMITED **Trial Balance** **July 31, 2004**			
	Debit	Credit	
Accounts payable		$ 37,000	B
Accounts receivable	$ 712,000		B
Accumulated amortization		147,000	B
Advertising and promotion payable		141,000	B
Buildings	365,000		B
Cash ($32,000 − $7,000 + $75,000)	100,000		B
Common shares		472,000	B
Cost of goods sold	2,384,000		E
Current portion of long-term debt		12,000	B
Income tax expense ($353,000 − $50,000)	303,000		E
Inventories	1,291,000		B
Land	110,000		B
Long-term debt ($873,000 − $472,000)		401,000	B
Machinery and equipment ($357,000 + $7,000)	364,000		B
Notes payable		495,000	B
Retained earnings		822,000	RE
Sales revenue		3,741,000	E
Salaries and wages payable		62,000	B
Selling and administrative expenses ($651,000 + $50,000)	701,000		E
	$6,330,000	$6,330,000	

Summary of Study Objectives

❶ Analyse the effect of business transactions on the basic accounting equation. Each business transaction must have a dual effect on the accounting equation. For example, if an individual asset is increased, there must be a corresponding (a) decrease in another asset, or (b) increase in a specific liability, or (c) increase in shareholders' equity.

❷ Explain what an account is and how it helps in the recording process. An account is an individual accounting record of increases and decreases in specific asset, liability, and shareholders' equity items.

❸ Define debits and credits and explain how they are used to record business transactions. The terms "debit" and "credit" are synonymous with "left" and "right." Assets, dividends, and expenses are increased by debits and decreased by credits. Liabilities, common shares, retained earnings, and revenues are increased by credits and decreased by debits.

❹ Identify the basic steps in the recording process. The basic steps in the recording process are (a) analysing each transaction in terms of its effect on the accounts, (b) entering the transaction information in a general journal, and (c) transferring the journal information to the appropriate accounts in the general ledger.

❺ Explain what a journal is and how it helps in the recording process. The initial accounting record of a transaction is entered in a general journal before the data are entered in the accounts. A general journal (a) discloses the complete effect of a transaction in one place, (b) provides a chronological record of transactions, and (c) prevents or helps locate errors because the debit and credit amounts for each entry can be readily compared.

❻ Explain what a ledger is and how it helps in the recording process. The entire group of accounts maintained by a company is referred to as a general ledger. The general ledger keeps all the information about changes in specific account balances in one place.

❼ Explain what posting is and how it helps in the recording process. Posting is the procedure of transferring journal entries to the general ledger accounts. This step of the recording process accumulates the effects of journalized transactions in the individual accounts.

❽ Explain the purposes of a trial balance. A trial balance is a list of accounts and their balances at a given time. The primary purpose of the trial balance is to prove the mathematical equality of debits and credits after posting. A trial balance also uncovers errors in journalizing and posting and is useful in preparing financial statements.

Decision
Toolkit
Summary

Decision Toolkit—A Summary

DECISION CHECKPOINTS	INFO NEEDED FOR DECISION	TOOL TO USE FOR DECISION	HOW TO EVALUATE RESULTS
Has an accounting transaction occurred?	Details of the event	Accounting equation	Determine the effect, if any, on assets, liabilities, and shareholders' equity.
How do you determine that debits equal credits?	All general ledger account balances	Trial balance	List the account titles and their balances; total the debit and credit columns; verify equality.

NAVIGATOR

Glossary

Account An individual accounting record of increases and decreases in specific asset, liability, and shareholders' equity items. (p. 108)

Accounting information system The system of collecting and processing transaction data and communicating financial information to interested parties. (p. 102)

Accounting transactions Events that require recording in the financial statements because they involve an exchange affecting assets, liabilities, or shareholders' equity. (p. 102)

Chart of accounts A list of a company's accounts. (p. 117)

Credit The right side of an account. (p. 109)

Debit The left side of an account. (p. 109)

Double-entry system A system that records the dual effect of each transaction in appropriate accounts. (p. 110)

General journal An accounting record in which transactions are initially recorded in chronological order. (p. 114)

General ledger A book or computer record that contains a company's asset, liability, and shareholders' equity accounts. (p. 116)

Posting The procedure of transferring journal entries to the ledger accounts. (p. 117)

T account The basic form of an account. (p. 108)

Trial balance A list of general ledger accounts and their balances at a given time. (p. 125)

Demonstration Problem

Additional
Demonstration
Problems

Campus Laundry Inc. opened on September 1, 2004. During the first month of operations the following transactions occurred:

Sept. 1 Shareholders invested $20,000 cash in the business.
   2 Paid $1,000 cash for store rent for the month of September.
   3 Purchased washers and dryers for $25,000, paying $10,000 in cash and signing a $15,000, six-month, 8% note payable.
   4 Paid $1,200 for a one-year accident insurance policy.
   10 Received a bill from the *Daily News* for advertising the opening of the laundromat, $200.
   15 Performed services on account for $6,200.
   20 Paid a $700 cash dividend to shareholders.
   30 Received $5,000 from customers billed on September 15.

The chart of accounts for the company is the same as for Sierra Corporation except for the following: Laundry Equipment and Advertising Expense.

Instructions

(a) Journalize the September transactions.
(b) Open general ledger accounts and post the September transactions.
(c) Prepare a trial balance at September 30, 2004.

Action Plan

- Make separate journal entries for each transaction.
- Note that debit entries precede credit entries
- In journalizing, make sure debits equal credits.
- In journalizing, use specific account titles taken from the chart of accounts.
- Provide an appropriate explanation of the journal entry.
- Arrange the general ledger in statement order, beginning with the balance sheet accounts.
- Post in chronological order.
- Prepare a trial balance which lists accounts in the order in which they appear in the ledger.
- In the trial balance, list debit balances in the left column and credit balances in the right column.

Solution to Demonstration Problem

(a)

GENERAL JOURNAL			
Date	Account Titles and Explanation	Debit	Credit
2004 Sept. 1	Cash	20,000	
	Common Shares		20,000
	(Invested cash in business)		
2	Rent Expense	1,000	
	Cash		1,000
	(Paid September rent)		

3	Laundry Equipment		25,000	
	Cash			10,000
	Notes Payable			15,000
	(Purchased laundry equipment for cash and six-month, 8% note payable)			
4	Prepaid Insurance		1,200	
	Cash			1,200
	(Paid one-year insurance policy)			
10	Advertising Expense		200	
	Accounts Payable			200
	(Received bill from *Daily News* for advertising)			
15	Accounts Receivable		6,200	
	Service Revenue			6,200
	(Record revenue for laundry services provided)			
20	Dividends		700	
	Cash			700
	(Declared and paid a cash dividend)			
30	Cash		5,000	
	Accounts Receivable			5,000
	(Record collection of cash on account)			

(b)

GENERAL LEDGER

Cash					Common Shares		
Sept. 1	20,000	Sept. 2	1,000			Sept. 1	20,000
30	5,000	3	10,000				
		4	1,200				
		20	700				
Bal.	12,100						

Accounts Receivable					Dividends	
Sept.15	6,200	Sept. 30	5,000	Sept.20	700	
Bal.	1,200					

Prepaid Insurance			Service Revenue		
Sept. 4	1,200			Sept. 15	6,200

Laundry Equipment			Advertising Expense	
Sept. 3	25,000		Sept.10	200

Notes Payable			Rent Expense	
	Sept. 3	15,000	Sept. 2	1,000

Accounts Payable		
	Sept. 10	200

(c)

CAMPUS LAUNDRY INC. Trial Balance September 30, 2004		
	Debit	Credit
Cash	$12,100	
Accounts receivable	1,200	
Prepaid insurance	1,200	
Laundry equipment	25,000	
Notes payable		$15,000
Accounts payable		200
Common shares		20,000
Dividends	700	
Service revenue		6,200
Advertising expense	200	
Rent expense	1,000	
	$41,400	$41,400

Multiple Choice Quiz

SELF-STUDY QUESTIONS

Answers are at the end of the chapter.

(SO 1) 1. The effects on the basic accounting equation of performing services for cash are to:
(a) increase assets and decrease shareholders' equity.
(b) increase assets and increase shareholders' equity.
(c) increase assets and increase liabilities.
(d) increase liabilities and increase shareholders' equity.

(SO 1) 2. Genesis Inc. buys a $900 machine on credit. This transaction will affect the:
(a) statement of earnings only.
(b) balance sheet only.
(c) statement of earnings and statement of retained earnings only.
(d) statement of earnings, statement of retained earnings, and balance sheet.

(SO 2) 3. Which statement about an account is *true*?
(a) In its simplest form, an account consists of two parts.
(b) An account is an individual accounting record of increases and decreases in specific asset, liability, and shareholders' equity items.
(c) There are separate accounts for specific assets and liabilities but only one account for shareholders' equity items.
(d) The left side of an account is the credit or decrease side.

4. Debits: (SO 3)
(a) increase both assets and liabilities.
(b) decrease both assets and liabilities.
(c) increase assets and decrease liabilities.
(d) decrease assets and increase liabilities.

5. A revenue account: (SO 3)
(a) is increased by debits.
(b) is decreased by credits.
(c) has a normal balance of a debit.
(d) is increased by credits.

6. Which accounts normally have debit balances? (SO 3)
(a) Assets, expenses, and revenues
(b) Assets, expenses, and retained earnings
(c) Assets, liabilities, and dividends
(d) Assets, dividends, and expenses

7. Which is *not* part of the recording process? (SO 4)
(a) Analysing transactions
(b) Preparing a trial balance
(c) Entering transactions in a general journal
(d) Posting transactions

8. Which of these statements about a general journal is *false*? (SO 5)
(a) It contains only revenue and expense accounts.
(b) It provides a chronological record of transactions.
(c) It helps to locate errors because the debit and credit amounts for each entry can be readily compared.
(d) It discloses the complete effect of a transaction in one place.

(SO 6) 9. A general ledger:
(a) contains only asset and liability accounts.
(b) should show accounts in alphabetical order.
(c) is a collection of the entire group of accounts maintained by a company.
(d) provides a chronological record of transactions.

(SO 7) 10. Posting:
(a) normally occurs before journalizing.
(b) transfers ledger transaction data to the journal.
(c) is an optional step in the recording process.
(d) transfers journal entries to ledger accounts.

(SO 8) 11. A trial balance:
(a) is a list of accounts with their balances at a given time.
(b) proves the mathematical accuracy of journalized transactions.

(c) will not balance if a correct journal entry is posted twice.
(d) proves that all transactions have been recorded.

12. A trial balance will not balance if: (SO 8)
(a) a journal entry to record a cash sale is posted twice.
(b) the purchase of supplies on account is debited to Supplies and credited to Cash.
(c) a $100 cash dividend is debited to Dividends for $1,000 and credited to Cash for $100.
(d) a $450 payment on account is debited to Accounts Payable for $45 and credited to Cash for $45.

Questions

(SO 1) 1. Can a business enter into a transaction that affects only the left side of the basic accounting equation? If so, give an example.

(SO 1) 2. Are the following events recorded in the accounting records? Explain your answer in each case.
(a) A major shareholder of the company dies.
(b) Supplies are purchased on account.
(c) An employee is fired.
(d) The company pays a cash dividend to its shareholders.

(SO 1) 3. Indicate how each business transaction affects the basic accounting equation:
(a) Paid cash for janitorial services.
(b) Purchased equipment on account.
(c) Issued common shares to investors in exchange for cash.
(d) Paid an account payable in full.

(SO 2) 4. Why is an account referred to as a T account?

(SO 3) 5. Charles Thon, a fellow student, contends that the double-entry system means each transaction must be recorded twice. Is Charles correct? Explain.

(SO 3) 6. Natalie Boudreau, an introductory accounting student, believes debit balances are favourable and credit balances are unfavourable. Is Natalie correct? Discuss.

(SO 3) 7. State the rules of debit and credit for (a) asset accounts, (b) liability accounts, and (c) the common shares account, revenue accounts, expense accounts, and dividend accounts.

(SO 3) 8. What is the normal balance for each of these accounts?
(a) Accounts Receivable (e) Service Revenue
(b) Cash   (f) Income Tax Expense
(c) Dividends   (g) Common Shares
(d) Accounts Payable   (h) Unearned Revenue

9. Indicate whether each account below is an asset, a li- (SO 3) ability, or a shareholders' equity account and whether it would have a normal debit or credit balance:
(a) Accounts Receivable (d) Dividends
(b) Accounts Payable   (e) Supplies
(c) Equipment   (f) Service Revenue

10. For the following transactions, indicate the ac- (SO 3) count debited and the account credited:
(a) Supplies are purchased on account.
(b) Cash is received on signing a note payable.
(c) Employees are paid salaries.

11. For each account listed, indicate whether it gen- (SO 3) erally will have debit entries only, credit entries only, or both debit and credit entries:
(a) Cash   (d) Accounts Payable
(b) Accounts Receivable (e) Salaries Expense
(c) Dividends   (f) Service Revenue

12. Should the balance in total shareholders' equity (SO 3) equal the balance in the Cash account? Explain why or why not.

13. A company received cash from a customer. It deb- (SO 3) ited the Cash account. Name two credit accounts that the company might have used to record a cash receipt from a customer.

14. Identify and describe the steps in the recording (SO 4) process.

15. An efficiency expert who was reviewing the steps (SO 5) in the recording process suggested dropping the general journal and recording and summarizing transactions directly into the general ledger instead. Comment on this suggestion.

16. Journalize these accounting transactions: (SO 5)
(a) $9,000 is invested in the business by shareholders in exchange for common shares.

(b) Insurance of $800 is paid for the year.

(c) Supplies of $1,500 are purchased on account.

(d) Cash of $7,500 is received for services performed.

(SO 6) 17. (a) What is a general ledger?

(b) Why is a chart of accounts important?

(SO 7) 18. Does it matter how frequently transactions are posted from the general journal to the general ledger? Explain.

(SO 8) 19. What is a trial balance? What are its purposes and limitations?

(SO 8) 20. Kap Shin is confused about how accounting information flows through the accounting system. He believes information flows in the following order:

1. Debits and credits are posted to the general ledger.

2. An accounting transaction occurs.

3. Information is entered in the general journal.

4. Financial statements are prepared.

5. A trial balance is prepared.

Indicate to Kap the proper flow of the information.

21. ⚒ Two students are discussing the use of a (SO 8) trial balance. They wonder whether the following errors, each considered separately, would prevent the trial balance from balancing. What would you tell the students?

(a) The bookkeeper debited Cash for $600 and credited Wages Expense for $600 for payment of wages.

(b) Cash collected on account was debited to Cash for $900, and Service Revenue was credited for $90.

Brief Exercises

Analyse effect of transactions.
(SO 1)

BE3-1 Presented here are six economic events. On a sheet of paper, list the letters (a) to (f) with columns for assets, liabilities, and shareholders' equity. In each column, indicate whether the event increased (+), decreased (−), or had no effect (NE) on assets, liabilities, and shareholders' equity.

(a) Purchased supplies on account.

(b) Provided a service on account.

(c) Paid expenses.

(d) Issued common shares to investors in exchange for cash.

(e) Paid a cash dividend to shareholders.

(f) Received cash from a customer who had previously been billed for services provided.

Indicate debit and credit effects.
(SO 3)

BE3-2 For each of the following accounts, indicate (a) the effect of a debit or credit on the account and (b) the normal balance:

1. Accounts Payable
2. Advertising Expense
3. Service Revenue
4. Accounts Receivable
5. Unearned Service Revenue
6. Dividends

Identify accounts to be debited and credited.
(SO 3)

BE3-3 Identify the accounts to be debited and credited for each of the following transactions.

June 1 Issued common shares to investors in exchange for $2,500 cash.

2 Purchased equipment on account for $900.

3 Paid $500 to landlord for June rent.

12 Billed J. Kronsnoble $300 for welding work done.

30 Paid $100 for income tax instalment.

Journalize transactions.
(SO 5)

BE3-4 Use the data in BE3-3 and journalize the transactions. (You may omit explanations.)

Identify steps in recording process.
(SO 4)

BE3-5 Tage Shumway, a fellow student, is unclear about the basic steps in the recording process. Identify and briefly explain the steps in the order in which they occur.

Indicate basic debit-credit analysis.
(SO 5)

BE3-6 Indicate (a) the basic analysis and (b) the debit-credit analysis similar to that shown in Illustrations 3-15 to 3-25 for the following transactions.

Aug. 1 Issues common shares to investors in exchange for $5,000.

4 Pays insurance in advance for six months, $2,100.

16 Receives $900 from clients for services provided.

27 Pays secretary $500 salary.

Journalize transactions.
(SO 5)

BE3-7 Use the data in BE3-6 and journalize the transactions. (You may omit explanations.)

BE3-8 Selected transactions are presented in journal form (without explanations). Post the transactions to T accounts.

Post journal entries.
(SO 7)

GENERAL JOURNAL

Date	Account Titles	Debit	Credit
May 5	Accounts Receivable	3,200	
	Service Revenue		3,200
12	Cash	1,900	
	Accounts Receivable		1,900
15	Cash	2,000	
	Service Revenue		2,000
15	Income Tax Expense	750	
	Income Tax Payable		750

BE3-9 From the ledger balances given below, prepare a trial balance for Carland Inc. at June 30, 2004. All account balances are normal.

Prepare trial balance.
(SO 8)

Accounts Payable	4,000	Income Tax Expense	640
Accounts Receivable	3,000	Rent Expense	1,000
Accumulated Amortization	3,400	Retained Earnings	1,090
Cash	8,400	Salaries Expense	4,000
Common Shares	20,000	Service Revenue	6,600
Dividends	1,200	Unearned Service Revenue	150
Equipment	17,000		

BE3-10 An inexperienced bookkeeper prepared the following trial balance, which does not balance. Prepare a correct trial balance, assuming all account balances are normal.

Prepare corrected trial balance.
(SO 8)

ING LIMITED
Trial Balance
December 31, 2004

	Debit	Credit
Cash	$17,600	
Prepaid insurance		$ 3,500
Accounts payable		3,000
Unearned revenue	2,200	
Common shares		10,000
Retained earnings		7,000
Dividends		4,500
Service revenue		25,600
Salaries expense	18,600	
Rent expense		2,400
Income tax expense	1,200	
	$39,600	$56,000

Exercises

E3-1 Selected transactions for Green Lawn Care Company, Ltd., follow:

Analyse effect of transactions.
(SO 1)

1. Issued common shares to investors in exchange for cash.
2. Paid monthly rent.
3. Purchased equipment on account.
4. Billed customers for services performed.
5. Paid a dividend to shareholders.
6. Received cash from customers billed in (4).
7. Incurred an advertising expense on account.
8. Purchased additional equipment, issuing cash and a note payable in payment.
9. Received cash from customers when service was provided.
10. Paid monthly income taxes.

Analyse effect of transactions.
(SO 1)

Interactive
Homework

Instructions

Describe the effect of each transaction on assets, liabilities, and shareholders' equity. For example, the first answer is "1. Increase in assets and increase in shareholders' equity."

E3-2 Wang Computer Corporation entered into these transactions during the month of May:

1. Purchased a computer for $19,000 from Digital Equipment on account.
2. Paid $4,000 cash for May rent on storage space.
3. Received $15,000 cash from customers for contracts billed in April.
4. Provided computer services to Brieske Construction Ltd. for $3,000 cash.
5. Paid BC Hydro $11,000 cash for energy usage in May.
6. Issued common shares to Li Wang in exchange for an additional $32,000 investment in the business.
7. Paid Digital Equipment for computers purchased in (1).
8. Purchased $1,000 of supplies on account.

Instructions

Indicate the effect each of the transactions listed above has on assets, liabilities, shareholders' equity, revenues, expenses, and net earnings as shown in the following schedule. Use "+" for increase, "−" for decrease, and "NE" for no effect. The first transaction is done for you as an example.

Trans-action	Assets	Liabilities	Shareholders' Equity	Revenues	Expenses	Net Earnings
1.	+19,000	+19,000	NE	NE	NE	NE

Analyse transactions and calculate net earnings.
(SO 1)

E3-3 A tabular analysis of the transactions made by Hagiwara Inc. during August 2004, its first month of operations, is shown below. Each increase and decrease in shareholders' equity is explained.

	Cash	+	Accounts Receivable	+	Supplies	+	Office Equipment	=	Accounts Payable	+	Shareholders' Equity
1.	$+15,000										+$15,000 Issued common shares
2.	−1,000						$+5,000		$+4,000		
3.	−750				$+750						
4.	+4,600		$+3,400								+8,000 Service revenue
5.	−1,500								−1,500		
6.	−2,000										−2,000 Dividends
7.	−800										−800 Rent expense
8.	+450		−450								
9.	−2,900										−2,900 Salaries expense
10.									+500		−500 Utilities expense
11.	−1,500										−1,500 Income tax expense

Instructions

(a) Describe each transaction.
(b) Determine how much shareholders' equity increased for the month.
(c) Calculate the net earnings for the month.

Prepare financial statements.
(SO 1)

E3-4 The tabular analysis of transactions for Hagiwara Inc. is presented in E3-3.

Instructions

Prepare a statement of earnings and a statement of retained earnings for the month of August and a classified balance sheet at August 31, 2004.

Identify normal account balance and financial statement.
(SO 3)

E3-5 You are presented with the following alphabetical list of accounts, selected from the financial statements of Krispy Kreme Doughnuts, Inc.:

Accounts payable	Interest expense
Accounts receivable	Interest income
Cash and cash equivalents	Inventories
Common stock	Prepaid expenses
Dividends	Property and equipment
Income taxes payable	Revenues

Instructions

For each account, indicate (a) whether the normal balance is a debit or a credit, (b) the financial statement—balance sheet, statement of earnings, or statement of retained earnings—where the account should be reported, and (c) the financial statement classification (e.g., current assets, long-term liabilities, revenues, etc.).

E3-6   Selected transactions for the Decorators Mill Ltd., an interior decorator corporation in its first month of business, are as follows:

1. Issued shares to investors for $10,000 in cash.
2. Purchased used car for $18,000 cash for use in business.
3. Purchased supplies on account for $500.
4. Billed customers $2,600 for services performed.
5. Paid $200 cash to advertise business opening.
6. Received $700 cash from customers billed in transaction (4).
7. Paid supplier $300 cash on account.
8. Paid dividends of $500 cash to shareholders.

Identify debits, credits, and normal balances.
(SO 3)

Interactive Homework

Instructions

For each transaction indicate: (a) The basic type of account debited and credited (asset, liability, shareholders' equity), (b) The specific account debited and credited (Cash, Rent Expense, Service Revenue, etc.), (c) Whether the specific account is increased or decreased, and (d) Whether the account would be debited or credited to record this transaction

Use the following format, in which transaction 1 is given as an example:

	Account Debited				Account Credited			
	(a)	(b)	(c)	(d)	(a)	(b)	(c)	(d)
Trans-action	Basic Type	Specific Account	Effect	Dr. / Cr.	Basic Type	Specific Account	Effect	Dr. / Cr.
1.	Asset	Cash	Increase	Debit	Share-holders' equity	Common Shares	Increase	Credit

E3-7   Data for the Decorators Mill Ltd. are presented in E3-6.

Journalize transactions.
(SO 5)

Instructions

Journalize the transactions.

E3-8   This information relates to Aubut Real Estate Agency Corporation:

Oct. 1 Shareholders invest $25,000 cash in exchange for common shares.
2 Hires an administrative assistant at an annual salary of $30,000.
3 Buys office furniture for $1,900, on account.
6 Sells a house and lot for B. Rollins; commissions due from Rollins, $6,200 (not paid by Rollins at this time).
10 Receives $140 cash commission for finding a tenant for an apartment.
27 Pays $700 on account for the office furniture purchased on October 3.
30 Pays the administrative assistant $2,500 in salary for October.

Indicate basic debit-credit analysis.
(SO 5)

Instructions

Prepare the debit-credit analysis for each transaction as shown in Illustrations 3-15 to 3-25.

E3-9   Transaction data for Aubut Real Estate Agency Corporation are presented in E3-8.

Journalize transactions.
(SO 5)

Instructions

Journalize the transactions.

E3-10   The transaction data and journal entries for the Aubut Real Estate Agency Corporation are presented in E3-8 and E3-9.

Post journal entries and prepare trial balance.
(SO 7, 8)

Instructions

(a) Post the transactions to T accounts.
(b) Prepare a trial balance at October 31, 2004.

Post journal entries and pre-pare trial balance.
(SO 7, 8)

E3-11   Selected transactions from the general journal of Kang, Inc., are presented here:

GENERAL JOURNAL

Date		Account Titles	Debit	Credit
Aug.	1	Cash	1,600	
		Common Shares		1,600
	10	Cash	2,900	
		Service Revenue		2,900
	12	Office Equipment	4,000	
		Cash		1,000
		Notes Payable		3,000
	25	Accounts Receivable	1,800	
		Service Revenue		1,800
	31	Cash	600	
		Accounts Receivable		600

Instructions

(a) Post the transactions to T accounts.
(b) Prepare a trial balance at August 31, 2004.

Journalize transactions from T accounts and prepare trial balance.
(SO 5, 7, 8)

E3-12   Here is the general ledger for Holly Corp.:

GENERAL LEDGER

	Cash							Common Shares		
Oct.	1	4,000	Oct.	4	400			Oct.	1	4,000
	10	750		12	1,500				25	2,000
	10	8,000		15	250					
	20	800		30	300					
	25	2,000		31	500					

	Accounts Receivable							Dividends	
Oct.	6	800	Oct.	20	800	Oct. 30	300		
	20	740							

	Supplies							Service Revenue		
Oct.	4	400	Oct.	31	180			Oct.	6	800
									10	750
									20	740

	Furniture				Store Wages Expense	
Oct.	3	3,000		Oct. 31	500	

	Notes Payable				Supplies Expense	
		Oct. 15	8,000	Oct. 31	180	

	Accounts Payable				Rent Expense	
Oct. 12	1,500	Oct.	3	3,000	Oct. 15	250

Instructions

(a) Reproduce the journal entries for the transactions that occurred during October, and provide explanations for each.
(b) Prepare a trial balance at October 31, 2004.

Analyse, journalize, and post transactions.
(SO 1, 5, 7)

Interactive Homework

E3-13   Selected transactions for the Basler Corporation during its first month in business are presented below:

Sept. 1 Issued common shares in exchange for $15,000 cash received from investors.
     5 Purchased equipment for $12,000, paying $5,000 in cash and the balance on account.
    25 Paid $3,000 cash on balance owed for equipment.
    30 Paid a $500 cash dividend.

Instructions

(a) Prepare a tabular analysis of the transactions. The headings over the three columns should be Cash + Equipment = Accounts Payable + Shareholder's Equity, with one column for each part of the equation. For transactions affecting shareholders' equity, provide explanations in the right margin.
(b) Journalize the transactions.
(c) Post the transactions to T accounts.

E3-14 The bookkeeper for Castle's Equipment Repair Corporation made these errors in journalizing and posting:

Analyse errors and their effects on trial balance. (SO 8)

1. A credit posting of $400 to Accounts Receivable was omitted.
2. A debit posting of $750 for Prepaid Insurance was debited to Insurance Expense.
3. A collection on account of $100 was journalized and posted as a debit to Cash $100 and a credit to Service Revenue $100.
4. A credit posting of $300 to Property Taxes Payable was made twice.
5. A cash purchase of supplies for $250 was journalized and posted as a debit to Supplies $25 and a credit to Cash $25.
6. A debit of $465 to Advertising Expense was posted as $456.

Instructions

For each error, indicate (a) whether the trial balance will balance, (b) the amount of the difference if the trial balance will not balance, and (c) the trial balance column that will have the larger total. Consider each error separately. Use the following form, in which error 1 is given as an example:

	(a)	(b)	(c)
Error	In Balance	Difference	Larger Column
1.	No	$400	Debit

E3-15 The accounts in the ledger of Speedy Delivery Service, Inc., contain the following balances on July 31, 2004:

Prepare trial balance and financial statements. (SO 8)

Interactive Homework

Accounts Payable	$ 7,390	Income Tax Expense	$ 1,500
Accounts Receivable	13,640	Insurance Expense	520
Accumulated Amortization	19,745	Notes Payable, due 2009	18,450
Amortization Expense	9,870	Prepaid Insurance	1,960
Cash	?	Repair Expense	1,200
Common Shares	40,000	Retained Earnings	4,630
Delivery Equipment	49,360	Salaries Expense	4,420
Dividends	700	Salaries Payable	815
Gas and Oil Expense	750	Service Revenue	20,610

Instructions

(a) Prepare a trial balance with the accounts arranged in financial statement order, and fill in the missing amount for Cash.
(b) Prepare a statement of earnings, statement of retained earnings, and classified balance sheet.

Problems: Set A

Analyse transactions, classify cash flows, and calculate net earnings.
(SO 1)

P3-1A Tony's Repair Shop, Inc., was started on May 1. A summary of the May transactions follows:

1. Issued Common shares for $15,000 cash.
2. Purchased equipment for $5,000 cash.
3. Paid $500 cash for May office rent.
4. Paid $400 cash for supplies.
5. Purchased $250 of advertising in the *Beacon News*, on account.
6. Received $4,100 in cash from customers for repair services provided.
7. Paid a $500 cash dividend.
8. Paid part-time employee salaries, $1,500.
9. Paid utility bills, $140.
10. Provided repair service on account to customers, $400.
11. Collected $120 cash from customers for services billed in transaction (10).
12. Paid income tax of $1,000.

Instructions

(a) Prepare a tabular analysis of the transactions using these column headings: Cash, Accounts Receivable, Supplies, Equipment, Accounts Payable, Common Shares, and Retained Earnings. Include margin explanations for any changes in Retained Earnings.
(b) From an analysis of the Cash column, identify where each transaction would be classified on the cash flow statement. Use "O" for operating activities, "I" for investing activities, and "F" for financing activities.
(c) From an analysis of the Retained Earnings column, calculate the net earnings or net loss for May.

Analyse transactions and prepare financial statements.
(SO 1)

P3-2A Corso Care Corp., a veterinary business, opened on August 1, 2004. On August 31, the balance sheet showed Cash $9,000; Accounts Receivable $1,700; Supplies $600; Office Equipment $6,000; Accounts Payable $3,600; Common Shares $13,000; and Retained Earnings $700. During September, the following transactions occurred:

1. Paid $3,100 cash for accounts payable due.
2. Received $1,600 from customers in payment of accounts receivable.
3. Purchased additional office equipment for $4,100, paying $1,000 in cash and the balance on account.
4. Earned revenue of $8,900, of which $2,300 is paid in cash and the balance is due in October.
5. Declared and paid a $600 cash dividend.
6. Paid salaries, $700; rent, $900; and advertising, $100, for the month.
7. Incurred utility expenses for the month on account, $170.
8. Received $7,000 from Canadian Western Bank; the money was borrowed on a note payable.
9. Paid income tax for the month, $2,500.

Instructions

(a) Prepare a tabular analysis of the September transactions beginning with the August 31 balances.
(b) Prepare a statement of earnings for September, a statement of retained earnings for September, and a classified balance sheet at September 30, 2004.

Identify normal account balance and associated financial statement.
(SO 3)

P3-3A You are presented with the following alphabetical list of accounts selected from Reitmans [Canada] Limited's financial statements:

Account	(a) Normal Balance	(b) Financial Statement	(c) Classification
Accounts payable and accrued items	Crebit	Balance Sheet	Current Liabilities
Accounts receivable			
Capital assets			
Cash and short-term deposits			

Cost of goods sold and selling, general,
   and administrative expenses
Depreciation and amortization expense
Dividends
Income tax expense
Income taxes payable
Investments
Investment income
Merchandise inventories
Prepaid expenses
Retained earnings
Sales
Share capital

Instructions

For each account, indicate (a) whether the normal balance is a debit or a credit, (b) the financial statement where the account should be reported (e.g., balance sheet, statement of earnings, or statement of retained earnings), and (c) the appropriate classification (e.g., current assets, long-term liabilities, revenues, etc.) The first one is done for you as an example.

P3-4A You are presented with the following transactions for Kailynn Corporation:

1. Issued $10,000 of common shares for cash.
2. Provided services for cash, $2,500.
3. Purchased a $35,000 truck for use in the business. Paid cash of $10,000 and issued a note payable for the remainder.
4. Received a $5,000 cash deposit from a customer for services to be provided in the future.
5. Paid $2,000 cash to employees on Friday for work done that week.
6. Billed customers $20,000 for services performed during the month.
7. Purchased $500 of supplies on account.
8. Collected cash from transaction (6) above.
9. Paid rent for the month, $1,500.
10. Paid income tax for the month, $800.

Identify debits, credits, and normal balances; calculate cash flow and net earnings. (SO 3)

Instructions

(a) For each transaction, indicate (1) the basic type of account debited and credited (asset, liability, shareholders' equity); (2) the specific account debited and credited (Cash, Service Revenue, etc.); (3) whether the specific account is increased or decreased; and (4) whether the account would be debited or credited to record this transaction. Use the following format, in which transaction 1 is given as an example:

	Account Debited				Account Credited			
	(1)	(2)	(3)	(4)	(1)	(2)	(3)	(4)
Trans-action	Basic Type	Specific Account	Effect	Dr. / Cr.	Basic Type	Specific Account	Effect	Dr. / Cr.
1.	Asset	Cash	Increase	Debit	Share-holders' Equity	Common Shares	Increase	Credit

(b) Calculate the cash flow and net earnings from these transactions.

P3-5A The North Park Corp. was formed on April 1. These selected events and transactions occurred during April:

Journalize transactions. (SO 5)

Apr. 1 Issued Common shares for $75,000 cash.
     4 Purchased land costing $50,000, for cash of $10,000. Issued a note payable for the remainder due.
     8 Purchased advertising space of $1,800 on account.
   11 Paid salaries to employees, $1,700.
   12 Hired park manager at a salary of $4,000 per month, effective May 1.
   13 Paid $3,000 for a one-year insurance policy.
   17 Paid $600 in cash dividends.
   20 Received $5,700 in cash from customers for admission fees.
   25 Sold 100 coupon books for $75 each. Each book contains 10 coupons that entitle

the holder to one admission to the park per coupon. [*Hint*: The revenue is not earned until the coupons are used.]

30 Received $7,875 in cash from customers for admission fees.

30 Paid $700 for the advertising purchased on account on April 8.

Instructions

Journalize the April transactions.

Journalize transactions, post, and prepare trial balance.
(SO 5, 7, 8)

P3-6A During the first month of operations, these events and transactions occurred for Astromech Accounting Services Inc.:

May 1 Common shares were issued for $52,000 cash.

2 A secretary-receptionist was hired at a salary of $1,000 per month.

3 Purchased $800 of supplies on account from Read Supply Company.

7 Paid office rent of $900 for the month.

11 Completed an income tax assignment and billed client $1,100 for services provided.

12 Received $4,200 in advance on a management consulting engagement.

17 Received cash of $4,200 for services completed for Arnold Corp.

31 Paid secretary-receptionist $1,000 salary for the month.

31 Paid 40% of balance due to Read Supply Company.

31 Paid monthly income tax instalment, $100.

Instructions

(a) Journalize the transactions.

(b) Post to the ledger T accounts.

(c) Prepare a trial balance at May 31, 2004.

Journalize transactions, post, and prepare trial balance.
(SO 5, 7, 8)

P3-7A Lake Theatre, Inc., started operations on March 31, 2004. At this time, the ledger showed Cash $6,000; Land $10,000; Buildings (concession stand, projection room, ticket booth, and screen) $8,000; Equipment $6,000; Accounts Payable $2,000; Mortgage Payable $8,000; and Common Shares $20,000. During April, the following events and transactions occurred:

Apr. 2 Paid film rental fee of $1,000 on first movie.

3 Ordered two additional films at $900 each.

9 Received $3,800 cash from admissions.

10 Paid $2,000 on mortgage and $1,000 on accounts payable.

11 Hired R. Thoms to operate concession stand. Thoms agrees to pay the Lake Theatre 17% of gross receipts, payable monthly.

12 Paid advertising expenses, $400.

20 Received one of the films ordered on April 3 and was billed $500. The film will be shown in April.

25 Received $3,000 cash from customers for admissions.

29 Paid salaries, $1,600.

30 Received statement from R. Thoms showing gross receipts of $1,000 and the balance due to the Lake Theatre of $170 for April. Thoms paid half of the balance due and will remit the remainder on May 5.

30 Prepaid $1,000 rental fee on special film to be run in May.

In addition to the accounts identified above, the chart of accounts shows Accounts Receivable, Prepaid Rentals, Admission Revenue, Concession Revenue, Advertising Expense, Film Rental Expense, and Salaries Expense.

Instructions

(a) Enter the beginning balances in the ledger T accounts as at April 1.

(b) Journalize the April transactions.

(c) Post the April journal entries to the ledger T accounts.

(d) Prepare a trial balance at April 30, 2004.

Analyse errors and their effects on trial balance.
(SO 8)

P3-8A A first year co-op student working for Insidz.com recorded the company's transactions for the month. He wasn't exactly sure about the recording process, but he did the best he could. He had a few questions, however, about the following transactions:

1. Cash received from a customer on account was recorded as a debit to Cash of $560 and a credit to Accounts Receivable of $650, instead of $560.

2. A service provided for cash was posted as a debit to Cash of $2,000 and a credit to

Accounts Receivable, instead of Fees Earned, of $2,000.

3. A credit of $750 for interest earned was neither recorded nor posted. The debit was recorded correctly.
4. The debit to record $1,000 of cash dividends was posted to the Salary Expense account.
5. The purchase, on account, of a computer that cost $2,500 was recorded as a debit to Supplies and a credit to Accounts Payable.
6. Insidz.com received advances from customers in the amount of $500 for work to be performed next month. The student debited Cash for $500 but didn't credit anything, as he wasn't sure what to credit.
7. A cash payment of $495 for salaries was recorded as a debit to Salary Expense and a credit to Salaries Payable.
8. Payment of rent for the month was debited to Rent Expense and credited to Cash, $850.

Instructions

(a) Indicate which of the above transactions are correct, and which are incorrect.
(b) For each error identified in (a), indicate (1) whether the trial balance will balance; (2) the amount of the difference if the trial balance will not balance; and (3) the trial balance column that will have the larger total. Consider each error separately. Use the following form, in which transaction 1 is given as an example:

	(a)	(b)	(c)
Error	In Balance	Difference	Larger Column
1.	No	$90	Credit

P3-9A This trial balance of Saginaw Ltd. does not balance:

Prepare corrected trial balance.
(SO 8)

SAGINAW LTD.
Trial Balance
May 31, 2004

	Debit	Credit
Cash	$ 7,490	
Accounts receivable		$ 2,750
Prepaid insurance	700	
Equipment	8,000	
Accumulated amortization		3,200
Accounts payable		4,500
Common shares		5,700
Retained earnings		6,000
Service revenue	6,690	
Salaries expense	4,200	
Advertising expense		1,100
Amortization expense	1,600	
Income tax expense	200	
	$28,880	$23,250

Your review of the ledger reveals that each account has a normal balance. You also discover the following errors:

1. The totals of the debit sides of Prepaid Insurance, Accounts Payable, and Income Tax Expense were each understated by $100.
2. Transposition errors were made in Accounts Receivable and Service Revenue. Based on postings made, the correct balances were $2,570 and $6,960, respectively.
3. A debit posting to Insurance Expense of $200 was omitted.
4. A $700 cash dividend was debited to Common Shares for $700 and credited to Cash for $700.
5. A $420 purchase of supplies on account was debited to Equipment for $420 and credited to Cash for $420.
6. A collection from a customer for $210 was debited to Cash for $210 and credited to Service Revenue for $210.

Instructions

Prepare the correct trial balance.

Prepare trial balance and financial statements.
(SO 8)

P3-10A   The Hudson's Bay Company has the following alphabetical list of accounts and balances (in thousands), as at January 31, 2003:

Capital Stock	$1,454,655	Other Accounts Payable and	
Cash in Stores	7,308	Accrued Expenses	$ 541,599
Credit Card Receivables	559,151	Other Accounts Receivable	117,412
Dividends	38,912	Other Assets	496,702
Fixed Assets	1,205,333	Other Long-Term Liabilities	230,824
Goodwill	152,294	Other Shareholders' Equity	
Income Tax Expense	42,421	Items	199,231
Interest Expense	45,428	Prepaid Expenses and Other	
Long-Term Debt	388,543	Current Assets	122,860
Long-Term Debt Due		Retained Earnings	668,304
Within One Year	258,870	Sales and Revenue	7,383,813
Long-Term Receivables	12,105	Short-Term Borrowings	24,744
Merchandise Inventories	1,551,104	Short-Term Deposits	51,418
Operating Expenses	7,184,503	Trade Accounts Payable	436,368

Instructions

(a) Prepare a trial balance, sorting each account balance into the debit column or the credit column.

(b) Prepare a statement of earnings and a statement of retained earnings for the year ended January 31, 2003, and a classified balance sheet as at January 31, 2003, for Hudson's Bay.

Problems: Set B

Analyse transactions, classify cash flows, and calculate net earnings.
(SO 1)

P3-1B   On April 1, the Seall Travel Agency, Inc., started operations. These transactions were completed during the month:

1. Issued common shares to shareholders for $20,000 cash.
2. Paid $700 cash for April office rent.
3. Purchased office equipment for $2,500 cash.
4. Purchased $300 of advertising in the *Halifax Herald*, on account.
5. Paid $600 cash for office supplies.
6. Earned $9,000 for services performed: cash of $1,000 is received from customers, and the balance of $8,000 is billed to customers on account.
7. Paid $400 cash dividends.
8. Paid *Halifax Herald* amount due in transaction (4).
9. Paid employees' salaries, $1,200.
10. Received $8,000 in cash from customers who had been billed in transaction (6).
11. Paid income tax of $2,000.

Instructions

(a) Prepare a tabular analysis of the transactions using these column headings: Cash, Accounts Receivable, Supplies, Office Equipment, Accounts Payable, Common Shares, and Retained Earnings. Include margin explanations for any changes in Retained Earnings.

(b) From an analysis of the Cash column, identify where each transaction would be reported on the cash flow statement. Use "O" for operating activities, "I" for investing activities, and "F" for financing activities.

(c) From an analysis of the Retained Earnings column, calculate the net earnings or net loss for April.

Analyse transactions and prepare financial statements.
(SO 1)

P3-2B   Ivan Izo created a corporation providing legal services, Ivan Izo, LLP, on July 1, 2004. On July 31, the balance sheet showed Cash $4,000; Accounts Receivable $2,500; Supplies $500; Office Equipment $5,000; Accounts Payable $4,200; Common Shares $6,500; and Retained Earnings $1,300. During August the following transactions occurred:

1. Collected $2,000 of accounts receivable due from customers.
2. Paid $2,700 cash for accounts payable due.

3. Earned revenue of $6,400, of which $3,000 is collected in cash and the balance is due in September.
4. Purchased additional office equipment for $2,000, paying $400 in cash and the balance on account.
5. Paid salaries, $1,500; rent, $900; and advertising, $350, for the month of August.
6. Declared and paid a cash dividend of $550.
7. Received $2,000 from Laurentian Bank; the money was borrowed on a note payable.
8. Incurred utility expenses for the month on account, $300.
9. Paid income tax for the month, $1,300.

Instructions

(a) Prepare a tabular analysis of the August transactions beginning with the July 31 balances.
(b) Prepare a statement of earnings for August, a statement of retained earnings for August, and a classified balance sheet at August 31.

P3-3B You are presented with the following alphabetical list of accounts for O'Laney's Welding Services Ltd.:

Identify normal account balance and associated financial statement.
(SO 3)

Account	(a) Normal Balance	(b) Financial Statement	(c) Classification
Accounts receivable	Debit	Balance Sheet	Current Asset
Amortization expense			
Common shares			
Cost of goods sold			
Equipment			
Income tax expense			
Income taxes payable			
Insurance expense			
Interest revenue			
Inventories			
Long-term debt			
Notes payable			
Prepaid insurance			
Retained earnings			
Sales revenue			
Unearned sales revenue			

Instructions

For each account, indicate (a) whether the normal balance is a debit or a credit, (b) the financial statement where the account should be reported (e.g., balance sheet or statement of earnings), and (c) the appropriate classification (e.g., current assets, long-term liabilities, revenues, etc.). The first one is done for you as an example.

P3-4B You are presented with the following transactions for Paddick Enterprises Ltd.:

Identify debits, credits, and normal balances; calculate cash flow and net earnings.
(SO 3)

1. Purchased supplies on account at a cost of $600.
2. Purchased furniture for $10,000 by signing a note that is due in three months.
3. Earned revenue of $90,000. Of this amount, $30,000 was received in cash. The balance was on account.
4. Paid $1,000 in cash dividends.
5. Paid the amount owing from transaction 1.
6. Collected $20,000 owing from the customers in transaction 3.
7. Paid operating expenses for the month, $12,000.
8. Recorded wages due to employees for work performed during the month, $4,000.

Instructions

(a) For each transaction indicate (1) the basic type of account debited and credited (asset, liability, shareholders' equity); (2) the specific account debited and credited (Cash, Service Revenue, etc.); (3) whether the specific account is increased or decreased; and (4) whether the account would be debited or credited to record this transaction. Use the following format, in which transaction 1 is given as an example:

	Account Debited				Account Credited			
	(1)	(2)	(3)	(4)	(1)	(2)	(3)	(4)
Trans-action	Basic Type	Specific Account	Effect	Dr. / Cr.	Basic Type	Specific Account	Effect	Dr. / Cr.
1.	Asset	Supplies	Increase	Debit	Liability	Accounts Payable	Increase	Credit

(b) Calculate the cash flow and net earnings from these transactions.

Journalize transactions.
(SO 5)

P3-5B Surepar Miniature Golf and Driving Range, Inc., was opened on March 1. These selected events and transactions occurred during March:

Mar. 1 Cash of $60,000 was invested in the business in exchange for common shares.
  3 Purchased Lee's Golf Land for $68,000 cash. The price consists of land $43,000, building $19,000, and equipment $6,000.
  5 Advertised the opening of the driving range and miniature golf course, paying advertising expenses of $1,600.
  6 Paid $1,800 cash for a one-year insurance policy.
  10 Purchased golf clubs and other equipment for $4,900 from Tiger Company, payable in 30 days.
  18 Received $1,200 in cash from customers for golf fees earned.
  19 Sold 100 coupon books for $50 each. Each book contains 10 coupons that enable the holder to play one round of miniature golf or to hit one bucket of golf balls per coupon. (*Hint*: The revenue is not earned until the customers use the coupons.)
  25 Declared and paid a $500 cash dividend.
  30 Paid salaries of $700.
  30 Paid Tiger Company in full for equipment purchased on March 10.
  31 Received $500 cash from customers for golf fees earned.

Instructions

Journalize the March transactions.

Journalize transactions, post, and prepare trial balance.
(SO 5, 7, 8)

P3-6B During the first month of operations, these events and transactions occurred for Virmani Architects Inc.:

Apr. 1 Cash of $16,000 was invested in exchange for common shares.
  1 A secretary-receptionist was hired at a salary of $400 per week, payable monthly.
  2 Paid office rent for the month, $800.
  3 Purchased architectural supplies on account from Halo Ltd., $1,500.
  10 Completed blueprints on a carport and billed client $1,100 for services.
  11 Received $500 cash advance from R. Welk for the design of a new home.
  20 Received $1,500 cash for services completed and delivered to P. Donahue.
  30 Paid secretary-receptionist for the month, $1,200.
  30 Paid $600 to Halo on account.

Instructions

(a) Journalize the transactions.
(b) Post to the ledger T accounts.
(c) Prepare a trial balance at April 30, 2004.

Journalize transactions, post, and prepare trial balance.
(SO 5, 7, 8)

P3-7B The Star Theatre, Inc. is unique in that it shows only triple features of sequential theme movies. As at February 28, Star's ledger showed Cash $16,000; Land $42,000; Buildings (concession stand, projection room, ticket booth, and screen) $18,000; Equipment $16,000; Accounts Payable $12,000; and Common Shares $80,000. During the month of March the following events and transactions occurred:

Mar. 2 Rented three *Scream* movies (*Scream, Scream 2*, and *Scream 3*) to be shown during the first three weeks of March. The film rental was $12,000; $4,000 was paid in cash and $8,000 will be paid on March 10.
  3 Ordered three *Star Trek* movies, to be shown the last 10 days of March. The film rental cost is $400 per night.
  9 Received $6,500 cash from customers for admissions.
  10 Paid balance due on *Scream* movies rental and $2,600 on February 28 accounts payable.
  11 Hired M. Brewer to operate concession stand. Brewer agrees to pay Star Theatre 15% of gross receipts, payable monthly.

12 Paid advertising expenses, $800.
20 Received $7,500 cash from customers for admissions.
20 Received the *Star Trek* movies and paid rental fee of $4,000.
31 Paid salaries of $3,800.
31 Received statement from M. Brewer, showing gross receipts from concessions of $8,000, and the balance due to Star Theatre of $1,200 for March. Brewer paid half the balance due and will remit the remainder on April 5.
31 Received $20,000 cash from admissions.

In addition to the accounts identified above, the chart of accounts includes Accounts Receivable, Admission Revenue, Concession Revenue, Advertising Expense, Film Rental Expense, and Salaries Expense.

Instructions

(a) Using T accounts, enter the beginning balances in the ledger as at March 1.
(b) Journalize the March transactions.
(c) Post the March journal entries to the ledger.
(d) Prepare a trial balance at March 31, 2004.

P3-8B The bookkeeper for Cater's Dance Studio Ltd. made the following errors in journalizing and posting:

Analyse errors and their effects on trial balance.
(SO 8)

1. A debit posting to Supplies of $600 was omitted.
2. A debit posting of $300 to Accounts Payable was inadvertently debited to Accounts Receivable.
3. A purchase of Supplies on account of $450 was debited to Supplies for $540 and credited to Accounts payable for $540.
4. A credit to Wages Payable for $1,200 was credited to Wages Expense.
5. A credit posting of $250 to Wages Payable was posted twice.
6. A debit posting for $1,000 of dividends was inadvertently posted to Dividends Expense instead.
7. A credit to Service Revenue for $400 was inadvertently posted as a credit to Unearned Service Revenue.
8. A credit to Accounts Receivable of $250 was omitted and was credited to Accounts Payable.

Instructions

For each error, indicate (a) whether the trial balance will balance; (b) the amount of the difference if the trial balance will not balance; and (c) the trial balance column that will have the larger total. Consider each error separately. Use the following format, in which error 1 is given as an example:

Error	(a) In Balance	(b) Difference	(c) Larger Column
1.	No	$600	Credit

P3-9B This trial balance of Wargo Ltd. does not balance:

Prepare corrected trial balance.
(SO 8)

WARGO LTD.
Trial Balance
June 30, 2004

	Debit	Credit
Cash		$ 5,652
Accounts receivable	$ 3,230	
Supplies	800	
Equipment	3,000	
Accumulated amortization	50	
Accounts payable		2,665
Unearned revenue	1,200	
Common shares		9,000
Dividends	800	
Service revenue		4,380
Salaries expense	3,400	
Office expense	910	
Income tax expense	200	
	$13,590	$21,697

Each of the listed accounts has a normal balance per the general ledger. An examination of the ledger and journal reveals the following errors:

1. Cash received from a customer on account was debited for $570, and Accounts Receivable was credited for the same amount. The actual collection was for $750.
2. The purchase of a scanner on account for $340 was recorded as a debit to Supplies for $340 and a credit to Accounts Payable for $340.
3. Services were performed on account for a client for $890. Accounts Receivable was debited for $890 and Service Revenue was credited for $89.
4. A debit posting to Amortization Expense of $50 was omitted.
5. A payment made by a customer on account for $206 was debited to Cash for $206 and credited to Accounts Receivable for $260.
6. Payment of a $600 cash dividend to Wargo's shareholders was debited to Salaries Expense for $600 and credited to Cash for $600.

Instructions

Prepare the correct trial balance.

Prepare trial balance and
financial statements.
(SO 8)

P3-10B You are presented with the following alphabetical list of accounts and balances for Taggar Enterprises Inc. at June 30, 2004:

Accounts Receivable	$ 500	Interest Expense	$ 225
Accumulated Amortization	300	Inventories	510
Amortization Expense	150	Land	800
Cash	180	Long-Term Debt	1,200
Common Shares	550	Long-Term Investment	495
Cost of Goods Sold	870	Notes Payable, due 2008	1,000
Equipment	1,500	Prepaid Insurance	90
Income Tax Expense	160	Retained Earnings,	
Income Tax Payable	160	July 1, 2003	400
Insurance Expense	130	Sales Revenue	2,000

Instructions

(a) Prepare a trial balance, sorting each account balance into the debit column or the credit column.
(b) Prepare a classified balance sheet as at June 30, 2004, and a statement of earnings and a statement of retained earnings for the year ended June 30, 2004, for Taggar Enterprises Inc.

BROADENING YOUR PERSPECTIVE

Financial Reporting and Analysis  Analysis Tools

---

FINANCIAL REPORTING PROBLEM: *Loblaw Companies Limited*

BYP3-1 The 2002 financial statements of Loblaw in Appendix A at the back of this book contain the following selected accounts (in millions):

Accounts payable and accrued liabilities	$2,336	Fixed assets	$ 5,587
		Interest expense	161
Accounts receivable	605	Sales	23,082
Depreciation expense	354		

Instructions

(a) What is the increase and decrease side for each account? What is the normal balance for each account?

(b) Identify the probable other account(s) in the transaction and the effect on that (those) account(s) when:

1. Accounts Payable is decreased.
2. Accounts Receivable is decreased.
3. Depreciation Expense is increased.
4. Fixed Assets is increased.
5. Interest Expense is increased.
6. Sales is increased.

COMPARATIVE ANALYSIS PROBLEM: *Loblaw and Sobeys*

BYP3-2 The financial statements of Sobeys Inc. are presented in Appendix B, following the financial statements for Loblaw in Appendix A.

Instructions

(a) Using Loblaw's balance sheet, statement of retained earnings, and statement of earnings, recast the accounts and amounts provided into a trial balance format as at December 28, 2002.

(b) Using Sobeys' balance sheet, statement of retained earnings, and statement of earnings, recast the accounts and amounts provided into a trial balance format as at May 3, 2003.

RESEARCH CASE

BYP3-3 The North American Industry Classification System (NAICS) provides a common-standard framework for the collection of economic and financial data for Canada, the United States, and Mexico. *NAICS Canada*, the Canadian version of the classification, groups economic activity into sectors and industries.

Instructions

At your library, find *NAICS Canada* (published by Statistics Canada, Standards Division) and answer these questions:

(a) The NAICS numbering system uses five levels of detail to identify company activities.
   What do the first two digits identify? The fourth digit? The sixth digit?

(b) Identify the sector, subsector, industry group, NAICS industry, and Canadian industry represented by the code 517210.

(c) Identify the sector code (first two digits) for the following industries:
   1. agriculture, forestry, fishing, and hunting
   2. information
   3. finance and insurance
   4. management of companies and enterprises
   5. arts, entertainment, and recreation

(d) Suppose that you are interested in examining several companies in the arts, entertainment, and recreation industry. Determine the appropriate six-digit codes for each of your chosen companies.

INTERPRETING FINANCIAL STATEMENTS

BYP3-4 Agricore United is one of Canada's leading agri-businesses. The following list of accounts and amounts were extracted from Agricore United's 2002 financial statements:

AGRICORE UNITED Trial Balance October 31, 2002 (in thousands)	
Accounts receivable and prepaid expenses	$ 212,454
Accounts payable and accrued expenses	344,836
Bank and other payable	388,722
Cash and cash equivalents	39,117
Cost of goods sold	3,669,961
Depreciation and amortization expense	82,958
Dividends	4,728
Dividends payable	4,728
Gain on disposal of assets	17,221
Income tax recovery	17,075
Interest expense	48,408
Inventories	469,172
Long-term debt	338,342
Operating, general, and administrative expense	382,420
Other assets	138,305
Other expenses	4,236
Property, plant, and equipment	724,926
Retained earnings	74,919
Sales and revenue from services	4,130,154
Share capital	460,688

Instructions

(a) Prepare a trial balance for Agricore United, with accounts reorganized in financial statement order.
(b) Present Agricore United's accounts and amounts in the form of the accounting equation: Assets = Liabilities + Shareholders' Equity.

A GLOBAL FOCUS

BYP3-5 Holmen AB is one of Europe's largest forest products companies, headquartered in Stockholm, Sweden. Its accounts are prepared in conformity with the standards issued by the Swedish Standards Board. Its financial statements are harmonized (that is, there is a minimal difference in methods) with those of member countries of the European Union.

The following trial balance lists Holmen's general ledger accounts as at December 31, 2002. In Canada, and in this chapter, trial balances normally list accounts in financial statement order to facilitate later preparation of the financial statements. Holmen also lists its accounts in financial statement order—that is, the order in which they appear in Holmen's financial statements—but financial statements in the European Union are presented in a different order than in Canada. To assist you in understanding this trial balance, the classification used by Holmen has also been included.

HOLMEN

Classification	Account	Debit	Credit
Intangible fixed assets	Goodwill, leases, and similar rights	$ 576	
Tangible fixed assets	Forest land	6,302	
	Buildings, other land, and land installations	2,552	
	Machinery and equipment	9,834	
	Fixed plants under construction and advance payments	124	
Financial fixed assets	Shares and participations	1,721	
	Financial receivables	54	
	Other long-term receivables	248	
Current assets	Inventories	2,244	
	Operating receivables	2,678	
	Short-term placements	306	
	Cash and bank	328	
Equity	Minority interest		$ 112
	Restricted equity (includes share capital)		7,889
	Non-restricted equity (includes retained earnings)		5,225
Provisions	Interest-bearing (includes pension liabilities)		25
	Non-interest bearing (includes future income tax payable)		4,631
Liabilities	Financial liabilities (includes current and long-term bank loans)		4,471
	Operating liabilities (includes current bills payable)		2,655
Revenues	Net turnover		16,081
	Other operating income		497
Expenses	Raw materials, goods for resale, and consumables	7,112	
	Personnel costs	2,346	
	Other external costs	3,188	
	Depreciation	1,153	
	Other	215	
	Income tax	605	
	Totals	$41,586	$41,586

HOLMEN AB Trial Balance December 31, 2002 (Swedish krona, in millions)

Instructions

List all differences that you notice between Holmen's trial balance presentation (order and terminology) and the normal presentation of trial balances in Canada, as shown in the chapter.

FINANCIAL ANALYSIS ON THE WEB

BYP3-6 Find liquidity, solvency, and profitability information for two competitor companies, and compare this information across companies in the same industry.

Instructions

Specific requirements of this Web case can be found on the Kimmel website.

Critical Thinking

COLLABORATIVE LEARNING ACTIVITY

BYP3-7   Andrée Boudreau operates Boudreau Riding Academy, Inc. The academy's primary sources of revenue are riding fees and lesson fees, which are provided on a cash basis. Andrée also boards horses and bills their owners monthly for boarding fees. In a few cases, boarders pay in advance of expected use. For its revenue-related transactions, the academy maintains these accounts: Cash, Boarding Accounts Receivable, Unearned Revenue, Riding Revenue, Lesson Revenue, and Boarding Revenue.

The academy owns 10 horses, a stable, a riding corral, riding equipment, and office equipment. These assets are accounted for in the following accounts: Horses, Building, Riding Arena, Riding Equipment, and Office Equipment.

The academy employs stable helpers and an office employee who are paid weekly. At the end of each month, the mail usually brings bills for advertising, utilities, and veterinary service. Other expenses include feed for the horses and insurance. For its expenses, the academy maintains the following accounts: Hay and Feed Supplies, Prepaid Insurance, Accounts Payable, Salaries Expense, Advertising Expense, Utilities Expense, Veterinary Expense, Hay and Feed Expense, and Insurance Expense.

The corporation pays periodic dividends. To record shareholders' investments in the business and dividends, two accounts are maintained: Common Shares and Dividends.

During the first month of operations an inexperienced bookkeeper was employed. Andrée Boudreau asks you to review the following eight of the 50 entries made during the month. In each case, the explanation for the entry is correct.

	GENERAL JOURNAL		
Date	Account Titles and Explanations	Debit	Credit
May 1	Cash	15,000	
	Common Shares		15,000
	(Issued common shares in exchange for $15,000 cash)		
5	Cash	250	
	Riding Revenue		250
	(Received $250 cash for lesson fees)		
7	Cash	500	
	Boarding Revenue		500
	(Received $500 for boarding of horses beginning June 1)		
9	Hay and Feed Expense	1,700	
	Cash		1,700
	(Purchased estimated five months' supply of feed and hay for $1,700 on account)		
14	Riding Equipment	80	
	Cash		800
	(Purchased desk and other office equipment for $800 cash)		
15	Salaries Expense	400	
	Cash		400
	(Paid dividend)		
20	Cash	145	
	Riding Revenue		154
	(Received $154 cash for riding fees)		
31	Veterinary Expense	75	
	Accounts Payable		75
	(Received bill of $75 from veterinarian for services provided)		

Instructions

With the class divided into groups, answer the following:

(a) Indicate each journal entry that is correct. For each journal entry that is incorrect, prepare the entry that should have been made by the bookkeeper.
(b) Which of the incorrect entries would prevent the trial balance from balancing?
(c) What was the correct net earnings for May, assuming the bookkeeper reported net earnings of $4,500 after posting all 50 entries?
(d) What was the correct balance for Cash at May 31, assuming the bookkeeper reported a balance of $12,475 after posting all 50 entries?

COMMUNICATION ACTIVITY

BYP3-8 White Glove Ltd. offers a home cleaning service. Two recurring transactions for the company are billing customers for services rendered and paying employee salaries. For example, on March 15, bills totalling $6,000 were sent to customers and $2,000 was paid in salaries to employees.

Instructions

Write a memorandum to your instructor that explains and illustrates the steps in the recording process for each of the March 15 transactions.

ETHICS CASE

BYP3-9 Vu Hung is the assistant chief accountant at Digitech Corporation, a manufacturer of computer chips and cellular phones. The company presently has total sales of $20 million. It is the end of the first quarter and Vu is hurriedly trying to prepare a trial balance so that quarterly financial statements can be prepared and released to management and the regulatory agencies. To Vu's dismay, the total credits on the trial balance exceed the debits by $1,000. In order to meet the 4 p.m. deadline, Vu decides to plug the difference! She believes that the difference is quite small and will not affect anyone's decisions, so she forces the debits and credits into balance by adding the amount of the difference to the Equipment account. She chose Equipment because it is one of the larger account balances; percentage-wise it will be the least misstated. She wishes that she had another few days to find the error but realizes that the financial statements are already late.

Ethics In
Accounting

Instructions

(a) Who are the stakeholders in this situation?
(b) What ethical issues are involved?
(c) What are Vu's alternatives?

Answers to Self-Study Questions

1. b   2. b   3. b   4. c   5. d   6. d   7. b   8. a   9. c   10. d
11. a   12. c

Answer to Loblaw Review It Question 4

Accounts Receivable (Asset-Dr.), Long-Term Debt (Liability-Cr.), Sales (Revenue-Cr.), and Interest Expense (Expense-Dr.).

Remember to go back to the Navigator box on the
chapter-opening page to check off your completed work.

Accrual Accounting Concepts

NAVIGATOR

Swapping Quarters

The accuracy of the financial reporting system depends on answers to a few fundamental questions. At what point has revenue been earned? At what point is the earnings process complete? When have expenses really been incurred?

To see the significance of these questions, consider a simple example. Early one morning a brother and sister opened a lemonade stand in front of their house. As their neighbour left for work, she bought a glass of lemonade for a quarter. Unfortunately, it was a cool day and the kids lived on a quiet cul-de-sac. In short, business was slow.

After an hour passed with no more customers, the brother decided to buy a glass of lemonade. He took the quarter received from the neighbour, passed it to his sister, and then enjoyed a glass of lemonade. A short time later, the sister decided to buy a glass of lemonade. She picked up the quarter, passed it to her brother, and enjoyed a glass.

Within an hour, after passing the quarter back and forth, they had finished off the lemonade. They walked into their house and told their parents how great business had been. They had sold the whole pitcher in less than two hours. The only thing they couldn't figure out was why, after so many transactions, they had only a quarter to show for their efforts.

Before you're too critical of these siblings consider this: During the 1990s' boom in the share prices of dot-com companies, many dot-coms earned most of their revenue from selling advertising space on their websites. To boost reported revenue, some began swapping website ad space. Company A would put an ad for its website on company B's website, and company B would put an ad for its website on company A's website. No money changed hands, but each company recorded revenues and expenses (for the value of the ad space). This practice did not change net earnings and resulted in no additional cash flow—but it did increase *reported revenue*.

Corel Corporation had to restate its results for part of 1997 after incorrectly reporting simi-

THE NAVIGATOR

Scan *Study Objectives* ☐

Read *Feature Story* ☐

Read *Chapter Preview* ☐

Read text and answer *Before You Go On*
p. 160 ☐ p. 165 ☐ p. 171 ☐ p. 180 ☐

Work *Using the Decision Toolkit* ☐

Review *Summary of Study Objectives*
and *Decision Toolkit* ☐

Work *Demonstration Problem* ☐

Answer *Self-Study Questions* ☐

Complete assignments ☐

larly bartered technology trades as revenue. Regulators eventually put an end to the practice.

Another type of transgression results from companies, recording revenue or expenses in the wrong year. In fact, shifting revenues and expenses is one of the most common abuses of financial accounting.

Xerox recently admitted reporting billions of dollars of lease revenue in periods earlier than it should have been reported, while WorldCom stunned the financial markets with its admission that it had boosted 2001 net earnings by billions of dollars by delaying the recognition of expenses until later years. Vancouver-based 360networks Inc., which underwent restructuring in 2002, had

claimed up-front revenue in 2001 from some long-term contracts. In fact, it was later discovered that much of the revenue on the company's books was for services that had not yet been provided.

One of the most high-profile Canadian cases involving allegations of revenue abuses is that of Livent Inc., the Toronto-based theatre company that filed for bankruptcy in 1998. The company's former executives have been accused, among other things, of inflating revenues by recording certain expenses as long-lived assets and understating other expenses to ensure that reported financial results met targets.

Unfortunately, revelations such as these have become all

too common. An Ipsos-Reid poll carried out in July 2002 revealed that only 58 percent of Canadians had confidence in the accuracy of a company's audited financial statements when released.

Why did so many companies violate basic financial reporting rules and sound ethics? Many speculate that as share prices climbed, executives were under greater pressure to meet higher and higher earnings expectations. Because of these pressures, regulators and standard-setters have made improving company practices for revenue recognition and disclosure a priority.

155

Making adjustments properly is important and necessary, as indicated in the feature story, because doing otherwise leads to a misstatement of revenues and expenses. In this chapter, we introduce you to the accrual accounting concepts that make such adjustments possible.

The content and organization of the chapter are as follows:

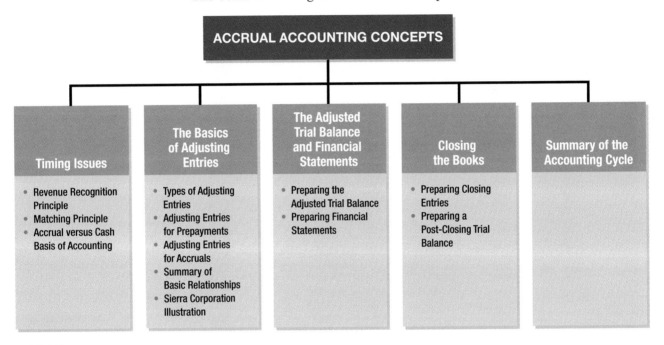

ACCRUAL ACCOUNTING CONCEPTS

Timing Issues	The Basics of Adjusting Entries	The Adjusted Trial Balance and Financial Statements	Closing the Books	Summary of the Accounting Cycle
• Revenue Recognition Principle • Matching Principle • Accrual versus Cash Basis of Accounting	• Types of Adjusting Entries • Adjusting Entries for Prepayments • Adjusting Entries for Accruals • Summary of Basic Relationships • Sierra Corporation Illustration	• Preparing the Adjusted Trial Balance • Preparing Financial Statements	• Preparing Closing Entries • Preparing a Post-Closing Trial Balance	

Timing Issues

STUDY OBJECTIVE

1

Explain the revenue recognition principle and the matching principle.

Consider the following story:

> A grocery store owner from the old country kept his accounts payable on a spindle, accounts receivable on a notepad, and cash in a shoebox. His daughter, a CA, chided him: "I don't understand how you can run your business this way. How do you know what your profits are?"
>
> "Well," the father replied, "when I got off the boat 40 years ago, I had nothing but the pants I was wearing. Today your brother is a doctor, your sister is a professor, and you are a CA. Your mother and I have a nice car, a well-furnished house, and a lake home. We have a good business and everything is paid for. So, you add all that together, subtract the pants, and there's your profit."

Although the old grocer may be correct in his evaluation of how to calculate earnings over his lifetime, most businesses need more immediate feedback about how well they are doing. For example, management needs monthly reports on financial results, large corporations present quarterly and annual financial statements to shareholders, and the Canada Customs and Revenue Agency requires all businesses to file annual tax returns. Consequently, **accounting divides the economic life of a business into artificial time periods.** As indicated in Chapter 1, this is the time period assumption. **Accounting time periods are generally a month, a quarter, or a year.**

Many business transactions affect more than one of these arbitrary time periods. For example, a new building purchased by Sears or a new airplane purchased by Air Canada will be used for many years. It doesn't make sense to expense the

Helpful Hint An accounting time period that is one year long is called a fiscal year.

full cost of the building or the airplane at the time of purchase because each will be used for many subsequent periods. Instead, we must determine the impact of each transaction on specific accounting periods.

Determining the amount of revenues and expenses to report in a given accounting period can be difficult. Proper reporting becomes possible, however, when the nature of a company's business is well understood. Generally accepted accounting principles include two principles that serve as guidelines in recognizing revenue and expense: the revenue recognition principle and the matching principle.

REVENUE RECOGNITION PRINCIPLE

The revenue recognition principle dictates that revenue must be recognized in the accounting period in which it is earned. In a service company, revenue is considered earned at the time the service is performed. To illustrate, assume a dry cleaning business cleans clothing on June 30, but customers do not claim and pay for their clothes until the first week of July. Under the revenue recognition principle, revenue is earned in June when the service is performed, not in July when the cash is received. At June 30, the dry cleaning service would report a receivable on its balance sheet and revenue in its statement of earnings for the service performed.

Improper application of the revenue recognition principle can have devastating consequences for investors. For example, the share price of the well-known outdoor clothing manufacturer North Face plunged when the company announced that $9 million of transactions that had been recorded in a previous year were reversed because North Face had repurchased the goods from the customer. This raised the question of whether a sale should have been recorded in the first place.

BUSINESS INSIGHT
MANAGEMENT PERSPECTIVE

There have been many highprofile cases highlighting the improper application of the revenue recognition principle. These include Livent, Enron, Lucent Technologies, Qwest Communications, Xerox, and AOL Time Warner, among others. Why did this happen? It happened because the revenue recognition principle has become increasingly difficult to apply as revenue generating activities have become more innovative and complex. These activities include "swap" transactions, "bill and hold" sales arrangements, risk sharing agreements, complex rights of return, price protection guarantees, and post-sale maintenance contracts.

The revenue recognition principle has been pushed to its limits by the variety of possible interpretations of these activities. In addition, many companies felt pressure to report increasing earnings and deliberately advanced the reporting of revenue, or inflated revenue, to make their companies appear more profitable than they actually were.

Regulators and standard-setters now have this difficult topic at the top of their agendas.

Decision Toolkit

DECISION CHECKPOINTS	INFO NEEDED FOR DECISION	TOOL TO USE FOR DECISION	HOW TO EVALUATE RESULTS
At what point should the company record revenue?	Need to understand the nature of the company's business	Revenue should be recorded when earned. For a service business, revenue is earned when a service is performed.	Recognizing revenue too early overstates current period revenue; recognizing it too late understates current period revenue.

MATCHING PRINCIPLE

In recognizing expenses, a simple rule is followed: "Let the expenses follow the revenues." Thus, expense recognition is tied to revenue recognition. With the preceding example, this means that the salary expense of performing the cleaning service on June 30 should be reported in the same period in which the service revenue is recognized. The critical issue in expense recognition is determining when the expense contributes to revenue. This may or may not be the same period in which the expense is paid. If the salary incurred on June 30 is not paid until July, the dry cleaner would report salaries payable on its June 30 balance sheet.

The practice of expense recognition is referred to as the matching principle because it dictates that efforts (expenses) must be matched with accomplishments (revenues).

Some expenses are easy to match with revenues. For example, the cost of goods sold can be directly matched to sales revenue in the period in which the sale occurs.

Other costs are more difficult to directly associate with revenue. For example, it is difficult to match administrative salary expense or interest expense with the revenue these help earn. Such costs are normally expensed in the period in which they are incurred. Other examples include costs that help generate revenue over multiple periods of time, such as the amortization of equipment. The association of these types of expense with revenue is less direct than that of cost of goods sold so we have to make assumptions as to how to best allocate these costs to each period. We will learn more about allocating expenses later in this chapter.

BUSINESS INSIGHT

ETHICS PERSPECTIVE

Numerous companies have dominated the news with stories of improper recognition of expense. The most significant of these was WorldCom, which disguised $3.9 billion in expenses as assets in 2001 and part of 2002, setting off a chain of events that resulted in its bankruptcy. By reclassifying operating expenses as long-lived assets, WorldCom was able to artificially inflate its earnings because long-lived assets aren't matched to revenue immediately but are instead allocated to each period over time as amortization expense. WorldCom executives have been charged with fraud, and if convicted they could face up to 65 years in prison. It doesn't pay to be unethical!

Decision Toolkit

DECISION CHECKPOINTS	INFO NEEDED FOR DECISION	TOOL TO USE FOR DECISION	HOW TO EVALUATE RESULTS
At what point should the company record expenses?	Need to understand the nature of the company's business	Expenses should "follow" revenues—that is, the effort (expense) should be matched with the result (revenue).	Recognizing expenses too early overstates current period expenses; recognizing them too late understates current period expenses.

STUDY OBJECTIVE

2

Differentiate between the cash basis and the accrual basis of accounting.

ACCRUAL VERSUS CASH BASIS OF ACCOUNTING

The combined application of the revenue recognition principle and the matching principle results in accrual basis accounting. Accrual basis accounting **means that transactions that affect a company's financial statements are recorded in the periods in which the events occur**, rather than when the company actually receives or pays cash. Using the accrual basis to determine net earnings means recognizing revenues when earned rather than when cash is received. Likewise, under the accrual basis, expenses are recognized in the period in which services or goods are used or consumed to produce these revenues, rather than when cash is paid. This results in revenues that have been earned being matched with the expenses incurred to earn these same revenues.

An alternative to the accrual basis is the cash basis. Under cash basis accounting, **revenue is recorded only when cash is received, and an expense is recorded only when cash is paid.** A statement of earnings presented under the cash basis of accounting does not satisfy generally accepted accounting principles. Why not? Because it fails to record revenue that has been earned but for which cash has not yet been received, thus violating the revenue recognition principle. Similarly a cash-basis statement of earnings fails to match expenses with earned revenues, which violates the matching principle.

Illustration 4-1 compares accrual-based numbers and cash-based numbers, using a simple example. Suppose that you own a painting company and you paint a large building during year 1. In year 1, you incur and pay total expenses of $50,000, which includes the cost of the paint and your employees' salaries. You bill your customer $80,000 at the end of year 1, but you aren't paid until year 2. On an accrual basis, you would report the revenue during the period earned— year 1—and the expenses would be matched to the period in which the revenues were earned. Thus, your net earnings for year 1 would be $30,000, and no revenue or expense from this project would be reported in year 2. The $30,000 of earnings reported for year 1 provides a useful indication of the profitability of your efforts during that period.

If, instead, you were reporting on a cash basis, you would report expenses of $50,000 in year 1 and revenues of $80,000 in year 2. Net earnings for year 1 would be a loss of $50,000, while net earnings for year 2 would be $80,000. While total earnings are the same over the two-year period ($30,000), cash basis measures are not very informative about the results of your efforts during year 1 or year 2.

⊕ **International Note**

Although different accounting standards are often used by companies in other industrialized countries, the accrual basis of accounting is central to all these standards.

Illustration 4-1
Accrual versus cash basis accounting

	Year One	**Year Two**
Activity	Purchased paint, painted building, paid employees	Received payment for work done in year 1
Accrual basis	Revenues $80,000 Expenses 50,000 Net earnings $30,000	Revenues $ 0 Expenses 0 Net earnings $ 0
Cash basis	Revenues $ 0 Expenses 50,000 Net loss ($50,000)	Revenue $80,000 Expense 0 Net earnings $80,000

Although most companies use the accrual basis of accounting, some small companies use the cash basis because they often have few receivables and payables.

● **REVIEW IT**

1. What are the revenue recognition and matching principles?
2. What are the differences between the cash and accrual bases of accounting?

The Basics of Adjusting Entries

STUDY OBJECTIVE

③

Explain why adjusting entries are needed, and identify the major types of adjusting entries.

Accounting
Cycle Tutorial

In order for revenues to be recorded in the period in which they are earned, and for expenses to be matched with the revenue they generate, adjusting entries are made to adjust accounts at the end of the accounting period. **Adjusting entries are needed to ensure that the revenue recognition and matching principles are followed.**

Adjusting entries make it possible to produce relevant financial statements at the end of the accounting period. Thus, the balance sheet reports appropriate assets, liabilities, and shareholders' equity at the statement date, and the statement of earnings shows the proper net earnings (or loss) for the period. Adjusting entries are necessary because the trial balance—the first pulling together of the transaction data—may not contain complete and up-to-date data. This is true for several reasons:

1. Some events are not journalized daily, because it would not be useful or efficient to do so. Examples are the use of supplies and the earning of wages by employees.
2. Some costs are not journalized during the accounting period, because these costs expire with the passage of time rather than as a result of recurring daily transactions. Examples of such costs are expenses to reflect the use of buildings and equipment, rent, and insurance.
3. Some items may be unrecorded. An example is a utility service bill that will not be received until the next accounting period.

Adjusting entries are required every time financial statements are prepared. Each account in the trial balance is analysed to determine whether it is complete and up-to-date for financial statement purposes.

TYPES OF ADJUSTING ENTRIES

Adjusting entries can be classified as either prepayments or accruals. Each of these classes has two subcategories as shown in Illustration 4-2.

Illustration 4-2
Categories of adjusting entries

> **Prepayments**
> 1. **Prepaid expenses:** Expenses paid in cash and recorded as assets before they are used or consumed
> 2. **Unearned revenues:** Cash received and recorded as liabilities before revenue is earned
>
> **Accruals**
> 1. **Accrued revenues:** Revenues earned but not yet received in cash or recorded
> 2. **Accrued expenses:** Expenses incurred but not yet paid in cash or recorded

Specific examples and explanations of each type of adjustment are provided over the following pages. Each example is based on the October 31 trial balance of Sierra Corporation, from Chapter 3, reproduced below in Illustration 4-3. Note that Retained Earnings has been added to this trial balance with a zero balance. We will explain its use later.

SIERRA CORPORATION Trial Balance October 31, 2004		
	Debit	Credit
Cash	$15,200	
Advertising supplies	2,500	
Prepaid insurance	600	
Office equipment	5,000	
Notes payable		$ 5,000
Accounts payable		2,500
Unearned service revenue		1,200
Common shares		10,000
Retained earnings		0
Dividends	500	
Service revenue		10,000
Salaries expense	4,000	
Rent expense	900	
	$28,700	$28,700

Illustration 4-3
Trial balance

We assume that Sierra Corporation uses an accounting period of one month. Thus, monthly adjusting entries need to be made.

ADJUSTING ENTRIES FOR PREPAYMENTS

Prepayments are either prepaid expenses or unearned revenues. Adjusting entries for prepayments record the portion of the prepayment that applies to the current accounting period. This means that for prepaid expenses the adjusting entry records the expenses which apply to the period. For unearned revenues, the adjusting entry records the revenues earned in the period.

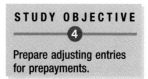

STUDY OBJECTIVE

④

Prepare adjusting entries for prepayments.

Prepaid Expenses

Payments of costs that will benefit more than one accounting period are identified as prepaid expenses or prepayments. When such a cost is incurred, an asset account is debited to show the service or benefit that will be received in the future. Examples of common prepayments are insurance, supplies, advertising, and rent. In addition, long-term prepayments are made when long-lived assets, such as buildings and equipment, are purchased.

Prepaid expenses are costs that expire either with the passage of time (e.g., rent and insurance) or through use (e.g., supplies). The expiration of these costs does not require daily entries, which would be impractical and unnecessary. Accordingly, we postpone the recognition of such cost expirations until financial statements are prepared. At each statement date, adjusting entries are made to record the expenses applicable to the current accounting period and to show the remaining amounts in the asset accounts.

Prior to adjustment, assets are overstated and expenses are understated. As shown in Illustration 4-4, **an adjusting entry for prepaid expenses results in an increase (a debit) to an expense account and a decrease (a credit) to an asset account.**

Helpful Hint A cost can be an asset or an expense. If the cost has future benefits (i.e., the benefits have not yet expired), it is an asset. If the cost has no future benefits (i.e., the benefits have expired), it is an expense.

Illustration 4-4
Adjusting entries for prepaid expenses

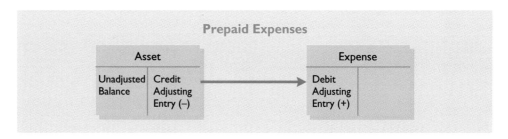

Let's look in more detail at some specific types of prepaid expenses, beginning with supplies.

Supplies. The purchase of supplies, such as paper, results in an increase (debit) to an asset account. During the accounting period, supplies are used. Rather than record supplies expense as the supplies are used, supplies expense is recognized at the end of the accounting period. At that time the company must count the remaining supplies. The difference between the balance in the Supplies (asset) account and the actual cost of supplies on hand represents the supplies used (an expense) for that period.

Recall from the facts presented in Chapter 3 that Sierra Corporation purchased advertising supplies costing $2,500 on October 6. The payment was recorded by increasing (debiting) the asset Advertising Supplies. This account shows a balance of $2,500 in the October 31 trial balance. A count at the close of business on October 31 reveals that $1,000 of supplies is still on hand. Thus, the cost of supplies used is $1,500 ($2,500 − $1,000). This use of supplies decreases an asset, Advertising Supplies. It also decreases shareholders' equity by increasing an expense account, Advertising Supplies Expense. The use of supplies is recorded as follows:

A = L + SE			
−1,500 −1,500			

Cash flows: no effect

Oct. 31	Advertising Supplies Expense	1,500	
	Advertising Supplies		1,500
	(To record supplies used)		

After the adjusting entry is posted, the two supplies accounts are as shown below in T account form:

Advertising Supplies				Advertising Supplies Expense		
Oct. 6	2,500	Oct. 31	Adj. 1,500	Oct. 31	Adj. 1,500	
Oct. 31	Bal. 1,000			Oct. 31	Bal. 1,500	

The asset account Advertising Supplies now shows a balance of $1,000, which is equal to the cost of supplies on hand at the statement date. In addition, Advertising Supplies Expense shows a balance of $1,500, which equals the cost of supplies used in October. If the adjusting entry is not made, October expenses will be understated and net earnings overstated by $1,500. Moreover, both assets and shareholders' equity will be overstated by $1,500 on the October 31 balance sheet.

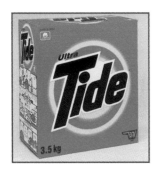

BUSINESS INSIGHT

MANAGEMENT PERSPECTIVE

The costs of advertising on radio, on television, and in magazines for burgers, bleaches, athletic shoes, and such products are normally considered an expense. Sometimes, however, they are considered prepayments. As a manager for Procter & Gamble noted, "If we run a long ad campaign for soap and bleach, we sometimes report the costs as prepayments if we think we'll receive sales benefits from the campaign down the road."

At present, whether these costs should be prepayments or expenses in the current period is a judgement call. The issue is important because the outlays for advertising can be substantial. For example, advertising expenditures in Canada are expected to reach $8.5 billion in 2003.

Insurance.   Companies purchase insurance to protect themselves from losses due to fire, theft, and unforeseen events. Insurance must be paid in advance, often for one year. Insurance payments (premiums) made in advance are normally recorded in the asset account Prepaid Insurance. At the financial statement date, it is necessary to make an adjustment to increase (debit) Insurance Expense and decrease (credit) Prepaid Insurance for the cost of insurance that has expired during the period.

On October 5, Sierra Corporation paid $600 for a one-year fire insurance policy. Coverage began on October 1. The payment was recorded by increasing (debiting) Prepaid Insurance when it was paid. This account shows a balance of $600 in the October 31 trial balance. An analysis of the insurance policy reveals that $50 of insurance expires each month ($600 ÷ 12 mos.). The expiration of Prepaid Insurance would be recorded as follows:

Oct. 31	Insurance Expense	50	
	Prepaid Insurance		50
	(To record insurance expired)		

$$A \ = \ L \ + \ SE$$
$$-50 \qquad\qquad -50$$

Cash flows: no effect

After the adjusting entry is posted, the accounts appear as follows:

Prepaid Insurance				Insurance Expense		
Oct. 5	600	Oct. 31	Adj. 50	Oct. 31	Adj. 50	
Oct. 31	Bal. 550			Oct. 31	Bal. 50	

The asset Prepaid Insurance shows a balance of $550, which represents the cost that applies to the remaining 11 months of insurance coverage. At the same time, the balance in Insurance Expense is equal to the insurance cost that was used in October. If this adjustment is not made, October expenses will be understated by $50 and net earnings overstated by $50. Moreover, as the accounting equation shows, both assets and shareholders' equity will be overstated by $50 on the October 31 balance sheet.

Amortization.   A company typically owns a variety of assets that have long lives, such as buildings, equipment, and motor vehicles. The period of service is referred to as the useful life of the asset. Because a building is expected to provide service for many years, it is recorded as an asset, rather than an expense, on the date it is acquired. As explained in Chapter 1, such assets are recorded at cost, as required by the cost principle. According to the matching principle, a portion of this cost should be reported as an expense during each period of the asset's useful life. Amortization is the process of allocating the cost of a long-lived asset to expense over its useful life.

Need for Adjustment.   From an accounting standpoint, the acquisition of long-lived assets is essentially a long-term prepayment for services. Similar to other prepaid expenses, there is a need to recognize the cost that has been used (an expense) during the period and to report the unused cost (an asset) at the end of the period. One point is very important to understand: **Amortization is an allocation concept, not a valuation concept. That is, we amortize an asset to allocate its cost to the periods over which we use it. We are not attempting to record the change in the value of the asset.**

Sierra Corporation purchased office equipment that cost $5,000 on October

4. Assume that amortization on this office equipment is estimated to be $1,000 a year, or $83 per month. Accordingly, amortization for October is recognized by this adjusting entry:

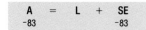

A   =   L   +   SE
-83   -83

Cash flows: no effect

Oct. 31	Amortization Expense	83	
	Accumulated Amortization—Office Equipment		83
	(To record monthly amortization)		

After the adjusting entry is posted, the accounts appear as follows:

Accumulated Amortization—Office Equipment			Amortization Expense		
	Oct. 31	Adj. 83	Oct. 31	Adj. 83	
	Oct. 31	Bal. 83	Oct. 31	Bal. 83	

The balance in the Accumulated Amortization account will increase by $83 each month.

Helpful Hint Every contra account has increases, decreases, and normal balances that are opposite to those of the account it relates to.

Statement Presentation.   Accumulated Amortization—Office Equipment is a contra asset account. That means it is offset against an asset account (Office Equipment on the balance sheet, and its normal balance is a credit. This separate account is used instead of decreasing (crediting) Office Equipment for a simple reason: to disclose both the original cost of the equipment and the total estimated cost that has expired to date. In the balance sheet, Accumulated Amortization—Office Equipment is deducted from the related asset account as shown in Illustration 4-5.

Illustration 4-5
Balance sheet presentation of accumulated amortization

Office equipment	$5,000
Less: Accumulated amortization—office equipment	83
Net book value	$4,917

Alternative Terminology *Book value* is also referred to as *carrying value*.

The difference between the cost of any asset requiring amortization and its related accumulated amortization is referred to as the net book value, or **book value**, of that asset. In Illustration 4-5, the book value of the equipment at the balance sheet date is $4,917. Be sure to understand that the book value and the market value of the asset are generally two different values. As noted earlier, the purpose of amortization is not to state an asset's value, but to allocate its cost over time.

Amortization expense identifies the portion of an asset's cost that expired during the period (in this case in October). The accounting equation shows that the omission of this adjusting entry would cause total assets, total shareholders' equity, and net earnings to be overstated and Amortization Expense to be understated.

Unearned Revenues

Cash received before revenue is earned is recorded by increasing (crediting) a liability account called Unearned Revenue. Items like rent, magazine subscriptions, and customer deposits for future service may result in unearned revenues. Airlines such as Air Canada, for instance, treat receipts from the sale of tickets as unearned revenue until the flight service is provided. Similarly, tuition fees received by universities and colleges prior to the academic session are considered unearned revenue. Unearned revenues are the opposite of prepaid expenses. Indeed, unearned revenue on the books of one company is likely to be a prepayment on the books of the company that has made the advance payment. For example, if identical accounting periods are assumed, a landlord will have unearned rent revenue when a tenant company has prepaid rent.

When the payment is received for services to be provided in a future accounting period, an unearned revenue (a liability) account should be increased (credited) to recognize the obligation that exists. Unearned revenues are subsequently earned by providing service to a customer. During the accounting period it is not practical to make daily entries as the revenue is earned. Instead, recognition of earned revenue is delayed until the adjustment process. Then an adjusting entry is made to record the revenue that has been earned during the period and to show the liability that remains at the end of the accounting period. Typically, prior to adjustment, liabilities are overstated and revenues are understated. Therefore, as shown in Illustration 4-6, **the adjusting entry for unearned revenues results in a decrease (a debit) to a liability account and an increase (a credit) to a revenue account.**

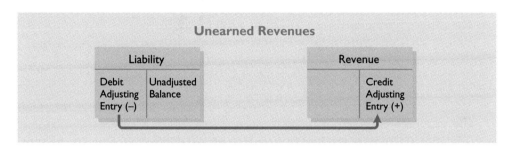

Illustration 4-6
Adjusting entries for unearned revenues

Sierra Corporation received $1,200 on October 4 from R. Knox for advertising services expected to be completed by December 31. The payment was credited to Unearned Revenue, and this liability account shows a balance of $1,200 in the October 31 trial balance. From an evaluation of the work performed by Sierra for Knox during October, it is determined that $400 has been earned in October.

The following adjusting entry is made:

Oct. 31	Unearned Service Revenue	400	
	Service Revenue		400
	(To record revenue earned)		

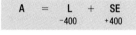

A = L + SE
       –400   +400

Cash flows: no effect

After the adjusting entry is posted, the accounts appear as below:

Unearned Service Revenue		Service Revenue	
Oct. 31 Adj. 400	Oct. 4 1,200		Oct. 5 10,000
	Oct. 31 Bal. 800		31 Adj. 400
			Oct. 31 Bal. 10,400

The liability Unearned Service Revenue now shows a balance of $800, which represents the remaining advertising services expected to be performed in the future. At the same time, Service Revenue shows total revenue earned in October of $10,400. If this adjustment is not made, revenues and net earnings will be understated by $400 in the statement of earnings. Moreover, liabilities will be overstated and shareholders' equity will be understated by $400 on the October 31 balance sheet.

BEFORE YOU GO ON . . .

● **REVIEW IT**

1. What are the four types of adjusting entries?
2. What is the effect on assets, shareholders' equity, expenses, and net earnings if a prepaid expense adjusting entry is not made?
3. What is the effect on liabilities, shareholders' equity, revenues, and net earnings if an unearned revenue adjusting entry is not made?

● **DO IT**

The ledger of Hammond, Inc., on March 31, 2004, includes these selected accounts before adjusting entries are prepared:

	Debit	Credit
Prepaid Insurance	$ 3,600	
Office Supplies	2,800	
Office Equipment	25,000	
Accumulated Amortization—Office Equipment		$5,000
Unearned Service Revenue		9,200

An analysis of the accounts shows the following:

1. Insurance expires at the rate of $100 per month.
2. Supplies on hand total $800.
3. The office equipment is amortized at $200 a month.
4. Half of the unearned service revenue was earned in March.

Prepare the adjusting entries for the month of March.

Action Plan

- Make adjusting journal entries at the end of the period for revenues earned and expenses incurred in the period.
- Adjusting entries for prepaid expenses require a debit to an expense account and a credit to an asset account.
- Adjusting entries for unearned revenues require a debit to a liability account and a credit to a revenue account.

Solution

1. Mar. 31	Insurance Expense		100	
	Prepaid Insurance			100
	(To record insurance expired)			
2. 31	Office Supplies Expense		2,000	
	Office Supplies			2,000
	(To record supplies used ($2,800 − $800))			
3. 31	Amortization Expense		200	
	Accumulated Amortization—Office Equipment			200
	(To record monthly amortization)			
4. 31	Unearned Service Revenue		4,600	
	Service Revenue			4,600
	(To record revenue earned ($9,200 × $\frac{1}{2}$))			

ADJUSTING ENTRIES FOR ACCRUALS

STUDY OBJECTIVE

5

Prepare adjusting entries for accruals.

The second category of adjusting entries is **accruals**. Adjusting entries for accruals are required in order to record revenues earned, and related expenses, in the current accounting period. Accruals have not been recognized through daily entries and thus are not yet reflected in the accounts. Prior to an accrual adjustment, the revenue account (and the related asset account), or the expense account (and the related liability account), is understated. Thus, adjusting entries for accruals will **increase both a balance sheet and statement of earnings account.**

Accrued Revenues

Alternative Terminology Ac-
crued revenues are also called
accrued receivables.

Revenues earned but not yet received in cash or recorded at the statement date are accrued revenues. Accrued revenues may accumulate (accrue) with the passing of time, as in the case of interest revenue. Or they may result from services that have been performed but neither billed nor collected, as in the case of commissions and fees. The former are unrecorded because the earning of interest does not involve daily transactions. The latter may be unrecorded because only a portion of the total service has been provided and the clients won't be billed until the service has been completed.

An adjusting entry is required to show the receivable that exists at the balance sheet date and to record the revenue that has been earned during the period. Prior to adjustment, both assets and revenues are understated. As shown in Illustration 4-7, **an adjusting entry for accrued revenues results in an increase (a debit) to an asset account and an increase (a credit) to a revenue account.**

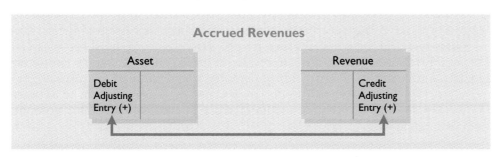

Illustration 4-7
Adjusting entries for accrued revenues

Helpful Hint For accruals, there may be no prior entry and the accounts requiring adjustment may both have zero balances prior to adjustment.

In October, Sierra Corporation earned $200 for advertising services that were not billed to clients before October 31. Because these services have not been billed, they have not been recorded. The adjusting entry would be as follows:

Oct. 31	Accounts Receivable	200	
	Service Revenue		200
	(To accrue revenue earned but not billed or collected)		

A = L + SE
+200 +200

Cash flows: no effect

After the adjusting entry is posted, the accounts appear as below:

Accounts Receivable		Service Revenue	
Oct. 31 Adj. 200		Oct. 5	10,000
Oct. 31 Bal. 200		31	400
		31 Adj. 200	
		Oct. 31 Bal. 10,600	

The asset Accounts Receivable shows that $200 is owed by clients at the balance sheet date. The balance of $10,600 in Service Revenue represents the total revenue earned during the month ($10,000 + $400 + $200). If the adjusting entry is not made, assets and shareholders' equity on the balance sheet, and revenues and net earnings on the statement of earnings, will be understated.

In the next accounting period, the clients will be billed. When this occurs, the entry to record the billing should recognize that $200 of revenue earned in October has already been recorded in the October 31 adjusting entry. To illustrate, assume that bills totalling $3,000 are mailed to clients on November 10. Of this amount, $200 represents revenue earned in October and recorded as Service Revenue in the October 31 adjusting entry. The remaining $2,800 represents revenue earned in November. Thus, the following entry is made:

Nov. 10	Accounts Receivable	2,800	
	Service Revenue		2,800
	(To record revenue earned)		

A = L + SE
+2,800 +2,800

Cash flows: no effect

This entry records the amount of revenue earned between November 1 and November 10. The subsequent collection of cash from clients (including the $200 earned in October) will be recorded with an increase (a debit) to Cash and a decrease (a credit) to Accounts Receivable.

Accrued Expenses

Alternative Terminology *Accrued expenses* are also called *accrued liabilities.*

Expenses incurred but not yet paid or recorded at the statement date are called accrued expenses. Interest, salaries, and income taxes are common examples of accrued expenses. Accrued expenses result from the same factors as accrued revenues. In fact, an accrued expense on the books of one company is an accrued revenue to another company. For example, the $200 accrual of service revenue for Sierra Corporation is an accrued expense for the client that received the service.

Adjustments for accrued expenses are necessary to record the obligations that exist at the balance sheet date and to recognize the expenses that apply to the current accounting period. Prior to adjustment, both liabilities and expenses are understated. Therefore, **an adjusting entry for accrued expenses results in an increase (a debit) to an expense account and an increase (a credit) to a liability account,** as in Illustration 4-8.

Illustration 4-8
Adjusting entries for accrued expenses

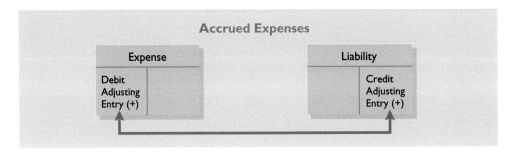

Let's look in more detail at some specific types of accrued expenses, beginning with accrued interest.

Helpful Hint To make the illustration easier to understand, a simplified method of interest calculation is used. In reality, interest is calculated using the exact number of days in the interest period and year (365).

Accrued Interest. Sierra Corporation signed a three-month note payable in the amount of $5,000 on October 1. The note requires interest at an annual rate of 6%. The amount of the interest accumulation is determined by three factors: (1) the face value of the note, (2) the interest rate, which is always expressed as an annual rate, and (3) the length of time the note is outstanding. In this instance, the total interest due on the $5,000 note at its due date, three months in the future, is $75 ($5,000 × 6% × $\frac{3}{12}$), or $25 for one month. Note that the time period is expressed as a fraction of a year. The formula for calculating interest and its application to Sierra Corporation for the month of October are shown in Illustration 4-9.

Illustration 4-9
Formula for calculating interest

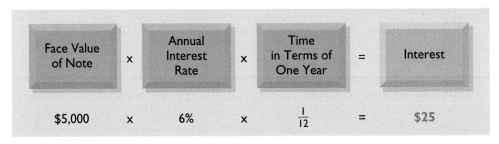

The accrual of interest at October 31 would be reflected in an adjusting entry as follows:

A	=	L	+	SE
		+25		−25

Cash flows: no effect

Oct. 31	Interest Expense	25	
	Interest Payable		25
	(To accrue interest on note payable)		

After the adjusting entry is posted, the accounts appear as shown below:

Interest Expense			Interest Payable		
Oct. 31	Adj. 25			Oct. 31	Adj. 25
Oct. 31	Bal. 25			Oct. 31	Bal. 25

Interest Expense shows the interest charges for the month of October. The amount of interest owed at the statement date is shown in Interest Payable. It will not be paid until the note comes due at the end of three months. The Interest Payable account is used, instead of crediting Notes Payable, to disclose the two different types of obligations—interest and principal—in the accounts and statements. If this adjusting entry is not made, liabilities and interest expense will be understated, and net earnings and shareholders' equity will be overstated.

Accrued Salaries.   Some types of expenses, such as employee salaries and commissions, are paid for after the services have been performed. At Sierra Corporation, salaries were last paid on October 22; the next payment of salaries will not occur until November 5. As shown on the calendar in Illustration 4-10, five as yet unpaid working days remain in October (October 25–29).

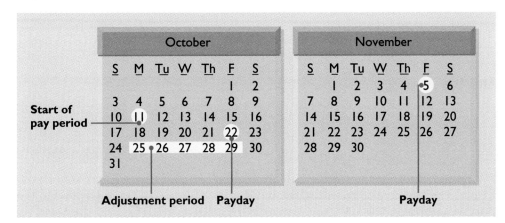

Illustration 4-10
Calendar showing Sierra Corporation's pay periods

At October 31, the salaries for these days represent an accrued expense and a related liability to Sierra. The four employees each receive a salary of $500 a week for a five-day work week, from Monday to Friday, or $100 a day. Thus, accrued salaries at October 31 are $2,000 (5 days × $100/day × 4 employees). This accrual increases a liability, Salaries Payable, and an expense account, Salaries Expense, and has the following adjusting entry:

Oct. 31	Salaries Expense	2,000	
	Salaries Payable		2,000
	(To record accrued salaries)		

A	=	L	+	SE
		+2,000		-2,000

Cash flows: no effect

After this adjusting entry is posted, the accounts are as indicated below:

Salaries Expense			Salaries Payable		
Oct. 22	4,000			Oct. 31	Adj. 2,000
Oct. 31	Adj. 2,000				
Oct. 31	Bal. 6,000			Oct. 31	Bal. 2,000

After this adjustment, the balance in Salaries Expense of $6,000 (15 days × $100/day × 4 employees) is the actual salary expense for October. The balance in Salaries Payable of $2,000 is the amount of the liability for salaries owed as at October 31. If the $2,000 adjustment for salaries is not recorded, Sierra's expenses will be understated $2,000 and its liabilities will be understated $2,000.

At Sierra Corporation, salaries are payable every two weeks. Consequently, the next payday is November 5, when total salaries of $4,000 will again be paid. The payment consists of $2,000 of salaries payable at October 31 plus $2,000 of salaries expense for November (5 days × $100/day × 4 employees). Therefore, the following entry is made on November 5:

Nov. 5	Salaries Payable	2,000	
	Salaries Expense	2,000	
	Cash		4,000
	(To record November 5 payroll)		

A = L + SE
-4,000   -2,000   -2,000

Cash flows: -4,000

This entry eliminates the liability for Salaries Payable that was recorded in the October 31 adjusting entry and records the proper amount of Salaries Expense for the period between November 1 and November 5.

Accrued Income Taxes.   For accounting purposes, corporate income taxes must be accrued based on the current period's earnings. Sierra's monthly income taxes payable are estimated to be $600. This accrual increases a liability, Income Tax Payable, and an expense account, Income Tax Expense. The adjusting entry is:

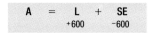

A = L + SE
    +600   -600

Cash flows: no effect

Oct. 31	Income Tax Expense	600	
	Income Tax Payable		600
	(To record accrued income taxes)		

After this adjusting entry is posted, the accounts are as shown below:

	Income Tax Expense			Income Tax Payable	
Oct. 31	Adj. 600			Oct. 31	Adj. 600
Oct. 31	Bal. 600			Oct. 31	Bal. 600

Corporations, such as Sierra, pay corporate income taxes in monthly instalments. The payment is based on the income tax that was actually payable in the prior year. If there was no prior year, as is the case with Sierra, or if there was no tax payable in the prior year, then no income tax instalment payments are required. However, the liability must still be accrued.

As noted in Chapter 1, income tax expense is reported separately from other expenses, following the subtotal earnings before income tax in order to emphasize the earnings generated from operations. The income tax payable is reported as a current liability on the balance sheet as it is normally paid in monthly instalments. Other taxes owing, such as commodity and property taxes, must also be estimated and accrued in a similar manner.

B U S I N E S S   I N S I G H T

INTERNATIONAL PERSPECTIVE

In Canada, the federal government, the ten provinces, and the three territories all impose income taxes on corporate earnings. The combined federal and provincial income tax rate averages 43%. For national companies, income taxes include tax payable to every province in which the company operates, in addition to the tax payable to the federal government. International companies are taxed on their worldwide earnings, and their income taxes include tax payable to every country in which they operate. Canada's corporate income taxes are generally lower than those in the United States and United Kingdom.

● **REVIEW IT**

1. What is the effect on assets, shareholders' equity, revenues, and net earnings if an accrued revenue adjusting entry is not made?
2. What is the effect on liabilities, shareholders' equity, expenses, and net earnings if an accrued expense adjusting entry is not made?
3. What was the amount of Loblaw's 2002 Depreciation Expense? Its Accumulated Depreciation as at December 28, 2002? (*Hint*: This amount is reported in the notes to the financial statements.) The answers to these questions are provided at the end of this chapter.

● **DO IT**

Micro Computer Services Inc. began operations on August 1, 2004. Management prepares monthly financial statements. This information relates to August:

1. Revenue earned but unrecorded for August totalled $1,100.
2. On August 1, the company borrowed $30,000 from a local bank on a one-year note payable. The annual interest rate is 5% and is payable at maturity.
3. At August 31, the company owed its employees $800 in salaries that will be paid on September 1.
4. Estimated income tax payable for August totalled $275.

Prepare the adjusting entries needed at August 31, 2004.

Action Plan

• Make adjusting journal entries at the end of the period for revenues earned and expenses incurred in the period.
• Remember that accruals are entries that were not previously recorded; therefore the adjustment pattern is different from that for prepayments.
• Adjusting entries for accrued revenues require a debit to a receivable account and a credit to a revenue account.
• Adjusting entries for accrued expenses require a debit to an expense account and a credit to a liability account.

Solution

1. Aug. 31	Accounts Receivable		1,100	
		Service Revenue		1,100
		(To accrue revenue earned but not billed or collected)		
2.	31	Interest Expense	125	
		Interest Payable		125
		(To record accrued interest: $30,000 \times 5\% \times \frac{1}{12}$)		
3.	31	Salaries Expense	800	
		Salaries Payable		800
		(To record accrued salaries)		
4.	31	Income Tax Expense	275	
		Income Tax Payable		275
		(To record accrued income taxes)		

SUMMARY OF BASIC RELATIONSHIPS

The four basic types of adjusting entries are summarized in Illustration 4-11. Take some time to study and analyse the adjusting entries. Be sure to note that **each adjusting entry affects one balance sheet account and one statement of earnings account.**

Illustration 4-11
Summary of adjusting
entries

	Type of Adjustment	Accounts Before Adjustment	Adjusting Entry
Prepayments	Prepaid expenses	Assets overstated Expenses understated	Dr. Expenses Cr. Assets
	Unearned revenues	Liabilities overstated Revenues understated	Dr. Liabilities Cr. Revenues
Accruals	Accrued revenues	Assets understated Revenues understated	Dr. Assets Cr. Revenues
	Accrued expenses	Liabilities understated Expenses understated	Dr. Expenses Cr. Liabilities

It is important to understand that **adjusting entries never involve the Cash account** (except for bank reconciliations, which we will study in Chapter 7). In the case of prepayments, cash has already been received or paid and recorded in the original journal entry. The adjusting entry simply reallocates or adjusts amounts between a balance sheet account (e.g., prepaid assets or unearned revenues) and a statement of earnings account (e.g., expenses or revenues). In the case of accruals, cash will be received or paid in the future and recorded then. The adjusting entry simply records the receivable or payable and related asset or expense.

SIERRA CORPORATION ILLUSTRATION

The journalizing and posting of the adjusting entries described in this chapter for Sierra Corporation on October 31 are shown in Illustrations 4-12 and 4-13. When reviewing the general ledger in Illustration 4-13, note that the adjustments are highlighted in colour.

Illustration 4-12
General journal showing
adjusting entries

	GENERAL JOURNAL		
Date	Account Titles and Explanation	Debit	Credit
2004 Oct. 31	Advertising Supplies Expense	1,500	
	Advertising Supplies		1,500
	(To record supplies used)		
31	Insurance Expense	50	
	Prepaid insurance		50
	(To record insurance expired)		
31	Amortization Expense	83	
	Accumulated Amortization—Office Equipment		83
	(To record monthly amortization)		
31	Unearned Service Revenue	400	
	Service Revenue		400
	(To record revenue earned)		
31	Accounts Receivable	200	
	Service Revenue		200
	(To accrue revenue earned but not billed or collected)		
31	Interest Expense	25	
	Interest Payable		25
	(To accrue interest on note payable)		
31	Salaries Expense	2,000	
	Salaries Payable		2,000
	(To record accrued salaries)		
31	Income Tax Expense	600	
	Income Tax Payable		600
	(To record accrued income taxes)		

Illustration 4-13
General ledger after
adjustments

GENERAL JOURNAL

	Cash				
Oct.	1	10,000	Oct.	4	5,000
	1	5,000		5	900
	4	1,200		5	600
	5	10,000		20	500
				22	4,000
Oct. 31	Bal. 15,200				

Common Shares			
	Oct.	1	10,000
	Oct. 31	Bal.	10,000

	Accounts Receivable		
Oct. 31	200		
Oct. 31	Bal. 200		

Retained Earnings			
	Oct.	1	0
	Oct. 31	Bal.	0

	Advertising Supplies		
Oct. 6	2,500	Oct. 31	1,500
Oct. 31	Bal. 1,000		

	Dividends		
Oct. 20	500		
Oct. 31	Bal. 500		

	Prepaid Insurance		
Oct. 5	600	Oct. 31	50
Oct. 31	Bal. 550		

Service Revenue			
	Oct.	5	10,000
		31	400
		31	200
	Oct. 31	Bal.	10,600

	Office Equipment		
Oct. 4	5,000		
Oct. 31	Bal. 5,000		

	Salaries Expense		
Oct. 22	4,000		
	31	2,000	
Oct. 31	Bal. 6,000		

Accumulated Amortization—Office Equipment			
	Oct. 31		83
	Oct. 31	Bal.	83

	Advertising Supplies Expense		
Oct. 31	1,500		
Oct. 31	Bal. 1,500		

Notes Payable			
	Oct.	1	5,000
	Oct. 31	Bal.	5,000

	Rent Expense		
Oct. 5	900		
Oct. 31	Bal. 900		

Accounts Payable			
	Oct.	6	2,500
	Oct. 31	Bal.	2,500

	Insurance Expense		
Oct. 31	50		
Oct. 31	Bal. 50		

Interest Payable			
	Oct. 31		25
	Oct. 31	Bal.	25

	Interest Expense		
Oct. 31	25		
Oct. 31	Bal. 25		

	Unearned Service Revenue		
Oct. 31	400	Oct. 4	1,200
		Oct. 31	Bal. 800

	Amortization Expense		
Oct. 31	83		
Oct. 31	83		

Salaries Payable			
	Oct. 31		2,000
	Oct. 31	Bal.	2,000

	Income Tax Expense		
Oct. 31	600		
Oct. 31	Bal. 600		

Income Tax Payable			
	Oct. 31		600
	Oct. 31	Bal.	600

The Adjusted Trial Balance and Financial Statements

After all adjusting entries have been journalized and posted, another trial balance is prepared from the ledger accounts. This trial balance is called an adjusted trial balance. It shows the balances of all accounts at the end of the accounting period, including those that have been adjusted. The purpose of an adjusted trial balance is to **prove the equality** of the total debit balances and the total credit balances in the ledger after all adjustments have been made. Because the accounts contain all the data that are needed for financial statements, the adjusted trial balance is the primary basis for the preparation of financial statements.

PREPARING THE ADJUSTED TRIAL BALANCE

The adjusted trial balance for Sierra Corporation presented in Illustration 4-14 has been prepared from the ledger accounts in Illustration 4-13. The amounts affected by the adjusting entries are highlighted in colour.

Illustration 4-14
Adjusted trial balance

SIERRA CORPORATION
Adjusted Trial Balance
October 31, 2004

	Debit	Credit
Cash	$15,200	
Accounts receivable	200	
Advertising supplies	1,000	
Prepaid insurance	550	
Office equipment	5,000	
Accumulated amortization— office equipment		$ 83
Notes payable		5,000
Accounts payable		2,500
Interest payable		25
Unearned service revenue		800
Salaries payable		2,000
Income tax payable		600
Common shares		10,000
Retained earnings		0
Dividends	500	
Service revenue		10,600
Salaries expense	6,000	
Advertising supplies expense	1,500	
Rent expense	900	
Insurance expense	50	
Interest expense	25	
Amortization expense	83	
Income tax expense	600	
	$31,608	$31,608

PREPARING FINANCIAL STATEMENTS

Financial statements can be prepared directly from an adjusted trial balance. The interrelationships of data in the adjusted trial balance of Sierra Corporation are presented in Illustrations 4-15 and 4-16.

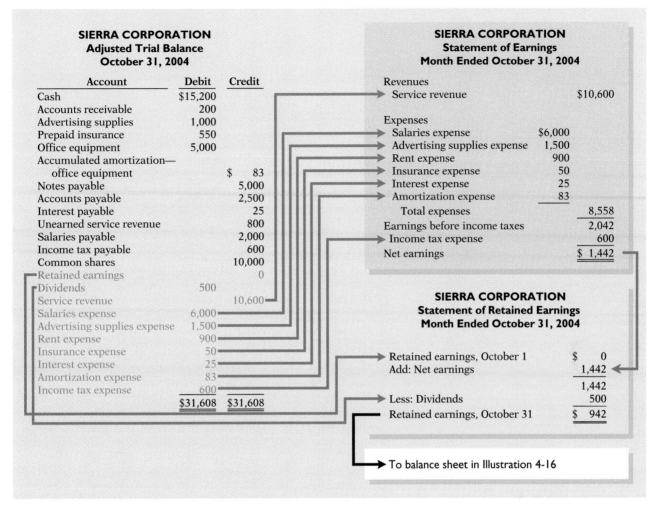

As Illustration 4-15 shows, the statement of earnings is prepared from the revenue and expense accounts. The statement of retained earnings is derived from the Retained Earnings account, Dividends account, and the net earnings (or net loss) shown in the statement of earnings. As shown in Illustration 4-16 on the following page, the balance sheet is then prepared from the asset and liability accounts and the ending retained earnings as reported in the statement of retained earnings.

Illustration 4-15
Preparation of the statement of earnings and statement of retained earnings from the adjusted trial balance

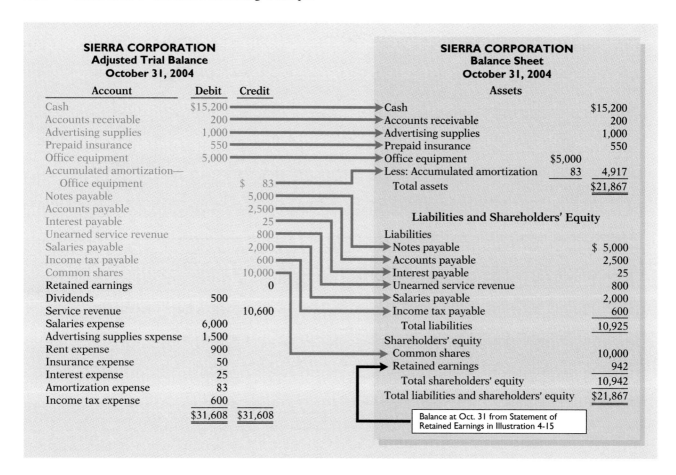

SIERRA CORPORATION Adjusted Trial Balance October 31, 2004		
Account	Debit	Credit
Cash	$15,200	
Accounts receivable	200	
Advertising supplies	1,000	
Prepaid insurance	550	
Office equipment	5,000	
Accumulated amortization— Office equipment		$ 83
Notes payable		5,000
Accounts payable		2,500
Interest payable		25
Unearned service revenue		800
Salaries payable		2,000
Income tax payable		600
Common shares		10,000
Retained earnings		0
Dividends	500	
Service revenue		10,600
Salaries expense	6,000	
Advertising supplies sxpense	1,500	
Rent expense	900	
Insurance expense	50	
Interest expense	25	
Amortization expense	83	
Income tax expense	600	
	$31,608	$31,608

SIERRA CORPORATION Balance Sheet October 31, 2004		
Assets		
Cash		$15,200
Accounts receivable		200
Advertising supplies		1,000
Prepaid insurance		550
Office equipment	$5,000	
Less: Accumulated amortization	83	4,917
Total assets		$21,867
Liabilities and Shareholders' Equity		
Liabilities		
Notes payable		$ 5,000
Accounts payable		2,500
Interest payable		25
Unearned service revenue		800
Salaries payable		2,000
Income tax payable		600
Total liabilities		10,925
Shareholders' equity		
Common shares		10,000
Retained earnings		942
Total shareholders' equity		10,942
Total liabilities and shareholders' equity		$21,867

Balance at Oct. 31 from Statement of Retained Earnings in Illustration 4-15

Illustration 4-16
Preparation of the balance sheet from the adjusted trial balance

Closing the Books

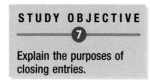

STUDY OBJECTIVE

7

Explain the purposes of closing entries.

In previous chapters, you learned that revenue and expense accounts and the dividends account are subdivisions of retained earnings, which is reported in the shareholders' equity section of the balance sheet. Because revenues, expenses, and dividends only relate to a given accounting period, they are considered temporary accounts. In contrast, all balance sheet accounts are considered permanent accounts because their balances are carried forward into future accounting periods. Illustration 4-17 identifies the accounts in each category.

Illustration 4-17
Temporary versus permanent accounts

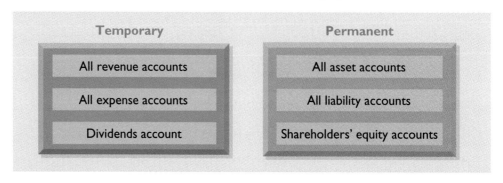

Temporary	Permanent
All revenue accounts	All asset accounts
All expense accounts	All liability accounts
Dividends account	Shareholders' equity accounts

PREPARING CLOSING ENTRIES

At the end of the accounting period, the temporary account balances are transferred to the permanent shareholders' equity account—Retained Earnings—through the preparation of closing entries. Closing entries transfer net earnings (or net loss) and dividends to Retained Earnings, so that the balance in the Retained Earnings account agrees with the balance reported in the statement of retained earnings. For example, notice that in Illustration 4-14, Retained Earnings has an adjusted balance of zero. Prior to the closing entries, the balance in Retained Earnings will be its beginning-of-the-period balance. For Sierra, this is zero because it is Sierra's first year of operations.

In addition to updating Retained Earnings to its ending balance, closing entries produce a **zero balance in each temporary account**. As a result, these accounts are ready to accumulate data about revenues, expenses, and dividends in the next accounting period separate from the data in the prior periods. Permanent accounts are not closed.

When closing entries are prepared, each statement of earnings account could be closed directly to Retained Earnings. However, to do so would result in excessive detail in the Retained Earnings account. Accordingly, the revenue and expense accounts are first closed to another temporary account, Income Summary. Only the resulting net earnings or net loss is transferred from this account to Retained Earnings. Illustration 4-18 shows the closing process.

Helpful Hint Income Summary is a very descriptive title. Total revenues are closed to Income Summary, total expenses are closed to Income Summary, and the balance in the Income Summary is the net earnings or net loss.

Illustration 4-18
Closing process

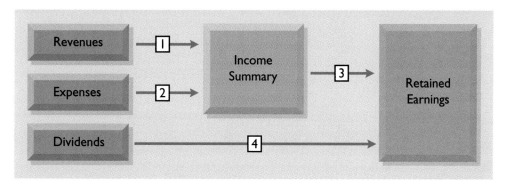

To prepare closing entries:

1. To close revenue accounts: Debit each individual revenue account for its balance, and credit Income Summary for total revenues.
2. To close expense accounts: Debit Income Summary for total expenses, and credit each individual expense account for its balance.
3. To close Income Summary: Debit Income Summary for the balance in the account (or credit if a net loss), and credit (debit) Retained Earnings.
4. To close Dividends: Debit Retained Earnings, and credit Dividends for its balance.

The closing entries for Sierra Corporation are shown in Illustration 4-19.

Illustration 4-19
Closing entries journalized

	GENERAL JOURNAL		
Date	Account Titles and Explanation	Debit	Credit
	Closing Entries		
2004			
	(1)		
Oct. 31	Service Revenue	10,600	
	Income Summary		10,600
	(To close revenue account)		
	(2)		
31	Income Summary	9,158	
	Salaries Expense		6,000
	Advertising Supplies Expense		1,500
	Rent Expense		900
	Insurance Expense		50
	Interest Expense		25
	Amortization Expense		83
	Income Tax Expense		600
	(To close expense accounts)		
	(3)		
31	Income Summary	1,442	
	Retained Earnings		1,442
	(To close net earnings to retained earnings)		
	(4)		
31	Retained Earnings	500	
	Dividends		500
	(To close dividends to retained earnings)		

BUSINESS INSIGHT

MANAGEMENT PERSPECTIVE

Technology has dramatically changed the process of closing the books. Closing the books used to take up to 10 days after the end of the accounting period for most companies. Now, according to the Hackett Group, companies that embrace best practices for managing information are able to close their books in just 2.9 days. This results in the production of 44% fewer manual journal entries and 60% fewer general ledger reports.

Source: The Hacket Group. *"2002 Book of Numbers–Finance,"* ©2002.

The posting of Sierra Corporation's closing entries is shown in Illustration 4-20.

Illustration 4-20
Posting of closing entries

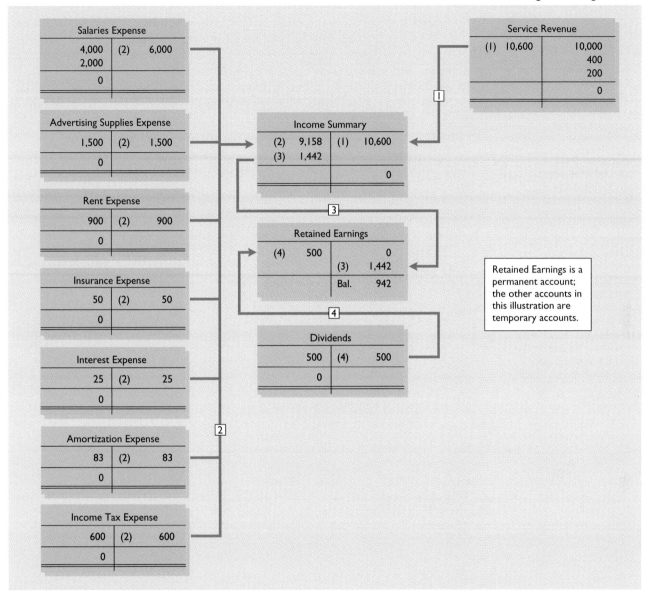

PREPARING A POST-CLOSING TRIAL BALANCE

After all closing entries are journalized and posted, another trial balance, called a post-closing trial balance, is prepared from the ledger. A post-closing trial balance is a list of all permanent accounts and their balances after closing entries are journalized and posted. **The purpose of this trial balance is to prove the equality of the permanent account balances that are carried forward into the next accounting period.** Since all temporary accounts will have zero balances, **the post-closing trial balance will contain only permanent—balance sheet—accounts.**

Summary of the Accounting Cycle

STUDY OBJECTIVE

⑧

Describe the required steps in the accounting cycle.

The required steps in the accounting cycle are shown in Illustration 4-21. You can see that the cycle begins with the analysis of business transactions and ends with the preparation of a post-closing trial balance. The steps in the cycle are performed in sequence and are repeated in each accounting period.

Steps 1–3 may occur daily during the accounting period, as explained in Chapter 3. Steps 4–7 are performed on a periodic basis, such as monthly, quarterly, or annually. Steps 8 and 9, closing entries and a post-closing trial balance, are usually prepared only at the end of a company's **annual** accounting period.

Illustration 4-21
Required steps in the accounting cycle

Helpful Hint Some accountants prefer to reverse certain adjusting entries at the beginning of a new accounting period to simplify the recording of later transactions related to the adjusting entries. A reversing entry is made at the beginning of the next accounting period and is the exact opposite of the adjusting entry made in the previous period.

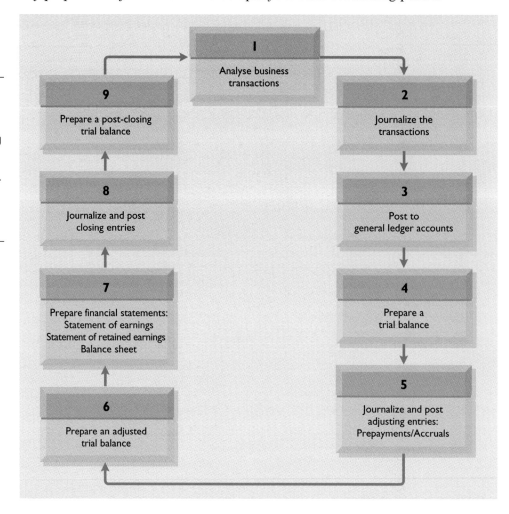

BEFORE YOU GO ON . . .

● **REVIEW IT**

1. How do permanent accounts differ from temporary accounts?
2. What are the two purposes of closing entries?
3. What four different types of entries are required in closing the books?
4. What financial statement amount will the balance in the Income Summary account equal immediately before it is closed into the Retained Earnings account?
5. What are the content and purpose of a post-closing trial balance?
6. What are the required steps in the accounting cycle?

Using the Decision Toolkit

FPI (Fishery Products International) Limited is the world's largest seafood supplier. A simplified version of FPI's December 31, 2002, year-end adjusted trial balance is shown below.

Instructions

From the adjusted trial balance, prepare a statement of earnings, statement of retained earnings, and classified balance sheet.

FISHERY PRODUCTS INTERNATIONAL

FPI LIMITED Trial Balance December 31, 2002 (in thousands)	Debit	Credit
Cash	$ 9,954	
Accounts receivable	86,484	
Inventories	145,844	
Prepaid expenses	5,754	
Other current assets	2,571	
Buildings, wharves, and land	71,518	
Machinery and equipment	118,382	
Vessels and vessel equipment	68,074	
Other long-term assets	30,025	
Accumulated amortization		
—Buildings and wharves		$ 37,342
—Machinery and equipment		78,347
—Vessels and vessel equipment		32,032
Bank indebtedness (short-term)		66,746
Accounts payable and accrued liabilities		53,953
Current portion of long-term debt		13,621
Long-term debt		55,607
Share capital		122,930
Other shareholders' equity items		537
Retained earnings		66,491
Dividends	2,771	
Sales		740,914
Commission income		3,647
Cost of goods sold	654,823	
Administrative and marketing expenses	52,530	
Amortization expense	9,877	
Interest expense	5,797	
Income tax expense	7,763	
	$1,272,167	$1,272,167

FISHERY PRODUCTS INTERNATIONAL

Solution

FPI LIMITED Statement of Earnings Year Ended December 31, 2002 (in thousands)	
Revenue	
Sales	$740,914
Commission income	3,647
Total revenue	744,561
Expenses	
Cost of goods sold	654,823
Administrative and marketing expenses	52,530
Amortization expense	9,877
Interest expense	5,797
Total expenses	723,027
Earnings before income taxes	21,534
Income tax expense	7,763
Net earnings	$ 13,771

FPI LIMITED Statement of Retained Earnings Year Ended December 31, 2002 (in thousands)	
Retained earnings, January 1	$66,491
Add: Net earnings	13,771
	80,262
Less: Dividends	2,771
Retained earnings, December 31	$77,491

FISHERY PRODUCTS INTERNATIONAL

FPI LIMITED
Balance Sheet
December 31, 2002
(in thousands)

Assets

Current assets		
Cash		$ 9,954
Accounts receivable		86,484
Inventories		145,844
Prepaid expenses		5,754
Other current assets		2,571
Total current assets		250,607
Property, plant, and equipment		
Buildings, wharves, and land	$71,518	
Less: Accumulated amortization	37,342	
	34,176	
Machinery and equipment	$118,382	
Less: Accumulated amortization	78,347	
	40,035	
Vessels and vessel equipment	$68,074	
Less: Accumulated amortization	32,032	
	36,042	110,253
Other long-term assets		30,025
Total assets		$390,885

Liabilities and Shareholders' Equity

Current liabilities	
Bank indebtedness	$ 66,746
Accounts payable and accrued liabilities	53,953
Current portion of long-term debt	13,621
Total current liabilities	134,320
Long-term debt	55,607
Total liabilities	189,927
Shareholders' equity	
Share capital	122,930
Other shareholders' equity items	537
Retained earnings	77,491
Total shareholders' equity	200,958
Total liabilities and shareholders' equity	$390,885

NAVIGATOR

Summary of Study Objectives

❶ Explain the revenue recognition principle and the matching principle. The revenue recognition principle dictates that revenue must be recognized in the accounting period in which it is earned. The matching principle dictates that expenses must be recognized when they make their contribution to revenues.

❷ Differentiate between the cash basis and the accrual basis of accounting. Accrual-based accounting means that events that change a company's financial statements are recorded in the periods in which the events occur. Under the cash basis, events are recorded only in the periods in which the company receives or pays cash.

❸ Explain why adjusting entries are needed, and identify the major types of adjusting entries. Adjusting entries are made at the end of an accounting period. They ensure that revenues are recorded in the period in which they are earned and that expenses are recognized in the period in which services or goods are used or consumed in order to match expenses with revenues. The major types of adjusting entries are prepaid expenses, unearned revenues, accrued revenues, and accrued expenses.

❹ Prepare adjusting entries for prepayments. Prepayments are either prepaid expenses or unearned revenues. Adjusting entries for prepayments are required to record the portion of the prepayment that applies to the expense incurred or revenue earned in the current accounting period.

❺ Prepare adjusting entries for accruals. Accruals are either accrued revenues or accrued expenses. Adjusting entries for accruals are required to record revenues and expenses applicable to the current accounting period that have not been recognized through daily entries.

❻ Describe the nature and purpose of the adjusted trial balance. An adjusted trial balance is a trial balance that shows the balances of all accounts at the end of an accounting period, including those that have been adjusted. The purpose of an adjusted trial balance is to show the effects of all financial events that have occurred during the accounting period.

❼ Explain the purposes of closing entries. One purpose of closing entries is to transfer the results of operations for the period to Retained Earnings. A second purpose is to enable all temporary accounts (revenue accounts, expense accounts, and dividends) to begin a new period with a zero balance. To accomplish this, entries are made to close each individual revenue and expense account to income summary, then income summary to retained earnings, and finally dividends to retained earnings. Only temporary accounts are closed.

❽ Describe the required steps in the accounting cycle. The required steps in the accounting cycle are to: (a) analyse business transactions, (b) journalize the transactions, (c) post to general ledger accounts, (d) prepare a trial balance, (e) journalize and post adjusting entries, (f) prepare an adjusted trial balance, (g) prepare financial statements, (h) journalize and post closing entries, and (i) prepare a post-closing trial balance.

Decision Toolkit—A Summary

Decision Toolkit Summary

DECISION CHECKPOINTS	INFO NEEDED FOR DECISION	TOOL TO USE FOR DECISION	HOW TO EVALUATE RESULTS
At what point should the company record revenue?	Need to understand the nature of the company's business	Revenue should be recorded when earned. For a service business, revenue is earned when a service is performed.	Recognizing revenue too early overstates current period revenue; recognizing it too late understates current period revenue.
At what point should the company record expenses?	Need to understand the nature of the company's business	Expenses should "follow" revenues—that is, the effort (expense) should be matched with the result (revenue).	Recognizing expenses too early overstates current period expenses; recognizing them too late understates current period expenses.

NAVIGATOR

Glossary

Accrual basis accounting Accounting basis in which transactions that change a company's financial statements are recorded in the periods in which the events occur, rather than in the periods in which the company receives or pays cash. (p. 158)

Accrued expenses Expenses incurred but not yet paid in cash or recorded. (p. 168)

Accrued revenues Revenues earned but not yet received in cash or recorded. (p. 166)

Adjusted trial balance A list of accounts and their balances after all adjustments have been made. (p. 174)

Adjusting entries Entries made at the end of an accounting period to ensure that the revenue recognition and matching principles are followed. (p. 160)

Amortization The process of allocating the cost of a long-lived asset to expense over its useful life. (p. 163)

Cash basis accounting An accounting basis in which revenue is recorded only when cash is received, and an expense is recorded only when cash is paid. (p. 159)

Closing entries Entries at the end of an accounting period to transfer the balances of temporary accounts (revenues, expenses, and dividends) to the permanent shareholders' equity account Retained Earnings. (p. 177)

Contra asset account An account that is offset against (reduces) an asset account on the balance sheet. (p. 164)

Fiscal year An accounting period that is one year long. (p. 156)

Income summary A temporary account used in closing revenue and expense accounts. (p. 177)

Matching principle The principle that dictates that efforts (expenses) must be matched with accomplishments (revenues). (p. 158)

Net book value (book value) The difference between the cost of an amortizable asset and its related accumulated amortization. (p. 164)

Permanent accounts Balance sheet accounts whose balances are carried forward to the next accounting period. (p. 176)

Post-closing trial balance A list of permanent accounts and their balances after closing entries have been journalized and posted. (p. 179)

Prepaid expenses (prepayments) Expenses paid in cash and recorded as assets before they are used or consumed. (p. 161)

Revenue recognition principle The principle that revenue must be recognized in the accounting period in which it is earned. (p. 157)

Temporary accounts Revenue, expense, and dividend accounts whose balances are transferred to Retained Earnings at the end of an accounting period. (p. 176)

Time period assumption An assumption that the economic life of a business can be divided into artificial time periods. (p. 156)

Unearned revenue Cash received before revenue is earned and recorded as a liability until it is earned. (p. 164)

Useful life The length of service of a productive facility. (p. 163)

Demonstration Problem

The Green Thumb Lawn Care Corporation was incorporated on April 1. At April 30, the trial balance shows the following balances for selected accounts:

Prepaid insurance	$ 3,600
Equipment	28,000
Income tax payable	0
Note payable	20,000
Unearned service revenue	4,200
Service revenue	1,800

Analysis reveals the following additional data pertaining to these accounts:

1. Prepaid insurance is the cost of a one-year insurance policy, effective April 1.
2. Amortization on the equipment is $500 per month.
3. The note payable is dated April 1. It is a six-month, 6% note. Interest is payable on the first of each month.
4. Seven customers paid for the company's $600 six-month lawn service package beginning in April. These customers were serviced in April.
5. Lawn services provided to other customers but not billed at April 30 totalled $1,500.

Additional
Demonstration
Problems

6. Income tax expense for April is estimated to be $100.

Instructions

Prepare the adjusting entries for the month of April. Show calculations.

Action Plan

- Note that adjustments are being made for only one month.
- Show your calculations.
- Select account titles carefully.
- Check that debits equal credits for each entry.
- Use T accounts to help plan, or check, your adjustments

Solution to Demonstration Problem

GENERAL JOURNAL				
Date	Account Titles and Explanation		Debit	Credit
	Adjusting Entries			
Apr. 30	Insurance Expense		300	
	Prepaid Insurance			300
	(To record insurance expired: $3,600 \times \frac{1}{12} = $300 per month)			
30	Amortization Expense		500	
	Accumulated Amortization—Equipment			500
	(To record monthly amortization)			
30	Interest Expense		100	
	Interest Payable			100
	(To accrue interest on notes payable: $20,000 \times 6\% \times \frac{1}{12} = $100)			
30	Unearned Service Revenue		700	
	Service Revenue			700
	(To record revenue earned: $600 \div 6 \text{ mos.} \times 7 = $700)			
30	Accounts Receivable		1,500	
	Service Revenue			1,500
	(To accrue revenue earned but not billed or collected)			
30	Income Tax Expense		100	
	Income Tax Payable			100
	(To accrue income taxes payable)			

Self-Study Questions

Multiple Choice Quiz

Answers are at the end of the chapter.

(SO 1) 1. Which one of these statements about the accrual basis of accounting is *false*?
 (a) Events that change a company's financial statements are recorded in the periods in which the events occur.
 (b) Revenue is recognized in the period in which it is earned.
 (c) The accrual basis is in accordance with generally accepted accounting principles.
 (d) Revenue is recorded only when cash is received, and an expense is recorded only when cash is paid.

(SO 1) 2. What is the time period assumption?
 (a) Revenue should be recognized in the ac-

counting period in which it is earned.
 (b) Expenses should be matched with revenues.
 (c) The economic life of a business can be divided into artificial time periods.
 (d) The fiscal year should correspond with the calendar year.

3. Which principle dictates that efforts (expenses) must (SO 1) be recorded with accomplishments (revenues)?
 (a) Matching principle
 (b) Cost principle
 (c) Periodicity principle
 (d) Revenue recognition principle

4. Adjusting entries are made to ensure that: (SO 3)
 (a) expenses are matched to revenues in the period in which the revenue is generated.

(b) revenues are recorded in the period in which they are earned.

(c) balance sheet and statement of earnings accounts have correct balances at the end of an accounting period.

(d) All of the above

(SO 4) 5. The trial balance shows Supplies $1,350 and Supplies Expense $0. If $600 of supplies are on hand at the end of the period, the adjusting entry is:

(a) Supplies | 600 |
     Supplies Expense | | 600

(b) Supplies | 750 |
     Supplies Expense | | 750

(c) Supplies Expense | 750 |
     Supplies | | 750

(d) Supplies Expense | 600 |
     Supplies | | 600

(SO 4) 6. Adjustments for unearned revenues:
(a) decrease liabilities and increase revenues.
(b) increase liabilities and increase revenues.
(c) increase assets and increase revenues.
(d) decrease revenues and decrease assets.

(SO 5) 7. Adjustments for accrued revenues:
(a) increase assets and increase liabilities.
(b) increase assets and increase revenues.
(c) decrease assets and decrease revenues.
(d) decrease liabilities and increase revenues.

(SO 5) 8. Kathy Kiska earned a salary of $400 for the last week of September. She will be paid on October 1. The adjusting entry for Kathy's employer at September 30 is:
(a) No entry is required.

(b) Salaries Expense | 400 |
     Salaries Payable | | 400

(c) Salaries Expense | 400 |
     Cash | | 400

(d) Salaries Payable | 400 |
     Cash | | 400

9. Which statement is *incorrect* concerning the adjusted trial balance? (SO 6)
(a) An adjusted trial balance proves the equality of the total debit balances and the total credit balances in the ledger after all adjustments are made.
(b) The adjusted trial balance provides the primary basis for the preparation of financial statements.
(c) The adjusted trial balance is prepared after the closing entries have been journalized and posted.
(d) The adjusted trial balance is prepared after the adjusting entries have been journalized and posted.

10. Which account will have a zero balance after closing entries have been journalized and posted? (SO 7)
(a) Service Revenue
(b) Advertising Supplies
(c) Unearned Revenue
(d) Accumulated Amortization

11. Which types of accounts will appear in the post-closing trial balance? (SO 7)
(a) Permanent accounts
(b) Temporary accounts
(c) Unearned Revenue
(d) None of the above

12. All of the following are required steps in the accounting cycle *except*: (SO 8)
(a) journalizing and posting closing entries.
(b) journalizing and posting reversing entries.
(c) preparing an adjusted trial balance.
(d) preparing a post-closing trial balance.

Questions

(SO 1) 1. (a) How does the time period assumption affect an accountant's analysis of accounting transactions?
(b) Explain the term "fiscal year."

(SO 1) 2. Identify and state two generally accepted accounting principles that relate to adjusting the accounts.

(SO 1) 3. ⚒ Tony Galego, a lawyer, accepts a legal engagement in March, performs the work in April, bills the client $8,000 in May, and is paid in June. If Galego's law firm prepares monthly financial statements, when should it recognize revenue from this engagement? Why?

(SO 1) 4. ⚒ In completing the engagement in question 3, Galego incurs $2,000 of expenses in March, $2,500 in April, and none in May and June. How much expense should be deducted from revenues in the month the revenue is recognized? Why?

5. (a) What information do accrual basis financial statements provide that cash basis statements do not? (SO 2)
(b) What information do cash basis financial statements provide that accrual basis statements do not?

6. Why may the financial information in a trial balance not be complete and up-to-date? (SO 3)

7. Distinguish between the two categories of adjusting entries and identify the types of adjustments applicable to each category. (SO 3)

8. What accounts are debited and credited in a prepaid expense adjusting entry? (SO 4)

9. "Amortization is a process of valuation that results (SO 4)

in the reporting of the fair market value of the asset." Do you agree? Explain.

(SO 4) 10. Explain the difference between amortization expense and accumulated amortization.

(SO 4) 11. Cheung Company purchased equipment for $12,000. Annual amortization expense is $4,000. Show the presentation of the equipment and the accumulated amortization on the balance sheet at the end of the first and second fiscal years.

(SO 4) 12. What accounts are debited and credited in an unearned revenue adjusting entry?

(SO 5) 13. A company fails to recognize revenue earned but not yet received. Indicate which of the following accounts is debited and which is credited in the adjusting entry: (a) asset, (b) liability, (c) revenue, and (d) expense?

(SO 5) 14. A company fails to recognize an expense incurred but not paid. Indicate which of the following accounts is debited and which is credited in the adjusting entry: (a) asset, (b) liability, (c) revenue, and (d) expense.

(SO 5) 15. A company makes an accrued revenue adjusting entry for $900 and an accrued expense adjusting entry for $600. How much was net earnings understated prior to these entries? Explain.

(SO 5) 16. On January 9, a company pays $5,000 for salaries, of which $1,700 was reported as Salaries Payable on December 31. Give the entry to record the adjusting entry on December 31 and the payment on January 9.

(SO 4, 5) 17. Half of the adjusting entry is given below. Indicate the account title for the other half of the entry.

(a) Salaries Expense is debited.
(b) Amortization Expense is debited.
(c) Interest Payable is credited.
(d) Supplies is credited.
(e) Accounts Receivable is debited.
(f) Unearned Service Revenue is debited.

18. "An adjusting entry may affect more than one balance sheet or statement of earnings account." Do you agree? Why or why not? (SO 4, 5)

19. Adjusting entries for prepayments *always* include the Cash account, and adjusting entries for accruals *never* include the Cash account. Do you agree? Explain why or why not. (SO 4, 5)

20. Why is it possible to prepare financial statements directly from an adjusted trial balance? (SO 6)

21. Identify the account(s) debited and credited in each of the four closing entries, assuming the company has (1) net earnings, and (2) a net loss for the year. (SO 7)

22. What items are disclosed on a post-closing trial balance and what is the purpose of this trial balance? (SO 7)

23. Which of these accounts would not appear in the post-closing trial balance: Interest Payable, Equipment, Amortization Expense, Dividends, Unearned Service Revenue, Accumulated Amortization—Equipment, and Service Revenue? (SO 7)

24. Indicate, in the sequence in which they are made, the three required steps in the accounting cycle that involve journalizing. (SO 8)

25. Identify, in the sequence in which they are prepared, the three trial balances that are required in the accounting cycle. (SO 8)

Brief Exercises

Discuss revenue recognition.
(SO 1)

BE4-1 The University of Higher Education collects tuition for the fall term from registered students on the first day of classes in September. The fall term runs from September to December. When should the university recognize the revenue earned from tuition fees? Explain your reasoning.

Indicate impact of transaction on cash and earnings.
(SO 2)

BE4-2 Transactions that affect earnings do not necessarily affect cash. Identify the impact, if any, each of the following transactions would have upon cash and net earnings. The first transaction has been completed for you as an example.

	Cash	Net Earnings
(a) Purchased supplies for cash, $100.	$-100	$0
(b) Made an adjusting entry to record use of $50 of the above supplies.		
(c) Made sales of $1,000, all on account.		
(d) Received $800 from customers in payment of their accounts.		
(e) Purchased equipment for cash, $2,500.		
(f) Recorded amortization of equipment, $500.		

Identify major types of adjusting entries.
(SO 3)

BE4-3 Riko Limited accumulates the following adjustment data at December 31. Indicate (1) the type of adjustment (prepaid expense, accrued revenues, and so on) and (2) the status of the accounts before adjustment (overstated or understated).

(a) Supplies of $600 are on hand. The unadjusted balance in the Supplies account is $1,900.
(b) Service Revenues earned but unbilled total $900.
(c) Interest of $200 is due on a note receivable.
(d) Rent collected in advance totalling $800 has been earned.
(e) Amortization of $100 is estimated on the office equipment.
(f) Income taxes owed are $750.

BE4-4 Sain Advertising Ltd.'s trial balance at December 31 shows Advertising Supplies $8,800 and Advertising Supplies Expense $0. On December 31, there is $1,500 of supplies on hand. Prepare the adjusting entry at December 31. Using T accounts, enter the balances in the accounts, post the adjusting entry, and indicate the adjusted balance in each account.

Prepare adjusting entry for supplies.
(SO 4)

BE4-5 At the end of its first year, the trial balance of Shah Corporation shows Equipment $22,000 and zero balances for Accumulated Amortization—Equipment and Amortization Expense. Amortization for the year is estimated to be $4,400. Prepare the adjusting entry for amortization at December 31, post the adjustments to T accounts, and indicate the balance sheet presentation of the equipment at December 31.

Prepare adjusting entry for amortization.
(SO 4)

BE4-6 On June 1, Bere Ltd. pays $12,000 to Marla Insurance Corp. for a one-year insurance contract. Both companies have fiscal years ending December 31. Journalize and post Bere's entry on June 1 and the adjusting entry on December 31.

Prepare adjusting entry for prepaid expense.
(SO 4)

BE4-7 Using the data in BE4-6, journalize and post the entry on June 1 and the adjusting entry on December 31 for Marla Insurance Corp.

Prepare adjusting entry for unearned revenue.
(SO 4)

BE4-8 The total payroll for Classic Autos Ltd. is $5,000 every Friday ($1,000 per day) for employee salaries earned during a five-day week (Monday through Friday, inclusive). Salaries were last paid on Friday, December 28. This year the company's year end, December 31, falls on a Monday. Salaries will be paid next on Friday, January 4, at which time employees will receive pay for the five-day work week (including the New Year's holiday). Prepare the journal entries required to record (a) the payment of the salaries on December 28, (b) the adjusting journal entry to accrue salaries at year end, and (c) the payment of salaries on January 4.

Prepare transaction and adjusting entries for salaries.
(SO 5)

BE4-9 On July 1, 2004, a company purchased a truck for use in its business for $40,000, paying $18,000 cash and signing a 6% note payable for the remainder. The interest and principal of the note are due on December 31, 2005. Prepare the journal entry to record (a) the purchase of the truck on July 1, 2004, (b) the accrual of the interest at year end, December 31, 2004, and (c) the repayment of the interest and the note on December 31, 2005.

Prepare transaction and adjusting entries for interest.
(SO 5)

BE4-10 Fill in the missing amounts in the following schedule. Assume that 2004 was the company's first year of operations.

Determine missing amounts for income taxes.
(SO 5)

	2004	2005	2006
Income tax expense	$2,500	$3,500	(c)
Income tax payable	(a)	1,500	$2,500
Income tax paid	0	(b)	2,000

BE4-11 The trial balance of Hoi Inc. includes the following balance sheet accounts. Identify the accounts that might require adjustment. For each account that requires adjustment, indicate (1) the type of adjusting entry (prepaid expenses, unearned revenues, accrued revenues, and accrued expenses) and (2) the related account in the adjusting entry.

Analyse accounts in trial balance.
(SO 4, 5)

(a) Accounts receivable
(b) Prepaid insurance
(c) Equipment
(d) Accumulated amortization—equipment

(e) Notes payable
(f) Interest payable
(g) Unearned service revenue

BE4-12 The adjusted trial balance of Lumas Corporation at December 31, 2004, includes the following accounts and balances: Retained Earnings $15,600; Dividends $6,000; Service Revenue $37,000; Salaries Expense $13,000; Insurance Expense $2,000; Rent Expense $3,500; Supplies Expense $1,500; Amortization Expense $1,000; and Income Tax Expense $6,400. Prepare a statement of earnings for the year.

Prepare statement of earnings.
(SO 6)

BE4-13 Partial adjusted trial balance data for Lumas Corporation are presented in BE4-12. Prepare a statement of retained earnings for the year.

Prepare statement of retained earnings.
(SO 6)

Identify post-closing trial balance accounts.
(SO 7)

BE4-14 The following selected accounts appear in the adjusted trial balance for Khanna Ltd. Identify which accounts would be included in a post-closing trial balance.

(a) Accumulated amortization
(b) Amortization expense
(c) Retained earnings
(d) Dividends

(e) Service revenue
(f) Supplies
(g) Accounts payable
(h) Income tax expense

Prepare and post closing entries.
(SO 7)

BE4-15 The statement of earnings for the Edgebrook Golf Club Ltd. for the month ended July 31 shows Green Fees Earnings $26,000; Salaries Expense $8,200; Maintenance Expense, $2,500; and Income Tax Expense $6,000. Retained Earnings has an opening balance of $50,000. Prepare the journal entries to close the revenue and expense accounts to Retained Earnings. Post the entries to each account.

Exercises

Identify point of revenue recognition.
(SO 1)

E4-1 The following independent situations require professional judgement for determining when to recognize revenue from the transactions:

(a) Air Canada sells you an advance purchase airline ticket in September for your flight home at Christmas.
(b) Leon's Furniture sells you a home theatre on a "no money down, no interest, and no payments for one year" promotional deal.
(c) The Toronto Blue Jays sell season tickets to games in the Skydome on-line. Fans can purchase the tickets at any time, although the season doesn't officially begin until April. It runs from April through October.
(d) You borrow money in August from the RBC Financial Group. The loan and the interest are repayable in full in November.
(e) In August, you order a sweater from Sears using its on-line catalogue. It arrives in September and you charge it to your Sears credit card. You receive and pay the Sears bill in October.

Instructions
Identify when revenue should be recognized in each of the above situations.

Identify violated assumption, principle, or constraint.
(SO 1)

Interactive
Homework

E4-2 Here are some accounting reporting situations:

(a) Tercek Ltd. recognizes revenue at the end of the production cycle but before sale. The price of the product, as well as the amount that can be sold, is not certain.
(b) Ravine Hospital Supply Corporation reports only current assets and current liabilities on its balance sheet. Property, plant, and equipment and bonds payable are reported as current assets and current liabilities, respectively.
(c) Ng Ltd. is in its fifth year of operation and has yet to issue financial statements. (Do not use the full disclosure principle.)
(d) Watts Company has inventory on hand that cost $400,000. Watts reports inventory on its balance sheet at its current market value of $425,000.
(e) Steph Wolfson, president of Classic Music Ltd., bought a computer for her personal use. She paid for the computer by using company funds and debited the Computers account.

Instructions
For each situation, list the assumption, principle, or constraint that has been violated, if any. List only one answer for each situation.

Determine cash basis and accrual basis earnings.
(SO 2)

E4-3 In its first year of operations, Brisson Corp. earned $26,000 in service revenue, of which $4,000 was on account. The remainder, $22,000, was collected in cash from customers. The company incurred operating expenses of $15,000, of which $13,500 was paid in cash. Of this amount, $1,500 was still owing on account at year end. In addition, late in the year, Brisson prepaid $2,500 for insurance coverage that would not be used until its second year of operations. Brisson expects to owe $4,400 for income tax when it files its corporate income tax return after year end.

Instructions

(a) Calculate the first year's net earnings under the cash basis of accounting.

(b) Calculate the first year's net earnings under the accrual basis of accounting.

(c) Which basis of accounting (cash or accrual) provides the most useful information for decision-makers?

E4-4   Rafael Limited accumulates the following adjustment data at December 31:

1. Service revenue earned but unbilled totals $600.
2. Store supplies of $300 are on hand. The Supplies account shows an unadjusted account balance of $2,000.
3. Income tax expense of $225 is owed.
4. Service revenue of $260 collected in advance has been earned.
5. Salaries of $800 are owed.
6. Prepaid insurance totalling $350 has expired.

Identify types of adjustments and accounts before adjust-ments.
(SO 3, 4, 5)

Instructions

For each item, indicate (1) the type of adjustment (prepaid expense, unearned revenue, accrued revenue, or accrued expense) and (2) the impact on the accounts before adjustment (include both the dollar amount and whether the account is overstated or understated).

E4-5   On March 31 of the current year, the trial balance of Easy Rental Agency Inc. includes these selected accounts:

Prepare adjusting entries.
(SO 4, 5)

	Debits	Credits
Prepaid insurance	$ 3,600	
Supplies	4,000	
Equipment	24,000	
Accumulated amortization—equipment		$ 6,000
Notes payable		20,000
Unearned rent revenue		10,200
Rent revenue		60,000
Interest expense	0	
Wage expense	14,000	
Income tax expense	0	

An analysis of the accounts shows the following:

1. The equipment is amortized at $500 per month.
2. One-third of the unearned rent revenue was earned during the quarter.
3. Interest of $600 is accrued on the notes payable.
4. Supplies on hand total $850.
5. Insurance expires at the rate of $200 per month.
6. Income tax is estimated to be $15,000.

Instructions

Prepare the adjusting entries at March 31, assuming that adjusting entries are made quarterly.

E4-6   Kay Ong, D.D.S., opened an incorporated dental practice on January 1, 2004. During the first month of operations, the following transactions occurred:

1. Performed services for patients who had dental plan insurance. At January 31, $900 of such services were earned but not yet billed to the insurance companies.
2. Utility expenses incurred but not paid prior to January 31 totalled $5,200.
3. Purchased dental equipment on January 1 for $80,000, paying $20,000 in cash and signing a $60,000, three-year, 8% note payable. The equipment is amortized at $600 per month. Interest is due the first of each month.
4. Purchased a one-year malpractice insurance policy on January 1 for $5,000.
5. Purchased $1,800 of dental supplies. On January 31, determined that $500 of supplies were on hand.

Prepare adjusting entries.
(SO 4, 5)

Interactive
Homework

Instructions

Prepare the adjusting entries at January 31.

E4-7   The statement of earnings of Weller Corp. for the month of July 2005 shows Service Revenue $5,500; Wages Expense $2,300; Supplies Expense $1,000; and Utilities Expense $800. In reviewing the statement, you discover the following:

Prepare corrected statement of earnings.
(SO 4, 5)

1. Insurance of $300 that expired during July was omitted.
2. Supplies expense includes $400 of supplies that are still on hand at July 31.
3. Amortization on equipment of $150 was omitted.
4. Accrued but unpaid wages at July 31 of $300 were not included.
5. Revenue earned but unrecorded totalled $750.
6. Income tax expense of $600 was not accrued.

Instructions

Prepare a correct statement of earnings for the month ended July 31, 2005.

Re-create transactions and adjusting entries from adjusted data.
(SO 4, 5)

E4-8   Selected accounts of Jasper Limited are shown here:

Supplies Expense			Supplies		
July 31	700		July 1	Bal. 1,100	July 31	700
			10	300	

Salaries Payable			Accounts Receivable	
	July 31	1,200	July 31	500

Salaries Expense			Unearned Service Revenue		
July 15	1,200		July 31	1,200	July 1	Bal. 1,500
31	1,200				20	700

Service Revenue		
	July 14	3,000
	31	1,200
	31	800
	31	500

Instructions

After analysing the accounts, journalize (a) the July transactions and (b) the adjusting entries that were made on July 31. (*Hint*: July transactions were for cash.)

Prepare adjusting entries and report accrued expenses.
(SO 5)

E4-9   Arseneault Corporation is in the process of determining its year-end balance in accrued liabilities for the following items:

1. Arseneault paid $750 in income tax instalments at the end of each month during the year, based on the prior year's income. At year end, Arseneault determines that its actual income tax for the current year is $12,000.
2. A $900 power bill was just received. It has not yet been paid.
3. Arseneault pays weekly salaries of $1,500 for a five-day work week from Monday to Friday. This year the year end falls on a Wednesday.
4. The company has a one-year $10,000 note payable outstanding, with 6% interest payable the first of each month.

Instructions

(a) Prepare the adjusting journal entries to record each of the above transactions.
(b) What amount should Arseneault report as accrued expenses in its classified balance sheet? What classification should the amount be under?

Analyse adjusted data.
(SO 4, 5, 6)

E4-10   This is a partial adjusted trial balance of Nolet Ltd.:

NOLET LTD.
Adjusted Trial Balance
January 31, 2004

	Debit	Credit
Supplies	$ 800	
Prepaid insurance	2,400	
Salaries payable		$1,200
Unearned service revenue		750
Supplies expense	950	
Insurance expense	600	
Salaries expense	1,800	
Service revenue		2,500

Instructions

Answer these questions, assuming the year begins January 1:

(a) If the amount in Supplies Expense is the January 31 adjusting entry, and $850 of supplies were purchased in January, what was the balance in Supplies on January 1?

(b) If the amount in Insurance Expense is the January 31 adjusting entry, and the original insurance premium was for one year, what was the total premium and when was the policy purchased?

(c) If $2,500 of salaries were paid in January, what was the balance in Salaries Payable at December 31, 2003?

(d) If $1,600 was received in January for services performed in January, what was the balance in Unearned Service Revenue at December 31, 2003?

E4-11 The trial balances below are before and after adjustment for Inuit Inc. at the end of its fiscal year:

Prepare adjusting entries from analysis of trial balances.
(SO 4, 5, 6)

INUIT INC.
Trial Balance
August 31, 2004

	Before Adjustment Dr.	Before Adjustment Cr.	After Adjustment Dr.	After Adjustment Cr.
Cash	$ 9,600		$ 9,600	
Accounts receivable	8,800		9,500	
Office supplies	2,300		700	
Prepaid insurance	4,000		2,500	
Office equipment	14,000		14,000	
Accumulated amortization—office equipment		$ 3,600		$ 4,800
Accounts payable		5,800		5,800
Salaries payable		0		1,000
Income tax payable		0		3,500
Unearned rent revenue		1,500		700
Common shares		10,000		10,000
Retained earnings		5,600		5,600
Dividends	800		800	
Service revenue		34,000		34,700
Rent revenue		11,000		11,800
Salaries expense	17,000		18,000	
Office supplies expense	0		1,600	
Rent expense	15,000		15,000	
Insurance expense	0		1,500	
Amortization expense	0		1,200	
Income tax expense	0		3,500	
	$71,500	$71,500	$77,900	$77,900

Instructions

Prepare the adjusting entries that were made.

E4-12 The adjusted trial balance for Inuit Inc. is given in E4-11.

Prepare financial statements.
(SO 6)

Instructions

Prepare the statements of earnings and retained earnings for the year ended August 31, 2004, and the classified balance sheet at August 31, 2004.

E4-13 The adjusted trial balance for Inuit Inc. is given in E4-11.

Prepare closing entries.
(SO 7)

Instructions

Prepare the closing entries at August 31.

Interactive Homework

Problems: Set A

Identify accounting assumptions, principles, and constraints.
(SO 1)

P4-1A Presented here are the assumptions, principles, and constraints used in this and previous chapters:

1. Economic entity assumption
2. Going concern assumption
3. Monetary unit assumption
4. Time period assumption
5. Full disclosure principle
6. Revenue recognition principle
7. Matching principle
8. Cost principle
9. Materiality
10. Cost-benefit

Instructions

In the space provided, write the number of the accounting assumption, principle, or constraint that describes each of these situations. Do not use a number more than once.

(a) _____ Assets are not stated at their selling value. (Do not use the cost principle.)
(b) _____ The death of the president is not recorded in the accounts.
(c) _____ Pencil sharpeners are expensed when purchased.
(d) _____ Reporting must be done at defined intervals.
(e) _____ Revenue is recorded when earned.
(f) _____ Some financial events do not need to be disclosed if the cost is immaterial.
(g) _____ Each entity is kept as a unit distinct from its owner or owners.
(h) _____ All important information is presented in the notes to the financial statements.

Convert earnings from cash to accrual basis.
(SO 2, 4, 5)

P4-2A Your examination of the records of a company that follows the cash basis of accounting tells you that the company's reported cash basis earnings in 2004 are $45,000. If the company had followed accrual basis accounting practices, it would have reported the following year-end balances:

	2004	2003
Accounts receivable	$3,600	$2,700
Prepaid insurance	1,500	1,300
Accounts payable	1,500	2,200
Unearned revenues	1,400	1,500

Instructions

Determine the company's net earnings on an accrual basis for 2004.

Convert earnings from cash to accrual basis; prepare accrual-based financial statements.
(SO 2, 4, 5)

P4-3A The Radical Edge Ltd., a ski tuning and repair shop, opened in November 2003. The company carefully kept track of all its cash receipts and cash payments. The following information is available at the end of the ski season, April 30, 2004:

	Cash Receipts	Cash Payments
Issue of common shares	$20,000	
Payment for repair equipment		$9,200
Rent payments		1,225
Newspaper advertising paid		375
Utility bills paid		970
Part-time helper's wages paid		2,600
Income tax paid		10,000
Cash receipts from ski and snowboard repair services	32,150	
Subtotals	52,150	24,370
Cash balance		27,780
Totals	$52,150	$52,150

You learn that the repair equipment has an estimated useful life of five years. The company rents space at a cost of $175 per month on a one-year lease. The lease contract requires payment of the first and last months' rent in advance, which was done. The part-timer helper is owed $220 at April 30, 2004, for unpaid wages. At April 30, 2004, customers owe The Radical Edge $650 for services they have received but have not yet paid for.

Instructions

(a) Prepare an accrual basis statement of earnings for the six months ended April 30, 2004.

(b) Prepare the April 30, 2004, classified balance sheet.

P4-4A Bourque Corporation began operations on January 1, 2004. Its fiscal year end is December 31, and it prepares financial statements and adjusts its accounts only annually. Selected transactions during 2004 follow:

Prepare original and adjusting entries.
(SO 4, 5)

1. On January 2, 2004, Bourque bought office supplies for $2,800 cash. A physical count at December 31, 2004, revealed that $300 of supplies were still on hand.
2. The company bought a $3,600 one-year insurance policy for cash on August 1, 2004. The policy came into effect on this date.
3. On December 15, the company paid $500 rent in advance for the month of January 2005.
4. On November 15, Bourque received a $1,200 advance cash payment from three clients for accounting services expected to be provided in the future. As at December 31, services had been performed for two of the clients ($400 each) and are now complete.

Instructions

Prepare the journal entry for the original transaction and any adjusting journal entry required at December 31, 2004, for each of the above situations.

P4-5A A review of the ledger of Greenberg Corporation at January 5, 2005, produces the following data pertaining to the preparation of annual adjusting entries:

Prepare adjusting entries.
(SO 4, 5)

1. Salaries Payable $0. There are eight salaried employees. Salaries are paid every Friday for the current week. Six employees receive a salary of $800 each per week, and two employees earn $500 each per week. January 31 is a Tuesday. Employees do not work weekends.
2. Unearned Rent Revenue $369,000. The company began subleasing office space in its new building on December 1. Each tenant is required to make a $5,000 security deposit that is not refundable until occupancy is terminated. At January 31 the company had the following rental contracts that are paid in full for the entire term of the lease:

Date	Term (in months)	Monthly Rent	Number of Leases
Dec. 1	6	$4,000	5
Jan. 1	6	8,500	4

3. Prepaid Advertising $13,200. This balance consists of payments on two advertising contracts. The contracts provide for monthly advertising in two trade magazines and the first advertisement runs in the month in which the contract is signed. The terms of the contracts are as follows:

Contract	Date	Amount	Number of Magazine Issues
A650	June 1	$6,000	12
B974	Sept. 1	$7,200	24

4. Notes Payable $80,000. This balance consists of a note for one year at an annual interest rate of 9%, dated June 1, 2004. Interest is payable at maturity.

Instructions

Prepare the adjusting entries at January 31, 2005.

P4-6A The following *independent* situations for the Repertory Theatre Ltd. during the year ended December 31, 2004, may require either an original journal entry or an adjusting journal entry, or both:

Prepare original and adjusting entries.
(SO 4, 5)

1. Office supplies on hand amounted to $300 at the beginning of the year. During the year, additional office supplies were purchased for cash at a cost of $1,500. At the end of the year, a physical count showed that supplies on hand amounted to $500.
2. At the beginning of June, the theatre borrowed $4,000 from La Caisse Populaire Desjardins at an annual interest rate of 8%. The principal and interest are to be repaid in a year's time.
3. Upon reviewing its books on December 31, it was noted that a utility bill for the month of December had not yet been received. A call to Hydro-Québec determined that the electricity bill was $1,400.

4. On July 1, 2004, the theatre purchased a truck for use in its business for $38,000, paying cash in full. The annual amortization on this truck is $7,600.

5. Annual income taxes are estimated to be $13,000 for the year, $10,000 of which has been paid to date.

Instructions

Prepare the journal entry for the original transaction and any adjusting journal entry required at December 31, 2004, for each of the above situations.

Prepare adjusting entries and corrected statement of earnings.
(SO 4, 5)

P4-7A   The Try-Us Travel Agency Ltd. was organized on January 1, 2004. Paul Volpé, the general manager and accountant, is a good manager but a poor accountant. Paul prepared the following statement of earnings for the quarter that ended March 31, 2004:

TRY-US TRAVEL AGENCY LTD.
Statement of Earnings
Quarter Ended March 31, 2004

Revenues		
Travel service fees		$50,000
Operating expenses		
Advertising	$2,600	
Amortization	400	
Income tax	1,500	
Salaries	6,000	
Utilities	400	10,900
Net earnings		$39,100

Paul thought that something was wrong with the statement because he didn't expect net earnings to exceed $7,500 in any one quarter. Knowing that you are an experienced accountant, he asks you to review the statement of earnings and other data.

You first look at the trial balance. In addition to the account balances reported above in the statement of earnings, the trial balance contains the following additional selected balances at March 31, 2004:

Supplies	$ 3,200
Prepaid Insurance	1,200
Note Payable	10,000

You then make inquiries and discover the following:

1. Travel service fees include advance payments for cruises, $28,000.
2. There were $800 of supplies on hand at March 31.
3. Prepaid insurance resulted from the payment of a one-year policy on January 1, 2004.
4. The mail on April 1, 2004, included the March utility bill for heat, light, and power, $180.
5. There are two employees who receive salaries of $175 each per day. At March 31, three days of salaries have been incurred but not paid.
6. The note payable is a six-month, 5% note dated February 1, 2004. Interest is payable on the first of each month.

Instructions

(a) Prepare any adjusting journal entries required as at March 31, 2004.
(b) Prepare a correct statement of earnings for the quarter ended March 31, 2004.
(c) Explain to Paul the generally accepted accounting principles that he did not recognize in preparing his statement of earnings, and their effect on his results.

Prepare adjusting entries, post, and prepare adjusted trial balance.
(SO 4, 5, 6)

P4-8A   Ortega Limo Service Ltd. began operations on January 1, 2004. At the end of the first year of operations, this is the trial balance before adjustment:

ORTEGA LIMO SERVICE LTD.
Trial Balance
December 31, 2004

	Debit	Credit
Cash	$ 12,400	
Accounts receivable	3,200	
Prepaid insurance	3,600	
Automobiles	58,000	
Notes payable		$ 45,000
Unearned service revenue		2,500
Common shares		18,000
Service revenue		96,000
Salaries expense	57,000	
Rent expense	12,000	
Repairs expense	6,000	
Gas and oil expense	9,300	
	$161,500	$161,500

Other data:

1. Service revenue earned but unbilled is $11,500 at December 31.
2. Insurance coverage began on January 1, under a two-year policy.
3. Automobile amortization is $11,600 for the year.
4. Interest of $2,250 accrued on notes payable for the year.
5. Of the unearned service revenue, $1,000 has been earned.
6. Drivers' salaries total $900 per day. At December 31, four days of salaries are unpaid.
7. Repairs to automobiles of $650 have been incurred, but bills have not been received prior to December 31. (Use Accounts Payable.)
8. Income taxes payable are $2,600.

Instructions

(a) Journalize the adjusting entries at December 31, 2004.
(b) Prepare a general ledger using T accounts. Enter the trial balance amounts and post the adjusting entries.
(c) Prepare an adjusted trial balance at December 31, 2004.

P4-9A Highland Cove Resort Inc. opened for business on June 1 with eight chalets available for rent. Its trial balance before adjustment at August 31 is presented here:

Prepare adjusting entries, post, prepare adjusted trial balance, financial statements, and closing entries.
(SO 4, 5, 6, 7)

HIGHLAND COVE RESORT INC.
Trial Balance
August 31, 2005

	Debit	Credit
Cash	$ 15,600	
Prepaid insurance	5,400	
Supplies	4,300	
Land	50,000	
Cottages	125,000	
Furniture	26,000	
Accounts payable		$ 6,500
Unearned rent revenue		6,800
Income tax payable		5,000
Mortgage payable		90,000
Common shares		100,000
Dividends	5,000	
Rent revenue		90,000
Salaries expense	51,000	
Utilities expense	9,400	
Repair expense	3,600	
Income tax expense	3,000	
	$298,300	$298,300

Other data:

1. Insurance expires at the rate of $300 per month.
2. A count on August 31 shows $1,200 of supplies on hand.
3. Annual amortization is $6,000 on cottages and $5,000 on furniture.
4. Unearned rent of $5,000 was earned prior to August 31.
5. Salaries of $400 were unpaid at August 31.
6. Rentals of $1,800 were due from tenants at August 31. (Use Accounts Receivable.)
7. The mortgage interest rate is 8% per year. (The mortgage was taken out August 1.) Interest is payable the first of each month.
8. Total income tax for the quarter is $4,000.

Instructions

(a) Journalize the adjusting entries at August 31 for the three-month period from June 1 to August 31.
(b) Prepare a general ledger using T accounts. Enter the trial balance amounts and post the adjusting entries.
(c) Prepare an adjusted trial balance at August 31.
(d) Prepare a statement of earnings and a statement of retained earnings for the three months ended August 31, and a classified balance sheet as at August 31.
(e) Journalize the closing entries on August 31, assuming the company closes its books quarterly.

Prepare adjusting entries and financial statements; identify accounts to be closed.
(SO 4, 5, 6, 7)

P4-10A Presented here are both the adjusted and unadjusted trial balances for the Grant Advertising Agency Limited as at December 31, 2004:

GRANT ADVERTISING AGENCY LIMITED
Trial Balance
December 31, 2004

	Unadjusted Debit	Unadjusted Credit	Adjusted Debit	Adjusted Credit
Cash	$ 11,000		$ 11,000	
Accounts receivable	18,000		21,500	
Art supplies	8,400		6,000	
Prepaid insurance	3,350		2,500	
Printing equipment	60,000		60,000	
Accumulated amortization		$ 28,000		$ 35,000
Accounts payable		5,000		5,000
Interest payable				225
Note payable		15,000		15,000
Unearned advertising revenue		6,000		5,600
Salaries payable				1,300
Income tax payable				2,500
Common shares		20,000		20,000
Retained earnings		11,650		11,650
Dividends	12,000		12,000	
Advertising revenue		58,600		62,500
Salaries expense	10,000		11,300	
Insurance expense			850	
Interest expense			225	
Amortization expense			7,000	
Art supplies expense			2,400	
Rent expense	14,000		14,000	
Income tax expense	7,500		10,000	
	$144,250	$144,250	$158,775	$158,775

Instructions

(a) Journalize the annual adjusting entries that were made.
(b) Prepare a statement of earnings and a statement of retained earnings for the year ended December 31, and a classified balance sheet at December 31.
(c) Identify which accounts should be closed on December 31.

(d) If the note has been outstanding three months, what is the annual interest rate on that note?

(e) If the company paid $13,500 in salaries in 2004, what was the balance in Salaries Payable on December 31, 2003?

P4-11A On September 1, 2004, the following were the account balances of Rijo Equipment Repair Corp.:

Complete accounting cycle through to preparation of financial statements.
(SO 4, 5, 6)

	Debit		Credit
Cash	$ 4,880	Accumulated amortization	$ 1,500
Accounts receivable	3,720	Accounts payable	3,100
Supplies	800	Unearned service revenue	400
Store equipment	15,000	Salaries payable	700
	$24,400	Common shares	10,000
		Retained earnings	8,700
			$24,400

During September, the following summary transactions were completed:

Sept. 8 Paid $1,100 for salaries due to employees, of which $400 is for September and $700 is for August salaries payable.
   10 Received $1,200 cash from customers in payment of accounts.
   12 Received $3,400 cash for services performed in September.
   15 Purchased store equipment on account, $3,000.
   17 Purchased supplies on account, $1,500.
   20 Paid creditors $4,500 of accounts payable due.
   22 Paid September rent, $500.
   25 Paid salaries, $1,200.
   27 Performed services on account and billed customers for services provided, $900.
   29 Received $650 from customers for services to be provided in future.
   30 Paid income tax for month, $500.

Adjustment data:

1. Supplies on hand, $1,800.
2. Accrued salaries payable, $400.
3. Amortization, $250 per month.
4. Unearned service revenue of $350 earned.

Instructions

(a) Enter the September 1 balances in the general ledger T accounts.
(b) Journalize the September transactions.
(c) Post to the T accounts.
(d) Prepare a trial balance at September 30.
(e) Journalize and post adjusting entries.
(f) Prepare an adjusted trial balance.
(g) Prepare a statement of earnings and a statement of retained earnings for September, and a classified balance sheet at September 30.

P4-12A Ewok's Carpet Cleaners Ltd. opened on March 1. During March, the following transactions were completed:

Complete all steps in accounting cycle.
(SO 4, 5, 6, 7, 8)

Mar. 1 Issued $10,000 of common shares for cash.
    1 Purchased used truck for $26,000, paying $6,000 cash, and signed a three-year 8% note payable for the balance. Interest is due the first of each month.
    2 Paid rent for the month, $500.
    3 Purchased cleaning supplies for $1,200 on account.
    5 Paid $1,800 cash on one-year insurance policy effective March 1.
   14 Billed customers $4,800 for cleaning services.
   18 Paid $500 on amount owed on cleaning supplies.
   20 Paid $1,500 cash for employee salaries.
   21 Collected $2,600 cash from customers billed on July 14.
   28 Billed customers $3,500 for cleaning services.
   31 Paid $350 for truck's gas and oil used during the month.
   31 Paid a $900 cash dividend.

Instructions

(a) Journalize the March transactions.
(b) Post to the general ledger T accounts.
(c) Prepare a trial balance at March 31.
(d) Journalize the following adjustments:

1. Earned but unbilled revenue at March 31 was $600.
2. Amortization on the truck for the month was $400.
3. Accrued interest on note.
4. One-twelfth of the insurance expired.
5. An inventory count shows $400 of cleaning supplies on hand at March 31.
6. Unpaid employee salaries were $500.
7. Income tax for the month is estimated to be $1,600.

(e) Post adjusting entries to the T accounts.
(f) Prepare an adjusted trial balance.
(g) Prepare a statement of earnings and a statement of retained earnings for March, and a classified balance sheet at March 31.
(h) Journalize and post closing entries, and complete the closing process.
(i) Prepare a post-closing trial balance at March 31.

Problems: Set B

Identify accounting assumptions, principles, and constraints.
(SO 1)

P4-1B Presented below are the assumptions, principles, and constraints used in this and previous chapters:

1. Economic entity assumption
2. Going concern assumption
3. Monetary unit assumption
4. Time period assumption
5. Full disclosure principle
6. Revenue recognition principle
7. Matching principle
8. Cost principle
9. Materiality
10. Cost-benefit

Instructions

In the space provided, write the number of the accounting assumption, principle, or constraint that describes each of these situations. Do not use a number more than once.

(a) _____ Requires recognition of expenses in the same period as related revenues.
(b) _____ Ensures that irrelevant financial information is not reported at a great expense.
(c) _____ Assumes that the dollar is the measuring stick used to report financial information.
(d) _____ Separates financial information into time periods for reporting purposes.
(e) _____ Market value changes after purchase are not recorded in the accounts. (Do not use the revenue recognition principle.)
(f) _____ Indicates that personal and business record keeping should be separately maintained.
(g) _____ Ensures that all relevant financial information is reported.
(h) _____ Repair tools are expensed when purchased. (Do not use cost-benefit.)

Convert earnings from cash to accrual basis.
(SO 2, 4, 5)

P4-2B Your examination of the records of a company that follows the cash basis of accounting tells you that the company's reported cash basis earnings in 2004 are $35,190. If this firm had followed accrual basis accounting practices, it would have reported the following year-end balances:

	2004	2003
Accounts receivable	$2,500	$3,400
Supplies on hand	1,160	1,300
Unpaid wages owing	2,400	1,200

Instructions

Determine the company's net earnings on an accrual basis for 2004.

P4-3B During the first week of January, Creative Designs Ltd. commenced operations. Although the company kept no formal accounting records, it did maintain a record of cash receipts and disbursements. Creative Designs approached the local bank for a $10,000 loan and was asked to submit a balance sheet and statement of earnings prepared on an accrual basis. The following information is available for the year ended December 31, 2004:

Convert earnings from cash to accrual basis; prepare accrual-based financial statements.
(SO 2, 4, 5)

	Cash Receipts	Cash Payments
Investments by common shareholders	$20,000	
Equipment		$16,400
Supplies		6,200
Rent		9,600
Income tax		4,000
Insurance		1,800
Advertising—all ads completed		3,600
Wages of assistant		18,400
Telephone		980
Dividend payments to shareholders		4,000
Design revenue received	61,500	
	81,500	64,980
Cash balance		16,520
	$81,500	$81,500

Additional information:

1. The equipment has an estimated five-year life.
2. Supplies on hand on December 31 were $1,800.
3. Rent payments included $750 per month rental and a $600 deposit refundable at the end of the two-year lease.
4. The insurance was paid for a one-year period expiring on December 31.
5. Wages earned the last week in December and to be paid in January 2005 amounted to $400.
6. Design revenue earned but not yet collected amounted to $3,800.
7. The company manager used her personal automobile for business purposes: 10,000 km at 30 cents per km. She was not paid for the use of her car but would like to be.

Instructions:

(a) Prepare an accrual basis statement of earnings for the year ended December 31, 2004.
(b) Prepare the December 31, 2004, classified balance sheet.

P4-4B Ouellette Corporation began operations on January 2, 2004. Its fiscal year end is December 31, and it prepares financial statements and adjusts its accounts only *annually*. Selected transactions during 2004 follow:

Prepare original and adjusting entries.
(SO 4, 5)

1. On January 2, 2004, bought office supplies for $4,500 cash. A physical count at December 31, 2004, revealed that $500 of supplies were still on hand.
2. Bought a $3,600 one-year insurance policy for cash on September 1, 2004. The policy came into effect on this date.
3. On November 15, Ouellette received a $1,200 advance cash payment from a client for accounting services expected to be provided in the future. As at December 31, half of these services had been performed and are now complete.
4. On December 1, the company rented out excess office space for a six-month period starting on this date and received a $920 cheque for two months of rent.

Instructions

Prepare the journal entry for the original transaction and any adjusting journal entry required at December 31, 2004, for each of the above situations.

P4-5B A review of the ledger of Come-By-Chance Company Limited at January 31, 2005, produces these data pertaining to the preparation of annual adjusting entries:

Prepare adjusting entries.
(SO 4, 5)

1. Prepaid Insurance $12,800. The company has separate insurance policies on its buildings and its motor vehicles. Policy B4564 on the building was purchased on August 1, 2003, for $9,600. The policy has a term of two years. Policy A2958 on the vehicles was purchased on February 1, 2004, for $4,800. This policy has a term of 18 months.

2. Unearned Subscription Revenue $49,000. The company began selling magazine subscriptions in 2004 on an annual basis. The selling price of a subscription is $50. A review of subscription contracts reveals the following:

Subscription Date	Number of Subscriptions
November 1	200
December 1	300
January 1	480
	980

3. Notes Payable, $50,000. This balance consists of a note for six months at an annual interest rate of 7%, dated September 1. Interest is payable at maturity.
4. Salaries Payable $0. There are eight salaried employees. Salaries are paid every Friday for a five-day work week (M–F). Five employees receive a salary of $600 each per week, and three employees earn $800 each per week. January 31 is a Tuesday.

Instructions

Prepare the adjusting entries at January 31, 2005.

Prepare original and adjusting entries.
(SO 4, 5)

P4-6B The following *independent* situations for the New Age Theatre Ltd. during the year ended December 31, 2004, require either an original journal entry, or an adjusting journal entry, or both:

1. Office supplies on hand amounted to $640 at the beginning of the year. During the year, additional office supplies were purchased for cash at a cost of $1,460. At the end of the year, a physical count showed that supplies on hand amounted to $740.
2. At the beginning of February, the theatre borrowed $10,000 from the Bank of Montreal at an annual interest rate of 6%. The principal is to be repaid in two years' time. The interest is payable the first of each month.
3. Upon reviewing its books on December 31, it was noted that the telephone bill for the month of December had not yet been received. A call to NBTel determined that the telephone bill was $400.
4. On January 1, 2004, the theatre purchased a used truck for use in its business for $28,000, paying cash in full. The annual amortization on this truck is $5,600.
5. The total payroll is $3,000 every Monday for employee wages earned during a six-day week (Tuesday–Sunday). This year, December 31 falls on a Friday.

Instructions:

Prepare the journal entry for the original transaction and any adjusting journal entry required at December 31, 2004, for each of the above situations.

Prepare adjusting entries and corrected statement of earnings.
(SO 4, 5)

P4-7B The Holiday Travel Court Ltd. was organized on April 1, 2003. The new accountant, Alice Adare, prepared the following statement of earnings for the fourth quarter, which ended March 31, 2004:

HOLIDAY TRAVEL COURT LTD.
Statement of Earnings
Quarter Ended March 31, 2004

Revenues		
Travel court rental fees		$95,000
Operating expenses		
Advertising	$ 5,200	
Wages	29,800	
Utilities	900	
Amortization	800	
Repairs	4,000	40,700
Net earnings		$54,300

Alice knew that something was wrong with the statement because net earnings had never exceeded $20,000 in any one quarter. Knowing that you are an experienced accountant, she asks you to review the statement of earnings and other data.

You first look at the trial balance. In addition to the account balances reported above in the statement of earnings, the ledger contains the following additional selected balances at March 31, 2004:

Supplies	$ 5,200
Prepaid Insurance	7,200
Note Payable	12,000

You then make inquiries and discover the following:

1. Travel court rental fees include advance rental payments for summer occupancy, in the amount of $28,000.
2. There were $1,300 of supplies on hand at March 31.
3. Prepaid insurance resulted from the payment of a one-year policy on June 1, 2003.
4. The mail in April brought the following bills: advertising for the week of March 24, $410; repairs made March 10, $4,260; and utilities for the month of March, $380.
5. There are four employees, who receive wages that total $350 per day. At March 31, three days of wages have been incurred but not paid.
6. The note payable is a 5% note dated January 1, 2004. Interest and principal are due on June 30, 2004.
7. Income tax of $6,000 for the quarter is due in April but has not yet been recorded.

Instructions

(a) Prepare any adjusting journal entries required as at March 31, 2004.
(b) Prepare a correct statement of earnings for the quarter ended March 31, 2004.
(c) Explain to Alice the generally accepted accounting principles that she did not recognize in preparing her statement of earnings and their effect on her results.

P4-8B The trial balance before adjustment of Scenic Tours Limited at the end of its first month of operations is presented here:

Prepare adjusting entries, post, and prepare adjusted trial balance.
(SO 4, 5, 6)

SCENIC TOURS LIMITED
Trial Balance
June 30, 2005

	Debit	Credit
Cash	$ 3,000	
Prepaid insurance	7,200	
Office equipment	1,800	
Buses	140,000	
Notes payable		$ 62,000
Unearned revenue		15,000
Common shares		70,000
Tour revenue		15,900
Salaries expense	9,000	
Advertising expense	800	
Gas and oil expense	1,100	
	$162,900	$162,900

Other data:

1. The insurance policy has a one-year term beginning June 1, 2005.
2. The monthly amortization is $50 on office equipment and $2,500 on buses.
3. Interest of $310 accrues on the notes payable each month.
4. Deposits of $1,500 each were received for advanced tour reservations from 10 school groups. At June 30, six of these deposits have been earned.
5. Bus drivers are paid a combined total of $400 per day. At June 30, four days of salaries are unpaid.
6. A senior citizens' organization that had not made an advance deposit took a tour on June 30 for $1,200. This group was not billed for the services provided until July.
7. Income taxes payable are $2,000.

Instructions

(a) Journalize the adjusting entries at June 30, 2005.
(b) Prepare a general ledger using T accounts. Enter the trial balance amounts and post the adjusting entries.
(c) Prepare an adjusted trial balance at June 30, 2005.

Prepare adjusting entries, post, prepare adjusted trial balance, financial statements, and closing entries.
(SO 4, 5, 6, 7)

P4-9B The River Run Motel Ltd. opened for business on May 1, 2004. Here is its trial balance before adjustment:

RIVER RUN MOTEL LTD.
Trial Balance
May 31, 2004

	Debit	Credit
Cash	$ 2,500	
Prepaid insurance	1,800	
Supplies	2,600	
Land	15,000	
Lodge	70,000	
Furniture	16,800	
Accounts payable		$ 4,700
Unearned rent revenue		4,500
Mortgage payable		35,000
Common shares		60,000
Rent revenue		9,000
Salaries expense	3,000	
Utilities expense	1,000	
Advertising expense	500	
	$113,200	$113,200

Other data:
1. Insurance expires at the rate of $300 per month.
2. An inventory of supplies shows $1,350 of unused supplies on May 31.
3. Annual amortization is $3,500 on the lodge and $3,360 on furniture.
4. The mortgage interest rate is 7%. (The mortgage was taken out on May 1.) Interest is payable the first of each month.
5. Unearned rent of $1,500 has been earned.
6. Salaries of $500 are accrued and unpaid at May 31.
7. Accrued income taxes are estimated to be $1,700.

Instructions

(a) Journalize the adjusting entries at May 31.
(b) Prepare a general ledger using T accounts. Enter the trial balance amounts and post the adjusting entries.
(c) Prepare an adjusted trial balance at May 31.
(d) Prepare a statement of earnings and a statement of retained earnings for the month of May and a classified balance sheet at May 31.
(e) Journalize the closing entries, assuming that the company closes its books monthly.

Prepare adjusting entries and financial statements; identify accounts to be closed.
(SO 4, 5, 6, 7)

P4-10B Ozaki Corp. was organized on July 1, 2004. Quarterly financial statements are prepared. The trial balance and adjusted trial balance at September 30 are shown here:

OZAKI CORP.
Trial Balance
September 30, 2004

	Before Adjustment		After Adjustment	
	Debit	Credit	Debit	Credit
Cash	$ 6,700		$ 6,700	
Accounts receivable	400		800	
Prepaid rent	2,000		900	
Supplies	1,200		1,000	
Equipment	15,000		15,000	
Accumulated amortization— equipment				$ 350
Note payable		$ 5,000		5,000
Accounts payable		1,710		1,710
Salaries payable				600

Interest Payable				50
Unearned Rent Revenue		1,000		700
Common Shares		14,000		14,000
Income Tax Payable				1,000
Dividends	600		600	
Commission Revenue		14,000		14,400
Rent Revenue		400		700
Salaries Expense	8,800		9,400	
Rent Expense	900		2,000	
Amortization Expense			350	
Supplies Expense			200	
Utilities Expense	510		510	
Interest Expense			50	
Income Tax Expense			1,000	
	$36,110	$36,110	$38,510	$38,510

Instructions

(a) Journalize the adjusting entries that were made.
(b) Prepare a statement of earnings and a statement of retained earnings for the three months ending September 30, and a classified balance sheet at September 30.
(c) Identify which accounts should be closed on September 30 if the books are closed quarterly.
(d) If the note bears interest at 6%, how many months has it been outstanding?

P4-11B   On November 1, 2004, the following were the account balances of Alou Equipment Repair Corp.:

Complete accounting cycle through to preparation of financial statements.
(SO 4, 5, 6)

	Debit			Credit
Cash	$ 2,790	Accumulated amortization	$ 500
Accounts receivable	2,910	Accounts payable	2,300
Supplies	1,000	Unearned service revenue	400
Store equipment	10,000	Salaries payable	500
	$16,700	Common shares	10,000
		Retained earnings	3,000
			$16,700

During November, the following summary transactions were completed:

Nov.   8 Paid $1,100 for salaries due employees, of which $600 is for November and $500 is for October salaries payable.
     10 Received $1,200 cash from customers in payment of accounts.
     12 Received $1,700 cash for services performed in November.
     15 Purchased store equipment on account, $3,000.
     17 Purchased supplies on account, $1,300.
     20 Paid creditors $2,500 of accounts payable due.
     22 Paid November rent, $300.
     25 Paid salaries, $1,100.
     27 Performed services on account and billed customers for services provided, $700.
     29 Received $550 from customers for services to be provided in future.

Adjustment data:

  1. Supplies on hand are valued at $1,600.
  2. Accrued salaries payable are $500.
  3. Amortization for the month is $250.
  4. Unearned service revenue of $300 is earned.

Instructions

(a) Enter the November 1 balances in the general ledger T accounts.
(b) Journalize the November transactions.
(c) Post to the T accounts.
(d) Prepare a trial balance at November 30.
(e) Journalize and post adjusting entries.
(f) Prepare an adjusted trial balance.

(g) Prepare a statement of earnings and a statement of retained earnings for November, and a classified balance sheet at November 30.

Complete all steps in accounting cycle.
(SO 4, 5, 6, 7, 8)

P4-12B   Corellian Window Washing Inc. opened on July 1, 2004. During July, the following transactions were completed:

July   1 Issued $24,000 of common shares for cash.
     1 Purchased used truck for $36,000, paying $16,000 cash and the balance with an 8% one-year note payable. Interest is due the first of each month.
     3 Purchased cleaning supplies for $800 on account.
     5 Paid $1,200 cash on a one-year insurance policy effective July 1.
    12 Billed customers $4,500 for cleaning services.
    18 Paid $500 on amount owed on cleaning supplies.
    20 Paid $1,600 cash for employee salaries.
    21 Collected $1,500 cash from customers billed on July 12.
    25 Billed customers $2,000 for cleaning services.
    31 Paid $250 for gas and oil used in the truck during the month.
    31 Paid monthly income taxes of $1,200.
    31 Declared and paid a $600 cash dividend.

Instructions

(a) Journalize the July transactions.
(b) Post to the general ledger T accounts.
(c) Prepare a trial balance at July 31.
(d) Journalize the following adjustments:

    1. Services provided but unbilled and uncollected at July 31 were $1,500.
    2. Amortization on equipment for the month was $300.
    3. One-twelfth of the insurance expired.
    4. An inventory count shows $600 of cleaning supplies on hand at July 31.
    5. Accrued but unpaid employee salaries were $400.
    6. Interest accrued on note payable.

(e) Post adjusting entries to the T accounts.
(f) Prepare an adjusted trial balance.
(g) Prepare a statement of earnings and a statement of retained earnings for July, and a classified balance sheet at July 31.
(h) Journalize and post closing entries and complete the closing process.
(i) Prepare a post-closing trial balance at July 31.

BROADENING YOUR PERSPECTIVE

Financial Reporting and Analysis

Analysis
Tools

FINANCIAL REPORTING PROBLEM: *Loblaw Companies Limited*

BYP4-1   The financial statements of Loblaw are presented in Appendix A at the end of this book.

Instructions

(a) Using the consolidated statement of earnings and the balance sheet, identify items that may result in adjusting entries for prepayments.

(b) Using the consolidated statement of earnings, identify items that may result in adjusting entries for accruals.

(c) What were the amounts of income tax expense for 2002 and 2001? Are there any taxes payable at December 28, 2002?

(d) What was the cash paid for interest during 2002? See the net interest paid amount reported in Note 2. What was the net interest expense reported on the statement of earnings for 2002? Where is the difference between the interest expense and cash paid for interest likely reported?

COMPARATIVE ANALYSIS PROBLEM: *Loblaw and Sobeys*

BYP4-2   The financial statements of Sobeys Inc. are presented in Appendix B, following the financial statements for Loblaw in Appendix A.

Instructions

(a) Identify two accounts on Sobeys' consolidated balance sheet that provide evidence that Sobeys uses accrual accounting. In each case, identify the statement of earnings account that would be affected by the adjustment process.

(b) Identify two accounts on Loblaw's balance sheet that provide evidence that Loblaw uses accrual accounting. In each case, identify the statement of earnings account that would be affected by the adjustment process.

RESEARCH CASE

BYP4-3   Cisco Systems, Inc., is a worldwide leader in networking for the Internet. Since Larry Carter became chief financial officer of Cisco Systems in 1995, Cisco's annual revenues have grown from $1.2 billion to $22.3 billion. The need to successfully manage the rapid growth at Cisco instigated the aggressive goal that Larry set for the company of closing the books within one day on any day. "Knowing exactly where you are all of the time," says Mr. Carter, "allows you to respond faster than your competitors." The June 26, 1999, issue of *The Economist* includes an article entitled "Cisco@Speed."

Instructions

Read the article and answer these questions:

(a) How often does Cisco close its books? How long does it take Cisco to close its books?

(b) How long did the closing process formerly take at Cisco?

(c) What is a "virtual close"? Identify two advantages of the virtual close.

INTERPRETING FINANCIAL STATEMENTS

BYP4-4   Rogers Cable Inc. is Canada's largest cable television service provider. Rogers is also a leading North American provider of high-speed Internet service. Rogers' interim balance sheet included a current liability of $33,961,000 at September 30, 2002, called Unearned Revenue. An excerpt from the notes to the interim financial statements follows:

ROGERS CABLE INC. **Notes to the Interim Financial Statements** **September 30, 2002**
Note 2 (k): Significant accounting policies—Revenue recognition The Company earns revenue from several sources. The principal sources of revenue to the Company and recognition of these revenues for financial statement purposes are as follows: (i) Installation revenues in connection with cable and high-speed Internet services are recorded as revenue to the extent of direct selling costs incurred. (ii) Monthly fees in connection with cable and high-speed Internet services are recorded as revenue on a pro rata basis over the month. (iii) Revenue from pay-per-view movies, video rentals and other transactional sales of products are recorded as revenue as the services or products are provided. Unearned revenue included subscriber deposits and amounts received from subscribers related to services and subscriptions to be provided in future periods.

Instructions

(a) Adjusting entries can be classified as either prepayments or accruals. Is Unearned Revenue an example of a prepayment or an accrual?

(b) When an amount is received from a subscriber for services to be provided in the future, what account would be debited? What account would be credited?

(c) When should the revenue be recognized from the subscriber deposits recorded in the Unearned Revenue account? When revenue is recognized, what account would be debited? What account would be credited? If this journal entry was omitted, what would be the effect on the company's financial position (use the basic accounting equation and explain what elements would be overstated or understated)?

(d) Rogers is following two generally accepted accounting principles with the policy disclosed above. Name the two principles and explain how they relate to each other.

A GLOBAL FOCUS

BYP4-5 Internet Initiative Japan Inc. (IIJ) is one of Japan's leading Internet-access and comprehensive Internet solution providers, mainly targeting high-end corporate customers. In its 2002 annual report it reported the following (in millions of yen).

	2002	2001
Cash	11,046	13,570
Net earnings (loss)	(7,446)	(4,700)
Cash provided (used) by operating activities	1,161	(271)

Instructions

(a) Explain how the company could have reported a net loss in 2002 and yet have a positive cash flow from operating activities in that year.

(b) Explain how the company's cash from operating activities could be 1,161 million yen in 2002, while its cash balance declined by 2,524 million yen from 2001 to 2002.

(c) During 2002, the company's revenues were 39,905 million yen. At the beginning of the year, it had 5,417 million yen of accounts receivable. At the end of the year, it had 8,982 million yen of accounts receivable. Based on this data, determine the amount of cash collected from customers during the year.

FINANCIAL ANALYSIS ON THE WEB

BYP4-6 SEDAR (System for Electronic Document Analysis and Retrieval) provides information about Canadian public companies and access to their documents. In this activity, we will use SEDAR to locate and identify recent corporate filings for Loblaw and Sobeys.

Instructions

Specific requirements of this Web case can be found on the Kimmel website.

Critical Thinking

COLLABORATIVE LEARNING ACTIVITY

BYP4-7 Air Canada sells tickets for airline flights to passengers at a number of differ-ent points of sale. For example, you can purchase a ticket in advance (seat sale fare) that may be non-refundable or include restrictions about making changes; you can purchase a fully refundable full fare ticket up to the time of flight departure; or you can fly standby at the last minute.

Air Canada's management team is brainstorming its options in terms of recognizing the revenue from its ticket sales. One person says they should record the revenue when they advertise the seat sale, because these are such great fares they just know that every seat will be sold. Another states that revenue should be recognized when passengers pick up their tickets and pay for the flight. "What about when the boarding passes are collected at the gate?" a third asks. "Or when passengers arrive at their destinations?" a fourth adds.

Instructions

With the class divided into groups, do the following:
(a) Each group will be assigned, or should choose, one of the above revenue recognition options. Evaluate the effect of the option on recorded revenues, expenses, and net earnings for the period in question.
(b) Briefly review your option and compare it to the other options described in the above case. After doing so, determine the point at which you think Air Canada should rec-ognize the revenue from flight ticket sales. Explain why you believe this point of rev-enue recognition to be the best, referring to relevant generally accepted accounting principles in your answer.

COMMUNICATION ACTIVITY

BYP4-8 There are many people today who believe that cash is a better indicator of a com-pany's future success than net earnings. This notion gained popularity when it was widely reported in a number of corporate financial scandals that management was easily able to manipulate estimates and accruals to influence net earnings.

Instructions

Write a memo discussing whether you believe cash is a more reliable performance measure than net earnings. Include in your memo the answers to the following questions:
(a) What is the difference between accrual-based net earnings and cash?
(b) Do you believe that it is possible for management to manipulate net earnings? If so, identify one way that management might be able to increase net earnings by ma-nipulating estimates or accruals.
(c) Do you believe that it is possible for management to manipulate cash? If so, identify one way that management might be able to increase cash flow.

ETHICS CASE

BYP4-9 Die Hard Corporation is a pesticide manufacturer. Its sales declined greatly this year due to the passage of legislation outlawing the sale of several of Die Hard's chemical pesticides. During the coming year, Die Hard will have environmentally safe and competi-tive chemicals to replace these discontinued products. Sales in the next year are expected to greatly exceed those of any prior year. The decline in this year's sales and profits appears, therefore, to be a one-year aberration.

Even so, the company president believes that a large dip in the current year's profits could cause a significant drop in the market price of Die Hard's shares and make it a takeover target. To avoid this possibility, he urges Carole Denton, controller, to accrue every possi-ble revenue and to defer as many expenses as possible when making this period's year-end adjusting entries. The president says to Carole, "We need the revenues this year, and next year can easily absorb expenses deferred from this year. We can't let our share price be ham-mered down!" Carole didn't get around to recording the adjusting entries until January 17, but she dated the entries December 31, as if they were recorded then. Carole also made every effort to comply with the president's request.

Ethics In
Accounting

Instructions

(a) Who are the stakeholders in this situation?
(b) What are the ethical considerations of the president's request and Carole's dating the adjusting entries December 31?
(c) Can Carole aggressively accrue revenues and defer expenses and still be ethical?

Answers to Self-Study Questions

1. d   2. c   3. a   4. d   5. c   6. a   7. b   8. b   9. c   10. a
11. a   12. b

Answer to Loblaw Review It Question 3

Depreciation Expense, $354 million (see Consolidated Statement of Earnings); Accumulated Depreciation, $2,270 million (see Note 7 in Notes to the Consolidated Financial Statements)

Remember to go back to the Navigator box on the chapter-opening page to check off your completed work.

CHAPTER 5

Merchandising Operations

STUDY OBJECTIVES

After studying this chapter, you should be able to:

1. Identify the differences between a service company and a merchandising company.

2. Explain the recording of purchases under a perpetual inventory system.

3. Explain the recording of sales under a perpetual inventory system.

4. Distinguish between a single-step and a multiple-step statement of earnings.

5. Explain the factors affecting profitability.

6. Explain the recording of purchases and sales under a periodic inventory system (Appendix 5A).

NAVIGATOR

Who Doesn't Shop at Wal-Mart?

Until the twentieth century, the word "consumption" evoked negative images. To be labelled a "consumer" was an insult. In fact, one of the deadliest diseases in history, tuberculosis, was often referred to as "consumption."

Today, however, consumption describes the lifestyle of the Western world in a nutshell. Merchants realized that, in order to prosper, they had to convince people that it was good—even necessary—to buy things that had not previously been considered essential. For example, General Motors began making annual changes to the design of its cars so that people would be discontented with the cars they already owned.

North America was thus the birthplace of consumerism, and has led the world in its devotion to the concept ever since. As North Americans, we consume twice as much today per person as we did at the end of World War II. It appears that we live to shop.

The story of retail shopping in Canada began over three centuries ago with the Hudson's Bay Company. Founded in 1670 to trade European goods for furs in the vast northern territories that would later become part of Canada, it is the oldest commercial organization in the world. Today, Hudson's Bay is Canada's largest department-store chain, accounting for 36% of all domestic department-store sales with its Bay, Zellers, Home Outfitters, and Fields stores.

Another early retail giant in

Canada was the T. Eaton Company, founded in 1869. Timothy Eaton revolutionized a fledgling retail industry with a simple guarantee that was then a new concept: "Goods satisfactory or money refunded." Eaton's expanded its operations to become a well-loved catalogue company, enabling people in rural areas to buy things by mail. For over a century it was a leader in Canadian merchandising and a household name. But in the 1990s Eaton's lost its edge, failing to recognize changes in consumer shopping patterns and tastes. After a decade of losses and unsuccessful restructuring attempts, Eaton's closed its doors in 1999.

Sears, another company that grew up on its catalogue business, joined the Canadian landscape in 1953 and continues to be a major retailer of general

Wal-Mart www.walmart.com

THE NAVIGATOR

Scan *Study Objectives* □

Read *Feature Story* □

Read *Chapter Preview* □

Read text and answer *Before You Go On*
p. 221 □ p. 224 □ p. 229 □ p. 232 □

Work *Using the Decision Toolkit* □

Review *Summary of Study Objectives*
and *Decision Toolkit* □

Work *Demonstration Problem* □

Answer *Self-Study Questions* □

Complete assignments □

merchandise in Canada. More than 4.5 million households receive the Sears Canada catalogue. The company, which acquired the assets of Eaton's in 2000, had revenues of over $6.5-billion in 2002.

However, the undisputed king of the Canadian shopping cart today is the U.S.-based discount chain Wal-Mart, which is larger than Hudson's Bay and Sears combined. Wal-Mart opened its first store in the United States in 1962. In 1970, it had 38 stores and sales of U.S.$44 million. In 1994, Wal-Mart entered Canada, acquiring 122 former Woolco stores and providing serious competition to Hudson's Bay and Sears. Today, it has 201 stores across the country, and is the number one retailer in Canada.

Wal-Mart also has operations in Mexico, South America, Asia, Japan, China, and Europe. It is the undisputed number one retailer in the world, with worldwide sales of U.S.$218 billion in 2002 from 4,570 Wal-Marts, Sam's Club warehouse stores, Wal-Mart Supercenters, and Neighborhood Markets.

Wal-Mart has grown rapidly in recent years, with average annual increases in sales of 20%, and increases in earnings of 15%, over the last decade. One key contributor to this success has been an amazing system of inventory control and distribution. Wal-Mart has a management information system that employs six satellite channels. Its computer system receives 8.4 million updates every minute on the items that customers take home and the relationship among the items in each basket. The result is an enormous database of purchasing information which is transmitted by computer to its accounting systems. This enables Wal-Mart to keep its shelves stocked with exactly what customers want, while still keeping its inventory under tight control.

In 1998, Wal-Mart brought its huge selection and rock-bottom prices on-line. It now sells 80,000 products on-line—about the same number as are stocked in an average Wal-Mart store. Internet retailing has opened up a whole new way for people to meet their basic—and not-so-basic—needs. According to a Léger Marketing survey carried out in 2002, 16% of Internet users in Canada now shop on-line. In the U.S., where the concept has been more warmly embraced, the figure has already reached 32%.

NAVIGATOR

213

Hudson's Bay, Sears, and Wal-Mart are called merchandising companies because they buy and sell merchandise (rather than perform services) as their primary source of revenue. Merchandising companies that purchase and sell directly to consumers are called **retailers**. Merchandising companies that sell to retailers are known as **wholesalers**. For example, retailer Sears might buy toys from Valley Trading Company, a Canadian hobby and toy wholesaler.

As merchandising is one of the largest and most influential industries in Canada, understanding the financial statements of these companies is important. In this chapter, you will learn the basics about reporting merchandising transactions. In addition, you will learn how to prepare and analyse a commonly used form of the statement of earnings—the multiple-step statement of earnings. The content and organization of the chapter are as follows:

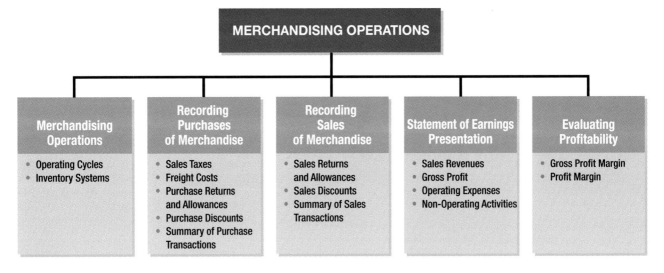

MERCHANDISING OPERATIONS				
Merchandising Operations	**Recording Purchases of Merchandise**	**Recording Sales of Merchandise**	**Statement of Earnings Presentation**	**Evaluating Profitability**
• Operating Cycles • Inventory Systems	• Sales Taxes • Freight Costs • Purchase Returns and Allowances • Purchase Discounts • Summary of Purchase Transactions	• Sales Returns and Allowances • Sales Discounts • Summary of Sales Transactions	• Sales Revenues • Gross Profit • Operating Expenses • Non-Operating Activities	• Gross Profit Margin • Profit Margin

NAVIGATOR

Merchandising Operations

STUDY OBJECTIVE

1

Identify the differences between a service company and a merchandising company.

The primary source of revenue for merchandising companies is the sale of merchandise, often referred to simply as sales revenue or **sales**. Expenses for a merchandising company are divided into two categories: the cost of goods sold and operating expenses.

The cost of goods sold is the total cost of merchandise sold during the period. This expense is directly related to the revenue recognized from the sale of goods. Sales revenue less cost of goods sold is called gross profit. After gross profit is calculated, operating expenses are deducted to determine net earnings (or net loss). Operating expenses are expenses that are incurred in the process of earning sales revenue.

The earnings measurement process for a merchandising company is shown in Illustration 5-1. The items in the two blue boxes are unique to a merchandising company; they are not used by a service company.

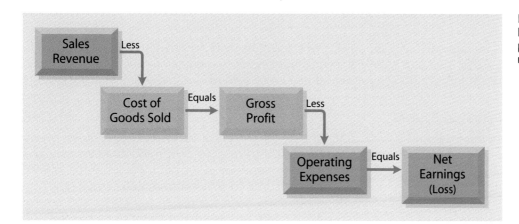

Illustration 5-1
Earnings measurement process for a merchandising company

OPERATING CYCLES

The operating cycle—the time it takes to go from cash to cash in producing revenues—of a merchandising company is usually longer than that of a service company. The purchase of merchandise inventory and the lapse of time until it is sold lengthen the cycle. The operating cycles of service and merchandising companies can be contrasted as shown in Illustration 5-2. Note that the added asset account for a merchandising company is the Merchandise Inventory account.

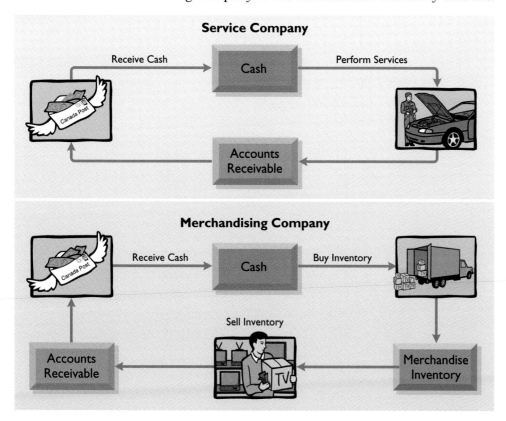

Illustration 5-2
Operating cycles for a service company and a merchandising company

INVENTORY SYSTEMS

A merchandising company keeps track of its inventory to determine what is available for sale and what has been sold. One of two kinds of systems is used to account for inventory: a **perpetual inventory system** or a **periodic inventory system**.

Perpetual System

In a perpetual inventory system, detailed records of the cost of each inventory purchase and sale are maintained. These records continuously—perpetually—show the inventory that should be on hand for every item. For example, a Ford dealership has separate inventory records for each automobile, truck, and van on its lot and showroom floor. Similarly, with the use of bar codes and optical scanners, a grocery store can keep a running record of every box of cereal and every jar of peanut butter that it buys and sells. Under a perpetual inventory system, the cost of goods sold is **determined each time a sale occurs**.

Periodic System

In a periodic inventory system, detailed inventory records of the goods on hand are not kept throughout the period. The cost of goods sold is **determined only at the end of the accounting period**—that is, periodically—when a physical inventory count is taken to determine the cost of goods on hand. To determine the cost of goods sold under a periodic inventory system, the following steps are necessary: (1) Determine the cost of goods on hand at the beginning of the accounting period. (2) Add to it the cost of goods purchased. (3) Subtract the cost of goods on hand at the end of the accounting period.

Illustration 5-3 compares the sequence of activities and the timing of the cost of goods sold calculation under the two inventory systems.

Illustration 5-3
Comparing periodic and perpetual inventory systems

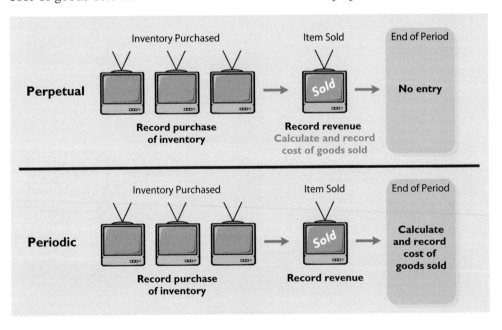

Helpful Hint For control purposes, a physical inventory count is also taken under the perpetual system to determine any discrepancies between the recorded inventory amount and that which is actually on hand.

Additional Considerations

A perpetual inventory system provides better control over inventories than a periodic system. Since the inventory records show the quantities that should be on hand, the goods can be counted at any time to see whether they actually exist. Any shortages uncovered can be investigated immediately. Although a perpetual inventory system requires additional clerical work and additional cost to maintain the subsidiary records, a computerized system can minimize this cost. As noted in the feature story, much of Wal-Mart's success is thanks to its sophisticated inventory system.

Some businesses find it either unnecessary or too expensive to invest in a perpetual inventory system. Many small merchandising businesses, in particular, find that a perpetual inventory system costs more than it is worth. By using a periodic inventory system, managers of these businesses can still control their merchandise and manage day-to-day operations without detailed inventory records. Periodically, they count their merchandise to determine quantities on hand and establish costs for accounting purposes.

Because the perpetual inventory system is the most widely used, we illustrate it in this chapter. The journal entries for the periodic system are described in the appendix to this chapter.

BUSINESS INSIGHT

INVESTOR PERSPECTIVE

Investors are often eager to invest in a company that has a hot new product. However, when snowboard maker Morrow Snowboards, Inc., issued shares to the public for the first time, some investors expressed reluctance to invest in Morrow because of a number of internal control problems. To reduce investor concerns, Morrow implemented a perpetual inventory system to improve its control over inventory. In addition, it stated that it would perform a physical inventory count every quarter to ensure that the perpetual inventory system was reliable.

Recording Purchases of Merchandise

Purchases of inventory may be made for cash or on account (credit). Purchases are normally recorded when the goods are received from the seller. Every purchase should be supported by a business document that provides written evidence of the transaction. Each cash purchase should be supported by a cash register receipt indicating the items purchased and amounts paid. Cash purchases are recorded by an increase in Merchandise Inventory and a decrease in Cash.

Each credit purchase should be supported by a purchase invoice that indicates the total purchase price and other relevant information. However, the purchaser does not prepare a separate purchase invoice. Instead, the copy of the sales invoice sent by the seller is used by the buyer as a purchase invoice. In Illustration 5-4 on the following page, for example, the sales invoice prepared by PW Audio Supply, Inc. (the seller) is used as a purchase invoice by Sauk Stereo Ltd. (the buyer).

STUDY OBJECTIVE

2

Explain the recording of purchases under a perpetual inventory system.

Illustration 5-4
Sales invoice used as purchase invoice by Sauk Stereo

Helpful Hint To better understand the contents of this invoice, identify these items:
1. Seller
2. Invoice date
3. Purchaser
4. Salesperson
5. Credit terms
6. Freight terms
7. Goods sold: catalogue number, description, quantity, price per unit
8. Total invoice amount

INVOICE NO. 731

PW Audio Supply, Inc.

277 Wellington Street, West
Toronto, Ontario, M5V 3H2

SOLD TO

Firm Name ___Sauk Stereo Ltd.___

Attention of ___James Hoover, Purchasing Agent___

Address ___21 King Street, West___

Hamilton	Ontario	L8P 4W7
City	Province	Postal Code

Date: May 4, 2004	Salesperson: Malone	Terms 2/10, n/30	Freight Paid by Buyer

Catalogue No.	Description	Quantity	Price	Amount
X572Y9820	Printed Circuit Board-prototype	1	2,300	$2,300
A2547Z45	Production Model Circuits	5	300	1,500

IMPORTANT: ALL RETURNS MUST BE MADE WITHIN 10 DAYS	**TOTAL**	$3,800

The entry for Sauk Stereo to record the purchase of merchandise from PW Audio Supply is:

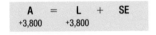

Cash flows: no effect

May	4	Merchandise Inventory	3,800	
		Accounts Payable		3,800
		(To record goods purchased on account per invoice #731, terms 2/10, n/30)		

Under the perpetual inventory system, purchases of merchandise for sale are recorded in the Merchandise Inventory account. Thus, Wal-Mart Canada would increase (debit) Merchandise Inventory for clothing, sporting goods, groceries, and anything else purchased for resale to customers. Not all purchases are debited to Merchandise Inventory, however. Purchases of assets acquired for use and not for resale, such as supplies and equipment, are recorded as increases to specific asset accounts rather than to Merchandise Inventory. For example, Wal-Mart would increase Supplies to record the purchase of materials used to make shelf signs or for cash register receipt paper.

SALES TAXES

Sales taxes are collected by most service and merchandising companies on the services they provide and the goods they sell. Sales taxes in Canada include the Goods and Services Tax (GST) and the Provincial Sales Tax (PST). The federal GST is assessed at a rate of 7% across Canada. Provincial sales tax rates vary throughout the provinces and territories. In the Atlantic provinces (except for P.E.I.), GST and PST have been combined into one 15% tax, called the Harmonized Sales Tax (HST).

Although a company collects these sales taxes when it makes a sale, sales taxes are not revenue to the company. These monies are collected on behalf of the federal and provincial governments and must be periodically remitted to the

Receiver General, their collecting authority. Until then, they are a current liability of the company.

Sales taxes add much complexity to the accounting process. In addition, not all companies and their goods and services are taxable. Accounting transactions described in this and other chapters are therefore presented without the added complication of sales taxes. That is why Invoice No. 731 in Illustration 5-4 omitted sales taxes, which would normally be added to the invoice price.

FREIGHT COSTS

The accounting treatment of freight costs depend on whether they've been incurred by the buyer or the seller.

Freight Costs Incurred by Buyer

The sales invoice indicates whether the seller or the buyer pays the cost of transporting the goods to the buyer's place of business. When the buyer pays the transportation costs, these costs are considered part of the cost of purchasing inventory. As a result, the account Merchandise Inventory is increased. For example, if upon delivery of the goods on May 4, Sauk Stereo (the buyer) pays Acme Freight Company $150 for freight charges, the entry on Sauk's books is:

May 4	Merchandise Inventory	150	
	Cash		150
	(To record payment of freight on goods purchased)		

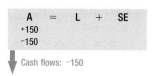

Freight Costs Incurred by Seller

In contrast, **freight costs incurred by the seller on outgoing merchandise are an operating expense to the seller.** These costs increase an expense account titled Freight-Out or Delivery Expense. For example, if the freight terms on the invoice in Illustration 5-4 had required that PW Audio Supply (the seller) pay the $150 freight charges, the entry by PW Audio would have been:

May 4	Freight-Out	150	
	Cash		150
	(To record payment of freight on goods sold)		

When the freight charges are paid by the seller, the seller will usually charge a higher invoice price for the goods to cover the expense of shipping.

PURCHASE RETURNS AND ALLOWANCES

A purchaser may be dissatisfied with the merchandise received because the goods are damaged or defective, of inferior quality, or do not meet the purchaser's specifications. In such cases, the purchaser may return the goods to the seller for credit if the purchase was made on credit, or for a cash refund if the purchase was for cash. This transaction is known as a purchase return. Alternatively, the purchaser may choose to keep the merchandise if the seller is willing to grant an allowance (deduction) from the purchase price. This transaction is known as a purchase allowance.

Assume that Sauk Stereo returned goods costing $300 to PW Audio Supply on May 8. The entry by Sauk Stereo for the returned merchandise is:

A	=	L	+	SE
-300		-300		

Cash flows: no effect

May 8	Accounts Payable		300	
	Merchandise Inventory			300
	(To record return of goods to PW Audio Supply)			

Because Sauk Stereo increased Merchandise Inventory when the goods were received, Merchandise Inventory is decreased when it returns the goods.

PURCHASE DISCOUNTS

The credit terms of a purchase on account may permit the buyer to claim a cash discount for fast payment. The buyer calls this cash discount a purchase discount. This incentive offers advantages to both parties: the purchaser saves money, and the seller is able to shorten the operating cycle by converting accounts receivable into cash earlier.

Helpful Hint So as not to miss purchase discounts, unpaid invoices should be filed by due dates. This procedure helps the purchaser remember the discount date, prevents early payment of bills, and maximizes the time that cash can be used for other purposes.

The **credit terms** specify the amount of the cash discount and the time period during which it is offered. They also indicate the date by which the purchaser is expected to pay the full invoice price. In the sales invoice in Illustration 5-4, credit terms are 2/10, n/30, which is read "two-ten, net thirty." This means that a 2% cash discount may be taken on the invoice price, less ("net of") any returns or allowances, if payment is made within 10 days of the invoice date (the **discount period**). Otherwise, the invoice price, less any returns or allowances, is due 30 days from the invoice date.

When the seller chooses not to offer a cash discount for fast payment, credit terms will specify only the maximum time period for paying the balance due. For example, the time period may be stated as n/30, meaning that the net amount must be paid in 30 days.

When an invoice is paid within the discount period, the amount of the discount decreases Merchandise Inventory because inventory is recorded at its cost. By paying within the discount period, the merchandiser has reduced its cost. To illustrate, assume Sauk Stereo pays the balance due of $3,500 (gross invoice price of $3,800 less purchase returns and allowances of $300) on May 14, the last day of the discount period. The cash discount is $70 ($3,500 × 2%), and the amount of cash paid by Sauk Stereo is $3,430 ($3,500 − $70). The entry to record the May 14 payment by Sauk Stereo is:

A	=	L	+	SE
-3,430		-3,500		
-70				

Cash flows: -3,430

May 14	Accounts Payable		3,500	
	Cash			3,430
	Merchandise Inventory			70
	(To record payment to PW Audio Supply within discount period)			

If Sauk Stereo fails to take the discount and instead makes full payment of $3,500 on June 3, Sauk's entry is:

A	=	L	+	SE
-3,500		-3,500		

Cash flows: -3,500

June 3	Accounts Payable		3,500	
	Cash			3,500
	(To record payment to PW Audio Supply with no discount taken)			

A merchandising company should usually take all available discounts. Passing up the discount may be viewed as paying interest for use of the money. For example, if Sauk Stereo passed up the discount, it would be paying 2% for the use of $3,500 for 20 days. This is the equivalent of an annual interest rate of 36.5% (2% × 365/20). Obviously, it would be better for Sauk Stereo to borrow at bank interest rates than to lose the discount.

SUMMARY OF PURCHASE TRANSACTIONS

A summary of the effect of the previous transactions on Merchandise Inventory is provided in the following T account (with transaction descriptions in parentheses). Sauk originally purchased $3,800 worth of inventory for resale. It paid $150 in freight charges. It then returned $300 worth of goods. Finally, it received a $70 discount off the balance owed because it paid within the discount period. This results in a balance in Merchandise Inventory of $3,580.

	Merchandise Inventory				
(Purchase)	May 4	3,800	May 8	300	(Purchase return)
(Freight-in)	4	150	14	70	(Purchase discount)
	Bal.	3,580			

BEFORE YOU GO ON . . .

● **REVIEW IT**

1. How does the measurement of net earnings in a merchandising company differ from its measurement in a service enterprise?
2. How does a perpetual inventory system differ from a periodic system?
3. Under the perpetual inventory system, what entries are made to record purchases, freight costs, purchase returns and allowances, and purchase discounts?

Recording Sales of Merchandise

Sales revenues, like service revenues, are recorded when earned in order to comply with the revenue recognition principle. Typically, sales revenues are earned when the goods are transferred from the seller to the buyer. At this point the sales transaction is completed and the sales price is established.

Sales may be made on credit or for cash. Every sales transaction should be supported by a business document that provides written evidence of the sale. Cash register tapes provide evidence of cash sales. A sales invoice, like the one that was shown in Illustration 5-4, provides support for a credit sale. The original copy of the invoice goes to the customer, and a copy is kept by the seller for use in recording the sale.

Two entries are made for each sale: (1) Accounts Receivable or Cash is increased and Sales is increased. (2) Cost of Goods Sold is increased and Merchandise Inventory is decreased. As a result, the Merchandise Inventory account will show at all times the amount of inventory that should be on hand.

To illustrate a credit sales transaction, PW Audio Supply's sale of $3,800 worth of goods on May 4 to Sauk Stereo is recorded as follows (assume the merchandise cost PW Audio Supply $2,400):

STUDY OBJECTIVE
③
Explain the recording of sales under a perpetual inventory system.

May 4	Accounts Receivable	3,800	
	Sales		3,800
	(To record credit sale to Sauk Stereo per invoice #731)		

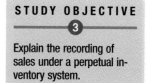

Cash flows: no effect

A	=	L	+	SE		May	4	Cost of Goods Sold	2,400	
−2,400				−2,400				Merchandise Inventory		2,400
								(To record cost of merchandise sold on		
Cash flows: no effect								invoice #731 to Sauk Stereo)		

For internal decision-making purposes, merchandising companies may use more than one sales account. For example, PW Audio Supply may decide to keep separate sales accounts for its sales of TV sets, DVD players, and microwave ovens. By using separate sales accounts for major product lines, rather than a single combined sales account, company management can monitor sales trends more closely and respond in a more strategic fashion to changes in sales patterns. For example, if TV sales are increasing while microwave oven sales are decreasing, the company should re-evaluate both its advertising and pricing policies on each of these items to ensure that they are optimal.

On its statement of earnings presented to outside investors, a merchandising company would normally provide only a single sales figure—the sum of all of its individual sales accounts. This is done for two reasons. First, providing detail on all of its individual sales accounts would add considerable length to its statement of earnings. Second, companies do not want their competitors to know the details of their operating results. Sometimes, however, companies go against this norm. Microsoft decided to expand the number of different types of revenue that it discloses in its statement of earnings from three to five in 2000. This disclosure enables users to better evaluate the growth of its consumer and Internet businesses.

SALES RETURNS AND ALLOWANCES

We now look at the "flip side" of purchase returns and allowances, which are recorded as sales returns and allowances on the books of the seller. PW Audio Supply's entries to record credits for returned goods involve (1) an increase in Sales Returns and Allowances and a decrease in Accounts Receivable at the $300 selling price, and (2) an increase in Merchandise Inventory (assume a $140 cost) and a decrease in Cost of Goods Sold. This second entry assumes that the merchandise is not damaged and is resaleable. Otherwise, a loss account would be debited rather than an inventory account.

A	=	L	+	SE		May	8	Sales Returns and Allowances	300	
−300				−300				Accounts Receivable		300
								(To record return of goods by Sauk Stereo)		
Cash flows: no effect										

A	=	L	+	SE		May	8	Merchandise Inventory	140	
+140				+140				Cost of Goods Sold		140
								(To record cost of merchandise returned		
Cash flows: no effect								by Sauk Stereo)		

Helpful Hint Remember that the increases, decreases, and normal balances of contra accounts are the opposite of the accounts they correspond to.

Sales Returns and Allowances is a contra revenue account to Sales. The normal balance of Sales Returns and Allowances is a debit. A contra account is used, instead of debiting Sales, to disclose in the accounts and in the statement of earnings the amount of sales returns and allowances. Disclosure of this information is important to management: excessive returns and allowances suggest problems—inferior merchandise, inefficiencies in filling orders, errors in billing customers, or mistakes in the delivery or shipment of goods. Moreover, a decrease (debit) recorded directly to Sales would obscure the relative importance of sales returns and allowances as a percentage of sales. It could also distort comparisons between total sales in different accounting periods.

SALES DISCOUNTS

As mentioned in our discussion of purchase transactions, the seller may offer the customer a cash discount—called a sales discount by the seller—for quick payment of the balance due. Like a purchase discount, a sales discount is based on the invoice price less returns and allowances, if any. The Sales Discounts account is increased (debited) for discounts that are taken. The entry by PW Audio Supply to record the cash receipt on May 14 from Sauk Stereo within the discount period is:

May 14	Cash	3,430	
	Sales Discounts	70	
	Accounts Receivable		3,500
	(To record collection from Sauk Stereo within		
	2/10, n/30 discount period)		

A	=	L	+	SE
+3,430				−70
−3,500				

Cash flows: +3,430

Like Sales Returns and Allowances, Sales Discounts is a **contra revenue account** to Sales. Its normal balance is a debit. This account is used, instead of debiting Sales, to disclose the amount of cash discounts taken by customers. If the discount is not taken, PW Audio Supply increases Cash by $3,500 and decreases Accounts Receivable by the same amount at the date of collection.

SUMMARY OF SALES TRANSACTIONS

A summary of the effect of the previous transactions on Sales, and its contra accounts, is provided in the following T accounts. PW Audio Supply sold merchandise for $3,800, with $300 of it later returned. A sales discount of $70 was granted when the invoice was paid within the discount period. In contrast to the purchase transactions illustrated on p. 221, which affected only one account, Merchandise Inventory, sales transactions are recorded in different accounts.

Sales		Sales Returns and Allowances	
	May 4 3,800	May 8 300	

Sales Discounts	
May 14 70	

BEFORE YOU GO ON . . .

- **REVIEW IT**
  1. Under a perpetual inventory system, what are the two entries that must be recorded for each sale?
  2. Why is it important to use the Sales Returns and Allowances account, rather than simply reduce the Sales account, when goods are returned?

- **DO IT**

On September 5, Guerette Corp. buys merchandise on account from Lalonde Ltd. The selling price of the goods is $1,500, and the cost to Lalonde was $800. On September 8, goods with a selling price of $300 and a cost of $140 are returned and restored to inventory. Record the transaction on the books of both companies.

Action Plan

- Buyer: Record purchases of inventory at cost. Reduce the Merchandise Inventory account for returned goods.
- Seller: Record two entries for the sale and return of goods: (1) record the selling price and (2) record the cost of the sale. Record the selling price of returns in a contra account, Sales Returns and Allowances.

Solution

Guerette Corp. (Buyer)

Sept. 5	Merchandise Inventory		1,500	
	Accounts Payable			1,500
	(To record goods purchased on account)			
8	Accounts Payable		300	
	Merchandise Inventory			300
	(To record return of goods)			

Lalonde Ltd. (Seller)

Sept. 5	Accounts Receivable		1,500	
	Sales			1,500
	(To record credit sale)			
5	Cost of Goods Sold		800	
	Merchandise Inventory			800
	(To record cost of goods sold)			
8	Sales Returns and Allowances		300	
	Accounts Receivable			300
	(To record credit granted for receipt of returned goods)			
8	Merchandise Inventory		140	
	Cost of Goods Sold			140
	(To record cost of goods returned)			

Statement of Earnings Presentation

Two forms of the statement of earnings are widely used by companies. One is the **single-step statement of earnings**. The statement is called this because only one step—subtracting total expenses from total revenues—is required in determining net earnings (or net loss). In a single-step statement, all data are classified into two categories: (1) **revenues**, which include both operating revenues and non-operating revenues (for example, interest revenue and a gain on sale of equipment); and (2) **expenses**, which include cost of goods sold, operating expenses, and non-operating expenses (for example, interest expense and a loss on the sale of equipment). Sometimes income tax expense is listed with the expenses, but more often it is disclosed separately. A condensed single-step statement for Leon's Furniture is shown in Illustration 5-5.

STUDY OBJECTIVE

④

Distinguish between a single-step and a multiple-step statement of earnings.

LEON'S FURNITURE Statement of Income Year Ended December 31, 2002 (in thousands)	
Revenues	
Sales	$449,693
Interest income	2,650
Other income	10,727
Total revenues	463,070
Expenses	
Cost of sales	261,265
Salaries and commissions	66,610
Advertising	27,306
Other operating expenses	25,807
Amortization	8,552
Rent and property taxes	7,316
Employee profit-sharing plan	2,483
Total expenses	399,339
Income before income taxes	63,731
Income tax expense	25,211
Net income	$ 38,520

Illustration 5-5
Single-step statement of earnings

Alternative Terminology Note that Leon's *statement of earnings* is entitled *Statement of Income.*

The single-step statement of earnings is the form we have used in the text so far. There are two main reasons for using the single-step form: (1) a company does not realize any type of profit or earnings until total revenues exceed total expenses, so it makes sense to divide the statement into these two categories; and (2) the single-step form is simple and easy to read.

A second form of the statement of earnings is the **multiple-step statement of earnings**. The multiple-step statement is often considered more useful because it highlights the components of net earnings. Leon's statement of earnings in Illustration 5-6 is an example.

Illustration 5-6
Multiple-step statement
of earnings

LEON'S FURNITURE Statement of Income Year Ended December 31, 2002 (in thousands)	
Sales	$449,693
Cost of sales	261,265
Gross profit	188,428
Operating expenses	
Salaries and commissions	66,610
Advertising	27,306
Other operating expenses	25,807
Amortization	8,552
Rent and property taxes	7,316
Employee profit-sharing plan	2,483
Total operating expenses	138,074
Income from operations	50,354
Other revenues	
Interest income	2,650
Other income	10,727
Total other revenues	13,377
Income before income taxes	63,731
Income tax expense	25,211
Net income	$ 38,520

The multiple-step statement of earnings (or income, as is the case with Leon's) has three important line items: **gross profit**, **earnings (income) from operations**, and **net earnings (income)**. They are determined as follows:

1. Cost of goods sold is subtracted from sales to determine gross profit.
2. Operating expenses are deducted from gross profit to determine earnings (income) from operations.
3. The results of activities not related to operations are added (other revenue) or subtracted (other expenses) to determine net earnings (income).

You should note that income tax expense is reported in a separate section of the statement of earnings (income) before net earnings. The following discussion provides more information about the components of a multiple-step statement of earnings.

SALES REVENUES

The statement of earnings for a merchandising company typically presents gross sales revenues for the period and provides details about deductions from that total amount. As contra revenue accounts, Sales Returns and Allowances, and Sales Discounts are deducted from Sales in the statement of earnings to arrive at net sales. The sales revenues section of the statement of earnings for PW Audio Supply is as follows:

Sales revenues		
Sales		$480,000
Less: Sales returns and allowances	$12,000	
Sales discounts	8,000	20,000
Net sales		460,000

GROSS PROFIT

Cost of goods sold is deducted from sales revenue to determine **gross profit**. As shown in Illustration 5-6, Leon's had a gross profit of $188,428 thousand in 2002. The sales revenue used for this calculation is **net sales**, which takes into account sales returns and allowances and sales discounts. On the basis of the sales data presented above (net sales of $460,000) and the cost of goods sold (assume a balance of $316,000), the gross profit for PW Audio Supply is $144,000, calculated as follows:

Alternative Terminology
Gross profit is sometimes referred to as *gross margin*.

Net sales	$460,000
Cost of goods sold	316,000
Gross profit	144,000

It is important to understand what gross profit is—and what it is not. Gross profit represents the **merchandising profit** of a company. It is *not* a measure of the overall profit of a company, because operating expenses have not been deducted. Nevertheless, the amount and trend of gross profit are closely watched by management and other interested parties. Comparisons of current gross profit with past amounts and rates, and with those in the industry, indicate the effectiveness of a company's purchasing and pricing policies.

OPERATING EXPENSES

Operating expenses are the next component in measuring net earnings for a merchandising company. At Leon's, operating expenses were $138,074 thousand in 2002. These expenses are similar in merchandising and service companies. At PW Audio Supply, operating expenses were $114,000. The firm's earnings from operations are calculated by subtracting operating expenses from gross profit. Thus, earnings from operations are $30,000, as shown below:

Gross profit	$144,000
Operating expenses	114,000
Earnings from operations	30,000

Sometimes operating expenses are subdivided into selling expenses and administrative expenses. **Selling expenses** are those associated with making sales. They include advertising expenses as well as the expenses of completing the sale, such as delivery and shipping expenses. **Administrative expenses** relate to general operating activities such as management, accounting, and legal.

NON-OPERATING ACTIVITIES

Non-operating activities consist of various revenues and expenses that are unrelated to the company's primary operations. When non-operating items are included, the label "Earnings from operations" precedes them. This clearly identifies the results of the company's normal operations, an amount determined by subtracting cost of goods sold and operating expenses from net sales. The results of non-operating activities are shown in **other revenues** and **other expenses**. Examples of each are listed in Illustration 5-7.

Illustration 5-7
Items reported in
non-operating sections

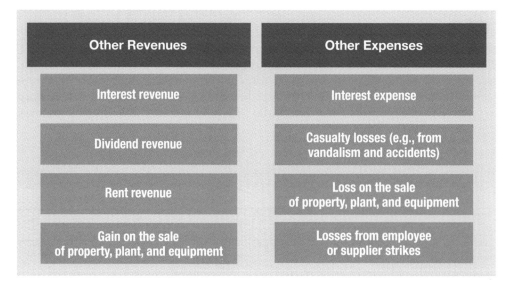

The distinction between operating and non-operating activities is crucial to many external users of financial data. Earnings from operations are viewed as sustainable and therefore long-term, and non-operating activities are viewed as non-recurring and therefore short-term.

BUSINESS INSIGHT

ETHICS PERSPECTIVE

After Enron, many companies were forced by increased investor criticism and regulator scrutiny to improve the clarity of their financial disclosures.

For example, IBM announced that it would begin providing more detail regarding its non-operating activities. It had previously included these items in its operating expenses, with little disclosure.

Disclosing other revenues and expenses in a separate line item on the statement of earnings won't have any effect on bottom-line earnings. However, analysts complained that burying these details in operating expenses reduced their ability to fully understand how well IBM was performing. For example, previously if IBM sold off one of its buildings at a gain, it would include this gain in the selling, general, and administrative expense line item, thus reducing that expense. This made it appear that the company had done a better job of controlling operating expenses than it actually had.

The non-operating activities are reported in the statement of earnings immediately after the operating activities. Included among these activities in Illustration 5-6 for Leon's is revenue earned from interest and other sources of $13,377 thousand in 2002. After adding the earnings (or income) from operations to non-operating revenues and then deducting income tax expense, the amount remaining is Leon's net earnings of $38,520 thousand. Note that the net earnings (income) in Illustrations 5-5 and 5-6 are the same. The differences between the two statements of earnings are the amount of detail displayed and the order of presentation.

In Illustration 5-8, we have provided the multiple-step statement of earnings for PW Audio supply, using assumed data. This statement provides more detail than that of Leon's.

Illustration 5-8
Multiple-step statement of earnings

PW AUDIO SUPPLY, INC.
Statement of Earnings
Year Ended December 31, 2004

Calculation of gross profit	Sales revenues		
	Sales		$480,000
	Less: Sales returns and allowances	$12,000	
	Sales discounts	8,000	20,000
	Net sales		460,000
	Cost of goods sold		316,000
	Gross profit		144,000
Calculation of earnings from operations	Operating expenses		
	Store salaries expense	$45,000	
	Administrative salaries expense	19,000	
	Utilities expense	17,000	
	Advertising expense	16,000	
	Amortization expense—store equipment	8,000	
	Freight-out	7,000	
	Insurance expense	2,000	
	Total operating expenses		114,000
	Earnings from operations		30,000
Calculation of activities not related to operations	Other revenues		
	Interest revenue	$ 3,000	
	Gain on sale of equipment	600	
		3,600	
	Other expenses		
	Interest expense	$ 1,800	
	Casualty loss from vandalism	200	
		2,000	1,600
	Earnings before income taxes		31,600
	Income tax expense		10,100
	Net earnings		$ 21,500

Helpful Hint Note the distinction between earnings from operations and the final figure on the statement of earnings, net earnings. Which figure should you use to assess the future profitability of the company?

BEFORE YOU GO ON . . .

● **REVIEW IT**

1. How are sales and contra revenue accounts reported in the statement of earnings?
2. What is the significance of gross profit?
3. Does Loblaw use a single-step or multiple-step statement of earnings? The answer to this question is provided at the end of the chapter.

Evaluating Profitability

GROSS PROFIT MARGIN

A company's gross profit may be expressed as a **percentage** by dividing the amount of gross profit by net sales; this is called the gross profit margin. For PW Audio Supply, the gross profit margin is 31.3% ($144,000 ÷ $460,000). The gross profit

STUDY OBJECTIVE
5

Explain the factors affecting profitability.

margin is generally considered more informative than the gross profit *amount*, because it expresses a more meaningful relationship between gross profit and net sales. For example, a gross profit amount of $1,000,000 may sound impressive. But if it is the result of sales of $100,000,000, the company's gross profit margin is only 1%. Illustration 5-9 presents gross profit margins for a variety of industries.

Illustration 5-9
Gross profit margin by industry

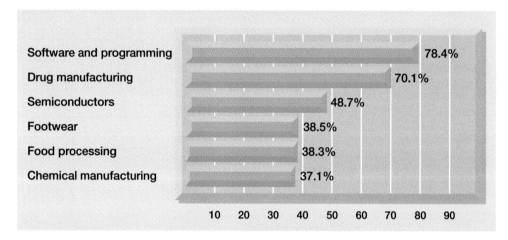

A decline in a company's gross profit margin might have several causes. The company may have begun to sell products with a lower "markup"—for example, budget blue jeans versus designer blue jeans. Increased competition may have resulted in a lower selling price. Or the company may be forced to pay higher prices to its suppliers without being able to pass these costs on to its customers. The gross profit margin for Leon's Furniture is presented in Illustration 5-10.

Illustration 5-10
Gross profit margin

$$\text{GROSS PROFIT MARGIN} = \frac{\text{GROSS PROFIT}}{\text{NET SALES}}$$

(in thousands)	2002	2001
Leon's Furniture	$\dfrac{\$188,428}{\$449,693} = 41.9\%$	$\dfrac{\$177,242}{\$425,687} = 41.6\%$
Industry Average	36.1%	35.9%

Leon's Funiture's gross profit margin improved marginally in 2002, and continued to exceed the industry average. Leon's attributes some of its success to its "pinpoint inventory accuracy." It takes particular pride in its product shipping and receiving efficiency.

Normally, we would compare Leon's gross profit margin to that of its nearest competitor, Sears Canada, which is the largest furniture and major appliance retailer in Canada. However, Sears, like many companies, does not report gross profit separately on its statement of earnings. Rather, it combines cost of merchandise sold with its operating, administrative, and selling expenses for reporting purposes. Gross profit is considered sensitive information that some companies do not wish to make available to their competitors. In fact, only about 15% of companies in Canada report a separate cost of goods sold figure on their statement of earnings. Even if we had been able to calculate Sears' gross profit margin, it would not have provided a meaningful comparison to Leon's Furniture as Sears' margin would have included all of its operations, not just its furniture and appliance sales. Companies often calculate and compare gross profit on each of their product lines, but this information is usually only reported internally.

Decision Toolkit

DECISION CHECKPOINTS	INFO NEEDED FOR DECISION	TOOL TO USE FOR DECISION	HOW TO EVALUATE RESULTS
Is the price of goods keeping pace with changes in the cost of inventory?	Gross profit and net sales	$\text{Gross profit margin} = \dfrac{\text{Gross profit}}{\text{Net sales}}$	A higher ratio suggests the average margin between the selling price and inventory cost is increasing. Too high a margin may result in lost sales.

PROFIT MARGIN

The profit margin ratio measures the percentage of each dollar of sales that results in net earnings. It is calculated by dividing net earnings by net sales (revenue) for the period.

How do the gross profit margin and profit margin differ? The gross profit margin measures the amount by which the selling price exceeds the cost of goods sold. The profit margin measures the extent by which the selling price covers *all expenses* (including the cost of goods sold). A company can improve its profit margin by increasing its gross profit margin or by controlling its operating expenses (or by doing both).

Profit margins vary across industries. Businesses with a high turnover of inventory, such as grocery stores (e.g., Loblaw), generally experience low profit margins. Low-turnover businesses, such as jewellery stores (e.g., Birks), have high profit margins. Profit margins from a variety of industries are provided in Illustration 5-11.

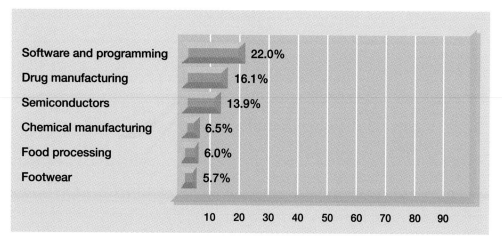

Illustration 5-11
Profit margin by industry

Profit margins for Leon's and Sears, and the industry average, are presented in Illustration 5-12.

Illustration 5-12
Profit margin

PROFIT MARGIN = $\dfrac{\text{NET EARNINGS}}{\text{NET SALES}}$		
(in thousands)	**2002**	**2002**
Leon's Furniture	$\dfrac{\$38,520}{\$449,693} = 8.6\%$	$\dfrac{\$36,323}{\$425,687} = 8.5\%$
Sears	0.8%	1.4%
Industry Average	3.3%	2.2%

Leon's Furniture's profit margin increased marginally from 8.5% to 8.6% in 2002. This means that in 2001, the company generated 8.5 cents on each dollar of sales, and in 2002, it generated 8.6 cents on each dollar of sales. How does Leon's compare to its competitors? Its profit margin is much higher than those of both Sears and the industry. Keep in mind, as mentioned earlier, that Sears sells much more than just furniture and appliances. These other product lines generally produce a lower margin than furniture and appliances.

BUSINESS INSIGHT

MANAGEMENT PERSPECTIVE

In its death spiral toward bankruptcy, Kmart appeared to make two very costly strategic errors. First, in an effort to attract customers, it decided to reduce selling prices on over 30,000 items. The problem was that this reduced its gross profit margin—and didn't even have the intended effect of increasing sales because Wal-Mart quickly matched these price cuts. Since Wal-Mart operates much more efficiently than Kmart, it could afford to absorb these price cuts and still operate at a profit. Kmart couldn't. Its second error was to try to increase its profit margin by reducing operating costs. Kmart decided to cut its advertising expenditures. This resulted in fewer customers—and less sales revenue.

Decision Toolkit

DECISION CHECKPOINTS	INFO NEEDED FOR DECISION	TOOL TO USE FOR DECISION	HOW TO EVALUATE RESULTS
Is the company maintaining an adequate margin between sales and expenses?	Net earnings and net sales	Profit margin $= \dfrac{\text{Net earnings}}{\text{Net sales}}$	A higher value suggests a favourable return on each dollar of sales.

BEFORE YOU GO ON . . .

● **REVIEW IT**
1. How is the gross profit margin calculated? What might cause it to decline?
2. What effect does improved efficiency of operations have on the profit margin?

A P P E N D I X   5 A

PERIODIC INVENTORY SYSTEM

As described in this chapter, there are two basic systems of accounting for inventories: (1) the perpetual inventory system and (2) the periodic inventory system. In the chapter we focused on the characteristics of the **perpetual inventory system**. In this appendix we discuss and illustrate the periodic inventory system. One key difference between the two systems is when cost of goods sold is calculated.

Recording Merchandise Transactions

There are some key differences for recording merchandise transactions under a periodic inventory system. First, in this kind of system, revenues from the sale of merchandise are recorded when sales are made but, unlike the perpetual system, no attempt is made on the date of sale to record the cost of the merchandise sold. Instead, a physical inventory count is taken at the end of the period to determine the cost of the merchandise on hand. This figure is then used to calculate the cost of the goods sold during the period.

Second, under a periodic system, purchases of merchandise are recorded in the Purchases account rather than the Merchandise Inventory account. In addition, purchase returns and allowances, purchase discounts, and freight costs paid by the buyer are recorded in separate accounts.

To illustrate the recording of merchandise transactions under a periodic inventory system, we will use purchase/sale transactions between PW Audio Supply, Inc. (the seller), and Sauk Stereo Ltd. (the buyer), as illustrated for the perpetual inventory system earlier in this chapter.

> **STUDY OBJECTIVE**
> **6**
> Explain the recording of purchases and sales under a periodic inventory system.

RECORDING PURCHASES OF MERCHANDISE

On the basis of the sales invoice (sales invoice No. 731 in Illustration 5-4, shown on page 218) and receipt of the merchandise ordered from PW Audio Supply, Sauk Stereo records the $3,800 purchase as follows:

May 4	Purchases	3,800	
	Accounts Payable		3,800
	(To record goods purchased on account per invoice #731, terms 2/10, n/30)		

> A   =   L   +   SE
>   +3,800   −3,800
> Cash flows: no effect

Purchases is a temporary account whose normal balance is a debit.

Freight Costs

When the purchaser directly incurs the freight costs, the account Freight-In is debited. For example, if upon delivery of the goods, Sauk pays Acme Freight Company $150 for freight charges on its purchases from PW Audio Supply, the entry on Sauk's books is:

May 4	Freight-In	150	
	Cash		150
	(To record payment of freight on goods purchased)		

> A   =   L   +   SE
> −150   −150
> Cash flows: −150

Like Purchases, Freight-in is a temporary account whose normal balance is a debit. **Freight-in is part of the cost of goods purchased.** The reason is that the cost of goods purchased should include any freight charges necessary to bring the goods to the purchaser. Freight costs are not subject to a purchase discount. Purchase discounts apply on the invoice cost of the merchandise.

Purchase Returns and Allowances

When $300 of merchandise is returned to PW Audio Supply, Sauk Stereo prepares the following entry to recognize the return:

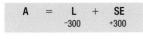

A = L + SE
   −300 +300

Cash flows: no effect

May 8	Accounts Payable	300	
	Purchase Returns and Allowances		300
	(To record return of goods to PW Audio Supply)		

Purchase Returns and Allowances is a contra expense account subtracted from the Purchases account. It is a temporary account whose normal balance is a credit.

Purchase Discounts

On May 14, Sauk Stereo pays the balance due on account to PW Audio Supply, taking the 2% cash discount allowed by PW Audio Supply for payment within 10 days. The payment and discount are recorded by Sauk Stereo as follows:

A = L + SE
−3,430 −3,500 +70

Cash flows: −3,430

May 14	Accounts Payable ($3,800 − $300)	3,500	
	Purchase Discounts ($3,500 × 2%)		70
	Cash		3,430
	(To record payment to PW Audio Supply		
	within discount period)		

Purchase Discounts is a contra expense account subtracted from the Purchases account along with any returns or allowances. It is a temporary account whose normal balance is a credit.

Determining Cost of Goods Purchased

As illustrated above, separate accounts are used to record the cost of goods purchased in a periodic inventory system. These four accounts—Purchases, Freight-In, Purchase Returns and Allowances, and Purchase Discounts—combine to determine the cost of goods purchased. First, purchase returns and allowances and purchase discounts are deducted from purchases to determine net purchases. Second, freight-in is added to net purchases to arrive at the cost of goods purchased.

We will demonstrate the calculations of net purchases, and the cost of goods purchased, using the assumed data for PW Audio Supply shown in Illustration 5A-1.

Illustration 5A-1
Calculation of net purchases and cost of goods purchased

Purchases		$325,000
Less: Purchase returns and allowances	$10,400	
Purchase discounts	6,800	17,200
Net purchases		307,800
Add: Freight-in		12,200
Cost of goods purchased		320,000

RECORDING SALES OF MERCHANDISE

The sale of $3,800 of merchandise to Sauk Stereo on May 4 is recorded by the seller, PW Audio Supply, as follows:

May 4	Accounts Receivable	3,800	
	Sales		3,800
	(To record credit sale to Sauk Stereo per invoice #731)		

A = L + SE
+3,800   +3,800
Cash flows: no effect

Sales Returns and Allowances

When Sauk Stereo returns merchandise on May 8, PW Audio Supply records the $300 sales return as follows:

May 8	Sales Returns and Allowances	300	
	Accounts Receivable		300
	(To record return of goods by Sauk Stereo)		

A = L + SE
-300   -300
Cash flows: no effect

Sales Discounts

On May 14, PW Audio Supply receives payment of $3,430 on account from Sauk Stereo. PW Audio Supply honours the 2% cash discount and records the payment of Sauk Stereo's account receivable in full as follows:

May 14	Cash	3,430	
	Sales Discounts ($3,500 × 2%)	70	
	Accounts Receivable ($3,800 − $300)		3,500
	(To record collection from Sauk Stereo within 2/10, n/30 discount period)		

A = L + SE
+3,430   -70
-3,500
Cash flows: +3,430

COMPARISON OF ENTRIES—PERPETUAL VS. PERIODIC

The periodic inventory system entries just seen are shown in Illustration 5A-2 next to those that were illustrated earlier in the chapter under the perpetual inventory system for both Sauk Stereo and PW Audio Supply.

ENTRIES ON SAUK STEREO'S BOOKS (BUYER)						
Transaction		Perpetual Inventory System			Periodic Inventory System	
May 4 Purchase of merchandise on credit		Merchandise Inventory Accounts Payable	3,800 3,800		Purchases Accounts Payable	3,800 3,800
May 4 Freight costs on purchases		Merchandise Inventory Cash	150 150		Freight-In Cash	150 150
May 8 Purchase returns and allowances		Accounts Payable Merchandise Inventory	300 300		Accounts Payable Purchase Returns and Allowances	300 300
May 14 Payment on account with a discount		Accounts Payable Cash Merchandise Inventory	3,500 3,430 70		Accounts Payable Cash Purchase Discounts	3,500 3,430 70

ENTRIES ON PW AUDIO SUPPLY'S BOOKS (SELLER)

Transaction	Perpetual Inventory System			Periodic Inventory System		
May 4 Sale of merchandise on credit	Accounts Receivable Sales	3,800	3,800	Accounts Receivable Sales	3,800	3,800
	Cost of Goods Sold Merchandise Inventory	2,400	2,400	No entry		
May 8 Return of merchandise sold	Sales Returns and Allowances Accounts Receivable	300	300	Sales Returns and Allowances Accounts Receivable	300	300
	Merchandise Inventory Cost of Goods Sold	140	140	No entry		
May 14 Cash received on account with a discount	Cash Sales Discounts Accounts Receivable	3,430 70	3,500	Cash Sales Discounts Accounts Receivable	3,430 70	3,500

Illustration 5A-2
Comparison of journal entries under perpetual and periodic inventory systems

Determining Cost of Goods Sold Under a Periodic System

Calculating cost of goods sold is different under the periodic system than under the perpetual system. When a company uses a perpetual inventory system, all transactions affecting inventory (such as freight cost, returns, and discounts) are recorded directly to the Merchandise Inventory account. In addition, at the time of each sale, the perpetual inventory system requires a reduction in Merchandise Inventory and an increase in Cost of Goods Sold. But under a periodic system, there is no running account of changes in inventory. Instead, the balance in ending inventory, as well as the cost of goods sold for the period, is calculated at the end of the period. The calculation of cost of goods sold for PW Audio Supply, using a periodic inventory system, is shown in Illustration 5A-3.

Illustration 5A-3
Cost of goods sold using a periodic inventory system

Helpful Hint The right column identifies the primary items that make up cost of goods sold of $316,000. The middle column explains cost of goods purchased of $320,000. The left column reports the contra purchased items of $17,200.

Cost of goods sold			
Inventory, January 1			$ 36,000
Purchases		$325,000	
Less: Purchases returns and allowances	$10,400		
Purchase discounts	6,800	17,200	
Net purchases		307,800	
Add: Freight-in		12,200	
Cost of goods purchased			320,000
Cost of goods available for sale			356,000
Inventory, December 31			40,000
Cost of goods sold			316,000

In a periodic inventory system, the multiple-step income statement includes the same level of detail about the calculation of goods sold as shown above. In a perpetual inventory system, a multiple-step income statement uses only one line to report cost of goods sold, as was shown in Illustration 5-8 in the chapter. Use of the periodic inventory system does not affect the content of the balance sheet. As under the perpetual system, merchandise inventory is reported in the current assets section, and at the same amount.

Using the Decision Toolkit

Costco Wholesale Corporation operates wholesale clubs in Canada, the U.S., Japan, Mexico, South Korea, Taiwan, and the UK. It competes head to head with Wal-Mart, offering discount prices on 4,500 different products. The following financial data (in U.S. millions) are available for Costco and Wal-Mart:

	Costco		Wal-Mart	
	2002	2001	2002	2001
Net sales	$38,762	$34,797	$217,799	$191,329
Cost of goods sold	33,983	30,598	171,562	150,255
Operating expenses	4,079	3,597	39,566	34,779

Instructions

(a) Wal-Mart is more than five times larger than Costco. Can a comparison of the financial results of these two companies be meaningful?

(b) Calculate the gross profit margin and profit margin for Costco and Wal-Mart for the 2002 and 2001 fiscal years.

(c) Using the profitability ratios calculated in (b), compare Costco's profitability to Wal-Mart's.

Solution

(a) It doesn't matter that Wal-Mart is more than five times larger than Costco. Ratio analysis puts both companies' financial information into the same perspective for a comparison. It is the relationship between the figures that is meaningful.

(b) (in U.S. millions)

Costco

	2002	2001
Gross profit margin	$\dfrac{(\$38,762 - \$33,983)}{\$38,762} = 12.3\%$	$\dfrac{(\$34,797 - \$30,598)}{\$34,797} = 12.1\%$
Profit margin	$\dfrac{(\$38,762 - \$33,983 - \$4,079)}{\$38,762} = 1.8\%$	$\dfrac{(\$34,797 - \$30,598 - \$3,597)}{\$34,797} = 1.7\%$

Wal-Mart

	2002	2001
Gross profit margin	$\dfrac{(\$217,799 - \$171,562)}{\$217,799} = 21.2\%$	$\dfrac{(\$191,329 - \$150,255)}{\$191,329} = 21.5\%$
Profit margin	$\dfrac{(\$217,799 - \$171,562 - \$39,556)}{\$217,799} = 3.1\%$	$\dfrac{(\$191,329 - \$150,255 - \$34,779)}{\$191,329} = 3.3\%$

(c) Costco's profitability has improved slightly from 2001 to 2002. Both its gross profit margin and profit margin improved. Wal-Mart's, on the other hand, declined slightly from 2001 to 2002. Still, Wal-Mart's profitability is significantly better than Costco's. Comparing Wal-Mart's gross profit margin of 21% to Costco's 12%, it appears that Wal-Mart has a higher mark-up on its goods. However, comparing Wal-Mart's declining profit margin to Costco's increasing profit margin could indicate that Costco is better able to control its operating costs. The changes are not significant between years, but this is something to keep an eye on.

Summary of Study Objectives

❶ Identify the differences between a service company and a merchandising company. A service company has service or fee revenue and operating expenses. Because it has inventory, a merchandising company has sales revenue, cost of goods sold, and gross profit in addition to operating expenses.

❷ Explain the recording of purchases under a perpetual inventory system. The Merchandise Inventory account is debited for all purchases of merchandise, and for freight costs, if paid by the buyer. It is credited for purchase discounts, and purchase returns and allowances.

❸ Explain the recording of sales under a perpetual inventory system. When inventory is sold, Accounts Receivable (or Cash) is debited and Sales is credited for the selling price of the merchandise. At the same time, Cost of Goods Sold is debited and Merchandise Inventory is credited for the cost of inventory items sold. Contra accounts are used to record sales returns and allowances and sales discounts. Two journal entries are also required for sales returns, to record both the selling price and the cost of the returned merchandise.

❹ Distinguish between a single-step and a multiple-step statement of earnings. In a single-step statement of earnings, all data are classified under two categories—revenues or expenses—and net earnings are determined in one step. A modified single-step statement separates income tax expense from the other expenses and reports it separately after earnings before income taxes. A multiple-step statement

of earnings shows numerous steps in determining net earnings: step 1 deducts cost of goods sold from net sales to determine gross profit. Step 2 deducts operating expenses from gross profit to determine earnings from operations. Step 3 adds or deducts any non-operating items to determine earnings before income taxes. Finally, step 4 deducts income taxes to determine net earnings.

❺ Explain the factors affecting profitability. Profitability is affected by gross profit, as measured by the gross profit margin, and by management's ability to control costs, as measured by the profit margin.

❻ Explain the recording of purchases and sales under a periodic inventory system (Appendix 5A). In contrast to recording purchases in a perpetual inventory system, separate temporary accounts are used to record (a) cash and credit purchases, (b) purchases returns and allowances, (c) purchase discounts, and (d) freight costs paid by the buyer. Sales entries are required for (a) cash and credit sales, (b) sales returns and allowances, and (c) sales discounts. Sales are recorded similar to those in a perpetual inventory system, except that the cost of goods sold is not recorded throughout the period. Instead, cost of goods sold is determined and recorded at the end of the period.

To determine cost of goods sold, first calculate cost of goods purchased by adjusting purchases for returns, allowances, discounts, and freight-in. Then, calculate cost of goods sold by adding cost of goods purchased to beginning inventory and subtracting ending inventory.

Decision Toolkit—A Summary

Decision Toolkit Summary

DECISION CHECKPOINTS	INFO NEEDED FOR DECISION	TOOL TO USE FOR DECISION	HOW TO EVALUATE RESULTS
Is the price of goods keeping pace with changes in the cost of inventory?	Gross profit and net sales	$\text{Gross profit margin} = \dfrac{\text{Gross profit}}{\text{Net sales}}$	A higher ratio suggests the average margin between the selling price and inventory cost is increasing. Too high a margin may result in lost sales.
Is the company maintaining an adequate margin between sales and expenses?	Net earnings and net sales	$\text{Profit margin} = \dfrac{\text{Net earnings}}{\text{Net sales}}$	A higher value suggests a favourable return on each dollar of sales.

NAVIGATOR

Glossary

Contra revenue account An account that is offset against a revenue account on the statement of earnings. (p. 222)

Cost of goods purchased The sum of net purchases and freight-in. (p. 234)

Cost of goods sold The total cost of merchandise sold during the period. (p. 214)

Gross profit The excess of net sales over the cost of goods sold. (p. 214)

Gross profit margin Gross profit expressed as a percentage of sales. It is calculated by dividing gross profit by net sales. (p. 229)

Net purchases Purchases less purchase returns and allowances and purchase discounts. (p. 234)

Net sales Sales less sales returns and allowances and sales discounts. (p. 226)

Operating cycle The time required to go from cash to cash in producing revenues. (p. 215)

Operating expenses Expenses incurred in the process of earning sales revenue. They are deducted from gross profit in the statement of earnings. (p. 214)

Periodic inventory system An inventory system in which detailed records are not maintained and the cost of goods sold is determined only at the end of an accounting period. (p. 216)

Perpetual inventory system A detailed inventory system in which the quantity and cost of each inventory item is always maintained. The records continuously show the inventory that should be on hand. (p. 216)

Profit margin Net earnings expressed as a percentage of net sales. It is calculated by dividing net earnings by net sales. (p. 231)

Purchase allowance A deduction granted by the seller on the selling price of unsatisfactory merchandise. (p. 219)

Purchase discount A cash discount claimed by a buyer for early payment of a balance due. (p. 220)

Purchase invoice A document that supports each credit purchase. (p. 217)

Purchase return A return of goods from the buyer to the seller for cash or credit. (p. 219)

Sales discount A reduction given by a seller for early payment of a credit sale. (p. 223)

Sales invoice A document that provides support for credit sales. (p. 221)

Sales returns and allowances A return of goods, or reduction in price, of unsatisfactory merchandise (purchase returns and allowances from the seller's perspective). (p. 222)

Sales revenue The primary source of revenue in a merchandising company. (p. 214)

Demonstration Problem

Additional Demonstration Problems

The adjusted trial balance for the year ended December 31, 2004, for Dykstra Inc. follows:

DYKSTRA INC. Adjusted Trial Balance December 31, 2004		
	Debit	Credit
Cash	$ 4,500	
Accounts receivable	11,100	
Merchandise inventory	29,000	
Prepaid insurance	2,500	
Store equipment	95,000	
Accumulated amortization		$ 18,000
Notes payable		25,000
Accounts payable		10,600
Common shares		70,000
Retained earnings		11,000
Dividends	12,000	
Sales		536,800
Sales returns and allowances	6,700	
Sales discounts	5,000	
Cost of goods sold	363,400	
Freight-out	7,600	
Advertising expense	12,000	
Salaries expense	56,000	
Utilities expense	18,000	
Rent expense	24,000	
Amortization expense	9,000	
Insurance expense	4,500	
Interest revenue	3,600	
Interest revenue		2,500
Income tax expense	10,000	
	$673,900	$673,900

Instructions

Prepare a multiple-step statement of earnings.

Solution to Demonstration Problem

DYKSTRA INC.
Statement of Earnings
Year Ended December 31, 2004

Sales revenues		
Sales		$536,800
Less: Sale returns and allowances	$ 6,700	
Sales discounts	5,000	11,700
Net sales		525,100
Cost of goods sold		363,400
Gross profit		161,700
Operating expenses		
Salaries expense	$56,000	
Rent expense	24,000	
Utilities expense	18,000	
Advertising expense	12,000	
Amortization expense	9,000	
Freight-out	7,600	
Insurance expense	4,500	
Total operating expenses		131,100
Earnings from operations		30,600
Other revenues		
Interest revenue	$ 2,500	
Other expenses		
Interest expense	3,600	1,100
Earnings before income taxes		29,500
Income tax expense		10,000
Net earnings		$ 19,500

NAVIGATOR ✔

Action Plan

- Remember the major subtotal headings in the statement of earnings: gross profit, earnings from operations, earnings before income taxes, and net earnings.
- Prepare this statement in steps:
  1. Net sales less cost of goods sold equals gross profit.
  2. Gross profit less operating expenses equals earnings from operations.
  3. Earnings from operations plus or minus other non-operating items equals earnings before income taxes.
  4. Earnings before income taxes less income tax expense equals net earnings.

Note: All questions, exercises, and problems with an asterisk relate to material in the chapter appendix.

 Multiple Choice Quiz

Self-Study Questions

Answers are at the end of the chapter.

(SO 1)   1. Which of the following statements about a perpetual inventory system is true?
(a) Cost of goods sold is only determined at the end of the accounting period.
(b) Detailed records of the cost of each inventory purchase and sale are maintained continuously.
(c) The periodic system provides better control over inventories than a perpetual system.
(d) A physical inventory count is not performed in a perpetual inventory system.

(SO 2)   2. Under a perpetual system, which of the following items does *not* result in an entry to the Merchandise Inventory account?
(a) A purchase of merchandise
(b) A return of merchandise inventory to the supplier

(c) Payment of freight costs by the buyer
(d) Payment of freight costs by the seller

3. Which sales accounts normally have a debit balance?   (SO 3)
(a) Sales Discounts
(b) Sales Returns and Allowances
(c) Both (a) and (b)
(d) Sales

4. A credit sale of $750 is made on June 13, terms   (SO 3) 2/10, n/30, on which a return of $50 is granted on June 16. What amount is received as payment in full on June 22?
(a) $685   (c) $700
(b) $686   (d) $735

5. Sales revenues are $400,000, cost of goods sold is   (SO 4) $310,000, and operating expenses are $60,000.

What is the gross profit?
(a) $30,000   (c) $340,000
(b) $90,000   (d) $400,000

(SO 4) 6. The multiple-step statement of earnings for a merchandising company shows each of the following features *except*:
(a) gross profit.
(b) cost of goods sold.
(c) a sales revenue section.
(d) operating activities.

(SO 5) 7. Which of the following would affect the gross profit margin?
(a) An increase in advertising expense
(b) A decrease in amortization expense
(c) An increase in cost of goods sold
(d) A decrease in insurance expense

(SO 5) 8. If net sales are $500,000, cost of goods sold $300,000, operating expenses $75,000, and other revenues $25,000, the profit margin is:

(a) 25%.   (c) 40%.
(b) 30%.   (d) 50%.

*9. When goods are purchased for resale by a company using a periodic inventory system: (SO 6)
(a) purchases are debited to Merchandise Inventory.
(b) purchases are debited to Purchases.
(c) purchase returns are debited to Purchase Returns and Allowances.
(d) freight costs are debited to Purchases.

*10. If beginning inventory is $60,000, cost of goods (SO 6)
purchased is $380,000, and ending inventory is $50,000, what is the cost of goods sold?
(a) $330,000   (c) $390,000
(b) $370,000   (d) $420,000

Multiple
Choice
Quiz

Questions

(SO 1) 1. (a) Explain the earnings measurement process in a merchandising company.
(b) How does earnings measurement differ between a merchandising company and a service company?
(c) How is earnings measurement the same for a merchandising company and a service company?

(SO 1) 2. Why is the normal operating cycle for a merchandising company likely to be longer than that of a service company?

(SO 1) 3. Distinguish between a perpetual and a periodic inventory system.

(SO 1) 4. Song Yee wonders why a physical inventory count is necessary in a perpetual inventory system. After all, the accounting records show how much inventory is on hand. Explain why a physical inventory count is required in a perpetual inventory system.

(SO 2) 5. Why are purchases of merchandise for resale recorded in a separate account from the purchases of other items, such as supplies or equipment? Wouldn't it make more sense to use one account to record all these purchases?

(SO 3) 6. Explain why sales returns are not debited directly to the Sales account.

(SO 3) 7. Using *X*s for amounts, give the journal entries to record (a) a cash sale and (b) a credit sale for both the purchaser and the seller, assuming a perpetual inventory system.

(SO 3) 8. Bao Tong believes revenues from credit sales must be collected in cash before they are earned. Do you agree? Explain.

(SO 4) 9. Identify the distinguishing features of a statement of

earnings for a merchandising company.

10. Identify the sections of a multiple-step statement of (SO 4)
earnings that relate to (a) operating activities, and (b) non-operating activities.

11. Chiasson Company Ltd. reports net sales of (SO 4)
$800,000, gross profit of $580,000, non-operating revenues of $20,000, and net earnings of $300,000. What are its operating expenses?

12. Huamei Corp. has sales revenue of $100,000, (SO 4, 5)
cost of goods sold of $70,000, and operating expenses of $20,000. What is its gross profit? Its gross profit margin? Its net earnings? Its profit margin?

13. What factors affect a company's gross profit (SO 5)
margin—that is, what can cause the gross profit margin to increase and what can cause it to decrease?

*14. Using *X*s for amounts, prepare the journal entries to (SO 6)
record (a) a cash sale and (b) a cash purchase, assuming (1) a periodic inventory system is used, and (2) a perpetual inventory system is used.

*15. Identify the accounts that are added to or deducted (SO 6)
from purchases to determine the cost of goods purchased. For each account, indicate (a) whether it is added or deducted and (b) its normal balance.

*16. In the following cases, use a periodic inventory system to identify the item(s) designated by the letters (SO 6)
X and *Y*:
(a) Purchases − X − Y = Net purchases
(b) Cost of goods purchased − Net purchases = X
(c) Beginning inventory + X = Cost of goods available for sale
(d) Cost of goods available for sale − Cost of goods sold = X

NAVIGATOR

Brief Exercises

BE5-1 Prepare the journal entries to record the following purchase transactions in Xiaoyan Ltd.'s books. The company uses a perpetual inventory system.

(a) On January 3, Xiaoyan purchased $900,000 of merchandise from Feng Corp., terms 2/10, n/30.
(b) On January 6, Xiaoyan returned $100,000 of the merchandise purchased on January 3 because it didn't need it.
(c) On January 12, Xiaoyan paid the balance owed to Feng.

Journalize purchase transactions.
(SO 2)

BE5-2 Prepare the journal entries to record the following sale transactions in Feng Corp.'s books. Feng uses a perpetual inventory system.

(a) On January 3, Feng sold $900,000 of merchandise to Xiaoyan Ltd., terms 2/10, n/30. The cost of the merchandise sold was $600,000.
(b) On January 6, Xiaoyan returned $100,000 of the merchandise purchased from Feng on January 3 because it didn't need it. The cost of the merchandise returned was $80,000, and it was restored to inventory.
(c) On January 12, Feng received the balance due from Xiaoyan.

Journalize sales transactions.
(SO 3)

BE5-3 Presented here are the components in Nam Inc.'s multiple-step statement of earnings. Determine the missing amounts.

Determine missing amounts.
(SO 4)

Sales	Cost of Goods Sold	Gross Profit	Operating Expenses	Non-Operating Revenues	Net Earnings
$75,000	(b)	$43,500	(d)	$2,700	$16,200
$108,000	$65,000	(c)	$15,000	(e)	$29,500
(a)	$71,900	$109,600	$39,500	$2,900	(f)

BE5-4 Cosby Inc. provides this information for the month ended October 31, 2004: credit sales $300,000; cash sales $100,000; sales discounts $5,000; and sales returns and allowances $18,000. Prepare the sales revenue section of the statement of earnings.

Prepare sales revenue section of statement of earnings.
(SO 4)

BE5-5 Explain where each of the following items would appear on (1) a multiple-step statement of earnings and (2) a single-step statement of earnings: gain on sale of equipment, cost of goods sold, amortization expense, interest expense, sales returns and allowances, and income tax expense.

Identify placement of items on statement of earnings.
(SO 4)

BE5-6 The Forzani Group Ltd. reports sales revenue of $923.8 million, cost of goods sold of $603.3 million, and net earnings of $30.5 for 2003. It reported sales revenue of $758.3 million, cost of goods sold of $497.8 million, and net earnings of $20.6 million for 2002. Calculate the gross profit margin and profit margin for each of 2003 and 2002. Comment on Forzani's changing profitability.

Calculate profitability ratios.
(SO 5)

*BE5-7 From the information in BE5-1, prepare the journal entries to record the purchase transactions on Xiaoyan Ltd.'s books, assuming a periodic inventory system is used instead of a perpetual inventory system.

Journalize purchase transactions.
(SO 6)

*BE5-8 From the information in BE5-2, prepare the journal entries to record the sale transactions on Feng Corp.'s books, assuming a periodic inventory system is used instead of a perpetual inventory system.

Journalize sales transactions.
(SO 6)

*BE5-9 Bassing Corp. uses a periodic inventory system and has these account balances: Purchases, $400,000; Purchase Returns and Allowances, $11,000; Purchase Discounts, $7,800; and Freight-In, $16,000. Determine net purchases and cost of goods purchased.

Calculate net purchases and cost of goods purchased.
(SO 6)

*BE5-10 In addition to the information given in BE5-9, Bassing Corp. has beginning inventory of $60,000, ending inventory of $90,000, and net sales of $630,000. Determine the amounts to report for cost of goods sold and gross profit.

Calculate cost of goods sold and gross profit.
(SO 6)

Exercises

Journalize purchase transactions.
(SO 2)

E5-1 This information relates to Olaf Corp.:

1. On April 5, purchased merchandise from DeVito Ltd. for $18,000, terms 2/10, n/30.
2. On April 6, paid freight costs of $900 on merchandise purchased from DeVito.
3. On April 7, purchased equipment on account for $26,000.
4. On April 8, returned $2,800 of the April 5 merchandise to DeVito.
5. On April 15, paid the amount due to DeVito in full.

Instructions

(a) Prepare the journal entries to record the transactions listed above in the books of Olaf Corp., assuming a perpetual inventory system is used.
(b) Assume that Olaf Corp. paid the balance due to DeVito on May 4 instead of April 15. Prepare the journal entry to record this payment.

Journalize purchase and sales transactions.
(SO 2, 3)

Interactive Homework

E5-2 On September 1, Campus Office Supply Ltd. had an inventory of 30 pocket calculators at a cost of $20 each. The company uses a perpetual inventory system. During September these transactions occurred:

Sept. 6 Purchased 60 calculators at $20 each from Digital Corp. on account, terms n/30.
     10 Returned two calculators to Digital for $40 credit because they did not meet specifications.
     12 Sold 26 calculators for $30 each to Campus Book Store, terms 2/10, n/30.
     14 Granted credit of $30 to Campus Book Store for the return of one calculator that was not ordered.
     20 Sold 30 calculators for $30 each to Student Card Shop, terms n/30.
     21 Received payment in full from Campus Book Store.

Instructions

Journalize the September transactions.

Journalize purchase and sales transactions.
(SO 2, 3)

E5-3 The following merchandise transactions occurred in December. Both companies use a perpetual inventory system.

1. On December 3, Pippen Ltd. sold $480,000 of merchandise to Thomas Corp., terms 2/10, n/30. The cost of the merchandise sold was $320,000.
2. On December 8, Thomas was granted an allowance of $24,000 for defective merchandise purchased on December 3. No merchandise was returned.
3. On December 13, Pippen received the balance due from Thomas.

Instructions

(a) Prepare the journal entries to record these transactions in the books of Pippen Ltd.
(b) Prepare the journal entries to record these transactions in the books of Thomas Corp.

Determine missing amounts and calculate profitability ratios.
(SO 4, 5)

Interactive Homework

E5-4 Financial information is presented here for two companies:

	Young Company	Rioux Company
Sales	$90,000	$ (4)
Sales returns	(1)	5,000
Net sales	81,000	95,000
Cost of goods sold	56,000	(5)
Gross profit	(2)	38,000
Operating expenses	15,000	(6)
Income tax expense	4,000	7,000
Net earnings	(3)	11,000

Instructions

(a) Fill in the missing amounts. Show all calculations.
(b) Calculate the gross profit margin and profit margin for each company.

E5-5   Presented is information related to Fortier Corp. for the month of January 2004:

Prepare statement of earnings and calculate profitability ratios.
(SO 4, 5)

Cost of goods sold	$208,000	Rent expense	$ 18,000
Freight-out	7,000	Sales discounts	8,000
Insurance expense	12,000	Sales returns and allowances	13,000
Salary expense	61,000	Sales	350,000
		Income tax expense	9,200

Instructions
(a) Prepare a multiple-step statement of earnings.
(b) Calculate the gross profit margin and profit margin.

E5-6   Danier Leather Inc. reports the following condensed data (in thousands except for share price) for the year ended June 29, 2002:

Prepare statements of earnings and calculate profitability ratios.
(SO 4, 5)

Revenue	$179,977	Interest expense	$ 461
Cost of sales	92,098	Income tax expense	7,429
Selling, general, and		Average number of common shares	6,850
administrative expenses	69,264	Market value per share	12.10

Instructions
(a) Prepare a single-step statement of earnings.
(b) Prepare a multiple-step statement of earnings.
(c) Calculate the following profitability ratios: gross profit margin, profit margin, earnings per share, and price-earnings ratio.

*E5-7**   Data for the Olaf Corp. are presented in E5-1.

Journalize purchase transactions.
(SO 6)

Instructions
Repeat the requirements for E5-1, assuming a periodic inventory system is used instead of a perpetual inventory system.

*E5-8**   On June 10, Pele Ltd. purchased $5,000 of merchandise from Duvall Ltd., terms 2/10, n/30. Pele pays the freight costs of $300 on June 11. Damaged goods totalling $300 are returned to Duvall for credit on June 12. On June 19, Pele pays Duvall in full.

Journalize purchase and sales transactions.
(SO 6)

Interactive Homework

Instructions
(a) Prepare journal entries for each transaction in the books of Pele Ltd., assuming (1) a perpetual inventory system is used, and (2) a periodic inventory system is used.
(b) Prepare journal entries for each transaction for Duvall Ltd., assuming (1) a perpetual inventory system is used, and (2) a periodic inventory system is used. The merchandise purchased by Pele on June 10 cost Duvall $3,000. The merchandise returned by Pele on June 12 cost Duvall $180. The merchandise was repaired and restored to inventory.

*E5-9**   Below is a series of cost of goods sold sections for four companies:

Determine missing amounts.
(SO 6)

Interactive Homework

	Co. 1	Co. 2	Co. 3	Co. 4
Beginning inventory	$ 250	$ 120	$1,000	$ (j)
Purchases	1,500	1,080	(g)	43,590
Purchase returns and allowances	40	(d)	290	700
Purchase discounts	25	20	150	(k)
Net purchases	(a)	1,030	7,210	42,090
Freight-in	110	(e)	(h)	2,240
Cost of goods purchased	(b)	1,230	7,940	(l)
Cost of goods available for sale	1,795	1,350	(i)	49,530
Ending inventory	310	(f)	1,450	6,230
Cost of goods sold	(c)	1,230	7,490	43,300

Instructions
Fill in the lettered blanks to complete the cost of goods sold sections.

Prepare cost of goods sold section of statement of earnings.
(SO 6)

*E5-10   The adjusted trial balance of Garbo Inc. at the end of its fiscal year, August 31, 2004, includes these accounts and balances: Merchandise Inventory $17,200; Purchases $144,000; Sales $190,000; Freight-In $4,000; Sales Returns and Allowances $3,000; Freight-Out $1,000; Purchase Discounts $2,200; and Purchase Returns and Allowances $2,000. The ending merchandise inventory is $25,000.

Instructions

Prepare a cost of goods sold section for the year ending August 31.

Problems: Set A

Classify accounts of merchandising company.
(SO 1)

P5-1A   The following list of accounts has been selected from the financial statements of Scott Paper Limited:

Accounts payable and accrued liabilities
Accumulated depreciation
Cash and cash equivalents
Cost of products sold
Current portion of long-term debt
Depreciation expense
Deficit
Goodwill and other intangible assets
Income taxes expense
Income taxes payable

Interest expense
Inventories
Long-term debt
Operating expenses
Prepaid expenses
Property, plant, and equipment
Sales and operating revenue
Selling, administrative, and general expenses
Share capital
Trade and other accounts receivable

Instructions

For each account listed above, indicate whether the account was reported on Scott Paper's balance sheet, statement of earnings, or statement of retained earnings. Specify where the account was most likely classified. For example, Accounts Payable and Acccrued Liabilities would be classified as a current liability on the balance sheet.

Journalize purchase and sales transactions.
(SO 2, 3)

P5-2A   Presented here are selected transactions for Shaoshi Inc. during October of the current year. Shaoshi uses a perpetual inventory system.

Oct. 1 Purchased merchandise on account from Microcell Ltd. at a cost of $75,000, terms n/30. Paid freight charges of $1,800 for the delivery of this merchandise.
   5 Returned for credit $6,000 of damaged goods purchased from Microcell on October 1.
   8 Sold merchandise costing $16,500 to Guidant Corp. on account for $22,000, terms 2/10, n/30.
   10 Guidant returned merchandise sold for $3,000 that originally cost $2,250. The merchandise was restored to inventory.
   12 Made cash purchase of supplies costing $5,000.
   15 Made cash purchase of merchandise for $7,500.
   17 Received the balance due from Guidant.
   20 Purchased delivery equipment on account for $44,000.
   25 Paid Microcell the balance due.
   28 Sold on account $30,000 of merchandise, costing $22,500, to Deux Ltée, terms 2/10, n/30.

Instructions

Journalize the October transactions for Shaoshi Inc.

Journalize, post, and prepare trial balance and partial statement of earnings.
(SO 2, 3, 4)

P5-3A   Jana Nejedly, a former professional tennis star, operates J's Tennis Shop. At the beginning of the current season, the ledger of J's Tennis Shop showed Cash $2,500; Merchandise Inventory $1,700; and Common Shares $4,200. The following transactions were completed during April:

Apr. 4 Purchased racquets and balls from Robert Corp. for $840, terms 2/10, n/30.
   6 Paid freight on Robert Corp. purchase, $60.
   8 Sold merchandise to members for $900, terms n/30. The merchandise cost $600.

Apr. 10 Received credit of $140 from Robert Corp. for a damaged racquet that was returned.

11 Purchased tennis shoes from Niki Sports for $300 cash.

13 Paid Robert Corp. in full.

14 Purchased tennis shirts and shorts from Martina's Sportswear for $700, terms 2/10, n/60.

15 Received $50 cash refund from Niki Sports for damaged merchandise that was returned.

17 Paid freight on Martina's Sportswear purchase, $80.

18 Sold merchandise to members for $800, terms n/30. The cost of the merchandise was $410.

20 Received $500 in cash from members in settlement of their accounts.

21 Paid Martina's Sportswear in full.

27 Granted an allowance of $50 to members for tennis clothing that did not fit properly.

30 Received cash payments on account from members, $350.

Instructions

(a) Journalize the April transactions.

(b) Using T accounts, enter the beginning balances in the ledger accounts and post the April transactions.

(c) Prepare a trial balance as at April 30, 2004.

(d) Prepare a multiple-step statement of earnings through gross profit.

P5-4A   Nisson Distributing Ltd. completed the following merchandising transactions in the month of April. At the beginning of April, Nisson's ledger showed Cash of $9,000 and Common Shares of $9,000.

Journalize, post, and prepare statement of earnings, and calculate ratios.
(SO 2, 3, 4, 5)

Apr. 2 Purchased merchandise on account from Kai Supply Corp. for $6,300, terms 2/10, n/30.

4 Sold $5,000 of merchandise on account, terms 2/10, n/30. The cost of the merchandise was $4,000.

5 Paid $200 freight on April 4 sale.

6 Received credit from Kai Supply Corp. for merchandise returned, $300.

11 Paid Kai Supply Corp. in full.

13 Received payment in full from customers billed on April 4.

14 Purchased merchandise for $4,400 cash.

16 Received refund from supplier for returned merchandise on cash purchase of April 14, $500.

18 Purchased merchandise from Pigeon Distributors for $4,200, terms 2/10, n/30.

20 Paid $100 freight on April 18 purchase.

23 Sold merchandise for cash, $8,100. The cost of the merchandise was $6,700.

26 Purchased merchandise for $2,300 cash.

27 Paid Pigeon Distributors in full.

29 Made cash refunds to customers for returned merchandise, $110. The returned merchandise had a cost of $75 and was restored to inventory.

30 Sold merchandise on account for $3,700, terms n/30. The cost of the merchandise was $3,000.

30 Operating expenses for the month were $1,400 and were paid in cash.

30 Income taxes of $1,000 were paid for the month.

Instructions

(a) Journalize the transactions.

(b) Using T accounts, enter the beginning Cash and Common Share balances. Post the April transactions

(c) Prepare a multiple-step statement of earnings.

(d) Calculate the gross profit margin and profit margin.

Journalize, post, and prepare adjusted trial balance and financial statements.
(SO 4)

P5-5A The trial balance of the Fashion Centre Ltd. contained the following accounts at November 30, the end of the company's fiscal year:

FASHION CENTRE LTD.
Trial Balance
November 30, 2004

	Debit	Credit
Cash	$ 16,700	
Accounts receivable	33,700	
Notes receivable, due 2006	51,000	
Merchandise inventory	45,000	
Store supplies	5,500	
Store equipment	72,000	
Accumulated amortization—store equipment		$ 18,000
Delivery equipment	30,000	
Accumulated amortization—delivery equipment		6,000
Accounts payable		39,500
Common shares		80,000
Retained earnings		30,000
Dividends	10,000	
Sales		757,200
Sales returns and allowances	4,200	
Cost of goods sold	469,400	
Salaries expense	100,000	
Advertising expense	26,400	
Utilities expense	14,000	
Repair expense	12,100	
Delivery expense	16,700	
Rent expense	24,000	
	$930,700	$930,700

Adjustment data:

1. Store supplies on hand total $2,500.
2. Amortization expense for the period is $9,000 on the store equipment and $6,000 on the delivery equipment.
3. Interest of $3,000 is accrued on notes receivable at November 30. Notes of $30,000 are due next year.
4. Income taxes of $30,000 are due and unpaid.

Instructions

(a) Journalize the adjusting entries.
(b) Prepare T accounts for all accounts used in part (a). Enter the trial balance amounts in the T accounts and post the adjusting entries.
(c) Prepare an adjusted trial balance.
(d) Prepare a multiple-step statement of earnings and a statement of retained earnings for the year, and a classified balance sheet at November 30, 2004.

Prepare financial statements and calculate profitability ratios.
(SO 4, 5)

P5-6A At the end of the fiscal year for N-Mart Department Store Ltd. on December 31, 2004, the following alphabetical list of accounts appeared in its adjusted trial balance:

Accounts payable	$ 89,300	Dividends	$ 8,000
Accounts receivable	50,300	Equipment	110,000
Accumulated amortization—		Income tax expense	46,000
building	38,000	Insurance expense	7,200
Accumulated amortization—		Interest expense	6,400
equipment	68,750	Interest payable	5,000
Amortization expense	21,350	Interest revenue	4,000
Building	190,000	Land	250,000
Cash	17,000	Merchandise inventory	75,000
Common shares	150,000	Mortgage payable	80,000
Cost of goods sold	412,700	Office salaries expense	32,000

Prepaid insurance	$ 2,400	Sales	$700,000
Property taxes expense	24,800	Sales commissions expense	14,500
Property taxes payable	24,800	Sales commissions payable	3,500
Retained earnings	199,300	Sales returns and allowances	8,000
Sales salaries expense	76,000	Utilities expense	11,000

Additional data: Of the mortgage payable, $20,000 is due for payment next year.

Instructions

(a) Prepare a multiple-step statement of earnings, a statement of retained earnings, and a classified balance sheet.
(b) Calculate the gross profit margin and profit margin.

P5-7A MacLean Corp. purchases all merchandise inventory on credit and uses a perpetual inventory system. The Accounts Payable account is used for recording merchandise inventory purchases only; all other current liabilities are accrued in separate accounts. You are provided with the following selected information for the fiscal years 2002 through 2005:

Calculate missing amounts and assess profitability.
(SO 2, 4, 5)

	2002	2003	2004	2005
Merchandise inventory (ending)	$13,000	$ 11,300	$ 14,700	$ 12,200
Accounts payable (ending)	20,000			
Net sales		225,700	227,600	219,500
Purchase of merchandise inventory on account		141,000	150,000	132,000
Cash payments to suppliers		135,000	161,000	127,000

Instructions

(a) Calculate cost of goods sold for each of the 2003, 2004, and 2005 fiscal years.
(b) Calculate the gross profit for each of the 2003, 2004, and 2005 fiscal years.
(c) Calculate the ending balance of Accounts Payable for each of the 2003, 2004, and 2005 fiscal years.
(d) Sales declined in fiscal 2005. Does that mean that profitability also declined? Explain, calculating the gross profit margin for each of the 2003, 2004, and 2005 fiscal years to help support your answer.

P5-8A You are presented with the following statement of earnings for Merigomish Mariners Inc. for the year ended July 31, 2004:

Consider impact of changes on profitability ratios.
(SO 5)

MERIGOMISH MARINERS INC.
Statement of Earnings
Year Ended July 31, 2004

Net sales		$450,000
Cost of goods sold		315,000
Gross profit		135,000
Operating expenses		
Salaries expense	$65,000	
Utilities expense	12,000	
Amortization expense	6,700	
Advertising expense	5,600	
Freight-out	1,500	
Insurance expense	1,200	
Total operating expenses		92,000
Earnings from operations		43,000
Other expense		
Interest expense		8,000
Earnings before income taxes		35,000
Income tax expense		14,000
Net earnings		$ 21,000

The sales manager has come to the company president with a proposal. He wants to increase advertising expense and salaries by 10% each. He also wants to cut the gross profit margin by three percentage points (that is, if the gross profit margin is 25%, it would have to be cut to 22%). The sales manager says that marketing research shows that net sales will increase by 12%! The sales manager is really pushing this new proposal: "This increase in sales will be great!"

Instructions

(a) Calculate the gross profit margin and profit margin for Merigomish Mariners.

(b) The president wants to make sure that the company's profit margin will not deteriorate if she follows the sales manager's proposal. She knows that income tax expense is 40% of earnings before income taxes. Do the following to help the president make her decision:

1. Prepare revised versions of the ratios listed in part (a).
2. Comment on the revised numbers and whether or not the president should agree to the sales manager's proposal.

Journalize purchase and sales transactions.
(SO 6)

*P5-9A Data for Shaoshi Inc. are presented in P5-2A.

Instructions

Journalize the September transactions for Shaoshi Inc., assuming a periodic inventory system is used instead of a perpetual inventory system.

Journalize purchase and sales transactions.
(SO 6)

*P5-10A Data for J's Tennis Shop are presented in P5-3A.

Instructions

Repeat the requirements for P5-3A, assuming a periodic inventory system is used instead of a perpetual inventory system. Ending merchandise inventory is $2,100.

Prepare partial statement of earnings.
(SO 6)

*P5-11A At the end of Abela Corporation's July 31, 2004, fiscal year, the following selected accounts appeared in its adjusted trial balance:

Freight-in	$ 5,060	Purchase returns and allowances	$ 3,000
Merchandise inventory	44,360	Sales	910,000
Purchases	630,000	Sales returns and allowances	20,000
Purchase discounts	7,000	Sales discounts	5,000

Abela uses a periodic inventory system. A physical inventory count at year end determined that its ending inventory on July 31 was $36,200.

Instructions

Prepare a multiple-step statement of earnings, through gross profit, for the year ended July 31, 2004.

Problems: Set B

Classify accounts of merchandising company.
(SO 1)

P5-1B You are provided with the following list of accounts from the adjusted trial balance of Swirsky Inc.:

Accounts payable	Income tax payable	Salaries expense
Accounts receivable	Insurance expense	Salaries payable
Accumulated amortization	Interest expense	Sales
Advertising expense	Interest payable	Sales discounts
Amortization expense	Land	Sales returns and
Cash	Merchandise inventory	allowances
Common shares	Mortgage payable	Store equipment
Dividends	Office building	Utilities expense
Freight-out	Prepaid insurance	Unearned sales revenue
Income tax expense	Retained earnings	Wages payable

Instructions

For each account, identify whether the account should be reported on the balance sheet, statement of earnings, or statement of retained earnings. Also, specify where the account should be classified. For example, Accounts Payable would be classified as a current liability on the balance sheet.

P5-2B   Presented here are selected transactions for Norlan Inc. during September of the current year. Norlan uses a perpetual inventory system.

Journalize purchase and sales transactions.
(SO 2, 3)

Sept. 2 Purchased delivery equipment on account for $28,000.

    4 Purchased merchandise on account from Hillary Company at a cost of $60,000, terms 2/10, n/30.

    5 Paid freight charges of $2,500 on merchandise purchased from Hillary Company on September 4.

    5 Returned damaged goods costing $8,000 received from Hillary Company on September 4.

    6 Sold merchandise costing $15,000 to Fischer Company on account for $20,000, terms 1/10, n/30.

    14 Paid Hillary balance due.

    15 Purchased supplies for $4,000 cash.

    16 Received balance due from Fischer Company.

    18 Purchased merchandise for $6,000 cash.

    22 Sold inventory costing $20,000 to Waldo Company on account for $27,000, terms 2/10, n/30.

    28 Waldo returned merchandise sold for $9,500 that cost $7,000. The merchandise was restored to inventory.

Instructions

Journalize the September transactions for Norlan Inc.

P5-3B   Joe Weir, a former professional golf star, operates Weir's Pro Shop at the Bay Golf Course. At the beginning of the current season, on April 1, the ledger of Weir's Pro Shop showed Cash $2,500; Merchandise Inventory $3,500; and Common Shares $6,000. The following transactions were completed during April 2004:

Journalize, post, and prepare trial balance and partial statement of earnings.
(SO 2, 3, 4)

Apr. 5 Purchased golf bags, clubs, and balls on account from Balata Corp. for $1,700, terms 2/10, n/30.

    7 Paid $80 freight on Balata purchase.

    9 Received $100 credit from Balata for merchandise returned.

    10 Sold merchandise on account to members for $950, terms n/30. The merchandise had a cost of $630.

    12 Purchased golf shoes, sweaters, and other accessories on account from Arrow Sportswear for $660, terms 1/10, n/30.

    14 Paid Balata in full.

    17 Received $60 credit from Arrow Sportswear for merchandise returned.

    20 Made sales on account to members for $700, terms n/30. The cost of the merchandise sold was $490.

    21 Paid Arrow Sportswear in full.

    27 Granted a $75 sales allowance to members for clothing that did not fit properly. No merchandise was returned.

    30 Received payments on account from members, $1,100.

Instructions

(a) Journalize the April transactions.

(b) Using T accounts, enter the beginning balances in the ledger accounts and post the April transactions.

(c) Prepare a trial balance as at April 30, 2004.

(d) Prepare a multiple-step statement of earnings through gross profit.

P5-4B   Eagle Hardware Store Ltd. completed the following merchandising transactions in the month of May. At the beginning of May, Eagle's ledger showed Cash of $5,000 and Common Shares of $5,000.

Journalize, post, and prepare statement of earnings, and calculate ratios.
(SO 2, 3, 4, 5)

May 1 Purchased merchandise on account from Depot Wholesale Supply for $5,000, terms 2/10, n/30.

    2 Sold merchandise on account for $4,500, terms 2/10, n/30. The cost of the merchandise sold was $3,000.

    5 Received credit from Depot Wholesale Supply for merchandise returned, $200.

    9 Received payment in full from customers billed for sales of $4,500 on May 2.

    10 Paid Depot Wholesale Supply in full.

May 11 Purchased supplies for $900 cash.
  12 Purchased merchandise for $3,100 cash.
  15 Received cash refund of $230 for return of poor-quality merchandise.
  17 Purchased merchandise from Harlow Distributors for $1,900, terms 2/10, n/30.
  19 Paid $250 freight on May 17 purchase.
  24 Sold merchandise for $6,200 cash. The cost of the merchandise was $4,340.
  25 Purchased merchandise from Horicon Inc. for $800, terms 2/10, n/30.
  27 Paid Harlow Distributors in full.
  29 Paid $100 cash refund to customers for returned merchandise. The cost of the returned merchandise was $70. It was restored to inventory.
  31 Sold merchandise on account for $1,600, terms n/30. The cost of the merchandise was $1,120.
  31 Operating expenses for the month were $1,500, and were paid in cash.
  31 Income tax expense of $500 was accrued.

Instructions

(a) Journalize the transactions.
(b) Using T accounts, enter the beginning Cash and Common Share balances. Post the May transactions.
(c) Prepare a multiple-step statement of earnings.
(d) Calculate the gross profit margin and profit margin.

Journalize, post, and prepare adjusted trial balance and financial statements.
(SO 4)

P5-5B The trial balance of Mesa Inc. at December 31, the end of the company's fiscal year, follows:

MESA INC.
Trial Balance
December 31, 2004

	Debit	Credit
Cash	$ 33,400	
Accounts receivable	37,600	
Merchandise inventory	110,000	
Land	92,000	
Buildings	197,000	
Accumulated amortization—buildings		$ 57,000
Equipment	83,500	
Accumulated amortization—equipment		42,400
Notes payable		52,000
Accounts payable		37,500
Common shares		200,000
Retained earnings		68,200
Dividends	12,000	
Sales		922,100
Sales discounts	5,000	
Cost of goods sold	709,900	
Salaries expense	69,800	
Utilities expense	9,400	
Repair expense	8,900	
Gas and oil expense	7,200	
Insurance expense	3,500	
	$1,379,200	$1,379,200

Adjustment data:
  1. Amortization is $10,000 on buildings and $9,000 on equipment.
  2. Interest of $3,640 is due and unpaid on notes payable at December 31. Of the notes payable, $15,000 is payable next year.
  3. Income taxes of $20,000 are due and unpaid.

Instructions

(a) Journalize the adjusting entries.
(b) Create T accounts for all accounts used in part (a). Enter the trial balance amounts in the T accounts and post the adjusting entries.

(c) Prepare an adjusted trial balance.
(d) Prepare a multiple-step statement of earnings and a statement of retained earnings for the year, and a classified balance sheet at December 31, 2004.

P5-6B At the end of the Metro Department Store Ltd.'s fiscal year on November 30, 2004, these accounts appeared, in alphabetical order, in its adjusted trial balance:

Prepare financial statements and calculate profitability ratios.
(SO 4, 5)

Accounts payable	$ 27,310	Income tax expense	$ 21,000
Accounts receivable	11,770	Insurance expense	9,000
Accumulated amortization—		Interest expense	2,850
delivery equipment	22,800	Interest revenue	7,000
Amortization expense—		Merchandise inventory	36,200
store equipment	15,625	Notes payable, due 2008	47,500
Accumulated amortization—		Prepaid insurance	6,000
store equipment	31,250	Retained earnings	34,785
Amortization expense—		Rent expense	29,000
delivery equipment	11,400	Salaries expense	110,000
Cash	8,000	Sales	910,000
Common shares	38,000	Sales commissions expense	14,000
Cost of goods sold	623,000	Sales commissions payable	6,000
Delivery expense	8,200	Sales returns and allowances	20,000
Delivery equipment	57,000	Store equipment	125,000
Dividends	6,000	Utilities expense	10,600

Instructions
(a) Prepare a multiple-step statement of earnings, a statement of retained earnings, and a classified balance sheet.
(b) Calculate the gross profit margin and profit margin.

P5-7B Psang Inc. purchases all merchandise inventory on credit and uses a perpetual inventory system. The Accounts Payable account is used for recording merchandise inventory purchases only; all other current liabilities are accrued in separate accounts. You are provided with the following selected information for the fiscal years 2003 through 2005:

Calculate missing amounts and assess profitability.
(SO 2, 4, 5)

	2003	2004	2005
Income Statement Data			
Net sales	$96,000	$ (c)	$82,000
Cost of goods sold	(a)	27,000	26,000
Gross profit	69,000	61,000	(g)
Operating expenses	63,000	(d)	51,000
Net earnings	$ (b)	$ 4,000	$ (h)
Balance Sheet Data			
Merchandise inventory	$11,000	$ (e)	$12,000
Accounts payable	6,000	4,000	(i)
Additional Information			
Purchase of merchandise			
inventory on account	$25,000	$30,000	$22,000
Cash payments to suppliers	24,000	(f)	24,000

Instructions
(a) Calculate the missing amounts.
(b) Sales declined over the three-year fiscal period, 2003–2005. Does that mean that profitability necessarily also declined? Explain, calculating the gross profit margin and profit margin for each fiscal year to help support your answer.

Consider how the timing of sales and purchases can affect ratios.
(SO 5)

P5-8B You are presented with the following information for La Crosse Inc. as at May 24, 2004. The company's year end is May 31.

LA CROSSE INC.
Balance Sheet
May 31, 2004

Current assets	$ 80,000
Other assets	29,000
Total assets	$109,000
Current liabilities	$ 35,000
Long-term liabilities	30,000
Total liabilities	65,000
Shareholders' equity	44,000
Total liabilities and shareholders' equity	$109,000

LA CROSSE INC.
Statement of Earnings
Year Ended May 31, 2004

Net sales	$24,000
Cost of goods sold	(16,000)
Operating expenses	(7,000)
Net earnings	$ 1,000

The company has debt covenants with the bank which require it to maintain a current ratio in excess of 2 to 1, a gross profit margin of 25%, a profit margin of 4%, and a debt to total assets ratio which cannot exceed 60%. The company wants to boost its financial performance by year end, as it may be going back to the bank to finance the purchase of some equipment.

The sales manager has come to you with a proposal. She says that she can purchase inventory on credit for $13,500. She has a customer who she can sell the inventory to, also on credit, for $16,000. "I know the gross profit on the deal is not as high as usual. But the beauty of this is that we should be able to collect the cash from our customer early next month, in time to pay the supplier. And the bank will be impressed by the $2,500 increase in earnings! So we can boost our profit without having to pay out any cash, which I know we're short of anyway!"

Instructions

(a) Calculate the following, based on the financial data presented as at May 31:

    1. Current ratio   3. Gross profit margin

    2. Debt to total assets   4. Profit margin

(b) 1. If you followed the sales manager's proposal, what would be the impact on each of the ratios you calculated in (a)?

    2. Make a recommendation about whether or not to proceed with the sales manager's suggestion.

Journalize purchase and sales transactions.
(SO 6)

P5-9B Data for Norlan Inc. are presented in P5-2B.

Instructions

Journalize the September transactions for Norlan Inc., assuming a periodic inventory system is used instead of a perpetual inventory system.

Journalize purchase and sales transactions.
(SO 6)

P5-10B Data for Weir's Pro Shop are presented in P5-3B.

Instructions

Repeat the requirements for P5-3B, assuming a periodic inventory system is used instead of a perpetual inventory system. Ending merchandise inventory is $4,500.

Prepare partial statement of earnings.
(SO 6)

P5-11B At the end of Alain Corporation's January 31, 2005, fiscal year, the following selected accounts appeared in its adjusted trial balance:

Freight-in	$ 5,600	Purchase returns and allowances	$ 6,400
Merchandise inventory	40,500	Sales	718,000
Purchases	442,000	Sales returns and allowances	8,000
Purchase discounts	12,000	Sales discounts	6,000

Alain uses a periodic inventory system. A physical inventory count at year end determined that its ending inventory on January 31 was $75,000.

Instructions

Prepare a multiple-step statement of earnings, through gross profit, for the year ended January 31, 2005.

BROADENING YOUR PERSPECTIVE

Financial Reporting and Analysis

Analysis Tools

FINANCIAL REPORTING PROBLEM: *Loblaw Companies Limited*

BYP5-1   The financial statements for Loblaw are presented in Appendix A at the end of this book.

Instructions

Answer these questions using the consolidated statement of earnings:
(a) What was the percentage change in sales and in net earnings from 2001 to 2002?
(b) Is there sufficient information in the statement to determine Loblaw's gross profit margin? If so, calculate it for each of the two years.
(c) What was the profit margin in each of the two years presented in the annual report? Comment on the trend.
(d) Are any non-operating revenues and non-operating expenses included in Loblaw's statement of earnings? If so, identify the accounts included.

COMPARATIVE ANALYSIS PROBLEM: *Loblaw and Sobeys*

BYP5-2   The financial statements of Sobeys Inc. are presented in Appendix B following the financial statements for Loblaw in Appendix A.

Instructions

(a) Based on the information contained in these financial statements, determine the following values for each company for each of the two most recent years presented in their annual reports:
 1. Percentage change in sales
 2. Percentage change in operating income
 3. Gross profit margin
 4. Profit margin
(b) What conclusions concerning the relative profitability of the two companies can be drawn from these data?

RESEARCH CASE

BYP5-3 The article "Wal Around the World," published in the December 8, 2001, issue of *The Economist*, discusses Wal-Mart as the world's largest retailer which still thinks of itself as a small-town outfit. The article states that perception may be Wal-Mart's greatest strength.

Instructions

Read the article and answer the following questions:
(a) Lacking customers, staff, and suppliers, what did Sam Walton have to do differently from established retailers to get his business going?
(b) Wal-Mart turns its inventory over twice as fast as the industry average. How is this accomplished?
(c) Suppliers are given full and free access to real-time data from Wal-Mart on how their products are selling store by store. Why is this an advantage to both Wal-Mart and its suppliers?
(d) Wall Street is pinning its hopes on Wal-Mart's overseas efforts. Has Wal-Mart been successful overseas in the past? Explain why or why not.

INTERPRETING FINANCIAL STATEMENTS

BYP5-4 Big Rock Brewery Ltd. is a western producer and marketer of premium quality beers. Selected information from Big Rock's statement of earnings for the past three years follows:

	2003	2002	2001
Sales	$30,463,010	$24,909,081	$23,199,678
Cost of sales	11,728,022	10,167,456	9,240,503
Operating expenses	15,694,624	12,772,839	11,951,602
Income tax expense	747,367	751,000	655,000

Instructions

(a) Calculate gross profit and net earnings for each of the three years.
(b) Calculate the percentage change in sales and net earnings from 2001 to 2003.
(c) Calculate the gross profit margin for each of the three years. Comment on any trend in this percentage.
(d) Calculate the profit margin for each of the three years. Comment on any trend in this percentage.
(e) How well has Big Rock managed operating expenses over the three-year period?

A GLOBAL FOCUS

BYP5-5 Carrefour, headquartered in Paris, is the world's second largest retailer—second only to Wal-Mart. Although Wal-Mart is still the world's #1 retailer, its international sales are far lower than Carrefour's. This is a concern for Wal-Mart, since its primary opportunity for future growth lies outside of North America.

Below are selected financial data for Carrefour (in euros) and Wal-Mart (in U.S. dollars). Even though their results are presented in different currencies, by employing ratios, we can make some basic comparisons.

	Carrefour (in billions)	Wal-Mart (in billions)
Sales	€69.5	$217.8
Cost of goods sold	53.9	171.6
Net earnings	1.3	6.7
Total assets	43.5	83.5
Average total assets	43.8	80.8
Current assets	16.9	28.2
Current liabilities	13.0	27.3
Total liabilities	32.8	48.3

Instructions

Compare the two companies by doing the following:

(a) Calculate the gross profit margin, profit margin, and return on assets ratios for each company. Discuss their relative profitability.
(b) Calculate the current ratios and the debt to total assets ratios for the two companies. Discuss their relative liquidity and solvency.
(c) What concerns might you have in relying on this comparison?

FINANCIAL ANALYSIS ON THE WEB

BYP5-6 Identify profitability ratios for Nortel Networks Corp., and compare this information to industry, sector, and market indices.

Instructions

Specific requirements for this Web case can be found on the Kimmel website.

Critical Thinking

COLLABORATIVE LEARNING ACTIVITY

BYP5-7 Three years ago, Kathy Webb and her brother-in-law, John Utley, formed the Wu Department Store Ltd. For the first two years, business was good, but the following results for 2004 were disappointing:

WU DEPARTMENT STORE LTD.
Statement of Earnings
Year Ended December 31, 2004

Net sales	$700,000
Cost of goods sold	546,000
Gross profit	154,000
Operating expenses	125,000
Earnings before income tax	29,000
Income tax expense	11,000
Net earnings	$ 18,000

Kathy believes the problem lies in the relatively low gross profit margin of 22%. John believes the problem is that operating expenses are too high. Kathy thinks the gross profit margin can be improved by making two changes: (1) Increase average selling prices by 17%. This increase is expected to lower sales volume so that total sales will increase only 6%. (2) Buy merchandise in larger quantities and take all purchase discounts. These changes are expected to increase the gross profit margin by 3%. Kathy does not expect these changes to have any effect on operating expenses.

John thinks expenses can be cut by making these two changes: (1) Cut sales salaries of $60,000 in half and give sales personnel a commission of 2% of net sales. (2) Reduce store deliveries to one day per week rather than twice a week. This change will reduce delivery expenses of $30,000 by 40%. John feels that these changes will not have any effect on net sales.

Kathy and John come to you for help in deciding the best way to improve net earnings. The income tax rate is anticipated to be 40% of earnings before income tax in 2005.

Instructions

With the class divided into groups, do the following:

(a) Prepare a projected statement of earnings for 2005 assuming (1) Kathy's changes are implemented and (2) John's ideas are adopted.
(b) What is your recommendation to Kathy and John?
(c) Prepare a projected statement of earnings for 2005 assuming both sets of proposed changes are made.
(d) Discuss the impact that other factors might have. For example, would increasing the quantity of inventory increase costs? Would a salary cut affect employee morale? Would decreased morale affect sales? Would decreased store deliveries decrease customer satisfaction? What other suggestions might be considered?

COMMUNICATION ACTIVITY

BYP5-8 Consider the following events, which are listed in chronological order:

1. Dexter Maersk decides to buy a custom-made snowboard and calls The Great Canadian Snowboard Company, Inc., to inquire about its products.
2. Dexter asks Great Canadian Snowboard to manufacture a custom board for him.
3. The company sends Dexter a purchase order to fill out, which he immediately completes, signs, and sends back with a required 25% down payment.
4. Great Canadian Snowboard receives Dexter's purchase order and down payment, and begins working on the board.
5. The Great Canadian Snowboard Company has its fiscal year end. At this time, Dexter's board is 75% completed.
6. The company completes the snowboard for Dexter and notifies him to take delivery.
7. Dexter picks up his snowboard from the company and takes it home.
8. Dexter tries the snowboard out and likes it so much that he carves his initials in it.

9. The Great Canadian Snowboard Company bills Dexter for the cost of the snowboard, less the 25% down payment.

10. The company receives payment of the balance due from Dexter.

Instructions

In a memo to the president of The Great Canadian Snowboard Company, answer these questions:

(a) When should The Great Canadian Snowboard Company record the revenue and cost related to the snowboard? Refer to the revenue recognition and matching principles in your answer.

(b) Suppose that with his purchase order Dexter was not required to make a down payment. Would that change your answer to part (a)?

ETHICS CASE

**Ethics In
Accounting**

BYP5-9   Rita Pelzer was just hired as the assistant treasurer of Zaz Stores Ltd., a specialty chain store company that has nine retail stores concentrated in one city. Among other things, the payment of all invoices is centralized in one of the departments Rita will manage. Her primary responsibility is to maintain the company's high credit rating by paying all bills when due and to take advantage of all cash discounts.

Jamie Caterino, the treasurer, is training Rita in her new duties. He instructs Rita that she is to continue the practice of preparing all cheques "net of discount" and dating the cheques the last day of the discount period. "But," Jamie continues, "we always hold the cheques at least four days beyond the discount period before mailing them. That way we get another four days of interest on our money. Most of our creditors need our business and don't complain. And, if they scream about our missing the discount period, we blame it on the mailroom or the post office. We've only lost one discount out of every hundred we take that way. I think everybody does it. By the way, welcome to our team!"

Instructions

(a) What are the ethical considerations in this case?

(b) What stakeholders are harmed or benefited?

(c) Should Rita continue the practice started by Jamie? Does she have any choice?

Answers to Self-Study Questions

1. b   2. d   3. c   4. b   5. b   6. d   7. c   8. b   *9. b   *10. c

Answer to Loblaw Review It Question 3

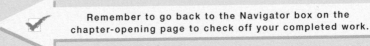

A passion for food... and a lot more!

Loblaw uses a multiple-step statement of earnings and reports its non-operating interest expense separate from operating income. However, the first portion of its statement of earnings is not the same as the multiple-step statements presented in this chapter. For competitive reasons, Loblaw does not report its cost of sales or its gross profit separately.

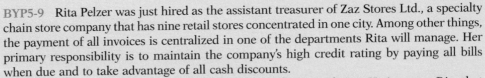

Remember to go back to the Navigator box on the chapter-opening page to check off your completed work.

C H A P T E R   6

Reporting and Analysing Inventory

STUDY OBJECTIVES

After studying this chapter, you should be able to:

1. Describe the steps in determining inventory quantities.
2. Explain the basis of accounting for inventories and apply the inventory cost flow assumptions under a periodic inventory system.
3. Explain the financial statement effects of each of the inventory cost flow assumptions.
4. Indicate the effects of inventory errors on the financial statements.
5. Explain the lower of cost and market basis of accounting for inventories.
6. Calculate and interpret inventory turnover.
7. Apply the inventory cost flow assumptions under a perpetual inventory system (Appendix 6A).

NAVIGATOR

How Many Dump Trucks Did You Want?

Let's talk inventory—BIG inventory. The world's largest dump truck, the Caterpillar 797B, is as tall as a three-storey building and has a capacity of over 345 tonnes. The first 19 units of its predecessor, the Cat 797, rolled off the production line back in 1998. Six of the square behemoths were promptly sent to Fort McMurray, Alberta—no easy feat, since many highways and bridges can't take their weight—to be tested at Syncrude Canada before Caterpillar began a full production cycle of 200 units per year.

Headquartered in Peoria, Illinois, Caterpillar Inc. is the world's largest manufacturer and retailer of construction and mining products. Its product line consists of more than 300 machines, it has manufacturing plants in 24 countries, and it sells its products around the world. Already a global organization—exports account for some 50% of its sales—Caterpillar is investing in new markets such as China, the former Soviet republics, Central Europe, and a number of other developing nations. In Canada, Caterpillar has manufacturing operations in Edmonton, Montreal, and Laval, as well as logistics operations in Edmonton, Guelph, Saskatoon, and Toronto. It also has its own financial services locations in Calgary and Toronto.

For Syncrude, the world's largest producer of crude oil from oil sands, the testing period allowed it to evaluate the Cat 797 for long-term production capability, durability, and maintenance in an oil sands mine, one of the toughest mining environments. Used at the company's Base and Aurora mines, the trucks haul massive quantities of oil sand, ore, and dirt to extraction plants at the mines for partial processing on-site. Not surprisingly, they scored top marks—Syncrude had in fact been a key collaborator with Caterpillar on the development of the truck for a number of years. By 2002, Syncrude had bought 15 more Cat 797s—it now has 21—and it expects to have 80 of the giants by 2008.

Now a Cat 797B retails for about U.S.$3.5 million, depending on the options—and requires one heck of a big garage for storage. You can imagine, therefore,

Caterpillar Inc. www.caterpillar.com

THE NAVIGATOR

Scan *Study Objectives* ☐

Read *Feature Story* ☐

Read *Chapter Preview* ☐

Read text and answer *Before You Go On*
p. 265 ☐ p. 274 ☐ p. 277 ☐ p. 280 ☐

Work *Using the Decision Toolkit* ☐

Review *Summary of Study Objectives*
and *Decision Toolkit* ☐

Work *Demonstration Problem* ☐

Answer *Self-Study Questions* ☐

Complete assignments ☐

that Caterpillar wants to avoid having too much of this kind of inventory sitting around tying up its resources. Conversely, it has to have enough inventory to meet its customers' demands. In short, Caterpillar is a big company that makes big products—and has big inventory challenges.

After a difficult period in the 1980s, Caterpillar today enjoys record sales, profits, and growth. While part of this turnaround can be attributed to diversification of its products and services, effective management of inventory has been a key factor. In the last 10 years, Caterpillar's sales increased by more than 97%, while its inventory increased by only 49%. The average item went from 87 days in inventory to 76 days.

To achieve this reduction in

the amount of resources tied up in inventory, while continuing to meet its customers' needs, Caterpillar used a two-pronged approach. First, it completed a factory modernization program in 1993, which dramatically increased its production efficiency: the time it takes to manufacture a part was reduced by an incredible 75%.

Second, Caterpillar vastly improved its distribution system. It ships 140,000 items daily from 20 distribution centres located around the world (facilities which add up to nearly 750,000 square metres of warehouse space—remember, we're talking dump trucks and bulldozers). The company even has a dedicated "Emergency Floor" to handle rush requests for parts around the clock—often shipping items

in less than four hours.

In fact, its distribution system is so advanced that Caterpillar has created a separate unit, Caterpillar Logistics Services, that warehouses and distributes other companies' products—from running shoes to software to auto parts. Using sophisticated probability models, Cat Logistics uses its inventory management know-how to help its clients improve their product availability while reducing costly inventory investments.

The bottom line is that Caterpillar's inventory management and accounting practices make a crucial contribution to its own and other companies' profitability.

In the previous chapter, we discussed the accounting for merchandise inventory using a perpetual inventory system. In this chapter, we explain the methods used to calculate the cost of goods sold during the period and the cost of inventory on hand at the end of the period. We conclude by illustrating methods for analysing inventory.

The content and organization of this chapter are as follows:

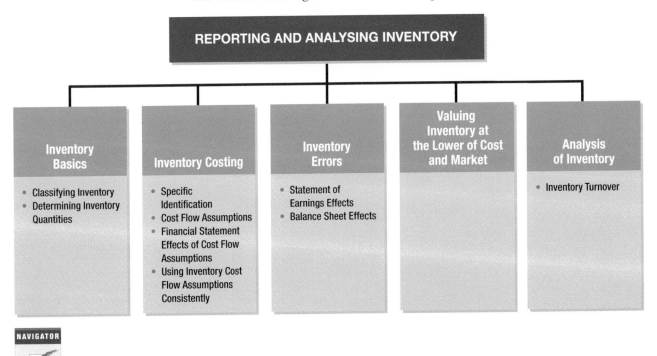

REPORTING AND ANALYSING INVENTORY

Inventory Basics	Inventory Costing	Inventory Errors	Valuing Inventory at the Lower of Cost and Market	Analysis of Inventory
• Classifying Inventory • Determining Inventory Quantities	• Specific Identification • Cost Flow Assumptions • Financial Statement Effects of Cost Flow Assumptions • Using Inventory Cost Flow Assumptions Consistently	• Statement of Earnings Effects • Balance Sheet Effects		• Inventory Turnover

NAVIGATOR

Inventory Basics

In our economy, inventories are an important barometer of business activity. The amount of inventories and the time required to sell the goods are two closely watched indicators. During downturns in the economy, there can be an initial buildup of inventories, as it takes longer to sell existing quantities. Inventories generally decrease with an upturn in business activity. A delicate balance must be maintained between too little inventory and too much.

BUSINESS INSIGHT

MANAGEMENT PERSPECTIVE

Inventory management for companies that make and sell high-tech products is very complex because the product life cycle is so short. The company wants to have enough inventory to meet demand, but doesn't want to have too much inventory, because the introduction of a new product can eliminate demand for the "old" product. Palm, Inc., maker of personal digital assistants (PDAs), learned this lesson the hard way in 2001. Sales of its existing products had been booming, and the company was frequently faced with shortages, so it started increasing its inventories. Then sales started to slow and inventories started to grow faster than wanted. Management panicked and decided to announce that its new product—one that would make its old one obsolete—would be coming out in two weeks. Sales of the old product quickly died—leaving a mountain of inventory. But the new product wasn't actually ready for six weeks, resulting in a loss of sales in the interim.

CLASSIFYING INVENTORY

How a company classifies its inventory depends on whether the firm is a merchandiser or a manufacturer. In a **merchandising company**, such as those described in Chapter 5, inventory consists of many different items. For example, in a grocery store, canned goods, dairy products, meats, and produce are just a few of the inventory items on hand. These items have two common characteristics: (1) they are owned by the company, and (2) they are in a form that is ready for sale to customers in the ordinary course of business. Thus, only one inventory classification, merchandise inventory, is needed to describe the many different items that make up the total inventory.

In a **manufacturing company**, some of its inventory may not yet be ready for sale. As a result, inventory is usually classified into three categories: finished goods, work in process, and raw materials. Finished goods inventory is manufactured items that are completed and ready for sale. Work in process is that portion of manufactured inventory that has been placed into the production process but is not yet complete. Raw materials are the basic goods that will be used in production but have not yet been sent into production. For example, Caterpillar classifies earth-moving trucks completed and ready for sale as finished goods. The trucks on the assembly line in various stages of production are classified as work in process. The steel, glass, tires, and other components that are on hand waiting to be used in the production of trucks are identified as raw materials.

By observing the levels and changes in the levels of these three inventory types, financial statement users can gain insight into management's production plans. For example, low levels of raw materials and high levels of finished goods could suggest that management believes it has enough inventory on hand and will slow down production—perhaps in anticipation of a recession. On the other hand, high levels of raw materials and low levels of finished goods probably indicate that management is planning to step up production.

The accounting concepts discussed in this chapter apply to the inventory classifications of both merchandising and manufacturing companies.

Helpful Hint Regardless of the classification, all inventories are reported as current assets on the balance sheet.

DETERMINING INVENTORY QUANTITIES

No matter whether they are using a perpetual or periodic inventory system, all companies need to determine inventory quantities at the end of the accounting period. If using a perpetual inventory system, companies take a physical inventory at year end for two purposes: (1) to check the accuracy of their perpetual inventory records and (2) to determine the amount of inventory lost due to wasted raw materials, shoplifting, or employee theft. Companies using a periodic inventory system must take a physical inventory for two different purposes: (1) to determine the inventory on hand at the balance sheet date and (2) to determine the cost of goods sold for the period.

Determining inventory quantities involves two steps: (1) taking a physical inventory of goods on hand and (2) determining the ownership of goods.

STUDY OBJECTIVE 1

Describe the steps in determining inventory quantities.

Taking a Physical Inventory

Taking a physical inventory involves actually counting, weighing, or measuring each kind of inventory on hand. In many companies, taking an inventory is a formidable task. Retailers such as Zellers, Canadian Tire, or Loblaw have thousands of different inventory items. An inventory count is generally more accurate when goods are not being sold or received during the counting. Consequently, companies often "take inventory" when the business is closed or when business is slow. The physical inventory is taken at the end of the accounting period.

Over the years, inventory has played a role in many fraud cases. A classic one involved salad oil. Management filled storage tanks mostly with water, and since oil rises to the top, the auditors thought the tanks were full of oil. In this instance, management also said they had more tanks than they really did—they repainted numbers on the tanks to confuse the auditors.

In recent years, the management of women's apparel maker The Leslie Fay Company, Inc., was convicted of falsifying inventory records to boost net earnings and management bonuses. In another case, Frost Fence Limited was forced into bankruptcy after it was discovered that $17 million in inventory was on the company's books but not in its storage yard.

Determining Ownership of Goods

One challenge in determining inventory quantities is making sure a company owns the inventory. To determine ownership of goods, two questions must be answered: (1) Do all of the goods included in the count belong to the company? (2) Does the company own any goods that were not included in the count?

Goods in Transit. Goods in transit at the end of the period (on board a truck, train, ship, or plane) make determining ownership a bit more complicated. The company may have purchased goods that have not yet been received, or it may have sold goods that have not yet been delivered. To arrive at an accurate count, ownership of these goods must be determined.

Goods in transit should be included in the inventory of the company that has legal title to the goods. Legal title is determined by the terms of the sale, as shown in Illustration 6-1 and described below:

> **Alternative Terminology**
> Other common shipping terms of sale include *FCA* (free carrier), *CIF* (cost, insurance, freight), and *CPT* (carriage paid to).

1. When the terms are FOB (free on board) shipping point, ownership of the goods passes to the buyer when the public carrier accepts the goods from the seller.
2. When the terms are FOB destination, ownership of the goods remains with the seller until the goods reach the buyer.

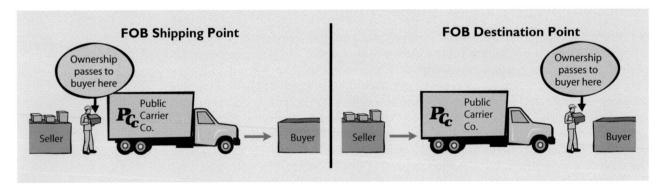

Illustration 6-1
Terms of sale

Consigned Goods. In some lines of business, it is customary to hold goods belonging to other parties and sell them, for a fee, without ever taking ownership of the goods. These are called consigned goods. For example, you might have a used car that you would like to sell. If you take it to a used car dealer, the dealer might be willing to put the car on a lot and charge you a commission if it is sold. Under this agreement the dealer **would not take ownership** of the car—it would still belong to you. Therefore, if an inventory count were taken, the car should not be included in the dealer's inventory. Many car, boat, craft, clothing, and antique dealers sell goods on consignment to keep their inventory costs down and to avoid the risk of purchasing an item they won't be able to sell.

BEFORE YOU GO ON . . .

- **REVIEW IT**

    1. What are the three inventory categories a manufacturing company would be likely to use? Why should financial statement users be aware of these categories?
    2. What steps are involved in determining inventory quantities?
    3. How is ownership determined for goods in transit?
    4. Who has title to consigned goods?

Inventory Costing

After the quantity of units of inventory has been determined, unit costs are applied to those quantities to determine the total cost of the goods sold and cost of the ending inventory. This process can be complicated if inventory items have been purchased at different times and at different prices. For example, assume that PDA Ltd. purchases three identical BlackBerry handheld wireless devices at costs of $600, $550, and $500. During the month, PDA sells two BlackBerries at $800 each. These facts are summarized below.

> **STUDY OBJECTIVE**
>
> **2**
>
> Explain the basis of accounting for inventories and apply the inventory cost flow assumptions under a periodic inventory system.

Purchases		
Feb. 3	1 BlackBerry Model 6720	$ 600
5	1 BlackBerry Model 6720	550
22	1 BlackBerry Model 6720	500
Total goods available for sale		$1,650
Sales		
Feb. 25	2 BlackBerry Model 6720	$1,600 ($800 × 2)

Cost of goods sold will differ depending on which of the units the company sold. For example, cost of goods sold might be $1,150 ($600 + $550) or $1,100 ($600 + $500) or $1,050 ($550 + $500). In this section, we discuss the different inventory costing assumptions PDA can use.

SPECIFIC IDENTIFICATION

If the BlackBerry models sold by PDA Ltd. are the ones it purchased February 3 and February 22, then its cost of goods sold is $1,100 ($600 + $500), and its ending inventory is $550. If PDA can positively identify which particular units were sold and which are still in ending inventory, it can use the specific identification method of inventory costing. In this case, ending inventory and cost of goods sold are easily and accurately determined.

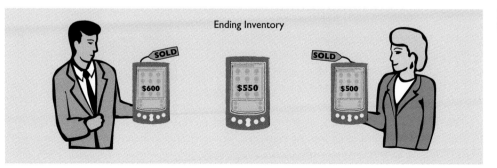

Illustration 6-2
Specific identification

Specific identification requires that records be kept of the original cost of each individual inventory item. In the past, specific identification could only be used when a company sold high-unit-cost items that could be identified clearly from the time of purchase through the time of sale. Cars are an example of such an item as a dealership can easily identify each car by its serial number.

Today, with bar coding, it is theoretically possible to use specific identification with nearly any type of product. The reality is, however, that this practice is still relatively rare. Instead, rather than keep track of the cost of each particular item sold, most companies make assumptions, called **cost flow assumptions**, about which units are sold. Even Caterpillar, in the feature story, uses a cost flow assumption instead of specific identification to track its sales of the Cat 797.

COST FLOW ASSUMPTIONS

Because specific identification is often impractical, other cost flow methods are allowed. These differ from specific identification as they assume flows of costs that may be unrelated to the physical flow of goods. There are three commonly assumed cost flow methods:

1. First-in, first-out (FIFO)
2. Average
3. Last-in, first-out (LIFO)

No accounting rule requires the cost flow assumption to be consistent with the physical movement of goods. Management should choose the cost flow method **which results in the fairest matching of costs against revenues** for the type of business.

These cost flow assumptions can be illustrated using the data of PDA Ltd. Under the FIFO cost flow assumption, the first goods purchased are assumed to be the first goods sold. Thus, PDA's cost of goods sold under FIFO would be $1,150 ($600 + $550). Under the average cost flow assumption, the cost of goods sold is calculated using the weighted average cost of all units purchased. In this case, the weighted average cost of each unit would be $550 [($600 + $550 + $500) ÷ 3]. The cost of goods sold for the two units sold would be $1,100 ($550 × 2). Finally, under the LIFO cost flow assumption, the last goods purchased are assumed to be the first goods sold. Thus, PDA's cost of goods sold under LIFO would be $1,050 ($500 + $550).

Any of the three cost flow assumptions can be applied within a perpetual inventory system or a periodic inventory system. Under a perpetual inventory system, the cost of goods available for sale is allocated to cost of goods sold and ending inventory as each item is sold. Under a periodic inventory system, the allocation is made only at the end of the period. Illustration 6-3 shows this allocation.

Illustration 6-3
Allocation of cost of goods available for sale

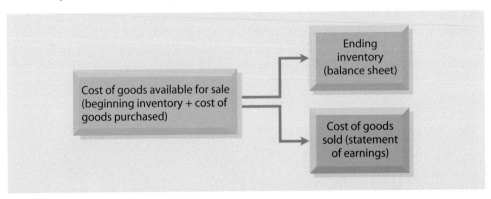

We will use the periodic inventory system to illustrate cost flow assumptions in this chapter, for a number of reasons. First, many companies that use a perpetual inventory system use it only to keep track of *quantities* on hand. They then determine cost of goods sold at the end of the period using one of the three cost flow assumptions under a periodic inventory system. Second, most companies that use the average cost flow assumption use it under a periodic inventory system. Third, the FIFO cost flow assumption gives the same results under the periodic and perpetual systems. Finally, it is simpler to demonstrate the cost flow assumptions under the periodic inventory system, which makes them easier to understand. (If you would like to expand your knowledge beyond the periodic inventory system, read the chapter appendix, as it explains the use of these cost flow assumptions under a perpetual inventory system.)

To illustrate these three inventory cost flow assumptions in a periodic inventory system, we will assume that Wynneck Electronics Ltd. has the information shown in Illustration 6-4 for one of its products, an Astro condenser.

WYNNECK ELECTRONICS LTD.				
Astro Condensers				
Date	Explanation	Units	Unit Cost	Total Cost
Jan. 1	Beginning inventory	100	$10	$ 1,000
Apr. 15	Purchase	200	11	2,200
Aug. 24	Purchase	300	12	3,600
Nov. 27	Purchase	400	13	5,200
	Total	1,000		$12,000

Illustration 6-4
Cost of goods available
for sale

The company had a total of 1,000 units available for sale during the period. The total cost of these units was $12,000. A physical inventory count at the end of the year determined that 550 units were sold during the year and 450 units remained in inventory at December 31. The question is how to determine what unit costs to use to calculate the cost of the goods sold and the ending inventory. Whatever the inventory cost flow assumption used, the cost allocated to the units sold and the units in inventory must add up to $12,000, the total cost of all goods available for sale.

First-In, First-Out (FIFO)

The first-in, first-out (FIFO) cost flow assumption assumes that the **earliest goods** purchased are the first to be sold. FIFO often parallels the actual physical flow of merchandise, because it is generally good business practice to sell the oldest units first. Under the FIFO method, therefore, the costs of the earliest goods purchased are the first to be recognized as cost of goods sold. (Note that this does not necessarily mean that the oldest units are actually sold first, only that the costs of the oldest units are recognized first. In a bin of picture hangers at the hardware store, for example, no one really knows, nor would it matter, which hangers are sold first.)

The allocation of the cost of goods available for sale at Wynneck Electronics under FIFO is shown in Illustration 6-5.

Illustration 6-5
Allocation of costs—FIFO

POOL OF COSTS COST OF GOODS AVAILABLE FOR SALE				
Date	Explanation	Units	Unit Cost	Total Cost
Jan. 1	Beginning inventory	100	$10	$ 1,000
Apr. 15	Purchase	200	11	2,200
Aug. 24	Purchase	300	12	3,600
Nov. 27	Purchase	400	13	5,200
	Total	1,000		$12,000

STEP 1: COST OF GOODS SOLD				STEP 2: ENDING INVENTORY			
Date	Units	Unit Cost	Total Cost	Date	Units	Unit Cost	Total Cost
Jan. 1	100	$10	$1,000	Nov. 27	400	$13	$5,200
Apr. 15	200	11	2,200	Aug. 24	50	12	600
Aug. 24	250	12	3,000	Total	450		$5,800
Total	550		$6,200				

Proof:
$6,200 + $5,800 = $12,000

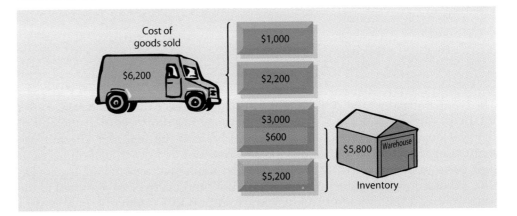

In the periodic inventory system, we ignore the different dates of each of the sales. Instead, **at the end of the period** we assume that the entire pool of costs is available for allocation.

To determine the cost of the 550 units sold, we use the costs of the first 550 units purchased, since FIFO assumes that the first goods sold were the first goods purchased. Simply start at the beginning of the period and count forward until the total number of units sold (550) is reached. The result is that of the 300 units purchased on August 24, only 250 units are assumed sold.

After calculating the cost of goods sold, we must next allocate a cost to the remaining inventory. Under FIFO, the cost of the ending inventory is obtained by taking the unit cost of the most recent purchase and working backward until all units of inventory have been costed. In this example, the 450 units of ending inventory must be costed using the most recent purchase costs. The last purchase was 400 units at $13 on November 27. The remaining 50 units are costed at the price of the second most recent purchase, $12, on August 24.

Another way of determining either the ending inventory or cost of goods sold is to calculate one of them and subtract it from the cost of goods available for sale. The result is the other amount. For example, if we wish to calculate only the ending inventory and use it to determine the cost of goods sold, we can proceed as shown in Illustration 6-6.

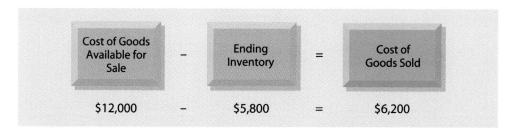

Illustration 6-6
Calculation of cost of
goods sold

Because of the potential for calculation errors, the authors prefer to calculate the ending inventory and cost of goods sold amounts separately. The advantage is that the total of these two amounts can then be compared to the cost of goods available for sale amount to check the accuracy of the calculations (e.g., $6,200 + $5,800 = $12,000).

Average

The average cost flow assumption assumes that the goods available for sale are homogeneous or nondistinguishable. Under this assumption, the allocation of the cost of goods available for sale is made on the basis of the weighted average unit cost incurred. The formula and calculation of the weighted average unit cost are given in Illustration 6-7.

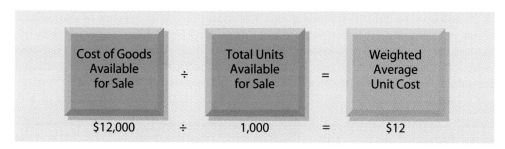

Illustration 6-7
Calculation of weighted
average unit cost

The weighted average unit cost is then applied to the units sold to determine the cost of goods sold and the units on hand to determine the cost of the ending inventory. The allocation of the cost of goods available for sale at Wynneck Electronics using weighted average cost is shown in Illustration 6-8.

Illustration 6-8
Allocation of costs—
average

POOL OF COSTS COST OF GOODS AVAILABLE FOR SALE				
Date	Explanation	Units	Unit Cost	Total Cost
Jan. 1	Beginning inventory	100	$10	$ 1,000
Apr. 15	Purchase	200	11	2,200
Aug. 24	Purchase	300	12	3,600
Nov. 27	Purchase	400	13	5,200
	Total	1,000		$12,000

STEP 1: COST OF GOODS SOLD			STEP 2: ENDING INVENTORY		
Units	Weighted Average Unit Cost	Total Cost	Units	Weighted Average Unit Cost	Total Cost
550 ×	$12	= $6,600	450 ×	$12	= $5,400

Proof:
$6,600 + $5,400 = $12,000

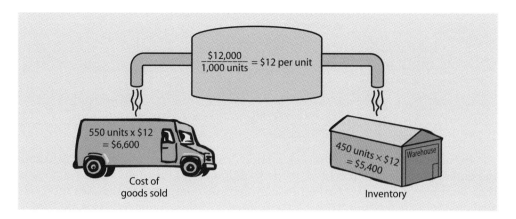

Note that this cost flow assumption does not use the average of the unit costs. That average is $11.50 [($10 + $11 + $12 + $13) ÷ 4 = $11.50]. The average cost flow assumption instead uses the average **weighted** by the quantities purchased at each unit cost.

Last-In, First-Out (LIFO)

The last-in, first-out (LIFO) cost flow assumption assumes that the **latest goods purchased** are the first to be sold. LIFO seldom matches the actual physical flow of inventory. (Exceptions include goods stored in piles, such as coal or hay, where goods are removed from the top of the pile as sold.) Under the LIFO cost flow assumption, the costs of the latest goods purchased are the first to be recognized when calculating cost of goods sold. The allocation of the cost of goods available for sale at Wynneck Electronics under LIFO is shown in Illustration 6-9.

Illustration 6-9
Allocation of costs—LIFO

POOL OF COSTS
COST OF GOODS AVAILABLE FOR SALE

Date	Explanation	Units	Unit Cost	Total Cost
Jan. 1	Beginning inventory	100	$10	$ 1,000
Apr. 15	Purchase	200	11	2,200
Aug. 24	Purchase	300	12	3,600
Nov. 27	Purchase	400	13	5,200
	Total	1,000		$12,000

STEP 1: COST OF GOODS SOLD				STEP 2: ENDING INVENTORY			
Date	Units	Unit Cost	Total Cost	Date	Units	Unit Cost	Total Cost
Nov. 27	400	$13	$5,200	Jan. 1	100	$10	$1,000
Aug. 24	150	12	1,800	Apr. 15	200	11	2,200
	550		$7,000	Aug. 24	150	12	1,800
				Total	450		$5,000

Proof:
$7,000 + $5,000 = $12,000

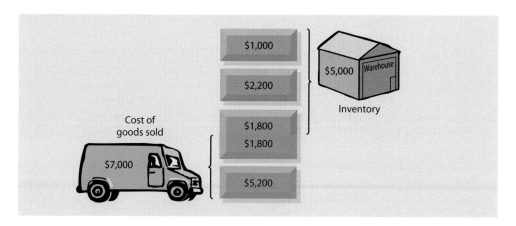

Remember that, under a periodic inventory system, all goods purchased during the period are assumed to be available for the first sale, even goods that are purchased after that sale. Under LIFO, the cost of the **last** goods in is the **first** to be assigned to cost of goods sold. Using our example, start at the end of the period and count backwards until you reach the total number of units sold (550). The result is that 400 units from the November 27, or last, purchase are assumed to be sold first, and only 150 units from the next purchase (August 24) are needed to reach the total 550 units sold.

Under LIFO, since it is assumed that the first goods sold were those that were most recently purchased, ending inventory is based on the costs of the oldest units purchased. That is, the cost of the ending inventory is obtained by taking the unit cost of the earliest goods available for sale and working forward until all units of inventory have been costed. In our example, therefore, the 450 units of ending inventory must be costed using the earliest purchase prices. The first purchase was 100 units at $10 in the January 1 beginning inventory. Then 200 units were purchased at $11. The remaining 150 units are costed at $12 per unit (the August 24 purchase price).

FINANCIAL STATEMENT EFFECTS OF COST FLOW ASSUMPTIONS

Companies can choose the specific identification method or any of the three cost flow assumptions—all are acceptable for use. For example, Ault Foods, Canadian Tire, and Sobeys currently use FIFO. Abitibi-Price, Andrés Wines, and Mountain Equipment Co-op use average. Alberta Natural Gas, Cominco, and Suncor use LIFO for part or all of their inventory. Indeed, a company may use more than one cost flow assumption at the same time. Finning International, for example, uses specific identification to account for its equipment inventory, FIFO to account for about two-thirds of its inventory of parts and supplies, and average to account for the remainder. Illustration 6-10 shows the use of the three assumed cost flow assumptions in Canada.

The reasons companies have for adopting different inventory cost flow assumptions are varied, but they usually involve one of two factors:

1. Statement of earnings effects
2. Balance sheet effects

Statement of Earnings Effects

To understand why companies might choose a particular cost flow assumption, let's examine the effects of the different cost flow assumptions on the financial statements of Wynneck Electronics. The condensed statements of earnings in Illustration 6-11

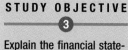

STUDY OBJECTIVE

③

Explain the financial statement effects of each of the inventory cost flow assumptions.

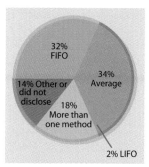

Illustration 6-10
Use of cost flow assumptions by Canadian public companies

Helpful Hint The management of companies in the same industry may reach different conclusions as to the most appropriate method for their respective companies.

assume that Wynneck sold its 550 units for $11,500, had operating expenses of $2,000, and is subject to an income tax rate of 30%.

Although the cost of goods available for sale ($12,000) is the same under each of the three inventory cost flow assumptions, the ending inventories and costs of goods sold are different. This difference is due to the unit costs that are allocated to cost of goods sold and to ending inventory. Each dollar of difference in ending inventory results in a corresponding dollar difference in earnings before income tax. For Wynneck, an $800 difference exists between the FIFO and LIFO cost of goods sold.

Illustration 6-11
Comparative effects of cost flow assumptions

WYNNECK ELECTRONICS LTD.
Condensed Statement of Earnings

	FIFO		Average		LIFO	
Sales		$11,500		$11,500		$11,500
Beginning inventory	$ 1,000		$ 1,000		$ 1,000	
Purchases	11,000		11,000		11,000	
Cost of goods available for sale	12,000		12,000		12,000	
Ending inventory	5,800		5,400		5,000	
Cost of goods sold		6,200		6,600		7,000
Gross profit		5,300		4,900		4,500
Operating expenses		2,000		2,000		2,000
Earnings before income tax		3,300		2,900		2,500
Income tax expense (30% except for LIFO)		990		870		990
Net earnings		$ 2,310		$ 2,030		$ 1,510

In periods of changing prices, the cost flow assumption can have a significant impact on earnings. In a period of inflation (rising prices), FIFO produces higher net earnings because the lower unit costs of the first units purchased are matched against revenues. When prices are rising (as is the case here for Wynneck), FIFO reports the highest net earnings ($2,310) and LIFO the lowest ($1,510). Average falls roughly in the middle ($2,030). If prices are falling, the results from the use of FIFO and LIFO are reversed: FIFO will report the lowest net earnings and LIFO the highest. To management, higher net earnings are an advantage: they cause external users to view the company more favourably. In addition, if management bonuses are based on net earnings, FIFO will provide the basis for higher bonuses.

Overall, **LIFO provides the best statement of earnings valuation. It matches** current costs with current revenues since, under LIFO, the cost of goods sold is assumed to be the cost of the most recently acquired goods. However, even though LIFO may produce the best match of revenues and expenses, it is seldom used in Canada. The method is subject to manipulation, depending on the timing of purchases. The use of LIFO is also not permitted for income tax purposes and most firms do not wish to maintain two sets of inventory records—one for accounting purposes and another for income tax purposes. Companies can use FIFO or average to determine their income tax, but not LIFO. That is why, in Illustration 6-11, it was assumed that the income tax expense amount was the same under both the FIFO and LIFO alternatives.

BUSINESS INSIGHT

INTERNATIONAL PERSPECTIVE

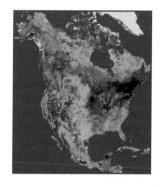

In the U.S., contrary to Canadian practice, the use of LIFO is permitted for income tax purposes. Not surprisingly, many U.S. corporations choose LIFO because it reduces inventory profits and taxes. It also increases after-tax cash flow, since less income tax has to be paid in the short term.

The international community has considered a rule that would ban LIFO entirely and force corporations to use FIFO. This proposed rule was defeated, but the issue is almost certain to reappear. As John Wulff, controller for Union Carbide, noted, "We were in support of the international effort up until the proposal to eliminate LIFO." Wulff says that if Union Carbide had been suddenly forced to switch from LIFO to FIFO, its reported $632 million pre-tax earnings would have jumped by $300 million. That would have increased Union Carbide's income tax bill by as much as $120 million.

Balance Sheet Effects

A major advantage of FIFO is that in a period of inflation, the costs allocated to ending inventory will approximate their current cost. For example, for Wynneck, 400 of the 450 units in the ending inventory are costed under FIFO at the higher November 27 unit cost of $13.

Conversely, a major shortcoming of LIFO is that in a period of inflation, the costs allocated to ending inventory may be significantly understated in terms of current cost. This is true for Wynneck, where the cost of the ending inventory includes the $10 unit cost of the beginning inventory. The understatement becomes greater over prolonged periods of inflation if the inventory includes goods purchased in one or more prior accounting periods.

Helpful Hint LIFO may provide the best statement of earnings valuation, but FIFO provides the best balance sheet valuation.

Summary of Effects

Illustration 6-12 summarizes the key financial statement differences that will result from the different choices of cost flow assumption during a period of rising prices. These effects will be the inverse if prices are falling, and equal if prices are constant. In all instances, the use of the average cost flow assumption will yield results that fall somewhere in between those produced by FIFO and LIFO.

	FIFO	LIFO
Cost of goods sold	Lowest	Highest
Gross profit/Net earnings	Highest	Lowest
Pre-tax cash flow	Same	Same
Ending inventory	Highest	Lowest

Illustration 6-12
Financial statement effects of cost flow assumptions during a period of inflation

We have seen that both inventory on the balance sheet and net earnings on the statement of earnings are highest when FIFO is used in a period of inflation. Do not confuse this with cash flow. All three cost flow assumptions produce exactly the same cash flow before income taxes. Sales and purchases are not affected by the choice of cost flow assumption. The only thing affected is the allocation between ending inventory and cost of goods sold, which does not involve cash.

It is also worth remembering that all three cost flow assumptions will yield exactly the same results over the life cycle of the business or its product. That is, the allocation between cost of goods sold and ending inventory may vary annually, but will produce the same cumulative results over time. Although much has been written about the impact of the choice of inventory cost flow assumption on a variety of performance measures, in reality there is little real economic distinction among the assumptions over time.

Decision Toolkit

DECISION CHECKPOINTS	INFO NEEDED FOR DECISION	TOOL TO USE FOR DECISION	HOW TO EVALUATE RESULTS
What is the impact of the choice of inventory cost flow assumption?	Are prices increasing, or are they decreasing?	Statement of earnings and balance sheet effects	It depends on the objective. In a period of rising prices, earnings and inventory are higher under FIFO. LIFO provides opposite results. Average can moderate the impact of changing prices.

USING INVENTORY COST FLOW ASSUMPTIONS CONSISTENTLY

Whatever cost flow assumption a company chooses, it should be used consistently from one accounting period to another. Consistent application enhances the comparability of financial statements over successive time periods. In contrast, using FIFO one year and average the next year would make it difficult to compare the net earnings of the two years.

Although consistent application is preferred, it does not mean that a company may *never* change its inventory cost flow assumption. When a company adopts a different assumption, the change and its effects on prior periods should be disclosed in the financial statements. This conforms with the **full disclosure principle**, which requires all relevant information to be disclosed.

BEFORE YOU GO ON . . .

● **REVIEW IT**

1. What inventory cost flow assumption does Loblaw use to account for its inventories? The answer to this question is provided at the end of the chapter.
2. Which inventory cost flow assumption produces the highest net earnings in a period of rising prices? The lowest ending inventory valuation? The highest cash flow?

● **DO IT**

The accounting records of Ag Implement Inc. show the following data:

Beginning inventory	4,000 units at $3
Purchases	6,000 units at $4
Sales	8,000 units at $8

Determine the cost of goods sold and ending inventory under a periodic inventory system using (a) FIFO, (b) average, and (c) LIFO.

Action Plan

- Ignore selling price in allocating cost.
- Allocate costs between goods sold and goods on hand for each cost flow assumption.
- For FIFO, allocate the earliest costs to the goods sold and the latest costs to the goods on hand.
- For average, determine the weighted average unit cost (cost of goods available for sale ÷ number of units available for sale). Multiply this cost by the number of units sold and the number of the units on hand.

- For LIFO, allocate the latest costs to the goods sold and the earliest costs to the goods on hand.
- Prove your work: Cost of goods sold + Ending inventory = Cost of goods available for sale.

Solution

(a) FIFO cost of goods sold: (4,000 × \$3) + (4,000 × \$4) = \$28,000
    FIFO ending inventory: 2,000 × \$4 = \$8,000
    Proof: \$28,000 + \$8,000 = \$36,000
(b) Weighted average unit cost: [(4,000 × \$3) + (6,000 × \$4)] ÷ 10,000 = \$3.60
    Average cost of goods sold: 8,000 × \$3.60 = \$28,800
    Average ending inventory: 2,000 × \$3.60 = \$7,200
    Proof: \$28,800 + \$7,200 = \$36,000
(c) LIFO cost of goods sold: (6,000 × \$4) + (2,000 × \$3) = \$30,000
    LIFO ending inventory: 2,000 × \$3 = \$6,000
    Proof: \$30,000 + \$6,000 = \$36,000

Inventory Errors

Unfortunately, errors occasionally occur in accounting for inventory. In some cases, errors are caused by a failure to count or cost the inventory correctly. In other cases, errors occur because proper recognition is not given to the transfer of legal title to goods that are in transit. When errors occur, they affect both the statement of earnings and the balance sheet.

STUDY OBJECTIVE
4
Indicate the effects of inventory errors on the financial statements.

STATEMENT OF EARNINGS EFFECTS

As you know, both the beginning and ending inventories appear in the statement of earnings of a company using the periodic inventory system. The ending inventory of one period automatically becomes the beginning inventory of the next period. Consequently, an error in ending inventory can affect the calculation of cost of goods sold and net earnings in two periods.

The formula in Illustration 6-13 makes it clear that inventory errors have a significant impact on the calculation of cost of goods sold. The effects of inventory errors can be calculated by entering data in the formula.

Illustration 6-13
Calculation of cost of goods sold

If beginning inventory is understated, cost of goods sold will be understated. On the other hand, understating ending inventory will overstate cost of goods sold. The effects of inventory errors on the current year's statement of earnings are shown in Illustration 6-14.

Illustration 6-14
Effects of inventory errors on statement of earnings

Inventory Error	Cost of Goods Sold	Net Earnings
Understate beginning inventory	Understated	Overstated
Overstate beginning inventory	Overstated	Understated
Understate cost of goods purchased	Understated	Overstated
Overstate cost of goods purchased	Overstated	Understated
Understate ending inventory	Overstated	Understated
Overstate ending inventory	Understated	Overstated

Illustration 6-15
Effects of inventory errors on statement of earnings for two years

An error in the *ending* inventory of the current period will have a **reverse effect on net earnings of the next accounting period**. This is shown in Illustration 6-15. Note that the $3,000 understatement of ending inventory in 2004 results in an overstatement of cost of goods sold and an understatement of net earnings in the same year. It also results in an understatement of beginning inventory and cost of goods sold and an overstatement of net earnings in 2005.

SAMPLE COMPANY
Statement of Earnings

	2004 Incorrect		2004 Correct		2005 Incorrect		2005 Correct	
Sales		$80,000		$80,000		$90,000		$90,000
Beginning inventory	$20,000		$20,000		$12,000		$15,000	
Cost of goods purchased	40,000		40,000		68,000		68,000	
Cost of goods available for sale	60,000		60,000		80,000		83,000	
Ending inventory	12,000		15,000		23,000		23,000	
Cost of goods sold		48,000		45,000		57,000		60,000
Gross profit		32,000		35,000		33,000		30,000
Operating expenses		10,000		10,000		20,000		20,000
Net earnings		$22,000		$25,000		$13,000		$10,000

Net earnings understated ($3,000)

Net earnings overstated $3,000

The errors cancel. Thus the combined total earnings for the two-year period are correct.

Over the two years, total net earnings are correct because the errors offset each other. Notice that total earnings using incorrect data are $35,000 ($22,000 + $13,000), which is the same as the total earnings of $35,000 ($25,000 + $10,000) using correct data. Also note in this example that an error in the beginning inventory does not result in a corresponding error in the ending inventory for that period. The correctness of the ending inventory depends entirely on the accuracy of taking and costing the inventory at the balance sheet date under the periodic inventory system.

BUSINESS INSIGHT

ETHICS PERSPECTIVE

Inventory fraud increases during recessions. Such fraud includes pricing inventory at amounts in excess of its actual value, or claiming to have inventory which doesn't exist. Inventory fraud is usually done to overstate ending inventory, thereby understating cost of goods sold and creating higher earnings.

BALANCE SHEET EFFECTS

The effect of ending inventory errors on the balance sheet can be calculated by using the basic accounting equation: Assets = Liabilities + Shareholders' Equity. Errors in the ending inventory have the effects shown in Illustration 6-16.

Ending Inventory Error	Assets	=	Liabilities	+	Shareholders' Equity
Overstated	Overstated		No effect		Overstated
Understated	Understated		No effect		Understated

Illustration 6-16
Effects of ending inventory errors on balance sheet

Recall from the previous section that errors in ending inventory affect net earnings. If net earnings is affected, then shareholders' equity will be affected by the same amount since net earnings is closed into the Retained Earnings account, which is part of shareholders' equity. Consequently, an error in ending inventory affects the asset account Inventory and the shareholders' equity account Retained Earnings equally.

The effect of an error in ending inventory on the next period was shown in Illustration 6-15. Recall that if the error is not corrected, the combined total net earnings for the two periods would be correct. In the example, therefore, the assets and shareholders' equity reported on the balance sheet at the end of 2005 will be correct.

BEFORE YOU GO ON . . .

● **REVIEW IT**

1. How do inventory errors affect the statement of earnings? Balance sheet?

● **DO IT**

On July 31, 2004, Zhang Inc. counted and recorded $600,000 of inventory. This count did not include $90,000 of goods in transit purchased on July 29 on account, shipped FOB shipping point. Identify any accounts that are in error at July 31, 2004. State the amount and direction (e.g., understated or overstated) of the error for each of these accounts.

Action Plan

- Use the cost of goods sold formula to determine the impact of the error on statement of earnings accounts.
- Use the accounting equation to determine the impact of the error on balance sheet accounts.

Solution

The correct inventory count should have been $690,000 ($600,000 + $90,000).

Statement of earnings accounts: Purchases are understated (U) by $90,000. However, since ending inventory is also understated, cost of goods sold and net earnings will be correct. [Beginning inventory + Cost of goods purchased (U $90,000) − Ending inventory (U $90,000) = Cost of goods sold]

Balance sheet accounts: Merchandise Inventory (ending) is understated by $90,000, as is Accounts Payable. [Assets (U $90,000) = Liabilities (U $90,000) + Shareholders' Equity]

Valuing Inventory at the Lower of Cost and Market

The value of the inventory of companies selling high-tech or fashion goods can drop very quickly due to changes in technology or in fashions. These circumstances sometimes call for inventory valuation methods other than those presented so far. For example, suppose you are the owner of a retail store that sells computers. During the recent 12-month period, the cost of the computers dropped almost 30%. At the end of your fiscal year, you have some of these computers in inventory. Do you think your inventory should be stated at cost, in accordance with the cost principle, or at its lower market value?

As you probably reasoned, this situation requires a departure from the cost basis of accounting. When the value of inventory is lower than its cost, the inventory is written down to its market value. This is done by valuing the inventory at the lower of cost and market (LCM) in the period in which the decline in value occurs. LCM is an example of the accounting concept of **conservatism**, which holds that the best choice among accounting alternatives is the method that is least likely to overstate assets and net earnings.

LCM is applied to the inventory after specific identification or one of the cost flow assumptions (FIFO, average, or LIFO) has been used to determine cost.

The term *market* in the phrase *lower of cost and market* is not specifically defined in Canada. It can mean replacement cost or net realizable value, among other things. The majority of Canadian companies use net realizable value to define market for LCM purposes. For a merchandising company, net realizable value is the selling price, less any costs required to make the goods ready for sale.

 International Note

Almost every country in the world applies the LCM rule; however, the definition of **market** can vary. The International Accounting Standards Commitee defines market as net realizable value, as do the UK, France, and Germany. The U.S., Italy, and Japan define it as replacement cost.

FALCONBRIDGE

BUSINESS INSIGHT

INVESTOR PERSPECTIVE

In its 2002 third quarter financial statements, Falconbridge Limited wrote down the value of its metal inventory by $11 million, after taxes. Falconbridge's president and chief executive officer, Aaron Regent, commented that global economic conditions were uncertain and business confidence low. He said that this had a negative impact on demand for metals, particularly copper and zinc. On receiving the news, analysts immediately cut share price targets by 12% for Falconbridge.

Analysis of Inventory

For companies that sell goods, managing inventory levels can be one of the most critical tasks. Having too much inventory on hand can cost the company money in storage costs, interest costs (on funds tied up in inventory), and costs associated with the obsolescence of technology-driven goods (e.g., computer memory) or shifts in fashion (e.g., clothes). But having too little inventory on hand can result in lost sales. In this section we discuss some issues related to evaluating inventory levels.

INVENTORY TURNOVER

The inventory turnover ratio is calculated as cost of goods sold divided by average inventory. Its complement, the days in inventory ratio, indicates the average age of the inventory. It is calculated as 365 days divided by the inventory turnover ratio. Both measures indicate how quickly a company sells its goods—how many times the inventory "turns over" (is sold) during the year.

Low inventory turnover or high days in inventory could indicate that the company has excessive carrying costs (e.g., interest, storage, insurance, taxes) or obsolete inventory. High inventory turnover or low days in inventory indicates the company is tying up little of its funds in inventory—i.e. that it has a minimal amount of inventory on hand at any one time. Although having minimal funds tied up in inventory suggests efficiency, too high an inventory turnover ratio may indicate that the company is losing sales opportunities because of inventory shortages. For example, investment analysts suggested recently that Office Depot had gone too far in reducing its inventory—they said they were seeing too many empty shelves. Management should closely monitor this ratio to achieve the best balance between too much and too little inventory.

We will use Office Depot, Inc., to illustrate the calculation of the inventory turnover and days in inventory ratios. Office Depot is the world's biggest chain of office supply stores, operating in 17 countries besides Canada. The following data are available for Office Depot:

(in U.S. millions)	2002	2001	2000
Ending inventory	$1,305.6	$1,253.4	$1,420.8
Cost of goods sold	8,022.7	7,940.1	8,435.9

Illustration 6-17 presents the inventory turnover and days in inventory for Office Depot.

Illustration 6-17
Inventory turnover and days in inventory

$$\text{INVENTORY TURNOVER} = \frac{\text{COST OF GOODS SOLD}}{\text{AVERAGE INVENTORY}}$$

$$\text{DAYS IN INVENTORY} = \frac{365 \text{ DAYS}}{\text{INVENTORY TURNOVER}}$$

(in U.S. millions)		2002	2001
Office Depot	Inventory turnover	$\frac{\$8,022.7}{(\$1,305.6 + \$1,253.4) \div 2} = 6.3$ times	$\frac{\$7,940.1}{(\$1,253.4 + \$1,420.8) \div 2} = 5.9$ times
	Days in inventory	$\frac{365 \text{ days}}{6.3} = 58$ days	$\frac{365 \text{ days}}{5.9} = 62$ days
Industry average	Inventory turnover	4.4 times	3.9 times
	Days in inventory	83 days	94 days

The calculations in Illustration 6-17 show that Office Depot has improved its inventory turnover from 2001 to 2002 and turns its inventory over more frequently than the industry in general. This suggests that Office Depot is more efficient in its inventory management. However, as mentioned earlier, it is a balancing act to keep minimum amounts of inventory on hand, while still keeping the shelves full of what customers are looking for. Turning over the inventory too often can result in empty shelves and unsatisfied customers.

BEFORE YOU GO ON . . .

- **REVIEW IT**

1. When should inventory be reported at a value other than cost?
2. What is the purpose of the inventory turnover ratio? What is the relationship between the inventory turnover and days in inventory ratios?

Decision Toolkit

DECISION CHECKPOINTS	INFO NEEDED FOR DECISION	TOOL TO USE FOR DECISION	HOW TO EVALUATE RESULTS
How long is an item in inventory?	Cost of goods sold; beginning and ending inventory	$\text{Inventory turnover} = \dfrac{\text{Cost of goods sold}}{\text{Average inventory}}$ $\text{Days in inventory} = \dfrac{365 \text{ days}}{\text{Inventory turnover}}$	A higher inventory turnover or lower days in inventory suggests that management is reducing the amount of inventory on hand, relative to sales.

APPENDIX 6A

INVENTORY COST FLOW ASSUMPTIONS IN PERPETUAL INVENTORY SYSTEMS

STUDY OBJECTIVE

7

Apply the inventory cost flow assumptions under a perpetual inventory system.

Each of the inventory cost flow assumptions described in the chapter for a periodic inventory system may be used in a perpetual inventory system. To show how to use the three cost flow assumptions (FIFO, average, and LIFO) under a perpetual system, we will use the data in Illustration 6A-1 and from earlier in this chapter for the Wynneck Electronics Astro Condenser.

Illustration 6A-1
Cost of goods available for sale

WYNNECK ELECTRONICS LTD. Astro Condensers						
Date	Explanation	Units	Unit Cost	Total Cost	Balance in Units
Jan. 1	Beginning inventory	100	$10	$ 1,000	100
Apr. 15	Purchases	200	11	2,200	300
Aug. 24	Purchases	300	12	3,600	600
Sept. 10	Sale	550			50
Nov. 27	Purchases	400	13	5,200	450
	Total			$12,000	

First-In, First-Out (FIFO)

Under FIFO, the cost of the earliest goods on hand before each sale is charged to cost of goods sold. The cost of goods sold on September 10 therefore consists of all of the units on hand on January 1, all of the units purchased on April 15, and

250 of the units purchased on August 24. Illustration 6A-2 shows the inventory under a FIFO perpetual system.

Date	Purchases	Cost of Goods Sold	Balance
Jan. 1			(100 @ $10) $1,000
Apr. 15	(200 @ $11) $2,200		(100 @ $10) ⎱ $3,200 (200 @ $11) ⎰
Aug. 24	(300 @ $12) $3,600		(100 @ $10) ⎫ (200 @ $11) ⎬ $6,800 (300 @ $12) ⎭
Sept. 10		(100 @ $10) ⎫ (200 @ $11) ⎬ $6,200 (250 @ $12) ⎭	(50 @ $12) $ 600
Nov. 27	(400 @ $13) $5,200		(50 @ $12) ⎱ $5,800 (400 @ $13) ⎰

As shown, the ending inventory in this situation is $5,800, and the cost of goods sold is $6,200.

The results under FIFO in a perpetual system are the **same as in a periodic system** (see Illustration 6-5 where, similarly, the ending inventory is $5,800 and the cost of goods sold is $6,200). Under both inventory systems, the first costs in are the ones assigned to cost of goods sold.

Average

The average cost flow assumption in a perpetual inventory system is often called the **moving average cost flow assumption**. Under this assumption, a new average is calculated after each purchase. The weighted average cost is calculated by dividing the cost of goods available for sale by the number of units on hand. The average cost is then applied to (1) the units sold, to determine the cost of goods sold, and (2) the remaining units on hand, to determine the cost of the ending inventory. Use of the average cost flow assumption by Wynneck Electronics is shown in Illustration 6A-3.

Date	Purchases	Cost of Goods Sold	Balance
Jan. 1			(100 @ $10.000) $1,000
Apr. 15	(200 @ $11) $2,200		(300 @ $10.667) $3,200
Aug. 24	(300 @ $12) $3,600		(600 @ $11.333) $6,800
Sept. 10		(550 @ $11.333) $6,233	(50 @ $11.333) $ 567
Nov. 27	(400 @ $13) $5,200		(450 @ $12.816) $5,767

As indicated in Illustration 6A-3, **a new average is calculated each time a purchase (or purchase return) is made.** On April 15, after 200 units are purchased for $2,200, a total of 300 units costing $3,200 ($1,000 + $2,200) are on hand. The average unit cost is $10.667 ($3,200 ÷ 300). On August 24, after 300 units are purchased for $3,600, a total of 600 units costing $6,800 ($1,000 + $2,200 + $3,600) are on hand. This results in an average cost per unit of $11.333 ($6,800 ÷ 600). This unit cost of $11.333 is used in determining the cost of goods sold until another purchase is made, and a new unit cost is again calculated. Accordingly, the unit cost of the 550 units sold on September 10 is $11.333, and the total cost of goods sold is $6,233. On November 27, following the purchase of

400 units for $5,200, there are 450 units on hand costing $5,767 ($567 + $5,200), resulting in a new average cost of $12.816 ($5,767 ÷ 450).

This moving average cost under the perpetual inventory system should be compared to Illustration 6-8 (shown earlier in the chapter) which presents the weighted average cost under a periodic inventory system.

Last-In, First-Out (LIFO)

With the LIFO cost flow assumption under a perpetual system, the cost of the most recent purchase prior to a sale is allocated to the units sold. Therefore, the cost of the goods sold on September 10 consists of all the units from the August 24 and April 15 purchases and 50 of the units in beginning inventory. For our example, the ending inventory under a LIFO cost flow assumption is calculated in Illustration 6A-4.

Illustration 6A-4
LIFO—perpetual system

Date	Purchases	Cost of Goods Sold	Balance
Jan. 1			(100 @ $10) $1,000
Apr. 15	(200 @ $11) $2,200		(100 @ $10) ⎱ $3,200 (200 @ $11) ⎰
Aug. 24	(300 @ $12) $3,600		(100 @ $10) ⎫ (200 @ $11) ⎬ $6,800 (300 @ $12) ⎭
Sept. 10		(300 @ $12) ⎫ (200 @ $11) ⎬ $6,300 (50 @ $10) ⎭	(50 @ $10) $ 500
Nov. 27	(400 @ $13) $5,200		(50 @ $10) ⎱ $5,700 (400 @ $13) ⎰

Use of LIFO in a perpetual system will usually produce cost allocations that differ from LIFO results in a periodic system. In a perpetual system, the latest units purchased before each sale are allocated to cost of goods sold. In contrast, in a periodic system, the latest units purchased during the period are allocated to cost of goods sold. Thus, when a purchase is made after the last sale, the LIFO periodic system will apply this purchase to the previous sale. See Illustration 6-9 where the 400 units at $13 purchased on November 27 are all allocated to the sale of 550 units on September 10. Compare this to Illustration 6A-4, where, under the LIFO perpetual system, the 400 units at $13 purchased on November 27 are all applied to the ending inventory.

The ending inventory in this example of LIFO perpetual is $5,700 and the cost of goods sold is $6,300, as compared to the LIFO periodic example in Illustration 6-9, where the ending inventory is $5,000 and the cost of goods sold is $7,000.

A comparison of the cost of goods sold and ending inventory figures for each of these cost flow assumptions under a perpetual inventory system yields the same proportionate outcomes that we saw in the application of cost flow assumptions under a periodic system. That is, in a period of rising prices (prices rose from $10 to $13 in this example), FIFO will always yield the highest ending inventory valuation and LIFO the lowest. On the other hand, LIFO will always result in the highest cost of goods sold figure (and lowest net earnings) and FIFO the lowest. Of course, if prices are falling, the inverse relationships will result. And, finally, remember that the sum of cost of goods sold and ending inventory always equals the cost of goods available for sale, which is the same regardless of the choice of cost flow assumption.

Illustration 6A-5 summarizes these effects under a perpetual inventory system.

	FIFO	Average	LIFO
Cost of goods sold	$ 6,200	$ 6,233	$ 6,300
Ending inventory	5,800	5,767	5,700
Cost of goods available for sale	$12,000	$12,000	$12,000

Illustration 6A-5
Financial statement effects of cost flow methods

Using the Decision Toolkit

IPSCO Inc., headquartered in Regina, Saskatchewan, manufactures and sells steel mill and fabricated products in Canada and the U.S. Selected financial information related to IPSCO Inc.'s inventories follows:

IPSCO INC. Selected Financial Information December 31, 2002 (in U.S. thousands)			
	2002	2001	2000
Inventories			
Finished goods	$ 99,489	$105,105	$ 89,394
Work in process	70,492	62,029	65,344
Raw materials and supplies	85,429	72,260	71,220
	$ 255,410	$239,394	$225,958
Sales	$1,081,709	$903,743	$949,263
Cost of sales	925,343	770,788	764,633
Net earnings	20,279	38,868	57,673

Selected industry data follow:

	2002	2001
Inventory turnover	6.1 times	6.3 times
Days in inventory	60 days	58 days
Gross profit margin	21.2%	18.7%
Profit margin	2.0%	1.0%

Instructions

(a) Why does the company report its inventory on its balance sheet in three components?
(b) IPSCO uses the average cost flow assumption. Steel prices have generally been falling over the last two years in response to excess global capacity. If IPSCO had used FIFO instead of average, would its earnings have been higher or lower than currently reported?
(c) Do each of the following:
  1. Calculate the inventory turnover and days in inventory for 2002 and 2001.
  2. Calculate the gross profit margin and profit margin for each of 2002 and 2001.
  3. Evaluate IPSCO's performance with inventories over the three years and compare to the industry.

Solution

(a) IPSCO is a manufacturer, so it purchases raw materials and makes them into finished products. At the end of each period, it has some goods that have been started but are not yet complete, referred to as work in process. By reporting all three components of inventory, the company reveals important information about its inventory position. For example, if amounts of raw materials have increased, and finished goods decreased, compared to the previous year, as they have for IPSCO, we might safely assume that the company is planning to step up production. On the other hand, if levels of finished goods have increased relative to last year and raw materials have declined, we might conclude that sales are slowing down and that the company therefore has too much inventory on hand and is cutting back production.

(b) If IPSCO used the FIFO cost flow assumption instead of the average cost flow assumption during a period of rising prices, its cost of goods sold would be higher and its net earnings lower than currently reported.

(c) 1.

Ratio	2002		2001	
Inventory turnover	$\dfrac{\$1,081,709}{(\$255,410 + \$239,394) \div 2}$	$=$ 4.4 times	$\dfrac{\$770,788}{(\$239,394 + \$225,958) \div 2}$	$=$ 3.3 times
Days in inventory	$\dfrac{365 \text{ days}}{4.4}$ = 83 days		$\dfrac{365 \text{ days}}{3.3}$ = 111 days	

2.

Ratio	2002		2001	
Gross profit margin	$\dfrac{\$1,081,709 - \$925,343}{\$1,081,709}$ = 14.5%		$\dfrac{\$903,743 - \$770,788}{\$903,743}$ = 14.7%	
Profit margin	$\dfrac{\$20,279}{\$1,081,709}$ = 1.9%		$\dfrac{\$38,868}{\$903,743}$ = 4.3%	

3. IPSCO's inventory turnover and days in inventory ratios improved significantly in 2002, although they remain below the industry averages. That means that IPSCO has more inventory on hand and is not selling it as fast as its competitors. This is a result, no doubt, of the price erosion IPSCO suffered on many of its products.

   IPSCO's profitability ratios declined in 2002, and are also below the industry averages. Although it's gross profit margin is quite a bit below the industry, its profit margin is comparable to that of the industry in 2002. This may be because of an unusual gain on the sale of assets, rather than better control of operating expenses.

Summary of Study Objectives

❶ Describe the steps in determining inventory quantities. The steps are (1) taking a physical inventory of goods on hand and (2) determining the ownership of goods in transit or on consignment.

❷ Explain the basis of accounting for inventories and apply the inventory cost flow assumptions under a periodic inventory system. The primary basis of accounting for inventories is cost. Cost includes all expenditures necessary to acquire goods and make them ready for sale. The cost of goods available for sale (beginning inventory + cost of goods purchased) may be allocated to cost of goods sold and ending inventory by specific identification or by one of the three cost flow assumptions—FIFO (first-in, first-out), average, or LIFO (last-in, first-out).

Specific identification allocates the exact cost of each merchandise item to cost of goods sold and ending inventory.

FIFO assumes a first-in, first-out cost flow for sales. The FIFO cost flow assumption allocates the cost of the earliest goods purchased to cost of goods sold. The cost of the most recent goods purchased is allocated to ending inventory.

Average uses goods available for sale in dollars and in units to calculate a weighted average cost per unit. This unit cost is then applied to the number of units sold and number of units remaining in ending inventory.

LIFO assumes a last-in, first-out cost flow for sales. The LIFO cost flow assumption allocates the cost of the most recent goods purchased to cost of goods sold. The cost of the earliest goods purchased is allocated to ending inventory.

❸ Explain the financial statement effects of each of the inventory cost flow assumptions. When prices are rising, FIFO results in a lower cost of goods sold and higher net earnings than average and LIFO. The reverse is true when prices are falling. In the balance sheet, FIFO results in an ending inventory that is closest to current (replacement) value, whereas the inventory under LIFO is the furthest from current value. All three cost flow assumptions result in the same cash flow before income taxes. LIFO is not permitted for income tax purposes in Canada.

❹ Indicate the effects of inventory errors on the financial statements. In the statement of earnings of the current year, (a) an error in beginning inventory will have a re-verse effect on net earnings (e.g., overstatement of inventory results in understatement of net earnings, and vice versa) and (b) an error in ending inventory will have a similar effect on net earnings (e.g., overstatement of inventory results in overstatement of net earnings). If ending inventory errors are not corrected in the following period, their effect on net earnings for that period is reversed, and total net earnings for the two years will be correct. In the balance sheet, ending inventory errors will have the same effects on total assets and total shareholders' equity, and no effect on liabilities.

❺ Explain the lower of cost and market basis of accounting for inventories. The lower of cost and market (LCM) basis is used when the market value (net realizable value) is less than cost. Under LCM, the loss is recognized in the period in which the price decline occurs.

❻ Calculate and interpret inventory turnover. The inventory turnover ratio is calculated as cost of goods sold divided by average inventory. It can be converted to days in inventory by dividing 365 days by the inventory turnover ratio. A higher turnover or lower days in inventory suggests that management is trying to keep inventory levels low relative to its sales level.

❼ Apply the inventory cost flow assumptions under a perpetual inventory system (Appendix 6A). Under FIFO, the cost of the earliest goods on hand is allocated to cost of goods sold. The cost of the most recent goods purchased is allocated to ending inventory. Under average, a new weighted (moving) average unit cost is calculated after each purchase and applied to the number of units sold and the number of units remaining in ending inventory. Under LIFO, the cost of the most recent purchase is allocated to cost of goods sold. The cost of the earliest goods purchased is allocated to ending inventory.

Each of these cost flow assumptions is applied in the same cost flow order as in a periodic inventory system. The main difference is that in a perpetual inventory system, the cost flow assumption is applied at the date of each sale to determine cost of goods sold. In a periodic inventory system, the cost flow assumption is applied only at the end of the period.

Decision
Toolkit
Summary

Decision Toolkit—A Summary

DECISION CHECKPOINTS	INFO NEEDED FOR DECISION	TOOL TO USE FOR DECISION	HOW TO EVALUATE RESULTS
What is the impact of the choice of inventory cost flow assumption?	Are prices increasing, or are they decreasing?	Statement of earnings and balance sheet effects	It depends on the objective. In a period of rising prices, earnings and inventory are higher under FIFO. LIFO provides opposite results. Average can moderate the impact of changing prices.
How long is an item in inventory?	Cost of goods sold; beginning and ending inventory	$$\text{Inventory turnover} = \frac{\text{Cost of goods sold}}{\text{Average inventory}}$$ $$\text{Days in inventory} = \frac{365 \text{ days}}{\text{Inventory turnover}}$$	A higher inventory turnover or lower days in inventory suggests that management is reducing the amount of inventory on hand, relative to sales.

NAVIGATOR

Glossary

Glossary

Average cost flow assumption An inventory cost flow assumption that assumes that the goods available for sale are homogeneous or nondistinguishable. Each good is assumed to have the same weighted average cost per unit. (p. 269)

Consigned goods Goods held for sale by one party (the consignee) although ownership of the goods is kept by another party (the consignor). (p. 264)

Days in inventory A measure of the average number of days inventory is held. It is calculated as 365 divided by the inventory turnover ratio. (p. 278)

Finished goods Manufactured items that are completed and ready for sale. (p. 263)

First-in, first-out (FIFO) cost flow assumption An inventory cost flow assumption that assumes that the costs of the earliest goods acquired are the first to be recognized as cost of goods sold. The costs of the latest goods acquired are assumed to remain in ending inventory. (p. 267)

FOB (free on board) destination Freight terms indicating that the goods are placed free on board at the buyer's place of business, and the seller pays the freight cost. Goods belong to the seller while in transit. (p. 264)

FOB (free on board) shipping point Freight terms indicating that the seller places the goods free on board the carrier, and the buyer pays the freight cost. Goods belong

to the buyer while in transit. (p. 264)

Inventory turnover A measure of the number of times, on average, inventory is sold during the period. It is calculated by dividing cost of goods sold by the average inventory during the period. (p. 278)

Last-in, first-out (LIFO) cost flow assumption An inventory cost flow assumption that assumes that the costs of the latest units purchased are the first to be allocated to cost of goods sold. The costs of the earliest goods acquired are assumed to remain in ending inventory. (p. 270)

Lower of cost and market (LCM) A basis for stating inventory at the lower of cost and market (net realizable value) at the end of the period. (p. 278)

Net realizable value The selling price of an inventory item, less any costs required to make the item saleable. (p. 278)

Raw materials Basic goods that will be used in production but have not yet been sent into production. (p. 263)

Replacement cost The cost of replacing an asset. (p. 278)

Specific identification method An actual physical flow costing method in which individual items are specifically costed to arrive at the cost of goods sold and cost of the ending inventory. (p. 265)

Weighted average unit cost Average cost that is weighted by the number of units purchased at each unit cost. It is calculated as cost of goods available for sale divided by the number of units available for sale. (p. 269)

Work in process Manufactured inventory that has begun the production process but is not yet complete. (p. 263)

Demonstration Problem

Additional
Demonstration
Problems

Englehart Ltd. has the following inventory, purchases, and sales data for the month of March:

Inventory, March 1	200 units @ $4.00	$800
Purchases		
Mar. 10	500 units @ $4.50	$2,250
Mar. 20	400 units @ $4.75	$1,900
Mar. 30	300 units @ $5.00	$1,500
Sales		
Mar. 15	500 units @ $8.00	$4,000
Mar. 25	400 units @ $8.00	$3,200

The physical inventory count on March 31 shows 500 units on hand.

Instructions

Under a periodic inventory system, determine the cost of goods sold for March and the cost of inventory on hand at March 31 under (a) FIFO; (b) average; and (c) LIFO.

Solution to Demonstration Problem

The cost of goods available for sale is $6,450:

Beginning inventory	200 units @ $4.00	$ 800	
Purchases			
Mar. 10	500 units @ 4.50	2,250	
Mar. 20	400 units @ 4.75	1,900	
Mar. 30	300 units @ 5.00	1,500	
Total cost of goods available for sale	1,400	$6,450	

(a) **FIFO**

Cost of goods sold:

	Units	Unit Cost	Total Cost
Beginning inventory	200	$4.00	$ 800
Mar. 10	500	4.50	2,250
Mar. 20	200	4.75	950
	900		$4,000

Ending inventory:

	Units		
Mar. 30	300	$5.00	$1,500
Mar. 20	200	4.75	950
	500		$2,450

Proof: $4,000 + $2,450 = $6,450

(b) **Average**

Weighted average unit cost: $6,450 ÷ 1,400 = $4.607

Cost of goods sold: 900 × $4.607 = $4,146.50 (rounded)

Ending inventory: 500 × $4.607 = $2,303.50

Proof: $4,146.50 + $2,303.50 = $6,450

Action Plan

- Ignore the dates of sale in a periodic inventory system. Assume everything happens at the end of the period.
- Allocate costs between goods sold and goods on hand for each cost flow assumption.
- For FIFO, allocate the earliest costs to the goods sold and the latest costs to the goods on hand.
- For average, calculate the weighted average unit cost. Multiply this cost by the number of units sold and the number of units on hand.
- For LIFO, allocate the latest costs to the goods sold and the earliest costs to the goods on hand.
- Prove your work: Cost of goods sold + Ending inventory = Cost of goods available for sale.

(a) LIFO

Cost of goods sold:

	Units	Unit Cost	Total Cost
Mar. 30	300	$5.00	$1,500
Mar. 20	400	4.75	1,900
Mar. 10	200	4.50	900
	900		$4,300

Ending inventory:

	Units	Unit Cost	Total Cost
Beginning inventory	200	$4.00	$ 800
Mar. 10	300	4.50	1,350
	500		$2,150

Proof: $4,300 + $2,150 = $6,450

NAVIGATOR

Note: All questions, exercises, and problems with an asterisk relate to material in the chapter appendix.

Multiple
Choice
Quiz

SELF-STUDY QUESTIONS

Answers are at the end of the chapter.

(SO 1) 1. A physical inventory count is normally taken:
   (a) in a periodic inventory system.
   (b) in a perpetual inventory system.
   (c) at the end of the company's fiscal year.
   (d) All of the above

(SO 1) 2. Which of the following should not be included in the physical inventory of a company?
   (a) Goods held on consignment from another company
   (b) Goods in transit sold to another company shipped FOB destination
   (c) Goods in transit purchased from another company shipped FOB shipping point
   (d) All of the above should be included.

(SO 2) 3. Kam Ltd. has the following units and costs, and uses a periodic inventory system:

	Units	Unit Cost
Inventory, Jan. 1	8,000	$11
Purchase, June 19	13,000	12
Purchase, Nov. 8	5,000	13

   If 9,000 units are on hand at December 31, what is the cost of the ending inventory under FIFO?
   (a) $100,000   (c) $196,000
   (b) $113,000   (d) $209,000

(SO 2) 4. From the data in question 3, what is the cost of the goods sold under LIFO?
   (a) $100,000   (c) $196,000
   (b) $113,000   (d) $209,000

(SO 3) 5. ⚒ In periods of declining prices, the average cost flow assumption will produce:
   (a) higher net earnings than FIFO.

   (b) the same net earnings as FIFO.
   (c) lower net earnings than FIFO.
   (d) higher net earnings than LIFO.

(SO 4) 6. Lavigne Ltd.'s ending inventory is understated by $4,000. The effects of this error on the current year's cost of goods sold and net earnings, respectively, are:
   (a) understated and overstated.
   (b) overstated and understated.
   (c) overstated and overstated.
   (d) understated and understated.

(SO 4) 7. From the data in question 6, what is the effect of this error in ending inventory on the subsequent year's cost of goods sold and net earnings, respectively?
   (a) Understated and overstated
   (b) Overstated and understated
   (c) Overstated and overstated
   (d) Understated and understated

(SO 5) 8. The lower of cost and market rule for inventory is an example of the application of:
   (a) the conservatism concept.
   (b) the historical cost principle.
   (c) the materiality constraint.
   (d) the economic entity assumption.

(SO 6) 9. ⚒ Which of these would cause the inventory turnover ratio to increase the most?
   (a) Increasing the amount of inventory on hand
   (b) Keeping the amount of inventory on hand constant but increasing sales
   (c) Keeping the amount of inventory on hand constant but decreasing sales
   (d) Decreasing the amount of inventory on hand and increasing sales

(SO 7) *10. In a perpetual inventory system:
(a) LIFO cost of goods sold will be the same as in a periodic inventory system.
(b) average costs are based entirely on straight unit cost averages.

(c) a new average is calculated after each purchase in the average cost flow assumption.
(d) FIFO cost of goods sold will be different than in a periodic inventory system.

Questions

(SO 1) 1. Mary Ann's Hat Shop Ltd. received a shipment of hats for which it paid the wholesaler $2,940. The price of the hats was $3,000, but Mary Ann's was given a $60 cash discount and required to pay freight charges of $70. In addition, Mary Ann's paid $100 to cover the travel expenses of an employee who negotiated the purchase of the hats. What amount should Mary Ann's include as the cost of its hat inventory?

(SO 1) 2. Your friend Tom Wetzel has been hired to help take the physical inventory in Kikujiro's Hardware Store. Explain to Tom what this job will entail, with particular instructions for determining the inventory quantities to which Kikujiro's has legal title.

(SO 1) 3. (a) Janine Ltd. ships merchandise to Fastrak Corporation on December 30. The merchandise reaches the buyer on January 5. Indicate the terms of sale (e.g. FOB shipping point or FOB desination) that will result in the goods being included in (1) Janine's December 31 inventory and (2) Fastrak's December 31 inventory.
(b) Under what circumstances should Janine Ltd. include consigned goods in its inventory?

(SO 2) 4. Dave Wier believes that the allocation of cost of goods available for sale should be based on the actual physical flow of the goods. Explain to Dave why this may be both impractical and inappropriate.

(SO 2) 5. Explain how cost of goods sold can be manipulated when the specific identification and LIFO cost flow assumptions are used.

(SO 2) 6. Which inventory cost flow assumption:
(a) assumes that goods available for sale during an accounting period are homogeneous?
(b) assumes that the latest units purchased are the first to be sold?
(c) usually parallels the actual physical flow of merchandise?

(SO 2) 7. ⚒ Compare the financial effects of using the FIFO and LIFO cost flow assumptions during a period of declining prices on (1) cash, (2) ending inventory, (3) cost of goods sold, and (4) net earnings.

(SO 3) 8. ⚒ In a period of rising prices, the inventory reported in Plato Ltd.'s balance sheet is close to the current cost of the inventory, whereas York Ltd.'s inventory is considerably below its current cost. Identify the inventory cost flow assumption used by each company. Which company has prob-

ably been reporting the higher gross profit?

(SO 3) 9. ⚒ Swift Corporation has been using the FIFO cost flow assumption during a prolonged period of inflation. During the same time period, Swift has been paying out all of its net earnings as dividends. What adverse effects may result from this policy?

(SO 3) 10. ⚒ "The selection of an inventory cost flow method depends on whether prices are rising or falling." Do you agree? Explain. Once a method has been selected, what accounting requirement applies?

(SO 4) 11. Mila Ltd. discovers in 2005 that its ending inventory at December 31, 2004, was understated by $5,000. What effect will this error have on (a) 2004 net earnings, (b) 2005 net earnings, and (c) 2005 retained earnings?

(SO 4) 12. A customer took merchandise home on a trial basis before deciding whether or not to purchase it on account. These goods were omitted during the physical inventory count at year end. What effect will this error have on the components of the accounting equation: assets, liabilities, and shareholders' equity?

(SO 5) 13. Lucy Ritter is studying for the next accounting mid-term examination. What should Lucy know about (a) departing from the cost basis of accounting for inventories and (b) the usual meaning of *market* in the lower of cost and market method?

(SO 5) 14. Today's Music Inc. has five CD players on hand at the balance sheet date that cost $400 each. The net realizable value is $320 per unit. Under the lower of cost and market basis of accounting for inventories, what value should be reported for the CD players on the balance sheet? Why?

(SO 6) 15. "The key to successful business operations is effective inventory management." Do you agree? Explain.

(SO 6) 16. ⚒ Under what circumstances might the inventory turnover ratio be too high—that is, what possible negative consequences might occur?

(SO 6) 17. ⚒ Would an increase in the days in inventory ratio from one year to the next be viewed as an improvement or a deterioration in the company's efficiency in managing its inventory?

(SO 7) *18. Your classmate doesn't understand the difference between the perpetual and periodic inventory systems. He says the same cost flow assumptions are used in both systems and a physical inventory count is required in both systems—so what's the difference? Explain to your confused classmate how the perpetual and periodic inventory systems differ.

(SO 7) *19. "When perpetual inventory records are kept, the results under the FIFO and LIFO methods are the same as they would be in a periodic inventory system." Do you agree? Explain.

*20. How does the average method of inventory cost- (SO 7) ing differ between a perpetual inventory system and a periodic inventory system?

Brief Exercises

Identify items in inventory.
(SO 1)

BE6-1   Helgeson Inc. identifies the following items for possible inclusion in the physical inventory count. For each item, indicate whether or not it should be included in the inventory.

(a) Goods shipped on consignment by Helgeson to another company
(b) Goods held on consignment from another company
(c) Goods sold but being held for customer pickup
(d) Goods in transit from a supplier shipped FOB destination
(e) Goods in transit to a customer shipped FOB shipping point

Apply cost flow assumptions in periodic inventory system.
(SO 2)

BE6-2   In its first month of operations, Quilt Inc. made three purchases and two sales of merchandise in the following sequence: (1) 300 units purchased at $6, (2) 200 units sold at $9, (3) 400 units purchased at $7, (4) 400 units sold at $10, and (5) 300 units purchased at $8. Calculate the cost of goods sold and ending inventory under (a) FIFO, (b) average, and (c) LIFO. Quilt uses a periodic inventory system.

Compare financial statement effects of inventory cost flow assumptions.
(SO 3)

BE6-3   Interactive.com just started business and is trying to decide which inventory cost flow assumption to use. Assuming prices are falling, as they often do in the information technology business, answer the following questions for Interactive.com:

(a) Which cost flow assumption will result in the highest ending inventory? Explain.
(b) Which cost flow assumption will result in the highest cost of goods sold? Explain.
(c) Which cost flow assumption will result in the highest pre-tax cash flow? Explain.
(d) What factors are important to Interactive.com in the selection of the most appropriate cost flow assumption?

Determine effect of inventory error.
(SO 4)

BE6-4   Creole Ltd. reports net earnings of $90,000 in 2004. However, ending inventory was overstated by $7,000. What is the correct net earnings for 2004? What effect, if any, will this error have on total assets reported in the balance sheet at December 31, 2004?

Determine effect of inventory error for two years.
(SO 4)

BE6-5   DuPlessis Corporation counted and recorded its ending inventory as at December 31, 2004, incorrectly, understating its correct value by $25,000. Assuming that this misstatement was not subsequently discovered and corrected, what is the impact of this error on assets, liabilities, and shareholders' equity at the end of 2004? At the end of 2005?

Determine LCM valuation.
(SO 5)

BE6-6   Hawkeye Video Centre Ltd. accumulates the following cost and market data at December 31:

Inventory Categories	Cost	Market
Cameras	$12,000	$10,200
Camcorders	9,000	9,500
VCRs	14,000	12,800

Calculate the lower of cost and market valuation for Hawkeye's total inventory.

Calculate inventory turnover and days in inventory.
(SO 6)

BE6-7   At December 31, 2002, the following information (in millions) is available for paper products manufacturer Cascades Inc.: Inventories, December 31, 2002, $478; Inventories, December 31, 2001, $438; Net Sales, $3,375; and Cost of Sales, $2,592. Calculate the inventory turnover and days in inventory ratios for Cascades.

Determine impact of transactions on inventory turnover.
(SO 6)

BE6-8 Indicate whether the following transactions would increase (+), decrease (–), or have no effect (NE) on the inventory turnover ratio:

(a) _____ Beginning inventory was understated.
(b) _____ Cost of goods purchased was reduced by moving to a new, cheaper supplier.
(c) _____ Operating expenses increased.

*BE6-9 Berthiaume Inc. uses a perpetual inventory system. Data for product E2-D2 include the following purchases:

Date	Units	Unit Cost
May 7	50	$10
July 28	30	$15

On June 1, Berthiaume sold 30 units for $20 each, and on August 27, 33 more units for $20 each. Calculate the cost of goods sold and ending inventory using (1) FIFO and (2) average.

Apply cost flow assumptions in perpetual inventory system.
(SO 7)

*BE6-10 Data for Quilt Inc. are presented in BE6-2. Calculate the cost of goods sold and ending inventory under (a) FIFO, (b) average, and (c) LIFO, assuming Quilt uses a perpetual inventory system.

Apply cost flow assumptions in perpetual inventory system.
(SO 7)

*BE6-11 At the beginning of the year, Seller Ltd. had 700 units with a cost of $3 per unit in its beginning inventory. The following inventory transactions occurred during the month of January:

Jan. 3 Sold 500 units on account for $5 each.
       9 Purchased 1,000 units on account for $4 per unit.
      15 Sold 800 units for $8 each, cash.

Prepare journal entries assuming that Seller Ltd. uses (a) FIFO under the periodic inventory assumption, and (b) FIFO under the perpetual inventory system.

Journalize transactions in periodic and perpetual inventory systems.
(SO 7)

Exercises

E6-1 Shippers Ltd. had the following inventory situations to consider at January 31, its year end:

(a) Goods held on consignment for MailBoxes Corp. since December 12
(b) Goods shipped on consignment to Rinehart Holdings Ltd. on January 5
(c) Goods shipped to a customer, FOB destination, on January 29 that are still in transit
(d) Goods shipped to a customer, FOB shipping point, on January 29 that are still in transit
(e) Goods purchased FOB destination from a supplier on January 25, that are still in transit
(f) Goods purchased FOB shipping point from a supplier on January 25, that are still in transit
(g) Office supplies on hand at January 31

Identify items in inventory.
(SO 1)

Instructions

Identify which of the above items should be included in inventory. If the item should not be included in inventory, state where it should be recorded.

E6-2 Gatineau Bank is considering giving Novotna Corporation a loan. Before doing so, it decides that further discussions with Novotna's accountant may be desirable. One area of particular concern is the inventory account, which has a year-end balance of $295,000. Discussions with the accountant reveal the following:

Determine correct inventory amount.
(SO 1)

1. Novotna sold goods costing $55,000 to India-based Moghul Company, FOB shipping point, on December 28. The goods are not expected to arrive in India until January 12. The goods were not included in the physical inventory because they were not in the warehouse.

2. The physical count of the inventory did not include goods costing $95,000 that were shipped to Novotna, FOB destination, on December 27 and were still in transit at year end.

3. Novotna received goods costing $25,000 on January 2. The goods were shipped FOB shipping point on December 26 by Cellar Corp. The goods were not included in the physical count.

4. Novotna sold goods costing $40,000 to UK-based Sterling of Britain Ltd., FOB destination, on December 30. The goods were received by Sterling on January 8. They were not included in Novotna's physical inventory.

Instructions

Determine the correct inventory amount on December 31.

Apply specific identification and FIFO in periodic inventory system.
(SO 2)

E6-3   On December 1, Discount Electronics Ltd. has three DVD players left in stock. All are identical, and all are priced to sell at $750. One of the three DVD players, serial #1012, was purchased on June 1 at a cost of $500. Another, serial #1045, was purchased on November 1 for $450. The last player, serial #1056, was purchased on November 30 for $400.

Instructions

(a) Calculate the cost of goods sold using the FIFO periodic inventory method assuming that two of the three players were sold by the end of December, Discount Electronics' year end.
(b) If Discount Electronics used the specific identification method instead of the FIFO method, how might it alter its earnings by "selectively choosing" which particular players to sell to the two customers? What would Discount Electronics' cost of goods sold be if the company wished to minimize earnings? Maximize earnings?
(c) Which inventory method do you recommend that Discount Electronics use? Explain why.

Apply cost flow assumptions in periodic inventory system.
(SO 2)

E6-4   Mawmey Inc. uses a periodic inventory system. Its records show the following for the month of May, in which 70 units were sold:

Date	Explanation	Units	Unit Cost	Total Cost
May 1	Inventory	30	$ 8	$240
15	Purchase	25	10	250
24	Purchase	35	12	420
	Total	90		$910

Instructions

Calculate the cost of goods sold and ending inventory using (a) FIFO, (b) average, and (c) LIFO.

Apply cost flow assumptions in periodic inventory system.
(SO 2, 3)

E6-5   At the end of June, Lakshmi Ltd. reports the following for the month:

Date	Explanation	Units	Unit Cost	Total Cost
June 1	Inventory	200	$5	$1,000
12	Purchase	300	6	1,800
23	Purchase	500	7	3,500
30	Inventory	160		

Instructions

(a) Calculate the cost of goods sold and the cost of the ending inventory under (1) FIFO, (2) average, and (3) LIFO.
(b) Which costing method gives the highest ending inventory? Why?
(c) Which method results in the highest cost of goods sold? Why?
(d) Which method results in the highest cash flow? Why?

Determine effects of inventory errors.
(SO 4)

E6-6   Seles Hardware Limited reported cost of goods sold as follows:

	2004	2005
Beginning inventory	$ 20,000	$ 30,000
Cost of goods purchased	160,000	175,000
Cost of goods available for sale	180,000	205,000
Ending inventory	30,000	35,000
Cost of goods sold	$150,000	$170,000

Seles made two errors:

1. Ending inventory for 2004 was overstated by $4,000.
2. Ending inventory for 2005 was understated by $3,000.

Instructions

(a) Calculate the correct cost of goods sold for each year.
(b) Describe impact of the error on each year, and in total for the two years.

E6-7   Aruba Inc. reported these statement of earnings data:

Prepare correct statements of earnings.
(SO 4)

	2004	2005
Sales	$210,000	$250,000
Beginning inventory	32,000	40,000
Cost of goods purchased	173,000	202,000
Cost of goods available for sale	205,000	242,000
Ending inventory	40,000	52,000
Cost of goods sold	165,000	190,000
Gross profit	$ 45,000	$ 60,000

Aruba Inc. uses a periodic inventory system. The inventories at January 1, 2004, and December 31, 2005, are correct. However, the ending inventory at December 31, 2004, is overstated by $4,000.

Instructions

(a) Prepare correct statements of earnings for the two years.
(b) What is the cumulative effect of the inventory error on total gross profit for the two years?
(c) Calculate the gross profit margin for each of the two years, before and after the correction.
(d) In a letter to the president of Aruba, explain what has happened—that is, the nature of the error and its effect on the financial statements.

E6-8   Cody Camera Shop Ltd. uses the lower of cost and market basis for its inventory. The following data are available at December 31:

Determine LCM valuation.
(SO 5)

	Units	Cost/Unit	Market Value/Unit
Cameras:			
Minolta	5	$175	$160
Canon	7	150	152
Light Meters:			
Vivitar	12	125	119
Kodak	10	115	135

Instructions

(a) Determine the total cost of the ending inventory.
(b) Determine the total market value of the ending inventory.
(c) What amount should be reported on Cody Camera Shop's financial statements, assuming the lower of cost and market rule is applied to total inventory?

E6-9   This information is available for Best Buy Inc., the owner of Future Shop Ltd., for the three most recent years (in U.S. millions):

Calculate inventory turnover, days in inventory, and gross profit margin.
(SO 6)

	2002	2001	2000
Inventory	$ 2,258.0	$ 1,766.9	$ 1,183.7
Sales	19,597.0	15,326.6	12,494.0
Cost of sales	14,858.0	12,100.1	9,991.1

Instructions

Calculate the inventory turnover, days in inventory, and gross profit margin for Future Shop for 2002 and 2001. Comment on any trends.

E6-10   Wal-Mart values its inventories using the LIFO cost flow assumption. If it valued its inventories using FIFO, they would be reported at a slightly higher value, as shown below (in U.S. millions):

Determine effect of cost flow assumption on inventory turnover.
(SO 6)

	January 31, 2003	
	LIFO	FIFO
Cost of goods sold	$191,838	$191,808
Average inventory	23,752	23,902

Instructions

(a) Wal-Mart's average inventory cost differs by only $150 million (less than 1%) when using the LIFO cost flow assumption, as opposed to the FIFO cost flow assumption.

Why do you suppose there is an insignificant difference between these two amounts?

(b) Calculate the inventory turnover under (1) LIFO and (2) FIFO. Round your answer to two decimal points.

(c) Which method gives you the highest inventory turnover?

(d) Does Wal-Mart's inventory really turn over faster with one cost flow assumption than the other? Explain.

Apply cost flow assumptions in perpetual inventory system.
(SO 7)

*E6-11   Inventory data for Lakshmi Ltd. are presented in E6-5.

Instructions

(a) Calculate the cost of goods sold and the cost of the ending inventory under (1) FIFO, (2) average, and (3) LIFO, using a perpetual inventory system. Assume sales of 400 units on June 15 for $8 each and 440 units on June 27 for $9 each.

(b) How do the results differ from E6-5?

(c) Why is the average unit cost not $6 (simple average) or $6.30 (weighted average)?

Apply cost flow assumptions in periodic and perpetual inventory systems.
(SO 2, 7)

*E6-12   Powder! sells an Xpert snowboard that is popular with snowboard enthusiasts. Below is information relating to Powder!'s purchases and sales of Xpert snowboards during September:

Date	Transaction	Units	Unit Price	Total Sales Price	Total Purchase Cost
Sept. 1	Beginning inventory	26	$ 97		$ 2,522
Sept. 5	Sale	(12)	199	$ 2,388	
Sept. 12	Purchase	45	102		4,590
Sept. 16	Sale	(50)	199	9,950	
Sept. 19	Purchase	28	104		2,912
	Totals	37		$12,338	$10,024

Instructions

(a) Calculate the cost of goods sold and the ending inventory using FIFO, average, and LIFO, assuming Powder! uses a perpetual inventory system.

(b) What would the cost of goods sold and ending inventory be if Powder! used each of these cost flow assumptions in a periodic inventory system?

Journalize transactions in perpetual and periodic inventory systems.
(SO 2, 7)

*E6-13   Refer to the data provided for Powder! in *E6-12.

Instructions

(a) Prepare journal entries to record purchases and sales for Powder! in a perpetual inventory system under each of the following cost flow assumptions: (1) FIFO, (2) average, and (3) LIFO.

(b) Prepare journal entries to record purchases and sales for Powder! in a periodic inventory system under each of the following cost flow assumptions: (1) FIFO, (2) average, and (3) LIFO.

Problems: Set A

Identify items in inventory.
(SO 1)

P6-1A   Banff Limited is trying to determine the value of its ending inventory as at February 28, 2005, the company's year end. The accountant counted everything that was in the warehouse, as at February 28, which resulted in an ending inventory valuation of $48,000. However, she didn't know how to treat the following transactions so she didn't include them in inventory.

(a) On February 26, Banff shipped goods costing $800 to a customer. The goods were shipped FOB shipping point. The receiving report indicates that the customer received the goods on March 2.

(b) On February 26, Seller Inc. shipped goods to Banff FOB destination. The selling price was $350 plus $25 for freight. The receiving report indicates that the goods were received by Banff on March 1.

(c) Banff had $500 of inventory at a customer's warehouse "on approval." The customer was going to let Banff know whether it wanted the merchandise by the end of the week, March 5.

(d) Banff also had $400 of inventory at a Jasper craft shop, on consignment from Banff.

(e) On February 26, Banff ordered goods costing $750. The goods were shipped FOB shipping point, and the receiving report indicates that Banff received them on March 1.

(f) On February 28, Banff packaged goods and had them ready for shipping to a customer FOB destination. The selling price was $400 plus $50 for freight; the cost of the items was $320. The receiving report indicates that the goods were received by the customer on March 2.

(g) Banff had damaged goods set aside in the warehouse because they were not saleable. These goods originally cost $400 and Banff had expected to sell them for $600.

Instructions

For each of the above transactions, specify whether the item should be included in ending inventory, and if so, at what amount. For each item that is not included in ending inventory, indicate who owns it and what account, if any, it should have been recorded in.

P6-2A Steward Inc. had a beginning inventory on January 1 of 400 units of Product MLN at a cost of $8 per unit. During the year, purchases were:

Feb. 20	700 units at $9	Aug. 12	300 units at $11
May 5	500 units at $10	Dec. 8	100 units at $12

Apply cost flow assumptions in periodic inventory system, and assess financial statement effects.
(SO 2, 3)

Steward uses a periodic inventory system. Sales totalled 1,600 units.

Instructions

(a) Determine the cost of goods available for sale.

(b) Determine the cost of goods sold and the ending inventory under each of the cost flow assumptions (FIFO, average, and LIFO).

(c) Which cost flow assumption results in the lowest inventory amount for the balance sheet? The lowest cost of goods sold for the statement of earnings? The lowest cash flow for the cash flow statement?

P6-3A The management of Real Novelty Inc. is re-evaluating the appropriateness of using the average cost flow assumption, as it now does. The company requests your help in determining the results of operations for 2004 if the FIFO, average, or LIFO periodic inventory assumption had been used. For 2004, the accounting records show these data:

Apply cost flow assumptions in periodic inventory system, prepare statements of earnings, and answer questions.
(SO 2, 3)

Inventories		Purchases and Sales	
Beginning (15,000 units)	$33,750	Total net sales (225,000 units)	$900,000
Ending (20,000 units)	?	Total cost of goods purchased	
		(230,000 units)	$578,500

Purchases were made quarterly as follows:

Quarter	Units	Unit Cost	Total Cost
1	60,000	$2.30	$138,000
2	50,000	2.50	125,000
3	50,000	2.60	130,000
4	70,000	2.65	185,500
	230,000		$578,500

Operating expenses were $147,000, and the company's income tax was $60,000 under all three assumptions.

Instructions

(a) Calculate cost of goods sold under FIFO, average, and LIFO.

(b) Prepare comparative condensed statements of earnings for 2004 under FIFO, average, and LIFO.

(c) Write a business letter to answer the following questions for management:

  1. Which cost flow assumption produces the most meaningful inventory amount for the balance sheet? Why?

  2. Which cost flow assumption produces the most meaningful net earnings? Why?

  3. Which assumption provides the most realistic gross profit figure?

4. Which cost flow assumption is most likely to approximate the actual physical flow of goods? Why?
5. How much cash will be available for management under each assumption?

Prepare journal entries for purchaser and seller using FIFO periodic; apply lower of cost and market.
(SO 2, 5, 6)

P6-4A You are provided with the following information concerning the transactions for Schwinghamer Inc. Schwinghamer purchases all items from Pataki Inc. and makes sales to a variety of customers. All transactions are settled on account. Returns are normally undamaged and are restored immediately to inventory for resale. Both companies use the periodic inventory method and the FIFO cost flow assumption.

Date	Description	Units	Unit Price
Oct. 1	Beginning inventory	60	$15
Oct. 9	Purchase	120	14
Oct. 11	Sale	150	35
Oct. 13	Sale return	25	35
Oct. 17	Purchase	70	13
Oct. 22	Purchase return	5	13
Oct. 29	Sale	75	30

Instructions
(a) Prepare all journal entries for the month of October for Schwinghamer Inc.
(b) Prepare all journal entries for the month of October for Pataki Inc.
(c) Determine the ending inventory amount for Schwinghamer, using the FIFO cost flow assumption.
(d) By October 31, Schwinghamer learns that the product has a net realizable value of $12 per unit. What amount should ending inventory be valued at on the October 31 balance sheet?
(e) What impact would the reduction in the ending inventory valuation (due to the application of the lower of cost and market rule) have on Schwinghamer's inventory turnover ratio?

Determine effects of inventory errors.
(SO 4, 6)

P6-5A The records of Pelletier Inc. show the following data:

	2004	2005
Sales	$300,000	$320,000
Beginning inventory	30,000	22,000
Cost of goods purchased	200,000	240,000
Ending inventory	22,000	31,000
Operating expenses	60,000	64,000
Income tax expense	12,000	0

After its July 31, 2005, year end, Pelletier Inc. discovers two errors. Its ending inventory was understated by $3,000 in 2004, and its cost of goods purchased was understated by $25,000 in 2005.

Instructions
(a) Prepare incorrect and corrected statements of earnings for Pelletier Inc. for 2004 and 2005.
(b) Calculate both the incorrect and corrected inventory turnover ratios for 2004 and 2005.

Determine effects of inventory errors.
(SO 4)

P6-6A Handspring Corporation included inventory that it held on consignment in its physical inventory count at March 31, 2004.

Instructions
Indicate the effect of this error (overstated, understated, or no effect) on the following:
(a) Cost of goods sold for each of 2004 and 2005
(b) Net earnings for each of 2004 and 2005
(c) Retained earnings for each of 2004 and 2005
(d) Ending inventory for each of 2004 and 2005
(e) Inventory turnover for each of 2004 and 2005

P6-7A The following information (in U.S. millions) is available for PepsiCo, Inc., for the year ended December 31:

Calculate ratios; comment on liquidity and effect of cost flow assumptions on ratios.
(SO 1, 3, 6)

	2002	2001	2000
Cost of goods sold	$11,497	$10,750	$10,226
Inventory	1,342	1,310	1,192
Current assets	6,413	5,853	5,617
Current liabilities	6,052	4,998	4,795

PepsiCo discloses the composition of its inventory, as follows:

	2002	2001	2000
Raw materials	$ 525	$ 535	$ 503
Work in process	214	205	160
Finished goods	603	570	529
	$1,342	$1,310	$1,192

Instructions

(a) Calculate the inventory turnover, days in inventory, and current ratios for 2002 and 2001. Comment on PepsiCo's liquidity.
(b) Comment on the changes in the composition of PepsiCo's inventories over the last three years. Do these changes give you any insight into PepsiCo's production plans?
(c) Are the changes you observed in (b) consistent with the trends you observed in the inventory turnover ratio in (a)?

*P6-8A You are provided with the following information for Lahti Inc. for the month ended October 31, 2004:

Apply average cost flow assumption in periodic and perpetual inventory systems.
(SO 2, 7)

Date	Description	Units	Unit Price
Oct. 1	Beginning inventory	60	$25
9	Purchase	120	26
11	Sale	150	35
22	Purchase	70	27
29	Sale	80	40

Instructions

(a) Calculate the cost of ending inventory and gross profit under average cost flow assumption in (1) a periodic inventory system, and (2) a perpetual inventory system.
(b) Compare your results for (a1) and (a2), commenting particularly on any differences or similarities between the two inventory systems.

*P6-9A The Family Appliance Mart Ltd. began operations on May 1 and uses a perpetual inventory system. During May, the company had the following purchases and sales for its Model 25 digital camera:

Apply cost flow assumptions in perpetual inventory systems, and assess financial statement effects.
(SO 3, 7)

Date	Purchases Units	Purchases Unit Cost	Units Sold
May 1	5	$ 90	
6			3
11	4	99	
14			5
21	3	103	
27			2
29	2	106	

Instructions

(a) Determine the cost of goods sold and ending inventory under a perpetual inventory system using (1) FIFO, (2) average, and (3) LIFO.
(b) Which cost flow assumption produces the highest gross profit and net earnings?
(c) Which cost flow assumption produces the highest ending inventory valuation?

Prepare journal entries under perpetual inventory system. Assess financial statement effects.
(SO 3, 7)

*P6-10A Yuan Ltd. uses the perpetual inventory method. Assume that all transactions are settled in cash. You are provided with the following information for Yuan Ltd. for the month of January 2005:

Date	Description	Units	Unit Price
Jan. 1	Beginning inventory	150	$17
Jan. 2	Purchase	100	21
Jan. 6	Sale	175	40
Jan. 9	Purchase	50	24
Jan. 15	Sale	75	45
Jan. 23	Purchase	100	28

Instructions

(a) Prepare all required journal entries using (1) FIFO and (2) average.

(b) Compare the results of each cost flow assumption for the impact on (1) ending inventory, (2) net cash flow, and (3) gross profit.

Problems: Set B

Identify items in inventory.
(SO 1)

P6-1B Kananaskis Limited is trying to determine the value of its ending inventory as at February 28, 2005, the company's year end. The following transactions occurred, and the accountant asked for your help in determining whether they should be included in inventory or not:

(a) On February 26, Kananaskis shipped goods costing $800 to a customer and charged the customer $1,000. The goods were shipped FOB destination. The receiving report indicates that the customer received the goods on March 2.

(b) On February 26, Custom Inc. shipped goods costing $350 plus $25 freight to Kananaskis FOB shipping point. The receiving report indicates that the goods were received by Kananaskis on March 2.

(c) Kananaskis had $500 of inventory set aside in the warehouse. The inventory is designated for a customer who has requested that the goods be shipped on March 10.

(d) Also in Kananaskis' warehouse is $400 of inventory that Craft Producers Ltd. shipped to Kananaskis on consignment.

(e) On February 26, Kananaskis purchased goods costing $750. The goods were shipped FOB destination and the receiving report indicates that Kananaskis received them on March 2.

(f) On February 26, Kananaskis shipped goods to a customer FOB shipping point. The selling price was $375 plus $25 for freight; the cost of the items sold was $280. The receiving report indicates that the goods were received by the customer on March 2.

Instructions

For each of the above transactions, specify whether the item should be included in ending inventory, and if so, at what amount. For each item that is not included in ending inventory, indicate who owns it and what account, if any, it should have been recorded in.

Apply cost flow assumptions in periodic inventory system and assess financial statement effects.
(SO 2, 3)

P6-2B Kane Ltd. had a beginning inventory on January 1 of 100 units of Product SXL at a cost of $20 per unit. During the year, purchases were:

Mar. 15	300 units at $24	Sept. 4	300 units at $28
July 20	200 units at $25	Dec. 2	100 units at $30

Kane sold 800 units during the year. It uses a periodic inventory system.

Instructions

(a) Determine the cost of goods available for sale.

(b) Determine the cost of goods sold and the ending inventory under each of the cost flow assumptions (FIFO, average, and LIFO).

(c) Which cost flow assumption results in the highest inventory amount for the balance sheet? The highest cost of goods sold for the statement of earnings? The highest cash flow for the cash flow statement?

P6-3B The management of Tumatoe Inc. asks for your help in determining the compara-tive effects of the FIFO, average, and LIFO periodic inventory cost flow assumptions. For 2004, the accounting records show these data:

Inventory, January 1 (10,000 units)	$ 35,000
Cost of 110,000 units purchased	462,500
Selling price of 95,000 units sold	665,000
Operating expenses	120,000
Income tax expense	50,000

Purchases consisted of 40,000 units at $4.00 on May 10; 50,000 units at $4.25 on August 15; and 20,000 units at $4.50 on November 20. Assume income tax expense remains the same under all three cost flow assumptions.

Instructions
(a) Calculate the cost of goods sold under FIFO, average, and LIFO.
(b) Prepare comparative condensed statements of earnings for 2004 under FIFO, aver-age, and LIFO.
(c) Write a business letter to answer the following questions for management:
  1. Which inventory cost flow assumption produces the most meaningful inventory amount for the balance sheet? Why?
  2. Which inventory cost flow assumption produces the most meaningful net earn-ings? Why?
  3. Which inventory cost flow assumption is most likely to approximate the actual physical flow of the goods? Why?
  4. How much cash will be available for management under each assumption?
  5. What factors should influence management's choice of cost flow assumption?

P6-4B You are provided with the following information for Amelia Inc. Amelia purchases all items from Karina Inc. and makes sales to a variety of customers. All transactions are settled in cash. Returns are usually undamaged and are restored immediately to inventory for resale. Both Amelia and Karina use the periodic inventory method and the average cost flow assumption.

Date	Description	Units	Unit Price
July 1	Beginning inventory	25	$10
July 5	Purchase	60	9
July 8	Sale	65	11
July 15	Sale return	10	11
July 25	Purchase	25	8
July 26	Purchase return	5	8

Instructions
(a) Prepare all journal entries for the month of July for Amelia Inc.
(b) Prepare all journal entries for the month of July for Karina Inc.
(c) Determine the ending inventory amount for Amelia, using the average cost flow as-sumption.
(d) By July 31, Amelia learns that the product has a net realizable value of $7 per unit. What amount should ending inventory be valued at on the July 31 balance sheet?
(e) If the lower of cost and market rate is applied, what impact would the reduction in the ending inventory valuation have on Amelia's days in inventory ratio?

P6-5B The records of Alyssa Inc. show the following data:

	2004	2005
Sales	$300,000	$320,000
Beginning inventory	30,000	22,000
Cost of goods purchased	200,000	240,000
Ending inventory	22,000	31,000
Operating expenses	60,000	64,000
Income tax expense	12,000	10,000

After the July 31, 2005, year end, Alyssa Inc. discovers that its inventory at the end of 2004 was actually $27,000, not $22,000.

Instructions
(a) Prepare incorrect and corrected statements of earnings for Alyssa Inc. for 2004 and 2005.
(b) What is the impact of this error on retained earnings at July 31, 2005?

Determine effects of inventory errors.
(SO 4)

P6-6B Appleby Corporation omitted to include inventory that was stored at an off-site warehouse in its physical inventory count at February 28, 2004.

Instructions
Indicate the effect of this error (overstated, understated, or no effect) on the following:
(a) Cost of goods sold for each of 2004 and 2005
(b) Net earnings for each of 2004 and 2005
(c) Retained earnings for each of 2004 and 2005
(d) Ending inventory for each of 2004 and 2005
(e) Days in inventory for each of 2004 and 2005

Calculate ratios; comment on liquidity and effect of cost flow assumptions on ratios.
(SO 3, 6)

P6-7B The following information (in thousands) is available for Markham-based Cool-Brands International Inc. for the year ended August 31:

	2002	2001	2000
Cost of goods sold	$129,246	$98,190	$47,569
Inventory	25,361	16,539	7,047
Current assets	131,839	93,937	57,104
Current liabilities	74,485	50,529	27,051

The industry averages for the inventory turnover, days in inventory, and current ratios are as follows:

	2002	2001
Inventory turnover	8 times	12 times
Days in inventory	45.6 days	30.4 days
Current ratio	1.42:1	1.35:1

Instructions
(a) Calculate the inventory turnover, days in inventory, and current ratios for 2002 and 2001. Comment on CoolBrands' liquidity.
(b) CoolBrands uses FIFO to determine the cost of its inventory. If prices are rising, how would you expect the inventory turnover, days in inventory, and current ratios to change (e.g., increase or decrease) if CoolBrands used LIFO instead of FIFO.

Apply FIFO cost flow assumption in periodic and perpetual inventory systems.
(SO 2, 7)

*P6-8B You are provided with the following information for Danielle Inc. for the month ended June 30, 2004.

Date	Description	Units	Unit Price
June 1	Beginning inventory	25	$60
June 4	Purchase	85	64
June 10	Sale	90	90
June 18	Purchase	35	68
June 25	Sale	50	95
June 28	Purchase	20	72

Instructions
(a) Calculate the cost of ending inventory and gross profit under the FIFO cost flow assumption in (1) a perpetual inventory system, and (2) a periodic inventory system.
(b) Compare your results for (a1) and (a2), commenting particularly on any differences or similarities between the two inventory systems.

Apply cost flow assumptions in perpetual inventory system, and assess financial statement effects.
(SO 3, 7)

*P6-9B Save-Mart Centre Inc. began operations on July 1. It uses a perpetual inventory system. During July, the company had the following purchases and sales:

Date	Purchases Units	Purchases Unit Cost	Units Sold
July 1	6	$90	
July 6			3
July 11	4	99	
July 14			5
July 21	5	106	

Instructions

(a) Determine the cost of goods sold and ending inventory under a perpetual inventory system using (1) FIFO, (2) average, and (3) LIFO.

(b) Which cost flow assumption produces the highest gross profit and net earnings?

(c) Which cost flow assumption produces the highest ending inventory valuation?

*P6-10B Matthew Inc. uses the perpetual inventory method. Assume that all transactions are on account. You are provided with the following information for Matthew Inc. for the month of January 2005:

Prepare journal entries under perpetual system. Assess financial statement effects.
(SO 3, 7)

Date	Description	Units	Unit Price
Jan. 1	Beginning inventory	50	$12
Jan. 5	Purchase	100	14
Jan. 7	Sale	110	25
Jan. 14	Purchase	30	16
Jan. 20	Sale	60	25
Jan. 25	Purchase	20	18

Instructions

(a) Prepare all required journal entries using (1) FIFO and (2) average.

(b) Compare the results of each cost flow assumption for the impact on (1) cash flow, (2) gross profit, and (3) ending inventory.

BROADENING YOUR PERSPECTIVE

Financial Reporting and Analysis

Analysis Tools

FINANCIAL REPORTING PROBLEM: *Loblaw Companies Limited*

BYP6-1 Refer to the financial statements of Loblaw Companies Ltd. in Appendix A.

Instructions

Answer the following questions:

(a) What did Loblaw report for the amount of inventories in its consolidated balance sheet at the end of 2002? 2001?

(b) Calculate the dollar amount of change and the percentage change in inventories between 2001 and 2002. Calculate inventory as a percentage of current assets for each of the two years.

(c) Does Loblaw report cost of sales separately on its consolidated statement of earnings? If not, what does it include with cost of sales? Why might Loblaw not wish to report its cost of sales separately?

COMPARATIVE ANALYSIS PROBLEM: *Loblaw and Sobeys*

BYP6-2 The financial statements of Sobeys Inc. are presented in Appendix B, following the financial statements for Loblaw in Appendix A.

Instructions

(a) Based on the information in these statements, calculate the following values for Loblaw for fiscal 2002 and 2001 and for Sobeys for fiscal 2003 and 2002.

   1. Inventory turnover, using "cost of sales, selling, and administrative expenses" instead of cost of goods sold and year-end inventory balances instead of averages.

   2. Days in inventory

(b) What conclusions about the management of inventory, and selling and administrative expenses can be drawn from your results in (a)?

RESEARCH CASE

BYP6-3 The March 29, 2002, issue of *Report on Business Magazine* contains an article by Patrick Brethour entitled, "The Worst Is Not Over in Telecom: Billions More in Write-Offs Loom as Backlogs of Components Pile Up." This article discusses the inventory write-offs of communications equipment makers.

Instructions

Read the article and answer the following questions:
(a) Explain how writing down the value of inventory follows the lower of cost and market rule.
(b) How much was Nortel Networks' inventory write-off in 2001?
(c) What was Nortel's inventory turnover in 2001 and 2000? Explain how the inventory write-off contributed to the change in Nortel's inventory turnover.
(d) What is the danger sign to watch out for concerning the value of inventories?

INTERPRETING FINANCIAL STATEMENTS

BYP6-4 The following information was taken from the December 31, 2002, financial statements of Cooper Tire and Rubber Company (in U.S. thousands):

	2002	2001	2000
Cost of goods sold	$2,839,757	$2,724,692	$2,939,815
Inventories			
Finished goods	$ 181,219	$ 207,484	$ 192,357
Work in process	33,457	32,838	32,882
Raw materials and supplies	65,965	66,156	71,221
	$ 280,641	$ 306,478	$ 296,460

Additional information:
1. From the notes to the financial statements:

   Inventories are valued at cost, which is not in excess of market. Inventory costs have been determined by the last-in, first-out (LIFO) method for substantially all domestic inventories. Costs of other inventories have been determined principally by the first-in, first-out (FIFO) method.

   Under the LIFO method, inventories have been reduced by approximately $52,336 thousand and $46,565 thousand at December 31, 2002 and 2001, respectively, from current cost which would be reported under the FIFO method.
2. The inventory turnover and days in inventory ratios for the industry are 6.8 times and 54 days for 2002, and 5.3 times and 69 days for 2001.

Instructions

(a) What does Cooper mean when it states that inventories are not valued "in excess of market?"
(b) The company experienced a decrease in finished goods inventory and raw materials inventory. Discuss the likely cause of this.
(c) What might explain why the company uses FIFO for its nondomestic inventories?
(d) Calculate the company's inventory turnover and days in inventory ratios for 2002 and 2001. Discuss the implications of any change in the ratios.
(e) If Cooper had used the FIFO cost flow assumption in 2002, what would be the cost of its inventory? Do you consider this difference a "material" amount from the perspective of an analyst? Which cost better represents the value of the company's inventory?

A GLOBAL FOCUS

BYP6-5 Japan-based Fuji Photo Film and arch-rival U.S.-based Eastman Kodak dominate the global market for film. The following information is from the financial statements of the two companies:

FUJI PHOTO FILM CO., LTD
Notes to the Financial Statements
March 31, 2002

Note 2. Summary of significant accounting policies

The Company and its domestic subsidiaries maintain their records and prepare their financial statements in accordance with accounting practices generally accepted in Japan... Certain reclassifications and adjustments have been incorporated in the consolidated financial statements to conform them with accounting principles generally accepted in the United States of America.

Inventories

Inventories are valued at the lower of cost or market, cost being determined generally by the moving average method.

Note 6. Inventories

Inventories at March 31, 2002 and 2001, consisted of the following:

	(in yen millions)		(in U.S. millions)	
	2002	2001	2002	2001
Finished goods	¥222,523	¥218,507	$1,673.1	$1,762.2
Work in process	65,714	67,399	494.1	543.5
Raw materials and supplies	70,266	68,415	528.3	551.7
	¥358,503	¥354,321	$2,695.5	$2,857.4

Additional information

2002 cost of goods sold, U.S.$9,537.8 million

EASTMAN KODAK COMPANY
Notes to the Financial Statements
December 31, 2001

Note 1. Summary of significant accounting policies

Inventories

Inventories are valued at the lower of cost or market. The cost of most inventories in the U.S. is determined by the last-in, first-out (LIFO) method. The cost of all of the Company's remaining inventories in and outside the U.S. is determined by the first-in, first-out (FIFO) or average cost method, which approximates current cost.

Note 3. Inventories

	(in U.S. millions)	
	2001	2000
At FIFO or average cost (approximates current cost)		
Finished goods	$ 851	$1,155
Work in process	318	423
Raw materials and supplies	412	589
Total inventories at FIFO or average	$1,581	$2,167
At LIFO		
Total inventories at LIFO	$1,137	$1,718

Additional information

2001 cost of goods sold, U.S.$8,670 million (at FIFO) and U.S.$8,675 million (at LIFO)

Instructions

(a) Why do you suppose Fuji makes reclassifications and adjustments to its accounts so that they conform with U.S. accounting principles and currency when it reports its results?

(b) Does Fuji use a perpetual or periodic inventory method to account for its inventories?

(c) Why do you think Eastman Kodak would use a different cost flow assumption to account for its nondomestic inventories?

(d) What are the 2001 (use March 31, 2002, figures for Fuji and December 31, 2001, figures for Kodak using its FIFO or average cost flow assumption) inventory turnover and days in inventory ratios of the two companies in U.S. dollars? How does this comparison change when you use Kodak's inventory figures at LIFO to calculate the inventory turnover and days in inventory? Explain which comparison is the most relevant for decision-making purposes.

(e) Calculate, as a percentage of total inventory, the portion that each of the components of 2001 inventory (raw materials, work in process, and finished goods) represents (use March 31, 2002, figures for Fuji and December 31, 2001, figures for Kodak). Comment on your findings.

FINANCIAL ANALYSIS ON THE WEB

BYP6-6 In this activity we use a company's annual report to calculate several key inventory-related ratios and to identify the company's inventory cost flow assumption.

Instructions

Specific requirements of this Web case can be found on the Kimmel website.

Critical Thinking

COLLABORATIVE LEARNING ACTIVITY

BYP6-7 Just-in-Time (JIT) Auto Parts Ltd. manufactures auto parts. The company's inventories reported on its balance sheet at July 31, 2004, total $1,094.7 million. Assume that the following transactions occurred during July and August 2004:

1. Office supplies were shipped to JIT Auto Parts by Office Maxx, FOB destination. The goods were shipped July 31 and received August 3.

2. JIT Auto Parts purchased specialty plastic from DuPont Canada for use in the manufacture of door mouldings. The goods were shipped FOB shipping point July 31 and received August 3.

3. Ford Motor Company of Canada, Limited, purchased 3,000 rear liftgate assemblies to be used in the manufacture of the Ford Windstar. They were shipped FOB shipping point July 29, and were received by Ford August 1.

4. Nadeau Furniture shipped office furniture to JIT Auto Parts, FOB destination, on July 27. The furniture was received August 3.

5. Inland Specialty Chemical shipped JIT Auto Parts chemicals that JIT Auto Parts uses in the manufacture of door mouldings and other items. The goods were sent FOB shipping point July 30 and received August 3.

6. JIT Auto Parts purchased new Cadillac Sevilles for its executives to drive. The cars were shipped FOB destination July 30 and received August 5.

7. JIT Auto Parts purchased steel, to be used in expanding its manufacturing plant, from IPSCO, FOB Regina (shipping point). The steel was shipped July 30, arrived in Ontario August 2, and at JIT Auto Parts' plant in Aurora on August 3.

8. JIT Auto Parts shipped instrument panels to Jaguar, FOB destination. The panels were shipped July 31, and arrived at Jaguar's headquarters in England August 7.

Instructions

With the class divided into groups, answer the following:

(a) Determine which of the above transactions affect JIT Auto Parts' Inventory account. For each item that has an effect, would the transaction result in an increase or a decrease in the Inventory account at July 31, 2004?

(b) For each transaction that does not affect JIT Auto Parts' Inventory account, indicate who owns the revelant items and how they should be reported.

COMMUNICATION ACTIVITY

BYP6-8 You are the controller of Small Toys Inc. Joy Small, the president, recently mentioned to you that she found an error in the 2003 financial statements which she believes has corrected itself. In discussions with the purchasing department, she determined that 2003 ending inventory was overstated by $1 million. Joy says that the 2004 ending inventory is correct, and she assumes that 2004 net earnings is correct. Joy says to you, "What happened happened—there's no point in worrying about it anymore."

Instructions

You conclude that Joy is incorrect. Write a brief, tactful memo to her, clarifying the situation.

ETHICS CASE

BYP6-9 You are provided with the following information for Discount Diamonds Ltd. Discount only carries one brand and size of diamond—all are identical. Each batch of diamonds purchased is carefully coded and marked with its purchase cost.

Ethics In
Accounting

Mar.	1	Beginning inventory is 150 diamonds at a cost of $300 per diamond.
	3	Purchased 200 diamonds at a cost of $350 each.
	5	Sold 180 diamonds for $600 each.
	10	Purchased 350 diamonds at a cost of $375 each.
	25	Sold 500 diamonds for $650 each.

Instructions

(a) Assume that Discount Diamonds uses the specific identification cost flow method.
  1. Demonstrate how Discount Diamonds could maximize its gross profit for the month by selecting which diamonds to sell on March 5 and March 25.
  2. Demonstrate how Discount Diamonds could minimize its gross profit for the month by selecting which diamonds to sell on March 5 and March 25.
(b) Assume that Discount Diamonds uses FIFO. How much gross profit would Discount Diamonds report under this cost flow assumption?
(c) Who are the stakeholders in this situation? Is there anything unethical in choosing which diamonds to sell in a month?
(d) Which cost flow assumption should Discount Diamonds select? Explain.

Answers to Self-Study Questions
1. d   2. a   3. b   4. d   5. a   6. b   7. a   8. a   9. d   *10. c

Answer to Loblaw Review It Question 1

Loblaw uses the FIFO (first-in, first-out) cost flow assumption to account for its inventories.

Remember to go back to the Navigator box on the
chapter-opening page to check off your completed work.

Internal Control and Cash

Counting Out the Money

Couples, students, locals just finished work—on any given evening you can find them all hanging out at the Granite Brewery, enjoying traditional pub food and a range of international cuisine, not to mention quality ale brewed by the owner himself.

The Brewery, which employs 25 people, has become something of a Halifax institution since it opened in 1987. In fact, it was so popular that in 1991 it opened a location in Toronto. In 2001, it added another location in Halifax just a few blocks away to house its brewing operations and a second restaurant.

The original Granite Brewery takes in over $1 million in annual sales, all of which flows in one way or another through the hands of its wait staff. General manager Denise Avery has a detailed system in place to track it all.

"There are two cash registers," explains Ms. Avery, "and up to three people might use each one on any given shift. Each server has a private code number that they punch into the register when they ring up a sale, and it tracks their totals separately." Everyone is given a float of $30 at the beginning of the shift to make change from, and is responsible for turning in that amount plus whatever his or her cash receipts total is at the end.

What if there's a discrepancy between the cash register machine's total and the amount in the till? "The machine prints two tapes—one we can use as receipts and one that stays inside," says Ms. Avery, "so we can look for the error." The register is preprogrammed with the cost of each item, so the staff need not enter any numbers—they just press a button labelled "domestic beer" or "fish and chips." "That and the cash register codes eliminate a lot of problems," Ms. Avery says.

The Brewery also has internal controls in place at its bar, where two bartenders work each day on two separate shifts. "When they come in to work in the morning, the first thing they do is count the inventory in the fridge—bottles of beer, pop,

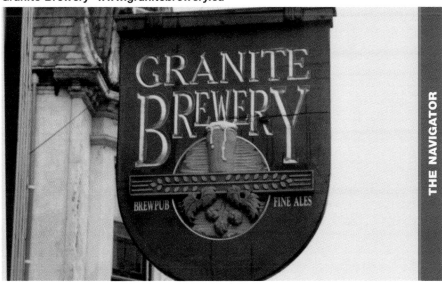

Granite Brewery www.granitebrewery.ca

THE NAVIGATOR

Scan *Study Objectives* ☐

Read *Feature Story* ☐

Read *Chapter Preview* ☐

Read text and answer *Before You Go On*
p. 313 ☐ p. 322 ☐ p. 327 ☐

Work *Using the Decision Toolkit* ☐

Review *Summary of Study Objectives*
and *Decision Toolkit* ☐

Work *Demonstration Problem* ☐

Answer *Self-Study Questions* ☐

Complete assignments ☐

juice, and wine—and read the meters on each ale," explains Ms. Avery. "At the end of the shift, they do another count with the next bartender, who in turn rings off at closing." When the adding and subtracting is done at the end of each shift, everything must correspond to the cash register tape. For example, if three beers are missing from the fridge, three beers should have been rung in. If they weren't, the bartender is responsible.

"With a good system, discrepancies just don't happen often," she continues. "If ever there is one, it's usually pretty easy to find the problem from looking at the cash tapes. Of course, theft is always the last thing you want to think of. The controls are there so that there is practically no opportunity for trouble. You assume your staff is honest, but you know there's such a thing as human nature, so you don't put temptation in their way."

Of course, these days, fewer and fewer customers pay with actual cash. Ms. Avery estimates that about 40% of sales are paid for by debit card, and another 20% by credit card, so that actual cash makes up less than half of a day's receipts.

"At the end of the day—or more realistically, the next morning," laughs Ms. Avery, "I prepare the deposit and take the cash to the bank." At the end of the month, "everything is reconciled on the computer. We use *Simply Accounting* computerized accounting software, which works just fine."

Cash control is crucial to a business like the Granite Brewery. "A place like this is basically a cash business," says Ms. Avery. But with a carefully thought-out system and the help of modern automation, cash can be controlled reliably and fairly easily. The owner doesn't like to be bothered with daily problems, Ms. Avery explains; it's her job to keep things running smoothly so he can spend his time brewing great beer.

Cash is the lifeblood of any company. Large and small companies alike must guard it carefully. Even companies that are in every other way successful can go bankrupt if they fail to manage cash. Managers must know both how to use cash efficiently and how to protect it, as described in the feature story. Due to its liquid nature, cash is the easiest asset to steal.

In this chapter, you will learn ways to reduce the risk of cash and other assets being stolen, how to report cash in the financial statements, and how to manage cash. The content and organization of this chapter are as follows:

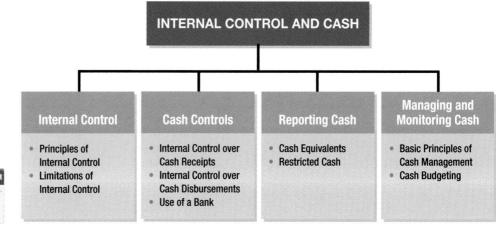

Internal Control

In the *Canadian Retail Security Report*, retailers report that customer theft amounts to $3 million in losses each day. Theft by dishonest employees increases this figure by another $3 million a day and paperwork errors add nearly $2 million more. Findings such as these emphasize the need for a good system of internal control.

Internal control consists of all the related methods and measures adopted within a business to:

1. **optimize the use of resources** to reduce inefficiencies and waste
2. **prevent and detect errors and irregularities** in the accounting process
3. **safeguard assets** from theft, robbery, and unauthorized use
4. **maintain reliable control systems** to enhance the accuracy and reliability of accounting records

Under the *Canada Business Corporations Act*, all federally incorporated companies are required to maintain an adequate system of internal control. The CICA's Criteria of Control Board stresses that this internal control should address not only external financial reporting, but also the reliability of internal reporting.

BUSINESS INSIGHT
ETHICS PERSPECTIVE

In response to the rash of corporate scandals that involved companies such as Enron, WorldCom, and Global Crossing, legislators around the world introduced wide-ranging reforms to improve accountability. One such example is the requirement for accounting firms to make a statement about the adequacy of the internal controls over financial reporting at the companies they audit.

"There is much more intensity around the adequacy of a company's internal control environment," said Dennis Nally, chair of PricewaterhouseCoopers—the world's largest accounting firm. "As a result of that, you're going to see much more auditing, not only by the external auditors but also by the internal auditors, directed at compliance."

Source: Deepa Babington, "Auditors Crack Whip, Preach Tough Love Post-Enron," *Reuters News,* December 30, 2002.

PRINCIPLES OF INTERNAL CONTROL

To optimize resources, prevent and detect errors and irregularities, safeguard assets, and maintain reliable systems, a company follows internal control principles. The specific control measures used vary with the size and nature of the business and with management's control philosophy. However, the six principles listed in Illustration 7-1 apply to most companies. These principles are explained in the following sections.

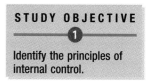

STUDY OBJECTIVE
1
Identify the principles of internal control.

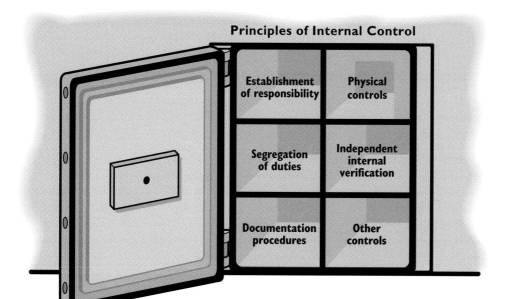

Illustration 7-1
Principles of internal control

Establishment of Responsibility

An essential characteristic of internal control is the assignment of responsibility to specific individuals. **Control is most effective when only one person is responsible for a given task.** To illustrate, assume that the cash on hand at the end of the day is $10 short of the cash rung up on the cash register. If only one person has operated the register, responsibility for the shortage can be attributed quickly. If two or more individuals have worked the register, it may be impossible to determine who is responsible for the error unless each person is assigned a separate cash drawer or code number, as is done at the Granite Brewery described in the feature story.

Responsibility must also be assigned for the authorization and approval of transactions. For example, the vice-president of sales should have the authority to establish policies for making credit sales. Typically, these policies require written credit department approval of credit sales.

Segregation of Duties

Segregation of duties is indispensable in a system of internal control. **The work of one employee should, without a duplication of effort, provide a reliable basis for** evaluating the work of another employee. There are two common applications of segregation of duties:

1. The responsibility for related activities should be assigned to different individuals.
2. The responsibility for accounting for an asset should be separate from the responsibility for physical custody of that asset.

Related Activities. Related activities should be assigned to different individuals in both the purchasing and selling areas. **When one individual is responsible for all of the related activities, the potential for errors and irregularities is increased.**

Related purchasing activities include ordering merchandise, receiving goods, and paying (or authorizing payment) for merchandise. In purchasing, for example, orders could be placed with friends or with suppliers who give kickbacks. In addition, payment might be authorized without a careful review of the invoice or, even worse, fictitious invoices might be approved for payment. When the responsibilities for ordering, receiving, and paying are assigned to different individuals, the risk of such abuses is minimized.

Related sales activities should also be assigned to different individuals. Related sales activities include making a sale, shipping (or delivering) the goods to the customer, and billing the customer. When one person is responsible for these related sales transactions, the risks that the following could happen increase: a salesperson could make sales at unauthorized prices to increase sales commissions, a shipping clerk could ship goods to him- or herself, or a billing clerk could understate the amount billed for sales made to friends and relatives. These abuses are less likely to occur when salespersons make the sale, shipping department employees ship the goods on the basis of the sales order, and billing department employees prepare the sales invoice after comparing the sales order with the report of goods shipped.

Custody of Assets. To make the accountability for an asset in an accounting system valid, the accountant (as record keeper) should not have physical custody of the asset or access to it. Similarly, the custodian of the asset should not maintain or have access to the accounting records. **The custodian of an asset is not likely to convert the asset to personal use if another employee maintains the record which states that the asset should be on hand.** The separation of accounting responsibility from the custody of assets is especially important for cash and inventories, because these assets are vulnerable to unauthorized use or misappropriation.

Documentation Procedures

Documents provide evidence that transactions and events have occurred. At the Granite Brewery, the cash register tape is documentation for the amount of cash received. Similarly, a shipping document indicates that goods have been shipped, and a sales invoice indicates that the customer has been billed for the goods. By adding a signature (or initials) to the documents, the individual responsible for the transaction or event can be identified.

Procedures should be established for documents. First, whenever possible, **documents should be prenumbered and all documents should be accounted for.** Prenumbering helps to prevent a transaction from being recorded more than once or, conversely, from not being recorded. Second, documents that are source documents for accounting entries should be promptly forwarded to the accounting department to help ensure timely recording of the transaction and event. This control measure contributes directly to the accuracy and reliability of the accounting records.

Physical Controls

Use of physical controls is essential. Physical controls include mechanical and electronic controls to safeguard assets and enhance the accuracy and reliability of the accounting records. Examples of these controls are shown in Illustration 7-2.

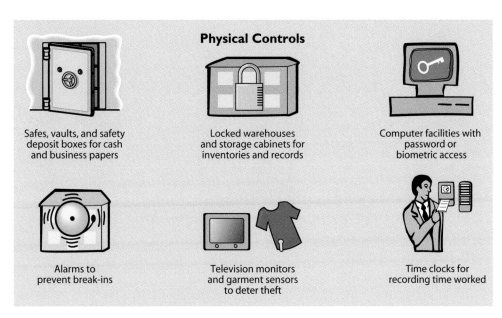

Illustration 7-2
Physical controls

Many books and movies have been produced with computer system tampering as a theme. A critical consideration in programming computers is building in controls that limit unauthorized or unintentional tampering. Program controls built into the computer prevent intentional or unintentional errors and unauthorized access. To prevent unauthorized access, the computer system may require that passwords be entered and random personal questions be correctly answered, or that biometric controls such as fingerprint or retinal scans be used, before system access is allowed. Once access has been allowed, other program controls identify data having a value higher or lower than a predetermined amount (limit checks), validate calculations (math checks), and detect improper processing orders (sequence checks).

Independent Internal Verification

Most systems of internal control provide for independent internal verification. This principle involves the review, comparison, and reconciliation of data prepared by employees. Three measures are recommended to obtain maximum benefit from independent internal verification:

1. The verification should be done periodically or on a surprise basis.
2. The verification should be done by an employee who is independent of the personnel responsible for the information.
3. Discrepancies and exceptions should be reported to a management level that can take appropriate corrective action.

Independent internal verification is especially useful in comparing accounting records with existing assets. The reconciliation by the two bartenders of the inventory with the cash register tape in the feature story about the Granite Brewery is an example. Another common example is the reconciliation by an independent person of the cash balance per books with the cash balance per bank. The relationship between this principle and the segregation of duties principle is shown in Illustration 7-3.

Illustration 7-3
Relationship of segregation of duties principle to independent internal verification principle

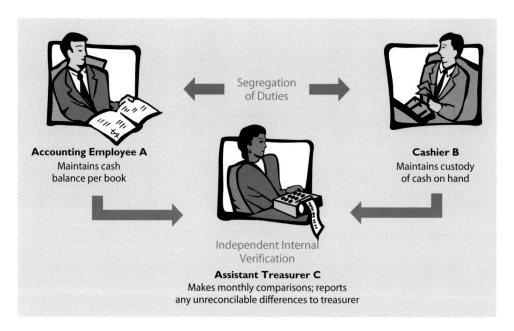

In large companies, independent internal verification is often assigned to internal auditors. Internal auditors are employees of the company who evaluate the effectiveness of the company's system of internal control. They periodically review the activities of departments and individuals to determine whether prescribed internal controls are being followed. The importance of this function is illustrated by the fact that most fraud is discovered by companies through internal mechanisms, such as existing internal controls and internal audits. The alleged fraud at WorldCom involving billions of dollars, for example, was uncovered by an internal auditor.

Other Controls

Here are two other control measures:

1. **Bonding of employees who handle cash.** Bonding involves obtaining insurance protection against misappropriation of assets by dishonest employees. This measure contributes to the safeguarding of cash in two ways: First, the insurance company carefully screens all individuals before adding them to the policy and may reject risky applicants. Second, bonded employees know that the insurance company will vigorously prosecute all offenders.
2. **Rotating employees' duties and requiring employees to take vacations.** These measures are designed to deter employees from attempting any thefts, since they will not be able to permanently conceal their improper actions. Many embezzlements, for example, have been discovered when the perpetrator was on vacation or assigned to a new position.

Decision Toolkit

DECISION CHECKPOINTS	INFO NEEDED FOR DECISION	TOOL TO USE FOR DECISION	HOW TO EVALUATE RESULTS
Are the company's financial statements supported by adequate internal controls?	Auditor's report, statement of management responsibility, management discussion and analysis, articles in the financial press	The required measures of internal control are to (1) establish responsibility, (2) segregate duties, (3) document procedures, (4) employ physical controls, and (5) use independent internal verification.	If any indication is given that these or other controls are lacking, the financial statements should be used with caution.

LIMITATIONS OF INTERNAL CONTROL

A company's system of internal control is generally designed to provide **reasonable assurance** that assets are properly safeguarded and that the accounting records are reliable—in other words, that a reliable control system is maintained. The concept of reasonable assurance rests on the premise that the costs of establishing control procedures should not exceed their expected benefit.

To illustrate, consider shoplifting losses in retail stores. Such losses could be completely eliminated by having a security guard stop and search customers as they leave the store. Store managers have concluded, however, that the negative effects of this procedure cannot be justified. Instead, stores have attempted to "control" shoplifting losses by using less costly procedures such as (1) posting signs saying, "We reserve the right to inspect all packages" and "All shoplifters will be prosecuted," (2) using hidden TV cameras and store detectives to monitor customer activity, and (3) using sensor equipment at exits.

The **human element** is an important factor in every system of internal control. A good system can become ineffective as a result of employee fatigue, carelessness, or indifference. For example, a receiving clerk may not bother to count goods received or may just "fudge" the counts. Occasionally, two or more individuals may work together to get around prescribed controls. Such collusion can significantly impair the effectiveness of a system because it eliminates the protection expected from segregation of duties. If a supervisor and a cashier collaborate to understate cash receipts, the system of internal control may be defeated (at least in the short run).

The **size of the business** may impose limitations on internal control. In a small company, for example, it may be difficult to apply the principles of segregation of duties and independent internal verification because of the small number of employees. In such instances, the owner usually either assumes responsibility for or oversees incompatible functions.

Computer systems provide unique internal control problems. In many instances, computerization has shifted the responsibility for internal control to programmers and end-users. For example, in point-of-sale systems, accountants are not required to record daily transactions. The computer automatically records the transaction when the cashier or clerk makes the sale. It is especially important to maintain effective control over authorization, documentation, and access in computerized systems.

International Note

Other countries also have control problems. For example, a judge in France issued a 36-page report detailing many widespread scams, such as kickbacks in public works contracts, the skimming of development aid money to Africa, and bribes on arms sales.

BUSINESS INSIGHT

ETHICS PERSPECTIVE

Unfortunately, computer-related frauds are a major concern. The average computer crime loss is nearly $1 million, compared with an average loss of only $30,000 resulting from other types of white-collar crime. Computer fraud can be perpetrated almost invisibly and done with electronic speed. Psychologically, stealing using a company computer seems far less criminal to some people than other types of theft. As a result, the moral threshold to commit computer fraud is lower than for fraud involving a person-to-person interaction. Nonetheless, computer crime is still illegal and the *Criminal Code of Canada* and the *Copyright Act* contain provisions to deal with computer crimes.

BEFORE YOU GO ON . . .

- **REVIEW IT**
  1. What are the four primary objectives of internal control?
  2. Identify and describe the principles of internal control.
  3. What are the limitations of internal control?

● **DO IT**

Li Song owns a small retail store. Li wants to establish good internal control procedures but is confused about the differences between segregation of duties and independent internal verification. Explain the differences to Li.

Action Plan

- Understand and explain the differences between (1) segregation of duties and (2) independent internal verification.

Solution

Segregation of duties relates to the assignment of responsibility so that (1) the work of one employee will evaluate the work of another employee and (2) the physical control of assets is separated from the accounting records that keep track of the assets. Segregation of duties occurs daily in using assets and in executing and recording transactions. In contrast, independent internal verification involves reviewing, comparing, and reconciling data prepared by one or several employees. Independent internal verification occurs after the fact, as in reconciling cash register totals at the end of the day with cash on hand.

Cash Controls

Just as cash is the beginning of a company's operating cycle, it is usually the starting point for a company's system of internal control. Cash is the one asset that is readily convertible into any other type of asset: it is easily concealed and transported, lacks owner identification, and is highly desired. Because of these characteristics, cash is susceptible to improper diversion and use. Moreover, because of the large volume of cash transactions, numerous errors may occur in executing and recording these transactions. To safeguard cash and to ensure the accuracy of the accounting records, effective internal control over cash is essential.

Cash consists of coins, currency (paper money), cheques, money orders, and money on hand or on deposit in a bank or similar depository. The general rule is that if the bank will accept it for deposit, it is cash. Debit card transactions and bank credit card receipts, such as VISA and MasterCard, are considered as cash but non-bank credit card receipts are not. (We will discuss the classification and accounting for these types of transactions in more detail in Chapter 8.) In addition, cash does *not* include postdated (payable in the future) cheques, staledated (in excess of six months old) cheques, or returned cheques (due to insufficient funds). Nor are postage stamps or IOUs from employees cash, because these items are not the current medium of exchange or acceptable at face value on deposit. The application of internal control principles to cash receipts and cash disbursements is explained in the next sections.

BUSINESS INSIGHT

ETHICS PERSPECTIVE

Canadians are among the world's most frequent users of debit cards. Cash, including debit cards, makes up half of all point-of-sale payments in Canada. Credit cards, such as VISA and MasterCard, account for less than one-quarter of payments. Only 2% of retail transactions are paid by personal cheque.

Unfortunately, debit card fraud now rivals credit card fraud. RCMP superintendent Ben Soave recently called such fraud a frightening development that threatened electronic commerce like never before.

Source: "Debit Card Fraud an 'Epidemic,'" CBC News, January 9, 2003.

INTERNAL CONTROL OVER CASH RECEIPTS

STUDY OBJECTIVE
2
Explain the applications of internal control to cash receipts.

Cash receipts result from a variety of sources: cash sales; collections on account from customers; the receipt of interest, rents, and dividends; investments by shareholders; bank loans; and proceeds from the sale of assets. Generally, internal control over cash receipts is more effective when **cash receipts are deposited intact into the bank account on a daily basis.** The internal control principles explained earlier apply to cash receipt transactions as shown in Illustration 7-4. As might be expected, companies vary considerably in how they apply these principles.

Illustration 7-4
Application of internal control principles to cash receipts

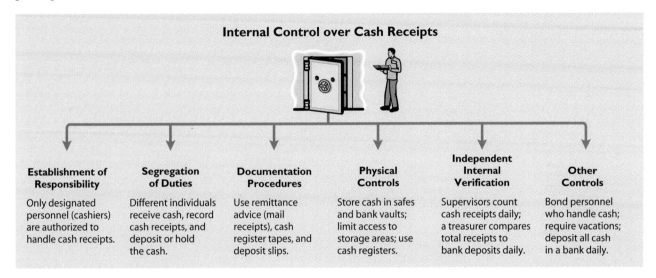

Internal Control over Cash Receipts

Establishment of Responsibility	Segregation of Duties	Documentation Procedures	Physical Controls	Independent Internal Verification	Other Controls
Only designated personnel (cashiers) are authorized to handle cash receipts.	Different individuals receive cash, record cash receipts, and deposit or hold the cash.	Use remittance advice (mail receipts), cash register tapes, and deposit slips.	Store cash in safes and bank vaults; limit access to storage areas; use cash registers.	Supervisors count cash receipts daily; a treasurer compares total receipts to bank deposits daily.	Bond personnel who handle cash; require vacations; deposit all cash in a bank daily.

INTERNAL CONTROL OVER CASH DISBURSEMENTS

STUDY OBJECTIVE
3
Explain the applications of internal control to cash disbursements.

Cash is disbursed for a variety of reasons, such as to pay expenses and liabilities or to purchase assets. Generally, internal control over cash disbursements is more effective when **payments are made by cheque rather than by cash.** Payment is generally made by cheque only after specified control procedures have been followed. In addition, once the cheque has been paid by the bank, it constitutes proof of payment. The principles of internal control apply to cash disbursements as shown in Illustration 7-5.

Illustration 7-5
Application of internal control principles to cash disbursements

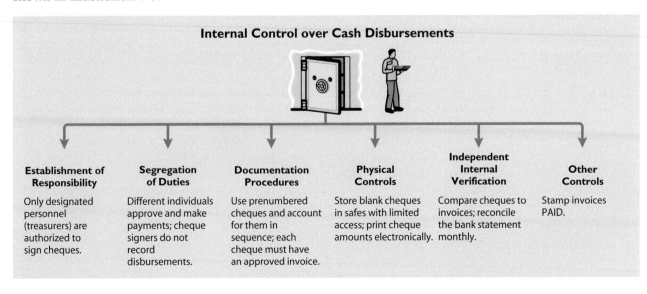

Internal Control over Cash Disbursements

Establishment of Responsibility	Segregation of Duties	Documentation Procedures	Physical Controls	Independent Internal Verification	Other Controls
Only designated personnel (treasurers) are authorized to sign cheques.	Different individuals approve and make payments; cheque signers do not record disbursements.	Use prenumbered cheques and account for them in sequence; each cheque must have an approved invoice.	Store blank cheques in safes with limited access; print cheque amounts electronically.	Compare cheques to invoices; reconcile the bank statement monthly.	Stamp invoices PAID.

USE OF A BANK

The use of a bank contributes significantly to good internal control over cash. A company can safeguard its cash by using a bank as a depository and clearing house for cash and cheques received and cheques written. The use of a bank minimizes the amount of currency that must be kept on hand. In addition, it makes it easier to control cash because a double record is maintained of all bank transactions—one by the business and the other by the bank. The asset account Cash maintained by the company is the "flip-side" of the bank's liability account for that company. It should be possible to **reconcile these accounts**—make them agree—at any time.

Many companies have more than one bank account. For efficiency of operations and better control, national retailers like Loblaw have regional bank accounts. Similarly, a company such as Bell Canada, with more than 150,000 employees, has a payroll bank account as well as one or more general bank accounts. In addition, a company may maintain several bank accounts in order to have more than one source for obtaining short-term loans when needed.

Bank Statements

Each month, the bank sends the company a bank statement showing the company's bank transactions and balances. For example, in Illustration 7-6, the statement for Laird Ltd. shows the following: (1) cheques paid and other debits that reduce the balance in the depositor's account, (2) deposits and other credits that increase the balance in the depositor's account, and (3) the account balance after each day's transactions. Remember that bank statements are prepared from the *bank's* perspective. For example, every deposit received by the bank is an increase in a liability (an account payable to the depositor). Therefore, every deposit received from Laird Ltd. by the Bank of Montreal is *credited* by the bank to Laird's account with the bank. The reverse occurs when the bank pays a cheque issued by Laird Ltd. on its chequing account balance. Payment reduces the bank's liability and is therefore *debited* to Laird's account with the bank.

All paid cheques are listed in chronological order on the bank statement along with the date the cheque was paid and its amount. Upon paying a cheque, the bank stamps the cheque "Paid"; a paid cheque is sometimes referred to as a **cancelled cheque**. In addition, the bank includes memoranda with the bank statement that explain other debits and credits made by the bank to the depositor's account.

Helpful Hint

Bank	Company
Credit	*Debit*
Debit	*Credit*

Illustration 7-6
Bank statement

Bank of Montreal ▲ Banque de Montréal

505 King Street
Fredericton, NB
E3B 1E7

Transit No de dom	Date D/J M/M Y/A	Account Title Désignation de compte	Account Type Type de compte	Account No. No de compte	Page
0123	30 04 04	Operating Account	FBOA	1050-800	58

TRANSACTION CODES*
*CODES DE TRANSACTIONS**

AD Adjustments
Rectification
CB Cheque Posted By Branch
Cheque inscrit par la succ.
CC Certified Cheque
Cheque certifié
CD Customer Deposit
Dépôt
CK Cheque
Cheque
CM Credit Memo
Avis de Crédit
CW Telephone Banking
Services bancaires par téléphone
DC Other Charges
Autres frais
DD Direct Deposit/
Pre-authorized Debit
Dépôt ou débit direct
DM Debit Memo
Avis de débit
DN Not Service Chargeable
Sans frais de gestion
DR Overdraft
Découvert
DS Service Chargeable
Avec frais de gestion
EC Error Correction
Correction d'erreur
FX Foreign Exchange
Change
GS Tax
Taxe
IB Instabank
Instabanque
IN Interest
Intérêt
LI Loan Interest
Intérêt sur prêt
LN Loan Payment
Vesement sur prêt
LP Loan Advance
Avance sur prêt
LT Large Volume Account
List Total
Liste de chèque - compte
superactif
MB Multi-Branch Banking
Inter-Service
NR Non-Resident Tax
Impôt de non-résident
NS Cheque returned NSF
Chèque retourné - provision
insuffisante
NT Nesbitt Burns Entry
Transaction de Nesbitt Burns
OM Other Machine
Autre machine
PR Purchase at Merchant
Achat chez le commerçant
RC NSF Charge
Frais pour provision insuffisante
RN Merchandise Return
Retour de marchandise
RT Returned Item
Article retourné
RV Merchant Reversal
Correction - Commerçant
SC Service Charge
Frais de gestion
SO Standing Order
Ordre de virement
ST Merchant Deposit
Dépôt du commerçant
TF Transfer of Funds
Virement
TX Tax
Taxe
WD Withdrawal
Retrait
Please see the reverse side
for the Account Types
Les types de compte
figurent au verso.

Laird Ltd.
500 Queen Street
Fredericton, NB   E3B 5C2

BALANCE FORWARD
SOLDE REPORTÉ

Date
03 31 13,256.90

CODE	Description/ Message justificatif	Debits/ Débits	Credits/Crédits	Mo.	Day Jour	Balance/Solde
CK	NO. 435	644.95			04 02	12,611.95
CK	NO. 438	776.65			04 03	11,835.30
CK	NO. 437	1,185.79			04 04	10,649.51
CK	NO. 436	3,260.00			04 05	7,389.51
CD			2,350.47		04 06	9,739.98
CK	NO. 440	1,487.90			04 09	8,252.08
CK	NO. 439	1,781.70			04 10	6,470.38
CK	NO. 441	2,420.00			04 10	4,050.38
CD			3,320.28		04 12	7,370.66
CM			1,035.00		04 13	8,405.66
CK	NO. 442	585.60			04 16	7,820.06
CD			2,720.00		04 18	10,540.06
CK	NO. 443	226.00			04 18	10,314.06
CD			757.41		04 20	11,071.47
CD			1,218.56		04 23	12.290.03
CD			715.42		04 25	13,005.45
RC		425.60			04 26	12,579.85
CK	NO. 444	1,080.30			04 26	11,499.55
CD			2,929.45		04 27	14,429.00
DM		30.00			04 30	14,399.00
CD			2,128.60		04 30	16,527.60
CK	NO. 448	620.15			04 30	15,907.45

Debit Memorandum. A debit memorandum (DM) is used by the bank when a previously deposited customer's cheque bounces because of insufficient funds. In such a case, the cheque is marked NSF (not sufficient funds) by the customer's bank, or **RC (returned cheque)**, as in the case of the Bank of Montreal, and is returned to the depositor's bank. The bank then debits (decreases) the depositor's account, as shown by the symbol RC on the bank statement in Illustration 7-6, and sends the NSF cheque and debit memorandum to the depositor as notification of the charge. The NSF cheque creates an account receivable for the depositor and reduces cash in the bank account.

Recording an account receivable assumes that the customer will honour the account due by replacing the bounced cheque with a valid cheque, or with cash. This happens in most cases. In the next chapter, we will discuss how to account for uncollectible accounts receivable when customers are unable to pay their accounts.

Debit memoranda are also used by banks to identify bank service charges, interest expense, electronic fund transfers from the depositor's account to another account, and other charges deducted from the depositor's account.

Credit Memorandum. Credit memoranda (CM) identify interest earned on the bank account, electronic fund transfers into the depositor's account, and other amounts added to the depositor's account. For example, some retailers enable electronic payment of merchandise sold on account. Funds are electronically transferred from the customer's account to the retailer's account in payment of the bill.

Reconciling the Bank Account

STUDY OBJECTIVE

④

Prepare a bank reconciliation.

Because the bank and the company maintain independent records of the company's chequing account, you might assume that the respective balances will always agree. In fact, the two balances are seldom the same at any given time. It is therefore necessary to make the balance per books agree with the balance per bank—a process called reconciling the bank account. The lack of agreement between the balances has two causes:

1. **Time lags** that prevent one of the parties from recording the transaction in the same period as the other party
2. **Errors** by either party in recording transactions

Alternative Terminology
When a cheque is paid by the bank, it is said to *clear* the bank.

Time lags occur frequently. For example, several days may elapse between the time a company pays a supplier by cheque and the date the cheque is presented to the bank for payment by the supplier. Similarly, when a company uses the bank's night depository to make its deposits, there will be a difference of one day (or more, if holidays intervene) between the time the receipts are recorded by the company and the time they are recorded by the bank. A time lag also occurs whenever the bank mails a debit or credit memorandum to the company.

The incidence of errors depends on the effectiveness of the internal controls maintained by the company and the bank. Bank errors are infrequent. However, either party could accidentally record a $450 cheque as $45 or $540. In addition, the bank might mistakenly charge a cheque to the wrong account if the code is missing or if is not scannable.

BUSINESS INSIGHT

MANAGEMENT PERSPECTIVE

Bank errors may be infrequent, but they can involve a story more suitable for Ripley's Believe It or Not than an accounting textbook. The Bank of Nova Scotia's discount brokerage arm accidentally put $17.1 million of somebody else's money into a Toronto doctor's Scotiabank account. It took four months to find and correct the error. Stories about banks misplacing customers' funds are a dime a dozen. But they usually involve misplaced debits, and rarely amounts as high as this.

Source: John Partridge, "Bank Error in Your Favour: Collect $17 Million," *Globe and Mail,* April 11, 2000, A1.

Reconciliation Procedure. In reconciling the bank account, it is customary to reconcile the balance per books and balance per bank to their adjusted (correct) cash balances. To obtain maximum benefit from a bank reconciliation, the reconciliation should be prepared by an employee who has no other responsibilities related to cash. When the internal control principle of independent internal verification is not followed in preparing the reconciliation, cash embezzlements may escape unnoticed.

The reconciliation is usually divided into two sections—one per the bank statement and one per the books—as shown in Illustration 7-7.

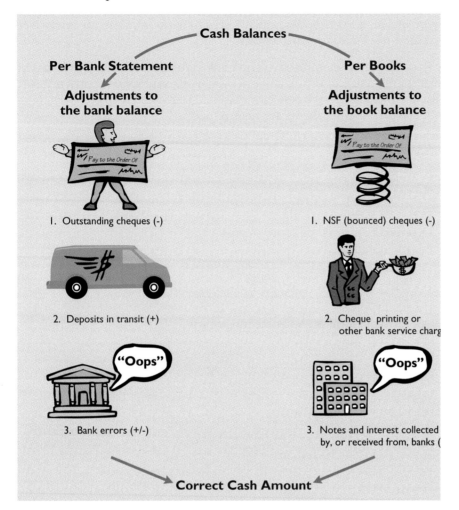

Illustration 7-7
Bank reconciliation procedures

The starting point in preparing the reconciliation is to enter the balance per bank statement and balance per books. The following steps should reveal all the reconciling items that cause the difference between the two balances:

1. Compare the individual deposits on the bank statement with (a) the deposits in transit from the preceding bank reconciliation and (b) the deposits per company records or copies of duplicate deposit slips. Deposits recorded by the depositor that have not been recorded by the bank represent deposits in transit. These deposits are added to the balance per bank.

2. Compare the paid cheques shown on the bank statement or the paid cheques returned with the bank statement with (a) cheques outstanding from the preceding bank reconciliation and (b) cheques issued by the company as recorded in the journal. Issued cheques recorded by the company that have not been paid by the bank represent outstanding cheques that are deducted from the balance per bank.

3. Note any **errors** discovered in the previous steps and list them in the appropriate section of the reconciliation schedule. For example, if a paid cheque correctly written by the company for $195 was mistakenly recorded by the company as $159, the error of $36 ($195 − $159) is deducted from the balance per books. All errors made by the depositor are reconciling items in determining the adjusted cash balance per books. All errors made by the bank are reconciling items in determining the adjusted cash balance per bank.

Helpful Hint Deposits in transit and outstanding cheques are reconciling items because of time lags.

4. Trace **bank memoranda** to the depositor's records. Any unrecorded memoranda should be listed in the appropriate section of the reconciliation. For example, a $25 debit memorandum for bank service charges is deducted from the balance per books, and a $3 credit memorandum for interest earned is added to the balance per books.

Bank Reconciliation Illustrated. The bank statement for Laird Ltd. was shown in Illustration 7-6. It shows a balance per the bank of $15,907.45 on April 30, 2004. On this date the balance of cash per books is $11,589.45. From the foregoing steps, the following reconciling items are determined:

Helpful Hint Note in the bank statement that cheques number 444 and 448 have been paid but cheques number 445, 446, and 447 are not listed. Thus, these cheques are outstanding. The amounts for these three cheques are obtained from the company's accounting records.

1. **Deposits in transit:** April 30 deposit (received by bank on May 1). $2,201.40
2. **Outstanding cheques:** No. 445: $3,000.00; No. 446: $1,401.30; No. 447: $1,502.70.   5,904.00
3. **Error:** Cheque No. 443 was correctly written by Laird for $226.00 and was correctly paid by the bank. However, it was recorded as $262.00 on Laird's books.   36.00
4. **Bank memoranda:**
    (a) Debit—Returned or NSF cheque from J.R. Baron   425.60
    (b) Debit—Cheque printing charge   30.00
    (c) Credit—Electronic payment by customer—V. Kinnear—on account   1,035.00

The bank reconciliation is shown in Illustration 7-8.

Illustration 7-8
Bank reconciliation

LAIRD LTD. Bank Reconciliation April 30, 2004			
Cash balance per bank statement			$ 15,907.45
Add: Deposits in transit			2,201.40
			18,108.85
Less: Outstanding cheques			
No. 445		$3,000.00	
No. 446		1,401.30	
No. 447		1,502.70	5,904.00
Adjusted cash balance per bank			$12,204.85
Cash balance per books			$11,589.45
Add: Electronic payment by customer on account		$1,035.00	
Error in recording cheque No. 443		36.00	1,071.00
			12,660.45
Less: Returned (NSF) cheque		$ 425.60	
Bank service charge		30.00	455.60
Adjusted cash balance per books			$12,204.85

BUSINESS INSIGHT

MANAGEMENT PERSPECTIVE

It would be easy to reconcile the bank statement for Mary Jane Lee, formerly of College Street, Toronto. Her account, with a balance of $14,007.60, was last touched in 1938! Mary Jane's inactive account is far from the only one. There are more than 770,000 unclaimed accounts at the Bank of Canada.

Chartered banks must transfer dormant accounts to the Bank of Canada if they have not been used in the last 10 years. Accounts with balances of less than $500 are kept up to an additional 10 years by the Bank of Canada, then written off. All other accounts remain with the Bank of Canada indefinitely until someone comes forward to claim the funds.

Entries for Bank Reconciliation.   Each reconciling item which arises from determining the adjusted cash balance per books should be recorded by the depositor. If these items are not journalized and posted, the Cash account will not show the correct balance. The adjusting entries for the Laird Ltd. bank reconciliation on April 30 are as follows:

Electronic Payment on Account.   A payment by a customer of their account is recorded in the same way, whether the cash is received through the mail or electronically. The entry is:

Apr. 30	Cash	1,035	
	Accounts Receivable—V. Kinnear		1,035
	(To record electronic payment on account)		

A = L + SE
+1,035
−1,035

Cash flows: +1,035

Book Error.   An examination of the journal shows that incorrectly recorded cheque No. 443 was a payment on account to Andrea Corporation, a supplier. The correcting entry is:

Apr. 30	Cash	36	
	Accounts Payable—Andrea Corporation		36
	(To correct error in recording cheque No. 443)		

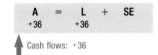

A = L + SE
+36 +36

Cash flows: +36

NSF Cheque.   As indicated earlier, an NSF (RC) cheque becomes an account receivable to the depositor. The entry is:

Apr. 30	Accounts Receivable—J.R. Baron	425.60	
	Cash		425.60
	(To record returned cheque)		

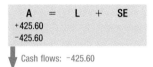

A = L + SE
+425.60
−425.60

Cash flows: −425.60

Bank Service Charges.   Cheque printing charges (DM) and other bank service charges (SC) are debited to the expense account Bank Charges. Some companies use the account Interest Expense; others use Miscellaneous Expense if charges are nominal in amount. The entry is:

Apr. 30	Bank Charges	30	
	Cash		30
	(To record charge for printing cheques)		

A = L + SE
−30 −30

Cash flows: −30

All of the entries above could also be combined into one compound entry. Our presentation assumes that all adjustments are made at the end of the month. In practice, a company may also make journal entries during the month as it receives information from the bank regarding its account.

After the entries are posted, the Cash account will appear as in the T account which follows. The adjusted cash balance in the ledger should agree with the adjusted cash balance per books in the bank reconciliation in Illustration 7-8.

		CASH			
Apr.	30	Bal. 11,589.45	Apr.	30	425.60
	30	1,035.00		30	30.00
	30	36.00			
Apr.	30	Bal. 12,204.85			

What entries does the bank make? **The bank cannot correct your errors on its books and you cannot correct the bank's errors on your books.** If any bank errors are discovered in preparing the reconciliation, the bank should be notified so it can make the necessary corrections on its records. The bank does not make any entries for deposits in transit or outstanding cheques. Only when these items reach the bank will it record them.

BEFORE YOU GO ON . . .

- **REVIEW IT**

1. How do the principles of internal control apply to cash receipts?
2. How do the principles of internal control apply to cash disbursements?
3. What steps are involved in the bank reconciliation procedure?

- **DO IT**

The new accountant of Kist Fabrics Inc. asks you to explain how the following reconciling items should be treated in reconciling the bank account at December 31: (1) a debit memorandum for an NSF cheque, (2) a credit memorandum for interest earned, (3) outstanding cheques from the prior period, (4) outstanding cheques from the current period, and (5) a deposit in transit.

Action Plan

- Understand the purpose of a bank reconciliation.
- Identify time lags and explain how they cause reconciling items.

Solution

In reconciling the bank account, the reconciling items are treated by Kist Fabrics as follows:

(a) NSF cheque: deducted from balance per books.
(b) Interest earned: added to balance per books.
(c) Outstanding cheques from the prior period: deducted from the balance per bank. Note that an outstanding cheque from a prior period means that the cheque was deducted from the books in the prior period, but not yet paid by the bank. If the cheque has been paid by the bank in the current month, both sides (books and bank) are now reconciled and no further reconciliation of this item is required. If the cheque continues to be outstanding, then it is still a reconciling item (deduction) for the bank side of the reconciliation since the bank has not yet recorded the transaction.

(d) Outstanding cheques from the current period: deducted from balance per bank.
(e) Deposit in transit: added to balance per bank.

Reporting Cash

STUDY OBJECTIVE

5

Explain the reporting of cash.

Cash is reported in two different statements: the balance sheet and the cash flow statement. The balance sheet reports the amount of cash available at a given point in time. The cash flow statement shows the sources and uses of cash during a period of time. The cash flow statement was introduced in Chapters 1 and 2 and will be discussed in detail in Chapter 13. In this section, we discuss some important points regarding the presentation of cash in the balance sheet.

When presented in a balance sheet, cash on hand and cash in banks is combined and reported simply as **Cash**. Because it is the most liquid asset owned by a company, cash is listed first in the current asset section of the balance sheet.

CASH EQUIVALENTS

Many companies combine cash with cash equivalents. Cash equivalents are short-term, highly liquid (easily sold) investments. These investments include short-term deposits, short-term investments such as treasury bills and money-market funds, and short-term notes that normally have maturities of three months or less when purchased. All are typically purchased with cash that is in excess of immediate needs.

More than 70% of Canadian public companies present cash in this manner. Examples of companies that combine cash with cash equivalents for reporting purposes include BCE, CBC, Canada Post, Canadian Pacific, Canadian Tire, George Weston, and Second Cup. As shown in Appendix A at the end of this textbook, Loblaw also combines its cash with cash equivalents on its balance sheet.

Some companies may be in a cash deficit or negative position at year end. This, hopefully, is a temporary situation and can occur when the company is in an overdraft position at the bank. Bank overdrafts occur when a cheque is written for more than the amount in the bank account. This, in effect, is a short-term loan from the bank. The cash account will show a credit balance in the general ledger and is reported as a current liability, as shown in an extract from Andrés Wines' balance sheet in Illustration 7-9.

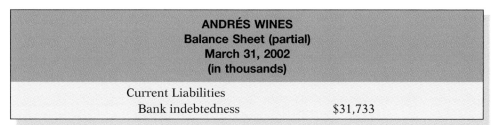

ANDRÉS WINES Balance Sheet (partial) March 31, 2002 (in thousands)	
Current Liabilities	
Bank indebtedness	$31,733

Illustration 7-9
Presentation of a cash credit balance

RESTRICTED CASH

A company may have cash that is not available for general use because it is restricted for a special purpose. For example, landfill companies are often required to maintain a fund of restricted cash to ensure they will have adequate resources to cover closing and clean-up costs at the end of a landfill site's useful life. Cash having restricted use should be reported separately on the balance sheet as restricted cash. If the restricted cash is expected to be used within the next year, the amount should be reported as a current asset. When this is not the case, the restricted funds should be reported as a noncurrent asset.

In making loans to depositors, banks commonly require borrowers to maintain minimum cash balances. These minimum balances, called compensating balances, provide the bank with support for the loans. They are a form of restriction on the use of cash. A compensating balance should be reported as a noncurrent asset and disclosed in the notes to the financial statements.

Decision Toolkit

DECISION CHECKPOINTS	INFO NEEDED FOR DECISION	TOOL TO USE FOR DECISION	HOW TO EVALUATE RESULTS
Is all of the company's cash available for general use?	Balance sheet and notes to financial statements	Does the company report any cash as being restricted?	A restriction on the use of cash limits management's ability to use those resources for general obligations. This might be considered when assessing liquidity.

Managing and Monitoring Cash

Many companies struggle, not because they can't generate sales, but because they can't manage their cash. A real-life example of this is a clothing manufacturing company owned by Sharon McCollick. McCollick gave up a stable, high-paying marketing job with Intel Corporation to start her own company. Soon she had more clothing orders than she could fill. Yet she found herself on the brink of financial disaster, owing three mortgage payments on her house and $2,000 in taxes. Her company could generate sales, but it wasn't collecting cash fast enough to support its operations. The bottom line is that a business must have cash.

To understand cash management, consider the operating cycle of Sharon McCollick's clothing manufacturing company. First, it purchases cloth. Let's assume that it purchases the cloth on credit provided by the supplier, so the company owes its supplier money. Next, employees convert the cloth to clothing. Now the company also owes its employees money. Next, it sells the clothing to retailers, on credit. McCollick's company will have no money to repay suppliers or employees until its customers pay. In a manufacturing operation, there may be a significant lag between the original purchase of raw materials and the ultimate receipt of cash from customers.

Managing the often precarious balance created by the ebb and flow of cash during the operating cycle is one of a company's greatest challenges. The objective is to ensure that a company has sufficient cash to meet payments as they come due, yet minimize the amount of nonrevenue-generating cash on hand.

BASIC PRINCIPLES OF CASH MANAGEMENT

Any company can improve its chances of having adequate cash by following five basic principles of cash management:

1. **Increase the speed of collection on receivables.** Money owed to Sharon McCollick by her customers is money that she can't use. The faster customers pay her, the faster she can use those funds. Thus, rather than have an average collection period of 30 days, she may want an average collection period of 20 days. However, any attempt to force her customers to pay earlier must be carefully weighed against the possibility that she may anger or alienate customers. Perhaps her competitors are willing to provide a 30-day grace period. As noted in Chapter 5, one common way to encourage customers to pay more quickly is to offer cash discounts for early payments under such terms as 2/10, n/30.
2. **Keep inventory levels low.** Maintaining a large inventory of cloth and finished clothing is costly. It ties up large amounts of cash, as well as warehouse space. Increasingly, firms are using techniques to reduce the inventory on hand, thus conserving their cash. Of course, if Sharon McCollick has inadequate inventory, she will lose sales. The proper level of inventory is an important decision.
3. **Delay payment of liabilities.** By keeping track of when her bills are due, Sharon McCollick's company can avoid paying bills too early. Let's say her supplier allows 30 days for payment. If she pays in 10 days, she has lost the use of cash for 20 days. Therefore, she should use the full payment period, but she should not "stretch" payment past the point that could damage her credit rating (and future borrowing ability).
4. **Plan the timing of major expenditures.** To maintain operations or to grow, all companies must make major expenditures which normally require some form of outside financing. In order to increase the likelihood of obtaining outside financing, McCollick should carefully consider the timing of major expenditures in light of her company's operating cycle. If at all possible, the expenditure should be made when the firm normally has excess cash—usually during the off-season.

5. **Invest idle cash.** Cash on hand earns nothing. Excess cash should be invested, even if it is only overnight. Many businesses, such as Sharon McCollick's clothing company, are seasonal. During her slow season, when she has excess cash, she should invest it. To avoid a cash crisis, however, it is very important that these investments be liquid and risk-free. A *liquid investment* is one with a market in which someone is always willing to buy or sell the investment. A risk-free investment means there is no concern that the party will default on its promise to pay its principal and interest.

For example, using excess cash to purchase shares in a small company because you heard that it was probably going to increase in value in the near term is inappropriate. First, the shares of small companies are often illiquid. Second, if the shares suddenly decrease in value, you might be forced to sell them at a loss in order to pay your bills as they come due. A common liquid, risk-free investment is treasury bills or money market funds.

BUSINESS INSIGHT

INVESTOR PERSPECTIVE

Is there such a thing as too much cash? Some companies are upsetting shareholders by not spending their excess cash. Unused cash hurts a company in a number of ways. Primarily, it is a lost opportunity—all that money sitting around is not producing the best return for shareholders.

Canadian oil and gas companies are struggling with just such a cash challenge. They have too much cash and too few places to spend it. The oil and gas sector produced an unprecedented $8 billion in surplus cash flow in 2000. "The question is, what do you do with the cash?" said Scott Inglis, managing director of research at FirstEnergy Capital Corp. "If high commodity prices are here to stay, the likelihood is that they are going to continue to have surplus cash flow, and you need to figure out ways to create value with that. Given the magnitude of the cash flow, it is unlikely there will be opportunities to use all of it up with acquisitions."

Source: Claudia Cattaneo, "New Problem for Oilpatch: Too Much Cash," *Financial Post*, February 22, 2001, C01.

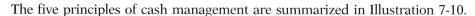

The five principles of cash management are summarized in Illustration 7-10.

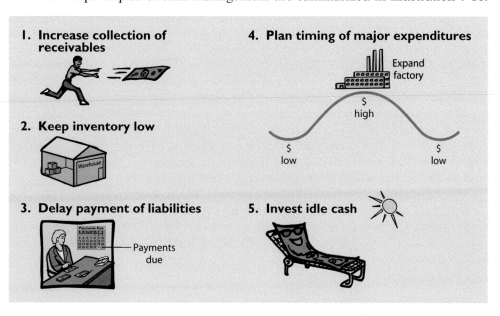

Illustration 7-10
Five principles of cash management

CASH BUDGETING

STUDY OBJECTIVE

7

Identify the primary elements of a cash budget.

Because cash is so vital to a company, planning the company's cash needs is a key business activity. It enables the company to plan ahead to cover possible cash shortfalls and to invest idle funds. The cash budget shows anticipated cash flows, usually over a one- to two-year period. In this section, we introduce the basics of cash budgeting. More advanced discussions of cash budgets and budgets in general are found in managerial accounting texts.

As shown in Illustration 7-11, the cash budget contains three sections—cash receipts, cash disbursements, and financing—and the beginning and ending cash balances.

Illustration 7-11
Basic form of a cash budget

ANY COMPANY LTD. Cash Budget	
Beginning cash balance	$x
Add: Cash receipts (itemized)	x
Total available cash	x
Less: Cash disbursements (itemized)	x
Excess (deficiency) of available cash over cash disbursements	x
Financing needed	x
Ending cash balance	$x

The **cash receipts section** includes expected receipts from the company's principal sources of revenue, such as cash sales and collections from customers on credit sales. This section also shows anticipated receipts of interest and dividends, and proceeds from planned sales of investments, property, plant, and equipment, and the company's share capital.

The **cash disbursements section** shows expected payments for purchases of merchandise, and selling and administrative expenses. This section also includes projected payments for income taxes, dividends, investments, and property, plant, and equipment.

The **financing section** shows expected borrowings and the repayment of the borrowed funds plus interest. This is needed when there is a cash deficiency or when the cash balance is less than management's minimum required balance.

Data in the cash budget must be prepared in sequence, because the ending cash balance of one period becomes the beginning cash balance for the next period. Data for preparing the cash budget are obtained from other budgets and from information provided by management. In practice, cash budgets are often prepared for the year, detailing cash receipts and disbursements by month or by quarter.

To minimize detail, we will assume that Hayes Ltd. prepares a quarterly cash budget. Preparing a cash budget requires making some assumptions. For example, the cash budget for Hayes Ltd. is based on the company's assumptions regarding the collection of accounts receivable, sales of investments, payments for merchandise and salaries, and purchases of property, plant, and equipment. The accuracy of the cash budget is dependent on the accuracy of these assumptions.

The cash budget for Hayes Ltd. is shown in Illustration 7-12. The budget indicates that $33,000 of financing will be needed in the second quarter to maintain a minimum cash balance of $5,000. Since there is an excess of available cash over disbursements of $47,700 at the end of the third quarter, the borrowing is repaid in this quarter.

Illustration 7-12
Cash budget

HAYES LTD. Cash Budget Year Ended December 31, 2004				
	Quarter			
	1	2	3	4
Beginning cash balance	$ 18,000	$ 5,500	$ 5,000	$ 14,700
Add: Receipts				
Collections from customers	168,000	198,000	263,200	258,000
Sale of investments	2,000	0	0	0
Total receipts	170,000	198,000	263,200	258,000
Total available cash	188,000	203,500	268,200	272,700
Less: Disbursements				
Purchases of merchandise	23,200	27,200	31,200	35,200
Salaries	62,000	72,000	82,000	92,000
Other operating expenses	94,300	99,300	104,300	109,300
Purchase of truck	0	30,000	0	0
Income tax expense	3,000	3,000	3,000	3,000
Total disbursements	182,500	231,500	220,500	239,500
Excess (deficiency) of available cash over disbursements	5,500	(28,000)	47,700	33,200
Financing				
Borrowings	0	33,000	0	0
Repayments	0	0	33,000	0
Ending cash balance	$ 5,500	$ 5,000	$ 14,700	$ 33,200

A cash budget contributes to more effective cash management. For example, it can show when additional financing will be necessary well before the actual need arises. Conversely, it can indicate when excess cash will be available for repayment of debts, for investments, or for other purposes. Consequently, creditors find a cash budget to be a critical tool for assessing a company's ability to repay its debts.

Decision Toolkit

DECISION CHECKPOINTS	INFO NEEDED FOR DECISION	TOOL TO USE FOR DECISION	HOW TO EVALUATE RESULTS
Will the company be able to meet its projected cash needs?	Cash budget (typically available only to management)	The cash budget shows projected sources and uses of cash. If cash uses exceed internal cash sources, then the company must look for outside sources.	Two issues: (1) Are management's projections reasonable? (2) If outside sources are needed, are they available?

BEFORE YOU GO ON . . .

- **REVIEW IT**
  1. What are the five principal elements of cash management?
  2. What are the three sections of the cash budget?
  3. What was Loblaw's balance in cash and cash equivalents as at December 28, 2002? How did Loblaw define cash equivalents (see Note 1)? The answers to these questions are provided at the end of this chapter.

● **DO IT**

The management of Staudinger Ltd. wants to maintain a minimum monthly cash balance of $5,000. At the beginning of March, the cash balance is $13,500; expected cash receipts for March are $210,000; and cash disbursements are expected to be $220,000. How much cash, if any, must be borrowed to maintain the desired minimum monthly balance?

Action Plan

• Insert the dollar data into the basic form of the cash budget.

Solution

Beginning cash balance	$ 13,500
Add: Cash receipts	210,000
Total available cash	223,500
Less: Cash disbursements	220,000
Excess of available cash over cash disbursements	3,500
Financing	1,500
Ending cash balance	$ 5,000

NAVIGATOR

To maintain the desired minimum cash balance of $5,000, Staudinger needs to borrow $1,500.

Using the Decision Toolkit

Presented below is financial information for Ming, Inc., a toy manufacturer. This information represents management's best estimate of its projected sources and uses of cash during the year ended December 31, 2005. This information is needed to prepare a cash budget.

MING, INC. Projected Sources and Uses of Cash (in millions)	
Beginning cash balance	$ 194.9
Cash collected from sales	3,922.1
Cash received from short-term investments sold	20.0
Cash disbursed for inventory	2,371.1
Cash disbursed for operating expenses	1,695.4
Cash paid for property, plant, and equipment	257.6
Cash paid for taxes	135.9

Ming's management believes it should maintain a balance of $100 million cash.

Instructions

(a) Using the projected sources and uses of cash information presented above, prepare a cash budget for the year ended December 31, 2005.
(b) Comment on Ming's cash adequacy, and discuss steps that might be taken to improve its cash position.

Solution

(a)

MING, INC. Cash Budget Year Ended December 31, 2005 (in millions)		
Beginning cash balance		$ 194.9
Add: Cash receipts		
Sales	$3,922.1	
Sale of short-term investments	20.0	3,942.1
Total cash available		4,137.0
Less: Cash disbursements		
Inventory	$2,371.1	
Operating expenses	1,695.4	
Property, plant, and equipment	257.6	
Taxes	135.9	4,460.0
Excess (deficiency) of available cash over disbursements		(323.0)
Financing needed		423.0
Ending cash balance		$ 100.0

(b) Ming's cash position appears to be inadequate. For 2005, it is projecting a cash shortfall. This is not necessarily of concern, but it should be investigated. Given that its primary line of business is toys, and that most toys are sold during the holiday season, we would expect Ming's cash position to vary significantly during the course of the year. Early in the new year, it probably has a lot of excess cash, and later in the year, when it is making and selling its product but has not yet been paid, it may need to borrow to meet any temporary cash shortfalls.

In the event that Ming's management is concerned with its cash position, it could take the following steps: (1) offer its customers cash discounts for early payment, such as 2/10, n/30; (2) implement inventory management techniques to reduce the need for large inventories of raw materials used to make its toys; (3) carefully time payments to suppliers by keeping track of when payments are due, so as not to pay too early; and (4) if it has plans for major expenditures, time those expenditures to coincide with its seasonal period of excess cash.

Summary of Study Objectives

❶ Identify the principles of internal control. The principles of internal control are establishment of responsibility; segregation of duties; documentation procedures; physical controls; independent internal verification; and other controls.

❷ Explain the applications of internal control to cash receipts. Internal controls over cash receipts include (a) designating only personnel such as cashiers to handle cash; (b) assigning the duties of receiving cash, recording cash, and having custody of cash to different individuals;

(c) obtaining remittance advices for mail receipts, cash register tapes for over-the-counter receipts, and deposit slips for bank deposits; (d) using company safes and bank vaults to store cash, with access limited to authorized personnel, and using cash registers in executing over-the-counter receipts; (e) depositing all cash intact daily in the bank account; (f) making independent daily counts of register receipts and daily comparisons of total receipts with total deposits; and (g) bonding personnel who handle cash and requiring them to take vacations.

③ *Explain the applications of internal control to cash disbursements.* Internal controls over cash disbursements include (a) making all payments by cheque; (b) having only specified individuals authorized to sign cheques; (c) assigning the duties of approving items for payment, paying the items, and recording the payments to different individuals; (d) using prenumbered cheques and accounting for all cheques; (e) storing each cheque in a safe or vault with access restricted to authorized personnel, and using electronic methods to print amounts on cheques; (f) comparing each cheque with the approved invoice before issuing the cheque, and making monthly reconciliations of bank and book balances; and (g) after payment, stamping each approved invoice "Paid."

④ *Prepare a bank reconciliation.* In reconciling the bank account, it is customary to reconcile the balance per books and the balance per bank to their adjusted balances. Reconciling items may include deposits in transit, outstanding cheques, errors by the depositor or the bank, and unrecorded bank memoranda. Adjusting entries must be made for any errors by the depositor and unrecorded bank memoranda.

⑤ *Explain the reporting of cash.* Cash is listed first in the current assets section of the balance sheet. Cash is often reported together with cash equivalents. Cash restricted for a special purpose is reported separately as a current asset or as a noncurrent asset, depending on when the cash is expected to be used.

⑥ *Discuss the basic principles of cash management.* (a) Increase collection of receivables, (b) keep inventory levels low, (c) delay payment of liabilities, (d) plan timing of major expenditures, and (e) invest idle cash.

⑦ *Identify the primary elements of a cash budget.* The three main elements of a cash budget are the cash receipts section, cash disbursements section, and financing section.

Decision Toolkit—A Summary

Decision Toolkit Summary

DECISION CHECKPOINTS	INFO NEEDED FOR DECISION	TOOL TO USE FOR DECISION	HOW TO EVALUATE RESULTS
Are the company's financial statements supported by adequate internal controls?	Auditor's report, statement of management responsibility, management discussion and analysis, articles in the financial press	The required measures of internal control are to (1) establish responsibility, (2) segregate duties, (3) document procedures, (4) employ physical controls, and (5) use independent internal verification.	If any indication is given that these or other controls are lacking, the financial statements should be used with caution.
Is all of the company's cash available for general use?	Balance sheet and notes to financial statements	Does the company report any cash as being restricted?	A restriction on the use of cash limits management's ability to use those resources for general obligations. This might be considered when assessing liquidity.
Will the company be able to meet its projected cash needs?	Cash budget (typically available only to management)	The cash budget shows projected sources and uses of cash. If cash uses exceed internal cash sources, then the company must look for outside sources.	Two issues: (1) Are management's projections reasonable? (2) If outside sources are needed, are they available?

NAVIGATOR

Glossary

Bank statement A statement received monthly from the bank that shows the depositor's bank transactions and balances. (p. 316)

Cash Resources that consist of coins, currency, cheques, money orders, and money on hand or on deposit in a bank or similar depository. (p. 314)

Cash budget A projection of anticipated cash flows, usually over a one- to two-year period. (p. 326)

Cash equivalents Short-term, highly liquid investments that can be readily sold. (p. 323)

Compensating balances Minimum cash balances required by a bank in support of bank loans. (p. 323)

Deposits in transit Deposits recorded by the depositor that have not yet been recorded by the bank. (p. 319)

Internal auditors Company employees who continously evaluate the effectiveness of the company's system of internal control. (p. 312)

Internal control All the related methods and measures adopted within a business to (1) optimize resources, (2) prevent and detect errors and irregularities, (3) safeguard assets, and (4) maintain reliable control systems. (p. 308)

NSF (not sufficient funds) cheque A cheque that is not paid by a bank because of insufficient funds in a customer's bank account. (p. 317)

Outstanding cheques Cheques issued and recorded by a company that have not yet been paid by the bank. (p. 319)

Restricted cash Cash that is not available for general use, but instead is restricted for a particular purpose. (p. 323)

Demonstration Problem

Trillo Ltd.'s bank statement for May shows these data:

Balance May 31	$14,280	
Debit memorandum:		Credit memorandum:
NSF cheque	175	Interest earned	40

Additional
Demonstration
Problems

The cash balance per books at May 31 is $13,784. Your review of the data reveals the following:

1. The NSF cheque was from Hup Corp., a customer.
2. Outstanding cheques at May 31 total $2,410, including a cheque for $300 that was also outstanding at April 30.
3. Deposits in transit at May 31 total $1,752.
4. A Trillo cheque for $352 dated May 10 cleared the bank on May 25. This cheque, which was a payment on account, was incorrectly journalized at $325.

Instructions

(a) Prepare a bank reconciliation at May 31.
(b) Journalize the entries required by the reconciliation.

Solution to Demonstration Problem

(a)			
	Cash balance per bank statement		$14,280
	Add: Deposits in transit		1,752
			16,032
	Less: Outstanding cheques		2,410
	Adjusted cash balance per bank		$13,622
	Cash balance per books		$13,784
	Add: Interest earned		40
			13,824
	Less: NSF cheque	$175	
	Error in recording cheque ($352 − $325)	27	202
	Adjusted cash balance per books		$13,622

Action Plan

- Identify reconciling items. Ask yourself whose books—the company's or the bank's—already include each reconciling item. Then adjust the other side accordingly.

- Be careful when you deal with any errors that have been made.

- All journal entries are based on the reconciling items per books.

- Make sure the cash ledger balance after posting the reconciling entries agrees with the adjusted cash balance per books.

(b)

May 31	Cash		40	
	Interest Revenue			40
	(To record interest earned)			
31	Accounts Receivable—Hup Corp.		175	
	Cash			175
	(To record NSF cheque from Hup Corp.)			
31	Accounts Payable		27	
	Cash			27
	(To correct error in recording cheque)			

Self-Study Questions

Answers are at the end of the chapter.

(SO 1) 1. Which of the following is *not* an objective of internal control?
(a) Optimize resources
(b) Eliminate errors
(c) Safeguard assets
(d) Maintain reliable control systems

(SO 1) 2. Which of the following items in a cash drawer at November 30 is *not* cash?
(a) Money orders
(b) Coins and currency
(c) A customer cheque dated December 1
(d) A customer cheque dated November 28

(SO 2) 3. Permitting only designated personnel, such as cashiers, to handle cash receipts is an application of the principle of:
(a) segregation of duties.
(b) establishment of responsibility.
(c) independent internal verification.
(d) other controls.

(SO 3) 4. The use of prenumbered cheques in disbursing cash is an application of the principle of:
(a) establishment of responsibility.
(b) segregation of duties.
(c) physical controls.
(d) documentation procedures.

(SO 3) 5. The control features of a bank account do *not* include:
(a) having bank auditors verify the correctness of the bank balance per books.
(b) minimizing the amount of cash that must be kept on hand.
(c) providing a double record of all bank transactions.
(d) safeguarding cash by using a bank as a depository.

6. In a bank reconciliation, deposits in transit are: (SO 4)
(a) deducted from the book balance.
(b) added to the book balance
(c) added to the bank balance.
(d) deducted from the bank balance.

7. A company erroneously recorded a $459 cheque written in payment of an account as $495. The adjusting journal entry required to correct this would be: (SO 4)
(a) debit Accounts Payable, $36; credit Cash, $36.
(b) debit Cash, $36; credit Accounts Payable, $36.
(c) debit Cash, $36; credit Accounts Receivable, $36.
(d) No journal entry is required.

8. ⚒ Which statement correctly describes the reporting of cash? (SO 5)
(a) Cash cannot be combined with cash equivalents.
(b) Restricted cash funds may be combined with cash.
(c) Cash is listed first in the current asset section.
(d) Restricted cash funds are always reported as a current asset.

9. The principles of cash management do *not* include: (SO 6)
(a) accelerating the collection of receivables.
(b) accelerating the payment of liabilities.
(c) keeping inventory low.
(d) investing idle cash.

10. ⚒ Which of the following is *not* one of the sections of a cash budget? (SO 7)
(a) Cash receipts section
(b) Cash disbursements section
(c) Financing section
(d) Cash from operating activities section

Questions

(SO 1) 1. "Internal control is only concerned with enhancing the accuracy of the accounting records." Do you agree? Explain.

(SO 1) 2. In the corner grocery store, all sales clerks make change out of one cash register drawer using the same password. Is this a violation of internal control? Why?

(SO 1) 3. J. Duma is reviewing the principle of segregation of duties. What are the two common applications of this principle?

(SO 1) 4. How do documentation procedures contribute to good internal control?

(SO 1) 5. What internal control objectives are met by physical controls?

(SO 1) 6. As the company accountant, explain the following ideas to the management of Cobo Corporation:
   (a) The concept of reasonable assurance in internal control
   (b) The importance of the human factor in internal control

(SO 1) 7. West Inc. owns these assets at the balance sheet date:

Cash in bank—savings account	$ 5,000
Cash on hand	100
Income tax refund due from CCRA	1,000
Chequing account balance	12,000
Postdated cheques	500

What amount should be reported as Cash in the balance sheet?

(SO 2) 8. What principle(s) of internal control is (are) involved in making daily cash counts and deposits of over-the-counter receipts?

(SO 2) 9. Dent Department Stores Ltd. has just installed new electronic cash registers with scanners in its stores. How do these cash registers improve internal control over cash receipts?

(SO 2) 10. At Allen Wholesale Ltd., two mail clerks open all mail receipts. How does this strengthen internal control?

(SO 3) 11. Why should the individual who receives cash not also be permitted to make cash payments or to record cash transactions?

(SO 3) 12. "To have maximum internal control over cash disbursements, all payments should be made by cheque." Is this true? Explain.

(SO 3) 13. Handy Inc.'s internal controls over cash disbursements require the treasurer to sign cheques printed by a computer after comparing the cheque with the approved invoice. Identify the internal control principles that underlie these controls.

(SO 4) 14. "The use of a bank contributes significantly to good internal control over cash." Is this true? Why?

(SO 4) 15. Paul Pascal is confused about the lack of agreement between the cash balance per books and the balance per bank. Explain the causes for the lack of agreement to Paul, and give an example of each cause.

(SO 4) 16. Mary Mora asks for your help concerning an NSF cheque. Explain to Mary (a) what an NSF cheque is, (b) how it is treated in a bank reconciliation, and (c) whether it will require an adjusting entry.

(SO 5) 17. "Cash equivalents are the same as cash." Do you agree? Explain.

(SO 5) 18. What is a compensating balance? How should compensating balances be reported in the financial statements?

(SO 6) 19. Describe the basic principles of cash management.

(SO 6) 20. Talisman Energy Inc. announced record cash flow in 2002—the best in the company's ten-year history. What cash management problems might this cause for Talisman?

(SO 7) 21.
   (a) What is a cash budget?
   (b) How does a cash budget contribute to effective cash management?

Brief Exercises

BE7-1   Gina Milan is the new owner of Plenty Parking Ltd.—a parking garage. She has heard about internal control but is not clear about its importance for her business. Explain to Gina the four purposes of internal control, and give her one application of each purpose for Plenty Parking.

Explain importance of internal control.
(SO 1)

BE7-2   The internal control procedures in Beaupré Ltée make the following provisions. Identify the principles of internal control that are being followed in each case.

(a) Employees who have physical custody of assets do not have access to the accounting records.

(b) Each month, the assets on hand are compared to the accounting records by an internal auditor.

(c) A prenumbered shipping document is prepared for each shipment of goods to customers.

Identify internal control principles.
(SO 1)

Identify internal control principles applicable to cash receipts.
(SO 2)

BE7-3 Tene Ltd. has the following internal control procedures over cash receipts. Identify the internal control principle that is applicable to each procedure.

(a) All over-the-counter receipts are recorded on cash registers.
(b) All cashiers are bonded.
(c) Daily cash counts are made by cashier department supervisors.
(d) The duties of receiving cash, recording cash, and having custody of cash are assigned to different individuals.
(e) Only cashiers may operate cash registers.
(f) All cash is deposited intact in the bank account every day.

Identify internal control principles applicable to cash disbursements.
(SO 3)

BE7-4 Rolling Hills Ltd. has the following internal control procedures over cash disbursements. Identify the internal control principle that is applicable to each procedure.

(a) Company cheques are prenumbered.
(b) The bank statement is reconciled monthly by an internal auditor.
(c) Blank cheques are stored in a safe in the treasurer's office.
(d) Only the treasurer may sign cheques.
(e) Cheque signers are not allowed to record cash disbursement transactions.
(f) All payments are made by cheque.

Indicate location of reconciling items in bank reconciliation.
(SO 4)

BE7-5 The following reconciling items are applicable to the bank reconciliation for Ashley Corp. Indicate how each item should be shown on a bank reconciliation.

(a) Outstanding cheques
(b) Bank debit memorandum for a service charge
(c) Bank credit memorandum for interest earned
(d) Deposit in transit
(e) Bank error, recording a deposit twice

Identify adjusting entries.
(SO 4)

BE7-6 Using the data in BE7-5, indicate (a) the items that will result in an adjustment to the depositor's records and (b) why the other items do not require adjustment.

Prepare bank reconciliation.
(SO 4)

BE7-7 At July 31, Dana Limited has the following information: cash balance per bank, $7,800; cash balance per books, $8,760; outstanding cheques, $760; deposits in transit, $1,700; and a bank service charge, $20. Determine the adjusted cash balance at July 31.

Prepare adjusting entries.
(SO 4)

BE7-8 Using the data in BE7-7, prepare the adjusting entries required on July 31 for Dana Limited.

Analyse outstanding deposits.
(SO 4)

BE7-9 For the months of January and February, Kahn Ltd. recorded cash deposits in its books of $2,500 and $2,800, respectively. For the same two months, the bank reported deposits totalling $2,300 and $2,000, respectively. Assuming that there were no outstanding deposits at the end of December, what was the amount of outstanding deposits at the end of January? At the end of February?

Analyse outstanding cheques.
(SO 4)

BE7-10 In the month of November, its first month of operations, Jayasinghe Inc. wrote cheques in the amount of $9,250. In December, cheques in the amount of $12,700 were written. In November, $8,600 of these cheques were presented to the bank for payment; $10,900, in December. What is the amount of outstanding cheques at the end of November? At the end of December?

Explain statement presentation of cash balances.
(SO 5)

BE7-11 Ouellette Ltée has these cash balances: cash in bank, $12,800; payroll bank account, $6,000; and plant expansion fund cash, $25,000. Ouellette also maintains a $3,000 compensating bank balance in a separate bank account. Explain how each balance should be reported on the balance sheet.

Discuss cash management issues.
(SO 6)

BE7-12 Identify and discuss the likely cash management issues faced by the following businesses:

(a) Toronto Maple Leafs hockey team   (d) WestJet Airlines Ltd.
(b) Imperial Tobacco Canada Limited   (e) McMaster University Bookstore
(c) Intrawest Corporation   (f) Tim Hortons

Prepare cash budget.
(SO 7)

BE7-13 The following information is available for Marais Limited for the month of January: expected cash receipts, $60,000; expected cash disbursements, $65,000; cash balance on January 1, $2,000. Management wishes to maintain a minimum cash balance of $5,000. Prepare a basic cash budget for the month of January.

Exercises

E7-1 A new accountant at La Maison Ltd. is trying to identify which of the following amounts should be reported as the current asset "Cash and Cash Equivalents" in the year-end balance sheet, as at April 30, 2004:

Identify reporting of cash.
(SO 1)

Interactive
Homework

1. $60 of currency and coin in a locked box used for incidental cash transactions
2. A $10,000 guaranteed investment certificate, due May 31, 2004
3. $300 of April-dated cheques that La Maison has received from customers but not yet deposited
4. An $85 cheque received from a customer in payment of its April account, but post-dated to May 1
5. $2,500 in the company's Royal Bank chequing account
6. $4,000 in its Royal Bank savings account
7. $75 of prepaid postage in its postage meter
8. A $25 IOU from the company receptionist

Instructions

(a) What balance should La Maison report as its "Cash and Cash Equivalents" balance at April 30, 2004?
(b) In what financial statement(s) and in what account(s) should the items not included in "Cash and Cash Equivalents" be reported?

E7-2 Bank employees use a system known as the "maker-checker" system. An employee records an entry in the appropriate journal and then a supervisor verifies and approves the entry. Since the bank's accounts are computerized, the entries are posted automatically to the general ledger account after the supervisor approves them on the computer system. Access to the computer system is password-protected and task-specific, which means that the computer system will not allow the employee to approve a transaction, or the supervisor to record a transaction.

Identify principles of internal control.
(SO 1)

Instructions

Identify the principles of internal control present in the "maker-checker" procedure used by banks.

E7-3 Marino's Pizza operates strictly on a takeout basis. Customers pick up their orders at a counter where a clerk exchanges the pizza for cash. While at the counter, the customer can see other employees making the pizzas and the large ovens in which the pizzas are baked.

Identify principles of internal control.
(SO 1)

Instructions

Identify the six principles of internal control and give an example of each principle that you might observe when picking up your pizza. (*Note*: It may not be possible to observe all the principles.)

E7-4 The following control procedures are used in Tolan Ltd. for over-the-counter cash receipts:

Identify internal control weaknesses for cash receipts and suggest improvements.
(SO 2)

1. Cashiers are experienced, so they are not bonded.
2. All over-the-counter receipts are registered by three clerks, who use a cash register with a single cash drawer.
3. To minimize the risk of robbery, cash in excess of $100 is stored in an unlocked strong-box in the stock room until it is deposited in the bank.
4. At the end of each day, the total receipts are counted by the cashier on duty and reconciled to the cash register total.
5. The company accountant makes the bank deposit and then records the day's receipts.

Instructions

(a) For each procedure, explain the weakness in internal control and identify the control principle that is violated.
(b) For each weakness, suggest a change in procedure that will result in good internal control.

Identify internal control weaknesses for cash disbursements and suggest improvements.
(SO 3)

E7-5 The following control procedures are used in Ann's Boutique Shoppe Ltd. for cash disbursements:

1. Company cheques are stored in an unmarked envelope on a shelf behind the cash register.
2. The store manager personally approves all payments before signing and issuing cheques.
3. When the store manager has to go away for extended periods of time, she pre-signs a number of cheques to be used in her absence.
4. The company cheques are unnumbered.
5. After payment, bills are filed in a paid invoice folder.
6. The company accountant prepares the bank reconciliation and reports any discrepancies to the store manager.

Instructions

(a) For each procedure, explain the weakness in internal control and identify the internal control principle that is violated.
(b) For each weakness, suggest a change in procedure that will result in good internal control.

Identify internal control weaknesses for cash disbursements and suggest improvements.
(SO 3)

E7-6 At O'Malley Inc., cheques are not prenumbered, because both the purchasing agent and the treasurer are authorized to issue cheques. Each signer has access to unissued cheques kept in an unlocked filing cabinet. The purchasing agent pays all bills pertaining to goods purchased for resale. Prior to payment, the purchasing agent determines that the goods have been received and verifies the mathematical accuracy of the vendor's invoice. After payment, the invoice is filed by the vendor and the purchasing agent records the payment in the cash disbursements journal. The treasurer pays all other bills after approval by authorized employees. After payment, the treasurer stamps all bills "Paid," files them by payment date, and records the cheques in the journal. O'Malley maintains one chequing account that is reconciled by the treasurer.

Instructions

(a) List the weaknesses in internal control over cash disbursements.
(b) Write a memo indicating your recommendations for improving company procedures.

Prepare bank reconciliation and adjusting entries.
(SO 4)

E7-7 LoKo Ltd. is unable to reconcile its bank balance at January 31. The bank reconciliation is shown here:

Cash balance per bank	$3,660.20		Cash balance per books	$3,975.20
Add: NSF cheque	430.00		Less: Deposits in transit	590.00
Less: Bank service charge	25.00		Add: Outstanding cheques	730.00
Adjusted balance per bank	$4,065.20		Adjusted balance per books	$4,115.20

Instructions

(a) Prepare a correct bank reconciliation.
(b) Journalize the entries required by the reconciliation.

Determine outstanding cheques.
(SO 4)

E7-8 At April 30, the bank reconciliation of Drofo Limited shows three outstanding cheques: No. 254, $650; No. 255, $800; and No. 257, $410. The May bank statement and the general journal are given here:

Bank Statement Cheques Paid May 31				General Journal Cheques Issued May 31		
Date	Cheque No.	Amount		Date	Cheque No.	Amount
May 4	254	$650		May 2	258	$159
May 2	257	410		May 5	259	275
May 17	258	159		May 10	260	925
May 12	259	275		May 15	261	500
May 20	261	500		May 22	262	750
May 29	263	480		May 24	263	480
May 30	262	750		May 29	264	360

Instructions

List the outstanding cheques at May 31.

E7-9 The following information is for Mohammed Ltd.:

1. Cash balance per bank, July 31, $7,238
2. Cash balance per books, July 31, $6,990
3. July bank service charge not recorded by the depositor, $40
4. Deposits in transit, July 31, $1,700
5. Electronic payment on account by customer, $1,216
6. Outstanding cheques, July 31, $772

Prepare bank reconciliation and adjusting entries.
(SO 4)

Interactive Homework

Instructions

(a) Prepare a bank reconciliation at July 31.
(b) Journalize the adjusting entries at July 31 on the books of Mohammed Ltd.

E7-10 Reston Ltd.'s Cash account shows a balance of $19,430 at September 30. The September bank statement shows a balance of $16,422 at September 30 and the following memoranda:

Prepare bank reconciliation and adjusting entries.
(SO 4)

Credit Memorandum		Debit Memoranda	
Interest earned	$45	NSF cheque: Hower Corp.	$410
		Safety deposit box fee	30

At September 30, deposits in transit were $4,996 and outstanding cheques totalled $2,383.

Instructions

(a) Prepare the bank reconciliation at September 30.
(b) Prepare the adjusting entries at September 30.

E7-11 The cash records of Lejeune Inc. show the following situations:

Deposits in transit

1. The June 30 bank reconciliation indicated that deposits in transit total $750. During July, the general ledger account Cash shows deposits of $16,200, but the bank statement indicates that only $15,600 in deposits were received during the month.
2. In September, deposits per bank statement totalled $25,900, deposits per books were $25,400, and deposits in transit at September 30 were $2,400.

Calculate deposits in transit and outstanding cheques.
(SO 4)

Interactive Homework

Outstanding cheques

1. The June 30 bank reconciliation also reported outstanding cheques of $920. During the month of July, the Lejeune books show that $17,200 of cheques were issued, yet the bank statement showed that $16,400 of cheques cleared the bank in July.
2. In September, cash disbursements per books were $23,700, cheques clearing the bank were $25,000, and outstanding cheques at September 30 were $2,100.

There were no bank debit or credit memoranda, and no errors were made by either the bank or Lejeune.

Instructions

(a) What were the deposits in transit at July 31? At August 31?
(b) What were the outstanding cheques at July 31? At August 31?

E7-12 Tory, Hachey, and Wedunn, three law students who have joined together to open a law practice, are struggling to manage their cash flow. They haven't yet built up sufficient clientele and revenues to support their legal practice's ongoing costs. Initial costs, such as advertising, renovations to their premises, and the like, all result in outgoing cash flow at a time when little is coming in! Tory, Hachey, and Wedunn haven't had time to establish a billing system since most of their clients' cases haven't yet reached the courts and the lawyers didn't think it would be right to bill them until "results were achieved." Unfortunately, Tory, Hachey, and Wedunn's suppliers don't feel the same way. Their suppliers expect them to pay their accounts payable within a few days of receiving their bills. So far, there hasn't even been enough money to pay the three lawyers, and they are not sure how long they can keep practicing law without getting some money into their pockets!

Review cash management practices.
(SO 6)

Instructions

Can you provide any suggestions for Tory, Hachey, and Wedunn to improve their cash management practices?

Prepare cash budget.
(SO 7)

Interactive
Homework

E7-13   Hanover Limited expects to have a cash balance of $36,000 on January 1, 2005. These are the relevant monthly budget data for the first two months of 2005:

1. Collections from customers: January, $70,000; February, $150,000
2. Payments to suppliers: January, $40,000; February, $75,000
3. Wages: January, $30,000; February, $40,000. Wages are paid in the month they are incurred.
4. Operating expenses: January, $35,000; February, $50,000. These costs include amortization of $1,000 per month. All other costs are paid as incurred.
5. Sales of short-term investments in January are expected to realize $10,000 in cash. Hanover has a line of credit at a local bank that enables it to borrow up to $25,000. The company wants to maintain a minimum monthly cash balance of $10,000.

Instructions
Prepare a cash budget for January and February.

Problems: Set A

Identify internal control weaknesses for cash receipts.
(SO 2)

P7-1A   The board of trustees of a local church is concerned about the internal controls for the offering collections made at weekly services. At a meeting of the board of trustees, you learn the following:

1. The church's board of trustees has delegated responsibility for the financial management and audit of the financial records to the finance committee. This group prepares the annual budget and approves major disbursements but is not involved in collections or record keeping. No audit has been done in recent years, because the same trusted employee has kept church records and served as financial secretary for 15 years. The church does not carry any fidelity insurance.
2. The collection at the weekly service is taken by a team of ushers who volunteer to serve for one month. The ushers take the collection plates to a basement office at the back of the church. They hand their plates to the head usher and return to the church service. After all plates have been turned in, the head usher counts the cash received. The head usher then places the cash in the church safe along with a notation of the amount counted. The head usher volunteers to serve for three months.
3. The next morning, the financial secretary opens the safe and recounts the collection. The secretary withholds $150 to $200 in cash, depending on the cash expenditures expected for the week, and deposits the remainder of the collections in the bank. To facilitate the deposit, church members who contribute by cheque are asked to make their cheques payable to "Cash."
4. Each month the financial secretary reconciles the bank statement and submits a copy of the reconciliation to the board of trustees. The reconciliations have rarely contained any bank errors and have never shown any errors per books.

Instructions
(a) Indicate the weaknesses in internal accounting control in the handling of collections.
(b) List the improvements in internal control procedures that you plan to make at the next meeting of the board of trustees for the (1) ushers, (2) head usher, (3) financial secretary, and (4) finance committee.
(c) What church policies should be changed to improve internal control?

Identify internal control principles for cash disbursements.
(SO 3)

P7-2A   Segal Office Supply Limited recently changed its system of internal control over cash disbursements. The system includes the following features:

1. Instead of being unnumbered and manually prepared, all cheques must now be prenumbered and written by a new computerized cheque-writing system purchased by the company.
2. Before a cheque can be issued, each invoice must have the approval of Cindy Morris, the purchasing agent, and Ray Mills, the receiving department supervisor.
3. Cheques must be signed by either Frank Malone, the treasurer, or Mary Arno, the assistant treasurer. Before signing a cheque, the signer is expected to compare the amount of the cheque with the amount on the invoice.

4. After signing a cheque, the signer stamps the invoice "Paid" and writes in the date, cheque number, and amount of the cheque. The paid invoice is then sent to the accounting department for recording.
5. Blank cheques are stored in a safe in the treasurer's office. The combination to the safe is known by only the treasurer and assistant treasurer.
6. Each month the bank statement is reconciled by the assistant chief accountant.

Instructions

Identify the internal control principles and their application to cash disbursements at Segal Office Supply Limited.

P7-3A Giant Inc. is a profitable small business. It has not, however, given much consideration to internal control. For example, in an attempt to keep clerical and office expenses to a minimum, the company has combined the jobs of cashier and bookkeeper. As a result, K. Kilgora handles all cash receipts, keeps the accounting records, and prepares the monthly bank reconciliations.

Prepare bank reconciliation and identify internal control deficiencies.
(SO 2, 3, 4)

The balance per bank statement on November 30, 2004, was $19,460. Outstanding cheques were No. 762 for $113.90, No. 783 for $160, No. 784 for $266.90, No. 862 for $170.73, No. 863 for $325.40, and No. 864 for $173.10. Included with the statement was a credit memorandum of $750 indicating the electronic payment of an account receivable by a customer on November 25.

The company's ledger showed one Cash account with a balance of $19,640.77. The balance included undeposited cash on hand. Because of the lack of internal controls, Kilgora took all of the undeposited receipts for personal use. He then prepared the following bank reconciliation in an effort to conceal his theft of cash:

Cash balance per books, November 30		$19,640.77
Add: Outstanding cheques		
No. 862	$170.73	
No. 863	325.40	
No. 864	173.10	569.23
Unadjusted balance per bank, November 30		20,210.00
Less: Bank credit memorandum		750.00
Cash balance per bank statement, November 30		$19,460.00

Instructions

(a) Prepare a correct bank reconciliation. (*Hint:* The theft is the difference between the adjusted balances per books and per bank.)
(b) Indicate the three ways that Kilgora attempted to conceal the theft and the dollar amount for each method.
(c) What principles of internal control were violated in this case?

P7-4A On May 31, 2004, Maloney Inc. had a cash balance per books of $8,821.50. The bank statement from Community Bank on that date showed a balance of $6,804.60. A comparison of the bank statement with the company's Cash account revealed the following facts:

Prepare bank reconciliation and adjusting entries.
(SO 4)

1. The statement included a debit memo of $40 for the printing of additional company cheques and a credit memo of $20 for interest earned.
2. Cash sales of $836.15 on May 12 were deposited in the bank. The journal entry and the deposit slip were incorrectly made out for $846.15. The bank credited Maloney for the correct amount.
3. Outstanding cheques at May 31 totalled $276.25, and deposits in transit were $936.15.
4. On May 18, the company issued cheque No. 1181 for $685 to Helms Corporation on account. The cheque, which cleared the bank in May, was incorrectly journalized and posted by Maloney for $658.
5. Included with the cancelled cheques was a cheque issued by Baloney Inc. for $600 that was incorrectly charged to Maloney by the bank.
6. On May 31, the bank statement showed an NSF charge of $700 for a cheque issued by W. Hoad, a customer, to Maloney on account.

Instructions

(a) Prepare the bank reconciliation as at May 31, 2004.
(b) Prepare the necessary adjusting entries at May 31, 2004.

Prepare bank reconciliation and adjusting entries.
(SO 4)

P7-5A You are provided with the following information for River Adventures Ltd.:

RIVER ADVENTURES LTD.
Bank Reconciliation
April 30, 2004

Cash balance per bank		$9,008.53
Add: Deposits in transit		846.33
		9,854.86
Less: Outstanding cheques		
#526	$1,357.99	
#533	89.78	
#541	363.44	
#555	78.82	1,890.03
Adjusted cash balance		$7,964.83

The adjusted cash balance per bank agreed with the cash balance per books at April 30, 2004. The May bank statement showed the following:

RIVER ADVENTURES LTD.
Bank Statement
May 31, 2004

Date	Cheque Number	Cheque Amount	Deposit Amount	Balance
Apr. 30				$9,008.53
May 3	526	$ 1,357.99	$ 846.33	8,496.87
May 4	541	363.44		8,133.43
May 6	556	223.46		7,909.97
May 6	557	1,800.00	1,250.00	7,359.97
May 10			980.00	8,339.97
May 10	559	1,650.00		6,689.97
May 13			426.00	7,115.97
May 13	CM		1,650.00	8,765.97
May 14	561	799.00		7,966.97
May 18	562	2,045.00		5,921.97
May 18			222.00	6,143.97
May 19	563	2,487.00		3,656.97
May 21	564	603.00		3,053.97
May 25	565	1,033.00		2,020.97
May 26			980.00	3,000.97
May 28			1,771.00	4,771.97
May 31	SC	25.00		4,746.97

Additional information: The bank statement contained two memoranda:
(a) Credit memo: Electronic payment by a customer on account of $1,650
(b) Debit memo: Service charge of $25
   The cash records per books for May showed the following:

Cash Receipts		Cash Disbursements		
Date	Amount	Date	Number	Amount
May 5	$1,250.00	May 4	556	$ 223.46
May 8	980.00	May 5	557	1,800.00
May 12	426.00	May 7	558	943.00
May 18	222.00	May 7	559	1,650.00
May 25	980.00	May 8	560	890.00
May 28	1,771.00	May 10	561	799.00
May 31	1,286.00	May 15	562	2,045.00
Total	$6,915.00	May 18	563	2,487.00
		May 20	564	603.00
		May 25	565	1,033.00
		May 31	566	950.00
		Total		$13,423.46

Instructions

(a) Calculate the unadjusted balance of cash at May 31, 2004, according to River Adventures Ltd.'s general ledger.

(b) Prepare a bank reconciliation for the month of May.

(c) Prepare necessary journal entries for River Adventures Ltd. as at May 31, 2004.

P7-6A The bank portion of the bank reconciliation for Racine Limited at November 30, 2004, is shown here:

Prepare bank reconciliation and adjusting entries.
(SO 4)

RACINE LIMITED
Bank Reconciliation
November 30, 2004

Cash balance per bank		$14,367.90
Add: Deposits in transit		2,530.20
		16,898.10
Less: Outstanding cheques		
#3451	$2,260.40	
#3470	1,100.00	
#3471	844.50	
#3472	1,426.80	
#3474	1,050.00	6,681.70
Adjusted cash balance		$10,216.40

The adjusted cash balance per bank agreed with the cash balance per books at November 30. The December bank statement showed the following cheques and deposits:

RACINE LIMITED
Bank Statement
December 31, 2004

Date	Deposits Amount	Cheques and Other Debits Number	Amount	Balance
Nov. 30				$14,367.90
Dec. 1	$2,530.20	3451	$2,260.40	14,637.70
Dec. 2		3471	844.50	13,793.20
Dec. 4	1,211.60	3475	1,640.70	13,364.10
Dec. 7		3472	1,426.80	11,937.30
Dec. 8	2,365.10	3476	1,300.00	13,002.40
Dec. 10		3477	2,130.00	10,872.40
Dec. 15	CM3,145.00	3479	3,080.00	10,937.40
Dec. 16	2,672.70			13,610.10
Dec. 21	2,945.00			16,555.10
Dec. 26	2,567.30	DM	1,027.10	18,095.30
Dec. 27		3480	600.00	17,495.30
Dec. 29	2,836.00	3483	1,140.00	19,191.30
Dec. 30	1,025.00	3482	475.50	19,740.80
Dec. 30		3485	540.80	19,200.00
Dec. 31		DM	45.00	19,155.00

The bank statement contained three memoranda:

1. A credit of $3,145 for the electronic payment by a customer, M. Sinnott, on account.
2. A debit of $1,027.10 for an NSF cheque written by A. Shoaib, a customer. At December 31, the account had still not been paid.
3. A debit of $45 for service charges for the month.

The cash records per books for December showed the following:

	Cash Receipts			Cash Disbursements	
Date	Amount		Date	Number	Amount
Dec. 3	$1,211.60		Dec. 1	3475	$ 1,640.70
Dec. 7	2,365.10		Dec. 2	3476	1,300.00
Dec. 15	2,672.70		Dec. 2	3477	2,130.00
Dec. 20	2,954.00		Dec. 4	3478	538.20
Dec. 25	2,567.30		Dec. 8	3479	3,080.00
Dec. 28	2,836.00		Dec. 10	3480	600.00
Dec. 30	1,025.00		Dec. 17	3481	807.40
Dec. 31	1,190.40		Dec. 20	3482	475.50
Total	$16,822.10		Dec. 22	3483	1,140.00
			Dec. 23	3484	832.00
			Dec. 24	3485	450.80
			Dec. 29	3486	1,389.50
				Total	$14,384.10

At December 31, the cash balance per books was $12,654.40. The bank did not make any errors, but two errors were made by Racine Limited.

Instructions

(a) Prove the calculation of the cash balance per books at December 31.

(b) Prepare a bank reconciliation at December 31, 2004.

(c) Prepare the adjusting entries based on the reconciliation. (*Note:* The correction of any errors pertaining to recording cheques should be made to Accounts Payable. The correction of any errors pertaining to recording cash receipts should be made to Accounts Receivable.)

Prepare bank reconciliation and adjusting entries.
(SO 4)

P7-7A Palmeiro Ltd. maintains a chequing account at the Canadian Western Bank. At July 31, selected data from the ledger balance and the bank statement are as follows:

	Cash in Bank	
	Per Books	Per Bank
Balance, July 1	$17,600	$19,200
July receipts	82,000	
July credits		80,070
July disbursements	76,900	
July debits		74,740
Balance, July 31	$22,700	$24,530

Analysis of the bank data reveals that the credits consist of $80,040 of July deposits and a credit memorandum of $30 for interest revenue. The July debits per bank consist of cheques cleared $74,700, and a debit memorandum of $40 for printing additional company cheques. You also discover the following errors involving July cheques: (1) a cheque for $250 to a creditor on account that cleared the bank in July was journalized and posted as $520, and (2) a salary cheque to an employee for $255 was recorded by the bank as $155. The June 30 bank reconciliation contained only two reconciling items: deposits in transit of $5,000, and outstanding cheques of $6,600.

Instructions

(a) Prepare a bank reconciliation at July 31.

(b) Journalize the adjusting entries to be made by Palmeiro Ltd. at July 31.

Calculate cash balance; prepare bank reconciliation and adjusting entries.
(SO 4, 5)

P7-8A On August 31, 2004, Dublin Ltd. had a cash balance per the general ledger of $2,112.97. The bank statement from the Royal Bank showed a balance of $1,523.47. A comparison of the bank statement with the Cash account revealed the following facts:

1. The company had $150 of traveller's cheques on hand. This amount was included in the book amount of cash, but had already been subtracted from the bank records. The traveller's cheques will be charged to travel expense by the company as they are used. There was a bank service charge of $16 related to the traveller's cheques which has not been recorded in the company's books.

in a bank account Roger had opened.

The day of the dance, Roger wrote a cheque from the account to pay Obnoxious Al. However, Al said that he accepted only cash and did not give receipts. So Roger took $200 out of the cash box and gave it to Al. At the dance, Roger had Sara Billings working at the entrance to the gymnasium, collecting tickets from students and selling tickets to those who had not prepurchased them. Roger estimated that 400 students attended the dance.

The following day Roger closed out the bank account, which had $250 in it, and gave that amount plus the $180 in the cash box to Principal Skinner. Principal Skinner seemed surprised that, after generating roughly $4,000 in sales, the dance netted only $430 in cash. Roger did not know how to respond.

Instructions

Identify as many internal control weaknesses as you can in this scenario. Suggest how each could be addressed.

P7-3B   Tarika Ltd. is a profitable small business. It has not, however, given much consideration to internal control. For example, in an attempt to keep clerical and office expenses to a minimum, the company has combined the jobs of cashier and bookkeeper. As a result, Rob Rowe handles all cash receipts, keeps the accounting records, and prepares the monthly bank reconciliations.

Prepare bank reconciliation and identify internal control deficiencies.
(SO 2, 3, 4)

The balance per bank statement on October 31, 2004, was $18,480. Outstanding cheques were No. 801 for $126.75, No. 883 for $150, No. 884 for $253.25, No. 900 for $190.71, No. 901 for $226.80, and No. 902 for $165.28. Included with the statement was a credit memorandum of $45 indicating interest earned for the month.

The company's ledger showed one cash account with a balance of $18,042.21. The balance included undeposited cash on hand. Because of the lack of internal controls, Rowe took all of the undeposited receipts for himself. He then prepared the following bank reconciliation in an effort to conceal his theft of cash:

Cash balance per books, October 31		$18,042.21
Add: Outstanding cheques		
No. 900	$190.71	
No. 901	226.80	
No. 902	165.28	482.79
Unadjusted balance per bank, October 31		18,525.00
Less: Bank credit memorandum		45.00
Cash balance per bank statement, October 31		$18,480.00

Instructions

(a) Prepare a correct bank reconciliation. (*Hint:* The theft is the difference between the adjusted balances per books and per bank.)
(b) Indicate the three ways that Rowe attempted to conceal the theft and the dollar amount involved in each method.
(c) What principles of internal control were violated in this case?

P7-4B   On July 31, 2004, Dubeau Ltd. had a cash balance per books of $7,380. The statement from the Caisse Populaire on that date showed a balance of $7,695.80. A comparison of the bank statement with the cash account revealed the following facts:

Prepare bank reconciliation and adjusting entries.
(SO 4)

1. The bank service charge for July was $25.
2. The bank recorded $1,238 received from a customer electronically in payment of its account.
3. The July 31 receipts of $1,824.30 were not included in the bank deposits for July. These receipts were deposited by the company in a night deposit vault on July 31.
4. Company cheque No. 2480 for $492, issued to J. Brokaw, a creditor, cleared the bank in July and was incorrectly entered in the general journal on July 10 as $429.
5. Cheques outstanding on July 31 totalled $1,480.10.
6. On July 31, the bank statement showed an NSF charge of $490 for a cheque received by the company from R. Chiasson, a customer, on account.

Instructions

(a) Prepare the bank reconciliation as at July 31.
(b) Prepare the necessary adjusting entries at July 31.

*Prepare bank reconciliation
and adjusting entries.*
(SO 4)

P7-5B Selected banking and book documents required to reconcile the bank account for Yap Ltd. as at March 31, 2004, are reproduced below:

BANK

The March bank statement showed the following:

YAP LTD.
Bank Statement
March 31, 2004

	Deposits	Cheques and Other Debits		
Date	Amount	Number	Amount	Balance
Feb. 29				$14,368
Mar. 1	$2,530	3451	$2,260	14,638
Mar. 2		3471	845	13,793
Mar. 5	1,212			15,005
Mar. 7		3472	1,427	13,578
Mar. 10		NSF–Jordan	550	13,028
Mar. 15		3473	1,641	11,387
Mar. 22		3474	2,130	9,257
Mar. 27	2,567			11,824
Mar. 30		SC	49	11,775

Additional information:
1. The bank statement contained two debit memoranda:
   (a) An NSF cheque in the amount of $550 that had previously been deposited by Yap had been returned due to insufficient funds in the payor's bank account. This cheque was originally given to Yap by Mr. Jordan, a customer, in payment of his account. Yap believes it will be able to collect this amount from Mr. Jordan in the future.
   (b) A service charge (SC) of $49 for bank services provided throughout the month
2. No errors were made by the bank.

BOOKS

The cash records on the books of the company for the month of March showed the following:

Cash Receipts		Cash Disbursements		
Date	Amount	Date	Cheque Number	Balance
Mar. 4	$2,121	Mar. 7	3472	$1,427
Mar. 26	2,567	Mar. 15	3473	1,641
Mar. 30	1,025	Mar. 22	3474	2,130
	$5,713	Mar. 29	3475	600
				$5,798

Additional information:
1. All cash receipts were deposited daily in the bank, using the night deposit slot. All cash payments were made by cheque.
2. A $909 error was made by Yap in recording cash receipts from cash sales on March 4.

FEBRUARY BANK RECONCILIATION

The bank portion of last month's bank reconciliation for Yap Ltd. at February 29, 2004, was as follows:

YAP LTD.
Bank Reconciliation
February 29, 2004

Cash balance per bank		$14,368
Add: Deposits in transit		2,530
		16,898
Less: Outstanding cheques		
#3451	$2,260	
#3470	720	
#3471	845	3,825
Adjusted cash balance		$13,073

Instructions

(a) Determine Yap Ltd.'s unadjusted cash balance in its general ledger on March 31.
(b) What is the amount of the deposits in transit, if any, at March 31?
(c) What is the amount of the outstanding cheques, if any, at March 31?
(d) Prepare a bank reconciliation for Yap Ltd. for the month of March 2004.
(e) Prepare any journal entries required to adjust the accounts at March 31, 2004.

P7-6B The bank portion of the bank reconciliation for London Inc. at October 31, 2004, is shown here:

Prepare bank reconciliation and adjusting entries.
(SO 4)

LONDON INC.
Bank Reconciliation
October 31, 2004

Cash balance per bank		$12,367.90
Add: Deposits in transit		1,530.20
		13,898.10
Less: Outstanding cheques		
#2451	$1,260.40	
#2470	720.10	
#2471	844.50	
#2472	426.80	
#2474	1,050.00	4,301.80
Adjusted cash balance		$ 9,596.30

The adjusted cash balance per bank agreed with the cash balance per books at October 31. The November bank statement showed the following cheques and deposits:

LONDON INC.
Bank Statement
November 30, 2004

Date	Deposits Amount	Cheques and Other Debits Number	Amount	Balance
Oct. 31				$12,367.90
Nov. 1	$1,530.20	2470	$ 720.10	13,178.00
Nov. 2		2471	844.50	12,333.50
Nov. 4	1,211.60	2475	1,640.70	11,904.40
Nov. 5		2474	1,050.00	10,854.40
Nov. 8	990.10	2476	2,830.00	9,014.50
Nov. 10		2477	600.00	8,414.50
Nov. 13	2,575.00			10,989.50
Nov. 15		2479	1,750.00	9,239.50
Nov. 18	1,472.70	2480	1,330.00	9,382.20
Nov. 21	2,945.00			12,327.20
Nov. 25	2,567.30	DM	110.00	14,784.50
Nov. 27		2481	695.40	14,089.10
Nov. 28	1,650.00			15,739.10
Nov. 29	CM 2,105.00	2486	900.00	16,944.10
Nov. 30	1,186.00	2483	575.50	17,554.60

The bank statement contained two memoranda:

1. A credit of $2,105 for the electronic payment of an account by a customer—K. Tanika.
2. A debit for the printing of additional company cheques, $110.

The bank did not make any errors. The cash records per books for November showed the following. Note that two errors were made by London Inc.

Cash Receipts			Cash Disbursements		
Date	Amount		Date	Number	Amount
Nov. 3	$ 1,211.60		Nov. 1	2475	$ 1,640.70
Nov. 7	990.10		Nov. 2	2476	2,830.00
Nov. 12	2,575.00		Nov. 2	2477	600.00
Nov. 17	1,472.70		Nov. 4	2478	538.20
Nov. 20	2,954.00		Nov. 8	2479	1,570.00
Nov. 24	2,567.30		Nov. 10	2480	1,330.00
Nov. 27	1,650.00		Nov. 15	2481	695.40
Nov. 29	1,186.00		Nov. 18	2482	612.00
Nov. 30	1,225.00		Nov. 20	2483	575.50
Total	$15,831.70		Nov. 22	2484	829.50
			Nov. 23	2485	974.80
			Nov. 24	2486	900.00
			Nov. 29	2487	398.00
			Nov. 30	2488	1,200.00
			Total		$14,694.10

Instructions

(a) Determine the unadjusted cash balance per books as at November 30, 2004, prior to reconciliation.

(b) Prepare a bank reconciliation at November 30.

(c) Prepare the required entries based on the reconciliation. (*Note:* The correction of any errors in the recording of cheques should be made to Accounts Payable. The correction of any errors in the recording of cash receipts should be made to Accounts Receivable.)

Prepare bank reconciliation and adjusting entries.
(SO 4)

P7-7B   Mayo Ltd.'s bank statement from Canadian Western Bank at August 31, 2004, gives this information:

Balance, August 1	$16,400	Bank debit memorandum:	
August deposits	73,000	Safety deposit box fee	$ 25
Cheques cleared in August	68,660	Service charge	50
Bank credit memorandum:		Balance, August 31	20,710
Interest earned	45		

A summary of the Cash account in the ledger for August shows the following: balance, August 1, $16,900; receipts, $77,000; disbursements, $73,570; and balance, August 31, $20,330. Analysis reveals that the only reconciling items on the July 31 bank reconciliation were a deposit in transit for $4,000 and outstanding cheques of $4,500. In addition, you determine that there were two errors involving company cheques drawn in August: (1) a cheque for $400 to a creditor on account that cleared the bank in August was journalized and posted for $40, and (2) a salary cheque to an employee for $275 was recorded by the bank as $257.

Instructions

(a) Prepare a bank reconciliation at August 31.

(b) Journalize the adjusting entries to be made by Mayo Ltd. at August 31.

Calculate cash balance.
(SO 1, 5)

P7-8B   A first year co-op student is trying to determine the amount of cash that should be reported on a company's balance sheet. The following information was provided to the student at year end:

1. Cash on hand in the cash registers totals $5,000.
2. The balance in the commercial bank savings account is $100,000 and in the commercial bank chequing account, $25,000. The company also has the equivalent of $45,000 Canadian dollars in a U.S. bank account.
3. A special bank account holds $150,000 cash that is restricted for equipment replacement.
4. A $50,000 line of credit is available at the bank on demand.
5. Amounts due from employees (travel advances) total $12,000.
6. Short-term investments held by the company include $32,000 in a money-market fund and $75,000 in a treasury bill fund.
7. The company has a supply of unused postage stamps totalling $50.

8. The company has NSF cheques from customers that were returned by the bank totalling $500.
9. The company has $7,500 of cash deposits (advances paid by customers) held in a special bank account.

Instructions

(a) Calculate the cash balance that should be reported on the year-end balance sheet.
(b) Would your answer in (a) change if the company combines its cash and cash equivalents?
(c) Identify where any items that were not reported in the cash balance in (a) should be reported.

P7-9B Hanover Ltd. expects to have a cash balance of $36,000 on January 1, 2005. Relevant monthly budget data for the first two months of 2005 are as follows:

Prepare cash budget.
(SO 7)

1. Collections from customers: January $70,000; February, $150,000
2. Payments to suppliers: January, $40,000; February, $75,000
3. Salaries: January, $30,000; February, $40,000. Salaries are paid in the month they are incurred.
4. Operating expenses: January, $34,000; February, $49,000. These costs do not include amortization and are paid as incurred.
5. Sales of short-term investments in January are expected to realize $10,000 in cash.
6. Hanover has a line of credit at a local bank that enables it to borrow up to $25,000. The company wants to maintain a minimum monthly cash balance of $10,000.

Instructions

(a) Prepare a cash budget for January and February.
(b) Explain how a cash budget contributes to effective management.

P7-10B Joplin Inc. prepares monthly cash budgets. Here are relevant data from operating budgets for January and February in 2005:

Prepare cash budget.
(SO 7)

	January	February
Sales	$360,000	$400,000
Purchases	100,000	110,000
Operating expenses	215,000	255,000

All sales are on account. Collections are expected to be 50% in the month of sale, 30% in the first month following the sale, and 20% in the second month following the sale. Forty percent of purchases are paid in cash in the month of purchase, and the balances are paid in the month following the purchase. All other items above are paid in the month incurred. Amortization has been excluded from operating expenses.

Other data are listed here:

1. Credit sales—November 2004, $200,000; December 2004, $280,000
2. Purchases—December 2004, $90,000
3. Other receipts—January: collection of December 31, 2004, interest receivable of $3,000; February: proceeds from sale of investments, $5,000
4. Other disbursements—February: payment of $20,000 for land

The company's cash balance on January 1, 2005, is expected to be $20,000. The company wants to maintain a minimum cash balance of $10,000.

Instructions

(a) Prepare schedules for (1) expected collections from customers and (2) expected payments for purchases.
(b) Prepare a cash budget for January and February.

Financial Reporting and Analysis

Analysis
Tools

FINANCIAL REPORTING PROBLEM: *Loblaw Companies Limited*

BYP7-1   Two reports are attached to Loblaw Companies Limited financial statements presented in Appendix A of this book: (1) Management's Statement of Responsibility for Financial Reporting and (2) the Independent Auditors' Report.

Instructions

(a) What comments, if any, concerning the company's system of internal control are included in Management's Statement of Responsibility? In the Auditors' Report?
(b) What reference, if any, is made to internal auditors in each of the above reports?
(c) Explain how Loblaw can have both cash and bank indebtedness on its balance sheet at the same time.

COMPARATIVE ANALYSIS PROBLEM: *Loblaw and Sobeys*

BYP7-2   The financial statements of Sobeys Inc. are presented in Appendix B, following the financial statements for Loblaw in Appendix A.

Instructions

Answer the following questions for each company:

(a) What is the balance in cash and cash equivalents for the current fiscal year?
(b) How much cash was provided by operating activities for the current year?
(c) Does either company have any compensating balances?
(d) What conclusions regarding the ability to generate cash and the companies' cash management can be made from the comparison of these results?

RESEARCH CASE

BYP7-3   *Report on Business Magazine* included an article by Patrick Brethour in its September 27, 2002, edition, p. 126, entitled "Money in the Bank: Some Tech Companies Actually Have Too Much Cash, and It's Weighing Down Their Share Price."

Instructions

Read the article and answer these questions:

(a) How did these tech companies amass so much cash?
(b) Does the market reflect the full value of cash holdings in the companies' share prices?
(c) What options are available to these tech companies to use this cash?
(d) Do tech companies normally pay dividends?

INTERPRETING FINANCIAL STATEMENTS

BYP7-4 Shown on the next page is selected information from Imperial Tobacco Canada Limited's December 31, 2002, balance sheet:

IMPERIAL TOBACCO CANADA LIMITED Balance Sheet (partial) December 31, 2002 (in millions)		
	2002	2001
Current assets		
Cash and cash equivalents	$ 402	$ 581
Trade and other accounts receivable	223	148
Future income taxes	59	71
Inventories	443	490
Total current assets	$1,127	$1,290
Total current liabilities	$ 932	$1,186

Instructions

(a) What is a cash equivalent? How do cash equivalents differ from other types of short-term investments?

(b) Calculate the (1) working capital and (2) current ratio for each year. The industry average for the current ratio is 1.61:1 in 2002 and 1.06:1 in 2001. Comment on your results.

(c) Is it possible to have too much cash? Explain why or why not.

A GLOBAL FOCUS

BYP7-5   The following information has been selected from the 2002 financial statements of Nestlé, the world's #1 food company:

NESTLÉ S.A. Selected Financial Information December 31, 2002 (in Swiss francs (CHF) millions)		
	2002	2001
Cash and cash equivalents	CHF 6,338	CHF 7,617
Cash flow provided by operating activities	10,248	8,614
Total current assets	35,342	39,045
Total current liabilities	33,737	41,492

Good Food, Good Life

Instructions

(a) Calculate Nestlé's (1) working capital and (2) current ratio for each year. Comment on the company's cash adequacy.

(b) As an international company, Nestlé is affected by economic and financial conditions in each of the countries where it operates. For example, when currencies devalue substantially, Nestlé's cash position is hit hard. In fact, Nestlé notes in its letter to shareholders that "evolution of foreign currencies against the Swiss franc... penalized our sales." Explain how Nestlé's operating cash flow is affected by devaluation of a foreign currency.

FINANCIAL ANALYSIS ON THE WEB

BYP7-6   KPMG's *2002 Fraud and Misconduct Diagnostic Survey* polls Canada's business leaders to determine how they are managing fraud and misconduct in their organizations. In this case, we review this report to determine how fraud risk is managed.

Instructions

Specific requirements of this Web case can be found on the Kimmel website.

Critical Thinking

COLLABORATIVE LEARNING ACTIVITY

BYP7-7 During its annual audit, Alternative Distributor Corp., a distributor of groceries and related products, was advised that existing internal controls necessary for the company to develop reliable financial statements were inadequate. The audit report stated that the current system of accounting for sales, receivables, and cash receipts constituted a material weakness. Among other items, the report focused on the non-timely depositing of cash receipts, exposing Alternative Distributor to potential loss or misappropriation; excessive past due accounts receivable due to a lack of collection efforts; a disregard of advantages offered by vendors for prompt payment of invoices; an absence of appropriate segregation of duties by personnel consistent with appropriate control objectives; inadequate procedures for applying accounting principles; a lack of qualified management personnel; a lack of supervision by an outside board of directors; and overall poor record keeping.

Instructions
With the class divided into groups, do the following:
(a) Identify the principles of internal control violated by Alternative Distributor Corp.
(b) Write a memo to the company's management. The memo should address the following points:
1. Which principles of internal control were violated by Alternative Distributor Corp.
2. Why these controls are important
3. Steps that could be taken to improve the situation

COMMUNICATION ACTIVITY

BYP7-8 Landry Corporation is a small family-owned company selling office supplies. Guylaine Lavoie has been with the company from the beginning, doing all the clerical work, including recording and depositing cash, paying the bills, and reconciling the bank account monthly. The company has grown in size from three employees to twenty and annual sales have gone from $200,000 to $7,000,000. Guylaine is still looking after the cash and says she doesn't require any assistance in completing her tasks.

Instructions

Write a letter to Lucette Landry, the president of Landry Corporation, explaining the weaknesses in internal control over cash and your recommendations for improving the system. In your answer, address the fact that the company was initially small but has now grown in both size and revenues.

ETHICS CASE

Ethics In
Accounting

BYP7-9 Banks charge fees of up to $25 for bounced cheques—that is, cheques that exceed the balance in the account. It has been estimated that processing bounced cheques costs a bank roughly $1.50 per cheque. Thus, the profit margin on bounced cheques is high. Recognizing this, banks process cheques from largest to smallest. By doing this, they maximize the number of cheques that bounce if a customer overdraws an account. One bank projected a $14-million increase in fee revenue as a result of processing the largest cheques first. In response to criticism, banks have responded that their customers prefer to have large cheques processed first, because those tend to be the most important. At the other extreme, some banks will cover their customers' bounced cheques, effectively extending them overdraft protection.

Instructions

(a) Who are the stakeholders in this case?
(b) Freeman Corp. had a balance of $1,200 in its chequing account on a day when the bank received the following five cheques for processing against that account:

Cheque Number	Amount
3150	$ 35
3158	510
3162	400
3165	550
3169	180

Assuming a $25 fee is assessed by the bank, how much fee revenue would the bank generate if it processed cheques from largest to smallest, (2) from smallest to largest, and (3) in the order of the cheque numbers?

(c) Do you think that processing cheques from largest to smallest is an ethical business practice?

(d) Besides ethical issues, what other considerations must a bank make in deciding whether to process cheques from largest to smallest?

(e) If you were managing a bank, what policy would you adopt on bounced cheques?

Answers to Self-Study Questions

1. b   2. c   3. b   4. d   5. a   6. c   7. b   8. c   9. b   10. d

Answer to Loblaw's Review It Question 3

Loblaw reported $823 million of cash and cash equivalents as at December 28, 2002. Loblaw's cash equivalents are defined in Note 1 as "highly liquid investments with a maturity of less than 90 days."

Remember to go back to the Navigator box on the chapter-opening page to check off your completed work.

CHAPTER 8

Reporting and Analysing Receivables

STUDY OBJECTIVES

After studying this chapter, you should be able to:

1. Identify the different types of receivables.

2. Explain how accounts receivable are recognized in the accounts.

3. Describe the method used to account for bad debts.

4. Explain how notes receivable are recognized and valued in the accounts.

5. Explain the statement presentation of receivables.

6. Describe the principles of sound accounts receivable management.

7. Identify the ratios used to analyse a company's receivables.

8. Describe the methods used to accelerate the receipt of cash from receivables.

NAVIGATOR

A Dose of Careful Management Keeps Receivables Healthy

For any large company, careful management of receivables is crucial to profitability. After all, receivables are generally a company's third-largest asset (after its property, plant, and equipment, and inventory). As Maria Cardoso knows, keeping tabs on the timely receipt of payments from hundreds of credit accounts can be a tough job, although a little flexibility sometimes goes a long way in maintaining good customer relationships.

Ms. Cardoso is supervisor of credit and collections at Mississauga-based Whitehall-Robins Inc. Canada. Whitehall-Robins is a Canadian subsidiary of global pharmaceutical company Wyeth, which distributes over-the-counter health-care products. Some of these products—such as Advil, Robitussin, and Centrum—are among the top-selling health-care brands in the world.

The company's sales terms are 1/15, n/30 (1% discount if paid within 15 days). Sometimes, if the customer pays several invoices—some under 15 days, some over—with one cheque, Ms. Cardoso might allow the discount for all of them. That's because smaller companies often only write cheques once a week, or even once a month.

"We always consider each case individually," she says. "With larger accounts, payments normally come through automatically, and we don't run into special circumstances very often. In other situations, we might give them a bit of a break when they ask."

In total, Whitehall-Robins records more than $180 million in sales a year, all of which comes in through the credit accounts Ms. Cardoso manages. The process starts with a decision to grant a customer an account in the first place. A sales rep gives the customer a credit application, which Ms. Cardoso then reviews. In addition to having to supply three good references, prospective accounts are also screened with a credit agency. Once accepted, they are assigned a credit limit based on their size and history.

After that, they are supervised closely. "We get an aging report every morning that shows

Whitehall-Robins Inc. Canada   www.wyeth.com

THE NAVIGATOR

Scan *Study Objectives* ▢

Read *Feature Story* ▢

Read *Chapter Preview* ▢

Read text and answer *Before You Go On*
p. 363 ▢ p. 367 ▢ p. 368 ▢ p. 376 ▢

Work *Using the Decision Toolkit* ▢

Review *Summary of Study Objectives*
and *Decision Toolkit* ▢

Work *Demonstration Problem* ▢

Answer *Self-Study Questions* ▢

Complete assignments ▢

exactly what each customer owes and what category the account falls into—current, 1–30 days, 31–60 days, 61–90, and over 90," says Ms. Cardoso. "Fortunately, our receivables are always at 95% current or better, so we have very few overdues." When it does happen, there's usually an explanation. That's why Ms. Cardoso tends to call as soon as a payment is late. "If the invoice has gone missing, for example, you want to find out right away," she says.

More typically, she points out, the challenge with bigger customers is trying to reconcile accounts for short payments. Whitehall-Robins often gives its customers rebates for displaying its products prominently. "What occasionally happens is they just take the rebate off their pay-

ment," she says. "It would be a lot better if they waited for us to actually give it to them!"

Other times, the sales rep has offered a price, and somehow it hasn't been communicated to Customer Service. And from time to time it does happen that payments are simply late. "We start to call them after about five days. We would then send a letter and after that a final notice. If we don't get any results we place it with a third party," Ms. Cardoso says. "But this is the last resort and it doesn't happen often."

Although the company's write-offs are minimal, Ms. Cardoso's boss, Terry Norton, records an estimate for them every year, based on a percentage of receivables. What percentage depends on the current aging history. He also watches the company's re-

ceivables turnover ratio. "I think of it in terms of collection period or DSO—days of sales outstanding," he says. "You want to keep that number as close to your terms as possible. But it varies over the year. In the fall, for example, we often extend more favourable terms to customers to allow them to do special promotions, and our DSO might reach 60-odd days." As Mr. Norton and Ms. Cardoso know, keeping customers happy and receivables healthy are both good for business.

In this chapter, we discuss some of the decisions related to reporting and analysing receivables. As indicated in the feature story, receivables are a significant asset on the books of pharmaceutical company Whitehall-Robins. Receivables are important to companies in other industries as well, because a large number of sales are made on credit in Canada. Companies must therefore pay close attention to their receivables balances and manage them carefully.

The content and organization of the chapter are as follows:

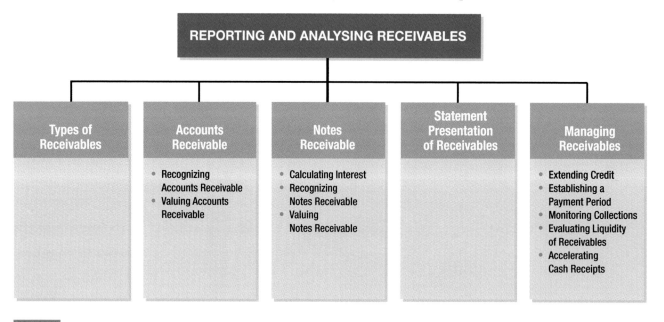

REPORTING AND ANALYSING RECEIVABLES

Types of Receivables	Accounts Receivable	Notes Receivable	Statement Presentation of Receivables	Managing Receivables
	• Recognizing Accounts Receivable • Valuing Accounts Receivable	• Calculating Interest • Recognizing Notes Receivable • Valuing Notes Receivable		• Extending Credit • Establishing a Payment Period • Monitoring Collections • Evaluating Liquidity of Receivables • Accelerating Cash Receipts

NAVIGATOR

Types of Receivables

STUDY OBJECTIVE

1

Identify the different types of receivables.

The term receivables refers to amounts due from individuals and companies. Receivables are claims that are expected to be collected in cash. The management of receivables is a very important activity for any company that sells goods on credit. Receivables are important because they represent one of a company's most liquid assets. As noted in our feature story, receivables are also important because of their size—they are often one of a company's largest assets.

The relative significance of a company's receivables as a percentage of its assets differs depending on the industry, the time of year, whether the company extends long-term financing, and its credit policies. To reflect important differences among receivables, they are frequently classified as (1) accounts receivable, (2) notes receivable, and (3) other receivables.

Accounts receivable are amounts owed by customers on account. They result from the sale of goods and services. These receivables generally are expected to be collected within 30 days or so and are classified as current assets. They are usually the most significant type of claim held by a company.

Notes receivable represent claims for which formal instruments of credit—a written promise to repay—are issued as evidence of the debt. The credit instrument normally requires the debtor to pay interest and extends for time periods of 30 days or longer. Notes receivable may be either current assets or long-term assets, depending on their due dates. Notes and accounts receivable that result from sales transactions are often called trade receivables.

Nontrade receivables include other receivables such as interest receivable, loans to company officers, advances to employees, and recoverable sales and income taxes. Nontrade receivables are generally classified and reported as separate items in the current or noncurrent assets section of the balance sheet, according to their due dates.

Accounts Receivable

We will now examine two accounting problems associated with accounts receivable:

1. Recognizing accounts receivable
2. Valuing accounts receivable

A third issue, accelerating cash receipts from receivables, is discussed later in the chapter.

RECOGNIZING ACCOUNTS RECEIVABLE

The initial recognition of accounts receivable is relatively straightforward. For a service organization, a receivable is recorded when service is provided on account. For a merchandiser, accounts receivable are recorded at the point of sale of merchandise on account.

Receivables are reduced as a result of sales discounts and sales returns. The seller may offer terms that encourage early payment by providing a discount. For example, terms of 2/10, n/30 provide the buyer with a 2% discount if the bill is paid within 10 days. If the buyer chooses to pay within the discount period, the seller's accounts receivable are reduced. Also, the buyer might find some of the goods unacceptable and choose to return them. This also results in a reduction of accounts receivable. For example, if $100 of merchandise purchased on account is returned, the seller reduces accounts receivable by $100 upon receipt of the returned merchandise.

STUDY OBJECTIVE

2

Explain how accounts receivable are recognized in the accounts.

BUSINESS INSIGHT

ETHICS PERSPECTIVE

Anticipating and recognizing sales returns is an important part of revenue recognition and valuing accounts receivable. Consider, for instance, the case of Take-Two Interactive Software, Inc., which makes video games for Sony's PlayStation, Microsoft's Xbox, and Nintendo's GameCube and GameBoy. After SEC inquiries, Take-Two reassessed its method of recognizing revenue from sales to distributors. The company had apparently recorded as revenue the sale of games that were later returned to, or repurchased by, Take-Two. Sales returns and allowances increased from U.S.$9.2 million for the three months ending Jan. 31, 2001, to U.S.$28.3 million for the six months ending April 30.

Source: Aaron Elstein, "Take-Two Restatement Lingers," *Wall Street Journal Online*, January 2, 2002.

VALUING ACCOUNTS RECEIVABLE

Once receivables are recorded in the accounts, the next question is, How should receivables be reported in the financial statements? They are reported on the balance sheet as an asset, but determining the amount to report is sometimes difficult because some receivables will become uncollectible.

Although each customer must satisfy the credit requirements of the seller before the credit sale is approved, inevitably some accounts receivable become uncollectible. For example, a corporate customer may not be able to pay because of a decline in sales due to a downturn in the economy. Similarly, individuals may be laid off from their jobs or faced with unexpected bills. Credit losses are

STUDY OBJECTIVE

3

Describe the method used to account for bad debts.

debited to the Bad Debts Expense account. Such losses are considered a normal and necessary risk of doing business on a credit basis.

The key issue in valuing accounts receivable is when to recognize these credit losses. If the company waits until it knows for sure that the specific account will not be collected, it could end up recording the bad debts expense in a different period than the revenue.

Consider the following example. In 2004, Quick Buck Computer Corporation decides it could increase its revenues by offering computers to students without requiring any money down, and with no credit approval process. It goes on campuses across the country and distributes 1 million computers with a selling price of $1,200 each. This increases Quick Buck's revenues and receivables by $1.2 billion. The promotion is a huge success! The 2004 balance sheet and statement of earnings look wonderful. Unfortunately, during 2005, nearly 40% of the student customers default on their accounts. This makes the year 2005 statement of earnings and balance sheet look terrible. Illustration 8-1 shows that the promotion in 2004 is not such a great success after all.

Illustration 8-1
Effects of mismatching
bad debts

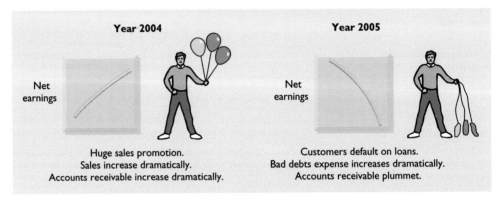

If credit losses are not recorded until they occur, no attempt is made to (1) match bad debts expense to sales revenues in the statement of earnings and (2) show the accounts receivable in the balance sheet at the amount actually expected to be received. Recording credit losses when they occur is called the direct write-off method. The direct write-off method does not provide useful information for decision-makers and is not acceptable for financial reporting purposes. There is, however, a method that estimates uncollectible accounts receivable and matches anticipated credit losses against sales in the accounting period in which the sales occur. This method is known as the allowance method.

Allowance Method for Uncollectible Accounts

The allowance method of accounting for bad debts involves estimating uncollectible accounts at the end of each period. This provides a better matching of expenses with revenues on the statement of earnings. It also ensures that receivables are stated at their net realizable value on the balance sheet. Net realizable value is the amount expected to be received in cash. It excludes amounts that the company estimates it will not collect. Receivables are therefore reduced by estimated uncollectible receivables on the balance sheet through the use of the allowance method.

The allowance method is required for financial reporting purposes. It has three essential features:

1. **Recording estimated uncollectibles:** Uncollectible accounts receivable are estimated and matched against sales in the accounting period in which the sales occur.

2. **Recording the write-off of an uncollectible account:** Actual uncollectibles are written off at the time the specific account is determined to be uncollectible.

3. **Recovery of an uncollectible account:** When an account previously written off

is subsequently collected, the original write-off is reversed and the collection recorded. Neither the write-off nor the subsequent recovery impact the statement of earnings, and thus matching is not distorted.

1. Recording Estimated Uncollectibles.

To illustrate the allowance method, assume that Abrams Furniture Ltd. has credit sales of $1,200,000 in 2004, of which $200,000 remains uncollected at December 31. The credit manager estimates that $10,000 will prove uncollectible. The adjusting entry to record the estimated uncollectibles is:

Dec. 31	Bad Debts Expense	10,000	
	Allowance for Doubtful Accounts		10,000
	(To record estimate of uncollectible accounts)		

A = L + SE
−10,000   −10,000

Cash flows: no effect

Note that a new account, Bad Debts Expense, is used instead of debiting a contra sales account. Bad Debts Expense is reported in the statement of earnings as an operating expense because credit and collections is a cost of doing business. With this debit entry to Bad Debts Expense, the estimated uncollectibles are matched with sales in 2004 because the expense is recorded in the same year the sales are made.

Allowance for Doubtful Accounts shows the estimated amount of claims on customers that are expected to become uncollectible in the future. A contra account is used instead of a direct credit to Accounts Receivable because we do not know which customers will not pay. The credit balance in the allowance account will absorb the specific write-offs when they occur.

Estimating the Allowance. For Abrams Furniture, the amount of the expected uncollectibles for the current period ($10,000) was given in the entry above. However, in actual practice, companies must estimate the amount of likely uncollectible accounts. While there are several acceptable ways to estimate uncollectible accounts, most companies apply a percentage to their outstanding receivables to determine the allowance for doubtful accounts.

Under the percentage of receivables basis, management establishes a percentage relationship between the amount of receivables and expected losses from uncollectible accounts. A schedule is prepared in which customer balances are classified by the length of time they have been unpaid. Because of its emphasis on time, this schedule is called an aging schedule, and its completion is called aging the accounts receivable.

After the accounts are arranged by age, the expected bad debt losses are determined by applying percentages, based on past experience, to the totals of each category. The longer a receivable is past due, the less likely it is to be collected. As a result, the estimated percentage of uncollectible debts increases as the number of days past due increases. An aging schedule for Abrams Furniture is shown in Illustration 8-2. Note the increasing uncollectible percentages from 2% to 50%.

| Customer | Total | Number of Days Outstanding | | | | |
		0–30	31–60	61–90	91–120	Over 120
T. E. Adert	$ 6,800	$3,800	$3,000			
R. C. Bortz	12,200	8,700	3,500			
B. A. Carl	9,400	6,400	3,000			
O. L. Diker	36,600	22,400	8,600	$4,000	$1,600	
T. O. Ebbet	2,500					$2,500
Others	132,500	70,200	23,300	34,000	5,000	
	$200,000	$111,500	$41,400	$38,000	$6,600	$2,500
Estimated percentage uncollectible		2%	5%	10%	25%	50%
Total estimated bad debts	$11,000	$2,230	$2,070	$3,800	$1,650	$1,250

Illustration 8-2
Aging schedule

Total estimated bad debts for Abrams Furniture ($11,000) represents the existing customer claims expected to become uncollectible in the future. Thus, this amount represents the required balance in allowance for doubtful accounts at the balance sheet date. Accordingly, **the amount of the bad debt adjusting entry is the difference between the required balance and the existing balance in the allowance account**. If the trial balance shows Allowance for Doubtful Accounts with a credit balance of $1,000, then an adjusting entry for $10,000 ($11,000 − $1,000) is necessary:

A	=	L	+	SE
−10,000				−10,000

Cash flows: no effect

Dec. 31	Bad Debts Expense		10,000	
	Allowance for Doubtful Accounts			10,000
	(To adjust allowance account to total estimated uncollectibles)			

After the adjusting entry is posted, the accounts of Abrams Furniture are as follows:

Bad Debts Expense	Allowance for Doubtful Accounts
Dec. 31 Adj. 10,000	Jan. 1 Bal. 1,000
	Dec. 31 Adj. 10,000
	Dec. 31 Bal. 11,000

An important aspect of accounts receivable management is simply maintaining a close watch on the accounts. Studies have shown that accounts more than 60 days past due lose approximately 50% of their value if no payment activity occurs within the next 30 days. For each additional 30 days that pass, the collectible value halves once again. As noted in our feature story, Maria Cardoso uses an aging schedule to closely monitor the collectibility of Whitehall-Robins' accounts receivable and to identify problem accounts.

Occasionally, the allowance account will have a debit balance prior to adjustment because write-offs during the year have exceeded previous provisions for bad debts. (We'll discuss write-offs in more detail in the next section.) If an opening debit balance exists, **the debit balance is added to the required balance** when the adjusting entry is made. Thus, if there had been a $500 debit balance in the allowance account before adjustment, the adjusting entry would have been for $11,500 ($11,000 + $500) to arrive at a credit balance of $11,000 in the Allowance account, as shown below:

Bad Debts Expense	Allowance for Doubtful Accounts	
Dec. 31 Adj. 11,500	Jan. 1 Bal. 500	Dec. 31 Adj. 11,500
		Dec. 31 Bal. 11,000

Net Realizable Value. The Allowance for Doubtful Accounts is deducted from accounts receivable in the current assets section of the balance sheet, as shown in Illustration 8-3.

Illustration 8-3
Presentation of allowance for doubtful accounts

ABRAMS FURNITURE LTD.
Balance Sheet (partial)
December 31, 2004

Current assets		
Cash		$ 14,800
Accounts receivable	$200,000	
Less: Allowance for doubtful accounts	11,000	189,000
Merchandise inventory		310,000
Prepaid expenses		25,000
Total current assets		$538,800

The $189,000 in Illustration 8-3 represents the expected **net realizable value** of the accounts receivable at the statement date. Illustration 8-4 shows the formula to calculate the net realizable value of accounts receivable.

Illustration 8-4
Formula for calculating net realizable value

2. Recording the Write-Off of an Uncollectible Account. Companies use various methods of collecting past-due accounts, such as letters, calls, collection agencies, and legal action. When all means of collecting a past-due account have been exhausted and collection appears unlikely, the account should be written off. To prevent premature or unauthorized write-offs, each write-off should be formally approved in writing by authorized management personnel. To maintain good internal control, authorization to write off accounts should not be given to someone who also has daily responsibilities related to cash or receivables.

To illustrate a receivables write-off, assume that Abrams Furniture's vice-president of finance authorizes a write-off of the $2,500 balance owed by T. O. Ebbet, a customer, on March 1, 2005. The entry to record the write-off is:

Mar. 1	Allowance for Doubtful Accounts	2,500	
	Accounts Receivable—T. O. Ebbet		2,500
	(Write-off of T. O. Ebbet account)		

A = L + SE
+2,500
−2,500

Cash flows: no effect

Bad Debts Expense is not increased when the write-off occurs. **Under the allowance method, every bad debt write-off is debited to the allowance account and not to Bad Debts Expense.** A debit to Bad Debts Expense would be incorrect because the expense was already recognized when the adjusting entry was made for estimated bad debts. Instead, the entry to record the write-off of an uncollectible account reduces both Accounts Receivable and the Allowance for Doubtful Accounts. After posting, using an assumed Accounts Receivable opening balance, the general ledger accounts will appear as follows:

Accounts Receivable			Allowance for Doubtful Accounts			
Feb. 28 Bal. 227,500	Mar. 1	2,500	Mar. 1	2,500	Jan. 1	Bal. 11,000
Mar. 1 Bal. 225,000					Mar. 1	Bal. 8,500

A write-off affects only balance sheet accounts. Net realizable value in the balance sheet, remains the same, as shown in Illustration 8-5.

	Before Write-off	After Write-off
Accounts receivable	$227,500	$225,000
Less: Allowance for doubtful accounts	11,000	8,500
Net realizable value	$216,500	$216,500

Illustration 8-5
Net realizable value comparison

As mentioned earlier, the Allowance account can sometimes end up in a debit balance position after a write-off of an uncollectible account. This occurs if the write-offs during the period exceed the opening balance. This is only a temporary situation: it will be corrected when the adjusting entry for estimated uncollectible accounts is made at the end of the period. After this adjusting entry is made, Allowance for Doubtful Accounts will again show its normal credit balance.

3. Recovery of an Uncollectible Account. Occasionally, a company collects from a customer after the account has been written off as uncollectible. Two entries are required to record the recovery of a bad debt: (1) the entry made in writing off the account is reversed to reinstate the customer's account; and (2) the collection is journalized in the usual manner. To illustrate, assume that on July 1, T. O. Ebbet pays the $2,500 amount that had been written off on March 1. These are the entries:

A	=	L	+	SE
+2,500				
−2,500				

Cash flows: no effect

		(1)		
July	1	Accounts Receivable—T. O. Ebbet	2,500	
		Allowance for Doubtful Accounts		2,500
		(To reverse write-off of T. O. Ebbet account)		
		(2)		
	1	Cash	2,500	
		Accounts Receivable—T. O. Ebbet		2,500
		(To record collection from T. O. Ebbet)		

A	=	L	+	SE
+2,500				
−2,500				

↑ Cash flows: +2,500

Note that the recovery of a bad debt, like the write-off of a bad debt, affects only balance sheet accounts. The net effect of the two entries is an increase in Cash and an increase in Allowance for Doubtful Accounts of $ 2,500. Accounts Receivable and Allowance for Doubtful Accounts both increase in entry (1) for two reasons: First, the account should not be written off after all. Second, T. O. Ebbet did pay, and therefore the Accounts Receivable account should show this collection for possible future credit purposes.

Summary of Allowance Method. In summary, there are three types of transactions that you may encounter when valuing accounts receivable using the allowance method:

1. Uncollectible accounts receivable are estimated using an aging schedule and recorded at the end of the period by debiting Bad Debts Expense and crediting Allowance for Doubtful Accounts.
2. Actual uncollectibles, or write-offs, are subsequently debited to Allowance for Doubtful Accounts and credited to an accounts receivable account.
3. Later recoveries, if any, are recorded in two separate entries. The first reverses the write-off by debiting Accounts Receivable and crediting Allowance for Doubtful Accounts. The second records the normal collection of the account by debiting Cash and crediting Accounts Receivable.

These entries are summarized and illustrated in T accounts below:

Accounts Receivable		Allowance for Doubtful Accounts	
Beginning balance	Collections	Write-offs	Beginning balance
Credit sales	Write-offs		Subsequent recoveries
Subsequent recoveries			Bad debt adjustment
Ending balance			Ending balance

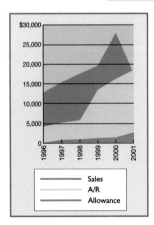

B U S I N E S S   I N S I G H T

MANAGEMENT PERSPECTIVE

How can you tell if a company is selling too much on credit? You must watch not only the company's sales, but also changes in accounts receivable and the allowance for doubtful accounts in order to assess the quality of a company's receivables.

For example, Nortel Networks Corp. saw its sales rocket 118% between 1996 and 2000. However, as these sales increased, the credit quality of the corresponding receivables deteriorated. During this same four-year period, Nortel's gross accounts receivable increased by 294% while its allowance for doubtful accounts increased by a staggering 450%.

The day of reckoning came in 2001. Even though Nortel's gross accounts receivable increased by only 14% between 2000 and 2001, its allowance increased by 80%. It was obvious that Nortel had loosened its credit policies in order to attract sales when, in 2001, Nortel had to write off a significant number of these accounts as uncollectible.

Decision Toolkit

DECISION CHECKPOINTS	INFO NEEDED FOR DECISION	TOOL TO USE FOR DECISION	HOW TO EVALUATE RESULTS
Is the amount of past-due accounts increasing? Which accounts require management's attention?	List of outstanding receivables and their due dates	Prepare an aging schedule showing the receivables in various stages: outstanding 0–30 days, 31–60 days, 61–90 days, 91–120 days, and over 120 days.	Accounts in the older categories require follow-up: letters, phone calls, e-mails, and possible renegotiations of terms.

BEFORE YOU GO ON . . .

● REVIEW IT

1. What type of receivables does Loblaw report in the current assets section of its balance sheet? The answer to this question is provided at the end of this chapter.
2. To maintain adequate internal controls over receivables, who should authorize receivables write-offs?
3. What are the essential features of the allowance method?

● DO IT

A partially prepared aging schedule for Holly Corporation to estimate its bad debts at year end, December 31, 2004, follows:

	Number of Days Outstanding				
	Total	0–30	31–60	61–90	Over 90
Accounts receivable	$230,000	$100,000	$60,000	$50,000	$20,000
Estimated percentage uncollectible		2%	5%	10%	20%
Total estimated bad debts					

Complete the aging schedule and prepare the journal entry required to record the estimated bad debts expense at year end. Assume that Allowance for Doubtful Accounts has an opening credit balance of $4,000.

Action Plan

- Apply percentages to outstanding receivables to determine total estimated bad debts.
- The total estimated bad debts determined in the aging schedule is the ending balance required in the Allowance account.
- Consider both the required ending balance and any existing balance in the Allowance account before determining the required adjustment amount.

Solution

Total estimated bad debts is $14,000 ($2,000 + $3,000 + $5,000 + $4,000). The following entry should be made to adjust Allowance for Doubtful Accounts $10,000 ($14,000 − $4,000) to equal the required ending balance of $14,000 :

Dec. 31	Bad Debts Expense	10,000	
	Allowance for Doubtful Accounts		10,000
	(To record estimate of uncollectible accounts)		

Notes Receivable

Credit may also be granted in exchange for a formal credit instrument known as a promissory note. A promissory note is a written promise to pay a specified amount of money on demand or at a definite time. Promissory notes may be used (1) when individuals and companies lend or borrow money, (2) when the amount of the transaction and the credit period exceed normal limits, and (3) in settlement of accounts receivable.

In a promissory note, the party making the promise to pay is called the maker; the party to whom payment is to be made is called the payee. The payee may be specifically identified by name or may be designated simply as the bearer of the note.

In the note shown in Illustration 8-6, Brent Ltd. is the maker and Tabusintac Inc. is the payee. For Tabusintac, the promissory note is a note receivable; for Brent, the promissory note is a note payable.

Illustration 8-6
Promissory note

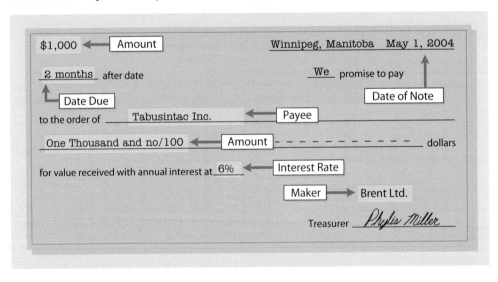

Helpful hint Note the similarities and differences between a note receivable and an account receivable.

Similarities: Both are credit instruments. Both are valued at net realizable value. Both can be sold to another party.

Differences: An account receivable is an informal promise to pay. A note receivable is secured by a formal, written promise to pay. An account receivable results from a credit sale. A note receivable arises from financing a purchase, lending money, or extending an account receivable beyond normal amounts or due dates. An account receivable is usually due within a short period of time (e.g., 30 days), while a note can extend for longer periods of time (e.g., 30 days to a number of years). An account receivable does not incur interest unless the account is overdue. A note usually bears interest for the entire period.

Notes receivable give the holder a stronger legal claim to assets than accounts receivable. Notes receivable can be readily sold to another party. Promissory notes are negotiable instruments (as are cheques), which means that they can be transferred to another party by endorsement.

Notes receivable are frequently accepted from customers who need to extend the payment of an outstanding account receivable. They are often required from high-risk customers. In some industries (e.g., the heavy equipment industry), all credit sales are supported by notes. The majority of notes, however, originate from lending transactions. There are two basic issues in accounting for notes receivable:

1. **Recognizing** notes receivable
2. **Valuing** notes receivable

We will look at each of these issues, but first we need to consider an issue that did not apply to accounts receivable—at least those paid within the period due—calculating interest.

CALCULATING INTEREST

The basic formula for calculating interest on an interest-bearing note is given in Illustration 8-7. You first learned this formula in Chapter 4.

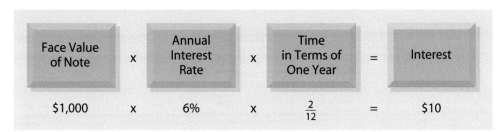

Illustration 8-7
Formula for calculating interest

Using the information given for the $1,000, two-month, 6% promissory note in Illustration 8-6, we can calculate that the interest on this note will total $10 for the two-month period. This interest will be recorded as interest revenue for Tabusintac Inc. and interest expense for Brent Ltd.

The interest rate specified on the note is an **annual** rate of interest. The time factor in the calculation represents the fraction of the year that the note is outstanding. When the maturity date is stated in days, the time factor is the number of days divided by 365. When the due date is stated in months, the time factor is usually simplified to the number of months divided by 12. As we did in past chapters, for simplicity we will continue to assume that interest is calculated in months, rather than days.

Note that interest on notes is sometimes due monthly. Often, however, especially for short-term notes, interest is collected along with the principal when the note matures.

RECOGNIZING NOTES RECEIVABLE

We will use Brent Ltd.'s promissory note to illustrate the basic entry for notes receivable. Assuming that the note was written to settle an open account, we record this entry for the receipt of the note by Tabusintac Inc.:

May 1	Notes Receivable—Brent Ltd.	1,000	
	Accounts Receivable—Brent Ltd.		1,000
	(To record acceptance of Brent Ltd. note)		

The note receivable is recorded at its **face value**, the value shown on the face of the note. No interest revenue is reported when the note is accepted because the revenue recognition principle does not recognize revenue until earned. As we learned in Chapter 4, interest is earned (accrued) as time passes.

If a note is exchanged for cash, the entry is a debit to Notes Receivable and a credit to Cash in the amount of the loan.

Notes are normally held to their maturity date, at which time the face value plus accrued interest is due. This is known as honouring (collecting) the note. In

STUDY OBJECTIVE

4

Explain how notes receivable are recognized and valued in the accounts.

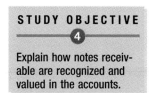

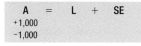
Cash flows: no effect

some situations, the maker of the note defaults and appropriate adjustment must be made. This is known as dishonouring (not collecting) the note.

Honour of Notes Receivable

A note is **honoured** when it is paid in full at its maturity date. To illustrate, assume that Wolder Corp. (the payee) lends Higley Inc. (the maker) $10,000 on June 1, accepting a four-month, 9% note. In this situation, interest is $300 ($10,000 × 9% × $\frac{4}{12}$) and payable at maturity. The amount due, the maturity value, is $10,300 ($10,000 face value + $300 interest). If Wolder presents the note to Higley for payment on October 1, the maturity date, the entry by Wolder to record the collection is:

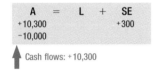

Oct. 1	Cash	10,300	
	Notes Receivable—Higley Inc.		10,000
	Interest Revenue		300
	(To record collection of Higley Inc. note and interest)		

Accrual of Interest Receivable

If Wolder prepares financial statements as at September 30, it is necessary to accrue interest. In this case, the adjusting entry by Wolder is for four months, or $300, as shown below:

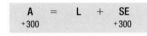

Sept. 30	Interest Receivable	300	
	Interest Revenue		300
	(To accrue four months' interest on Higley note)		

When interest has been accrued, it is necessary to credit Interest Receivable at maturity. The entry by Wolder to record the honouring of the Higley note on October 1 is:

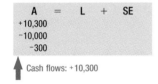

Oct. 1	Cash	10,300	
	Notes Receivable—Higley Inc.		10,000
	Interest Receivable		300
	(To record collection of Higley Inc. note and interest)		

In this case, Interest Receivable is credited because the receivable was established in the adjusting entry.

Dishonour of Notes Receivable

A dishonoured note is a note that is not paid in full at maturity. A dishonoured note receivable is no longer negotiable. However, the payee still has a claim against the maker of the note for both the face value and any unpaid interest. Therefore, the Notes Receivable account is usually transferred to an account receivable by debiting Accounts Receivable for both the face value of the note and the interest due.

If there is no hope of collection, the face value of the note and any accrued interest should be written off. No interest revenue would be recorded because collection will not occur.

BUSINESS INSIGHT

INTERNATIONAL PERSPECTIVE

Nessim Gaon isn't easily intimidated. He says that the Russian government owes him $600 million, and he is determined to get it one way or another. Back in 1991, he provided loans to the Russian Federation—when it was part of the Soviet Union—to buy food, pesticides, medicine, and other items. Russia was to repay the loan with oil. Shortly thereafter, the Soviet Union collapsed, and Gaon has been trying to get his money ever since. He convinced courts to freeze Russian bank accounts in Europe, tried to intercept U.S. payments to Russia for decommissioned nuclear warheads, and even tried to confiscate Russian president Vladimir Putin's plane as it landed in Paris.

Source: Andrew Higgins, "Bad-Risk Russia Is in Debt to a Guy Who Finds Creative Ways to Collect," *Wall Street Journal Online,* April 24, 2001.

VALUING NOTES RECEIVABLE

Like accounts receivable, notes receivable are reported at their **net realizable value**. Valuing short-term notes receivable is the same as valuing accounts receivable. The calculations and estimations involved in determining net realizable value and in recording the proper amount of bad debts expense and related allowance are similar.

Long-term notes receivable, however, pose additional estimation problems. As an example, we need only look at the problems a number of banks are having in collecting their receivables. The TD Bank, Canada's fourth-largest, recorded a $2.9-billion allowance for doubtful accounts in 2002, resulting in the first loss by any Canadian bank in a decade. TD ended the year with the largest net realizable value of loans receivable of any bank at $975 million. This figure represents the total amount of loans outstanding to struggling debtors, minus the allowance for doubtful accounts recorded by the bank. Scotiabank, which faces considerable South American exposure in its loan portfolio, was the second highest of the banks, with $620 million in net realizable value for its loans. Determining the proper allowance for doubtful accounts is understandably difficult for these types of long-term receivables.

BEFORE YOU GO ON ...

● **REVIEW IT**

1. What is the formula for calculating interest?
2. At what value are notes receivable reported on the balance sheet?
3. Explain the difference between honouring and dishonouring a note receivable.

● **DO IT**

Gambit Stores Ltd. accepts from Leonard Corp. a $3,400, three-month, 6% note dated May 10 in settlement of Leonard's overdue open account. What entry is made by Gambit at the maturity date, on August 10, assuming Leonard pays the note and interest in full at that time? No interest was previously accrued.

Action Plan

• Calculate the accrued interest. The formula is Face value × Annual interest rate × Time in terms of one year.
• Prepare the entry to record the collection of the note and any interest earned. Use separate accounts for the face value of the note and the interest.

Solution

The following entry is recorded by Gambit Stores at the maturity date:

Aug. 10	Cash	3,451	
	Notes Receivable—Leonard Corp.		3,400
	Interest Revenue ($3,400 \times 6\% \times \frac{3}{12}$)		51
	(To record collection of Leonard note and interest)		

Statement Presentation of Receivables

STUDY OBJECTIVE

5

Explain the statement presentation of receivables.

Each of the major types of receivables should be identified in the balance sheet or in the notes to the financial statements. Short-term receivables are reported in the current assets section of the balance sheet following short-term investments. Short-term investments appear before short-term receivables because they are more like cash. Although only the net amount of receivables less any allowance for doubtful accounts must be disclosed, it is helpful to report both the gross amount of receivables and the allowance for doubtful accounts either in the statement or in the notes to the financial statements.

Illustration 8-8 shows the current assets presentation of receivables for Bell Canada International Inc. Note that notes receivable are often listed before accounts receivable because notes are more easily converted to cash.

Illustration 8-8
Balance sheet presentation of receivables

BELL CANADA INTERNATIONAL INC.
Balance Sheet (partial)
December 31, 2002
(in thousands)

Current assets		
Cash and cash equivalents		$ 2,617
Temporary investments		146,488
Notes receivable		268,532
Accounts receivable	$1,989	
Less: Allowance for doubtful accounts	429	1,560
Prepaid expenses and other current assets		1,317
		$420,514

In the statement of earnings, bad debts expense is reported in the operating expenses section. Interest revenue is shown under other revenues in the non-operating section of the statement of earnings. If a company has significant risk of uncollectible accounts or other problems with its receivables, it is required to disclose this possibility in the notes to the financial statements.

BEFORE YOU GO ON . . .

● **REVIEW IT**

1. Explain where receivables are classified on the balance sheet.
2. Where are bad debts expense and interest revenue reported on the statement of earnings?

Managing Receivables

Managing accounts receivable involves five steps:

1. Determine who to extend credit to.
2. Establish a payment period.
3. Monitor collections.
4. Evaluate the liquidity of receivables.
5. Accelerate cash receipts from receivables when necessary.

EXTENDING CREDIT

A critical part of managing receivables is determining who should receive credit and who should not. Many companies increase sales by being generous with their credit policy, but they may end up extending credit to risky customers who do not pay. If the credit policy is too tight, the company will lose sales. If it is too loose, it may sell to "deadbeats" who will pay either very late or not at all.

Certain steps can be taken to help minimize losses as credit standards are relaxed. Risky customers might be required to provide letters of credit or bank guarantees. Then if the customer does not pay, the bank that provided the guarantee will do so. Particularly risky customers might be required to pay cash on delivery. In addition, companies should ask potential customers for references from banks and suppliers to determine their payment history. It is important to check these references on potential new customers and, periodically, to check the financial health of existing customers. Many resources are available for investigating customers. For example, to aid in lending decisions, companies such as Canadian Credit Reporting Limited provide credit opinions on companies around the world.

BUSINESS INSIGHT

MANAGEMENT PERSPECTIVE

Give the man credit. Like most of us, John Galbreath receives piles of unsolicited, "pre-approved" credit card applications in the mail. Galbreath doesn't just toss them out, though. In April 1995 he filled out a credit card application on which he stated he was 97 years old and had no income and no telephone. In a space inviting him to let the credit card company pay off his other credit card balances, Galbreath said he owed money to the Mafia.

Back came a credit card and a letter welcoming John to the fold with a $1,500 credit limit. Galbreath had requested the card under a false name, John C. Reath, an alias under which he had received two other credit cards—earning exemplary credit. John C. Reath might be a bit "long in the tooth," but it seems he paid his bills on time.

Source: Kate Bohner Lewis, "Forbes Informer," *Forbes*, August 14, 1995, 19.

ESTABLISHING A PAYMENT PERIOD

Companies that extend credit should determine a required payment period and communicate that policy to their customers. It is important to make sure that your company's payment period is consistent with that of your competitors. For example, if you decide to require payment within 15 days, but your competitors require payment within 45 days, you may lose sales to your competitors. However, as noted in Chapter 5, you might allow up to 45 days to pay but offer a sales discount for people paying within 15 days to match competitors' terms yet still encourage prompt payment of accounts.

MONITORING COLLECTIONS

An accounts receivable aging schedule should be prepared often—at least monthly. In addition to its use in estimating the allowance for doubtful accounts, the aging schedule has other uses for management. It helps estimate the timing of future cash inflows, which is important information to know before preparing a cash budget. It provides information about the overall collection experience of the company, and it identifies problem accounts.

Problem accounts need to be pursued with phone calls, letters, and occasionally legal action. In the feature story, Maria Cardoso uses the aging schedule to identify problem accounts early for Whitehall-Robins. Late-paying customers are telephoned when they are five days overdue. Subsequently, a letter and a final notice are sent, if required.

Credit risk increases during periods of economic downturns. Credit policies and collection experience must always be monitored not only in comparison to past experience, but also in light of current economic conditions. This is especially important when a company has a significant level of receivables from few customers.

If a company has significant concentrations of credit risk, it is required to discuss this risk in the notes to its financial statements. A concentration of credit risk is a threat of nonpayment from a single customer or class of customers that could adversely affect the company's financial health. An excerpt from the credit risk note from the financial statements of Research In Motion is shown in Illustration 8-9.

Illustration 8-9
Concentration of credit risk

> **RESEARCH IN MOTION LIMITED**
> **Notes to the Financial Statements**
> **March 2, 2002**
>
> **Credit Risk:** The Company, in the normal course of business, monitors the financial condition of its customers and reviews the credit history of each new customer. The Company establishes an allowance for doubtful accounts that corresponds to the specific credit risk of its customers, historical trends, and economic circumstances.
>
> While the Company sells to a variety of customers, two customers comprised 16% and 15% of trade receivables as at March 2, 2002 (2001—one customer comprised 25%). Additionally, two customers comprised 17% and 11% of the Company's sales (2001—one customer comprised 18%).

The note to Research In Motion's financial statements suggests that it has some credit risk concentrated in two customers. It is important for management to monitor the collectibility of receivables from these two customers carefully.

Decision Toolkit

DECISION CHECKPOINTS	INFO NEEDED FOR DECISION	TOOL TO USE FOR DECISION	HOW TO EVALUATE RESULTS
Is the company's credit risk increasing?	Customer account balances and due dates	Accounts receivable aging schedule	Calculate and compare the percentage of receivables overdue in each age classification
Does the company have significant concentrations of credit risk?	Note to the financial statements on concentrations of credit risk	If risky credit customers are identified, the financial health of those customers should be evaluated to gain an independent assessment of the potential for a material credit loss.	If a material loss appears likely, the potential negative impact of that loss on the company should be carefully evaluated, along with the adequacy of the allowance for doubtful accounts.

EVALUATING LIQUIDITY OF RECEIVABLES

Investors and managers keep a watchful eye on the relationship between sales, accounts receivable, and cash collections. If sales increase, then accounts receivable are also expected to increase. But a disproportionate increase in accounts receivable might signal trouble. Perhaps the company increased its sales by loosening its credit policy, and these receivables may be difficult or impossible to collect. Such receivables are considered less liquid. Recall that liquidity is measured by how quickly certain assets can be converted to cash.

The ratio used to assess the liquidity of the receivables is the receivables turnover ratio. This ratio measures the number of times, on average, receivables are collected during the period. The receivables turnover is calculated by dividing net credit sales by the average gross accounts receivable during the year. Unless seasonal factors are significant, **average** accounts receivable can be calculated from the beginning and ending balances of the accounts receivable.[1]

A popular variant of the receivables turnover is to convert it into an average collection period in terms of days. This is done by dividing 365 days by the receivables turnover. The average collection period is frequently used to assess the effectiveness of a company's credit and collection policies. As Terry Norton mentions in the feature story, the general rule is that the average collection period should not greatly exceed the credit term period (i.e., the time allowed for payment).

Receivables turnover ratios can vary significantly by industry. Illustration 8-10 shows common receivables turnover ratios for different industries.

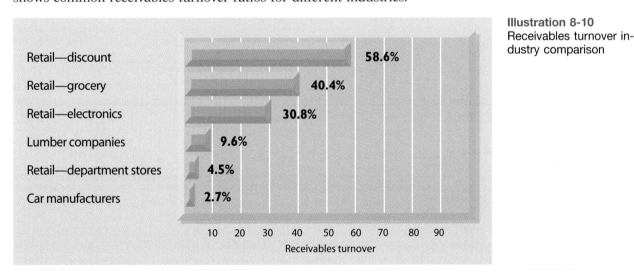

Illustration 8-10
Receivables turnover industry comparison

The following data (in U.S. millions) are available for Wyeth—Whitehall-Robins' parent company. Data are not available for Whitehall-Robins. We have assumed that all sales are credit sales for the purposes of this illustration. This is often done because few companies disclose the proportion of their sales that are credit rather than cash.

	2002	2001	2000
Sales	$14,584.0	$13,983.7	$13,081.3
Accounts receivable (gross)	2,512.2	2,873.8	2,884.4
Allowance for doubtful accounts	132.3	130.7	144.2

The receivables turnover and average collection period for Wyeth are shown in Illustration 8-11, along with comparative industry data.

---

[1]If seasonal factors are significant, the average accounts receivable balance might be determined by using monthly amounts.

Illustration 8-11
Receivables turnover

$$\text{RECEIVABLES TURNOVER} = \frac{\text{NET CREDIT SALES}}{\text{AVERAGE GROSS ACCOUNTS RECEIVABLE}}$$

$$\text{AVERAGE COLLECTION PERIOD} = \frac{\text{365 DAYS}}{\text{RECEIVABLES TURNOVER}}$$

(in U.S. millions)	Ratio	2002	2001
Wyeth	Receivables turnover	$\frac{\$14,584.0}{(\$2,512.2 + \$2,873.8) \div 2} = 5.4$ times	$\frac{\$13,983.7}{(\$2,873.8 + \$2,884.4) \div 2} = 4.9$ times
	Average collection period	$\frac{365}{5.4} = 68$ days	$\frac{365}{4.9} = 74$ days
Industry average	Receivables turnover	6.0 times	6.7 times
	Average collection period	61 days	54 days

Wyeth's receivables turnover was 5.4 times in 2002, with a corresponding average collection period of 68 days. This was an improvement over its 2001 collection period of 74 days. Still, Wyeth's collection experience is worse than the industry average of 61 days. It is interesting that while Wyeth's collection experience is improving, the industry's is deteriorating. Wyeth must continue to work to close this gap between itself and its competitors.

BUSINESS INSIGHT

MANAGEMENT PERSPECTIVE

In some cases, receivables turnover may be misleading. Some companies, especially large retail chains, encourage credit and revolving charge sales. However, they slow collections in order to earn a healthy return on the outstanding receivables in the form of interest at rates of up to 28.8%. This may explain why Sears Canada's receivables turnover is only 7.4 times (an average collection period of 49 days), for example. In general, the faster the turnover, the greater the reliance that can be placed on the current ratio for assessing liquidity.

Decision Toolkit

DECISION CHECKPOINTS	INFO NEEDED FOR DECISION	TOOL TO USE FOR DECISION	HOW TO EVALUATE RESULTS
Are collections being made in a timely fashion?	Net credit sales and average accounts receivable balance	$\text{Receivables turnover} = \dfrac{\text{Net credit sales}}{\text{Average gross receivables}}$ $\text{Average collection period} = \dfrac{\text{365 days}}{\text{Receivables turnover}}$	Average collection period should be consistent with corporate credit policy. An increase may suggest a decline in the financial health of customers.

ACCELERATING CASH RECEIPTS

In the normal course of events, receivable are collected in cash and removed from the books. However, as credit sales and receivables have grown in size and significance, the "normal course of events" has changed. Two common expressions apply to the collection of receivables: (1) Time is money—that is, waiting for the normal collection process costs money. (2) A bird in the hand is worth two in the bush—that is, getting the cash now is better than getting it later. Two typical ways to accelerate the receipt of cash from receivables are using the receivables to secure a loan and selling receivables.

STUDY OBJECTIVE

8

Describe the methods used to accelerate the receipt of cash from receivables.

Loans Secured by Receivables

One of the most common ways to speed up cash flow from receivables is to go to a bank and borrow money using receivables as collateral. While this does have a cost (interest has to be paid to the bank on the loan), the cash can be used sooner, and the loan can be repaid as the receivables are collected. Generally, banks are willing to provide financing for up to 75% of receivables that are less than 90 days old. Quite often, these arrangements occur through an **operating line of credit** (discussed in a later chapter).

Sale of Receivables

Companies also frequently sell their receivables to another company for cash, thereby shortening the cash-to-cash operating cycle.

There are three reasons for the sale of receivables. The first is their size. For competitive reasons, **sellers (retailers, wholesalers, and manufacturers) often provide financing to purchasers of their goods.** For example, many major companies in the automobile, truck, equipment, computer, and appliance industries have created companies that accept responsibility for accounts receivable financing. Ford has Ford Credit Canada, Sears has Sears Acceptance Company Inc., and Bombardier has Bombardier Capital. These companies are referred to as captive finance companies because they are wholly owned by the company selling the product. The purpose of captive finance companies is to encourage the sale of the product by assuring financing to buyers without the parent companies involved having to hold large amounts of receivables.

Second, **receivables may be sold because they may be the only reasonable source of cash.** When credit is tight, companies may not be able to borrow money in the usual credit markets. Even if credit is available, the cost of borrowing may be prohibitive.

A final reason for selling receivables is that **billing and collection are often time-consuming and costly.** As a result, it is often easier for a retailer to sell the receivable to another party that has expertise in billing and collection matters. Credit card companies such as MasterCard, VISA, American Express, and Diners Club specialize in billing and collecting accounts receivable.

Sale of Receivables to a Factor. A common way to accelerate receivables collection is by sale to a factor. A factor is a finance company or bank that buys receivables from businesses for a fee. If the customer does not pay, normally the company is responsible for reimbursing the factor for the uncollected amounts. This is known as selling receivables on a **recourse** basis.

Companies such as Sears Canada regularly sell their accounts receivable to speed up collection. For the year ended December 31, 2002, Sears sold more than half of its receivables.

Factoring arrangements vary widely, but typically the factor will advance up to 90% of the net realizable value of approved invoices, less the factor's fee. Fees are negotiable and can range from 16% to 36% of the amount of receivables purchased.

TCE
CAPITAL CORPORATION

BUSINESS INSIGHT

MANAGEMENT PERSPECTIVE

TCE Capital is one of a growing number of companies that help companies with their cash crunch by purchasing outstanding receivables at a discount. They don't call themselves factors; they prefer to be called invoice discounters and transaction financiers. "It seems that almost everyone takes at least 30 days to pay, and many companies are edging up through 60 days to 90 days," says Jim Shoniker, TCE's vice-president of business development. "By discounting invoices, businesses get the money today, when it's needed. That makes it possible for them to take on orders or projects they simply couldn't have done otherwise because of a lack of financing." TCE will finance transactions of up to $1,500,000. It advances up to 90% of the face value of an invoice. The remaining balance (known as a holdback) is returned, net of TCE fees, once the invoice has been paid. TCE fees work out to 3% for 30 days, or about 36% per year.

Source: Terrence Belford, "Sell Your Invoices," *CAmagazine*, May 1999, 25.

Credit Card Sales. Nearly 50 million VISA and MasterCard credit cards were estimated to be in use in Canada recently. Still more credit cards are issued by large department stores, gasoline companies, and other issuers such as American Express and Diners Club/enRoute. Three parties are involved when credit cards are used in making retail sales: (1) the credit card issuer, who is independent of the retailer, (2) the retailer, and (3) the customer. A retailer's acceptance of a national credit card is another form of selling (factoring) the receivable by the retailer.

The use of credit cards translates to more sales and zero bad debts for the retailer. Both are powerful reasons for a retailer to accept such cards. The major advantages of national credit cards to the retailer are shown in Illustration 8-12. In exchange for these advantages, the retailer pays the credit card issuer a fee of 1% to 3% of the invoice price for its services.

Illustration 8-12
Advantages of credit
cards to the retailer

Ethics Note
On-line credit card fraud occurs
three times as often as regular
credit card fraud. VISA recently
instituted new security rules for
transactions over the Internet
to combat on-line fraud and
boost consumer confidence in
electronic commerce.

Sales resulting from the use of **bank cards**, such as VISA and MasterCard, are considered cash sales by the retailer. As soon as the credit card is electronically swiped, or when it receives credit card sales slips from a retailer, the bank that issued the card adds the amount to the seller's bank balance. These credit card sales slips are therefore recorded in the same manner as cheques deposited from a cash sale.

To illustrate, assume that MuchMusic Corp. sells $100 of CDs to Anita Ferreri on January 19. Anita pays for this purchase with her Royal Bank VISA card. The service fee that Royal Bank charges MuchMusic is 3%. The entry by MuchMusic to record this transaction is:

Jan. 19	Cash	97	
	Service Charge Expense	3	
	Sales		100
	(To record VISA credit card sales)		

```
A    =    L    +    SE
+97                     -3
                      +100
```
Cash flows: +97

Nonbank cards, such as American Express, Diners Club/enRoute, and Petro-Canada, are reported as credit sales, not cash sales. Conversion into cash does not occur until the financing company remits the net amount to the seller.

BUSINESS INSIGHT
MANAGEMENT PERSPECTIVE

The average interest rate on a bank credit card in Canada is 18%. Nonbank cards, such as The Bay, can be as high as 21%. The Bank of Canada interest rate is 2%. Why are credit card rates so much higher than other interest rates?

The Bank of Canada interest rate is called the "risk-free" rate. This means that, theoretically, money can be borrowed at 2% if there is no other credit risk. The difference between the Bank of Canada rate and credit card rates is called a "risk premium." Banks justify this higher interest rate by saying that credit cards pose a greater risk. They argue that they have to cover their losses from fraud as well as their administrative costs. Given the amount of risk premium, the annual fee many consumers have to pay for their credit cards, and the service fee that banks charge retailers, banks appear to be well compensated for this risk.

Debit Card Sales. Canadians are the world's second most frequent users of debit cards, with only the inhabitants of the Netherlands using them more often. What's the difference between a debit card and a credit card? Debit cards allow customers to spend only what is in their bank account. Credit cards give a customer access to money made available by a bank or other financial institution, just like a loan. Credit cards are issued with the understanding that the amount charged will be repaid, with interest, if the account is not paid in full each month.

When a debit card sale is transacted, the bank immediately deducts the cost of the purchase from the customer's bank account. This amount is electronically transferred into the retailer's bank account, less a service fee. The entries to record a debit card sale are identical to those illustrated earlier for bank credit card sales.

BEFORE YOU GO ON . . .

● **REVIEW IT**

1. What is meant by a concentration of credit risk?
2. What do the receivables turnover and the average collection period reveal?
3. Why do companies accelerate cash receipts from receivables?
4. What's the difference between a credit card sale and a debit card sale, if any?

● **DO IT**

Joy Corporation is in its third year of operations, selling the "World's Best Doormat." The corporation is selling doormats faster than it can make them. Indeed, it has been selling the product on credit, telling customers to "pay when they can." Oddly, even though sales are tremendous, Joy is having trouble paying its bills. What might Joy Corporation do to lessen its cash shortage?

Action Plan

- Review options available to manage receivables.
- Compare cost of each option.

Solution

Joy Corporation needs to improve its collection of accounts receivable. Some options the company may wish to consider include:

- setting credit terms (e.g., n/30) and charging interest on overdue accounts
- offering sales discounts to encourage early payment
- using credit cards (compare benefits to cost)
- selling its receivables (compare benefits to cost)

Using the Decision Toolkit

French-based Aventis is one of Wyeth's top competitors. Selected financial information taken from Aventis' December 31, 2002, financial statements follows:

AVENTIS Selected Financial Information December 31, 2002 (in € millions)		
	2002	2001
Sales	€20,622	€22,941
Accounts and notes receivable	2,680	3,861
Allowance for doubtful accounts	136	339
Total current assets	9,646	12,785
Total current liabilities	10,478	13,939

Instructions

Comment on Aventis' accounts receivable management and liquidity relative to that of Wyeth for 2002, by considerating the current ratio, receivables turnover, and average collection period. Wyeth's current ratio was 2.1:1; the industry average, 1.4:1. Wyeth's receivables turnover and average collection period were calculated earlier in the chapter.

Solution

Current Ratio

Aventis	Wyeth	Industry
$\dfrac{€9,646}{€10,478} = 0.9:1$	2.1:1	1.4:1

Aventis' current ratio is significantly lower than that of Wyeth and the industry. However, a high current ratio does not always mean that a company has more liquidity. Wyeth's current ratio could be artificially high because of uncollectible receivables or slow-moving inventory. So, further investigation is warranted before we can fully compare Aventis' and Wyeth's liquidity.

Receivables Turnover and Average Collection Period

	Aventis	Wyeth	Industry
Receivables turnover	$\dfrac{€20,622}{(€2,680 + €3,861) \div 2} = 6.3$ times	5.4 times	6.0 times
Average collection period	$\dfrac{365 \text{ days}}{6.3} = 58$ days	68 days	61 days

Despite Aventis' current ratio being lower than that of Wyeth and the industry, it is collecting its receivables faster than both. Therefore, it is not uncollectible receivables that is influencing Aventis' lower current ratio. We would have to investigate Aventis' and Wyeth's inventory turnover ratios to determine whether Wyeth's current ratio is artificially high because of slow-moving inventory.

NAVIGATOR

Summary of Study Objectives

❶ *Identify the different types of receivables.* Receivables are frequently classified as accounts, notes, and nontrade or other. Accounts receivable are amounts owed by customers on account. Notes receivable are claims that are supported by formal instruments of credit. Nontrade receivables include other receivables such as interest receivable, loans to company officers, advances to employees, and recoverable sales and income taxes.

❷ *Explain how accounts receivable are recognized in the accounts.* Accounts receivable are recorded at invoice price. They are reduced by sales returns and allowances. Cash discounts reduce the amount received on accounts receivable.

❸ *Describe the method used to account for bad debts.* The allowance method, using a percentage of receivables, is used to match anticipated credit losses against sales, in the period in which the sales occurred. This method emphasizes the net realizable value of the accounts receivable. An aging schedule is used to estimate uncollectible accounts.

❹ *Explain how notes receivable are recognized and valued in the accounts.* Notes receivable are recorded at their face value. Interest is earned from the date the note is issued until it matures. Like accounts receivable, notes receivable are reported at their net realizable value. The calculation and estimations involved in recording the proper amount of bad debt expense and related allowance are similar to those required for accounts receivable.

Notes can be held to maturity, at which time the face value plus any unpaid interest is due and the note is removed from the accounts. In some situations, the maker of the note dishonours the note (defaults). If the amount is not expected to be repaid, the note is written off.

❺ *Explain the statement presentation of receivables.* Each major type of receivable should be identified in the balance sheet or in the notes to the financial statements. Short-term receivables are current assets. The gross amount of receivables and allowance for doubtful accounts should be reported. Bad debts and service charge expenses are reported in the statement of earnings as operating expenses, and interest revenue is shown as other revenues in the non-operating section of the statement.

❻ *Describe the principles of sound accounts receivable management.* To properly manage receivables, management must (a) determine who to extend credit to, (b) establish a payment period, (c) monitor collections, (d) evaluate the liquidity of receivables, and (e) accelerate cash receipts from receivables when necessary.

❼ *Identify the ratios used to analyse a company's receivables.* The receivables turnover ratio and the average collection period are both useful for analysing management's effectiveness in managing receivables. The accounts receivable aging schedule also provides useful information.

❽ *Describe the methods used to accelerate the receipt of cash from receivables.* If the company needs additional cash resources, management can accelerate the collection of cash from receivables by borrowing money from a bank, using the receivables as collateral for the loan, or by selling its receivables.

Decision
Toolkit
Summary

Decision Toolkit—A Summary

DECISION CHECKPOINTS	INFO NEEDED FOR DECISION	TOOL TO USE FOR DECISION	HOW TO EVALUATE RESULTS
Is the amount of past-due accounts increasing? Which accounts require management's attention?	List of outstanding receivables and their due dates	Prepare an aging schedule showing the receivables in various stages: outstanding 0–30 days, 31–60 days, 61–90 days, 91–120 days, and over 120 days.	Accounts in the older categories require follow-up: letters, phone calls, e-mails, and possible renegotiations of terms.
Is the company's credit risk increasing?	Customer account balances and due dates	Accounts receivable aging schedule	Calculate and compare the percentage of receivables overdue in each classification.
Does the company have significant concentrations of credit risk?	Note to the financial statements on concentrations of credit risk	If risky credit customers are identified, the financial health of those customers should be evaluated to gain an independent assessment of the potential for a material credit loss.	If a material loss appears likely, the potential negative impact of that loss on the company should be carefully evaluated, along with the adequacy of the allowance for doubtful accounts.
Are collections being made in a timely fashion?	Net credit sales and average accounts receivable balance	$$\text{Receivables turnover} = \frac{\text{Net credit sales}}{\text{Average gross receivables}}$$ $$\text{Average collection period} = \frac{365 \text{ days}}{\text{Receivables turnover}}$$	Average collection period should be consistent with corporate credit policy. An increase may suggest a decline in the financial health of customers.

NAVIGATOR

Glossary

Glossary

Accounts receivable   Amounts owed by customers on account. (p. 356)

Aging the accounts receivable   The analysis of customer balances by the length of time they have been unpaid. (p. 359)

Allowance method   A method of accounting for bad debts that involves estimating uncollectible accounts at the end of each period. (p. 358)

Average collection period   The average amount of time that a receivable is outstanding. It is calculated by dividing 365 days by the receivables turnover. (p. 371)

Concentration of credit risk   The threat of nonpayment from a single customer or class of customers that could adversely affect the financial health of the company. (p. 370)

Dishonoured note   A note that is not paid in full at maturity. (p. 366)

Factor   A finance company or bank that buys receivables from businesses for a fee. (p. 374)

Maker   The party to a promissory note who is making the promise to pay. (p. 364)

Net realizable value   The net amount expected to be received in cash. (p. 358)

Notes receivable   Claims for which formal instruments of credit are issued as evidence of the debt. (p. 356)

Payee   The party who receives payment under a promissory note. (p. 364)

Percentage of receivables basis   A percentage relationship established by management between the amount of receivables and the expected losses from uncollectible accounts. (p. 359)

Promissory note A written promise to pay a specified amount of money on demand or at a definite time. (p. 364)

Receivables Amounts due from individuals and companies that are expected to be collected in cash. (p. 356)

Receivables turnover A measure of the liquidity of re-

ceivables, calculated by dividing net credit sales by average gross accounts receivable. (p. 371)

Trade receivables Notes and accounts receivable that result from sales transactions. (p. 356)

Demonstration Problem

Additional
Demonstration
Problems

Presented here are selected transactions related to O'Reilly Corp.:

Mar. 1 Sold $20,000 of merchandise to Potter Company, terms 2/10, n/30.
11 Received payment in full from Potter Company for balance due.
12 Accepted Juno Company's $20,000 four-month 6% note for balance due. Interest is payable at maturity.
13 Made O'Reilly Corp. credit card sales for $13,200.
15 Made VISA credit sales totalling $6,700. A 3% service fee is charged by VISA.

Apr. 13 Received collections of $8,200 on O'Reilly Corp. credit card sales and added interest charges of 1.5% to the remaining balances.

May 10 Wrote off as uncollectible $16,000 of accounts receivable.

June 30 The balance in accounts receivable at the end of the first six months is $200,000. Using an aging schedule, estimated uncollectible accounts are determined to be $20,000. At June 30, the credit balance in the allowance account prior to adjustment is $3,500.

July 12 Collected Juno Company note (see March 12 transaction).
16 One of the accounts receivable written off in May paid the amount due, $4,000, in full.

Instructions

Prepare the journal entries for the transactions.

Action Plan

- Record accounts receivable at invoice price.
- Recognize that sales returns and allowances and cash discounts reduce the amount received on accounts receivable.
- Record a service charge expense when credit cards are used.
- Calculate interest by multiplying the interest rate by the face value, adjusting for the portion of the year that has passed.
- Consider any existing balance in the allowance account when making the adjustment for uncollectible accounts.
- Record write-offs of accounts receivable only in balance sheet accounts.

Solution to Demonstration Problem

Mar. 1	Accounts Receivable—Potter Company	20,000	
	Sales		20,000
	(To record sales on account)		
11	Cash	19,600	
	Sales Discounts (2% × $20,000)	400	
	Accounts Receivable—Potter Company		20,000
	(To record collection of accounts receivable)		
12	Notes Receivable—Juno Company	20,000	
	Accounts Receivable—Juno Company		20,000
	(To record acceptance of Juno Company note)		
13	Accounts Receivable	13,200	
	Sales		13,200
	(To record company credit card sales)		
15	Cash	6,499	
	Service Charge Expense (3% × $6,700)	201	
	Sales		6,700
	(To record credit card sales)		

Apr. 13	Cash	8,200	
	Accounts Receivable		8,200
	(To record collection of accounts receivable)		
	Accounts Receivable [($13,200 − $8,200) × 1.5%]	75	
	Interest Revenue		75
	(To record interest charges on overdue receivables)		
May 10	Allowance for Doubtful Accounts	16,000	
	Accounts Receivable		16,000
	(To record write-off of accounts receivable)		
June 30	Bad Debts Expense ($20,000 − $3,500)	16,500	
	Allowance for Doubtful Accounts		16,500
	(To record estimate of uncollectible accounts)		
July 12	Cash	20,400	
	Notes Receivable—Juno Company		20,000
	Interest Revenue ($20,000 × 6% × $\frac{4}{12}$)		400
	(To record collection of Juno note receivable)		
16	Accounts Receivable	4,000	
	Allowance for Doubtful Accounts		4,000
	(To reverse write-off of accounts receivable)		
	Cash	4,000	
	Accounts Receivable		4,000
	(To record collection of accounts receivable)		

Self-Study Questions

Multiple
Choice
Quiz

Answers are at the end of the chapter.

(SO 2) 1. On June 15, Jones Ltd. sells merchandise on account to Bullock Co. for $1,000, terms 2/10, n/30. On June 20, Bullock returns merchandise worth $300 to Jones. On June 24, payment is received from Bullock for the balance due. What is the amount of cash received?
(a) $680   (c) $700
(b) $686   (d) $1,000

(SO 3) 2. Sanderson Corporation has a *credit* balance of $5,000 in its Allowance for Doubtful Accounts before any adjustments are made. Based on an aging of its accounts receivable at the end of the period, the company estimates that $60,000 of its receivables are uncollectible. The amount of bad debts expense which should be reported for this accounting period is:
(a) $5,000.   (c) $60,000.
(b) $55,000.   (d) $65,000.

(SO 3) 3. Sanderson Corporation has a *debit* balance of $5,000 in its Allowance for Doubtful Accounts before any adjustments are made. Based on an aging of its ac-

counts receivable at the end of the period, the company estimates that $60,000 of its receivables are uncollectible. The amount of bad debts expense which should be reported for this accounting period is:
(a) $5,000.   (c) $60,000.
(b) $55,000.   (d) $65,000.

4. In 2004 Lawrence Inc. had net credit sales of   (SO 3)
$750,000. On January 1, 2004, Allowance for Doubtful Accounts had a credit balance of $18,000. During 2004, $30,000 of uncollectible accounts receivable were written off. Aging indicates that uncollectible accounts are $20,000. What is the required adjustment to Allowance for Doubtful Accounts at December 31, 2004?
(a) $2,000   (c) $20,000
(b) $8,000   (d) $32,000

5. Sorenson Corp. accepts a $1,000 three-month 7%   (SO 4)
promissory note in settlement of Parton Co. account. The entry to record this transaction on Sorenson's books is:
(a) Notes Receivable   1,017
         Accounts Receivable   1,017

(b) Notes Receivable

Accounts Receivable	1,000	1,000

(c) Notes Receivable

Sales	1,000	1,000

(d) Accounts Payable

Notes Payable	1,000	1,000

(SO 4) 6. Schlicht Corp. holds Osgrove Inc.'s $10,000, four-month, 9% note. The entry made by Schlicht Corp. when the note is collected, assuming no interest has previously been recorded, is:

(a) Cash

Notes Receivable	10,300	10,300

(b) Cash

Notes Receivable	10,000	10,000

(c) Accounts Receivable

Notes Receivable	10,300	10,000
Interest Revenue		300

(d) Cash

Notes Receivable	10,300	10,000
Interest Revenue		300

(SO 5) 7. Accounts and notes receivable are reported in the asset section of the balance sheet at:
(a) net realizable value.
(b) invoice cost.
(c) lower of cost and market value.
(d) net book value.

8. The principles of sound accounts receiv- (SO 6)
able management do not include:
(a) instituting a "cash only" policy.
(b) establishing a payment period.
(c) monitoring collections.
(d) evaluating the liquidity of receivables.

9. Moore Corporation had net credit sales dur- (SO 7)
ing the year of $800,000 and cost of goods sold of $500,000. The balance in accounts receivable at the beginning of the year was $100,000 and at the end of the year it was $150,000. What was the receivables turnover?
(a) 4.0   (b) 5.3   (c) 6.4   (d) 8.0

10. Hoffman Corporation sells its goods on terms (SO 7)
of 2/10, n/30. It has a receivables turnover ratio of 7. What is its average collection period (in days)?
(a) 30   (b) 52   (c) 210   (d) 2,555

11. Morgan Retailers accepted a Bank One VISA credit (SO 8)
card for $5,000 of merchandise sold on July 1. Bank One charges 3% for use of its credit card. The entry to record this transaction by Morgan Retailers will include a credit to Sales of $5,000 and a debit(s) to:
(a) Cash of $4,850 and Service Charge Expense of $150.
(b) Accounts Receivable of $4,850 and Service Charge Expense of $150.
(c) Cash of $5,000.
(d) Accounts Receivable of $5,000.

Questions

(SO 1) 1. What is the difference between an account receivable and a note receivable?

(SO 1) 2. What are some common types of receivables other than accounts receivable or notes receivable?

(SO 2) 3. On December 29, you sell $10,000 of merchandise to a company, with terms of sale 1/10, n/30. The company, a frequent customer, always takes the discount. However, you won't know for sure in this instance until January 8. Should you record the receivable and sale at $10,000, or at $9,900 ($10,000 – $100 discount), on December 29?

(SO 3) 4. What is the purpose of the account Allowance for Doubtful Accounts? Although the normal balance of this account is a credit balance, it sometimes has a debit balance. Explain how this can happen.

(SO 3) 5. Soo Eng cannot understand why the net realizable value does not decrease when an uncollectible account is written off under the allowance method. Clarify this point for Soo Eng.

(SO 3) 6. Should a company's attempts to collect a specific account receivable stop when it writes off the account as uncollectible? Explain why or why not.

7. When an account receivable that was previously (SO 3)
written off is subsequently collected, two journal entries are usually made. Explain why.

8. Danielle doesn't understand why a note receivable (SO 4)
isn't immediately recorded at its maturity value (face plus interest), rather than its face value. After all, you know you are going to collect both the face value and the interest and you know how much each will be. Explain to Danielle why notes are not recorded at their maturity value.

9. If a $30,000 ten-month note is issued on May 1 (SO 4)
with a 5% interest rate payable at maturity, how much interest will the note earn in total? If financial statements are prepared at the company's year end, December 31, how much interest will be recorded for the year ended December 31?

10. May Ltd. dishonours a note at maturity. Assum- (SO 4)
ing eventual payment is intended, what entries should the payee and the maker (May Ltd.) of the note make on their respective books?

(SO 5) 11. Saucier Ltd. has accounts receivable, notes receivable, and an allowance for doubtful accounts. How should the receivables be reported on the balance sheet?

(SO 6) 12. ⚒ What are the steps in having good receivables management?

(SO 6) 13. ⚒ What is meant by a concentration of credit risk?

(SO 7) 14. ⚒ Does an increase in the receivables turnover indicate a faster or slower collection of receivables? What does an increase in the collection period indicate?

(SO 7) 15. ⚒ Clearly Canadian Beverage Corporation's receivables turnover ratio was 11.6 times in 2002. If average accounts receivable were $1,762.5 million, what was the amount of sales for the period?

16. ⚒ The president of Ho Inc. proudly announces (SO 7) her company's improved liquidity since its current ratio had increased substantially. Does an increase in the current ratio always indicate improved liquidity? What other ratio or ratios might you review to determine whether or not the increase in the current ratio indicates an improvement in financial health?

17. ⚒ During the year ended January 31, 2002, (SO 8) Bombardier Inc. sold $3,860 million of receivables. Why might a company such as Bombardier sell its receivables?

18. ⚒ Sears accepts its own credit card, bank (SO 8) credit cards, and debit cards. What are the advantages of accepting each type of card? Explain how the accounting for sales differs for each type.

Brief Exercises

BE8-1 Presented below are four receivables transactions. Indicate whether these receivables are reported as accounts receivable, notes receivable, or nontrade receivables on a balance sheet.

Identify types of receivables.
(SO 1)

(a) Advanced $10,000 to an employee.
(b) Received a promissory note of $5,000 for services performed.
(c) Sold merchandise on account to a customer for $60,000.
(d) Estimated $5,000 of income tax to be refunded.

BE8-2 Record the following transactions on the books of Essex Corp., which uses a perpetual inventory system:

Record receivables transactions.
(SO 2)

(a) On July 1, Essex Corp. sold merchandise on account to Cambridge Inc. for $14,000, terms 2/10, n/30. The cost of the merchandise sold was $10,000.
(b) On July 8, Cambridge Inc. returned merchandise worth $2,400 to Essex Corp. Its original cost was $1,440. The merchandise was restored to inventory.
(c) On July 10, Cambridge Inc. paid for the merchandise.

BE8-3 Using an aging schedule, Massey Corp. estimates that $7,500 of total accounts receivable will become uncollectible. Accounts receivable are $500,000 at the end of the year, and Allowance for Doubtful Accounts has a credit balance of $3,000.

Prepare bad debts entry.
(SO 3)

(a) Prepare the adjusting journal entry to record bad debts expense for the year.
(b) If Allowance for Doubtful Accounts had a debit balance of $800 instead of a credit balance of $3,000, determine the amount to be reported for bad debts expense.

BE8-4 At the end of 2004, Searcy Corp. has accounts receivable of $700,000 and an allowance for doubtful accounts of $54,000. On January 24, 2005, it is learned that the company's $18,000 receivable from Hutley Inc. is not collectible. Management authorizes a write-off.

Prepare entry for write-off, and compare net realizable value.
(SO 3)

(a) Prepare the journal entry to record the write-off.
(b) What is the net realizable value of the accounts receivable (1) before the write-off and (2) after the write-off?

BE8-5 Assume the same information as in BE8-4. On March 4, 2005, Searcy Corp. receives payment of $18,000 in full from Hutley Inc., after the write-off. Prepare the journal entries to record this transaction.

Prepare entries for collection of bad debt written off.
(SO 3)

Calculate interest on note.
(SO 4)

BE8-6   Presented below are three promissory notes. Determine the missing amounts.

Date of Note	Term	Principal	Annual Interest Rate	Total Interest
Apr. 1	2 months	$90,000	10%	(b)
July 2	1 month	60,000	(a)	$400
Mar. 7	6 months	56,000	6%	(c)

Record receivables transactions.
(SO 4)

BE8-7   On January 10, 2004, Raja Corp. sold merchandise on account to R. Opal for $12,000, terms n/30, costing $8,000. On February 9, R. Opal gave Raja Corp. a 7% promissory note in settlement of this account. Prepare the journal entry to record the sale and the settlement of the accounts receivable on Raja's books. Raja uses a perpetual inventory system.

Record notes receivable transactions.
(SO 4)

BE8-8   Lee Corporation accepts a $10,000, 7%, three-month note receivable in settlement of an account receivable on April 1, 2004.

(a) Prepare the journal entries required to record the issue of the note on April 1, and the settlement of the note on July 1, assuming the note is honoured. No interest has previously been accrued.
(b) Repeat part (a) assuming that the note is dishonoured, but eventual collection is expected.

Prepare bad debts entry and balance sheet presentation, and calculate ratios.
(SO 3, 5, 7)

BE8-9   During its first year of operations, Kwon Ltd. had credit sales of $3,000,000, of which $600,000 remained uncollected at year end. The credit manager estimates that $35,000 of these receivables will become uncollectible.

(a) Prepare the journal entry to record the estimated uncollectibles.
(b) Prepare the current assets section of the balance sheet for Kwon Ltd., assuming that in addition to the receivables it has cash of $90,000, merchandise inventory of $130,000, and prepaid expenses of $13,000.
(c) Calculate the receivables turnover and average collection period.

Identify principles of receivables management.
(SO 6)

BE8-10   The following is a list of activities that companies perform in relation to their receivables:

1. Accept bank credit cards.
2. Review company credit ratings.
3. Collect information about competitors' payment period policies.
4. Prepare the accounts receivable aging schedule.
5. Calculate the receivables turnover and average collection period.

Instructions

Match each of the activities listed above with a purpose listed below:
(a) Determine who to extend credit to.
(b) Establish a payment period.
(c) Monitor collections.
(d) Evaluate the receivables balance.
(e) Accelerate cash receipts from receivables when necessary.

Calculate ratios.
(SO 7)

BE8-11   The financial statements of Maple Leaf Foods Inc. report net sales of $5,075.9 million for the year ended December 31, 2002. Accounts receivable were $248.1 million at the beginning of the year, and $243.1 million at the end of the year. Calculate Maple Leaf's receivables turnover and average collection period.

Prepare entries for credit and debit card sales.
(SO 8)

BE8-12   St. Pierre Restaurant accepted a VISA card in payment of a $100 lunch bill. The bank charges a 3% fee. What entry should St. Pierre make to record the sale? How would this entry differ if a nonbank card had been used in payment of the bill? A debit card? Assume that a 3% service charge is processed for each type of card.

Exercises

Record receivables and payables transactions.
(SO 2)

E8-1   On January 6, Nicklaus Corp. sells merchandise on account to Watson Inc. for $6,000, terms 2/10, n/30. The merchandise originally cost Nicklaus $3,600. On January 16, Watson pays the amount due. Both Nicklaus and Watson use a perpetual inventory system.

Instructions

(a) Prepare the entries on Nicklaus Corp.'s books to record the sale and related collection.

(b) Prepare the entries on Watson Inc.'s books to record the purchase and related payment.

E8-2   At the end of the current year, the ledger of Patillo Inc. shows Accounts Receivable $80,000; Sales $940,000; and Sales Returns and Allowances $40,000.

Record bad debts expense.
(SO 3)

Instructions

(a) If Allowance for Doubtful Accounts has a credit balance of $800 in the trial balance, journalize the adjusting entry at December 31, assuming uncollectible accounts are expected to be $9,000.

(b) If Allowance for Doubtful Accounts has a debit balance of $500 in the trial balance, journalize the adjusting entry at December 31, assuming uncollectible accounts are expected to be $7,000.

E8-3   Grevina Ltd. has accounts receivable of $92,500 at March 31, 2004. An analysis of the accounts shows these amounts:

Determine bad debts expense, prepare entry, and discuss implications.
(SO 3)

Month of Sale	Balance, March 31	
	2004	2003
March	$65,000	$75,000
February	12,600	8,000
January	8,500	2,400
October—December	6,400	1,100
	$92,500	$86,500

Credit terms are 2/10, n/30. At March 31, 2004, there is a $2,200 credit balance in Allowance for Doubtful Accounts prior to adjustment. The company uses an aging schedule for estimating uncollectible accounts. The company's estimates of uncollectible accounts are as follows:

Age of Accounts in Days	Estimated Percentage Uncollectible
0–30	2%
31–60	7%
61–90	30%
Over 90	50%

Instructions

(a) Prepare an aging schedule to determine the total estimated uncollectibles at March 31, 2004.

(b) Prepare the adjusting entry at March 31, 2004, to record bad debts expense.

(c) Discuss the implications of the changes in the age of receivables from 2003 to 2004.

E8-4   On December 31, 2004, when its Allowance for Doubtful Accounts had a debit balance of $1,000, Ceja Corp. estimated that $8,400 of its accounts receivable would become uncollectible and recorded the necessary adjustment. On May 11, 2005, Ceja determined that Robert Worthy's account was uncollectible and wrote off $900. On June 12, 2005, Worthy paid the amount previously written off.

Prepare entries for bad debts, write-off, and recovery.
(SO 3)

Instructions

Prepare the journal entries on December 31, 2004, May 11, 2005, and June 12, 2005.

E8-5   Passara Supply Corp. has the following transactions related to notes receivable during the last two months of the year:

Journalize notes receivable transactions.
(SO 4)

Nov. 1 Loaned $24,000 cash to A. Bouchard on a one-year, 8% note.

Dec. 1 Sold goods to Wright, Inc., receiving a $3,600, three-month, 6% note. These goods cost $2,500. Passara uses a perpetual inventory system to record sales of merchandise.

     15 Received an $8,000, six-month, 7% note on account from B. Barnes.

     31 Accrued interest revenue on all notes receivable.

Instructions

Journalize the transactions for Passara Supply Corp.

Journalize notes receivable transactions.
(SO 4)

E8-6 The following note-related transactions took place for Rather Corp.:

May 1 Received a $6,000, six-month, 5% note on account from Jioux Company. Interest is due at maturity.
June 30 Accrued interest on the Jioux note on this date, which is Rather's year end.
July 31 Lent $10,000 cash to an employee, issuing a three-month, 7% note. Interest is due at maturity
Oct. 31 Received payment in full for employee note.
Nov. 1 Wrote off Jioux note as Jioux defaulted. Future payment is not expected.

Instructions

Journalize the transactions for Rather Corp.

Prepare balance sheet presentation of receivables.
(SO 5)

E8-7 Deere and Company had the following balances in receivable accounts at October 31, 2002 (in U.S. millions): Allowance for Doubtful Accounts, $45; Trade Accounts and Notes Receivable, $2,779; Other Receivables, $426.4; and Financing Receivables, $9,068 (net of $136 Allowance for Doubtful Financing Receivables).

Instructions

Prepare the balance sheet presentation of Deere and Company's receivables in proper format as at October 31, 2002.

Discuss concentration of credit risk.
(SO 6)

E8-8 Bombardier Inc. reported the following in the notes to its January 31, 2003, financial statements:

[Bombardier's] receivables were concentrated in the transportation and aerospace segments, 77% and 19%, respectively, as at January 31, 2003 (86% and 9%, respectively, as at January 31, 2002). They were mainly located in Europe and North America, 56% and 34%, respectively, as at January 31, 2003 (72% and 19%, respectively, as at January 31, 2002).

Instructions

Does Bombardier have an industry or geographic concentration of credit risk that would concern users of its financial statements?

Calculate ratios.
(SO 7)

E8-9 The following information was taken from the December 31 financial statements of the Canadian National Railway Company:

(in millions)	2002	2001	2000
Accounts receivable, gross	$ 781	$ 726	$ 800
Allowance for doubtful accounts	59	81	63
Accounts receivable, net	722	645	737
Revenues	6,110	5,652	5,446
Total current assets	1,163	1,164	1,125
Total current liabilities	2,134	1,638	1,915

Instructions

(a) Calculate the 2002 and 2001 current ratios.
(b) Calculate the receivables turnover and average collection period for each of 2002 and 2001.
(c) Are accounts receivable a material component of the company's current assets?
(d) Comment upon any improvement or deterioration in CN's management of its receivables.

Indicate effect of transactions on receivables turnover.
(SO 7)

E8-10 Indicate whether the following transactions would increase (+), decrease (−), or have no effect (NE) on Bakbone Ltd.'s receivables turnover ratio of 8 times.

(a) _____ Recorded sales on account.
(b) _____ Collected amounts owing from customers.
(c) _____ Recorded bad debts expense for the year.
(d) _____ Wrote off an account from a customer as uncollectible.

Journalize credit and debit card sales and indicate statement presentation.
(SO 5, 8)

E8–11 Kasko Stores accepts both its own and bank credit cards, in addition to debit cards. During the year, the following selected summary transactions occurred:

Jan. 15 Made Kasko credit card sales totalling $15,000.
20 Made VISA credit card sales (service charge fee, 2%) totalling $4,500.
30 Made debit card sales (service charge fee, 3%) totalling $1,000.

Feb. 10 Collected $12,000 on Kasko credit card sales.
      15 Added interest charges of 18% to Kasko credit card balances.

Instructions

(a) Journalize the transactions for Kasko Stores.
(b) Indicate the statement presentation of the interest charges and the service charge expense for Kasko Stores.

E8-12   In the notes to its financial statements, the Canadian National Railway Company states that it has a five-year revolving agreement to sell eligible freight trade receivables up to a maximum of $350 million of receivables outstanding at any point in time.

Identify reason for sale of receivables.
(SO 8)

Instructions

Explain why CN, a financially stable company with positive cash flow, might wish to sell its receivables.

Problems: Set A

P8-1A   At the beginning of the current period, Huang Corp. had balances in Accounts Receivable of $200,000 and in Allowance for Doubtful Accounts of $9,000 (credit). During the period, it had net credit sales of $800,000 and collections of $743,000. It wrote off as uncollectible accounts receivable of $7,000. However, a $4,000 account written off as uncollectible was recovered before the end of the current period. Uncollectible accounts are estimated to total $25,000 at the end of the period.

Journalize receivables transactions.
(SO 2, 3)

Instructions

(a) Prepare the entry to record sales and collections during the period.
(b) Prepare the entry to record the write-off of uncollectible accounts during the period.
(c) Prepare the entries to record the recovery of the uncollectible account during the period.
(d) Prepare the entry to record bad debts expense for the period.
(e) Determine the ending balances in Accounts Receivable and Allowance for Doubtful Accounts.
(f) What is the net realizable value of the receivables at the end of the period?

P8-2A   Yasukuni Corporation reported the following information in its general ledger at June 30:

Determine missing amounts.
(SO 2, 3)

Accounts Receivable		
Beg. bal.	(f)	46,350
	45,000	(e)
End. bal.	4,500	

Sales	
	(d)

Allowance for Doubtful Accounts		
		Beg. bal. 350
	150	(b)
		End. bal. (a)

Bad Debts Expense	
(c)	

All sales were on account. At the end of the year, uncollectible accounts were estimated to total $425 based on an aging schedule.

Instructions

Using your knowledge of receivables transactions, determine the missing amounts. (*Hint:* You may find it helpful to reconstruct the journal entries.)

Journalize bad debts transactions.
(SO 3)

P8-3A   Image.com produced the following aging of the accounts receivable at year end:

	Total	Number of Days Outstanding				
		0–30	31–60	61–90	91–120	Over 120
Accounts receivable	$375,000	$220,000	$90,000	$40,000	$10,000	$15,000
% uncollectible		1%	4%	8%	16%	30%
Estimated bad debts						

Instructions

(a) Calculate the total estimated uncollectible accounts based on the above information.
(b) Prepare the year-end adjusting journal entry to record the bad debts using the estimated uncollectible accounts receivable determined in (a). Assume the opening balance in Allowance for Doubtful Accounts is a $10,000 debit.
(c) Of the amounts in the above accounts, $5,000 is determined to be specifically uncollectible. Prepare the journal entry to write off the uncollectible amount.
(d) The company subsequently collects $5,000 on the account that had previously been determined to be uncollectible in (c). Prepare the journal entry or entries to restore the account and record the cash collection.
(e) Comment on how your answers in (a) to (d) would change if Image.com used 4% of total accounts receivable, rather than aging the accounts receivable. What are the advantages to the company of aging the accounts receivable rather than applying a percentage to total accounts receivable?

Journalize bad debts transactions.
(SO 3)

P8-4A   Presented here is an aging schedule for Deep Woods Ltd.:

Customer	Total	Number of Days Outstanding				
		0–30	31–60	61–90	91–120	Over 120
Anita	$ 22,000		$10,000	$12,000		
Barry	40,000	$ 40,000				
Chagnon	57,000	16,000	6,000		$35,000	
David	34,000					$34,000
Others	126,000	96,000	16,000	14,000		
	$279,000	$152,000	$32,000	$26,000	$35,000	$34,000
% uncollectible		4%	9%	15%	25%	50%
Estimated bad debts	$ 38,610	$ 6,080	$ 2,880	$ 3,900	$ 8,750	$17,000

At December 31, 2004, the unadjusted balance in Allowance for Doubtful Accounts is a credit of $20,000.

Instructions

(a) Journalize the adjusting entry for bad debts at December 31, 2004.
(b) Journalize these events and transactions for 2005:
   1. March 31, an $800 customer balance originating in 2004 is judged uncollectible.
   2. May 31, a cheque for $800 is received from the customer whose account was written off as uncollectible on March 31.
(c) Journalize the adjusting entry for bad debts on December 31, 2005, assuming that the 2005 aging schedule indicates that total estimated uncollectible accounts will be $45,000.

Calculate bad debt amounts.
(SO 3)

P8-5A   Here is information related to Volkov Ltd. for 2004:

Total credit sales	$2,000,000
Accounts receivable	800,000
Bad debts written off	36,000

Instructions

(a) What amount of bad debts expense will Volkov Ltd. report if it does not use the allowance method of accounting for bad debts?
(b) Assume that Volkov decides to estimate its uncollectible accounts using the allowance

method and an aging schedule. Uncollectible accounts are estimated to be $32,000. What amount of bad debts expense will Volkov record if it has an Allowance for Doubtful Accounts credit balance of $3,000?

(c) Assume the same facts as in part (b) except that there is a $3,000 debit balance in Allowance for Doubtful Accounts. What amount of bad debts expense will Volkov record?

(d) What are the advantages of using the allowance method of reporting bad debts expense?

P8-6A On January 1, 2004, Vu Ltd. had Accounts Receivable $146,000; Notes Receivable $11,000; and Allowance for Doubtful Accounts $13,200. The note receivable is a four-month, 8% note from Annabelle Company dated December 31, 2003. Interest is due at maturity. Vu Ltd. prepares financial statements annually and uses a perpetual inventory system. During the year, the following selected transactions occurred:

Journalize receivables transactions.
(SO 2, 4)

Jan. 5 Sold $16,000 of merchandise to George Company, terms n/15. The merchandise cost $9,600.

 20 Accepted George Company's $16,000, three-month, 9% note for balance due. Interest is due at maturity.

Feb. 18 Sold $8,000 of merchandise costing $5,000 to Swaim Company. Accepted Swaim's six-month, 5% note in payment. Interest is due at maturity.

Apr. 20 Collected George Company note in full.

 30 Received payment in full from Annabelle Company on the amount due.

May 25 Accepted Avery Inc.'s $6,000, three-month, 8% note in settlement of a past-due balance on account. Interest is due at maturity.

Aug. 18 Received payment in full from Swaim Company on note due.

 25 The Avery note was dishonoured. Avery Inc. is not bankrupt and future payment is anticipated.

Sept. 1 Sold $10,000 of merchandise costing $6,000 to Young Company and accepted a six-month, 5% note in payment.

Instructions

Journalize the transactions.

P8-7A At December 31, 2004, Bordeaux Inc. reported this information on its balance sheet:

Journalize receivables transactions and calculate ratios.
(SO 2, 3, 7)

Accounts receivable	$960,000
Allowance for doubtful accounts	70,000

During 2005 the company had the following transactions related to receivables:

1. Sales on account, $3,200,000.
2. Sales returns and allowances, $50,000.
3. Collections of accounts receivable, $3,000,000.
4. Write-offs of accounts receivable deemed uncollectible, $90,000.
5. Recovery of bad debts previously written off as uncollectible, $40,000.

Instructions

(a) Prepare the journal entries to record each of these five summary transactions. Assume that no cash discounts were taken on the collections of accounts receivable.

(b) Enter the January 1, 2005, balances in Accounts Receivable and Allowance for Doubtful Accounts, post the entries to the two accounts, and determine the balances.

(c) Prepare the journal entry to record bad debts expense for 2005, assuming that aging the accounts receivable indicates that expected uncollectible accounts amount to $110,000.

(d) Calculate the receivables turnover and average collection period.

P8-8A On July 31, 2004, a company accepted a two-month, $50,000, 5% note from a customer in settlement of the customer's account. Interest is due at maturity. The company makes adjusting entries at the end of each month.

Journalize notes receivable transactions.
(SO 4)

Instructions

(a) Prepare all journal entries for the company over the life of the note. Assume that the customer settles the note in full on the maturity date.

(b) Assume that instead of honouring the note at maturity, the customer dishonours the note. Assuming that the entries made in part (a) for July and August have already been recorded, record the necessary entry at the maturity date, September 30, 2004. Eventual collection of the note is expected.

Journalize credit card and notes receivable transactions; show balance sheet presentation.
(SO 4, 5)

P8-9A   Selica Inc. closes its books on October 31. On September 30, the Interest Receivable account balance is $123.66 and the Notes Receivable account balance is $23,400. Notes receivable include the following:

Date	Maker	Face Value	Term	Interest Rate
Aug. 1	Foran Inc.	$ 8,000	2 months	7%
Sept. 1	Drexler Co.	5,200	2 months	7%
Sept. 30	MGH Corp.	10,200	6 months	9%
		$23,400		

Interest is due at maturity for all notes. During October the following transactions were completed:

Oct.   1 Received payment in full from Foran Inc. on the amount due.
      7 Made sales of $6,900 on Selica credit cards.
    12 Made sales of $750 on VISA credit cards. The credit card service charge is 2%.
    21 Made sales of $1,500 on debit cards. The debit card service charge is 2%.
    31 Received notice that Drexler Co. note will be dishonoured. (Assume that Drexler Co. is expected to pay in the future.)

Instructions

(a) Journalize the October transactions and the October 31 adjusting entry for accrued interest receivable.
(b) Enter the balances at October 1 in the receivable accounts and post the entries to all of these accounts.
(c) Show the balance sheet presentation of the receivable accounts at October 31.

Calculate and interpret ratios.
(SO 7)

P8-10A   Presented here is basic financial information (in millions) from the 2002 annual reports of Rogers Communications Inc. and Shaw Communications Inc.:

	Rogers	Shaw
Sales	$4,323.0	$1,888.6
Allowance for doubtful accounts, Jan. 1	63.4	19.2
Allowance for doubtful accounts, Dec. 31	65.5	19.3
Accounts receivable (gross), Jan. 1	558.8	208.8
Accounts receivable (gross), Dec. 31	577.6	206.8

Instructions

Calculate the receivables turnover and average collection period for both companies. The industry average for the receivables turnover was 9.6 times and the average collection period was 38 days. Comment on the difference in their collection experiences.

Evaluate liquidity.
(SO 7, 8)

P8-11A   The following ratios are available for Tianjin Inc.:

	2004	2003
Current ratio	1.3:1	1.5:1
Receivables turnover	12 times	10 times
Inventory turnover	11 times	9 times

Instructions

(a) Is Tianjin's short-term liquidity improving or deteriorating in 2004? Be specific in your answer, referring to relevant ratios.
(b) Do changes in turnover ratios affect profitability? Explain.
(c) Identify any steps Tianjin might have taken, or might wish to take, to improve its management of its receivables and inventory turnover.

Problems: Set B

P8-1B At the beginning of the current period, Fassi Corp. had balances in Accounts Receivable of $400,000 and in Allowance for Doubtful Accounts of $10,000 (credit). During the period, it had net credit sales of $900,000 and collections of $1,069,000. It wrote off as uncollectible accounts receivable of $6,000. However, a $3,000 account written off as uncollectible was recovered before the end of the current period. Uncollectible accounts are estimated to total $18,000 at the end of the period.

Journalize receivables transactions.
(SO 2, 3)

Instructions
(a) Prepare the entry to record sales and collections during the period.
(b) Prepare the entry to record the write-off of uncollectible accounts during the period.
(c) Prepare the entries to record the recovery of the uncollectible account during the period.
(d) Prepare the entry to record bad debts expense for the period.
(e) Determine the ending balance in Accounts Receivable and Allowance for Doubtful Accounts.
(f) What is the net realizable value of the receivables at the end of the period?

P8-2B Wilton Corporation reported the following information in its general ledger at December 31:

Determine missing amounts.
(SO 2, 3)

Accounts Receivable			
Beg. bal.	8,300	32,000	
	(d)	(e)	
End. bal.	(f)		

Sales	
	30,000

Allowance for Doubtful Accounts		
	Beg. bal.	750
105		(b)
	End. bal.	(a)

Bad Debts Expense	
(c)	

All sales were on account. At the end of the year, uncollectible accounts were estimated to total $930 based on an aging schedule.

Instructions
Using your knowledge of receivables transactions, determine the missing amounts. (*Hint:* You may find it helpful to reconstruct the journal entries.)

P8-3B The following represents selected information taken from a company's aging schedule to estimate uncollectible accounts receivable at year end:

Journalize bad debts transactions.
(SO 3)

	Total	Number of Days Outstanding				
		0–30	31–60	61–90	91–120	Over 120
Accounts receivable	$260,000	$100,000	$60,000	$50,000	$30,000	$20,000
% uncollectible		1%	5%	10%	20%	30%
Estimated bad debts						

Instructions
(a) Calculate the total estimated uncollectible accounts based on the above information.
(b) Prepare the year-end adjusting journal entry to record the bad debts using the estimated uncollectible accounts receivable determined in (a). Assume the opening balance in Allowance for Doubtful Accounts is a $15,000 credit.
(c) Of the amounts in the above accounts, $2,000 is determined to be specifically uncollectible. Prepare the journal entry to write off the uncollectible amount.
(d) The company subsequently collects $1,000 on a specific account that had previously been determined to be uncollectible in (c). Prepare the journal entry or entries to restore the account and record the cash collection.
(e) Explain how establishing an allowance satisfies the matching principle.

Journalize and post bad debts transactions.
(SO 3)

P8-4B This is an aging schedule for Stoiko Ltd. for the year ended December 31, 2004:

Customer	Total	Number of Days Outstanding				
		0–30	31–60	61–90	91–120	Over 120
Aber	$ 20,000		$ 9,000	$11,000		
Bohr	30,000	$ 30,000				
Case	50,000	15,000	5,000		$30,000	
Datz	38,000					$38,000
Others	120,000	92,000	15,000	13,000		
	$258,000	$137,000	$29,000	$24,000	$30,000	$38,000
% uncollectible		3%	5%	15%	25%	50%
Estimated bad debts	$ 35,660	$ 4,110	$ 1,450	$ 3,600	$ 7,500	$19,000

At December 31, 2004, the unadjusted balance in Allowance for Doubtful Accounts is a credit of $19,000.

Instructions

(a) Journalize and post the adjusting entry for bad debts at December 31, 2004.
(b) Journalize and post to the allowance account these events and transactions for 2005:
   1. March 1, an $800 customer balance originating in 2004 is judged uncollectible.
   2. May 1, a cheque for $800 is received from the customer whose account was written off as uncollectible on March 1.
(c) Journalize and post the adjusting entry for bad debts at December 31, 2005, assuming that the 2005 aging schedule indicates that total estimated uncollectible accounts will be $40,000.

Calculate bad debt amounts.
(SO 3)

P8-5B Here is information related to Aris Ltd. for 2004:

Total credit sales	$1,500,000
Accounts receivable	600,000
Bad debts written off	28,000

Instructions

(a) What amount of bad debts expense will Aris Ltd. report if it does not use the allowance method of accounting for bad debts?
(b) Assume that Aris decides to estimate its uncollectible accounts using the allowance method and an aging schedule. Uncollectible accounts are estimated to total $20,000. What amount of bad debts expense will Aris record if Allowance for Doubtful Accounts has a credit balance of $4,000?
(c) Assume the same facts as in part (b), except that there is a $2,000 debit balance in Allowance for Doubtful Accounts. What amount of bad debts expense will Aris record?
(d) What are the advantages of using the allowance method of reporting bad debts expense?

Journalize receivables transactions.
(SO 2, 4)

P8-6B On January 1, 2004, Comaneci Ltd. had Accounts Receivable of $54,200 and Allowance for Doubtful Accounts of $4,700. Comaneci prepares financial statements annually and uses a perpetual inventory system. During the year the following selected transactions occurred:

Jan. 5 Sold $6,000 of merchandise to Brooks Company, terms n/30. Cost of merchandise sold, $4,000.

Feb. 2 Accepted a $6,000, four-month, 6% promissory note from Brooks Company for balance due. Interest is payable at maturity.

12 Sold $7,800 of merchandise costing $5,000 to Gage Company and accepted Gage's two-month, 6% note in payment. Interest is payable at maturity.

26 Sold $5,000 of merchandise to Mathias Co., terms n/30. Cost of merchandise sold was $3,750.

Apr. 5 Accepted a $5,000, three-month, 7% note from Mathias Co. for balance due. Interest is payable at maturity.

12 Collected Gage Company note in full.

June 2 Collected Brooks Company note in full.

July 5 Mathias Co. dishonours its note of April 5. It is expected that Mathias will eventually pay the amount owed.

   15 Sold $2,000 of merchandise costing $1,500 to Tritt Inc., and accepted Tritt's three-month, 7%, note in payment. Interest is payable at maturity.

Oct. 15 The Tritt Inc. note was paid in full.

Instructions

Journalize the transactions.

P8-7B At December 31, 2004, Underwood Imports Inc. reported this information on its balance sheet:

Accounts receivable	$1,000,000
Allowance for doubtful accounts	50,000

Journalize receivables transactions and calculate ratios.
(SO 2, 3, 7)

During 2005 the company had the following transactions related to receivables:

1. Sales on account, $2,600,000.
2. Sales returns and allowances, $40,000.
3. Collections of accounts receivable, $2,200,000.
4. Write-offs of accounts receivable deemed uncollectible, $80,000.
5. Recovery of bad debts previously written off as uncollectible, $25,000.

Instructions

(a) Prepare the journal entries to record each of these five summary transactions. Assume that no cash discounts were taken on the collections of accounts receivable.
(b) Enter the January 1, 2005, balances in Accounts Receivable and Allowance for Doubtful Accounts, post the entries to the two accounts, and determine the balances.
(c) Prepare the journal entry to record bad debts expense for 2005, assuming that aging the accounts receivable indicates that estimated uncollectible accounts amount to $70,000.
(d) Calculate the receivables turnover and average collection period.

P8-8B On November 1, 2004, a company accepted a three-month, $20,000, 7% note from a customer in settlement of the customer's account. Interest is payable at maturity. The company's year end is December 31. The company makes adjusting entries at the end of each month.

Journalize notes receivable transactions.
(SO 4)

Instructions

(a) Prepare all journal entries for the company over the life of the note. Assume that the customer settles the note in full on the maturity date.
(b) Assume that instead of honouring the note at maturity, the customer dishonours the note. Assuming that the entries made in part (a) for November, December, and January have already been recorded, record the necessary entry at the maturity date, February 1, 2005. Eventual collection of the note is expected.

P8-9B Bon Ton Ltd. closes its books on July 31. On June 30, the Interest Receivable account balance is $84, and the Notes Receivable account balance is $19,800. Notes Receivable include the following:

Journalize credit card and notes receivable transactions; show balance sheet presentation.
(SO 4, 5)

Date	Maker	Face Value	Term	Interest Rate
May 1	Alder Inc.	$ 6,000	2 months	6%
June 1	Dorn Co.	4,800	2 months	6%
June 30	MJH Corp.	9,000	6 months	5%
		$19,800		

Interest is payable at maturity for all notes. During July the following transactions were completed:

July 1 Received payment in full from Alder Inc. on the amount due.
    5 Made sales of $7,800 on Bon Ton credit cards.
   14 Made sales of $700 on VISA credit cards. The credit card service charge is 3%.
   31 Received notice that Dorn Co. cannot pay its note on August 1. (Assume that Dorn Co. is not expected to pay in the future.)

Instructions

(a) Journalize the July transactions and the July 31 adjusting entry for accrued interest receivable.

(b) Enter the balances at July 1 in the receivable accounts and post the entries to all of these accounts.

(c) In proper format, show the balance sheet presentation of the receivable accounts at July 31.

Calculate and interpret ratios.
(SO 7)

P8-10B   Presented here is basic financial information (in U.S. millions) from the 2002 financial statements of Nike and Reebok:

	Nike	Reebok
Sales	$9,893.0	$3,127.9
Allowance for doubtful accounts, Jan. 1	72.1	55.2
Allowance for doubtful accounts, Dec. 31	77.4	60.9
Accounts receivable (gross), Jan. 1	1,693.5	438.6
Accounts receivable (gross), Dec. 31	1,884.5	482.7

Instructions

Calculate the receivables turnover and average collection period for both companies. The industry average for the receivables turnover was 8 times and the average collection period was 46 days. Comment on the difference in the two companies' collection experiences.

Evaluate liquidity.
(SO 7, 8)

P8-11B   The following ratios are available for Hawryluk Corporation:

	2004	2003
Current ratio	1.8:1	1.5:1
Receivables turnover	8 times	10 times
Inventory turnover	7 times	9 times

Instructions

(a) Is Hawryluk's short-term liquidity improving or deteriorating in 2004? Be specific in your answer, referring to relevant ratios.

(b) Do changes in turnover ratios affect cash flow? Explain.

(c) Identify any steps Hawryluk may wish to consider to better manage its receivables and inventory turnover.

BROADENING YOUR PERSPECTIVE

Financial Reporting and Analysis

Analysis
Tools

FINANCIAL REPORTING PROBLEM: *Loblaw Companies Limited*

A passion for food... *and a lot more!*

BYP8-1   Refer to the financial statements of Loblaw and the accompanying notes to its financial statements in Appendix A.

Instructions

(a) Assuming that all sales are credit sales, and using net receivables instead of gross receivables, calculate the receivables turnover and average collection period for 2002.

(b) What is Loblaw's policy with respect to writing off uncollectible credit card receivables. (*Hint*: Review Note 1 to the financial statements.)

(c) Does Loblaw sell its receivables? (*Hint*: Review Note 1 to the financial statements.)

(d) What conclusions can you draw about Loblaw's management of its receivables from parts (a) to (c)?

COMPARATIVE ANALYSIS PROBLEM: *Loblaw and Sobeys*

BYP8-2 The financial statements of Sobeys Inc. are presented in Appendix B, following the financial statements for Loblaw in Appendix A.

Instructions

(a) What types of receivables does each company report in its balance sheets?
(b) Calculate the following for each company for its most recent fiscal year:
   1. Current ratio
   2. Receivables turnover (Assume all sales were credit sales and use net receivables instead of gross receivables.)
   3. Average collection period for receivables
(c) The industry averages for each of the above ratios are provided below:

Current ratio	1:1
Receivables turnover	40.4 times
Average collection period	9 days

What conclusions concerning each company's liquidity and management of accounts receivable can be drawn from your calculations in (b) and the industry data?

RESEARCH CASE

BYP8-3 The August 23, 2002, edition of *The Globe and Mail* includes an article on page A1 by Bruce Little entitled "Moody's to Give Credit to Our Plastic Habits." In this article, Moody's Investors Service studies the use of credit cards in Canada.

Instructions

Read the article and answer the following questions:

(a) What percentage of credit card balances do Canadians pay off each month?
(b) What percentage of balances are overdue by more than 30 days?
(c) What percentage of uncollectible accounts were written off in the first quarter of 2002?
(d) How do Canadian experiences with credit cards as described in parts (a), (b), and (c) above compare to American experiences?

INTERPRETING FINANCIAL STATEMENTS

BYP8-4 Suncor Energy Inc. reported the following information (in millions) in its financial statements for the fiscal years 2000 through 2002:

	2002	2001	2000
Revenues (assume all credit)	$4,902	$4,194	$3,385
Accounts receivable (gross)	406	309	410
Allowance for doubtful accounts	3	3	3
Total current assets	722	622	665
Total current liabilities	797	773	837

Additional detail about Suncor's receivables includes the following:

The company has a securitization program in place to sell, on a revolving, fully serviced, and limited recourse basis, up to $170 million of accounts receivable having a maturity of 45 days or less to a third party. As at December 31, 2002, $170 million in outstanding accounts receivable had been sold under the program.

Industry averages for the current ratio, receivables turnover, and average collection period are 1:1, 6.3 times, and 58 days, respectively.

Instructions

(a) Calculate the current ratio, receivables turnover ratio, and average collection period for fiscal 2002 and 2001. Comment on Suncor's liquidity for each of the years and compared to the industry.
(b) Suncor has not changed the dollar amount of its allowance for doubtful accounts for a number of years. Comment on the relevance of this as a percentage of accounts receivable.
(c) Suncor regularly sells a portion of its accounts receivable. Comment on this practice as part of Suncor's management of its accounts receivable.

A GLOBAL FOCUS

BYP8-5 Sears, Roebuck & Co. is one of the world's largest retailers. Sears, Roebuck owns about 55% of Sears Canada. Until 2003, Sears, Roebuck was a huge provider of credit to 59 million cardholders through its Sears credit card. In July 2003, Sears, Roebuck sold its $29 billion credit card portfolio to Citigroup, a global financial services company.

In some instances, to acquire cash when needed, the company sells its receivables. In 2002, Sears, Roebuck sold $8.1 billion of its receivables.

The following information (in U.S. millions) was reported in Sears, Roebuck's financial statements:

	2002	2001	2000
Credit card receivables (gross)	$32,595	$29,321	$18,003
Allowance for doubtful accounts	1,836	1,166	686
Merchandise sales	35,698	35,755	36,277
Credit revenues	5,668	5,235	4,571
Bad debts expense	2,261	1,866	884

Instructions

(a) Discuss whether the sale of receivables in 2002 by Sears, Roebuck represents a significant portion of its receivables. Why might it have sold these receivables? As an investor, what concerns might you have about these sales?

(b) Calculate and discuss the receivables turnover and average collection period for Sears, Roebuck for 2002 and 2001.

(c) Calculate the ratio of bad debts expense to merchandise sales for 2002 and 2001. Did this ratio improve or worsen?

(d) Do you think Sears, Roebuck originally provided its own credit card as a revenue-generating activity, as a data-mining source, or as a convenience for its customers?

(e) Why do you think Sears, Roebuck decided to sell its credit card portfolio?

FINANCIAL ANALYSIS ON THE WEB

BYP8-6   This case examines the Credit Card Costs Calculator, provided by the Office of Consumer Affairs, Industry Canada. Based on how a credit card is used, we will determine which cards cost the least in interest and fees over a year. The cost of borrowing from a bank is then compared to the cost of using a credit card.

Instructions

Specific requirements of this Web case can be found on the Kimmel website.

Critical Thinking

COLLABORATIVE LEARNING ACTIVITY

BYP8-7   From its inception, Campus Fashions Ltd. has sold merchandise on either a cash or credit basis, but no credit cards have been accepted. During the past several months, the management of Campus Fashions has begun to question its credit-sales policies. First, Campus Fashions has lost some sales because management refuses to accept credit cards. Second, representatives of two banks have convinced management to accept their national credit cards for a credit card fee of 3%.

Management decided that it should determine the cost of carrying its own credit sales. These data are from the accounting records of the past three years:

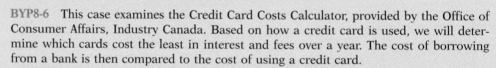

	2004	2003	2002
Net credit sales	$500,000	$600,000	$400,000
Collection agency fees for slow-paying customers	2,450	2,500	1,600
Salary of part-time accounts receivable clerk	3,800	3,800	3,800

Credit and collection expenses as a percentage of net credit sales are as follows: uncollectible accounts 1.6%; billing and mailing costs 0.5%; and credit investigation fee on new customers 0.15%.

The company also determines that the average accounts receivable balance outstanding during the year is 5% of net credit sales. Management estimates that it could earn an average of 5% annually on cash invested in other business opportunities.

Instructions

With the class divided into groups, so the following:

(a) Prepare a table for each year showing total credit and collection expenses in dollars and as a percentage of net credit sales.

(b) Determine the net credit and collection expenses in dollars and as a percentage of sales after considering the revenue not earned from other investment opportunities.

(c) Discuss both the financial and non-financial factors that are relevant to the decision.

COMMUNICATION ACTIVITY

BYP8-8 Toys for Big Boys sells snowmobiles, personal watercraft, ATVs, and the like. Recently, the credit manager of Toys for Big Boys retired. The sales staff threw him a big retirement party—they were glad to see him go, because they felt his credit policies restricted their selling ability. The sales staff convinced the management that there was no need to replace the credit manager, since they could handle this responsibility in addition to their sales positions.

Management was thrilled at year end when sales doubled. However, gross accounts receivables quadrupled and cash flow halved. Its average collection period increased from 30 days to 120 days.

Instructions

In a memo to the sales staff, explain the financial impact of allowing the sales staff to manage the credit function. Has the business assumed any additional credit risk? What would you recommend the company do to better manage its increasing accounts receivable?

ETHICS CASE

BYP8-9 Shady Corporation's bank will only accept accounts receivable under 90 days old as collateral for the company's operating line of credit. The president says to the controller, "I've been discussing the overdue accounts with our customers. All intend to pay; they just need a bit more time. I suggest you issue credit notes for all the accounts over 90 days and reissue invoices with today's date. That will improve the increasing age of our receivables and allow us to meet the bank's requirements for our line of credit."

Ethics In
Accounting

Instructions

(a) Who are the stakeholders in this case?

(b) What are the ethical dilemmas?

(c) What do you recommend the controller do?

Answers to Self-Study Questions

1. b   2. b   3. d   4. d   5. b   6. d   7. a   8. a   9. c   10. b   11. a

Answer to Loblaw Review It Question 1

Loblaw reports accounts receivable in the current assets section of its balance sheet. It also reports future income taxes, which represent recoverable amounts expected to be received in the future.

Remember to go back to the Navigator box on the chapter-opening page to check off your completed work.

Reporting and Analysing Long-Lived Assets

Tumult in the Skies

Since Air Canada acquired Canadian Airlines back in 2000, a lot has changed at Canada's major airline. After some initial turbulence, the two companies combined their resources and integrated their operations. Today, Air Canada holds 75% of market share in this country and is the world's twelfth largest commercial airline.

But the twists and turns this story has taken in the past three years have left everyone wondering just what's going to happen next.

Not long after the merger, the combined carrier launched a family of assorted sub-brands with names like Tango, Zip, Jazz, and Jetz. The new airlines—with Tango and Zip aimed at the dis-count market—made their debut in 2002 amid talk of more to come. The move was part of a strategy intended to reduce costs and make the airline more efficient and profitable.

First on the runway was Tango, a no-frills service featuring lower fares, on-line booking, and paperless ticketing, and without the usual free meals and head sets—customers pay extra for those. By the end of its first year, Tango had flown two million passengers.

Zip Air, the company's discount short-haul carrier for Western Canada, launched in September 2002, was slower to take off, with Calgary-based WestJet providing stiff competition. Although three months after its launch its flights were still nearly half empty, the company announced plans to expand its destinations to include Montreal and Ottawa.

In a bid to further improve its bottom line, Air Canada also began streamlining its equipment, selling off or reassigning older F-28, DC-9, B737, and B767 aircraft in its 357-strong fleet and replacing them with newer, more fuel-efficient Airbus models—notably the A330 and A321 as well as the longer-range, larger capacity A340. In doing so, it reduced the number of aircraft types to save on maintenance, spare parts inventory, and crew training.

At the beginning of 2003, however, the company still had more debt on its balance sheet than assets—$9.9 billion versus $8.4 billion, respectively. In contrast, its Western rival WestJet Airlines is debt-free.

Despite the new measures, in

in the feature story, in order to purchase newer, more fuel-efficient aircraft.

Many companies have substantial investments in property, plant, and equipment. Illustration 9-1 shows the percentages of net property, plant, and equipment in relation to total assets in several companies.

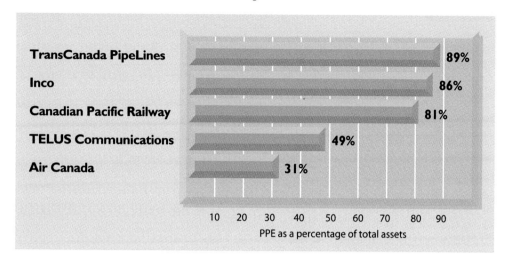

Illustration 9-1
Percentages of property, plant, and equipment (PPE) to total assets

DETERMINING THE COST OF PROPERTY, PLANT, AND EQUIPMENT

The **cost principle** requires that property, plant, and equipment be recorded at cost. Thus, the new planes that Air Canada purchased are recorded at cost. **Cost consists of all expenditures necessary to acquire an asset and make it ready for its intended use.** For example, the purchase price, the freight costs paid by Air Canada, and any testing or installation costs are all considered part of the cost of the aircraft. All these costs are **capitalized** (recorded as property, plant, and equipment), rather than expensed, because they will provide benefits over more than one period.

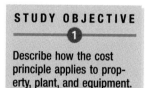

STUDY OBJECTIVE

Describe how the cost principle applies to property, plant, and equipment.

Determining which costs to include in a long-lived asset account and which costs not to include is very important. Costs which benefit only the current period are expensed. Such costs are referred to as operating expenditures. Costs that benefit future periods are included in a long-lived asset account. These are referred to as capital expenditures.

This distinction is important because it has immediate, and often material, implications for the statement of earnings. In order to boost current earnings, some companies have been known to improperly capitalize expenditures that should have been expensed. For example, suppose that $10,000 of maintenance costs are improperly capitalized to a building account; that is, they are included in the asset account Buildings rather than being expensed immediately. If the cost of the building is being allocated as an expense (amortized) over a 40-year life, then the maintenance cost of $10,000 will be incorrectly spread across 40 years instead of being expensed in the current year. Current-year expenses will be understated, and net earnings and total assets will be overstated. Thus, determining which costs to capitalize and which to expense is very important.

In what will likely be heralded as one of the largest accounting frauds in history, WorldCom, a global communications company operating in more than 65 countries, improperly capitalized U.S.$7.2 billion of expenses. This accounting fraud artificially boosted WorldCom's net earnings by U.S.$5 billion for fiscal 2001 and the first quarter of 2002. If these expenses had been recorded properly as operating expenditures, WorldCom would have reported a net loss for 2001, as well as for the first quarter of 2002. Instead, WorldCom reported net earnings of $1.4 billion for 2001 and $130 million for the first quarter of 2002. As a result of these, and other, problems, WorldCom declared bankruptcy, to the dismay of its investors and creditors. Several WorldCom executives have since been indicted for fraud.

Cost is measured by the cash paid in a cash transaction or by the cash equivalent price paid when noncash assets are used in payment. **The cash equivalent price is equal to the fair market value of the asset given up.** If the fair market value of the asset given up is not determinable, the cash equivalent price is considered to be the fair market value of the asset received.

Once cost is established, it becomes the basis of accounting for the property, plant, or equipment over its useful life. Current market values are not used to increase the recorded value after acquisition. If, however, an asset's market value permanently declines below its book value, an impairment loss should be recorded.

Unlike inventories, the lower of cost and market rule does not apply automatically to property, plant, and equipment. Because inventory is expected to be converted into cash within the year, it is important to value it annually at the lesser of its cost and saleable, or market, value. In contrast, property, plant, and equipment are used in operations over a longer term and are not available for resale. The going concern assumption assumes that a company will recover at least the cost of its long-lived assets. So, it is only when a permanent impairment occurs in the value of the asset, that long-lived assets are written down to market. This does not happen often, and this writedown is subject to certain recoverability tests before doing so. Fewer than 2% of the companies surveyed by *Financial Reporting in Canada* in 2001 wrote down any property, plant, and equipment. If the value of the asset later increases, the book value is **not** subsequently adjusted for any recovery in value.

Property, plant, and equipment are often subdivided into four classes:

1. **Land**, such as a building site
2. **Land improvements**, such as driveways, parking lots, fences, and underground sprinkler systems
3. **Buildings**, such as stores, offices, factories, and warehouses
4. **Equipment**, such as store checkout counters, cash registers, coolers, office furniture, factory machinery, and delivery equipment

The application of the cost principle to each of the major classes of property, plant, and equipment is explained in the following sections.

 International Note

The United Kingdom is flexible regarding asset valuation. Companies revalue to fair value when they believe this information is more relevant. Switzerland and the Netherlands also permit revaluations.

Land

The cost of land includes (1) the cash purchase price, and (2) closing costs such as survey and legal fees. For example, if the cash price is $50,000 and closing costs are $5,000, the cost of the land is $55,000.

All necessary costs incurred in making land **ready for its intended use** increase (debit) the Land account. When vacant land is acquired, its cost includes expenditures for clearing, draining, filling, and grading. If the land has a building on it that must be removed to make the site suitable for construction of a new building, all demolition and removal costs, less any proceeds from salvaged materials, are chargeable to the Land account.

To illustrate, assume that Hayes Manufacturing Corporation acquires real estate at a cash cost of $100,000. The property contains an old warehouse that is torn down at a net cost of $6,000 ($7,500 in costs less $1,500 in proceeds from salvaged materials). Additional expenditures are incurred for the legal fee of $1,000. Given these factors, the cost of the land is $107,000, calculated as shown in Illustration 9-2.

Land	
Cash price of property	$100,000
Net cost of removing warehouse	6,000
Legal fee	1,000
Cost of land	$107,000

Illustration 9-2
Calculation of cost of land

When the acquisition is recorded, Land is debited for $107,000 and Cash is credited for $107,000. Once the land is ready for its intended use, recurring costs, such as annual property taxes, are recorded as expenditures—in other words, these costs are matched against the revenues the land helps generate.

Land Improvements

Land is a unique long-lived asset. Its cost is not amortized—allocated over its useful life—because land has an unlimited useful life. However, costs are incurred for certain items to improve the land that do have limited useful lives. The costs of structural additions made to land are recorded separately as Land Improvements.

The cost of land improvements includes all expenditures necessary to make the improvements ready for their intended use. For example, the cost of a parking lot includes amounts paid for grading, paving, fencing, and lighting. Land improvements, such as parking lots, decline in service potential over time, and require maintenance and replacement to maintain their value to the company. Because of this, the cost of land improvements is amortized over their limited useful lives.

Buildings

All necessary expenditures related to the purchase or construction of a building are charged to the Buildings account. When a building is **purchased**, such costs include the purchase price and closing costs (e.g., legal fees). Costs to make the building ready for its intended use consist of expenditures for remodelling rooms and offices, and for replacing or repairing the roof, floors, electrical wiring, and plumbing. When a new building is **constructed**, its cost consists of the contract price plus payments made for architects' fees, building permits, and excavation costs.

In addition, interest costs incurred to finance a construction project are included in the cost of the asset when a significant period of time is required to get the asset ready for use. In these circumstances, interest costs are considered as necessary as materials and labour. However, the inclusion of interest costs in the cost of a constructed building is limited to interest costs incurred during the construction period. When construction has been completed, subsequent interest payments on funds borrowed to finance the construction are recorded as operating expenditures by increases (debits) to Interest Expense.

Equipment

The cost of equipment consists of the cash purchase price and the provincial sales tax (where applicable). Unlike other long-lived assets, provincial sales tax is normally charged on equipment purchases. Any GST (or HST) paid is not a capital cost, as it is normally recoverable. As mentioned earlier in this textbook, sales tax regulations are complicated and are ignored in the chapter material in order to focus on fundamental concepts. The cost of equipment also includes freight charges, insurance during transit paid by the purchaser, and expenditures required in assembling, installing, and testing the unit.

Costs such as motor vehicle licences and accident insurance on company trucks and cars are treated as operating expenditures as they are incurred, because they represent annual recurring expenditures and do not benefit future periods. Two criteria apply in determining the cost of equipment: (1) the frequency of the cost (one-time or recurring) and (2) the benefit period (the life of the asset or one year).

To illustrate, assume that Lenard Ltd. purchases a used delivery truck at a cash price of $22,000. Related expenditures are for painting and lettering, $500, motor vehicle licence, $80, and a one-year accident insurance policy, $1,600. The cost of the delivery truck is $22,500, calculated as shown in Illustration 9-3.

Illustration 9-3
Calculation of cost of delivery truck

Delivery Truck	
Cash price	$22,000
Painting and lettering	500
Cost of delivery truck	$22,500

The cost of a motor vehicle licence is treated as an expense, and the cost of an insurance policy is considered a prepaid expense (a current asset). The entry to record the purchase of the truck and related expenditures is as follows:

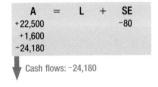

A	=	L	+	SE
+22,500				-80
+1,600				
-24,180				

Cash flows: -24,180

Delivery Truck	22,500	
Licence Expense	80	
Prepaid Insurance	1,600	
Cash		24,180
(To record purchase of delivery truck and related expenditures)		

To Buy or Lease?

In this chapter, we focus on assets that are purchased, but we would like to give you a brief look at an alternative to purchasing—leasing. In many industries, leasing is quite common. For example, nearly half of the vehicles used in Canada are leased. In a lease, a party that owns an asset (the lessor) agrees to allow another party (the lessee) to use the asset for an agreed period of time at an agreed price.

Some advantages of leasing an asset versus purchasing it are:

1. **Reduced risk of obsolescence.** Frequently, lease terms allow the party using the asset (the lessee) to exchange the asset for a more modern one if it becomes outdated. This is much easier than trying to sell an obsolete asset.
2. **Little or no down payment.** To purchase an asset, most companies must borrow money, which usually requires a down payment of at least 20%. Leasing an asset requires little or no down payment.
3. **Income tax advantages.** When a company owns an amortizable asset, it can only deduct the amortization expense (called capital cost allowance for income tax purposes) on its income tax return. We will learn more about capital cost allowance in a later section of this chapter. However, when a company leases an asset, it can deduct 100% of the lease payment on its income tax return.
4. **Assets and liabilities not reported.** Many companies prefer to keep assets and, especially, liabilities off their books. Certain types of leases, called operating leases, allow the lessee to account for the transaction as a rental with neither an asset nor a liability recorded.

Under another type of lease, a capital lease, both the asset and the liability are shown on the balance sheet. Under a capital lease, for the lessee, long-term lease agreements are accounted for in a way that is very similar to purchases. On the lessee's balance sheet, the leased item is shown as an asset and the obligation owed to the lessor is shown as a liability. The leased asset is amortized by the lessee in a manner similar to purchased assets.

Airlines often lease their airplanes in long-term lease agreements. Air Canada, for example, leases the majority of its airplanes. In 2002, it reporting having 9 aircraft under capital lease. These aircraft appear on Air Canada's balance sheet as Flight Equipment and are amortized along with its other property and equipment. The majority of Air Canada's planes, however, are accounted for under operating leases. Because operating leases are accounted for as rentals, these planes do not appear on its balance sheet and are instead disclosed in the notes to the financial statements as a commitment. There will be additional discussion of leasing in Chapter 10 with regard to liabilities.

BUSINESS INSIGHT

MANAGEMENT PERSPECTIVE

Leasing is big business. The Canadian Finance & Leasing Association estimated that nearly 25% of new property, plant, and equipment purchased in a recent year was financed by lease. The Canadian leasing industry has more than $100 billion of financing in place. The reasons often stated for leasing include favourable tax treatment, increased flexibility, keeping pace with technological improvements, driving down expense ratios, and increased cash flow.

BEFORE YOU GO ON . . .

● **REVIEW IT**

1. What are long-lived assets? What are the major classes of property, plant, and equipment? At what value should property, plant, and equipment be recorded?
2. What are operating expenditures? What are capital expenditures?
3. What are the primary advantages of leasing?

● **DO IT**

Assume that $50,000 of factory machinery is purchased on February 4. A $20,000 down payment is made and a $30,000 note is issued for the balance. Cash expenditures incurred that relate to this purchase include insurance during shipping, $100; the annual insurance policy, $750; and installation and testing costs, $500. Prepare the journal entry to record these expenditures.

Action Plan

- Capitalize expenditures made to get the machinery ready for its intended use.
- Expense operating costs that benefit only the current period, or which are recurring expenditures.

Solution

Feb. 3	Factory Machinery ($50,000 + $100 + $500)	50,600	
	Prepaid Insurance	750	
	Cash ($20,000 + $100 + $750 + $500)		21,350
	Note Payable		30,000
	(To record purchase of factory machinery and related expenditures)		

AMORTIZATION

As explained in Chapter 4, **amortization is the process of allocating the cost of a long-lived asset to expense over the asset's useful (service) life.** Such cost allocation is designed to properly match expenses with revenues in accordance with the matching principle.

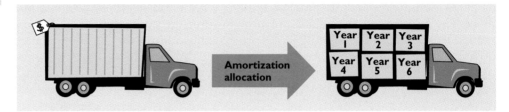

Illustration 9-4
Amortization as an allocation concept

As we learned in Chapter 4, amortization is allocated through an adjusting journal entry which debits Amortization Expense and credits Accumulated Amortization. Amortization Expense is a statement of earnings account; Accumulated Amortization appears on the balance sheet as a contra asset account.

Recognizing amortization for an asset does not result in the accumulation of cash for replacement of the asset. The balance in Accumulated Amortization represents the total amount of the asset's cost that has been allocated to expense to date: it is not a cash fund. The Cash account is not affected by the adjusting entry to record amortization.

It is important to understand that **amortization is a process of cost allocation, not a process of asset valuation.** No attempt is made to measure the change in an asset's market value during ownership because property, plant, and equipment are not held for resale. Thus, the net book value—cost less accumulated amortization—of a long-lived asset may differ significantly from its market value. In fact, if an asset is fully amortized, it can have zero book value but still have a significant market value.

Amortization applies to three classes of property, plant, and equipment: land improvements, buildings, and equipment. Each of these classes is considered an amortizable asset because the usefulness to the company and the revenue-producing ability of each class declines over the asset's useful life. Amortization does not apply to land because its usefulness and revenue-producing ability generally remain intact as long as the land is owned. In fact, in many cases, the usefulness of land increases over time because of the scarcity of good sites. Thus, **land is not an amortizable asset.**

During an amortizable asset's useful life, its revenue-producing ability declines because of **physical factors** such as wear and tear. A delivery truck that has been driven 100,000 kilometres will be less useful to a company than one driven only 800 kilometres.

A decline in revenue-producing ability may also occur because of **economic factors** such as obsolescence. Obsolescence is the process by which an asset becomes out of date before it physically wears out. For example, many companies replace their computers long before they wear out, because improvements in hardware and software make their old computers obsolete. It is important to understand that amortization only approximates the decline in revenue-producing ability. It cannot measure the true effects of physical or economic factors.

Factors in Calculating Amortization

Three factors affect the calculation of amortization, as shown in Illustration 9-5:

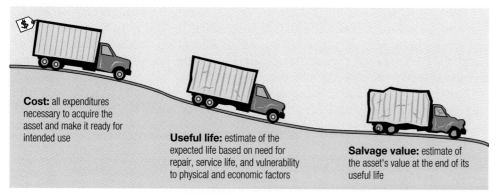

1. **Cost.** Considerations that affect the cost of an amortizable asset were explained earlier in this chapter. Remember that property, plant, and equipment are recorded at cost, in accordance with the cost principle.
2. **Useful life.** Useful life is an estimate of the expected productive life, also called "service life," of the asset. Useful life may be expressed in terms of time, units of activity (such as machine hours), or units of output. Useful life is an estimate. In making the estimate, management considers such factors as the intended use of the asset, repair and maintenance policies, and vulnerability of the asset to wear out or become obsolete. The company's past experience with similar assets is often helpful in determining expected useful life.
3. **Salvage value.** Salvage value is an estimate of the asset's value at the end of its useful life. The value may be based on the asset's worth as scrap or salvage, or on its expected trade-in value. Like useful life, salvage value is an estimate. In making the estimate, management considers how it plans to dispose of the asset and its experience with similar assets.

Alternative Terminology
Salvage value is also known as *residual value*.

BEFORE YOU GO ON . . .

● **REVIEW IT**

1. What is the relationship, if any, of amortization to (a) cost allocation, (b) asset valuation, and (c) cash accumulation?
2. Explain the factors that affect the calculation of amortization.
3. What does Loblaw use as its estimated useful life range for its buildings? For its equipment and fixtures? For its leasehold improvements? The answer to these questions is provided at the end of this chapter.

Amortization Methods

Amortization is generally calculated using one of these three methods:

1. Straight-line
2. Declining-balance
3. Units-of-activity

Like the alternative inventory cost flow assumptions discussed in Chapter 6, each amortization method is acceptable under generally accepted accounting principles. Management selects the method which it believes best measures an asset's contribution to revenue over its useful life. Once a method is chosen, it should be applied consistently over the useful life of the asset. Consistency enhances the comparability of financial statements.

Illustration 9-6 shows the distribution of the primary amortization methods in 200 Canadian companies. Clearly, straight-line amortization is the most widely used method.

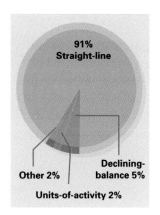

Illustration 9-6
Use of amortization methods in Canadian public companies

For this reason, we will illustrate the procedures for straight-line amortization and simply discuss the alternative approaches. In this manner, we introduce you to the basic idea of amortization as an allocation concept without entangling you in too much procedural detail. Details on the alternative approaches are presented in the appendix to this chapter.

Our illustration of amortization methods, both here and in the appendix, is based on the following data for a delivery truck purchased by Perfect Pizzas Ltd. on January 1, 2004:

Cost	$33,000
Expected salvage value	$3,000
Estimated useful life (in years)	5
Estimated useful life (in kilometres)	100,000

Straight-Line. Under the straight-line method, an equal amount of amortization is expensed each year of the asset's useful life. To calculate the annual amortization expense, we divide amortizable cost by the estimated useful life. Amortizable cost represents the total amount subject to amortization and is calculated as the cost of the asset less its salvage value. The amortizable cost is then divided by the asset's useful life to determine amortization expense. The calculation of amortization expense in the first year for Perfect Pizzas' delivery truck is shown in Illustration 9-7.

Illustration 9-7
Formula for straight-line method

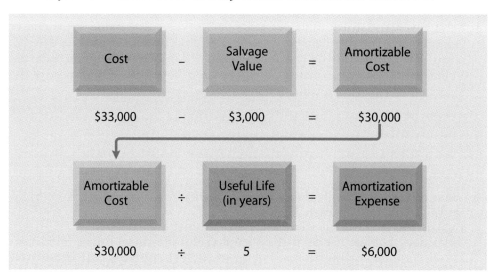

Alternatively, we can calculate an annual rate at which the delivery truck is to be amortized. In this case, the rate is 20% (100% ÷ 5 years). When an annual rate is used under the straight-line method, the percentage rate is applied to the amortizable cost of the asset, as shown in the **amortization schedule** in Illustration 9-8.

				End of Year	
	Amortizable	Amortization	Amortization	Accumulated	Book
Year	Cost	Rate	Expense	Amortization	Value
					$33,000
2004	$30,000	20%	$6,000	$ 6,000	27,000
2005	30,000	20%	6,000	12,000	21,000
2006	30,000	20%	6,000	18,000	15,000
2007	30,000	20%	6,000	24,000	9,000
2008	30,000	20%	6,000	30,000	3,000
			$30,000		

PERFECT PIZZAS LTD.

Illustration 9-8
Straight-line amortization
schedule

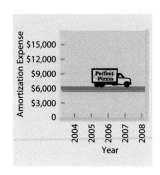

Note that the amortization expense of $6,000 is the same each year, and that the book value at the end of the useful life is equal to the estimated $3,000 salvage value.

What happens when an asset is purchased during the year, rather than on January 1, as in our example? In that case, it is necessary to **prorate the annual amortization for the proportion of the year used.** If Perfect Pizzas had purchased the delivery truck on April 1, 2004, the truck would be used for nine months in 2004. The amortization for 2004 would be $4,500 ($30,000 × 20% × $\frac{9}{12}$ of a year).

Some companies establish a convention for partial period amortization for simplicity, rather than calculating amortization monthly. Companies may choose to allocate a full year's amortization in the year of acquisition and none in the year of disposal. Other companies record a half year's amortization in the year of acquisition, and a half year's amortization in the year of disposition. Whatever company policy is used for partial-year amortization, the impact is not significant in the long run if the policy is applied consistently. We will assume that amortization is calculated monthly in the remainder of this chapter and in the end-of-chapter material.

As indicated earlier, the straight-line method predominates in practice. For example, such large companies as Air Canada, Bombardier, Domtar, and Loblaw use the straight-line method. It is simple to apply, and it matches expenses with revenues appropriately when the use of the asset is reasonably uniform throughout the service life. The types of assets that give equal benefits over their useful lives generally are those for which daily use does not affect productivity. Examples are office furniture and fixtures, buildings, warehouses, and garages for motor vehicles.

Declining-Balance. The declining-balance method is called an "accelerated method" because it results in more amortization in the early years of an asset's life than does the straight-line approach. However, because the total amount of amortization (the amortizable cost) taken over an asset's life is the same no matter what approach is used, the declining-balance method produces a decreasing annual amortization expense over the useful life of the asset. That is, in early years, declining-balance amortization expense will exceed straight-line, but in later years, it will be less than straight-line. Managers might choose an accelerated approach in order to match higher cost with higher revenue-producing ability in the early years, or if they think that an asset's utility will decline very quickly.

The declining-balance approach can be applied at different rates, which result in varying speeds of amortization. A common declining-balance rate is double the straight-line rate. If we apply the declining-balance method to Perfect Pizzas' delivery truck using double the straight-line rate and a five-year life, we get the pattern of amortization shown in Illustration 9-9.

Illustration 9-9
Declining-balance
amortization schedule

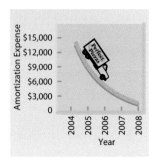

		End of Year	
Year	Amortization Expense	Accumulated Amortization	Book Value
			$33,000
2004	$13,200	$13,200	19,800
2005	7,920	21,120	11,880
2006	4,752	25,872	7,128
2007	2,851	28,723	4,277
2008	1,277	30,000	3,000
	$30,000		

PERFECT PIZZAS LTD.

The chapter's appendix presents the calculations behind these numbers. Again, note that total amortization over the life of the truck is $30,000, the amortizable cost.

Units-of-Activity. As indicated earlier, useful life can be expressed in ways other than a time period. Under the units-of-activity method, useful life is expressed in terms of either the total units of production or total use expected from the asset. The units-of-activity method is ideally suited to factory machinery: production can be measured in terms of units of output or machine hours used in operating the machinery. It is also possible to use the method for such items as delivery equipment (kilometres driven) and airplanes (hours in use). The units-of-activity method is generally not suitable for such assets as buildings or furniture, because activity levels are difficult to measure for these types of assets.

Applying the units-of-activity method to the delivery truck owned by Perfect Pizzas, we first must know some basic information. Perfect Pizzas expects to be able to drive the truck a total of 100,000 kilometres, with ongoing repairs and maintenance. Assuming that the mileage occurs in the pattern given over its five-year life, amortization in each year is shown in Illustration 9-10. The calculations used to arrive at these results are presented in the chapter's appendix.

Illustration 9-10
Units-of-activity
amortization schedule

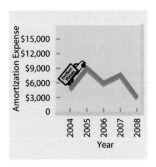

PERFECT PIZZAS LTD.

	Units-of-Activity (km)	Amortization Expense	End of Year	
Year			Accumulated Amortization	Book Value
				$33,000
2004	15,000	$ 4,500	$ 4,500	28,500
2005	30,000	9,000	13,500	19,500
2006	20,000	6,000	19,500	13,500
2007	25,000	7,500	27,000	6,000
2008	10,000	3,000	30,000	3,000
	100,000	$30,000		

As the name implies, under units-of-activity amortization, the amount of amortization is proportional to the activity that took place during that period. For example, the delivery truck was driven twice as many kilometres in 2005 as in 2004, and amortization was exactly twice as much in 2005 as in 2004.

Management's Choice: Comparison of Methods. Illustration 9-11 presents a comparison of annual and total amortization expense for Perfect Pizzas under the three methods. In addition, if we assume (as we have in Illustration 9-11) that net earnings, prior to deducting amortization expense, were $45,000 for each of the five years, we can clearly see the impact the choice of method has on net earnings.

| Year | Straight-Line | | Declining-Balance | | Units-of-Activity | |
	Amortization Expense	Net Earnings	Amortization Expense	Net Earnings	Amortization Expense	Net Earnings
2004	$6,000	$39,000	$13,200	$ 31,800	$4,500	$40,500
2005	6,000	39,000	7,920	37,080	9,000	36,000
2006	6,000	39,000	4,752	40,248	6,000	39,000
2007	6,000	39,000	2,851	42,149	7,500	37,500
2008	6,000	39,000	1,277	43,723	3,000	42,000
	$30,000	$195,000	$30,000	$195,000	$30,000	$195,000

Illustration 9-11
Comparison of amortization methods and effects on earnings

As discussed earlier, straight-line amortization results in a constant amount of expense and earnings impact each year. Declining-balance results in a higher expense in the early years, and correspondingly lower earnings, and a lower expense in later years, with correspondingly higher earnings. The units-of-activity method results vary depending on actual usage each year. While periodic amortization and net earnings vary considerably each year under the different methods, *total* amortization and *total* net earnings are the same for a five-year period.

Each method is acceptable in accounting because each recognizes the decline in service potential of the asset in a rational and systematic manner.

Amortization and Income Taxes

The Canada Customs and Revenue Agency (CCRA) allows corporate taxpayers to deduct a specified amount of amortization expense when calculating taxable income. For accounting purposes, a company should choose the amortization method that best matches revenue to expense. Tax regulations have different objectives. Income tax regulations require the taxpayer to use a defined amortization method—declining-balance—on the tax return, regardless of which method is used in preparing financial statements.

The Canada Customs and Revenue Agency also does not permit corporations to estimate the useful lives, or amortization rates, of assets. It groups assets into various classes and provides maximum amortization rates for each class. Amortization allowed for income tax purposes is calculated on a class (group) basis, and is termed capital cost allowance (CCA). Capital cost allowance is an optional deduction from taxable income, so you may see some businesses deducting amortization for accounting purposes (required to fulfill the matching principle) while deducting no CCA for tax purposes.

Helpful Hint Amortization per GAAP is usually different from amortization per CCRA.

⊕ **International Note**
In Germany, tax laws have a strong influence on financial accounting. The amortization expense determined by the tax code must also be used for preparing financial statements.

Amortization Disclosure in the Notes

The choice of amortization method must be disclosed in a company's financial statements or in the related notes that accompany the statements. Illustration 9-12 shows the "property and equipment" note from Air Canada's financial statements.

Illustration 9-12
Disclosure of amortization policies

AIR CANADA

AIR CANADA
Notes to the Financial Statements
December 31, 2002

Property and Equipment Operating property and equipment, including property under capital lease, are depreciated to estimated residual values based on the straight-line method over their estimated service lives. Mainline aircraft and operating flight equipment are depreciated over 20 to 25 years, with 10 to 15% estimated residual values. Regional aircraft and flight equipment are depreciated over 20 years, with 20% estimated residual values. Aircraft reconfiguration costs are amortized over 3 years. Aircraft introduction costs are amortized over 4 years. Betterments to owned aircraft are capitalized and amortized over the remaining service life of the aircraft. Betterments to aircraft on operating leases are amortized over the term of the lease.

From this note, we learn that Air Canada uses the straight-line method of amortization (also known as depreciation, which is the terminology that Air Canada uses in its note). It uses varying useful lives and residual, or salvage, values. Its regional aircraft (e.g., used by carriers such as Jazz) are amortized over a shorter useful life, and have a higher residual value, than its mainline aircraft.

Revising Periodic Amortization

STUDY OBJECTIVE

4

Describe the procedure for revising periodic amortization.

Annual amortization expense should be reviewed periodically by management. If wear and tear or obsolescence indicates that annual amortization is inadequate or excessive, the amortization expense amount should be changed.

When a change in an estimate is required, the change is made in **current and future years but not to prior periods.** Thus, when a change is made, (1) there is no correction of previously recorded amortization expense, and (2) amortization expense for current and future years is revised. The rationale for this treatment is that continual restatement of prior periods would adversely affect the user's confidence in financial statements. The revised amortization is calculated using the net book value at the time of the change in estimate, the revised salvage value, and the remaining useful life.

Significant changes in estimates must be disclosed in the financial statements. Illustration 9-13 shows an example of the disclosure of a change in estimate. Air Canada extended the estimated useful life of its aircraft in 2001, which decreased amortization expense, and reduced their salvage value, which increased amortization expense. The combined effect of this change in estimates was to decrease total amortization expense and increase net earnings.

Illustration 9-13
Disclosure of change in amortization estimate

AIR CANADA

AIR CANADA **Notes to the Financial Statements** **December 31, 2001**
Depreciation and Amortization   In the second quarter 2001, consistent with industry practices and in order to more accurately reflect the expected useful life of owned aircraft, the Corporation changed its estimate of the useful life of Airbus aircraft from 20 to 25 years, with a corresponding reduction in estimated residual values from 15% to 10%. As a result of this change, operating expenses were reduced by $9 [million] for the year ended December 31, 2001.

BEFORE YOU GO ON . . .

● REVIEW IT

1. Why is amortization an allocation concept rather than a valuation concept?
2. What is the formula for calculating annual amortization under the straight-line method?
3. How do the three amortization methods differ in their effects on annual amortization expense over the useful life of an asset? Total amortization expense?
4. Are revisions of periodic amortization made to prior periods? Explain.

● DO IT

On January 1, 2004, Iron Mountain Ski Corporation purchased a new snow grooming machine for $50,000. The machine is estimated to have a 10-year life with a $2,000 salvage value.

(a) What journal entry would Iron Mountain Ski Corporation make to record amortization at December 31, 2004, if it uses the straight-line method of amortization?

(b) Would amortization expense and net earnings in 2004 be higher or lower if the declining balance method had been used instead of the straight-line method of amortization?

Action Plan

- Calculate amortizable cost (Cost – Salvage value).
- Divide the amortizable cost by the asset's estimated useful life.
- Compare the effects of straight-line and declining-balance amortization methods.
- Remember that amortization expense reduces net earnings, so the impact on net earnings is the opposite of the impact on the expense.

Solution

(a)

$$\text{Amortization expense} = \frac{\text{Cost} - \text{Salvage value}}{\text{Useful life}} = \frac{\$50,000 - \$2,000}{10} = \$4,800$$

The entry to record amortization expense would be:

Dec. 31	Amortization Expense	4,800	
	Accumulated Amortization		4,800
	(To record annual amortization on snow grooming machine)		

(b) The straight-line method of amortization results in an equal amount of amortization expense each year. The declining-balance method results in higher amortization expense in the early years than straight-line. This would result in a lower net earnings amount.

EXPENDITURES DURING USEFUL LIFE

During the useful life of a long-lived asset, a company may incur costs for ordinary repairs, additions, and improvements. Ordinary repairs are expenditures to maintain the operating efficiency and expected productive life of the unit. They are usually fairly small amounts that occur frequently throughout the service life. Motor tune-ups and oil changes, the painting of buildings, and the replacement of worn-out gears on factory machinery are examples. They are debited to Repair (or Maintenance) Expense as incurred. Because they are immediately matched against revenues as an expense, these costs are **operating expenditures**.

Additions and improvements are costs incurred to increase the operating efficiency, productive capacity, or expected useful life of the asset. These expenditures are usually material in amount and occur infrequently during the period of ownership. Expenditures for additions and improvements increase the company's investment in productive facilities and are generally debited to the property, plant, and equipment account affected. Accordingly, they are **capital expenditures**. The accounting for capital expenditures varies, depending on the nature of the expenditure.

Additions and improvements are amortized over the remaining life of the original structure (for example, in the case of a new roof on a building) or the useful life of the addition, if it is not dependent on the original asset.

As described in the note to the financial statements displayed in Illustration 9-12, Air Canada incurs costs to reconfigure (called a betterment by Air Canada) its aircraft. These costs are recorded as capital expenditures, and amortized over their remaining useful lives.

Helpful Hint These expenditures occur after all costs have been incurred to make the asset ready for its intended use when it was acquired.

Illustration 9-14
Methods of property,
plant, and equipment
disposal

DISPOSALS OF PROPERTY, PLANT, AND EQUIPMENT

Companies dispose of property, plant, and equipment that is no longer useful to them. Illustration 9-14 shows three methods of disposal.

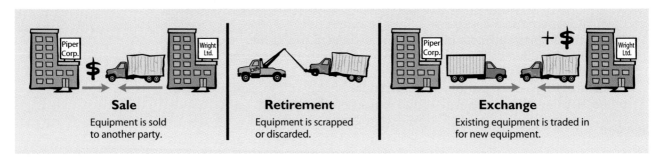

Sale	Retirement	Exchange
Equipment is sold to another party.	Equipment is scrapped or discarded.	Existing equipment is traded in for new equipment.

STUDY OBJECTIVE

5

Explain how to account for the disposal of property, plant, and equipment.

Whatever the disposal method, the company must determine the book value of the asset at the time of disposal. Recall that the book value is the difference between the cost of the asset and the accumulated amortization to date. If the disposal occurs at any time during the year, amortization for the fraction of the year to the date of disposal must be recorded. The book value is then eliminated by reducing (debiting) Accumulated Amortization for the total amortization associated with that asset to the date of disposal, and reducing (crediting) the asset account for the cost of the asset.

Sale of Property, Plant, and Equipment

In a disposal by sale, the book value of the asset is compared with the proceeds received from the sale. If the proceeds from the sale exceed the book value of the asset, a **gain on disposal** occurs. If the proceeds from the sale are less than the book value of the asset sold, **a loss on disposal** occurs.

Helpful Hint
Proceeds − Book value = Gain (loss)

Only by coincidence will the book value and the fair market value of the asset be the same at the time the asset is sold. Gains and losses on sales of property, plant, and equipment are therefore quite common. As an example, Air Canada reported a $42 million loss on the sale of assets in 2002.

Gain on Sale. To illustrate a gain on sale of property, plant, and equipment, assume that on July 1, 2004, Wright Ltd. sells office furniture for $25,000 cash. The office furniture originally cost $60,000 and as at January 1, 2004, had accumulated amortization of $33,000. Amortization for the first six months of 2004 is $5,500. The entry to record amortization expense and update accumulated amortization to July 1 is as follows:

A	=	L	+	SE
−5,500				−5,500

Cash flows: no effect

July 1	Amortization Expense	5,500	
	Accumulated Amortization—Office Furniture		5,500
	(To record amortization expense for the first six months of 2004)		

After the accumulated amortization balance is updated, a gain on disposal of $3,500 is calculated as shown in Illustration 9-15.

Illustration 9-15
Calculation of gain on disposal

Cost of office furniture	$60,000
Less: Accumulated amortization ($33,000 + $5,500)	38,500
Book value at date of disposal	21,500
Proceeds from sale	25,000
Gain on disposal	$ 3,500

The entry to record the sale of the office furniture is as follows:

July 1	Cash	25,000	
	Accumulated Amortization—Office Furniture	38,500	
	Office Furniture		60,000
	Gain on Disposal		3,500
	(To record sale of office furniture at a gain)		

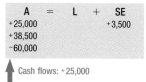

The gain on disposal is usually reported in the Other Revenues section of the statement of earnings.

Loss on Sale. Assume that instead of selling the office furniture for $25,000, Wright sells it for $20,000. In this case, a loss of $1,500 is calculated as in Illustration 9-16.

Cost of office furniture	$60,000
Less: Accumulated amortization	38,500
Book value at date of disposal	21,500
Proceeds from sale	20,000
Loss on disposal	$ 1,500

Illustration 9-16
Calculation of loss on disposal

The entry to record the sale of the office furniture is as follows:

July 1	Cash	20,000	
	Accumulated Amortization—Office Furniture	38,500	
	Loss on Disposal	1,500	
	Office Furniture		60,000
	(To record sale of office furniture at a loss)		

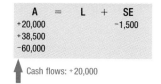

The loss on disposal is usually reported in the Other Expenses section of the statement of earnings.

Retirement of Property, Plant, and Equipment

Some assets are simply retired by the company at the end of their useful lives rather than sold. For example, some productive assets used in manufacturing may have very specific uses and consequently have no ready market when the company no longer needs them. In this case, the asset is simply retired.

Retirement of an asset is recorded as a special case of a sale where no cash is received. Accumulated Amortization is decreased (debited) for the full amount of amortization taken over the life of the asset. The asset account is reduced (credited) for the original cost of the asset. The loss (a gain is not possible on a retirement) is equal to the asset's book value on the date of retirement.

Air Canada retired 20 DC-9s, three B747s, three B767s, four B737s, and 28 F28 aircraft in 2002. These aircraft were retired from active service and no gain or loss was recorded.

Exchanges of Property, Plant, and Equipment

Some long-lived assets are sold for cash when they are no longer needed. Others are commonly exchanged for new assets. In an exchange of assets, a new asset is typically purchased by trading in an old asset, on which a **trade-in allowance** is given toward the purchase price of the new asset. An additional cash payment is usually also required for the difference between the trade-in allowance and the purchase price of the new asset.

Accounting for exchange transactions is complex. Further discussion of exchanges is left for future accounting courses.

BEFORE YOU GO ON . . .

- **REVIEW IT**

    1. What is the difference between an ordinary repair and an addition or improvement? Why is this distinction important to financial reporting?
    2. What is the proper accounting for sales and retirements of property, plant, and equipment?
    3. What is the formula for calculating a gain or loss on disposal?

- **DO IT**

Overland Trucking Ltd. has a truck that cost $30,000 and has accumulated amortization of $16,000. Assume two different situations: (1) the company sells the truck for $17,000 cash, and (2) the truck is worthless, so the company simply retires it. What entry should Overland use to record each scenario?

Action Plan

- Update any unrecorded amortization for partial periods.
- Compare the proceeds to the book value to determine whether any gain or loss has occurred.
- Record any proceeds received and any gain or loss. Remove both the asset and accumulated amortization accounts.

Solution

1. Sale of truck for cash:

Cash	17,000	
Accumulated Amortization—Truck	16,000	
Truck		30,000
Gain on Disposal [$17,000 − ($30,000 − $16,000)]		3,000
(To record sale of truck at a gain)		

2. Retirement of truck:

Accumulated Amortization—Truck	16,000	
Loss on Disposal	14,000	
Truck		30,000
(To record retirement of truck at a loss)		

Intangible Assets

STUDY OBJECTIVE

6

Identify the basic issues related to reporting intangible assets.

Intangible assets are rights, privileges, and competitive advantages that result from ownership of long-lived assets that do not possess physical substance. Many companies' most valuable assets are intangible. Some widely known intangibles are Alexander Graham Bell's patent on the telephone, the franchises of Tim Hortons, the trade name of President's Choice, and the trademark CBC.

    As you will learn in this section, although financial statements do report many intangibles, many other financially significant intangibles are not reported. To give an example, according to its 2002 financial statements, Research In Motion had a net book value of $876,745. But its *market* value—the total market price of all its shares on that same date—was $2,963,330. Thus, its actual market value was more than $2 million greater than what its balance sheet said the company was worth at that time. It is not uncommon for a company's reported book value to differ from its market value, because balance sheets are reported at historical cost. But such an extreme difference seriously diminishes the usefulness of the balance sheet to decision-makers. In the case of Research In Motion the difference is due to unrecorded intangibles. For many high-tech or intellectual property companies, most of their value is from intangibles such as knowledge assets, many of which are not reported under current accounting rules.

Intangibles must be evidenced by contracts, licences, and other documents. Intangibles may arise from the following sources:

1. Government grants such as patents, copyrights, franchises, trademarks, and trade names
2. Acquisition of another business in which the purchase price includes a payment for goodwill
3. Private monopolistic arrangements arising from contractual agreements, such as franchises and leases

ACCOUNTING FOR INTANGIBLE ASSETS

Similar to tangible assets, **intangible assets are recorded at cost**. Cost includes all costs of acquisition and other costs necessary to make the intangible asset ready for its intended use. Only certain types of intangible assets, however, are amortized. To distinguish between those intangibles that are amortizable and those that are not, we categorize intangible assets as having either a limited life or an indefinite life.

If an intangible asset has a **limited life**, its amortizable cost (cost less salvage value) should be allocated over the shorter of the (1) estimated useful life and (2) legal life. Normally, the useful life of an intangible asset is the shorter period, so it is the one most often used as the amortization period.

Intangible assets are typically amortized on a straight-line basis. To record amortization, Amortization Expense is increased (debited) and the specific intangible asset account is decreased (credited). Unlike tangible assets, no contra account (e.g., Accumulated Amortization) is usually used. This is because, contrary to tangible assets, most intangible assets cannot be replaced. It is therefore not as relevant for financial statement users to know the original cost and the proportion that the intangible asset has been amortized.

When analysing a company that has significant intangibles, the reasonableness of the estimated useful life should be evaluated. In determining useful life, the company should consider obsolescence, inadequacy, and other factors; these may cause an intangible to become economically ineffective before the end of its legal life. For example, suppose a computer hardware manufacturer obtains a patent on a new computer chip that it has developed (we will discuss patents in the next section). The legal life of the patent is 20 years. From experience, we know that the useful life of a computer chip is not more than four to five years, and often less—because new, superior chips are developed so rapidly, existing chips quickly become obsolete. Consequently, we would question the amortization expense of a company if it amortized its patent on a computer chip for longer than five years. Amortizing an intangible over a period that is too long will understate amortization expense, overstate the company's net earnings, and overstate its assets.

If an intangible has an **indefinite life**, it is not amortized. However, its cost is reviewed and tested for an impairment loss annually, or more often as circumstances dictate. Recall from earlier in this chapter that an impairment occurs if the asset's market value permanently falls below its book value. If any impairment is evident, the asset must be written down to its market value and an impairment loss recorded. If no impairment has occurred, the asset remains at its current value until the following year, when it is evaluated again.

At disposal, just as with tangible assets, the book value of the intangible asset is eliminated, and a gain or loss, if any, is recorded.

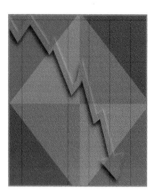

BUSINESS INSIGHT

INVESTOR PERSPECTIVE

AOL Time Warner Inc. wrote down its intangible assets by a staggering U.S.$54 billion in the first quarter of 2002. AOL blamed the introduction of a new accounting standard requiring intangible assets with indefinite lives, such as goodwill, to be tested annually for impairment, rather than amortized. This write-off is the largest asset impairment loss recorded in corporate history. However, it is not expected to be the last. Most companies paid high prices for acquisitions during the high-tech boom. The market value of these acquisitions—many of which were over-valued—have since fallen with the bear market.

Decision Toolkit

DECISION CHECKPOINTS	INFO NEEDED FOR DECISION	TOOL TO USE FOR DECISION	HOW TO EVALUATE RESULTS
Is the company's amortization of intangibles reasonable?	Estimated useful life of intangibles with definite lives from notes to financial statements of this company and its competitors	If the company's estimated useful life significantly exceeds that of competitors, or does not seem reasonable in light of the circumstances, the reason for the difference should be investigated.	Too high an estimated useful life will result in understating amortization expense and overstating net earnings.
Does the company have impairment losses?	Impairment loss recorded on statement of earnings; book value of intangible assets with indefinite lives	Review the impairment losses recorded by the company. Compare book and market values in light of current business conditions and company performance.	If book value is higher than market value, assets and net earnings will be overstated in the current period. Watch for earnings management—the deliberate timing of the recognition of impairment losses.

TYPES OF INTANGIBLE ASSETS

As mentioned in the previous section, intangible assets are segregated into two categories—those with limited lives and those with indefinite lives—in order to determine whether or not the intangible asset should be amortized. Examples of intangible assets with limited lives include patents and copyrights. We also include research and development costs in this section because these costs often lead to the creation of patents and copyrights. Examples of intangible assets with indefinite lives include trademarks and trade names, franchises and licences, and goodwill. Intangible assets do not always fit perfectly in a specific category. Sometimes trademarks, trade names, franchises, or licences do have limited lives. In such cases, they would be amortized over their useful lives. It is more usual, however, for these intangible assets, along with goodwill, to have indefinite lives.

Intangible Assets with Limited Lives

Patents. A patent is an exclusive right issued by the Canadian Intellectual Property Office of Industry Canada that enables the recipient to manufacture, sell, or otherwise control an invention for a period of 20 years from the date of the application. **The initial cost of a patent is the cash or cash equivalent price paid to acquire the patent.**

The cost of a patent should be amortized over its 20-year legal life or its useful life, whichever is shorter. To illustrate the calculation of patent amortization, assume that National Labs purchases a patent at a cost of $60,000. If the useful life of the patent is estimated to be eight years and there is no salvage value, the annual amortization expense is $7,500 ($60,000 ÷ 8). The following entry records the annual amortization:

Dec. 31	Amortization Expense	7,500	
	Patent		7,500
	(To record patent amortization)		

A	=	L	+	SE
-7,500				-7,500

Cash flows: no effect

The saying "A patent is only as good as the money you're prepared to spend defending it" is very true. Most patents are subject to some type of litigation by competitors. An example is the $25-million patent infringement suit won by Nortel Networks against Ciena Corp. in protecting fibre optics patents. If the owner incurs legal costs in successfully defending the patent in an infringement suit, such costs are considered necessary to establish the patent's validity. Thus, **they are added to the Patent account and amortized over the remaining life of the patent.**

Copyrights. A copyright is granted by the Canadian Intellectual Property Office, giving the owner the exclusive right to reproduce and sell an artistic or published work. Copyrights extend for the life of the creator plus 50 years. The cost of the copyright consists of the cost of acquiring and defending it. The cost may be only the fee paid, or it may amount to a great deal more if a copyright infringement suit is involved. Generally, the useful life of a copyright is significantly shorter than its legal life, and the copyright is therefore amortized over its useful life.

Research and Development Costs. Research and development (R & D) costs are not intangible assets per se. But they may lead to patents, copyrights, new processes, and new products. Many companies spend considerable sums of money on research and development in an ongoing effort to develop new products or processes. For example, in a recent year Nortel Networks spent nearly $5 billion on research and development. There are many uncertainties in identifying the extent and timing of the future benefits of these expenditures. As a result, research costs are **always recorded as an expense when incurred,** whether the research and development is successful or not. Certain development costs can be capitalized if it is reasonably certain that they will provide future benefits; otherwise, they too must be expensed.

To illustrate, assume that Laser Scanner Inc. spent $3 million on research and $2 million on development that resulted in two highly successful patents. The $3-million research cost cannot be included in the cost of the patent. Rather, it is recorded as an expense when incurred. The development cost of $2 million would be capitalized and included in the cost of the patent since the development was successful.

International Note

Accounting for R & D differs dramatically across nations. U.S. GAAP, as well as German, does not allow any R & D expenses to be capitalized, while other nations such as Canada, Great Britain, Japan, and Korea permit limited capitalization of some development costs. Still other countries, such as Italy, Sweden, and Brazil, have much more liberal R & D policies allowing full capitalization.

BUSINESS INSIGHT

INTERNATIONAL PERSPECTIVE

A survey by Research Infosource consulting group of Canada's top R & D spenders reveals that companies continue to spend money on research and development despite declining business prospects. In all, 581 companies invested $13.3 billion in R & D, an increase of nearly 5% from the prior year. Nortel Networks and JDS Uniphase were the top two spenders in Canada. This suggests that Canadian companies are responding to the federal government's innovation strategy to move Canada from fifteenth place in global R & D spending to fifth place by 2010.

Source: Showwei Chu, "R & D Spending Jumps," *The Globe and Mail,* September 5, 2002, B3.

Intangible Assets with Indefinite Lives

Trademarks and Trade Names. A trademark or trade name is a word, phrase, jingle, or symbol that distinguishes or identifies a particular enterprise or product. Trade names like the Blue Jays, Kleenex, Big Mac, President's Choice, the Habs, and TSN create immediate product identification and generally enhance the sale of the product. The creator or original user may obtain the exclusive legal right to the trademark or trade name by registering it with the Canadian Intellectual Property Office. Such registration provides continuous protection and may be renewed every 15 years as long as the trademark or trade name is in use.

If the trademark or trade name is purchased, the cost is the purchase price. If it is developed by the enterprise itself, the cost includes legal fees, registration fees, design costs, successful legal defence costs, and other expenditures directly related to securing it.

Because trademarks and trade names normally have indefinite lives, they are not amortized. The book value must be tested annually for impairment and a loss recognized if appropriate.

BUSINESS INSIGHT

MANAGEMENT PERSPECTIVE

Domain names are a good example of a trade name. Buying domain names is a hot business these days. While the cost of registration is negligible, if a company has to purchase its name from a cybersquatter—someone who registers names in the hopes of reselling them for a profit—the cost can rise quickly.

When eBay Inc. tried to register <www.ebay.ca>, it discovered that the name had been registered previously by a Dartmouth, N.S., entrepreneur. eBay then had two options to consider. Since eBay is a registered trademark around the world, the company could take legal action, or it could negotiate to buy the name from the current registrant. The entrepreneur eventually gave up the name without a fight rather than go to court and face huge legal bills.

Franchises and Licences. When you drive down the street in your Protegé purchased from a Mazda dealer, fill up your tank at the corner Petro-Canada station, eat lunch at Wendy's, and buy coffee from Tim Hortons, you are dealing with franchises. A franchise is a contractual arrangement under which the franchisor grants the franchisee the right to sell certain products, to render specific services, or to use certain trademarks or trade names, usually within a designated geographic area.

Another type of franchise, granted by a government body, permits the company to use public property in performing its services. Examples are the use of city streets for a bus line or taxi service; the use of public land for telephone, power, and cable television lines; and the use of airwaves for radio or TV broadcasting. Such operating rights are referred to as licences.

Franchises and licences may be granted for a definite period of time, an indefinite period, or perpetually. **When costs can be identified with the acquisition of the franchise or licence, an intangible asset should be recognized.** Annual payments made under a franchise agreement should be recorded as **operating expenses** in the period in which they are incurred. In the case of a limited life, the cost of a franchise (or licence) should be amortized over the useful life. If the life is indefinite, it is not amortized, but is tested annually for impairment.

Air Canada reports operating rights with a carrying value of $84 million on its balance sheet for route rights and landing and departure slot purchase costs. These rights have indefinite lives and are not amortized. Air Canada states that no impairment losses are evident on these operating rights.

Goodwill. Usually the largest intangible asset that appears on a company's balance sheet is goodwill. Goodwill represents the value of all favourable attributes that relate to a company. These include exceptional management, a desirable location, good customer relations, skilled employees, high-quality products, fair pricing policies, and harmonious relations with labour unions. Unlike other assets such as investments or property, plant, and equipment, which can be sold *individually* in the marketplace, goodwill can be identified only with the business *as a whole*.

If goodwill can only be identified with the business as a whole, how can it be determined? Certainly, many businesses have many of the factors cited above (exceptional management, a desirable location, and so on). However, to determine the amount of goodwill in these situations would be difficult and very subjective. In other words, to recognize goodwill without an exchange transaction that puts a value on it would lead to subjective valuations that do not contribute to the reliability of financial statements. **Therefore, goodwill is recorded only when there is an exchange transaction that involves the purchase of an entire business.**

Because goodwill has an indefinite life, just as the company has an indefinite life, it is not amortized. Since goodwill is measured using the market value of a company—a subjective valuation which can easily change—it must be tested regularly for impairment.

When Air Canada tested its goodwill and other intangible assets with indefinite lives for impairment, it found that the fair market value of these assets exceeded their book value. Consequently, no impairment loss was recorded.

BEFORE YOU GO ON . . .

● **REVIEW IT**

1. What are the main differences between accounting for property, plant, and equipment and for intangible assets?
2. Give some examples of intangible assets in your everyday surroundings.
3. Explain the accounting for research and development costs.
4. Distinguish between the amortization policy for intangible assets with limited lives and the policy for those with indefinite lives.

Statement Presentation of Long-Lived Assets

BALANCE SHEET PRESENTATION

Long-lived assets are normally reported in the balance sheet under the headings Property, Plant, and Equipment, and Intangible Assets. Sometimes intangible assets are listed separately, following Property, Plant, and Equipment, with no separate caption. Goodwill must be separately disclosed; other intangibles can be grouped together for reporting purposes. Some companies combine property, plant, and equipment and intangible assets under one heading called Capital Assets.

STUDY OBJECTIVE 7

Indicate how long-lived assets are reported on the balance sheet.

Either on the balance sheet or in the notes, the balances of the major classes of assets should be disclosed, as well as the accumulated amortization by major classes or in total. In addition, the amortization methods used should be described and the amount of amortization expense for the period for the amortizable assets should be disclosed.

Illustration 9-17 is an excerpt from Air Canada's 2002 financial statements. Long-lived assets are summarized in the balance sheet and detailed in the notes.

Illustration 9-17
Balance sheet presentation
of long-lived assets

AIR CANADA

AIR CANADA Balance Sheet (partial) December 31, 2002 (in millions)	
Property and equipment (note 3)	$2,279
Goodwill	510
Other assets (note 5)	1,071

Note 3 details the cost and accumulated amortization for flight equipment and other property and equipment. Note 5 details the cost of Air Canada's indefinite life route rights and slot purchase costs, in addition to other assets. The accounting policy note to the financial statements reports the amortization policy and period used for amortization. This note was provided earlier in Illustration 9-12.

CASH FLOW STATEMENT PRESENTATION

It is also interesting to examine the cash flow statement to determine the amount of cash received and spent on the purchase and sale of long-lived assets. For example, the investing activities section of Air Canada's cash flow statement reports the following:

Illustration 9-18
Cash flow statement
presentation of long-lived
assets

AIR CANADA

AIR CANADA Cash Flow Statement (partial) Year Ended December 31, 2002 (in millions)	
Investing Activities	
Proceeds from sale of assets	$ 17
Additions to property and equipment, net of recovered progress payments	(109)

As indicated, Air Canada made significant investments in property and equipment as part of its fleet modernization program. The level of investment suggests that Air Canada believes it can earn a reasonable rate of return on these assets.

Analysing Assets

STUDY OBJECTIVE
8

Describe the methods for
evaluating the use of assets.

The presentation of financial statement information about long-lived assets enables decision-makers to analyse a company's use of its total assets. We will use two ratios to analyse assets: return on assets and asset turnover.

RETURN ON ASSETS

An overall measure of profitability is the return on assets ratio. This ratio is calculated by dividing net earnings by average total assets. The return on assets ratio indicates the amount of net earnings generated by each dollar invested in assets. Thus, the higher the return on assets, the more profitable the company.

The following data are provided for Air Canada and WestJet Airlines Ltd. for the fiscal years 2002 and 2001:

(in millions)	Air Canada		WestJet	
	2002	2001	2002	2001
Net sales	$9,826	$ 9,611	$680	$478
Net earnings (loss)	(828)	(1,315)	52	37
Total assets	7,416	8,744	784	393

Total assets at the end of 2000 were $9,732 million for Air Canada and $337 million for WestJet.

The 2002 and 2001 return on assets of Air Canada, WestJet, and the industry averages are presented in Illustration 9-19.

Illustration 9-19
Return on assets

$$\text{RETURN ON ASSETS} = \frac{\text{NET EARNINGS}}{\text{AVERAGE TOTAL ASSETS}}$$

($ in millions)	2002	2001
Air Canada	$\dfrac{(\$828)}{(\$7,416 + \$8,744) \div 2} = (10.2\%)$	$\dfrac{(\$1,315)}{(\$8,744 + \$9,732) \div 2} = (14.2\%)$
WestJet	8.8%	10.1%
Industry average	(4.0%)	1.6%

As shown from the information provided, Air Canada had a miserable year in 2001, reporting a negative 14.2% return on assets. Despite continuing pressures on the airline industry, Air Canada was able to improve its return on assets in 2002 to negative 10.2%. Still, these ratios are both negative compared to positive—albeit declining—returns reported by WestJet. Air Canada also continues to report returns below that of the industry, even though the industry also reported a negative return in 2002. It is easy to see that the airline industry is in financial distress.

ASSET TURNOVER

The asset turnover ratio indicates how efficiently a company is able to generate sales with a given amount of assets—that is, how many dollars of sales are generated by each dollar invested in assets. It is calculated by dividing net sales by average total assets. When we compare two companies in the same industry, the one with the higher asset turnover ratio is operating more efficiently. It is generating more sales per dollar invested in assets.

The asset turnover ratios for Air Canada and WestJet Airlines for 2002 and 2001 are calculated in Illustration 9-20.

Illustration 9-20
Asset turnover

$$\text{ASSET TURNOVER} = \frac{\text{NET SALES}}{\text{AVERAGE TOTAL ASSETS}}$$

(in millions)	2002	2001
Air Canada	$\dfrac{\$9,826}{(\$7,416 + \$8,744) \div 2} = 1.2 \text{ times}$	$\dfrac{\$9,611}{(\$8,744 + \$9,732) \div 2} = 1.0 \text{ times}$
WestJet	1.2 times	1.3 times
Industry average	0.6 times	0.6 times

The asset turnover ratios in the illustration mean that for each dollar invested in assets, both Air Canada and WestJet generate sales of $1.20. While Air Canada's return on assets is declining, its asset turnover is improving—no doubt due to its equipment streamlining efforts. Air Canada's asset turnover of 1.2 times in 2002 is consistent with that of WestJet. Both companies, turnover ratios double the industry average.

Asset turnover ratios vary considerably across industries. The average asset turnover for utility companies is 0.6 times, and the grocery store industry has an average asset turnover of 2.4. Asset turnover ratios, therefore, are only comparable within—not between—industries.

PROFIT MARGIN REVISITED

For a complete picture of the sales-generating ability of assets, one would also want to look at the company's profit margin ratio. In Chapter 5, you learned about profit margin. Profit margin is calculated by dividing net earnings by net sales. It tells how effective a company is in turning its sales into earnings—that is, how much earnings are generated by each dollar of sales.

Together, the profit margin and asset turnover explain the return on assets ratio. Illustration 9-21 shows how return on assets can be calculated from the profit margin and asset turnover ratios for WestJet in 2002.

Illustration 9-21
Composition of WestJet's return on assets

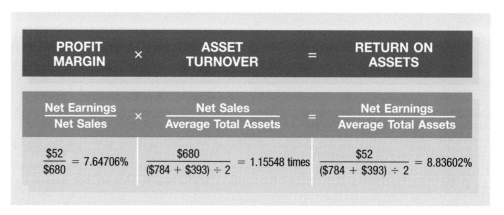

This relationship has important implications for management. From Illustration 9-21, we can see that if a company wants to increase its return on assets, it can do so either by increasing the margin it generates from each dollar of goods that it sells (profit margin), or by trying to increase the volume of goods that it sells (asset turnover).

We extended the ratios in Illustration 9-21 to five digits, in order to illustrate the calculation effect without the impact of rounding. The profit margin, 7.64706%, multiplied by the asset turnover of 1.15548 times, equals the return on assets of 8.83602%.

We chose WestJet to illustrate, rather than Air Canada, because WestJet reported a profit. As indicated from this information, WestJet Airlines has a solid profit margin, which suggests that it has good control of its cost structure. The profit margin is particularly impressive when compared to the industry average of (6.5%). As a result, WestJet was one of the few airlines to earn a profit in 2002. WestJet pursued a growth strategy in 2002—adding 10 new airplanes. If WestJet can increase its turnover in the future by generating more sales through this expanded capacity, it should attain a high level of profitability relative to its competitors and earn a higher return on its assets.

Decision Toolkit

DECISION CHECKPOINTS	INFO NEEDED FOR DECISION	TOOL TO USE FOR DECISION	HOW TO EVALUATE RESULTS
Is the company using its assets effectively?	Net earnings and average total assets	$\text{Return on assets} = \dfrac{\text{Net earnings}}{\text{Average total assets}}$	Higher value suggests favourable efficiency (use of assets).
How effective is the company at generating sales from its assets?	Net sales and average total assets	$\text{Asset turnover} = \dfrac{\text{Net sales}}{\text{Average total assets}}$	Indicates the sales dollars generated per dollar of assets. A high value suggests the company is effective in using its resources to generate sales.

BEFORE YOU GO ON . . .

● **REVIEW IT**

1. How are long-lived assets presented on the balance sheet? The cash flow statement?
2. What information related to long-lived assets is disclosed in the notes to the financial statements?
3. What is the purpose of the return on assets? Of the asset turnover? How are these ratios calculated?
4. What are the two components that explain the return on assets ratio?

NAVIGATOR

A P P E N D I X   9 A

CALCULATIONS OF AMORTIZATION USING OTHER METHODS

In this appendix, we show the calculations of the amortization expense amounts used in the chapter for the declining-balance and units-of-activity methods.

STUDY OBJECTIVE

⑨

Calculate periodic amortization using the declining-balance method and the units-of-activity method.

Declining-Balance

The **declining-balance method** produces a decreasing annual amortization expense over the useful life of the asset. It is called the "declining-balance" method because the calculation of periodic amortization is based on a declining book value of the asset (cost less accumulated amortization). Annual amortization expense is calculated by multiplying the book value at the beginning of the year by the declining-balance amortization rate. **The amortization rate remains constant from year to year, but the book value to which the rate is applied declines each year.**

Book value for the first year is the cost of the asset, because the balance in accumulated amortization at the beginning of the asset's useful life is zero. In subsequent years, book value is the difference between cost and accumulated amortization at the beginning of the year. **Unlike other amortization methods, salvage value is ignored in determining the amount to which the declining-balance rate is applied.** Salvage value does, however, limit the total amortization that can be taken. Amortization stops when the asset's book value equals its expected salvage value.

Varying rates of amortization may be used, depending on how fast the company wishes to accelerate amortization. You will find rates such as one time (single), two times (double), and even three times (triple) the straight-line rate of amortization used. An amortization rate that is often used is double the straight-line rate—a method often referred to as the **double-declining-balance method**. If Perfect Pizzas uses double the straight-line rate, the amortization rate is 40% (2 × the straight-line rate of 20%). Illustration 9A-1 presents the formula and calculation of the first year's amortization on the delivery truck, which cost $33,000.

Helpful Hint The straight-line rate is determined by dividing 100% by the estimated useful life. In this case, it is 100% ÷ 5 = 20%.

Illustration 9A-1
Formula for declining-balance method

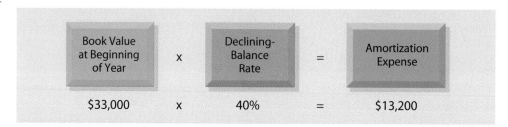

The amortization schedule under this method is given in Illustration 9A-2.

Illustration 9A-2
Double-declining-balance amortization schedule

					End of Year	
Year	Book Value Beginning of Year	× Amortization Rate	= Amortization Expense		Accumulated Amortization	Book Value
						$33,000
2004	$33,000	40%	$13,200		$13,200	19,800
2005	19,800	40%	7,920		21,120	11,880
2006	11,880	40%	4,752		25,872	7,128
2007	7,128	40%	2,851		28,723	4,277
2008	4,277	40%	1,277¹		30,000	3,000

PERFECT PIZZAS LTD.

¹ Calculation of $1,711 ($4,277 × 40%) is adjusted to $1,277 so book value will equal salvage value.

Helpful Hint Amortization stops when the asset's book value equals its expected salvage value.

You can see that the delivery equipment is 64% amortized ($21,120 ÷ $33,000) at the end of the second year. Under the straight-line method, it would be amortized 36% ($12,000 ÷ $33,000) at that time. Because the declining-balance method produces higher amortization expense in the early years than in the later years, it is considered an **accelerated amortization method**. The declining-balance method is compatible with the matching principle. The higher amortization expense in early years is matched with the higher benefits received in these years. Conversely, lower amortization expense is recognized in later years when the asset's contribution to revenue is less. Also, some assets lose their usefulness rapidly because of obsolescence. In these cases, the declining-balance method provides a more appropriate amortization amount.

When an asset is purchased during the year, it is necessary to prorate the declining-balance amortization in the first year on a time basis. For example, if Perfect Pizzas had purchased the delivery equipment on April 1, 2004, amortization for 2004 would be $9,900 ($33,000 × 40% × $\frac{9}{12}$) if amortization is calculated monthly. The book value for calculating amortization in 2005 then becomes $23,100 ($33,000 − $9,900), and the 2005 amortization is $9,240 ($23,100 × 40%).

Units-of-Activity

Under the **units-of-activity method**, useful life is expressed in terms of the estimated total units of production or use expected from the asset. The units-of-activity method is ideally suited to equipment whose activity can be measured in units of output, kilometres driven, or hours in use. The units-of-activity method is generally not suitable for assets for which amortization is a function more of time than of use.

To use this method, the total units of activity for the entire useful life are estimated and that amount is divided into the amortizable cost to determine the amortization cost per unit. The amortization cost per unit is then multiplied by the units of activity during the year and the result is the annual amortization. To illustrate, assume that the delivery truck of Perfect Pizzas is driven 15,000 kilometres in the first year of a total estimated useful life of 100,000 kilometres. Using this distance, Illustration 9A-3 presents the formula and calculation of amortization expense in the first year.

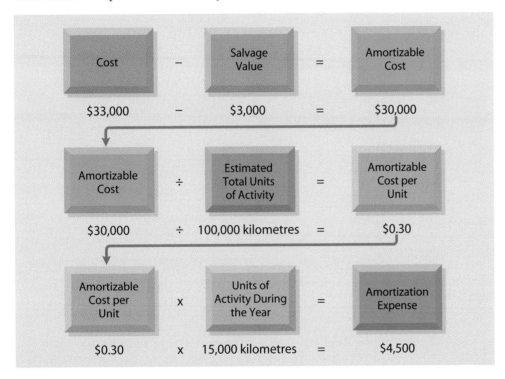

Illustration 9A-3
Formula for units-of-activity method

The amortization schedule, using assumed distance data for the later years, is shown in Illustration 9A-4.

Illustration 9A-4
Units-of-activity amortization schedule

| | | | | | End of Year | |
| PERFECT PIZZAS LTD. | | | | | | |
Year	Units of Activity	× Amortization Cost/Unit	=	Amortization Expense	Accumulated Amortization	Book Value
						$33,000
2004	15,000	$0.30		$4,500	$ 4,500	28,500
2005	30,000	0.30		9,000	13,500	19,500
2006	20,000	0.30		6,000	19,500	13,500
2007	25,000	0.30		7,500	27,000	6,000
2008	10,000	0.30		3,000	30,000	3,000

When the productivity of an asset varies significantly from one period to another, the units-of-activity method results in the best matching of expenses with revenues. This method is easy to apply when assets are purchased during the year. In such a case, the productivity of the asset for the partial year is used in calculating the amortization.

Using the Decision Toolkit

Krispy Kreme Doughnuts, Inc. is a specialty retailer of doughnuts which entered the Canadian market in 2001. Krispy Kreme's principal business is owning and franchising Krispy Kreme doughnut stores.

Many stock analysts have recently strongly recommended buying Krispy Kreme's shares. A friend of yours, Seth Bloomer has an interest in investing in Krispy Kreme and has asked you some questions about the financial statements. Excerpts from the accounting policy note to Krispy Kreme's 2002 financial statements follow:

Instructions

Review the excerpts from the company's financial statements and then answer the questions Seth asked:

1. What method does the company use to amortize (depreciate) its property and equipment? Over what period are these assets being amortized (depreciated)?
2. Why are Krispy Kreme's recently acquired intangible assets not being amortized?
3. Why is interest capitalized on major capital expenditures during construction, whereas most interest is expensed as incurred?
4. What does the term "impairment" mean in relation to accounting for intangible assets?
5. Seth was able to get the following information related to Krispy Kreme:

	Krispy Kreme	Industry average
Profit margin	7.1%	7.9%
Return on assets	12.2%	10.4%

Seth does not understand how Krispy Kreme can have a lower profit margin than the industry average but a higher return on assets. Explain to Seth how this can happen.

KRISPY KREME DOUGHNUTS, INC.
Excerpts from Summary of Significant Accounting Policies
February 3, 2002

Property and Equipment Property and equipment are stated at cost less accumulated depreciation. Major renewals and betterments are charged to the property accounts while replacements, maintenance, and repairs which do not improve or extend the lives of the respective assets are expensed currently. Interest is capitalized on major capital expenditures during the period of construction.

Depreciation of property and equipment is provided on the straight-line method over the estimated useful lives: Buildings—15 to 35 years; Machinery and equipment—3 to 15 years; Leasehold improvements—lesser of useful lives of assets or lease term.

Intangible Assets Intangible assets include goodwill recorded in connection with a business acquisition and the value assigned to reacquired franchise agreements in connection with the acquisition of the rights to certain markets from franchisees. Goodwill and reacquired franchise agreements associated with acquisitions completed on or before June 30, 2001, were amortized on a straight-line basis over an estimated life of 15 years. Reacquired franchise agreements associated with acquisitions completed after June 30 were not amortized. The Company periodically evaluates the recoverability of goodwill and reacquired franchise agreements and will adjust recorded amounts for impairment losses. The Company believes that no impairment of intangible assets existed at February 3, 2002.

Solution

1. Property and equipment are amortized on the straight-line method over the estimated useful lives: Buildings—15 to 35 years; Machinery and equipment—3 to 15 years; Leasehold improvements—lesser of useful lives of assets or lease term.
2. Goodwill and, apparently, the reacquired franchise agreements are viewed as having an indefinite life. The cost of intangible assets with indefinite lives should not be amortized.
3. Interest costs incurred to finance construction projects are included in the cost of the asset when a significant period of time is required to get the asset ready for use. In these circumstances, interest costs are considered to be as necessary as materials and labour. However, the inclusion of interest costs in the cost of a constructed building is limited to the construction period.
4. A permanent decline in the market value of an asset is referred to as an impairment. To ensure that the asset is not overstated on the books, it is written down to its new market value during the year in which the decline in value occurs. Given that the intangible assets for Krispy Kreme have an indefinite life, it is important that they be tested periodically for impairment.
5. The return on assets is a function of two factors: profit margin and asset turnover. The formula to calculate return on assets is:

$$\text{Return on assets} = \text{Profit margin} \times \text{Asset turnover}$$

Because Krispy Kreme has a lower profit margin but a higher rate of return than the industry average, its asset turnover must be higher than the industry average. In this case Krispy Kreme's asset turnover is 1.7 times (12.2% ÷ 7.1%), whereas the industry average is 1.3 times (10.4% ÷ 7.9%). This analysis indicates that Krispy Kreme is selling a lot of doughnuts relative to its assets.

Summary of Study Objectives

① Describe how the cost principle applies to property, plant, and equipment. The cost of property, plant, and equipment includes all expenditures necessary to acquire the assets and make them ready for their intended use. Cost is measured by the cash or cash equivalent price paid.

② Explain the concept of amortization. Amortization is the process of allocating to expense the cost of a long-lived asset over the asset's useful (service) life. Amortization is not a process of valuation, and it is not a process that results in an accumulation of cash.

③ Calculate periodic amortization using the straight-line method, and contrast its expense pattern with those of other methods. The formula for straight-line amortization is:

$$\frac{\text{Cost} - \text{Salvage value}}{\text{Useful life (in years)}}$$

The expense patterns of the three amortization methods are as follows:

Method	Annual Amortization Pattern
Straight-line	Constant amount
Declining-balance	Decreasing amount
Units-of-activity	Varying amount

④ Describe the procedure for revising periodic amortization. Revisions of periodic amortization are made in present and future periods, not retroactively. The new annual amortization is determined by dividing the amortizable cost at the time of the revision (net book value less any revised salvage value) by the remaining useful life.

⑤ Explain how to account for the disposal of property, plant, and equipment. The procedure for accounting for the disposal of property, plant, and equipment through sale or retirement is:
 (a) Update any unrecorded amortization.
 (b) Eliminate the asset and accumulated amortization accounts at the date of disposal.
 (c) Record the cash proceeds, if any.
 (d) Account for the difference between the cash proceeds and the book value as a gain (proceeds less book value) or loss (book value less proceeds) on disposal.

⑥ Identify the basic issues related to reporting intangible assets. Intangible assets are reported at cost, which includes all expenditures necessary to prepare the asset for its intended use. Intangible assets with limited lives are amortized on a straight-line basis over the shorter of their useful lives or legal lives. Accumulated amortization is normally credited directly to the intangible asset account, rather than to a separate contra asset account. Intangible assets with indefinite lives are not amortized, but are tested annually for impairment.

7 *Indicate how long-lived assets are reported on the balance sheet.* Land, land improvements, buildings, and equipment are usually shown under the heading Property, Plant, and Equipment. Intangible assets are sometimes combined under the headings Intangible Assets or Other Assets, or are listed separately. Either on the balance sheet or in the notes, the balances of the major classes of assets—such as land, buildings, and equipment—are presented and accumulated amortization by major classes, or in total, is disclosed. The amortization methods used should be described, and the amount of amortization expense for the period should be disclosed for any amortizable assets.

8 *Describe the methods for evaluating the use of assets.* These assets may be analysed using the return on assets and

asset turnover ratios. Return on assets is composed of the asset turnover and the profit margin.

9 *Calculate periodic amortization using the declining-balance method and the units-of-activity method (Appendix 9A).* The calculation for each of these methods is as follows:

Declining-balance:

$$\text{Book value at beginning of year} \times \text{Declining-balance rate} = \text{Amortization expense}$$

Units-of-activity:

$$\text{Cost} - \text{Salvage value} = \text{Amortizable cost}$$

$$\text{Amortizable cost} \div \text{Estimated total units of activity} = \text{Amortizable cost per unit}$$

$$\text{Amortizable cost per unit} \times \text{Units of activity during year} = \text{Amortization expense}$$

Decision Toolkit—A Summary

Decision Toolkit Summary

DECISION CHECKPOINTS	INFO NEEDED FOR DECISION	TOOL TO USE FOR DECISION	HOW TO EVALUATE RESULTS
Is the company's amortization of intangibles reasonable?	Estimated useful life of intangibles with definite lives from notes to financial statements of this company and its competitors	If the company's estimated useful life significantly exceeds that of competitors, or does not seem reasonable in light of the circumstances, the reason for the difference should be investigated.	Too high an estimated useful life will result in understating amortization expense and overstating net earnings.
Does the company have impairment losses?	Impairment loss recorded on the statement of earnings; book value of intangible assets with indefinite lives	Review the impairment losses recorded by the company. Compare book and market values in light of current business conditions and company performance.	If book value is higher than market value, assets and net earnings will be overstated in the current period. Watch for earnings management—the deliberate timing of the recognition of impairment losses.
Is the company using its assets effectively?	Net earnings and average total assets	$\text{Return on assets} = \dfrac{\text{Net earnings}}{\text{Average total assets}}$	Higher value suggests favourable efficiency (use of assets).
How effective is the company at generating sales from its assets?	Net sales and average total assets	$\text{Asset turnover} = \dfrac{\text{Net sales}}{\text{Average total assets}}$	Indicates the sales dollars generated per dollar of assets. A high value suggests the company is effective in using its resources to generate sales.

NAVIGATOR

Glossary

Additions and improvements   Costs incurred to increase the operating efficiency, productive capacity, or expected useful life of property, plant, and equipment. (p. 413)

Amortizable cost   The cost of a long-lived asset less its salvage value. (p. 408)

Asset turnover   Measure of sales volume, calculated as net sales divided by average total assets. (p. 423)

Capital expenditures   Expenditures that benefit future periods. They are recorded as a long-lived asset. (p. 401)

Capital lease   A long-term agreement allowing one party (the lessee) to use another party's (the lessor's) asset. The arrangement is accounted for as a purchase. (p. 404)

Cash equivalent price   An amount equal to the fair market value of the asset given up. If this is not determinable, the fair market value of the asset received is used. (p. 402)

Copyright   An exclusive right granted by the federal government allowing the owner to reproduce and sell an artistic or published work. (p. 419)

Declining-balance method   An amortization method that applies a constant rate (100% divided by useful life) to the declining book value of an asset. This method produces a decreasing annual amortization expense over the useful life of the asset. (p. 409)

Franchise   A contractual arrangement under which the franchisor grants the franchisee the right to sell certain products, to render specific services, or to use certain trademarks or trade names, usually within a designated geographic area. (p. 420)

Goodwill   The value of all favourable attributes that relate to a business enterprise. (p. 421)

Impairment loss   An impairment loss results when the market value of an asset permanently declines below its book value. (p. 402)

Intangible assets   Rights, privileges, and competitive advantages that result from the ownership of long-lived assets that do not possess physical substance. (p. 416)

Lessee   A party that has made contractual arrangements to use another party's asset without purchasing it. (p. 404)

Lessor   A party that has agreed contractually to let another party use its asset. (p. 404)

Licences   Operating rights to use public property, granted by a government agency to a business enterprise. (p. 420)

Net book value   Cost less accumulated amortization. (p. 406)

Operating expenditures   Expenditures that benefit only the current period. They are immediately matched against revenues as an expense. (p. 401)

Operating lease   An arrangement allowing one party (the lessee) to use the asset of another party (the lessor). The arrangement is accounted for as a rental. (p. 404)

Ordinary repairs   Expenditures to maintain the operating efficiency and expected productive life of the asset. (p. 413)

Patent   An exclusive right issued by the federal government that enables the recipient to manufacture, sell, or otherwise control an invention for a period of 20 years from the date of the grant. (p. 418)

Property, plant, and equipment   Long-lived, tangible assets, such as land, land improvements, buildings, and equipment. (p. 400)

Research and development (R & D) costs   Expenditures that may lead to patents, copyrights, new processes, and new products. (p. 419)

Return on assets   A profitability measure that indicates the amount of net earnings generated by each dollar invested in assets. It is calculated as net earnings divided by average total assets. (p. 422)

Straight-line method   An amortization method in which the amortizable cost of an asset is divided by its estimated useful life. This method produces the same amortization expense for each year of the asset's useful life. (p. 408)

Tangible assets   These are long-lived tangible resources that have physical substance, are used in the operations of the business, and are not intended for sale to customers. Tangible assets include property, plant, and equipment, and natural resources. (p. 400)

Trademark (trade name)   A word, phrase, jingle, or symbol that distinguishes or identifies a particular business or product. (p. 420)

Units-of-activity method   An amortization method in which useful life is expressed in terms of the total units of production or total use expected from the asset. Amortization expense (amortizable cost multiplied by actual activity during the year divided by estimated total activity) will vary each period depending on activity. (p. 410)

Demonstration Problem 1

Additional
Demonstration
Problems

DuPage Ltd. purchased a factory machine at a cost of $18,000 on January 1, 2004. The machine was expected to have a salvage value of $2,000 at the end of its four-year useful life. During its useful life, the machine was expected to be used 16,000 hours. Actual annual hourly use was as follows: 2001, 4,500 hours; 2002, 4,000 hours; 2003, 3,500 hours; and 2004, 4,000 hours.

Instructions

(a) Prepare an amortization schedule using the straight-line method.
(b) Prepare amortization schedules for the following methods: (1) units-of-activity and (2) declining-balance using double the straight-line rate (Appendix 9A).

Action Plan

• Deduct the salvage value in the straight-line and units-of-activity methods, but not in the declining-balance method.

• In the declining-balance method, the amortization rate is applied to the net book value (Cost – Accumulated amortization).

• Amortization should never reduce the book value of the asset below its expected salvage value.

Solution to Demonstration Problem

(a)

					End of Year	
Year	Amortizable Cost	× Amortization Rate	= Amortization Expense	Accumulated Amortization	Book Value
						$18,000
2004	$16,000 [1]	25% [2]	$4,000	$ 4,000	14,000 [3]
2005	16,000	25%	4,000	8,000	10,000
2006	16,000	25%	4,000	12,000	6,000
2007	16,000	25%	4,000	16,000	2,000

DUPAGE LTD.
Amortization Schedule—Straight-Line Method

[1] $18,000 − $2,000 = $16,000
[2] 100% ÷ 4 years = 25%
[3] $18,000 − $4,000 = $14,000

(b) (1)

DUPAGE LTD.
Amortization Schedule—Units-of-Activity Method

					End of Year	
Year	Units of Activity	× Amortization Cost/Unit	= Amortization Expense	Accumulated Amortization	Book Value
						$18,000
2004	4,500	$1 [1]	$4,500	$ 4,500	13,500
2005	4,000	1	4,000	8,500	9,500
2006	3,500	1	3,500	12,000	6,000
2007	4,000	1	4,000	16,000	2,000

[1] $18,000 − $2,000 = $16,000 ÷ 16,000 hours = $1

(b) (2)

	Book Value Beginning of Year		Amortization Rate		Amortization Expense	Accumulated Amortization	Book Value
Year		×		=			

DUPAGE LTD.
Amortization Schedule—Double-Declining-Balance Method

Year	Book Value Beginning of Year	×	Amortization Rate	=	Amortization Expense	End of Year Accumulated Amortization	Book Value
							$18,000
2004	$18,000		50% [1]		$9,000	$ 9,000	9,000
2005	9,000		50%		4,500	13,500	4,500
2006	4,500		50%		2,250	15,750	2,250
2007	2,250		50%		250 [2]	16,000	2,000

[1] 25% × 2 = 50%
[2] Adjusted to $250 because ending book value should not be less than expected value.

Demonstration Problem 2

On January 1, 2002, Skyline Limousine Corp. purchased a used limousine at an acquisition cost of $28,000. The vehicle has been amortized by the straight-line method using a four-year service life and a $4,000 salvage value. The company's fiscal year ends on December 31.

Instructions

Prepare the journal entry or entries to record the disposal of the limousine assuming that it was:
(a) retired and scrapped with no salvage value on January 1, 2006.
(b) sold for $8,000 on July 1, 2005.

Solution to Demonstration Problem

(a)

Jan. 1, 2006	Accumulated Amortization—Limousine [($28,000 − $4,000) ÷ 4 × 4)]	24,000	
	Loss on Disposal	4,000	
	Limousine		28,000
	(To record retirement of limousine)		

(b)

July 1, 2005	Amortization Expense [($28,000 − $4,000) ÷ 4 = $6,000 × $\frac{6}{12}$]	3,000	
	Accumulated Amortization—Limousine		3,000
	(To record amortization to date of disposal)		
	Cash	8,000	
	Accumulated Amortization—Limousine ($6,000 × 3.5 yrs)	21,000	
	Gain on Disposal		1,000
	Limousine		28,000
	(To record sale of limousine)		

Action Plan

- Update the amortization to the date of the disposal for any partial period.
- Determine the book value of the asset at the time of disposal.
- Calculate any gain or loss by comparing proceeds to book value.
- Remove the book value of the asset from the records by debiting accumulated amortization (for the total amortization to the date of disposal) and crediting the asset account for the cost of the asset. Record proceeds and any gain or loss.

NAVIGATOR

Note: All questions, exercises, and problems with an asterisk relate to material in the chapter appendix.

Multiple Choice Quiz

Self-Study Questions

Answers are at the end of the chapter.

(SO 1) 1. Corrieten Ltd. purchased equipment and incurred these costs:

Cash price	$24,000
Shipping—FOB shipping point	1,000
Insurance during transit	200
Installation and testing	400
Total costs	$25,600

What amount should be recorded as the cost of the equipment?
(a) $24,000   (c) $24,600
(b) $24,200   (d) $25,600

(SO 1) 2. Harrington Corporation recently leased a number of trucks from André Corporation. In inspecting the books of Harrington Corporation, you notice that the trucks have not been recorded as assets on its balance sheet. From this you can conclude that Harrington is accounting for this transaction as a(n):
(a) operating lease.   (c) impairment.
(b) capital lease.   (d) None of the above

(SO 2) 3. Amortization is a process of:
(a) valuation.   (c) cash accumulation.
(b) cost allocation.   (d) appraisal.

(SO 3) 4. Cuso Ltd. purchased equipment on January 1, 2003, at a total invoice cost of $400,000. The equipment has an estimated salvage value of $10,000 and an estimated useful life of five years. What is the amount of accumulated amortization at December 31, 2004, if the straight-line method of amortization is used?
(a) $78,000   (c) $156,000
(b) $80,000   (d) $160,000

(SO 3) 5. A company would minimize its amortization expense in the first year of owning an asset if it:
(a) used a low estimated life, a low salvage value, and straight-line amortization.
(b) used a high estimated life, a high salvage value, and straight-line amortization.
(c) used a low estimated life, a low salvage value, and declining-balance amortization.
(d) used a high estimated life, a high salvage value, and declining-balance amortization.

(SO 4) 6. When there is a change in estimated amortization:
(a) previous amortization should be corrected.
(b) current and future years' amortization should be revised.
(c) only future years' amortization should be revised.
(d) None of the above

(SO 4) 7. Additions to property, plant, and equipment:
(a) are operating expenditures.
(b) increase a Repair Expense account.
(c) increase an Inventory account.
(d) are capital expenditures.

(SO 5) 8. Oviatt Ltd. sold equipment for $10,000 cash. At the time of disposition, the equipment had a cost of $45,000 and accumulated amortization of $30,000. Oviatt should record a:
(a) $5,000 loss on disposal.
(b) $5,000 gain on disposal.
(c) $15,000 loss on disposal.
(d) $15,000 gain on disposal.

(SO 6) 9. Pierce Inc. incurred $150,000 of research costs in its laboratory to develop a new product. It spent $20,000 in legal fees for a patent granted on January 2, 2004. On July 31, 2004, Pierce paid $15,000 for legal fees in a successful defence of the patent. What is the total amount that should be debited to Patents through July 31, 2004?
(a) $15,000   (c) $35,000
(b) $20,000   (d) $185,000

(SO 7) 10. Indicate which one of these statements is *true*:
(a) Since intangible assets lack physical substance, they need to be disclosed only in the notes to the financial statements.
(b) Goodwill should be reported as a contra account in the Shareholders' Equity section of the balance sheet.
(c) Totals of major classes of assets can be shown in the balance sheet, with asset details disclosed in the notes to the financial statements.
(d) Intangible assets are typically combined with property, plant, and equipment, and natural resources and then shown in the Property, Plant, and Equipment section of the balance sheet.

(SO 8) 11. Which of the following ratios provides an indication of how efficient a company is in employing its assets?
(a) Current ratio   (c) Debt to total assets
(b) Profit margin   (d) Asset turnover

(SO 9) *12. Kant Enterprises Ltd. purchases a truck for $32,000 on July 1, 2004. The truck has an estimated salvage value of $2,000, an estimated useful life of five years, and an estimated total mileage of 300,000 km. If 50,000 km are driven in 2004, what amount of amortization expense would Kant record at December 31, 2004, assuming it uses the units-of-activity method?
(a) $2,500   (c) $5,000
(b) $3,000   (d) $5,333

(SO 9) *13. Refer to the data provided for Kant Enterprises in question 12. If Kant uses the double-declining-balance method of amortization, what amount of amortization expense would be recorded at December 31, 2004?
(a) $6,000   (c) $12,000
(b) $6,400   (d) $12,800

NAVIGATOR

Questions

(SO 1) 1. Susan Leung is uncertain about how the cost and matching principles apply to long-lived assets. Explain these principles to Susan.

(SO 1) 2. Market values of property, plant, and equipment are more relevant than historical cost for decisions made by users, including creditors, investors, and managers. Why do you suppose the cost principle has persisted even though it doesn't appear very useful?

(SO 1) 3. How is the cost of property, plant, and equipment measured in a cash transaction? In a noncash transaction?

(SO 1) 4. What is an impairment loss? Under what circumstances does it arise?

(SO 1) 5. What are the primary advantages of leasing?

(SO 2) 6. In a recent newspaper release, the president of Lawsuit Inc. asserted that something has to be done about amortization. The president said, "Amortization does not come close to accumulating the cash needed to replace the asset at the end of its useful life." What is your response to the president?

(SO 3) 7. Contrast the straight-line, declining-balance, and units-of-activity methods in relation to (a) useful life and (b) the pattern of periodic amortization over useful life.

(SO 3) 8. Contrast the effects of the three amortization methods on annual amortization expense, net earnings, and book value (1) in the early years of an asset's life, and (2) over the total life of the asset.

(SO 3) 9. Morgan Corporation and Fairchild Corporation both operate in the same industry. Morgan uses the straight-line method to account for amortization, whereas Fairchild uses the declining-balance method. Explain what complications might arise in trying to compare the results of these two companies.

(SO 3) 10. Lucille Corporation uses straight-line amortization for financial reporting purposes but the declining-balance method for income tax purposes. Is it acceptable to use different methods for the two purposes? What is Lucille Corporation's motivation for doing this?

(SO 4) 11. Distinguish between operating expenditures and capital expenditures during an asset's useful life.

(SO 4) 12. In the fourth year of an asset's five-year useful life, the company decides that the asset will have a six-year total service life. How should the revision of amortization be recorded? Why?

(SO 5) 13. How is a gain or a loss on the sale of property, plant, or equipment calculated?

(SO 5) 14. Rashid Corporation owns a machine that is fully amortized but is still being used. How should Rashid account for this asset and report it in the financial statements?

(SO 6) 15. Heflin Corporation hires an accounting student who says that intangible assets should always be amortized. Is the student correct? Explain.

(SO 6) 16. Bob Leno, a business major, is working on a case for one of his classes. In this case, the company needs to raise cash to market a new product it developed. Saul Cain, an engineering major, takes one look at the company's balance sheet and says, "This company has an awful lot of goodwill. Why don't you recommend that they sell some of it to raise cash?" How should Bob respond to Saul?

(SO 6) 17. Often research and development costs provide companies with benefits that last a number of years. (For example, these costs can lead to the development of a patent that will increase the company's earnings for many years.) However, generally accepted accounting principles require that research costs be recorded as expenses when incurred and that development costs be expensed except in certain circumstances. Why?

(SO 7) 18. Explain how long-lived assets should be reported on the balance sheet. Are any transactions related to long-lived assets reported on the statement of earnings? Cash flow statement?

(SO 7) 19. What information related to long-lived assets should be disclosed in the notes to the financial statements?

(SO 8) 20. 🔧 Give an example of an industry that would be characterized by (a) a high asset turnover and a low profit margin, and (b) a low asset turnover and a high profit margin.

(SO 8) 21. 🔧 Tim Hortons reported net sales of U.S.$572 million, pre-tax earnings of U.S.$132 million, and average total assets of U.S.$521 million in a recent year. Use pre-tax earnings as a proxy for net earnings. Calculate Tim Hortons' return on assets and asset turnover ratios.

(SO 8) 22. 🔧 Explain how the profit margin and asset turnover ratios can be used to help explain return on assets.

(SO 9) *23. Why is amortizable cost (cost less salvage value) used in the straight-line and units-of-activity methods but not in the declining-balance method?

Brief Exercises

Determine cost of land.
(SO 1)

BE9-1 These expenditures were incurred by Shumway Ltd. in purchasing land: cash price, $50,000; legal fees, $2,500; and clearing and grading, $3,500. What is the cost of the land?

Determine cost of truck.
(SO 1)

BE9-2 Basler Ltd. incurs these expenditures in purchasing a truck: cash price, $18,000; one-year accident insurance policy, $2,000; motor vehicle licence, $100; and painting and lettering, $400. What is the cost of the truck?

Calculate straight-line amortization.
(SO 3)

BE9-3 Cunningham Ltd. acquires a delivery truck at a cost of $42,000. The truck is expected to have a salvage value of $2,000 at the end of its four-year useful life. Calculate annual amortization for the first and second years using the straight-line method.

Calculate revised amortization.
(SO 4)

BE9-4 On January 1, 2004, the Asler Corporation ledger shows Equipment, $32,000, and Accumulated Amortization, $15,000. The amortization resulted from using the straight-line method with a useful life of eight years and a salvage value of $2,000. On this date, the company concludes that the equipment has a remaining useful life of only two more years with the same salvage value. Calculate the revised annual amortization.

Identify operating and capital expenditures.
(SO 4)

BE9-5 Indicate whether each of the following items is an operating expenditure (O) or a capital expenditure (C). If the expenditure is neither, insert NA (not applicable) in the space provided.

(a) _____ Repaired building roof, $500   (f) _____ Purchased oil and gas for truck, $75
(b) _____ Replaced building roof, $7,500   (g) _____ Replaced tires on truck, $500
(c) _____ Purchased building, $80,000   (h) _____ Rebuilt engine on truck, $5,000
(d) _____ Purchased supplies, $350   (i) _____ Added a new wing to building, $250,000
(e) _____ Purchased truck, $35,000   (j) _____ Painted interior of building, $1,500

Record retirement of equipment.
(SO 5)

BE9-6 Ruiz Ltd. retires its delivery equipment which cost $41,000. Prepare journal entries to record the transaction if (a) accumulated amortization is also $41,000 on this delivery equipment and no salvage value is received; and (b) the accumulated amortization is $38,000 instead of $41,000.

Record sale of equipment.
(SO 5)

BE9-7 Wiley Inc. sells office equipment on September 30, 2004, for $21,000 cash. The office equipment originally cost $72,000 and as at December 31, 2003, had accumulated amortization of $42,000. Annual amortization is $14,000. Prepare the journal entries to (a) update amortization to September 30, 2004, and (b) record the sale of the equipment.

Calculate goodwill.
(SO 6)

BE9-8 The Descartes Systems Group Inc., a global logistics company in Waterloo, Ontario, has, in its unadjusted trial balance, goodwill of U.S.$104.3 million at January 31, 2003. At year end, it was determined that the market value of the goodwill—related to five companies purchased by Descartes in prior years—was $17.6 million. At what value should goodwill be reported on Descartes' balance sheet at January 31, 2003? Explain why.

Classify long-lived assets.
(SO 7)

BE9-9 Indicate whether each of the following assets is property, plant, and equipment (PPE), or an intangible asset (I). If the asset doesn't fit one of these categories, insert NA (not applicable) in the space provided.

(a) _____ Building   (h) _____ Land held for sale
(b) _____ Cash   (i) _____ Licence right
(c) _____ Franchise   (j) _____ Machinery
(d) _____ Goodwill   (k) _____ Parking lot
(e) _____ Inventory   (l) _____ Patent
(f) _____ Investment in common shares   (m) _____ Timber tract
(g) _____ Land   (n) _____ Trademark

Prepare partial balance sheet.
(SO 7)

BE9-10 Canadian Tire Corporation, Limited reports the following selected information about long-lived assets at December 28, 2002 (in millions): accumulated amortization—assets under capital lease, $7.2; accumulated amortization—buildings, $558.8; accumulated amortization—computer software, $116.9; accumulated amortization—fixtures and equipment, $270.5; accumulated amortization—leasehold improvements, $57.2; assets under capital lease, $23.5; buildings, $1,806.3; computer software, $172.4; fixtures and equipment, $392.9; goodwill, $32.8; land, $613.9; and leasehold improvements, $179.2.

Included in land and buildings are property held for disposal at a cost of $87.5 and accumulated amortization of $37.3. Prepare a partial balance sheet for Canadian Tire.

BE9-11 Hudson's Bay Company reports the following in its 2003 financial statements: net sales, $7,383.8 million; net earnings, $111.5 million; total assets, January 31, 2003, $4,275.7; and total assets, January 31, 2002, $4,534.2 million. Calculate Hudson's Bay's return on assets and asset turnover for 2003.

Calculate ratios.
(SO 8)

*BE9-12   Amortization information for Cunningham Ltd. is given in BE9-3. Assuming the amortization rate is equal to (one times) the straight-line rate, calculate annual amortization for the first and second years under the single declining-balance method.

Calculate declining-balance amortization.
(SO 9)

*BE9-13   Englehart Taxi Service uses the units-of-activity method to calculate amortization on its taxicabs. Each cab is expected to be driven 125,000 km. Taxi 10 cost $34,500 and is expected to have a salvage value of $500. Taxi 10 was driven 50,000 km in 2003 and 40,000 km in 2004. Calculate the amortization for each year.

Calculate units-of-activity amortization.
(SO 9)

Exercises

E9-1   The following expenditures relating to property, plant, and equipment were made by Kosinki Ltd.:

Determine acquisition cost.
(SO 1)

1. Paid $45,000 for new delivery truck.
2. Paid $250 to have company name and advertising slogan painted on new delivery truck.
3. Paid $75 motor vehicle licence fee on new truck.
4. Paid $850 for winter tires for new delivery truck.
5. Paid $900 for a one-year accident insurance policy on new delivery truck.
6. Paid $100,000 for plant site.
7. Paid $17,500 for parking lot on new plant site.
8. Paid $5,000 of property taxes after plant site was acquired.

Instructions

(a) Explain the application of the cost principle in determining the acquisition cost of property, plant, and equipment.
(b) List the numbers of the preceding transactions, and opposite each indicate the account title to which the expenditure should be debited.

E9-2   Orbis Inc. paid $100,000 cash for land on which it planned to construct a small office building. An old warehouse on the property was razed at a cost of $6,600; the salvaged materials were sold for $1,700. Additional expenditures before construction began included a $1,300 legal fee for work concerning the land purchase, a $7,800 architect's fee, and $14,000 to put in driveways and a parking lot.

Determine cost of land.
(SO 1)

Instructions

(a) Determine the amount to be reported as the cost of the land.
(b) For each cost not used in part (a), indicate the account to be debited.

E9-3   Costello Limited purchased a new machine on April 1, 2004, at a cost of $96,000. The company estimated that the machine has a salvage value of $12,000. The machine is expected to be used for 40,000 working hours during its six-year life.

Calculate straight-line amortization.
(SO 3)

Interactive Homework

Instructions

Calculate the amortization expense under the straight-line method for 2004 and 2005, assuming a December 31 year end.

E9-4   Lindy Weink, the new controller of Lafreniere Inc., has reviewed the expected useful lives and salvage values of selected amortizable assets at the beginning of 2004. Here are her findings and proposed changes:

Calculate revised annual amortization.
(SO 4)

Interactive Homework

Type of Asset	Date Acquired	Cost	Accumulated Amortization, Jan. 1, 2004	Useful Life (in years)		Salvage Value	
				Current	Proposed	Current	Proposed
Building	Jan. 1, 1995	$800,000	$342,000	20	25	$40,000	$62,000
Equipment	Jan. 1, 2002	120,000	46,000	5	4	5,000	3,600

All assets are amortized by the straight-line method. Lafreniere uses a calendar year in preparing annual financial statements. After discussion, management has agreed to accept Lindy's proposed changes. (The "Current" and "Proposed" useful life are for total life, not remaining life.)

Instructions

(a) Calculate the revised annual amortization on each asset in 2004.
(b) Prepare the entry (or entries) to record amortization in 2004.

Discuss implications of amortization period.
(SO 4)

E9-5 **Alliance Atlantis Communications Inc.** changed its accounting policy to amortize a program's broadcast rights over the contracted exhibition period, which is based on the estimated useful life of the program. Previously, the company amortized broadcast rights over the lesser of two years or the contracted exhibition period.

Instructions

Write a short memo to your client explaining the implications this has for the analysis of Alliance Atlantis' results. Also discuss whether this change in amortization period appears reasonable.

Record disposal of equipment.
(SO 5)

Interactive
Homework

E9-6 Presented here are selected transactions for Beck Corporation for 2004:

Jan. 1 Retired a piece of machinery that was purchased on January 1, 1994. The machine cost $62,000 and had a useful life of 10 years with no salvage value.

June 30 Sold a computer that was purchased on January 1, 2002. The computer cost $33,000 and had a useful life of three years with no salvage value. The computer was sold for $5,000 cash.

Dec. 31 Sold a delivery truck for $9,000 cash. The truck cost $27,000 when it was purchased on January 1, 2001, and was amortized based on a five-year useful life with a $3,000 salvage value.

Instructions

Journalize all entries required on the above dates, including entries to update amortization on assets disposed of, where applicable. Beck Corporation uses straight-line amortization.

Apply accounting concepts.
(SO 1, 6)

E9-7 The following situations are independent of one another:

1. An accounting co-op student can't understand why the company is only amortizing its buildings and equipment, but not its land. The student prepared journal entries to amortize all the company's property, plant, and equipment for the current year end.

2. The same co-op student also thinks the company's amortization policy on its intangible assets is wrong. The company is currently amortizing its patents but not its goodwill. The student fixed that for the current year end by adding goodwill to her adjusting entry for amortization. She told a fellow student that she felt she had improved the consistency of the company's accounting policies by making these changes.

3. The same company has a building still in use that has a zero book value but a substantial market value. The co-op student felt that this practice didn't benefit the company's users—especially the bank—and wrote the building up to its market value. After all, she reasoned, you can write down assets if market values are lower. Writing them up if market value is higher is yet another example of the improved consistency that her employment has brought to the company's accounting practices.

Instructions

Explain whether or not the accounting treatment in each of the above situations is in accordance with generally accepted accounting principles. Explain what accounting principle or assumption, if any, has been violated and what the appropriate accounting treatment should be.

Record acquisition and amortization of intangible assets.
(SO 6)

E9-8 Organized in 2004, Collins Ltd. has these transactions related to intangible assets in that year:

Jan. 2 Purchased patent (five-year life), $450,000.
Apr. 1 Goodwill acquired (indefinite life), $360,000.
July 1 Acquired 10-year franchise (expiration date is July 1, 2014), $250,000.
Sept. 1 Incurred research costs, $185,000.
    30 Development costs of $50,000 are incurred. No marketable products have yet been identified.

Instructions

(a) Prepare the necessary entries to record these intangibles. Assume all costs incurred were for cash.

(b) Make the entries as at December 31, 2004, recording any necessary amortization. There was no impairment of goodwill.

(c) Indicate what the balance in each intangible asset account is on December 31, 2004.

E9-9 BCE Inc. reported the following selected information as at December 31, 2002 (in millions):

Classify long-lived assets.
(SO 7)

Accounts	Amounts
Accumulated amortization—buildings	$ 1,307
Accumulated amortization—finite-life intangible assets	1,335
Accumulated amortization—machinery and equipment	3,253
Accumulated amortization—other property, plant, and equipment	139
Accumulated amortization—telecommunications assets	21,848
Amortization expense	3,146
Buildings	2,585
Cash and cash equivalents	306
Cash paid for capital expenditures	3,771
Common shares	16,520
Finite-life intangible assets	3,021
Goodwill	10,103
Impairment charge	770
Indefinite-life intangible asset	900
Land	99
Machinery and equipment	6,144
Other long-term assets	4,355
Other property, plant, and equipment	357
Plant under construction	1,743
Telecommunications assets	34,573

Instructions

(a) Identify in which financial statement (balance sheet, statement of earnings, or cash flow statement) and which section (e.g., current assets) each of the above items should be reported.

(b) Prepare the tangible and intangible assets sections of the balance sheet as at December 31, 2002.

E9-10 Empire Company Limited reports the following information (in millions) at April 30, 2002: net sales, $9,926.5; net earnings, $195.9; total assets, April 30, 2002, $4,312.6; and total assets, April 30, 2001, $4,254.3.

Calculate ratios.
(SO 8)

Instructions

(a) Calculate the (1) return on assets, (2) asset turnover, and (3) profit margin ratios for the year ended April 30, 2002.

(b) Prove mathematically how the profit margin and asset turnover work together to explain return on assets, by showing the appropriate calculation.

(c) Empire Company owns Sobeys, Empire Theatres, Lawton Drugstores, and Wajax, and manages commercial real estate, among other activities. Does this diversity of activities affect your ability to interpret the ratios you calculated in (a)? Explain.

*E9-11 Stojko Ltd. purchased a new machine on January 1, 2004, at a cost of $89,000. The company estimated that the machine will have a salvage value of $12,000. The machine is expected to be used for 10,000 working hours during its six-year life. Stojko uses a calendar year end.

Calculate amortization using three methods.
(SO 3, 9)

Instructions

(a) Calculate the amortization expense under the following methods for each of the years ended December 31, 2004 and 2005: (1) straight-line, (2) units-of-activity, assuming machine usage was 1,700 hours for 2004 and 1,500 hours for 2005, and (3) declining-balance using double the straight-line rate.

(b) Which method results in the highest net earnings for the first two years?

(c) Which method results in the highest cash flow for the first two years?

Determine effect of choice of amortization method over life of asset.
(SO 3, 9)

Interactive
Homework

*E9-12   Rahim Corporation purchased a computer for $10,000. The company planned to keep it for four years, after which it expected to sell it for $3,000.

Instructions

(a) Calculate the amortization expense for each of the first three years under the (1) straight-line method, and (2) double-declining-balance method.

(b) Assuming Rahim sold the computer for $2,500 at the end of the third year, calculate the gain or loss on disposal under each amortization method.

(c) Determine the impact on earnings (total amortization plus loss on disposal or less gain on disposal) of each method for use of the computer over the entire three-year period.

Problems: Set A

Determine acquisition cost.
(SO 1)

P9-1A   Kadlec Company Inc. was organized on January 1. During the first year of operations, the following payments and receipts were recorded in random order:

Expenditures

1. Cost of real estate purchased as a plant site (land, $180,000, and building, $70,000)	$ 250,000
2. Legal fees paid for title search	4,900
3. Cost of demolishing building to make land suitable for construction of new building	27,000
4. Cost of filling and grading the land	7,000
5. Excavation costs for new building	20,000
6. Architect's fees on building plans	30,000
7. Full payment to building contractor	700,000
8. Cost of parking lots and driveways	34,000
9. Property taxes paid on land for the current year	15,000
	$1,087,900

Receipts

10. Proceeds for salvage of demolished building	$12,700

Instructions

Analyse the transactions using the following column headings: Item; Land; Building; Land Improvements; Other Accounts. Enter the number of each transaction in the Item column, and enter the amounts in the appropriate columns. For amounts in the Other Accounts column, also indicate the account title.

Classify expenditures.
(SO 1, 6)

P9-2A   The following expenditures were made for Cohlmeyer Corporation, as it was getting ready to commence its first year of operations:

Jan. 10 Land was purchased for $65,000.
Jan. 15 The land was surveyed at a cost of $3,000.
Feb.   1 An existing building on the land was razed at a cost of $5,500 to provide room for the new structure.
Feb. 10 A security fence was built around the land for $2,500.
Feb. 23 An architectural firm was paid $10,500 for plans for the new building.
Mar. 15 In preparation for construction of the new building, $3,500 was spent to remove trees and level the land.
Mar. 17 A building permit was acquired for $1,000, and construction of the building began.
Apr. 10 Cohlmeyer paid $5,000 in legal and application costs for a patent on a newly developed product that it will sell.
May   1 The building was completed for a total cost of $460,000.
May 15 Landscaping was done for $4,000.
May 20 A parking lot was constructed for $8,000.
May 25 The company's domain name, <www.cohlmeyer.ca>, was registered for $150.
May 28 Cohlmeyer paid $4,000 to the lawyer for organizing the new company.
June 1 The building was occupied and business began.

Instructions

For each of the above expenditures, indicate the account title to which the expenditure should be recorded.

P9-3A At December 31, 2004, Yount Corporation reported the following property, plant and equipment:

Record property, plant, and equipment transactions; prepare partial balance sheet.
(SO 3, 5, 7)

Land		$ 4,000,000
Buildings	$28,500,000	
Less: Accumulated amortization—buildings	10,687,500	17,812,500
Equipment	$48,000,000	
Less: Accumulated amortization—equipment	35,000,000	13,000,000
		$34,812,500

During 2005, the following selected transactions occurred:

Apr. 1 Purchased land for $2,630,000. Paid $630,000 cash and issued an 8% note payable for the balance.

May 1 Sold equipment that cost $750,000 when purchased on January 1, 2001. The equipment was sold for $350,000 cash.

June 1 Sold land purchased on June 1, 1991, for $1,800,000 cash. The land cost $300,000.

July 1 Purchased equipment for $1,000,000. Paid $250,000 cash and issued an 8% note payable for the balance.

Dec. 31 Retired equipment that cost $470,000 when purchased on December 31, 1995. No salvage value was received.

Yount uses straight-line amortization for buildings and equipment. The buildings are estimated to have a 40-year life and no salvage value; the equipment is estimated to have a 10-year useful life and no salvage value. Interest is payable at maturity on all notes.

Instructions

(a) Journalize the transactions.

(b) Record adjusting entries for amortization and interest for 2005.

(c) Prepare the property, plant and equipment section of Yount's balance sheet at December 31, 2005.

P9-4A Tashia's Interior Decorators Ltd. operates out of an office building that it purchased 25 years ago for $185,000. Tashia estimates that the building has a useful life of 40 years and no salvage value. Tashia has been using straight-line amortization for the 25 years that the building has been in use.

Revise amortization; calculate gain or loss on disposal.
(SO 4, 5)

Shortly after the beginning of the current year, Tashia installed an air conditioning system for the building. The air conditioning unit cost $29,125 and is embedded in the structure of the building; it cannot be easily removed. The air conditioning unit has a 20-year useful life.

Instructions

(a) What was the book value of the building at the beginning of the current year?

(b) How much amortization expense should be recorded in the current year, which is the twenty-sixth year of using the building?

(c) What is the book value of the building at the end of the thirtieth year?

(d) Assume that the building is disposed of at the end of the thirtieth year for $50,000. What is the gain or loss on disposal?

P9–5A The transactions below involve expenditures for a forklift:

Classify operating and capital expenditures.
(SO 4)

1. Rebuilding of the diesel engine as it has over 20,000 hours, $10,000
2. New tires, $6,000
3. New safety cab, $5,000
4. Replacement of a windshield (not covered by insurance), $1,200
5. Training the operator, $1,600
6. New paint job after the company changed its logo and colours, $2,000

Instructions

For each of the transactions listed above, indicate the title of the account that you think should be debited in recording the transaction. Briefly explain your reasoning.

Record disposal of equipment.
(SO 5)

P9-6A Walker Corp. has office furniture that cost $80,000 and has been amortized $48,000.

Instructions

Record entries for the disposal under these assumptions:
(a) It was scrapped as having no value.
(b) It was sold for $30,000.
(c) It was sold for $35,000.

*Correct errors in recording
and amortizing intangible
assets.*
(SO 6)

P9-7A Due to rapid employee turnover in the accounting department, the following transactions involving intangible assets were improperly recorded by Cher Ltd. in 2004:

1. Cher developed a new manufacturing process, incurring research costs of $153,000. The company also purchased a patent for $62,000. In early January, Cher capitalized $215,000 as the cost of the patents. Patent amortization expense of $10,750 was recorded based on a 20-year useful life.
2. On July 1, Cher purchased a small company and, as a result, acquired goodwill of $76,000. Cher recorded a half year's amortization in 2004 based on a 50-year life ($760 amortization).
3. The company purchased the right to operate the airport taxi service for $25,000 on December 31 for the next three years. The company capitalized this right in its Vehicles account.

Instructions

Prepare all journal entries necessary to correct any errors made during 2004.

*Record intangible asset
transactions; prepare
intangible assets section.*
(SO 6, 7)

P9-8A The intangible assets section of the balance sheet for Ip Inc. at December 31, 2004, is presented here:

Patent ($70,000 cost less $7,000 amortization)	$ 63,000
Copyright ($48,000 cost less $19,200 amortization)	28,800
Goodwill	210,000
Total	$301,800

The patent was acquired in January 2004 and has a useful life of 10 years. The copyright was acquired in January 2001 and also has a useful life of 10 years. The following cash transactions may have affected intangible assets during 2005:

Jan. 2 Paid $22,500 in legal costs to successfully defend the patent against infringement by another company.

July 1 Developed a new product, incurring $220,000 in research costs and $60,000 in development costs. A patent was granted for the product on July 1, and its useful life is equal to its legal life.

Sept. 1 Paid $110,000 to an Olympic rower to appear in commercials advertising the company's products. The commercials will air in September.

Oct. 1 Acquired a copyright for $160,000. The copyright has a useful life of 50 years.

Dec. 31 The company determined the fair market value of the goodwill to be $150,000. It believes this to be a permanent impairment.

Instructions

(a) Prepare journal entries to record the transactions.
(b) Prepare journal entries to record the 2005 amortization expense.
(c) Prepare the intangible assets section of the balance sheet at December 31, 2005.

Calculate and evaluate ratios.
(SO 8)

P9-9A Sleeman Breweries Ltd. and Big Rock Brewery Ltd. reported the following information in 2002:

(in thousands)	Sleeman Breweries	Big Rock Brewery
Total assets, fiscal 2002	$220,081	$33,061
Total assets, fiscal 2001	197,642	31,346
Net sales	157,053	24,909
Net earnings	12,321	1,218

Industry averages are as follows: profit margin, 9.2%; return on assets, 7.4%; and asset turnover, 0.8 times.

Instructions

(a) For each company, calculate the profit margin, return on assets, and asset turnover ratios for 2002.

(b) Based on your calculations in part (a), comment on the relative effectiveness of the two companies in using their assets to generate sales and produce net earnings. What complicates your ability to compare the two companies?

P9-10A The following ratios are available for a company operating in the computer industry:

Evaluate ratios.
(SO 8)

	Company	Industry Average
Return on assets	12.4%	(1.7%)
Profit margin	31.0%	(3.4%)
Asset turnover	0.4 times	0.5 times

Instructions

(a) The company's asset turnover is close to the industry average. However, its return on assets and profit margin are far higher than the industry averages. Explain what is primarily driving the company's return on assets compared to that of the industry: margin (profit margin) or volume (asset turnover).

(b) Speculate on this company's strategy for computer sales, compared to that of its competitors in the industry.

*P9-11A Scott Piper Corporation purchased machinery on January 1, 2005, at a cost of $243,000. The estimated useful life of the machinery is five years, with an estimated salvage value at the end of that period of $12,000. The company is considering different amortization methods that could be used for financial reporting purposes.

Calculate amortization under straight-line and declining-balance methods.
(SO 3, 9)

Instructions

(a) Prepare two amortization schedules for the life of the machinery: one using the straight-line method, and a second under the declining-balance method using one times the straight-line rate.

(b) Which method would result in the higher reported 2005 earnings? In the higher total reported earnings over the five-year period?

(c) Which method would result in the higher reported 2005 cash flow? In the higher total reported cash flow over the five-year period?

*P9-12A Rapid Transportation Ltd. purchased a new bus at a cost of $80,000. The bus has an estimated useful life of three years with an estimated salvage value at the end of the three years of $8,000. Management is contemplating the merits of using the units-of-activity method of amortization, as opposed to the straight-line method which it currently uses.

Under the units-of-activity method, management estimates a total estimated useful life of 300,000 km: 120,000 km driven in year 1; 100,000 km in year 2; and 80,000 km in year 3.

Calculate amortization under straight-line and units-of-activity methods; calculate total expense over life of asset.
(SO 3, 5, 9)

Instructions

(a) Prepare a schedule comparing the amortization expense and the book values for each of the three years, and in total for the three years, under the straight-line method and the units-of-activity method.

(b) Assume that the bus is sold at the end of its second year for $25,000.
1. Calculate the gain or loss on the sale of equipment, under (a) the straight-line method and (b) the units-of-activity method.
2. Prepare a schedule to show the overall impact of the total amortization expense combined with the gain or loss on sale for the two-year period under each method of amortization (consider the total effect on net earnings over the two-year period). Comment on your results.

Problems: Set B

Determine acquisition cost.
(SO 1)

P9-1B Weiseman Ltd. was organized on January 1. During the first year of operations, the following payments and receipts were recorded in random order:

Expenditures

1. Cost of real estate purchased as a plant site (land, $235,000, and building, $25,000)	$260,000
2. Installation cost of fences around property	7,200
3. Cost of demolishing building to make land suitable for construction of new building	19,000
4. Excavation costs for new building	23,000
5. Insurance while under construction	2,000
6. Cost of parking lots and driveways	12,000
7. Architect's fees on building plans	38,000
8. Property taxes paid for the current year on land	5,800
9. Full payment to building contractor	600,000
	$967,000

Receipts

10. Proceeds from salvage of demolished building	$5,000

Instructions

Analyse the preceding transactions using the following column headings: Item; Land; Land Improvements; Building; Other Accounts. Enter the number of each transaction in the Item column, and enter the amounts in the appropriate columns. For amounts in the Other Accounts column, also indicate the account title.

Classify expenditures.
(SO 1, 6)

P9-2B Cumby Inc. incurred the following expenditures in a recent year:

1. Architect fees
2. Cost to demolish an old building on a piece of land intended for a new building
3. Lawyer's fees associated with a successful patent application
4. Lawyer's fees associated with an unsuccessful patent application
5. Cost of a grease and oil change on the company's truck
6. Cost of installing a new roof on the company's building
7. Cost of painting the president's office
8. Cost of CDs and toner for the office computer
9. Payment to a celebrity for endorsement of a product. The celebrity's endorsement is featured in television advertisements which have been airing for the past three months and will continue to be televised for another six months after year end.
10. Cost of new tires for the company delivery van
11. Cost to rebuild the engine on the company delivery van
12. Cost to pave the company parking lot
13. Cost of painting the corporate logo on the sides of the company delivery van

Instructions

For each of the above expenditures, indicate the account title to which the expenditure should be recorded.

Record property, plant, and equipment transactions; prepare partial balance sheet.
(SO 3, 5, 7)

P9-3B At December 31, 2004, Hamsmith Corporation reported the following property, plant and equipment:

Land		$ 3,000,000
Buildings	$26,500,000	
Less: Accumulated amortization—buildings	13,250,000	13,250,000
Equipment	$40,000,000	
Less: Accumulated amortization—equipment	8,000,000	32,000,000
		$48,250,000

During 2005, the following selected transactions occurred:

Apr. 1 Purchased land for $2,200,000. Paid $200,000 cash and issued a 6% note payable for the balance.

May 1 Sold equipment that cost $600,000 when purchased on January 1, 2003. The equipment was sold for $450,000 cash.

June 1 Sold land for $1,800,000 cash. The land cost $500,000.

July 1 Purchased equipment for $1,200,000. Paid $200,000 cash and issued a 6% note payable for the balance.

Dec. 31 Sold equipment that cost $500,000 when purchased on December 31, 1995. The equipment was sold for $4,000.

Hamsmith uses straight-line amortization for buildings and equipment. The buildings are estimated to have a 40-year useful life and no salvage value; the equipment is estimated to have a 10-year useful life and no salvage value. Interest is payable at maturity on all notes.

Instructions

(a) Journalize the transactions.

(b) Record adjusting entries for 2005.

(c) Prepare the property, plant and equipment section of Hamsmith's balance sheet at December 31, 2005.

P9-4B On January 1, 2002, Harrington Corporation acquired equipment costing $40,000. It was estimated at that time that this equipment would have a useful life of five years and a salvage value of $4,000. The straight-line method of amortization is used by Harrington for its equipment; and its fiscal year end is December 31.

Revise amortization.
(SO 4)

At the beginning of 2004, the company's engineers reconsidered their expectations, and estimated that the equipment's useful life would more likely be six years in total, instead of the previously estimated five years. The estimated salvage value was also reduced to $2,500.

Instructions

(a) Indicate how much amortization expense should be recorded each year for this equipment by completing the following table:

Year	Amortization Expense	Accumulated Amortization	Book Value
2002			
2003			
2004			
2005			
2006			
2007			
Totals			

(b) If Harrington Corporation had not revised the equipment's remaining useful life, what would its total amortization expense and accumulated amortization have been? The book value of the asset on December 31, 2007?

P9-5B The transactions below involve expenditures related to property, plant, and equipment:

Classify operating and capital expenditures.
(SO 4)

1. Operator controls on equipment were replaced for $7,000, because the original control devices were not adequate.

2. A total of $4,600 was spent for decorative landscaping (planting flowers and shrubs, etc.).

3. A new air conditioning system for the factory offices was bought for $36,000.

4. Windows broken in a labour dispute (not covered by insurance) were replaced for $2,400.

5. A fee of $1,500 was paid for adjusting and testing new machinery prior to its use.

6. Machinery damaged by a fork-lift was repaired for $5,000.

Instructions

For each of the transactions listed above, indicate the title of the account that you think should be debited in recording the transaction. Briefly explain your reasoning.

P9-6B Express Corp. has delivery equipment that cost $50,000 and accumulated amortization of $20,000.

Record disposal of equipment.
(SO 5)

Instructions

Record entries for the disposal under the following assumptions:

(a) It was scrapped as having no value.

(b) It was sold for $37,000.

(c) It was sold for $28,000.

*Correct errors in recording
and amortizing intangible
assets.*
(SO 6)

P9-7B Due to rapid employee turnover in the accounting department, the following trans-actions involving intangible assets were improperly recorded by Riley Corporation:

1. Riley developed a new manufacturing process, incurring research costs of $120,000. The company also purchased a patent for $37,400. In early January 2004, Riley capi-talized $157,400 as the cost of the patent. Patent amortization expense of $7,870 was recorded based on a 20-year useful life.
2. On July 1, 2004, Riley purchased a small company and as a result acquired goodwill of $60,000. Riley recorded a half year's amortization for the goodwill in 2004, based on a 50-year life ($600 amortization).
3. The company made a $5,000 charitable donation on December 1, 2004, which it deb-ited to Goodwill.

Instructions

Prepare all necessary journal entries to correct any errors made during 2004.

*Record intangible asset
transactions; prepare
intangible assets section.*
(SO 6, 7)

P9-8B The intangible assets section of Ghani Corporation's balance sheet at December 31, 2004, is presented here:

Patent ($60,000 cost less $6,000 amortization)	$ 54,000
Copyright ($36,000 cost less $25,200 amortization)	10,800
Goodwill	125,000
Total	$189,800

The patent was acquired in January 2004 and has a useful life of 10 years. The copyright was acquired in January 2001 and also has a useful life of 10 years. The following cash transactions may have affected intangible assets during 2005:

Jan. 2   Paid $27,000 in legal costs to successfully defend the patent against infringe-ment by another company.

Jan.–June   Developed a new product, incurring $210,000 in research and $50,000 in development costs. A patent was granted for the product on July 1, and its useful life is equal to its legal life.

Sept. 1   Paid $60,000 to a popular hockey player to appear in commercials advertising the company's products. The commercials will air in September and October.

Oct. 1   Acquired a copyright for $180,000. The copyright has a useful life of 50 years.

Dec. 31   The company determined the fair value of goodwill to be $85,000. This is believed to represent a permanent impairment.

Instructions

(a) Prepare journal entries to record the transactions.
(b) Prepare journal entries to record the 2005 amortization expense.
(c) Prepare the intangible assets section of the balance sheet at December 31, 2005.

*Calculate and evaluate
ratios.*
(SO 8)

P9-9B Green Mountain Coffee, Inc. and Starbucks Corporation reported the following information in 2002:

(in U.S. millions)	Green Mountain	Starbucks
Total assets, fiscal 2002	$ 54.7	$2,292.7
Total assets, fiscal 2001	34.5	1,851.0
Net sales	100.0	3,288.9
Net earnings	6.0	215.1

Industry averages are as follows: profit margin, 6.4%; return on assets, 9.6%; and asset turnover, 1.5 times.

Instructions

(a) For each company, calculate the profit margin, return on assets, and asset turnover ratios for 2002.
(b) Based on your calculations in part (a), comment on the relative effectiveness of the two companies in using their assets to generate sales and produce net earnings. What complicates your ability to compare the two companies?

P9-10B The following ratios are available for a company operating in the restaurant industry:

Evaluate ratios.
(SO 8)

	Company	Industry Average
Return on assets	4.2%	7.4%
Profit margin	6.0%	6.2%
Asset turnover	0.7 times	1.2 times

Instructions

(a) The company's profit margin is very close to that of the industry. Yet, its return on assets and asset turnover are lower than the industry average. Explain what is primarily driving the company's return on assets, compared to that of the industry—margin (profit margin) or volume (asset turnover).

(b) Explain how the company might be able to improve its return on assets ratio.

P9-11B Whitley Corporation purchased machinery on January 1, 2004, at a cost of $170,000. The estimated useful life of the machinery is four years, with an estimated salvage value at the end of that period of $10,000. The company is considering different amortization methods that could be used for financial reporting purposes.

Calculate amortization under straight-line and declining-balance methods.
(SO 3, 9)

Instructions

(a) Prepare separate amortization schedules for the life of the machinery using the straight-line method and the declining-balance method using double the straight-line rate.

(b) Which method would result in the higher reported 2004 earnings? In the higher total reported earnings over the four-year period?

(c) Which method would result in the higher reported 2004 cash flow? In the higher total reported cash flow over the four-year period?

P9-12B Forristal Farmers Inc. purchased a piece of equipment at a cost of $21,000. The equipment has an estimated useful life of four years with an estimated salvage value at the end of the four years of $1,000. The president is debating the merits of using the single-declining-balance method of amortization as opposed to the straight-line method of amortization. The president feels that the straight-line method will have a more favourable impact on the statement of earnings.

Calculate amortization under straight-line and declining-balance methods; calculate total expense over life of asset.
(SO 3, 5, 9)

Instructions

(a) Prepare a schedule comparing the amortization expense and book values for each of the four years, and in total for the four years, under the straight-line method and the declining-balance method.

(b) Assume that the equipment is sold at the end of the third year for $7,500.
   1. Calculate the gain or loss on the sale of the equipment, under (a) the straight-line method and (b) the declining-balance method.
   2. Prepare a schedule to show the overall impact of the total amortization expense combined with the gain or loss on sale for the three-year period under each method of amortization (consider the total effect on net earnings over the three-year period). Comment on your results.

Financial Reporting and Analysis

Analysis Tools

FINANCIAL REPORTING PROBLEM: *Loblaw Corporation Limited*

BYP9-1   Refer to the financial statements and the Notes to Consolidated Financial Statements of Loblaw, in Appendix A.

Instructions

Answer the following questions:
(a) What were the total cost and net book value of fixed assets at December 28, 2002?
(b) What amortization method is used by Loblaw?
(c) What was the amount of amortization expense and accumulated amortization for each of the two fiscal years 2001 and 2002?
(d) Using the cash flow statement, what are the amounts of fixed assets purchased in 2001 and 2002?
(e) Read Loblaw's "Note 7 Fixed Assets" and "Note 15. Contingencies and Commitments." Does the company primarily engage in capital leases or operating leases? What are the implications for analysis of its financial statements?

COMPARATIVE ANALYSIS PROBLEM: *Loblaw and Sobeys*

BYP9-2   The financial statements of Sobeys Inc. are presented in Appendix B, following the financial statements for Loblaw in Appendix A.

Instructions
(a) Based on the information in these financial statements, calculate the following values for each company for its most recent fiscal year:
   1. Profit margin   3. Asset turnover
   2. Return on assets
(b) Industry averages for the above three ratios are as follows: profit margin, 1.3%; return on assets, 3.0%; and asset turnover, 2.4 times. What conclusions concerning the management of assets can be drawn from your results in (a) and these data?

RESEARCH CASE

BYP9-3 The January/February 2003 issue of *CAmagazine* includes an article by Stephen Cole and Paula White entitled "Accounting for Goodwill." This article discusses the new governance and accounting rules for reporting intangible assets.

Instructions

Read the article and answer these questions:
(a) Goodwill is described as a residual amount. Explain what this means.
(b) Will the initial writedown (impairment) of goodwill to fair market value impact earnings per share if the adjustment is made in the first fiscal year starting after January 1, 2002? Will subsequent writedowns impact earnings per share? If so, explain why.
(c) What valuation technique should be used to determine market value of goodwill?
(d) In most cases, management will undertake to test impairment annually. It is expected that companies will retain independent valuation specialists to review management's reports. For what areas should these specialists give independent opinions?

INTERPRETING FINANCIAL STATEMENTS

BYP9-4   Early in 1998, labour disputes occurred at Maple Leaf Foods Inc.'s meat products plants—one of which was a fresh pork facility. Prior to the labour dispute, the fresh pork facility in Burlington processed about 32,000 hogs per week on a single shift. Following resolution of the dispute, the facility initially processed only about 18,000 hogs per week. The hog supply was gradually increased over the balance of the year, to process 44,000 hogs per week.

This dispute had an adverse financial impact on Maple Leaf's financial results. Maple Leaf paid $37 million of labour dispute–related costs and payments to employees upon settlement of the strike at the Burlington fresh pork facility.

Subsequently, Maple Leaf invested $40-million to add a second shift capacity to the facility. After its completion, Maple Leaf was able to process 85,000 hogs per week on a double shift.

Instructions

(a) Identify and discuss the advantages and disadvantages of each amortization method for Maple Leaf Foods' pork facilities. Which method would you recommend Maple Leaf use to amortize its property, plant, and equipment at its Burlington plant? Explain why you chose this method.

(b) How should Maple Leaf have accounted for the $37 million of labour dispute–related costs? Determine which financial statement this amount should have been reported in, and where.

(c) How should Maple Leaf have accounted for the $40-million investment it made to create more capacity at its prepared-meats facility? Discuss whether these costs should have been treated as operating expenditures or capital expenditures.

A GLOBAL FOCUS

BYP9-5 Vivendi Universal, S.A., with headquarters in France, is a world leader in media and communications. The following discussion of impairment in goodwill was taken from the notes to the financial statements.

VIVENDI UNIVERSAL, S.A.
Notes to the Financial Statements
June 30, 2002

Note 2 Goodwill: *Exceptional Impairment of Goodwill and Assets*

In view of the deterioration of the economy since December 2001 and the impact of the increase in the cost of capital, the group has taken the decision to take a provision against goodwill on certain acquisitions of €11 billion as at June 30, 2002. This preliminary adjustment has been calculated using the group's accounting principles for long-term assets. Long-term assets are subject to an exceptional impairment of goodwill if events result in, or show a risk of, an unexpected reduction in the value of the assets. In this situation, their fair value is re-assessed and a provision is made to cover any eventual, significant difference between the book value and the realizable value.

This exceptional goodwill impairment is broken down as follows:

- €3.8 billion for Canal+
- €3.5 billion for Universal Music Group
- €2.6 billion for Vivendi Universal Entertainment
- €1.1 billion for international telecoms and Internet assets

Standard evaluation methods have allowed us to establish fair market values, notably:

- Business units involved in recent transactions or ones that are currently under discussion have been assessed at the value attributed to them in the transaction.
- Investments in listed companies have been valued at the stock market price.
- In all other cases, the fair market value of business units has been determined by the analysis of discounted cash flows or, whenever possible, by comparison to similar listed companies.

Instructions

Answer the following questions:

(a) What evaluation method(s) did Vivendi use to calculate fair market value of goodwill?

(b) How does Vivendi's recording of the goodwill impairment loss compare with accounting practices in Canada?

(c) Would this writedown affect Vivendi's current earnings? Would it affect future earnings?

(d) How will this goodwill writedown affect Vivendi's balance sheet?

FINANCIAL ANALYSIS ON THE WEB

BYP9-6 SEDAR (System for Electronic Document Analysis and Retrieval) provides information about Canadian public companies and access to some of their documents. We will use SEDAR to select a public company, examine its annual report, and identify the company's long-lived assets, profitability, amortization method, and current year capital expenditures.

Instructions

Specific requirements of this Web case can be found on the Kimmel website.

Critical Thinking

COLLABORATIVE LEARNING ACTIVITY

*BYP9-7 Ty Corporation and Hamline Corporation are two companies that are similar in many respects except that for amortization Ty uses the straight-line method and Hamline uses the declining-balance method at double the straight-line rate. On January 2, 2002, both companies acquired the amortizable assets listed below.

Asset	Cost	Salvage Value	Useful Life
Building	$320,000	$20,000	30 years
Equipment	110,000	10,000	5 years

Including the appropriate amortization expense, annual net earnings for the companies in the years 2002, 2003, and 2004 and total earnings for the three years were as follows:

	2002	2003	2004	Total
Ty Corporation	$184,000	$188,400	$190,000	$562,400
Hamline Corporation	168,000	176,000	185,000	529,000

At December 31, 2004, the balance sheets of the two companies are similar except that Hamline has lower assets and retained earnings than Ty.

Dawna Tucci is interested in investing in one of the companies, and she comes to you for advice.

Instructions

With the class divided into groups, do the following:

(a) Determine the annual and total amortization recorded by each company during the three years.

(b) Assuming that Hamline Company uses the straight-line method of amortization instead of the declining-balance method, prepare comparative earnings data for the three years.

(c) Which company should Dawna Tucci buy shares in? Why?

COMMUNICATION ACTIVITY

BYP9-8 The chapter presented some concerns regarding the current accounting standards for research and development expenditures.

Instructions

Pretend that you are either (a) the president of a company that is very dependent on ongoing research and development, and that you are writing a memo to the CICA complaining about the current accounting standards regarding research and development, or (b) the CICA member defending the current standards regarding research and development. Your letter should address these questions:

1. By requiring expensing of research costs, do you think companies will spend less on R & D? Why or why not? What are the possible implications for the competitiveness of Canadian companies?

2. If a company makes a commitment to spend money for R & D, it must believe it has future benefits. Shouldn't these costs all be capitalized just like the purchase of any long-lived asset that you believe will have future benefits?

ETHICS CASE

BYP9-9 Imporia Container Ltd. is suffering declining sales of its principal product, non-biodegradable plastic cartons. The president, Benny Benson, instructs his controller, John Straight, to lengthen asset lives to reduce amortization expense. A processing line of automated plastic extruding equipment, purchased for $2.7 million in January 2003, was originally estimated to have a useful life of five years and a salvage value of $300,000. Amortization has been recorded for two years on that basis. Benny wants the estimated life changed to eight years total and the straight-line method continued. John is hesitant to make the change, believing it is unethical to increase net earnings in this manner. Benny says, "Hey, the life is only an estimate, and I've heard that our competition uses an eight-year life on their production equipment."

**Ethics In
Accounting**

Instructions

(a) Who are the stakeholders in this situation?
(b) Is the proposed change in asset life unethical or simply a good business practice by an astute president?
(c) What is the effect of Benny Benson's proposed change on earnings before taxes in the year of the change?

Answers to Self-Study Questions
1. d 2. a 3. b 4. c 5. b 6. b 7. d 8. a 9. c 10. c
11. d *12. c *13. b

Answers to Loblaw Review It Question 3

Loblaw amortizes its buildings over a period of 20 to 40 years and its equipment and fixtures over a period of 3 to 10 years. It amortizes its leasehold improvements over the lesser of the asset's useful life and the lease term plus one renewal period to a maximum of 10 years (see Note 1).

 Remember to go back to the Navigator box on the chapter-opening page to check off your completed work.

CHAPTER 10

Reporting and Analysing Liabilities

STUDY OBJECTIVES

After studying this chapter, you should be able to:

1. Distinguish between current and long-term liabilities.

2. Explain the accounting for current liabilities.

3. Prepare the entries for the issue of bonds.

4. Prepare the entries for the retirement of bonds.

5. Explain the accounting for long-term notes payable.

6. Identify the requirements for the financial statement presentation and analysis of liabilities.

7. Apply the straight-line method of amortizing bond discounts and premiums (Appendix 10A).

8. Apply the effective-interest method of amortizing bond discounts and premiums (Appendix 10B).

NAVIGATOR

Borrowing Money to Make Money

"Neither a borrower nor a lender be," says Polonius in Shakespeare's *Hamlet*. But such a philosophy wouldn't get him far in the world of modern business! Take, for example, the case of Pierre Péladeau, who borrowed $1,500 in 1950 to start a small newspaper business. At the time of Mr. Péladeau's death 47 years later, he had turned this small business, through shrewd management and aggressive acquisitions, into one of the largest and most respected companies in Canada—a conglomerate operating on five continents, with over 60,000 employees worldwide and yearly sales in the billions.

Mr. Péladeau was often rferred to by colleagues as "le grand bâtisseur"—the great builder. The first stone of his company, Quebecor Inc., was laid when he purchased the financially troubled *Le Journal de Rosemont* with that first loan. Fifteen hundred dollars was a large sum for a 25-year-old law student in 1950. Mr. Péladeau borrowed it from his mother, who had her doubts about the wisdom of the loan.

However, Mr. Péladeau was able to turn the neighbourhood weekly's finances around, and soon purchased several others. The next step was to acquire a printing firm, which printed his papers—and others—at a profit. In 1964, when the major Montreal daily was on strike, he founded *Le Journal de Montréal*, which grew to become one of the largest newspapers in the country and the "jewel" in Quebecor's crown.

Shortly thereafter, Quebecor began to grow more rapidly. In the 1970s, it expanded beyond newspapers and printing into other communications media. In the 1980s, it grew beyond the Canadian border, purchasing several U.S. printing plants in 1985 and then an international printing group in 1988.

In the 1990s, Quebecor's growth became exponential. By then in his seventies, Mr. Péladeau continued to preside over a dizzying series of acquisitions. The company continued on this path after his death in 1997 and, by 1999, Quebecor was the largest commercial printer in the world, with major subsidiaries in several related

THE NAVIGATOR

Scan *Study Objectives* ☐

Read *Feature Story* ☐

Read *Chapter Preview* ☐

Read text and answer *Before You Go On*
p. 460 ☐   p. 466 ☐   p. 468 ☐
p. 471 ☐   p. 478 ☐

Work *Using the Decision Toolkit* ☐

Review *Summary of Study Objectives*
and *Decision Toolkit* ☐

Work *Demonstration Problem* ☐

Answer *Self-Study Questions* ☐

Complete assignments ☐

markets: lumber, pulp, and newsprint marketing; publications for CD-ROM and the Internet (notably the CANOE network of Internet sites); cable TV networks; magazine and book publication; music retailing; and, of course, newspaper publishing (Sun Media, which as the second-largest newspaper publisher in Canada owns eight metropolitan dailies, is 70% owned by Quebecor).

With its diverse array of holdings, Quebecor has created a huge convergence-driven media group, placing it at the forefront of a sweeping trend that is changing the Canadian business landscape. Today, the activities of its two major subsidiaries span the globe. Quebecor Media, whose operations are concentrated mostly in Quebec, ac-

counts for 30% of advertising revenues in the French-language market in that province and boasts 1.5 million cable TV subscribers. Quebecor World, which groups together the company's worldwide printing activities, has 160 plants in 16 countries in North America, Europe, Latin America, and Asia. Together, the revenue for Quebecor and its subsidiaries for 2002 was in excess of $12 billion.

Clearly, that first loan was a smart move. Mr. Péladeau learned early that borrowing money can make good business sense. As the story of Quebecor shows, strategic acquisitions can be a wildly successful way of making a business grow quickly—and going into debt is one of the ways to finance such acquisitions.

Too much debt, of course, can be dangerous. The return on the investment made with the debt must be enough to cover the cost of the debt. Measures of immediate liquidity, in addition to measures of longer-term solvency, help test a company's strength in this area.

But too little debt can also be a problem. If you can invest only the cash you currently have on hand, you may be missing out on significant opportunities for profit. Pierre Péladeau knew this at age 25, and turned this knowledge into an empire that is envied worldwide.

The feature story suggests that Quebecor has grown rapidly. It is unlikely that it could have grown so large without debt, but at times debt can threaten a company's very existence. Given this risk, why do companies borrow money? Why do they sometimes borrow for the short term and other times long-term? Besides bank borrowings, what other kinds of debt might a company incur? In this chapter, we answer these questions.

The content and organization of this chapter are as follows:

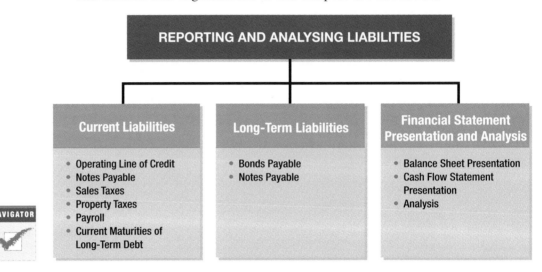

REPORTING AND ANALYSING LIABILITIES

Current Liabilities
- Operating Line of Credit
- Notes Payable
- Sales Taxes
- Property Taxes
- Payroll
- Current Maturities of Long-Term Debt

Long-Term Liabilities
- Bonds Payable
- Notes Payable

Financial Statement Presentation and Analysis
- Balance Sheet Presentation
- Cash Flow Statement Presentation
- Analysis

NAVIGATOR

Current Liabilities

STUDY OBJECTIVE

1

Distinguish between current and long-term liabilities.

As explained in Chapter 2, a current liability is a debt that will be paid (1) from existing current assets or through the creation of other current liabilities, and (2) within one year. Most companies pay current liabilities out of current assets, rather than by creating other liabilities (e.g., paying an account payable by issuing a note payable). Debts that do not meet both criteria are classified as **long-term liabilities**.

Financial statement users want to know whether a company's obligations are current or long-term. A company, for example, that has more current liabilities than current assets often lacks liquidity, or short-term debt-paying ability. In addition, users want to know the types of liabilities a company has. If a company declares bankruptcy, a specific, predetermined order of payment to creditors exists. Thus, the amount and type of liabilities are of critical importance.

The different types of current liabilities include notes payable, accounts payable, unearned revenues, accrued liabilities such as taxes, salaries and wages, and interest, and the current portion of long-term debt. Entries for many of these liabilities have been explained in previous chapters. In this section we discuss operating lines of credit, notes payable, sales taxes, property taxes, payroll, and current maturities of long-term debt in more detail. All current liabilities that are material should be reported in a company's balance sheet.

OPERATING LINE OF CREDIT

Current assets (such as accounts receivable) do not always turn into cash at the exact time that current liabilities (such as accounts payable) must be paid. Consequently, most companies have an operating line of credit at their bank to help them manage temporary cash shortfalls. This means that the company has been pre-authorized by the bank to borrow money, up to a pre-set limit, when it is needed. Quebecor, for example, has a $300-million line of credit.

Security, called collateral, is usually required by the bank as protection in the event of a default on the loan. Collateral normally includes some, or all, of the company's current assets (e.g., accounts receivable or inventories), investments, or property, plant, and equipment.

Line of credit borrowings are normally on a short-term basis, repayable immediately upon request—that is, on demand—by the bank. In reality, repayment is seldom demanded without notice. A line of credit makes it very easy for a company to borrow money. It doesn't have to call or visit its bank to actually arrange the transaction. The bank simply covers any cheques written in excess of the bank account balance, up to the approved credit limit.

A number of companies show a negative, or overdrawn, cash balance at year end as a result of using their line of credit. This amount is usually termed **bank indebtedness, bank overdraft**, or **bank advances**. No special entry is required to record the overdrawn amount. The normal credits to cash will simply accumulate and be reported as a current liability with a suitable note disclosure. Interest is usually charged on the overdrawn amount at a floating rate, such as prime plus a specified percentage rate. The prime rate is the interest rate that banks charge their best customers. This rate is usually increased by a specified percentage that reflects the risk profile of the company.

STUDY OBJECTIVE

2

Explain the accounting for current liabilities.

NOTES PAYABLE

Obligations in the form of written notes are recorded as notes payable. Notes payable are often used instead of accounts payable because they give the lender written documentation of the obligation, which helps if legal remedies are needed to collect the debt. Notes payable are frequently issued to meet short-term financing needs and usually require the borrower to pay interest.

Notes are issued for varying periods of time. **Those due for payment within one year of the balance sheet date are classified as current liabilities.** To illustrate the accounting for notes payable, assume that the HSBC Bank agrees to lend $100,000 on March 1, 2004, if Williams Ltd. signs a $100,000, 6%, four-month note maturing on July 1. Interest is payable at maturity. When Williams signs the note, it receives $100,000 cash and makes the following journal entry:

Mar. 1	Cash	100,000	
	Notes Payable		100,000
	(To record issue of 6%, four-month note to the HSBC Bank)		

A = L + SE
+100,000 +100,000

Cash flows: +100,000

Interest accrues over the life of the note and must be recorded periodically. If Williams has a March 31 year end, an adjusting entry is required to recognize interest expense and interest payable of $500 ($100,000 × 6% × $\frac{1}{12}$) at March 31. The adjusting entry is:

Mar. 31	Interest Expense	500	
	Interest Payable		500
	(To accrue interest for one month on the HSBC Bank note)		

A = L + SE
+500 −500

Cash flows: no effect

In the March 31 financial statements, the current liability section of the balance sheet will show notes payable of $100,000, and interest payable of $500. In addition, interest expense of $500 will be reported in the statement of earnings.

At maturity (July 1), Williams Ltd. must pay the face value of the note ($100,000) plus $2,000 interest ($100,000 $\times$ 6% $\times \frac{4}{12}$), $500 of which has already been accrued. The entry to record payment of the note and interest is:

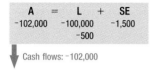

A   =   L   +   SE
-102,000   -100,000   -1,500
          -500

Cash flows: -102,000

July 1	Notes Payable	100,000	
	Interest Payable	500	
	Interest Expense ($100,000 $\times$ 6% $\times \frac{3}{12}$)	1,500	
	Cash		102,000
	(To record payment of HSBC note and interest at maturity)		

SALES TAXES

As consumers, we are well aware that many of the products we purchase at retail stores are subject to sales taxes. The taxes are expressed as a percentage of the sales price. Sales taxes may take the form of the Goods and Services Tax (GST), Provincial Sales Tax (PST), or Harmonized Sales Tax (HST). In Quebec, the PST is known as the Quebec Sales Tax (QST). Federal GST is assessed at 7%. Provincial sales tax rates vary from 0% to 10% across Canada. In Newfoundland and Labrador, Nova Scotia, and New Brunswick, the PST and GST have been combined into one 15% Harmonized Sales Tax.

The retailer (or selling company) collects the sales tax from the customer when the sale occurs, and periodically (normally monthly) remits (sends) the GST or HST collected to the Receiver General of Canada, and PST collected to the provincial Minister of Finance or Treasurer, as the case may be. In the case of GST and HST, collections may be offset against payments and only the net amount owing must be remitted.

The amount of the sale and the amount of the sales tax collected are usually rung up separately on the cash register. The cash register readings are then used to credit the Sales and Sales Taxes Payable accounts. For example, assuming that the March 25 cash register readings for the Setthawiwat Corporation show sales of $10,000, federal sales taxes of $700 (7% GST rate), and provincial sales taxes of $800 (PST rate of 8%), the entry is:

A   =   L   +   SE
+11,500   +700   +10,000
          +800

Cash flows: +11,500

Mar. 25	Cash	11,500	
	Sales		10,000
	GST Payable ($10,000 $\times$ 7%)		700
	PST Payable ($10,000 $\times$ 8%)		800
	(To record sales and sales taxes)		

When the taxes are remitted to the Receiver General and/or Minister of Finance/Treasurer, GST and PST (or HST) Payable is debited and Cash is credited. The company does not report sales taxes as an expense; it simply forwards the amount paid by the customer to the government. Thus, Setthawiwat Corporation serves only as a collection agent for the governments.

Some businesses account for their sales on a tax inclusive basis, not separating sales taxes from their sales price. When this occurs, sales taxes must still be recorded apart from sales revenues. Total receipts can be divided by 100% plus the sales tax percentage to determine sales. To illustrate, assume in the above example that Setthawiwat records total receipts, which are $11,500. Because the amount received from the sale is equal to the sales price, 100%, plus 15% (7% + 8%) of sales, or 1.15 times the sales total, we can calculate sales as follows: $11,500 $\div$ 1.15 = $10,000.

Helpful Hint Watch how sales are rung up at local retailers to see whether the sales tax is calculated separately.

Thus, the total sales tax amount of $1,500 ($700 + $800) can be found by subtracting sales from total receipts ($11,500 − $10,000). The components of this total can be found by multiplying sales by the respective sales tax rates ($10,000 × 7% and $10,000 × 8%).

In some provinces, PST is charged on GST. For example, in Quebec a $100 sale would result in $7 GST (7%) and $8.02 QST [($100 + $7) × 7.5%]. The escalated sales tax rate is slightly over 15% [($7 + $8.02) ÷ $100] rather than 14.5% (7% GST + 7.5% QST). Caution must be exercised when extracting sales tax amounts from total receipts because of the varying rate combinations that may be in use.

PROPERTY TAXES

Businesses pay property taxes annually. These taxes are charged by the municipal and provincial governments, and are calculated at a specified rate for every $100 of the assessed value of the property (i.e., land and building). It is difficult to determine the property tax expense because the amount due for the current year is unknown until the bill is received, usually sometime in the spring of each year. Until that time, property taxes must be estimated and accrued.

To illustrate, assume that Tantramar Management Ltd. owns land and a building in the city of Regina. Tantramar's year end is December 31 and it makes monthly adjusting entries. Tantramar receives its property tax bill of $6,000 on March 1, and it is due to be paid on May 31.

For the months of January and February, Tantramar accrues the monthly property tax expense based on last year's property tax bill of $5,520 as follows:

Jan. 31 to Feb. 28	Property Tax Expense ($5,520 ÷ 12)
	    Property Tax Payable
	    (To accrue estimated property tax)
		460	460

$$A = L + SE$$
$$+460 \quad -460$$
Cash flows: no effect

In March, when Tantramar receives the property tax bill, it records the liability owed for its property taxes. Note that Tantramar has already accrued $920 ($460 × 2 months) of this liability, so it need only record the difference between the total property tax bill of $6,000 and the amount already accrued. In addition, the $80 shortfall in estimated expense for the first two months of the year, calculated as shown below, must also be adjusted.

Actual property tax expense ($6,000 ÷ 12 = $500 × 2 months)	$1,000
Less: Amount accrued to date ($5,520 ÷ 12 = $460 × 2 months)	920
Unrecorded expense	$ 80

Mar. 1	Property Tax Expense
	Prepaid Property Tax
	    Property Tax Payable ($6,000 − $460 − $460)
	    (To adjust, and record, property tax payable)
		80
		5,000
			5,080

$$A = L + SE$$
$$+5,000 \quad +5,080 \quad -80$$
Cash flows: no effect

At this point, Tantramar has both a prepaid asset and a liability. For the remaining ten months of the year, March through December, Tantramar adjusts the prepaid expense for the portion of the property tax that expires each month as follows:

Mar. 31 to Dec. 31	Property Tax Expense
	    Prepaid Property Tax
	    (To record property tax expense)
		500	500

$$A = L + SE$$
$$-500 \quad -500$$
Cash flows: no effect

Part way through the year, in May when Tantramar pays the property tax bill, the entry is a simple payment of the liability:

May 31	Property Tax Payable	6,000	
	Cash		6,000
	(To record payment of property tax)		

At year-end, the Prepaid Property Tax and Property Tax Payable accounts have a nil balance. The Property Tax Expense account has a balance of $6,000. There are other ways to adjust property tax throughout the period; however, all should result in the same ending balances.

PAYROLL

Assume that Linfang Wang works 40 hours this week for Pepitone Inc., earning $10 per hour. Will Linfang receive a $400 cheque at the end of the week? No, she won't. The reason: Pepitone is required to withhold amounts known as **payroll deductions** from her wages to pay various other parties. For example, Pepitone must withhold amounts for federal and provincial income taxes, Canada Pension Plan (CPP) contributions, and employment insurance (EI) premiums. It might also withhold voluntary deductions for charitable, insurance, and other purposes.

Until these payroll deductions are remitted to the third parties on whose behalf Pepitone collected the amounts, they are reported as a current liability in Pepitone's balance sheet. Illustration 10-1 summarizes the types of payroll deductions that normally occur for most companies.

Illustration 10-1
Payroll deductions

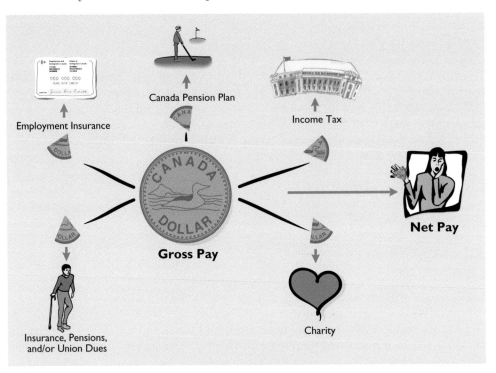

The following illustrates the accrual and payment of a $100,000 payroll on which Pepitone Inc. withholds assumed deductions from its employees' wages.

Mar. 7	Wages Expense	100,000	
	CPP Payable		4,950
	EI Payable		2,100
	Income Taxes Payable		20,427
	United Way Payable		2,445
	Union Dues Payable		667
	Wages Payable		69,411
	(To record payroll and employee deductions for the week ending March 7)		
7	Wages Payable	69,411	
	Cash		69,411
	(To record payment of the March 7 payroll)		

A = L + SE
      +4,950 −100,000
      +2,100
      +20,427
      +2,445
      +667
      +69,411

Cash flows: no effect

A = L + SE
−69,411 −69,411

Cash flows: −69,411

In this case, Pepitone reports $100,000 in wages expense. In addition, it reports liabilities to its employees for the wages payable as well as liabilities to others, such as the government, United Way, and the union. Rather than pay its employees $100,000, Pepitone is instead required to withhold amounts such as income taxes, CPP, and EI and make these payments directly. In summary, Pepitone is essentially serving as a collection agency for the government and other third parties.

In addition to the liabilities incurred as a result of payroll deductions, employers also incur a second type of payroll-related liability. With every payroll, the employer incurs liabilities to pay various payroll costs that are levied, such as the employer's share of CPP and EI. In addition, the provincial governments mandate employer funding of a Workplace Health, Safety and Compensation Plan. Each of these contributions, plus items such as paid vacations and employer-sponsored pensions, are collectively referred to as **employee benefits**.

Based on the $100,000 payroll in our Pepitone Inc. example, the following entry would be made to record the employer's expense and liability for these employee benefits:

Mar. 7	Employee Benefits Expense	12,465	
	CPP Payable		4,950
	EI Payable		2,940
	Worker's Compensation Payable		575
	Vacation Pay Payable		4,000
	(To record employer's payroll costs on March 7 payroll)		

A = L + SE
      +4,950 −12,465
      +2,940
      +575
      +4,000

Cash flows: no effect

The payroll and payroll liability accounts are classified as current liabilities because they must either be paid to employees or remitted to government authorities or other third parties both periodically and in the near term.

CURRENT MATURITIES OF LONG-TERM DEBT

Companies often have a portion of long-term debt that comes due in the current year. As an example, assume that Cudini Construction issues a five-year, interest-bearing, $25,000 note on January 1, 2004. This note specifies that each January 1, starting January 1, 2005, $5,000 of the note should be repaid. When financial statements are prepared on December 31, 2004, $5,000 should be reported as a current liability and $20,000 as a long-term liability. Current maturities of long-term debt are often identified on the balance sheet as **long-term debt due within one year**. Illustration 10-2 shows that at December 31, 2002, Quebecor had $643.5 million of such debt.

Illustration 10-2
Current liability section—
Quebecor Inc.

QUEBECOR INC.

QUEBECOR INC. Balance Sheet (Partial) December 31, 2002 (in millions)	
Current liabilities	
Bank indebtedness	$ 13.6
Accounts payable and accrued charges	2,397.2
Income and other taxes	121.1
Future income taxes	1.0
Current portion of long-term debt	643.5
Total current liabilities	$3,176.4

It is not necessary to prepare an adjusting entry to recognize the current maturity of long-term debt. The proper statement classification of each balance sheet account is recognized when the balance sheet is prepared.

BUSINESS INSIGHT

MANAGEMENT PERSPECTIVE

An interesting example of a current liability is the airlines' frequent flier programs. An expert on frequent-flier programs calculated that at the end of 2001, the world's airlines had issued nearly 12 trillion frequent flier miles, with two-thirds of those yet to be redeemed. About 36% of all miles are earned from airline travel. The remainder are earned from partners to whom airlines sell their frequent flier miles, such as hotels, credit cards, and, yes, even ginger ale companies. Toronto university student Jeff McKinnon consumed a litre of ginger ale a day over four months— 132 litres all told—when the soft-drink company offered free Aeroplan points.

Aeroplan, Air Canada's frequent flier program, has 100 billion points outstanding. The airline has recorded a $384-million current liability on its balance sheet for anticipated redemptions. In 2002, Aeroplan redemptions accounted for 8.9% of Air Canada's seats.

Source: Keith McArthur and Gordon Pitts, "Fliers, Airlines Love Their Point Programs," *The Globe and Mail*, February 1, 2003, B1.

BEFORE YOU GO ON . . .

● **REVIEW IT**

1. What are the two criteria for classifying a debt as a current liability?
2. What are some examples of current liabilities?
3. What are three items generally withheld from employees' wages or salaries?
4. Identify the liabilities classified as current by Loblaw. The answer to this question is provided at the end of this chapter.

● **DO IT**

Prepare the journal entries to record the following transactions:

1. Accrue interest on December 31 (year end) for a $10,000, 8%, three-month note payable issued November 1. Interest is payable at maturity.
2. The cash register total for a four-day craft sale was $256,000. This total included sales taxes. The GST tax rate is 7% and the PST is 8%. Record the sales and sales taxes.
3. A company's gross wages amount to $10,000. Amounts deducted from the employees' wages are CPP of $495, EI of $210, income tax of $3,965, and

health insurance of $950. The employer's portion of CPP is $495 and of EI, $294. Record the weekly payroll, assuming that cash is paid to the employees but the withholdings are still due.

Action Plan

- Remember the formula for interest: Face value × Annual interest rate × Time.
- Before recording any amounts, separate sales taxes from sales. Divide the total proceeds by 100% plus the sales tax rates.
- Record both the employees' portion of the payroll and the benefits owed by the employer. Employee deductions are not an expense to the employer.

Solution

1.	Interest Expense ($10,000 × 8% × $\frac{2}{12}$)	133	
	Interest Payable		133
	(To accrue interest on note payable)		
2.	Cash	256,000	
	Sales ($256,000 ÷ 115%)		222,608
	GST Payable ($222,608 × 7%)		15,583
	PST Payable ($222,608 × 8%)		17,809
	(To record sales and sales taxes)		
3.	Wages Expense	10,000	
	CPP Payable		495
	EI Payable		210
	Income Tax Payable		3,965
	Health Insurance Payable		950
	Wages Payable		4,380
	(To record payment of wages)		
	Employee Benefits Expense	789	
	CPP Payable		495
	EI Payable		294
	(To record employee benefits)		

Long-Term Liabilities

A long-term liability is an obligation expected to be paid after one year. In this section, we explain the accounting for the principal types of obligations reported in the long-term liability section of the balance sheet. These obligations are often in the form of bonds or long-term notes. Bonds are explained in the next section; followed by long-term notes.

STUDY OBJECTIVE

3

Prepare the entries for the issue of bonds.

BONDS PAYABLE

A bond is a form of interest-bearing note payable issued by corporations, universities, and government agencies. Bonds, like common shares, are sold in small denominations (usually $1,000 or multiples of $1,000). As a result, they attract many investors.

Types of Bonds

Bonds may have many different features. Some commonly issued types of bonds are described in the following sections.

Secured and Unsecured Bonds.   Secured bonds have specific assets of the issuer pledged as collateral for the bonds. Unsecured bonds are issued against the general credit of the borrower. These bonds, called debenture bonds, are used extensively by large corporations with good credit ratings. For example, in its 2002 financial statements, Quebecor reported $470.8 million of debenture bonds outstanding, $235.4 million of which mature in 2007 and $235.4 million of which mature in 2027.

BUSINESS INSIGHT
INVESTOR PERSPECTIVE

Bond credit-rating agencies help investors assess the risk level or creditworthiness of bonds. The highest quality bonds are graded as AAA bonds; superior quality, AA; good quality, A; medium grade, BBB. Bonds rated below BBB are commonly referred to as "junk bonds." They are considered to be of higher credit risk; that is, the chance of default is higher for them than for bonds of better credit quality.

One of the rating agencies downgraded Air Canada's credit rating to "B," or junk bond status, early in 2003. "The downgrade reflects Air Canada's continuing operating losses, the gradual reduction of its sources of backup liquidity and the increasingly competitive dynamics in the domestic market," analysts wrote. Immediately after this downgrade, Air Canada's share price fell 14% and its unsecured bonds sold at between 35 and 45 cents, close to where they were trading after the September 11, 2001, terrorist attacks in the United States.

Source: Keith McArthur, "Air Canada Credit Ratings Cut After Big Losses," *The Globe and Mail,* February 8, 2003, B3.

Convertible and Redeemable/Retractable Bonds.   Bonds that can be converted into common shares at the bondholder's option are called convertible bonds. Bonds that can be retired at a stated dollar amount prior to maturity at the option of the issuer are known as redeemable (callable) bonds. Retractable bonds are bonds which can be redeemed prior to maturity at the option of the bondholder.

Convertible bonds have features that are attractive both to bondholders and to the issuer. The conversion often gives bondholders an opportunity to benefit if the market price of the common shares increases substantially. Furthermore, until conversion, the bondholder receives interest on the bond. For the issuer, the bonds sell at a higher price and pay a lower rate of interest than comparable debt securities that do not have a conversion option. Quebecor reported $235.4 million of redeemable debentures in its 2002 financial statements. These debentures mature on August 1, 2027, and are redeemable at the option of the bondholder at their face value on August 1, 2004.

Issuing Procedures

A bond certificate is issued to investors to provide evidence of an investor's credit claim against the company. The certificate provides information such as the name of the company that issued the bonds, the face value of the bonds, the maturity date of the bonds, and the contractual interest rate. The face value is the amount due at the maturity date. The maturity date is the date that the final payment is due to the investor from the company. The contractual interest rate is the rate used to determine the amount of cash interest the borrower pays and the investor receives. Usually, the contractual rate is stated as an annual rate, and interest is paid semi-annually.

Alternative Terminology
Face value is often referred to as the *par value;* and the *contractual rate* is often referred to as the *stated rate.*

Determining the Market Value of Bonds

If you were an investor interested in purchasing a bond, how would you determine how much to pay? To be more specific, assume that Coronet, Inc. issues a zero-interest bond (pays no interest) with a face value of $1,000,000 due in 20 years. For this bond, the only cash you receive is $1 million at the end of 20 years. Would you pay $1 million for this bond? We hope not, because $1 million received 20 years from now is not the same as $1 million received today.

You should not pay $1 million, because of what is called the **time value of money.** If you had $1 million today, you would invest it and earn interest such that after 20 years, your investment could be worth much more than $1 million. Thus, if someone is going to pay you $1 million 20 years from now, you would want to find its equivalent today, or its present value. In other words, you would want to determine how much must be invested today at current interest rates to have $1 million in 20 years.

The current market value (present value) of a bond is a function of three factors: (1) the dollar amounts to be received, (2) the length of time until the amounts are received, and (3) the market rate of interest. The market interest rate is the rate investors demand for loaning funds to a corporation. The process of finding the present value is referred to as **discounting** the future amounts.

To illustrate, assume that on January 1, 2004, Daoust Ltd. issues $100,000 of 4% bonds, due in five years, with interest payable semi-annually. The purchaser of the bonds would receive the following two cash inflows: (1) **principal** of $100,000 to be paid at maturity, and (2) ten $2,000 **interest payments** ($100,000 × 4% × $\frac{6}{12}$ months) over the term of the bonds. A time diagram for both cash flows is shown in Illustration 10-3.

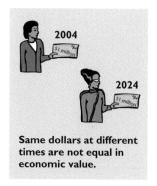

Same dollars at different times are not equal in economic value.

Alternative Terminology The *market interest rate* is also known as the *effective interest rate.*

Illustration 10-3
Time diagram of cash flows

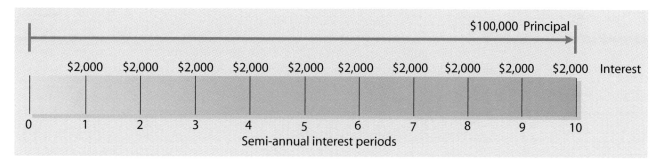

The current market value of a bond is equal to the present value of all the future cash payments promised by the bond. The present values of these amounts are listed in Illustration 10-4.

Illustration 10-4
Calculating the present value (market price) of bonds

Present value of $100,000 received at the end of 10 periods	
$100,000 × 0.82035 (*n* = 10, *i* = 2%)*	$ 82,035
Present value of $2,000 received semi-annually for 10 periods	
$2,000 × 8.98259 (*n* = 10, *i* = 2%)	17,965
Present value (market price) of bonds	$100,000
* *n* = number of interest periods and *i* = interest rate	

Tables are available to provide the present value numbers to be used, or these values can be determined mathematically. Further discussion of the concepts and the mechanics of the time value of money calculations is provided on the CD that accompanies this book.

Study
Tools

Accounting for Bond Issues

A corporation records bond transactions when it issues or buys back bonds, or when bondholders convert bonds into common shares. If a bondholder sells a bond to another investor, the issuing firm receives no money on the transaction, **nor is the transaction journalized by the issuing corporation** (similar to what happens when shares are traded among investors).

Bonds may be issued at face value, below face value (discount), or above face value (premium). Bond prices for both new issues and existing bonds are quoted as a **percentage of the face value of the bond, which is usually $1,000.** Thus, a $1,000 bond with a quoted price of 97 means that the selling price of the bond is 97% of face value, or $970.

Issuing Bonds at Face Value. To illustrate the accounting for bonds issued at face value, assume that Devor Corporation issues 100 five-year, 9%, $1,000 bonds dated January 1, 2004, at 100 (100% of face value). The entry to record the sale is:

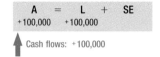

Jan. 1	Cash	100,000	
	Bonds Payable		100,000
	(To record sale of bonds at face value)		

These bonds payable are reported in the long-term liability section of the balance sheet because the maturity date is January 1, 2009 (more than one year away).

Over the term (life) of the bonds, entries are required for bond interest. Interest on bonds payable is calculated in the same manner as interest on notes payable, explained earlier. If it is assumed that interest is payable semi-annually on January 1 and July 1 on the bonds described above, interest of $4,500 ($100,000 $\times 9\% \times \frac{6}{12}$) must be paid on July 1, 2004. The entry for the payment is:

July 1	Bond Interest Expense	4,500	
	Cash		4,500
	(To record payment of bond interest)		

At December 31, Devor's year-end, an adjusting entry is required to recognize the $4,500 of interest expense incurred since July 1. The entry is:

Dec. 31	Bond Interest Expense	4,500	
	Bond Interest Payable		4,500
	(To accrue bond interest)		

Bond interest payable is classified as a current liability because it is scheduled for payment within the next year. When the interest is paid on January 1, 2005, Bond Interest Payable is decreased (debited) and Cash is also decreased (credited) for $4,500.

Discount or Premium on Bonds. The previous illustrations assumed that the interest rate paid on the bonds—referred to as the contractual interest rate—and the market interest rate were the same. Recall that the contractual interest rate is the rate applied to the face value to arrive at the interest paid in a year. The market interest rate is the rate investors demand for loaning funds to the corporation. When the contractual interest rate and the market interest rate are the same, bonds sell at face value, as illustrated above.

However, market interest rates change daily. They are influenced by the type of bond issued, the state of the economy, current industry conditions, and the company's individual performance. As a result, the contractual and market interest rates often differ, and bonds therefore sell below or above face value.

To illustrate, suppose that a company issues 6% bonds at a time when other bonds of similar risk are paying 8%. Investors will not be interested in buying the 6% bonds, so their price will fall below their face value. In this case, we say the 6% bonds are selling at a discount. As a result of the decline in the bonds' selling price, the actual interest rate incurred by the company increases to the level of the current market interest rate.

Conversely, if the market interest rate is **lower** than the contractual interest rate, investors will have to pay more than face value for the bonds. That is, if the market

Helpful Hint Bond prices vary inversely with changes in the market interest rate. As market interest rates decline, bond prices increase. When a bond is issued, if the market interest rate is below the contractual rate, the price will be higher than the face value.

interest rate is 4% but the contractual interest rate on the bonds is 6%, everyone will want to buy the bonds and the price will rise above their face value. In these cases, bonds sell at a premium. These relationships are shown in Illustration 10-5.

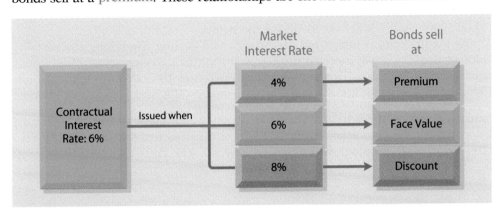

Illustration 10-5
Interest rates and bond prices

Issuing bonds at an amount different from face value is quite common. By the time a company prints the bond certificates and markets the bonds, it will be a coincidence if the market rate and the contractual rate are the same. Thus, the issue of bonds at a discount does not mean that the financial strength of the issuer is suspect. Conversely, the sale of bonds at a premium does not indicate that the financial strength of the issuer is exceptional.

Issuing Bonds at a Discount. To illustrate the issue of bonds at a discount, assume that on January 1, 2004, Candlestick Inc., sells $1 million of five-year, 5% bonds at 95.7345 (95.7345% of face value) with interest payable on July 1 and January 1. The entry to record the issue is:

Jan.	1	Cash ($1,000,000 × 95.7345%)	957,345	
		Discount on Bonds Payable	42,655	
		Bonds Payable		1,000,000
		(To record sale of bonds at a discount)		

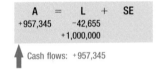

A = L + SE
+957,345   −42,655
         +1,000,000

Cash flows: +957,345

Although Discount on Bonds Payable has a debit balance, **it is not an asset**. Rather, it is a **contra liability account** which is **deducted from Bonds Payable** on the balance sheet as in Illustration 10-6.

CANDLESTICK INC.
Balance Sheet (partial)
January 1, 2004

Long-term liabilities		
Bonds payable	$1,000,000	
Less: Discount on bonds payable	42,655	$957,345

Illustration 10-6
Statement presentation of discount on bonds payable

The $957,345 represents the **carrying (or book) value** of the bonds. On the date of issue, this amount equals the market price of the bonds.

When bonds are issued below face value, the total cost of borrowing is higher than the contractual bond interest paid. That is, at maturity, the issuing corporation must pay not only the contractual interest rate over the term of the bonds, but also the face value (rather than the issue price). Therefore, the difference between the issue price and the face value of the bonds—the discount—is an **additional cost of borrowing** that should be recorded as **bond interest expense** over the life of the bonds.

To follow the matching principle, the bond discount should be allocated to expense over the life of the bonds. This is referred to as **amortizing the discount**.

Illustration 10-7
Amortization of bond
discount

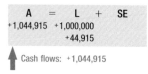

A = L + SE
+1,044,915 +1,000,000
           +44,915

↑ Cash flows: +1,044,915

Amortization of the discount increases the amount of interest expense reported each period. That is, after amortizing the discount, the amount of interest expense reported in a period will exceed the contractual amount. For the bonds issued by Candlestick Inc., total interest expense will exceed the contractual interest by $42,655 ($1,000,000 − $957,345) over the life of the bonds.

As the discount is amortized, its balance will decline. Therefore, the carrying value of the bonds will increase until at maturity the carrying value of the bonds equals their face value. This is shown in Illustration 10-7. Procedures for amortizing bond discounts are discussed in Appendices 10A and 10B to this chapter.

Issuing Bonds at a Premium. The issue of bonds at a premium can be illustrated by assuming the Candlestick Inc. bonds described earlier are sold at 104.4915 (104.4915% of face value) rather than at 95.7345. The entry to record the sale is:

Jan.	1	Cash	1,044,915	
		Bonds Payable		1,000,000
		Premium on Bonds Payable		44,915
		(To record sale of bonds at a premium)		

Premium on Bonds Payable is **added to Bonds Payable** on the balance sheet, as shown in Illustration 10-8.

Illustration 10-8
Statement presentation of
bond premium

| **CANDLESTICK INC.** |
| **Balance Sheet (partial)** |
| **January 1, 2004** |

Long-term liabilities		
Bonds payable	$1,000,000	
Add: Premium on bonds payable	44,915	$1,044,915

The sale of bonds above face value causes the total cost of borrowing to be **less than the bond interest paid**, because the borrower is not required to pay the bond premium at the maturity date of the bonds. Thus, the premium is considered to be **a reduction in the cost of borrowing** that reduces bond interest expense over the life of the bonds.

Illustration 10-9
Amortization of bond
premium

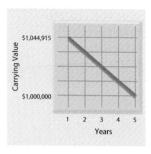

Similar to bond discounts, the bond premium should be allocated to expense over the life of the bonds. The is referred to as **amortizing the premium**. Amortization of the premium decreases the amount of interest expense reported each period. That is, after amortizing the premium, the amount of interest expense reported in a period will be less than the contractual amount. For the bonds issued by Candlestick Inc., contractual interest will exceed the interest expense by $44,915 ($1,044,915 − $1,000,000) over the life of the bonds.

As the premium is amortized, its balance will decline. Therefore, the carrying value of the bonds will decrease, until at maturity the carrying value of the bonds equals their face value. This is shown in Illustration 10-9. Procedures for amortizing bond premiums are discussed in Appendices 10A and 10B to this chapter.

BEFORE YOU GO ON...

● **REVIEW IT**

1. What journal entry is made to record the issue of bonds payable of $100,000 at 100? At 96? At 102?
2. Why do bonds sell at face value? At a discount? At a premium?
3. Explain why bond discounts and premiums are amortized.

4. When bonds are issued at a discount, does the carrying value increase or decrease over the life of the bond? When issued at a premium?

● DO IT

Over the total life of recently issued bonds, contractual interest is determined to be $50,000 and interest expense, $52,000. Answer the following questions: (1) Were the bonds sold at face value, a discount, or a premium? (2) After recording the interest expense, will the bond carrying value increase or decrease until maturity?

Action Plan

• Understand the effects that the amortization of a bond discount or premium has on bond interest expense and on the carrying value of the bond.
• Remember that bond discount amortization increases both bond interest expense and the carrying value of the bond.
• Remember that bond premium amortization decreases both bond interest expense and the carrying value of the bond.

Solution

Interest expense is $2,000 greater than the interest paid. This difference is equal to the discount amount that must be amortized. (1) The bonds were sold at a discount. (2) Recording interest expense and amortizing the bond discount will decrease the Discount on Bonds Payable account and increase the carrying value of the bonds.

Accounting for Bond Retirements

Bonds are retired when they are purchased (redeemed) by the issuing corporation. The appropriate entries for these transactions are explained next.

Redeeming Bonds at Maturity. Regardless of the issue price of bonds, the carrying value of the bonds at maturity will equal their face value. Assuming that the interest for the last interest period is paid and recorded separately, the entry to record the redemption of the Candlestick bonds at maturity, on January 1, 2009, is:

Jan. 1	Bonds Payable	1,000,000	
	Cash		1,000,000
	(To record redemption of bonds at maturity)		

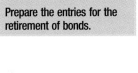
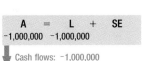

Redeeming Bonds Before Maturity. Bonds may be redeemed before maturity. A company may decide to retire bonds before maturity in order to reduce interest costs and remove debt from its balance sheet. A company should only retire debt early if it has sufficient cash resources.

When bonds are retired before maturity, it is necessary to (1) update any unrecorded interest of amortization, (2) eliminate the carrying value of the bonds at the redemption date, (3) record the cash paid, and (4) recognize the gain or loss on redemption. The carrying value of the bonds is the face value of the bonds less the unamortized bond discount, or plus the unamortized bond premium, at the redemption date.

To illustrate, assume that at the end of the fourth year (eighth period), Candlestick Inc., having originally sold its bonds at a premium of $44,915, as described in the last section, now retires them at 103 after paying the semi-annual interest. Assume that the carrying value of the bonds at the redemption date is $1,008,983. That is, the face value of the bonds is $1,000,000 and the unamortized premium, $8,983. The entry to record the redemption at the end of the eighth interest period (January 1, 2008) is:

A	=	L	+	SE
−1,030,000		−1,000,000		−21,017
		−8,983		

Cash flows: −1,030,000

Jan.	1	Bonds Payable	1,000,000	
		Premium on Bonds Payable	8,983	
		Loss on Bond Redemption	21,017	
		Cash		1,030,000
		(To record redemption of bonds at 103)		

Note that the loss of $21,017 is the difference between the cash paid of $1,030,000 and the carrying value of the bonds of $1,008,983. Losses and gains on bond redemption are reported in the statement of earnings, often as Other Expenses or Revenues.

This is very similar to the calculation of a loss or gain on the sale of property, plant, and equipment where cash is also compared to carrying value. However, the determination of whether a loss or a gain results naturally differs, depending on whether you are selling property, plant, and equipment (assets) or purchasing bonds (liabilities).

Illustration 10-10
Comparison of asset and liability gain and loss

Property, Plant, and Equipment	Bonds Payable
Sale price	Purchase price
− Carrying (book) value	− Carrying value
Gain (loss)	Loss (gain)

BUSINESS INSIGHT

INVESTOR PERSPECTIVE

University bonds are a relatively new phenomenon in Canada. Since 2001, Canadian universities have issued bonds totalling three-quarters of a billion dollars. The bond issues range in size from $125 million (University of British Columbia) to $225 million (Concordia University).

Years of putting off much-needed maintenance work, and rising enrolments, have made universities about as desperate for cash as students. And, considering how poorly the equity markets have performed, investors are eagerly purchasing university bonds as a safe way to invest in their own futures. University bonds are currently paying about 6.5%, for 40 years.

Source: Mark Brown, "Schools of Higher Earnings," *Canadian Business*, September 16, 2002, 20.

BEFORE YOU GO ON . . .

● **REVIEW IT**

1. Explain the accounting for a redemption of bonds at maturity and before maturity.
2. Distinguish between the calculation of gains (losses) from the sale of property, plant, and equipment and the redemption of bonds.

● **DO IT**

R & B Inc. issues $500,000 of 10-year bonds at a premium. Prior to maturity, on June 30 when the carrying value of the bonds is $508,000, the company redeems the bonds at 101. Prepare the entry to record the redemption of the bonds.

Action Plan

• Update any partial period interest and amortization.
• Eliminate the carrying value of the bonds. Remove the balances from the Bonds Payable account and any Discount or Premium account.

- Record the cash paid.
- Calculate and record the gain or loss (the difference between the cash paid and the carrying value).

Solution

There is a $3,000 gain on redemption. The cash paid, $505,000, is lower than the carrying value of $508,000 ($500,000 + $8,000). The entry is as follows:

June 30	Bonds Payable	500,000	
	Premium on Bonds Payable	8,000	
	Gain on Bond Redemption		3,000
	Cash ($500,000 × 101%)		505,000
	(To record redemption of bonds at 101)		

NOTES PAYABLE

The use of long-term notes payable in debt financing is common. For example, Quebecor has $3.6 billion of long-term notes payable. Long-term notes payable are similar to short-term notes payable except that the terms of the notes exceed one year. In periods of unstable interest rates, the interest rate on long-term notes may be tied to changes in the market rate.

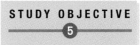

STUDY OBJECTIVE
5
Explain the accounting for long-term notes payable.

A long-term note may be unsecured or secured. A secured note pledges title to specific assets as security for the loan. Secured notes are commonly known as mortgages. A mortgage note payable is widely used by individuals to purchase homes. It is also used by many companies to acquire property, plant, and equipment.

While short-term notes are normally repayable in full at maturity, most long-term notes are repayable in a series of periodic payments. These payments are known as **instalments** and are paid monthly, quarterly, semi-annually, or at another defined period. Each payment consists of (1) interest on the unpaid balance of the loan, and (2) a reduction of loan principal. Payments generally take one of two forms: (1) fixed principal payments plus interest, or (2) blended principal and interest payments. Let's look at each of these payment patterns in more detail.

Fixed Principal Payments

Instalment notes with fixed principal payments are repayable in **equal periodic amounts, plus interest**. Interest may be either **fixed** or **floating**. A fixed interest rate will be constant over the term of the note. A floating (or variable) interest rate will change with fluctuating market rates. Generally, floating rates are tied to changes in the **prime rate**. As explained earlier in the chapter, prime is the rate that banks use to loan money to their most creditworthy customers.

To illustrate, assume that, on January 1, 2004, Belanger Ltée issues a $120,000, 7%, five-year note payable to obtain financing for a new research laboratory. The terms provide for equal monthly instalment payments of $2,000 ($120,000 ÷ 60 periods) on the first of each month, plus interest of 7% on the outstanding principal balance. Monthly interest expense is calculated by multiplying the outstanding principal balance by the interest rate. For the first payment date—February 1—interest expense is $700 ($120,000 × 7% × $\frac{1}{12}$ mos.). Note that the 7% is an annual interest rate and must be adjusted for the monthly time period. The cash payment of $2,700 for the month of February is the total of the instalment payment, $2,000, which is applied against the principal, plus the interest, $700.

An instalment payment schedule is a useful tool to help organize this information and to provide information to assist in the preparation of journal entries. The instalment payment schedule for the first few months for Belanger Ltée, rounded to the nearest dollar, is shown in Illustration 10-11.

		BELANGER LTÉE		
		Instalment Payment Schedule—Fixed Principal Payment		
	(A)	(B)	(C)	(D)
	Cash		Reduction of	Principal
	Payment	Interest Expense	Principal	Balance
Interest Period	(B + C)	(D × 7% × $\frac{1}{12}$)	($120,000 ÷ 60)	(D − C)
Jan. 1				$120,000
Feb. 1	$2,700	$700	$2,000	118,000
Mar. 1	2,688	688	2,000	116,000
Apr. 1	2,677	677	2,000	114,000

With fixed principal payments, the interest decreases each period (as the principal decreases). The portion applied to the reduction of loan principal stays constant, but because of the decreasing interest, the total payment decreases.

The entries to record the note payable and the first instalment payment one month later are as follows:

A	=	L	+	SE
+120,000		+120,000		

↑ Cash flows: +120,000

Jan. 1	Cash	120,000	
	Notes Payable		120,000
	(To record five-year, 7% note payable)		

A	=	L	+	SE
−2,700		−2,000		−700

↓ Cash flows: −2,700

Feb. 1	Interest Expense	700	
	Notes Payable	2,000	
	Cash		2,700
	(To record monthly payment on note)		

Blended Principal and Interest Payments

Instalment notes with blended principal and interest payments are repayable in **equal periodic amounts, including interest.** Blended principal and interest payments result in changing amounts of interest and principal applied to the loan. As with fixed principal payments, the interest decreases each period (as the principal decreases). In contrast to fixed principal payments, the portion applied to the loan principal increases each period.

To illustrate, assume that instead of fixed principal payments, Belanger Ltée repays its $120,000, 7% note payable in equal monthly instalments of $2,376. Illustration 10-12 shows the instalment payment schedule for the first few months for Belanger Ltée, rounded to the nearest dollar.

		BELANGER LTÉE		
		Instalment Payment Schedule—Blended Principal and Interest Payment		
	(A)	(B)	(C)	(D)
			Reduction of	Principal
	Cash	Interest Expense	Principal	Balance
Interest Period	Payment	(D × 7% × $\frac{1}{12}$)	(A − B)	(D − C)
Jan. 1				$120,000
Feb. 1	$2,376	$700	$1,676	118,324
Mar. 1	2,376	690	1,686	116,638
Apr. 1	2,376	680	1,696	114,942

The entries to record the note payable and the first instalment payment one month later are as follows:

Jan.	1	Cash	120,000	
		Notes Payable		120,000
		(To record five-year, 7% note payable)		

A = L + SE
+120,000 +120,000

Cash flows: +120,000

Feb.	1	Interest Expense	700	
		Notes Payable	1,676	
		Cash		2,376
		(To record monthly payment on note)		

A = L + SE
-2,376 -1,676 -700

Cash flows: -2,376

With both types of instalment notes payable, as with any other long-term note payable, **the reduction in principal for the next year must be reported as a current liability. The remaining unpaid principal is classified as a long-term liability.**

BEFORE YOU GO ON . . .

● **REVIEW IT**

1. Distinguish between short-term and long-term notes payable.
2. Explain the accounting for long-term notes payable.

● **DO IT**

On December 31, 2004, Tian Inc. issued a $500,000, 8%, 15-year mortgage note payable. The terms provide for semi-annual blended instalment payments of $28,915, principal and interest, on June 30 and December 31. Prepare the journal entries required to record the issue of the note on December 31, 2004, and the first two payments on June 30, 2005, and December 31, 2005.

Action Plan

- Multiply the semi-annual interest rate by the principal balance at the beginning of the period to determine interest expense.
- Record mortgage payments, recognizing that each payment consists of (1) interest on the unpaid loan balance, and (2) a reduction of the loan principal.

Solution

Dec.31, 2004	Cash	500,000	
	Mortgage Notes Payable		500,000
	(To record issue of 8%, 15-year mortgage note payable)		

June 30, 2005	Interest Expense ($500,000 $\times$ 8% $\times$ $\frac{6}{12}$)	20,000	
	Mortgage Notes Payable ($28,915 − $20,000)	8,915	
	Cash		28,915
	(To record semi-annual mortgage payment)		

Dec. 31, 2005	Interest Expense [($500,000 − $8,915) $\times$ 8% $\times$ $\frac{6}{12}$)]	19,643	
	Mortgage Notes Payable ($28,915 − $19,643)	9,272	
	Cash		28,915
	(To record semi-annual mortgage payment)		

NAVIGATOR

Financial Statement Presentation and Analysis

BALANCE SHEET PRESENTATION

STUDY OBJECTIVE

6

Identify the requirements for the financial statement presentation and analysis of liabilities.

Current liabilities are reported as the first category in the Liabilities section of the balance sheet. Each of the principal types of current liabilities is listed separately within the category.

Similar to current assets, current liabilities are generally listed in their order of maturity. However, this is not always possible because of the varying maturity dates that may exist for specific obligations such as notes payable. Long-term liabilities are reported separately immediately following current liabilities. An example is shown in Illustration 10-13. Disclosure of debt is very important. Because of numerous corporate failures, investors have become very concerned about companies' debt obligations. Summary data regarding debts may be presented in the balance sheet while detailed data (such as interest rates, maturity dates, conversion privileges, and assets pledged as collateral) should be shown in the notes.

Illustration 10-13
Balance sheet presentation of long-term liabilities

MARAIS COMPANY Balance Sheet (partial) December 31, 2004		
Liabilities		
Current liabilities		
Notes payable	$ 250,000	
Accounts payable	125,000	
Accrued liabilities	75,000	
Current portion of long-term debt	300,000	
Total current liabilities		$ 750,000
Long-term liabilities		
Bonds payable	$1,000,000	
Less: Discount on bonds payable	80,000	920,000
Notes payable		500,000
Lease liability		540,000
Total long-term liabilities		1,960,000
Total liabilities		$2,710,000

CASH FLOW STATEMENT PRESENTATION

The balance sheet presents the balances of a company's debts at a point in time. Information regarding cash inflows and outflows during the year that resulted from the principal portion of debt transactions is provided in the financing activities section of the cash flow statement. Interest expense is reported in the operating activities section even though it resulted from debt transactions.

Illustration 10-14 presents the cash flows from financing activities from Quebecor's cash flow statement. From this we learn that Quebecor decreased its borrowing on its operating line of credit (bank indebtedness). It issued long-term debt of $231.8 million and repaid long-term debt of $1,110.4 million. Other financing activities relate to equity transactions. Quebecor's subsidiary companies issued capital stock of $50.8 million. Quebecor also paid dividends during the year of $76.0 million.

QUEBECOR INC. Cash Flow Statement (partial) Year Ended December 31, 2002 (in millions)	
Financing activities	
Net (decrease) increase in bank indebtedness	$ (24.6)
Issuance of long-term debt and convertible notes	231.8
Repayment of long-term debt	(1,110.4)
Issuance of capital stock by subsidiaries	50.8
Dividends	(76.0)
Cash used by financing activities	$ (928.4)

Illustration 10-14
Cash flow statement presentation of financing activities—Quebecor

QUEBECOR INC.

ANALYSIS

A careful examination of debt obligations makes it easier to assess a company's ability to pay its current obligations. It also helps to determine whether a company can obtain long-term financing in order to grow. The condensed information in Illustration 10-15 from Quebecor's financial statements will be used to illustrate the analysis of a company's liquidity and solvency.

QUEBECOR INC. Balance Sheet December 31, 2002 (in millions)		
	2002	2001
Assets		
Current assets		
Cash and cash equivalents	$ 190.9	$ 340.1
Short-term investments	323.0	49.5
Accounts receivable	1,067.3	928.1
Other receivables	62.8	24.8
Inventories	799.5	766.4
Prepaid expenses	58.1	61.6
Future income taxes	75.5	114.7
Total current assets	2,577.1	2,285.2
Noncurrent assets	14,553.3	17,217.8
Total assets	$17,130.4	$19,503.0
Liabilities and Shareholders' Equity		
Liabilities		
Current liabilities	$ 3,176.4	$ 2,530.1
Noncurrent liabilities	12,475.2	14,407.0
Total liabilities	15,651.6	16,937.1
Shareholders' equity	1,478.8	2,565.9
Total liabilities and shareholders' equity	$17,130.4	$19,503.0

Illustration 10-15
Quebecor balance sheet

QUEBECOR INC.

Liquidity

Liquidity ratios measure the short-term ability of a company to pay its maturing obligations and to meet unexpected needs for cash. A commonly used measure of liquidity was examined in Chapter 2: the **current ratio** (Current assets ÷ Current liabilities). In this section, we add a second measure of liquidity, the acid-test ratio.

The current ratio is frequently used, but it can be misleading. Consider the current ratio's numerator, which can include some items in current assets that are not very liquid. For example, when a company is having a difficult time selling its merchandise, its inventory and current ratio increase even though its liquidity has actually declined. Similarly, prepaid expenses increase assets but generally cannot be sold and therefore do not contribute to liquidity. Consequently, the current ratio is often supplemented by the acid-test ratio.

Alternative Terminology
The *acid-test ratio* is often referred to as the *quick ratio.*

The acid-test ratio is a measure of a company's immediate short-term liquidity. It is calculated by dividing the sum of cash, short-term investments, and accounts receivable by current liabilities. Cash, short-term investments, and accounts receivable are usually highly liquid compared to inventory and prepaid expenses. Thus, because it measures **immediate** liquidity, the acid-test ratio should be calculated along with the current ratio. The current ratios and acid-test ratios for Quebecor and its industry are provided in Illustration 10-16.

Illustration 10-16
Liquidity measures

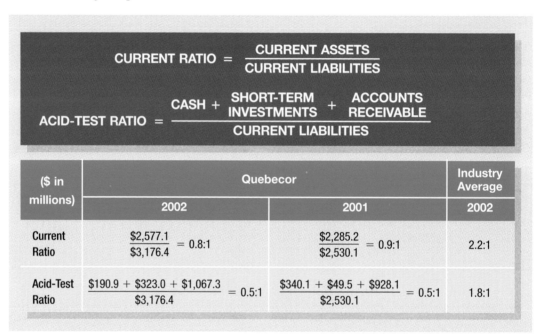

Quebecor's current ratio declined marginally from 2001 to 2002, even though its acid-test ratio remained constant in both years at 0.5:1. This means that Quebecor did not have enough current assets to pay its current liabilities, and only had $0.50 of immediately liquid current assets for every $1 of liabilities. Both Quebecor's current and acid-test ratios are far below those of the industry.

In recent years many companies have intentionally reduced their liquid assets, because they cost too much to hold. Companies that keep fewer liquid assets on hand must rely on other sources of liquidity. One such source is an **operating line of credit**, as discussed earlier in this chapter. To the extent that its low amount of liquid assets causes a cash shortfall, a company may borrow money on its available short-term lines of credit.

Quebecor's operating lines of credit exceed $1 billion and amount to more than the sum of its existing cash, short-term investments, and accounts receivable. Thus, while Quebecor's ratios are significantly below the industry average, its available lines of credit appear adequate to meet any short-term cash deficiency it might experience as its continues on its acquisition spree.

Decision Toolkit

DECISION CHECKPOINTS	INFO NEEDED FOR DECISION	TOOL TO USE FOR DECISION	HOW TO EVALUATE RESULTS
Can the company meet its current obligations?	Cash, accounts receivable, short-term investments, and other highly liquid assets, and current liabilities	$$\text{Acid-test ratio} = \frac{\text{(Cash} + \text{Short-term investments} + \text{Accounts receivable)}}{\text{Current liabilities}}$$	Ratio should be compared to others in the same industry. High ratio indicates good liquidity.
Can the company obtain short-term financing when necessary?	Available lines of credit from notes to the financial statements	Compare available lines of credit to current liabilities. Also, evaluate liquidity ratios.	If liquidity ratios are low, then lines of credit should be high to compensate.

Solvency

Solvency ratios measure the ability of a company to repay its long-term debt and survive over a long period of time. One of Quebecor's subsidiary companies, Sun Media Inc., improved its solvency rating in February 2003. It refinanced its debt, and was then removed from its "credit watch with negative implications" status, which the credit rating agencies had given it in September 2002. This highlights the fact that even large companies such as Quebecor must ensure that they don't impair their solvency.

In Chapter 2 you learned that one measure of a company's solvency is **debt to total assets**. It is calculated by dividing total liabilities by total assets. This ratio indicates the extent to which a company's debt could be repaid by liquidating its assets.

The debt to total assets ratio should be interpreted in light of the company's ability to handle its debt. That is, a company might have a high debt to total assets ratio, but still be able to easily cover its interest payments. Alternatively, a company may have a low debt to total assets ratio, and struggle to cover its interest payments. A useful ratio to supplement the information provided by the debt to total assets ratio is the times interest earned ratio. The times interest earned ratio provides an indication of a company's ability to meet interest payments as they come due. It is calculated as follows: earnings before interest expense and income tax expense divided by interest expense. It uses earnings before interest and taxes (often abbreviated as EBIT) because this number best represents the amount available to cover interest.

We can use the balance sheet information in Illustration 10-15 and the additional information below to calculate solvency ratios for Quebecor:

($ in millions)	2002	2001
Net earnings (loss)	$ 91.9	$(248.7)
Interest expense	624.1	665.4
Income tax expense	156.2	76.1

The debt to total assets and times interest earned ratios for Quebecor and averages for the industry are shown in Illustration 10-17.

International Note

The use of debt financing varies considerably across countries. One measure of the degree of debt financing is the ratio of national debt to gross national product. In a recent survey, this ratio was 49% in Canada, 145% in Japan, 100% in Italy, and 75% in the U.S.

Alternative Terminology The *times interest earned ratio* is also known as the *interest coverage ratio.*

			DEBT TO TOTAL ASSETS $= \dfrac{\text{TOTAL DEBT}}{\text{TOTAL ASSETS}}$			
			TIMES INTEREST EARNED $= \dfrac{\text{EBIT}}{\text{INTEREST EXPENSE}}$			

($ in millions)	Quebecor		Industry Average
	2002	**2001**	**2002**
Debt to Total Assets	$\dfrac{\$15{,}651.6}{\$17{,}130.4} = 91.4\%$	$\dfrac{\$16{,}937.1}{\$19{,}503.0} = 86.8\%$	35.9%
Times Interest Earned	$\dfrac{\$91.9 + \$624.1 + \$156.2}{\$624.1} = 1.4 \text{ times}$	$\dfrac{\$(248.7) + \$665.4 + \$76.1}{\$665.4} = 0.7 \text{ times}$	2.5 times

Illustration 10-17
Solvency ratios

Debt to total assets varies across industries, because different capital structures are appropriate for different industries. The debt to total assets ratio for the communications and media industry is 35.9%—2.5 times less than that of Quebecor. Quebecor's ratio increased from 2001 to 2002, reflecting higher debt incurred to finance business acquisitions during 2002. One should be very careful when interpreting debt to assets ratios. In Quebecor's case, its consolidated financial statements include 100% of its subsidiaries' debt, which Quebecor is not responsible for in the event of default.

Quebecor appears to be equipped to handle the additional debt created by its acquisitions, as its improving times interest earned ratio indicates. These acquisitions led to increased earnings, which help to cover the additional financing costs. Yet, Quebecor is still below the industry average in its ability to cover its interest charges. Management is of the opinion that future cash flows generated by the combined operations will be adequate to cover debt reimbursement and interest payments.

Decision Toolkit

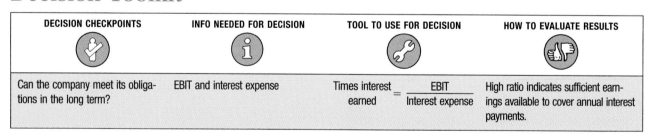

DECISION CHECKPOINTS	INFO NEEDED FOR DECISION	TOOL TO USE FOR DECISION	HOW TO EVALUATE RESULTS
Can the company meet its obligations in the long term?	EBIT and interest expense	Times interest earned $= \dfrac{\text{EBIT}}{\text{Interest expense}}$	High ratio indicates sufficient earnings available to cover annual interest payments.

Other Analysis Issues—Unrecorded Debt

A concern for analysts when they evaluate a company's liquidity and solvency is whether that company has properly recorded all of its obligations. The bankruptcy of Enron Corporation—the largest bankruptcy in corporate history—demonstrated how much damage can result when a company does not properly record or disclose all of its debts. Two examples are discussed here—contingencies and off–balance sheet financing.

Contingencies. Sometimes a company's balance sheet does not fully disclose its actual obligations. One reason this occurs is that the company's balance sheet might not fully reflect its potential obligations which may result from contingencies. Contingencies are events with uncertain outcomes. For users of financial statements, contingencies are often very important to understanding a company's financial position. Lawsuits are a common type of contingency. Suppose, for example, that you were analysing the financial statements of a cigarette manufacturer and did not consider the possible negative implications of existing unsettled lawsuits. Your analysis of the company's financial position would certainly be misleading. Other common types of contingencies are product warranties and environmental problems.

Accounting rules require that contingencies be disclosed in the notes; in some cases they must be accrued as liabilities. If the company can determine **a reasonable estimate** of the expected loss, and if it is **likely** to occur, then the company should accrue for the loss. The loss is recorded by increasing (debiting) a loss account and increasing (crediting) a liability account. If *both* of these conditions are not met, then the company discloses the basic facts regarding the contingent loss in the notes to its financial statements.

Off–Balance Sheet Financing. A second reason that a company's balance sheet might understate its actual obligations is that the company might have "off–balance sheet financing." Off–balance sheet financing refers to a situation where liabilities are not recorded on the balance sheet. This situation occurs when a company is able to finance its operations or asset acquisitions with what many analysts would consider to be debt financing, yet the terms of the deal are structured in a way that allows the company to avoid recording debt while still following GAAP. One very common type of off–balance sheet financing results from leasing transactions.

In most lease contracts, the lessee makes a periodic payment that is recorded as rent expense in the statement of earnings. The renting of an apartment and the rental of a car are examples of this type of lease, often referred to as an operating lease. In an operating lease, the intent is temporary use of the property by the lessee with continued ownership of the property by the lessor. In some cases, however, the lease contract transfers substantially all the benefits and risks of ownership to the lessee, so that the lease is in effect a purchase of the property. This type of lease is called a capital lease because the fair value of the leased asset is *capitalized* on the lessee's balance sheet.

Accounting standards have precise criteria that determine whether or not a lease should be accounted for as a capital lease. We won't review the criteria here, but their purpose is to help determine whether the lease transaction more closely resembles a purchase transaction or a rental transaction.

If the lease is a capital lease, the lessee's books must contain entries to record the asset and a related liability for the lease payments. Otherwise, the lessee would account for the transaction as an operating lease, meaning that neither an asset nor a liability is shown on the books.

Critics of off–balance sheet financing contend that many operating leases represent unavoidable obligations that meet the definition of a liability, and they should therefore be reported as liabilities on the balance sheet. To reduce these concerns, companies are required to report their operating lease obligations in a note to the financial statements. This allows analysts and other financial statement users to adjust ratios such as debt to total assets by adding leased assets and lease liabilities if they feel that this treatment is more appropriate.

Quebecor's obligations under operating leases total $934.2 million and are disclosed in the notes to the financial statements. The total increase in assets and liabilities that would result if these leases were recorded on the balance sheet is $934.2 million. However, this amount is not very significant relative to Quebecor's total assets of $17,130.4 million or total liabilities of $15,651.6 million. Thus, the

 International Note

Different countries use different criteria to determine whether a lease should be recorded as operating or capital. Brazil, Italy, and Japan classify all leases as operating. France, Spain, and Sweden require a purchase option to exist or to be exercised before capitalization occurs.

potential unrecorded off–balance sheet assets and liabilities resulting from Quebecor's leases do not appear to be a concern.

Decision Toolkit

DECISION CHECKPOINTS	INFO NEEDED FOR DECISION	TOOL TO USE FOR DECISION	HOW TO EVALUATE RESULTS
Does the company have any contingent liabilities?	Knowledge of events with uncertain negative outcomes	Financial statements and notes to financial statements	If negative outcomes are possible, determine the probability, the amount of loss, and the potential impact on financial statements.
Does the company have significant off–balance sheet financing, such as unrecorded lease obligations?	Information on unrecorded obligations, such as minimum lease payments from lease note	Compare liquidity and solvency ratios with and without unrecorded obligations included.	If ratios differ significantly after including unrecorded obligations, these obligations should not be ignored in analysis.

BUSINESS INSIGHT

INVESTOR PERSPECTIVE

New and innovative "off–balance sheet" financing arrangements are surfacing every day, all designed to help companies deal with deregulation, foreign exchange and interest rate volatility, income tax changes, and other factors. These types of arrangements include loan commitments, financial guarantees, options, synthetic leases, and asset securitizations. Accounting standard-setters are struggling to keep up with disclosure requirements for these evolving financial instruments as investors and regulators increasingly question the merits of these transactions. One senior analyst noted, "I look at off–balance sheet financing from an investor's point of view. All material liabilities must be front and centre."

Source: "CFO Roundtable Webcast Debates the Future of Off–Balance Sheet Financing," *Business Wire*, January 21, 2003.

BEFORE YOU GO ON . . .

- ● **REVIEW IT**
  1. How are liabilities presented on the balance sheet and cash flow statement?
  2. Distinguish between liquidity and solvency.
  3. What information do the acid-test and times interest earned ratios provide? How are these two ratios calculated?
  4. What is off–balance sheet financing? Give some examples of off–balance sheet financing.

APPENDIX 1 0 A

STRAIGHT-LINE AMORTIZATION

To follow the matching principle, bond discounts or premiums must be allocated to expense in each period in which the bonds are outstanding. There are two commonly used amortization methods to do so: the straight-line method and the effective-interest method (discussed in Appendix 10B). The straight-line method of amortization is the simpler of the two. It allocates the same amount to interest expense in each interest period. The amount is determined as shown in Illustration 10A-1.

STUDY OBJECTIVE

7

Apply the straight-line method of amortizing bond discounts and premiums.

Illustration 10A-1
Formula for straight-line method of bond discount/premium amortization

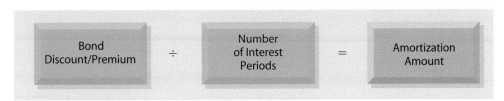

Amortizing a Bond Discount

To illustrate the straight-line method of amortization, we will continue to use Candlestick Inc., illustrated earlier in the chapter, as an example. As you recall, Candlestick issued $1,000,000 of five-year, 5% bonds at $957,345. Interest is payable semi-annually on July 1 and January 1.

In this example, the bond discount is $42,655. Semi-annual amortization of this discount is $4,265.50 ($42,655 ÷ 10 six-month periods), using straight-line method. The entry to record the payment of bond interest and the amortization of bond discount on the first interest date (July 1, 2004) is as follows:

July 1	Bond Interest Expense	29,265.50	
	Discount on Bonds Payable		4,265.50
	Cash ($1,000,000 × 5% × $\frac{6}{12}$)		25,000.00
	(To record payment of bond interest and		
	amortization of bond discount)		

A = L + SE
−25,000.00 +4,265.50 −29,265.50

Cash flows: −25,000

Note that it is the *interest payment*, and not the *interest expense*, that is calculated by applying the contractual interest rate for the period (5% × $\frac{6}{12}$) to the face value of the bonds. The interest expense includes both the interest payment ($25,000) and the bond discount amortization ($4,265.50). Recall from our chapter discussion that the bond discount is part of the cost of borrowing.

At December 31, Candlestick's year end, the adjusting entry is recorded as follows:

Dec. 31	Bond Interest Expense	29,265.50	
	Discount on Bonds Payable		4,265.50
	Bond Interest Payable		25,000.00
	(To record accrued bond interest and		
	amortization of bond discount)		

A = L + SE
+4,265.50 −29,265.50
+25,000.00

Cash flows: no effect

Over the term of the bonds, the balance in Discount on Bonds Payable will decrease semi-annually by the same amortization amount until it reaches zero at maturity. The carrying value of the bonds at maturity will be equal to the face value.

A bond discount amortization schedule, as shown in Illustration 10A-2, is a useful tool to organize and summarize this information. The schedule shows the interest payment, interest expense, discount amortization, and carrying value of the bond for each interest period. Note that the carrying value of the bond increases by $4,265.50 each period until it reaches its face value of $1,000,000 at the end of period 10 (January 1, 2009).

	CANDLESTICK INC. Bond Discount Amortization Schedule Straight-Line Method				
Semi-Annual Interest Period	(A) Interest Payment ($1,000,000 × 5% × $\frac{6}{12}$)	(B) Interest Expense (A + C)	(C) Discount Amortization ($42,655 ÷ 10)	(D) Unamortized Discount (D − C)	(E) Bond Carrying Value ($1,000,000 − D)
Issue date				$42,655.00	$ 957,345.00
1	$ 25,000	$ 29,265.50	$ 4,265.50	38,389.50	961,610.50
2	25,000	29,265.50	4,265.50	34,124.00	965,876.00
3	25,000	29,265.50	4,265.50	29,858.50	970,141.50
4	25,000	29,265.50	4,265.50	25,593.00	974,407.00
5	25,000	29,265.50	4,265.50	21,327.50	978,672.50
6	25,000	29,265.50	4,265.50	17,062.00	982,938.00
7	25,000	29,265.50	4,265.50	12,796.50	987,203.50
8	25,000	29,265.50	4,265.50	8,531.00	991,469.00
9	25,000	29,265.50	4,265.50	4,265.50	995,734.50
10	25,000	29,265.50	4,265.50	0.00	1,000,000.00
	$250,000	$292,655.00	$42,655.00		

Column (A) remains constant because the face value of the bonds ($1,000,000) is multiplied by the semi-annual contractual interest rate each period.
Column (B) is calculated as the interest paid (Column A) plus the discount amortization (Column C).
Column (C) indicates the discount amortization each period.
Column (D) decreases each period by the same amount of discount amortization until it reaches zero at maturity.
Column (E) increases each period by the same amount of discount amortization until it equals the face value at maturity.

Illustration 10A-2
Bond discount amortization schedule—straight-line method

Amortizing a Bond Premium

The amortization of bond premium parallels that of bond discount. In the chapter example, Candlestick issued $1,000,000 of 5% bonds at a premium of $44,915. The premium amortization for each interest period is $4,491.50 ($44,915 ÷ 10). The entry to record the first payment of interest on July 1 follows:

A = L + SE
−25,000.00   −4,491.50 −20,508.50

Cash flows: −25,000

July 1	Bond Interest Expense	20,508.50	
	Premium on Bonds Payable	4,491.50	
	Cash ($1,000,000 × 5% × $\frac{6}{12}$)		25,000.00
	(To record payment of bond interest and amortization of bond premium)		

At December 31, the adjusting entry is:

A = L + SE
     −4,491.50 −20,508.50
    +25,000.00

Cash flows: no effect

Dec. 31	Bond Interest Expense	20,508.50	
	Premium on Bonds Payable	4,491.50	
	Bond Interest Payable		25,000.00
	(To record accrued bond interest and amortization of bond premium)		

Over the term of the bonds, the balance in Premium on Bonds Payable will decrease semi-annually by the same amount until it reaches zero at maturity. Carrying values *increase* to maturity value with a bond discount and *decrease* to maturity value with a bond premium.

A bond premium amortization schedule, as shown in Illustration 10A-3, shows interest expense, premium amortization, and the carrying value of the bond for each interest period. The interest expense recorded each period for the Candlestick bond is $20,508.50 under the straight-line method. This is the amount of the interest payment ($25,000) reduced by the premium amortization ($4,491.50). Note also that the carrying value of the bonds decreases by $4,491.50 each period until it reaches the face value of $1,000,000 at the end of period 10.

Illustration 10A-3
Bond premium amortization schedule—straight-line method

		CANDLESTICK INC.			
		Bond Premium Amortization Schedule			
		Straight-Line Method			
	(A)	(B)	(C)	(D)	(E)
Semi-Annual	Interest	Interest	Premium	Unamortized	Bond
Interest	Payment	Expense	Amortization	Premium	Carrying Value
Period	($1,000,000 × 5% × $\frac{6}{12}$)	(A − C)	($44,915 ÷ 10)	(D − C)	($1,000,000 + D)
Issue date				$44,915.00	$1,044,915.00
1	$ 25,000	$ 20,508.50	$ 4,491.50	40,423.50	1,040,423.50
2	25,000	20,508.50	4,491.50	35,932.00	1,035,932.00
3	25,000	20,508.50	4,491.50	31,440.50	1,031,440.50
4	25,000	20,508.50	4,491.50	26,949.00	1,026,949.00
5	25,000	20,508.50	4,491.50	22,457.50	1,022,457.50
6	25,000	20,508.50	4,491.50	17,966.00	1,017,966.00
7	25,000	20,508.50	4,491.50	13,474.50	1,013,474.50
8	25,000	20,508.50	4,491.50	8,983.00	1,008,983.00
9	25,000	20,508.50	4,491.50	4,491.50	1,004,491.50
10	25,000	20,508.50	4,491.50	0.00	1,000,000.00
	$250,000	$205,085.00	$44,915.00		

Column (A) remains constant because the face value of the bonds ($1,000,000) is multiplied by the semi-annual contractual interest rate each period.
Column (B) is calculated as the interest paid (Column A) less the premium amortization (Column C).
Column (C) indicates the premium amortization each period.
Column (D) decreases each period by the same amount of premium amortization until it reaches zero at maturity.
Column (E) decreases each period by the same amount of premium amortization until it equals the face value at maturity.

A P P E N D I X   1 0 B

EFFECTIVE-INTEREST AMORTIZATION

To follow the matching principle, bond discounts or premiums must be allocated to expense in each period in which the bonds are outstanding. There are two commonly used amortization methods to do so: the straight-line method (discussed in Appendix 10A) and the effective-interest method. The effective-interest method of amortization calculates interest expense by multiplying the carrying value of the bonds by the market interest rate in effect at the time the bonds were issued. This market interest rate, expressed as a percentage, is also known as the effective interest rate.

Under the effective-interest method, the amortization of a bond discount or bond premium results in periodic interest expense equal to a constant percentage of the carrying value of the bonds. The effective-interest method results in varying amounts of amortization and interest expense per period but a constant percentage rate. The straight-line method results in constant amounts of amortization and interest expense per period but a varying percentage rate. The effective-interest method is considered conceptually superior to the straight-line method.

STUDY OBJECTIVE
8

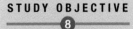

Apply the effective-interest method of amortizing bond discounts and premiums.

Both the straight-line and effective-interest methods of amortization result in the same total amount of interest expense over the term of the bonds. However, **when the amounts are materially different each interest period, the effective-interest method is required under generally accepted accounting principles.**

The following steps are required under the effective-interest method:

1. Calculate the **bond interest expense:** Multiply the carrying value of the bonds at the beginning of the interest period by the effective interest rate.
2. Calculate the **bond interest paid** (or accrued): Multiply the face value of the bonds by the contractual interest rate.
3. Calculate the **amortization amount:** Determine the difference between the amounts calculated in steps (1) and (2).

These steps are shown in Illustration 10B-1.

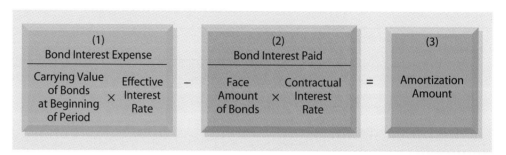

Amortizing a Bond Discount

To illustrate the effective-interest method of bond discount amortization, we will continue to use Candlestick Inc., illustrated earlier in the chapter, as an example. As you recall, Candlestick issued $1,000,000 of five-year, 5% bonds. Interest is payable semi-annually on July 1 and January 1.

The bonds are issued to yield a market interest rate of 6% (the effective interest rate). Using time value of money techniques, we determine that the bonds will sell for $957,345 (95.7345% of face value). This sale price results in a bond discount of $42,655 ($1,000,000 − $957,345).

For the first interest period, the bond interest expense is $28,720, calculated by multiplying the carrying value of the bonds by the effective interest rate ($957,345 × 6% × $\frac{6}{12}$). The interest payment, $25,000, is the same regardless of which method is used. It is calculated by multiplying the face value of the bonds by the contractual interest rate ($1,000,000 × 5% × $\frac{6}{12}$). The amortization is not a specific calculation as it is in the straight-line amortization method. It is simply the difference between the interest expense and the interest paid ($28,720 − $25,000 = $3,720). The interest payment will remain constant each period while the interest expense and amortization will change with the carrying value.

A bond discount amortization schedule, as shown in Illustration 10B-2, makes it easier to record the interest expense and the discount amortization. For simplicity, amounts have been rounded to the nearest dollar in this schedule.

CANDLESTICK INC.
Bond Discount Amortization Schedule
Effective-Interest Method

Semi-Annual Interest Period	(A) Interest Payment ($1,000,000 × 5% × $\frac{6}{12}$)	(B) Interest Expense (Preceding bond carrying value × 6% × $\frac{6}{12}$)	(C) Discount Amortization (B − A)	(D) Unamortized Discount (D − C)	(E) Bond Carrying Value ($1,000,000 − D)
Issue date				$42,655	$ 957,345
1	$ 25,000	$ 28,720	$ 3,720	38,935	961,065
2	25,000	28,832	3,832	35,103	964,897
3	25,000	28,947	3,947	31,156	968,844
4	25,000	29,065	4,065	27,091	972,909
5	25,000	29,187	4,187	22,904	977,096
6	25,000	29,313	4,313	18,591	981,409
7	25,000	29,442	4,442	14,149	985,851
8	25,000	29,576	4,576	9,573	990,427
9	25,000	29,713	4,713	4,860	995,140
10	25,000	29,860*	4,860	0	1,000,000
	$250,000	$292,655	$42,655		

Column (A) remains constant because the face value of the bonds ($1,000,000) is multiplied by the semi-annual contractual interest rate each period.
Column (B) is the bond carrying value at the end of the preceding period multiplied by the semi-annual market interest rate.
Column (C) indicates the discount amortization each period.
Column (D) decreases each period by the amortization amount until it reaches zero at maturity.
Column (E) increases each period by the amortization amount until it equals the face value at maturity.
* $6 difference due to rounding.

Note that interest expense as a percentage of carrying value remains constant at 3% (6% × $\frac{6}{12}$ mos.).

For the first interest period, the entry to record the payment of interest and amortization of bond discount by Candlestick is as follows:

Illustration 10B-2
Bond discount amortization schedule—effective-interest method

July 1	Bond Interest Expense ($957,345 × 6% × $\frac{6}{12}$)	28,720	
	Discount on Bonds Payable		3,720
	Cash ($1,000,000 × 5% × $\frac{6}{12}$)		25,000
	(To record payment of bond interest and amortization of bond discount)		

A	=	L	+	SE
−25,000		+3,720		−28,720

Cash flows: −25,000

For the second interest period, at Candlestick's year end, the following adjusting entry is made:

Dec. 31	Bond Interest Expense ($961,065 × 6% × $\frac{6}{12}$)	28,832	
	Discount on Bonds Payable		3,832
	Bond Interest Payable ($1,000,000 × 5% × $\frac{6}{12}$)		25,000
	(To record accrued bond interest and amortization of bond discount)		

A	=	L	+	SE
		+3,832		−28,832
		+25,000		

Cash flows: no effect

Amortizing a Bond Premium

The amortization of a bond premium by the effective-interest method is similar to the procedures described for a bond discount.

Using our previous example, assume that Candlestick Inc. issues its $1,000,000 of five-year, 5% bonds on January 1, 2004, with interest payable on July 1 and January 1. In this case, the bonds are issued to yield a market (effective) interest rate of

Illustration 10B-3
Bond premium amortization schedule— effective-interest method

4%. Using time value of money techniques, we determine that the bonds will sell for $1,044,915. This sale price results in a premium of $44,915.

The bond premium amortization schedule is shown in Illustration 10B-3. Figures have been rounded to the nearest dollar for simplicity.

	(A)	(B)	(C)	(D)	(E)
Semi-Annual Interest Period	Interest Payment ($1,000,000 × 5% × $\frac{6}{12}$)	Interest Expense (Preceding bond carrying value × 4% × $\frac{6}{12}$)	Premium Amortization (A − B)	Unamortized Premium (D − C)	Bond Carrying Value ($1,000,000 + D)
Issue date				$44,915	$1,044,915
1	$ 25,000	$ 20,898	$ 4,102	40,813	1,040,813
2	25,000	20,816	4,184	36,629	1,036,629
3	25,000	20,733	4,267	32,362	1,032,362
4	25,000	20,647	4,353	28,009	1,028,009
5	25,000	20,560	4,440	23,569	1,023,569
6	25,000	20,471	4,529	19,040	1,019,040
7	25,000	20,381	4,619	14,421	1,014,421
8	25,000	20,288	4,712	9,709	1,009,709
9	25,000	20,194	4,806	4,903	1,004,903
10	25,000	20,097*	4,903	0	1,000,000
	$250,000	$205,085	$44,915		

Column (A) remains constant because the face value of the bonds ($1,000,000) is multiplied by the semi-annual contractual interest rate each period.
Column (B) is the bond carrying value at the end of the preceding period multiplied by the semi-annual market interest rate.
Column (C) indicates the premium amortization each period.
Column (D) decreases each period by the amortization amount until it reaches zero at maturity.
Column (E) decreases each period by the amortization amount until it equals the face value at maturity.
* $1 difference due to rounding.

The entry on the first interest date is as follows:

A = L + SE
−25,000 −4,102 −20,898

Cash flows: −25,000

July 1	Bond Interest Expense ($1,044,915 × 4% × $\frac{6}{12}$)	20,898	
	Premium on Bonds Payable	4,102	
	Cash ($1,000,000 × 5% × $\frac{6}{12}$)		25,000
	(To record payment of bond interest and amortization of bond premium)		

For the second period, the following adjusting entry is made. While the interest expense and amortization amounts vary, the cash payment is a constant $25,000 every interest period.

A = L + SE
−4,184 −20,816
+25,000

Cash flows: no effect

Dec. 31	Bond Interest Expense ($1,040,813 × 4% × $\frac{6}{12}$)	20,816	
	Premium on Bonds Payable	4,184	
	Bond Interest Payable ($1,000,000 × 5% × $\frac{6}{12}$)		25,000
	(To record accrued bond interest and amortization of bond premium)		

Note that the amount of periodic interest expense decreases over the life of the bond when the effective interest method is applied to bonds issued at a premium. The reason is that a constant percentage is applied to a decreasing bond carrying value to calculate interest expense. The carrying value is decreasing because of the amortization of the premium.

Using the Decision Toolkit

CanWest Global Communications Corp. is the country's largest media conglomerate. Its holdings include television and radio stations, newspapers, and Internet publishing operations and it is one of Quebecor's biggest competitors. Selected financial information for CanWest is provided below as at August 31, 2002 and 2001.

CANWEST GLOBAL COMMUNICATIONS CORP. Balance Sheet August 31, 2002 (in millions)		
	2002	2001
Assets		
Current assets		
Cash	$ 61.1	$ 19.5
Accounts receivable	470.2	475.6
Inventory	19.8	30.8
Other current assets	175.2	147.5
Total current assets	726.3	673.4
Noncurrent assets	4,994.8	5,625.8
Total assets	$5,721.1	$6,299.2
Liabilities and Shareholders' Equity		
Liabilities		
Current liabilities	$ 690.3	$ 668.2
Long-term liabilities	3,854.9	4,325.0
Total liabilities	4,545.2	4,993.2
Total shareholders' equity	1,175.9	1,306.0
Total liabilities and shareholders' equity	$5,721.1	$6,299.2
Other information		
Net earnings	$ 13.0	$ 46.6
Interest expense	376.6	356.8
Income tax expense (recovery)	7.1	(59.0)

Available lines of credit: Credit facilities provide for revolving and term loans in the maximum amounts of $600 million and $1,796.5 million, respectively. $30 million of the revolving loan is available as an operating line of credit. As at August 31, 2002, none of the revolving loan had been utilized, but all of the term loan had been used.

Instructions

1. Evaluate CanWest's liquidity using appropriate ratios, and compare them to those of Quebecor and to industry averages.
2. Evaluate CanWest's solvency using appropriate ratios, and compare them to those of Quebecor and to industry averages.

Solution

1. CanWest's liquidity can be measured using the current and acid-test ratios:

Ratio	2002	2001	Industry Average
Current	$\frac{\$726.3}{\$690.3} = 1.1{:}1$	$\frac{\$673.4}{\$668.2} = 1.0{:}1$	2.2:1

Acid-test $\dfrac{\$61.1 + \$470.2}{\$690.3} = 0.8{:}1$ $\dfrac{\$19.5 + \$475.6}{\$668.2} = 0.7{:}1$ 1.8:1

CanWest Global's current and acid-test ratios are better than Quebecor's (recall that Quebecor's current ratios were 0.8:1 and 0.9:1 and its acid-test ratios 0.5:1 and 0.5:1, in 2002 and 2001 respectively). CanWest's liquidity has improved marginally from fiscal 2001 to 2002. However, both companies' liquidity is lower than the industry average.

CanWest's current ratio is still greater than 1:1, which means that it has enough current assets to pay its current liabilities. Taken in conjunction with its available line of credit, CanWest's liquidity is adequate.

2. CanWest's solvency can be measured with the debt to total assets and times interest earned ratios:

Ratio	2002	2001	Industry Average
Debt to total assets	$\dfrac{\$4,545.2}{\$5,721.1} = 79.4\%$	$\dfrac{\$4,993.2}{\$6,299.2} = 79.3\%$	35.9%
Times interest earned	$\dfrac{\$13.0 + \$376.6 + \$7.1}{\$376.6} = 1.1 \text{ times}$	$\dfrac{\$46.6 + \$356.8 - \$59.0}{\$356.8} = 1.0 \text{ times}$	2.5 times

CanWest Global's debt to total assets ratio is relatively unchanged from 2001 to 2002. In addition, it is better than Quebecor's (recall that Quebecor's debt to total assets was 91.4% and 86.8% in 2002 and 2001, respectively).

It is interesting to note, however, that although CanWest Global's debt to total assets is better than Quebecor's, Quebecor is better able to handle its debt—at least in 2002. Quebecor's times interest earned ratio improved from 0.7 times to 1.4 times between 2001 and 2002. CanWest Global's times interest earned ratio improved only marginally from 1.0 times to 1.1 times between 2001 and 2002.

One might have expected to see more of an improvement in CanWest's solvency. In September 2001, the company suspended the payment of dividends in favour of debt reduction. However, it also made several large acquisitions in 2002, including a purchase of the remaining 50% interest in *The National Post*. Both companies' solvency is significantly lower than the industry average.

Summary of Study Objectives

① *Distinguish between current and long-term liabilities.* A current liability is a debt that will be paid (1) from existing current assets or through the creation of other current liabilities, and (2) within one year. Liabilities that do not meet both criteria are long-term.

② *Explain the accounting for current liabilities.* Operating lines of credit, if drawn, are reported as bank indebtedness and disclosed in the notes to the financial statements. Sales taxes payable (GST, PST, HST) are recorded at the time the sale occurs. Sales taxes, payroll deductions, and employee benefits are current liabilities until remitted to the appropriate third party. The company serves as a collection agent for other parties for these liabilities. Property taxes and interest on notes payable must be accrued until paid. The portion of long-term debt due within the next

year must be deducted from the long-term liability and reported as a current liability.

③ *Prepare the entries for the issue of bonds.* When bonds are issued, Cash is debited for the cash proceeds and Bonds Payable is credited for the face value of the bonds. In addition, the accounts Discount on Bonds Payable and Premium on Bonds Payable are used to show the bond discount and bond premium, respectively, if the bonds are issued for less or more than their face value. Bond discounts and bond premiums are amortized to interest expense over the life of the bond.

④ *Prepare the entries for the retirement of bonds.* When bonds are redeemed at maturity, Cash is credited, Bonds Payable is debited for the face value of the bonds, and any unamortized discount or premium account is credited or debited, respectively. When bonds are redeemed before maturity, it is necessary to (a) eliminate the carrying value of the bonds at the redemption date, (b) record the cash paid, and (c) recognize any gain or loss on redemption.

⑤ Explain the accounting for long-term notes payable. Long-term notes payable are repayable in a series of payments. Each payment consists of (1) interest on the unpaid balance of the note, and (2) a reduction of the principal balance. These payments can be either (1) fixed principal payments or (2) blended principal and interest payments.

⑥ Identify the requirements for the financial statement presentation and analysis of liabilities. Current liabilities are reported first, followed by long-term liabilities. The nature and amount of each liability should be reported in the balance sheet or in the notes accompanying the financial statements. Inflows and outflows of cash related to the principal portion of long-term debt are reported in the financing activities section of the cash flow statement. The liquidity of a company may be analysed by calculating the current and acid-test ratios. The solvency of a company may be analysed by calculating the debt to total assets and times interest earned ratios. Other factors to consider are contingent liabilities and lease obligations.

⑦ Apply the straight-line method of amortizing bond discounts and premiums (Appendix 10A). Amortization is calculated under the straight-line method by dividing the bond discount or premium by the number of interest periods. Interest expense is calculated by multiplying the face value of the bonds by the contractual interest rate. The straight-line method of amortization results in a constant amount of amortization and interest expense each period, but a varying percentage rate.

⑧ Apply the effective-interest method of amortizing bond discounts and premiums (Appendix 10B). Amortization is calculated under the effective-interest method as the difference between the interest paid and the interest expense. Interest paid is calculated by multiplying the face value of the bonds by the contractual interest rate. Interest expense is calculated by multiplying the carrying value of the bonds at the beginning of the interest period by the effective interest rate. The effective-interest method of amortization results in varying amounts of amortization and interest expense each period, but a constant percentage rate of interest.

Decision
Toolkit
Summary

Decision Toolkit—A Summary

DECISION CHECKPOINTS	INFO NEEDED FOR DECISION	TOOL TO USE FOR DECISION	HOW TO EVALUATE RESULTS
Can the company meet its current obligations?	Cash, accounts receivable, short-term investments and other highly liquid assets, and current liabilities	$$\text{Acid-test ratio} = \frac{(\text{Cash} + \text{Short-term investments} + \text{Accounts receivable})}{\text{Current liabilities}}$$	Ratio should be compared to others in the same industry. High ratio indicates good liquidity.
Can the company obtain short-term financing when necessary?	Available lines of credit from notes to the financial statements	Compare available lines of credit to current liabilities. Also, evaluate liquidity ratios.	If liquidity ratios are low, then lines of credit should be high to compensate.
Can the company meet its obligations in the long term?	EBIT and interest expense	$$\text{Times interest earned} = \frac{\text{EBIT}}{\text{Interest expense}}$$	High ratio indicates sufficient earnings available to cover annual interest payments.
Does the company have any contingent liabilities?	Knowledge of events with uncertain negative outcomes	Financial statements and notes to financial statements	If negative outcomes are possible, determine the probability, the amount of loss, and the potential impact on financial statements.
Does the company have significant off–balance sheet financing, such as unrecorded lease obligations?	Information on unrecorded obligations, such as minimum lease payments from lease note	Compare liquidity and solvency ratios with and without unrecorded obligations included.	If ratios differ significantly after including unrecorded obligations, these obligations should not be ignored in analysis.

NAVIGATOR

Glossary

Acid-test ratio A measure of a company's immediate short-term liquidity, calculated by dividing the sum of cash, short-term investments, and accounts receivable by current liabilities. (p. 474)

Bond A form of interest-bearing note payable issued by corporations, universities, and government entities. (p. 461)

Bond certificate A legal document that indicates the name of the issuer, the face value of the bonds, and such other data as the contractual interest rate and the maturity date of the bonds. (p. 462)

Capital lease A type of lease whose characteristics make it similar to a debt-financed purchase, which is consequently accounted for as an asset and a liability. (p. 477)

Collateral Assets pledged as a security for the payments of a debt (e.g., land, buildings, and equipment in the case of mortgage bonds or notes; accounts receivable or inventory in the case of a bank loan). (p. 455)

Contingencies Events with uncertain outcomes, such as a potential liability that may become an actual liability sometime in the future. (p. 477)

Contractual interest rate Rate used to determine the amount of interest the borrower pays and the investor receives. (p. 462)

Convertible bonds Bonds that permit bondholders to convert them into common shares at their option. (p. 462)

Current liability A debt that will be paid (1) from existing current assets or through the creation of other current liabilities, and (2) within one year. (p. 454)

Debenture bonds Bonds issued against the general credit of the borrower; also called unsecured bonds. (p. 462)

Discount (on a bond) The difference between the face value of a bond and its selling price when a bond is sold for less than its face value. (p. 464)

EBIT Earnings before interest expense and income tax expense. (p. 475)

Effective-interest method of amortization A method of amortizing a bond discount or premium that results in periodic interest expense equal to a constant percentage of the carrying value of the bond. (p. 481)

Effective interest rate A market rate established when bonds are issued that remains constant in each interest period. (p. 481)

Face value Amount of principal due at the maturity date of the bond. (p. 462)

Long-term liability An obligation expected to be paid more than one year in the future. (p. 461)

Market interest rate The rate investors demand for loaning funds to a corporation. (p. 463)

Maturity date The date on which the final payment on a bond is due from the bond issuer to the investor. (p. 462)

Mortgage note payable A long-term note secured by a mortgage that pledges title to property as security for the loan. (p. 469)

Notes payable Obligations in the form of written notes. (p. 455)

Off–balance sheet financing The intentional effort by a company to structure its financing arrangements so as to avoid showing liabilities on its books. (p. 477)

Operating lease A contractual arrangement giving the lessee temporary use of the property with continued ownership of the property by the lessor, and accounted for as a rental. (p. 477)

Operating line of credit A pre-arranged agreement to borrow money at a bank, up to an agreed-upon amount. (p. 455)

Premium (on a bond) The difference between the selling price and the face value of a bond when a bond is sold for more than its face value. (p. 465)

Present value The value today of an amount to be received at some date in the future after taking into account current interest rates. (p. 463)

Redeemable (callable) bonds Bonds that are subject to retirement at a stated dollar amount prior to maturity at the option of the issuer. (p. 462)

Retractable bonds Bonds that are subject to retirement at a stated dollar amount prior to maturity at the option of the bondholder. (p. 462)

Secured bonds Bonds that have specific assets of the issuer pledged as collateral. (p. 462)

Straight-line method of amortization A method of amortizing a bond discount or bond premium that allocates the same amount to interest expense in each interest period. (p. 479)

Times interest earned A measure of a company's solvency, calculated by dividing earnings before interest expense and income tax expense (EBIT) by interest expense. (p. 475)

Unsecured bonds Bonds issued against the general credit of the borrower; also called debenture bonds. (p. 462)

Demonstration Problem

On January 1, 2004, Feng Software Inc. issued $500,000 of 7%, 10-year bonds at 93. Interest is payable semi-annually on January 1 and July 1. Feng's year end is June 30. Five years later, on January 1, 2009, Feng redeemed all of these bonds at 90. The carrying value of the bonds at that time was $482,500.

Instructions

(a) Prepare the journal entry to record the issue of the bonds on January 1, 2004.
(b) Prepare the journal entry to accrue the first interest payment on June 30. Assume that the amortization amount for the first interest period is $1,750.
(c) Show the presentation of the liability on Feng's balance sheet on June 30, 2004.
(d) Prepare the journal entry to record the redemption of the bonds on January 1, 2009.

Additional
Demonstration
Problems

Solution to Demonstration Problem

Action Plan
- Compare the face value of the bonds to the proceeds to determine if the bonds are issued at a discount or premium. A discount occurs when the proceeds are less than the face value.
- To calculate the proceeds, multiply the face value by the issue price, expressed as a percentage (e.g., 93%).
- Record and report the discount on bonds as a contra liability account.
- Record the amortization of the bond discount as an increase in interest expense.
- Compare the redemption price of the bonds to their carrying value to determine if a gain or a loss resulted.

(a)

Jan. 1, 2004	Cash ($500,000 × 93%)	465,000	
	Discount on Bonds Payable	35,000	
	Bonds Payable		500,000
	(To record issue of 7%, 10-year bonds)		

(b)

June 30, 2004	Bond Interest Expense ($1,750 + $17,500)	19,250	
	Discount on Bonds Payable		1,750
	Bond Interest Payable ($500,000 × 7% × 6/12)		17,500
	(To record accrual of semi-annual interest)		

(c)

FENG SOFTWARE INC.
Balance Sheet (Partial)
June 30, 2004

Long-term liabilities	
Bonds payable	$500,000
Less: Discount on bonds payable ($35,000 − $1,750)	33,250
	$466,750

(d)

Jan. 1, 2009	Bonds Payable	500,000	
	Discount on Bonds Payable ($500,000 − $482,500)		17,500
	Cash ($500,000 × 90%)		450,000
	Gain on Bond Redemption ($482,500 − $450,000)		32,500
	(To record redemption of bonds)		

Note: All of the questions, exercises, and problems with an asterisk relate to material in the chapter appendices.

Self-Study Questions

Multiple
Choice
Quiz

Answers are at the end of the chapter.

(SO 1) 1. To be classified as a current liability, a debt must be expected to be paid:
(a) out of existing current assets.
(b) by creating other current liabilities.
(c) within two years.
(d) Either (a) or (b)

(SO 2) 2. Reeves Ltd. has total proceeds of $4,515 from sales. If the proceeds include HST of 15%, what is the amount to be credited to Sales?
(a) $589   (c) $3,926
(b) $677   (d) $4,515

(SO 2) 3. On January 1, 2004, Swift Current Ltd. estimates that its property taxes for the current year will be $12,000. On March 1, Swift Current received its property tax assessment for 2004 of $14,000. The property tax bill is due May 1. If Swift Current prepares quarterly financial statements, how much property tax expense should the company report for the quarter ended March 31, 2004?
(a) $3,000   (c) $3,500
(b) $3,200   (d) $14,000

(SO 3) 4. If bonds are issued at a premium, this indicates that:
(a) the contractual interest rate exceeds the market interest rate.
(b) the market interest rate exceeds the contractual interest rate.
(c) the contractual interest rate and the market interest rate are the same.
(d) no relationship exists between the two rates.

(SO 3) 5. On January 1, 2004, Scissors Corp. issues $200,000 of five-year, 7% bonds at 97. The entry to record the issue of the bonds would include a:
(a) debit to Cash for $200,000.
(b) debit to Bonds Payable for $200,000.
(c) debit to Discount on Bonds Payable for $6,000.
(d) credit to Premium on Bonds Payable for $6,000.

(SO 4) 6. Gester Corporation retires its $100,000 of face value bonds at 105 on January 1, following the payment of semi-annual interest. The carrying value of the bonds at the redemption date is $103,745. The entry to record the redemption will include a:
(a) debit of $1,255 to Loss on Bond Redemption.
(b) credit of $1,255 to Gain on Bond Redemption.
(c) credit of $3,745 to Premium on Bonds Payable.
(d) debit of $105,000 to Cash.

(SO 5) 7. Zhang Inc. issues a $497,000, 10%, three-year instalment note payable on January 1. The note will be paid in three annual blended instalments of $200,000, each payable at the end of the year. What is the amount of interest expense that should be recognized by Zhang in the second year?
(a) $16,567   (c) $49,700
(b) $34,670   (d) $347,600

(SO 6) 8. Which of the following would not be included in the numerator of the acid-test ratio?
(a) Accounts receivable
(b) Cash
(c) Short-term investments
(d) Inventory

(SO 6) 9. In a recent year, Kennedy Corporation had net earnings of $150,000, interest expense of $30,000, and income tax expense of $20,000. What was Kennedy Corporation's times interest earned ratio for the year?
(a) 5.0 times   (c) 6.0 times
(b) 5.7 times   (d) 6.7 times

(SO 6) 10. Which of the following items is not an example of off–balance sheet financing?
(a) Contingent liabilities
(b) Operating line of credit
(c) Operating leases
(d) Loan guarantee

(SO 7) *11. On January 1, Hurley Corporation issues $500,000 of five-year, 6% bonds at 96 with interest payable on July 1 and January 1. The entry on July 1 to record the payment of bond interest and the amortization of a bond discount using the straight-line method will include a:
(a) debit to Interest Expense, $13,000.
(b) debit to Interest Expense, $15,000.
(c) debit to Discount on Bonds Payable, $2,000.
(d) credit to Discount on Bonds Payable, $2,000.

(SO 8) *12. On January 1, Daigle Corporation issued $2,000,000 of five-year, 7% bonds with interest payable on January 1 and July 1. The bonds sold for $1,918,880, at a market (effective) interest rate of 8%. Assuming the effective interest-method is used, the debit entry to Bond Interest Expense (rounded to the nearest dollar) on July 1 is for:
(a) $67,161.   (c) $76,755.
(b) $70,000.   (d) $80,000.

NAVIGATOR

Questions

(SO 1) 1. Li Feng believes a current liability is a debt that can be expected to be paid in one year. Is Li correct? Explain.

(SO 2) 2. What is the difference between accounts payable and notes payable? Notes payable and an operating line of credit?

(SO 2) 3. The Fraiser Corporation obtains $25,000 in cash by signing a 9%, six-month, $25,000 note payable to First Bank on July 1. Fraiser's fiscal year ends on September 30. What information should be reported for the note payable in the financial statements?

(SO 2) 4. Your roommate says, "Sales taxes and employee payroll deductions are reported as expenses in the statement of earnings." Do you agree? Explain.

(SO 2) 5. Explain how recording property taxes can result in both a liability (property tax payable) and an asset (prepaid property tax) in the same period.

(SO 2) 6. Where in the financial statements does the employer report payroll deductions withheld from employees' pay that are paid by the employees? By the employer?

(SO 3) 7. Describe the two major obligations incurred by a company when bonds are issued.

(SO 3) 8. Assume that Stoney Inc. sold bonds with a face value of $100,000 for $104,000. Was the market interest rate equal to, less than, or greater than the bonds' contractual interest rate? Explain.

(SO 3) 9. La Mi and Jack Dalton are discussing how the market price of a bond is determined. La believes that the market price of a bond is solely a function of the amount of the principal payment at the end of the term of a bond. Is she right? Discuss.

(SO 3) 10. If the Bonds Payable account has a balance of $900,000 and the Discount on Bonds Payable account has a balance of $40,000, what is the carrying value of the bonds? How would your answer change if there was a $40,000 Premium in Bonds Payable, rather than a discount?

(SO 4) 11. Which accounts are debited and which are credited if a bond issue originally sold at a premium is redeemed before maturity at 97?

(SO 5) 12. Distinguish between instalment notes payable with fixed principal payments and those with blended principal and interest payments.

(SO 5) 13. Doug Bareak, a friend of yours, has recently purchased a building for $125,000. He paid $25,000 down and financed the remainder with a 10.5%, 20-year mortgage, payable in blended payments of principal and interest at $998 per month. At the end of the first month, Doug received a statement

from the bank indicating that only $123 of principal was paid during the month. At this rate, he calculated that it would take over 67 years to pay off the mortgage. Explain why this is not the case.

14. 🔧   (SO 6)
(a) In general, what are the requirements for the financial statement presentation of current liabilities?
(b) In general, what are the requirements for the financial statement presentation of long-term liabilities?
(c) What ratios may be calculated to evaluate a company's liquidity and solvency?

15. 🔧 Lincoln Corporation has a current ratio of   (SO 6)
1:1. Joe Investor has always been told that a corporation's current ratio should exceed 1:1. Lincoln argues that its ratio is low because it has a minimal amount of inventory on hand so as to reduce operating costs. Is Joe still correct? What other measures might he check?

16. 🔧 What is off–balance sheet financing? Provide two examples of off–balance sheet financing.   (SO 6)

17. 🔧 What is the primary difference between an operating lease and a capital lease? What is the difference in how they are recorded?   (SO 6)

18. 🔧 What criteria must be met before a contingency has to be recorded as a liability? How should the contingency be disclosed if the criteria are not met?   (SO 6)

19. 🔧 Six years ago, Air Canada owned half of its air fleet and leased the remainder. Today, it owns only 4% of its aircraft and leases the remainder. What are the implications of this change in ownership when performing a trend analysis of Air Canada's solvency?   (SO 6)

*20. Distinguish between the effective-interest and straight-line methods of amortizing discounts and premiums on bonds payable.   (SO 7, 8)

*21. Brent Corporation issues $200,000 of 8%, five-year bonds on January 1, 2004, at 104. Assuming that the straight-line method is used to amortize the premium, what is the total amount of interest expense for 2004? Interest paid?   (SO 7)

*22. Summit Corporation issues $400,000 of 9%, five-year bonds on January 1, 2004, at 104. If Summit uses the effective-interest method in amortizing the premium, will the annual interest expense increase or decrease over the life of the bonds? Explain.   (SO 8)

Brief Exercises

Identify current liabilities.
(SO 1)

BE10-1 Identify which of the following transactions would be classified as a current liability. For those that are not current liabilities, identify where they should be classified.

1. A demand loan
2. Cash received in advance by WestJet Airlines for airline tickets
3. PST collected on sales
4. GST collected on sales
5. Current portion of long-term debt
6. Interest owing on an overdue account payable
7. Interest due on an overdue account receivable
8. A nuisance lawsuit pending against the company
9. Amounts withheld from the employees' weekly pay
10. Property tax payable

Prepare entries for note payable.
(SO 2)

BE10-2 Romez Limited borrows $60,000 on July 1 from the bank by signing a $60,000, 5%, one-year note payable. Prepare the journal entries to record (a) the issue of the note and (b) accrued interest at December 31, assuming adjusting entries are made only at the end of the year.

Prepare entries for sales taxes.
(SO 2)

BE10-3 Grandy Auto Supply Inc. does not segregate sales and sales taxes at the time of sale. The register total for March 16 is $9,975. All sales are subject to GST of 7% and PST of 7%. PST is not charged on GST. Prepare the entry to record sales and sales taxes payable.

Determine amounts reported for property tax.
(SO 2)

BE10-4 Pierce Corp. has a June 30 fiscal year end. It estimated its annual property taxes to be $24,000, based on last year's property tax bill, and accrued $2,000 of property tax each month to March 31. Its actual property tax assessment, received on April 30, is $25,200 for the calendar year. The property tax bill is payable on July 15. How much property tax expense will Pierce report on its June 30 statement of earnings? How much property tax payable and/or prepaid property tax will Pierce report at June 30 on its balance sheet?

Compare bond financing to share financing.
(SO 3)

BE10-5 Olga Inc. is considering these two alternatives to finance its construction of a new $2-million plant:

(a) Issue 200,000 common shares at the market price of $10 per share. 700,000 shares are currently issued.
(b) Issue $2 million of 8% bonds at face value.

Complete the table and indicate which alternative is preferable.

	Issue Shares	Issue Bonds
Earnings before interest and taxes	$1,000,000	$1,000,000
Interest expense from bonds	0	
Earnings before income taxes	1,000,000	
Income tax expense (30%)	300,000	
Net earnings	$ 700,000	$
Number of shares		700,000
Earnings per share	$	$

Prepare entries for issue of bonds. Show balance sheet presentation.
(SO 3)

BE10-6 Keystone Corporation issued one thousand 9%, five-year, $1,000 bonds dated March 1, 2004.

(a) Prepare the journal entry to record the sale of these bonds assuming that the bonds were issued at 100.
(b) Prepare the journal entry to record the sale of these bonds assuming that the bonds were issued at 98, rather than 100.
(c) Prepare the journal entry to record the sale of these bonds assuming that the bonds were issued at 102, rather than 100.
(d) Show the balance sheet presentation of the bonds under each of the above three assumptions.
(e) What will the carrying value be at maturity, March 1, 2009, under each of the above three assumptions ((a) – (c))?

BE10-7 The balance sheet for Hathaway Ltd. reports the following information:

Prepare entry for redemption of bonds.
(SO 4)

HATHAWAY LTD.
Balance Sheet (partial)
November 30, 2004

Long-term liabilities
  Bonds payable $1,000,000
  Less: Discount on bonds payable   60,000 $940,000

Hathaway decides to redeem these bonds at 98 after paying semi-annual interest. Prepare the journal entry to record the redemption on November 30, 2004.

BE10-8 You qualify for a $10,000 loan from the Canada Student Loans Program to help finance your education. Once you graduate, you start repaying this note payable at an interest rate of 7% and with a monthly cash payment of $116.11, principal and interest, for 120 payments (10 years). Prepare an instalment payment schedule for the first three payments.

Prepare instalment payment schedule for note payable.
(SO 5)

BE10-9 Eyre Inc. issues a $300,000, 8%, 10-year mortgage note payable on November 30, 2004, to obtain financing for a new building. The terms provide for monthly payments. Prepare the entries to record the mortgage loan on November 30, 2004, and the first two payments on December 31, 2004, and January 31, 2005, assuming:

Prepare entries for mortgage note payable.
(SO 5)

(a) the payment is a fixed principal payment of $2,500.
(b) the payment is a blended principal and interest payment of $3,639.83.

BE10-10 Presented here are liability items for Warner Ltd. at December 31, 2004. Prepare the liabilities section of Warner's balance sheet.

Prepare liabilities section of balance sheet.
(SO 6)

Accounts payable	$135,000	Employee benefits payable	$ 7,800
Bank indebtedness	20,000	Interest payable	40,000
Bonds payable, due 2008	900,000	Notes payable, due 2006	80,000
Current portion of		Property tax payable	3,500
long-term debt	240,000	Sales taxes payable	1,400
Discount on bonds payable	45,000		

BE10-11 Molson Canada's 2002 financial statements contain the following selected data (in millions):

Analyse liquidity and solvency.
(SO 6)

Accounts receivable	$ 90.3	Other current assets	$ 257.6
Cash and short-term investments	4.9	Prepaid expenses	42.3
Income tax expense	0.5	Total assets	2,178.9
Interest expense	52.1	Total current liabilities	458.2
Inventories	121.2	Total liabilities	1,261.3
Net earnings	246.7		

Calculate these values:
(a) Working capital   (d) Debt to total assets
(b) Current ratio   (e) Times interest earned
(c) Acid-test ratio

BE10-12 The Canadian National Railway Company's (CN) total assets in 2002 were $18,924 million and its total liabilities were $12,297 million. That year, CN reported operating lease commitments for its locomotives, freight cars, and equipment totalling $1,154 million. If these assets had been recorded as capital leases, assume that assets and liabilities would have risen by approximately $1,154 million.

Analyse liquidity and solvency.
(SO 6)

(a) Calculate CN's debt to total assets ratio, first using the figures reported, and then after increasing assets and liabilities for the unrecorded operating leases.
(b) Discuss the potential effect of these operating leases on your assessment of CN's solvency.

*BE10-13** On January 1, 2004, Dominic Ltd. issues $2 million of 10-year, 9% bonds at 96, with interest payable on July 1 and January 1. The straight-line method is used to amortize the bond discount.

Prepare entries for bonds, using straight-line amortization.
(SO 3, 7)

(a) Prepare the journal entry to record the sale of these bonds on January 1, 2004.
(b) Prepare the journal entry to record interest expense and bond discount amortization on July 1, 2004.

Prepare entries for bonds, using straight-line amortization.
(SO 3, 7)

*BE10-14   Abela Inc. issues $5 million of five-year, 8% bonds at 103 on January 1, 2004, with interest payable on July 1 and January 1. The straight-line method is used to amortize the bond premium.

(a) Prepare the journal entry to record the sale of these bonds on January 1, 2004.
(b) Prepare the journal entry to record interest expense and bond premium amortization on July 1, 2004.

Prepare entries for bonds, using effective-interest amortization.
(SO 3, 8)

*BE10-15   Presented below is the partial bond amortization schedule for Chiasson Corporation, which uses the effective-interest method of amortization:

Semi-Annual Interest Periods	Interest Payment	Interest Expense	Discount/ Premium Amortization	Unamortized Discount/ Premium	Bond Carrying Value
Issue date				$62,311	$937,689
1	$45,000	$46,884	$1,884	60,427	939,573
2	45,000	46,979	1,979	58,448	941,552

(a) Prepare a journal entry to record the sale of the bond at the issue date.
(b) Prepare the journal entry to record the payment of interest and the amortization at the end of period 1.
(c) Explain why interest expense is greater than interest paid.
(d) Explain why interest expense will increase each period.
(e) What will be the carrying value of the bond on its maturity date?

Exercises

Prepare entries for note payable.
(SO 2)

E10-1   On June 1, Microchip Ltd. borrows $50,000 from First Bank on a six-month, $50,000, 8% note. Interest is payable at maturity.

Instructions

(a) Prepare the entry on June 1.
(b) Prepare the adjusting entry on June 30.
(c) Prepare the entry at maturity (December 1), assuming monthly adjusting entries have been made through November 30.
(d) What was the total financing cost (interest expense)?

Prepare entries for note receivable and note payable.
(SO 2)

Interactive Homework

E10-2   Valerio Construction Ltd. borrows $250,000 from the TD Bank on October 1, 2004. It signs a two-year, 5% note payable. Interest is payable monthly.

Instructions

(a) Prepare the journal entries to record the transactions on October 1, 2004, and the first interest payment on November 1 for Valerio Construction.
(b) Prepare the journal entries to record the transactions on October 1, 2004, and the first interest receipt on November 1 for the TD Bank. (*Hint*: You might find it helpful to review accounting for notes receivable in Chapter 8.)

Prepare entries for sales taxes.
(SO 2)

E10-3   In providing accounting services to small businesses, you encounter the following situations pertaining to cash sales. Assume in both situations that PST is *not* charged on GST.

1. Jintao Ltd. rings up sales and sales taxes separately on its cash register. On April 10, the register totals are sales, $25,000; GST, $1,750; and PST, $2,000.
2. Gan Ltd. does not separate sales and sales taxes. Its register total for April 15 is $11,700, which includes 7% GST and 10% PST.

Instructions

Prepare the entries to record the sales transactions and related taxes for (a) Jintao Ltd. and (b) Gan Ltd.

Prepare entries for property tax.
(SO 2)

Interactive Homework

E10-4   Seaboard Corp. receives its property tax bill for the calendar year for $26,400 on May 1, payable July 1. Prior to receiving this bill, it had estimated that its property taxes would be $24,000. Seaboard accrues property taxes monthly and has a September 30 year end.

Instructions

(a) Prepare the journal entry necessary to record the accrual of the property tax expense for each of the months from October through April.

(b) Prepare the journal entry to record the property tax expense for the months of May and June.

(c) Prepare the journal entry to record the payment of the property tax bill on July 1.

(d) Prepare the journal entry to record the property tax expense for the months of July, August and September.

E10-5 The following are independent situations recently reported in *The Globe and Mail*:

1. Bank of Montreal 7% bonds, maturing January 28, 2010, were issued at 111.12.
2. Bell Canada 7% bonds, maturing September 24, 2027, were issued at 99.08.

Prepare entries for issue of bonds.
(SO 3)

Instructions

(a) Were the Bank of Montreal and Bell Canada bonds issued at a premium or a discount?

(b) Explain how bonds, both paying the same contractual interest rate, could be issued at different prices.

(c) Prepare the journal entry to record the issue of each of these two bonds, assuming $500,000 of bonds were issued in total.

E10-6 On September 1, 2004, Mooney Corporation issued $400,000 of 9%, 10-year bonds at face value. Interest is payable semi-annually on September 1 and February 1. Mooney's year end is December 31.

Prepare entries for bonds.
(SO 3)

Interactive
Homework

Instructions

Prepare journal entries to record the following:

(a) The issue of the bonds on September 1, 2004

(b) The accrual of interest on December 31, 2004

(c) The payment of interest on February 1, 2005

E10-7 Ernst Corporation redeemed $120,000 of 7% bonds on June 30, 2004. The carrying value of the bonds at the redemption date was $107,500.

Prepare entries for redemption of bonds.
(SO 4)

Instructions

(a) Prepare the journal entry to record the redemption of the bonds assuming Ernst paid 102 to repurchase them.

(b) Prepare the journal entry to record the redemption of the bonds assuming Ernst paid 98 to repurchase them.

E10-8 Ste. Anne Corp. issues a $150,000, 8%, 20-year mortgage note payable to finance the construction of a building at December 31, 2004. The terms provide for semi-annual instalment payments on June 30 and December 31.

Prepare entries for mortgage note payable.
(SO 5)

Interactive
Homework

Instructions

Prepare the journal entries to record the mortgage note payable and the first two instalment payments assuming:

(a) the payment is a fixed principal payment of $3,750.

(b) the payment is a blended principal and interest payment of $7,578.52.

E10-9 Bombardier Inc. reports the following liabilities (in millions) on its January 31, 2003, balance sheet and notes to the financial statements:

Prepare liabilities section of balance sheet.
(SO 1,6)

Accounts payable	$3,263.9	Notes payable—long-term	$5,746.7
Accrued benefit liability	1,215.2	Operating leases	1,641.7
Accrued liabilities	1,258.1	Other liabilities	1,498.7
Bonds payable	1,961.2	Other loans payable	335.6
Current portion of		Payroll-related liabilities	558.1
long-term debt	1,992.2	Short-term borrowings	2,563.6
Deferred income taxes	206.4	Unused operating line of credit	3,337.6
Income taxes payable	28.8	Warranty provision	1,417.3

Instructions

(a) Identify which of the above liabilities are likely current and which are likely long-term. Say if an item fits in neither category. Explain the reasoning for your selection.

(b) Prepare the liabilities section of Bombardier's balance sheet as at January 31, 2003.

Calculate current and acid-test ratios before and after paying accounts payable.
(SO 6)

E10-10 The following financial data were reported by the Calgary Exhibition & Stampede:

CALGARY EXHIBITION AND STAMPEDE LIMITED
Balance Sheet (partial)
December 31, 2002
(in thousands)

	2002	2001
Current assets		
Cash and short-term deposits	$ 1,834	$ 2,247
Accounts receivable	4,616	7,545
Contributions receivable	448	612
Inventories	1,401	1,393
Prepaid expenses	735	839
Total current assets	$ 9,034	$12,636
Current liabilities	$15,944	$18,162

Instructions

(a) Calculate the current and acid-test ratios for the Calgary Stampede for 2002 and 2001.

(b) Suppose that at the end of 2002 the Stampede used $1 million cash to pay off $1 million of accounts payable. How would its current ratio and acid-test ratio change?

(c) At December 31, 2002, the Stampede has an undrawn operating line of credit of $12.5 million. Would this affect any assessment that you might make of the Stampede's short-term liquidity? Explain.

Analyse liquidity and solvency.
(SO 6)

E10-11 Maple Leaf Foods Inc.'s financial statements for 2002 contain the following selected data (in thousands):

Cash	$ 156,866	Current liabilities	$ 597,003
Accounts receivable	243,121	Total liabilities	1,457,346
Inventories	266,889	Net earnings	84,686
Prepaid expenses and		Income tax expense	54,947
other assets	14,806	Interest expense	56,289
Total assets	2,189,247		

Instuctions

(a) Calculate the following values:

1. Working capital
2. Current ratio
3. Acid-test ratio
4. Debt to total assets
5. Times interest earned

(b) The notes to Maple Leaf Foods' financial statements show that the company has future operating lease commitments totalling $250,229 thousand. Discuss the implications these unrecorded obligations have for the analysis of Maple Leaf Foods' liquidity and solvency.

Discuss contingent liabilities.
(SO 6)

E10-12 Wal-Mart was sued 4,851 times last year—about once every two hours every day of the year. Wal-Mart has been sued for everything imaginable—ranging from falls on icy parking lots to injuries sustained in shoppers' stampedes to a murder with a rifle purchased at Wal-Mart.

Wal-Mart does not adhere to the legal strategy many businesses use of "Settle quickly and cut your losses." Instead, Wal-Mart aggressively fights lawsuits, even when it would be cheaper to settle. The company reports the following in the notes to its financial statements:

> The Company and its subsidiaries are involved from time to time in claims, proceedings, and litigation arising from the operation of its business. The Company does not believe that any such claim, proceeding, or litigation, either alone or in the aggregate, will have a material adverse effect on the Company's financial position or results of its operations.

Instructions

(a) Explain why Wal-Mart does not have to record these contingent liabilities.

(b) Comment on any implications for analysis of the financial statements.

Prepare entries for bonds, using straight-line method of amortization.
(SO 3, 4, 7)

*E10-13 Pueblo Limited issued $300,000 of 9%, 20-year bonds on January 1, 2004, at 103. Interest is payable semi-annually on July 1 and January 1. Pueblo uses straight-line amortization for bond premiums or discounts and has a December 31 year end.

Instructions

Prepare the journal entries to record these events:
(a) The issue of the bonds
(b) The payment of interest and the amortization on July 1, 2004
(c) The accrual of interest and the amortization on December 31, 2004
(d) The redemption of the bonds at maturity on January 1, 2024, assuming interest for the last interest period has been paid and recorded

*E10-14   Cotter Ltd. issued $180,000 of 6%, 10-year bonds on December 31, 2004, for $172,000. Interest is payable semi-annually on June 30 and December 31. Cotter uses the straight-line method to amortize bond premiums or discounts and has a December 31 year end.

Prepare entries for bonds, using straight-line method of amortization.
(SO 3, 4, 7)

Instructions

Prepare the journal entries to record these events:
(a) The issue of the bonds
(b) The payment of interest and the amortization on June 30, 2005
(c) The payment of interest and the amortization on December 31, 2005
(d) The redemption of the bonds at maturity, assuming interest for the last interest period has been paid and recorded

*E10-15   Tagawa Corporation issued $600,000 of 10-year, 7% bonds on January 1, 2004, for $559,231. This price resulted in an effective interest rate of 8% on the bonds. Interest is payable semi-annually, on July 1 and January 1. Tagawa uses the effective-interest method to amortize any bond premium or discount and has a December 31 year end.

Prepare entries for bonds, using effective-interest method of amortization.
(SO 8)

Instructions

Prepare the journal entries (rounded to the nearest dollar) to record the following:
(a) The issue of the bonds on January 1, 2004
(b) The payment of interest and the amortization on July 1, 2004
(c) The accrual of interest and the amortization on December 31, 2004

Problems: Set A

P10-1A   The following transactions occurred in Iqaluit Ltd. Iqaluit's fiscal year end is April 30.

Identify liabilities.
(SO 1)

1. Iqaluit purchased goods for $10,000 on April 29, terms n/30, FOB destination. The goods arrived on May 3.
2. The company chief executive officer is to be paid a bonus equal to 6% of net earnings, six months after year end. Net earnings are estimated to be $600,000.
3. Weekly salaries of $10,000 are paid every Friday for a five-day work week (Monday to Friday). This year, April 30 is a Thursday. Payroll deductions include CPP of 4.95% and EI of 2.10% of gross salaries, and income tax withholdings of $3,000.
4. Iqaluit received $25,000 from customers on April 27 for services to be performed in May.
5. Iqaluit was named in a lawsuit alleging negligence for an oil spillage that leaked into the neighbouring company's water system. Iqaluit's legal counsel estimates that the company will likely lose the suit. Restoration costs are anticipated to total $250,000.
6. The company purchased equipment for $25,000 on April 1. It issued an 8%, six-month note in payment. Interest is payable monthly, on the first of each month.
7. Iqaluit paid income tax instalments of $240,000 throughout the year. After the preparation of its year-end corporate income tax return, it was determined that the total income tax payable for the year was $250,000.

Instructions

(a) Identify which of the above transactions should be presented in the current liabilities section, and which should be recorded in the long-term liabilities section of Iqaluit's balance sheet on April 30. Identify the account title(s) and amount(s) for each reported liability.
(b) Indicate any information that should be disclosed in the notes to Iqaluit's financial statements.

Prepare current liability entries and section of balance sheet.
(SO 2, 6)

P10-2A On January 1, 2004, the ledger of Burlington Inc. contained these liability accounts:

Accounts Payable	$52,000	PST Payable	$ 8,570
GST Payable	7,500	Unearned Service Revenue	16,000

During January, the following selected transactions occurred. Burlington uses a perpetual inventory system.

Jan. 5 Sold merchandise for cash totalling $26,632, which includes 7% GST and 8% PST. The cost of goods sold was $15,000.

12 Provided services for customers who had made advance payments of $16,000.

14 Paid Receiver General and Minister of Finance for sales taxes collected in December 2003 ($7,500 GST and PST $8,570, respectively).

20 Sold 500 units of a new product on credit at $150 per unit, plus 7% GST and 8% PST. The cost of this product was $90 per unit.

21 Borrowed $18,000 from HSBC Bank on a three-month, 6%, $18,000 note. Interest is payable monthly, on the 21st of each month.

25 Sold merchandise for cash totalling $31,340, which includes 7% GST and 8% PST. The cost of goods sold was $12,500.

31 Paid monthly payroll of $75,000. Accrued payroll deductions include CPP, $3,713; EI, $1,575; income tax, $15,000; and workers' compensation, $750. Accrued employee benefits under CPP, $3,713 and EI, $2,205.

Instructions

(a) Journalize the January transactions. Round all amounts to the nearest dollar.

(b) Journalize the adjusting entry at January 31 for the interest on the note payable. Use one-third of a month for the period January 21–31.

(c) Prepare the current liabilities section of the balance sheet at January 31, 2004.

Prepare entries for note payable; show balance sheet presentation.
(SO 2, 6)

P10-3A MileHi Mountain Bikes Ltd. markets mountain-bike tours to clients vacationing in various locations in the mountains of British Columbia. In preparation for the upcoming summer biking season, MileHi entered into the following transactions related to notes payable.

Mar. 2 Purchased Mongoose bikes for use as rentals by issuing an $8,000, 9%, three-month note payable. Interest is payable at maturity.

31 Recorded accrued interest for the Mongoose note.

Apr. 1 Issued a $21,000 nine-month note for the purchase of mountain property on which to build bike trails. The note bears 9% interest. Interest is payable monthly.

30 Recorded accrued interest for the Mongoose note.

May 1 Paid interest on the mountain property note.

2 Issued a four-month note to Western Bank for $20,000 at 6%. The funds will be used for working capital for the beginning of the season; interest is payable at maturity.

31 Recorded accrued interest for Mongoose and Western bank notes.

June 1 Paid interest on the mountain property note.

2 Paid principal and interest on the Mongoose note.

30 Recorded accrued interest for the mountain property note and the Western Bank note, on the company's year end.

Instructions

(a) Prepare journal entries for the transactions above.

(b) Show the balance sheet presentation of Notes Payable and Interest Payable at June 30.

(c) How much interest expense relating to notes payable did MileHi incur during the year?

Prepare entries for bonds.
(SO 3, 4)

P10-4A The following section is taken from Disch Corp.'s balance sheet at December 31, 2003.

Current liabilities	
Bond interest payable	$ 72,000
Long-term liabilities	
Bonds payable, 9%, due January 1, 2008	1,600,000

Interest is payable semi-annually on January 1 and July 1.

Instructions

(a) Journalize the payment of the bond interest on January 1, 2004.

(b) Assume that on January 1, 2004, after paying interest, Disch redeems bonds having a face value of $400,000. The redemption price is 104. Record the redemption of the bonds.

(c) Journalize the payment of the bond interest on July 1, 2004, on the remaining bonds.

(d) Prepare the adjusting entry on December 31, 2004, to accrue the interest on the remaining bonds.

P10-5A On May 1, 2003, MEM Corp. issued $800,000 of 9%, five-year bonds at face value. The bonds were dated May 1, 2003, and pay interest annually on May 1. Financial statements are prepared annually on December 31.

Prepare entries for bonds; show balance sheet presentation.
(SO 3, 4, 6)

Instructions

(a) Prepare the journal entry to record the issue of the bonds.

(b) Prepare the adjusting entry to record the accrual of interest on December 31, 2003.

(c) Show the balance sheet presentation on December 31, 2003.

(d) Prepare the journal entry to record the payment of interest on May 1, 2004.

(e) Prepare the adjusting entry to record the accrual of interest on December 31, 2004.

(f) Assume that on January 1, 2005, MEM pays the accrued bond interest and redeems all of the bonds. The redemption price is 101. Record the payment of interest and redemption of the bonds.

P10-6A Myron Corporation is building a new, state-of-the-art production and assembly facility for $15,000,000. To finance the facility, it issued $12,000,000 of 6%, 10-year bonds at face value on September 1, 2004. They pay interest September 1 and March 1. Myron has a December 31 year end.

Prepare entries for bonds and mortgage note payable. Show balance sheet presentation.
(SO 3, 5, 6)

Myron also purchased a new piece of equipment to be used in its new facility. The $750,000 piece of equipment was purchased with a $50,000 down payment and with cash received through the issue of a $700,000, 6%, four-year mortgage note payable issued on October 1, 2004. The terms provide for quarterly blended instalment payments of $49,536 on December 31, March 31, June 30, and September 30.

Instructions

Round all calculations to the nearest dollar.

(a) Prepare all necessary journal entries to record the issue of the bonds and bond interest expense for 2004.

(b) Prepare all necessary journal entries related to the notes payable at December 31, 2004.

(c) Show the balance sheet presentation for these obligations for December 31, 2004. (*Hint*: Be sure to distinguish between the current and long-term portions of the note.)

P10-7A Isabelle Moreau has just approached a venture capitalist for financing for her new business venture, the development of a local ski hill. On April 1, 2004, the lenders loaned the company $100,000 at an annual interest rate of 10%. The loan is repayable over five years in annual instalments of $26,380, principal and interest, due each March 31. The first payment is due March 31, 2005. The ski hill company's year end will be March 31.

Prepare entries for note payable. Show balance sheet presentation.
(SO 5, 6)

Instructions

(a) Prepare all journal entries for the ski hill company for the first two fiscal years ended March 31, 2005, and March 31, 2006.

(b) Show the balance sheet presentation of the note payable as at March 31, 2006. (*Hint*: Don't forget to distinguish between the current and long-term portions of the note).

Analyse liquidity and solvency.
(SO 6)

P10-8A The following selected information was taken from WestJet Airlines Ltd.'s financial statements:

WESTJET AIRLINES LTD.
Balance Sheet
December 31, 2002
(in thousands)

	2002	2001	2000
Current assets			
Cash and cash equivalents	$100,410	$ 58,942	$ 79,025
Accounts receivable	20,532	12,211	6,447
Income taxes recoverable	—	779	—
Prepaid expenses and deposits	19,759	11,643	6,099
Inventory	2,314	2,155	604
Total current assets	143,015	85,730	92,175
Long-term assets	641,190	308,173	244,997
Total assets	$784,205	$393,903	$337,172
Current liabilities	$175,064	$ 95,095	$ 90,780
Long-term liabilities	253,385	76,638	65,300
Total liabilities	428,449	171,733	156,080
Shareholders' equity	355,756	222,170	181,092
Total liabilities and shareholders' equity	$784,205	$393,903	$337,172

Selected information:	2002	2001	2000
Interest expense	$ 3,960	$ 2,249	$ 474
Income tax	31,064	21,079	22,452
Net earnings	51,780	36,710	30,254
Cash provided by operating activities	161,624	67,361	87,413

Instructions

(a) Calculate each of the following ratios for 2002 and 2001. Industry ratios have been included in parentheses where available.
1. Current ratio (0.8:1)
2. Acid-test ratio (0.5:1)
3. Cash current debt coverage (n/a)
4. Debt to total assets (82.9%)
5. Times interest earned (-2.6 times)
6. Cash total debt coverage (n/a)
(b) Comment on WestJet's liquidity and solvency.
(c) WestJet has operating lease commitments totalling $632,466 thousand. Recalculate the debt to total assets and cash total debt coverage ratios in light of this information and discuss the implications for analysis.

Analyse liquidity and solvency.
(SO 6)

P10-9A The following selected liquidity and solvency ratios are available for two companies operating in the fast food industry:

Ratio	Grab 'N Gab	Chick 'N Lick	Industry Average
Acid-test ratio	0.7:1	0.9:1	0.4:1
Current ratio	1.1:1	1.0:1	0.7:1
Receivables turnover	18.9 times	29.9 times	29.4 times
Inventory turnover	66.9 times	50.4 times	49.4 times
Debt to total assets	57.9%	50.4%	66.5%
Times interest earned	7.1 times	8.2 times	6.1 times

Instructions

Assume that you are the credit manager of the local bank. Answer the following questions, citing relevant ratios to justify your answer:

(a) Both Grab 'N Gab and Chick 'N Lick have applied for a short-term loan from your bank. Which of the two companies is the most liquid and merits more consideration for a short-term loan? Explain.
(b) Both Grab 'N Gab and Chick 'N Lick have applied for a long-term loan from your bank. Are you concerned with the solvency of either company? Explain why or why not.

*P10-10A Diego Ltd. issued $1,500,000 of 7%, 10-year bonds on July 1, 2004. The bonds were dated July 1, 2004, and pay interest on July 1 and January 1. Diego Company uses the straight-line method to amortize any bond premium or discount and has a December 31 year end.

Prepare entries for bonds, using straight-line amortization. Show balance sheet presentation.
(SO 3, 6, 7)

Instructions

(a) Prepare all the necessary journal entries to record the issue of the bonds and bond interest expense for 2004, assuming that the bonds sold at 102.

(b) Prepare journal entries as in part (a) assuming that the bonds sold at 94.

(c) Show the balance sheet presentation at December 31, 2004 for each bond issue under the assumptions in (a) and (b).

*P10-11A The following section is taken from Walenda Oil Ltd.'s balance sheet:

Prepare entries for bonds, using straight-line amortization.
(SO 3, 4, 7)

WALENDA OIL LTD.
Balance Sheet (partial)
December 31, 2004

Current liabilities		
Bond interest payable		$ 108,000
Long-term liabilities		
Bonds payable, 6% due January 1, 2015	$3,600,000	
Add: Premium on bonds payable	300,000	3,900,000

Interest is payable semi-annually on January 1 and July 1. Walenda uses straight-line amortization for any bond premium or discount and has a December 31 year end.

Instructions

Round all calculations to the nearest dollar.

(a) Journalize the payment of bond interest on January 1, 2005.

(b) Prepare the entry to record the amortization and to pay the interest due on July 1, 2005.

(c) Assume on July 1, 2005, after paying interest, that Walenda redeems bonds having a face value of $1,800,000. The redemption price is 101. Record the redemption of the bonds.

(d) Prepare the adjusting entry at December 31, 2005, to record the amortization and to accrue interest on the remaining bonds.

*P10-12A On July 1, 2004, Ponasis Corporation issued $1,500,000 of face value, 6%, 10-year bonds at $1,616,917. This price resulted in an effective interest rate of 5% on the bonds. Ponasis uses the effective-interest method to amortize any bond premium or discount. The bonds pay semi-annual interest on July 1 and January 1. Ponasis has a December 31 year end.

Prepare entries for bonds, using effective-interest amortization.
(SO 3, 8)

Instructions

Round all calculations to the nearest dollar.

(a) Prepare the journal entry to record the issue of the bonds on July 1, 2004.

(b) Prepare an amortization table through December 31, 2005 (three interest periods) for this bond issue.

(c) Prepare the journal entry to record the accrual of interest and amortization on December 31, 2004.

(d) Prepare the journal entry to record the payment of interest and amortization on July 1, 2005.

(e) Prepare the journal entry to record the accrual of interest and amortization on December 31, 2005.

*P10-13A On July 1, 2004, Waubonsee Ltd. issued $2,200,000 of face value, 5%, 10-year bonds at $2,036,357. This price resulted in an effective interest rate of 6% on the bonds. Waubonsee uses the effective-interest method to amortize any bond premium or discount. The bonds pay semi-annual interest on July 1 and January 1. Waubonsee has a December 31 year end.

Prepare entries for bonds, using effective-interest amortization. Show balance sheet presentation and answer questions.
(SO 3, 6, 8)

Instructions

(a) Prepare the journal entries to record the following transactions:
1. The issue of the bonds on July 1, 2004
2. The accrual of interest and amortization on December 31, 2004
3. The payment of interest and amortization on July 1, 2005
4. The accrual of interest and amortization on December 31, 2005

(b) Show the proper balance sheet presentation for the liability for the bonds payable on the December 31, 2005, balance sheet.

(c) Answer the following questions:
1. What amount of interest expense is reported for 2005?
2. Would the bond interest expense reported in 2005 be the same as, greater than, or less than the amount that would be reported if the straight-line method of amortization were used?
3. Determine the total cost of borrowing over the life of the bonds.
4. Would the total bond interest expense be greater than, the same as, or less than the total interest expense that would be reported if the straight-line method of amortization were used?

Problems: Set B

Identify liabilities.
(SO 1)

P10-1B The following transactions occurred in Wendell Corporation. Wendell's fiscal year end is December 31.

1. Wendell purchased goods for $150,000 on December 23, terms n/30.
2. The Wendell chief executive is to be paid a bonus of $35,000 six months after year end.
3. Weekly salaries of $5,000 are paid every Friday for a five-day work week (Monday to Friday). This year, December 31 is a Wednesday. Payroll deductions include CPP of 4.95% and EI of 2.10% of gross salaries, and income tax withholdings of $1,800.
4. Property taxes of $40,000 were assessed on October 1 for the upcoming calendar year. They are payable by March 1.
5. Wendell is the defendant in a negligence suit. Wendell's legal counsel estimates that Wendell may suffer a $40,000 loss if it loses the suit. In legal counsel's opinion, the likelihood of success in the case is not determinable at this time.
6. Wendell entered into a $500,000, 5% note payable on July 1. The note requires fixed principal payments of $100,000, each June 30, for the next five years. Interest is due monthly, on the first of each month.
7. Wendell made income tax instalments of $60,000 throughout the year. After the preparation of its corporate income tax return at year end, it was determined that total income tax payable for the year was $50,000.

Instructions

(a) Identify which of the above transactions should be presented in the current liabilities section and which should be recorded in the long-term liabilities section of Wendell's balance sheet on December 31. Identify the account title(s) and amount(s) for each reported liability.

(b) Indicate any information that should be disclosed in the notes to Wendell's financial statements.

Prepare current liability
entries and section of
balance sheet.
(SO 2, 6)

P10-2B On January 1, 2004, the ledger of Molega Software Ltd. contains the following liability accounts:

Accounts Payable	$42,500	Provincial Sales Tax Payable	$ 5,800
Goods and Services Tax Payable	5,800	Unearned Service Revenue	15,000

During January the following selected transactions occurred:

Jan. 1 Borrowed $15,000 in cash on a four-month, 5%, $15,000 note. Interest is payable at maturity.

5 Sold merchandise for cash totalling $47,752, which included 7% GST and 7% PST. The cost of goods sold was $28,600. Molega Software uses a perpetual inventory system.

12 Provided services for customers who had made advance payments of $15,000.
14 Paid the Receiver General and Provincial Treasurer for sales taxes collected in December 2003, $11,600 ($5,800 GST + $5,800 PST).
25 Sold merchandise for cash totalling $54,820, which included sales taxes (7% GST and 7% PST). The cost of this sale was $39,000.
31 Paid monthly payroll of $62,000. Accrued payroll deductions include CPP, $3,069; EI, $1,302; income tax $12,400; and union dues, $800. Accrued employee benefits of CPP, $3,069 and EI, $1,823.

Instructions

(a) Journalize the January transactions.
(b) Journalize any required adjusting entries at January 31.
(c) Prepare the current liabilities section of the balance sheet at January 31, 2004.

P10-3B Cling-on Ltd. sells rock-climbing products and also operates an indoor climbing facility for climbing enthusiasts. During the last part of 2004, Cling-on had the following transactions related to notes payable:

Prepare entries for notes payable; show balance sheet presentation.
(SO 2, 6)

Sept. 1 Issued a $15,000 note to Black Diamond to purchase inventory. The three-month note payable bears interest of 8%. Interest is payable monthly, on the first of each month.
Oct. 1 Paid interest on the Black Diamond note.
Oct. 2 Issued a $10,000, 8%, two-month note to Montpelier Bank to finance the building of a new climbing area for advanced climbers. Interest is payable monthly, on the first of each month.
Nov. 1 Paid interest on the Black Diamond note and the Montpelier Bank note.
Nov. 2 Issued a one-month, $18,000 note and paid $8,000 in cash to purchase a vehicle to transport clients to nearby climbing sites as part of a new series of climbing classes. This note bears interest of 9%. Interest is payable at maturity.
Nov. 30 Recorded accrued interest for the vehicle note issued November 2.
Dec. 1 Paid principal and interest on the Black Diamond note.
Dec. 1 Paid interest on the Montpelier Bank note.
Dec. 31 Recorded accrued interest for the Montpelier Bank note and the vehicle note, at the company's year end.

Instructions

(a) Prepare journal entries for the transactions above.
(b) Show the balance sheet presentation of Notes Payable and Interest Payable at December 31.
(c) How much interest expense relating to notes payable did Cling-on incur during the year?

P10-4B The following section is taken from Peppermint Patty Ltd.'s balance sheet at December 31, 2003:

Prepare entries for bonds.
(SO 3, 4)

Current liabilities	
Bond interest payable	$ 8,000
Long-term liabilities	
Bonds payable, 8%, due January 1, 2010	200,000

Interest is payable semi-annually on January 1 and July 1.

Instructions

(a) Journalize the payment of the bond interest on January 1, 2004.
(b) Assume that on January 1, 2004, after paying interest, Peppermint Patty redeems bonds having a face value of $50,000. The redemption price is 102. Record the redemption of the bonds.
(c) Journalize the payment of the bond interest on July 1, 2004, on the remaining bonds.
(d) Prepare the adjusting entry on December 31, 2004, to accrue the interest on the remaining bonds.

P10-5B On October 1, 2003, PFQ Corp. issued $600,000 of 6%, 10-year bonds at face value. The bonds were dated October 1, 2003, and pay interest annually on October 1. Financial statements are prepared annually on December 31.

Prepare entries for bonds; show balance sheet presentation.
(SO 3, 4, 6)

Instructions

(a) Prepare the journal entry to record the issue of the bonds on October 1, 2003.
(b) Prepare the adjusting entry to record the accrual of interest on December 31, 2003.
(c) Show the balance sheet presentation on December 31, 2003.
(d) Prepare the journal entry to record the payment of interest on October 1, 2004.
(e) Prepare the adjusting entry to record the accrual of interest on December 31, 2004.
(f) Assume that on January 1, 2005, PFQ pays the accrued bond interest and redeems all of the bonds. The redemption price is 103. Record the payment of interest and redemption of the bonds.

Prepare entries for bonds, and mortgage note payable. Show balance sheet presentation. (SO 3, 5, 6)

P10-6B Atwater Corporation is building a new, state-of-the-art production and assembly facility for $10,000,000. To finance the facility, it issued $10,000,000 of 8%, five-year bonds at face value on August 1, 2004. They pay interest on August 1 and February 1. Atwater has a December 31 year end.

Atwater also purchased a new piece of equipment to be used in its new facility. The $550,000 piece of equipment was purchased with a $50,000 down payment and with cash received through the issue of a $500,000, 8%, three-year mortgage note payable issued on October 1, 2004. The terms provide for quarterly blended instalment payments of $47,280 on December 31, March 31, June 30, and September 30.

Instructions

Round all calculations to the nearest dollar.
(a) Prepare all necessary journal entries to record the issue of the bonds and the bond interest expense for 2004.
(b) Prepare all necessary journal entries related to the notes payable for 2004.
(c) Show the balance sheet presentation for these obligations for December 31, 2004. (*Hint*: Be sure to distinguish between the current and long-term portions of the note.)

Prepare entries for note payable. Show balance sheet presentation. (SO 5, 6)

P10-7B Peter Furlong has just approached a venture capitalist for financing for his sailing school. The lenders are willing to loan Peter $50,000 at a high-risk annual interest rate of 18%. The loan is payable over three years in instalments of $3,635, blended as to principal and interest. Payments are due every other month (that is, six times per year). Peter receives the loan on May 1, 2004, the first day of his fiscal year. Peter makes the first payment on June 30, 2004. The sailing school's year-end is April 30.

Instructions

(a) Prepare all journal entries for the sailing school for the first six months of the fiscal year beginning May 1, 2004 through to October 31, 2004.
(b) Show the balance sheet presentation of the note payable at October 31, 2004. (*Hint*: Don't forget to distinguish between the current and long-term portions of the note).

Analyse liquidity and solvency. (SO 6)

P10-8B You have been presented with the following selected information taken from the financial statements of Air Canada:

AIR CANADA
Balance Sheet (partial)
December 31, 2002
(in millions)

	2002	2001	2000
Current assets			
Cash and cash equivalents	$ 558	$ 1,067	$ 437
Accounts receivable	760	764	909
Spare parts, materials, and supplies	367	344	403
Prepaid expenses	86	60	33
Future income taxes	0	0	447
Total current assets	$1,771	$ 2,235	$2,229
Current liabilities	$2,592	$ 2,869	$3,560
Long-term liabilities	7,112	7,335	5,856
Total liabilities	9,704	10,204	9,416
Shareholders' equity (deficit)	(2,288)	(1,460)	316
Total liabilities and shareholders' equity	$7,416	$ 8,744	$9,732

Selected information (in millions):	2002	2001	2000
Net (loss) earnings	$(828)	$(1,315)	$ (82)
Income tax (recovery) expense	(384)	(330)	45
Interest expense	221	275	210
Cash provided (used) by operating activities	(95)	(1,072)	140

Instructions

(a) Calculate each of the following ratios for 2002 and 2001. Industry ratios have been included in parentheses where available.

1. Current ratio (0.8:1)   4. Debt to total assets (82.9)
2. Acid-test ratio (0.5:1)   5. Times interest earned (-2.6 times)
3. Cash current debt coverage (n/a)   6. Cash total debt coverage (n/a)

(b) Comment on Air Canada's liquidity and solvency.

(c) Air Canada has operating lease commitments totalling $7,697 million in 2002 and $7,591 million in 2001. Recalculate the debt to total assets and cash total debt coverage ratios in light of this information, and discuss the implications for analysis.

P10-9B The following selected liquidity and solvency ratios are available for two companies operating in the petroleum industry:

Analyse liquidity and solvency.
(SO 6)

Ratio	Petro-Zoom	Sun-Oil	Industry
Acid-test ratio	0.6:1	0.8:1	0.7:1
Current ratio	1.1:1	1.5:1	1.0:1
Receivables turnover	8.1 times	11.9 times	9.9 times
Inventory turnover	5.9 times	8.0 times	7.1 times
Debt to total assets	34.5%	62.1%	46.3%
Times interest earned	3.3 times	2.1 times	3.4 times
Cash current debt coverage	1.5 times	1.7 times	1.4 times
Cash total debt coverage	1.4 times	1.9 times	1.3 times

Instructions

Assume that you are the credit manager of the local bank. Answer the following questions, citing relevant ratios to justify your answer:

(a) Both Petro-Zoom and Sun-Oil have applied for a short-term loan from your bank. Which of the two companies is the most liquid and merits more consideration for a short-term loan? Explain.

(b) Both Petro-Zoom and Sun-Oil have applied for a long-term loan from your bank. Are you concerned with the solvency of either company? Explain why or why not.

*P10-10B Beatrice Corporation sold $1,500,000 of 8%, 10-year bonds on April 1, 2004. The bonds were dated April 1, 2001, and pay interest on April 1 and October 1. Beatrice Corporation uses the straight-line method to amortize bond premiums or discounts and has a December 31 year end.

Prepare entries for bonds, using straight-line amortization. Show balance sheet presentation.
(SO 3, 6, 7)

Instructions

(a) Prepare all the necessary journal entries to record the issue of the bonds and bond interest expense for 2004, assuming that the bonds sold at 102.

(b) Prepare journal entries as in part (a) assuming that the bonds sold at 97.

(c) Show the balance sheet presentation at December 31, 2004 for each bond issue under the assumptions in (a) and (b).

*P10-11B The following section is taken from Bermuda Corporation's balance sheet:

Prepare entries for bonds, using straight-line amortization.
(SO 3, 4, 7)

BERMUDA CORPORATION
Balance Sheet (partial)
December 31, 2004

Current liabilities		
Bond interest payable		$ 96,000
Long-term liabilities		
Bonds payable, 8%, due January 1, 2015	$2,400,000	
Less: Discount on bonds payable	84,000	2,316,000

Interest is payable semi-annually on January 1 and July 1. Bermuda uses straight-line amortization for any bond premium or discount.

Instructions

Round all calculations to the nearest dollar.

(a) Journalize the payment of bond interest on January 1, 2005.

(b) Prepare the entry to record the amortization and to pay the interest due on July 1, 2005.

(c) Assume on July 1, 2005, after paying interest, that Bermuda redeems bonds having a face value of $800,000. The redemption price is 102. Record the redemption of the bonds.

(d) Prepare the adjusting entry at December 31, 2005, to record amortization and to accrue interest on the remaining bonds.

Prepare entries for bonds, using effective-interest amortization.
(SO 3, 8)

*P10-12B   On July 1, 2004, Global Satellites Corporation issued $1,200,000 of face value, 7%, 10-year bonds at $1,118,462. This price resulted in an effective interest rate of 8% on the bonds. Global uses the effective-interest method to amortize any bond premium or discount. The bonds pay semi-annual interest on July 1 and January 1.

Instructions

Round all calculations to the nearest dollar.

(a) Prepare the journal entry to record the issue of the bonds on July 1, 2004.

(b) Prepare an amortization table through December 31, 2005 (three interest periods) for this bond issue.

(c) Prepare the journal entry to record the accrual of interest and amortization on December 31, 2004.

(d) Prepare the journal entry to record the payment of interest and amortization on July 1, 2005.

(e) Prepare the journal entry to record the accrual of interest and amortization on December 31, 2005.

Prepare entries for bonds, using effective-interest amortization. Show balance sheet presentation and answer questions.
(SO 3, 6, 8)

*P10-13B   On July 1, 2004, Imperial Ltd. issued $2,000,000 of face value, 6%, 10-year bonds at $2,155,890. This price resulted in a 5% effective interest rate on the bonds. Imperial uses the effective-interest method to amortize any bond premium or discount. The bonds pay semi-annual interest on each July 1 and January 1.

Instructions

(a) Prepare the journal entries for the following transactions:
   1. The issue of the bond on July 1, 2004
   2. The accrual of interest and amortization on December 31, 2004
   3. The payment of interest and amortization on July 1, 2005
   4. The accrual of interest and amortization on December 31, 2005

(b) Show the proper balance sheet presentation for the liability for bonds payable on December 31, 2005.

(c) Answer the following questions:
   1. What amount of interest expense is reported for 2005?
   2. Would the bond interest expense reported in 2005 be the same as, greater than, or less than the amount that would be reported if the straight-line method of amortization were used?
   3. Determine the total cost of borrowing over the life of the bonds.
   4. Would the total bond interest expense be greater than, the same as, or less than the total interest expense that would be reported if the straight-line method of amortization were used?

Financial Reporting and Analysis

Analysis Tools

FINANCIAL REPORTING PROBLEM: *Loblaw Companies Limited*

BYP10-1   Refer to the financial statements of Loblaw Companies Limited and the Notes to Consolidated Financial Statements in Appendix A.

Instructions

(a) What current liabilities were reported in Loblaw's balance sheet at December 28, 2002?
(b) What long-term liabilities were reported in Loblaw's balance sheet at December 28, 2002?
(c) What financing activities related to liabilities were reported in Loblaw's cash flow statement for the year ended December 28, 2002?
(d) Does Loblaw have any contingent liabilities and commitments that are expected to have a material impact on its financial position?

COMPARATIVE ANALYSIS PROBLEM: *Loblaw and Sobeys*

BYP10-2   The financial statements of Sobeys Inc. are presented in Appendix B, following the financial statements of Loblaw Companies Limited in Appendix A.

Instructions

(a) Based on the information contained in the financial statements, calculate the following ratios for each company for its most recent fiscal year. Industry ratios are shown in parentheses where available.

1. Current ratio. (1.1:1)
2. Acid-test ratio (0.3:1)
3. Cash current debt coverage (n/a)
4. Debt to total assets (61.5%)
5. Cash total debt coverage (n/a)
6. Times interest earned (2.8 times)

(b) What conclusions concerning the companies' liquidity can be drawn from the ratios calculated in (a)?
(c) What conclusions concerning the companies' solvency can be drawn from the ratios calculated in (a)?

RESEARCH CASE

BYP10-3 The May 4, 2002, issue of *The Economist* magazine contains an article on page 66 entitled "Company Accounts: Badly in Need of Repair."

Instructions

Read the article and answer the following questions:

(a) What are some examples of off–balance sheet financing? Can this be a risky practice? Explain.
(b) Operating leases make up most off–balance sheet financing. Why are operating leases so popular with the airline companies? What effect does using operating leases instead of capital leases have on net earnings? On the balance sheet?
(c) Is off–balance sheet financing in accordance with generally accepted accounting principles? What are standard-setters doing to try to curb abuses?

INTERPRETING FINANCIAL STATEMENTS

BYP10-4 **Reitmans (Canada) Limited** and **La Senza Corporation** are two specialty women's clothing merchandisers. Here are financial data for both companies at February 1, 2003 (in thousands):

	Reitmans	La Senza
Cash and cash equivalents	$ 30,885	$ 20,361
Accounts receivable	5,089	5,743
Short-term investments	0	32,615
Total current assets	134,185	109,562
Beginning total assets	279,336	245,258
Ending total assets	419,570	234,609
Beginning current liabilities	50,258	53,777
Ending current liabilities	79,915	61,171
Beginning total liabilities	53,757	97,133
Ending total liabilities	176,049	90,253
Net sales	752,494	289,100
Interest expense	2,656	2,094
Income tax expense	12,548	5,945
Net earnings (loss)	24,535	(3,775)
Cash provided by operating activities	32,235	33,690
Total operating lease commitments for next five years and subsequently	347,144	270,759

Instructions

Using the data, perform the following analysis:

(a) Calculate the working capital, current ratio, acid-test ratio, and cash current debt coverage for each company. Discuss their relative liquidity.

(b) Calculate the debt to total assets, times interest earned, and cash total debt coverage for each company. Discuss their relative solvency.

(c) The notes to the financial statements indicate that many of the retail stores' furniture and fixtures and the like are leased using operating leases. Discuss the implications of these operating leases for each company's solvency.

(d) Calculate return on assets and profit margin for each company. Note that La Senza actually reported net earnings of $15,445 thousand, before taking into consideration a $19,220 thousand expense due to discontinuing the operations of its Suzy Shier stores. Comment on each company's relative profitability.

A GLOBAL FOCUS

BYP10-5 **Swedish Match AB** is the world's largest maker of matches and the third largest producer of disposable lighters. It produces a wide range of other tobacco products, including Red Man chewing tobacco, which is a market leader in the United States.

Swedish Match reports the following information about contingencies in the notes to its financial statements:

> **SWEDISH MATCH AB**
> **Notes to the Financial Statements**
> **December 31, 2002**
>
> The Company is involved in a number of legal proceedings of a routine character. Among others, there are proceedings against General Cigar, where Cubatobaco is claiming that General Cigar does not have the right to use the Cohiba brand. Subsidiaries of Swedish Match in Brazil and France are subject to claims concerning alleged unfair dismissal of employees....
>
> Claims for damages against subsidiaries of Swedish Match for injuries that allegedly were caused by Swedish Match lighter products have been filed in Brazil and the U.S. In addition, subsidiaries of Swedish Match in the U.S. are the defendants in cases where it is claimed that the use of tobacco products has caused health problems... Although management cannot in any meaningful way estimate the damages that might be awarded, if any, in any ongoing or anticipated disputes, it holds the view that there are good defences against all the claims and each case will be defended vigorously.

Instructions

(a) Why would Swedish Match disclose information about these legal disputes in the notes to the financial statements, instead of accruing them as liabilities in its accounting records?

(b) Where should Swedish Match record the legal costs incurred to date on the disputes (e.g., the costs before proceeding to trial)?

(c) Swedish Match's debt to total assets ratio is higher than that of the industry. Its times interest earned ratio is lower than that of the industry. What implications do these contingent liabilities have for an analysis of Swedish Match's solvency?

FINANCIAL ANALYSIS ON THE WEB

BYP10-6 Bonds have complex terminology associated with them. Bonds Online is a useful site that provides a glossary of bond terms to explore.

Instructions

Specific requirements of this Web case can be found on the Kimmel website.

Critical Thinking

COLLABORATIVE LEARNING ACTIVITY

BYP10-7 On January 1, 2003, Landry Corporation issued $1,200,000 of five-year, 8% bonds at 97; the bonds pay interest semi-annually on July 1 and January 1. By January 1, 2005, the market rate of interest for bonds of risk similar to those of Landry Corporation had risen. As a result, the market value of these bonds was $1,000,000 on January 1, 2005, which was well below their carrying value of $1,178,400.

Barbara Landry, president of the company, suggests repurchasing all of these bonds in the open market at the $1,000,000 price. To do so, the company will have to issue $1,000,000 (face value) of new 10-year, 6% bonds. The president asks you as controller, "What is the feasibility of my proposed repurchase plan?"

Instructions

With the class divided into groups, do the following:

(a) Prepare the journal entry to retire the five-year bonds on January 1, 2005. Prepare the journal entry to issue the new 10-year bonds.

(b) Prepare a short memo to the president in response to her request for advice. List the economic factors that you believe should be considered for her repurchase proposal.

COMMUNICATION ACTIVITY

BYP10-8 Just about everywhere nowadays, companies are offering "rewards" to ensure customer loyalty. Hotels offer free nights. Airlines offer free travel. Supermarkets, phone companies, department stores—you name it—all encourage customers to collect points which can be redeemed for merchandise, travel, or other goods.

Instructions

Write a memorandum explaining whether or not unredeemed loyalty points should be recorded as current liabilities, be disclosed in the notes to the financial statements, or not be recorded and reported until redeemed. Be sure to include the reasoning for your answer.

ETHICS CASE

Ethics In Accounting

BYP10-9 Enron Corporation—formerly one of the world's largest electronic traders in natural gas and electricity—was one of the largest corporate bankruptcies in American history. Just weeks before it filed for bankruptcy, the company admitted that it had shifted billions of dollars in debt off its balance sheets and into a variety of complex partnerships.

One journalist wrote that "The Enron practice of shifting liabilities off the books to more than 3,500 subsidiaries raised so many red flags that you'd think you were in a military parade somewhere in China." Yet, Enron and its auditors argued vehemently that the "special purpose entity" partnerships they used were in accordance with U.S. GAAP and fully disclosed, even if not recorded in the books.

Instructions

(a) Who are the stakeholders in this situation?
(b) Explain how shifting debt off the balance sheet might mislead investors.
(c) Do you think that management has an obligation to ensure that its accounting and disclosure is relevant to users, even if this means going beyond GAAP?

Answers to Self-Study Questions

1. d   2. c   3. c   4. a   5. c   6. a   7. b   8. d   9. d   10. b
*11. d   *12. c

Answer to Loblaw Review It Question 4

Loblaw has the following current liabilities, totalling $3,154 million as at December 28, 2002: bank indebtedness; commercial paper; accounts payable and accrued liabilities; income taxes; and long-term debt due within one year.

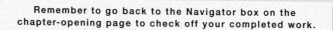

Remember to go back to the Navigator box on the chapter-opening page to check off your completed work.

CHAPTER 11

Reporting and Analysing Shareholders' Equity

STUDY OBJECTIVES

After studying this chapter, you should be able to:

1 Identify and discuss the major characteristics of a corporation and its shares.

2 Record the issue of common shares.

3 Differentiate preferred shares from common shares.

4 Prepare the entries for cash dividends, stock dividends, and stock splits, and understand their financial impact.

5 Identify the items that affect retained earnings.

6 Indicate how shareholders' equity is presented in the financial statements.

7 Evaluate dividend and earnings performance.

Race You to the Corner

Here's a riddle for you: What major world corporation had its first big breakthrough in the 1970s with a waffle iron? Hint: It doesn't sell food. Another hint: Swoosh. Final hint: "Just do it."

That's right—Nike Inc. In 1971 Nike co-founder Bill Bowerman put a piece of rubber in a kitchen waffle iron, and the Waffle™ sole was born. The rest, as they say, is history.

Nike was founded by Bowerman and Phil Knight, an accounting student and member of Bowerman's university track team. Each got into the shoe business independently during the early 1960s. Bowerman made handcrafted running shoes for his university track team, and Knight, after completing graduate school, started a small business importing low-cost, high-quality shoes from Japan. In 1964 the two became partners in Blue Ribbon Sports.

At first the pair marketed Japanese shoes. It wasn't until 1971 that the company began manufacturing its own line. With these new shoes—and their waffle-textured soles—came a new corporate name: Nike, the Greek goddess of victory.

Today Nike is a household name across North America and worldwide. It now boasts a stable full of world-class athletes as promoters. But, at one time it had part-time employees selling shoes out of car trunks at track meets. The company's success has been achieved through continual innovation combined with relentless promotion.

By 1980 Nike was sufficiently established to issue its first shares to the public. From the beginning, it offered a share ownership program for its employees, allowing them to take part in the company's success. Since then Nike has enjoyed phenomenal growth, with 2002 sales reaching U.S.$9.9 billion throughout the world—the highest in the company's history. The dividend paid to shareholders has increased every year for the last 13 years. Today, Nike is the world's number 1 shoe company, selling its products in 141 countries, and on-line.

Nike is not alone in its quest for the top spot in the sport shoe world. Reebok International Ltd. pushes Nike every

512

Nike www.nike.com
Reebok www.reebok.com

THE NAVIGATOR

Scan *Study Objectives* ☐

Read *Feature Story* ☐

Read *Chapter Preview* ☐

Read text and answer *Before You Go On*
p. 522 ☐ p. 523 ☐ p. 525 ☐
p. 530 ☐ p. 533 ☐ p. 537 ☐

Work *Using the Decision Toolkit* ☐

Review *Summary of Study Objectives*
and *Decision Toolkit* ☐

Work *Demonstration Problem* ☐

Answer *Self-Study Questions* ☐

Complete assignments ☐

step of the way. Reebok was clearly outstripped by its giant rival in the last few years—Reebok's 2002 sales of U.S.$3.2 billion are only about a third of Nike's, and Reebok has issued no dividends since 1996. But its unwillingness to give up the race is boldly symbolized in its recent ad campaign: "This is my planet." Reebok recently revamped its mission statement around the core value of "delighting our customers."

Shares of both Nike and Reebok have fluctuated considerably over the years, both reaching highs in the late 1990s. Nike, which peaked in 1998 at U.S.$76, was trading at U.S.$47 at the beginning of 2003. The company issued two-for-one stock splits in 1990, 1995, and 1996. Shares of Reebok, which hit U.S.$53 in

1997, currently trade around U.S.$32. The company's last stock split was in 1987.

The race is far from over. Nike has seen revenues in the U.S. and South America drop recently. In addition, its largest single customer, Foot Locker Inc., which accounted for 10.9% of Nike's worldwide revenues in 2002, announced its intention to focus on more moderately priced footwear, sharply reducing its orders. The company is also facing ongoing PR challenges in the face of increasing awareness of globalization-related labour issues among its prime youth market.

The shoe market is notoriously fickle, with new styles becoming popular almost daily. And there is still plenty of room for expansion in international

markets. As well, both companies are taking steps to attract more female customers in what has traditionally been a male-dominated market. In 2001, Reebok launched its "It's a woman's world" campaign; while in 2002, Nike, which owns few retail outlets of its own, opened its first two Nike Goddess stores, aimed specifically at women. It plans to use the shops to study new ways to approach the women's market.

As these two Olympians thunder down the track of the marketplace, shareholders sit anxiously in the stands. But in business, as in life, as another famed Nike ad proclaims, "There is no finish line."

NAVIGATOR ✔

Corporations like Nike and Reebok have substantial resources at their disposal. In fact, corporations are the dominant form of business organization throughout the world in terms of sales, earnings, and number of employees. All of the largest Canadian companies are corporations. In this chapter, we look at the essential features of a corporation and explain the accounting for a corporation's share capital transactions.

The content and organization of this chapter are as follows:

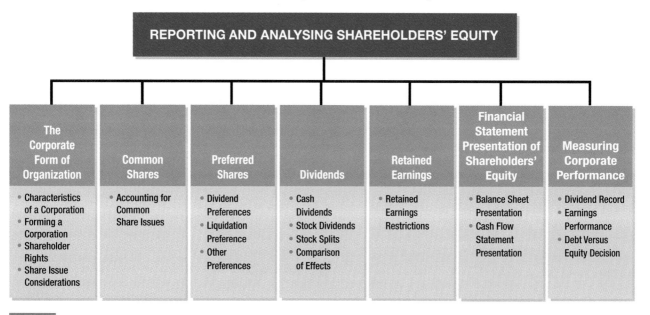

The Corporate Form of Organization

A corporation is created by law. As a legal entity, a corporation has most of the rights and privileges of a person. The major exceptions relate to privileges that can be exercised only by a living person, such as the right to vote or to hold public office. Similarly, a corporation is subject to the same duties and responsibilities as a person. For example, it must abide by the laws and it must pay taxes.

Corporations may be classified in a variety of ways. Two common classifications are **by purpose** and **by ownership**. A corporation may be organized for the purpose of making a profit (such as Nike and Reebok), or it may be a not-for-profit charitable or educational institution (such as the Canadian Cancer Society or McGill University).

Classification by ownership differentiates public and private corporations. A public corporation may have thousands of shareholders, and its shares are regularly traded on a securities market such as the Toronto Stock Exchange. Examples are BCE, Canadian Pacific Railway, and Sears Canada. In contrast, a private corporation, often referred to as a closely held corporation, usually has only a few shareholders. It does not offer its shares for sale to the general public. Private companies are generally much smaller than public companies, although some notable exceptions exist such as McCain Foods, The Jim Pattison Group and the Irving companies.

CHARACTERISTICS OF A CORPORATION

In 1964, when Nike's founders, Knight and Bowerman, were just getting started in the running shoe business, they formed their original organization as a partnership. In 1968, they reorganized the company as a corporation. A number of characteristics distinguish corporations from proprietorships and partnerships. The most important of these characteristics are explained below.

STUDY OBJECTIVE

1

Identify and discuss the major characteristics of a corporation and its shares.

Separate Legal Existence

As an entity separate and distinct from its owners, the corporation acts under its own name rather than in the name of its shareholders. Nike, for example, may buy, own, and sell property, borrow money, and enter into legally binding contracts in its own name. It may also sue or be sued. It pays income taxes as a separate entity.

In contrast to a proprietorship or partnership, in which the acts of the owners bind the proprietorship or partnership, the acts of a corporation's owners (shareholders) do not bind the corporation unless these owners are also agents of the corporation. For example, if you owned Nike shares, you would not have the right to purchase inventory for the company unless you were designated as an agent of the corporation.

Limited Liability of Shareholders

Since a corporation is a separate legal entity, creditors ordinarily only have recourse to corporate assets to satisfy their claims. The liability of shareholders is normally limited to their investment in the corporation. Creditors have no legal claim on the personal assets of the shareholders unless fraud has occurred. Even in bankruptcy, shareholders' losses are generally limited to the amount of capital they have invested in the corporation.

Transferable Ownership Rights

Ownership of a corporation is held in shares of capital, which are transferable units. Shareholders may dispose of part or all of their interest in a corporation simply by selling their shares. The transfer of shares is entirely up to the shareholder. It does not require the approval of either the corporation or other shareholders.

The transfer of ownership rights among shareholders has no effect on the operating activities of the corporation. Nor does it affect the corporation's assets, liabilities, or shareholders' equity. The transfer of ownership rights is a transaction between individual shareholders. The corporation does not participate in the transfer of these ownership rights; it is only involved in the original sale of the share capital.

Ability to Acquire Capital

It is relatively easy for a corporation to obtain capital by issuing shares. Buying shares in a corporation is often attractive to an investor because a shareholder has limited liability and shares are readily transferable. Also, because only small amounts of money need to be invested, many individuals can become shareholders. In sum, the ability of a successful corporation to obtain capital is virtually unlimited.

Continuous Life

Corporations have an unlimited life. Since a corporation is a separate legal entity, its continuance as a going concern is not affected by the withdrawal, death, or incapacity of a shareholder, employee, or officer. As a result, a successful corporation can have a continuous and indefinite life.

Corporation Management

Although shareholders legally own the corporation, they manage it indirectly through a board of directors they elect. Philip Knight is the chair of Nike's board of directors. The board, in turn, formulates the operating policies for the company. The board also selects officers, such as a president and one or more vice-presidents, to execute policy and to perform daily management functions.

The organizational structure of a corporation enables a company to hire professional managers to run the business. On the other hand, some view this separation as a weakness. The separation of ownership and management prevents owners from having an active role in managing the company, which some owners would like to have.

BUSINESS INSIGHT

ETHICS PERSPECTIVE

In the wake of Enron's collapse, many people have asked, "Where was the Board of Directors?" The Enron Board claimed that it was kept in the dark by management and the auditors. Some have speculated that the collapse of Enron was not so much because of problems with accounting standards, as because of board culture and leadership. This situation highlighted the need for the election and training of independent directors. Corporate governance reforms now encourage directors to ask the hard questions of management and the auditors and to work with management to set the ethical tone for the corporation.

Government Regulations

Canadian companies may be incorporated federally, under the terms of the *Canada Business Corporations Act*, or provincially, under the terms of a provincial business corporations act. Federal and provincial laws usually prescribe the requirements for issuing and reacquiring shares and distributing earnings. Similarly, provincial securities commissions regulations govern the sale of share capital to the general public. When a corporation's shares are listed and traded on foreign securities markets, the corporation must comply with the reporting requirements of these exchanges. Compliance with federal, provincial, and securities regulations increases the cost and complexity of the corporate form of organization.

Income Taxes

For proprietorships and partnerships, the owner's (or partner's) share of earnings is reported on his or her personal income tax return. Taxes are then paid on this amount by the individual. Corporations, on the other hand, must pay income taxes as separate legal entities. These taxes can be substantial. They can amount to as much as 45% of taxable income.

There are, however, income tax deductions available to some corporations. With eligible deductions, or other corporate tax incentives, a corporation's tax rate may be reduced to between 15% and 25%. This tax rate is much lower than the tax rate for the same amount of income earned by an individual.

In some circumstances, an advantage of incorporation is the deferral of personal income tax. The shareholders of a corporation do not pay tax on the corporate earnings until they are distributed to them. Shareholders pay tax on cash dividends, which are pro rata distributions of net earnings. Many people argue that corporate earnings are taxed twice (double taxation)—at the corporate level and again at the individual level. This is not exactly true, however, as individuals receive a dividend tax credit to reduce some of the tax burden.

To determine whether incorporating will result in more or less income tax than operating as a proprietorship or partnership, it is wise to seek expert advice. Income tax laws are complex, and care in tax planning is essential for any business venture.

The advantages and disadvantages of a corporation compared to a proprietorship and partnership are shown in Illustration 11-1.

Advantages	Disadvantages
• Corporation management— professional managers • Separate legal existence • Limited liability of shareholders • Potential for deferred or reduced income taxes • Transferable ownership rights • Ability to acquire capital • Continuous life	• Corporation management— separation of ownership and management • Increased costs and complexity of adhering to government regulations • Potential for additional income taxes

Illustration 11-1
Advantages and disadvantages of a corporation

Decision Toolkit

DECISION CHECKPOINTS	INFO NEEDED FOR DECISION	TOOL TO USE FOR DECISION	HOW TO EVALUATE RESULTS
Should the company incorporate?	Capital needs, growth expectations, type of business, tax status	Corporations have limited liability, easier capital-raising ability, and professional managers. They may suffer from additional government regulations and separation of ownership from management. Income taxes may be higher or lower for a corporation.	Carefully weigh the costs and benefits in light of the particular circumstances.

FORMING A CORPORATION

As previously mentioned, a company can incorporate federally, under the *Canada Business Corporations Act*, or provincially. The federal government and the majority of provinces file **articles of incorporation**, although other methods of incorporation also exist. Upon receipt of its articles of incorporation—essentially the constitution of the corporation—the corporation establishes by-laws. The by-laws establish the internal rules and procedures for conducting the affairs of the corporation. Corporations engaged in interprovincial commerce must also obtain a licence from each province in which they do business. The licence subjects the corporation's operating activities to the general corporation laws of the province.

The costs of forming a corporation are called organization costs. These costs include legal fees, accounting fees, and registration costs. It may be argued that organization costs should be capitalized as an intangible asset as they have a useful life equal to the life of the corporation. However, most companies expense organization costs in the year they occur. Determining the amount and timing of future benefits is so difficult that the conservative approach of expensing these costs immediately is more justifiable.

Corporations in North America are identified by "Ltd.," "Inc.," "Corp.," or in some cases, "Co."—all of these either abbreviated or spelled out—following their names. In Brazil and France, the letters used are "SA" (Sôciedade Anonima, Société Anonyme); in Japan, "KK" (Kabushiki Kaisha); in the Netherlands, "NV" (Naamloze Vennootschap); in Italy, "SpA" (Società per Azioni); and in Sweden, "AB" (Aktiebolag).

In the UK, public corporations are identified by "Plc" (public limited company), while private corporations are denoted by "Ltd." The parallel designations in Germany are "AG" (Aktiengesellschaft) for public corporations and "GmbH" (Gesellschaft mit beschränkter Haftung) for private corporations.

SHAREHOLDER RIGHTS

Alternative Terminology
Shares are also commonly known as *stock*.

After incorporation, a corporation sells ownership rights in the form of shares. When a corporation has only one class of shares, that class is identified as **common shares**. Each common share gives the shareholder the ownership rights pictured in Illustration 11-2. The share ownership rights are stated in the articles of incorporation or in the by-laws.

Illustration 11-2
Ownership rights of shareholders

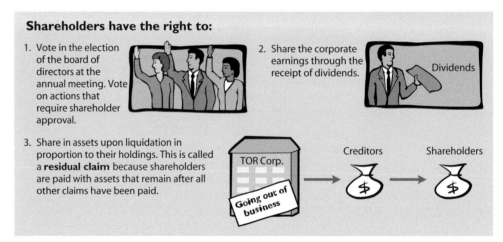

Shareholders have the right to:

1. Vote in the election of the board of directors at the annual meeting. Vote on actions that require shareholder approval.

2. Share the corporate earnings through the receipt of dividends.

3. Share in assets upon liquidation in proportion to their holdings. This is called a **residual claim** because shareholders are paid with assets that remain after all other claims have been paid.

Proof of ownership is evidenced by a printed or engraved form known as a **share certificate**. The face of the certificate shows the number and type of shares owned, the name of the corporation, the shareholder's name, the date, the corporate seal, and signatures of authorized corporate officials. Certificates are pre-numbered to facilitate their accountability; they may be issued for any quantity of shares.

SHARE ISSUE CONSIDERATIONS

Although Nike incorporated in 1968, it did not sell shares to the public until 1980. At that time, Nike evidently decided it would benefit from the infusion of cash that a public sale of its shares would bring. When a corporation decides to issue share capital, it must resolve a number of basic questions: How many shares should be authorized for sale? How should the shares be issued? What value should be assigned to the shares? These questions are answered in the following sections.

Authorized Share Capital

The amount of share capital that a corporation is authorized to sell is indicated in its articles of incorporation. It may be specified as an unlimited amount or a certain number (e.g., 500,000 shares authorized). More than 85% of public companies in Canada have an unlimited amount of authorized shares. If a number is specified, the amount of authorized shares normally anticipates a company's initial and later capital needs. If a corporation has sold all of its authorized shares, it must obtain legislative approval to amend its articles of incorporation before it can issue additional shares.

To determine the number of unissued shares that can be issued without amending the articles of incorporation, the total shares issued are subtracted from the total authorized. For example, if Advanced Micro Corp. is authorized to sell 100,000 common shares but has issued only 80,000 shares, 20,000 shares remain unissued. If Advanced Micro had an unlimited amount of common shares authorized, an unlimited number of shares would remain unissued.

The authorization of share capital does not result in a formal accounting entry because the event has no immediate effect on either corporate assets or shareholders' equity. However, disclosure of the number of shares authorized and issued is required in the shareholders' equity section of the balance sheet.

Issue of Shares

A corporation can issue common shares directly to investors or indirectly through an investment banking firm that specializes in bringing securities to the attention of potential investors. Direct issue is typical in closely held companies. Indirect issue is customary for a publicly held corporation. The first time a corporation's shares are offered to the public, the offer is called an initial public offering (IPO). The company receives the cash (less any issue fees) from the sale of the IPO shares whether done by a direct or indirect issue. The company's assets (cash) increase, and its shareholders' equity (share capital) also increases.

Once these shares have been initially issued, they continue trading on the **secondary market**. That is, investors buy and sell shares from each other, rather than from the company. When shares are sold among investors, there is no impact on the company's financial position. The company receives no additional assets, and issues no additional shares. The only change in the company records is the name of the shareholder, not the number of shares issued.

In Canada, shares are offered for sale to the public (whether through an IPO or through the secondary market) using organized securities exchanges, such as the Toronto Stock Exchange (TSX) or the Montreal Exchange (ME).

⊕ **International Note**

The United States has the world's largest market capitalization. Nearly half of all companies in the world list their shares on U.S. stock exchanges. Europe has 24%, Japan and the UK each 10%, and Canada and the rest of the Pacific less than 3% each of the world's market capitalization.

Market Value of Shares

After the initial issue of new shares, the subsequent market price per share is established by the interaction between buyers and sellers. In general, the price follows the trend of a company's earnings and dividends. Factors beyond a company's control (such as an embargo on oil, changes in interest rates, the outcome of an election, and war) can also influence market prices.

For each listed security, the financial press reports the highs and lows of the shares for the year; the annual dividend rate; the high, low, and closing prices for the day; and the net change over the previous day. The total volume of shares traded on a particular day, the dividend yield, and price-earnings ratios are also reported. A recent listing for Bank of Montreal common shares is shown in Illustration 11-3:

Illustration 11-3
Stock market listing for Bank of Montreal

| 365-day | | stock | sym | div | high /bid | low /ask | close | chg | vol 100s | yld | p/e ratio |
high	low										
43.40	31.00	Bank of Montreal	BMO	1.32	43.39	42.00	42.00	-1.25	14545	3.14	15.2

The Bank of Montreal has an annual dividend of $1.32 per common share. The high, low, and closing prices for the date shown were $43.39, $42.00, and $42.00 per share, respectively. The high and low share prices for the year (shown in the first two columns) were $43.40 and $31.00 per share, respectively. The closing share price decreased by $1.25 from the previous day. The trading volume was 1,454,500 shares. The dividend yield (dividend divided by closing share price) is 3.14% ($1.32 ÷ $42.00). The dividend yield reports the rate of return an investor earned from dividends. The price-earnings ratio was 15.2, indicating that the market price ($42.00) is 15.2 times the Bank's earnings per share.

No Par Value Shares

Years ago, par or stated value was used to determine the legal capital per share that must remain invested in a business for the protection of corporate creditors. Corporations with par or stated value shares were required to sell their shares at par or stated value or above. Consequently, most companies assigned their par or stated value shares a very low value.

The usefulness of par or stated value as a protective device for creditors was questionable because this assigned value was usually immaterial relative to the actual value of the company's shares—even at the time of issue. For example, Reebok's par value is one cent per share, yet a new share issue by Reebok would sell today at a market value of $31 per share. Thus, par or stated value had no relationship with market value and in the vast majority of cases was an immaterial amount. Today, the use of par or stated values for shares is either not required or prohibited in Canada. Par value shares are still issued in some other countries, however, including the United States.

No par value shares are shares that have not been assigned a pre-set value. Instead, the entire proceeds received upon issue of the shares are considered to be legal capital. If shares have no par value, then the questionable practice of using par value as a basis for legal capital never arises. Whenever shares are issued in the chapter, we will assume that they are no par value.

Reacquisition of Shares

Companies can purchase their own shares on the open market. A corporation may acquire its own shares to:

- increase trading of the company's shares in the securities market in the hopes of enhancing its market value
- reduce the number of shares issued and thereby increase earnings per share
- have additional shares available to issue to officers and employees under bonus and stock compensation plans
- have additional shares available for use in acquiring other companies

Another reason for purchasing one's own shares is that management may want to eliminate hostile shareholders by buying them out. Canadian Occidental Petroleum Ltd. (CanOxy) repurchased nearly half, roughly $600 million, of its shares held by Los Angeles–based Occidental Petroleum Corp. in 2000 to stop Occidental from taking over its huge Syncrude oil sands project in northern Alberta.

When a federally incorporated company reacquires its own shares, the repurchased shares must be retired and cancelled. This effectively restores the shares to the status of authorized but unissued shares.

Stock Compensation Plans

We mentioned above that a company sometimes repurchases shares so it can issue them to officers and employers under stock compensation plans. Stock compensation plans reward employees with shares, encouraging them to act in a way that maximizes the share price and benefits shareholders. A stock option is a right granted by a company to an employee to purchase a specified number of the company's shares at a specified price during a specified time period. When the market price of the shares exceeds the option price, the employee gains by exercising the option to buy the shares.

Stock option plans are a common form of supplementing compensation—especially for corporate executives. Of the companies surveyed in a recent year, 98% reported the use of stock-based compensation plans. It has been estimated that stock options account, on average, for up to 80% of executive compensation. In some instances, stock options account for significantly more. For example, Frank Stronach, Chair of Magna International Inc., earned a salary of $314,000 in 2002 and received stock options valued at $57,686,000.

Over the last few years, no subject in financial accounting has received as much press as accounting for stock options. While there is no doubt in anyone's mind that stock options have an intrinsic value, it is very difficult to measure the actual value of the compensation. Consequently, stock options have not, to date, been recorded in the financial statements. This has resulted in a situation where literally billions of dollars of compensation provided to employees has not been recorded as compensation expense, significantly overstating earnings. A recent study surveyed 167 companies and concluded that 25 of them would see net earnings entirely eliminated if stock options cost had been recorded.

All of this is about to change. Accounting standard-setting bodies in Canada and Europe have made proposals that would require public companies to estimate and report the costs of employee stock option compensation packages on their financial statements. These proposals are considered to be timely by many, given the increasing demand for greater transparency in financial reporting.

Others have concerns that these proposals are premature until issues about the measurement and comparability of the stock option values are resolved. The issue of options accounting continues to be controversial and it will likely be some time before the standards are finalized. Nonetheless, several companies have already announced their intention to voluntarily expense stock options, in advance of the standards coming into effect. Standard-setters may have to play catch-up as companies try to do the right thing.

BUSINESS INSIGHT

INVESTOR PERSPECTIVE

Lavish executive options packages of the late 1990s may have provided too much incentive for senior executives to manage share prices. Some speculate that the steps taken to boost revenues and hide losses in the corporate scandals of the past few years were taken in order to allow executives time to cash in their stock options before the signs of decline became apparent. At the very least, stock options forced executives to focus on short-term results, at the expense of long-term consequences and the company's survival.

This may be a moot point in the future. Plummeting share values and closer scrutiny of stock options once they are recorded in the financial statements will certainly mean that the portion of executive compensation derived from stock options will decline in relation to other forms of compensation. Right now, most stock options granted in the past three to five years are worth far less than their current option price. Re-pricing options for company employees has all but been ruled out by irate shareholders who would not benefit from such a move. And buying back options is not viable for cash-strapped companies.

This has made stock options unattractive to those who hold them and of questionable value as a long-term financial reward that ties together shareholder and management interests.

BEFORE YOU GO ON . . .

● **REVIEW IT**

1. What are the advantages and disadvantages of a corporation compared to a proprietorship or a partnership?
2. To a corporation, what is the significance of the amount of authorized shares? Issued shares?
3. How does the sale of shares affect a company in an initial public offering? Subsequently, in the secondary market?
4. Why might a company wish to repurchase its own shares?

Common Shares

The shareholders' equity section of a corporation's balance sheet includes (1) **share capital (contributed capital)** and (2) **retained earnings (earned capital)**. The distinction between share capital and retained earnings is important from both a legal and an economic point of view. Share capital is the amount contributed to the corporation by shareholders in exchange for shares of ownership. Retained earnings is earned capital held for future use in the business. In this section, we discuss the accounting for share capital. In a later section, we discuss retained earnings.

ACCOUNTING FOR COMMON SHARE ISSUES

STUDY OBJECTIVE

2

Record the issue of common shares.

A	=	L	+	SE
+6,000				+6,000

↑ Cash flows: +6,000

If a corporation only issues one class of shares, this class is known as common shares. As shown below, **the issue of common shares affects only share capital accounts.** To illustrate, assume that Hydro-Slide, Inc. issues 1,000 common shares for cash at $6 per share. The entry to record this transaction is:

Cash	6,000	
Common Shares		6,000
(To record issue of 1,000 common shares)		

If Hydro-Slide, Inc. has retained earnings of $27,000, the shareholders' equity section of the balance sheet is as shown in Illustration 11-4.

Illustration 11-4
Shareholders' equity

HYDRO-SLIDE, INC.
Balance Sheet (partial)
Decembeer 31, 2004

Shareholders' equity	
Common shares	$ 6,000
Retained earnings	27,000
Total shareholders' equity	$33,000

Common shares may also be issued for considerations other than cash, such as services (e.g., compensation to lawyers, consultants) or noncash assets (e.g., land, buildings, equipment). To comply with the cost principle in a noncash transaction, **cost is the cash equivalent price.** Thus, cost is the fair market value of the consideration (common shares) given up. If the common shares do not have a ready market, we then look to the fair market value of the consideration received to determine cost.

BEFORE YOU GO ON . . .

- **REVIEW IT**

    1. Explain the accounting for common shares issued for cash.
    2. How are common shares valued when they are issued for services or non-cash assets?

- **DO IT**

Cayman Corporation begins operations on March 1 by issuing 10,000 common shares for $12 cash per share. Journalize the share issue.

Action Plan

- In issuing shares for cash, credit the Common Shares account for the proceeds.

Solution

Mar. 1	Cash	120,000	
	Common Shares		120,000
	(To record issue of 10,000 shares at $12 per share)		

Preferred Shares

A corporation may issue an additional class of shares, called preferred shares. Preferred shares have contractual provisions that give them preference or priority over common shares in certain areas. Typically, preferred shareholders have a priority in relation to (1) dividends and (2) assets in the event of liquidation. However, they often do not have voting rights. A recent survey indicated that nearly one-third of Canadian companies have one or more classes of preferred shares.

Like common shares, preferred shares may be issued for cash or for noncash considerations. The entries for these transactions are similar to the entries for common shares. When a corporation has more than one class of shares, separate account titles should be used (e.g., Preferred Shares, Common Shares).

Assume that Stine Corporation issues 10,000 preferred shares for $12 cash per share. The entry to record the issue is:

Cash	120,000	
Preferred Shares		120,000
(To record issue of 10,000 preferred shares)		

In the shareholders' equity section of the balance sheet, preferred shares are shown first because of their dividend and liquidation preferences over common shares.

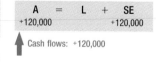
DIVIDEND PREFERENCES

As indicated earlier, **preferred shareholders have the right to share in the distribution of dividends before common shareholders do.** For example, if the dividend rate on preferred shares is $5 per share, common shareholders will not receive any dividends in the current year until preferred shareholders have received $5 per share. The first claim to dividends does not, however, **guarantee** dividends. Dividends depend on many factors, such as adequate retained earnings and the availability of cash.

Cumulative Dividend

Preferred shares may contain a cumulative dividend feature. This right means that preferred shareholders must be paid both current-year dividends and any unpaid prior-year dividends before common shareholders receive dividends. Preferred shares without this feature are called noncumulative. The majority of preferred shares issued today are noncumulative.

When preferred shares are cumulative, preferred dividends not declared in a given period are called dividends in arrears. To illustrate, assume that Scientific-Leasing has 5,000 cumulative preferred shares. The annual dividend is $35,000 (5,000 × $7 per share). If dividends are two years in arrears, preferred shareholders are entitled to receive the dividends in the current year, as shown below.

Dividends in arrears ($35,000 × 2)	$ 70,000
Current-year dividends	35,000
Total preferred dividends	$105,000

No distribution can be made to common shareholders until this entire preferred dividend is paid. In other words, dividends cannot be paid to common shareholders while any preferred share dividends are in arrears.

Dividends in arrears are not considered a liability. No obligation exists until a dividend is declared by the board of directors. However, the amount of dividends in arrears should be disclosed in the notes to the financial statements. Doing so enables investors to assess the potential impact of this commitment on the corporation's financial position. Of the Canadian companies disclosing cumulative preferred in a recent year, 11% had dividends in arrears.

Companies that are unable to meet their dividend obligations—whether cumulative or noncumulative—are not looked upon favourably by the investment community. As a financial officer noted in discussing one company's failure to pay its preferred dividend for a period of time, "Not meeting your obligations on something like that is a major black mark on your record."

LIQUIDATION PREFERENCE

Most preferred shares have a preference on corporate assets if the corporation fails. This feature provides security for the preferred shareholder. The preference on assets may be for the legal value of the shares or for a specified liquidating value. The liquidation preference is used in bankruptcy lawsuits involving the respective claims of creditors and preferred shareholders.

OTHER PREFERENCES

The attractiveness of preferred shares as an investment is sometimes enhanced by adding a conversion privilege. Convertible preferred shares allow the exchange of preferred shares for common shares at a specified ratio, at the shareholder's option. Convertible preferred shares are purchased by investors who want the greater security of preferred shares, but who also desire the added option of conversion if the market value of the common shares increases significantly.

Many preferred shares are also issued with a redemption or call feature. Redeemable (or callable) preferred shares grant the issuing corporation the right to purchase the shares from shareholders at specified future dates and prices. The redemption feature offers some flexibility to a corporation by enabling it to eliminate this type of equity security when it is advantageous to do so.

Retractable preferred shares are similar to redeemable or callable preferred shares, except that it is at the *shareholder's* option rather than the corporation's option that the shares are redeemed. This usually occurs at an arranged price and date.

Companies are issuing an increasing number of shares with innovative preferences. Some have the attributes of both debt and equity; others have the attributes of both common and preferred shares. Accounting for complex share preferences—sometimes known as financial instruments—presents unique challenges for accountants. Further detail is left for another course.

BEFORE YOU GO ON . . .

● **REVIEW IT**

1. Compare the normal rights and privileges of common and preferred shares.
2. Distinguish between convertible, redeemable, and retractable preferred shares.

Dividends

A dividend is a distribution on a pro rata basis made by a corporation to its shareholders. "Pro rata" means that if you own, say, 10% of the common shares, you will receive 10% of the dividend. Cash dividends, which predominate in practice, and stock dividends, which are declared with some frequency, are the focus of our discussion about dividends.

Investors are very interested in a company's dividend practices. However, fewer and fewer companies are consistently paying dividends. According to the Toronto Stock Exchange, only 57 Canadian companies have paid dividends nonstop for the past 25 years, compared to 100 companies 20 years ago. The Bank of Montreal has the longest unbroken dividend record, having begun paying dividends in 1829—175 years ago. In the financial press, **dividends are generally reported quarterly as a dollar amount per share**, although sometimes they are reported on an annual basis. For example, the Bank of Montreal has a quarterly dividend rate of $0.33 on its common shares, and $0.30 on one of its classes of preferred shares.

> **STUDY OBJECTIVE**
> **④**
> Prepare the entries for cash dividends, stock dividends, and stock splits, and understand their financial impact.

CASH DIVIDENDS

A cash dividend is a pro rata distribution of cash to shareholders. For a corporation to pay a cash dividend, it must have the following:

1. **Retained earnings.**   In most jurisdictions, payment of dividends from legal capital is prohibited. Payment of dividends from retained earnings is permitted.
2. **Adequate cash.**   Recently, Nike had a balance in retained earnings of $3,839 million but a cash balance of only $576 million. If it had wanted to pay a dividend equal to its retained earnings, Nike would have had to raise $3,263 million more in cash. It would have been unlikely for Nike to do this because a dividend of this size would not be sustainable in the future (that is, Nike would not be able to pay this much in dividends in future years). In addition, such a dividend would completely deplete Nike's balance in retained earnings, so it would not be able to pay a dividend in the next year unless it had positive net earnings.
3. **Declared dividends.**   The board of directors has full authority to determine the amount of earnings to be distributed in the form of dividends and the amount to be retained in the business. Dividends do not accrue like interest on a note payable, and they are not a liability until they are declared.

The amount and timing of a dividend are important issues for management to consider. The payment of a large cash dividend could lead to liquidity problems for the company. Conversely, a small dividend or a missed dividend may cause unhappiness among shareholders who expect to receive a reasonable cash payment from the company on a periodic basis. On the other hand, a number of high-growth companies pay no dividends, preferring to retain earnings and use them to finance capital expenditures.

In order to remain in business, companies must honour their interest payments to creditors, bankers, and bondholders. But the payment of dividends to shareholders is another matter. Many companies can survive, and even thrive, without such payouts. Investors must keep an eye on the company's dividend policy and understand what it may mean. For most companies, for example, regular dividend boosts in the face of irregular earnings can be a warning signal. Companies with high dividends and rising debt may be borrowing money to pay shareholders. On the other hand, low dividends may not be a negative sign, because they may mean high returns through market appreciation. Presumably, investors for whom regular dividends are important tend to buy shares in companies that pay periodic dividends, and those for whom growth in the share price (capital gains) is more important tend to buy shares in companies that retain earnings.

BUSINESS INSIGHT

INVESTOR PERSPECTIVE

As the economy continues to deteriorate, a growing number of blue-chip Canadian companies are facing reduced profits and have slashed their dividends in order to conserve cash. Reducing or eliminating dividends has made the shares much less attractive to investors.

This was evident when Sherritt International Corp.'s share price dropped 14% as investors expressed their dismay at the news that the natural resources company planned to discontinue its quarterly dividend because its earnings had been hurt by the declining price of commodities. "If you start to cut [the dividend], you're pulling the rug out from under investors," said one market analyst. "It's a tough time to be taking that stability away from your investors."

Source: Caroline Alphonso, "Dividend Cuts Raise Investor Ire," *The Globe and Mail*, November 28, 2001, B1.

Entries for Cash Dividends

Three dates are important in connection with dividends: (1) the declaration date, (2) the record date, and (3) the payment date. Accounting entries are required on the declaration date and the payment date.

On the declaration date, the board of directors formally authorizes the cash dividend and announces it to shareholders. The declaration of a cash dividend commits the corporation to a binding legal obligation. Thus, an entry is required to recognize the increase in Cash Dividends (which results in a decrease in Retained Earnings) and the increase in the liability Dividends Payable.

To illustrate, assume that on December 1, 2004, the directors of Media General Inc. declare a $0.50 per share cash dividend on 100,000 common shares. The dividend is $50,000 (100,000 × $0.50), and the entry to record the declaration is:

A = L + SE
+50,000 −50,000

Cash flows: no effect

		Declaration Date		
Dec. 1	Cash Dividends		50,000	
	Dividends Payable			50,000
	(To record declaration of cash dividend)			

Dividends Payable is a current liability: it will normally be paid within the next month or so.

At the record date, ownership of the shares is determined to establish who should be paid the dividend. The shareholders' records maintained by the corporation supply this information. For Media General, the record date is December 22. No entry is required on the record date because the corporation's liability recognized on the declaration date is unchanged:

Helpful Hint The record date is important in determining the dividend to be paid to each shareholder but not the total dividend.

	Record Date		
Dec. 22	No entry necessary		

On the payment date, dividend cheques are mailed to the shareholders and the payment of the dividend is recorded. If January 20 is the payment date for Media General, the entry on that date is:

	Payment Date		
Jan. 20	Dividends Payable	50,000	
	Cash		50,000
	(To record payment of cash dividend)		

A   =   L   +   SE
−50,000   −50,000

Cash flows: −50,000

Note that payment of the dividend reduces both current assets and current liabilities, but it has no effect on shareholders' equity. The cumulative effect of the declaration and payment of a cash dividend on a company's financial statements is to **decrease both shareholders' equity and total assets**.

STOCK DIVIDENDS

A stock dividend is a pro rata distribution of the corporation's own shares to shareholders. Whereas a cash dividend is paid in cash, a stock dividend is distributed in shares. **A stock dividend results in a decrease in retained earnings and an increase in share capital.** Unlike a cash dividend, a stock dividend does not change total shareholders' equity or total assets.

Note that since a stock dividend neither increases nor decreases the assets in the company, investors are not receiving anything they didn't already own. In a sense, it is like ordering a piece of pie and cutting it into smaller pieces. You are not initially better off, but you have your pieces of pie.

To illustrate a stock dividend, assume that you have a 2% ownership interest in Cetus Inc.; you own 20 of its 1,000 common shares. If Cetus declares a 10% stock dividend, 100 shares (1,000 × 10%) would be issued. You would receive two shares (2% × 100), but your ownership interest would remain at 2% (22 ÷ 1,100). You now own more shares, but your ownership interest has not changed.

What then are the purposes and benefits of a stock dividend? Corporations generally issue stock dividends for one of the following reasons:

1. To satisfy shareholders' dividend expectations while conserving cash.
2. To increase the marketability of the shares by increasing the number of shares and thereby decreasing the market price per share. Decreasing the market price of the shares makes it easier for smaller investors to purchase them.
3. To emphasize that a portion of shareholders' equity has been permanently reinvested in the business and is therefore unavailable for cash dividends.

The size of the stock dividend and the value to be assigned to each dividend share are determined by the board of directors when the dividend is declared. The *Canada Business Corporations Act* recommends that stock dividends be valued based on the **fair market value per share** at the declaration date, and it is widespread practice to do so.

Entries for Stock Dividends

To illustrate the accounting for stock dividends, assume that Medland Corporation has a balance of $300,000 in retained earnings and declares a 10% stock dividend on its 50,000 common shares. The fair market value of its shares is $15 per share. The number of shares to be issued is 5,000 (10% × 50,000), and the total amount to be debited to Stock Dividends is $75,000 (5,000 × $15). The entry to record this transaction at the declaration date is:

A = L + SE
-75,000
+75,000

Cash flows: no effect

Stock Dividends	75,000	
Common Stock Dividends Distributable		75,000
(To record declaration of 10% stock dividend)		

Note that at the declaration date the Stock Dividends account is increased by the fair market value of the shares issued; Common Stock Dividends Distributable is increased by the same amount.

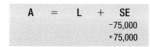

Helpful Hint Note that the dividend account title is "Distributable" not "Payable."

Common Stock Dividends Distributable is a shareholders' equity account reported in the Share Capital section. It is not a liability, because assets will not be used to pay the dividend.

As with cash dividends, no entry is required at the record date. When the dividend shares are issued, Common Stock Dividends Distributable is decreased and Common Shares is increased as follows:

A = L + SE
-75,000
+75,000

Cash flows: no effect

Common Stock Dividends Distributable	75,000	
Common Shares		75,000
(To record issue of 5,000 shares in a stock dividend)		

Effects of Stock Dividends

How do stock dividends affect shareholders' equity? They change the composition of shareholders' equity, because a portion of retained earnings is transferred to share capital. However, **total shareholders' equity remains the same.** These effects are shown in Illustration 11-5 for Medland Corporation.

Illustration 11-5
Stock dividend effects

	Before Stock Dividend	After Stock Dividend
Shareholders' equity		
Common shares	$500,000	$575,000
Retained earnings	300,000	225,000
Total shareholders' equity	$800,000	$800,000
Number of shares	50,000	55,000

In this example, total share capital is increased by $75,000 and retained earnings is decreased by the same amount. Note also that total shareholders' equity remains unchanged at $800,000.

STOCK SPLITS

A stock split, like a stock dividend, involves the issue of additional shares to shareholders according to their percentage ownership. However, a stock split results in a reduction in the legal capital per share and is usually much larger than a stock dividend. The purpose of a stock split is to increase the marketability of the shares by lowering the market value per share. A lower market value increases investor interest and makes it easier for the corporation to issue additional shares.

The effect of a split on market value is generally inversely proportional to the size of the split. For example, after a two-for-one stock split, the market value of Scotiabank common shares fell from $70 to $35. In announcing the split, Robert Chisholm, Scotiabank vice-chair, said, "This share split makes the bank's shares more affordable for the average Canadian investor."

In a stock split, the number of shares is increased by a specified proportion. For example, in a two-for-one split, one no par value share is exchanged for two no par value shares. **A stock split does not have any effect on total share capital, retained earnings, or total shareholders' equity.** However, the number of shares increases. These effects are shown in Illustration 11-6, assuming that instead of issuing a 10% stock dividend, Medland splits its 50,000 common shares on a two-for-one basis.

	Before Stock Split	After Stock Split
Shareholders' equity		
Common shares	$500,000	$500,000
Retained earnings	300,000	300,000
Total shareholders' equity	$800,000	$800,000
Number of shares	50,000	100,000

Illustration 11-6
Stock split effects

Because a stock split does not affect the balances in any shareholders' equity accounts, **it is not necessary to journalize a stock split.** However, a memorandum entry explaining the effect of the split is typically made.

BUSINESS INSIGHT

INVESTOR PERSPECTIVE

A wave of reverse stock splits is underway as many companies—particularly in the struggling technology sector—try to turn around sinking share prices. Some companies have seen their share prices fall to the point where they're in jeopardy of being delisted from stock market exchanges. Reverse stock splits—where the number of shares is reduced by exchanging a multiple of shares for a single share—appear to be an attractive and inexpensive method of boosting a company's share price. Handheld maker Palm, Inc. was forced to take this route to ensure its shares didn't fall into penny stock status and trade below the Nasdaq's $1 minimum price in 2002. Palm's reverse stock split exchanged twenty shares for one.

COMPARISON OF EFFECTS

Significant differences between cash dividends, stock dividends, and stock splits are shown in Illustration 11-7. In the illustration, "NE" means "no effect."

Item	Cash Dividend	Stock Dividend	Stock Split
Total assets	Decrease	NE	NE
Total liabilities	NE	NE	NE
Total shareholders' equity	Decrease	NE	NE
Total share capital	NE	Increase	NE
Total retained earnings	Decrease	Decrease	NE
Number of shares	NE	Increase	Increase

Illustration 11-7
Effects of cash dividends, stock dividends, and stock splits

A passion for food... *and a lot more!*

BEFORE YOU GO ON...

● **REVIEW IT**

1. What factors affect the size of a company's cash dividend?
2. Why do companies issue stock dividends? Why do companies declare stock splits?
3. Did Loblaw repurchase any common shares in 2002? Did it declare any dividends? Stock splits? The answers to these questions are provided at the end of this chapter.
4. Contrast the effects of a stock dividend and a two-for-one stock split on (a) shareholders' equity and (b) the number of shares.

● **DO IT**

Due to five years of record earnings at Sing CD Corporation, the market price of its 500,000 common shares tripled from $15 per share to $45. During this period, share capital remained the same at $2,000,000. Retained earnings increased from $1,500,000 to $10,000,000. President Joan Elbert is considering either a 10% stock dividend or a two-for-one stock split. She asks you to show the before-and-after effects of each option on the Common Shares and Retained Earnings accounts.

Action Plan

- Calculate the stock dividend effects on retained earnings by multiplying the stock dividend percentage by the number of existing shares to determine the number of new shares to be issued. Multiply the number of new shares by the market price of the shares.
- A stock dividend increases the number of shares and affects both the Common Shares and Retained Earnings account.
- A stock split increases the number of shares but does not affect the Common Shares or Retained Earnings accounts.

Solution

The stock dividend amount is $2,250,000 [(500,000 × 10%) × $45]. The effects in the shareholders' equity accounts of each option are as follows:

	Original Balances	After Stock Dividend	After Stock Split
Common shares	$ 2,000,000	$ 4,250,000	$ 2,000,000
Retained earnings	10,000,000	7,750,000	10,000,000
Total shareholders' equity	$12,000,000	$12,000,000	$12,000,000
Number of shares	500,000	550,000	1,000,000

Retained Earnings

STUDY OBJECTIVE
5

Identify the items that affect retained earnings.

Retained earnings are net earnings that are retained in the business. That is, retained earnings consist of the cumulative total of net earnings less dividends since incorporation. The balance in retained earnings is part of the shareholders' claim on the total assets of the corporation. It does not, however, represent a claim on any specific asset. Nor can the amount of retained earnings be associated with the balance of any asset account. For example, a $100,000 balance in retained earnings does not mean that there should be $100,000 in cash. Illustration 11-8 shows the amounts of retained earnings and cash in selected companies for 2002.

Illustration 11-8
Retained earnings and
cash balances

	(in millions)	
Company	Retained Earnings	Cash
BCE	$712.0	$569.0
Canadian Tire	973.0	578.8
Corel (USD)	(318.0)	18.9
Noranda	896.0	285.0

When expenses exceed revenues, a **net loss** results. In contrast to net earnings, a net loss decreases retained earnings. If cumulative losses exceed cumulative earnings over a company's life, a debit balance in Retained Earnings results. A debit balance in retained earnings, such as that of Research In Motion Limited, is identified as a deficit and is reported as a deduction in the shareholders' equity section of the balance sheet, as shown in Illustration 11-9.

Illustration 11-9
Shareholders' equity with
deficit

RESEARCH IN MOTION LIMITED **Balance Sheet (partial)** **March 1, 2003** **(in U.S. thousands)**	
Shareholders' equity	
Capital stock	$874,377
Deficit	(169,643)
Total shareholders' equity	$704,734

RETAINED EARNINGS RESTRICTIONS

The balance in retained earnings is generally available for dividend declarations. In some cases, however, there may be retained earnings restrictions. These make a portion of the balance currently unavailable for dividends. Restrictions result from one or more of these types of causes: legal or contractual obligations or voluntary choices. Retained earnings restrictions are generally disclosed in the notes to the financial statements.

Financial Statement Presentation of Shareholders' Equity

BALANCE SHEET PRESENTATION

In the shareholders' equity section of the balance sheet, **contributed capital** and **retained earnings** are reported, and the specific sources of contributed capital are identified if multiple sources exist. Within contributed capital, share capital is normally the only classification that is disclosed, unless additional contributed capital is present, as it was for Corel in Illustration 11-9. **Share capital** consists of preferred and common shares. Preferred shares are shown before common shares because of the former's preferential rights. Information about the legal capital, shares authorized, and shares issued is reported for each class of shares.

The shareholders' equity section of the balance sheet of Graber Inc. is presented in Illustration 11-10.

STUDY OBJECTIVE
6

Indicate how shareholders' equity is presented in the financial statements.

Illustration 11-10
Shareholders' equity
section of the balance
sheet

GRABER INC. Balance Sheet (partial) December 31, 2004		
Shareholders' equity		
Share capital		
$9 preferred shares, no par value, cumulative, redeemable at $120, 10,000 shares authorized, 6,000 shares issued		$ 630,000
Common shares, no par value, unlimited number of shares authorized, 400,000 shares issued	$2,000,000	
Common stock dividends distributable	50,000	2,050,000
Total share capital		2,680,000
Retained earnings (Note R)		1,160,000
Total shareholders' equity		$3,840,000

Note R: Loan agreements contain, among other covenants, a restriction on the payment of dividends, which limits future dividend payments to 75% of net earnings.

The shareholders' equity section for Graber Inc. includes most of the accounts discussed in this chapter. Graber has 6,000 preferred shares issued, which have a $9 per share annual dividend rate and, are redeemable by the company at $120 per share. The disclosures pertaining to Graber's common shares indicate that 400,000 shares are issued with an unlimited number authorized. Note that Common Stock Dividends Distributable is shown under Share Capital. A retained earnings restriction is disclosed in the notes. In published annual reports, subclassifications within the shareholders' equity section are seldom presented.

CASH FLOW STATEMENT PRESENTATION

The balance sheet presents the balances of a company's shareholders' equity accounts at a point in time. Information about cash inflows and outflows during the year that resulted from equity transactions is reported in the financing activities section of the cash flow statement. Illustration 11-11 presents the cash flows from financing activities from Nike's cash flow statement.

From the equity-related information, we learn that the company's repurchase of shares exceeded its issues of new shares, including those from the exercise of stock options. Nike also paid cash dividends to its common and preferred shareholders during the year.

Illustration 11-11
Financing activities
section of the cash flow
statement

NIKE INC. Cash Flow Statement (partial) Year Ended May 31, 2002 (in U.S. millions)	
Cash provided (used) by financing activities	
Proceeds from long-term debt issue	$ 329.9
Reductions in long-term debt	(80.3)
Decrease in notes payable	(431.5)
Proceeds from exercise of stock options and other share issues	59.5
Repurchase of shares	(226.9)
Dividends—common	(128.9)
Cash used by financing activities	$(478.2)

BEFORE YOU GO ON...

● REVIEW IT

1. Identify the classifications within the shareholders' equity section of a balance sheet.
2. Where are shareholders' equity transactions reported in a cash flow statement?

Measuring Corporate Performance

Investors are interested in both a company's dividend record and its earnings performance. Although they are often parallel, that is not always the case. Thus, each should be investigated separately.

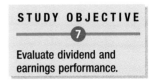

STUDY OBJECTIVE

⑦

Evaluate dividend and earnings performance.

DIVIDEND RECORD

One way that companies reward investors for their investment is to pay them dividends. The payout ratio measures the percentage of earnings distributed in the form of cash dividends. It is calculated by dividing cash dividends by net earnings. From the information shown below, the payout ratios for Nike in 2002 and 2001 are calculated in Illustration 11-12.

(in U.S. millions)	2002	2001
Dividends	$128.6	$129.6
Net earnings	663.3	589.7

Illustration 11-12
Nike payout ratio

$$\text{PAYOUT RATIO} = \frac{\text{CASH DIVIDENDS}}{\text{NET EARNINGS}}$$

(in U.S. millions)	2002	2001
Payout Ratio	$\frac{\$128.6}{\$663.3} = 19.4\%$	$\frac{\$129.6}{\$589.7} = 22.0\%$
Industry average	61.1%	64.9%

Companies that have high growth rates are characterized by low payout ratios because they reinvest most of their net earnings in the business. Thus, a low payout ratio is not necessarily bad news. Companies that believe they have many good opportunities for growth, such as Nike, will reinvest those funds in the company rather than pay high dividends. So it is not surprising that Nike's payout ratio is far lower than the industry's. In fact it is difficult to compare a specific company's payout ratio to industry averages because so many individual factors affect a company's dividend policy.

Dividend payout ratios are currently low relative to historical payout rates. However, low dividend payments, or a cut in dividend payments, might also signal that a company has liquidity or solvency problems and is trying to free up cash by not paying dividends. In other words, the reason for low dividend payments should always be investigated.

Listed in Illustration 11-13 are payout ratios in recent years of four well-known companies.

Ilustration 11-13
Variability of payout ratios among companies

Company	Payout Ratio
Bank of Montreal	48.5%
Bombardier	34.0%
Molson	19.9%
Corel	0.0%

BUSINESS INSIGHT

INVESTOR PERSPECTIVE

Traditionally, technology companies have not paid dividends, arguing they need to conserve their cash for innovation and expansion. Less than 10% of technology companies pay a regular dividend, compared to 50% of non-technology companies. Analysts have argued for years that technology heavyweights should eliminate this double standard.

The worst offender, Microsoft, finally caved in early in 2003 when it announced it would start paying dividends. Microsoft will still have lots of cash to hoard. It will pay out a mere U.S.$850 million a year in dividends, while still generating U.S.$7 billion in excess cash a year. This will put a great deal of pressure on other cash-rich technology companies to start doing the same.

Source: Fabrice Taylor, "Dividend Trend Will Expose Worst Techs for What They Are," *The Globe and Mail*, January 21, 2003, B17.

EARNINGS PERFORMANCE

Another way to measure corporate performance is through profitability. A widely used ratio that measures profitability from the common shareholders' viewpoint is the return on common shareholders' equity. This ratio shows how many dollars were earned for each dollar invested by common shareholders. It is calculated by dividing net earnings available to common shareholders (Net earnings − Preferred share dividends) by average common shareholders' equity. Common shareholders' equity is total shareholders' equity less the legal capital of any preferred shares.

From the additional information presented below, Nike's return on common shareholders' equity ratios are calculated for 2002 and 2001 in Illustration 11-14.

(in U.S. millions)	2002	2001	2000
Net earnings	$ 663.3	$ 589.7	$ 579.1
Common shareholders' equity	3,839.0	3,494.5	3,136.0

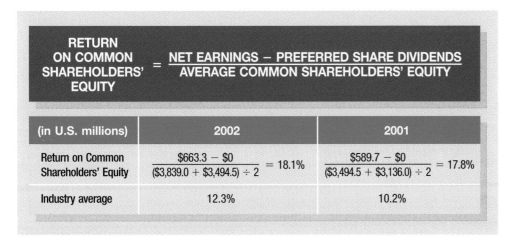

Illustration 11-14
Nike return on common
shareholders' equity

From 2001 to 2002, Nike's return on common shareholders' equity increased slightly, from 17.8% to 18.1%. It continues to exceed the industry average. Return on equity is a widely published figure. Recently, the highest return on equity among Canada's top 500 corporations was reported by Calgary-based Hurricane Hydrocarbons Ltd.—66%.

DEBT VERSUS EQUITY DECISION

To obtain large amounts of long-term capital, corporate managers must decide whether to issue bonds or to sell common shares. Bonds have three primary advantages relative to common shares, as shown in Illustration 11-15.

Bond Financing	Advantages
	1. **Shareholder control is not affected.** Bondholders do not have voting rights, so shareholders retain full control of the company.
	2. **Tax savings result.** Bond interest is deductible for income tax purposes; dividends are not.
	3. **The return on common shareholders' equity may be higher.** Although bond interest expense reduces net earnings, the return on common shareholders' equity is often higher under bond financing because no additional shares are issued.

Illustration 11-15
Advantages of bond
financing over common
shares

How does the debt versus equity decision affect the return on common shareholders' equity ratio? Illustration 11-16 shows that the return on common shareholders's equity is affected by the return on assets ratio and the amount of leverage a company uses—that is, by the company's reliance on debt (often measured by the debt to total assets ratio). If a company wants to increase its return on common shareholders' equity, it can either increase its return on assets or increase its reliance on debt financing.

Illustration 11-16
Components of the return on common shareholders' equity

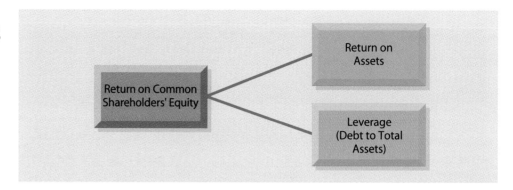

To illustrate the potential effect of debt financing on the return on common shareholders' equity, assume that Microsystems Inc. is considering two plans for financing the construction of a new $5-million plant: Plan A involves issuing 200,000 common shares at the current market price of $25 per share. Plan B involves issuing $5 million of 6% bonds at face value. Earnings before interest and taxes on the new plant will be $1.5 million; income taxes are expected to be 30%. Microsystems currently has 100,000 common shares issued at $25 per share. The alternative effects on the return on common shareholders' equity are shown in Illustration 11-17.

Illustration 11-17
Effects on return on common shareholders' equity of issuing debt vs. shares

	Plan A: Issue shares	Plan B: Issue bonds
Earnings before interest and taxes	$1,500,000	$1,500,000
Interest (6% × $5,000,000)	—	300,000
Earnings before income taxes	1,500,000	1,200,000
Income tax expense (30%)	450,000	360,000
Net earnings	$1,050,000	$ 840,000
Common shareholders' equity	$7,500,000	$2,500,000
Return on common shareholders' equity	14%	34%

Note that with long-term debt financing (bonds), net earnings is $210,000 lower ($1,050,000 − $840,000). However, the return on common shareholders' equity increases from 14% to 34% with the use of debt financing because there is less common shareholders' equity to spread the earnings across. In general, as long as the return on assets rate exceeds the rate paid on debt, the return on common shareholders' equity will be increased by the use of debt.

After seeing this illustration, one might ask why companies don't rely almost exclusively on debt financing, rather than equity. Debt has one major disadvantage: The company locks in fixed payments that must be made in good times and bad. **Interest must be paid on a periodic basis, and the principal (face value) of the bonds must be paid at maturity.** A company with fluctuating earnings and a relatively weak cash position may experience great difficulty in meeting interest requirements in periods of low earnings. In the extreme, this can result in bankruptcy. With common share financing, on the other hand, the company can decide to pay low (or no) dividends if earnings are low.

BEFORE YOU GO ON . . .

● **REVIEW IT**

1. What measure can be used to evaluate a company's dividend record, and how is it calculated?
2. What factors affect the return on common shareholders' equity ratio?
3. What are the advantages and disadvantages of debt and equity financing?

Decision Toolkit

DECISION CHECKPOINTS	INFO NEEDED FOR DECISION	TOOL TO USE FOR DECISION	HOW TO EVALUATE RESULTS
What portion of its earnings does the company pay out in dividends?	Net earnings and total cash dividends	$$\frac{\text{Payout}}{\text{ratio}} = \frac{\text{Cash dividends}}{\text{Net earnings}}$$	A low ratio suggests that the company is retaining its earnings for investment in future growth.
What is the company's return on its common shareholders' investment?	Earnings available to common shareholders and average common shareholders' equity	$$\frac{\text{Return on}}{\substack{\text{common}\\\text{shareholders'}\\\text{equity}}} = \frac{\substack{\text{Net earnings}\\-\ \text{Preferred}\\\text{share dividends}}}{\substack{\text{Average common}\\\text{shareholders'}\\\text{equity}}}$$	A high measure suggests a strong earnings performance from the common shareholders' perspective.

Using the Decision Toolkit

Reebok is one of Nike's fiercest competitors. After bottoming out at the end of 1999, Reebok's shares have rebounded sharply.

Instructions

The following facts are available for Reebok. Using this information, evaluate its (1) dividend record and (2) earnings performance, and contrast them with those of Nike for 2001 and 2002. Nike's earnings per share and price-earnings ratios at the end of 2002 were $2.61 and 17.8 times, respectively:

(in U.S. millions except per share data)	2002	2001	2000
Dividends	$ 0	$ 0	$ 0
Net earnings	126.5	102.7	80.9
Common shareholders' equity	884.6	719.9	607.9
Average number of common shares	59.6	58.5	56.9
Share price	29.40	26.50	27.34

Solution

1. One measure to evaluate a company's dividend record is the payout ratio. For Reebok, this measure in 2002 and 2001 is calculated as shown here:

	2002	2001
Payout ratio	$\dfrac{\$0}{\$126.5} = 0\%$	$\dfrac{\$0}{\$102.7} = 0\%$

Nike's payout ratio declined slightly in 2002, from 22.0% to 19.4%, while Reebok paid no dividends. Both companies' payout ratios are far less than the industry average.

2. There are many measures of earnings performance. Some of those presented in the book so far include earnings per share (Chapter 2), the price-earnings ratio (Chapter 2), and the return on common shareholders' equity ratio (this chapter). These measures for Reebok in 2002 and 2001 are calculated as shown here:

	2002	2001
Earnings per share	$\dfrac{\$126.5 - \$0}{59.6} = \$2.12$	$\dfrac{\$102.7 - \$0}{58.5} = \$1.76$
Price-earnings ratio	$\dfrac{\$29.40}{\$2.12} = 13.9$ times	$\dfrac{\$26.50}{\$1.76} = 15.1$ times
Return on common shareholders' equity	$\dfrac{\$126.5 - \$0}{(\$884.6 + \$719.9) \div 2} = 15.8\%$	$\dfrac{\$102.7 - \$0}{(\$719.9 + \$607.9) \div 2} = 15.5\%$

From 2001 to 2002, Reebok's earnings increased on both a total and per share basis. However, Reebok's price-earnings ratio decreased to 13.9 times, perhaps hinting that investors believe that the shares are overpriced. Investors appear to be favouring Nike, with its higher P-E ratio of 17.8 times.

Reebok's return on shareholders' equity increased only marginally in 2002. This means that Reebok's shareholders' equity increased roughly proportionately to its increase in net earnings. Reebok's 15.8% return on shareholders' equity is lower than Nike's 18.1%. Both companies' returns exceed the industry average.

NAVIGATOR

Summary of Study Objectives

① *Identify and discuss the major characteristics of a corporation and its shares.* The major characteristics of a corporation are separate legal existence, limited liability of shareholders, transferable ownership rights, the ability to acquire capital, continuous life, corporation management, government regulations, and corporate income taxes.

Companies issue shares for sale to the public. After the initial share offering, the shares trade amongst investors and do not affect the company's financial position. A company can also reacquire its own shares from investors, but must cancel the shares upon acquisition.

② *Record the issue of common shares.* When no par value common shares are issued for cash, the entire proceeds from the issue become legal capital and are credited to the Common Shares account.

③ *Differentiate preferred shares from common shares.* Preferred shares have contractual provisions that give them priority over common shares in certain areas. Typically, preferred shareholders have a preference as to (a) dividends and (b) assets in the event of liquidation. However, they do not have voting rights.

In addition, preferred shares may be cumulative, convertible, redeemable, and/or retractable. Cumulative preferred shares give preferred shareholders the right to receive the current-year dividend and any unpaid prior-year dividends before common shareholders can receive any dividend. Convertible preferred shares entitle the holder to convert those shares to common shares at a specified ratio. The redemption feature gives the issuing corporation the right to purchase these shares from shareholders at specified future dates and prices. Retractable preferred shares give the shareholder the option of selling the shares to the corporation at specified future dates and prices.

④ *Prepare the entries for cash dividends, stock dividends, and stock splits, and understand their financial impact.* Entries for both cash and stock dividends are required at the declaration date and the payment or distribution date. There is no entry (other than a memo entry) for a stock split. Cash dividends reduce assets (cash) and shareholders' equity (retained earnings). Stock dividends increase common shares and decrease retained earnings but do not affect assets, liabilities, or shareholders' equity *in total*. Stock splits also have no impact on assets, liabilities, or shareholders' equity. The number of shares increases with both stock dividends and stock splits.

⑤ *Identify the items that affect retained earnings.* Additions to retained earnings consist of net earnings. Deductions consist of net loss, and cash and stock dividends. In some instances, portions of retained earnings are restricted, making them unavailable for the payment of dividends.

⑥ *Indicate how shareholders' equity is presented in the financial statements.* In the shareholders' equity section of the balance sheet, share capital and retained earnings are reported separately. Cash inflows and outflows for the issue or reacquisition of shares, or a payment of dividends, are reported in the financing section of the cash flow statement. Notes to the financial statements explain restrictions to retained earnings, and dividends in arrears, if any.

7 *Evaluate dividend and earnings performance.* A company's dividend record can be evaluated by looking at what percentage of net earnings it chooses to pay out in dividends, as measured by the dividend payout ratio (dividends divided by net earnings). Earnings performance is measured with the return on common shareholders' equity ratio (earnings available to common shareholders divided by average common shareholders' equity).

Decision Toolkit—A Summary

Decision Toolkit Summary

DECISION CHECKPOINTS	INFO NEEDED FOR DECISION	TOOL TO USE FOR DECISION	HOW TO EVALUATE RESULTS
Should the company incorporate?	Capital needs, growth expectations, type of business, tax status	Corporations have limited liability, easier capital-raising ability, and professional managers. They may suffer from additional government regulations and separation of ownership from management. Income taxes may be higher or lower for a corporation.	Carefully weigh the costs and benefits in light of the particular circumstances.
What portion of its earnings does the company pay out in dividends?	Net earnings and total cash dividends	$\text{Payout ratio} = \dfrac{\text{Cash dividends}}{\text{Net earnings}}$	A low ratio suggests that the company is retaining its earnings for investment in future growth.
What is the company's return on its common shareholders' investment?	Earnings available to common shareholders and average common shareholders' equity	$\text{Return on common shareholders' equity} = \dfrac{\text{Net earnings} - \text{Preferred share dividends}}{\text{Average common shareholders' equity}}$	A high measure suggests a strong earnings performance from the common shareholders' perspective.

NAVIGATOR

Glossary

Authorized shares The amount of share capital that a corporation is authorized to sell. The amount may be unlimited or specified. (p. 519)

Cash dividend A pro rata distribution of cash to shareholders. (p. 525)

Convertible preferred shares Preferred shares that the shareholder can convert into common shares at a specified ratio. (p. 524)

Corporation A company organized as a separate legal entity, with most of the rights and privileges of a person. Shares are evidence of ownership. (p. 514)

Cumulative A feature of preferred shares entitling the shareholder to receive current and unpaid prior-year dividends before common shareholders receive any dividends. (p. 524)

Declaration date The date the board of directors formally declares a dividend and announces it to shareholders. (p. 526)

Deficit A debit balance in retained earnings. (p. 531)

Dividend A distribution by a corporation to its shareholders on a pro rata (proportional) basis. (p. 525)

Dividends in arrears Preferred dividends that were scheduled to be declared but were not declared during a given period. (p. 524)

Initial public offering (IPO) The initial offering of a corporation's shares to the public. (p. 519)

Legal capital The amount per share that must be retained in the business for the protection of corporate creditors. (p. 520)

Leverage A measure of the company's reliance on debt financing. (p. 535)

Noncumulative Preferred shares that are entitled to the current dividend, but not to any unpaid amounts from prior years. (p. 524)

No par value shares Share capital that has not been pre-assigned a legal capital value. (p. 520)

Organization costs Costs (e.g., legal, accounting, etc.) of forming a corporation. (p. 517)

Payment date The date dividend cheques are mailed to shareholders. (p. 527)

Payout ratio A measure of the percentage of earnings distributed in the form of cash dividends to common shareholders. It is calculated by dividing cash dividends by net earnings. (p. 533)

Preferred shares Share capital that has contractual preferences over common shares in certain areas. (p. 523)

Private corporation A corporation that has only a few shareholders and whose shares are not available for sale to the general public. (p. 514)

Public corporation A corporation that may have many shareholders and whose shares are regularly traded on a stock exchange. (p. 514)

Record date The date when ownership of shares is determined for dividend purposes. (p. 527)

Redeemable (callable) preferred shares Preferred shares that grant the issuer the right to purchase the shares from shareholders at specified future dates and prices. (p. 524)

Retained earnings Net earnings that are retained in the business. (p. 530)

Retained earnings restrictions Circumstances that make a portion of retained earnings currently unavailable for dividends. (p. 531)

Retractable preferred shares Preferred shares that grant the shareholder the right to redeem the shares at specified future dates and prices. (p. 524)

Return on common shareholders' equity A measure of profitability from the shareholders' point of view. It is calculated by dividing net earnings minus preferred dividends by average common shareholders' equity. (p. 534)

Share capital The amount paid to the corporation by shareholders in exchange for shares of ownership. (p. 522)

Stock dividend A pro rata distribution of the corporation's own shares to shareholders. (p. 527)

Stock option A right granted to purchase a specified number of shares at a specified price during a specified time period. (p. 521)

Stock split The issue of additional shares to shareholders accompanied by a reduction in the legal capital per share. (p. 528)

Demonstration Problem

Rolman Corporation is authorized to issue 1,000,000 common shares. In its first year, the company has the following share transactions:

Jan. 10   Issued 400,000 shares at $8 per share.
Sept. 1   Declared a 5% stock dividend to shareholders of record on September 15, distributable September 30. The fair market value of the shares on this date was $10 per share.
Dec. 24   Declared a cash dividend of $0.10 per share to shareholders of record on January 15, payable January 31.

Instructions

(a) Journalize the transactions.
(b) Prepare the shareholders' equity section of the balance sheet assuming the company had net earnings of $392,600 for the year ended December 31, 2004.

Solution to Demonstration Problem

(a)

Jan. 10	Cash (400,000 × $8)	3,200,000	
	Common Shares		3,200,000
	(To record issue of 400,000 common shares)		
Sept. 1	Stock Dividends (400,000 × 5% = 20,000 × $10)	200,000	
	Stock Dividends Distributable		200,000
	(To record declaration of 5% stock dividend)		
Sept. 30	Stock Dividends Distributable	200,000	
	Common Shares		200,000
	(To record issue of 5% stock dividend)		
Dec. 24	Cash Dividends (400,000 + 20,000 = 420,000 × $0.10)	42,000	
	Dividends Payable		42,000
	(To record declaration of $0.10 per share cash dividend)		

Action Plan

• Credit Common Shares for the full amount of the proceeds.
• Apply the stock dividend percentage to the number of shares issued. Multiply the new shares to be issued by the fair market value of the shares.
• Recall that the Stock Dividends Distributable account is not a liability.
• Keep a running total of the number of shares issued. Make sure you calculate the cash dividend on the total number of shares issued to date.

(b)

ROLMAN CORPORATION
Balance Sheet (partial)
December 31, 2004

Shareholders' equity		
Common shares, no par value, 1,000,000 shares authorized, 420,000 shares issued	$3,400,000[1]	
Retained earnings	150,600[2]	
Total shareholders' equity	$3,550,600	

[1] $3,200,000 + $200,000 = $3,400,000
[2] $392,600 − $200,000 − $42,000 = $150,600

Self-Study Questions

Answers are at the end of the chapter.

(SO 1)   1. Which of these is *not* a major advantage of a corporation?
   (a) Separate legal existence
   (b) Separation of ownership and management
   (c) Government regulations
   (d) Transferable ownership rights

(SO 1)   2. Which of these statements is *false*?
   (a) Ownership of common shares gives the owner a voting right.
   (b) The shareholders' equity section begins with share capital.
   (c) The authorization of share capital results in a formal accounting entry.
   (d) The market value of a share is the same as its no par value on the issue date.

(SO 1)   3. A company will buy back its own shares:
   (a) to force the share price up.
   (b) to force the share price down.
   (c) to increase the number of shares available for dividends.
   (d) to save cash.

(SO 2)   4. ABC Corporation issues 1,000 common shares at $12 per share. When the transaction is recorded, credits are made to:
   (a) Investments, $12,000.
   (b) Common Shares, $12,000.
   (c) Retained Earnings, $12,000.
   (d) Gain on Sale of Shares, $12,000.

(SO 3)   5. Preferred shares may have priority over common shares *except* in:
   (a) dividends.
   (b) assets in the event of liquidation.
   (c) conversion.
   (d) voting.

(SO 4)   6. Entries for cash dividends are required on the:
   (a) declaration date and record date.
   (b) record date and payment date.
   (c) declaration date, record date, and payment date.
   (d) declaration date and payment date.

7. Which of these statements about stock dividends   (SO 4)
is *true*?
   (a) A debit should be made to Cash Dividends for the market value of the shares issued.
   (b) Market value per share should be assigned to the dividend shares.
   (c) A stock dividend decreases total shareholders' equity.
   (d) A stock dividend ordinarily will have no effect on total share capital.

8. Which of the following is not reported in a state-   (SO 5)
ment of retained earnings?
   (a) Cash dividend   (c) Stock split
   (b) Stock dividend   (d) Net earnings

9. The cash received on issuing shares would be re-   (SO 6)
ported in what section of the cash flow statement?
   (a) Operating activities
   (b) Investing activities
   (c) Financing activities
   (d) It is not reported in the cash flow statement.

10. The return on common shareholders' eq-   (SO 7)
uity is increased by all of the following except:
   (a) an increase in the return on assets.
   (b) an increase in the use of debt financing.
   (c) an increase in the company's share price.
   (d) an increase in net earnings.

11. Herb Fischer is nearing retirement and   (SO 7)
would like to invest in shares that will provide a good, steady income. Herb should choose shares with a:
   (a) high current ratio.
   (b) high payout ratio.
   (c) high earnings per share.
   (d) high price-earnings ratio.

Questions

(SO 1) 1. Pat Kabza, a student, asks for your help in understanding some corporation characteristics. Explain each of these to Pat:
(a) Separate legal existence
(b) Limited liability of shareholders
(c) Transferable ownership rights
(d) Continous life

(SO 1) 2. (a) Your friend R. Cedras cannot understand how income taxation can be both an advantage and a disadvantage for a corporation. Explain why this is true.
(b) Identify and explain two other advantages and disadvantages of a corporation.

(SO 1) 3. What are the basic ownership rights of common shareholders?

(SO 1) 4. WAT Inc.'s common shares have no par value and a current market value of $15. Explain why these amounts are different.

(SO 1) 5. Peter Ma purchases 100 common shares of Innovate.com for $10 per share from the company's initial public offering. Subsequently, Peter purchases 200 more Innovate.com shares for $15 each on the Toronto Stock Exchange, using his own Web Broker account. Explain the impact each of these transactions will have on Innovate.com's assets, liabilities, and shareholders' equity.

(SO 1) 6. Bombardier Inc.'s share price fell 9% when the company announced that it would not meet expected financial targets for the year ended January 31, 2003. Explain the effects of this decline in share price on Bombardier's financial statements.

(SO 1) 7. Letterman Corporation is authorized to issue 100,000 common shares. During its first two years of operation, Letterman issued 60,000 shares to shareholders and reacquired and cancelled 7,000 of these shares. After these transactions, how many shares are authorized and issued?

(SO 1) 8. For what reasons might a company repurchase some of its shares?

(SO 1) 9. Why is there so much controversy about the recording of stock options issued as executive compensation?

(SO 2) 10. Land with a fair market value of $125,000 is acquired by issuing common shares with a fair market value of $100,000. What value would this land be recorded at in the company's records?

(SO 3) 11. (a) What are the principal differences between common shares and preferred shares?
(b) Preferred shares may be cumulative. Discuss this feature.
(c) How are dividends in arrears presented in the financial statements?

(SO 4) 12. What three conditions must be met before a cash dividend is paid?

(SO 4) 13. Galena Ltd. declared a cash dividend on May 1, for shareholders of record on May 15, payable on May 31. Discuss the significance of each date and give the entry at each date.

(SO 4) 14. Contrast the effects of a cash dividend, stock dividend and stock split on (a) a corporation's balance sheet and (b) an individual shareholder's personal financial position.

(SO 4) 15. Jill Sims asks, "Since stock dividends don't change anything, why declare them?" What is your answer to Jill?

(SO 4) 16. Bella Corporation has 500,000 common shares authorized and 10,000 common shares issued, when it announces a two-for-one split. Before the split, the shares had a market price of $140 per share. After the split, how many shares will be authorized and issued? What will be the approximate market price per share?

(SO 5) 17. Identify the events that result in credits and debits to retained earnings.

(SO 5) 18. (a) What is the purpose of a retained earnings restriction?
(b) Identify the possible causes of retained earnings restrictions.

(SO 6) 19. Indicate how each of these accounts should be classified in the shareholders' equity section of the balance sheet:
(a) Common Shares
(b) Retained Earnings
(c) Stock Dividends Distributable
(d) Preferred Shares

(SO 6) 20. Explain where share transactions and dividend transactions are reported in the (a) cash flow statement, (b) balance sheet, and (c) statement of earnings.

(SO 7) 21. ⚒ Indicate whether each of the following is generally considered favourable or unfavourable by a potential investor:
(a) An increase in the payout ratio
(b) An increase in the return on common shareholders' equity
(c) An increase in debt to total assets
(d) An increase in the return on assets

(SO 7) 22. ⚒ Under what circumstances will the return on assets and return on common shareholders' equity ratios be equal?

(SO 7) 23. ⚒ Quan Corp. has a return on assets of 15%. It plans to issue bonds at 8% and use the cash to retire debt. What effect will this have on its debt to total assets and on its return on common shareholders' equity?

Brief Exercises

Cite advantages and dis-
advantages of a corporation.
(SO 1)

BE11-1   Tracy Bono is studying for her accounting mid-term examination. Identify for Tracy the advantages and disadvantages of the corporate form of business organization.

Evaluate impact of share
price on financial position.
(SO 1)

BE11-2   The share prices of technology companies started dropping like stones near the middle of the year 2000. Nortel Networks' share price, for example, dropped from a 52-week high of $124.50 in July 2000 to a low of $0.70 in September 2002. What is the impact of this drop in share price on Nortel's financial position?

Journalize issue of common
shares.
(SO 2)

BE11-3   On May 10, Armada Corporation issues 1,000 common shares for cash at $15 per share. Journalize the share issue.

Analyse noncash share issue.
(SO 2)

BE11-4   Intrawest Corporation issued 325,000 common shares to acquire the Raven golf resorts and Alpine Helicopters. The fair market value of these common shares at the time of acquisition was $9.1 million. If the fair market value of Raven and Alpine was $10 million at the time of acquisition, at what value did Intrawest record these assets and the issue of common shares?

Journalize issue of preferred
shares.
(SO 3)

BE11-5   Ozark Inc. issues 5,000 preferred shares for cash at $110 per share. Journalize the share issue.

Prepare entries for cash divi-
dend.
(SO 4)

BE11-6   The Seabee Corporation has 10,000 common shares. It declares a $1 per share cash dividend on November 1 to shareholders of record on December 1. The dividend is paid on December 31. Prepare the entries on the appropriate dates to record the cash dividend.

Prepare entries for stock divi-
dend.
(SO 4)

BE11-7   Satina Corporation has 100,000 common shares. It declares a 5% stock dividend on December 1, when the market value per share is $12. The dividend shares are issued on December 31. Prepare the entries for the declaration and distribution of the stock dividend.

Show before-and-after effects
of stock dividend.
(SO 4)

BE11-8   The shareholders' equity section of Chew Corporation's balance sheet consists of 100,000 common shares for $1,000,000, and retained earnings of $400,000. A 10% stock dividend is declared when the market value per share is $9. Show the before-and-after effects of the dividend on (1) share capital, (2) the number of shares, and (3) retained earnings.

Analyse impact of stock split.
(SO 4)

BE11-9   In April 2002, Call-Net Enterprises Inc., parent of Sprint Canada, announced a 20-to-1 reverse stock split. If a shareholder owned 100 shares before the split, how many Call-Net shares would he or she own immediately after the split? If the share price was $0.50 before the split, what would you anticipate the share price to be immediately after the split? Explain why Call-Net might have undertaken a reverse stock split.

Compare impact of cash divi-
dend, stock dividend, and
stock split.
(SO 4)

BE11-10   Indicate whether each of the following transactions would increase (+), decrease (−), or not affect (N/A) total assets, total liabilities, and total shareholders' equity.

Transaction	Assets	Liabilities	Shareholders' Equity
(a) Declared cash dividend.			
(b) Paid cash dividend declared in (a).			
(c) Declared stock dividend.			
(d) Distributed stock dividend declared in (c).			
(e) Split stock three-for-one.			

Prepare shareholders' equity
section.
(SO 6)

BE11-11   Kaposi Corporation has the following accounts at December 31, 2004: Common Shares, no par value, unlimited number of shares authorized, 5,000 shares issued, $50,000; Preferred Shares, $8 cumulative, no par value, unlimited number of shares authorized, 800 shares issued, $20,000; and Retained Earnings, $29,000. Prepare the shareholders' equity section of the balance sheet.

Calculate return on share-
holders' equity.
(SO 7)

BE11-12   Sleeman Breweries Ltd. reported the following selected information for the year ended December 31, 2002 (in thousands): net sales, $157,053; net earnings, $12,321; beginning common shareholders' equity, $73,088; and ending common shareholders' equity, $90,197. Calculate the return on common shareholders' equity.

Evaluate dividend record.
(SO 7)

BE11-13   Paul Schwartz, president of Schwartz Corporation, believes that it is good practice to maintain a constant payout of dividends relative to earnings. Last year, net earnings were $600,000, and the corporation paid $150,000 in dividends. This year, due to some unusual circumstances, the corporation had net earnings of $2,000,000. Paul expects next year's net earnings to be about $700,000. What was Schwartz Corporation's payout ratio last year? If it is to maintain the same payout ratio, what amount of dividends would it pay this year? Is this necessarily a good idea—that is, what are the pros and cons of maintaining a constant payout ratio in this scenario?

BE11-14 The share prices of dozens of high-tech companies soared in early to mid-2000. Take, for example, NHC Communications Inc., located in Quebec. Its share price went from a low of $0.08 to a high of $22, an increase of 27,500%! Yet NHC reported a loss of $2,180,000 and a 33% negative return on common shareholders' equity in this same period. Why do you think shareholders were anxious to pay increasing amounts for NHC's shares?

Evaluate factors affecting share price.
(SO 7)

Exercises

E11-1 Presented below is a stock market listing for Research In Motion's common shares:

Interpret stock market listing.
(SO 1)

365-day		stock	sym	div	high /bid	low /ask	close	chg	vol 100s	yld	p/e ratio
high	low										
32.35	13.19	RIM LTD.	RIM	0	32.35	31.33	32.05	+0.66	5509	0	N/A

Instructions
(a) What is the highest price RIM's shares traded for during the last year? The lowest?
(b) How many of RIM's common shares were sold on the trading day in question?
(c) If you had purchased 1,000 common shares at RIM's high price of the day of the above listing, what would the total cost of your share purchase be?
(d) What would be your likely motivation for purchasing these shares—future dividend income or price increase?
(e) What was the closing price of RIM's common shares on the previous day?

E11-2 Wendy's International, Inc. repurchased 525,000 common shares in February 2003 for U.S.$13.2 million. Wendy's also has a stock option plan for employees and outside directors to purchase the company's common shares. It makes no recognition of the options in its financial statements until they are exercised.

Discuss share repurchase and stock options.
(SO 1)

Instructions
(a) Explain how a repurchase of shares affects the number of shares authorized and issued, and the market value of the remaining shares.
(b) Speculate on why Wendy's may have repurchased its shares.
(c) What is the financial impact of not recognizing stock options in the financial statements when the options are first issued? That is, identify any accounts that you believe are understated or overstated.

E11-3 Santiago Corp. had these transactions during a recent period:

Journalize issue of shares.
(SO 2, 3)

June 12 Issued 60,000 common shares for $375,000 cash.
July 11 Issued 1,000 preferred shares for cash at $105 per share.
Oct. 1 Issued 10,000 common shares for land. The common shares had a market value of $7 per share on that date. The fair market value of the land was estimated to be $75,000.

Instructions
Prepare the journal entries for the transactions.

E11-4 During the first month, a new accountant made the following entries for a corporation's share capital:

Correct entries for share transactions.
(SO 2, 3)

May 2	Cash	144,000	
	Gain on Sale of Shares		144,000
	(Issued 12,000 common shares at $12 per share)		

10	Loss on Repurchase of Shares	600,000	
	Cash		600,000
	(Repurchased 10,000 preferred shares at $60 per share. The shares were originally issued at an average price of $60 per share)		

Instructions

Based on the explanation for each entry, prepare entries to correct the transactions.

Journalize share transactions and indicate statement presentation.
(SO 2, 4, 6)

Interactive
Homework

E11-5   On January 1, Tarow Corporation had 75,000 common shares. During the year, the following transactions occurred:

Apr. 1 Issued 5,000 common shares at $10 per share.
June 15 Declared a cash dividend of $1 per share to shareholders of record on June 30.
July 10 Paid the $1 cash dividend.
Dec. 1 Issued 3,000 common shares at $12 per share.
     15 Declared a cash dividend of $1.25 per share to shareholders of record on December 31.

Instructions

(a) Prepare the entries, if any, to record the above transactions.
(b) How are dividends and dividends payable reported in the financial statements prepared at December 31?

Answer questions about shareholders' equity section
(SO 2, 3, 4)

E11-6   The shareholders' equity section of Shumway Corporation's balance sheet is presented here:

SHUMWAY CORPORATION
Balance Sheet (partial)
December 31, 2004

Shareholders' equity	
Share capital	
Preferred shares, $5 cumulative, no par value, unlimited number of shares authorized, 10,000 shares issued	$ 600,000
Common shares, no par value, 750,000 shares authorized, 600,000 shares issued	1,800,000
Total share capital	2,400,000
Retained earnings	1,158,000
Total shareholders' equity	$3,558,000

Instructions

From a review of the shareholders' equity section, answer these questions:

(a) What was the average per share selling price of the preferred shares? Common shares?
(b) How many additional common shares will Shumway be able to sell if it wishes to raise additional equity financing?
(c) What is the annual dividend on preferred shares in total?
(d) If dividends of $100,000 were in arrears on the preferred shares, what would be the balance reported for retained earnings?

Journalize stock dividend.
(SO 4)

E11-7   On March 4, 2003, Dominion Citrus Limited, Ontario's largest wholesale distributor of fruit and vegetables, declared a 5% preferred stock dividend to shareholders of record on March 14, distributable on March 28. At that time, there were 16,408,880 shares and the stock dividend was valued at $2.25 per share.

Instructions

Prepare any required journal entries to record the stock dividend.

Compare effects of stock dividend and stock split.
(SO 4)

Interactive
Homework

E11-8   On October 31, the shareholders' equity section of Lane Corporation's balance sheet consists of 60,000 common shares for $600,000, and retained earnings of $400,000. Sarah Lane is considering the following two courses of action: (1) declaring a 10% stock dividend or (2) effecting a two-for-one stock split. The current market price is $15 per share.

Instructions

Prepare a tabular summary of the effects of the alternative actions on these components: total shareholders' equity, share capital, retained earnings, and number of shares. Use these column headings: "Before Action," "After Stock Dividend," and "After Stock Split."

E11-9   Before preparing financial statements for the current year, the chief accountant for Koo Ltd. discovered the following errors in the accounts:

Prepare correcting entries for dividends and stock split.
(SO 4)

1. The declaration and payment of a $25,000 cash dividend was recorded as a debit to Interest Expense, $25,000, and a credit to Cash, $25,000.
2. A 10% stock dividend (1,000 shares) was declared when the market value per share was $17. The only entry made was Retained Earnings (Dr.), $10,000, and Dividend Payable (Cr.), $10,000. The shares have not yet been distributed.
3. A four-for-one stock split involving the issue of 400,000 new common shares for 100,000 old common shares was recorded as a debit to Retained Earnings, $2,000,000, and a credit to Common Shares, $2,000,000.

Instructions

Prepare the necessary correcting entries.

E11-10   The ledger of Val d'Or Corporation contains the following selected accounts:

Classify financial statement accounts.
(SO 6)

 Interactive Homework

1. Cash
2. Common Shares
3. Gain on Sale of Property, Plant, and Equipment
4. Patents
5. Preferred Shares
6. Retained Earnings
7. Organization Costs
8. Dividends
9. Stock Dividends Distributable

Instructions

Using the table headings below, indicate whether or not each of the above accounts should be reported in the shareholders' equity section of the balance sheet. If yes, indicate whether the account should be reported as share capital or retained earnings. If not, indicate in which financial statement (balance sheet, statement of earnings, or cash flow statement) and in which section the account should be reported. The first account has been done for you as an example.

| | Shareholders' Equity | | Other | |
| | Share | Retained | Financial | |
Account	Capital	Earnings	Statement	Classification
1. Cash			Balance Sheet	Current asset

E11-11   The following accounts appear in the ledger of Ozabal Inc. after the books are closed at December 31, 2004:

Prepare shareholders' equity section.
(SO 6)

Common Shares (no par value, unlimited number of shares authorized, 300,000 shares issued)	$300,000
Common Stock Dividends Distributable	75,000
Preferred Shares ($8, no par value, 40,000 shares authorized, 30,000 shares issued)	150,000
Retained Earnings	900,000

Instructions

Prepare the shareholders' equity section at December 31, 2004, assuming $100,000 of retained earnings is restricted for plant expansion.

E11-12   Intrawest Corporation reported the following selected accounts and information, as at June 30, 2002:

Prepare statement of retained earnings and shareholders' equity section.
(SO 6)

	(in U.S. thousands)
Dividends	$ 4,737
Common shares, unlimited number without par value authorized, 47,255,062 shares issued	453,299
Net earnings	58,480
NRP* common shares, 50,000,000 shares without par value authorized, 5,163,436 shares issued	13,600

Preferred shares, unlimited number without par value authorized, nil shares issued	0
Retained earnings, July 1, 2001	187,922

*The NRP shares are a special class of common shares related to non-resort real estate assets.

Instructions

Prepare a statement of retained earnings and the shareholders' equity section of the balance sheet for Intrawest, as at June 30, 2002.

Calculate ratios to evaluate dividend and earnings performance.
(SO 7)

Interactive
Homework

E11-13 This financial information is available for CIBC at October 31:

(in millions)	2002	2001	2000
Dividends paid to common shareholders	$ 577	$ 536	$ 501
Dividends paid to preferred shareholders	161	121	128
Net earnings	653	1,686	2,060
Preferred shares	3,088	2,299	1,876
Common shares	2,868	2,827	2,868
Retained earnings	6,377	6,774	6,625

Instructions

Calculate the payout ratio for the common shareholders and the return on common shareholders' equity ratio for 2002 and 2001. Comment on your results.

Calculate ratios to evaluate profitability and solvency.
(SO 7)

E11-14 Pyongyang Corporation issued common shares for $400,000. It used the entire proceeds to retire its bonds on January 1, 2004. The following information is available for the company for 2003 and 2004:

	2004	2003
Net earnings	$ 250,000	$ 200,000
Total assets	1,200,000	1,200,000
Current liabilities	100,000	100,000
Total liabilities	100,000	500,000
Average common shareholders' equity	1,100,000	700,000

Instructions

(a) Calculate the return on common shareholders' equity for both years.
(b) Explain how it is possible that net earnings increased but the return on common shareholders' equity decreased.
(c) Calculate the debt to total assets for both years. Comment on the implications of this change in the company's solvency.

Problems: Set A

Journalize share transactions and prepare share capital section. Discuss financing choice.
(SO 2, 3, 6)

P11-1A Wetland Corporation was organized on January 1, 2004. It is authorized to issue an unlimited number of $8, no par value preferred shares and an unlimited number of no par value common shares. The following share transactions were completed during the first year:

Jan. 10 Issued 80,000 common shares for cash at $3 per share.
Mar. 1 Issued 5,000 preferred shares for cash at $102 per share.
May 1 Issued 80,000 common shares for cash at $4 per share.
Aug. 2 Issued 5,000 common shares in exchange for a piece of equipment. The asking price of the equipment was $27,500. The fair market value of the shares was $5 per share.
Sept. 1 Issued 10,000 common shares for cash at $6 per share.
Nov. 1 Issued 2,000 preferred shares for cash at $105 per share.

Instructions

(a) Journalize the transactions.
(b) Post to the shareholders' equity accounts.
(c) Prepare the share capital section of shareholders' equity at December 31, 2004.
(d) Explain why Wetland may have chosen to finance its operations by issuing share capital rather than debt.

P11-2A Cattrall Corporation has been authorized to issue an unlimited number of no par value, $10, noncumulative preferred shares and an unlimited number of no par value common shares. During the first year of operations, ended December 31, 2004, the following transactions occurred:

Journalize transactions, and prepare shareholders' equity section.
(SO 2, 3, 6)

1. Issued 1,200 preferred shares for $150,000 cash.
2. Issued 200,000 common shares for $1,000,000 cash.
3. Issued 5,000 common shares in exchange for land. At the time of the exchange, the land was valued at $40,000 and the common shares at $30,000.
4. Declared and paid annual preferred dividends.
5. Net earnings for the year were $712,000.

Instructions

(a) Prepare journal entries to record the above transactions.
(b) Prepare the shareholders' equity section of the balance sheet at December 31, 2004.

P11-3A The shareholders' equity accounts of Capozza Corporation on January 1, 2004, were as follows:

Journalize transactions and prepare shareholders' equity section; calculate profitability ratios.
(SO 2, 3, 4, 6, 7)

Preferred Shares ($12, no par value, cumulative, unlimited number of shares authorized, 4,000 shares issued)	$ 480,000
Common Shares (no par value, unlimited number of shares authorized, 480,000 shares issued)	2,400,000
Retained Earnings	1,756,000

During 2004, the corporation had these transactions and events pertaining to its shareholders' equity:

Feb. 1 Issued 15,000 common shares for $90,000.
June 1 Declared a $0.30 per share cash dividend to common shareholders of record on June 15, payable June 30.
Nov. 15 Declared a $10 cash dividend on preferred shares to shareholders of record on November 30, payable December 15.
Dec. 31 Determined that net earnings for the year were $408,000. The market price of the common shares on this date was $9 per share.

Instructions

(a) Journalize the transactions.
(b) Enter the beginning balances in T accounts, and post the journal entries to the shareholders' equity accounts.
(c) Prepare the shareholders' equity section of the balance sheet at December 31, 2004, including the disclosure of any dividends in arrears.
(d) Calculate the dividend payout, earnings per share, price-earnings, and return on common shareholders' equity ratios.

P11-4A Dofasco Inc. reported the following selected information in its 2002 financial statements:

Evaluate impact of stock option plan.
(SO 2)

DOFASCO INC.
Notes to the Financial Statements
Year Ended December 31, 2002

2. Accounting Changes

c) Stock-based Compensation and Other Stock-based Payments

Effective January 1, 2002, the Corporation adopted the new recommendations of the CICA with respect to the recognition, measurement, and disclosure of stock-based compensation and other stock-based payments at fair value.

Stock options without attached stock appreciation rights, granted after January 1, 2002, are accounted for under the fair value method.... Stock options granted prior to January 1, 2002, continue to be accounted for using the intrinsic value method which does not give rise to compensation expense. The effect of the change was a decrease in net income of $0.8 million ($0.01 per share) for the year ended December 31, 2002.

For stock options with attached stock appreciation rights and other awards to be settled in cash, compensation expense is calculated as the amount by which the quoted market price exceeds the option price with ongoing re-measurement of the outstanding liability. This change was adopted on a retroactive basis without restatement of prior periods. As a result of this change, retained earnings at January 1, 2002, decreased by $3.5 million, accounts payable increased by $5.2 million, and future income tax assets increased by $1.7 million to recognize the liability for stock appreciation rights owing on January 1, 2002. Previously, compensation expense was recognized when the Corporation made cash payments to holders upon exercise of their stock appreciation rights. The effect of the change was a reduction in net income of $1.4 million ($0.02 per share) for the year ended December 31, 2002.

10. Stock-Based Compensation Plans

At December 31, 2002, the Corporation has four stock-based compensation plans... The Corporation accounts for its grants under those plans in accordance with the fair value based method of accounting for stock-based compensation. The compensation charge recognized for these awards for the year ended December 31, 2002, was an expense of $9.1 million.

Instructions

Discuss the financial impact of Dofasco's accounting for stock options.

Compare impact of equity transactions.
(SO 2, 4)

P11-5A   Gull Lake Enterprises Inc. has 100,000 common shares at July 1, 2004, the beginning of its current fiscal year. Mark Bradbury is the president and largest shareholder and owns 25% of the common shares. On July 1, the common shares were trading on the Toronto Stock Exchange for $25 per share. Gull Lake Enterprises' Common Share and Retained Earnings accounts had opening balances of $2,000,000 and $350,000, respectively.

You are provided with the following information about selected events and transactions that occurred during the year:

1. On August 31, Gull Lake declared and issued a 4% stock dividend. The shares were trading at $28 per share on that day.
2. On December 1, the company issued another 20,000 common shares. This issue was needed in order to finance new product development. Mark Bradbury acquired 5,000 of these shares in order to maintain his 25% interest in the shares of the company. The market value of the shares was $30 per share.
3. On March 31, 2005, the company's shares were trading at $26 per share and the company effected a two-for-one stock split. After the stock split, each share was trading at $13.
4. The share price at the close of business on June 30, 2005, was $10.50.

Instructions

Prepare a schedule illustrating the impact of each transaction on:
(a) The balance of retained earnings
(b) The number of shares issued
(c) The number of shares held by Mark Bradbury
(d) The share price
(e) The market value of Mark Bradbury's portfolio of common shares

Reproduce retained earnings account, and prepare shareholders' equity section.
(SO 4, 5, 6)

P11-6A   The post-closing trial balance of Maggio Corporation at December 31, 2004, contains these shareholders' equity accounts:

Preferred Shares (12,000 shares issued)	$ 850,000
Common Shares (250,000 shares issued)	3,200,000
Common Stock Dividends Distributable	400,000
Retained Earnings	758,600

A review of the accounting records reveals this information:

1. Preferred shares are $10 cumulative shares.
2. There is an unlimited number of no par value preferred and common shares authorized.
3. The January 1 balance in Retained Earnings was $980,000.
4. On July 1, 20,000 common shares were sold for cash at $16 per share.

5. A cash dividend of $240,000 was declared and paid to preferred shareholders on October 1. No dividends were paid to preferred shareholders in 2003.
6. On December 31, an 8% common stock dividend was declared when the market price per share was $20. The stock dividend was distributed on January 25.
7. Net earnings for the year were $418,600.
8. On December 31, the directors authorized a $200,000 restriction on retained earnings in accordance with a debt covenant.

Instructions

(a) Reproduce the Retained Earnings T account for the year.
(b) Prepare the shareholders' equity section of the balance sheet at December 31, including any required note disclosure.

P11-7A On January 1, 2004, Stengel Corporation had these shareholders' equity accounts:

Common Shares (no par value, unlimited number of shares authorized, 60,000 shares issued)	$1,400,000
Retained Earnings	600,000

Journalize dividend transactions, prepare shareholders' equity section, and calculate profitability ratios.
(SO 4, 6, 7)

During the year, the following transactions occurred:

Feb. 1 Declared a $0.50 per share cash dividend to shareholders of record on February 15, payable March 1.
Mar. 1 Paid the dividend declared in February.
July 1 Declared a 5% stock dividend to shareholders of record on July 15, distributable July 31. On July 1, the market price was $28 per share.
　31 Issued the shares for the stock dividend.
Dec. 1 Declared a $1 per share cash dividend to shareholders of record on December 15, payable January 5, 2005.
　31 Determined that net earnings for the year were $410,000. The market price of the common shares on this date was $35.

Instructions

(a) Journalize the transactions.
(b) Enter the beginning balances and post the entries to the shareholders' equity T accounts. (*Note:* Open additional shareholders' equity accounts as needed.)
(c) Prepare the shareholders' equity section of the balance sheet at December 31.
(d) Calculate the dividend payout, earnings per share, price-earnings, and return on common shareholders' equity ratios.

P11-8A On December 31, 2003, Schipper Ltd. had 1,000,000 common shares issued. The shareholders' equity accounts at December 31, 2003, had the balances listed here:

Common Shares	$1,000,000
Retained Earnings	700,000

Prepare shareholders' equity section of balance sheet and financing activities section of cash flow statement.
(SO 6)

Transactions during 2004 and other information related to shareholders' equity accounts were as follows:

1. On January 9, Schipper issued 100,000 noncumulative $4.50 preferred shares of no par value at $26 per share.
2. On June 10, Schipper declared a cash dividend of $1 per share on the common shares, payable on July 10, to shareholders of record on July 1.
3. On December 15, Schipper declared the yearly cash dividend on the preferred shares, payable December 28, to shareholders of record on December 15.
4. Net earnings for the year were $2,400,000.

Instructions

(a) Prepare the shareholders' equity section of Schipper's balance sheet at December 31, 2004.
(b) Prepare the financing activities section of Schipper's cash flow statement for the year ended December 31, 2004.

Evaluate dividend policy.
(SO 7)

P11-9A The following five-year summary of dividend-related information is available for the years ended March 31 for Molson Inc.:

	Earnings per Share	Dividends per Common Share	Payout Ratio
1998	$0.94	$0.36	38.3%
1999	1.44	0.36	25.0%
2000	(0.37)	0.36	n/a
2001	1.12	0.36	32.1%
2002	1.48	0.38	25.7%

Instructions

(a) Evaluate Molson's dividend policy.
(b) If you were an investor seeking dividend income, would you be happy with Molson's dividend policy? Explain.
(c) If you were one of Molson's creditors, what would you think about Molson's policy of maintaining a consistent dividend regardless of whether the company reports net earnings or a net loss?

Calculate profitability ratios and comment.
(SO 7)

P11-10A The following selected information is available for the National Bank of Canada for the year ended October 31:

(in millions, except for market price)	2002	2001
Average number of common shares	186.6	189.9
Net earnings	$ 429	$ 563
Common cash dividends	174	156
Preferred cash dividends	21	35
Average common shareholders' equity	3,612	3,480
Market price per common share	29.39	24.25

Industry averages for selected ratios in 2002 are as follows:

Payout ratio	45.6%	Price-earnings ratio	23.2 times
Earnings per share	$0.83	Return on common shareholders' equity	9.6%

Instructions

(a) Calculate the following ratios for 2002 and 2001:

   1. Payout ratio   3. Price-earnings ratio
   2. Earnings per share   4. Return on common shareholders' equity

(b) Comment on the above ratios for 2002, in comparison to the prior year, and in comparison to the industry.

Evaluate profitability.
(SO 7)

P11-11A Selected ratios for two retailers follow:

Ratio	Bargain Hunters	Discount Paradise	Industry Average
Profit margin	3.8%	3.3%	2.9%
Return on common shareholders' equity	21.2%	18.9%	17.6%
Return on assets	8.4%	5.8%	7.3%
Asset turnover	2.7 times	1.7 times	2.5 times
Earnings per share	$1.31	$1.00	$1.33
Price-earnings ratio	26.6 times	14.8 times	27.8 times
Payout ratio	16.6%	23.3%	17.3%

Instructions

(a) Compare the profitability of Bargain Hunters to that of Discount Paradise and of the industry. Which company is more profitable? Explain.
(b) You are interested in investing in the shares of one of the two companies in order to secure regular income from your investment to pay your tuition fees for the next few years. Which of the two companies is a better choice for you? Explain.
(c) Assume that instead of seeking regular income, you are interested in investing in the shares of one of the companies to secure growth in the share value so that you can resell the shares at a gain in the future. Now which of the two companies is the better for you? Explain.

P11-12A During 2004 Jiye Corporation decided to issue bonds at 7% interest and then used the cash to repurchase a significant amount of its own common shares. The following information is available for Jiye:

Evaluate profitability and solvency.
(SO 7)

	2004	2003
Sales	$3,000,000	$3,000,000
Net earnings	850,000	1,000,000
Interest expense	125,000	50,000
Income tax expense	100,000	142,000
Total assets	5,000,000	5,625,000
Average total assets	5,312,500	6,250,000
Total liabilities	2,000,000	1,000,000
Average total common shareholders' equity	3,312,500	5,250,000
Dividends	340,000	400,000

Instructions

(a) Use the information above to calculate the following ratios for both years: (1) return on assets, (2) return on common shareholders' equity, (3) dividend payout, (4) debt to total assets, and (5) times interest earned.

(b) Referring to your findings in part (a), discuss the changes in the company's profitability from 2003 to 2004.

(c) Referring to your findings in part (a), discuss the changes in the company's solvency from 2003 to 2004.

(d) Based on your findings in (b), was the decision to issue debt to purchase common shares wise?

Problems: Set B

P11-1B Remmers Corporation was organized on January 1, 2004. It is authorized to issue 200,000 $3, noncumulative, no par value preferred shares and an unlimited number of no par value common shares. The following share transactions were completed during the first year:

Journalize share transactions and prepare share capital section. Discuss financing choice.
(SO 2, 3, 6)

Jan. 10 Issued 100,000 common shares for cash at $3 per share.
Mar. 1 Issued 12,000 preferred shares for cash at $52 per share.
May 1 Issued 70,000 common shares for cash at $5 per share.
Sept. 1 Issued 5,000 common shares for cash at $6 per share.
Nov. 1 Issued 2,000 preferred shares for cash at $63 per share.
Dec. 12 Issued 400 preferred shares for a patent. The asking price of the patent was $25,000. The fair market value of the shares was $60 per share.

Instructions

(a) Journalize the transactions.

(b) Post to the shareholders' equity accounts.

(c) Prepare the share capital portion of the shareholders' equity section at December 31, 2004.

(d) Explain why Remmers may have chosen to finance its operations by issuing share capital rather than debt.

P11-2B Largent Corporation is authorized to issue 200,000 no par value, $8, cumulative preferred shares and an unlimited number of no par value common shares. During the first year of operations, ended December 31, 2004, the following transactions occurred:

Journalize transactions, and prepare shareholders' equity section.
(SO 2, 3, 6)

1. Issued 1,000 preferred shares for $150,000 cash.
2. Issued 400,000 common shares for $3,850,000 cash.
3. Issued 10,000 common shares in exchange for a building. At the time of the exchange, the building was valued at $110,000 and the common shares at $100,000.
4. Declared and paid annual preferred dividend.
5. Net earnings for the year were $582,000.

Instructions

(a) Prepare the journal entries to record the above transactions.

(b) Prepare the shareholders' equity section of the balance sheet at December 31, 2004.

Journalize transactions and prepare shareholders' equity section; calculate profitability ratios.
(SO 2, 3, 4, 6, 7)

P11-3B The shareholders' equity accounts of Chung Corporation on January 1, 2004, were as follows:

Preferred Shares ($10, no par value, noncumulative, 25,000 shares authorized, 3,000 shares issued)	$ 320,000
Common Shares (unlimited number authorized, no par value, 200,000 shares issued)	1,425,000
Retained Earnings	488,000

During 2004, the corporation had the following transactions and events pertaining to its shareholders' equity:

Feb. 1 Issued 3,000 common shares for $18,000.
Oct. 1 Declared a $5 cash dividend on preferred shares to shareholders of record on October 15, payable November 1.
Dec. 1 Declared a $0.50 per share cash dividend to common shareholders of record on December 15, payable December 31.
     31 Determined that net earnings for the year were $280,000. At December 31, the market price of the common shares was $10 per share.

Instructions

(a) Journalize the transactions.
(b) Enter the beginning balances in T accounts and post the journal entries to the shareholders' equity accounts.
(c) Prepare the shareholders' equity section of the balance sheet at December 31, 2004, including the disclosure of any dividends in arrears.
(d) Calculate the dividend payout, earnings per share, price-earnings, and return on common shareholders' equity ratios.

Evaluate impact of stock option plan and repurchase of shares.
(SO 2)

P11-4B Canadian Tire Corporation reported the following selected information in its third quarter report in 2002:

CANADIAN TIRE CORPORATION
Notes to the Financial Statements
39 Weeks Ended September 28, 2002

3. Stock-Based Compensation Plans

Effective December 30, 2001, the Corporation elected early adoption, on a prospective basis, of the new recommendations issued by The Canadian Institute of Chartered Accountants relating to stock-based compensation and other stock-based payments. The standard requires that all stock-based awards made to non-employees be measured and recognized using a fair value based method. The standard encourages the use of a fair value based method for all stock-based awards made to employees, but only requires it for direct awards of stock, stock appreciation rights, and awards that call for settlement in cash or other assets. As no compensation expense is recognized when stock options are granted to employees, the Corporation discloses pro forma net earnings... as if the fair value method had been used (see Note 9).

9. Pro Forma Stock Option Disclosure

Had the fair value based method been used for stock options granted in 2002, the Corporation's net earnings for the 39 weeks ended September 29, 2002, would have decreased by $0.9 million.

Operating Highlights: Equity

Canadian Tire has a policy of repurchasing enough Class A Non-Voting Shares each year to offset the effects of shares issued to fulfill employee profit sharing, stock option and share purchase plans and the dividend reinvestment plan.

Instructions

(a) Discuss the financial impact of Canadian Tire's accounting for stock options.
(b) During 2002, Canadian Tire repurchased 310,504 Class A Non-Voting Shares. Explain the impact this repurchase had on Canadian Tire's financial position, including the number of authorized and issued shares.

P11-5B   The condensed balance sheet of Laporte Corporation reports the following amounts:

Compare impact of cash dividend, stock dividend, and stock split.
(SO 4)

LAPORTE CORPORATION
Balance Sheet (partial)
June 30, 2004

Assets		$13,500,000
Liabilities and shareholders' equity		
Liabilities		$ 1,500,000
Shareholders' equity		
Common shares, unlimited number authorized,		
400,000 issued, no par value	$ 2,000,000	
Retained earnings	10,000,000	12,000,000
Total liabilities and shareholders' equity		$13,500,000

Laporte Corporation wishes to assess the impact of three possible alternatives on the corporation and its shareholders. The market price of the common shares is currently $40 per share. The alternatives are:

1. Payment of a $2 per share cash dividend   3. Two-for-one stock split
2. Distribution of a 5% stock dividend

Instructions

(a) Determine the impact on assets, liabilities, shareholders' equity (common shares and retained earnings), and the number of shares involved under each of the three alternatives for Laporte Corporation.
(b) Assume a Laporte shareholder currently owns 1,000 common shares, at a cost of $35,000. Which alternative is most beneficial for the shareholder? Assess the impact of each alternative.

P11-6B After the books have been closed at Robichaud Corporation on December 31, 2004, the ledger contains the following shareholders' equity accounts:

Reproduce retained earnings account, and prepare shareholders' equity section.
(SO 4, 5, 6)

Preferred Shares (10,000 shares issued)	$1,000,000
Common Shares (420,000 shares issued)	3,700,000
Common Stock Dividends Distributable	147,000
Retained Earnings	3,613,000

A review of the accounting records reveals this information:

1. Preferred shares are $10, no par value, noncumulative, and redeemable at $125. An unlimited number of preferred shares are authorized.
2. Common shares are no par value. An unlimited number of common shares are authorized.
3. The January 1 balance in Retained Earnings was $2,980,000.
4. On October 1, 100,000 common shares were sold for cash at $8 per share.
5. A cash dividend of $100,000 was declared and paid to preferred shareholders on November 1. No dividends were paid to preferred shareholders in 2003.
6. On December 31, a 5% common stock dividend was declared on common shares when the market price per share was $7. The stock dividend is distributable on January 20.
7. Net earnings for the year were $880,000.
8. On December 31, 2004, the directors authorized a $100,000 restriction on retained earnings for a plant expansion.

Instructions

(a) Reproduce the Retained Earnings T account for the year.
(b) Prepare the shareholders' equity section of the balance sheet at December 31, including any required note disclosure.

P11-7B   On January 1, 2004, Wirth Corporation had these shareholders' equity accounts:

Journalize dividend transactions, prepare shareholders' equity section, and calculate profitability ratios.
(SO 4, 6, 7)

Common Shares (no par value, unlimited number	
of shares authorized, 80,000 shares issued)	$1,000,000
Retained Earnings	540,000

During the year, the following transactions occurred:

Jan. 15 Declared a $0.60 per share cash dividend to shareholders of record on January 31, payable February 15.

Feb. 15 Paid the dividend declared in January.
Apr. 15 Declared a 10% stock dividend to shareholders of record on April 30, distributable May 15. On April 15, the market price of the shares was $20 per share.
May 15 Issued the shares for the stock dividend.
Dec. 1 Declared a $0.75 per share cash dividend to shareholders of record on December 15, payable January 10, 2005.
    31 Determined that net earnings for the year were $370,000. On December 31, the market price of the shares was $25 per share.

Instructions

(a) Journalize the transactions.
(b) Enter the beginning balances and post the entries to the shareholders' equity T accounts. (*Note*: Open additional shareholders' equity accounts as needed.)
(c) Prepare the shareholders' equity section of the balance sheet at December 31.
(d) Calculate the dividend payout, earnings per share, price-earnings, and return on common shareholders' equity ratios.

Prepare shareholders' equity section of balance sheet and financing activities section of cash flow statement.
(SO 6)

P11-8B On December 31, 2003, Conway Ltd. had 1,500,000 no par value common shares issued. The shareholders' equity accounts at December 31, 2003, had the balances listed here:

Common Shares	$16,500,000
Retained Earnings	900,000

Transactions during 2004 and other information related to shareholders' equity accounts were as follows:

1. On January 10, 2004, Conway issued, at $110 per share, 100,000 shares of no par value, $8, noncumulative preferred stock.
2. On June 8, 2004, Conway declared a cash dividend of $1 per share on the common shares to shareholders of record on July 1, payable on July 10.
3. On December 15, 2004, Conway declared the yearly cash dividend on the preferred shares to shareholders of record on December 31, 2004, payable January 10, 2005.
4. Net earnings for the year were $3,600,000.

Instructions

(a) Prepare the shareholders' equity section of Conway's balance sheet at December 31, 2004.
(b) Prepare the financing activities section of Conway's cash flow statement for the year ended December 31, 2004.

Evaluate dividend policy.
(SO 7)
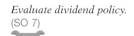

P11-9B The following five-year summary of dividend-related information is available for the years ended January 31 for Bombardier Inc.:

	Earnings per Share	Dividends per Common Share	Payout Ratio
1998	$0.29	$0.075	25.9%
1999	0.39	0.085	21.8%
2000	0.51	0.110	21.6%
2001	0.70	0.135	19.3%
2002	0.27	0.180	66.7%

Instructions

(a) Evaluate Bombardier's dividend policy.
(b) Speculate on why Bombardier's dividend payout ratio jumped to 66.7% in 2002. What does this mean?
(c) If you were an investor seeking dividend income, would you be happy with Bombardier's dividend policy? Explain.

Calculate profitability ratios and comment.
(SO 7)

P11-10B The following selected information is available for the Canadian National Railway Company (CN) for the year ended December 31:

(in millions, except for market price)	2002	2001
Average number of common shares	199	195
Net earnings	$ 571	$ 727
Common cash dividends	170	150
Preferred cash dividends	6	12
Average common shareholders' equity	6,494	6,000
Market price per common share	65.27	76.70

Industry averages for selected ratios in 2002 were as follows:

Payout ratio	20.1%	Return on common	
Earnings per share	$1.89	shareholders' equity	8.8%
Price-earnings ratio	14.4 times		

Instructions

(a) Calculate the following ratios for 2002 and 2001:
1. Payout ratio   3. Price-earnings ratio
2. Earnings per share   4. Return on common shareholders' equity
(b) Comment on the above ratios for 2002 in comparison to the prior year, and in comparison to the industry.

P11-11B Selected ratios for two companies operating in the petroleum industry follow:

Evaluate profitability.
(SO 7)

Ratio	Petro-Boost	World Oil	Industry Average
Profit margin	7.9%	14.5%	8.5%
Return on common shareholders' equity	11.7%	17.3%	9.7%
Return on assets	6.4%	6.5%	6.8%
Asset turnover	0.5 times	1.8 times	1.3 times
Earnings per share	$0.52	$0.81	$1.34
Price-earnings ratio	14.2 times	26.8 times	23.5 times
Payout ratio	65.3%	14.8%	61.9%

Instructions

(a) Compare the profitability of Petro-Boost to that of World Oil, and to the industry average. Which company is more profitable? Explain.
(b) You are interested in investing in the shares of one of the two companies in order to secure regular income from your investment to pay your tuition fees for the next few years. Which of the companies is a better choice for you? Explain.
(c) Assume that instead of seeking regular income, you are interested in the shares of one of the two companies to secure growth in the share value so that you can resell the shares at a gain in the future. Now which of the two companies is the better choice for you? Explain.

P11-12B During 2004 Extralite Corporation issued bonds at 8% interest and used the cash proceeds to repurchase common shares. The following financial information is available for Extralite for the years 2004 and 2003:

Evaluate profitability and solvency.
(SO 7)

	2004	2003
Sales	$ 9,000,000	$ 9,000,000
Net earnings	2,550,000	3,000,000
Interest expense	400,000	150,000
Income tax expense	700,000	826,000
Dividends	1,020,000	1,200,000
Total assets (year end)	14,500,000	16,875,000
Average total assets	14,937,500	17,647,000
Total liabilities (year end)	6,000,000	3,000,000
Average total common shareholders' equity	9,400,000	14,100,000

Instructions

(a) Use the information above to calculate the following ratios for both years: (1) return on assets, (2) return on common shareholders' equity, (3) dividend payout, (4) debt to total assets, and (5) times interest earned.
(b) Referring to your findings in part (a), discuss the changes in the company's profitability from 2003 to 2004.
(c) Referring to your findings in part (a), discuss the changes in the company's solvency from 2003 to 2004.
(d) Based on your findings in (b), was the decision to issue debt to purchase common shares a wise one?

BROADENING YOUR PERSPECTIVE

Financial Reporting and Analysis

Analysis
Tools

FINANCIAL REPORTING PROBLEM: *Loblaw Companies Limited*

BYP11-1   The shareholders' equity section of Loblaw's balance sheet is shown in the Consolidated Balance Sheet in Appendix A. You will also find data relative to this problem in the Notes to the Consolidated Financial Statements.

Instructions

Answer the following questions:

(a) How many common shares has Loblaw authorized? How many common shares were issued at the end of the 2002 and 2001 fiscal years?
(b) Did Loblaw repurchase any shares in 2002 and 2001? If so, how much cash did it spend on this activity in each year?
(c) How much cash did Loblaw pay out in dividends in each of 2002 and 2001?
(d) How does Loblaw account for its stock options?
(e) Calculate the payout ratio and return on common shareholders' equity for 2002 and 2001. Loblaw's shareholders' equity was $3,124 million at the end of 2000.

COMPARATIVE ANALYSIS PROBLEM: *Loblaw and Sobeys*

BYP11-2   The financial statements of Sobeys Inc. are presented in Appendix B, following the financial statements for Loblaw in Appendix A.

Instructions

(a) Based on the information in these financial statements, calculate the return on common shareholders' equity, debt to total assets, and return on assets ratios for each company for the most recent fiscal year.
(b) Which company relies more on debt to boost its return to common shareholders?
(c) What conclusions concerning the companies' profitability can be drawn from these ratios?

RESEARCH CASE

BYP11-3   The January 21, 2003, issue of *The Globe and Mail* included an article on page B17 by Fabrice Taylor entitled "Dividend Trend Will Expose Worst Techs for What They Are."

Instructions

Read the article and answer the following questions:

(a) Tech companies don't usually pay dividends. Why not?
(b) Are there any disadvantages for a tech company if it does pay dividends?
(c) The article says that accounting rules boost the return on common shareholders' equity in technology. Explain the reasoning behind this statement.
(d) Tech companies make use of stock options to compensate employees. Does this practice affect net earnings? Explain why or why not.

INTERPRETING FINANCIAL STATEMENTS

BYP11-4   Intrawest Corporation, headquartered in Vancouver, is the leading developer and operator of village-centred destination resorts across North America. Intrawest has an unlimited number of common shares authorized. During the year ended June 30, 2002, Intrawest repurchased 292,182 of its common shares. The following additional information is also available for the year ended June 30 (in U.S. thousands except for per share information).

	2002	2001
Interest expense	$ 43,072	$ 44,490
Income tax expense	9,549	10,014
Net earnings	58,602	63,529
Total assets	2,166,917	1,956,312
Average total assets	2,061,615	1,836,834
Average common shareholders' equity	609,037	523,876
Total liabilities	1,489,648	1,387,950
Average total liabilities	1,438,799	1,297,017
Cash provided by (used in) operating activities	5,706	(47,645)
Cash dividend	4,737	4,618
Average number of common shares	44,206	43,665
Cash dividend per common share	0.16	0.16

Instructions

(a) What are some of the reasons why management repurchases its own shares?

(b) Calculate the earnings per share, return on common shareholders' equity, and return on assets ratios for 2002 and 2001. Discuss the change in the company's profitability over this period.

(c) Calculate the dividend payout ratio. Discuss any change in this ratio from 2001 to 2002 and the implications for the company's dividend policy.

(d) Calculate the debt to total assets, times interest earned, and cash total debt coverage ratios. Discuss the change in the company's solvency over this period.

(e) Based on your findings in (a) and (c), discuss to what extent any change in the return on common shareholders' equity was due to an increased reliance on debt.

A GLOBAL FOCUS

BYP11-5 UK-based cosmetics retailer The Body Shop International plc operates nearly 2,000 stores in 50 countries.

The Body Shop reported the following selected information for fiscal 2002 and 2001:

(in millions of £, except share price)	2002	2001
Average number of common shares	195.0	190.5
Average common shareholders' equity	£122.9	£130.9
Dividends	11.4	10.9
Net earnings	5.4	9.5
Closing share price	0.965	0.735

Instructions

Calculate the dividend payout, earnings per share, price-earnings, and return on common shareholders' equity ratios for each year. Comment on The Body Shop's profitability.

FINANCIAL ANALYSIS ON THE WEB

BYP11-6 The Toronto Stock Exchange (TSX) is Canada's premier stock exchange and one of the top ten exchanges in the world. The TSX is Canada's largest capital market, accounting for over 80% of the value of shares traded on Canadian exchanges. This case explores the information available on the TSX website.

Instructions

Specific requirements of this Web case can be found on the Kimmel website.

Critical Thinking

COLLABORATIVE LEARNING ACTIVITY

BYP11-7 The shareholders' meeting for Mantle Corporation has been in progress for some time. The chief financial officer for Mantle is presently reviewing the company's financial statements and is explaining the items that make up the shareholders' equity section of the balance sheet for the current year. The shareholders' equity section for Mantle Corporation is presented here:

MANTLE CORPORATION
Balance Sheet (partial)
December 31, 2004

Shareholders' equity	
Share capital	
Preferred shares, 1,000,000 shares authorized,	
$8 cumulative, no par value, 6,000 shares issued	$ 650,000
Common shares, unlimited number authorized,	
no par value, 3,000,000 shares issued	28,000,000
Total share capital	28,650,000
Retained earnings	900,000
Total shareholders' equity	$29,550,000

A number of questions regarding the shareholders' equity section of Mantle Corporation's balance sheet have been raised at the meeting by different people.

Instructions

With the class divided into groups, answer the following questions that were asked as if your group were Mantle Corporation's chief financial officer:
(a) "What does the cumulative provision related to the preferred shares mean?"
(b) "I thought the common shares were presently selling at $29.75, and yet the company has an average share price of $9.33 ($28,000,000 ÷ 3,000,000). How can that be?"
(c) The CFO mentions that the company repurchased 300,000 common shares during 2004. "Why is the company buying back its common shares?"
(d) The CFO also mentions that $50,000 of the retained earnings is restricted for a plant expansion. "I know that retained earnings aren't cash. How can retained earnings finance a plant expansion?"

COMMUNICATION ACTIVITY

BYP11-8 Most companies do not record stock options as compensation expense in their statement of earnings. Rather, they disclose their stock options in a note to the financial statements. But financial scandals involving big stock option packages for executives have led to a renewed call for changes to how options are accounted for. Dozens of companies have recently announced plans to report stock options as expenses.

Other companies are against this accounting proposal. Some say reporting options as an expense would be too complicated to measure. Others say recording stock options as an expense would cut billions of dollars from their reported net earnings.

Instructions

Acting as an investor, write a memo to the Accounting Standards Board explaining the benefits to investors of recording stock options as an expense.

ETHICS CASE

Ethics In
Accounting

BYP11-9 Flambeau Corporation has paid 60 consecutive quarterly cash dividends (15 years' worth). The last six months have been a real cash drain on the company, however, as profit margins have been greatly narrowed by increasing competition. With a cash balance sufficient to meet only day-to-day operating needs, the president, Vince Ramsey, has decided that a stock dividend instead of a cash dividend should be declared. He tells Flambeau's financial vice-president, Janice Rahn, to issue a press release stating that the company is extending its consecutive dividend record with the declaration of a 5% stock dividend. "Write the press release convincing the shareholders that the stock dividend is just as good as a cash dividend," he orders. "Just watch our share price rise when we announce the stock dividend; it must be a good thing if that happens."

Instructions

(a) Who are the stakeholders in this situation?

(b) Is there anything unethical about President Ramsey's intentions or actions?

(c) What is the effect of a stock dividend on a corporation's shareholders' equity accounts? Which would you rather receive as a shareholder—a cash dividend or a stock dividend? Why?

Answers to Self-Study Questions

1. c   2. c   3. a   4. b   5. d   6. d   7. b   8. c   9. c   10. c   11. b

Answer to Loblaw Review It Question 3

Loblaw repurchased and cancelled 309,000 common shares in 2002. It did not declare any stock splits, but it did declare a $133-million ($0.48 per share) dividend to its common shareholders.

Remember to go back to the Navigator box on the chapter-opening page to check off your completed work.

Reporting and Analysing Investments

NAVIGATOR

Birth of a Giant

Every day you read about mergers and acquisitions in the corporate world. In fact, in any given year hundreds of these deals take place in Canada, many of them in the oil and gas industry. In the fiscal year ended September 30, 2002, 97 out of 860 Canadian mergers and acquisitions were in the oil patch, according to Toronto investment bank Crosbie and Co. Those deals accounted for $22 billion of a total $90 billion for all sectors.

By far the biggest merger of 2002 was the $8.7-billion marriage between Alberta Energy Co. (AEC) and PanCanadian Energy Corp., two of Canada's leading oil and gas producers. The "super independent" they've created, Calgary-based EnCana Cor-

poration, is now North America's number one independent oil and gas producer and one of the biggest independent oil companies in the world.

The story behind this mega-merger underlines the role of strategic acquisitions in the growth of corporations. AEC was launched in 1975 as a provincially owned Crown corporation. Initially, the Alberta government owned half the shares, with the rest held by the public. Over the years, AEC invested in other industries in addition to oil and gas, including coal and steel, forest products, and petrochemicals.

By 1993, the government had divested itself of its shares. Amid rumours of an impending takeover, AEC hit the acquisition trail again, but not before shed-

ding many of its non–oil and gas assets. Between 1995 and 2001, the company made four large acquisitions, among them Conwest Exploration, Amber Energy, and McMurray Oil. As well, it expanded to the U.S. and Ecuador, doubling in size along the way. By 2001, it was the largest independent gas storage operator in North America.

PanCanadian Energy has an interesting history, too. In 1881, the Government of Canada commissioned the Canadian Pacific Railway (CPR) to build a cross-country railroad. As partial payment, CPR received 25 million acres of land. In 1883, a CPR crew drilling for water near Medicine Hat made Alberta's first natural gas discovery, which marked the beginning of the petroleum industry. In 1958, CPR created

EnCana Corporation www.encana.com

THE NAVIGATOR

Scan *Study Objectives* ☐

Read *Feature Story* ☐

Read *Chapter Preview* ☐

Read text and answer *Before You Go On*
p. 568 ☐ p. 573 ☐ p. 579 ☐

Work *Using the Decision Toolkit* ☐

Review *Summary of Study Objectives*
and *Decision Toolkit* ☐

Work *Demonstration Problem* ☐

Answer *Self-Study Questions* ☐

Complete assignments ☐

Canadian Pacific Oil and Gas Company to hold and exploit the subsurface mineral rights that came with the 25 million acres. When Canadian Pacific Oil and Gas amalgamated with Central-Del Rio Oils in 1971, the name changed to PanCanadian Energy and the company went on to become a huge exploration and production firm.

Fast-forward to 2002. In April of that year, AEC and Pan-Canadian combined their assets in a "friendly merger" to create a new company with an enter-prise value of $31 billion. With about 2.9 billion barrels of proven oil equivalent reserves in-cluding those of Syncrude, En-Cana is twice the size of its nearest Canadian competitor and ranks alongside giants such as Exxon Mobil, ChevronTexaco, and Royal Dutch/Shell. In addi-tion to the emerging offshore oil activities off Canada's eastern coast, the company has major operations in the U.S. Rockies, Ecuador, the Gulf of Mexico, and the UK's North Sea.

By the end of 2002, En-Cana's sales of oil and gas reached 623,170 barrels of oil per day, an increase of 115% over the results of PanCanadian one year earlier. The company also generated more than $10 billion of revenues during the year. Its earnings were $1,224 million, or $2.92 per share.

Looking forward, it will be interesting to see how EnCana develops. In 2003, the company expanded its oil production in Ecuador, where it is building a U.S.$1.4-billion, 500-km pipeline from the country's oil-rich inte-rior across the Andes to a Pa-cific Ocean port. To raise cash in 2003, the company sold its Cold Lake and Express oil pipelines for $1.6 billion, and its 10% stake in Syncrude for $1 billion.

Which other assets will it sell and which will it keep? What kinds of acquisitions will it make? How will its financial situation evolve over time? Much will depend, of course, on what happens with oil and gas prices. In the meantime, in-vestors and competitors alike are sure to be watching closely as this story unfolds.

EnCana grew through a policy of aggressive growth by investing in the equity securities (shares) of other companies. In addition to purchasing equity securities, companies also purchase other securities, such as debt securities issued by corporations or by governments. Investments can be purchased for a short or long period of time, and as a passive investment or with the intent to control another company. As you will see later in the chapter, the way in which a company accounts for its investments is determined by a number of factors.

The content and organization of this chapter are as follows:

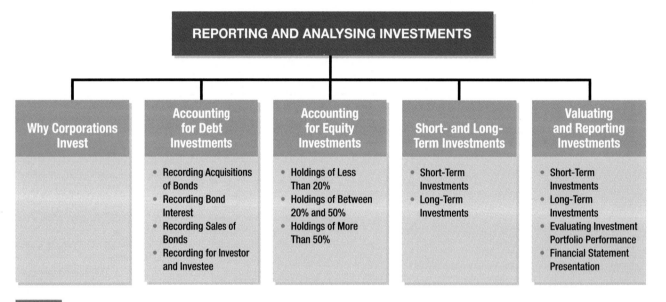

Why Corporations Invest

STUDY OBJECTIVE

①

Identify the reasons corporations invest in debt and equity securities.

Corporations generally purchase investments in debt or equity securities for one of three reasons. First, a corporation may have **excess cash** that it will not need for the purchase of operating assets until a future period. For example, many companies experience seasonal fluctuations in sales which can lead to idle cash until purchases are made for the next busy season. A marina has more sales in the spring and summer than in the fall and winter. The reverse is true for a ski shop.

At the end of an operating cycle, many companies have cash on hand that is idle until the start of another operating cycle. Until the cash is needed, these companies may invest the excess funds to earn a greater return than they would get by just holding the funds in the bank.

When investing excess cash for short periods of time, corporations invest in low-risk, highly liquid securities—most often short-term government securities. Generally, it is unwise to invest short-term excess cash in shares, because equity investments such as these can experience rapid price changes. If a company does invest its short-term excess cash in shares and the price of the shares declines significantly just before the company needs the cash again, it will be forced to sell its equity investment at a loss.

A second reason some companies purchase investments is to generate **earnings from investment income**. Companies generate earnings from interest and dividends by investing in debt and equity securities. Debt securities generate earnings from interest. Although some common shares pay dividends, most companies purchase preferred shares to generate such earnings.

Companies also invest in debt and equity securities hoping they can sell them at a higher price than was originally paid. They speculate that the investment will increase in value and result in a gain when sold.

A third reason companies invest is for **strategic purposes**. A company may purchase a noncontrolling interest in another company in a related industry in which it wishes to establish a presence. Alternatively, a company can exercise some influence over one of its customers or suppliers by purchasing a significant, but not controlling, interest in that company. For example, EnCana has a 31% indirect equity investment in Oleoducto de Crudos Pesados Ltd., the owner of the pipeline that will ship crude oil in Ecuador.

A corporation may also choose to purchase a controlling interest in the common shares of another company. This might be done to enter a new industry without incurring the tremendous costs and risks associated with starting from scratch. Or a company might purchase another company in its industry. The purchase of a company that is in the industry, but involved in a different activity, is called a **vertical acquisition**. In a **horizontal acquisition**, the purchase is of a company that does the same activity as the purchasing company.

In summary, businesses invest in other companies for the reasons shown in Illustration 12-1.

Reason	Typical Investment
To house excess cash until needed	Low-risk, high-liquidity short-term securities such as government-issued securities
To generate earnings *I need 1,000 Treasury bills by tonight*	Debt securities (money market instruments and bonds), and equity securities (preferred and common shares)
To meet strategic goals	Common shares of companies in a related industry or an unrelated industry that the company wishes to enter

Illustration 12-1
Why corporations invest

BUSINESS INSIGHT

MANAGEMENT PERSPECTIVE

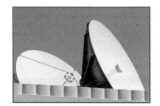

Giant deals were commonplace in the 1990s as mature companies consolidated operations to achieve the scale and scope necessary to dominate global markets. The bear market of the early 2000s quickly sobered this enthusiasm for growth, and squashed non-strategic acquisitions. Today companies are improving their earnings by cost cutting and spinning off divisions, rather than by acquisition.

"Sixty to seventy percent of acquisitions fail to create economic value...the market is not tolerant of people buying the more speculative deals," said Denis Lemieux, a finance specialist with Ernst & Young. Nortel Networks was Canada's acquisition king in the late 1990s, using shares and a small amount of cash to buy 20 companies for about U.S.$33.7 billion. Most of these companies have since been written down or sold at a fraction of their original value as Nortel refocuses on its core business.

Source: Ian Karleff, "Rules of M&A Game Change during a Bear Market: Tables Have Turned," *Financial Post*, November 11, 2002, DM1.

Accounting for Debt Investments

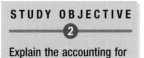

STUDY OBJECTIVE

2

Explain the accounting for debt investments.

Debt investments include investments in money market instruments,[1] as well as investments in government and corporation bonds. In accounting for debt investments, entries are required to record (1) the acquisition, (2) the interest revenue, and (3) the sale. Although we will focus our attention in this section on entries for bonds, the entries for money market instruments are similar.

RECORDING ACQUISITIONS OF BONDS

At acquisition, the **cost principle** applies. Cost includes all expenditures made to acquire these investments, such as the price paid plus brokerage fees (commissions), if any. For example, if Kuhl Corporation acquires 50 Doan Inc. 6%, 10-year, $1,000 bonds on January 1, 2004, for $51,000, including brokerage fees of $1,000, the entry to record the investment is:

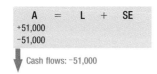

A = L + SE
+51,000
−51,000

Cash flows: −51,000

Jan.	1	Debt Investments—Doan Bonds	51,000	
		Cash		51,000
		(To record purchase of 50 Doan Inc. bonds)		

Kuhl Corporation, as the bondholder, is known as the investor. Doan Inc., as the issuer of the bonds, is known as the investee.

BUSINESS INSIGHT

INVESTOR PERSPECTIVE

Corporate bonds, like shares, are traded on securities exchanges. They can be bought and sold at any time. Bond prices and trading activity are published daily in the financial press, in the format shown below:

	Coupon	Maturity	Price	Yield
Hydro One	5.770	Nov. 15/12	100.50	5.70

This information indicates that Hydro One Inc. has issued 5.77%, $1,000 bonds (default amount), maturing November 15, 2012. These bonds currently are yielding a 5.70% market interest rate. Investors are willing to pay 100.50% of face value, or $1,005 for each bond, on this particular day. Note that since the coupon (contractual) interest rate is higher than the market interest rate, Hydro One's bonds are trading at a premium.

RECORDING BOND INTEREST

Kuhl Corporation's investment in Doan bonds pays interest of $1,500 semi-annually on July 1 and January 1 ($50,000 × 6% × $\frac{6}{12}$). Note that interest is calculated using the face value of the bonds, $50,000, and not on the cost of the bonds, $51,000. The entry for the receipt of interest on July 1 is:

A = L + SE
+1,500   +1,500

Cash flows: +1,500

July	1	Cash	1,500	
		Interest Revenue		1,500
		(To record receipt of interest on Doan Inc. bonds)		

---

[1]Money market instruments include (1) certificates of deposit issued by banks, (2) money market certificates issued by banks, (3) Treasury bills issued by the government, and (4) short-term debt issued by corporations with good credit ratings.

If Kuhl Corporation's fiscal year ends on December 31, it is necessary to accrue the interest of $1,500 earned since July 1. The adjusting entry is:

Dec. 31	Interest Receivable	1,500	
	Interest Revenue		1,500
	(To accrue interest on Doan Inc. bonds)		

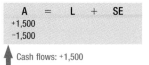

A   =   L   +   SE
+1,500   +1,500

Cash flows: no effect

Interest receivable is reported as a current asset in the balance sheet; interest revenue is reported in the statement of earnings. When the interest is received on January 1, the entry is:

Jan. 1	Cash	1,500	
	Interest Receivable		1,500
	(To record receipt of accrued interest)		

A   =   L   +   SE
+1,500
–1,500

⬆ Cash flows: +1,500

A credit to the Interest Revenue account at this time is incorrect because the interest revenue was earned and accrued in the preceding accounting period.

RECORDING SALES OF BONDS

When bonds are sold, it is necessary to (1) update any unrecorded interest up to the date of the sale, and (2) credit the investment account for the cost of the bonds. Any difference between the net proceeds from the sale (sales price less brokerage fees) and the cost of the bonds is recorded as a gain or loss.

Assume, for example, that Kuhl Corporation receives net proceeds of $55,000 on the sale of the Doan Inc. bonds on January 1, 2005, after receiving the interest due. Since the securities cost $51,000, a gain of $4,000 has been realized. The entry to record the sale is:

Jan. 1	Cash	55,000	
	Debt Investments—Doan bonds		51,000
	Gain on Sale of Debt Investment		4,000
	(To record sale of Doan bonds)		

A   =   L   +   SE
+55,000   +4,000
–51,000

⬆ Cash flows: +55,000

The gain on the sale of debt investments is reported as other revenue in the statement of earnings.

RECORDING FOR INVESTOR AND INVESTEE

Recording an investment in bonds (an asset) is essentially the inverse of recording long-term bonds payable (a liability), discussed in Chapter 10. Using the Kuhl Corporation example introduced earlier, Illustration 12-2 compares the recording of the bonds as an investment for Kuhl (the investor) and the recording of the bonds as a liability for Doan (the investee). For the purposes of this illustration, we have assumed that the bonds have been issued at face value.

Helpful Hint The accounting for short-term debt investments and long-term debt investments is similar. Exceptions are discussed in more advanced courses.

Illustration 12-2
Comparison of bond investment and liability

Kuhl Corporation—Investor				Doan Inc.—Investee		
Jan. 1	Debt Investment—Doan Bonds	51,000		Cash	50,000	
	Cash		51,000	Bonds Payable		50,000
	(To record purchase of 6%, 10-year Doan bonds)			(To record issue of 6%, 10-year bonds)		
July 1	Cash ($50,000 × 6% × $\frac{6}{12}$)	1,500		Interest Expense	1,500	
	Interest Revenue		1,500	Cash ($50,000 × 6% × $\frac{6}{12}$)		1,500
	(To record receipt of semi-annual interest)			(To record payment of semi-annual interest)		

BEFORE YOU GO ON . . .

- **REVIEW IT**

  1. What are the reasons corporations invest in debt and equity securities?
  2. What entries are required in accounting for debt investments?
  3. Compare the accounting for bond investments and liabilities.

- **DO IT**

The Wang Corporation had the following transactions pertaining to debt investments:

Jan. 1 Purchased 30 $1,000, 5% Hillary Corp. bonds for $30,000 plus brokerage fees of $900. Interest is payable semi-annually on July 1 and January 1.
July 1 Received semi-annual interest on Hillary bonds.
     1 Sold 15 Hillary bonds for $15,000, less $400 of brokerage fees.

(a) Journalize the transactions.
(b) Prepare the adjusting entry for the accrual of interest on December 31.

Action Plan

- Record the bond investment at cost, including brokerage fees.
- When bonds are sold, (1) update any unrecorded interest and (2) credit the investment account for the cost of the bonds.
- Record any difference between the cost of the bonds and the net proceeds as a gain or loss: Gain = Proceeds > Cost; Loss = Proceeds < Cost.

Solution

(a)

Jan.	1	Debt Investments—Hillary Bonds	30,900	
		Cash ($30,000 + $900)		30,900
		(To record purchase of 5% Hillary Corp. bonds)		
July	1	Cash	750	
		Interest Revenue ($30,000 × 5% × $\frac{6}{12}$)		750
		(To record receipt of semi-annual interest on Hillary bonds)		
July	1	Cash ($15,000 − $400)	14,600	
		Loss on Sale of Debt Investments	850	
		Debt Investments—Hillary Bonds ($30,900 × $\frac{15}{30}$)		15,450
		(To record sale of 15 Hillary bonds)		

(b)

Dec. 31		Interest Receivable	375	
		Interest Revenue ($15,000 × 5% × $\frac{6}{12}$)		375
		(To accrue semi-annual interest on Hillary bonds)		

Accounting for Equity Investments

STUDY OBJECTIVE

3

Explain the accounting for equity investments.

Equity investments are investments in the share capital—common and/or preferred— of other corporations. When a company holds shares and/or debt of several different corporations, the group of securities is identified as an **investment portfolio.**

The accounting for investments in common shares is based on the extent of the investor's influence over the operating and financial affairs of the issuing corporation (the investee) as shown in Illustration 12-3.

Illustration 12-3
Accounting guidelines
for equity investments

Investor's Ownership Interest in Investee's Common Shares	Presumed Influence on Investee	Accounting Guidelines
Less than 20%	Insignificant	Cost method
Between 20% and 50%	Significant	Equity method
More than 50%	Controlling	Equity method for accounting; consolidated financial statements for reporting

In some cases, depending on the degree of investor influence, net earnings of the investee are considered to be earnings to the investor. When an investor owns 20% or more of the common shares of another company, it is generally presumed to exercise a significant influence over the decisions of the investee company. The presumed influence may be negated by extenuating circumstances. For example, a company that acquires a 25% interest in another company in a "hostile" takeover may not have any significant influence over the investee.

Among the questions that should be considered in determining an investor's influence are whether (1) the investor has representation on the investee's board of directors, (2) the investor participates in the investee's policy-making process, (3) there are material transactions between the investor and the investee, and (4) the common shares held by other shareholders are concentrated or dispersed. Companies are required to use judgment instead of blindly following the guidelines. We now explain and illustrate the application of each guideline.

HOLDINGS OF LESS THAN 20%

In accounting for equity investments of less than 20%, the cost method is used. Under the cost method, the investment is recorded at cost, and revenue is only recognized when cash dividends are received. EnCana's 10% investment in Syncrude Canada mentioned in the feature story would have been accounted for using the cost method before EnCana sold this investment in 2003.

Recording Acquisitions of Shares

The **cost principle** applies when shares are purchased. Cost includes all expenditures made to acquire these investments, such as the price paid plus brokerage fees, if any. Assume, for example, that on July 1, 2004, Passera Corporation (the investor) acquires 1,000 common shares (10% ownership) of Beal Corporation (the investee) at $40 per share plus brokerage fees of $500. The entry for the purchase is:

July 1	Equity Investments—Beal Common	40,500	
	Cash		40,500
	(To record purchase of 1,000 common shares of Beal)		

A = L + SE
+40,500
−40,500

Cash flows: −40,500

While the investor, Passera Corporation, must make an entry to record this acquisition, no entry is required by Beal Corporation. Recall that shares, once issued, are traded among investors. Passera did not purchase these shares directly from Beal. It purchased them from investors on organized stock exchanges, such as the Toronto Stock Exchange.

Recording Dividend Revenue

During the time the shares are held, entries are required for any cash dividends received. Thus, if a $2-per-share dividend is received by Passera Corporation on December 31, the entry is:

Dec. 31	Cash (1,000 × $2)	2,000	
	Dividend Revenue		2,000
	(To record receipt of cash dividend)		

Dividend revenue is reported as other revenue in the statement of earnings.

Recording Sales of Shares

When shares are sold, the difference between the net proceeds from the sale (sales price less brokerage fees) and the cost of the shares is recognized as a gain or loss. Assume that Passera Corporation receives net proceeds of $39,500 on the sale of its Beal Corporation shares on February 10, 2005. Because the shares cost $40,500, there has been a loss of $1,000. The entry to record the sale is:

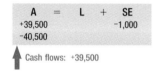

Feb. 10	Cash	39,500	
	Loss on Sale of Equity Investments	1,000	
	Equity Investments—Beal Common		40,500
	(To record sale of Beal common shares)		

The loss is reported as other expenses in the statement of earnings, whereas a gain on sale is shown as other revenues.

HOLDINGS OF BETWEEN 20% AND 50%

When an investor owns only a small portion of the common shares of another company, the investor cannot exercise control over the investee. But when an investor owns between 20% and 50% of the common shares of a corporation, it is presumed that the investor has **significant influence** over the investee's financial and operating activities. The investor probably has a representative on the investee's board of directors. Through that representative, the investor begins to exercise some control over the investee. The investee company, to some extent, becomes part of the investor company.

As mentioned earlier in the chapter, EnCana has a 31% equity investment in Oleoducto de Crudos Pesados Ltd., the owner of a crude pipeline in Ecuador. Because it exercises significant influence over major decisions made by Oleoducto, EnCana uses an approach called the equity method to account for its investment. Under the equity method, **the investor records its share of the net earnings of the investee in the year the earnings occur**. An alternative might be to delay recognizing the investor's share of net earnings until a cash dividend is declared. But that approach would ignore the fact that the investor and investee are, in some sense, one company, making the investee's earnings an immediate improvement to the investor's situation.

Under the equity method, the investment in common shares is initially recorded at cost. After that, the investment account is adjusted annually to show the investor's equity in the investee. Each year, the investor does the following: It (1) increases (debits) its investment account and increases (credits) revenue for its share of the investee's net earnings,[2] and (2) decreases (credits) the investment account for the amount of dividends received. The investment account is reduced for dividends received because the net assets of the investee are decreased when a dividend is paid.

Recording Acquisitions of Shares

Assume that Milar Corporation (the investor) acquires 30% of the common shares of Beck Inc. (the investee) for $120,000 on January 1, 2004. The entry to record this transaction is:

Jan. 1	Equity Investments—Beck Common	120,000	
	Cash		120,000
	(To record purchase of Beck common shares)		

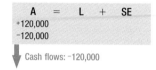

Recording Investment Revenue and Dividends

For the year ended December 31, 2004, Beck reports net earnings of $100,000. It declares and pays a $40,000 cash dividend. Milar is required to record (1) its share of Beck's earnings, $30,000 (30% × $100,000), and (2) the reduction in the investment account for the dividends received, $12,000 ($40,000 × 30%). The entries are:

(1)

Dec. 31	Equity Investments—Beck Common	30,000	
	Revenue from Investment in Beck Company		30,000
	(To record 30% equity in Beck's net earnings)		

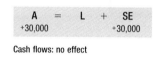

(2)

Dec. 31	Cash	12,000	
	Equity Investments—Beck Common		12,000
	(To record dividends received)		

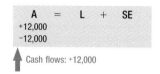

After the transactions for the year are posted, the investment and revenue accounts show the following:

Equity Investments—Beck Common				Revenue from Investment in Beck Company	
Jan. 1	120,000	Dec. 31	12,000		
Dec. 31	30,000			Dec. 31	30,000
Dec. 31 Bal.	138,000				

During the year, the investment account has increased by $18,000 ($30,000 − $12,000). This $18,000 is Milar's 30% equity in the $60,000 increase in Beck's retained earnings ($100,000 − $40,000). In addition, Milar reports $30,000 of revenue from its investment, which is 30% of Beck's net earnings of $100,000.

The difference between reported earnings under the cost method and under the equity method can be significant. For example, Milar would report only the $12,000 of dividend revenue (30% × $40,000) if the cost method were used.

Illustration 12-4 compares the journal entries used to record these investment transactions. First, it is assumed that the cost method (no significant influence) is used by Milar. Then we assume that the equity method (as discussed in this section) is used.

---

[2] Conversely, the investor increases (debits) a loss account and decreases (credits) the investment account for its share of the investee's net loss.

	Cost Method				Equity Method		
Acquisition							
Equity Investments—Beck	120,000			Equity Investments—Beck	120,000		
Cash		120,000		Cash		120,000	
Investee reports earnings							
No entry				Equity Investments—Beck	30,000		
				Revenue from Investment		30,000	
Investee pays dividends							
Cash	12,000			Cash	12,000		
Dividend Revenue		12,000		Equity Investments—Beck		12,000	

Illustration 12-4
Comparison of cost and equity methods

Helpful Hint From the viewpoint of the shareholders of the parent company, if the parent (A) has three wholly owned subsidiaries (B, C, and D), there are four separate legal entities but only one economic entity.

HOLDINGS OF MORE THAN 50%

A company that owns more than 50% of, or controls, the common shares of another entity is known as the parent company. The entity whose shares are owned by the parent company is called the subsidiary (affiliated) company. Because of its share ownership, the parent company has a controlling interest in the subsidiary company. Voting control can occur with share ownership of less than 50%, depending on how widely dispersed the share ownership is, and other factors mentioned previously.

When a company controls another company, consolidated financial statements are prepared for financial reporting purposes. Consolidated financial statements present the assets and liabilities controlled by the parent company. They also present the total revenues and expenses of the subsidiary companies. They are prepared in addition to the financial statements for the individual parent and subsidiary companies. For example, EnCana has a number of subsidiaries—one of which is the Alberta Energy Company Ltd. (AEC). It uses the equity method to account for its investment in AEC in its own accounting records and internal financial statements. But, for external reporting, EnCana consolidates AEC's results with its own. Under this approach, the individual assets and liabilities of AEC are included with those of EnCana.

Consolidated financial statements are useful to the shareholders, board of directors, and management of the parent company. Consolidated statements indicate to creditors, prospective investors, and regulatory agencies the magnitude and scope of operations of the companies under common control. Consolidation is a complex topic which is usually dealt with in advanced accounting courses.

BUSINESS INSIGHT

MANAGEMENT PERSPECTIVE

The top five subsidiary companies in Canada, ranked by revenue, are listed below. In all cases, the major shareholder controls (owns more than 50%) of the subsidiary's shares. The percentage ownership is indicated in parentheses.

Rank	Subsidiary	Parent
1	Loblaw, Toronto	George Weston (61%)
2	Power Financial, Montreal	Power Corp. of Canada (67%)
3	Great-West Lifeco, Winnipeg	Power Financial (82%)
4	Celestica, Toronto	Onex (84%)
5	Bell Canada, Montreal	BCE (100%)

BEFORE YOU GO ON...

● REVIEW IT

1. Compare the accounting entries for equity investments in common shares with ownership of (a) less than 20% with no significant influence, and (b) more than 20% with significant influence.
2. What entries are made under the equity method when (a) the investor receives a cash dividend from the investee and (b) the investee reports net earnings for the year?
3. What is the purpose of consolidated financial statements?

● DO IT

CJW, Inc., purchased 20% of North Sails' 60,000 common shares at a cost of $10 per share on January 1, 2004. On April 15, North Sails declared and paid a cash dividend of $45,000. On December 31, North Sails reported net earnings of $120,000 for the year.

Prepare all necessary journal entries assuming (a) no significant influence exists and (b) significant influence exists.

Action Plan

- Use the cost method when significant influence is not present (normally less than 20% ownership).
- Under the cost method, recognize income when dividends are declared.
- Use the equity method when significant influence exists (normally 20% or more ownership).
- Under the equity method, recognize income when the investee declares net earnings. The distribution of dividends is not income; rather, it reduces the equity investment.

Solution

(a) Cost Method

Jan. 1	Equity Investments—North Sails Common	120,000	
	(12,000 × $10)		
	Cash		120,000
	(To record purchase of 12,000		
	[20% × 60,000] North Sails shares)		
Apr. 15	Cash	9,000	
	Dividend Revenue ($45,000 × 20%)		9,000
	(To record receipt of cash dividend)		

(b) Equity Method

Jan. 1	Equity Investments—North Sails Common	120,000	
	(12,000 × $10)		
	Cash		120,000
	(To record purchase of 12,000		
	[20% × 60,000] North Sails shares)		
Apr. 15	Cash	9,000	
	Equity Investments—North Sails Common		
	($45,000 × 20%)		9,000
	(To record receipt of cash dividend)		
Dec. 31	Equity Investments—North Sails Common	24,000	
	($120,000 × 20%)		
	Revenue from Investment in North Sails		24,000
	(To record 20% equity in North Sails' net		
	earnings)		

Short- and Long-Term Investments

In addition to being classified as debt or equity investments, investments are also categorized as short-term and long-term investments.

SHORT-TERM INVESTMENTS

Short-term investments ordinarily consist of money market instruments, debt securities (government and corporate bonds), and equity securities (preferred and common shares). However, in order to be classified as short-term, these investments must be (1) **readily marketable** and (2) **intended to be converted into cash** in the near future.

Readily Marketable

An investment is "readily marketable" if it can be easily sold whenever the need for cash arises. Money market instruments meet this criterion, as they can be sold readily to other investors. Shares and bonds traded on organized securities markets, such as the Toronto Stock Exchange, are readily marketable because they can be bought and sold daily. In contrast, there may be only a limited market for the securities issued by small corporations and no market for the securities of a privately held company.

Intent to Convert

"Intent to convert" means that management intends to sell the investment whenever the need for cash arises. It is the intention to sell that determines whether or not the investment is classified as temporary, not the length of time it is held. For example, a ski resort may invest idle cash during the summer months and intend to sell the securities to buy supplies and equipment shortly before the next winter season. This investment is considered temporary even if lack of snow cancels the next ski season and eliminates the need to convert the securities into cash as intended.

LONG-TERM INVESTMENTS

Long-term investments can also consist of debt securities (government and corporate bonds) and equity securities (preferred and common shares), among other items. To determine whether a debt or equity security is short-term or long-term, we test the investment against the short-term investment criteria. Investments that do not meet *both* short-term investment criteria—readily marketable and intent to convert—are long-term investments.

Valuating and Reporting Investments

The value of debt and equity investments may fluctuate greatly during the time they are held. Bond and share equity prices may jump dramatically with favourable economic events and drop drastically with unfavourable economic developments. For example, in the first full week of trading following the September 11, 2001, terrorist attack on the U.S., the Dow Jones Industrial Average had its biggest drop in nearly 70 years. The Dow Jones is the oldest and best-known index of the U.S. stock market, measuring the price movements of the 30 large and well-known companies that best represent the American economy.

If prices fluctuate so much, how should investments be valued at the balance sheet date? Valuation could be at cost, at market value, or at the lower of cost and market value. Some argue that market value is the best valuation because it is the expected realizable value. Market value is the amount for which a security can be sold in a normal market. Others say, however, that unless the investment is going to be sold soon, the market value is not relevant because the price will likely change again. **Conservatism** resolves this issue by requiring the application of the lower of cost and market (LCM) rule.

You were first introduced to the lower of cost and market rule in Chapter 6 with respect to inventories. Just as inventories are reported at the lower of their cost and market value, so too are investments. If the market value of the investments falls below their cost, this potential loss should be recognized as soon as it becomes known in order to minimize any negative impact on decision-makers. Application of the LCM rule varies depending on whether the investment is short-term or long-term.

SHORT-TERM INVESTMENTS

To illustrate the valuation of short-term debt and equity investments, assume that on December 31, 2004, Plano Corporation has the following costs and market values:

Investments	Cost	Market Value	LCM Value
Bell Canada bonds	$ 50,000	$ 48,000	$(2,000)
Nexfor shares	90,000	91,000	1,000
Total	$140,000	$139,000	$(1,000)

The LCM rule is normally applied to the total portfolio and not to individual investments. Applying LCM individually results in an overly conservative valuation with what is already a conservative rule.

The adjusting entry for Plano is as follows:

Dec. 31	Loss on Decline in Value of Investment	1,000	
	Allowance to Reduce Cost to Market Value		1,000
	(To record loss in value of short-term investments)		

A	=	L	+	SE
−1,000				+1,000

Cash flows: no effect

The decline in value from cost to market is reported as an other expense on the statement of earnings. A valuation allowance account, Allowance to Reduce Cost to Market Value, is used to record the difference between the cost and market value of the securities. The use of this **contra asset** account, enables the company to maintain a record of the investment cost. Actual cost is needed to determine the gain or loss realized when individual securities are sold. The allowance account balance is deducted from the cost of the investments to arrive at the lower of cost and market valuation reported on the balance sheet for the short-term investments.

The allowance account is carried forward into future accounting periods, in a manner similar to the Allowance for Doubtful Accounts, which offsets Accounts Receivable. No entries are made to the Allowance to Reduce Cost to Market Value account during the period. At the end of each reporting period, the balance in the account is adjusted to the difference between cost and market value. If the market value recovers above the cost, the allowance account can be adjusted to a zero balance. The valuation allowance should never have a debit balance; this would result in the recognition of a gain. Remember that while conservatism allows losses to be recognized in advance of realization, gains are not recognized until they are realized.

LONG-TERM INVESTMENTS

Helpful Hint Note that while an allowance is used to record declines in market value below cost in the *total portfolio* of short-term investments, *individual* long-term investments are directly written down if the decline is permanent.

Because long-term investments have longer maturities than short-term investments, **their carrying values are not adjusted to reflect short-term fluctuations in market values.** If market value falls substantially below cost and the decline is considered permanent, the investment must be reduced to its market value. This value becomes the investment's new cost base. Any write-down to market value is directly credited to the investment account as no subsequent recovery in value is anticipated.

To illustrate, assume that Hébert Corporation purchased 10,000 shares of Bre-X Minerals Ltd., at a cost of $20 per share, as a long-term investment. These shares are now worthless as Bre-X no longer exists. The adjusting entry for Hébert to record the realized loss of $200,000 is as follows:

A	=	L	+	SE
-200,000				-200,000

Cash flows: no effect

Dec. 31	Loss on Decline in Value of Investment	200,000	
	Equity Investment—Bre-X Minerals Shares		200,000
	(To record loss in value of long-term		
	investment in Bre-X shares)		

BUSINESS INSIGHT

INVESTOR PERSPECTIVE

JDS Uniphase Corporation's eye-popping U.S.$56 billion loss in 2001 represented a hangover from a high-priced acquisition binge to build up the optical equipment market—a spending spree that came back to haunt it. This loss amounts to the equivalent of a stack of U.S.$10,000 bills 2.3 times the height of the CN Tower.

Massive write-offs of investments contributed to the fibre-optics supplier's loss. In hindsight, the company grossly overpaid for its acquisitions. A senior technology analyst said at the time, "The market has devalued the companies significantly, so they're revaluating those assets at current market valuations."

Source: Showwei Chu, "Buying Binge Blamed for Startling JDS Loss," *The Globe and Mail,* July 27, 2001, B1.

EVALUATING INVESTMENT PORTFOLIO PERFORMANCE

The potential for earnings management in valuating and reporting investments is readily apparent. Companies can easily "window dress" their reported earnings results—that is, make net earnings look better or worse than they really are. Refer back to the values of Plano Corporation's short-term investments. Assume Plano has a large net earnings amount this year and wants to minimize demands from shareholders for more dividends, or from employees for increased wages. It could simply choose to sell those investments that have losses (Bell Canada bonds) before the year end. This would have the effect of reducing earnings by $2,000, compared to the $1,000 LCM loss that would be recorded if Plano retained all of its investments.

Another way that earnings can be managed is by altering a company's classification of investments as short-term or long-term. Remember that classification depends on management's intent—a subjective concept. If the investment portfolio contains some investments whose market value is greater than cost and some whose market value is less than cost, classifying them as short-term allows increases to be offset against decreases. Only the net cost and net market values are taken into consideration when applying the LCM rule to short-term investments. One can see that companies could have an incentive to classify their investments as short-term rather than long-term depending on the investment's performance.

Alternatively, if the investments are classified as long-term, companies can potentially defer recognition of losses by simply assuming that the criterion of a permanent decline is not met. Clearly, it is important to consider the impact of actual and potential losses on current and future earnings when evaluating the performance of a company's investment portfolio.

Decision Toolkit

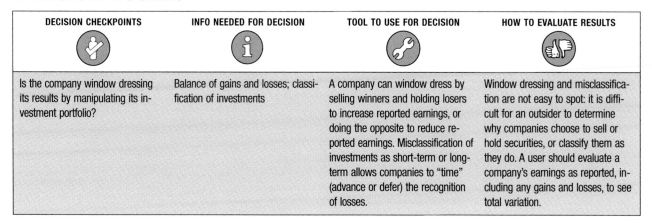

DECISION CHECKPOINTS	INFO NEEDED FOR DECISION	TOOL TO USE FOR DECISION	HOW TO EVALUATE RESULTS
Is the company window dressing its results by manipulating its investment portfolio?	Balance of gains and losses; classification of investments	A company can window dress by selling winners and holding losers to increase reported earnings, or doing the opposite to reduce reported earnings. Misclassification of investments as short-term or long-term allows companies to "time" (advance or defer) the recognition of losses.	Window dressing and misclassification are not easy to spot: it is difficult for an outsider to determine why companies choose to sell or hold securities, or classify them as they do. A user should evaluate a company's earnings as reported, including any gains and losses, to see total variation.

FINANCIAL STATEMENT PRESENTATION

Balance Sheet Presentation

For balance sheet presentation, investments must be classified as either short-term or long-term. No distinction is usually made between debt and equity securities for financial reporting purposes. These securities are usually combined and reported as one portfolio amount for each of the short-term or long-term classifications in the balance sheet.

Short-Term Investments. Cash, the most liquid asset, is listed first in the current assets section of the balance sheet. Highly liquid investments of a very short-term duration (typically less than three months) are viewed as cash equivalents and often combined with cash for reporting purposes.

Other short-term investments are presented next in order of liquidity. Short-term investments are reported on the balance sheet at the lower of cost and market value. Because of the importance of market value to the reader of the financial statements, the market value is also disclosed, either in parentheses or in a note.

Long-Term Investments. Long-term investments are generally reported in a separate section of the balance sheet. The following illustration presents the assets section of a balance sheet, detailing the presentation of its short- and long-term investments.

Statement of Earnings Presentation

Gains and losses on investments must be presented in the financial statements. In the statement of earnings, gains and losses, as well as interest and dividend revenue, are reported in the non-operating section, normally as other revenue and expense.

Illustration 12-5
Balance sheet presentation
of investments

PACE CORPORATION Balance Sheet (partial) December 31, 2004			
Assets			
Current assets			
Cash and cash equivalents			$ 21,000
Short-term investments, at lower of cost and market (market $75,000)			60,000
Accounts receivable		$ 84,000	
Less: Allowance for doubtful accounts		4,000	80,000
Merchandise inventory			130,000
Prepaid insurance			23,000
Total current assets			314,000
Investments			
Debt investments		$100,000	
Equity investments at cost		150,000	
Equity investments at equity		150,000	
Total investments			400,000
Property, plant, and equipment			
Land		$200,000	
Buildings	$800,000		
Less: Accumulated amortization	200,000	600,000	
Equipment	$180,000		
Less: Accumulated amortization	54,000	126,000	926,000
Goodwill			170,000
Total assets			$1,810,000

Cash Flow Statement Presentation

As shown in Illustration 12-5, the balance sheet presents the balances in a company's investment accounts at a point in time. Information on the cash inflows and outflows that resulted from investment transactions during the period is reported in the investing activities section of the cash flow statement.

Illustration 12-6 presents the cash flows from investing activities from EnCana's 2002 cash flow statement. From this information, we learn that EnCana spent a total of $4,062 million on investing activities in 2002. These activities included spending $128 million to merge with Alberta Energy Company Ltd. This cash outflow was offset by $93 million in cash received from corporate dispositions (selling other companies) and $64 million net cash received from investments and other assets.

Illustration 12-6
Cash flow statement
presentation of investments

ENCANA CORPORATION Cash Flow Statement (partial) Year Ended December 31, 2002 (in millions)	
Investing activities	
Business combination with Alberta Energy Company Ltd.	$ (128)
Capital expenditures	(4,940)
Proceeds on disposal of capital assets	566
Corporate dispositions	93
Net change in investments and other	64
Net change in noncash working capital from continuing operations	293
Discontinued operations	(10)
	$(4,062)

BEFORE YOU GO ON . . .

- ● **REVIEW IT**

1. What are the proper valuation and reporting for short-term and long-term investments on the balance sheet? Statement of earnings? Cash flow statement?
2. How might a company window dress its reported earnings?
3. What do Loblaw's short-term investments consist of? Are they carried at cost, market, or LCM? Does Loblaw have any long-term investments? The answers to these questions are provided at the end of this chapter

Using the Decision Toolkit

EnCana's largest competitor is Exxon Mobil Corporation. Exxon Mobil is the world's largest integrated oil company, engaged in oil and gas exploration, production, supply, transportation, and marketing around the world. Exxon Mobil reported the following selected information about its long-term investments in 2002:

EXXON MOBIL CORPORATION Consolidated Balance Sheet (partial) December 31, 2002 (in U.S. millions)	
Investments and advances	
Companies carried at equity	$9,859
Companies carried at cost	1,088

Exxon Mobil has a long history of acquisitions. In 1999, it acquired Mobil for U.S.$81 billion. It also owns 70% of Imperial Oil Limited—Canada's largest oil company— in addition to interests in many other subsidiaries. On a smaller scale, Exxon Mobil owns a 19% interest in Guangzhou Petrochemical (a subsidiary of China Petroleum & Chemical Corp.), with which it began negotiations in 2002 to jointly expand capacity at Guangzhou's refinery.

Instructions

1. In addition to what is shown in the consolidated balance sheet, Exxon Mobile also reports Cash and Cash Equivalents of U.S.$7,229 million. What are cash equivalents?
2. What method—cost or equity—should Exxon Mobil use to record its ownership interest in Guangzhou Petrochemical? Explain the impact that using the method you chose has on the recognition of earnings.
3. What method—cost or equity—should Exxon Mobil use to record its ownership interest in Imperial Oil? Explain the impact that using the method you chose has on the recognition of earnings.
4. How should Exxon Mobil report its investment in Imperial Oil on its financial statements?

Solution

1. Cash equivalents are short-term investments that are highly liquid and have maturities of less than three months. They are considered to be "near cash" items and combined with cash for reporting purposes.

2. Exxon Mobil's 19% ownership interest in Guangzhou Petrochemical should be accounted for using the cost method, assuming significant influence is not present. Use of the cost method means that Exxon Mobil does not record any investment earnings until Guangzhou Petrochemical declares dividends. If significant influence exists—it may, given the ongoing negotiations to expand capacity—then Exxon Mobil's ownership interest should be accounted for using the equity method.

3. Exxon Mobil's 70% ownership interest in Imperial Oil should be accounted for using the equity method. Use of the equity method means that Exxon Mobil records its proportionate share of investment earnings (or losses) when Imperial Oil declares its own earnings (or losses) and increase the value of its investment in Imperial Oil. Any dividends paid by Imperial Oil would reduce the value of Exxon Mobil's investment. Because Exxon Mobil controls (exerts significant influence over) Imperial Oil, it is not appropriate to wait until dividends are distributed to recognize the earnings.

4. Exxon Mobil must use the equity method to account for its investment in Imperial Oil in its internal accounting records. For external reporting purposes, Exxon Mobil must consolidate (combine) the activities of its subsidiaries such as Imperial Oil with its own, and report the combined activities as though they were one entity.

Summary of Study Objectives

❶ Identify the reasons corporations invest in debt and equity securities. Corporations invest for three common reasons: (1) They have excess cash. (2) They view investments as a significant revenue source. (3) They have strategic goals such as gaining control of a competitor or moving into a new line of business.

❷ Explain the accounting for debt investments. Entries for investments in debt securities are required when (1) bonds are purchased, (2) interest is received or accrued, and (3) bonds are sold.

❸ Explain the accounting for equity investments. Entries for investments in shares are required when (1) the shares are purchased, (2) dividends are received, and (3) shares are sold. When the investor company is not able to exert significant influence (ownership usually < 20%) over the operating and financial policies of the investee company, the cost method should be used. When significant influence exists (ownership usually > 20%), the equity method should be used.

❹ Describe the purpose and usefulness of consolidated financial statements. When a company controls (owner-ship usually > 50%) the voting shares of another company, consolidated financial statements detailing the financial position of the combined entity must also be prepared. These statements are especially useful to the shareholders, board of directors, and management of the parent company.

❺ Distinguish between short-term and long-term investments. Short-term investments are securities held by a company that are readily marketable and intended to be converted to cash in the near future as the need for cash arises. Investments that do not meet both criteria are classified as long-term investments.

❻ Indicate how debt and equity investments are valued and reported in the financial statements. Short-term investments in debt and equity securities are valuated at the lower of cost and market, with market values separately disclosed. Long-term investments are valuated at cost. If market value is anticipated to be less than cost on a permanent basis, the investment should be written down to market, which now becomes its new cost base.

Decision
Toolkit
Summary

Decision Toolkit—A Summary

DECISION CHECKPOINTS	INFO NEEDED FOR DECISION	TOOL TO USE FOR DECISION	HOW TO EVALUATE RESULTS
Is the company window dressing its results by manipulating its investment portfolio?	Balance of gains and losses; classification of investments	A company can window dress by selling winners and holding losers to increase reported earnings, or doing the opposite to reduce reported earnings. Misclassification of investments as short-term or long-term allows companies to "time" (advance or defer) the recognition of losses.	Window dressing and misclassification are not easy to spot: it is difficult for an outsider to determine why companies choose to sell or hold securities, or classify them as they do. A user should evaluate a company's earnings as reported, including any gains and losses, to see total variation.

NAVIGATOR

Glossary

Glossary

Consolidated financial statements Financial statements that present the assets and liabilities controlled by the parent company and the collective profitability of the affiliated companies. (p. 572)

Controlling interest Ownership of more than 50%, or voting control, of the common shares of another entity. (p. 572)

Cost method An accounting method in which the equity investment in shares is recorded at cost and revenue is recognized only when cash dividends are received. (p. 569)

Debt investments Investments in money market instruments, and government and corporation bonds. (p. 566)

Equity investments Investments in the share capital of corporations. (p. 568)

Equity method An accounting method in which the investment in common shares is initially recorded at cost. The investment account is then adjusted annually (increased for share of investee's net earnings and decreased for dividends received) to show the investor's equity in the investee. (p. 570)

Investee The corporation that issues the debt or equity securities. (p. 566)

Investor The corporation that purchases (owns) the debt or equity securities. (p. 566)

Long-term investments Investments that are not readily marketable or that management does not intend to convert into cash in the near future. (p. 574)

Lower of cost and market (LCM) A conservative rule that states that investments must be carried at the lower of their cost and market value. (p. 575)

Market value Amount for which a security could be sold in a normal market. (p. 575)

Parent company A company that controls, or owns more than 50% of the common shares of, another entity. (p. 572)

Short-term investments Investments that are readily marketable and intended to be converted into cash in the near future when the need for cash arises. (p. 574)

Subsidiary (affiliated) company A company which has another company controlling its common shares (usually owning more than 50%). (p. 572)

Demonstration Problem

Additional
Demonstration
Problems

In its first year of operations, DeMarco Ltd. had these selected transactions in short-term equity investments:

June   1   Purchased for cash 600 Sanburg common shares at $24 per share plus $300 of brokerage fees.
July   1   Purchased for cash 800 Cey common shares at $33 per share plus $600 of brokerage fees.
Sept. 1   Received a $1-per-share cash dividend from Cey Corporation.
Nov.   1   Sold 200 Sanburg common shares for cash at $27 per share less $150 of brokerage fees.
Dec. 15   Received a $0.50-per-share cash dividend on Sanburg common shares.

At December 31, the market values per share were Sanburg, $25, and Cey, $30.

Instructions

(a) Journalize the transactions, assuming DeMarco uses the cost method to account for them.
(b) Prepare the adjusting entry at December 31 to report the securities at their lower of cost and market value.

Action Plan

- Recall that cost includes the price paid plus brokerage fees.
- Record dividend revenue when received (or declared).
- Keep a running balance of the number of shares purchased and sold for each company.
- Calculate the gain or loss by subtracting the cost of the securities from the net selling price.
- Determine the adjustment to LCM based on the difference between the total cost and total market value of the securities.

Solution to Demonstration Problem

(a)

June 1	Equity Investments—Sanburg Common	14,700	
	Cash [(600 × $24) + $300]		14,700
	(To record purchase of 600 Sanburg common shares)		
July 1	Equity Investments—Cey Common	27,000	
	Cash [(800 × $33) + $600]		27,000
	(To record purchase of 800 Cey common shares)		
Sept. 1	Cash (800 × $1)	800	
	Dividend Revenue		800
	(To record receipt of $1-per-share cash dividend from Cey)		
Nov. 1	Cash [(200 × $27) − $150]	5,250	
	Equity Investments—Sanburg Common (200 ÷ 600 × $14,700)		4,900
	Gain on Sale of Equity Investments		350
	(To record sale of 200 Sanburg common shares)		
Dec. 15	Cash [(600 − 200) × $0.50]	200	
	Dividend Revenue		200
	(To record receipt of $0.50-per-share dividend from Sanburg)		

(b)

Dec. 31	Loss on Decline in Value of Short-Term Investments	2,800	
	Allowance to Reduce Cost to Market Value		2,800
	(To record loss on short-term investments)		

Investment	Cost	Market Value	Gain (Loss)
Sanburg common shares (400)	$ 9,800	$10,000	$ 200
Cey common shares (800)	27,000	24,000	(3,000)
Total	$36,800	$34,000	$(2,800)

NAVIGATOR

Self-Study Questions

Multiple Choice

Answers are at the end of the chapter.

(SO 1) 1. Which of the following is not a reason that corporations invest in debt and equity securities?
(a) They have excess cash.
(b) They wish to lose money and generate losses to reduce taxable income.
(c) They wish to generate investment income.
(d) They invest to meet strategic goals.

(SO 2) 2. Debt investments are initially recorded at:
(a) cost.
(b) lower of cost and market value.
(c) market value.
(d) book value.

(SO 2) 3. Hanes Ltd. sells debt investments costing $26,000 for $28,000. In journalizing the sale, credits are:
(a) Debt Investments and Loss on Sale of Debt Investments.
(b) Debt Investments and Gain on Sale of Debt Investments.
(c) Debt Investments and Interest Revenue.
(d) The correct answer is not given.

(SO 3) 4. Pryor Ltd. receives net proceeds of $37,000 on the sale of equity investments that cost $39,500. This transaction will result in reporting in the statement of earnings a:
(a) loss of $2,500 under Other Expenses.
(b) loss of $2,500 under Operating Expenses.
(c) gain of $2,500 under Other Revenues.
(d) gain of $2,500 under Operating Revenues.

(SO 3) 5. The equity method of accounting for long-term investments in shares should be used when the investor owns:
(a) less than 20% of the investee's common shares.
(b) more than 20% of the investee's common shares.
(c) more than 20% of the investee's bonds.
(d) between 20% and 50% of the investee's common shares.

(SO 3) 6. The Big K Ranch owns 20% of the Little L Ranch. The Little L Ranch reported net earnings of $150,000 and paid dividends of $40,000 this year. How much investment revenue would the Big K Ranch report if it used the cost method to account for this investment? The equity method?
(a) $8,000 cost method; $22,000 equity method

(b) $8,000 cost method; $30,000 equity method
(c) $40,000 cost metod; $110,000 equity method
(d) $150,000 under both methods

(SO 4) 7. Consolidated financial statements do not:
(a) determine the profitability of specific subsidiaries.
(b) determine the collective profitability of enterprises under common control.
(c) determine the breadth of a parent company's operations.
(d) determine the full extent of collective obligations of enterprises under common control.

(SO 5) 8. Short-term investments must be readily marketable and be expected to be sold:
(a) within three months.
(b) within the next year.
(c) when the need for cash arises.
(d) within the operating cycle.

(SO 6) 9. At the end of the first year of operations, the total cost of the short-term investment portfolio is $120,000 and the total market value is $115,000. What should the financial statements show?
(a) A $5,000 increase in an asset and a $5,000 gain
(b) A $5,000 reduction in an asset and a $5,000 loss in share capital
(c) A $5,000 reduction in an asset in the current asset section and a $5,000 loss under other expenses
(d) No reduction and no loss

(SO 6) 10. In the balance sheet, the Allowance to Reduce Cost to Market Value is reported as a:
(a) contra asset account.
(b) contra shareholders' equity account.
(c) loss in the statement of earnings.
(d) loss in the retained earnings statement.

(SO 6) 11. ⚙ If a company wants to increase its reported income by manipulating its investment accounts, which should it do?
(a) Sell its "winner" securities and hold its "loser" securities
(b) Hold its "winner" securities and sell its "loser" securities
(c) Reclassify its profitable short-term investments as long-term investments
(d) Reclassify its unprofitable long-term investments as short-term investments

Questions

(SO 1)   1. What are the reasons that corporations invest in debt and equity securities?

(SO 2)   2. (a) What is the cost of an investment in bonds?
(b) When is interest on bonds recorded?

(SO 2)   3. Ann Adler is confused about losses and gains on the sale of investments. Explain these issues to Ann:
(a) How the gain or loss is calculated
(b) The statement presentation of gains and losses

(SO 2)   4. Compare the accounting for an investment in bonds to that for a bond liability.

(SO 3)   5. What is the cost of an investment in shares using the cost method? Equity method?

(SO 3)   6. To acquire Mega Corporation shares, Duran Corp. pays $65,000 in cash plus $1,500 of broker's fees.
(a) What entry should be made for this investment, assuming the shares are readily marketable and the company intends to sell them when the need for cash arises?
(b) How should this investment be reported on Duran's balance sheet?

(SO 3)   7. (a) When should a long-term investment in common shares be accounted for using the cost method? Equity method?
(b) When is revenue recognized under each method?

(SO 3)   8. Malon Corporation uses the equity method to account for its ownership of 35% of the common shares of Flynn Packing. During 2004, Flynn reports net earnings of $80,000 and declares and pays cash dividends of $10,000. What recognition should Malon Corporation give to these events?

(SO 3)   9. What constitutes "significant influence"? Is it safe to conclude that significant influence exists when a company owns more than 20% of the common shares of another company?

(SO 4)   10. What are consolidated financial statements? When must they be prepared?

(SO 5)   11. Kirk Wholesale Supply Ltd. owns shares in Corel Corporation, which it intends to hold indefinitely because of some negative tax consequences if they are sold. Should the investment in Corel be classified as a short-term investment? Why?

(SO 6)   12. Wendy Walner is the controller of G-Products, Inc. At December 31, the company's investments in short-term securities cost $74,000 and have a market value of $70,000. Indicate how G-Products would report these data in its December 31 financial statements.

(SO 6)   13. Using the data in question 12, how would G-Products report them if the investments were long-term and the decline was thought to be temporary? Permanent?

(SO 6)   14. Rioux Corporation's investment portfolio in securities at November 30, its year end, shows a total cost of $192,000 and a total market value of $150,000. Prepare the adjusting entry to record the investments at the lower of cost and market under these three different assumptions:
(a) Assume the investments are temporary.
(b) Assume the investments are long-term and the decline is temporary.
(c) Assume the investments are long-term and the decline is permanent.

(SO 6)   15. What is the proper statement presentation of the account Loss on Decline in Value of Investment?

(SO 6)   16. What purposes are served by reporting the Allowance to Reduce Cost to Market Value as a contra asset in the balance sheet?

(SO 6)   17. Hollinger Inc. reported the following selected data (in thousands) in fiscal 2002: Cash and cash equivalents, $188,852; Investment in associated companies, at equity, $48,975; Marketable investments, at cost, $91,476; Other investments, $69,694; Investment and other income, $29,729; Net loss in equity accounted companies, $1,233; Proceeds on sale of investment in subsidiary, $38,637; and Proceeds on disposal of investment, $7,188. Identify on which financial statement each of these amounts should be reported and give the relevant classification.

Brief Exercises

Journalize debt investment transactions.
(SO 2)

BE12-1   Phelps Corporation purchased debt investments for $41,500 on January 1, 2004. On July 1, 2004, Phelps received cash interest of $1,245. Journalize the purchase and the receipt of interest. Assume no interest has been accrued.

Journalize debt investment and liability transactions.
(SO 2)

BE12–2   Assume that 10-year, 7% bonds are issued at their face value of $50,000 on June 30. Interest is payable semi-annually each June 30 and December 31.

(a) Prepare the journal entries to record the purchase of the debt investment on June 30 and the receipt of the first interest payment on December 31 on the books of the investor.
(b) Prepare the journal entries to record the issue of the debt on June 30 and the first interest payment on December 31 on the books of the issuer.

BE12-3 On August 1, McLain Ltd. buys 1,000 Datawave common shares for $36,000 cash plus brokerage fees of $600. On December 1, the equity investments are sold for $38,000 cash. Journalize the purchase and sale of the common shares.

Journalize equity investment transactions.
(SO 3)

BE12-4 Harmon Corporation owns 25% of Hook Ltd. For the current year, Hook reports net earnings of $180,000 and declares and pays a $50,000 cash dividend. Record Harmon's equity in Hook's net earnings and the receipt of dividends from Hook. How much revenue was reported by Harmon?

Journalize transactions under equity method.
(SO 3)

BE12-5 For the data presented in BE12-4, assume that Harmon owns only 10% of Hook Ltd. Prepare the required journal entries to record Harmon's investment earnings. How much revenue was reported by Harmon? Explain why this differs from the answer obtained in BE12-4.

Journalize transactions under cost method.
(SO 3)

BE12-6 Chan Inc. owns 20% of Dong Ltd.'s common shares. During the year, Dong reported net earnings and paid a dividend. Indicate whether using the equity method instead of the cost method would result in an increase (+), a decrease (−), or no effect (NE) in each of the following categories:

Compare financial impact of cost and equity methods.
(SO 3)

Balance Sheet			Statement of Earnings		
		Shareholders'			Net
Assets	Liabilities	Equity	Revenues	Expenses	Earnings

BE12-7 Cost and market data for the short-term investments of Deal.com Ltd. at December 31, 2004, are $64,000 and $61,000, respectively. Prepare the adjusting entry to record the securities at the lower of cost and market value, if one is required.

Journalize LCM for short-term investment.
(SO 6)

BE12-8 For the data presented in BE12-7, show the financial statement presentation of the short-term investment and related accounts.

Indicate statement presentation.
(SO 6)

BE12-9 In its first year of operations, Duggen Corporation holds equity securities costing $72,000 as a long-term investment. At December 31, 2004, the market value of the securities is $60,000. Prepare the adjusting entry to record the securities at market value assuming the decline is permanent.

Journalize LCM for long-term investment.
(SO 6)

BE12-10 For the data presented in BE12-9, show the financial statement presentation of the long-term investment and related accounts.

Indicate statement presentation.
(SO 6)
Prepare investments section of balance sheet.
(SO 6)

BE12-11 Sabre Corporation has the following long-term investments at November 30, 2004: (1) common shares of Sword Corp. (10% ownership), cost $108,000, market value $120,000; (2) common shares of Epee Inc. (30% ownership), cost $210,000, equity $250,000; and (3) bonds of Ghoti Ltd., cost $150,000, market value $175,000. Prepare the investments section of the balance sheet.

BE12-12 Indicate whether each of the following transactions would increase or decrease earnings:

Identify impact of earnings manipulation.
(SO 6)

(a) Reclassification of short-term investments with temporary declines in market value as long-term investments
(b) Sale of long-term investments with market value less than cost. The decline was not anticipated to be permanent.

Exercises

E12-1 Piper Corporation had these transactions pertaining to debt investments:

Journalize debt investment transactions.
(SO 2)

Jan.   1 Purchased 60 $1,000, 6% Harris Corp. bonds for $60,000 cash plus brokerage fees of $900. Interest is payable semi-annually on July 1 and January 1.
July   1 Received semi-annual interest on Harris bonds.
         1 Sold 30 Harris bonds for $32,000 less $500 of brokerage fees.
Dec. 31 Acccrued interest at Piper's year-end.

Interactive
Homework

Instructions
Journalize the transactions.

Journalize equity investment transactions.

(SO 3)

Interactive Homework

E12-2   McCormick Inc. had the following transactions pertaining to investments in common shares:

Jan.   1 Purchased 1,000 Starr Corporation common shares (5%) for $105,000 cash plus a $3,000 broker's commission.

July   1 Received a cash dividend of $9 per share.

Dec.   1 Sold 500 Starr common shares for $57,000 cash less a $1,000 broker's commission.

       31 Received a cash dividend of $9 per share.

Instructions

Journalize the transactions.

Journalize entries under cost and equity methods.

(SO 3)

Interactive Homework

E12-3   These are two independent situations:

1. Visage Cosmetics Ltd. acquired 10% of the 200,000 common shares of Bell Fashion Ltd. at a total cost of $12 per share on March 18, 2004. On June 30, Bell declared and paid a $75,000 dividend. On December 31, Bell reported net earnings of $122,000 for the year. At December 31, the market price of Bell Fashion was $14 per share. The shares are classified as short-term.

2. Digital Ventures, Inc. acquired 40% of Diner Corporation's 30,000 common shares at a cost of $9 per share on January 1, 2004. On June 15, Diner declared and paid a cash dividend of $35,000. On December 31, Diner reported net earnings of $80,000 for the year.

Instructions

Prepare all the necessary journal entries for 2004 for (a) Visage Cosmetics Ltd. and (b) Digital Ventures, Inc.

Identify method of accounting for equity investments.

(SO 3, 4)

E12-4   Hollinger Inc. reports the following selected long-term equity investments:

Investment	Percentage Ownership	Method
Hollinger International Inc.	36.0%	_____
Jerusalem Post Publications Limited	100.0%	_____
Hollinger Canadian Publishing Holdings Co.	100.0%	_____
Cayman Free Press Ltd.	40.0%	_____
CanWest Global Communications Corp.	15.6%	_____

Instructions

(a) Indicate whether each of the above investments should be accounted for using the cost method or the equity method by writing the words "cost" or "equity" in the space provided.

(b) Which of the above investments, if any, should be consolidated with Hollinger's operations?

Identify and journalize cost and equity methods of accounting.

(SO 3, 4)

E12-5 Shaw Communications Inc. held a 9.5% ownership interest in Canadian Satellite Communications Corporation (Cancom) until August 31, 1999. On August 31, Shaw acquired additional shares in Cancom and increased its ownership interest to 35%. During 2000 and 2001, Shaw purchased the remaining shares of Cancom, owning 100% by the end of 2001.

Instructions

(a) What method of accounting—cost or equity—should Shaw have used to account for its 9.5% equity interest in Cancom until 1999?

(b) What method of accounting—cost or equity—should Shaw have used to account for its 35% interest in Cancom in 1999?

(c) What method of accounting—cost or equity—should Shaw use to account for its 100% investment in Cancom? Is Shaw required to prepare its financial statements any differently now that it owns 100% compared to 35% of Cancom?

(d) Prepare the journal entries (using Xs for amounts) that Shaw would have made to record this investment in Cancom (1) first at cost, (2) then at equity. Assume that Cancom reported net earnings and paid dividends each year.

Journalize equity investment transactions, including LCM.

(SO 3, 6)

E12-6 On November 1, 2004, Lalonde Lteé purchases 1,000 shares of Lyman Corporation for $60 per share and 2,000 shares of Kaur Inc. for $40 per share as a short-term equity investment. On December 15, Lalonde sells 400 shares of Lyman for $80 per share. At December 31, the company's year end, the market value of the Lyman shares is $70 per share and the market value of the Kaur shares is $20 per share. On March 31, 2005, Lalonde sells the remaining Lyman shares for $65 per share. On December 31, 2005, the market value of the Kaur shares is $35 per share.

Instructions

Prepare journal entries to record all transactions, including any required adjusting entries, related to short-term equity investments for Lalonde Lteé for 2004 and 2005.

E12-7 At December 31, 2004, the short-term investments for Nielson, Inc., are as follows:

Journalize LCM for short-term investments.
(SO 6)

Security	Cost	Market Value
A	$17,500	$16,000
B	12,500	14,000
C	23,000	19,000
Total	$53,000	$49,000

Instructions

(a) Prepare the adjusting entry at December 31, 2004, to report the investment portfolio at the lower of cost and market value.
(b) Show the balance sheet and statement of earnings presentation at December 31, 2004.

E12-8 Data for investments in shares classified as short-term investments are presented in E12-7. Assume instead that the investments are classified as long-term with the same cost and market value.

Journalize LCM for long-term investments, indicate statement presentation, and prepare memo.
(SO 6)

Instructions

(a) Prepare the adjusting entry at December 31, 2004, to report the securities at the lower of cost and market value, assuming that any declines in value are permanent.
(b) Show the balance sheet and statement of earnings presentation at December 31, 2004.
(c) J. Arnet, a member of the board of directors, does not understand why a loss is recorded when nothing has been sold. Write a letter to Ms. Arnet explaining the reporting and the purposes it serves.

E12-9 Shaw Communications Inc. reports the following selected information related to investments (in thousands) in its financial statements for the year ended August 31, 2002:

Indicate statement presentation.
(SO 6)

Interactive Homework

Account	Amount	Financial Statement	Classification
Investment in Terayon Communication Systems, at cost	$ 45,872	___	___
Investments in specialty channel networks, at equity	2,918	___	___
Write-down of investments	330,466	___	___
Equity loss on investees	53,487	___	___
Cash paid for cable and MDU business acquisitions	40,454	___	___
Cash paid for acquisition of investments	28,158	___	___

Instructions

Indicate on which financial statement (i.e., balance sheet, statement of earnings, or cash flow statement) each of the above accounts would be reported. Also note the appropriate classification (e.g., long-term investments, other expenses, investing activities, etc.).

E12-10 Accounting for investments hinges on the classification of short-term and long-term investments.

Discuss classification of investments.
(SO 5, 6)

Instructions

(a) Explain why companies usually have an investment portfolio composed of both short-term and long-term investments.
(b) Explain why companies usually have an investment portfolio composed of both debt and equity investments.
(c) Explain how management could manipulate earnings simply by changing the classification between short-term and long-term. What impact would this reclassification have on the company's financial position?

Problems: Set A

*Journalize debt investment
transactions for investor and
investee. Show statement
presentation.*
(SO 2, 6)

P12-1A The following bond transactions occurred during the year ended February 1, 2005, for the University of Higher Learning (UHL) and Otutye Ltd.:

Feb. 1, 2004   UHL sold $3 million of 8%, five-year bonds at 100 to Otutye Ltd. The bonds were dated February 1, 2004, with interest payable semi-annually each August 1 and February 1. The University's and Otutye's year ends are also February 1.

Aug. 1, 2004   Paid the semi-annual interest on the bonds.

Feb. 1, 2005   Paid the semi-annual interest on the bonds.

Aug. 1, 2005   1. Paid the semi-annual interest on the bonds.
2. After paying the semi-annual interest on the bonds on this date, UHL decided to repurchase the bonds and retire them. UHL repurchased all $3 million of the bonds from Otutye at a cash price of $3.1 million.

Instructions

(a) Prepare journal entries for UHL (investee) to record the above bond transactions.

(b) Show how the bond liability would be presented on UHL's February 1, 2005, balance sheet, immediately after the second semi-annual interest payment date.

(c) Prepare journal entries for Otutye Ltd. (investor) to record the above bond transactions.

(d) Show how the debt investment would be presented on Otutye's February 1, 2005, balance sheet.

*Journalize debt investment
transactions, including LCM.
Show statement presentation.*
(SO 2, 6)

P12-2A The following Givarz Corporation transactions relate to long-term bonds:

2004

Jan.   1 Purchased $100,000 of Leslye Corporation 5% bonds at 100.

July   1 Received interest on Leslye bonds.

Dec. 31 Accrued interest on Leslye bonds.

2005

Jan.   1 Received interest on Leslye bonds.
       1 Sold $25,000 of Leslye bonds for $23,000.

July   1 Received interest on Leslye bonds.

Instructions

(a) Journalize the transactions.

(b) Assume that the market value of the bonds at December 31, 2004, was $97,000. Prepare the adjusting entry required (if any) to record these bonds at the lower of cost and market value, assuming that any decline in market value is permanent.

(c) Show the balance sheet presentation of the bonds and interest receivable at December 31, 2004, and indicate where any gain or loss is reported in the statement of earnings.

(d) Show the cash flow statement presentation of the investment transactions for the year ended December 31, 2004.

*Journalize debt and equity
investment transactions,
including LCM. Show
statement presentation.*
(SO 2, 3, 6)

P12-3A In January 2004, the management of Mead Ltd. concludes that it has sufficient cash to permit some short-term investments in debt and equity securities. During the year, these transactions occurred:

Feb.   1 Purchased 600 CBF common shares for $32,000 plus brokerage fees of $600.

Mar.   1 Purchased 800 RSD common shares for $20,000 plus brokerage fees of $400.

Apr.   1 Purchased 50 $1,000, 6% MRT bonds for $50,000 plus $1,000 of brokerage fees. Interest is payable semi-annually on April 1 and October 1.

July   1 Received a cash dividend of $1 per share on the CBF common shares.

Aug.   1 Sold 200 CBF common shares at $60 per share less brokerage fees of $200.

Sept. 1 Received a $1-per-share cash dividend on the RSD common shares.

Oct.   1 Received the semi-annual interest on the MRT bonds.
       1 Sold the MRT bonds for $49,000 less $1,000 of brokerage fees.

At December 31, the market values of the CBF and RSD common shares were $50 and $21 per share, respectively.

Instructions

(a) Journalize and post the transactions.

(b) Prepare the adjusting entry at December 31, 2004, to report the investment securities at the lower of cost and market.

(c) Show the balance sheet presentation of investment securities at December 31, 2004.

(d) Identify the statement of earnings accounts and give the statement classification of each account.

P12-4A DFM Services Ltd. acquired 25% of the common shares of BNA Ltd. on January 1, 2004, by paying $800,000 for 40,000 shares. BNA declared and paid $0.20 per share cash dividends on March 15, June 15, September 15, and December 15, 2004. BNA reported net earnings of $350,000 for the year.

Journalize entries under cost and equity methods, and compare balances.
(SO 3)

Instructions

(a) Prepare the journal entries for DFM Services for 2004, assuming DFM cannot exercise significant influence over BNA.

(b) Prepare the journal entries for DFM Services for 2004, assuming DFM can exercise significant influence over BNA.

(c) Compare the investment and revenue account balances at December 31, 2004, under each method of accounting.

P12-5A McReynolds Mariners Inc. has 150,000 common shares and a fiscal year which begins on October 1. On October 1, 2004, LeTourneau Enterprises Inc. purchases 30% of McReynolds Mariners' common shares from another shareholder for $40 per share. LeTourneau intends to hold the shares as a long-term investment. On December 31, 2004, McReynolds Mariners issues a 4% common stock dividend when the shares are trading for $42 per share. On May 31, 2005, McReynolds Mariners pays a cash dividend of $2 per share to common shareholders. McReynolds Mariners' net earnings for the year ended September 30, 2005, were $350,000. The market value of each share of McReynolds Mariners at September 30, 2005, was $50.

Journalize entries under cost and equity methods. Compare statement presentations.
(SO 3, 4, 6)

Instructions

(a) Prepare all entries for LeTourneau Enterprises for the year ended September 30, 2005, assuming that it exercises significant influence over McReynolds Mariners.

(b) Prepare all entries for LeTourneau Enterprises for the year ended September 30, 2005, assuming that it is unable to exercise significant influence over McReynolds Mariners.

(c) Compare the balance sheet and statement of earnings accounts of LeTourneau Enterprises at September 30, 2005, under the two assumptions.

(d) If LeTourneau had purchased 100% of McReynolds' common shares, what method of accounting for this investment would LeTourneau use? What kind of financial statements would it issue? Whose name would be on the financial statements—LeTourneau's, McReynolds', or both?

P12-6A Outer Cove Outfitters Ltd.'s shareholders' equity section at the beginning of the current fiscal year was as follows:

Journalize equity investment transactions for investor and investee. Show statement presentation.
(SO 3, 6)

OUTER COVE OUTFITTERS LTD.
Balance Sheet (partial)
May 1, 2004

Shareholders' Equity
  Common shares, no par value;
    50,000 shares authorized; 30,000 shares issued $600,000
  Retained earnings   325,000
    Total shareholders' equity $925,000

Listed below are selected transactions that occurred during the year:

1. On May 1, Outer Cove Outfitters sold 10,000 shares to Cumby Inc. for $25 per share. The total number of shares issued is now 40,000. Cumby is not able to exercise significant influence over Outer Cove Outfitters and intends to hold the investment for the long term.

2. On September 1, Outer Cove Outfitters issued a 5% common stock dividend. The market value of the common shares on that date was $30 per share.

3. On November 1, Outer Cove Outfitters paid a $0.50-per-share cash dividend.

4. Outer Cove Outfitters recorded net earnings of $200,000 for the year.
5. The market value of Outer Cove Outfitters' common shares on April 30, 2005, was $30 per share.

Instructions

(a) Prepare all journal entries for Outer Cove Outfitters and for Cumby.
(b) Show the balance sheet presentation for Outer Cove Outfitters and for Cumby at April 30, 2005.

Analyse information for cost and equity methods.
(SO 3, 6)

P12-7A You are presented with the following selected information for Khalil Travel Agency:

KHALIL TRAVEL AGENCY LTD.
Balance Sheet (partial)
December 31, 2004

Shareholders' equity		
Common shares, 500,000 shares		
authorized, 180,000 shares issued	$ 900,000	
Retained earnings	300,000	
Total shareholders' equity	$1,200,000	

On January 1, 2004, Stewart Inc. purchased shares of Khalil Travel Agency when the shares were trading at $15 per share. The market value of each share of Khalil Travel Agency at December 31, 2004, was $18.

Stewart Inc. intends to hold these shares as a long-term investment. Stewart's bookkeeper prepared an unadjusted trial balance as at December 31, 2004, under the assumption that it could not exercise significant influence over Khalil. Accordingly, the bookkeeper presented the following information:

STEWART INC.
Trial Balance (partial)
December 31, 2004

Investment in shares of Khalil Travel Agency (market value $648,000)	$540,000
Dividend revenue from investment in shares of Khalil Travel Agency	72,000

Instructions

(a) How many shares of Khalil Travel Agency did Stewart Inc. purchase? What percentage of the Khalil shares does Stewart own?
(b) What was the cash dividend paid per share of Khalil Travel Agency?
(c) Stewart determines that it is now able to exercise significant influence over Khalil Travel Agency. The investment will now be carried on Stewart's balance sheet at $600,000 at December 31, 2004. What were the net earnings of Khalil Travel Agency for the year ended December 31, 2004?
(d) Assuming that Stewart is able to exercise significant influence over Khalil Travel Agency, what amount will Stewart report on its statement of earnings for 2004?

Journalize equity transactions and show statement presentation.
(SO 3, 6)

P12-8A The following data are in Big Head Todd Corporation's portfolio of short-term securities at December 31, 2003:

	Quantity	Cost
Aglar Corporation common shares	500	$26,000
BAL Corporation common shares	700	42,000
Hicks Corporation preferred shares	400	16,800

On December 31, the total cost of the portfolio equalled total market value. Big Head Todd had the following transactions related to the securities during 2004:

Jan.   7 Sold 500 Aglar Corporation common shares at $56 per share less brokerage fees of $700.
      10 Purchased 400 Miley Corporation common shares at $78 per share, plus brokerage fees of $780.
      26 Received a cash dividend of $1.15 per share on BAL Corporation common shares.
Feb. 2 Received cash dividend of $4 per share on Hicks Corporation preferred shares.
      10 Sold all 400 Hicks Corporation preferred shares at $40 per share less brokerage fees of $180.
Sept. 1 Purchased an additional 200 Miley Corporation common shares at $82 per share, plus brokerage fees of $400.

Dec. 15 Received a cash dividend of $1.50 per share on Miley Corporation common shares.

At December 31, 2004, the market values of the securities were:

BAL Corporation common shares $65 per share
Miley Corporation common shares $70 per share

Instructions

(a) Prepare journal entries to record the transactions.
(b) Post to the investment accounts.
(c) Prepare the adjusting entry at December 31, 2004, to report the portfolio at the lower of cost and market value.
(d) Show the balance sheet presentation at December 31, 2004.

P12-9A The following table summarizes information about the short- and long-term investment portfolio of Daoust Corporation at year end:

Determine valuation of investments.
(SO 3, 6)

Short-Term Investments	Quantity Purchased	Cost/Security	Market Value/Security
Bank of Montreal	1,000	$31	$41
Bombardier	5,000	15	4
Nortel Networks	5,000	75	3
T-Bills	10,000	1	1
Long-Term Investments			
CIBC bonds	2,000	98	100
Government of Canada bonds	1,000	100	140

Instructions

(a) At what value should the short-term investment portfolio be reported at year end? The long-term investment portfolio?
(b) Prepare any required adjusting entries to apply the lower of cost and market rule at year end.
(c) The president of Daoust Corporation is speculating about holding Bombardier and Nortel for the long term, rather than the short term. She doesn't believe there is any point in selling these shares in the near term until their values recover. What impact would it have on Daoust's statement of earnings if the Bombardier and Nortel shares were classified as long-term investments and the declines in market values were assumed to be due to temporary considerations? If the declines in market values were assumed to be permanent? What advice can you offer the president about this situation?

P12-10A Lai Inc. had the following investment transactions:

Identify statement impact of investment transactions.
(SO 6)

1. Purchased Chang Corporation preferred shares for cash, as a short-term equity investment.
2. Received a stock dividend on Chang preferred shares.
3. Purchased Government of Canada bonds for cash, as a short-term debt investment.
4. Accrued interest on Government of Canada bonds.
5. Sold Government of Canada bonds for cash at a price less than originally paid.
6. Purchased 10% of Xing Ltd. common shares, as a long-term equity investment, for cash.
7. Received Xing's financial statements, which reported a net loss for the year.
8. Xing declared and paid a cash dividend.
9. Prepared an adjusting entry to record a decline in the market value of the investment portfolio below cost.

Instructions

Using the following table format, indicate whether each of the above transactions would result in an increase (+), a decrease (−), or no effect (NE). The first one has been done for you as an example.

	Balance Sheet			Statement of Earnings			Cash Flow Statement
	Assets	Liabilities	Shareholders' Equity	Revenues	Expenses	Net Earnings	Investing Activities
1.	NE(+/−)	NE	NE	NE	NE	NE	−

Problems: Set B

Journalize debt investment transactions for investor and investee.
(SO 2)

P12-1B CASB Incorporated is establishing a new business venture in western Canada. In order to secure the necessary start-up capital, it has issued 10-year, 8% bonds which pay interest semi-annually on June 30 and December 31. On January 1, 2004, Densmore Consulting Ltd. paid $100,000 face value for CASB bonds. On January 1, 2005, Densmore Consulting sold its CASB bonds on the TSX Venture Exchange for $99,000. CASB has a December 31 year end. Densmore Consulting has an October 31 year end.

Instructions

(a) Prepare all required entries for the investor—Densmore Consulting.
(b) Prepare all required entries for the investee—CASB.
(c) Comment on the differences in recording that you observe between the investor and the investee.

Journalize debt investment transactions, including LCM. Show statement presentation.
(SO 2, 6)

P12-2B The following Liu Corporation transactions relate to long-term bonds:

2004
Jan. 1 Purchased $50,000 RAM Corporation 6% bonds at 100.
July 1 Received interest on RAM bonds.
Dec. 31 Accrued interest on RAM bonds.

2005
Jan. 1 Received interest on RAM bonds.
       1 Sold $25,000 of RAM bonds for $27,500.
July 1 Received interest on RAM bonds.

Instructions

(a) Journalize the transactions.
(b) Assume that the market value of the bonds at December 31, 2004, was $47,000. Prepare the adjusting entry required (if any) to record the bonds at the appropriate value, assuming any decline in market value is temporary.
(c) Show the balance sheet presentation of the bonds and interest receivable at December 31, 2004.
(d) Identify the statement of earnings accounts involved, and give the statement classification of each account.
(e) Show the cash flow statement presentation of the investment transactions for the year ended December 31, 2004.

Journalize debt and equity investment transactions, including LCM. Show statement presentation.
(SO 2, 3, 6)

P12-3B In January 2004, the management of Rakai Ltd. concludes that it has sufficient cash to purchase some short-term investments in debt and equity securities. During the year, these transactions occurred:

Feb. 1 Purchased 800 IBF common shares for $40,000 plus brokerage fees of $800.
Mar. 1 Purchased 500 RST common shares for $18,000 plus brokerage fees of $500.
Apr. 1 Purchased 70 $1,000, 6% CRT bonds for $70,000 plus $1,200 of brokerage fees. Interest is payable semi-annually on April 1 and October 1.
July 1 Received a cash dividend of $0.60 per share on the IBF common shares.
Aug. 1 Sold 200 IBF common shares at $42 per share less brokerage fees of $350.
Sept.1 Received $2-per-share cash dividend on the RST common shares.
Oct. 1 Received the semi-annual interest on the CRT bonds.
       1 Sold the CRT bonds for $68,000 less $1,000 of brokerage fees.

At December 31, the market values of the IBF and RST common shares were $39 and $30 per share, respectively.

Instructions

(a) Journalize and post the transactions.
(b) Prepare the adjusting entry at December 31, 2004, to report the investments at the lower of cost and market value.
(c) Show the balance sheet presentation of investment securities at December 31, 2004.
(d) Identify the statement of earnings accounts and give the statement classification of each account.

P12-4B Cardinal Concrete Corp. acquired 20% of the common shares of Edra Inc. on January 1, 2004, by paying $1,200,000 for 50,000 shares. Edra declared and paid an $0.80-per-share cash dividend on June 30 and again on December 31, 2004. Edra reported net earnings of $800,000 for the year.

Journalize entries under cost and equity methods, and prepare memo.
(SO 3)

Instructions

(a) Prepare the journal entries for Cardinal Concrete for 2004, assuming Cardinal cannot exercise significant influence over Edra.

(b) Prepare the journal entries for Cardinal Concrete for 2004, assuming Cardinal can exercise significant influence over Edra.

(c) The board of directors of Cardinal Concrete is confused about the differences between the cost and equity methods. Prepare a memorandum for the board that (1) explains each method, and (2) shows the investment and revenue account balances under each method at December 31, 2004.

P12-5B Sub Corporation has 200,000 common shares issued. On January 10, 2004, Par Inc. purchased a block of these shares in the open market at $20 cash per share. At the end of 2004, Sub Corporation reported net earnings of $210,000 and declared and paid a $0.50-per-share dividend.

This problem assumes three independent situations related to the accounting for the purchase of the block of shares by Par Company:

Journalize entries under cost and equity methods. Compare statement presentations.
(SO 3, 4 6)

  Situation A: Par Company purchased 20,000 Sub common shares.
  Situation B: Par Company purchased 70,000 Sub common shares.
  Situation C: Par Company purchased all 200,000 Sub common shares.

Instructions

(a) For each situation, identify the accounting method that should be used by Par Inc. to account for its investment.

(b) For each situation, prepare the journal entries for Par Inc. for the year ended December 31, 2004, to record all transactions related to the investment.

(c) Compare Par's balance sheet and statement of earnings accounts related to these investments at year end for each situation.

(d) In Situation C, what kind of financial statements should be prepared to report the operations of Par and Sub? Whose name will be on the financial statements?

P12-6B The following transactions occurred during the year ended November 30, 2004:

Journalize equity investment transactions for investor and investee. Show statement presentation.
(SO 3, 6)

Dec. 1, 2003 Mountain View Corp. purchased 20,000 shares on the open market, representing a 40% interest in Lakeside Corp. for $5 cash per share.
Dec. 31, 2003 Lakeside paid a $0.25-per-share dividend.
Nov. 30, 2004 Lakeside reported net earnings of $150,000.

Instructions

(a) Prepare all journal entries to record these transactions on (1) Mountain View's books and (2) Lakeside's books.

(b) Show the presentation of the equity investment for Mountain View on its November 30, 2004, balance sheet.

P12-7B On January 1, 2003, Landriault Ltée purchased a 40% (400,000 common shares) equity interest in Groth Inc. for $7,500,000. On December 31, 2004, the Equity Investment—Groth Common Shares account was reported on Landriault's balance sheet at $10,750,000. Over the last two years, Groth had paid a constant annual cash dividend of $500,000 ($0.50 per share).

Analyse information for cost and equity methods.
(SO 3, 6)

Instructions

(a) Determine the total earnings of Groth Inc. during the period January 1, 2003, through December 31, 2004.

(b) If Landriault had accounted for its investment in Groth using the cost method rather than the equity method, what would the balance in its Equity Investment account be at December 31, 2004?

Journalize equity investment transactions, and show statement presentation.
(SO 3, 6)

P12-8B Here is Hi-Tech Company's portfolio of long-term investments at December 31, 2003:

	Quantity	Cost
Awixa Corporation common shares	500	$26,000
HAL Corporation common shares	700	42,000
Renda Corporation preferred shares	400	16,800

On December 31, the total cost of the portfolio equalled the total market value. Hi-Tech had these transactions related to the securities during 2004:

Jan. 7 Sold 500 Awixa Corporation common shares at $56 per share less brokerage fees of $700.
     10 Purchased 200 of Mintor Corporation's common shares at $78 per share plus brokerage fees of $240.
     26 Received a cash dividend of $1.15 per share on HAL Corporation common shares.
Feb. 2 Received a cash dividend of $0.40 per share on Renda Corporation preferred shares.
     10 Sold all 400 Renda Corporation preferred shares at $35 per share less brokerage fees of $180.
July 1 Received a cash dividend of $1 per share on HAL Corporation common shares.
Aug. 23 Received 20 Mintor Corporation common shares as a result of a 10% stock dividend.
Sept. 1 Purchased an additional 400 common shares of Mintor Corporation at $75 per share plus brokerage fees of $400.
Dec. 15 Received a cash dividend of $1.50 per share on Mintor Corporation common shares.

At December 31, 2004, the market values of the securities were:

HAL Corporation common shares	$32 per share
Mintor Corporation common shares	$72 per share

Instructions

(a) Prepare journal entries to record the transactions.
(b) Post to the investment accounts.
(c) Prepare the adjusting entry at December 31, 2004, to report the portfolio at the lower of cost and market value. Assume that any declines are not due to temporary market declines.
(d) Show the balance sheet presentation at December 31, 2004.

Determine valuation of equity investments.
(SO 3, 6)

P12-9B On January 1, 2004, Sturge Enterprises Inc. held the following equity investments:

Company	Shares	Cost Per Share
X Corporation	1,500	$11
Y Corporation	2,000	8

During the year, Sturge made the following purchases:

Company	Shares	Cost Per Share
X Corporation	1,500	$10
X Corporation	1,000	8
X Corporation	1,000	7
Y Corporation	500	9
Z Corporation	3,000	12

The market values of the various securities at year end, December 31, 2004, were as follows: X Corporation: $6; Y Corporation: $10; and Z Corporation: $12. Any declines in market value are considered to be temporary.

Instructions

(a) Calculate the cost of Sturge Enterprises' equity investment portfolio at December 31, 2004.
(b) Calculate the market value of Sturge Enterprises' equity investment portfolio at December 31, 2004.
(c) If Sturge Enterprises considers its entire portfolio to be a short-term investment, what is the LCM valuation?
(d) If Sturge Enterprises decides to classify the X Corporation shares as a long-term investment and the Y Corporation and Z Corporation shares as short-term investments, what would be the impact on the statement of earnings?

P12-10B Olsztyn Inc. had the following investment transactions:

Identify statement impact of investment transactions.
(SO 6)

1. Purchased Arichat Corporation common shares for cash, as a short-term equity investment.
2. Received a cash dividend on Arichat common shares.
3. Purchased Bombardier bonds for cash, as a short-term debt investment.
4. Received interest on Bombardier bonds.
5. Sold Bombardier bonds for cash at a price greater than originally paid.
6. Purchased 40% of LaHave Ltd.'s common shares, as a long-term equity investment, for cash.
7. Received LaHave's financial statements, which reported net earnings for the year.
8. LaHave paid a cash dividend.
9. Prepared an adjusting entry to record a decline in the market value of the investment portfolio below cost.

Instructions

Using the following table format, indicate whether each of the above transactions would result in an increase (+), a decrease (−), or no effect (NE). The first one has been done for you as an example.

Balance Sheet			Statement of Earnings			Cash Flow Statement
Assets	Liabilities	Shareholders' Equity	Revenues	Expenses	Net Earnings	Investing Activities
1. NE(+/−)	NE	NE	NE	NE	NE	−

B R O A D E N I N G   Y O U R   P E R S P E C T I V E

Financial Reporting and Analysis

Analysis Tools

FINANCIAL REPORTING PROBLEM: *Loblaw Companies Limited*

BYP12-1 The financial statements of Loblaw are presented in Appendix A.

Instructions

(a) What information about investments is reported in the consolidated balance sheet?
(b) Based on the information in Note 4 to Loblaw's financial statements, how much interest income was earned on short-term investments in 2002? 2001?
(c) Note 1 to the financial statements identifies Loblaw's effective interest in the voting equity share capital of its subsidiaries. What is this percentage?

COMPARATIVE ANALYSIS PROBLEM: *Loblaw and Sobeys*

BYP12-2 The financial statements of Sobeys Inc. are presented in Appendix B, following the financial statements for Loblaw in Appendix A.

Instructions

Compare the investing activities sections of the cash flow statements of the two companies for the most recent two fiscal years. What conclusions concerning the nature of investment activities can be drawn from these data?

RESEARCH CASE

BYP12-3 The November 30, 2001, issue of *Computer Dealer News* includes an article on page 6 entitled "Canadian Merger Successes are Both Few and Far Between" by Liam Lahey. The article provides information on a study of Canadian mergers and acquisitions by the Toronto firm A.T. Kearney.

Instructions

Read the article and answer these questions:

(a) What percentage of mergers or acquisitions will actually create a merged company that will outperform its industry peers?

(b) In Canada, which is usually more successful: a merger or an acquisition? Explain.

(c) What drives a successful integration?

(d) Are larger companies easier or more difficult to merge than smaller companies?

(e) What are the key success factors to any merger or acquisition, according to A.T. Kearney?

INTERPRETING FINANCIAL STATEMENTS

BYP12-4   Canadian Tire Corporation, Limited supplies merchandise to dealer-operated Canadian Tire Stores across Canada which retail automotive parts, accessories, and service; sports and leisure products; and hardware and home products. In February 2002, CTC Acquisition Limited, a wholly owned subsidiary of Canadian Tire, acquired all of the common shares of Mark's Work Wearhouse Ltd. for $110.8 million, including acquisition costs. Mark's retails work-related casual apparel through stores across Canada.

Instructions

(a) Prepare the journal entry that CTC Acquisition Limited made to record the acquisition of Mark's Work Wearhouse's common shares. Assume the complete purchase was made in cash. What entry would Mark's make on its books?

(b) Which method—cost or equity—should CTC use to account for its investment in Mark's?

(c) Which company is the parent company and which company is the subsidiary?

(d) Mark's financial results have been included in CTC's consolidated financial statements. CTC's results have been included in Canadian Tire's consolidated financial statements. Explain why these results are consolidated in each company's statements for reporting purposes.

A GLOBAL FOCUS

BYP12-5   Xerox Corporation has a 25% investment interest in a joint venture with the Japanese corporation Fuji, called Fuji Xerox. Xerox accounts for this investment using the equity method and reports it in its 2002 financial statements as follows (in U.S. millions):

Investment in Fuji Xerox $563

Instructions

(a) What alternative approaches are available for accounting for long-term equity investments? Discuss whether Xerox is correct in using the equity method to account for this investment.

(b) Explain what type of transactions are recorded in the account, Investment in Fuji Xerox.

(c) The use of joint ventures is a fairly common practice. Why might companies like Xerox and Fuji prefer to participate in a joint venture rather than own a majority share?

FINANCIAL ANALYSIS ON THE WEB

BYP12-6   The Ontario Securities Commission (OSC) is the regulatory agency of Canada's largest capital market. Its job is to administer and enforce securities legislation in the province of Ontario. The OSC site provides useful information for investors.

Instructions

Specific requirements for this Web case can be found on the Kimmel website.

Critical Thinking

COLLABORATIVE LEARNING ACTIVITY

BYP12-7 At the beginning of the question and answer portion of the annual shareholders' meeting of Réno-Déco Corporation, shareholder Carol Finstrom asks, "Why did management sell the holdings in AHM Company at a loss when this company was very profitable during the period its shares were held by Réno-Déco?"

Since president Nathalie Clément has just concluded her speech on the recent success and bright future of Réno-Déco, she is taken aback by this question and responds, "I remember we paid $1,000,000 for those shares some years ago, and I am sure we sold the shares at a higher price. You must be mistaken."

Finstrom retorts, "Well, right here in note number 7 to the financial statements, it shows that 240,000 shares, a 30% interest in AHM, were sold on the last day of the year. Also, it states that AHM earned $550,000 this year and paid out $150,000 in cash dividends. Further, a summary statement indicates that in past years, while Réno-Déco held AHM shares, AHM earned $1,200,000 and paid out $500,000 in dividends. Finally, the statement of earnings for this year shows a loss on the sale of AHM shares of $180,000. So, I doubt that I am mistaken."

Red-faced, president Clément turns to you.

Instructions

With the class divided into groups, help out president Clément: What dollar amount did Réno-Déco receive upon the sale of the AHM shares? Explain why both Finstrom and Clément are correct.

COMMUNICATION ACTIVITY

BYP12-8 Chapperal Corporation has purchased two securities for its portfolio. The first is an equity investment in Ray Corporation, one of its suppliers. Chapperal purchased 10% of Ray with the intention of holding it for a number of years. The second investment is a purchase of debt securities. Chapperal purchased the debt securities because its analysts believe that changes in market interest rates will cause these securities to increase in value in a short period of time. Chapperal intends to sell the securities as soon as they have increased in value.

Instructions

Write a memo to Jean Talon, the chief financial officer, explaining how to account for each of these investments and the implications for reported earnings from this accounting treatment. Include in your memo any potential for earnings management that the CFO should be aware of.

ETHICS CASE

BYP12-9 Kreiter Financial Services Ltd. holds a large portfolio of debt and equity investments. The total market value of the portfolio at December 31, 2004, is lower than total cost, with some securities having increased in value and others having decreased. Vicki Lemke, the financial vice-president, and Ula Greenwood, the controller, are in the process of classifying the securities in the portfolio for the first time.

Lemke suggests classifying the securities that have increased in value as short-term investments in order to increase net earnings for the year. She wants to classify the securities that have decreased in value as long-term investments so that the temporary decreases in value will not affect the 2004 net earnings.

Greenwood disagrees. She recommends classifying the securities that have decreased in value as short-term investments and those that have increased in value as long-term investments. Greenwood argues that the company is having a good earnings year and that recognizing the losses now will help to smooth earnings for this year. Moreover, for future years, when the company may not be as profitable, the company will have built-in gains "held in reserve."

Ethics In
Accounting

Instructions

  (a) Will classifying the investments as Lemke and Greenwood suggest actually affect earnings as each says it will?

  (b) Is there anything unethical in what Lemke and Greenwood propose? Who are the stakeholders affected by their proposals?

  (c) Assume that Lemke and Greenwood classify the portfolio properly. Now, at year end, Lemke proposes to sell the securities that will increase net earnings for 2004, and Greenwood proposes to sell the securities that will decrease net earnings for 2004. Is this unethical?

Answers to Self-Study Questions

1. b   2. a   3. b   4. a   5. b   6. a   7. a   8. c   9. c   10. a   11. a

Answer to Loblaw Review It Question 3

Loblaw's short-term investments, totalling $304 million, are detailed in Note 1. They consist of U.S. government securities, commercial paper, and bank deposits. They are carried at the lower of cost and quoted market value. Loblaw has long-term investments in franchised stores (see Note 8: Other Assets).

Remember to go back to the Navigator box on the chapter-opening page to check off your completed work.

CHAPTER 13

Cash Flow Statement

STUDY OBJECTIVES

After studying this chapter, you should be able to:

1. Indicate the primary purpose of the cash flow statement.

2. Distinguish among operating, investing, and financing activities.

3. Prepare a cash flow statement using one of two approaches: (a) the indirect method or (b) the direct method.

4. Use the cash flow statement to evaluate a company.

NAVIGATOR

"I've Got $40 Billion Dollars Burning a Hole in My Pocket!"

Things move fast in the high technology sector. Very fast. The business story of the turn-of-the-millennium period was surely the explosion of activity in areas such as software, Internet-based services, and high-speed communications. Everyone knows stories of software companies started in basements that were sold for millions, and of young entrepreneurs who become dot.com millionaires on the day of their initial public offerings.

And everyone also knows stories of companies that were wiped out when the high-flying tech bubble burst in the spring of 2000. Whether the economy is booming or not, keeping lots of cash available is a real challenge for a young company. It requires great cash management and careful attention to cash flow.

One technique for cash management that is common in young high-tech companies is paying employees in part through stock options. This frees up cash for business activities, especially in the crucial early years of the company.

Microsoft, at 28 years of age the great-granddaddy of the software industry, was a pioneer of this and other cash management strategies. By some estimates, more than 1,000 Microsoft employees became millionaires through stock options in the first 20 years of the company's operations.

The story of Microsoft's phenomenal growth—how it was founded in 1975 by Bill Gates and, by 2000, had grown so large and powerful that a U.S. judge ordered it to be broken up, before the ruling was over-turned—is well known. But the numbers are nonetheless startling.

Seattle-based Microsoft's 2002 cash flow statement reported cash provided by operating activities in excess of U.S.$14.5 billion. Its net earnings were only a little more than half that amount, at U.S.$7.8 billion. Its cash and short-term investments reached U.S.$38.7 billion on its balance sheet at its fiscal year end of June 30, 2002. Microsoft's cash flow is triple the industry average.

That kind of money is astounding, even in this big-money

Microsoft Corporation www.microsoft.com

THE NAVIGATOR

Scan *Study Objectives* ☐

Read *Feature Story* ☐

Read *Chapter Preview* ☐

Read text and answer *Before You Go On*
p. 606 ☐ p. 609 ☐ p. 620 ☐
p. 633 ☐ p. 637 ☐

Work *Using the Decision Toolkit* ☐

Review *Summary of Study Objectives*
and *Decision Toolkit* ☐

Work *Demonstration Problem* ☐

Answer *Self-Study Questions* ☐

Complete assignments ☐

sector. As a comparison, consider Corel Corporation. Based in Ottawa, Corel is an internationally recognized developer of graphics and business applications, such as CorelDRAW and WordPerfect. Founded in 1985 by Dr. Michael Cowpland, Corel is younger than Microsoft by 10 years—eons in the computing world.

Cowpland may not be the worldwide household name that Bill Gates is, but Corel is certainly a major player. It generated cash from operating activities of U.S.$19.7 million for the year ending November 30, 2002, down 136% from a high of U.S.$55 million in 1997, which is still only a drop in the bucket compared with Microsoft's billions.

It is impossible to predict what the future will hold for either of these companies. The antitrust settlement finally reached with the U.S. Department of Justice in 2002 was a relief for Microsoft and its investors, but the company still faces legal challenges to its market position in other jurisdictions.

For its part, Corel has struggled financially in recent years, resulting in some changes. The company has exited the Linux market to develop more products for Macintosh. And following its acquisitions of Micrografx Inc. and SoftQuad Software Ltd., it has shifted its focus toward new kinds of software.

Interestingly, as part of a strategic alliance with Corel for the development and marketing of products related to Microsoft's .NET platform, Microsoft invested U.S.$135 million in its rival back in 2000. Microsoft subsequently sold its investment in Corel at a significant loss to Vector Capital in 2003.

Cash management is sure to continue to be an important factor for both companies, as for their ever-growing list of upstart competitors. Anything is possible in this sector where change is the only constant. After all, in 1975 who could've predicted that 19-year-old Bill Gates would become the world's best-known billionaire?

601

The balance sheet, statement of earnings, and statement of retained earnings do not always show the whole picture of the financial condition of a company. In fact, looking at the financial statements of some well-known companies, a thoughtful investor might ask questions like these: How did Andrés Wines pay cash dividends in a year in which it had no cash but only bank indebtedness? How did the Student Centre of McGill University purchase more than $97,000 of property, plant, and equipment in a year in which it reported a loss of $114,000? How did Capital Sports & Entertainment Inc. finance its purchase of the Ottawa Senators? Answers to these and similar questions can be found in this chapter, which presents the cash flow statement.

The content and organization of this chapter are as follows:

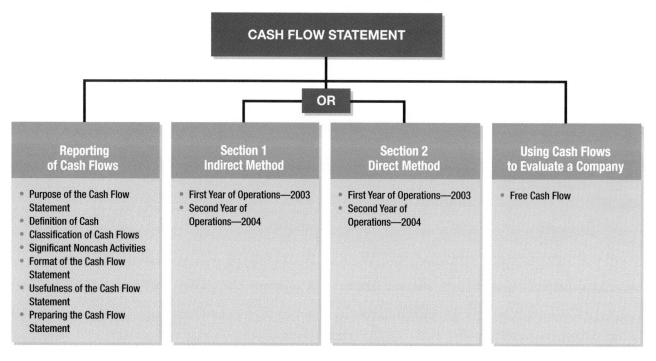

CASH FLOW STATEMENT			
Reporting of Cash Flows	**Section 1 Indirect Method**	**Section 2 Direct Method**	**Using Cash Flows to Evaluate a Company**
• Purpose of the Cash Flow Statement • Definition of Cash • Classification of Cash Flows • Significant Noncash Activities • Format of the Cash Flow Statement • Usefulness of the Cash Flow Statement • Preparing the Cash Flow Statement	• First Year of Operations—2003 • Second Year of Operations—2004	• First Year of Operations—2003 • Second Year of Operations—2004	• Free Cash Flow

NAVIGATOR

Reporting of Cash Flows

The basic financial statements we have presented so far provide only limited information about a company's cash flows (cash receipts and cash payments). For example, comparative balance sheets show the increase in property, plant, and equipment during the year, but they do not show how the additions were financed or paid for. The statement of earnings shows net earnings, but it does not indicate the amount of cash generated by operating activities. The statement of retained earnings shows cash dividends declared but not the cash dividends paid during the year. None of these statements reports the change in cash as a result of operating, investing, and financing activities during the period.

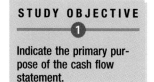

STUDY OBJECTIVE

1

Indicate the primary purpose of the cash flow statement.

PURPOSE OF THE CASH FLOW STATEMENT

The primary purpose of the cash flow statement is to provide information about cash receipts, cash payments, and the net change in cash resulting from the operating, investing, and financing activities of a company during a specific period. These cash activities are reported in a format that reconciles the beginning and ending cash balances.

Reporting the causes of changes in cash is useful because investors, creditors, and other interested parties want to know what is happening to a company's most liquid resource, its cash. As the feature story about Microsoft and Corel demonstrates, to understand a company's financial position, it is essential to understand its cash flows. The cash flow statement provides answers to the following simple but important questions about an enterprise:

- Where did the cash come from during the period?
- What was the cash used for during the period?
- What was the change in the cash balance during the period?

The answers provide important clues about whether dynamic companies like Microsoft will be able to continue to thrive and invest in new opportunities. The cash flow statement also provides clues about whether struggling companies like Corel will survive or perish.

DEFINITION OF CASH

The cash flow statement is often prepared using **cash and cash equivalents** as its basis. Cash equivalents are short-term highly liquid investments that are readily convertible to cash within a very short period of time. Generally, only investments due within three months qualify with this definition. Examples of cash equivalents are treasury bills, commercial paper (high-quality corporate short-term debt), and money-market funds. Sometimes short-term or demand loans are also deducted from this amount. Because of the varying definitions of "cash" that can be used in this statement, companies must clearly define *cash equivalents* when they are included. Since cash and cash equivalents are viewed as the same, transfers between the cash account and the cash equivalent accounts are not reported in the cash flow statement.

CLASSIFICATION OF CASH FLOWS

The cash flow statement classifies cash receipts and cash payments into operating, investing, and financing activities. Transactions within each activity are as follows:

1. Operating activities include the cash effects of transactions that create revenues and expenses. They affect net earnings.
2. Investing activities include (a) purchasing and disposing of investments and productive long-lived assets using cash and (b) lending money and collecting the loans. They affect short-term investments that are not cash equivalents in addition to affecting long-term asset accounts.
3. Financing activities include (a) obtaining cash from issuing debt and repaying the amounts borrowed and (b) obtaining cash from shareholders and paying them dividends. They affect short-term notes payable, and long-term liability and shareholders' equity accounts.

STUDY OBJECTIVE
2
Distinguish among operating, investing, and financing activities.

The operating activities category is the most important because it shows the cash provided or used by company operations. Ultimately, a company must generate cash from its operating activities in order to continue as a going concern and to expand.

Illustration 13-1 lists typical cash receipts and cash payments within each of the three activities. Study the list carefully. It will assist you in doing your assignments.

As you can see, some cash flows relating to investing or financing activities are classified as operating activities. For example, receipts of investment revenue (interest and dividends) are classified as operating activities. So are payments of interest to lenders. Why are these considered operating activities? Because these items are reported in the statement of earnings, where results of operations are shown.

Illustration 13-1
Cash receipts and payments classified by activity

Operating activities

Investing activities

Financing activities

Types of Cash Inflows and Outflows
Operating activities
Cash inflows:
From the sale of goods or services
From interest and dividends received
Cash outflows:
To suppliers for inventory
To employees for services
To governments for taxes
To lenders for interest
To others for expenses
Investing activities
Cash inflows:
From the sale of property, plant, and equipment
From the sale of investments (debt or equity securities of other companies)
From the collection of principal on loans to other companies
Cash outflows:
To purchase property, plant, and equipment
To purchase investments (debt or equity securities of other companies)
To make loans to other companies
Financing activities
Cash inflows:
From issues of equity securities (company's own shares)
From issues of debt securities (bonds and notes)
Cash outflows:
To shareholders as dividends
To redeem long-term debt or reacquire share capital

Note the following general guidelines: (1) Operating activities involve income determination (statement of earnings and noncash working capital) items. (2) Investing activities involve cash flows resulting from changes in investments and long-term asset items. (3) Financing activities involve cash flows resulting from changes in notes payable, and long-term liability and shareholders' equity items.

SIGNIFICANT NONCASH ACTIVITIES

Not all of a company's significant activities involve cash. The following are examples of significant noncash activities:

1. Issues of common shares to purchase assets
2. Conversions of debt into equity
3. Issues of debt to purchase assets
4. Exchanges of assets

Significant financing and investing activities that do not affect cash are not reported in the body of the cash flow statement. However, these activities are reported in a note to the financial statements. The reporting of these activities in a note satisfies the **full disclosure principle.**

FORMAT OF THE CASH FLOW STATEMENT

The general format of the cash flow statement is organized around the three activities—operating, investing, and financing—discussed above. A widely used form of the cash flow statement is shown in Illustration 13-2.

Illustration 13-2
Format of cash flow
statement

COMPANY NAME Cash Flow Statement Period Covered		
Operating activities		
(List of individual inflows and outflows)	$x	
Net cash provided (used) by operating activities		$x
Investing activities		
(List of individual inflows and outflows)	$x	
Net cash provided (used) by investing activities		x
Financing activities		
(List of individual inflows and outflows)	$x	
Net cash provided (used) by financing activities		x
Net increase (decrease) in cash		x
Cash, beginning of period		x
Cash, end of period		$x

Alternative Terminology The *cash flow statement* is also commonly known as the *statement of changes in financial position.*

The cash flow statement covers the same period of time as the statements of earnings and retained earnings. The section reporting cash flows from operating activities always appears first. It is followed by the investing activities section and then the financing activities section. Note also that the individual inflows and outflows from investing and financing activities are reported separately. The cash outflow for the purchase of equipment is reported separately from the cash inflow from the sale of equipment. Similarly, the cash inflow from the issue of debt securities is reported separately from the cash outflow for the retirement of debt. If a company did not report the inflows and outflows separately, it would obscure the investing and financing activities. This would make it more difficult for the user to assess future cash flows.

The reported operating, investing, and financing activities result in net cash either provided or used by each activity. The amounts of net cash provided or used by each activity are then totalled. The result is the net increase or decrease in cash for the period. This amount is then added to or subtracted from the beginning-of-period cash balance to obtain the end-of-period cash balance. The end-of-period cash balance should agree with the cash balance reported on the balance sheet. Finally, any significant noncash investing and financing activities are reported in a note to the statement.

USEFULNESS OF THE CASH FLOW STATEMENT

Many investors believe that "Cash is cash and everything else is accounting." Cash flow is less susceptible to management manipulation and fraud than traditional accounting measures such as net earnings. Although we suggest that relying on cash flows only and ignoring accrual accounting is inappropriate, comparing cash provided (used) by operating activities to net earnings can reveal important information about the "quality" of reported net earnings—that is, the extent to which net earnings provide a good measure of actual performance.

The information in a cash flow statement should help investors, creditors, and others evaluate the following aspects of the firm's financial position:

1. **The company's ability to generate future cash flows.** By examining relationships between items in the cash flow statement, investors and others can predict the amounts, timing, and uncertainty of future cash flows better than they can from accrual-based data.
2. **The company's ability to pay dividends and meet obligations.** If a company does not have adequate cash, it cannot pay employees, settle debts, or

pay dividends. Employees, creditors, shareholders, and customers should be particularly interested in this statement because it alone shows the flows of cash in a business.

3. **The reasons for the difference between net earnings and net cash provided (used) by operating activities.** Net earnings are important because they provide information on the success or failure of a business enterprise. However, some analysts are critical of accrual-based net earnings because these earnings require many estimates. As a result, the reliability of net earnings is often challenged. Such is not the case with cash. Many financial statement users investigate the reasons for the difference between net earnings and net cash provided by operating activities. Then they can assess for themselves the reliability of the earnings number.

4. **The investing and financing transactions during the period.** By examining a company's investing and financing activities, a financial statement reader can better understand why assets and liabilities increased or decreased during the period.

In summary, the information in the cash flow statement is useful in answering the following questions:

- How did cash increase when there was a net loss for the period?
- How were the proceeds of the bond issue used?
- How was the plant expansion financed?
- Why were dividends not increased?
- How was the retirement of debt accomplished?
- How much money was borrowed during the year?
- Is cash flow greater or less than net earnings?

BUSINESS INSIGHT

INVESTOR PERSPECTIVE

During the 1990s, analysts increasingly used cash-based measures, such as cash provided by operating activities, instead of, or in addition to, net earnings. The reason for the change was that they had lost faith in accrual-based measures. Sadly, these days even cash flow isn't always what it seems to be.

Take, for example, Alliance Atlantis Communications Inc. The company reported cash flow *provided* by operating activities of $686.5 million in 2001. Looks impressive, right? However, in 2002, the company's cash flow statement for 2001 was restated to report cash *used* by operating activities of $59.9 million. What happened? Accounting standard-setters decided that money spent to acquire, develop, and produce films and television programs was an operating expense, not an investment. Cash flow didn't actually change, but its reporting did. The moral of this story is that accounting assumptions can alter not only reported earnings, but also cash flow.

Source: Fabrice Taylor, "Show Me the Real Money," *Report on Business Magazine,* November 2002, 109.

BEFORE YOU GO ON . . .

● REVIEW IT

1. What is the primary purpose of a cash flow statement?
2. What are cash equivalents?
3. What are the three major activities classified in the cash flow statement? Give an example of each.
4. Why is the cash flow statement useful? What key information does it convey?

● **DO IT**

During the first week of its existence, Plano Molding Corp. had these transactions:

1. Issued 100,000 common shares for $800,000 cash.
2. Borrowed $200,000 from the HSBC Bank, signing an 8%, five-year note.
3. Purchased two semi-trailer trucks for $170,000 cash.
4. Paid employees $12,000 for salaries and wages.
5. Collected $20,000 cash for services provided.

Classify each of these transactions by type of cash flow activity. Indicate whether the transaction would be reported as a cash inflow or cash outflow.

Action Plan

- Identify the three types of activities used to report all cash inflows and outflows.
- Report as operating activities the cash effects of transactions that create revenues and expenses and enter into the determination of net earnings.
- Report as investing activities the transactions that (a) acquire and dispose of investments and productive long-lived assets, and (b) lend money and collect loans.
- Report as financing activities the transactions that (a) either obtain cash by issuing debt or repay the amounts borrowed, and (b) either obtain cash from shareholders or pay them dividends.

Solution:

1. Financing activity; cash inflow
2. Financing activity; cash inflow
3. Investing activity; cash outflow
4. Operating activity; cash outflow
5. Operating activity; cash inflow

PREPARING THE CASH FLOW STATEMENT

The cash flow statement is prepared differently from the other three financial statements. First, it is not prepared from an adjusted trial balance. The statement requires detailed information concerning the changes in account balances that occurred between two periods of time. An adjusted trial balance does not provide the necessary data. Second, the cash flow statement deals with cash receipts and payments. As a result, **the accrual concept is not used in the preparation of a cash flow statement.**

The information to prepare this statement usually comes from three sources:

STUDY OBJECTIVE

3

Prepare a cash flow statement using one of two approaches: (a) the indirect method or (b) the direct method.

1. **Comparative balance sheet.** Information in the comparative balance sheet indicates the amount of the changes in assets, liabilities, and shareholders' equity from the beginning to the end of the period.
2. **Statement of earnings.** Information in the statement of earnings helps the reader determine the amount of cash provided or used by operating activities during the period.
3. **Additional information.** Additional information includes transaction data that are needed to determine how cash was provided or used during the period.

Preparing the cash flow statement from these data sources involves the three major steps explained in Illustration 13-3. First, to see where you are headed, start by identifying the change in cash during the period. Has cash increased or decreased during the year? Second, determine the net cash provided (used) by operating activities. Third, determine the net cash provided (used) by investing and financing activities.

Illustration 13-3
Steps in preparing the
cash flow statement

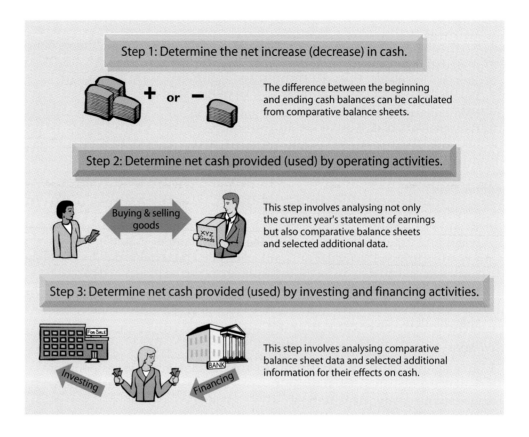

Indirect and Direct Methods

In order to perform step 2 and determine the cash provided (used) by operating activities, **net earnings must be converted from an accrual basis to a cash basis**. This conversion may be done by either of two methods: indirect or direct. The indirect method converts total net earnings from an accrual basis to a cash basis. The direct method converts each individual revenue and expense account to a cash basis, thereby identifying specific cash receipts and payments. **Both methods arrive at the same total amount** for "Net cash provided (used) by operating activities." They differ in disclosing the items that make up the total amount. Note that the two different methods affect only the operating activities section. The investing activities and financing activities sections are not affected by the choice of method.

Companies tend to favour the indirect method for three reasons: (1) it is easier to prepare; (2) it focuses on the differences between net earnings and net cash flow from operating activities; and (3) it tends to reveal less company information to competitors.

Others, however, favour the direct method. This method is more consistent with the objective of a cash flow statement because it shows operating cash receipts and payments. The CICA has expressed a preference for the direct method but allows the use of either method.

Despite the CICA's preference for the direct method, it is rarely used in Canadian practice. Less than 1% of the companies in Canada use the direct method. The authors of *Financial Reporting in Canada* state, "We continue to be surprised by the failure to use the direct method for presenting this important figure. It is difficult to believe that investors would not find information on the various functional cash flows (e.g., payments to employees) more useful than the information on the adjustments required to convert Net Income into Cash flows from Operating Activities (e.g., amortization expense)."

 International Note

International accounting requirements are quite similar with regard to the cash flow statement. But there are some exceptions. In Japan, operating and investing activities are combined. In Australia, the direct method is mandatory. In Spain, the indirect method is mandatory. Also, in a number of European countries, a cash flow statement is not required at all, although in practice most publicly traded companies provide one.

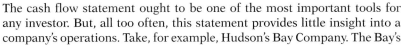

BUSINESS INSIGHT

INVESTOR PERSPECTIVE

The cash flow statement ought to be one of the most important tools for any investor. But, all too often, this statement provides little insight into a company's operations. Take, for example, Hudson's Bay Company. The Bay's business is pretty simple. It buys clothes, housewares, and other products, puts them in its stores, and sells them.

When you look at the operating activities section of the Bay's cash flow statement, however, you find references to amortization and "net change in operating working capital." Nowhere does it tell you how much cash The Bay received from shoppers or how much it paid its suppliers.

So why don't companies report this information in their cash flow statement? "It gives material information, so managements don't want to use it," says Richard Rooney, president of Burgundy Asset Management. Rooney would like to see the direct method of preparing the operating activities section of the cash flow statement become mandatory. "Something like this is comprehensible, easy to understand, and I think it would be harder to fudge—though where there's a will, there's a way."

Source: Derek DeCloet, "Show Investors the Cash Flow," *Financial Post*, March 28, 2002, IN3.

BEFORE YOU GO ON . . .

● **REVIEW IT**

1. Explain the difference between the indirect method and the direct method.
2. How much cash flow did Loblaw report as being provided by operating activities in 2002? Does Loblaw use the indirect or direct method to report its cash flow provided by operating activities?

On the following pages, in two separate sections, we describe the use of the two methods. Section 1 illustrates the indirect method, and section 2 illustrates the direct method. These sections are independent of each other. When you have finished the section(s) assigned by your instructor, turn to the next topic on page 635—"Using Cash Flows to Evaluate a Company."

S E C T I O N   1

Indirect Method

To explain and illustrate the indirect method, we will use the transactions of a service company, Computer Services Corporation, for two years: 2003 and 2004. We will show basic transactions in the first year. Additional transactions will be added in the second year.

STUDY OBJECTIVE

3a

Prepare a cash flow statement using the indirect method.

FIRST YEAR OF OPERATIONS—2003

Computer Services Corporation started up on January 1, 2003, when it issued 50,000 common shares for $50,000 cash. The company rented its office space and sold computers throughout the first year. The comparative balance sheet for the beginning and end of 2003, showing increases and decreases, appears in Illustration 13-4.

COMPUTER SERVICES CORPORATION Balance Sheet			
Assets	Dec. 31, 2003	Jan. 1, 2003	Change Increase/Decrease
Cash	$34,000	$0	$34,000 increase
Accounts receivable	30,000	0	30,000 increase
Inventory	25,000	0	25,000 increase
Equipment	10,000	0	10,000 increase
Total	$99,000	$0	
Liabilities and Shareholders' Equity			
Accounts payable	$15,000	$0	$15,000 increase
Acccrued expenses payable	4,000	0	4,000 increase
Common shares	60,000	0	60,000 increase
Retained earnings	20,000	0	20,000 increase
Total	$99,000	$0	

The statement of earnings and additional information for Computer Services Corporation are shown in Illustration 13-5.

COMPUTER SERVICES CORPORATION Statement of Earnings Year Ended December 31, 2003	
Sales revenue	$150,000
Cost of goods sold	65,000
Gross profit	85,000
Operating expenses	40,000
Earnings before income taxes	45,000
Income tax expense	10,000
Net earnings	$ 35,000

Additional information:
1. A dividend of $15,000 was declared and paid during the year.
2. The equipment was purchased at the end of 2003. No amortization was taken in 2003.

Step 1: Determining the Net Increase (Decrease) in Cash

To prepare a cash flow statement, the first step is to **determine the net increase or decrease in cash.** This is a simple calculation. For example, Computer Services Corporation had no cash on hand at the beginning of 2003. It had $34,000 on hand at the end of the year. Thus, the change in cash for 2003 was an increase of $34,000.

Step 2: Determining Net Cash Provided (Used) by Operating Activities

To determine net cash provided or used by operating activities under the indirect method, **net earnings are adjusted for items that did not affect cash.** A useful starting point in determining net cash provided (used) by operating activities is to understand why net earnings must be converted. Under generally accepted accounting principles, companies use the accrual basis of accounting. As you have learned, this basis requires that revenue be recorded when earned and that expenses be matched against the revenue they were incurred to generate. Earned revenues may include credit sales that have not been collected in cash. Expenses incurred, such as amortization, may not have been paid in cash. Under the accrual basis of accounting, net earnings do not indicate the net cash provided by operating activities. Therefore, under the indirect method, accrual-based net earnings must be adjusted to convert certain items to the cash basis.

The indirect method starts with net earnings and converts them to net cash provided by operating activities. In other words, **the indirect method adjusts net earnings for items that affected reported net earnings but did not affect cash**. That is, noncash expenses and other charges in the statement of earnings are added back to net earnings. Likewise, noncash revenues and other credits are deducted from net earnings. The result is net cash provided (used) by operating activities.

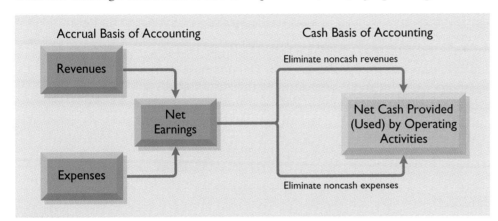

Illustration 13-6
Net earnings versus net cash provided (used) by operating activities

A useful starting point in identifying the adjustments to net earnings are the current asset and current liability accounts other than cash. Those accounts—receivables, payables, prepaid expenses, and inventories—should be analysed for their effects on cash. We will now do this for various accounts.

Increase in Accounts Receivable.   When accounts receivable increase during the year, revenues on an accrual basis are higher than revenues on a cash basis. In other words, operating activities of the period lead to revenues, **but not all of these revenues result in an increase in cash.** Some of the revenues result in an increase in accounts receivable.

The statement of earnings in Illustration 13-5 shows that Computer Services Corporation earned, on an accrual basis, $150,000 in revenues. On a cash basis, we would record only the cash received during the period. To determine how much cash was received from sales revenue, it is useful to analyse the Accounts Receivable account.

Accounts Receivable			
Jan. 1 Balance	0		
Sales revenue	150,000	Receipts from customers	120,000
Dec. 31 Balance	30,000		

$30,000 net increase

The ending balance of Accounts Receivable is $30,000 and revenues (assumed to be sales on account) journalized during the period were $150,000 (Dr. Accounts Receivable; Cr. Sales Revenue). Cash receipts from customers (Dr. Cash; Cr. Accounts Receivable) must have been $120,000 ($150,000 − $30,000). Revenues reported on the accrual-based statement of earnings are higher than cash collections. To convert net earnings to net cash provided by operating activities, the $30,000 increase in accounts receivable must be deducted from net earnings because $30,000 less cash was collected than reported in the accrual-based revenues section of the statement of earnings.

Increases in all noncash current asset accounts, not just accounts receivable, must be deducted from net earnings to convert an accrual basis figure to a cash basis figure. **An increase in a noncash current asset is deducted from net earnings**

Helpful Hint Once you understand why and how changes in noncash current account balances affect revenues and expenses, you will find it faster to simply look at the difference between ending and beginning balances, and at the direction of the change.

to determine net cash provided (used) by operating activities. Conversely, a decrease in a noncash current asset is added to net earnings to determine net cash provided (used) by operating activities.

Increase in Inventory. Assuming a perpetual inventory system is in use, the merchandise inventory account is increased by the cost of goods purchased. It is decreased by the cost of goods sold. When inventory increases during the year, the cost of goods purchased is greater than the cost of goods sold recorded in the statement of earnings. Any increase in the Inventory account must be deducted from net earnings, in a manner similar to the increase in the Accounts Receivable account explained above.

Inventory increased by $25,000 for Computer Services Corporation. Because the Inventory account is increased by the purchase of goods (Dr. Inventory; Cr. Accounts Payable) and is decreased by the cost of goods sold (Dr. Cost of Goods Sold; Cr. Inventory), Computer Services must have purchased $25,000 more inventory than it sold.

Inventory				
Jan.	1	Balance	0	
		Purchases	90,000	Cost of goods sold 65,000
Dec.	31	Balance	25,000	

$25,000 net increase

Cost of goods sold, reported on the statement of earnings, is $65,000. Purchases of merchandise during the year must therefore have been $90,000 ($65,000 + $25,000). To convert net earnings to net cash provided by operating activities, the $25,000 increase in inventory must be deducted from net earnings. The increase in Inventory means that the cash-based expense must have increased, which has the effect of reducing cash-based net earnings.

This deduction does not completely convert an accrual-based figure to a cash-based figure. It does not tell us how much cash was paid for the goods purchased. It just converts the cost of goods sold to the cost of goods purchased during the year. The analysis of accounts payable—shown next—completes this analysis by converting the cost of goods purchased from an accrual basis to a cash basis.

Increase in Accounts Payable. In the first year of operations, Computer Services' purchases of merchandise on account were credited to Accounts Payable. The Accounts Payable account is increased by purchases (Dr. Inventory; Cr. Accounts Payable) and decreased by payments to suppliers (Dr. Accounts Payable; Cr. Cash). We determined the amount of purchases made by Computer Services in the Inventory analysis above: $90,000. Using this figure, we can now determine that payments to suppliers must have been $75,000.

Accounts Payable				
		Jan.	1	Balance 0
Payments to suppliers 75,000				Purchases 90,000
		Dec.	31	Balance 15,000

$15,000 net increase

To convert net earnings to net cash provided by operating activities, the $15,000 increase in Accounts Payable must be added to net earnings. The increase in Accounts Payable means that less cash was paid for the purchases than the amount deducted in the accrual-based expenses section of the statement of earnings. Decreasing an expense has the effect of increasing net earnings. **An increase in a current liability is added to net earnings to determine net cash provided (used) by operating activities. Conversely, a decrease in a current liability is deducted from net earnings to determine net cash provided (used) by operating activities.**

Previously, cost of goods sold was converted to cost of goods purchased. The addition of $15,000 completes the adjustment required to convert the cost of goods purchased to the cash paid for these goods. In summary, the conversion of the cost of goods sold on the accrual-based statement of earnings to the cash paid for goods purchased involves two steps. First, the change in the Inventory account adjusts the cost of goods sold to the accrual-based figure, cost of goods purchased. Second, the change in the Accounts Payable account adjusts the accrual-based cost of goods purchased to the cash-based payments to suppliers.

Cost of goods sold	$65,000
Add: Increase in inventory	25,000
Cost of goods purchased	90,000
Less: Increase in accounts payable	15,000
Cash payments to suppliers	$75,000

Remember that adjustments to accrual-based expense accounts result in an adjustment in the opposite direction to net earnings. That is, when an expense account such as Cost of Goods Sold is increased because of an increase in Inventory, this amount must be *deducted* from net earnings. This is because expenses reduce net earnings. Likewise, when Cost of Goods Sold is decreased because of an increase in Accounts Payable, this amount must be *added* to net earnings.

If a periodic inventory system was in use, the Purchases and related expense accounts, rather than the Cost of Goods Sold account, would be adjusted in a similar manner for any change in accounts payable. There would be no change in the Inventory account throughout the period in a periodic inventory system.

Increase in Accrued Expenses Payable. In the first year, operating expenses on account were debited to Operating Expenses and credited to Accrued Expenses Payable.

Accrued Expenses Payable			
	Jan. 1 Balance	0	
Payments for operating expenses 36,000	Operating expenses	40,000	$4,000 net increase
	Dec. 31 Balance	4,000	

When Accrued Expenses Payable increases during the year, operating expenses on an accrual basis are higher than they are on a cash basis. For Computer Services Corporation, operating expenses reported in the statement of earnings were $40,000. But, since Accrued Expenses Payable increased by $4,000, only $36,000 of the expenses were paid in cash. To adjust net earnings to net cash provided by operating activities, the $4,000 increase in Accrued Expenses Payable must be added to net earnings to reflect the fact that operating expenses deducted on the accrual-based statement of earnings did not use as much cash.

For Computer Services Corporation, the changes in Accounts Receivable, Accounts Payable, and Accrued Expenses Payable were the only changes in noncash current asset and current liability accounts. This means that any other revenues or expenses reported in the statement of earnings were received or paid in cash. Thus, Computer Services Corporation's income tax expense of $10,000 was paid in cash, and no adjustment of net earnings is necessary.

The operating activities section of the cash flow statement for Computer Services Corporation is shown in Illustration 13-7.

Illustration 13-7
Operating activities
section for 2003—indirect
method

COMPUTER SERVICES CORPORATION Cash Flow Statement—Indirect Method (partial) Year Ended December 31, 2003		
Operating activities		
Net earnings		$35,000
Adjustments to reconcile net earnings to net cash provided by operating activities		
Increase in accounts receivable	$(30,000)	
Increase in inventory	(25,000)	
Increase in accounts payable	15,000	
Increase in accrued expenses payable	4,000	(36,000)
Net cash used by operating activities		$(1,000)

Helpful Hint Whether the indirect or direct method (section 2) is used, net cash provided (used) by operating activities will be the same.

Step 3: Determining Net Cash Provided (Used) by Investing and Financing Activities

The third and final step in preparing the cash flow statement begins with a study of the balance sheet. We look at it to determine changes in noncurrent accounts. The change in each noncurrent account is then analysed to determine what effect, if any, it had on cash.

For Computer Services Corporation, the three noncurrent accounts are Equipment, Common Shares, and Retained Earnings. All three accounts have increased during the year. What caused these increases? No transaction data are given for the increases in Equipment of $10,000 and Common Shares of $60,000. When other explanations are lacking, we assume that any differences involve cash. Thus, the increase in Equipment is assumed to be a purchase of equipment for $10,000 cash. This purchase is reported as a cash outflow in the investing activities section. The increase in Common Shares is assumed to result from the issue of common shares for $60,000 cash. It is reported as an inflow of cash in the financing activities section of the cash flow statement.

The reasons for the net increase of $20,000 in the Retained Earnings account are determined by analysis. First, net earnings increased Retained Earnings by $35,000. Second, the additional information provided at the bottom of the statement of earnings in Illustration 13-5 indicates that a cash dividend of $15,000 was declared and paid. The $35,000 increase due to net earnings is reported in the operating activities section. The $15,000 cash dividend paid is reported in the financing activities section.

This analysis can also be done directly from the Retained Earnings account as shown below:

Retained Earnings				
		Jan. 1	Balance	0
Cash dividends	15,000		Net earnings	35,000
		Dec. 31	Balance	20,000

$20,000 net increase

The $20,000 increase in Retained Earnings is a *net* change. When a net change in a noncurrent balance sheet account has occurred during the year, it is generally necessary to report the causes of this change separately in the cash flow statement. Note that this is different from our practice with current asset and current liability balance sheet accounts, where we report only the net change.

Cash Flow Statement

Having completed the three steps, we can prepare the cash flow statement. The statement starts with the operating activities section, continues with the investing activities section, and ends with the financing activities section. The 2003 cash flow statement for Computer Services Corporation is shown in Illustration 13-8.

Illustration 13-8
Cash flow statement for 2003—indirect method

COMPUTER SERVICES CORPORATION Cash Flow Statement—Indirect Method Year Ended December 31, 2003		
Operating activities		
Net earnings		$35,000
Adjustments to reconcile net earnings to net cash		
provided by operating activities		
Increase in accounts receivable	$(30,000)	
Increase in inventory	(25,000)	
Increase in accounts payable	15,000	
Increase in accrued expenses payable	4,000	(36,000)
Net cash used by operating activities		(1,000)
Investing activities		
Purchase of equipment	$(10,000)	
Net cash used by investing activities		(10,000)
Financing activities		
Issue of common shares	$ 60,000	
Payment of cash dividend	(15,000)	
Net cash provided by financing activities		45,000
Net increase in cash		34,000
Cash, January 1		0
Cash, December 31		$34,000

Helpful Hint Note that in the investing and financing activities sections, positive numbers indicate cash inflows (receipts) and negative numbers indicate cash outflows (payments).

Computer Services' cash flow statement shows that operating activities **used** $1,000 cash; investing activities **used** $10,000 cash; and financing activities **provided** $45,000 cash. The increase in cash of $34,000 reported in the cash flow statement agrees with the increase of $34,000 shown as the change in the Cash account in the comparative balance sheet.

Notice how the cash flow statement links the statement of earnings with the beginning and ending balance sheets. Net earnings from the statement of earnings is the starting point in determining operating activities. The changes in the balance sheet accounts are explained in terms of their impact on cash. These changes lead to end-of-period cash balances in the balance sheet and on the cash flow statement.

SECOND YEAR OF OPERATIONS—2004

Illustrations 13-9 and 13-10 present information related to the second year of operations for Computer Services Corporation.

Illustration 13-9
Comparative balance
sheet

COMPUTER SERVICES CORPORATION
Balance Sheet
December 31

Assets	2004	2003	Change Increase/Decrease
Cash	$ 56,000	$34,000	$ 22,000 increase
Accounts receivable	20,000	30,000	10,000 decrease
Inventory	75,000	25,000	50,000 increase
Prepaid expenses	4,000	0	4,000 increase
Land	130,000	0	130,000 increase
Building	160,000	0	160,000 increase
Accumulated amortization—building	(11,000)	0	11,000 increase
Equipment	27,000	10,000	17,000 increase
Accumulated amortization—equipment	(3,000)	0	3,000 increase
Total	$458,000	$99,000	
Liabilities and Shareholders' Equity			
Accounts payable	$115,000	$15,000	$100,000 increase
Accrued expenses payable	9,000	4,000	5,000 increase
Bonds payable	130,000	0	130,000 increase
Common shares	60,000	60,000	0
Retained earnings	144,000	20,000	124,000 increase
Total	$458,000	$99,000	

Illustration 13-10
Statement of earnings
and additional information

COMPUTER SERVICES CORPORATION
Statement of Earnings
Year Ended December 31, 2004

Revenues		$900,000
Cost of goods sold		393,000
Gross profit		507,000
Operating expenses (excluding amortization)	$261,000	
Amortization expense	15,000	
Loss on sale of equipment	3,000	279,000
Earnings from operations		228,000
Income tax expense		89,000
Net earnings		$139,000

Additional information:
1. In 2004, the company declared and paid a $15,000 cash dividend.
2. The company obtained land through the issue of $130,000 of long-term bonds.
3. An office building costing $160,000 was purchased for cash. Equipment costing $25,000 was also purchased for cash.
4. During 2004, the company sold equipment with a book value of $7,000 (cost of $8,000 less accumulated amortization of $1,000) for $4,000 cash.

Step 1: Determining the Net Increase (Decrease) in Cash

To prepare a cash flow statement from this information, the first step is to determine the net increase or decrease in cash. As indicated from the information presented in Illustration 13-9, cash increased by $22,000 ($56,000 − $34,000).

Step 2: Determining Net Cash Provided (Used) by Operating Activities

As in step 2 in 2003, net earnings on an accrual basis must be adjusted to arrive at net cash provided (used) by operating activities. Remember from the previous section that increases in noncash current assets and decreases in current liabilities are deducted from net earnings. Decreases in noncash current assets and increases in current liabilities are added to net earnings. Explanations for the adjustments to net earnings for Computer Services Corporation in 2003 follow:

Decrease in Accounts Receivable. Accounts receivable decreased during the period because cash receipts were higher than revenues reported on an accrual basis. To adjust net earnings to net cash provided by operating activities, the $10,000 decrease in the Accounts Receivable account must be added to net earnings to determine cash receipts from customers.

Increase in Inventory. Inventory increases during a period when the cash paid for goods purchased is greater than the expense reported on an accrual basis. In other words, the cost of goods purchased is greater than the cost of goods sold. Just as described in the first year of operations, the increase in Inventory must be deducted from net earnings to determine the cash paid for the goods purchased.

Increase in Prepaid Expenses. Prepaid expenses increase during a period when cash paid for expenses is greater than expenses reported on an accrual basis. In other words, cash payments have been made in the current period, but costs have been deferred to future periods. To adjust net earnings to net cash provided by operating activities, the $4,000 increase in the Prepaid Expenses account must be deducted from net earnings to determine the cash paid for expenses.

Increase in Accounts Payable. Like the increase in 2003, the $100,000 increase in Accounts Payable in 2004 must be added to net earnings to determine the cash payments to suppliers.

Increase in Accrued Expenses Payable. Like the increase in 2003, the $5,000 increase in Accrued Expenses Payable during the year must be added to adjust net earnings to cash paid for operating expenses.

Amortization Expense. During 2004, Computer Services Corporation reported amortization expense of $15,000. Of this amount, $11,000 related to the building and $4,000 to the equipment. These two amounts were determined by analysing the accumulated amortization accounts in the balance sheet as follows:

> **Helpful Hint** Amortization is similar to any other expense in that it reduces net earnings. It differs in that it does not involve a current cash outflow; that is why it must be added back to net earnings to arrive at cash provided by operating activities.

Increase in Accumulated Amortization—Building. As shown in Illustration 13-9, accumulated amortization on the building increased by $11,000. This change represents the amortization expense on the building for the year. **Amortization expense is a noncash charge.** It is added back to net earnings in order to arrive at net cash provided by operating activities.

It is important to recognize that this amount is not added to operating activities as if it were a source of cash. Amortization does not involve cash. It is added to cancel the deduction created by the amortization expense in the determination of net earnings.

Increase in Accumulated Amortization—Equipment. Accumulated Amortization—Equipment increased by $3,000. But this change does not represent the total amortization expense for the year. The additional information in Illustration 13-10 indicates that this account was decreased (debited $1,000) as a result of the sale of some equipment. Thus, amortization expense for 2004 was $4,000 ($3,000 + $1,000). This amount is added to net earnings to determine net cash provided by operating activities.

The T account that follows provides information about the changes that occurred in this account in 2004:

$3,000 net increase

Accumulated Amortization—Equipment			
Accumulated amortization on equipment sold	1,000	Jan. 1 Balance	0
		Amortization expense	4,000
		Dec. 31 Balance	3,000

Amortization expense of $11,000 on the building plus amortization expense of $4,000 on the equipment equals the amortization expense of $15,000 reported on the statement of earnings. Amortization and similar noncash charges are frequently listed in the cash flow statement as the first adjustments to net earnings.

Loss on Sale of Equipment. On the statement of earnings, Computer Services Corporation reported a $3,000 loss on the sale of equipment (book value of $7,000 less cash proceeds of $4,000). Like amortization, the loss reduced net earnings but did not reduce cash. Thus, the loss is **added to net earnings** in determining net cash provided by operating activities.

If we did not add back a loss to remove it from net earnings, we would count the loss twice—once in the operating activities section (as part of net earnings), and again in the investing activities section (as part of the cash proceeds from the sale). As a result, a loss must be added to net earnings to calculate net cash provided by operating activities. If there is a gain on sale, the reverse occurs.

As a result of the previous adjustments, Computer Services' net cash provided by operating activities is $218,000, as calculated in Illustration 13-11.

Illustration 13-11
Operating activities section for 2004—indirect method

COMPUTER SERVICES CORPORATION		
Cash Flow Statement—Indirect Method (partial)		
Year Ended December 31, 2004		
Operating activities		
Net earnings		$139,000
Adjustments to reconcile net earnings to net cash provided by operating activities		
Amortization expense	$ 15,000	
Loss on sale of equipment	3,000	
Decrease in accounts receivable	10,000	
Increase in inventory	(50,000)	
Increase in prepaid expenses	(4,000)	
Increase in accounts payable	100,000	
Increase in accrued expenses payable	5,000	79,000
Net cash provided by operating activities		$218,000

Summary of Conversion to Net Cash Provided by Operating Activities—Indirect Method. The cash flow statement prepared by the indirect method starts with net earnings and adds or deducts items not affecting cash to arrive at net cash provided by operating activities. The additions and deductions consist of (1) changes in specific noncash current assets and current liabilities and (2) noncash items reported in the statement of earnings. A summary of the adjustments for the changes in the account balances of the noncash current assets and current liabilities is provided in Illustration 13-12.

Illustration 13-12
Adjustments for noncash current assets and current liabilities

	Adjustments to Convert Net Earnings to Net Cash Provided (Used) by Operating Activities	
Current Assets	Add to Net Earnings a(n):	Deduct from Net Earnings a(n):
Accounts receivable	Decrease	Increase
Inventory	Decrease	Increase
Prepaid expenses	Decrease	Increase
Other current assets	Decrease	Increase
Current Liabilities		
Accounts payable	Increase	Decrease
Accrued expenses payable	Increase	Decrease
Other current liabilities	Increase	Decrease

Helpful Hint Decreases in noncash current assets are added to net earnings. Increases are deducted. Increases in current liabilities are added to net earnings. Decreases are deducted.

Adjustments for the noncash items reported in the statement of earnings are made as shown in Illustration 13-13.

Illustration 13-13
Adjustments for noncash items

Noncash Items	Adjustments to Convert Net Earnings to Net Cash Provided (Used) by Operating Activities
Amortization expense	Add
Loss on sale of asset	Add
Gain on sale of asset	Deduct

Helpful Hint Noncash expenses (debits) are added to net earnings. Noncash revenues (credits) are deducted.

Step 3: Determining Net Cash Provided (Used) by Investing and Financing Activities

The third and final step involves analysing the remaining changes in balance sheet accounts to determine net cash provided (used) by investing and financing activities.

Increase in Land. As indicated from the change in the Land account and the additional information provided in Illustration 13-10, land worth $130,000 was purchased through the issue of long-term bonds. The issue of bonds payable for land has no effect on cash. But it is a significant noncash investing and financing activity that merits disclosure. As indicated earlier, these activities are disclosed in a note to the financial statements.

Increase in Building. The additional information indicates that an office building was acquired using $160,000 of cash. This transaction is a cash outflow reported in the investing activities section.

Increase in Equipment. The equipment account increased by $17,000. Based on the additional information, this was a net increase that resulted from two transactions: (1) a purchase of equipment for $25,000 and (2) the sale of equipment costing $8,000 for $4,000 cash proceeds.

The T account below shows the reasons for the change in this account during the year:

Equipment			
Jan. 1 Balance	10,000		
Purchase of equipment	25,000	Cost of equipment sold	8,000
Dec. 31 Balance	27,000		

$17,000 net increase

These transactions are classified as investing activities. Each transaction should be reported separately. Thus, the purchase of equipment should be reported as an $25,000 outflow of cash, and the sale should be reported as a $4,000 inflow of cash. Note that it is the *cash flow* that is important here, not the cost or book value of the equipment.

Increase in Bonds Payable. The Bonds Payable account increased by $130,000. As shown in the additional information, land was acquired through the issue of these bonds. As indicated earlier, this noncash transaction is reported in a note to the statement.

Increase in Retained Earnings. Retained Earnings increased by $124,000 during the year. This increase can be explained by two factors: (1) Net earnings of $139,000 increased Retained Earnings. (2) A dividend of $15,000 decreased Retained Earnings. Net earnings are adjusted to net cash provided by operating activities in the operating activities section. Payment of the dividend is a cash outflow that is reported as a financing activity.

Cash Flow Statement

Combining the previous items, we obtain a cash flow statement for 2004 for Computer Services Corporation as presented in Illustration 13-14.

Illustration 13-14
Cash flow statement for 2004—indirect method

COMPUTER SERVICES CORPORATION Cash Flow Statement—Indirect Method Year Ended December 31, 2004		
Operating activities		
Net earnings		$139,000
Adjustments to reconcile net earnings to net cash provided by operating activities		
Amortization expense	$ 15,000	
Loss on sale of equipment	3,000	
Decrease in accounts receivable	10,000	
Increase in inventory	(50,000)	
Increase in prepaid expenses	(4,000)	
Increase in accounts payable	100,000	
Increase in accrued expenses payable	5,000	79,000
Net cash provided by operating activities		218,000
Investing activities		
Purchase of building	$(160,000)	
Purchase of equipment	(25,000)	
Sale of equipment	4,000	
Net cash used by investing activities		(181,000)
Financing activities		
Payment of cash dividend	$ (15,000)	
Net cash used by financing activities		(15,000)
Net increase in cash		22,000
Cash, January 1		34,000
Cash, December 31		$ 56,000
Note X: Noncash investing and financing activities		
Issue of bonds payable to purchase land		$130,000

BEFORE YOU GO ON . . .

● **REVIEW IT**

1. What is the format of the operating activities section of the cash flow statement using the indirect method?
2. Explain how increases and decreases in noncash current assets and current liabilities are reported in the operating activities section of the cash flow statement.

3. Is amortization expense added to the operating activities section of the cash flow statement because it is a source of cash?

● **DO IT**

The following information relates to Reynolds Inc., a merchandising company. Use it to prepare a cash flow statement using the indirect method.

REYNOLDS INC.
Balance Sheet
December 31

Assets	2004	2003	Change Increase/Decrease
Cash	$ 54,000	$ 37,000	$ 17,000 increase
Accounts receivable	68,000	26,000	42,000 increase
Inventories	54,000	0	54,000 increase
Prepaid expenses	4,000	6,000	2,000 decrease
Land	45,000	70,000	25,000 decrease
Buildings	200,000	200,000	0
Accumulated amortization— buildings	(21,000)	(11,000)	10,000 increase
Equipment	193,000	68,000	125,000 increase
Accumulated amortization— equipment	(28,000)	(10,000)	18,000 increase
Total	$569,000	$386,000	
Liabilities and Shareholders' Equity			
Accounts payable	$ 23,000	$ 40,000	$ 17,000 decrease
Accrued expenses payable	10,000	0	10,000 increase
Bonds payable	110,000	150,000	40,000 decrease
Common shares	220,000	60,000	160,000 increase
Retained earnings	206,000	136,000	70,000 increase
Total	$569,000	$386,000	

REYNOLDS INC.
Statement of Earnings
Year Ended December 31, 2004

Sales revenue		$890,000
Cost of goods sold	$465,000	
Operating expenses	221,000	
Interest expense	12,000	
Loss on sale of equipment	2,000	700,000
Earnings from operations		190,000
Income tax expense		65,000
Net earnings		$125,000

Additional information:
1. Operating expenses include amortization expense of $33,000.
2. Land was sold for its book value.
3. Equipment with a cost of $166,000 was purchased for cash. Equipment with a cost of $41,000 and a book value of $36,000 was sold for $34,000 cash.
4. Bonds of $10,000 were redeemed at their carrying value for cash. Bonds of $30,000 were converted into common shares.
5. Accounts payable pertain to merchandise suppliers.

Action Plan

- Determine the net increase (decrease) in cash.
- Determine net cash provided (used) by operating activities. Operating activities generally relate to revenues and expenses which are affected by changes in noncash current assets and current liabilities and noncash items in the statement of earnings.
- Determine net cash provided (used) by investing activities. Investing activities generally relate to changes in noncurrent assets.
- Determine net cash provided (used) by financing activities. Financing activities generally relate to changes in noncurrent liabilities and shareholders' equity accounts.

Solution

REYNOLDS INC.		
Cash Flow Statement—Indirect Method		
Year Ended December 31, 2004		
Operating activities		
Net earnings		$125,000
Adjustments to reconcile net earnings to net cash		
provided by operating activities		
Amortization expense	$ 33,000	
Loss on sale of equipment	2,000	
Increase in accounts receivable	(42,000)	
Increase in inventories	(54,000)	
Decrease in prepaid expenses	2,000	
Decrease in accounts payable	(17,000)	
Increase in accrued expenses payable	10,000	(66,000)
Net cash provided by operating activities		59,000
Investing activities		
Sale of land	$ 25,000	
Sale of equipment	34,000	
Purchase of equipment	(166,000)	
Net cash used by investing activities		(107,000)
Financing activities		
Redemption of bonds	$(10,000)	
Sale of common shares	130,000	
Payment of dividends	(55,000)	
Net cash provided by financing activities		65,000
Net increase in cash		17,000
Cash, January 1		37,000
Cash, December 31		$ 54,000
Note X: Noncash investing and financing activities		
Conversion of bonds into common shares		$ 30,000

Note: This concludes section 1 on the preparation of the cash flow statement using the indirect method. Unless your instructor assigns section 2, you should turn to the concluding section of the chapter, "Using Cash Flows to Evaluate a Company," on page 635.

Direct Method

To illustrate the direct method, we will use the transactions of a merchandising company, Jiang Limited, for two years: 2003 and 2004. We will show basic transactions in the first year, with additional transactions added in the second year.

STUDY OBJECTIVE

3b

Prepare a cash flow statement using the direct method.

FIRST YEAR OF OPERATIONS—2003

Jiang Limited began business on January 1, 2003, when it issued common shares for $300,000 cash. The company purchased land for a future office site and rented office and sales space along with equipment. The comparative balance sheet at the beginning and end of 2003 and the changes in each account are shown in Illustration 13-15. The statement of earnings and additional information for Jiang are shown in Illustration 13-16.

JIANG LIMITED Balance Sheet			
Assets	Dec. 31, 2003	Jan. 1, 2003	Change Increase/Decrease
Cash	$159,000	$0	$159,000 increase
Accounts receivable	15,000	0	15,000 increase
Inventory	160,000	0	160,000 increase
Prepaid expenses	8,000	0	8,000 increase
Land	80,000	0	80,000 increase
Total	$422,000	$0	
Liabilities and Shareholders' Equity			
Accounts payable	$ 60,000	$0	$ 60,000 increase
Accrued expenses payable	20,000	0	20,000 increase
Common shares	300,000	0	300,000 increase
Retained earnings	42,000	0	42,000 increase
Total	$422,000	$0	

Illustration 13-15
Comparative balance sheet

JIANG LIMITED Statement of Earnings Year Ended December 31, 2003	
Sales revenue	$780,000
Cost of goods sold	450,000
Gross profit	330,000
Operating expenses	170,000
Earnings before income taxes	160,000
Income tax expense	48,000
Net earnings	$112,000

Additional information:
1. Dividends of $70,000 were declared and paid in cash.
2. The accounts payable increase resulted from the purchase of merchandise.

Illustration 13-16
Statement of earnings and additional information

Step 1: Determining the Net Increase (Decrease) in Cash

The comparative balance sheet for Jiang Limited shows a zero cash balance at January 1, 2003, and a cash balance of $159,000 at December 31, 2003. Therefore, the change in cash for 2003 was a net increase of $159,000.

Step 2: Determining Net Cash Provided (Used) by Operating Activities

Under the direct method, net cash provided by operating activities is calculated by **adjusting each item in the statement of earnings** from the accrual basis to the cash basis. To simplify and condense the operating activities section, **only major classes of operating cash receipts and cash payments are reported**. The difference between these major classes of cash receipts and cash payments is the net cash provided by operating activities, as shown in Illustration 13-17.

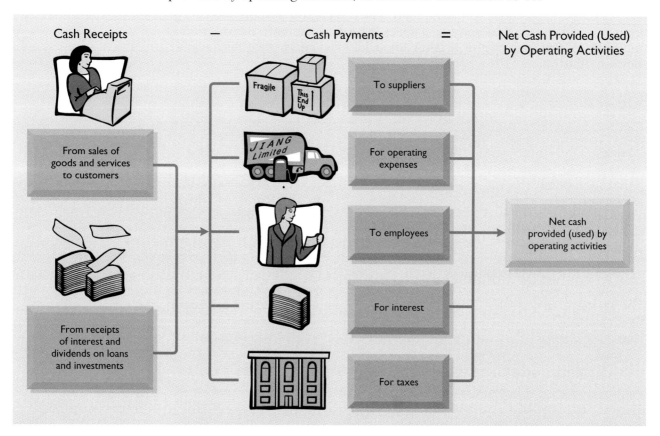

Illustration 13-17
Major classes of cash receipts and payments

An efficient way to apply the direct method is to analyse the revenues and expenses reported in the statement of earnings in the order in which they are listed. Cash receipts and cash payments related to these revenues and expenses are then determined by adjusting for changes in the related current balance sheet accounts.

For example, increases in current asset accounts are deducted from revenues and added to expenses to adjust accrual-based statement of earnings amounts to cash-based amounts. Conversely, decreases in current asset accounts are added to revenues and deducted from expenses. Increases in current liability accounts are added to revenues and deducted from expenses to adjust accrual-based statement of earnings amounts to cash-based amounts. Conversely, decreases in current liability accounts are deducted from revenues and added to expenses.

In the following sections, we explain the reasoning behind the adjustments that are needed to determine cash provided by operating activities for Jiang Limited.

Cash Receipts from Customers.   The statement of earnings for Jiang Limited reported revenues from customers of $780,000. How much of that was cash receipts from customers? To answer that, it is necessary to consider the change in accounts receivable during the year. When accounts receivable increase during the year, revenues on an accrual basis are higher than cash receipts from customers. In other words, revenues increased, but not all of these revenues resulted in cash receipts. To determine the amount of cash receipts, the increase in accounts receivable is deducted from sales revenues. On the other hand, there may be a decrease in accounts receivable. That would occur if cash receipts from customers exceeded sales revenues. In that case, the decrease in accounts receivable is added to sales revenues.

For Jiang, accounts receivable increased by $15,000. Thus, cash receipts from customers were $765,000, calculated as shown in Illustration 13-18.

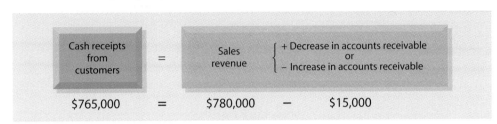

Illustration 13-18
Formula to calculate cash receipts from customers—direct method

Cash receipts from customers may also be determined from an analysis of the Accounts Receivable account, as shown below:

Accounts Receivable				
Jan. 1 Balance	0			
Sales revenue	780,000	Receipts from customers	765,000	} $15,000 net increase
Dec. 31 Balance	15,000			

Cash Receipts from Interest and Dividends. Jiang does not have any cash receipts from any source other than customers. If a statement of earnings reports other revenues, such as interest or dividend revenue, these amounts must be adjusted for any accrued amounts receivable to determine cash receipts. As in Illustration 13-18, increases in accrued receivables would be deducted from accrual-based revenues. Decreases in accrued receivables would be added to accrual-based revenues.

Cash Payments to Suppliers. Jiang reported cost of goods sold on its statement of earnings of $450,000, using the perpetual inventory system. How much of that amount was cash payments to suppliers? To answer that, it is first necessary to find purchases for the year. To find purchases, cost of goods sold is adjusted for the change in the Inventory account. When inventory increases during the year, the cost of goods purchased exceeds the cost of goods sold. To determine the cost of goods purchased, the increase in inventory is added to the cost of goods sold. Any decrease in the inventory would be deducted from the cost of goods sold. Jiang's cost of goods purchased is $610,000 ($450,000 + $160,000).

After the cost of goods purchased is calculated, cash payments to suppliers can be determined. This is done by adjusting the cost of goods purchased for the change in accounts payable (this assumes that only purchases of inventory on account are recorded in the Accounts Payable account). When accounts payable increase during the year, purchases on an accrual basis are higher than they are on a cash basis. To determine cash payments to suppliers, an increase in accounts payable is deducted from the cost of goods purchased. On the other hand, there may be a decrease in accounts payable. That would occur if cash payments to suppliers exceeded the cost of goods purchased. In that case, the decrease in accounts payable is added to the cost of goods purchased.

For Jiang, cash payments to suppliers were $550,000 ($610,000 − $60,000), calculated as shown in Illustration 13-19.

Illustration 13-19
Formula to calculate cash payments to suppliers—direct method

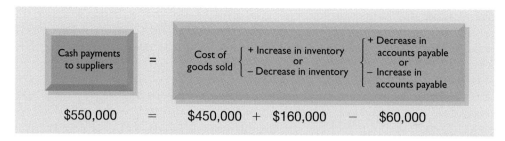

Cash payments to suppliers may also be determined from an analysis of the Inventory and Accounts Payable accounts, as shown below:

$160,000 net increase

Inventory			
Jan. 1 Balance	0		
Purchases	610,000	Cost of goods sold	450,000
Dec. 31 Balance	160,000		

$60,000 net increase

Accounts Payable			
		Jan. 1 Balance	0
Payments to suppliers	550,000	Purchases	610,000
		Dec. 31 Balance	60,000

Cash Payments for Operating Expenses. Operating expenses of $170,000 were reported on Jiang's statement of earnings. How much of that amount was cash paid for operating expenses? To answer that, we must adjust operating expenses for any changes in prepaid expenses and accrued expenses payable.

If prepaid expenses increase during the year, cash paid for operating expenses will be higher than operating expenses reported on the statement of earnings. To adjust operating expenses to cash payments for services, the increase in any prepaids must be added to operating expenses. On the other hand, if prepaid expenses decrease during the year, the decrease must be deducted from operating expenses.

Operating expenses must also be adjusted for changes in accrued expenses payable. While some companies record accrued expenses payable separately, others combine them with accounts payable. In a merchandising company, such as Jiang Limited, the Accounts Payable account is often used only for purchases of merchandise inventory on account. Accrued expense accounts are used for all other payables.

When accrued expenses payable increase during the year, operating expenses on an accrual basis are higher than they are on a cash basis. To determine cash payments for operating expenses, an increase in accrued expenses payable is deducted from operating expenses. On the other hand, a decrease in accrued expenses payable is added to operating expenses because cash payments exceed operating expenses.

Jiang's cash payments for operating expenses were $158,000, calculated as shown in Illustration 13-20.

Illustration 13-20
Formula to calculate cash payments for operating expenses—direct method

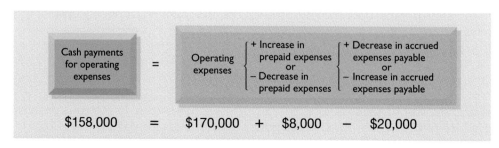

Cash payments for operating expenses can also be determined from an analysis of the Prepaid Expenses and Accrued Expenses Payable accounts, as shown below:

	Prepaid Expenses		
Jan. 1 Balance	0		
Payments for operating expenses	8,000		
Dec. 31 Balance	8,000		

$8,000 net increase

	Accrued Expenses Payable		
		Jan. 1 Balance	0
Payments for operating expenses	150,000	Operating expenses	170,000
		Dec. 31 Balance	20,000

$20,000 net increase

Cash Payments to Employees. Some companies report payments to employees separately, removing these payments from operating expenses. To determine payments to employees, you would have to know the salary (or wage) expense amount on the statement of earnings and any salaries payable on the balance sheet. Cash payments to employees would equal salary expense plus any decrease (or less any increase) during the period in salaries payable.

Other companies condense their statements of earnings in such a manner that cash payments to suppliers and employees cannot be separated from cash payments for operating expenses (i.e., they do not disclose cost of goods sold or salary expense separately). Although the disclosure will not be as informative, for reporting purposes it is acceptable to combine these sources of cash payments.

Cash Payments for Interest and Income Taxes. Jiang has no interest expense. The statement of earnings shows income tax expense of $48,000. This amount equals the cash paid. The comparative balance sheet indicates no income taxes payable at either the beginning or the end of the year. If Jiang needed to determine the cash paid for income taxes (or interest), assuming an Income Tax (or Interest) Payable account existed, it would simply adjust the expense for any decrease (+) or increase (−) in the account as shown in Illustration 13-21.

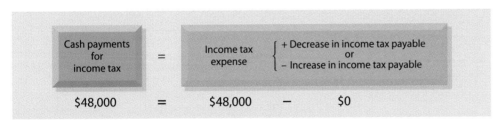

Illustration 13-21
Formula to calculate cash payments for income tax—direct method

A similar formula can be used for interest expense, if there is any. Amounts for income tax and interest should be reported separately.

All of the revenues and expenses in the 2003 statement of earnings have now been adjusted to a cash basis. The operating activities section of the cash flow statement is presented in Illustration 13-22.

Illustration 13-22
Operating activities section—direct method

JIANG LIMITED Cash Flow Statement—Direct Method (partial) Year Ended December 31, 2003		
Operating activities		
Cash receipts from customers		$765,000
Cash payments		
To suppliers	$550,000	
For operating expenses	158,000	
For income taxes	48,000	756,000
Net cash provided by operating activities		$ 9,000

Helpful Hint Whether the indirect (section 1) or direct method is used, net cash provided by operating activities will be the same.

Step 3: Determining Net Cash Provided (Used) by Investing and Financing Activities

Preparing the investing and financing activities sections of the cash flow statement begins by determining the changes in noncurrent accounts reported in the comparative balance sheet. The change in each account is then analysed to determine the effect, if any, the change had on cash.

Increase in Land. No additional information is given for the increase in Land. In such a case, you should assume that the increase affected cash. The purchase of land is an investing activity. Thus, an outflow of cash of $80,000 for the purchase of land should be reported in the investing activities section.

Increase in Common Shares. As indicated earlier, common shares were sold for $300,000 cash. A cash inflow of $300,000 from the issue of common shares is reported in the financing activities section.

Increase in Retained Earnings. What caused the net increase of $42,000 in the Retained Earnings account? First, net earnings increased retained earnings by $112,000. Second, the additional information provided in Illustration 13-16 indicates that cash dividends of $70,000 were declared and paid. The cash dividends paid are reported as an outflow of cash in the financing activities section.

This analysis can also be done directly from the Retained Earnings account, as shown below:

	Retained Earnings			
		Jan. 1	Balance	0
$42,000 net increase	Cash dividends 70,000		Net earnings	112,000
		Dec. 31	Balance	42,000

The $42,000 increase in Retained Earnings is a net change. When a net change in a noncurrent balance sheet account has occurred during the year, it is generally necessary to report the individual items that cause it.

Cash Flow Statement

We can now prepare the cash flow statement. The operating activities section is reported first, followed by the investing and financing activities sections. The cash flow statement for Jiang Limited for 2003 is presented in Illustration 13-23.

Illustration 13-23
Cash flow statement for 2003—direct method

Helpful Hint Note that in the investing and financing activities sections, positive numbers indicate cash inflows (receipts) and negative numbers indicate cash outflows (payments).

JIANG LIMITED Cash Flow Statement—Direct Method Year Ended December 31, 2003		
Operating activities		
Cash receipts from customers		$765,000
Cash payments		
To suppliers	$550,000	
For operating expenses	158,000	
For income taxes	48,000	756,000
Net cash provided by operating activities		9,000
Investing activities		
Purchase of land	$(80,000)	
Net cash used by investing activities		(80,000)
Financing activities		
Issue of common shares	$300,000	
Payment of cash dividend	(70,000)	
Net cash provided by financing activities		230,000
Net increase in cash		159,000
Cash, January 1		0
Cash, December 31		$159,000

The cash flow statement shows the following: Operating activities **provided** $9,000 of the net increase in cash of $159,000. Investing activities **used** $80,000 of cash. Financing activities **provided** $230,000 of cash. The net increase in cash for the year of $159,000 agrees with the $159,000 increase in cash reported in the comparative balance sheet in Illustration 13-15.

SECOND YEAR OF OPERATIONS—2004

Illustrations 13-24 and 13-25 present the comparative balance sheet, the statement of earnings, and additional information pertaining to the second year of operations for Jiang Limited.

Illustration 13-24
Comparative balance sheet

JIANG LIMITED
Balance Sheet
December 31

Assets	2004	2003	Change Increase/Decrease
Cash	$191,000	$159,000	$ 32,000 increase
Accounts receivable	12,000	15,000	3,000 decrease
Inventory	130,000	160,000	30,000 decrease
Prepaid expenses	6,000	8,000	2,000 decrease
Land	180,000	80,000	100,000 increase
Equipment	160,000	0	160,000 increase
Accumulated amortization— equipment	(16,000)	0	16,000 increase
Total	$663,000	$422,000	
Liabilities and Shareholders' Equity			
Accounts payable	$ 52,000	$ 60,000	$ 8,000 decrease
Accrued expenses payable	15,000	20,000	5,000 decrease
Income taxes payable	12,000	0	12,000 increase
Bonds payable	90,000	0	90,000 increase
Common shares	400,000	300,000	100,000 increase
Retained earnings	94,000	42,000	52,000 increase
Total	$663,000	$422,000	

Illustration 13-25
Statement of earnings and additional information

JIANG LIMITED
Statement of Earnings
Year Ended December 31, 2004

Sales revenue		$975,000
Cost of goods sold	$660,000	
Operating expenses (excluding amortization)	176,000	
Amortization expense	18,000	
Loss on sale of equipment	1,000	855,000
Earnings before income taxes		120,000
Income tax expense		36,000
Net earnings		$ 84,000

Additional information:
1. In 2004, the company declared and paid $32,000 of cash dividends.
2. Bonds were issued at face value for $90,000 in cash.
3. Equipment costing $180,000 was purchased for cash.
4. Equipment costing $20,000 was sold for $17,000 cash when the book value of the equipment was $18,000.
5. Common shares of $100,000 were issued to acquire land.

Step 1: Determining the Net Increase (Decrease) in Cash

The comparative balance sheet shows a beginning cash balance of $159,000 and an ending cash balance of $191,000. Thus, there was a net increase in cash in 2004 of $32,000.

Step 2: Determining Net Cash Provided (Used) by Operating Activities

Cash Receipts from Customers.   Sales revenue was $975,000. Since accounts receivable decreased by $3,000, cash receipts from customers were greater than sales revenue. Cash receipts from customers were $978,000, calculated as shown in Illustration 13-26.

Illustration 13-26
Calculation of cash
receipts from customers

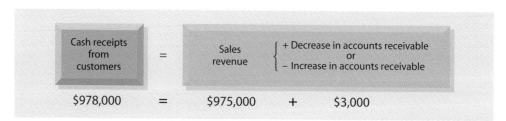

Cash Payments to Suppliers.   The conversion of (1) cost of goods sold to cost of goods purchased and (2) cost of goods purchased to cash payments to suppliers uses the same procedure as for 2003. For 2004, the cost of goods purchased is calculated using cost of goods sold of $660,000 from the statement of earnings and the decrease in inventory of $30,000 from the comparative balance sheet. The cost of goods purchased of $630,000 ($660,000 − $30,000) is then adjusted by the $8,000 decrease in accounts payable. Cash payments to suppliers were $638,000 ($630,000 + $8,000), as shown in Illustration 13-27.

Illustration 13-27
Calculation of cash
payments to suppliers

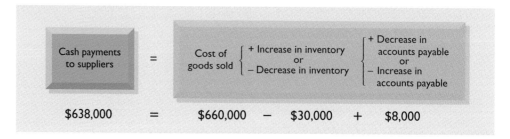

Cash Payments for Operating Expenses.   Operating expenses (exclusive of amortization expense) for 2004 were reported at $176,000. This amount is adjusted for changes in prepaid expenses and accrued expenses payable to determine cash payments for operating expenses.

As shown in the comparative balance sheet, prepaid expenses decreased by $2,000 during the year. This means that cash payments for expenses were less than the operating expense amount. To determine cash payments for operating expenses, the decrease in prepaid expenses is deducted from operating expenses.

Accrued expenses payable decreased by $5,000 during the period. As a result, cash payments were higher by $5,000 than the amount reported for operating expenses. The decrease in accrued expenses payable is added to operating expenses. Cash payments for operating expenses were $179,000, calculated as shown in Illustration 13-28.

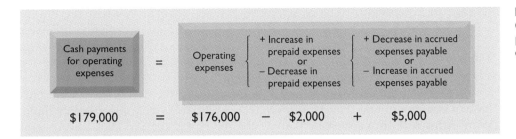

Illustration 13-28
Calculation of cash payments for operating expenses

Amortization Expense and Loss on Sale of Equipment.
Amortization expense in 2004 was $18,000. Amortization expense is not shown on a cash flow statement under the direct method because it is a noncash charge. If amortization expense is included in operating expenses, operating expenses must be reduced by the amount of amortization to determine cash payments for operating expenses.

The $1,000 loss on the sale of equipment is also a noncash charge. The loss reduces net earnings, but it does not reduce cash. Thus, a loss on the sale of equipment is not reported on a cash flow statement prepared using the direct method.

Cash Payments for Interest and Income Taxes.
Once again, Jiang had no interest payments. Income tax expense reported on the statement of earnings was $36,000. Income taxes payable, however, increased by $12,000. This increase means that $12,000 of the income taxes have not been paid. As a result, income taxes paid were less than income taxes reported on the statement of earnings. Cash payments for income taxes were therefore $24,000, as shown in Illustration 13-29.

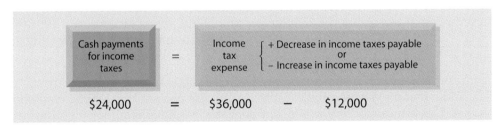

Illustration 13-29
Calculation of cash payments for income taxes

Summary of Conversion to Net Cash Provided by Operating Activities—Direct Method.
The direct method classifies operating activities into major categories of cash receipts (e.g., from customers, from investments) and cash payments (e.g., to suppliers, for operating expenses, to employees, for interest, for income tax). To find cash receipts and payments, accrual-based revenues and expenses must be adjusted for changes in noncash current asset and current liability accounts.

Increases in related current liability accounts and decreases in related current asset accounts are added to accrual-based revenues to determine cash receipts. Increases in related current asset accounts and decreases in related current liability accounts are added to accrual-based expenses to determine cash payments. Noncash items, such as amortization expense, do not affect cash and are therefore excluded from the cash flow statement.

Step 3: Determining Net Cash Provided (Used) by Investing and Financing Activities

Increase in Land. Land increased by $100,000. The additional information provided in Illustration 13-25 indicates that common shares were issued to purchase the land. The issue of common shares for land has no effect on cash. But it is a **significant noncash investing and financing transaction.** This transaction requires disclosure in a note to the cash flow statement.

Increase in Equipment. The comparative balance sheet shows that the Equipment account increased by $160,000 in 2004. The additional information indicates that the increase resulted from two investing transactions: (1) Equipment costing $180,000 was purchased for cash. (2) Equipment costing $20,000 was sold for $17,000 cash when its book value was $18,000.

The relevant data for the cash flow statement are the cash paid for the purchase of equipment and the cash proceeds from the sale of equipment. For Jiang, the investing activities section will show the following: the $180,000 purchase of equipment, as an outflow of cash, and the $17,000 sale of equipment, as an inflow of cash. The two amounts **should not be netted because one is an outflow of cash and the other is an inflow of cash.**

The analysis of the changes in Equipment should include the related Accumulated Amortization account. These two accounts for Jiang Limited are shown below:

	Equipment			
Jan. 1 Balance	0			
Purchase of equipment	180,000	Cost of equipment sold	20,000
Dec. 31 Balance	160,000			

$160,000 net increase

Accumulated Amortization—Equipment			
		Jan. 1 Balance	0
Sale of equipment	2,000	Amortization expense	18,000
		Dec. 31 Balance	16,000

$16,000 net increase

Increase in Bonds Payable. Bonds Payable increased by $90,000. The additional information in Illustration 13-25 indicates that bonds with a face value of $90,000 were issued for $90,000 cash. The issue of bonds is a financing activity. For Jiang, there is an inflow of cash of $90,000 from the issue of bonds payable.

Increase in Common Shares. The Common Shares account increased by $100,000. The additional information indicates that land was acquired by issuing common shares. This transaction is a **significant noncash investing and financing transaction** that should be reported in a note to the statement.

Increase in Retained Earnings. The $52,000 net increase in Retained Earnings resulted from net earnings of $84,000 and the declaration and payment of cash dividends of $32,000. Net earnings are not reported in the cash flow statement under the direct method. Instead, the individual components that make up net earnings are reported when they affect cash flows. The cash dividends paid of $32,000 are reported in the financing activities section as an outflow of cash.

Cash Flow Statement

The cash flow statement for Jiang Limited is shown in Illustration 13-30.

Illustration 13-30
Cash flow statement for
2004—direct method

JIANG LIMITED
Cash Flow Statement—Direct Method
Year Ended December 31, 2004

Operating activities		
Cash receipts from customers		$978,000
Cash payments		
To suppliers	$ 638,000	
For operating expenses	179,000	
For income taxes	24,000	841,000
Net cash provided by operating activities		137,000
Investing activities		
Purchase of equipment	$(180,000)	
Sale of equipment	17,000	
Net cash used by investing activities		(163,000)
Financing activities		
Issue of bonds payable	$ 90,000	
Payment of cash dividends	(32,000)	
Net cash provided by financing activities		58,000
Net increase in cash		32,000
Cash, January 1		159,000
Cash, December 31		$191,000
Note X: Noncash investing and financing activities		
Issue of common shares to purchase land		$100,000

BEFORE YOU GO ON . . .

● **REVIEW IT**

1. What is the format of the operating activities section of the cash flow statement using the direct method?
2. Does the net cash provided or used by operating activities differ depending on whether the direct method or the indirect method is used to prepare the cash flow statement?
3. Why is amortization expense not reported on the cash flow statement?

● **DO IT**

The following information relates to Reynolds Inc., a merchandising company. Use it to prepare a cash flow statement using the direct method.

REYNOLDS INC.
Balance Sheet
December 31

Assets	2004	2003	Change Increase/Decrease
Cash	$ 54,000	$ 37,000	$ 17,000 increase
Accounts receivable	68,000	26,000	42,000 increase
Inventories	54,000	0	54,000 increase
Prepaid expenses	4,000	6,000	2,000 decrease
Land	45,000	70,000	25,000 decrease
Buildings	200,000	200,000	0
Accumulated amortization—buildings	(21,000)	(11,000)	10,000 increase
Equipment	193,000	68,000	125,000 increase
Accumulated amortization—equipment	(28,000)	(10,000)	18,000 increase
Total	$569,000	$386,000	
Liabilities and Shareholders' Equity			
Accounts payable	$ 23,000	$ 40,000	$ 17,000 decrease
Accrued expenses payable	10,000	0	10,000 increase
Bonds payable	110,000	150,000	40,000 decrease
Common shares	220,000	60,000	160,000 increase
Retained earnings	206,000	136,000	70,000 increase
Total	$569,000	$386,000	

REYNOLDS INC.
Statement of Earnings
Year Ended December 31, 2004

Sales revenue		$890,000
Cost of goods sold	$465,000	
Operating expenses	221,000	
Interest expense	12,000	
Loss on sale of equipment	2,000	700,000
Earnings from operations		190,000
Income tax expense		65,000
Net earnings		$125,000

Additional information:
1. Operating expenses include amortization expense of $33,000 and charges from prepaid expenses of $2,000.
2. Land was sold for its book value.
3. Equipment with a cost of $166,000 was purchased for cash. Equipment with a cost of $41,000 and a book value of $36,000 was sold for $34,000 cash.
4. Bonds of $10,000 were redeemed at their carrying value for cash. Bonds of $30,000 were converted into common shares.
5. Accounts payable pertain to merchandise suppliers.

Action Plan

- Determine the net increase (decrease) in cash.
- Determine net cash provided (used) by operating activities. Operating activities report cash receipts and payments for the statement of earnings. Accrual-based amounts are adjusted for changes in noncash current assets and current liabilities to arrive at cash-based amounts.
- Determine net cash provided (used) by investing activities. Investing activities generally relate to changes in noncurrent assets.

• Determine net cash provided (used) by financing activities. Financing activities generally relate to changes in noncurrent liabilities and shareholders' equity accounts.

Solution

REYNOLDS INC. Cash Flow Statement—Direct Method Year Ended December 31, 2004		
Operating activities		
Cash receipts from customers		$848,000[a]
Cash payments		
To suppliers	$536,000[b]	
For operating expenses	176,000[c]	
For interest expense	12,000	
For income taxes	65,000	789,000
Net cash provided by operating activities		59,000
Investing activities		
Sale of land	$ 25,000	
Sale of equipment	34,000	
Purchase of equipment	(166,000)	
Net cash used by investing activities		(107,000)
Financing activities		
Redemption of bonds	$(10,000)	
Sale of common shares	130,000	
Payment of dividends	(55,000)[d]	
Net cash provided by financing activities		65,000
Net increase in cash		17,000
Cash, January 1		37,000
Cash, December 31		$ 54,000
Note X: Noncash investing and financing activities		
Conversion of bonds into common shares		$ 30,000

Calculations:
[a] $848,000 = $890,000 − $42,000
[b] $536,000 = $465,000 + $54,000 + $17,000
[c] $176,000 = $221,000 − $33,000 − $2,000 − $10,000
[d] $55,000 = $136,000 + $125,000 − $206,000

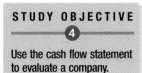

Note: This concludes section 2 on the preparation of the cash flow statement using the direct method. You should now turn to the next—and concluding—section of the chapter, "Using Cash Flows to Evaluate a Company."

Using Cash Flows to Evaluate a Company

Traditionally, the ratios most commonly used by investors and creditors have been based on accrual accounting. In Chapter 2, we introduced some cash-based ratios that are gaining increased acceptance among analysts (e.g., cash current debt coverage and cash total debt coverage). In this section, we introduce free cash flow to supplement the cash coverage ratios introduced earlier.

STUDY OBJECTIVE
4

Use the cash flow statement to evaluate a company.

FREE CASH FLOW

In the cash flow statement, cash provided by operating activities is supposed to indicate the company's ability to generate cash. Analysts have noted, however, that cash provided by operating activities fails to take into account the fact that a company must invest in new assets just to maintain its current level of operations. Companies must also at least maintain dividends at current levels to satisfy investors. One solvency-based measure that helps investors and management understand how much discretionary cash flow a company has is free cash flow. Free cash flow is the term used to describe the cash remaining from operating activities after adjustments for capital expenditures and dividends.

Consider the following example. Suppose that MPC Ltd. produces and sells 10,000 personal computers this year. It reports $100,000 cash provided by operating activities. In order to maintain production at 10,000 computers, MPC then invests $15,000 in equipment. It also chooses to pay $5,000 in dividends. Its free cash flow is therefore $80,000 ($100,000 − $15,000 − $5,000). The company could use this $80,000 to purchase new assets to expand the business or to pay an $80,000 dividend, amongst other alternatives, while continuing to produce 10,000 computers a year.

We will now use data from Microsoft, compared to Corel, to further illustrate the calculation of free cash flow. Selected information from the 2002 cash flow statement of Microsoft Corporation is shown in Illustration 13-31. Data for Corel have been extracted from Corel's cash flow statement, which is not shown here.

Illustration 13-31
Microsoft cash flow information

MICROSOFT CORPORATION Cash Flow Statement (partial) Year Ended June 30, 2002 (in U.S. millions)		
Net cash provided by operating activities		$ 14,509
Investing activities		
Additions to property and equipment	$ (770)	
Purchase of investments	(89,386)	
Sale of investments	79,311	
Net cash used by investing activities		(10,845)
Cash paid for dividends		(0)

In practice, free cash flow is often calculated with the formula applied to Microsoft and Corel in Illustration 13-32. Alternative definitions, and calculations, also exist.

Illustration 13-32
Free cash flow

FREE CASH FLOW =	CASH PROVIDED (USED) BY OPERATING ACTIVITIES	− CAPITAL EXPENDITURES	− DIVIDENDS PAID

(in U.S. millions)	Free Cash Flow	Cash Provided (Used) by Operating Activities	Capital Expenditures	Dividends Paid
Microsoft	$13,739 =	$14,509 −	$770 −	$0
Corel	$(22,978) =	$(19,742) −	$3,236 −	$0

U.S.$13,739 million is a tremendous amount of cash generated in a single year. It is available for the acquisition of new assets, the retirement of debt or equity securities, or the payment of dividends.

On the other hand, Corel Corporation's free cash flow for 2002 was a negative value of nearly U.S.$23 billion. So, while Microsoft still has cash available for future acquisitions, divestitures, or other purposes, Corel has used its cash capacity to date and is selling its investments to finance its operations.

Decision Toolkit

DECISION CHECKPOINTS	INFO NEEDED FOR DECISION	TOOL TO USE FOR DECISION	HOW TO EVALUATE RESULTS
How much cash did the company generate to either expand operations or pay dividends?	Cash provided by operating activities, cash spent on long-lived assets, and cash dividends.	$\text{Free cash flow} = \text{Cash provided by operating activities} - \text{Capital expenditures} - \text{Dividends paid}$	Significant free cash flow indicates greater potential to finance new investments and pay additional dividends.

BUSINESS INSIGHT

INVESTOR PERSPECTIVE

Until recently, many companies reported the cash flow per share ratio, in addition to earnings per share, in their financial statements. However, concerns with the wide range of calculations used to determine cash flow per share resulted in the prohibition of this ratio in the financial statements. For example, some companies used cash flow from operating activities, some companies used cash flow from operating activities without adjusting for changes in working capital items, and some companies used total cash flow as their numerator in calculating this ratio. Few companies disclosed their basis of calculation.

The CICA concluded that investors were being unnecessarily confused by terms used differently by different companies and even by the same company from one period to another. The CICA was also concerned that inclusion of cash flow per share information was perceived as an alternative performance measure to earnings per share figures by investors who favoured "hard cash data."

Investing Activities	
Oil and Gas Properties	(12,177,115)
Proceeds on Sales of Oil and Gas Properties	870,745
Acquisition of Subsidiary, Net of Cash Acquired	(2,953,904)
Loans to Officers and Directors	–
Investments	(600,000)
Furniture and Equipment	(80,284)
Change in Non-Cash Working Capital	1,655,728
	(13,284,830)
Increase in Cash During the Year	329
Cash: Beginning of Year	17,257
Cash: End of Year	17,586
Funds from Operations per Share *(Note 12)*	
Basic	0.34
Diluted	0.33

BEFORE YOU GO ON . . .

● **REVIEW IT**

1. What is the difference between cash from operating activities and free cash flow?
2. What does it mean if a company has negative free cash flow?
3. Why might an analyst want to supplement accrual-based ratios with cash-based ratios? What are some cash-based ratios?

Using the Decision Toolkit

Rogers Communications Inc. is Canada's number one cable company. The company also operates wireless communications systems and a multimedia group which includes radio and television broadcasting and the publication of magazines and newspapers. Shaw Communications Inc. is also one of Canada's top cable companies and its core business is providing broadband cable television and Internet services.

    The defining feature of today's cable and telecommunications market is change spurred by technological advances and deregulation. With such constant change, it is important to examine various cash-based measures for companies like Rogers and Shaw.

Instructions

Calculate the following cash-based measures for Rogers for 2002, and compare them with those provided here for Shaw:

1. Free cash flow
2. Cash current debt coverage
3. Cash total debt coverage

Selected financial statement data for Rogers and comparative data for Shaw follow:

ROGERS COMMUNICATIONS INC. Balance Sheet (partial) December 31, 2002 (in thousands)		
Assets	2002	2001
Current assets	$ 932,834	$ 909,835
Noncurrent assets	7,591,669	7,900,544
Total assets	$8,524,503	$8,810,379
Liabilities and Shareholders' Equity		
Current liabilities	$1,300,461	$ 1,329,354
Long-term liabilities	5,687,471	4,990,357
Total liabilities	6,987,932	6,319,711
Shareholders' equity	1,536,571	2,490,668
Total liabilities and shareholders' equity	$8,524,503	$8,810,379

ROGERS COMMUNICATIONS INC. Cash Flow Statement Year Ended December 31, 2002 (in thousands)		
	2002	2001
Cash provided by operating activities	$768,549	$ 418,949
Cash provided (used) by financing activities	(636,074)	1,310,446
Cash used by investing activities	(122,792)	(2,011,345)
Increase (decrease) in cash and cash equivalents	$ 9,683	$ (281,950)

Cash spent on property, plant, and equipment in 2002 was $1,261,983 thousand. Cash paid for dividends was $33,000 thousand.

Here are the comparative data for Shaw (also in thousands):

1. Free cash flow $(461,308)
2. Cash current debt coverage ratio   0.54 times
3. Cash total debt coverage ratio   0.06 times

Solution

1. Rogers' free cash flow is actually not "free" at all. It is a negative $526,434 thousand ($768,549 − $1,261,983 − $33,000). Shaw's is also a negative $461,308 thousand. In both companies, capital expenditures exceeded cash flow from operating activities.

2. Rogers' cash current debt coverage is calculated as follows:

$$\frac{\$768,549}{(\$1,300,461 + \$1,329,354) \div 2} = 0.58 \text{ times}$$

Rogers is slightly more liquid than Shaw, but neither company is generating enough cash from operating activities to meet its current obligations.

3. Rogers' cash total debt coverage is calculated as follows:

$$\frac{\$768,549}{(\$6,987,932 + \$6,319,711) \div 2} = 0.12 \text{ times}$$

Rogers is significantly more solvent than Shaw, with a cash total debt coverage ratio double Shaw's. However, neither company is reporting a strong coverage ratio in this regard. Neither company is generating enough cash from operating activities to finance its current obligations, much less its long-term, or total, obligations.

Summary of Study Objectives

❶ Indicate the primary purpose of the cash flow statement. The cash flow statement provides information about the cash receipts and cash payments resulting from the operating, investing, and financing activities of a company during a specific period.

❷ Distinguish among operating, investing, and financing activities. In general, operating activities include the cash effects of transactions that enter into the determination of net earnings. Investing activities involve cash flows resulting from changes in investments and long-term asset items. Financing activities involve cash flows resulting from changes in long-term liability and shareholders' equity items.

● Prepare a cash flow statement using the indirect method. The preparation of a cash flow statement involves three major steps: (1) Determine the net increase or decrease in cash. (2) Determine net cash provided (used) by operating activities. (3) Determine net cash provided (used) by investing and financing activities. Under the indirect method, accrual-based net earnings are adjusted to net cash provided by operating activities.

● Prepare a cash flow statement using the direct method. The preparation of the cash flow statement involves three major steps: (1) Determine the net increase or decrease in cash. (2) Determine net cash provided (used) by operating activities. (3) Determine net cash provided (used) by investing and financing activities. The direct method reports cash receipts less cash payments to arrive at net cash provided by operating activities.

❹ Use the cash flow statement to evaluate a company. Free cash flow is a measure of solvency that indicates the amount of cash a company generated during the current year that is available for the payment of dividends or for expansion. It is calculated by subtracting capital expenditures and dividends from cash provided by operating activities.

Decision Toolkit—A Summary

Decision
Toolkit
Summary

DECISION CHECKPOINTS	INFO NEEDED FOR DECISION	TOOL TO USE FOR DECISION	HOW TO EVALUATE RESULTS
How much cash did the company generate to either expand operations or pay dividends?	Cash provided by operating activities, cash spent on long-lived assets, and cash dividends.	Free cash flow = Cash provided by operating activities − Capital expenditures − Dividends paid	Significant free cash flow indicates greater potential to finance new investments and pay additional dividends

Glossary

Glossary

Direct method   A method of determining net cash provided by operating activities by adjusting each item in the statement of earnings from the accrual basis to the cash basis. (p. 608)

Financing activities   Cash flow activities that include (a) obtaining cash from issuing debt and repaying the amounts borrowed and (b) obtaining cash from shareholders and providing them with a return on their investment. (p. 603)

Free cash flow   Cash provided by operating activities less dividends and capital expenditures. (p. 636)

Indirect method   A method of determining net cash provided by operating activities in which net earnings are adjusted for items that do not affect cash. (p. 608)

Investing activities   Cash flow activities that include (a) purchasing and disposing of investments and productive long-lived assets using cash and (b) lending money and collecting on those loans. (p. 603)

Operating activities   Cash flow activities that include the cash effects of transactions which create revenues and expenses and thus enter into the determination of net earnings. (p. 603)

Demonstration Problem

Additional
Demonstration
Problems

The statement of earnings for Kosinski Manufacturing Inc. contains the following condensed information:

KOSINSKI MANUFACTURING INC.
Statement of Earnings
Year Ended December 31, 2004

Sales		$6,583,000
Cost of goods sold		3,427,000
Gross profit		3,156,000
Operating expenses	$1,493,000	
Amortization expense	880,000	2,373,000
Earnings before income taxes		783,000
Income tax expense		353,000
Net earnings		$ 430,000

Included in operating expenses is a $24,000 loss resulting from the sale of old machinery for $270,000 cash. New machinery was purchased during the year at a cost of $750,000. Dividends declared and paid in 2004 totalled $200,000. The following current asset and current liability balances are reported on Kosinski's comparative balance sheet at December 31:

	2004	2003	Increase (Decrease)
Cash	$672,000	$130,000	$542,000
Accounts receivable	775,000	610,000	165,000
Inventories	834,000	867,000	(33,000)
Accounts payable	521,000	501,000	20,000

Instructions

(a) Prepare the cash flow statement using the indirect method.
(b) Prepare the cash flow statement using the direct method.

Solution to Demonstration Problem

(a)

KOSINSKI MANUFACTURING INC.
Cash Flow Statement—Indirect Method
Year Ended December 31, 2004

Operating activities		
Net earnings		$ 430,000
Adjustments to reconcile net earnings to		
net cash provided by operating activities		
Amortization expense	$ 880,000	
Loss on sale of machinery	24,000	
Increase in accounts receivable	(165,000)	
Decrease in inventories	33,000	
Increase in accounts payable	20,000	792,000
Net cash provided by operating activities		1,222,000
Investing activities		
Sale of machinery	$ 270,000	
Purchase of machinery	(750,000)	
Net cash used by investing activities		(480,000)
Financing activities		
Payment of cash dividends	$(200,000)	
Net cash used by financing activities		(200,000)
Net increase in cash		542,000
Cash, January 1		130,000
Cash, December 31		$ 672,000

Action Plan

- Apply the same data to the cash flow statement under both the indirect and direct methods.
- Note the similarities of the two methods: Both methods report the same information in the investing and financing sections.
- Note the difference between the two methods: The cash flows from operating activities sections report different information (however, the *amount* of net cash provided by operating activities is the same for both methods).

(b)

KOSINSKI MANUFACTURING INC. Cash Flow Statement—Direct Method Year Ended December 31, 2004		
Operating activities		
Cash receipts from customers		$6,418,000 [a]
Cash payments to suppliers		(3,374,000)[b]
Cash payments for operating expenses		(1,469,000)[c]
Cash payment for income taxes		(353,000)
Net cash provided by operating activities		1,222,000
Investing activities		
Sale of machinery	$270,000	
Purchase of machinery	(750,000)	
Net cash used by investing activities		(480,000)
Financing activities		
Payment of cash dividends	$(200,000)	
Net cash used by financing activities		(200,000)
Net increase in cash		542,000
Cash, January 1		130,000
Cash, December 31		$ 672,000

Direct Method Calculations

[a] Cash receipts from customers:	
Sales per the statement of earnings	$6,583,000
Deduct: Increase in accounts receivable	165,000
Cash collections from customers	$6,418,000
[b] Cash payments to suppliers:	
Cost of goods sold per the statement of earnings	$3,427,000
Deduct: Decrease in inventories	33,000
Increase in accounts payable	20,000
Cash payments to suppliers	$3,374,000
[c] Cash payments for operating expenses:	
Operating expenses per the statement of earnings	$1,493,000
Deduct: Loss on sale of machinery	24,000
Cash payments for operating expenses	$1,469,000

Multiple
Choice
Quiz

Self-Study Questions

(SO 1)   1. Which of the following is *incorrect* about the cash flow statement?
   (a) It is a fourth basic financial statement.
   (b) It provides information about a company's cash receipts and cash payments during a period.
   (c) It reconciles the ending cash account balance to the balance per the bank statement.
   (d) It provides information about the operating, investing, and financing activities of the business.

(SO 2)   2. The cash flow statement classifies cash receipts and cash payments by these activities:
   (a) operating and non-operating.
   (b) operating, investing, and financing.
   (c) financing, operating, and non-operating.
   (d) investing, financing, and non-operating.

(SO 2)   3. Which is an example of a cash flow from an operating activity?
   (a) A payment of cash to lenders for interest
   (b) A receipt of cash from the sale of common shares
   (c) A payment of cash dividends to shareholders
   (d) A receipt of cash from the issue of a short-term note payable

(SO 2)   4. Which is an example of a cash flow from an investing activity?
   (a) A receipt of cash from the issue of bonds payable
   (b) A payment of cash to repurchase common shares
   (c) A receipt of cash from the sale of equipment
   (d) A payment of cash to suppliers for inventory

(SO 2)   5. Which is an example of a cash flow from a financing activity?
   (a) A receipt of cash from the sale of land
   (b) An issue of debt for cash
   (c) A purchase of equipment for cash
   (d) A purchase of inventory on credit

(SO 2)   6. Cash dividends paid to shareholders are classified on the cash flow statement under:
   (a) operating activities.
   (b) investing activities.
   (c) financing activities.
   (d) a note to the financial statements.

(SO 2)   7. Which of the following is *incorrect* about the cash flow statement?
   (a) The direct method may be used to report cash provided by operating activities.

   (b) The indirect method may be used to report cash provided by operating activities.
   (c) The statement shows the cash provided (used) by three categories of activity.
   (d) Significant noncash activities are reported in the body of the statement.

Questions 8 and 9 apply only to the indirect method.

(SO 3a)   8. Net earnings are $132,000. During the year, accounts payable increased by $10,000, inventory decreased by $6,000, and accounts receivable increased by $12,000. Under the indirect method, what is net cash provided by operating activities?
   (a) $102,000   (c) $124,000
   (b) $112,000   (d) $136,000

(SO 3a)   9. In determining cash provided by operating activities under the indirect method, noncash items that are added back to net earnings do *not* include:
   (a) amortization expense.
   (b) a decrease in inventory.
   (c) a gain on the sale of equipment.
   (d) a loss on the sale of equipment.

Questions 10 and 11 apply only to the direct method.

(SO 3b)   10. The beginning balance in Accounts Receivable is $44,000. The ending balance is $42,000. Sales during the period are $129,000. What are the cash receipts from customers?
   (a) $127,000   (c) $131,000
   (b) $129,000   (d) $141,000

(SO 3b)   11. Which of the following items is reported in the operating activities section of a cash flow statement prepared by the direct method?
   (a) A loss on the sale of a building
   (b) An increase in accounts receivable
   (c) Amortization expense
   (d) Cash payments to suppliers

(SO 4)   12. ⚙ Free cash flow provides an indication of a company's ability to:
   (a) generate net earnings.
   (b) generate cash to pay dividends.
   (c) generate cash to invest in new capital expenditures.
   (d) both (b) and (c).

Questions

(SO 1) 1. (a) What is a cash flow statement?
(b) Elisa Botelho maintains that the cash flow statement is an optional financial statement. Do you agree? Explain.

(SO 1) 2. What questions about cash are answered by the cash flow statement that are not answered by the other financial statements?

(SO 1) 3. What are cash equivalents? Why might the cash flow statement be prepared to explain the increase (decrease) in cash and cash equivalents rather than just cash?

(SO 2) 4. Distinguish among the three activities reported in the cash flow statement.

(SO 2) 5. Why is it important to disclose significant non-cash transactions? How should they be disclosed?

(SO 2) 6. Darren and Adriana were discussing the format of the cash flow statement of Rock Candy Corp. A note to Rock Candy's cash flow statement was entitled "Noncash investing and financing activities." Give examples of significant noncash transactions that might be reported in this note.

(SO 2) 7. Why is it necessary to use a comparative balance sheet, a statement of earnings, and certain transaction data in preparing a cash flow statement?

(SO 2) 8. The president of Pets.com Inc. is puzzled. During the last year, the company experienced a net loss of $800,000, yet its cash increased by $300,000 during the same period of time. Explain to the president how this could occur.

(SO 3) 9. Contrast the advantages and disadvantages of the direct and indirect methods of preparing the cash flow statement. Are both methods acceptable? Which method is preferred by the CICA? Which method is more popular? Why?

(SO 3) 10. Why is it necessary to convert accrual-based net earnings to cash-based earnings when preparing a cash flow statement?

(SO 3) 11. In 2004, Goh Corporation changed its method of reporting operating activities from the indirect method to the direct method in order to make its cash flow statement more informative to its readers. Will this change increase, decrease, or not affect the net cash provided by operating activities?

(SO 3a) 12. Identify four items that are adjustments to convert net earnings to net cash provided by operating activities under the indirect method.

(SO 3a) 13. Why and how is amortization expense reported in a cash flow statement prepared using the indirect method?

(SO 3a) 14. Explain how the sale of equipment at a gain is reported on a cash flow statement using the indirect method.

(SO 3b) 15. Give the formulas under the direct method for calculating (a) cash receipts from customers and (b) cash payments to suppliers.

(SO 3b) 16. Crawford Inc. reported sales of $2 million for 2004. Accounts receivable decreased by $100,000 and accounts payable increased by $300,000. Calculate cash receipts from customers.

(SO 3b) 17. In the direct method, why is amortization expense not reported in the operating activities section?

(SO 4) 18. ⬥━⬥ A company's free cash flow has been declining steadily over the last five years. What does this decline likely mean to shareholders?

(SO 4) 19. ⬥━⬥ AOL Time Warner Inc.'s free cash flow was negative in fiscal 2002. Analysts expect it to be positive in 2003. How is free cash flow calculated? What does this potential increase in free cash flow mean to the company?

(SO 4) 20. ⬥━⬥ Give one or more examples of a cash-based ratio that measures (a) liquidity, and (b) solvency.

Brief Exercises

Indicate statement presentation.
(SO 2)

BE13-1 Each of these items must be considered in preparing a cash flow statement for Murphy Corp. for the year ended December 31, 2004. For each item, state how it should be shown in the statement, if at all.

(a) Issued bonds for $200,000 cash.
(b) Purchased equipment for $150,000 cash.
(c) Sold land costing $20,000 for $30,000 cash.
(d) Paid a $50,000 cash dividend.
(e) Distributed a $75,000 stock dividend.

Classify activities.
(SO 2)

BE13-2 Classify each of the following items as an operating, investing, or financing activity. Assume all items involve cash.

(a) Purchase of equipment
(b) Sale of building
(c) Purchase of inventory

(d) Issue of bonds payable
(e) Payment of dividends
(f) Issue of common shares

BE13-3 The following T account is a summary of the cash account of Baker Ltd.:

Identify cash provided by financing activities.
(SO 2)

Cash (Summary Form)

Balance, Jan. 1	8,000	Payments to suppliers	200,000
Receipts from customers	364,000	Payments for operating expenses	140,000
Dividends on equity investments	6,000	Interest paid	10,000
Proceeds from sale of equipment	36,000	Income taxes paid	8,000
Proceeds from issue of bonds	200,000	Dividends paid	50,000
Balance, Dec. 31	206,000		

What amount of net cash provided (used) by financing activities should be reported in the cash flow statement?

BE13-4 The T accounts for Equipment and Accumulated Amortization—Equipment for Trevis Ltd. are shown here:

Calculate cash received from sale of equipment.
(SO 3)

Equipment

Beg. bal.	80,000	Disposals	22,000
Acquisitions	41,600		
End. bal.	99,600		

Accumulated Amortization—Equipment

Disposals	5,500	Beg. bal.	44,500
		Amortization	12,000
		End. bal.	51,000

In addition, Trevis' statement of earnings reported a loss of $7,500 on the sale of equipment. What amount was reported on the cash flow statement as "cash provided by sale of equipment"?

BE13-5 Canadian Tire Corporation, Limited reported net earnings of $202.4 million for fiscal 2002. Its retained earnings were $973.1 million on January 1 and $1,138.0 million on December 31. It also repurchased shares, which resulted in a $5.9-million reduction to retained earnings in 2002. What amount of dividends was paid by Canadian Tire in 2002?

Calculate dividends paid.
(SO 3)

BE13-6 Indicate whether each of the following transactions would be added (+) to or subtracted (–) from net earnings in determining cash provided by operating activities using the indirect method:

Determine impact on net earnings—indirect method.
(SO 3a)

1. _____ Amortization Expense
2. _____ Increase in Accounts Receivable
3. _____ Decrease in Inventory
4. _____ Increase in Accounts Payable
5. _____ Decrease in Income Tax Payable

BE13-7 Crystal, Inc. reported net earnings of $2.5 million. Amortization expense for the year was $260,000, accounts receivable decreased by $350,000, accounts payable decreased by $280,000, and the company incurred a loss on the sale of equipment of $10,000. Calculate net cash provided by operating activities using the indirect approach.

Calculate cash provided by operating activities—indirect method.
(SO 3a)

BE13-8 The comparative balance sheet for Dupigne Corporation shows these changes in noncash current asset accounts: Accounts Receivable, decrease of $80,000; Prepaid Expenses, increase of $18,000; and Inventories, increase of $30,000. Calculate net cash provided by operating activities using the indirect method assuming that net earnings are $200,000.

Calculate cash provided by operating activities—indirect method.
(SO 3a)

BE13-9 Depeche Corporation reported income tax expense of $70,000 on its 2004 statement of earnings, and income taxes payable of $9,000 at December 31, 2003, and $12,000 at December 31, 2004. What amount of cash payments was made for income taxes during 2004?

Calculate cash payments for income taxes—direct method.
(SO 3b)

BE13-10 Idol Corporation has accounts receivable of $24,000 at January 1, 2004, and of $14,000 at December 31, 2004. Sales revenues were $480,000 for the year 2004. What is the amount of cash receipts from customers in 2004?

Calculate receipts from customers—direct method.
(SO 3b)

BE13-11 Excel Corporation reports operating expenses of $75,000 including amortization expense of $15,000 for 2004. During the year, prepaid expenses decreased by $6,600 and accrued expenses payable increased by $4,400. Calculate the cash payments for operating expenses in 2004.

Calculate cash payments for operating expenses—direct method.
(SO 3b)

Calculate cash payments to suppliers—direct method.
(SO 3b)

BE13-12 Columbia Sportswear Company reported cost of goods sold of U.S.$438.8 million on its 2002 statement of earnings. It also reported a decrease in inventory of U.S.$20.0 million and an increase in accounts payable of U.S.$17.3 million. What amount of cash payments was made to suppliers in 2002?

Calculate cash-based ratios.
(SO 4)

BE13-13 Jain Corporation reported cash provided by operating activities of $300,000, cash used by investing activities of $250,000, and cash provided by financing activities of $70,000. In addition, cash spent for property, plant, and equipment during the period was $200,000. Average current liabilities were $150,000 and average total liabilities were $225,000. No dividends were paid. Calculate these values:

(a) Free cash flow
(b) Cash current debt coverage
(c) Cash total debt coverage

Calculate free cash flow.
(SO 4)

BE13-14 Alliance Atlantis Communications Inc. reported cash provided by operating activities of $44.6 million for its third quarter in 2003. Cash spent on property, plant, and equipment during the quarter was $1.6 million. No dividends were paid. Calculate the free cash flow for Alliance Atlantis.

Exercises

Classify activities.
(SO 2)

E13-1 Li Eng Corporation had the following transactions:

(a) Purchased a machine for $30,000, giving a long-term note in exchange.
(b) Issued $50,000 of common shares for cash.
(c) Collected $16,000 of accounts receivable.
(d) Paid a cash dividend of $25,000.
(e) Sold a long-term investment with a cost of $15,000 for $10,000 cash.
(f) Retired bonds with a carrying value of $200,000 for $175,000 cash.
(g) Paid $18,000 on accounts payable.
(h) Distributed a $45,000 stock dividend.

Instructions

Analyse the transactions and indicate whether each transaction resulted in a cash flow provided (used) by operating activities, investing activities, financing activities, or noncash investing and financing activities.

Classify activities.
(SO 2)

Interactive
Homework

E13-2 An analysis of the comparative balance sheet, statement of earnings, and general ledger accounts of Brosnan Corp. uncovered the following items. Assume all items involve cash unless there is information to the contrary.

(a) Purchase of land
(b) Payment of dividends
(c) Sale of building at a loss
(d) Exchange of land for patent
(e) Amortization expense
(f) Redemption of bonds at carrying value
(g) Receipt of interest on notes receivable
(h) Issue of share capital
(i) Collection of accounts receivable
(j) Issue of bonds for land
(k) Payment of interest on notes payable
(l) Conversion of bonds into common shares
(m) Sale of land at a gain
(n) Receipt of dividends on equity investment

Instructions

Indicate how each item should be classified in the cash flow statement using these four major classifications: operating activity (specify indirect or direct method), investing activity, financing activity, and noncash investing or financing activity.

Prepare operating activities section—indirect method.
(SO 3a)

E13-3 Pesci Company Ltd. reported net earnings of $195,000 for the year ended July 31, 2004. Pesci also reported amortization expense of $45,000 and a loss of $5,000 on the sale of equipment. The comparative balance sheet shows a decrease in accounts receivable of $15,000 for the year, a $10,000 increase in accounts payable, and a $4,000 decrease in prepaid expenses.

Instructions

Prepare the operating activities section of the cash flow statement for 2004. Use the indirect method.

Prepare operating activities section—indirect method.
(SO 3a)

E13-4   The current sections of Barth Inc.'s balance sheets at December 31, 2003 and 2004, are presented here:

	2004	2003
Current assets		
Cash	$105,000	$ 99,000
Accounts receivable	120,000	89,000
Inventory	161,000	186,000
Prepaid expenses	27,000	22,000
Total current assets	$413,000	$396,000
Current liabilities		
Accrued expenses payable	$ 15,000	$ 5,000
Accounts payable	85,000	92,000
Total current liabilities	$100,000	$ 97,000

Barth's net earnings for 2004 were $153,000. Amortization expense was $19,000.

Instructions

Prepare the operating activities section of Barth Inc.'s cash flow statement for the year ended December 31, 2004, using the indirect method.

Calculate cash flows— indirect method.
(SO 3a)

E13-5   These three accounts appear in the general ledger of Dupré Corp. during 2004:

Equipment

Date		Debit	Credit	Balance
Jan. 1	Balance			160,000
July 31	Purchase of equipment	70,000		230,000
Sept. 2	Purchase of equipment	53,000		283,000
Nov. 10	Cost of equipment sold		39,000	244,000

Accumulated Amortization—Equipment

Date		Debit	Credit	Balance
Jan. 1	Balance			71,000
Nov. 10	Accumulated amortization on equipment sold	30,000		41,000
Dec. 31	Amortization for year		28,000	69,000

Retained Earnings

Date		Debit	Credit	Balance
Jan. 1	Balance			105,000
Aug. 23	Dividends (cash)	14,000		91,000
Dec. 31	Net earnings		67,000	158,000

Instructions

From the postings in the accounts, indicate how the information is reported on a cash flow statement using the indirect method. Note that the loss on the sale of equipment was $6,000.

Prepare cash flow statement—indirect method—and calculate cash-based ratios.
(SO 3a, 4)

E13-6 Here is a comparative balance sheet for Puffy Ltd.:

PUFFY LTD.
Balance Sheet
December 31

Assets	2004	2003
Cash	$ 63,000	$ 22,000
Accounts receivable	85,000	76,000
Inventories	180,000	189,000
Land	75,000	100,000
Equipment	260,000	200,000
Accumulated amortization	(66,000)	(32,000)
Total	$597,000	$555,000

Liabilities and Shareholders' Equity		
Accounts payable	$ 39,000	$ 47,000
Bonds payable	150,000	200,000
Common shares	209,000	174,000
Retained earnings	199,000	134,000
Total	$597,000	$555,000

Additional information:

1. Net earnings for 2004 were $105,000.
2. No equipment was sold during 2004.
3. Bonds payable amounting to $50,000 were redeemed for $50,000 cash.
4. Common shares were issued for $35,000 cash.
5. Sales for 2004 were $978,000.
6. Cost of goods sold for 2004 was $588,000.
7. Accounts payable pertain only to purchases of merchandise.
8. Operating expenses for 2004 were $285,000.

Instructions

(a) Prepare a cash flow statement for the year ended December 31, 2004, using the indirect method.
(b) Calculate the following cash-based ratios:
   1. Free cash flow   3. Cash total debt coverage
   2. Cash current debt coverage

Calculate cash payments—direct method.
(SO 3b)

E13-7 The 2002 statement of earnings for Clearly Canadian Beverage Corporation shows (in U.S. thousands) cost of goods sold, $14,535, and operating expenses (exclusive of amortization), $8,068. The comparative balance sheet for the year shows that inventory increased by $135, prepaid expenses increased by $160, trade accounts payable (merchandise suppliers) decreased by $800, and accrued liabilities decreased by $10.

Instructions

Using the direct method, calculate (a) cash payments to suppliers and (b) cash payments for operating expenses.

Calculate cash flows—direct method.
(SO 3b)

E13-8 The following information is taken from the 2004 general ledger of Robinson Limited:

Rent:	Rent expense	$ 31,000
	Prepaid rent, January 1	5,900
	Prepaid rent, December 31	9,000
Salaries:	Salaries expense	54,000
	Salaries payable, January 1	10,000
	Salaries payable, December 31	8,000
Sales:	Revenue from sales	180,000
	Accounts receivable, January 1	12,000
	Accounts receivable, December 31	7,000

Instructions

In each case, calculate the amounts that should be reported in the operating activities section of the cash flow statement under the direct method.

E13-9 McGillis Ltd. completed its first year of operations on December 31, 2004. Its statement of earnings showed that McGillis had revenues of $182,000, operating expenses of $78,000, and income tax expense of $31,000. Accounts receivable and accounts payable at year end were $52,000 and $21,000, respectively. Assume that accounts payable related to operating expenses.

Calculate cash provided by operating activities—direct method.
(SO 3b)

Instructions

Calculate net cash provided by operating activities using the direct method.

E13-10 The 2004 accounting records of Flypaper Airlines Inc. reveal these transactions and events:

Calculate cash flow from operating activities—direct method.
(SO 3b)

Payment of interest	$10,000	Collection of accounts receivable	$192,000
Cash sales	48,000	Payment of salaries and wages	53,000
Receipt of dividend revenue	14,000	Amortization expense	16,000
Payment of income taxes	12,000	Proceeds from sale of aircraft	812,000
Net earnings	38,000	Purchase of equipment for cash	22,000
Payment of accounts payable		Loss on sale of aircraft	3,000
for merchandise	90,000	Payment of dividends	14,000
Payment for land	74,000	Payment of operating expenses	28,000

Instructions

Prepare the cash flows from operating activities section using the direct method. (Not all of the items will be used.)

E13-11 Refer to the comparative balance sheet and additional information provided in E13-6 for Puffy Ltd.

Prepare statement of cash flows—direct method—and calculate cash-based ratios.
(SO 3b, 4)

Interactive Homework

Instructions

(a) Prepare a cash flow statement for the year ended December 31, 2004, using the direct method.
(b) Calculate the following cash-based ratios:
 1. Free cash flow
 2. Cash current debt coverage
 3. Cash total debt coverage

E13-12 Information for two companies in the same industry, Ria Corporation and Les Corporation, is presented here:

Use cash-based ratios to compare two companies.
(SO 4)

Interactive Homework

	Ria Corporation	Les Corporation
Cash provided by operating activities	$200,000	$200,000
Average current liabilities	50,000	100,000
Average total liabilities	200,000	250,000
Capital expenditures	20,000	35,000
Dividends paid	14,000	18,000

Instructions

Using the cash-based ratios presented in this chapter and in Chapter 2, compare the (a) liquidity, and (b) solvency of the two companies.

E13-13 Presented here is 2002 information for PepsiCo, Inc. and The Coca-Cola Company:

Use cash-based ratios to compare two companies.
(SO 4)

(in U.S.millions)	PepsiCo	Coca-Cola
Cash provided by operating activities	$ 4,627	$ 4,742
Average current liabilities	5,525	7,885
Average total liabilities	13,612	11,876
Capital expenditures	1,788	1,395
Dividends paid	1,041	1,987

Instructions

Using the cash-based ratios presented in this chapter and in Chapter 2, compare the (a) liquidity, and (b) solvency of the two companies.

Problems: Set A

Classify activities.
(SO 2)

P13-1A You are provided with the following transactions that took place during a recent fiscal year:

Transaction	Classification	Cash Inflow or Outflow?
(a) Recorded amortization expense.		
(b) Incurred a gain on sale of land.		
(c) Recorded cash proceeds for a sale of land.		
(d) Acquired land by issuing common shares.		
(e) Paid a cash dividend to preferred shareholders.		
(f) Distributed a stock dividend to common shareholders.		
(g) Recorded cash sales.		
(h) Recorded sales on account.		
(i) Purchased inventory for cash.		
(j) Purchased inventory on account.		
(k) Paid income taxes.		

Instructions

Complete the table, indicating whether each item (1) should be classified as an operating activity (O), investing activity (I), financing activity (F), or noncash transaction (NC), and (2) represents a cash inflow or cash outflow. If the transaction does not affect the statement or notes in any way, state that there is no effect (NE).

Calculate cash flows.
(SO 3)

P13-2A The following selected account balances relate to the shareholders' equity accounts of Wood Corp. at year end:

	2004	2003
Common shares, 10,500 and 10,000 shares for 2004 and 2003, respectively	$168,000	$140,000
Cash dividends	10,000	10,000
Preferred shares, 5,000 shares	125,000	125,000
Stock dividends	8,400	0
Retained earnings	300,000	240,000

Instructions

(a) What was the amount of net earnings reported by Wood Corp. in 2004?
(b) Determine the amounts of any cash inflows or outflows related to the share capital and dividend accounts in 2004.
(c) Indicate where each of the cash inflows or outflows identified in (b) would be classified on the cash flow statement.

*Prepare cash flow
statement—indirect method.*
(SO 3a)

P13-3A Presented here is the comparative balance sheet for Cortina Limited at December 31:

CORTINA LIMITED
Balance Sheet
December 31

Assets	2004	2003
Cash	$ 30,000	$ 57,000
Accounts receivable	77,000	64,000
Inventory	192,000	140,000
Prepaid expenses	12,140	16,540
Land	105,000	150,000
Equipment	200,000	175,000
Accumulated amortization—equipment	(60,000)	(42,000)
Building	250,000	250,000
Accumulated amortization—building	(75,000)	(50,000)
Total	$731,140	$760,540

Liabilities and Shareholders' Equity

Accounts payable	$ 33,000	$ 45,000
Bonds payable	235,000	265,000
Common shares	280,000	250,000
Retained earnings	183,140	200,540
Total	$731,140	$760,540

Additional information:

1. Operating expenses include amortization expense of $70,000 and charges from prepaid expenses of $4,400.
2. Land was sold for cash at a gain of $5,000.
3. Cash dividends of $44,290 were paid.
4. Net earnings for 2004 were $26,890.
5. Equipment was purchased for $65,000 cash. In addition, equipment costing $40,000 with a book value of $13,000 was sold for $12,000 cash.
6. Bonds were converted at face value by issuing 30,000 common shares.

Instructions

Prepare a cash flow statement for the year ended December 31, 2004, using the indirect method.

P13-4A   The statement of earnings of Gum San Ltd. is presented here:

Prepare operating activities section—indirect method and direct method.
(SO 3a, 3b)

GUM SAN LTD.
Statement of Earnings
Year Ended December 31, 2004

Sales		$5,400,000
Cost of goods sold		3,290,000
Gross profit		2,110,000
Operating expenses	$925,000	
Amortization expense	145,000	1,070,000
Earnings before income taxes		1,040,000
Income tax expense		312,000
Net earnings		$ 728,000

Additional information:

1. Accounts receivable decreased by $510,000 during the year.
2. Prepaid expenses increased by $170,000 during the year.
3. Inventory increased by $220,000 during the year.
4. Accounts payable to merchandise suppliers increased by $50,000 during the year.
5. Accrued expenses payable decreased by $165,000 during the year.
6. Income taxes payable decreased by $26,000 during the year.

Instructions

(a) Prepare the operating activities section of the cash flow statement for the year ended December 31, 2004, using the indirect method.
(b) Prepare the operating activities section of the cash flow statement for the year ended December 31, 2004, using the direct method.

P13-5A   The statement of earnings of Hanalei International Inc. reported the following condensed information:

Prepare operating activities section—indirect method and direct method.
(SO 3a, 3b)

HANALEI INTERNATIONAL INC.
Statement of Earnings
Year Ended December 31, 2004

Revenues	$545,000
Operating expenses	370,000
Earnings from operations	175,000
Income tax expense	43,750
Net earnings	$131,250

Hanalei's balance sheet contained these comparative data at December 31:

	2004	2003
Accounts receivable	$50,000	$60,000
Accounts payable	30,000	41,000
Income taxes payable	8,000	4,000

Hanalei has no amortizable assets. Accounts payable pertain to operating expenses.

Instructions

(a) Prepare the operating activities section of the cash flow statement for the year ended December 31, 2004, using the indirect method.

(b) Prepare the operating activities section of the cash flow statement for the year ended December 31, 2004, using the direct method.

Prepare cash flow statement—indirect method and direct method.
(SO 3a, 3b)

P13-6A Financial data for Norway Inc. follow:

NORWAY INC.
Balance Sheet
December 31

Assets	2004	2003
Cash	$ 92,700	$ 47,250
Accounts receivable	90,800	37,000
Inventories	121,900	102,650
Investments	84,500	107,000
Property, plant, and equipment	290,000	205,000
Accumulated amortization	(49,500)	(40,000)
Total	$630,400	$458,900

Liabilities and Shareholders' Equity	2004	2003
Accounts payable	$ 52,700	$ 48,280
Accrued expenses payable	12,100	18,830
Bonds payable	140,000	70,000
Common shares	250,000	200,000
Retained earnings	175,600	121,790
Total	$630,400	$458,900

NORWAY INC.
Statement of Earnings
Year Ended December 31, 2004

Revenues		
Sales		$297,500
Gain on sale of equipment		8,750
		306,250
Expenses		
Cost of goods sold	$99,460	
Amortization expense	58,700	
Operating expenses	14,670	
Income tax expense	39,000	
Interest expense	2,940	214,770
Net earnings		$ 91,480

Additional information:

1. New equipment costing $141,000 was purchased for cash during the year.
2. Investments were sold at cost.
3. Equipment costing $56,000 was sold for $15,550, resulting in a gain of $8,750.
4. Accounts payable pertain to merchandise suppliers.

Instructions

(a) Prepare a cash flow statement for the year ended December 31, 2004, using the indirect method.

(b) Prepare a cash flow statement for the year ended December 31, 2004, using the direct method.

P13-7A DesRoches Inc. incorporated a repair business on January 1, 2005, by selling common shares for $5,000. On the same day, it borrowed $15,000 from a local bank at a 7% interest rate. Principal and interest are repayable in full in two years. DesRoches rented space on January 5, paying rent in advance for three months—January, February, and March—at the rate of $1,000 a month. The company also purchased insurance, effective January 1, for a 12-month period, paying $1,200 in cash.

Prepare statement of earnings and cash flow statement—direct method.
(SO 3b)

The company rented repair and office equipment on January 1 for $750 a month. It paid January's rent and hopes to be able to purchase this equipment at a later date when its cash flow improves.

In January, the company purchased $1,000 of supplies on account. The cost of the supplies remaining at the end of the month was $300. Cash paid on accounts payable during the month totalled $800. During the month, the company provided repair services of $2,500 for cash and $15,000 on account. Cash collected from customers during January was $12,200. Other operating expenses paid during the month totalled $2,000. Unpaid salaries at the end of the month were $500.

Instructions

(a) Prepare a statement of earnings and a cash flow statement, using the direct method, for the month ended January 31, 2005. (You may ignore income taxes.)

(b) Compare the results of the accrual-based statement and the cash-based statement. Which do you think is more useful to decision-makers?

P13-8A Here are the financial statements of Seymor Limited:

Prepare cash flow statement—indirect method and direct method—and calculate cash-based ratios.
(SO 3a, 3b, 4)

SEYMOR LIMITED
Balance Sheet
December 31

Assets	2004	2003
Cash	$ 26,000	$ 33,000
Accounts receivable	28,000	14,000
Merchandise inventory	38,000	25,000
Property, plant, and equipment	70,000	78,000
Accumulated amortization	(30,000)	(24,000)
Total	$132,000	$126,000
Liabilities and Shareholders' Equity		
Accounts payable	$ 29,000	$ 43,000
Income taxes payable	15,000	20,000
Bonds payable	20,000	10,000
Common shares	25,000	25,000
Retained earnings	43,000	28,000
Total	$132,000	$126,000

SEYMOR LIMITED
Statement of Earnings
Year Ended December 31, 2004

Sales	$286,000
Cost of goods sold	194,000
Gross profit	92,000
Operating expenses	34,000
Earnings from operations	58,000
Interest expense	7,000
Earnings before income taxes	51,000
Income tax expense	15,000
Net earnings	$ 36,000

The following additional data were provided:

1. During the year, equipment was sold for $10,000 cash. This equipment originally cost $15,000 and had a book value of $10,000 at the time of sale.
2. Additional equipment was purchased for cash.

3. All amortization expense is included in operating expenses.
4. Accounts payable pertain only to merchandise suppliers.

Instructions

(a) Prepare a cash flow statement for the year ended December 31, 2004, using the indirect method.
(b) Prepare a cash flow statement for the year ended December 31, 2004, using the direct method
(c) Calculate these cash-based measures:
    1. Cash current debt coverage
    2. Cash total debt coverage
    3. Free cash flow

Use cash-based ratios to compare two companies.
(SO 4)
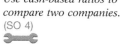

P13-9A Selected information (in millions) for Air Canada and WestJet Airlines Ltd. for fiscal 2002 follows:

	Air Canada	WestJet
Cash provided (used) by operating activities	$ (95)	$ 161
Cash provided (used) by investing activities	104	(345)
Cash provided (used) by financing activities	(310)	225
Average current liabilities	2,730	135
Average total liabilities	9,954	300
Capital expenditures	109	345
Dividends	0	0

Instructions

Using the cash-based ratios presented in this chapter and Chapter 2, compare the (a) liquidity and (b) solvency of the two companies.

Use ratios to compare two companies.
(SO 4)

P13-10A Selected ratios for two companies are as follows:

	Burrard	Pender
Acid-test ratio	0.8:1	0.5:1
Current ratio	1:1	0.8:1
Receivables turnover	6 times	4 times
Inventory turnover	5 times	4 times
Cash current debt coverage	0.5 times	0.4 times
Debt to assets	75%	50%
Times interest earned	6 times	2 times
Cash total debt coverage	0.4 times	0.3 times

Instructions

(a) Which company is the more liquid of the two? Explain.
(b) Which company is the more solvent of the two? Explain.

Discuss cash position.
(SO 4)

P13-11A Toronto-based Nexfor Inc. produces specialty papers and pulp, wooden panels, and building products. The company has more than 40 mills and production facilities in Canada, the UK, and the U.S.

    The company reported U.S.$13 million in net earnings in 2002, an increase of 8% over the U.S.$12 million in net earnings reported in 2001. It generated cash flow from operating activities of U.S.$146 million, an increase of 38% over the U.S.$106 million generated in 2001. Free cash flow totalled U.S.$102 million in 2002, an increase of 1,600% over free cash flow of U.S.$6 million in 2001.

Instructions

(a) How is it possible that Nexfor can only have U.S.$13 million of net earnings, but reports cash flow from operating activities of U.S.$146 million?
(b) Explain how Nexfor can increase its cash flow provided by operating activities by 38% when net earnings only increased 8%.
(c) Explain how Nexfor might have been able to increase its free cash flow by such a large percentage, 1,600%, in one year.

Problems: Set B

P13-1B   You are provided with the following transactions that took place during a recent fiscal year:

Classify activities.
(SO 2)

Transaction	Classification	Cash Inflow or Outflow?
(a) Recorded amortization expense.		
(b) Removed from the accounting records accumulated amortization on equipment that was sold during the year.		
(c) Incurred a loss on sale of equipment.		
(d) Acquired a building by paying 10% in cash and signing a mortgage payable for the balance.		
(e) Made principal repayments on the mortgage.		
(f) Issued common shares.		
(g) Purchased shares of another company to be held as a long-term equity investment.		
(h) Paid dividends to common shareholders.		
(i) Sold inventory on credit. The company uses a perpetual inventory system.		
(j) Purchased inventory on credit.		
(k) Paid wages owing to employees.		

Instructions

Complete the table indicating whether each item (1) should be classified as an operating activity (O), investing activity (I), financing activity (F), or noncash transaction (NC), and (2) represents a cash inflow or cash outflow. If the transaction does not affect the statement or notes in any way, state that there is no effect (NE).

P13-2B   The following selected account balances relate to the property, plant, and equipment accounts of Trudeau Inc. at year end:

Calculate cash flows.
(SO 3)

	2004	2003
Accumulated amortization—buildings	$337,500	$300,000
Accumulated amortization—equipment	144,000	96,000
Amortization expense	101,500	85,500
Buildings	750,000	750,000
Equipment	300,000	240,000
Land	100,000	70,000
Gain on sale of equipment	1,000	0

Additional information:

Trudeau purchased $80,000 of equipment and $30,000 of land for cash in 2004.

Instructions

(a) Determine the amounts of any cash inflows or outflows related to the property, plant, and equipment accounts in 2004.

(b) Indicate where each of the cash inflows or outflows identified in (a) would be classified on the cash flow statement.

Prepare cash flow statement—indirect method.
(SO 3a)

P13-3B This comparative balance sheet is for Cousin Tommy's Toys Ltd. as at December 31:

COUSIN TOMMY'S TOYS LTD.
Balance Sheet
December 31

Assets	2004	2003
Cash	$ 81,000	$ 45,000
Accounts receivable	47,500	62,000
Inventory	151,450	142,000
Prepaid expenses	16,780	21,000
Land	90,000	130,000
Equipment	228,000	155,000
Accumulated amortization—equipment	(45,000)	(35,000)
Building	200,000	200,000
Accumulated amortization—building	(60,000)	(40,000)
Total	$709,730	$680,000
Liabilities and Shareholders' Equity		
Accounts payable	$ 53,730	$ 40,000
Bonds payable	260,000	300,000
Common shares	200,000	160,000
Retained earnings	196,000	180,000
Total	$709,730	$680,000

Additional information:

1. Operating expenses include amortization expense of $42,000 and charges from prepaid expenses of $4,220.
2. Land was sold for cash at book value.
3. Cash dividends of $22,000 were paid.
4. Net earnings for 2004 were $38,000.
5. Equipment was purchased for $95,000 cash. In addition, equipment costing $22,000 with a book value of $10,000 was sold for $8,100 cash.
6. Bonds were converted at face value by issuing 50,000 common shares.

Instructions

Prepare a cash flow statement for the year ended December 31, 2004, using the indirect method.

Prepare operating activities section—indirect method and direct method.
(SO 3a, 3b)

P13-4B The statement of earnings of Breckenridge Ltd. is presented here:

BRECKENRIDGE LTD.
Statement of Earnings
Year Ended November 30, 2004

Sales		$7,200,000
Cost of goods sold		
Beginning inventory	$1,900,000	
Purchases	4,400,000	
Goods available for sale	6,300,000	
Ending inventory	1,400,000	
Total cost of goods sold		4,900,000
Gross profit		2,300,000
Operating expenses		1,050,000
Earnings before income taxes		1,250,000
Income tax expense		375,000
Net earnings		$ 875,000

Additional information:

1. Accounts receivable increased by $200,000 during the year.
2. Prepaid expenses increased by $150,000 during the year.
3. Accounts payable to suppliers of merchandise decreased by $300,000 during the year.
4. Accrued expenses payable decreased by $100,000 during the year.

5. Income tax payable increased by $20,000 during the year.
6. Operating expenses include amortization expense of $90,000.

Instructions

(a) Prepare the operating activities section of the cash flow statement for the year ended November 30, 2004, using the indirect method.
(b) Prepare the operating activities section of the cash flow statement for the year ended November 30, 2004, using the direct method.

P13-5B   Vail Limited's statement of earnings contained the condensed information below:

Prepare operating activities section—indirect method and direct method.
(SO 3a, 3b)

VAIL LIMITED
Statement of Earnings
Year Ended December 31, 2004

Revenues		$900,000
Operating expenses	$624,000	
Amortization expense	60,000	
Loss on sale of equipment	26,000	710,000
Earnings before income taxes		190,000
Income tax expense		47,500
Net earnings		$142,500

Vail's balance sheet contained these comparative data at December 31:

	2004	2003
Accounts receivable	$47,000	$57,000
Accounts payable	41,000	36,000
Income taxes payable	4,000	9,000

Accounts payable pertain to operating expenses.

Instructions

(a) Prepare the operating activities section of the cash flow statement for the year ended December 31, 2004, using the indirect method.
(b) Prepare the operating activities section of the cash flow statement for the year ended December 31, 2004, using the direct method.

P13-6B   Financial data for E-Perform, Inc. follow:

Prepare cash flow statement—indirect method and direct method.
(SO 3a, 3b)

E-PERFORM, INC.
Balance Sheet
December 31

Assets	2004	2003
Cash	$ 97,800	$ 48,400
Accounts receivable	95,800	33,000
Inventories	112,500	102,850
Prepaid expenses	18,400	6,000
Investments	113,000	94,000
Property, plant, and equipment	270,000	242,500
Accumulated amortization	(50,000)	(52,000)
Total	$657,500	$474,750

Liabilities and Shareholders' Equity	2004	2003
Accounts payable	$102,000	$ 67,300
Accrued expenses payable	16,500	17,000
Bonds payable	85,000	110,000
Common shares	220,000	175,000
Retained earnings	234,000	105,450
Total	$657,500	$474,750

E-PERFORM, INC.
Statement of Earnings
Year Ended December 31, 2004

Sales		$392,780
Cost of goods sold		135,460
Gross profit		257,320
Operating expenses	$12,410	
Amortization expense	46,500	
Interest expense	4,730	
Loss on sale of equipment	7,500	71,140
Earnings before income tax		186,180
Income tax expense		45,000
Net earnings		$141,180

Additional information:

1. Accounts payable pertain to merchandise suppliers.
2. New equipment costing $85,000 was purchased for cash during the year.
3. Old equipment having an original cost of $57,500 was sold for $1,500 cash.
4. Bonds matured and were paid off at face value for cash.

Instructions

(a) Prepare a cash flow statement for the year ended December 31, 2004, using the indirect method.
(b) Prepare a cash flow statement for the year ended December, 31, 2004, using the direct method.

Prepare statement of earnings and cash flow statement—direct method.
(SO 3b)

P13-7B You are provided with the following transactions for Great Big Sea Inc. during the year ended July 31, 2005:

1. Sold 1,000 common shares for $75 each.
2. Purchased recording equipment by signing a $200,000, 6% note payable.
3. Recorded amortization for the year on the recording equipment assuming a four-year life, zero residual value, and use of the straight-line method of amortization.
4. Recorded amount owing for interest on the note payable. Interest is owing for the full year.
5. Paid the amount of interest owing plus $15,000 on the principal of the note.
6. Purchased an inventory of CDs on credit. The invoice was for $75,000.
7. Sold CDs to customers for $200,000. Immediately collected $150,000 from the customers, with the balance on credit.
8. The cost of the CDs that were sold was $42,000.
9. Collected another $8,000 from the customers.
10. Sold a piece of equipment with a cost of $10,000 and accumulated amortization of $2,500 for $6,000. Collected the full $6,000 immediately.

Instructions

(a) Prepare a statement of earnings and a cash flow statement, using the direct method, for the year ended July 31, 2005. (You may ignore income taxes.)
(b) Compare the results of the accrual-based statement and the cash-based statement. Which do you think is more useful to decision-makers?

Prepare cash flow statement—indirect method and direct method—and calculate cash-based ratios.
(SO 3a, 3b, 4)

P13-8B These are the financial statements of Swayze Inc.:

SWAYZE INC.
Balance Sheet
December 31

Assets	2004	2003
Cash	$ 29,000	$ 20,000
Accounts receivable	38,000	14,000
Merchandise inventory	27,000	20,000
Property, plant, and equipment	60,000	78,000
Accumulated amortization	(30,000)	(24,000)
Total	$124,000	$108,000

Liabilities and Shareholders' Equity

Accounts payable	$ 17,000	$ 15,000
Income taxes payable	1,000	8,000
Bonds payable	27,000	33,000
Common shares	18,000	14,000
Retained earnings	61,000	38,000
Total	$124,000	$108,000

SWAYZE INC.
Statement of Earnings
Year Ended December 31, 2004

Sales	$242,000
Cost of goods sold	180,000
Gross profit	62,000
Operating expenses	24,000
Earnings from operations	38,000
Interest expense	2,000
Earnings before income taxes	36,000
Income tax expense	9,000
Net earnings	$ 27,000

Additional data:

1. During the year, equipment was sold for $8,500 cash. This equipment originally cost $18,000 and had a book value of $8,500 at the time of sale.
2. Bonds payable of $6,000 were redeemed for $6,000 cash.
3. A $4,000 stock dividend was distributed.
4. Amortization expense is included in operating expenses.
5. Accounts payable pertain only to merchandise suppliers.

Instructions

(a) Prepare a cash flow statement for the year ended December 31, 2004, using the indirect method.
(b) Prepare a cash flow statement for the year ended December 31,2004, using the direct method.
(c) Calculate these cash-based measures:

   1. Cash current debt coverage
   2. Cash total debt coverage
   3. Free cash flow

P13-9B Selected information (in thousands) for Reitmans (Canada) Limited and La Senza Corporation for fiscal 2002 follow:

Use cash-based ratios to compare two companies.
(SO 4)

	Reitmans	La Senza
Cash provided by operating activities	$42,742	$18,528
Cash used by investing activities	25,026	14,455
Cash used by financing activities	3,862	15,743
Average current liabilities	45,284	47,808
Average total liabilities	47,153	93,948
Capital expenditures	41,010	16,040
Dividends	6,749	781

Instructions

Using the cash-based ratios presented in this chapter and Chapter 2, compare the (a) liquidity and (b) solvency of the two companies.

Use ratios to compare two companies.
(SO 4)

P13-10B Selected ratios for two companies are as follows:

	Grenville	Robson
Acid-test ratio	0.5:1	0.4:1
Current ratio	1.7:1	1.2:1
Receivables turnover	10 times	20 times
Inventory turnover	4 times	2 times
Cash current debt coverage	0.4 times	0.3 times
Debt to assets	60%	20%
Times interest earned	5 times	20 times
Cash total debt coverage	0.2 times	0.1 times

Instructions

(a) Which company is the more liquid of the two? Explain.

(b) Which company is the more solvent of the two? Explain.

Discuss cash position.
(SO 4)

P13-11B Sleeman Breweries Ltd. is the largest craft brewer in Canada. The 2002 balance sheet of Sleeman Breweries showed current assets of $53 million and current liabilities of $48 million, including bank indebtedness (a negative cash balance) of more than $10 million. On a more positive note, Sleeman increased its earnings 26% in 2002, from $9.8 million in 2001 to $12.3 million in 2002. In addition, its cash flow statement indicates that Sleeman generated $13.4 million of cash from operating activities in 2002. Its free cash flow was a negative $4 million.

Instructions

(a) Do you believe that Sleeman's creditors should be worried about the bank overdraft? Explain why or why not.

(b) Why do you think Sleeman generated $13.4 million cash from operating activities but has no cash?

(c) If you were a creditor of Sleeman, what additional information might you request to help you assess the company's liquidity and solvency?

BROADENING YOUR PERSPECTIVE

Financial Reporting and Analysis

 Analysis Tools

FINANCIAL REPORTING PROBLEM: *Loblaw Companies Limited*

BYP13-1 Refer to the financial statements of Loblaw in Appendix A to answer the following questions:

 A passion for food... *and a lot more!*

Instructions

(a) How does Loblaw define "cash" for the purpose of its cash flow statement?

(b) What was the amount of increase or decrease in cash for the year ended December 28, 2002? For the year ended December 29, 2001?

(c) What was the amount of net cash flows from operating activities for 2002? For 2001? What were the primary causes of any significant changes in cash provided (used) by operating activities between 2002 and 2001?

(d) From your analysis of the 2002 cash flow statement, what were the significant investing activities? Financing activities?

(e) Did Loblaw report any significant noncash investing and financing activities?

COMPARATIVE ANALYSIS PROBLEM: *Loblaw and Sobeys*

BYP13-2   The financial statements of Sobeys, Inc. are presented in Appendix B, following the financial statements for Loblaw in Appendix A.

Instructions

(a) Based on the information in the financial statements, calculate these 2002 ratios for Loblaw and 2003 ratios for Sobeys:

  1. Cash current debt coverage
  2. Cash total debt coverage
  3. Free cash flow

(b) What conclusions concerning the management of cash can be drawn from these data?

RESEARCH CASE

BYP13-3   The November 2002 issue of *Report on Business Magazine* includes an article by Fabrice Taylor entitled "Show Me the Real Money," on page 109. This article discusses whether cash flow or earnings is a better indicator of a company's performance.

Instructions

Read the article and answer these questions:

(a) What are the three major components of a company's financial results?
(b) Cash flow from operating activities can be altered by accounting assumptions. What did Alliance Atlantis do in the year 2002 to alter its cash flow from operating activities in the years 2000 and 2001?
(c) Bombardier's 2002 cash flow statement showed an $88.5 million contribution to the company's pension and benefit plan. The statement of earnings showed an expense of $179.7 million. Why would the two amounts differ?
(d) Do consolidated financial statements of a holding company reflect the same percentage share of profits and losses as the cash flow provided from operating activities?
(e) Cash flow is often thought of as a more reliable indicator of a company's performance than earnings are. Would you agree with this statement? Why or why not?

INTERPRETING FINANCIAL STATEMENTS

BYP13-4 WestJet Airlines Ltd., headquartered in Calgary, provides scheduled short-haul passenger jet airline service to cities across Canada. The airline industry was a challenging one in 2002. Rising and unpredictable fuel prices and a decrease in the demand for air travel challenged all airlines. Throughout this period, WestJet expanded its capacity, adding Boeing 737-700 aircraft to its fleet.

The following information (in thousands) was available from the 2002 financial statements of WestJet:

	2002	2001
Cash and cash equivalents	$ 100,410	$ 58,942
Accounts receivable	20,532	12,211
Inventories	2,314	2,155
Prepaid expenses and other current assets	19,759	12,422
Total current assets	143,015	85,730
Total assets	784,205	393,413
Total current liabilities	175,064	95,095
Total liabilities	428,449	171,733
Cash provided by operating activities	161,624	67,361
Cash used by investing activities	(344,668)	(86,095)
Cash provided (used) by financing activities	244,512	(1,349)
Capital expenditures	344,902	86,789
Dividends paid	0	0

Instructions

(a) Calculate the current ratio and cash current debt coverage ratio for WestJet for 2002 and 2001 and discuss the airline's liquidity. (*Note:* Current liabilities at December 31, 2000, were $90,780 thousand.)

(b) Calculate the cash total debt coverage ratio and the debt to total assets ratio for West-Jet for 2002 and 2001 and discuss the airline's solvency. (*Note:* Total liabilities at December 31, 2000, were $156,080 thousand.)

(c) Calculate free cash flow for WestJet for 2002 and 2001 and discuss the airline's ability to finance expansion from internally generated cash.

A GLOBAL FOCUS

BYP13-5   The format of the cash flow statement varies across countries throughout the world. The following cash flow statement is from the 2001 financial statements of French building materials manufacturer Saint-Gobain Group:

SAINT-GOBAIN GROUP Cash Flow Statement December 31, 2001 (in millions of euro)		
	2001	**2000**
Net income	€1,134	€1,517
Minority interests	40	125
Excess of income of equity investees over dividends	7	(46)
Depreciation and amortization	1,636	1,631
Profit on sales of noncurrent assets	(84)	(584)
Cash flows from operations	2,733	2,643
Increase in inventories	(167)	(224)
Decrease in trade accounts and other accounts receivable	219	40
Decrease in trade accounts payable, other payables and accrued expenses	(92)	(73)
Changes in income taxes payable and deferred taxes	8	141
Other	(159)	(115)
Net change in working capital	(191)	(231)
Cash flows from operating activities	2,542	2,412
Purchases of property, plant and equipment	(1,430)	(1,722)
Acquisitions of businesses in 2001: (764); in 2000: (2,913), net of cash acquired	(717)	(2,709)
Disposals of consolidated investments, net of cash	140	943
Disposals of investments at cost	379	497
Acquisitions of investments at cost	(52)	(59)
Disposals of tangible and intangible assets	141	105
Decrease in marketable securities	115	67
Other	(68)	114
Cash flows from investing activities/divestments	(1,492)	(2,764)
Issue of capital stock	129	213
Minority interests' portion in capital stock increases of subsidiaries	13	28
Increases in treasury stock	(31)	(375)
Dividends paid	(357)	(284)
Dividends paid to minority shareholders of consolidated subsidiaries	(30)	(91)
(Increase) decrease in short-term loans	(16)	61
Increase (decrease) in long-term debt	(805)	1,152
Increase (decrease) in bank overdrafts and other short-term debt	335	(425)
Cash flows from financing activities	(762)	279
Net effect of exchange rate changes on cash and cash equivalents	4	10
Increase (decrease) in cash and cash equivalents	292	(63)
Cash and cash equivalents at beginning of year	666	729
Cash and cash equivalents at end of year	€ 958	€ 666

Instructions

(a) What similarities to Canadian cash flow statements do you notice in terms of general format, as well as terminology?
(b) What differences do you notice in terms of general format, as well as terminology?
(c) Using the data provided in the cash flow statement, calculate free cash flow. Does the difference in the format of the statement or the terminology complicate your efforts to calculate this measure?

FINANCIAL ANALYSIS ON THE WEB

BYP13-6   The software industry presents some unique challenges regarding cash flow. The industry is highly competitive, with a practice of providing free, or heavily discounted, products as a market-entry technique. This case reviews the sources and uses of cash flows of a major company in the software industry. The changing share price of this company is evaluated against its cash and earnings (loss) position, and other relevant cash-based ratios.

Instructions

Specific requirements of this Web case can be found on the Kimmel website.

Critical Thinking

COLLABORATIVE LEARNING ACTIVITY

BYP13-7   Greg Nord and Debra Gee are examining the following cash flow statement for Tuktoyaktuk Trading Company Limited for the year ended January 31, 2005:

TUKTOYAKTUK TRADING COMPANY LIMITED Cash Flow Statement Year Ended January 31, 2005	
Sources of cash	
From sales of merchandise	$370,000
From sale of common shares	420,000
From sale of investment (purchase recorded below)	80,000
From amortization	55,000
From issue of note for truck	20,000
From interest on investments	6,000
Total sources of cash	951,000
Uses of cash	
For purchase of fixtures and equipment	340,000
For merchandise purchased for resale	258,000
For operating expenses (including amortization)	170,000
For purchase of investment	75,000
For purchase of truck by issue of note	20,000
For interest on note payable	3,000
Total uses of cash	866,000
Net increase in cash	$ 85,000

Greg claims that Tuktoyaktuk's cash flow statement is an excellent portrayal of a superb first year, with cash increasing by $85,000. Debra replies that it was not a superb first year. Rather, she says that the year was an operating failure, that the statement is presented incorrectly, and that $85,000 is not the actual increase in cash. The cash balance at the beginning of the year was $140,000.

Instructions

With the class organized into groups, answer the following questions:

(a) With whom do you agree, Greg or Debra? Explain your position.

(b) Using the data provided, prepare a cash flow statement in proper form using the *indirect* method.

(c) Prepare a cash flow statement in proper form using the *direct* method.

(d) Would you recommend the payment of a dividend this year?

COMMUNICATION ACTIVITY

BYP13-8   Many investors today prefer the cash flow statement to the statement of earnings. These people believe that cash-based data are a better measure of performance than accrual-based data because it is less susceptible to possible earnings management.

Instructions

Write a brief memo explaining whether or not cash-based data is less susceptible to earnings management than accrual-based data. In your answer, include an assessment of which financial statement you believe to be the better measure of a company's performance.

ETHICS CASE

Ethics In
Accounting

BYP13-9   Paradis Corporation is a medium-sized wholesaler of automotive parts. It has 10 shareholders who have been paid a total of $1 million in cash dividends for eight consecutive years. The board of directors' policy requires that in order for a dividend to be declared, cash provided by operating activities as reported in the current year's cash flow statement must exceed $1 million. The job of president and CEO Phil Monat is secure so long as Phil produces annual operating cash flows to support the usual dividend.

At the end of the current year, controller Rick Rodgers presents president Monat with some disappointing news. The cash provided by operating activities is calculated by the indirect method to be only $970,000. The president says to Rick, "We must get that amount above $1 million. Isn't there some way to increase operating cash flow by another $30,000?" Rick answers, "These figures were prepared by my assistant. I'll go back to my office and see what I can do." The president replies, "I know you won't let me down, Rick."

Upon close scrutiny of the cash flow statement, Rick concludes that he can get the operating cash flows above $1 million by reclassifying a $60,000, two-year note payable listed in the financing activities section as "Proceeds from bank loan—$60,000." He will report the note instead as "Increase in payables—$60,000" and treat it as an adjustment of net earnings in the operating activities section. He returns to the president, saying, "You can tell the board to declare their usual dividend. Our net cash flow provided by operating activities is $1,030,000." "Good man, Rick! I knew I could count on you," exults the president.

Instructions

(a) Who are the stakeholders in this situation?

(b) Was there anything unethical about the president's actions? Was there anything unethical about the controller's actions?

(c) Are the board members or anyone else likely to discover the misclassification?

Answers to Self-Study Questions

1. c   2. b   3. a   4. c   5. b   6. c   7. d   8. d   9. c   10. c   11. d   12. d

Answer to Loblaw Review It Question 2

Loblaw reported $981 million of cash flow provided by operating activities in 2002. Loblaw uses the indirect method to report these cash flows.

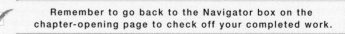

Remember to go back to the Navigator box on the chapter-opening page to check off your completed work.

Performance Measurement

After studying this chapter, you should be able to:

1. Understand the concept of sustainable earnings and indicate how irregular items are presented.

2. Discuss the need for comparative analysis and identify the tools of financial statement analysis.

3. Explain and apply horizontal analysis.

4. Explain and apply vertical analysis.

5. Identify and calculate ratios used to analyse liquidity, solvency, and profitability.

6. Understand the concept of quality of earnings.

NAVIGATOR

Brewery Produces Sparkling Report

Few companies in Canada have been around as long as Molson. The Montreal-based beer maker has been brewing ale for more than two hundred years. Founded by John Molson in 1786, the company is still 50% owned by the founder's great-great-great-grandson, Eric Molson, and his family. Today, it holds 45% of the Canadian domestic market with its Molson Canadian, Molson Export, and Molson Dry beers. It has also expanded significantly into the U.S. and Brazil, where it recently acquired the Bavaria and Kaiser brands.

Molson was one of several companies to be recognized by the Canadian Institute of Chartered Accountants at the Institute's

2002 Corporate Reporting Awards, where Molson garnered the Gold Award in the consumer products and services category for its 2002 annual report.

The judges for the Gold Award described Molson's report as "extremely comprehensive and informative" yet not overwhelming to readers. They gave it top marks for its description of corporate strategy, and praised the company's message to shareholders for its focus on ethical practices and employee contributions.

Like all annual reports, Molson's document presents the year's financial results, a message from the chairman and CEO, management discussion and analysis, as well as information about the company's directors. But it also includes a statement about the company's

vision, information about its growth strategies, marketing programs, and sponsorship activities, and an overview of its "responsible use" community initiatives.

Because of the information it contains, the annual report is the single most important document a company produces. It is a crucial tool for investors, creditors, and regulators in gathering information required to make important decisions about a company. While some companies may be tempted to overplay positive indicators or minimize poor results, Molson's report thoroughly details the company's corporate strategy and performance against stated goals.

Where the report really stands out is with its statement of the company's corporate strategy. In its message to shareholders, the

Molson *www.molson.com*

THE NAVIGATOR

Scan *Study Objectives* ☐

Read *Feature Story* ☐

Read *Chapter Preview* ☐

Read text and answer *Before You Go On*
p. 673 ☐   p. 681 ☐   p. 683 ☐   p. 687 ☐

Work *Using the Decision Toolkit* ☐

Review *Summary of Study Objectives*
and *Decision Toolkit* ☐

Work *Demonstration Problem* ☐

Answer *Self-Study Questions* ☐

Complete assignments ☐

company presents five main corporate objectives. In the subsequent section, it goes on to provide detailed discussions of how it has performed against each of them. For example, its first listed objective is to "grow operating profit by 14.5% annually." Molson reports how it exceeded this figure in 2002 and the different steps it is taking to meet its target in the future. In its discussion of its second objective, "to grow market share annually," the company explains its specific strategic growth initiatives for the Canadian market, the U.S., and Brazil.

In Canada, Molson is in stiff competition for number one spot with rival Interbrew, which owns Canada's Labatt Brewing—which also accounts for 45% of domestic beer sales. The annual report discusses Molson's re-

gional growth strategies to boost market share: "emphasis will be placed on beer sales through the LCBO [Liquor Control Board of Ontario]. Current share of this distribution channel stands at 38%, well below the average national share. To capture this potential, a sales team was put in place."

The second part of the annual report features an extensive financial review, with highlights up front, followed by in-depth tables and discussion. Molson clearly identifies its sustainable earnings by segregating the financial impact of its continuing operations from those of discontinued operations. It also fully details any changes in accounting principles that affect continuing operations.

In addition to content, a report's format and presentation

play an important role in how effectively a company's information is delivered to readers. Molson's 80-page report is well organized with a bright, attractive design. The different sections are distinctly identified and are interspersed with colourful charts, photographs, and diagrams, including an overview of the brewing process.

In short, Molson's thoroughness and clarity provide a "pleasing, high quality report," the judges wrote. In taking care to communicate effectively with its shareholders and other parties, the company demonstrates its commitment to keeping investors and other stakeholders informed—one of the most important issues in corporate governance today.

A n important lesson can be learned from Molson's annual report described in our feature story: Effective communication is the key to understanding. This has become even more important in the aftermath of corporate scandals which resulted in a climate of scepticism about the usefulness of financial reporting. The purpose of this chapter is to explain the importance of performance measurement in serving the interests of users. In addition, we highlight the difficulties of developing high-quality financial numbers, given the complexities of modern business transactions.

The content and organization of this chapter are as follows:

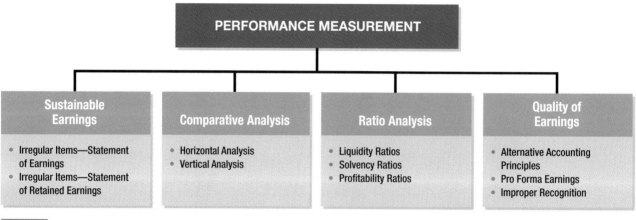

Sustainable Earnings

STUDY OBJECTIVE

1

Understand the concept of sustainable earnings and indicate how irregular items are presented.

Ultimately, the value of a company is a function of its future cash flows. When analysts use this year's net earnings to estimate future cash flows, they must make sure that the net earnings do not include irregular revenues, expenses, gains, or losses. Net earnings adjusted for irregular items are referred to as sustainable earnings. **Sustainable earnings are the most likely level of earnings to be obtained in the future**; that is, they indicate how accurately the year's net earnings predict future years' net earnings. Sustainable earnings differ from actual net earnings by the amount of irregular revenues, expenses, gains, and losses included in the year's net earnings.

Users are interested in sustainable earnings because the amount helps them estimate future earnings without the "noise" of irregular items. For example, suppose Rye Corporation reports that this year's net earnings are $500,000, but included in that amount is a once-in-a-lifetime gain of $400,000. In estimating next year's net earnings for Rye Corporation, we would likely ignore this $400,000 gain and estimate that next year's net earnings will be in the neighbourhood of $100,000, plus or minus any expected changes. That is, based on this year's results, the company's sustainable earnings are roughly $100,000. Identifying irregular items is important if you are going to use reported earnings to estimate a company's value.

In earlier chapters, you learned that earnings are presented on both the statement of earnings and the statement of retained earnings. In this chapter, we will explain how irregular items affect the presentation of these two financial statements.

IRREGULAR ITEMS—STATEMENT OF EARNINGS

To help determine sustainable earnings, irregular items are identified by type on the statement of earnings. Two types of irregular items are reported: (1) discontinued operations and (2) extraordinary items.

Irregular items are reported net of income taxes; that is, the applicable income tax expense or tax savings is shown for earnings before income taxes and for each of the irregular items. The general concept is "Let the tax follow earnings or loss."

Discontinued Operations

Discontinued operations refers to the disposal of a significant component of a business, such as the elimination of a major class of customers or an entire activity. The phasing out of a model or part of a line of business, however, is *not* considered a disposal of a business component. For example, Shaw Communications Inc.'s sale of its specialty television and radio media businesses to Corus Entertainment Inc. was reported as discontinued operations. On the other hand, Shaw's sale of its cable operations in Southern Ontario and New Brunswick to Rogers Communications was not reported as discontinued operations, since Shaw continues to operate in the cable industry in other areas of Canada.

When the disposal of a significant business component occurs, the statement of earnings should report the earnings (or loss) from discontinued operations, net of tax. **The earnings (loss) from discontinued operations consist of the earnings (loss) from operations and the gain (loss) on disposal of the segment.**

To illustrate, assume that Rozek Inc. has earnings from continuing operations of $560,000. During 2004, the company discontinues and sells its unprofitable chemical division. The loss in 2004 from chemical operations is $140,000 ($200,000 less $60,000 income tax savings, assuming a 30% income tax rate). The loss on disposal of the chemical division is $70,000 ($100,000 less $30,000 income tax savings). The statement of earnings appears in Illustration 14-1.

ROZEK INC. Statement of Earnings Year Ended December 31, 2004		
Sales		$2,500,000
Cost of goods sold		1,300,000
Gross profit		1,200,000
Operating expenses		400,000
Earnings before income taxes		800,000
Income tax expense		240,000
Earnings from continuing operations		560,000
Discontinued operations		
Loss from operations of chemical division, net of $60,000 income tax savings	$140,000	
Loss from disposal of chemical division, net of $30,000 income tax savings	70,000	(210,000)
Net earnings		$ 350,000

Illustration 14-1
Presentation of discontinued operations

Note that the caption "Earnings from continuing operations" is used and the section "Discontinued operations" is added. **Within the new section, both the operating loss and the loss on disposal are reported net of applicable income taxes.** In addition, the cash flow impact of the discontinued operations must also be reported separately on the cash flow statement. This presentation clearly indicates the separate effects of continuing operations and discontinued operations on net earnings. Discontinued operations are fairly common. In a recent year, 17% of the companies surveyed by *Financial Reporting in Canada* reported discontinued operations.

Molson reported a $2-million gain from discontinued operations in its March 31, 2002, statement of earnings. The company further details in the notes to the financial statements that this gain resulted from the sale of its Sports and Entertainment business, consisting of the Montreal Canadiens and the Molson Centre, and from the sale of Beaver Lumber to Home Hardware. Molson also reported that cash provided by discontinued operations affected operating activities by $12.6 million and investing activities by $188.6 million.

Extraordinary Items

Extraordinary items are events and transactions that meet three conditions. They are (1) not expected to occur frequently, (2) not typical of normal business activities, and (3) not subject to management's discretion.

To be infrequent, the item should be unlikely to happen again in the fore-seeable future. To be atypical, the item should be only incidentally related to the customary activities of the entity. To be outside of management's discretion, the item should not depend on decisions by management.

All three criteria must be evaluated in terms of the environment in which the business operates. Thus, Alcan Aluminium Limited reported the government cancellation of a contract to supply power to B.C. Hydro as an extraordinary item because the event was infrequent, unusual, and not determined by management. In contrast, Canada West Tree Fruits Ltd. of the Okanagan Valley does not report frost damage to its fruit crop as an extraordinary item because frost damage is not infrequent there.

In reality, extraordinary items are rare. *Financial Reporting in Canada* notes that no public company reported an extraordinary item in 2001. Illustration 14-2 shows the appropriate classification of extraordinary and ordinary items.

Illustration 14-2
Classification of extraordinary and ordinary items

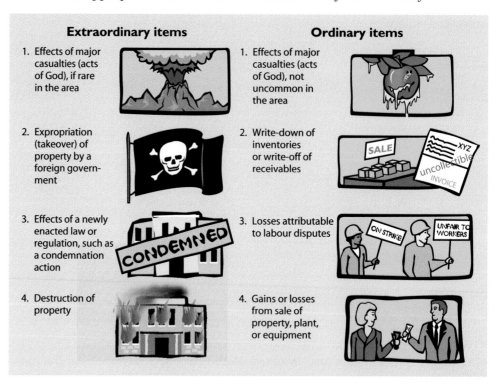

Extraordinary items	Ordinary items
1. Effects of major casualties (acts of God), if rare in the area	1. Effects of major casualties (acts of God), not uncommon in the area
2. Expropriation (takeover) of property by a foreign government	2. Write-down of inventories or write-off of receivables
3. Effects of a newly enacted law or regulation, such as a condemnation action	3. Losses attributable to labour disputes
4. Destruction of property	4. Gains or losses from sale of property, plant, or equipment

Extraordinary items are reported net of taxes in a separate section of the statement of earnings immediately below discontinued operations. Further information about the extrordinary item is usually detailed in a note to the financial statement.

To illustrate, assume that in 2004 a revolutionary foreign government expropriates property Rozek Inc. held as an investment. If the loss is $70,000 before an income tax saving of $21,000, the statement of earnings presentation will show a deduction of $49,000, as in Illustration 14-3.

Illustration 14-3
Presentation of
extraordinary item

ROZEK INC.
Statement of Earnings
Year Ended December 31, 2004

Sales		$2,500,000
Cost of goods sold		1,300,000
Gross profit		1,200,000
Operating expenses		400,000
Earnings before income taxes		800,000
Income tax expense		240,000
Earnings from continuing operations		560,000
Discontinued operations		
Loss from operations of chemical division, net of		
$60,000 income tax savings	$140,000	
Loss from disposal of chemical division, net of		
$30,000 income tax savings	70,000	(210,000)
Earnings before extraordinary item		350,000
Extraordinary item		
Expropriation of property, net of $21,000		
income tax savings		(49,000)
Net earnings		$301,000

As illustrated, the caption "Earnings before extraordinary item" is added immediately before the listing of extraordinary items. This presentation clearly indicates the effect of the extraordinary item on net earnings. If there were no discontinued operations, the seventh line of the statement of earnings in Illustration 14-3 would be "Earnings before extraordinary item."

If a transaction or event meets one, but not all, of the criteria for an extraordinary item, it should be reported in a separate line item in the upper half of the statement of earnings, rather than in the bottom half as an extraordinary item. Usually, these items are reported under either "Other revenues" or "Other expenses" at their gross amount (not net of tax). This is true, for example, of gains (losses) resulting from the sale of property, plant, and equipment, as explained in Chapter 9.

We have shown in this section that the determination of the most relevant earnings number can be elusive. In assessing the future prospects of a company, some investors focus on earnings from operations and ignore other revenue, other expenses, and irregular items. Others use measures such as net earnings, or some modified version of one of these amounts. To ensure comparability, it is important to be consistent with whatever measures are used.

BUSINESS INSIGHT

INTERNATIONAL PERSPECTIVE

The criteria used to determine whether an item is extraordinary or not differ across countries. For example, in the United States extraordinary items do not rule out management involvement. Consequently, in the U.S., extraordinary items are far more frequent than in Canada and can include items such as losses from the retirement of debt that involve decisions made by management.

Canada, Australia, the U.S., and the UK report extraordinary items (they are called "exceptional" in the UK) separately from ordinary items. Many other countries, however, do not distinguish extraordinary and ordinary items.

IRREGULAR ITEMS—STATEMENT OF RETAINED EARNINGS

Another type of irregular item, one that affects prior period earnings, is a change in accounting principle. Since prior period earnings are affected, a change in accounting principle is reported on the statement of retained earnings rather than on the current period statement of earnings.

Change in Accounting Principle

Financial statements are normally prepared on a basis consistent with that used for the preceding period. This enhances comparability. That is, where a choice of accounting principles is available, the principle chosen should be applied consistently from period to period. This does not mean, however, that changes can never occur. A change in accounting principle occurs when the principle used in the current year is different from the one used in the preceding year. A change is permitted when management can show that there has been a change in the reporting circumstances and that the new principle is preferable to the old principle.

A change in accounting principle affects reporting in these four ways:

Alternative Terminology *Accounting principles* are also known as *accounting policies.*

1. The new principle should be used for reporting the results of operations of the current year.
2. The cumulative effect of the change in accounting principle should be reported (net of income tax) as an adjustment to opening retained earnings.
3. All prior period financial statements should be restated to facilitate comparison.
4. The effects of the change should be detailed and disclosed in a note.

Examples of a change in accounting principle include a change in amortization methods (such as declining-balance to straight-line) and a change in inventory costing methods (such as FIFO to average cost). Often a change in accounting principle is mandated by the CICA. One of the most significant recent changes was the introduction of the requirement whereby goodwill and other intangible assets with indefinite lives are no longer amortized, but are instead tested annually for impairment. The effect of a change in an accounting principle on prior period earnings can be significant. When Molson adopted new accounting principles in 2001, including the new intangible asset standard, it resulted in a $320-million restatement of the company's opening retained earnings. This reduced previously reported retained earnings from $557.1 million to $237.1 million.

We will use our earlier illustration of Rozek Inc. to illustrate how changes in accounting principles are reported. Assume that at the beginning of 2004, Rozek changes from the straight-line method to the declining-balance method of amortization for equipment which had been purchased on January 1, 2001. The cumulative effect on prior year statements of earnings (for 2001–2003) is to increase amortization expense and decrease earnings before income taxes by $24,000. If the company had a 30% tax rate, the net of tax effect of the change on prior period net earnings would be $16,800 ($24,000 − $7,200 [$24,000 × 30%] in income tax savings).

The presentation of this change in the statement of retained earnings is shown in Illustration 14-4. The opening retained earnings balance is assumed to be $500,000.

ROZEK INC. Statement of Retained Earnings Year Ended December 31, 2004	
Retained earnings, January 1, 2004, as previously reported	$500,000
Deduct: Cumulative effect on prior years of change in	
amortization method, net of $7,200 income tax savings	(16,800)
Retained earnings, January 1, 2004, as adjusted	483,200
Add: Net earnings	301,000
Retained earnings, December 31, 2004	$784,200

Illustration 14-4
Presentation of a change in accounting principle

A financial statement from any prior year which is presented for comparative purposes would be restated using the declining-balance method of amortization. Rozek's statement of earnings will also show amortization expense for the current year on a declining-balance basis (i.e., using the new method of amortization). Accumulated amortization on the balance sheet will be calculated as though declining-balance had always been used. An appropriately cross-referenced note to the statements should detail the impact of the change and the fact that prior years' statements have been restated.

Decision Toolkit

DECISION CHECKPOINTS	INFO NEEDED FOR DECISION	TOOL TO USE FOR DECISION	HOW TO EVALUATE RESULTS
Has the company sold any major components of its business?	Discontinued operations section of statement of earnings	Anything reported in this section indicates that the company has discontinued a major component of its business.	If a major component of the company's business has been discontinued, its results in the current period should not be included in estimates of future net earnings.
Has the company experienced any extraordinary events or transactions?	Extraordinary item section of statement of earnings	Anything reported in this section indicates that the company experienced an event that was infrequent, unusual, and not determined by management.	These items should usually be ignored in estimating future net earnings.
Has the company changed any of its accounting principles?	Cumulative effect of change in accounting principle in statement of retained earnings	Anything reported in this manner indicates that the company has changed an accounting principle during the current year.	Financial statements are restated using the new principle for comparability.

BEFORE YOU GO ON...

● REVIEW IT

1. What are sustainable earnings?
2. What irregular items affect the statement of earnings? What effect do they have on future earnings and future cash flows?
3. What irregular item affects the statement of retained earnings? What impact does this item have on the comparability of prior period earnings?
4. Did Loblaw report any irregular items in 2002? The answer to this question is provided at the end of this chapter.

A passion for food... and a lot more!

NAVIGATOR

Comparative Analysis

As indicated, in assessing financial performance, investors and creditors are interested in the sustainable earnings of a company. In addition, they are interested in making comparisons from period to period. Throughout this book, we have relied on three types of comparisons to improve the usefulness of financial information for decisions:

1. **Intracompany basis.** Comparisons within a company are often useful to detect changes in financial relationships and significant trends. For example, a comparison of Molson's current year cash amount with its prior year cash amount shows either an increase or a decrease. Likewise, a comparison of Molson's year-end cash amount with the amount of its total assets at year end shows the proportion of total assets in the form of cash.
2. **Intercompany basis.** Comparisons with other companies provide insight into a company's competitive position. For example, Molson's total sales for the year can be compared with the total sales of Interbrew, or one of its other competitors in the beverages/brewers industry.
3. **Industry averages.** Comparisons with industry averages provide information about a company's relative position within the industry. For example, Molson's financial data can be compared with the averages for its industry compiled by financial ratings organizations such as Dun & Bradstreet, the *Financial Post*, or Statistics Canada.

Three basic tools are used in financial statement analysis to highlight the significance of financial statement data:

1. Horizontal analysis
2. Vertical analysis
3. Ratio analysis

In previous chapters, we relied primarily on ratio analysis, supplemented with some basic horizontal and vertical analysis. In the remainder of this section, we introduce more formal methods of horizontal and vertical analysis. A summary review of ratio analysis then follows.

But before we examine each of these forms of analysis, it is important to understand that the results must be interpreted in light of the economic circumstances a company is operating in. Economic measures such as the rate of interest, inflation, and unemployment—to list just a few—can have a significant impact on a company's performance. For example, it would be difficult to properly interpret declining performance if one didn't know that an industry had been affected by an economic recession.

Financial analysis must also include non-financial performance measures in addition to financial performance measures. Some argue that non-financial performance measures are even more important than financial performance measures in assessing success. Financial measures can only evaluate past performance. Non-financial measures may be better predictors of future performance. Non-financial performance measures include factors such as customer satisfaction, employee satisfaction, product reputation, innovation, knowledge resources, and the like.

The annual report includes a wealth of both financial and non-financial information. In addition to the financial statement package, other financial information usually includes a management discussion and analysis (MD&A) of the company's financial position and a summary of historical key financial figures and ratios.

Non-financial information includes a discussion of the company's mission, goals and objectives, market position, people, and products. Understanding a company's goals and objectives is important when interpreting financial performance. As mentioned in our feature story, Molson's award-winning annual report not only presents the brewer's corporate objectives, but also compares its performance to those objectives.

A complete description of an annual report, using Loblaw's 2002 report, is available on the CD that accompanies this text.

The annual report's status as the company's primary means of communication with its shareholders is being challenged. Increasingly, companies are using other methods such as websites and conference calls to communicate with their shareholders on a more timely basis. Because of "continuous" disclosure, the annual report is just one part of a series of information disclosures that a company makes to its current and future shareholders.

Annual Report
Walkthrough

BUSINESS INSIGHT

INVESTOR PERSPECTIVE

Companies preparing their annual reports are piling on the paper in order to ease Enron-type worries on the part of investors. In 2002, U.S.-based natural gas producer Williams Companies, Inc. turned out an eye-glazing annual report 1,234 pages in length. Here in Canada, Nortel Networks Corporation added an extra two dozen pages to its annual report. Other companies have followed suit.

The trend to fuller disclosure has been a long time coming, observers say. But they caution that more paper does not necessarily mean more information that the average investor will understand. In addition, it is important to remember that annual reports are just one piece of the puzzle as to how information is presented to decision-makers.

Source: Elizabeth Church, "No Item Too Small as Firms Cave to Enron Disclosure Craze," *The Globe and Mail,* April 1, 2002, B1.

HORIZONTAL ANALYSIS

Horizontal analysis is a technique for evaluating a series of financial statement data over a period of time. Its purpose is to determine the increase or decrease that has taken place, expressed as either an amount or a percentage.

As an example, here are Molson's recent revenue figures:

Illustration 14-5
Molson revenue

MOLSON INC.				
Sales and Other Revenues				
Year Ended March 31				
(in millions)				
2002	2001	2000	1999	1998
$2,830.8	$2,483.4	$2,375.0	$2,120.1	$1,071.8

If we assume that 1998 is the base year, we can measure all percentage increases or decreases from this base period amount with the formula shown in Illustration 14-6.

$$\text{CHANGE SINCE BASE YEAR} = \frac{\text{CURRENT YEAR AMOUNT} - \text{BASE YEAR AMOUNT}}{\text{BASE YEAR AMOUNT}}$$

Illustration 14-6
Horizontal analysis of changes since base period

We can, for example, determine that sales and other revenues for Molson increased approximately 14% [($2,830.8 − $2,483.4) ÷ $2,483.4] from 2001 to 2002. Similarly, we can also determine that sales and other revenues increased 164% [($2,830.8 − $1,071.8) ÷ $1,071.8] from 1998 to 2002.

Alternatively, we can express current year sales as a percentage of the base period. To do so, we would divide the current year amount by the base year amount. The percentage of the base period for each of five years, assuming 1998 is the base period, is shown for net sales in Illustration 14-7.

Illustration 14-7
Horizontal analysis of
Molson revenue

MOLSON INC. Sales and Other Revenues Year Ended March 31 (in millions)				
2002	2001	2000	1999	1998
$2,830.8	$2,483.4	$2,375.0	$2,120.1	$1,071.8
264%	232%	222%	198%	100%

Balance Sheet

To further illustrate horizontal analysis, we will use Molson's financial statements. Condensed balance sheets for 2002 and 2001, showing dollar and percentage changes, are presented in Illustration 14-8.

Illustration 14-8
Horizontal analysis of
balance sheet

MOLSON INC. Balance Sheet March 31 (in millions)				
			Increase (Decrease)	
	2002	2001	Amount	Percent
Assets				
Current assets	$ 501.8	$ 363.1	$ 138.7	38.2%
Current assets of discontinued operations	8.4	69.3	(60.9)	(87.9%)
Noncurrent assets	3,980.7	2,526.7	1,454.0	57.5%
Noncurrent assets of discontinued operations	30.1	321.7	(291.6)	(90.6%)
Total assets	$4,521.0	$3,280.8	$1,240.2	37.8%
Liabilities and Shareholders' Equity				
Current liabilities	$ 871.7	$ 573.8	$ 297.9	51.9%
Current liabilities of discontinued operations	3.8	44.6	(40.8)	(91.5%)
Noncurrent liabilities	2,368.3	1,710.6	657.7	38.4%
Noncurrent liabilities of discontinued operations	103.3	156.4	(53.1)	(34.0%)
Total liabilities	3,347.1	2,485.4	861.7	34.7%
Shareholders' equity	1,173.9	795.4	378.5	47.6%
Total liabilities and shareholders' equity	$4,521.0	$3,280.8	$1,240.2	37.8%

Helpful Hint It is difficult to grasp the significance of a change when only the dollar amount is examined. When the change is expressed in percentage form, it is easier to grasp its true magnitude.

The comparative balance sheet shows that a number of changes occurred in Molson's financial position from 2001 to 2002. In the assets section, current assets increased by $138.7 million or 38.2% [($501.8 − $363.1) ÷ $363.1]. Note that discontinued operations are segregated so that comparisons can be made without the potential distortion of the results of non-continuing operations. The increase in current assets was likely due to increases in receivables and inventories, resulting from an increase in sales volume.

Noncurrent assets increased by $1,454.0 million or 57.5%. The large increase in noncurrent assets was primarily due to upgrades in Toronto and Montreal breweries and an increase in intangible assets.

In the liabilities section, current liabilities increased by $297.9 million or 51.9%. This was due to an increase in accounts payable from the increased inventory purchases and the addition of the current portion of long-term debt. Long-term liabilities increased by $657.7 million or 38.4%, reflecting the acquisition of Kaiser, the second largest brewery in Brazil.

Shareholders' equity also increased by $378.5 million or 47.6%. This was due to increased net earnings and a new share issue as part of the purchase price for Kaiser.

Statement of Earnings

Presented in Illustration 14-9 is a two-year comparative statement of earnings for Molson, for 2002 and 2001, in a condensed format.

MOLSON INC. Statement of Earnings Year Ended March 31 (in millions)			Increase (Decrease)	
	2002	2001	Amount	Percent
Sales and other revenues	$2.830.8	$2,483.4	$ 347.4	14.0%
Brewing excise and sales taxes	728.5	626.3	102.2	16.3%
	2,102.3	1,857.1	245.2	13.2%
Costs and expenses	1,725.9	1,505.6	220.3	14.6%
Earnings before interest, income taxes, and amortization	376.4	351.5	24.9	7.1%
Amortization expense	54.6	87.9	(33.3)	(37.9%)
Earnings before interest and income taxes	321.8	263.6	58.2	22.1%
Net interest expense	65.5	68.7	(3.2)	(4.7%)
Earnings before income taxes	256.3	194.9	61.4	31.5%
Income tax expense	80.7	57.7	23.0	39.9%
Earnings from continuing operations	175.6	137.2	38.4	28.0%
Earnings (loss) from discontinued operations	2.0	(3.3)	5.3	n/a
Net earnings	$ 177.6	$ 133.9	$ 43.7	32.6%

Illustration 14-9
Horizontal analysis of statement of earnings

> **Helpful Hint** Note that, in a horizontal analysis, while the amount column is additive (the total is an increase of $43.7 million), the percentage column is not additive (32.6% is **not** a total).

A horizontal analysis of the statement of earnings shows that sales and other revenues increased by $347.4 million, or 14.0%. Costs and expenses increased by $220.3 million, or roughly the same percentage at 14.6%. Amortization expense, of course, declined significantly because of the new accounting standard of not amortizing intangible assets with indefinite lives. Interest expense decreased by $3.2 million, or 4.7%. This is primarily due to lower debt levels after the sale of Molson's Sports and Entertainment businesses. This will change in the upcoming year with the additional increase in debt assumed with the purchase of Kaiser. Earnings from continuing operations increased by $38.4 million, or 28.0%. This is notable given the modest earnings growth experienced by companies in Canada in 2002.

> **Helpful Hint** When using horizontal analysis, both dollar amount changes and percentage changes need to be examined. It is not necessarily bad if a company's earnings are growing at a declining rate. The **amount** of increase may be the same as or more than the base year, but the **percentage** change may be less because the base is greater each year.

The measurement of changes from period to period in percentages is relatively straightforward and quite useful. However, the calculations can be affected by complications. If an item has no value in a base year or preceding year and a value in the next year, no percentage change can be determined. And, if a negative amount appears in the base or preceding period, and a positive amount in the following year, or vice versa, no percentage change can be calculated. For example, no percentage could be calculated for the "Earnings (loss) from discontinued operations" category in Molson's statement of earnings.

We haven't provided a horizontal analysis of Molson's cash flow statement as this is not as useful as horizontal analyses performed on the balance sheet and statement of earnings. The amounts presented in the cash flow statement (except in the operating activities section) detail the changes between two periods (opening and ending balance sheets). The value of this statement comes from the analysis of where cash came from and what it was used for rather than from comparing these changes to a base amount.

Decision Toolkit

DECISION CHECKPOINTS	INFO NEEDED FOR DECISION	TOOL TO USE FOR DECISION	HOW TO EVALUATE RESULTS
How do the company's financial position and operating results compare with those of previous periods?	Statement of earnings and balance sheet	Comparative financial statements should be prepared over at least two years, with the first year reported as the base year. Changes in each line item relative to the base year should be presented both by amount and by percentage. This is called horizontal analysis.	A significant change should be investigated to determine what caused it.

VERTICAL ANALYSIS

Vertical analysis is a technique for evaluating financial statement data that expresses each item in a financial statement as a percentage of a base amount. For example, on a balance sheet we might say that current assets are 11% of total assets (total assets being the base amount). Or, on a statement of earnings we might say that operating expenses are 82% of net sales (net sales being the base amount).

Balance Sheet

Presented in Illustration 14-10 is Molson's comparative balance sheet for 2002 and 2001, analysed vertically. The base for the asset items is **total assets**, and the base for the liability and shareholders' equity items is **total liabilities and shareholders' equity**.

Illustration 14-10
Vertical analysis of a balance sheet

MOLSON INC.
Balance Sheet
March 31
(in millions)

	2002		2001	
	Amount	Percent	Amount	Percent
Assets				
Current assets	$ 501.8	11.1%	$ 363.1	11.1%
Current assets of discontinued operations	8.4	0.2%	69.3	2.1%
Noncurrent assets	3,980.7	88.0%	2,526.7	77.0%
Noncurrent assets of discontinued operations	30.1	0.7%	321.7	9.8%
Total assets	$4,521.0	100.0%	$3,280.8	100.0%
Liabilities and Shareholders' Equity				
Current liabilities	$ 871.7	19.3%	$ 573.8	17.5%
Current liabilities of discontinued operations	3.8	0.0%	44.6	1.4%
Noncurrent liabilities	2,368.3	52.4%	1,710.6	52.1%
Noncurrent liabilities of discontinued operations	103.3	2.3%	156.4	4.8%
Total liabilities	3,347.1	74.0%	2,485.4	75.8%
Shareholders' equity	1,173.9	26.0%	795.4	24.2%
Total liabilities and shareholders' equity	$4,521.0	100.0%	$3,280.8	100.0%

Vertical analysis shows the relative size of each category in the balance sheet. It also allows us to compare the percentage sizes of the individual asset, liability, and shareholders' equity items. For example, we can see that even though current assets increased 38.2% from 2001 to 2002 (see Illustration 14-8), they remained constant at 11.1% as a percentage of total assets in the same period. Noncurrent assets increased as a percentage of total assets, from 77% in 2001 to 88% in 2002.

Current liabilities increased slightly from 17.5% to 19.3% of total assets from 2001 to 2002. Noncurrent liabilities, even though they increased 38.4% (see Illustration 14-8), remained relatively constant as a percentage of total assets at 52.1% and 52.4% in 2001 and 2002, respectively. What this means is that although debt increased due to the Kaiser acquisition, assets increased proportionately. Shareholders' equity also changed only marginally from 2001 to 2002, increasing from 24.2% to 26.0%.

Statement of Earnings

Illustration 14-11
Vertical analysis of
statement of earnings

MOLSON INC. Statement of Earnings Year Ended March 31 (in millions)				
	2002		**2001**	
	Amount	Percent	Amount	Percent
Net sales and other revenues	$2,102.3	100.0%	$1,857.1	100.0%
Costs and expenses	1,725.9	82.1%	1,505.6	81.1%
Earnings before interest, income taxes, and amortization	376.4	17.9%	351.5	18.9%
Amortization expense	54.6	2.6%	87.9	4.7%
Earnings before interest and income taxes	321.8	15.3%	263.6	14.2%
Net interest expense	65.5	3.1%	68.7	3.7%
Earnings before income taxes	256.3	12.2%	194.9	10.5%
Income tax expense	80.7	3.8%	57.7	3.1%
Earnings from continuing operations	175.6	8.4%	137.2	7.4%
Earnings (loss) from discontinued operations	2.0	0.0%	(3.3)	(0.2%)
Net earnings	$ 177.6	8.4%	$ 133.9	7.2%

Although costs and expenses increased 14.6%, as shown in Illustration 14-9, they remained relatively constant as a percentage of sales at 81.1% in 2001 and 82.1% in 2002. Consistent with our horizontal analysis findings, amortization expense and interest expense both declined. Earnings from continuing operations also increased, as was noted in Illustration 14-9.

An associated benefit of vertical analysis is that it makes it possible to compare companies of different sizes. For example, Molson's main competitor is a much larger company—Interbrew. Using vertical analysis, we can make a more meaningful comparison of the condensed statements of earnings of Molson and Interbrew, as shown in Illustration 14-12.

Illustration 14-12
Intercompany comparison
by vertical analysis

Statement of Earnings				
	Molson Inc. Year Ended March 31, 2002 (in CAD millions)		Interbrew S.A. Year Ended December 31, 2002 (in millions of euro)	
	Amount	Percent	Amount	Percent
Sales and other revenues	$2,102.3	100.0%	€6,992	100.0%
Cost and expenses	1,675.9	79.7%	5,481	78.4%
Restructuring charges	50.0	2.4%	108	1.5%
Earnings before interest, income taxes, and amortization	376.4	17.9%	1,403	20.1%
Amortization expense	54.6	2.6%	640	9.2%
Earnings before interest and income taxes	321.8	15.3%	763	10.9%
Net interest expense	65.5	3.1%	134	1.9%
Earnings before income taxes	256.3	12.2%	629	9.0%
Income tax expense	80.7	3.8%	162	2.3%
Earnings from continuing operations	175.6	8.4%	467	6.7%
Earnings from discontinued operations	2.0	0.0%	0	0.0%
Net earnings	$ 177.6	8.4%	€ 467	6.7%

Although Interbrew's operating revenues are more than five times as large as Molson's (one Canadian dollar currently equals about 0.64 euros), and are reported in a different currency, vertical analysis eliminates these differences. Both companies have relatively the same proportionate costs and expenses. Molson has more restructuring charges, proportionately, than does Interbrew. Molson's amortization expense is lower than Interbrew's; however, its interest and income tax expense are higher. Molson's earnings from continuing operations, at 8.4% of sales, are higher than Interbrew's 6.7% of sales. This is primarily due to lower amortization, however, which is a timing difference only and not a significant difference between the two companies.

Although vertical analysis can also be performed on the cash flow statement, this is seldom done. As mentioned earlier, the value of this statement comes from the analysis it allows of where cash came from and what it was used for, not from the preparation of percentage comparisons of these changes against a base amount.

Decision Toolkit

DECISION CHECKPOINTS	INFO NEEDED FOR DECISION	TOOL TO USE FOR DECISION	HOW TO EVALUATE RESULTS
How do the relationships between items in this year's financial statements compare with last year's relationships or those of competitors?	Statement of earnings and balance sheet	Each line item on the statement of earnings should be presented as a percentage of net sales, and each line item on the balance sheet should be presented as a percentage of total assets (total liabilities and shareholders' equity). This is called vertical analysis.	Any difference, either across years or between companies, should be investigated to determine the cause.

● **REVIEW IT**

1. What are the different tools used to compare financial information?
2. What is horizontal analysis?
3. What is vertical analysis?

● **DO IT**

Summary financial information for Bonora Ltd. is as follows:

	December 31, 2005	December 31, 2004
Current assets	$234,000	$180,000
Noncurrent assets	756,000	420,000
Total assets	$990,000	$600,000

Calculate the amount and percentage changes in 2005, using (a) horizontal analysis, assuming 2004 is the base year, and (b) vertical analysis, assuming total assets is the base.

Action Plan

• Horizontal analysis: Find the percentage change by dividing the amount of the increase by the 2004 amount (base year).
• Vertical analysis: Find the percentage change by dividing the specific asset amount by total assets, for each of 2005 and 2004.

Solution

	Increase in 2005	
(a) Horizontal analysis:	Amount	Percentage
Current assets	$ 54,000	30% [($234,000 − $180,000) ÷ $180,000]
Noncurrent assets	336,000	80% [($756,000 − $420,000) ÷ $420,000]
Total assets	$390,000	65% [($990,000 − $600,000) ÷ $600,000]

(b) Vertical analysis:	2005		2004	
Current assets	23.6%	($234,000 ÷ $990,000)	30%	($180,000 ÷ $600,000)
Noncurrent assets	76.4%	($756,000 ÷ $990,000)	70%	($420,000 ÷ $600,000)
Total assets	100.0%		100%	

NAVIGATOR

Ratio Analysis

In previous chapters, we presented many ratios used for evaluating the financial health and performance of a company. In this section, we provide a summary listing of those ratios. Chapter and page references to prior discussions are included in case you wish to review any individual ratios. In addition, an example of a comprehensive financial analysis employing these ratios is provided in the appendix to this chapter.

For analysis of the primary financial statements, ratios can be classified into three types:

1. **Liquidity ratios.** These measure the short-term ability of the company to pay its maturing obligations and to meet unexpected needs for cash.
2. **Solvency ratios.** These measure the ability of the company to survive over a long period of time.
3. **Profitability ratios.** These measure the earnings or operating success of a company for a given period of time.

STUDY OBJECTIVE
5

Identify and calculate ratios used to analyse liquidity, solvency, and profitability.

As analysis tools, ratios can provide clues to underlying conditions that may not be apparent from an inspection of the individual components of a particular ratio. But a single ratio by itself is not very meaningful. Accordingly, ratios must be interpreted along with the information gained from a detailed review of the financial information, including horizontal and vertical analyses. Ratios must also be assessed in light of **intracompany, intercompany, and industry average comparisons**.

LIQUIDITY RATIOS

Liquidity ratios measure the short-term ability of a company to pay its maturing obligations and to meet unexpected needs for cash. Short-term creditors, such as bankers and suppliers, are particularly interested in assessing liquidity. Illustration 14-13 lists the liquidity ratios we have covered in this textbook. It is important to remember that these are only examples of commonly used liquidity ratios. You will find more examples as you expand your knowledge of financial analysis.

Illustration 14-13
Summary of liquidity ratios

Ratio	Formula	Purpose	Discussion
Working capital	Current assets − Current liabilities	Measures short-term debt-paying ability	Ch. 2, p. 68
Current ratio	$\dfrac{\text{Current assets}}{\text{Current liabilities}}$	Measures short-term debt-paying ability	Ch. 2, p. 69
Cash current debt coverage ratio	$\dfrac{\text{Cash provided by operating activities}}{\text{Average current liabilities}}$	Measures short-term debt-paying ability (cash basis)	Ch. 2, p. 73
Inventory turnover	$\dfrac{\text{Cost of goods sold}}{\text{Average inventory}}$	Measures liquidity of inventory	Ch. 6, p. 278
Days in inventory	$\dfrac{\text{365 days}}{\text{Inventory turnover}}$	Measures the number of days inventory is on hand	Ch. 6, p. 278
Receivables turnover	$\dfrac{\text{Net credit sales}}{\text{Average gross receivables}}$	Measures liquidity of receivables	Ch. 8, p. 371
Average collection period	$\dfrac{\text{365 days}}{\text{Receivables turnover}}$	Measures number of days receivables are outstanding	Ch. 8, p. 371
Acid-test ratio	$\dfrac{\text{Cash + Short-term investments + Accounts receivable}}{\text{Current liabilities}}$	Measures immediate short-term liquidity	Ch. 10, p. 474

SOLVENCY RATIOS

Solvency ratios measure the ability of a company to survive over a long period of time. Long-term creditors and shareholders are interested in a company's long-run solvency, particularly its ability to pay interest as it comes due and to repay the face value of debt at maturity.

Illustration 14-14
Summary of solvency
ratios

Ratio	Formula	Purpose	Discussion
Debt to total assets	$\dfrac{\text{Total liabilities}}{\text{Total assets}}$	Measures percentage of total assets provided by creditors	Ch. 2, p. 70
Cash total debt coverage	$\dfrac{\text{Cash provided by operating activities}}{\text{Average total liabilities}}$	Measures long-term debt-paying ability (cash basis)	Ch. 2, p. 73
Times interest earned	$\dfrac{\text{Earnings before interest expense and income tax expense (EBIT)}}{\text{Interest expense}}$	Measures ability to meet interest payments as they come due	Ch. 10, p. 475
Free cash flow	Cash provided by operating activities − Capital expenditures − Dividends paid	Measures cash available for paying more dividends or for expanding operations	Ch. 13, p. 642

PROFITABILITY RATIOS

Profitability ratios measure the earnings or operating success of a company for a given period of time. A company's earnings, or lack of them, affect its ability to obtain debt and equity financing, its liquidity position, and its growth. As a consequence, creditors and investors alike are interested in evaluating profitability. Profitability is frequently used as the ultimate test of management's operating effectiveness.

Illustration 14-15
Summary of profitability
ratios

Ratio	Formula	Purpose	Discussion
Earnings per share	$\dfrac{\text{Net earnings − Preferred dividends}}{\text{Average number of common shares}}$	Measures net earnings earned on each common share	Ch. 2, p. 64
Price-earnings ratio	$\dfrac{\text{Market price per share}}{\text{Earnings per share}}$	Measures relationship between market price per share and earnings per share	Ch. 2, p. 65
Gross profit margin	$\dfrac{\text{Gross profit}}{\text{Net sales}}$	Measures margin between selling price and cost of goods sold	Ch. 5, p. 229
Profit margin	$\dfrac{\text{Net earnings}}{\text{Net sales}}$	Measures net earnings generated by each dollar of sales	Ch. 5, p. 231
Return on assets	$\dfrac{\text{Net earnings}}{\text{Average total assets}}$	Measures overall profitability of assets	Ch. 9, p. 422
Asset turnover	$\dfrac{\text{Net sales}}{\text{Average total assets}}$	Measures how efficiently assets are used to generate sales	Ch. 9, p. 423
Payout ratio	$\dfrac{\text{Cash dividends}}{\text{Net earnings}}$	Measures percentage of earnings distributed as cash dividends	Ch. 11, p. 533
Return on common shareholders' equity	$\dfrac{\text{Net earnings − Preferred dividends}}{\text{Average common shareholders' equity}}$	Measures profitability of shareholders' investment	Ch. 11, p. 534

BEFORE YOU GO ON . . .

● **REVIEW IT**

1. What are liquidity ratios? Explain working capital, the current ratio, cash current debt coverage, inventory turnover, days in inventory, receivables turnover, average collection period, and the acid-test ratio.

2. What are solvency ratios? Explain debt to total assets, cash total debt coverage, times interest earned, and free cash flow.
3. What are profitability ratios? Explain earnings per share, the price-earnings ratio, gross profit margin, profit margin, return on assets, asset turnover, return on common shareholders' equity, and the payout ratio.

Quality of Earnings

STUDY OBJECTIVE

6

Understand the concept of quality of earnings.

In evaluating the financial performance of a company, the quality of earnings is of extreme importance to analysts. A company that has a high quality of earnings provides full and transparent information that will not confuse or mislead users of the financial statements. Molson, described in our feature story, has a high quality of earnings, providing thoroughness and clarity in the information it gives users.

BUSINESS INSIGHT

ETHICS PERSPECTIVE

In the wake of a proliferation of corporate scandals, many companies have been scared straight—or at the very least hiring ethics officers to help keep them straight. Regulation has tightened the requirement for ethical financial reporting, including requiring some chief executive officers and chief financial officers to vouch personally for the accuracy of their financial reports. Ethics officers conduct training courses for employees and watch over potential conflicts of interest. And they work with auditors and the board of directors to help make sure financial statements are accurate.

Of course, ethics programs aren't foolproof. "There isn't much even the most astute ethics officer can do when the board is asleep and senior management is corrupt," says Edward Petry, executive director of the Ethics Officer Association. However, it is a step in the right direction.

Source: Richard Schmitt, "Firms Scared Straight on Ethics," *The Globe and Mail,* November 4, 2002, B9.

Accounting
Irregularities and
Financial Fraud

The issue of quality of earnings has taken on increasing importance because recent corporate scandals suggest that some companies are spending too much time managing their earnings and not enough time managing their business. Some of the factors that can affect the quality of earnings include the choice of accounting principles, pro forma earnings, and improper recognition of revenues and expenses. Each of these topics is discussed in the next sections.

ALTERNATIVE ACCOUNTING PRINCIPLES

Variations among companies in the application of generally accepted accounting principles may hamper comparability and reduce the quality of earnings. For example, Molson chose to adopt the new accounting standard on amortizing goodwill early and therefore did not amortize its goodwill in its current fiscal year. On the other hand, Interbrew amortized the goodwill related to its acquisition of Labatt's over five years, on a straight-line basis. Consequently, Interbrew's earnings and assets will be lower than Molson's, which will affect comparisons.

Companies may choose from a host of acceptable accounting principles, such as different inventory cost flow assumptions (FIFO or average) or amortization methods (straight-line, declining-balance, or units-of-activity). Different choices result in differing financial positions, which again affect comparability. All of these are what we call "artificial," or timing, differences. Although there may be differences year by year, in total, over the life of the asset, there is no difference.

As well, in an increasing number of industries, competition is global. To evaluate a company's standing, an investor must make comparisons to companies from other countries just as we did by comparing Canadian-based Molson with Belgian-based Interbrew. Although differences in accounting methods might be detectable from reading the notes to the financial statements, adjusting the financial data to compensate for different methods is difficult, if not impossible, in some cases.

Even if we are able to adequately compare different accounting principles, we must also recognize that management discretion exists in choosing the most appropriate principle for the circumstances. In addition, numerous estimates are required in preparing financial information. Estimates are used, for example, in determining the allowance for uncollectible receivables, periodic amortization, and contingent losses. To the extent that managers are able to choose accounting principles and estimates to manage earnings, the quality of the earnings information content will decrease. Fortunately, audit committees today are held responsible for quizzing management on the degree of aggressiveness/conservatism applied and the quality of underlying accounting principles, key estimates, and judgments.

PRO FORMA EARNINGS

Publicly traded companies are required to present their earnings in accordance with generally accepted accounting principles. Many companies also report another measure of earnings in addition to GAAP earnings, called pro forma earnings. Pro forma earnings are a non-GAAP earnings measure that often excludes unusual or nonrecurring items. Companies use varying definitions of pro forma earnings. They have been known to exclude costs such as interest expense, stock compensation expenses, and impairment losses.

For example, fibre-optics manufacturer JDS Uniphase Corporation, with headquarters in Ottawa and San Jose, reported U.S.$67 million of pro forma earnings for fiscal 2001. These pro forma earnings excluded things like goodwill, stock-option charges, and losses on investments. Once these costs were added back, they resulted in a staggering U.S.$50.6 billion loss—a difference of nearly U.S.$50.7 billion! Such a large difference in earnings between GAAP numbers and pro forma numbers is not all that unusual. At one time, the 100 largest companies on the Nasdaq stock exchange reported total pro forma earnings of U.S.$19.1 billion. This was U.S.$101.4 billion more than GAAP-based numbers adding up to a loss of U.S.$82.3 billion.

There are no rules as to how to prepare pro forma earnings. Companies have free rein to exclude any items they deem inappropriate for measuring their performance. Many analysts and regulators are critical of the practice of using pro forma earnings because these numbers often make companies look better than they really are. Companies, on the other hand, argue that pro forma numbers more clearly indicate sustainable earnings because unusual and nonrecurring items are excluded.

Recently, Canadian securities regulators have started cracking down on companies that use creative accounting to artificially inflate poor earnings results. Publicly traded companies are now expected to provide GAAP numbers alongside non-GAAP earnings, explain how pro forma numbers are calculated, and detail why they exclude certain items required by GAAP. So far, these recommendations are guidelines, rather than rules, but regulators caution that they will take regulatory action if companies publish earnings that are judged misleading to investors.

BUSINESS INSIGHT

INVESTOR PERSPECTIVE

Pro forma terminology blossomed in Canada until recently. Montreal-based telephone utility BCE Inc., for example, coined the term "cash baseline earnings" to describe its operating performance. Telus Corporation, Canada's second largest telecommunications company, used the term "core baseline earnings"; the TD Bank, "cash operating earnings." These, and other companies, are now abandoning this methodology in favour of more traditional reporting.

Jim Hall, a Calgary-based portfolio manager, believes companies will always try to use any means at their disposal in stating results and will always interpret GAAP in their own best interest. "It's human nature, but I guess the pendulum has probably swung too far," he says. "The wary and thoughtful investor is the best defence against the corporate proclivity to focus on the positive."

Source: Michael Lewis, "Pro Forma Lingo," *CAmagazine*, March 2002, 16.

IMPROPER RECOGNITION

There is intense pressure, especially in a bear market in which stock prices are falling, to meet earnings forecasts. When managers feel pressured to meet expectations, they sometimes manipulate earnings which fall short of forecast expectations. According to a recent doctoral study in accounting, 270 companies restated their financial statements in 2001, up from 116 in 1997. It is commonly held that the increase in restatements reflects the number of new economy–type companies that pushed the limits of generally accepted accounting principles.

The leading cause of restatements is the improper recognition of revenue. Companies such as Quest Communications, Global Crossing, EnCana, Lucent Technologies, Xerox, Merck, Bristol-Myers Squibb, K-Mart, AOL-Time Warner, and a host of others have all been alleged to misapply the revenue recognition principle.

One practice that companies have used to distort revenue is called channel stuffing. Offering deep discounts on their products to customers, companies encourage their customers to buy early (stuff the channel) rather than later. This lets the company report good earnings in the current period, but it can lead to disaster in later periods because customers have no need for additional goods and may even end up returning the excess goods purchased. To illustrate, Bristol-Myers Squibb was forced to restate earnings three times because the company used sales incentives to encourage wholesalers to buy more drugs than necessary to meet patients' needs.

Another common practice in misapplying GAAP is the improper capitalization of expenses. WorldCom is the classic case, having capitalized more than U.S.$7 billion of operating expenses to ensure that it would report a positive earnings figure.

In other situations, companies fail to report all of their liabilities. For example, Enron had promised to make payments on certain contracts if financial difficulty developed, but these guarantees were not reported as liabilities. In addition, disclosure was so lacking in transparency, that it was impossible to understand what was happening. Both Tyco and IBM were also alleged to have abused disclosures at the cost of clarity and fairness. Regulators and standard-setters worldwide are currently re-evaluating the quality, completeness, and fairness of disclosure requirements.

Decision Toolkit

DECISION CHECKPOINTS	INFO NEEDED FOR DECISION	TOOL TO USE FOR DECISION	HOW TO EVALUATE RESULTS
Are efforts to evaluate the company helped or hampered by the quality of earnings?	Financial statements as well as other information disclosed	Review accounting principles, estimates, and pro forma earnings for reasonableness. Assess strength of corporate governance processes.	If there are any irregularities, the analysis should be relied upon with caution.

BEFORE YOU GO ON . . .

● **REVIEW IT**

1. Describe factors that reduce the quality of earnings.
2. Explain how alternative accounting principles can affect the comparability and quality of earnings.
3. Explain what is meant by "pro forma earnings."
4. Give an example of improper recognition of revenue and of expense.

A P P E N D I X   1 4 A

COMPREHENSIVE ILLUSTRATION OF RATIO ANALYSIS

In previous chapters, we calculated many ratios that are used to evaluate the financial health and performance of a company. In this appendix, we provide a comprehensive review of these ratios and discuss some important relationships among them. In this review, we use the following comparisons:

1. **Intracompany comparisons** covering two years (2001 and 2002) for Molson Inc.
2. **Intercompany comparisons** for the year ended December 31, 2002, for Interbrew S.A., Molson's principal competitor
3. **Industry average comparisons** for 2002 for the "beverages/brewers" industry. For some of the ratios that we use, industry comparisons are not available. These are marked "n/a."

The financial information in Illustrations 14A-1 through 14A-4 has been used to calculate Molson's ratios. Although the calculations are not shown, you can use these data to calculate each ratio yourself to make sure you understand where the numbers came from. Detailed financial data are not shown for either Interbrew or the industry.

Illustration 14A-1
Molson's balance sheet

MOLSON INC. Balance Sheet March 31 (in millions)	2002	2001
Assets		
Current assets		
Cash and short-term investments	$ 71.0	$ 70.1
Accounts receivable	192.1	102.3
Inventories	183.5	138.9
Prepaid expenses	55.2	51.8
Current assets of discontinued operations	8.4	69.3
Total current assets	510.2	432.4
Investments and other assets	122.5	93.0
Property, plant, and equipment	1,186.5	914.9
Intangible assets	2,671.7	1,518.8
Noncurrent assets of discontinued operations	30.1	321.7
Total assets	$4,521.0	$3,280.8
Liabilities and Shareholders' Equity		
Current liabilities		
Accounts payable and other current liabilities	$ 812.8	$ 573.8
Current portion of long-term debt	58.9	0
Current liabilities of discontinued operations	3.8	44.6
Total current liabilities	875.5	618.4
Long-term liabilities	2,368.3	1,710.6
Noncurrent liabilities of discontinued operations	103.3	156.4
Total liabilities	3,347.1	2,485.4
Shareholders' equity	1,173.9	795.4
Total liabilities and shareholders' equity	$4,521.0	$3,280.8

Illustration 14A-2
Molson's statement of earnings

MOLSON INC. Statement of Earnings Year Ended March 31 (in millions)	2002	2001
Sales and other revenues	$2,102.3	$1,857.1
Cost of sales, selling, and administrative costs	1,675.9	1,505.6
Provision for rationalization	50.0	0
Earnings before interest, income taxes, and amortization	376.4	351.5
Amortization expense	54.6	87.9
Earnings before interest and income taxes	321.8	263.6
Net interest expense	65.5	68.7
Earnings before income taxes	256.3	194.9
Income tax expense	80.7	57.7
Earnings from continuing operations	175.6	137.2
Earnings (loss) from discontinued operations	2.0	(3.3)
Net earnings	$ 177.6	$ 133.9

MOLSON INC. Cash Flow Statement Year Ended March 31 (in millions)				
		2002		2001
Cash provided by operating activities		$ 321.6		$ 228.2
Investing activities				
Business acquisitions	$(1,136.3)		$(374.5)	
Net proceeds from sale of investments	36.8		128.2	
Additions to property, plant,				
and equipment and intangible assets	(65.0)	(1,164.5)	(57.0)	(303.3)
Financing activities				
Net increase in long-term debt	$ 440.2		$ 94.8	
Issue of shares on business acquisition	238.2			
Cash dividends	(45.0)		(40.6)	
Other	2.4	635.8	63.8	118.0
Increase (decrease) in cash from				
continuing operations		(207.1)		42.9
Increase in cash from discontinued operations		201.2		8.8
Increase (decrease) in cash and cash equivalents		(5.9)		51.7
Cash and cash equivalents, April 1		76.9		25.2
Cash and cash equivalents, March 31		$ 71.0		$ 76.9

	2002	2001
Average number of shares (in millions)	120.1	119.0
Share price at year end	$34.92	$42.55

LIQUIDITY RATIOS

Liquidity ratios measure the ability of a company to pay its current liabilities. Consequently, liquidity ratios focus primarily on the relationships between current assets and current liabilities reported on the balance sheet and related accounts on the statement of earnings. Cash provided by operating activities, reported on the cash flow statement, is also useful in assessing liquidity. Liquidity ratios include working capital, the current ratio, acid-test ratio, cash current debt coverage, receivables turnover, average collection period, inventory turnover, and days in inventory.

Working Capital

Working capital is the difference between current assets and current liabilities. It is one measure of liquidity. However, as we learned in Chapter 2, the current ratio—which expresses current assets and current liabilities as a ratio rather than as an amount—is a more useful indicator of liquidity. Consequently, we will not illustrate working capital again here, but focus instead on the current ratio.

Current Ratio

The current ratio expresses the relationship of current assets to current liabilities, calculated by dividing current assets by current liabilities. It is widely used for evaluating a company's liquidity and short-term debt-paying ability. The 2002 and 2001 current ratios for Molson and comparative data are shown in Illustration 14A-5.

Ratio	Formula	Indicates	Molson 2002	2001	Interbrew 2002	Industry 2002
Current ratio	Current assets / Current liabilities	Short-term debt-paying ability	0.6:1	0.6:1	0.6:1	1.1:1

What does the measure actually mean? The 2002 ratio of 0.6:1 means that for every dollar of current liabilities, Molson has $0.60 of current assets. It is usual to remove the impact of discontinued operations when calculating ratios. In this particular case, Molson's current ratio of 0.6:1 in 2002 doesn't change whether current assets and liabilities from discontinued operations are included or not. However, its current ratio drops from 0.7:1 to 0.6:1 in 2001 when discontinued operations are excluded from the calculation.

Molson's current ratio remained consistent between 2001 and 2002. It is comparable to Interbrew's current ratio of 0.6:1. Both companies were significantly below the industry average. However, it is too early in our analysis to draw any conclusions about Molson's liquidity.

The current ratio is only one measure of liquidity. As it does not take into account the composition of current assets, a satisfactory current ratio could conceal the fact that a portion of current assets may be tied up in uncollectible accounts receivable or slow-moving inventory. The next ratio, the acid-test ratio, tightens the definition of liquidity, removing inventory and prepaid expenses from the mix.

Acid-Test Ratio

The acid-test ratio is a measure of a company's immediate short-term liquidity. It is calculated by dividing the sum of cash, short-term investments, and accounts receivable by current liabilities. Thus, it is an important complement to the current ratio. Note that it does not include inventory or prepaid expenses (or the current assets of discontinued operations). Cash, short-term investments, and accounts receivable are much more liquid than inventory and prepaid expenses. The inventory may not be readily saleable, and the prepaid expenses may not be transferable to others. The acid-test ratio for Molson is shown in Illustration 14A-6.

Ratio	Formula	Indicates	Molson 2002	2001	Interbrew 2002	Industry 2002
Acid-test ratio	(Cash + Short-term investments + Accounts receivable) / Current liabilities	Immediate short-term liquidity	0.3:1	0.3:1	0.8:1	0.7:1

Molson's acid-test ratio is unchanged from 2001 to 2002. However, it is much lower than both Interbrew's and the industry average. When liquidity is this tight, it is important to have access to operating lines of credit. Molson does have a $50-million general operating line of credit, which had a $30-million balance still available at March 31, 2002.

It is interesting that Molson's and Interbrew's current ratios are similar but their acid-test ratios are not. Further analysis regarding the companies' receivables and inventory situations will shed light on this difference.

Cash Current Debt Coverage

A disadvantage of the current and acid-test ratios is that they use year-end balances of current asset and current liability accounts. These year-end balances may not be representative of the company's position during most of the year. A ratio that partially corrects for this problem is the ratio of cash provided by operating activities to average current liabilities, called the cash current debt coverage ratio.

Because it uses cash provided by operating activities rather than a balance at one point in time, it may provide a better representation of liquidity. Molson's cash current debt coverage ratio is shown in Illustration 14A-7.

Ratio	Formula	Indicates	Molson 2002	2001	Interbrew 2002	Industry 2002
Cash current debt coverage	Cash provided by operating activities / Average current liabilities	Short-term debt-paying ability (cash basis)	0.4	0.4	0.3	n/a

Molson's cash provided by operating activities increased from $228.2 million in 2001 to $321.6 million in 2002. However, its current liabilities also increased proportionately. Consequently, Molson's cash current debt coverage ratio remained unchanged at 0.4 times. Molson's cash current debt coverage ratio is higher than Interbrew's. No industry comparison is available.

Receivables Turnover

We mentioned earlier that a high current ratio is not always a good indication of liquidity. The high result could be due to high receivable or inventory balances resulting from uncollectible accounts or slow-moving inventory. The ratio used to assess the liquidity of the receivables is the receivables turnover, which measures the number of times, on average, receivables are collected during the period. Receivables turnover is calculated by dividing net credit sales (net sales less cash sales) by average gross accounts receivable (before the allowance for doubtful accounts is deducted) during the year. The receivables turnover ratio for Molson is shown in Illustration 14A-8.

Ratio	Formula	Indicates	Molson 2002	2001	Interbrew 2002	Industry 2002
Receivables turnover	Net credit sales / Average gross accounts receivable	Liquidity of receivable	14.3	14.5	4.0	7.2

Since companies don't normally disclose the proportions of their sales that were made for cash and for credit, we normally assume that all sales are credit sales. In addition, not all companies report gross and net accounts receivable separately. In such cases, it is appropriate to use net accounts receivable. The important thing is to be consistent in your input data to ensure that the resulting ratios are comparable. Molson's receivables turnover declined marginally in 2002. However, 14.3 days is still an excellent turnover rate, and far better than both Interbrew's and the industry average.

Average Collection Period

A popular variant of the receivables turnover ratio converts it into an average collection period in days. This is done by dividing 365 days by the receivables turnover. The average collection period for Molson is shown in Illustration 14A-9.

Ratio	Formula	Indicates	Molson 2002	2001	Interbrew 2002	Industry 2002
Average collection period	365 days / Receivables turnover	Liquidity of receivables and collection success	25.5	25.2	91.2	50.7

Molson's 2002 receivables turnover of 14.3 times is divided into 365 days to obtain an average collection period of 25.5 days. Analysts frequently use the average collection period to assess the effectiveness of a company's credit and collection policies. The general rule is that the collection period should not greatly exceed the credit period (i.e., the time allowed for payment).

Molson's collection period is far superior to that of Interbrew and that of the industry. So, despite earlier concerns about Molson's liquidity, receivables management appears to be in good shape. One reason that Interbrew's receivables turnover and collection period may be far worse than Molson's is because of the global nature of its business and differences in worldwide collection practices. Interbrew operates in 120 countries. Molson operates primarily in Canada, the U.S., and Brazil.

Inventory Turnover

The inventory turnover ratio measures the number of times on average the inventory is sold during the period. Its purpose is to measure the liquidity of the inventory. Inventory turnover is calculated by dividing the cost of goods sold by the average inventory during the period. Unless seasonal factors are significant, average inventory can be calculated from the beginning and ending inventory balances. Molson's inventory turnover is shown in Illustration 14A-10.

Illustration 14A-10
Inventory turnover

Ratio	Formula	Indicates	Molson 2002	Molson 2001	Interbrew 2002	Industry 2002
Inventory turnover	Cost of goods sold / Average inventory	Liquidity of inventory	10.4	11.1	6.8	4.4

Like many other Canadian companies, Molson does not separately disclose its cost of goods sold. However, by using the cost of sales, selling, and administrative costs as a proxy for cost of goods sold, we can at least determine whether Molson's inventory turnover improved or deteriorated, assuming that cost of goods sold is the largest proportion of these costs.

Molson's inventory turnover declined slightly in 2002. However, even with the selling and administrative costs included, Molson's inventory turnover is still a reasonable one, and significantly better than both Interbrew's and the industry average. This is notable, especially since neither Interbrew nor the industry includes selling and administrative expenses in the numerator of this calculation.

Days in Inventory

A variant of the inventory turnover ratio is days in inventory, which measures the average number of days it takes to sell the inventory. It is calculated by dividing 365 days by the inventory turnover. The days in inventory for Molson is shown in Illustration 14A-11.

Illustration 14A-11
Days in inventory

Ratio	Formula	Indicates	Molson 2002	Molson 2001	Interbrew 2002	Industry 2002
Days in inventory	365 days / Inventory turnover	Liquidity of inventory and inventory management	35.1	32.9	53.7	83

Molson's 2002 inventory turnover of 10.4 times is divided into 365 days to obtain 35.1 days in inventory. This means that, on average, it takes Molson 35 days to sell its inventory. This average is significantly better than those of Interbrew and the industry. Generally, the faster inventory is sold, the less cash there is tied up in inventory and the less chance there is of inventory becoming obsolete.

Why might Molson's inventory turnover be so much better than that of Interbrew? Some of this difference might be explained by differences in product lines across the two companies. For example, Interbrew has over 100 brands—67 brands in Canada alone—while Molson has fewer than 10 brands. Also, in addition to dealing with a labour lock-out in Canada and a strike in Montenegro, Interbrew reorganized logistics in the UK and in Western Europe. All of these activities should lead to improved days in inventory in the future.

It is worth noting here that these interpretations are based not only on the financial data, but also on the knowledge gained from an understanding of Molson and Interbrew, their businesses, and their activities over the last year. As mentioned in the chapter, non-financial information is important in assessing the impact of the financial results.

Liquidity Conclusion

In an intracompany comparison, Molson's current, acid-test, and cash current debt coverage ratios were unchanged from 2001 to 2002. Its receivables and inventory turnover ratios declined slightly.

In an intercompany/industry comparison, Molson's current and acid-test ratios were generally lower than both Interbrew's and the industry average. However, all of its other liquidity ratios were better than both Interbrew's and the industry average. Interbrew's and the industry average current and acid-test ratios were likely inflated because of slower moving receivables and inventory.

To conclude, Molson's liquidity is tight. Its current and acid-test ratios are both less than one. However, it has a strong collection record and its inventory is moving. It also has access to an operating line of credit. Although it bears close watching, Molson's liquidity appears acceptable.

SOLVENCY RATIOS

While liquidity ratios measure the ability of a company to pay its current liabilities, solvency ratios measure the ability of a company to pay its total liabilities. The debt to total assets, times interest earned, and cash total debt coverage ratios provide information about debt-paying ability. In addition, free cash flow provides information about the company's ability to pay additional dividends or invest in new projects.

Debt to Total Assets

The debt to total assets ratio measures the percentage of the total assets provided by creditors. It is calculated by dividing total liabilities (both current and long-term) by total assets. This ratio indicates the degree of financial leveraging; it thus provides some indication of the company's ability to withstand losses without hurting the interests of its creditors. The higher the percentage of debt to total assets, the greater the risk that the company may be unable to meet its maturing obligations. The lower the ratio, the more equity "buffer" there is available to creditors if the company becomes insolvent. So, from the creditors' point of view, a low ratio of debt to total assets is desirable. Molson's debt to total assets is shown in Illustration 14A-12.

			Molson		Interbrew	Industry
Ratio	Formula	Indicates	2002	2001	2002	2002
Debt to total assets	Total liabilities / Total assets	Percentage of total assets provided by creditors	72.3%	79.1%	57.9%	50.0%

Illustration 14A-12
Debt to total assets

Molson's debt to total assets ratio of 72.3% (which excludes discontinued operations) means that creditors have provided financing to cover 72.3% of the company's total assets. Molson's solvency improved during the year, from 79.1% to 72.3%, as a result of the company's focus on restructuring its Canadian operations. Molson notes in its management discussion and analysis that its debt increased primarily because of the Kaiser acquisition. The cash received from the sale of a portion of its Brazilian operations to Heineken will be used to reduce $348 million of this debt, further improving its debt to total assets ratio. Still, Molson's debt to total assets ratio has a long way to improve. Its 72.3% debt to total assets ratio is significantly above Interbrew's 57.9% and the industry average of 50.0%.

Another ratio with a similar meaning is the debt to equity ratio. It shows the relative use of borrowed funds compared with resources invested by the shareholders. Because this ratio can be calculated in several ways, care should be taken when making comparisons. Debt may be defined to include only the noncurrent portion of liabilities, and intangible assets may be excluded from shareholders' equity (which would then equal tangible net worth). If debt and shareholders' equity are defined to include all liabilities and all equity, then when the debt to total assets ratio equals 50%, the debt to equity ratio is 1:1 (because total liabilities plus shareholders' equity equals total assets).

Using this definition, Molson's debt to equity ratio for 2002 is 2.9:1 ($3,347.1 ÷ $1,173.9) or 2.8:1 ($3,240.0 ÷ $1,173.9) if discontinued items are excluded from the liabilities. This means that Molson has financed its operations with 2.9 times as much debt as equity.

Times Interest Earned

The debt level of a company is not as important as its ability to service the debt—that is, pay the interest. The times interest earned ratio (also called interest coverage) indicates the company's ability to meet interest payments as they come due. It is calculated by dividing earnings before interest expense and income taxes by interest expense. Note that this ratio uses earnings before interest expense and income taxes because this amount represents what is available to cover interest. Molson's times interest earned ratio is shown in Illustration 14A-13.

Illustration 14A-13
Times interest earned

Ratio	Formula	Indicates	Molson 2002	Molson 2001	Interbrew 2002	Industry 2002
Times interest earned	$\dfrac{\text{Earnings before interest expense and income tax expense (EBIT)}}{\text{Interest expense}}$	Ability to meet interest payments as they come due	4.9	3.8	5.7	5.2

Molson's 2002 times interest earned ratio was 4.9 times. That is, earnings before interest and taxes were 4.9 times the amount needed for interest expense. The earnings figure excluded the earnings from discontinued operations. Molson's times interest earned ratio improved from 2001 to 2002. However, it is still slightly less than the industry average of 5.2 times, and less than Interbrew's ratio of 5.7 times.

Cash Total Debt Coverage

The ratio of cash provided by operating activities to average total liabilities, called the cash total debt coverage ratio, is a cash-based measure of solvency. This ratio indicates a company's ability to repay its liabilities from cash provided by operating activities, without having to liquidate the assets used in its operations. Illustration 14A-14 shows Molson's cash total debt coverage.

Ratio	Formula	Indicates	Molson 2002	Molson 2001	Interbrew 2002	Industry 2002
Cash total debt coverage	Cash provided by operating activities / Average total liabilities	Long-term debt-paying ability (cash basis)	0.1	0.1	0.2	n/a

Illustration 14A-14
Cash total debt coverage

An industry ratio for this measure is not available, but Molson's cash total debt coverage ratio remained constant at 0.1 times. One way of interpreting the cash total debt coverage ratio is to say that cash provided from one year of operating activities would be sufficient to pay off 10% of Molson's total liabilities. If 10% of liabilities were retired each year, it would take approximately nine more years to retire all debt.

Note that Molson's cash current debt coverage ratio was also unchanged, as shown in Illustration 14A-7. Since the cash total debt coverage ratio remained constant, we can deduce that Molson's long-term liabilities must have increased proportionately to its operating cash position in 2002.

Molson's cash total debt coverage ratio was slightly below Interbrew's 0.2 times. A general rule of thumb is that a measure above 0.2 times is acceptable.

Free Cash Flow

One indication of a company's solvency, as well as of its ability to pay additional dividends or expand operations, is the amount of excess cash it generates after investing to maintain its current productive capacity and after paying current dividends. This amount is referred to as free cash flow. Molson's free cash flow is shown in Illustration 14A-15.

Illustration 14A-15
Free cash flow

Ratio	Formula	Indicates	Molson 2002 (in millions)	Molson 2001 (in millions)	Interbrew 2002 (in millions)	Industry 2002
Free cash flow	Cash provided by operating activities − Capital expenditures − Dividends paid	Cash available for paying more dividends or expanding operations	$211.6	$130.6	$296.0	n/a

Although Molson's free cash flow has improved considerably from 2001 to 2002, Interbrew's sheer size and global coverage allow it to generate cash at a much faster rate than Molson can.

Solvency Conclusion

In an intracompany comparison, all of Molson's solvency ratios improved in 2002 except for its cash total debt coverage ratio, which remained constant. Although improvement was apparent, in an intercompany/industry comparison, Molson's solvency was significantly lower than that of Interbrew and the industry.

PROFITABILITY RATIOS

For a company to be successful, assets must be used to generate revenue efficiently and expenses must be controlled effectively. Consequently, profitability ratios focus primarily on the relationships between statement of earnings items and balance sheet items. Understanding these relationships can help management determine where to focus efforts on improving profitability.

Illustration 14A-16 diagrams these relationships and will structure our discussion of Molson's profitability. Profitability ratios include the return on common shareholders' equity, return on assets, profit margin, asset turnover, and gross profit margin ratios, as shown in Illustration 14A-16. In addition, we will review three

Illustration 14A-16
Relationships among
profitability measures

other commonly used measures of profitability of specific interest to investors—
earnings per share, price-earnings ratio, and the payout ratio.

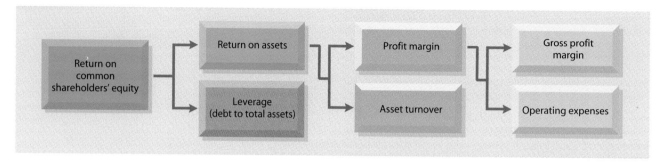

Return on Common Shareholders' Equity

A widely used measure of profitability from the common shareholders' viewpoint
is the return on common shareholders' equity ratio. This ratio shows how many
dollars of net earnings were earned for each dollar invested by the shareholders. It
is calculated by dividing net earnings minus any preferred share dividends—that
is, earnings available to common shareholders—by average common shareholders'
equity. The return on common shareholders' equity for Molson is shown in Illustration 14A-17.

Illustration 14A-17
Return on common
shareholders' equity

Ratio	Formula	Indicates	Molson 2002	Molson 2001	Interbrew 2002	Industry 2002
Return on common shareholders' equity	$\dfrac{\text{Net earnings} - \text{Preferred dividends}}{\text{Average common shareholders' equity}}$	Profitability of common shareholders' investment	17.8%	15.1%	9.8%	21.7%

Molson's 2002 return on shareholders' equity improved over that of 2001, and is
significantly better than Interbrew's. Both companies' ratios are less than the industry average. For the purpose of this illustration, we have assumed that there
are no preferred shareholders and have removed the impact of the discontinued
operations from the net earnings figure.

Return on Assets

Return on common shareholders' equity is affected by two factors: the return on
assets ratio and the degree of leverage. Return on assets measures the overall profitability of assets in terms of the income earned on each dollar invested in assets.
It is calculated by dividing net earnings by average total assets. Molson's return on
assets is shown in Illustration 14A-18.

Illustration 14A-18
Return on assets

Ratio	Formula	Indicates	Molson 2002	Molson 2001	Interbrew 2002	Industry 2002
Return on assets	$\dfrac{\text{Net earnings}}{\text{Average total assets}}$	Overall profitability of assets	4.8%	4.9%	4.1%	7.3%

Molson's return on assets of 4.8% is relatively unchanged from its return of 4.9%
in 2001. Although its return on assets is significantly below the industry average,
it is better than Interbrew's.

Note that Molson's rate of return on common shareholders' equity (17.8%)
is substantially higher than its rate of return on assets (4.8%). The reason is that

Molson has made effective use of **leverage**. Leveraging or trading on the equity at a gain means that the company has borrowed money at a lower rate of interest than the rate of return it earns on the assets it purchased with the borrowed funds. Leverage enables management to use money supplied by non-shareholders (non-owners) to increase the return to shareholders.

A comparison of the rate of return on assets with the rate of interest paid for borrowed money indicates the profitability of trading on the equity. If you borrow money at 3% and your rate of return on assets is 5%, you are trading on the equity at a gain. Note, however, that trading on the equity is a two-way street: for example, if you borrow money at 5% and earn only 3% on it, you are trading on the equity at a loss.

Molson earns more on its borrowed funds than it has to pay in interest. Thus, the return to shareholders exceeds the return on the assets because of the positive benefit of leverage. Recall from our earlier discussion that Molson's percentage of debt financing as measured by the ratio of debt to total assets is very high—72.3% in 2002 (see Illustration 14A-12). In contrast, Interbrew had a much lower debt to total assets ratio of 57.9%. It appears that Molson's high return on shareholders' equity, compared to Interbrew's, is largely a function of its use of leverage.

Profit Margin

Return on assets is affected by two factors, the first of which is the profit margin. The profit margin ratio, or rate of return on sales, measures the percentage that each dollar of sales produces of net earnings. It is calculated by dividing net earnings by net sales for the period. Molson's profit margin is shown in Illustration 14A-19.

			Molson		Interbrew	Industry
Ratio	Formula	Indicates	2002	2001	2002	2002
Profit margin	Net earnings / Net sales	Net earnings generated by each dollar of sales	8.4%	7.4%	6.7%	9.3%

Illustration 14A-19
Profit margin

Molson had an 8.4% profit margin, exclusive of discontinued operating items. This profit margin exceeded both Molson's for 2001, and that of Interbrew for 2002. Consistent with other profitability ratios we've analysed, both companies' profit margins are less than the industry average.

Asset Turnover

The other factor that affects the return on assets ratio is asset turnover. The asset turnover ratio measures how efficiently a company uses its assets to generate sales. It is determined by dividing net sales by average total assets for the period. The resulting number shows the dollars of sales produced by each dollar invested in assets. Illustration 14A-20 shows the asset turnover for Molson.

			Molson		Interbrew	Industry
Ratio	Formula	Indicates	2002	2001	2002	2002
Asset turnover	Net sales / Average total assets	How efficiently assets are used to generate sales	0.6	0.7	0.6	0.8

Illustration 14A-20
Asset turnover

The asset turnover ratio shows that Molson generated $0.60 of sales in 2002 for each dollar it had invested in assets, exclusive of discontinued operations. Although the asset turnover declined slightly from 2001, it is consistent with Interbrew's. Both companies' asset turnover ratios of 0.6 times fall below that of the industry at 0.8 times.

In summary, Molson's return on assets changed only marginally from 2001 to 2002, declining from 4.9% to 4.8%. However, underlying this relative stability was an increased profitability on each dollar of sales, as measured by the increase in the profit margin from 7.4% to 8.4%. This increase was offset by a decline in the sales-generating efficiency of its assets, as measured by the asset turnover ratio. The combined effects of the profit margin and asset turnover on return on assets for Molson can be analysed as shown in Illustration 14A-21.

Illustration 14A-21
Composition of return on assets

RATIOS:	PROFIT MARGIN: $\dfrac{\text{NET EARNINGS}}{\text{NET SALES}}$	ASSET TURNOVER: $\times \dfrac{\text{NET SALES}}{\text{AVERAGE TOTAL ASSETS}}$	RETURN ON ASSETS: $= \dfrac{\text{NET EARNINGS}}{\text{AVERAGE TOTAL ASSETS}}$
Molson			
2002	8.35%	× 0.57 times	= 4.76%
2001	7.39%	× 0.66 times	= 4.88%

The ratios presented earlier for the profit margin, asset turnover, and return on assets in Illustrations 14A-18 through 14A-20 were rounded to one digit. In Illustration 14A-21, the ratios have been extended to two digits in order to show more clearly how profit margin and asset turnover combine to produce return on assets, without the impact of rounding differences.

Gross Profit Margin

Two factors strongly influence the profit margin. One is the gross profit margin. The other is the company's ability to control its operating expenses. The gross profit margin is determined by dividing gross profit (net sales less cost of goods sold) by net sales. This ratio indicates a company's ability to maintain an adequate selling price above its cost of goods sold. Gross profit margins should be closely monitored over time. Illustration 14A-22 shows that Molson's gross profit margin is not available.

Illustration 14A-22
Gross profit margin

			Molson		Interbrew	Industry
Ratio	Formula	Indicates	2002	2001	2002	2002
Gross profit margin	$\dfrac{\text{Gross profit}}{\text{Net sales}}$	Margin between selling price and cost of goods sold	n/a	n/a	51.1%	56.9%

Similar to most Canadian companies, Molson does not separately disclose its cost of goods sold. Instead, it reports one combined figure for cost of sales, selling, and administrative costs. Consequently, the gross profit margin cannot be calculated for Molson. Interbrew's gross profit margin is 51.1%, slightly less than the industry average of 56.9%. For Interbrew, this means that 48.9% (100% − 51.1%) of each dollar of sales goes to cover operating expenses and generate a profit. Because we cannot calculate Molson's gross profit margin, we are unable to comment on its ability to control its operating expenses, compared to its cost of goods sold.

Profitability Conclusion

In an intracompany comparison, Molson's profitability measures have either improved or remained relatively constant (with only a marginal decline) from 2001 to 2002. In an intercompany comparison, Molson's profitability ratios have consistently exceeded those of Interbrew (except for asset turnover, which was the same). Both companies fell short of industry averages on all measures.

There are still three profitability ratios to review and all are externally reported measures of the profitability we have just assessed. These three ratios are earnings per share, the price-earnings ratio, and the payout ratio. They are of more interest to investors than to management.

Earnings Per Share (EPS)

Shareholders usually think in terms of the number of shares they own or plan to buy or sell. Expressing net earnings on a per share basis provides a useful perspective for determining profitability. Earnings per share is a measure of the net earnings realized on each common share. It is calculated by dividing net earnings by the average number of common shares issued during the year.

When we use "earnings per share," it refers to the amount of net earnings applicable to each common share. Therefore, when we calculate earnings per share, if there are preferred dividends declared for the period, they must be deducted from net earnings to arrive at earnings available to the common shareholders.

In reality, the average number of shares is not calculated by adding together the beginning and ending share balances and dividing by two. Instead, a weighted average, weighted by the number of months any new shares have been issued for during the year, is used. In addition, there are a number of other complexities involved in calculating earnings per share. Further details about these matters are left to a subsequent accounting course.

Molson's earnings per share is shown in Illustration 14A-23.

Illustration 14A-23
Earnings per share

Ratio	Formula	Indicates	Molson 2002	Molson 2001	Interbrew 2002	Industry 2002
Earnings per share (EPS)	$\dfrac{\text{Net earnings} - \text{Preferred dividends}}{\text{Average number of common shares}}$	Net earnings earned on each common share	$1.46	$1.15	$1.08	n/a

Note that no industry average is presented in Illustration 14A-23. Industry data for earnings per share are not reported and, in fact, Molson's and Interbrew's earnings per share ratios should not be compared. Such comparisons are not meaningful, because of the wide variations in number of shares among companies. Molson's earnings per share (exclusive of nonrecurring items) increased substantially in 2002. This represents a 27% increase over the 2001 EPS of $1.15.

Price-Earnings Ratio

The price-earnings ratio is an oft-quoted statistic that measures the ratio of the market price of each common share to the earnings per share. The price-earnings (P-E) ratio is a reflection of investors' assessments of a company's future earnings. It is calculated by dividing the market price per share by earnings per share. Molson's price-earnings ratio is shown in Illustration 14A-24.

Illustration 14A-24
Price-earnings ratio

Ratio	Formula	Indicates	Molson 2002	Molson 2001	Interbrew 2002	Industry 2002
Price-earnings ratio	$\dfrac{\text{Market price per share}}{\text{Earnings per share}}$	Relationship between market price per share and earnings per share	23.9	37.0	20.8	25.5

In 2002, each Molson common share sold for 23.9 times the amount that was earned on each share. In 2001, each share sold for 37.0 times earnings. Molson's price-earnings ratio is higher than Interbrew's. Both companies fell below the industry average of 25.5 times in 2002. This intercompany/industry comparison is consistent with our earlier profitability comparisons.

It is interesting to note that although Molson's profitability increased in 2002, investors do not appear quite as keen to purchase Molson's shares as they were in 2001. The higher P-E ratio in 2001 suggests that the market was more optimistic about Molson a year earlier. Or, it might also signal that Molson's shares were overpriced in 2001.

Payout Ratio

The payout ratio measures the percentage of earnings distributed in the form of cash dividends. It is calculated by dividing cash dividends by net earnings. Companies that have high growth rates are characterized by low payout ratios, because they reinvest most of their net earnings in the business. The payout ratio for Molson is shown in Illustration 14A-25.

Illustration 14A-25
Payout ratio

Ratio	Formula	Indicates	Molson 2002	Molson 2001	Interbrew 2002	Industry 2002
Payout ratio	Cash dividends / Net earnings	Percentage of earnings distributed as cash dividends	25.6%	29.6%	30.4%	65.7%

Molson's payout ratio declined in 2002, and is relatively low compared to those of Interbrew and the industry.

Management has some control over the amount of dividends paid each year, and companies are generally reluctant to reduce a dividend below the amount paid in a previous year. Therefore, the payout ratio will actually decrease if a company's net earnings increase but the company keeps its total dividend payment the same or more.

Before drawing any conclusions regarding Molson's payout ratio, we should calculate this ratio over a longer period of time to evaluate any trends, and also to try to find out whether management's philosophy regarding dividends has changed recently. In Molson's case, it has paid a dividend for six straight years and has increased its dividend each of the past three fiscal years.

This concludes our comprehensive analysis illustration using Molson. In terms of the types of financial information available and the ratios used by various industries, what can be practically covered in a textbook gives you only the tip of the iceberg. The availability of information is not a problem. The real trick is to be discriminating enough to perform relevant analyses and select pertinent comparative data.

Using the Decision Toolkit

When analysing a company, you should always investigate an extended period of time in order to determine whether the condition and performance of the company are changing. The condensed financial statements of Molson Inc. for 1999 and 2000 follow. They supplement the data presented earlier in the chapter for 2001 and 2002.

MOLSON INC.
Balance Sheet
March 31
(in millions)

	2000		1999	
	Amount	Percent	Amount	Percent
Assets				
Current assets	$ 433.2		$ 392.1	
Current assets of discontinued operations	19.2		143.8	
Noncurrent assets	2,639.6		2,794.3	
Noncurrent assets of discontinued operations	19.8		109.4	
Total assets	$3,111.8		$3,439.6	
Liabilities and Shareholders' Equity				
Current liabilities	$ 592.6		$ 514.8	
Current liabilities of discontinued operations	6.1		141.2	
Noncurrent liabilities	1,430.1		1,556.7	
Noncurrent liabilities of discontinued operations	57.3		118.8	
Total liabilities	2,086.1		2,331.5	
Shareholders' equity	1,025.7		1,108.1	
Total liabilities and shareholders' equity	$3,111.8		$3,439.6	

MOLSON INC.
Statement of Earnings
Year Ended March 31
(in millions)

	2000		1999	
	Amount	Percent	Amount	Percent
Sales and other revenues	$1,895.8		$1,584.1	
Costs and expenses	1,793.4		1,374.5	
Earnings before interest, income taxes, and amortization	102.4		209.6	
Amortization expense	100.3		82.8	
Earnings before interest and income taxes	2.1		126.8	
Net interest expense	77.8		62.7	
Earnings (loss) before income taxes	(75.7)		64.1	
Income tax expense (recovery)	(4.9)		36.1	
Earnings (loss) from continuing operations	(70.8)		28.0	
Earnings (loss) from discontinued operations	26.8		141.9	
Net earnings (loss)	$ (44.0)		$ 169.9	

Instructions

1. Prepare a vertical analysis of Molson's balance sheet and statement of earnings, inserting the appropriate percentages in the spaces provided above.
2. Comment on any relevant trends between 1999 and 2000, and in comparison to the vertical analysis for 2001 and 2002 presented earlier in the chapter in Illustrations 14-10 and 14-11.

Solution

1. Vertical analysis: The following lists the percentages for each of the four years—1999 and 2000 that you calculated above, and 2001 and 2002 presented in Illustrations 14-10 and 14-11 in the chapter—in a side-by-side format for easier reference.

MOLSON INC. Percentage Balance Sheet March 31				
	2002	2001	2000	1999
Assets				
Current assets	11.1%	11.1%	13.9%	11.4%
Current assets of discontinued operations	0.2%	2.1%	0.6%	4.2%
Noncurrent assets	88.0%	77.0%	84.8%	81.2%
Noncurrent assets of discontinued operations	0.7%	9.8%	0.7%	3.2%
Total assets	100.0%	100.0%	100.0%	100.0%
Liabilities and Shareholders' Equity				
Current liabilities	19.3%	17.5%	19.0%	15.0%
Current liabilities of discontinued operations	0.0%	1.4%	0.2%	4.1%
Long-term liabilities	52.4%	52.1%	46.0%	45.3%
Noncurrent liabilities of discontinued operations	2.3%	4.8%	1.8%	3.4%
Total liabilities	74.0%	75.8%	67.0%	67.8%
Shareholders' equity	26.0%	24.2%	33.0%	32.2%
Total liabilities and shareholders' equity	100.0%	100.0%	100.0%	100.0%

MOLSON INC. Percentage Statement of Earnings Year Ended March 31				
	2002	2001	2000	1999
Sales and other revenues	100.0%	100.0%	100.0%	100.0%
Costs and expenses	82.1%	81.1%	94.6%	86.8%
Earnings before interest, income taxes, and amortization	17.9%	18.9%	5.4%	13.2%
Amortization expense	2.6%	4.7%	5.3%	5.2%
Earnings before interest and income taxes	15.3%	14.2%	0.1%	8.0%
Net interest expense	3.1%	3.7%	4.1%	4.0%
Earnings (loss) before income taxes	12.2%	10.5%	(4.0%)	4.0%
Income tax expense (recovery)	3.8%	3.1%	(0.3%)	2.3%
Earnings (loss) from continuing operations	8.4%	7.4%	(3.7%)	1.7%
Earnings (loss) from discontinued operations	0.0%	(0.2%)	1.4%	9.0%
Net earnings (loss)	8.4%	7.2%	(2.3%)	10.7%

2. Current assets have remained relatively constant since 1999, except for a one-time increase in 2000. Molson's current liabilities represent a higher percentage of its total assets than do current assets. Current liabilities have generally been increasing, except in 2001. Except for that same year, 2001, Molson's noncurrent assets have also been increasing as a percentage of total assets. Long-term liabilities have been increasing steadily, although less so between 2001 and 2002.

Molson's liquidity and solvency would appear to be declining over the four years, with increasing percentages of liabilities. We would have to perform further analysis (e.g., ratio analysis as detailed in Appendix 14A) to determine whether this is actually the case and, if so, the reasons for this decline.

In terms of profitability, Molson appears to be controlling its costs and expenses, which declined substantially in 2001 and increased only marginally in 2002. Its profitability (earnings from continuing operations) also appears to be on the increase over the last three years.

It is interesting to note the impact that discontinued operations have on Molson's financial position. While these have been excluded from our analysis, one might question whether they are really a nonrecurring item since discontinued operations appear to be the norm rather than the exception over the last four years. However, except in 1999, the discontinued operations have not significantly impacted Molson's profitability.

Summary of Study Objectives

❶ Understand the concept of sustainable earnings and indicate how irregular items are presented. Sustainable earnings refer to a company's ability to sustain its profits from operations. Irregular items—discontinued operations and extraordinary items—are presented on the statement of earnings, net of tax, below "Earnings from continuing operations" to highlight their infrequent nature. Another irregular item—the cumulative effect on prior period earnings of a change in accounting principle—is presented on the statement of retained earnings, net of tax, as an adjustment to opening retained earnings. For comparability, all prior period financial statements presented are restated using the new principle.

❷ Discuss the need for comparative analysis and identify the tools of financial statement analysis. Comparative analysis is performed to evaluate a company's liquidity, profitability, and solvency. Comparisons can detect changes in financial relationships and significant trends, and provide insight into a company's competitiveness and relative position in its industry.

There are three bases of comparison: (1) intracompany, which compares an item or financial relationship to other data within a company; (2) intercompany, which compares an item or financial relationship of a company to data of one or more competing companies; (3) industry, which compares company data to industry averages. In addition, financial statements may be analysed horizontally, vertically, and with ratios.

❸ Explain and apply horizontal analysis. Horizontal analysis is a technique for evaluating a series of data over a period of time to determine the increase or decrease that has taken place, expressed as either an amount or a percentage.

❹ Explain and apply vertical analysis. Vertical analysis is a technique that expresses each item in a financial statement as a percentage of a relevant total or base amount.

❺ Identify and calculate ratios used to analyse liquidity, solvency, and profitability. Financial ratios are provided in Illustration 14-13 (liquidity), Illustration 14-14 (solvency), and Illustration 14-15 (profitability).

❻ Understand the concept of quality of earnings. A high quality of earnings provides full and transparent information that will not confuse or mislead users of the financial statements. Issues related to quality of earnings are (1) alternative accounting principles, (2) pro forma earnings, and (3) improper recognition of revenues and expenses.

Decision Toolkit—A Summary

Decision
Toolkit
Summary

DECISION CHECKPOINTS	INFO NEEDED FOR DECISION	TOOL TO USE FOR DECISION	HOW TO EVALUATE RESULTS
Has the company sold any major component of its business?	Discontinued operations section of statement of earnings	Anything reported in this section indicates that the company has discontinued a major component of its business.	If a major component of the company's business has been discontinued, its results in the current period should not be included in estimates of future net earnings.
Has the company experienced any extraordinary events or transactions?	Extraordinary item section of statement of earnings	Anything reported in this section indicates that the company experienced an event that was infrequent, unusual, and not determined by management.	These items should usually be ignored in estimating future net earnings.
Has the company changed any of its accounting principles?	Cumulative effect of change in accounting principle in statement of retained earnings	Anything reported in this manner indicates that the company has changed an accounting principle during the current year.	Financial statements are restated using the new principle for comparability.
How do the company's financial position and operating results compare with those of previous periods?	Statement of earnings and balance sheet	Comparative financial statements should be prepared over at least two years, with the first year reported as the base year. Changes in each line item relative to the base year should be presented both by amount and by percentage. This is called horizontal analysis.	A significant change should be investigated to determine what caused it.
How do the relationships between items in this year's financial statements compare with last year's relationships or those of competitors?	Statement of earnings and balance sheet	Each line item on the statement of earnings should be presented as a percentage of net sales, and each line item on the balance sheet should be presented as a percentage of total assets (total liabilities and shareholders' equity). This is called vertical analysis.	Any difference, either across years or between companies, should be investigated to determine the cause.
Are efforts to evaluate the company helped or hampered by the quality of earnings?	Financial statements as well as other information disclosed	Review accounting principles, estimates, and pro forma earnings for reasonableness. Assess strength of corporate governance processes.	If there are any irregularities, the analysis should be relied upon with caution.

NAVIGATOR

Glossary

Change in accounting principle Use of an accounting principle in the current year different from the one used in the preceding year. (p. 672)

Debt to equity A measure of the relationship between resources provided by the creditors compared to resources provided by the shareholders. It is calculated by dividing total liabilities by total shareholders' equity. (p. 694)

Discontinued operations The disposal of a significant component of a business. (p. 669)

Extraordinary items Events and transactions that meet these three conditions: they are (1) infrequent in occurrence, (2) unusual in nature, and (3) not the result of a management determination. (p. 670)

Horizontal analysis A technique for evaluating a series of financial statement data over a period of time to determine the increase (decrease) that has taken place, expressed as either an amount or a percentage. (p. 675)

Leveraging (trading on the equity) Borrowing money at a lower rate of interest than can be earned by using the borrowed money; also referred to as "trading on the equity." (p. 697)

Pro forma earnings A non-GAAP-based measure of earnings that usually excludes items that a company thinks are unusual or nonrecurring. (p. 685)

Quality of earnings An indicator of the level of full and transparent information that is provided to users of the financial statements. (p. 684)

Sustainable earnings The most likely level of earnings to be obtained in the future, determined by adjusting net earnings for irregular items. (p. 668)

Vertical analysis A technique for evaluating financial statement data that expresses each item in a financial statement as a percentage of a base amount. (p. 678)

Demonstration Problem

The events and transactions of Dever Corporation for the year ending December 31, 2004, resulted in these data:

Cost of goods sold	$2,600,000
Net sales	4,400,000
Operating expenses	1,100,000
Other expenses	9,600
Other revenues	5,600
Earnings from operations of plastics division (discontinued operations)	70,000
Gain on sale of plastics division (discontinued operations)	500,000
Loss from flood disaster (extraordinary loss)	600,000
Cumulative effect of changing from straight-line amortization to double declining-balance (increase in amortization expense)	300,000
Retained earnings, Jan. 1	3,926,000
Dividends	40,000

All items are before the applicable income tax rate of 30%.

Instructions

Prepare statements of earnings and retained earnings for the year ended December 31, 2004.

Additional
Demonstration
Problems

Solution to Demonstration Problem

DEVER CORPORATION
Statement of Earnings
Year Ended December 31, 2004

Net sales		$4,400,000
Cost of goods sold		2,600,000
Gross profit		1,800,000
Operating expenses		1,100,000
Earnings from operations		700,000
Other revenues	$ 5,600	
Other expenses	(9,600)	(4,000)
Earnings before income taxes		696,000
Income tax expense ($696,000 × 30%)		208,800
Earnings from continuing operations		487,200
Discontinued operations		
Earnings from operations of plastics division, net of $21,000 income taxes ($70,000 × 30%)	$ 49,000	
Gain on sale of plastics division, net of $150,000 income taxes ($500,000 × 30%)	350,000	399,000
Earnings before extraordinary item		886,200
Extraordinary item		
Flood loss, net of income tax savings of $180,000 ($600,000 × 30%)		(420,000)
Net earnings		$ 466,200

DEVER CORPORATION
Statement of Retained Earnings
Year Ended December 31, 2004

Retained earnings, January 1	$3,926,000
Cumulative effect on prior years of change in amortization method, net of $90,000 income tax savings ($300,000 × 30%)	(210,000)
Retained earnings, January 1, as restated	3,716,000
Add: Net earnings	466,200
	4,182,200
Less: Dividends	40,000
Retained earnings, December 31	$4,142,200

NAVIGATOR

Self-Study Questions

Answers are at the end of the chapter.

All of the self-study questions in this section employ decision tools.

(SO 1) 1. In reporting discontinued operations, a special section in the statement of earnings should show:
 (a) gains and losses on the disposal of the discontinued segment.
 (b) gains and losses from operations of the discontinued segment.
 (c) neither (a) nor (b).
 (d) both (a) and (b).

(SO 1) 2. The Dhillon Corporation has net earnings of $400,000, including an after-tax extraordinary loss of $100,000. If the income tax rate is 25% on all items, the statement of earnings should show earnings before and after extraordinary items, respectively, of:
 (a) $300,000 and $400,000.
 (b) $375,000 and $300,000.
 (c) $415,000 and $400,000.
 (d) $500,000 and $400,000.

(SO 2) 3. Comparisons of data within a company are an example of the following comparative basis:
 (a) industry averages.
 (b) intracompany comparisons.
 (c) intercompany comparisons.
 (d) both (b) and (c).

(SO 3) 4. In a horizontal analysis, each item is expressed as a percentage of the:
 (a) net earnings amount.
 (b) shareholders' equity amount.
 (c) total assets amount.
 (d) base year amount.

(SO 3) 5. Leland Corporation reported net sales of $300,000, $330,000, and $360,000 in the years 2002, 2003, and 2004, respectively. If 2002 is the base year, what is the trend percentage for 2004?
 (a) 77%   (c) 120%
 (b) 108%   (d) 130%

(SO 4) 6. In a vertical analysis, the base amount for amortization expense is generally:
 (a) net sales.
 (b) amortization expense in a previous year.
 (c) total assets.
 (d) property, plant, and equipment.

(SO 4) 7. The following schedule is a display of what type of analysis?

	Amount	Percent
Current assets	$200,000	25%
Noncurrent assets	600,000	75%
Total assets	$800,000	100%

 (a) Horizontal analysis   (c) Vertical analysis
 (b) Differential analysis (d) Ratio analysis

(SO 5) 8. Which of these is *not* a liquidity ratio?
 (a) Current ratio   (c) Inventory turnover
 (b) Asset turnover   (d) Receivables turnover

(SO 5) 9. Which of the following situations would be the most likely indicator that Wang Corporation might have a solvency problem?
 (a) Increasing debt to total assets and times interest earned ratios
 (b) Increasing debt to total assets and decreasing times interest earned ratios
 (c) Decreasing debt to total assets and times interest earned ratios
 (d) Decreasing debt to total assets and increasing times interest earned ratios

(SO 5) 10. Which of the following situations is a likely indicator of profitability?
 (a) Increasing price-earnings ratio
 (b) Increasing return on assets, asset turnover, and profit margin ratios
 (c) Decreasing return on common shareholders' equity and payout ratios
 (d) Decreasing gross profit margin and increasing profit margin

(SO 6) 11. Which situation below might indicate that a company has a low quality of earnings?
 (a) The same accounting principles are used each year.
 (b) Revenue is recognized when earned.
 (c) Recurring maintenance costs are capitalized and amortized.
 (d) The financial statements are prepared in accordance with generally accepted accounting principles.

(SO 6) 12. When completing a financial analysis of a company:
 (a) non-financial performance measures are not required.
 (b) both financial and non-financial performance measures should be reviewed.
 (c) the current state of the economy is not relevant to a financial analysis.
 (d) a company's goals and objectives are important qualitative factors, but not relevant to a financial analysis.

Questions

All of the questions in this section employ decision tools.

(SO 1) 1. Explain the concept of sustainable earnings. What relationship does this concept have to the treatment of irregular items on the statement of earnings?

(SO 1) 2. Indicate which of the following items would be reported as an extraordinary item on Thought for Food Corporation's statement of earnings:
(a) A loss from the sale of short-term investments
(b) A loss attributable to a labour strike
(c) A loss caused when the Canadian Food Inspection Agency prohibited the manufacture and sale of a product
(d) A loss of inventory from flood damage to a warehouse located on a flood plain that floods every few years
(e) A loss on the write-down of outdated inventory
(f) A loss from a foreign government's expropriation of a production facility
(g) A loss from damage to a warehouse from a minor earthquake

(SO 1) 3. Ingots Inc. reported earnings per share of $3.26 for 2004 and had no extraordinary items. In 2005, earnings per share based on earnings before extraordinary items was $2.99, and earnings per share based on net earnings was $3.49. Do you consider this trend to be favourable? Why or why not?

(SO 1) 4. Robotics Inc. has been in operation for three years. All of its manufacturing equipment, which has a useful life of 10 years, has been amortized on a straight-line basis. During the fourth year, Robotics changes to the declining-balance method of amortization for all of its equipment.
(a) Will Robotics likely record a positive or negative effect due to this change?
(b) How will this change be reported?

(SO 2) 5. (a) Distinguish among the following bases of comparison: intracompany, industry averages, and intercompany.
(b) Give the principal value of using each of the three bases of comparison.

(SO 3, 4) 6. Two popular methods of financial statement analysis are horizontal analysis and vertical analysis. Explain the difference between these two methods.

(SO 3, 4) 7. (a) If Roe Corporation had net earnings of $540,000 in 2004, and it experienced a 5% increase in net earnings for 2005, what are its net earnings for 2005?
(b) If six cents of every dollar of Roe's revenue in 2004 is net earnings, what is the dollar amount of 2004 revenue?

(SO 5) 8. What does each of the following types of ratios measure?
(a) Liquidity ratios   (c) Profitability ratios
(b) Solvency ratios

(SO 5) 9. Is a high current ratio always indicative of a company's liquidity? Name two situations in which a high current ratio might be hiding liquidity problems.

(SO 5) 10. What is the difference between the current ratio and the acid-test ratio? The cash current debt coverage ratio and the cash total debt coverage ratio?

(SO 5) 11. Bullock Ltd., a retail store, has a receivables turnover of 8.5 times. The industry average is 12.5 times. Does Bullock have a collection problem with its receivables?

(SO 5) 12. Tony Robins is puzzled. His company had a gross profit margin of 40% and profit margin of 10% in 2004. He feels that this is an indication that the company is doing well. Joan Graham, his accountant, says that more information is needed to determine the company's financial well-being. Who is correct? Why?

(SO 5) 13. Recently, the price-earnings ratio of the Bank of Nova Scotia was 11.8 times, and the price-earnings ratio of the Bank of Montreal was 14.6 times. Which company did investors favour? Explain.

(SO 5) 14. The return on assets for Windsor Corporation is 7.6%. During the same year, Windsor's return on common shareholders' equity is 12.8%. What is the explanation for the difference in the two rates?

(SO 5) 15. Do you expect the payout ratio to be high or low for a growth company?

(SO 5) 16. Which ratios should be used to help answer each of these questions?
(a) How efficient is a company in using its assets to produce sales?
(b) How near to sale is the inventory on hand?
(c) How many dollars of net earnings were earned for each dollar invested by the shareholders?
(d) How able is a company to meet interest charges as they fall due?

(SO 5) 17. Holding all other factors constant, indicate whether each of the following changes generally signals good or bad news about a company:
(a) An increase in the profit margin
(b) A decrease in inventory turnover
(c) An increase in the current ratio
(d) A decrease in earnings per share
(e) An increase in the price-earnings ratio
(f) An increase in debt to total assets
(g) A decrease in times interest earned

(SO 5) 18. Which ratio do you think should be of greatest interest in each of the following cases?
(a) A pension fund considering the purchase of 20-year bonds
(b) A bank contemplating a short-term loan
(c) A common shareholder

(SO 5) 19. What ratios are dependent on cash-based data rather than accrual-based data?

20. Give an example of how management might deliberately try to increase earnings by changing an accounting estimate.

21. Explain how earnings management can affect earnings quality.

22. Explain how the choice of one of the following accounting methods over the others raises or lowers a company's net earnings during a period of continuing inflation:
(a) Use of FIFO instead of average cost for inventory costing
(b) Use of a six-year life for machinery instead of a nine-year life
(c) Use of straight-line amortization instead of declining-balance amortization

Brief Exercises

All of the brief exercises in this section employ decision tools.

BE14-1 On June 30, 2004, Osborn Corporation discontinued a business component of its operations in Mexico. During the year, the operating loss from these operations was $300,000 before taxes. On September 1, Osborn disposed of the Mexican facility at a pretax loss of $160,000. The applicable tax rate is 35%. Show the discontinued operations section of Osborn's statement of earnings for the year ended December 31, 2004.

Prepare discontinued operations section of statement of earnings. (SO 1)

BE14-2 An inexperienced accountant for Lima Corporation showed the following in Lima's 2004 statement of earnings: Earnings before income taxes and extraordinary item, $300,000, and extraordinary loss from flood (before taxes), $60,000. The extraordinary loss and taxable earnings are both subject to a 25% tax rate. Prepare a statement of earnings in good format for the year ended November 30, 2004.

Prepare extraordinary item section of statement of earnings. (SO 1)

BE14-3 On January 1, 2005, Shirli Inc. changed from the straight-line method of amortization to the declining-balance method. The cumulative effect of the change was to increase the prior years' accumulated amortization by $40,000 and 2005 amortization expense by $8,000. Show how the change in accounting principle would be presented in the statement of retained earnings for the year ended June 30, 2005, assuming the income tax rate is 40% and opening retained earnings, $350,000.

Prepare change in accounting principles section of statement of retained earnings. (SO 1)

BE14-4 Using these selected data from the comparative balance sheet of Rioux Ltd., perform a horizontal analysis:

Prepare horizontal analysis. (SO 3)

	2004	2003
Cash	$ 150,000	$ 175,000
Accounts receivable	600,000	400,000
Inventory	780,000	600,000
Noncurrent assets	3,220,000	2,800,000

BE14-5 Horizontal analysis (trend analysis) percentages for Tilden Ltd.'s sales, cost of goods sold, and operating expenses are listed here:

Calculate change in net earnings. (SO 3)

Horizontal Analysis	2005	2004	2003
Sales	96.2%	106.8%	100.0%
Cost of goods sold	102.0%	97.0%	100.0%
Operating expenses	110.6%	95.4%	100.0%

Explain whether Tilden's net earnings increased, decreased, or remained unchanged over the three-year period.

BE14-6 Using the data presented in BE14-4 for Rioux Ltd., perform a vertical analysis.

Prepare vertical analysis. (SO 4)

BE14-7 Vertical analysis percentages for Waubons Corp.'s sales, cost of goods sold, and operating expenses are listed here:

Calculate change in net earnings. (SO 4)

Vertical Analysis	2005	2004	2003
Sales	100.0%	100.0%	100.0%
Cost of goods sold	59.2%	62.4%	64.5%
Operating expenses	25.0%	26.6%	27.5%

Did Waubons' net earnings as a percentage of sales increase, decrease, or remain unchanged over the three-year period? Provide figures that support your answer.

Calculate liquidity ratios.
(SO 4)

BE14-8 The Jean Coutu Group Inc. is one of the top three drugstore chains in Canada. Selected condensed financial data are taken from a recent interim balance sheet:

THE JEAN COUTU GROUP INC.
Balance Sheet (partial)
November 30, 2002
(in thousands)

Current assets	
Accounts receivable	$228,402
Inventories	588,178
Future income taxes	23,888
Prepaid expenses	5,215
Total current assets	$845,683
Total current liabilities	$448,606

What are its (a) working capital, (b) current ratio, and (c) acid-test ratio?

Evaluate liquidity.
(SO 5)

BE14-9 Holysh Inc. reported a current ratio of 1.5:1 in the current fiscal year, which is higher than last year's current ratio of 1.3:1. It also reported a receivables turnover of 8 times, which is less than last year's receivables turnover of 12 times. Is Holysh's liquidity improving or deteriorating? Explain.

Evaluate collection of accounts receivable.
(SO 5)

BE14-10 The following data are taken from the quarterly report of Maple Leaf Foods Inc.:

MAPLE LEAF FOODS INC.
September 30
(in thousands)

	2002	2001	2000
Accounts receivable	$ 263,135	$ 262,682	$ 241,527
Sales (assume on account)*	1,268,710	1,197,874	1,063,189

*Assume terms for all sales are n/60.

Calculate, for 2002 and 2001, the (a) receivables turnover and (b) average collection period. What conclusions about the management of accounts receivable can be drawn from these data?

Evaluate management of inventory.
(SO 5)

BE14-11 The following data were taken from the statement of earnings of Shumway Ltd.:

	2004	2003
Sales revenue	$6,420,000	$6,240,000
Cost of goods sold	4,580,000	4,538,000
Beginning inventory	960,000	837,000
Ending inventory	1,020,000	960,000

For each year, calculate the (a) inventory turnover and (b) days in inventory. What conclusions concerning the management of the inventory can be drawn from these data?

Calculate profitability ratios.
(SO 5)

BE14-12 Staples, Inc. is a large supplier of office products. The company had net earnings of $446.1 million and net revenue of $11,596.1 million for the year ended January 31, 2003. Its total assets were $4,093.0 million at the beginning of the year and $5,721.4 million at the end of the year. What are Staples, Inc.'s (a) asset turnover, (b) return on assets, and (c) profit margin?

Calculate profitability ratios.
(SO 5)

BE14-13 Haymark Products Corporation has shareholders' equity of $400,000 and net earnings of $56,000. It has a payout ratio of 20% and a return on assets of 16%. How much did Haymark Products pay in cash dividends, and what were its average assets?

Calculate cash-based liquidity and solvency ratios.
(SO 5)

BE14-14 The Topps Company, Inc. is a trading-card and bubble gum company, whose products are sold in more than 50 countries. Selected data taken from the 2003 financial statements are as follows (in U.S. thousands):

Net sales	$290,079
Current liabilities, March 3, 2002	47,183
Current liabilities, March 1, 2003	42,259
Net cash provided by operating activities	6,200
Total liabilities, March 3, 2002	63,896
Total liabilities, March 1, 2003	64,860
Capital expenditures	3,807

Calculate these ratios at March 1, 2003: (a) cash current debt coverage, (b) cash total debt coverage, and (c) free cash flow.

BE14-15 The management of Fujen Corporation is thinking about increasing the estimated useful life of its equipment when calculating straight-line amortization. Would this change in estimate increase, decrease, or have no effect on the following ratios: (a) profit margin, (b) asset turnover, and (c) debt to total assets?

Evaluate impact of change in estimate on ratios.
(SO 6)

Exercises

⚊ All of the exercises in this section employ decision tools.

E14-1 Davis Ltd. has earnings from continuing operations of $270,000 for the year ended December 31, 2004. It also has the following items (before considering income taxes): (1) an extraordinary fire loss of $60,000, (2) a gain of $40,000 from the discontinuance of a division, which includes a $110,000 gain from the operation of the division and a $70,000 loss on its disposal, and (3) a cumulative change in accounting principle that resulted in a $30,000 increase in the prior years' amortization. Assume all items are subject to a 40% income tax rate.

Prepare irregular items portion of statement of earnings.
(SO 1)

Instructions
(a) Prepare Davis's statement of earnings for the year ended December 31, 2004, beginning with "Earnings from continuing operations."
(b) Indicate the statement presentation of any items not included in (a).

E14-2 The *Financial Post* routinely publishes summaries of quarterly and annual earnings reports in a feature called "Earnings Summary." A typical report looks like the following one for Mazarin Inc.:

Evaluate effects of irregular items.
(SO 1, 5)

MAZARIN INC. C$ (MAZ/TSX)

	Current	Yr. Ago	% chg
		Dec. 31–4th Q	
Revenue (000s)	9,349	11,029	–15
Net income (000s)	(8,980)	107	–8,493
EPS	(0.20)	0.00	
		12 mos.	
Revenue (000s)	41,408	29,113	42
Net income (000s)	(10,317)	1,111	–1,029
EPS	(0.23)	0.02	

Net losses for the quarter and the year ended December 31, 2002, include a loss from discontinued operations of $6.5 million for the quarter and $8.1 million for the year.

The letters in parentheses following the company name indicate the company's share symbol and the exchange on which Mazarin Inc.'s shares are traded—in this case, the Toronto Stock Exchange. The first section reports results for the fourth quarter ended December 31, 2002, compared to the fourth quarter ended December 31, 2001. The second section reports results for the twelve months to date, compared to the twelve months ended a year before, December 31, 2001.

Instructions

(a) Why did the *Financial Post* list the discontinued operations separately?

(b) By what percentage did Mazarin's revenue and net income improve (or deteriorate) in the quarter ended December 31, 2002, compared to the previous year? Show how the percentage changes were calculated.

(c) As an investor, what numbers should you use to determine Mazarin's profit margin? Calculate the profit margin ratio for 2002 and 2001, using the numbers that you consider most useful. Explain your decision.

(d) What was the average number of shares in 2002? Did this number change from December 31, 2001, to December 31, 2002?

Prepare horizontal analysis.
(SO 3)

E14-3 Here is financial information for Merchandise.Com Inc.:

	2004	2003
Current assets	$120,000	$ 80,000
Noncurrent assets	400,000	350,000
Current liabilities	91,000	70,000
Long-term liabilities	144,000	95,000
Common shares	150,000	115,000
Retained earnings	135,000	150,000

Instructions

Prepare a schedule showing a horizontal analysis for 2004 using 2003 as the base year.

Prepare vertical analysis.
(SO 4)

E14-4 Operating data for Fleetwood Corporation are presented here:

	2004	2003
Sales	$800,000	$600,000
Cost of goods sold	500,000	390,000
Operating expenses	200,000	156,000
Income tax expense	25,000	13,500
Net earnings	$ 75,000	$ 40,500

Instructions

Prepare a schedule showing a vertical analysis for 2004 and 2003.

Prepare horizontal and vertical analyses of statement of earnings.
(SO 3)

E14-5 Here are the comparative statements of earnings of Olympic Corporation:

OLYMPIC CORPORATION
Statement of Earnings
Year Ended December 31

	2004	2003
Net sales	$550,000	$550,000
Cost of goods sold	440,000	450,000
Gross profit	110,000	100,000
Operating expenses	58,000	55,000
Earnings before income tax	52,000	45,000
Income tax	20,800	18,000
Net earnings	$ 31,200	$ 27,000

Instructions

(a) Prepare a horizontal analysis of the statement of earnings data for Olympic Corporation using 2003 as a base.

(b) Prepare a vertical analysis of the statement of earnings data for Olympic Corporation for both years.

Prepare horizontal and vertical analyses of balance sheet.
(SO 3, 4)

E14-6 The condensed comparative balance sheets of the Mountain Equipment Co-operative, an outdoor equipment supplier, are presented here:

MOUNTAIN EQUIPMENT CO-OPERATIVE
Balance Sheet
December 31
(in thousands)

	2002	2001
Assets		
Current assets	$40,927	$38,729
Deferred store pre-opening costs	417	0
Property, plant, and equipment	38,197	39,015
Total assets	$79,541	$77,744
Liabilities and Members' Equity		
Current liabilities	$23,560	$25,110
Long-term liabilities	348	399
Total liabilities	23,908	25,509
Members' equity	55,633	52,235
Total liabilities and members' equity	$79,541	$77,744

Instructions

(a) Prepare a horizontal analysis of the balance sheet data for Mountain Equipment Co-op using 2001 as a base.
(b) Prepare a vertical analysis of the balance sheet data for Mountain Equipment Co-op for 2002 and 2001, using total assets as your base.
(c) Comment on any significant changes from 2001 to 2002.

E14-7   Carleton University had the following selected financial statement data as at April 30, for 2002 and 2001 (in thousands).

Calculate liquidity ratios and comment.
(SO 5)

	2002	2001
Current assets		
Cash and cash equivalents	$62,915	$58,272
Accounts receivable	15,182	15,444
Student loans receivable	95	75
Prepaid expenses	1,083	1,214
Total current assets	79,275	75,005
Total current liabilities	80,186	70,219
Revenues	271,356	243,963
Cash provided by operating activities	8,180	17,196

Instructions

(a) Calculate Carleton's current ratio, acid-test ratio, cash current debt coverage, receivables turnover, and average collection period for 2002. Use total revenues as a substitute for credit sales in the receivables turnover ratio.
(b) Comment on Carleton's liquidity.

E14-8   Firpo Incorporated had the following transactions involving current assets and current liabilities during February 2005:

Determine effect of transactions on current and acid-test ratios.
(SO 5)

Feb. 3 Collected accounts receivable of $15,000.
       7 Purchased equipment for $25,000 cash.
      11 Paid $3,000 for a 12-month insurance policy.
      14 Paid accounts payable of $14,000.
      18 Paid cash dividends of $6,000.
      24 Sold merchandise on account for $4,500. The cost of the merchandise sold was $2,700.

Additional information:

1. As at February 1, 2005, current assets were $130,000 and current liabilities were $40,000.
2. As at February 1, 2005, current assets included $15,000 of inventory and $5,000 of prepaid expenses.

Instructions

(a) Calculate the current ratio as at the beginning of the month and after each transaction.

(b) Calculate the acid-test ratio as at the beginning of the month and after each transaction.

Evaluate liquidity.
(SO 5)

E14-9 The following selected ratios are available for Pampered Pets Inc. for the most recent three years:

Ratio	2004	2003	2002
Current ratio	2.6:1	1.4:1	2.1:1
Acid-test ratio	0.8:1	1.1:1	1.2:1
Receivables turnover	6.7 times	7.4 times	8.2 times
Inventory turnover	7.5 times	8.7 times	9.9 times

Instructions

(a) Has the company's collection of its receivables improved or deteriorated over the last three years?

(b) Is the company selling its inventory faster or slower than in past years?

(c) Overall, has the company's liquidity improved or deteriorated over the last three years? Explain.

Calculate ratios.
(SO 5)

E14-10   Georgette Ltd. has these comparative balance sheet data:

GEORGETTE LTD.
Balance Sheet
December 31

	2004	2003
Cash	$ 20,000	$ 30,000
Receivables (net)	65,000	60,000
Inventories	60,000	50,000
Property, plant, and equipment (net)	200,000	180,000
	$345,000	$320,000
Accounts payable	$ 50,000	$ 60,000
Mortgage payable	100,000	100,000
Common shares	140,000	120,000
Retained earnings	55,000	40,000
	$345,000	$320,000

Additional information for 2004:

1. Net earnings were $15,000.
2. Sales on account were $420,000. Sales returns and allowances amounted to $20,000.
3. The allowance for doubtful accounts was $10,000 on December 31, 2004, and $8,000 on December 31, 2003.
4. Cost of goods sold was $198,000.
5. Net cash provided by operating activities was $41,000.

Instructions

Calculate the following ratios at December 31, 2004:

(a) Current

(b) Acid-test

(c) Receivables turnover

(d) Average collection period

(e) Inventory turnover

(f) Days in inventory

(g) Cash current debt coverage

(h) Cash total debt coverage

(i) Debt to total assets

(j) Return on common shareholders' equity

Calculate ratios.
(SO 5)

E14-11   Selected comparative statement data of Shoppers Drug Mart Corporation are presented here (in millions):

	2002	2001
Revenue	$4019.4	$3,634.6
Cost of goods sold and other operating expenses	3,518.3	3,217.5
Interest expense	79.0	209.1
Income tax expense	135.7	74.5
Net earnings	208.6	7.2
Total assets	3,131.1	3,043.3
Total common shareholders' equity	1,419.8	1,418.6
Cash provided by operating activities	315.4	243.7
Number of common shares	209.6	183.3

Instructions

Calculate the following ratios for 2002:

(a) Profit margin
(b) Asset turnover
(c) Return on assets

(d) Return on common shareholders' equity
(e) Times interest earned
(f) Earnings per share

E14-12   Here is the statement of earnings for LeFay, Inc:

Calculate ratios.
(SO 5)

LEFAY, INC.
Statement of Earnings
Year Ended December 31, 2004

Sales	$425,000
Cost of goods sold	230,000
Gross profit	195,000
Expenses (including $35,000 of amortization, $15,000 of interest, and $36,000 of income taxes)	150,000
Net earnings	$ 45,000

Additional information:
  1. There were 30,000 common shares.
  2. The market price of LeFay, Inc. shares was $15 in 2004.
  3. Cash dividends of $21,000 were paid, $5,000 of which went to preferred shareholders.

Instructions

Calculate the following measures for 2004:

(a) Earnings per share
(b) Price-earnings ratio
(c) Payout ratio

(d) Times interest earned
(e) Gross profit margin
(f) Profit margin

E14-13   Mahat Corporation started the year with the following ratios:

Determine effect of transactions on ratios.
(SO 5)

Current ratio	1.5:1	Debt to total assets	30%
Cash current debt coverage	0.4 times	Return on assets	20%

Instructions

Determine the effect each of the following transactions during the year had on these ratios. Indicate whether the transaction causes each ratio to improve (I) or deteriorate (D), or if the transaction has no effect (NE).

(a) Mahat purchased merchandise inventory on account from a supplier. Mahat uses a perpetual inventory system.
(b) Mahat paid cash on an account payable.
(c) Mahat sold merchandise on account to a customer.
(d) The customer paid its account.
(e) Mahat purchased equipment, issuing a long-term note payable in payment.
(f) Mahat paid interest expense and a portion of the principal on the note payable.

Calculate amounts from ratios.
(SO 5)

E14-14 Shaker Corporation experienced a fire on December 31, 2004, in which its financial records were partially destroyed. It has been able to salvage some of the records and has ascertained the following December 31 balances:

	2004	2003
Cash	$ 30,000	$ 10,000
Receivables (gross)	72,500	126,000
Inventory	200,000	180,000
Accounts payable	50,000	10,000
Notes payable	30,000	20,000
Common shares	400,000	400,000
Retained earnings	113,500	101,000

Additional information:

1. The inventory turnover is 3.6 times.
2. The return on common shareholders' equity is 19%.
3. The receivables turnover is 9.4 times.
4. The return on assets is 14%.
5. Total assets at December 31, 2003, were $605,000.

Instructions

Calculate the following for Shaker Corporation:

(a) Cost of goods sold for 2004
(b) Net sales for 2004
(c) Net earnings for 2004
(d) Total assets at December 31, 2004

Discuss quality of earnings.
(SO 6)

E14-15 General Electric Company has met analysts' expectations nearly every quarter in the last ten years, missing only once by a penny in the fourth quarter of 1997. Year after year, its earnings have consistently been about 10% higher than the previous year. Instead of being lauded for "making the numbers," GE's chief executive officer, Jeffrey Immelt, has been put on the defensive and has had to tell interviewer after interviewer that no, he has not managed earnings.

Instructions

(a) Explain why GE's performance has raised questions about its quality of earnings?
(b) Why are users concerned that GE "makes its numbers" so consistently?

Problems: Set A

⚒ All of the problems in this section employ decision tools.

Perform horizontal analysis and comment.
(SO 3)

P14-1A Over the past few years, the airline industry has faced a number of significant challenges. The economic slowdown of 2001, the terrorist attacks of September 11, 2001, the growth of low-cost competition, high oil prices, and the war in Iraq have all contributed to the decline in fortunes that Air Canada and several other airlines face today. This decline continued through 2003, and on April 1, Air Canada filed for bankruptcy protection.

The following selected financial information (in millions) for the most recent five-year period is available for Air Canada:

	2002	2001	2000	1999	1998
Operating revenues	$ 9,826	$ 9,611	$9,296	$6,443	$5,898
Operating expenses	10,018	10,342	9,035	6,066	5,803
Nonrecurring expenses (revenues)	31	(21)	178	(38)	(1)
Interest expense	221	275	210	154	174
Income tax expense (recovery)	384	330	(45)	121	(34)
Net earnings (loss)	$ (828)	$(1,315)	$ (82)	$ 140	$ (44)

	2002	2001	2000	1999	1998
Total current assets	$ 1,771	$ 2,235	$2,229	$1,258	$1,092
Total assets	7,416	8,744	9,732	6,705	6,422
Current liabilities	2,592	2,869	3,560	1,405	1,279
Total liabilities	9,704	10,204	9,416	5,980	4,965
Share capital	992	992	992	990	1,305
Retained earnings (deficit)	(3,280)	(2,452)	(676)	(265)	152

Instructions

(a) Prepare a horizontal analysis for Air Canada.

(b) What components found in Air Canada's balance sheet and statement of earnings have been the primary drivers of the airline's decline?

(c) How has Air Canada been primarily financing its operations?

P14-2A Here are comparative statement data at December 31 for Breau Ltd. and Shields Ltd., two competitors:

Prepare vertical analyses, calculate selected ratios, and comment.
(SO 4, 5)

	Breau Ltd.		Shields Ltd.	
	2004	2003	2004	2003
Net sales	$350,000		$1,400,000	
Cost of goods sold	180,000		720,000	
Operating expenses	51,000		272,000	
Interest expense	3,000		10,000	
Income tax expense	29,000		100,000	
Current assets	130,000	$110,000	700,000	$650,000
Noncurrent assets	405,000	270,000	1,000,000	750,000
Current liabilities	60,000	52,000	250,000	275,000
Long-term liabilities	50,000	68,000	200,000	150,000
Common shares	288,000	210,000	677,000	700,000
Retained earnings	137,000	50,000	573,000	275,000

Instructions

(a) Prepare a vertical analysis of the 2004 statement of earnings data for Breau and Shields.

(b) Calculate the return on assets and the return on common shareholders' equity ratios for both companies.

(c) Comment on the relative profitability of the companies.

P14-3A The comparative statements of Rosen Inc. are presented here:

Calculate ratios.
(SO 5)

ROSEN INC.
Statement of Earnings
Year Ended December 31

	2004	2003
Net sales	$780,000	$624,000
Cost of goods sold	440,000	405,600
Gross profit	340,000	218,400
Operating expenses	143,880	149,760
Earnings from operations	196,120	68,640
Interest expense	9,920	7,200
Earnings before income taxes	186,200	61,440
Income tax expense	46,550	24,000
Net earnings	$139,650	$ 37,440

ROSEN INC.
Balance Sheet
December 31

	2004	2003
Assets		
Current assets		
Cash	$ 23,100	$ 21,600
Short-term investments	34,800	33,000
Accounts receivable (net of allowance for doubtful accounts of $3,200 and $2,800, respectively)	106,200	93,800
Inventory	122,400	64,000
Total current assets	286,500	212,400
Property, plant, and equipment	465,300	459,600
Total assets	$751,800	$672,000
Liabilities and Shareholders' Equity		
Current liabilities		
Accounts payable	$200,850	$132,000
Income taxes payable	15,300	24,000
Total current liabilities	216,150	156,000
Bonds payable	0	120,000
Total liabilities	216,150	276,000
Shareholders' equity		
Common shares	150,000	150,000
Retained earnings	385,650	246,000
Total shareholders' equity	535,650	396,000
Total liabilities and shareholders' equity	$751,800	$672,000

Additional information:
1. All sales were on account.
2. Cash provided by operating activities was $36,000.
3. There are 15,000 common shares.

Instructions

Calculate the following ratios for 2004:

(a) Current
(b) Acid-test
(c) Receivables turnover
(d) Average collection period
(e) Inventory turnover
(f) Days in inventory
(g) Cash current debt coverage
(h) Debt to total assets

(i) Times interest earned
(j) Cash total debt coverage
(k) Gross profit margin
(l) Profit margin
(m) Return on assets
(n) Asset turnover
(o) Return on common shareholders' equity
(p) Earnings per share

Calculate ratios and comment.
(SO 5)

P14-4A Here are condensed balance sheets and statement of earnings data for Colinas Corporation:

COLINAS CORPORATION
Balance Sheet
December 31

	2004	2003	2002
Cash	$ 40,000	$ 24,000	$ 20,000
Accounts receivable	73,000	45,000	48,000
Other current assets	80,000	75,000	62,000
Investments	90,000	70,000	50,000
Property, plant, and equipment	650,000	400,000	360,000
	$933,000	$614,000	$540,000

Current liabilities	$ 98,000	$ 75,000	$ 70,000
Long-term liabilities	250,000	75,000	65,000
Common shares	400,000	340,000	300,000
Retained earnings	185,000	124,000	105,000
	$933,000	$614,000	$540,000

COLINAS CORPORATION
Statement of Earnings
Year Ended December 31

	2004	2003
Sales	$800,000	$750,000
Less: Sales returns and allowances	40,000	50,000
Net sales	760,000	700,000
Cost of goods sold	420,000	400,000
Gross profit	340,000	300,000
Operating expenses	194,000	237,000
Earnings before income taxes	146,000	63,000
Income tax expense	65,700	28,350
Net earnings	$ 80,300	$ 34,650

Additional information:

1. The market price of Colinas' common shares was $10 and $8 for 2003 and 2004, respectively.
2. All dividends were paid in cash. (*Hint:* Analyse retained earnings to determine dividends.)
3. On July 1, 2003, 4,000 common shares were issued, and on July 1, 2004, 7,500 shares were issued. At the end of 2004, 40,000 shares have been issued in total.

Instructions

(a) Calculate the following ratios for 2003 and 2004:
   1. Profit margin   5. Price-earnings
   2. Gross profit margin   6. Payout
   3. Asset turnover   7. Debt to total assets
   4. Earnings per share   8. Current
(b) Based on the ratios calculated, briefly discuss the improvement or lack of improvement in the financial position and operating results of Colinas Corporation from 2003 to 2004.

P14-5A   Financial information for Star Track Ltd. is presented here:

Calculate ratios.
(SO 5)

STAR TRACK LTD.
Balance Sheet
December 31

	2004	2003
Assets		
Cash and cash equivalents	$ 130,000	$ 92,000
Receivables (net of allowance for doubtful accounts of $5,000 and $4,000, for 2004 and 2003, respectively)	100,000	87,000
Inventories	440,000	300,000
Prepaid expenses	25,000	31,000
Land, building, and equipment	645,000	475,000
Total assets	$1,340,000	$985,000
Liabilities and Shareholders' Equity		
Notes payable	$ 125,000	$ 25,000
Accounts payable	160,000	90,000
Accrued liabilities	48,750	50,000
Bonds payable, due 2008	200,000	100,000
Common shares (100,000 shares)	500,000	500,000
Retained earnings	306,250	220,000
Total liabilities and shareholders' equity	$1,340,000	$985,000

STAR TRACK LTD.
Statement of Earnings
Year Ended December 31

	2004	2003
Sales	$1,000,000	$940,000
Cost of goods sold	650,000	635,000
Gross profit	350,000	305,000
Operating expenses	235,000	215,000
Earnings before income taxes	115,000	90,000
Income tax expense	28,750	22,500
Net earnings	$ 86,250	$ 67,500

Additional information:

1. Inventory at the beginning of 2003 was $350,000.
2. Receivables at the beginning of 2003 were $80,000, net of an allowance for doubtful accounts of $3,000.
3. Total assets at the beginning of 2003 were $1,175,000.
4. Current liabilities at the beginning of 2003 were $300,000.
5. Total shareholders' equity at the beginning of 2003 was $740,000.
6. All sales were on account.
7. Cash provided by operating activities was $80,000 in 2004, and $65,000 in 2003.

Instructions

(a) Indicate, by using ratios, the change in Star Track's liquidity, profitability, and solvency from 2003 to 2004. (*Note:* Not all ratios can be calculated.)

(b) Given below are three independent situations and a ratio that may be affected. For each situation, calculate the affected ratio (1) as at December 31, 2004, and (2) as at December 31, 2005. Net earnings for 2005 were $125,000. Total assets on December 31, 2005, were $1,450,000.

Situation	Ratio
1. On July 1, 2005, 6,500 common shares were sold.	Earnings per share
2. All of the notes payable were paid in 2005.	Debt to total assets
3. The market price of common shares on December 31, 2005, was $6.25. The market price on December 31, 2004, was $5.	Price-earnings

Calculate ratios, and compare liquidity, profitability, and solvency for two companies.
(SO 5)

P14-6A Inco Limited and Falconbridge Limited are two of the world's leading producers of nickel and other metals and minerals. Selected financial data of these two close competitors are presented here (in U.S. and CDN millions, respectively) for a recent year:

	Inco	Falconbridge
	Statement of Earnings	
Net sales	$ 2,161	$2,394
Cost of sales and operating expenses	1,377	1,733
Selling, general, and administrative expenses	136	136
Interest expense	50	88
Other expenses	2,718	389
Earnings (loss) before income taxes	(2,120)	48
Income and mining tax recovery	639	25
Net earnings (loss)	$(1,481)	$ 73
Earnings (loss) per share	$ (8.27)	$ 0.34

	Inco	Falconbridge
	Balance Sheet	
Current assets		
Cash and cash equivalents	$1,087	$ 260
Accounts receivable	251	342
Inventories	576	448
Other current assets	73	0
Total current assets	1,987	1,050
Property, plant, and equipment	6,345	3,955
Other assets	208	199
Total assets	$8,540	$5,204
Current liabilities	$ 930	$ 424
Long-term liabilities	3,805	2,494
Total liabilities	4,735	2,918
Shareholders' equity	3,805	2,286
Total liabilities and shareholders' equity	$8,540	$5,204
	Other Data	
Average accounts receivable	$ 264	$ 301
Average inventories	538	454
Average total assets	9,064	5,136
Average total shareholders' equity	4,550	2,283
Cash provided by operating activities	599	341
Dividends	26	83

Instructions

(a) Calculate liquidity, solvency, and profitability ratios, as appropriate, for each company.

(b) Compare Inco's liquidity, solvency, and profitability to those of Falconbridge and of the industry. Selected industry averages are available for the following ratios

Current ratio	1.2:1	Profit margin	1.6%
Acid-test ratio	0.7:1	Return on assets	0.8%
Receivables turnover	8.3 times	Earnings per share	$0.13
Inventory turnover	4.9 times	Return on common	
Debt to total assets	40.1%	shareholders' equity	2.3%
Times interest earned	2.0 times	Asset turnover	0.6 times

P14-7A You are presented with the following comparative financial information for two Canadian airline companies whose identities have been disguised. One of these companies is in financial trouble and was acquired by another airline company (Company C).

Calculate ratios and compare two companies, one on the verge of bankruptcy.
(SO 5)

Balance Sheet
(in millions)

	Company A		Company B	
	Current Year	Prior Year	Current Year	Prior Year
Assets				
Cash and cash equivalents	$ 302.4	$ 193.9	$ 50.7	$ 13.5
Accounts receivable	267.7	221.9	5.2	5.2
Other current assets	176.3	176.9	4.6	4.0
Total current assets	746.4	592.7	60.5	22.7
Noncurrent assets	1,352.2	1,318.5	126.1	85.5
Total assets	$2,098.6	$1,911.2	$186.6	$108.2
Liabilities and Shareholders' Equity				
Total current liabilities	$ 953.6	$ 877.1	$ 49.9	$ 29.0
Total long-term liabilities	1,304.8	1,057.3	42.2	29.9
Total liabilities	2,258.4	1,934.4	92.1	58.9
Total shareholders' equity (deficit)	(159.8)	(23.2)	94.5	49.3
Total liabilities and shareholders' equity	$2,098.6	$1,911.2	$186.6	$108.2

Statement of Earnings
(in millions)

	Company A		Company B	
	Current Year	Prior Year	Current Year	Prior Year
Operating revenues (assume all on credit)	$3,171.3	$3,077.5	$203.6	$125.4
Operating expenses	3,193.1	2,980.4	173.1	112.3
Operating earnings (loss)	(21.8)	97.1	30.5	13.1
Other expenses	113.5	89.9	1.2	0.7
Earnings (loss) before income taxes	(135.3)	7.2	29.3	12.4
Income tax expense	2.3	1.8	13.5	5.9
Net earnings (loss)	$ (137.6)	$ 5.4	$ 15.8	$ 6.5

Instructions

(a) Prepare each of the following ratios for both Company A and Company B for the current year:

1. Current ratio
2. Acid-test ratio
3. Receivables turnover
4. Average collection period

5. Debt to total assets
6. Return on assets
7. Profit margin
8. Asset turnover

(b) Which company do you think is in financial trouble? Provide support for your conclusion.

Analyse ratios.
(SO 5)

P14-8A The following ratios are available for tool makers The Black & Decker Corporation and Snap-on Incorporated for fiscal 2002:

Ratio	Black & Decker	Snap-on	Industry
Liquidity			
Current ratio	1.5:1	1.9:1	2.1:1
Acid test ratio	0.9:1	1.0:1	1.2:1
Receivables turnover	6.1 times	3.6 times	5.1 times
Inventory turnover	3.8 times	2.9 times	3.1 times
Solvency			
Debt to total assets	67.5%	30.1%	35.9%
Times interest earned	4.6 times	6.6 times	6.1 times
Profitability			
Gross profit margin	37.5%	48.2%	37.9%
Profit margin	5.2%	4.9%	4.8%
Return on common shareholders' equity	38.3%	12.4%	12.0%
Return on assets	5.6%	5.2%	4.8%
Asset turnover	1.1 times	1.1 times	1.0 times
Payout ratio	16.9%	55.1%	34.5%
Earnings per share	$2.84	$1.76	$1.39
Price-earnings ratio	15.1 times	16.0 times	n/a

Instructions

(a) Which company is more liquid? Explain.
(b) Which company is more solvent? Explain.
(c) Which company is more profitable? Explain.
(d) Which company do investors favour? Is your answer consistent with your findings in (c)?

P14-9A Presented here are an incomplete statement of earnings and balance sheet for Vienna Corporation:

Calculate missing information using ratios.
(SO 5)

VIENNA CORPORATION
Statement of Earnings
Year ended December 31, 2004

Sales	$11,000,000
Cost of goods sold	(a)
Gross profit	(b)
Operating expenses	1,665,000
Earnings from operations	(c)
Interest expense	(d)
Earnings before income taxes	(e)
Income tax expense	560,000
Net earnings	$ (f)

VIENNA CORPORATION
Balance Sheet
December 31, 2004

Assets	
Current assets	
Cash	$ (g)
Accounts receivable	(h)
Inventory	(i)
Total current assets	(j)
Property, plant, and equipment	4,620,000
Total assets	$ (k)
Liabilities	
Current liabilities	$ (l)
Long-term liabilities	(m)
Total liabilities	(n)
Shareholders' Equity	
Common shares	3,000,000
Retained earnings	400,000
Total shareholders' equity	3,400,000
Total liabilities and shareholders' equity	$ (o)

Additional information:
1. The receivables turnover for 2004 is 10 times.
2. All sales are on account.
3. The gross profit margin is 36%.
4. The profit margin for 2004 is 14.5%.
5. The return on assets is 22%.
6. The current ratio on December 31, 2004, is 3:1.
7. The inventory turnover for 2004 is 8 times.

Instructions

Calculate the missing information using the ratios. Use ending balances instead of average balances where averages are required for ratio calculations. Show your calculations. (*Hint:* Start with one ratio and derive as much information as possible from it before trying another ratio. You will not be able to calculate the missing amounts in the same sequence as they are presented above.)

Determine effect of transactions on ratios.
(SO 5)

P14-10A The management of Konotopsky Venture Inc. would like to better understand the impact of the following transactions on specific ratios:

Transaction	Ratio
(a) Issued bonds payable at face value to finance an expansion.	Cash total debt coverage
(b) Paid interest on bonds.	Times interest earned
(c) Reacquired common shares.	Return on common shareholders' equity
(d) Distributed a stock dividend.	Payout ratio; return on common shareholders' equity
(e) Purchased inventory on credit (perpetual inventory system).	Current ratio
(f) Sold inventory for cash (perpetual inventory system).	Inventory turnover; gross profit margin
(g) Collected a previously written off account receivable.	Receivables turnover
(h) Decreased the estimated useful life of a building.	Return on assets

Instructions

Indicate whether each of the above transactions will increase (I), decrease (D), or have no effect (NE) on the ratio(s) listed next to the transaction. Explain your reasoning.

Analyse ratios.
(SO 5, 6)

P14-11A Selected ratios for the current year for two companies operating in the beverage industry follow, in alphabetical order. Industry ratios, where available, have also been included ("n/a" indicates that the ratio was not available).

Ratio	Refresh Corp.	Taste.Com	Industry
Acid-test ratio	0.4:1	0.7:1	0.4:1
Asset turnover	1.0 times	1.0 times	0.9 times
Cash total debt coverage	32%	20%	n/a
Current ratio	0.6:1	1.1:1	0.8:1
Debt to total assets	56%	72%	n/a
Earnings per share	$0.98	$1.37	$1.08
Gross profit margin	73.8%	60.0%	57.7%
Inventory turnover	5.8 times	9.9 times	8.3 times
Price-earnings	50.3 times	24.3 times	32.2 times
Profit margin	12.3%	11.2%	8.1%
Receivables turnover	11.4 times	9.8 times	9.3 times
Return on assets	11.2%	9.3%	7.2%
Return on common shareholders' equity	25.7%	29.8%	26.4%
Times interest earned	15.3 times	7.9 times	5.3 times

Instructions

Answer the following questions, citing relevant ratios to justify your answer:
(a) Which company appears to be the most liquid?
(b) As a potential investor, are you concerned with the debt levels of either company?
(c) Which company is the most profitable?
(d) One should always be cautious in interpreting ratios. Identify any *two* facts that you should keep in mind as you interpret the ratios in this question.

Assess effect of alternative accounting principles on ratios.
(SO 5, 6)

P14-12A The president of Dot.Com is debating the selection of generally accepted accounting principles. She would like you to advise her about the impact that selected accounting principles will have on the various company ratios listed in the following table:

Accounting Principle	Current ratio (1.5:1)	Gross profit margin (40%)	Earnings per share ($1.50)	Debt to total assets (25%)	Times interest earned (5×)	Return on total assets (10%)
(a) It is a period of deflation and the president would like to use the average inventory cost flow assumption instead of FIFO.						
(b) The company is considering using the straight-line method of amortization, instead of the declining-balance method. This will result in a lower amortization expense.						
(c) The company is leasing equipment and is setting up the lease as an operating lease. Its rent expense under an operating lease will be lower than interest and amortization expenses under a capital lease.						

Instructions

Indicate whether the above policy choices will increase (I), decrease (D), or have no effect (NE) on each of the ratios presented.

Problems: Set B

All of the problems in this section employ decision tools.

P14-1B Nortel Networks Corporation experienced rapid growth in the 1990s, as did most technology-based companies, followed by rapid declines in the 2000s after the market collapsed. The following selected information is available for the three most recent years of this maker of telecommunication products:

Prepare horizontal analysis and comment.
(SO 3)

NORTEL NETWORKS CORPORATION
Statement of Operations
Year Ended December 31
(in U.S. millions)

	2002	2001	2000
Revenues	$10,560	$ 17,511	$27,948
Cost of revenues	6,953	14,167	15,114
Gross profit	3,607	3,344	12,834
Operating expenses	5,184	27,353	9,435
Research and development expense	2,230	3,239	5,048
Interest expense	256	311	169
Net loss from continuing operations before income taxes	(4,063)	(27,559)	(1,818)
Income tax recovery (expense)	478	3,252	(1,177)
Net loss from continuing operations	(3,585)	(24,307)	(2,995)
Net loss from discontinued operations	0	(2,995)	(475)
Net loss	$(3,585)	$(27,302)	$(3,470)
Loss per share	$(0.93)	$(7.62)	$(1.01)
Market price per share	$2.52	$11.90	$48.25

NORTEL NETWORKS CORPORATION
Balance Sheet (partial)
December 31
(in U.S. millions)

	2002	2001	2000
Current assets of discontinued operations	$ 223	$ 708	$ 1,522
Total current assets	8,476	11,762	16,530
Total assets	15,971	21,137	42,180
Current liabilities	6,982	9,457	9,058
Total liabilities	14,011	16,313	13,071
Common shares	35,696	34,975	31,835
Deficit	33,736	30,151	2,726

Instructions

(a) Prepare a horizontal analysis for Nortel.
(b) What components found in Nortel's balance sheet and statement of earnings (operations) have been the primary drivers of the company's deterioration?
(c) How has Nortel been primarily financing its operations?

Prepare vertical analysis, calculate selected ratios, and comment.
(SO 4, 5)

P14-2B Here are comparative statement data at December 31 for Chen Corporation and Couric Ltd., two competitors:

	Chen Corporation		Couric Ltd.	
	2004	2003	2004	2003
Net sales	$1,849,035		$539,038	
Cost of goods sold	1,080,490		338,006	
Operating expenses	502,275		79,000	
Interest expense	6,800		1,252	
Income tax expense	103,800		48,300	
Current assets	325,975	$312,410	83,336	$ 79,467
Noncurrent assets	651,115	500,000	214,010	125,812
Current liabilities	66,325	75,815	35,348	30,281
Long-term liabilities	108,500	90,000	29,620	25,000
Common shares	500,000	500,000	120,000	120,000
Retained earnings	302,265	146,595	112,478	29,998

Instructions

(a) Prepare a vertical analysis of the 2004 statement of earnings data for Chen and Couric.
(b) Calculate the 2004 return on assets and the return on common shareholders' equity ratios for both companies.
(c) Comment on the relative profitability of the companies.

Calculate ratios.
(SO 5)

P14-3B The comparative statements of Johnson Ltd. are presented here:

JOHNSON LTD.
Statement of Earnings
Year Ended December 31

	2004	2003
Net sales	$1,918,500	$1,750,500
Cost of goods sold	1,005,500	996,000
Gross profit	913,000	754,500
Operating expenses	506,000	479,000
Earnings from operations	407,000	275,500
Interest expense	28,000	19,000
Earnings before income taxes	379,000	256,500
Income tax expense	113,700	77,000
Net earnings	$ 265,300	$ 179,500

JOHNSON LTD.
Balance Sheet
December 31

	2004	2003
Assets		
Current assets		
Cash	$ 60,100	$ 64,200
Short-term investments	54,000	50,000
Accounts receivable (net of allowance for doubtful		
accounts of $5,000 and $5,300, respectively)	107,800	102,800
Inventory	143,000	115,500
Total current assets	364,900	332,500
Property, plant, and equipment	625,300	520,300
Total assets	$990,200	$852,800
Liabilities and Shareholders' Equity		
Current liabilities		
Accounts payable	$170,000	$145,400
Income taxes payable	43,500	42,000
Total current liabilities	213,500	187,400
Bonds payable	66,000	200,000
Total liabilities	279,500	387,400
Shareholders' equity		
Common shares (56,000 and 60,000		
shares, respectively)	280,000	300,000
Retained earnings	430,700	165,400
Total shareholders' equity	710,700	465,400
Total liabilities and shareholders' equity	$990,200	$852,800

Additional information:

1. On July 1, 2004, 4,000 shares were repurchased and cancelled.
2. All sales were on account.
3. Net cash provided by operating activities for 2004 was $280,000.

Instructions

Calculate the following ratios for 2004:

(a) Current
(b) Acid-test
(c) Receivables turnover
(d) Average collection period
(e) Inventory turnover
(f) Days in inventory
(g) Cash current debt coverage
(h) Debt to total assets

(i) Times interest earned
(j) Cash total debt coverage
(k) Gross profit margin
(l) Profit margin
(m) Return on assets
(n) Asset turnover
(o) Return on common shareholders' equity
(p) Earnings per share

Calculate ratios and
comment.
(SO 5)

P14-4B Condensed balance sheet and statement of earnings data for Pitka Corporation are presented here:

PITKA CORPORATION
Balance Sheet
December 31

	2005	2004	2003
Cash	$ 25,000	$ 20,000	$ 18,000
Accounts receivable	50,000	45,000	48,000
Other current assets	90,000	85,000	64,000
Investments	55,000	70,000	45,000
Property, plant, and equipment	500,000	370,000	258,000
	$720,000	$590,000	$433,000
Current liabilities	$ 90,000	$ 75,000	$ 30,000
Long-term liabilities	170,000	85,000	20,000
Common shares	325,000	325,000	300,000
Retained earnings	135,000	105,000	83,000
	$720,000	$590,000	$433,000

PITKA CORPORATION
Statement of Earnings
Year Ended December 31

	2005	2004
Sales	$740,000	$700,000
Less: Sales returns and allowances	40,000	50,000
Net sales	700,000	650,000
Cost of goods sold	420,000	400,000
Gross profit	280,000	250,000
Operating expenses	236,000	218,000
Earnings before income taxes	44,000	32,000
Income tax expense	11,000	8,000
Net earnings	$ 33,000	$ 24,000

Additional information:

1. The market prices of Pitka's common shares were $4, $5, and $8 for 2003, 2004, and 2005, respectively.
2. All dividends were paid in cash. (*Hint:* Analyse retained earnings to calculate dividends.)
3. On July 1, 2004, 5,000 common shares were issued, bringing the total number of shares to 35,000.

Instructions

(a) Calculate the following ratios for 2004 and 2005:

1. Profit margin	5. Price-earnings
2. Gross profit margin	6. Payout
3. Asset turnover	7. Debt to total assets
4. Earnings per share	8. Current

(b) Based on the ratios calculated, discuss briefly the improvement or lack of improvement in the financial position and operating results for Pitka Corporation from 2004 to 2005.

Calculate ratios.
(SO 5)

P14-5B This financial information is for Click and Clack Ltd.:

CLICK AND CLACK LTD.
Balance Sheet
December 31

	2004	2003
Assets		
Cash	$ 70,000	$ 65,000
Short-term investments	45,000	40,000
Receivables (net of allowance for doubtful accounts of $5,000 and $4,000 in 2004 and 2003, respectively)	94,000	90,000
Inventories	230,000	125,000
Prepaid expenses	25,000	23,000
Land, building, and equipment	390,000	305,000
Total assets	$854,000	$648,000
Liabilities and Shareholders' Equity		
Notes payable	$170,000	$100,000
Accounts payable	45,000	42,000
Accrued liabilities	40,000	40,000
Bonds payable, due 2008	250,000	150,000
Common shares, 20,000 shares	200,000	200,000
Retained earnings	149,000	116,000
Total liabilities and shareholders' equity	$854,000	$648,000

CLICK AND CLACK LTD.
Statement of Earnings
Year Ended December 31

	2004	2003
Sales	$900,000	$840,000
Cost of goods sold	620,000	575,000
Gross profit	280,000	265,000
Operating expenses (including amortization expense of $15,000 and $11,000, respectively, for each year)	194,000	180,000
Earnings before income taxes	86,000	85,000
Income tax expense	30,000	30,000
Net earnings	$ 56,000	$ 55,000

Additional information:

1. Inventory at the beginning of 2003 was $115,000.
2. Receivables at the beginning of 2003 were $88,000, net of an allowance for doubtful accounts of $3,000.
3. Total assets at the beginning of 2003 were $630,000.
4. All sales were on account.

Instructions

(a) Indicate, by using ratios, the change in Click and Clack's liquidity, profitability, and solvency from 2003 to 2004. (*Note*: Not all ratios can be calculated.)
(b) Below are three independent situations and a ratio that may be affected. For each situation, calculate the affected ratio (1) as at December 31, 2004, and (2) as at December 31, 2005. Net earnings for 2005 were $40,000. Total assets on December 31, 2005, were $900,000.

Situation	Ratio
1. On July 1, 2005, 1,800 common shares were sold at $12 per share.	Return on common shareholders' equity
2. All of the notes payable were paid in 2005.	Debt to total assets
3. The market price of common shares was $10 and $12 on December 31, 2004 and 2005, respectively.	Price-earnings

Calculate ratios, and compare liquidity, profitability, and solvency for two companies.
(SO 5)

P14-6B Future Shop Ltd., now owned by U.S. retailer Best Buy Co., Inc., is Canada's largest consumer electronics retailer. InterTAN, Inc. also sells consumer electronics, through Radio Shack and Rogers AT&T stores in Canada. Selected financial data of these two close competitors are presented here (in CAD and U.S. millions, respectively) for a recent year:

	Future Shop	InterTAN
	Statement of Earnings	
Sales	$1,985.2	$468.8
Cost of sales	1,534.4	281.0
Gross profit	450.8	187.8
Selling, general, and administrative expenses	398.3	150.0
Unusual item expense (revenue)	0.7	(4.1)
Earnings before income taxes	51.8	41.9
Income tax expense	19.4	18.4
Net earnings	$ 32.4	$ 23.5
	Balance Sheet	
Current assets	$241.7	$192.7
Noncurrent assets	199.9	22.8
Total assets	$441.6	$215.5
Current liabilities	$275.2	$ 64.1
Long-term liabilities	51.5	7.1
Total liabilities	326.7	71.2
Shareholders' equity	114.9	144.3
Total liabilities and shareholders' equity	$441.6	$215.5
	Other Data	
Average gross accounts receivable	$ 13.5	$ 12.7
Average inventories	207.2	106.2
Average total assets	405.4	211.8
Average total shareholders' equity	97.6	131.6
Net cash provided by operating activities	34.9	18.8

The unusual item for Future Shop involved the closure of its Computer City stores and an unsuccessful bid to purchase Chapters Inc. The unusual item for InterTAN involved the sale of an Australian subsidiary company to Woolworths.

Instructions

(a) For each company, calculate the following ratios. Industry averages are provided in parentheses following each ratio, where available.

1. Current ratio (1.6:1)
2. Receivables turnover (use net accounts receivable) (23.7×)
3. Average collection period (15 days)
4. Inventory turnover (5.5×)
5. Days in inventory (66 days)
6. Cash current debt coverage (n/a)
7. Debt to total assets (n/a)
8. Cash total debt coverage (n/a)
9. Profit margin (2.1%)
10. Asset turnover (2.6×)
11. Return on assets (5.2%)
12. Return on common shareholders' equity (9.8%)
13. Gross profit margin (27.4%)

(b) Compare the liquidity, solvency, and profitability of the two companies.

Calculate ratios and compare two companies, one on the verge of bankruptcy.
(SO 5)

P14-7B You are presented with the following comparative financial information for two Canadian retailers whose identities have been disguised. At the end of the current year, one of these retailers was liquidated and purchased by another retailer (Company C).

Balance Sheet
(in millions)

	Company A		Company B	
	Current Year	Prior Year	Current Year	Prior Year
Assets				
Cash and cash equivalents	$ 22.0	$ 32.4	$ 7.5	$ 91.2
Credit card receivables	718.7	645.0	0	0
Other accounts receivable	169.7	181.9	56.7	28.1
Merchandise inventory	1,655.6	1,416.6	350.6	272.5
Other current assets	122.1	94.1	469.6	0
Total current assets	2,688.1	2,370.0	884.4	391.8
Noncurrent assets	1,916.0	1,510.2	200.3	1,252.5
Total assets	$4,604.1	$3,880.2	$1,084.7	$1,644.3
Liabilities and Shareholders' Equity				
Total current liabilities	$1,230.9	$ 869.0	$ 837.8	$ 441.2
Total long-term liabilities	1,314.9	1,301.0	116.1	976.4
Total liabilities	2,545.8	2,170.0	953.9	1,417.6
Total shareholders' equity	2,058.3	1,710.2	130.8	226.7
Total liabilities and shareholders' equity	$4,604.1	$3,880.2	$1,084.7	$1,644.3

Statement of Earnings
(in millions)

	Company A		Company B	
	Current Year	Prior Year	Current Year	Prior Year
Revenues (assume all on credit)	$7,075.0	$6,446.7	$1,688.2	$1,666.5
Earnings (loss) before interest, unusual items, and taxes	$ 187.2	$ 19.9	$ (108.6)	$ (92.5)
Interest expense	(97.2)	(88.3)	(17.3)	(20.7)
Unusual items	0.0	(243.0)	(124.5)	(80.4)
Income tax (expense) recovery	(50.3)	41.7	(83.2)	23.4
Net earnings (loss) from continuing operations	$ 39.7	$ (269.7)	$ (333.6)	$ (170.2)

Instructions

(a) Prepare each of the following ratios for both Company A and Company B for the current year:

    1. Current ratio   5. Debt to total assets
    2. Acid-test ratio   6. Times interest earned
    3. Receivables turnover   7. Return on assets
    4. Average collection period   8. Asset turnover

(b) Which company do you think is in financial trouble? Provide support for your conclusion.

Analyse ratios.
(SO 5)

P14-8B The following ratios are available for fast-food competitors McDonald's Corporation and Wendy's International, Inc. for fiscal 2002:

Ratio	McDonald's	Wendy's	Industry
Liquidity			
Current ratio	0.7:1	0.9:1	0.7:1
Acid-test ratio	0.5:1	0.7:1	0.4:1
Receivables turnover	17.7 times	28.4 times	30.7 times
Inventory turnover	60.9 times	52.3 times	30.1 times
Solvency			
Debt to total assets	49.2%	32.0%	44.8%
Times interest earned	5.4 times	9.3 times	6.3 times

Ratio	McDonald's	Wendy's	Industry
Profitability			
Gross profit margin	57.0%	29.3%	38.9%
Profit margin	6.4%	8.0%	5.4%
Return on common shareholders' equity	9.6%	15.1%	14.6%
Return on assets	4.1%	8.2%	6.3%
Asset turnover	0.7 times	1.2 times	1.2 times
Payout ratio	31.2%	9.5%	10.6%
Earnings per share	$0.77	$1.89	$1.04
Price-earnings ratio	20.9 times	14.3 times	n/a

Instructions

(a) Which company is more liquid? Explain.

(b) Which company is more solvent? Explain.

(c) Which company is more profitable? Explain.

(d) Which company do investors favour? Is your answer consistent with your findings in (c)?

Calculate missing information using ratios. (SO 5)

P14-9B Presented here are an incomplete statement of earnings and balance sheet for Schwenke Corporation:

SCHWENKE CORPORATION
Statement of Earnings
Year Ended December 31, 2004

Sales	$	(a)
Cost of goods sold		(b)
Gross profit		(c)
Operating expenses		287,500
Earnings from operations		(d)
Interest expense		4,167
Earnings before income taxes		(e)
Income tax expense		(f)
Net earnings		$125,000

SCHWENKE CORPORATION
Balance Sheet
December 31, 2004

Assets

Current assets

Cash	$	54,000
Accounts receivable		(g)
Inventory		(h)
Total current assets		(i)
Property, plant, and equipment		(j)
Total assets	$	(k)

Liabilities

Current liabilities	$	(l)
Long-term liabilities		210,000
Total liabilities		(m)

Shareholders' Equity

Common shares		320,000
Retained earnings		330,000
Total shareholders' equity		650,000
Total liabilities and shareholders' equity	$	(n)

Additional information:

1. The profit margin is 10%.
2. The gross profit margin is 40%.
3. The income tax rate is 40%.
4. The asset turnover is 1.25 times.
5. The current ratio is 2:1.
6. The acid-test ratio is 1.1:1.

Instructions

Calculate the missing information using the ratios. Use ending balances instead of average balances, where averages are required for ratio calculations. Show your calculations. (*Hint:* Start with one ratio and derive as much information as possible from it before trying another ratio.)

P14-10B The management of Bella Coola Inc. would like to better understand the impact of the following transactions on specific ratios:

Determine effect of transactions on ratios.
(SO 5)

Transaction	Ratio
(a) Issued bonds payable at face value to finance an expansion.	Debt to total assets; times interest earned
(b) Issued common shares to finance an expansion.	Return on common shareholders' equity
(c) Paid dividends.	Payout ratio
(d) Purchased inventory on credit (perpetual inventory system).	Current ratio; inventory turnover
(e) Sold inventory on credit (perpetual inventory system).	Acid-test ratio; gross profit margin
(f) Increased the allowance for doubtful accounts.	Receivables turnover
(g) Wrote off an uncollectible account.	Current ratio; receivables turnover
(h) Increased the estimated useful life of a building.	Return on assets

Instructions

Indicate whether the above transactions will increase (I), decrease (D), or have no effect (NE) on the ratio(s) listed next to the transaction. Explain your reasoning.

P14-11B Nextec Corp. has been in business for five years. Nextec has plans to create a new software package intended to allow users with limited computer knowledge to easily navigate the Internet by using their television sets and a control box that plugs into the cable jack.

Analyse ratios.
(SO 5, 6)

You are the loan officer at a Canadian chartered bank. The manager has asked you to analyse Nextec's financial statements and recommend whether or not the bank should lend Nextec additional funds for the project, based on its historical financial statements. Comparative financial statements follow:

NEXTEC CORP.
Balance Sheet
March 31

	2004	2003
Assets		
Cash	$ 45,000	
Accounts receivable	535,000	$470,000
Inventory	150,000	140,000
Prepaid expenses	5,000	10,000
Patents	40,000	0
Accumulated amortization	(2,000)	0
Total assets	$773,000	$620,000
Liabilities and Shareholders' Equity		
Bank indebtedness		$ 20,000
Accounts payable	$ 50,200	60,000
Current portion of long-term debt	60,000	50,000
Long-term debt	184,000	160,000
Common shares	100,000	100,000
Retained earnings	378,800	230,000
Total liabilities and shareholders' equity	$773,000	$620,000

NEXTEC CORP.
Statement of Earnings
Year Ended March 31

	2004	2003
Sales (all on credit)	$1,600,000	$1,400,000
Cost of goods sold	900,000	800,000
Gross profit	700,000	600,000
Operating expenses		
Salaries	370,000	340,000
Office	20,000	20,000
Rent	40,000	40,000
Interest	20,000	30,000
Amortization	2,000	
	452,000	430,000
Earnings before taxes	248,000	170,000
Income taxes (40%)	99,200	68,000
Net earnings	$ 148,800	$ 102,000

Selected comparative ratios and industry averages follow:

	2004	2003	2004 Industry Average
Current ratio	6.7:1	4.8:1	3:1
Average collection period	115 days	123 days	60 days
Inventory turnover	6.2 times	5.7 times	5 times
Return on common shareholders' equity	37%	31%	30%
Debt to total assets	38%	47%	40%
Times interest earned	13.4 times	6.7 times	10.9 times

Instructions

(a) Indicate whether the 2004 ratios presented above are favourable or unfavourable compared to the industry averages.

(b) Based on a comparison of Nextec Corp.'s ratios with the industry averages, identify one significant area that Nextec Corp. must improve and what it should do to improve it.

(c) The president of Nextec Corp. estimates that the company needs $1,000,000 to ensure the new software project's success. Based on the ratios given, and the financial statements presented, determine whether or not you would lend $1,000,000 to Nextec Corp. Explain your decision.

(d) Identify one additional thing Nextec could do (other than borrow) to raise the money it needs.

(e) In addition to the financial statements of Nextec Corp., list non-financial factors that should be considered when evaluating Nextec Corp.

Assess effect of alternative accounting principles on ratios.
(SO 5, 6)

P14-12B   Fly-by-Night Inc. is in its first year of operations. Obtaining financing has been difficult. The president of the company is debating the selection of generally accepted accounting principles. She would like you to advise her about the impact that selected accounting principles will have on the various company ratios listed below:

Accounting Principle	Current ratio (1.5:1)	Gross profit margin (40%)	Earnings per share ($1.50)	Debt to total assets (25%)	Times interest earned (5×)	Return on total assets (10%)
(a) It is a period of inflation and the president would like to use the FIFO inventory cost flow assumption instead of average cost.						
(b) The company is considering using double declining-balance amortization, which will produce a higher expense than other methods.						
(c) The company will be leasing automobiles and is setting up the lease as a capital lease. Its interest expense and amortization expense under the capital lease will be higher this year than the rent expense would be under an operating lease.						

Instructions

Indicate whether the above policy choices will increase (I), decrease (D), or have no effect (NE) on each of the ratios presented.

BROADENING YOUR PERSPECTIVE

Financial Reporting and Analysis

FINANCIAL REPORTING PROBLEM: *Loblaw Companies Limited*

BYP14-1   You are considering investing in Loblaw Companies Limited's common shares. Before doing so, you wish to analyse the company further, using Loblaw's financial statements presented in Appendix A of this textbook.

Instructions

(a) Prepare a two-year horizontal trend analysis, using 2001 as the base year. Comment on the significance of any trends you observe.

(b) For 2002, calculate the (1) debt to total assets, (2) times interest earned, and (3) cash total debt coverage ratios. What is your assessment of Loblaw's long-term solvency?

(c) For 2002, calculate the (1) profit margin, (2) asset turnover, (3) return on assets, and (4) return on common shareholders' equity ratios. What is your assessment of Loblaw's profitability?

(d) What information not included in the financial statements may also be useful to you in making a decision about Loblaw?

COMPARATIVE ANALYSIS PROBLEM: *Loblaw and Sobeys*

BYP14-2 The financial statements of Sobeys Inc. are presented in Appendix B, following the financial statements for Loblaw Companies Limited in Appendix A.

Instructions

(a) Based on the information in the financial statements, determine each of the following for each company:
   1. The percentage increase in sales and in net earnings from 2002 to 2003 for Sobeys and from 2001 to 2002 for Loblaw
   2. The percentage increase in total assets and in total shareholders' equity from 2002 to 2003 for Sobeys and from 2001 to 2002 for Loblaw
   3. The earnings per share for each of these two years
(b) What conclusions concerning the two companies can be drawn from these data?

RESEARCH CASE

BYP14-3 The November 12, 2001, issue of *Canadian Business* includes an article by Al Rosen on page 39 entitled "It's Extraordinary." The article discusses how companies will account for one-time, nonrecurring events, such as the September 11, 2001, terrorist attacks in the United States.

Instructions

Read the article and answer these questions:

(a) As an investor, would you be better informed about the magnitude of gains and losses resulting from the September 11 attacks by reading financial statements prepared using Canadian accounting principles or by reading financial statements prepared using American accounting principles? Explain.
(b) How might Air Canada report a multi-million-dollar aid package from Ottawa to help defray the costs incurred from airport restrictions on and after September 11?
(c) How might Air Canada report losses for flight delays and cancellations due to severe weather?
(d) Quebecor Inc. has provided an extra level of disclosure in its financial statements for 2000 and the first half of 2001. How has it done this?

INTERPRETING FINANCIAL STATEMENTS

BYP14-4 The Coca-Cola Company and PepsiCo, Inc. provide refreshments to every corner of the world. Selected data from the 2002 consolidated financial statements for Coca-Cola and PepsiCo are presented here (in U.S. millions):

	Coca-Cola	PepsiCo
Total current assets (including cash, accounts receivable, and short-term investments totalling $4,442 for Coca-Cola and $4,376 for PepsiCo)	$ 7,352	$ 6,413
Total current liabilities	7,341	6,052
Net sales	19,564	25,112
Cost of goods sold	7,105	11,497
Net earnings	3,050	3,313
Average gross accounts receivable	1,990	2,337
Average inventories	1,175	1,326
Average total assets	23,459	22,585
Average common shareholders' equity	11,583	8,973
Average current liabilities	7,885	5,525
Average total liabilities	11,876	13,602
Total assets	24,501	23,474
Total liabilities	12,701	14,183
Income tax expense	1,523	1,555
Interest expense	199	178
Cash provided by operating activities	4,742	4,627

Instructions

(a) Calculate the following liquidity ratios for Coca-Cola and PepsiCo and comment on the relative liquidity of the two competitors:

1. Current
2. Acid-test
3. Receivables turnover
4. Average collection period
5. Inventory turnover
6. Days in inventory
7. Cash current debt coverage

(b) Calculate the following solvency ratios for the two companies and comment on the relative solvency of the two competitors:

1. Debt to total assets
2. Times interest earned
3. Cash total debt coverage

(c) Calculate the following profitability ratios for the two companies and comment on the relative profitability of the two competitors:

1. Profit margin
2. Gross profit margin
3. Asset turnover
4. Return on assets
5. Return on common shareholders' equity

A GLOBAL FOCUS

BYP14-5 Canadian National Railway Company (CN) is the only railroad in North America to cross the continent from east to west and north to south. The Burlington Northern Santa Fe Corporation (BNSF), through its subsidiary The Burlington Northern and Santa Fe Railway Company, operates another of North America's largest railways in two provinces and 28 states. At one time, CN planned to merge with BNSF, until a U.S. moratorium on rail mergers was introduced. The following data were taken from the December 31, 2002, financial statements of each company:

Financial Highlights	CN (in CDN millions)		BNSF (in U.S. millions)	
	2002	2001	2002	2001
Cash and cash equivalents	$ 25	$ 53	$ 28	$ 26
Accounts receivable	722	645	141	172
Total current assets	1,163	1,164	791	723
Total assets	18,924	18,788	25,767	24,721
Total current liabilities	2,134	1,638	2,091	2,161
Total liabilities	12,297	12,427	17,835	16,872
Total shareholders' equity	6,627	6,034	7,932	7,849
Revenues	6,110		8,979	
Operating expenses	4,994		7,323	
Interest expense	353		428	
Income tax expense	268		456	
Net earnings	571		760	
Cash provided by operating activities	1,173		2,106	
Capital expenditures	571		1,358	
Dividends	179		183	

Instructions

Where available, industry averages are shown in parentheses next to each ratio below.

(a) Calculate the following liquidity ratios for 2002 and discuss the relative liquidity of the two companies and of the railroad industry:
1. Current ratio (0.7:1)
2. Acid-test ratio (0.4:1)
3. Cash current debt coverage (n/a)
4. Receivables turnover (13.0×)

(b) Calculate the following solvency ratios for 2002 and discuss the relative solvency of the two companies and of the railroad industry:
1. Debt to total assets (46.8%)
2. Times interest earned (3.3×)
3. Cash total debt coverage (n/a)
4. Free cash flow (n/a)

(c) Calculate the following profitability ratios for 2002 and discuss the relative profitability of the two companies and of the railroad industry:
1. Asset turnover (0.4×)
2. Profit margin (8.1%)
3. Return on assets (2.9%)
4. Return on common shareholders' equity (8.8%)
(d) What factors might contribute to the differences that you found?

FINANCIAL ANALYSIS ON THE WEB

BYP14-6 In this problem, comparative data and industry data are employed to evaluate the performance and financial position of two integrated oil and gas companies, Petro-Canada and Suncor.

Instructions

Specific requirements of this Web case can be found on the Kimmel website.

Critical Thinking

COLLABORATIVE LEARNING ACTIVITY

BYP14-7 You are a loan officer for a bank in Hamilton, Ontario. Ted Bourcier, president of Bourcier Corporation, has just left your office. The company is interested in a five-year loan for expansion purposes. The borrowed funds would be used to purchase new equipment. As evidence of the company's creditworthiness, Bourcier provided you with the following facts:

	2005	2004
Current ratio	3.1:1	2.1:1
Acid-test ratio	0.8:1	1.4:1
Asset turnover	2.8 times	2.2 times
Cash total debt coverage	0.1 times	0.2 times
Net earnings	Up 32%	Down 8%
Earnings per share	$3.30	$2.50

Ted Bourcier is a very insistent (some would say pushy) man. When you told him that you would need additional information before making your decision, he acted offended, and said, "What more could you possibly want to know?" You responded that, at a minimum, you would need complete, audited financial statements.

Instructions

(a) Explain why you would want the financial statements to be audited.
(b) Discuss the implications of the ratios provided for the lending decision you are to make. That is, does the information paint a favourable picture? Are these ratios relevant to the decision?
(c) List other ratios that you would want to calculate for this company, and explain why you would use each.
(d) What are the limitations of ratio analysis for credit and investing decisions?

COMMUNICATION ACTIVITY

BYP14-8 You are a new member of the board of directors of Shifty.com Inc. You are preparing for your first meeting of the audit committee and wish to reassure yourself about the quality of the company's earnings.

Instructions

Write a memo to yourself, listing questions that you should raise at the audit committee meeting to satisfy any concerns you may have about Shifty.com's earnings quality.

ETHICS CASE

**Ethics In
Accounting**

BYP14-9 Vern Fairly, president of Fairly Industries Inc., wishes to issue a press release to bolster the company's image and its share price, which has been gradually falling. As controller, you have been asked to provide a list of financial ratios along with some other operating statistics relative to Fairly Industries' first-quarter operations.

Two days after you provide the ratios and data requested, you are asked by Anne Saint-Onge, Fairly's public relations director, to prove the accuracy of the financial and operating data contained in the press release written by the president and edited by Anne. In the news release, the president highlights the sales increase of 25% over last year's first quarter and the positive change in the current ratio from 1.5:1 last year to 3:1 this year. He also emphasizes that production was up 50% over the prior year's first quarter. You note that the release contains only positive or improved ratios and none of the negative or deteriorated ratios. For instance, there is no mention of the fact that the debt to total assets ratio has increased from 35% to 55%, that inventories are up 89%, and that although the current ratio improved, the acid-test ratio fell from 1:1 to 0.5:1. Nor is there any mention that the reported profit for the quarter would have been a loss had the estimated lives of Fairly's machinery not been increased by 30%. Anne emphasized, "The Prez wants this release by early this afternoon."

Instructions

(a) Who are the stakeholders in this situation?
(b) Is there anything unethical in President Fairly's actions?
(c) Should you as controller remain silent? Does Anne have any responsibility?

Answers to Self-Study Questions

1. d   2. d   3. b   4. d   5. c   6. a   7. c   8. b   9. b
10. b   11. c   12. b

Answer to Loblaw Review It Question 4

Loblaw did not report any discontinued or extraordinary items on its statement of earnings in 2002. However, it did report a change in accounting principle on its 2002 statement of retained earnings due to implementing the new CICA standard on goodwill and other intangible assets. This resulted in a $25-million decrease in opening retained earnings.

Remember to go back to the Navigator box on the
chapter-opening page to check off your completed work.

Specimen Financial Statements: Loblaw Companies Limited

Loblaw Companies Limited
www.loblaw.com

Annual Report Walkthrough

In this appendix, and the next, we illustrate current financial reporting with two comprehensive sets of corporate financial statements that are prepared in accordance with generally accepted accounting principles. We are grateful for permission to use the actual financial statements of Loblaw Companies Limited in Appendix A and Sobeys Inc. in Appendix B.

The financial statement package for each company includes the statement of earnings, statement of retained earnings, balance sheet, cash flow statement, and notes to the financial statements. The financial statements are preceded by two reports: management's statement of responsibility for the financial statements and the auditors' report on these statements.

Loblaw's complete annual report, including the financial statements, is reviewed in detail on The Toolkit CD that accompanies this textbook. We encourage students to use these financial statements in conjunction with relevant material in the textbook, and to solve the Review It questions in the Before You Go On section of your chapter and the Financial Reporting Problem and Comparative Analysis Problem in the Broadening Your Perspective section of the end of chapter material.

MANAGEMENT'S STATEMENT OF RESPONSIBILITY FOR FINANCIAL REPORTING

The management of Loblaw Companies Limited is responsible for the preparation, presentation and integrity of the accompanying consolidated financial statements, Management's Discussion and Analysis and all other information in this Annual Report. This responsibility includes the selection and consistent application of appropriate accounting principles and methods in addition to making the judgements and estimates necessary to prepare the consolidated financial statements in accordance with Canadian generally accepted accounting principles. It also includes ensuring that the financial information presented elsewhere in this Annual Report is consistent with the consolidated financial statements.

To provide reasonable assurance that assets are safeguarded and that relevant and reliable financial information is produced, management maintains a system of internal controls reinforced by the Company's standards of conduct and ethics set out in written policies. Internal auditors, who are employees of the Company, review and evaluate internal controls on management's behalf, coordinating this work with the independent auditors. KPMG LLP, whose report follows, were appointed as independent auditors by a vote of the Company's shareholders to audit the consolidated financial statements.

The Board of Directors, acting through an Audit Committee comprised solely of directors who are unrelated and independent to the Company, is responsible for determining that management fulfills its responsibilities in the preparation of the consolidated financial statements and the financial control of operations. The Audit Committee recommends the independent auditors for appointment by the shareholders. The Audit Committee meets regularly with financial management, internal auditors and the independent auditors to discuss internal controls, auditing matters and financial reporting issues. The independent auditors and internal auditors have unrestricted access to the Audit Committee. These consolidated financial statements and Management's Discussion and Analysis have been approved by the Board of Directors for inclusion in this Annual Report based on the review and recommendation of the Audit Committee.

Toronto, Canada
March 4, 2003

John A. Lederer
PRESIDENT

Richard P. Mavrinac
EXECUTIVE VICE PRESIDENT

Stephen A. Smith
EXECUTIVE VICE PRESIDENT

INDEPENDENT AUDITORS' REPORT

To the Shareholders of Loblaw Companies Limited:

We have audited the consolidated balance sheets of Loblaw Companies Limited as at December 28, 2002 and December 29, 2001 and the consolidated statements of earnings, retained earnings and cash flow for the 52 week periods then ended. These consolidated financial statements are the responsibility of the Company's management. Our responsibility is to express an opinion on these consolidated financial statements based on our audits.

We conducted our audits in accordance with Canadian generally accepted auditing standards. Those standards require that we plan and perform an audit to obtain reasonable assurance whether the consolidated financial statements are free of material misstatement. An audit includes examining, on a test basis, evidence supporting the amounts and disclosures in the consolidated financial statements. An audit also includes assessing the accounting principles used and significant estimates made by management, as well as evaluating the overall consolidated financial statement presentation.

In our opinion, these consolidated financial statements present fairly, in all material respects, the financial position of the Company as at December 28, 2002 and December 29, 2001 and the results of its operations and its cash flow for the periods then ended in accordance with Canadian generally accepted accounting principles.

KPMG
KPMG LLP

Toronto, Canada
March 4, 2003

Chartered Accountants

43

CONSOLIDATED STATEMENTS OF EARNINGS

52 Weeks Ended December 28, 2002 ($ millions except where otherwise indicated)	2002	2001
SALES	$ 23,082	$ 21,486
OPERATING EXPENSES		
Cost of sales, selling and administrative expenses	21,425	20,035
Depreciation	354	315
	21,779	20,350
OPERATING INCOME	1,303	1,136
Interest Expense (note 2)	161	158
EARNINGS BEFORE INCOME TAXES	1,142	978
Income Taxes (note 6)	414	372
EARNINGS BEFORE GOODWILL CHARGES	728	606
Goodwill Charges (2001 – net of tax of $1) (note 1)		43
NET EARNINGS	$ 728	$ 563
EARNINGS PER COMMON SHARE ($) (note 3)		
Basic		
Net earnings	$ 2.64	$ 2.04
Earnings before goodwill charges	$ 2.64	$ 2.20
Diluted		
Net earnings	$ 2.62	$ 2.03
Earnings before goodwill charges	$ 2.62	$ 2.19

See accompanying notes to the consolidated financial statements.

CONSOLIDATED STATEMENTS OF RETAINED EARNINGS

52 Weeks Ended December 28, 2002 ($ millions except where otherwise indicated)	2002	2001
RETAINED EARNINGS, BEGINNING OF PERIOD	$ 2,375	$ 1,930
Impact of implementing new accounting standard (note 1)	(25)	
Net earnings	728	563
Premium on common shares purchased for cancellation (note 12)	(16)	(1)
Net stock option plan cash payments (note 13)		(7)
Dividends declared per common share – 48¢ (2001 – 40¢)	(133)	(110)
RETAINED EARNINGS, END OF PERIOD	$ 2,929	$ 2,375

See accompanying notes to the consolidated financial statements.

CONSOLIDATED BALANCE SHEETS

As at December 28, 2002 ($ millions)	2002	2001
ASSETS		
Current Assets		
Cash and cash equivalents (note 4)	$ 823	$ 575
Short term investments (note 4)	304	426
Accounts receivable (note 5)	605	472
Inventories	1,702	1,512
Future income taxes (note 6)	68	73
Prepaid expenses and other assets	24	28
Total Current Assets	3,526	3,086
Fixed Assets (note 7)	5,587	4,931
Goodwill	1,599	1,599
Future Income Taxes (note 6)	15	26
Other Assets (note 8)	383	383
TOTAL ASSETS	$ 11,110	$ 10,025
LIABILITIES		
Current Liabilities		
Bank indebtedness		$ 95
Commercial paper	$ 533	191
Accounts payable and accrued liabilities	2,336	2,291
Income taxes	179	138
Long term debt due within one year (note 10)	106	81
Total Current Liabilities	3,154	2,796
Long Term Debt (note 10)	3,420	3,333
Future Income Taxes (note 6)	68	49
Other Liabilities (note 11)	344	278
TOTAL LIABILITIES	6,986	6,456
SHAREHOLDERS' EQUITY		
Common Share Capital (note 12)	1,195	1,194
Retained Earnings	2,929	2,375
TOTAL SHAREHOLDERS' EQUITY	4,124	3,569
TOTAL LIABILITIES AND SHAREHOLDERS' EQUITY	$ 11,110	$ 10,025

See accompanying notes to the consolidated financial statements.

Approved on behalf of the Board

W. Galen Weston
DIRECTOR

T. Iain Ronald
DIRECTOR

CONSOLIDATED CASH FLOW STATEMENTS

52 Weeks Ended December 28, 2002 ($ millions)	2002	2001
OPERATING ACTIVITIES		
Net earnings	$ 728	$ 563
Depreciation and amortization	354	359
Future income taxes	37	44
Change in non-cash working capital	(142)	(102)
Acquisition restructuring and other charges,		
including income tax recoveries	(26)	(50)
Other	30	4
CASH FLOWS FROM OPERATING ACTIVITIES	981	818
INVESTING ACTIVITIES		
Fixed asset purchases	(1,079)	(1,108)
Short term investments	122	(62)
Proceeds from fixed asset sales	63	44
Franchise investments, other receivables		
and credit card receivables	(107)	(128)
Other	23	(27)
CASH FLOWS USED IN INVESTING ACTIVITIES	(978)	(1,281)
FINANCING ACTIVITIES		
Bank indebtedness	(95)	(108)
Commercial paper	342	(236)
Long term debt (note 10)		
– Issued	200	1,040
– Retired	(77)	(252)
Common share capital (note 12)		
– Issued	2	
– Retired	(17)	(1)
Dividends	(127)	(110)
Other	17	19
CASH FLOWS FROM FINANCING ACTIVITIES	245	352
Change in Cash and Cash Equivalents	248	(111)
Cash and Cash Equivalents, Beginning of Period	575	686
CASH AND CASH EQUIVALENTS, END OF PERIOD	$ 823	$ 575

See accompanying notes to the consolidated financial statements.

NOTES TO THE CONSOLIDATED FINANCIAL STATEMENTS
52 Weeks Ended December 28, 2002 ($ millions except where otherwise indicated)

NOTE 1. SUMMARY OF SIGNIFICANT ACCOUNTING POLICIES

The consolidated financial statements were prepared in accordance with Canadian generally accepted accounting principles ("GAAP").

BASIS OF CONSOLIDATION The consolidated financial statements include the accounts of Loblaw Companies Limited and its subsidiaries (the "Company"). The Company's interest in the voting share capital of its subsidiaries is 100%.

FISCAL PERIOD The fiscal period of the Company consists of a 52 or 53 week period ending on the Saturday closest to December 31. Each of the periods ended December 28, 2002 and December 29, 2001 contain 52 weeks.

REVENUE RECOGNITION Sales include revenues from customers through corporate stores operated by the Company and sales to and service fees from its franchised store, associated store and independent account customers, but exclude intercompany sales. The Company recognizes revenue at the time the sale is made to its customer.

EARNINGS PER SHARE ("EPS") Basic EPS is calculated by dividing the earnings available to common shareholders by the weighted average number of common shares outstanding during the period. Diluted EPS is calculated using the treasury stock method, which assumes that all stock options with an exercise price below average market price are exercised and the assumed proceeds are used to purchase common shares of the Company at the average market price during the period.

CASH, CASH EQUIVALENTS AND BANK INDEBTEDNESS Cash balances for which the Company has the ability and intent to offset are used to reduce reported bank indebtedness. Cash equivalents are highly liquid investments with a maturity of less than 90 days.

SHORT TERM INVESTMENTS Short term investments are carried at the lower of cost or quoted market value and consist primarily of United States government securities, commercial paper and bank deposits.

CREDIT CARD RECEIVABLES The Company, through President's Choice Bank ("PC Bank"), a wholly owned subsidiary of the Company, has credit card receivables that are stated net of an allowance for credit losses. Any credit card receivable that has a payment that is contractually 180 days in arrears or where the likelihood of collection is considered remote is written off. Interest charges are recorded when billed to customers and recognized in the Company's operating income.

ALLOWANCE FOR CREDIT LOSSES PC Bank maintains a general allowance for credit losses which, in management's opinion, is considered adequate to absorb all credit-related losses in its credit card receivable portfolio, based upon an analysis of past performance and market conditions. The allowance for credit losses is deducted from the credit card receivable balance.

The amount of the allowance for credit losses recognized in the Company's operating income is the net credit loss experience for the period.

SECURITIZATION PC Bank securitizes credit card receivables through the sale of a portion of the total interest in these receivables to an independent Trust and does not exercise any control over the Trust's management, administration or assets. When PC Bank sells credit card receivables in a securitization transaction, it has a retained interest in the securitized receivables represented by a cash reserve account and the right to future cash flows after obligations to investors have been met. Although PC Bank remains responsible for servicing all credit card receivables, it does not receive additional compensation for servicing those credit card receivables sold to the Trust. Any gain or loss on the sale of these receivables depends, in part, on the previous carrying amount of receivables involved in the securitization allocated between the receivables sold and the retained interest based on the relative fair values at the date of securitization. The fair values are determined using a financial model. Any gain or loss on a sale is recognized in operating income at the time of the securitization.

INVENTORIES Retail store inventories are stated at the lower of cost and estimated net realizable value less normal profit margin. Wholesale inventories are stated at the lower of cost and estimated net realizable value. Cost is determined substantially using the first-in, first-out method.

FIXED ASSETS Fixed assets are recorded at cost including capitalized interest. Depreciation commences when the assets are put into use and is recognized principally on a straight-line basis to depreciate the cost of these assets over their estimated useful lives. Estimated useful lives range from 20 to 40 years for buildings and from 3 to 10 years for equipment and fixtures. Leasehold improvements are depreciated over the lesser of the applicable useful life and the term of the lease plus one renewal period to a maximum of 10 years.

GOODWILL Goodwill represents the excess of the purchase price of a business acquired over the fair value of the underlying net assets acquired at the date of acquisition.

Effective December 30, 2001, the Company prospectively implemented the new standard issued by the Canadian Institute of Chartered Accountants (the "CICA") on goodwill and intangible assets. Under the new standard, goodwill is no longer amortized but instead the carrying value of goodwill must be tested annually for impairment. In addition, the amortization of intangible assets is no longer required unless the intangible asset has a limited life, in which case it will be amortized over its estimated useful life. Intangible assets not subject to amortization must be tested annually for impairment. Any impairment in the carrying value of goodwill or intangible assets will be recognized in net earnings.

A review of the business combinations completed prior to July 1, 2001 was performed and no change was required to the carrying value of goodwill and no previously unrecognized intangible assets were recorded. The Company performed the annual impairment test for goodwill and determined that there was no impairment to the carrying value of goodwill.

Goodwill in 2001 was amortized on a straight-line basis over the estimated useful life of the benefit determined for each acquisition. Any permanent impairment in value, based on projected cash flows, was recognized in net earnings.

FOREIGN CURRENCY TRANSLATION Assets and liabilities denominated in foreign currencies are translated into Canadian dollars at the exchange rates in effect at each period end date. Exchange gains or losses arising from the translation of these balances denominated in foreign currencies are recognized in net earnings. Revenues and expenses denominated in foreign currencies are translated into Canadian dollars at the average exchange rates for the period.

FINANCIAL DERIVATIVE INSTRUMENTS The Company uses derivative agreements in the form of cross currency basis swaps, interest rate swaps and equity forwards to manage its current and anticipated exposure to fluctuations in exchange rates, interest rates and the market price of the Company's common shares. The Company does not enter into financial derivative agreements for speculative purposes.

Cross currency basis swaps are identified as a hedge against the foreign currency exchange rate fluctuations on the Company's United States dollar denominated net assets, principally cash, cash equivalents and short term investments. Realized and unrealized foreign currency exchange rate adjustments on cross currency basis swaps are offset by realized and unrealized foreign currency exchange rate adjustments on the Company's United States dollar denominated net assets and are recognized in operating income. Unrealized foreign currency exchange rate adjustments are recorded in other liabilities. The exchange of interest payments on the cross currency basis swaps is recognized on an accrual basis.

Interest rate swaps are identified as a hedge against interest rate fluctuations because they offset the interest rate exposure on the underlying hedged items. The exchange of interest payments on the interest rate swaps is recognized on an accrual basis and unrealized gains or losses are not recognized.

Equity forwards partially offset fluctuations in the Company's stock-based compensation cost because they change in value as the market price of the underlying common shares changes. Market price adjustments are recognized in operating income and recorded in accounts receivable. Interest on the equity forwards is recognized on an accrual basis.

The Company entered into an electricity forward purchase contract to purchase a portion of its electricity needs in the province of Ontario. This contract is identified as a hedge of an anticipated transaction as it partially offsets the volatility in the price of electricity.

INCOME TAXES The Company uses the asset and liability method of accounting for income taxes. Under the asset and liability method, future income tax assets and liabilities are recognized for the future income tax consequences attributable to differences between the financial statement carrying values of existing assets and liabilities and their respective income tax bases. Future income tax assets and liabilities are measured using enacted or substantively enacted income tax rates expected to apply to taxable income in the periods in which those temporary differences are expected to be recovered or settled. The effect on future income tax assets and liabilities of a change in income tax rates is recognized in net earnings in the period that includes the date of enactment or substantive enactment. Future income tax assets are evaluated and a valuation allowance, if required, is recorded against any future income tax asset if it is more likely than not that the asset will not be realized.

PENSION, POST-RETIREMENT AND POST-EMPLOYMENT BENEFITS The cost of the Company's defined benefit pension plans, post-retirement and post-employment benefits is accrued based on actuarial valuations, which are determined using the projected benefit method pro-rated on service and management's best estimate of expected plan investment performance, salary escalation, retirement ages and expected health care costs. Market values are used to value pension and other benefit plan assets. Employee future benefits are measured using current market interest rates assuming a portfolio of Corporate AA bonds with terms to maturity that, on average, match the terms of the liabilities. Past service costs from plan amendments and the excess net actuarial gain or loss over 10% of the greater of the accrued benefit plan obligation and the market value of the plan assets are amortized on a straight-line basis over the average remaining service period of the active employees, ranging from 6 to 18 years with a weighted average of 13 years at period end. The cost of pension benefits for defined contribution plans and the multi-employer defined benefit pension plans are expensed as the contributions are paid.

STOCK-BASED COMPENSATION Effective December 30, 2001, the Company implemented the new standard issued by the CICA on stock-based compensation and other stock-based payments. The standard was implemented retroactively without restatement of the prior period consolidated financial statements. The cumulative effect of implementation was a decrease to retained earnings of $25 ($80 less future income tax recoverable of $23 and the $32 fair value impact of the equity forwards).

The Company recognizes in operating income a compensation cost related to employee stock option grants that allow for settlement in shares or in the share appreciation value in cash at the option of the employee, which is accounted for using the intrinsic value method. A change in the intrinsic value between the grant date and period end date will result in a change in the compensation cost recognized.

The Company accounts for stock option grants issued prior to December 30, 2001 that will be settled by issuing common shares as capital transactions. Consideration paid by employees on the exercise of this type of stock option is credited to common share capital. This type of option was last issued in 2001 and represents 4% of all options outstanding.

During 2001, consideration paid by employees on the exercise of a stock option grant that was settled by issuing common shares was credited to common share capital. The cash payment (net of applicable taxes), for those stock option grants that employees exercised and elected to receive in cash the share appreciation value equal to the excess of the market price of the common shares at the date of exercise over the specified stock option price, was charged to retained earnings.

The Company maintains an Employee Share Ownership Plan for its employees. The Company contributes 15% of each employee's contribution to the plan, which is recognized in operating income as a compensation cost when the contribution is made.

Outside members of the Company's Board of Directors may elect annually to receive all or a portion of their annual retainer(s) and fees in the form of deferred share units. The deferred share unit obligation is accounted for using the intrinsic value method and the period over period change in the deferred share unit obligation is recognized in operating income.

USE OF ESTIMATES AND ASSUMPTIONS The preparation of the consolidated financial statements in conformity with Canadian GAAP requires management to make estimates and assumptions that affect the amounts reported in the consolidated financial statements and accompanying notes. These estimates and assumptions are based on management's best knowledge of current events and actions that the Company may undertake in the future. Actual results could differ from these estimates.

COMPARATIVE INFORMATION Certain prior period's information was reclassified to conform with the current period's presentation.

NOTE 2. INTEREST EXPENSE

	2002	2001
Interest on long term debt	$ 246	$ 223
Other long term interest	(38)	(15)
	208	208
Net short term interest	(17)	(23)
Capitalized to fixed assets	(30)	(27)
Interest expense	$ 161	$ 158

Net interest paid in 2002 was $185 (2001 – $191).

NOTES TO THE CONSOLIDATED FINANCIAL STATEMENTS   49

NOTE 3. BASIC AND DILUTED NET EARNINGS PER COMMON SHARE

	2002	2001
Net earnings	$ 728	$ 563
Weighted average common shares outstanding (in millions)	276.2	276.2
Dilutive effect of stock-based compensation (in millions)	1.7	1.9
Diluted weighted average common shares outstanding (in millions)	277.9	278.1
Basic net earnings per common share ($)	$ 2.64	$ 2.04
Dilutive effect of stock-based compensation per common share ($)	(0.02)	(0.01)
Diluted net earnings per common share ($)	$ 2.62	$ 2.03

NOTE 4. CASH, CASH EQUIVALENTS AND SHORT TERM INVESTMENTS

At period end, the Company had $1.1 billion (2001 – $993) in cash, cash equivalents and short term investments held by Glenhuron Bank Limited ("Glenhuron"), a wholly owned subsidiary of the Company in Barbados. The $24 (2001 – $50) of income from the cash, cash equivalents and short term investments was recognized in net short term interest.

NOTE 5. CREDIT CARD RECEIVABLES

During 2002, the Company, through PC Bank securitized $244 (2001 – $112) of credit card receivables, yielding a minimal gain in both years, inclusive of a $2 (2001 – $3) servicing liability, on the initial sale. Servicing liabilities expensed during the year were $4 (2001 – nil) and the fair value of recognized servicing liabilities was $4 (2001 – $3). The Trust's recourse to PC Bank's assets is limited to PC Bank's retained interest and is further supported by the Company through a standby letter of credit for 15% of the securitized amount.

	2002	2001
Credit card receivables	$ 502	$ 166
Amount securitized	(356)	(112)
Net credit card receivables	$ 146	$ 54
Net credit loss experience	$ 6	$ 5

For 2002, the key economic assumptions used in measuring the securitization gain and the sensitivity of the current fair value of retained interests to an immediate 10% and 20% adverse change in those assumptions were as follows:

		Change in Assumptions	
	2002	(10%)	(20%)
Carrying amount of retained interests	$ 5		
Payment rate (monthly)	51.0%		
Weighted average life (in years)	0.5		
Expected credit losses (annual)	3.4%	$ (0.2)	$ (0.4)
Discounted residual cash flows (annual)	17.4%	$ (0.7)	$ (1.5)

The details on the cash flows from securitization were as follows:

	2002	2001
Proceeds from new securitizations	$ 244	$ 112
Net cash flows received on retained interests	$ 23	$ 1

NOTE 6. INCOME TAXES

The Company's effective income tax rate in the consolidated statements of earnings is reported at a rate less than the weighted average basic Canadian federal and provincial statutory income tax rate for the following reasons:

	2002	2001
Weighted average basic Canadian federal and provincial statutory income tax rate	38.6%	41.2%
Net decrease resulting from:		
Operating in countries with lower effective income tax rates	(2.9)	(3.0)
Non-taxable amounts (including capital gains/losses)	(0.1)	(0.9)
Large corporation tax	0.7	0.7
Substantively enacted changes in income tax rates		(0.1)
Effective income tax rate before goodwill charges	36.3	37.9
Non-deductible goodwill charges		1.8
Effective income tax rate	36.3%	39.7%

Net income taxes paid in 2002 were $323 (2001 – $277).

In 2001, the effect of the reduction in the Ontario provincial income tax rate of 1.5% in each of 2002, 2003, 2004 and 2005 was recognized as a $1 reduction to the future income tax expense. The deferral by one year of the reduction in the Ontario provincial income tax rate, which was announced in 2002, did not have a significant impact on the future income tax expense.

The income tax effects of temporary differences that gave rise to significant portions of the future income tax assets and future income tax liabilities were as follows:

	2002	2001
FUTURE INCOME TAX ASSETS		
Accounts payable and accrued liabilities	$ 62	$ 69
Long term debt (including amounts due within one year)	11	14
Other liabilities	55	51
Losses carried forward (expiring 2008)	20	20
	$ 148	$ 154
FUTURE INCOME TAX LIABILITIES		
Fixed assets	$ 132	$ 97
Other	1	7
	$ 133	$ 104

NOTE 7. FIXED ASSETS

	2002			2001		
	Cost	Accumulated Depreciation	Net Book Value	Cost	Accumulated Depreciation	Net Book Value
Properties held for development	$ 336		$ 336	$ 248		$ 248
Properties under development	234		234	206		206
Land	1,201		1,201	1,067		1,067
Buildings	2,983	$ 552	2,431	2,576	$ 476	2,100
Equipment and fixtures	2,421	1,415	1,006	2,153	1,221	932
Leasehold improvements	599	233	366	565	205	360
	7,774	2,200	5,574	6,815	1,902	4,913
Capital leases – buildings and equipment	83	70	13	83	65	18
	$ 7,857	$ 2,270	$ 5,587	$ 6,898	$ 1,967	$ 4,931

NOTES TO THE CONSOLIDATED FINANCIAL STATEMENTS   51

NOTE 8. OTHER ASSETS

	2002	2001
Franchise investments and other receivables	$ 300	$ 285
Accrued pension and other benefit plans (note 9)	37	37
Deferred charges and other	46	61
	$ 383	$ 383

NOTE 9. PENSION, POST-RETIREMENT AND POST-EMPLOYMENT BENEFITS

The Company has a number of defined benefit and defined contribution plans providing pension and other retirement and post-employment benefits to certain employees. The Company also contributes to various multi-employer defined benefit plans providing pension benefits.

Information about the Company's defined benefit plans other than the multi-employer defined benefit plans, in aggregate, was as follows:

	2002		2001	
	Pension Benefit Plans	Other Benefit Plans	Pension Benefit Plans	Other Benefit Plans
BENEFIT PLAN ASSETS				
Fair value, beginning of period	$ 690	$ 16	$ 834	$ 13
Actual return on plan assets	(19)	4	(95)	1
Employer contributions	13	13	6	10
Employees' contributions	2		2	
Benefits paid	(51)	(10)	(51)	(8)
Settlement gain			(3)	
Other	(7)		(3)	
Fair value, end of period	$ 628	$ 23	$ 690	$ 16
ACCRUED BENEFIT PLAN OBLIGATIONS				
Balance, beginning of period	$ 692	$ 103	$ 690	$ 99
Current service cost	21	2	21	5
Interest cost	52	7	48	7
Benefits paid	(51)	(10)	(51)	(8)
Actuarial loss (gain)	106	64	(18)	
Plan amendments	(1)		5	
Settlement gain			(3)	
Other	(2)			
Balance, end of period	$ 817	$ 166	$ 692	$ 103
DEFICIT OF PLAN ASSETS VERSUS PLAN OBLIGATIONS	$ (189)	$ (143)	$ (2)	$ (87)
Unamortized past service costs	3		4	
Unamortized net actuarial losses (gains)	168	56	(11)	(5)
Net accrued benefit plan liability	$ (18)	$ (87)	$ (9)	$ (92)
Accrued benefit plan asset included in other assets	$ 31	$ 6	$ 37	
Accrued benefit plan liability included in other liabilities	(49)	(93)	(46)	$ (92)
Net accrued benefit plan liability	$ (18)	$ (87)	$ (9)	$ (92)

At period end 2002, the deficit of plan assets versus plan obligations for those pension benefit plans and post-employment benefit plans where the accrued benefit plan obligations exceeded the fair value of benefit plan assets were $193 and $14, respectively (2001 – $54 and $4). There were no plan assets in non-registered pension plans. All the Company's post-retirement benefit plans also had no plan assets and, at period end 2002, had an aggregate accrued benefit plan obligation of $129 (2001 – $83).

The significant annual weighted average actuarial assumptions were as follows:

	2002		2001	
	Pension Benefit Plans	Other Benefit Plans	Pension Benefit Plans	Other Benefit Plans
Discount rate	6.5%	6.2%	7.5%	6.9%
Expected long term rate of return on plan assets	8.0%	5.0%	8.0%	6.0%
Rate of compensation increase	3.5%		3.5%	

The expected long term rates of return on pension benefit plans and other benefit plans assets used in calculating the Company's net defined benefit plan expense were 8.0% and 6.0%, respectively (2001 – 8.0% and 6.0%).

The Company's growth rate of health care costs, primarily drug costs, was estimated at 9.0% (2001 – 9.0%), with the rate trending to 5.0% in 2010 and remaining at that level thereafter.

The accrued benefit plan obligations and the fair value of the benefit plan assets were determined using a September 30 measurement date.

The total net expense for the Company's benefit plans and the multi-employer defined benefit plans was as follows:

	2002		2001	
	Pension Benefit Plans	Other Benefit Plans	Pension Benefit Plans	Other Benefit Plans
Current service cost	$ 19	$ 2	$ 19	$ 5
Interest cost on plan liabilities	52	7	48	7
Expected return on plan assets	(54)	(1)	(65)	(1)
Amortization of net actuarial gains			(6)	(1)
Other	1			
Net defined benefit plan expense (income)	18	8	(4)	10
Defined contribution plan expense	5		5	
Multi-employer defined benefit plans expense	33		30	
Net benefit plan expense	$ 56	$ 8	$ 31	$ 10

NOTES TO THE CONSOLIDATED FINANCIAL STATEMENTS   53

NOTE 10. LONG TERM DEBT

	2002	2001
LOBLAW COMPANIES LIMITED DEBENTURES		
Series 8, 10%, due 2007, redeemed in 2002 (i)		$ 61
PROVIGO INC. DEBENTURES		
Series 1997, 6.35%, due 2004	$ 100	100
Series 1996, 8.70%, due 2006	125	125
Other (ii)	13	17
LOBLAW COMPANIES LIMITED NOTES		
6.20%, BA Range Note, due 2002 (i)		10
6.60%, due 2003	100	100
6.95%, due 2005	200	200
6.00%, due 2008	390	390
5.75%, due 2009	125	125
7.10%, due 2010	300	300
6.50%, due 2011	350	350
6.00%, due 2014	100	100
7.10%, due 2016	300	300
6.65%, due 2027	100	100
6.45%, due 2028	200	200
6.50%, due 2029	175	175
11.40%, due 2031		
– principal	151	151
– effect of coupon repurchase	(4)	1
6.85%, due 2032 (i)	200	
8.75%, due 2033	200	200
6.45%, due 2039	200	200
7.00%, due 2040	150	150
Other at a weighted average interest rate of 10.74%, due 2003 to 2040	51	59
Total long term debt	3,526	3,414
Less amount due within one year	106	81
	$ 3,420	$ 3,333

The five year schedule of repayment of long term debt based on maturity is as follows: 2003 – $106; 2004 – $106; 2005 – $215; 2006 – $129; 2007 – $5.

(i) During 2002, the Company repaid its $10 6.20% BA Range Note as it matured, redeemed its $61 Series 8, 10% Debentures in accordance with their terms and issued $200 of Medium Term Notes ("MTN") with an interest rate of 6.85% due 2032.

(ii) **PROVIGO INC. DEBENTURES** – Other of $13 (2001 – $17) represents the unamortized portion of the adjustment to fair value the Provigo Inc. Debentures. This adjustment was recorded as part of the Provigo purchase equation and was calculated using the Company's average credit spread applicable to the remaining life of the Provigo Inc. Debentures. The adjustment is being amortized over the remaining term of the Provigo Inc. Debentures.

(iii) Subsequent to period end 2002, the Company issued $200 of 6.54% MTN due 2033.

NOTE 11. OTHER LIABILITIES

	2002	2001
Accrued pension and other benefit plans (note 9)	$ 142	$ 138
Unrealized currency adjustment (note 14)	131	96
Stock-based compensation	54	
Other	17	44
	$ 344	$ 278

NOTE 12. COMMON SHARE CAPITAL (authorized – unlimited)

The changes in the common shares issued and outstanding during the period were as follows:

	2002		2001	
	Number of Common Shares	Common Share Capital	Number of Common Shares	Common Share Capital
Issued and outstanding, beginning of period	276,252,714	$ 1,194	276,245,314	$ 1,194
Issued for stock options exercised (note 13)	75,000	2	20,000	
Purchased for cancellation	(309,000)	(1)	(12,600)	
Issued and outstanding, end of period	276,018,714	$ 1,195	276,252,714	$ 1,194
Weighted average outstanding	276,209,323		276,247,689	

NORMAL COURSE ISSUER BIDS ("NCIB") ($) During 2002, the Company purchased for cancellation 309,000 (2001 – 12,600) of its common shares for $17 million (2001 – $1 million) and entered into equity forwards to buy 390,100 (2001 – 601,600) of its common shares pursuant to its NCIB. In addition, the Company intends to renew its NCIB to purchase on the Toronto Stock Exchange or enter into equity forwards to purchase up to 5% of its common shares outstanding. The Company, in accordance with the rules and by-laws of the Toronto Stock Exchange, may purchase its shares at the then market prices of such shares.

Subsequent to period end, the Company purchased for cancellation 730,000 of its common shares for $41 million and entered into equity forwards to buy 1,103,500 of its common shares, at an average forward price of $56.39 with an initial term of 10 years, pursuant to its NCIB.

NOTE 13. STOCK-BASED COMPENSATION ($)

STOCK OPTION PLAN The Company maintains a stock option plan for certain employees. Under the plan, the Company may grant options for up to 20.4 million common shares. Stock options have up to a seven year term, vest 20% cumulatively on each anniversary date of the grant and are exercisable at the designated common share price, which is 100% of the market price of the Company's common shares on the last trading day prior to the effective date of the grant. Each stock option is exercisable into one common share of the Company at the price specified in the terms of the option or option holders may elect to receive in cash the share appreciation value equal to the excess of the market price at the date of exercise over the specified option price.

In 2002, the Company recognized in operating income a compensation cost of $14 million ($21 million less the $7 million fair value impact of the equity forwards) related to the stock option plan. The Company issued 75,000 (2001 – 20,000) common shares for cash consideration of $2 million (2001 – $.4 million) on the exercise of stock options issued prior to December 30, 2001 and paid the share appreciation value of $13 million (2001 – $8 million), net of tax of $9 million (2001 – $6 million), on 685,447 stock options (2001 – 513,970).

During 2002, the Company granted 80,000 stock options under its current stock option plan, that allow for settlement in shares or in the share appreciation value in cash at the option of the employee, to four employees, with an exercise price of $55.40 per common share.

At period end, the Company had a total of 4,055,237 (2001 – 4,832,900) stock option grants outstanding, which represented approximately 1.5% (2001 – 1.7%) of its issued and outstanding common shares and was within regulatory guidelines.

A summary of the status of the Company's stock option plan and activity was as follows:

	2002		2001	
	Options (number of shares)	Weighted Average Exercise Price/Share	Options (number of shares)	Weighted Average Exercise Price/Share
Outstanding options, beginning of period	4,832,900	$ 30.680	5,033,280	$ 28.676
Granted	80,000	$ 55.400	386,190	$ 48.664
Exercised	(760,447)	$ 25.857	(533,970)	$ 24.699
Forfeited/cancelled	(97,216)	$ 32.477	(52,600)	$ 31.653
Outstanding options, end of period	4,055,237	$ 32.029	4,832,900	$ 30.680
Options exercisable, end of period	1,491,119	$ 28.192	1,083,424	$ 25.541

Of the 4,055,237 outstanding options, 3,901,497 relate to stock option grants that allow for settlement in shares or in the share appreciation value in cash at the option of the employee and 153,740 relate to stock option grants, issued prior to December 30, 2001, that will be settled by issuing common shares.

	2002 Outstanding Options			2002 Exercisable Options	
Range of Exercise Prices	Number of Options Outstanding	Weighted Average Remaining Contractual Life (years)	Weighted Average Exercise Price/Share	Number of Exercisable Options	Weighted Average Exercise Price/Share
$ 14.250 – $ 24.500	783,109	2	$ 20.681	572,509	$ 19.276
$ 32.000 – $ 35.600	2,782,938	4	$ 32.157	832,372	$ 32.273
$ 43.800 – $ 55.400	489,190	6	$ 49.469	86,238	$ 47.993

Subsequent to period end 2002, the Company granted 2,367,746 stock options under its current stock option plan, that allow for settlement in shares or in the share appreciation value in cash at the option of the employee, to 196 employees with an exercise price of $53.60 per common share. Including stock option grants issued subsequent to period end, total stock option grants outstanding represent approximately 2.3% of the Company's issued and outstanding common shares.

EMPLOYEE SHARE OWNERSHIP PLAN ("ESOP") The Company maintains an ESOP for its employees, which allows its employees to acquire the Company's common shares through regular payroll deductions for up to 5% of their gross regular earnings. The Company contributes 15% of each employee's contribution. The ESOP is administered through a Trust, which purchases the Company's common shares on the open market on behalf of its employees. A compensation cost of $2 million (2001 – $1 million) related to the Company's ESOP was recognized in operating income.

DEFERRED SHARE UNITS Outside members of the Board of Directors may elect annually to receive all or a portion of their annual retainer(s) and fees in the form of deferred share units, the value of which is determined by the market price of the Company's common shares at the time of payment of the director's annual retainer(s) or fees. Upon termination of Board service, the common shares due to the director, as represented by the deferred share units, will be purchased on the open market on the director's behalf. At period end, 12,941 (2001 – 8,556) deferred share units were outstanding. The period over period change in the deferred share unit obligation was minimal and was recognized in operating income.

NOTE 14. FINANCIAL INSTRUMENTS

As at period end, a summary of the Company's outstanding financial instruments was as follows:

	Notional Amounts Maturing in						2002 Total	2001 Total
	2003	2004	2005	2006	2007	Thereafter		
Cross currency basis swaps	$ 49	$ 344	$ 64	$ 11	$ 67	$ 583	$ 1,118	$ 1,021
Interest rate swaps	$ 188	$ 282	$ 161	$ (43)		$ 279	$ 867	$ 883
Equity forwards						$ 150	$ 150	$ 129
Electricity forward purchase contract	$ 43	$ 47	$ 16				$ 106	

CROSS CURRENCY BASIS SWAPS The Company enters into cross currency basis swaps to manage its exposure to fluctuations in exchange rates, on United States dollar denominated net assets, principally cash, cash equivalents and short term investments.

The Company entered into cross currency basis swaps to exchange an amount of $1.1 billion (2001 – $1.0 billion) of Canadian dollar debt for United States dollar debt, which mature by 2016. Currency adjustments receivable or payable arising from these swaps may be settled in cash on maturity or the term may be extended. At period end, an unrealized foreign currency exchange rate adjustment of $131 (2001 – $96) was recorded in other liabilities.

INTEREST RATE SWAPS The Company enters into interest rate swaps to manage its exposure to fluctuations in interest rates and market liquidity.

The Company entered into interest rate swaps converting a net notional $867 (2001 – $883) of its 6.88% (2001 – 6.88%) fixed rate debt into floating rate debt, which mature by 2013.

EQUITY FORWARDS ($) The Company enters into equity forwards to manage its exposure to fluctuations in its stock-based compensation cost as a result of changes in the market price of its common shares.

The Company entered into equity forwards to buy 3.7 million (2001 – 3.3 million) of its common shares at an average forward price of $44.88 (2001 – $42.70) per common share, including $3.47 (2001 – $2.97) per common share of interest expense net of dividends that will be paid at redemption, with an average initial term of 10 (2001 – 10) years. The equity forwards allow for settlement in cash, common shares or net settlement. The Company has included an unrealized market adjustment of $34 million in accounts receivable relating to these equity forwards.

ELECTRICITY FORWARD PURCHASE CONTRACT The Company entered into an electricity forward purchase contract to maintain a portion of the Company's electricity costs in the province of Ontario at approximately 2001 rates. This electricity forward purchase contract, with a company that has a long term debt rating of A (low) from Dominion Bond Rating Service, had an initial term of three years and expires in May 2005.

COUNTERPARTY RISK The Company may be exposed to losses should any counterparty to its derivative agreements fail to fulfill its obligations. The Company has sought to minimize potential counterparty losses by transacting with counterparties that have at a minimum an A rating and by placing risk adjusted limits on its exposure to any single counterparty. The Company has internal policies, controls and reporting processes, which permit ongoing assessment and corrective action with respect to its derivative activity. In addition, principal amounts on cross currency basis swaps and equity forwards are netted by agreement and there is no exposure to loss of the notional principal amounts on the interest rate swaps and equity forwards.

FAIR VALUE OF FINANCIAL INSTRUMENTS The fair value of a financial instrument is the estimated amount that the Company would receive or pay to terminate the instrument agreement at the reporting date. The following methods and assumptions were used to estimate the fair value of each type of financial instrument by reference to various market value data and other valuation techniques as appropriate.

The fair values of cash, cash equivalents, short term investments, accounts receivable, bank indebtedness, commercial paper, accounts payable and accrued liabilities approximated their carrying values given their short term maturities.

The fair value of the cross currency basis swaps was estimated based on the market spot and forward exchange rates and approximated carrying value.

The fair value of long term debt issues was estimated based on the discounted cash flows of the debt at the Company's estimated incremental borrowing rates for debt of the same remaining maturities.

The fair value of the interest rate swaps was estimated by discounting net cash flows of the swaps at market rates for swaps of the same remaining maturities.

The fair value of the equity forwards was estimated by multiplying the total outstanding forwards based on the Company's common shares by the difference between the market price of its common shares and the average forward price of the outstanding forwards at period end.

The fair value of the electricity forward purchase contract was estimated by discounting the net cash flows at market rates for a contract of the same remaining maturity.

	2002		2001	
	Carrying Value	Estimated Fair Value	Carrying Value	Estimated Fair Value
Long term debt liability	$ 3,526	$ 3,890	$ 3,414	$ 3,550
Interest rate swaps net asset		$ 32		$ 48
Equity forwards net asset	$ 34	$ 34		$ 30
Electricity forward purchase contract net asset		$ 15		

NOTE 15. CONTINGENCIES AND COMMITMENTS

The Company is involved in and potentially subject to various claims and litigation arising out of the normal course and conduct of its businesses including product liability, labour and employment, environmental and tax. Although such matters cannot be predicted with certainty, management considers the Company's exposure to such litigation, to the extent not provided for through insurance or otherwise, not to be material to these consolidated financial statements.

The Company is committed to various operating leases. Future minimum lease payments related to these operating leases were as follows:

	Amounts Maturing in							
	2003	2004	2005	2006	2007	Thereafter to 2049	2002 Total	2001 Total
Operating lease payments	$ 161	$ 150	$ 137	$ 123	$ 109	$ 580	$ 1,260	$ 1,192
Expected sub-lease income	(49)	(43)	(39)	(36)	(30)	(61)	(258)	(232)
Net operating lease payments	$ 112	$ 107	$ 98	$ 87	$ 79	$ 519	$ 1,002	$ 960

Gross rentals under leases assigned to others for which the Company is contingently liable amount to $204 (2001 – $230).

At period end, capital projects-in-process which the Company has effectively committed to complete totaled approximately $179 (2001 – $109).

The Company has provided a guarantee, on behalf of PC Bank, to MasterCard International Incorporated for $50 U.S. (2001 – $12 U.S.) relating to PC Bank's obligation to meet its settlement commitments arising from its credit card program.

In connection with the purchase of Provigo, the Company has committed to support Quebec small business and farming communities as follows: for a period of seven years commencing 1999 and, subject to business dispositions, the aggregate amount of goods and services purchased from Quebec suppliers in the ordinary course of business will not fall below those of 1998. The Company has fulfilled its commitment in each year from 1999 to and including 2002.

NOTE 16. OTHER INFORMATION

SEGMENTED INFORMATION The Company's only reportable operating segment is food distribution. All sales to external parties were generated in Canada and all fixed assets and goodwill were attributable to Canadian operations.

RELATED PARTY TRANSACTIONS The Company's majority shareholder, George Weston Limited, its subsidiaries and its affiliates are related parties. It is the Company's policy to conduct all transactions and settle balances with related parties on normal trade terms. Total purchases from related parties represented about 3% (2001 – 3%) of the cost of sales, selling and administrative expenses.

Pursuant to an investment management agreement, the Company, through Glenhuron, manages certain United States cash, cash equivalents and short term investments on behalf of wholly owned non-Canadian subsidiaries of George Weston Limited. Management fees were based on market rates and were included in interest expense.

Specimen Financial Statements: Sobeys Inc.

Sobeys Inc.
www.sobeys.ca

In this appendix, we illustrate current financial reporting with a comprehensive set of corporate financial statements that are prepared in accordance with generally accepted accounting principles. We are grateful for permission to use the actual financial statements of Canada's second largest food distributor, Sobeys Inc.

The financial statement package includes the balance sheet, statement of retained earnings, statement of earnings, cash flow statement, and notes to the financial statements. The financial statements are preceded by two reports: a statement summarizing management's responsibility for the financial statements and the auditors' report on these statements.

We encourage students to use these financial statements in conjunction with relevant material in the textbook, and to solve the Comparative Analysis Problems in the Broadening Your Perspective section of the end of chapter material.

MANAGEMENT'S RESPONSIBILITY FOR FINANCIAL REPORTING

Preparation of the consolidated financial statements accompanying this annual report and the presentation of all other information in the report is the responsibility of management. The financial statements have been prepared in accordance with appropriate Canadian generally accepted accounting principles and reflect management's best estimates and judgements. All other financial information in the report is consistent with that contained in the financial statements.

Management of the Company has established and maintains a system of internal control that provides reasonable assurance as to the integrity of the financial statements, the safeguarding of Company assets, and the prevention and detection of fraudulent financial reporting.

The Board of Directors, through its Audit Committee, which is chaired by and consists of non-management directors, meets regularly with financial management and external auditors to satisfy itself as to the reliability and integrity of financial information. The Audit Committee reports its findings to the Board of Directors for consideration in approving the annual financial statements to be issued to the shareholders. The external auditors have full and free access to the Audit Committee.

BILL MᶜEWAN
President &
Chief Executive Officer
June 25, 2003

R. GLENN HYNES, C.A.
Executive Vice President &
Chief Financial Officer
June 25, 2003

AUDITORS' REPORT

To the Shareholders of Sobeys Inc.

We have audited the consolidated balance sheets of Sobeys Inc. as at May 3, 2003 and May 4, 2002, and the consolidated statements of earnings, retained earnings, and cash flows for the fiscal years then ended. These consolidated financial statements are the responsibility of the Company's management. Our responsibility is to express an opinion on these consolidated financial statements based on our audits.

We conducted our audits in accordance with Canadian generally accepted auditing standards. Those standards require that we plan and perform an audit to obtain reasonable assurance whether the consolidated financial statements are free of material misstatement. An audit includes examining, on a test basis, evidence supporting the amounts and disclosures in the consolidated financial statements. An audit also includes assessing the accounting principles used and significant estimates made by management, as well as evaluating the overall consolidated financial statement presentation.

In our opinion, these consolidated financial statements present fairly, in all material respects, the financial position of the Company as at May 3, 2003 and May 4, 2002, and the results of its operations and its cash flows for the fiscal years then ended in accordance with Canadian generally accepted accounting principles.

GRANT THORNTON LLP
Chartered Accountants
New Glasgow, Nova Scotia
June 6, 2003

CONSOLIDATED BALANCE SHEETS

(in millions)	May 3, 2003	May 4, 2002
ASSETS		
Current		
Cash and cash equivalents	$ 123.1	$ 196.7
Temporary investments, at cost (quoted market value $191.4, 2002 $79.0)	191.4	77.7
Receivables	285.4	251.0
Inventories	444.0	394.6
Prepaid expenses	30.5	30.4
Future tax assets (Note 10)	2.7	5.4
Mortgages and loans receivable	15.4	23.2
Assets of discontinued operations (Note 2)	1.9	5.8
	1,094.4	984.8
Mortgages and loans receivable (Note 3)	134.6	117.0
Property and equipment (Note 4)	1,243.9	1,072.1
Goodwill	555.6	553.1
Future tax assets (Note 10)	28.5	31.2
Deferred costs (Note 5)	135.5	117.0
	$ 3,192.5	$ 2,875.2
LIABILITIES		
Current		
Accounts payable and accrued liabilities	$ 971.9	$ 922.9
Income taxes payable	37.4	18.8
Future tax liabilities (Note 10)	21.1	–
Long-term debt due within one year	150.1	48.7
	1,180.5	990.4
Long-term debt (Note 7)	435.3	474.9
Employee future benefit obligation (Note 16)	75.5	70.4
Future tax liabilities (Note 10)	57.7	43.4
Deferred revenue	6.7	12.8
	1,755.7	1,591.9
SHAREHOLDERS' EQUITY		
Capital stock (Note 8)	903.4	901.3
Retained earnings	533.4	382.0
	1,436.8	1,283.3
	$ 3,192.5	$ 2,875.2

See accompanying notes to consolidated financial statements.

On Behalf of the Board

[signature]

Director

[signature]

Director

CONSOLIDATED STATEMENTS OF RETAINED EARNINGS

Year Ended May 3, 2003 (in millions)	2003	2002
Balance, beginning of year	$ 382.0	$ 192.5
Net earnings	179.0	210.6
	561.0	403.1
Dividends declared	23.8	15.8
Premium on common shares purchased for cancellation (Note 8)	3.8	5.3
Balance, end of year	$ 533.4	$ 382.0

See accompanying notes to consolidated financial statements.

CONSOLIDATED STATEMENTS OF EARNINGS

Year Ended May 3, 2003 (in millions)	2003	2002
Sales	$ 10,414.5	$ 9,732.5
Cost of sales, selling and administrative expenses	9,964.4	9,334.9
Depreciation	124.0	101.0
Operating income	326.1	296.6
Interest expense		
Long-term debt	41.7	54.9
Short-term debt	–	2.1
	41.7	57.0
	284.4	239.6
Capital loss and other items (Note 9)	–	(19.4)
Earnings before the following items:	284.4	220.2
Income taxes (Note 10)		
Operating activities	105.4	96.5
Capital loss and other items	–	(7.6)
	105.4	88.9
Earnings before goodwill charges and discontinued operations	179.0	131.3
Goodwill charges, net of tax (Note 1)	–	15.4
Earnings before discontinued operations	179.0	115.9
Discontinued operations, net of tax (Note 2)		
Earnings from operations	–	14.0
Gain on sale	–	80.7
	–	94.7
Net earnings	$ 179.0	$ 210.6
Earnings per share, basic and diluted (Note 11)		
Earnings before discontinued operations	$ 2.72	$ 1.76
Net earnings	$ 2.72	$ 3.20

See accompanying notes to consolidated financial statements.

CONSOLIDATED STATEMENTS OF CASH FLOWS

Year Ended May 3, 2003 (in millions)	2003	2002
OPERATIONS		
Net earnings before discontinued operations	$ **179.0**	$ 115.9
Items not affecting cash (Note 12)	**187.6**	211.0
Capital loss and other items not affecting cash	**–**	11.5
	366.6	338.4
Net change in non-cash working capital	**(18.5)**	156.3
Cash flows from operating activities	**348.1**	494.7
INVESTMENT		
Property and equipment purchases	**(342.3)**	(424.2)
Proceeds on disposal of property and equipment	**48.0**	49.1
Long-term investments and advances	**(9.8)**	17.1
Increase in deferred costs	**(41.6)**	(30.0)
Business acquisitions, net of cash acquired	**(2.5)**	(3.6)
Decrease in deferred foreign currency translation gains	**–**	(1.2)
Cash flows used in investing activities	**(348.2)**	(392.8)
FINANCING		
Bankers' acceptances	**–**	(25.0)
Issue of long-term debt	**118.6**	14.1
Repayment of long-term debt	**(56.8)**	(147.5)
Revolving securitization	**–**	(150.0)
Increase of share purchase loan	**(2.5)**	(0.3)
Issue of capital stock	**6.7**	8.6
Repurchase of capital stock	**(5.9)**	(8.4)
Dividends	**(23.8)**	(15.8)
Cash flows from (used in) financing activities	**36.3**	(324.3)
Increase (decrease) in cash from continuing operations	**36.2**	(222.4)
Discontinued operations (Note 2)	**3.9**	412.7
Increase in cash	**40.1**	190.3
Cash, beginning of year	**274.4**	84.1
Cash, end of year	$ **314.5**	$ 274.4

Cash is defined as cash, treasury bills, guaranteed investments, and temporary investments.

See accompanying notes to consolidated financial statements.

NOTES TO CONSOLIDATED FINANCIAL STATEMENTS
May 3, 2003 (in millions, except share capital)

Note 1. Summary of significant accounting policies

PRINCIPLES OF CONSOLIDATION
These consolidated financial statements include the accounts of the Company and its subsidiary companies. All of the Company's subsidiaries are wholly owned.

DEPRECIATION
Depreciation is recorded on a straight line basis over the estimated useful lives of the assets as follows:

Equipment and vehicles	3–10 years
Buildings	15–40 years
Leasehold improvements	7–10 years

CASH AND CASH EQUIVALENTS
Cash and cash equivalents are defined as cash, treasury bills, and guaranteed investments.

INVENTORIES
Warehouse inventories are valued at the lower of cost and net realizable value with cost being determined substantially on a first-in, first-out basis. Retail inventories are valued at the lower of cost and net realizable value, less normal profit margins as determined by the retail method of inventory valuation.

LEASES
Leases meeting certain criteria are accounted for as capital leases. The imputed interest is charged against income and the capitalized value is depreciated on a straight line basis over its estimated useful life. Obligations under capital leases are reduced by rental payments net of imputed interest. All other leases are accounted for as operating leases with rental payments being expensed as incurred.

GOODWILL
Goodwill represents the excess of the purchase price of the business acquired over the fair value of the underlying net tangible assets acquired at the date of acquisition.

Effective May 5, 2002, the Company prospectively adopted the requirements of the new standard issued by the CICA on accounting for Goodwill and Other Intangible Assets, Section 3062. Under the new standard, goodwill and intangible assets with indefinite useful lives are no longer amortized but are subject to an annual impairment review. Any permanent impairment in the book value of goodwill or intangible assets will be written off against earnings. The Company has completed its review, and determined the book value of existing goodwill is not impaired.

Goodwill charges are net of income tax recovery of $0.6 for fiscal 2002.

STOCK-BASED COMPENSATION
Members of the Board of Directors may elect to receive all or any portion of their fees in Deferred Share Units ("DSU") in lieu of cash. The number of DSUs received is determined by the market value of Sobeys Inc. common shares on each directors fee payment date. Additional DSUs are received as dividend equivalents. DSUs cannot be redeemed for cash until the holder is no longer a director of the Company. The redemption value of a DSU equals the market value of a Sobeys Inc. common share at the time of the redemption. On an ongoing basis, the Company values the DSU obligation at the current market value of a common share, and records any increase in the DSU obligation as an operating expense. At May 3, 2003, there were 26,617 (2002 12,496) DSUs outstanding.

REVENUE RECOGNITION
Sales are recognized at the point-of-sale. Sales include revenues from customers through corporate stores operated by the Company, and revenue from sales to franchised stores, associated stores, and independent accounts.

INTEREST CAPITALIZATION
Interest related to the period of construction is capitalized as part of the cost of the related property and equipment. The amount of interest capitalized to construction in progress in the current year was $1.3 (2002 $0.7).

DEFERRED REVENUE
Deferred revenue consists of long-term supplier purchase agreements, and rental revenue arising from the sale of subsidiaries. Deferred revenue is being taken into income over the term of the related agreement and leases.

NOTES TO CONSOLIDATED FINANCIAL STATEMENTS

STORE OPENING EXPENSES

Store opening expenses of new stores and store conversions are written off during the first year of operation.

FINANCIAL INSTRUMENTS

The Company uses interest rate instruments to manage exposure to fluctuations in interest rates. The realized gain or loss arising from the instruments is included in interest expense.

ACCOUNTING ESTIMATES

The preparation of consolidated financial statements, in conformity with Canadian generally accepted accounting principles, requires management to make estimates and assumptions that affect the amounts reported in the consolidated financial statements and accompanying notes. These estimates are based on management's best knowledge of current events and actions that the Company may undertake in the future.

FUTURE INCOME TAXES

CICA Handbook Section 3465 requires the difference between the tax basis of assets and liabilities and their carrying value on the balance sheet be used to calculate future tax assets and liabilities. The future tax assets and liabilities have been measured using substantially enacted tax rates that will be in effect when the differences are expected to reverse.

EARNINGS PER SHARE

Earnings per share is calculated by dividing the earnings available to common shareholders by the weighted average number of common shares outstanding, during the year.

Note 2. Discontinued operations

On March 30, 2002, Sobeys Inc. completed the sale of substantially all of the assets of its SERCA Foodservice operations. SERCA Foodservice distributed foodservice products to hospitality, institutional, and commercial customers throughout Canada.

The revenues of discontinued operations were $2,003.6 for the forty-seven weeks ended March 30, 2002.

Interest on debt that is not directly attributable to the discontinued operations has not been allocated to the discontinued operations. May 3, 2003, and May 4, 2002, current assets of discontinued operations consist of assets for resale.

Cash flows from discontinued operations for the 52 weeks ended May 3, 2003, includes cash generated by investing activities of $3.9. Cash flows from discontinued operations for the 11 months ended March 30, 2002, includes cash used by operating activities of $2.2, cash generated by investing activities of $3.8, and cash used by financing activities of $0.3.

GAIN ON SALE

On March 30, 2002, predominately all of the assets of SERCA Foodservice were sold to SYSCO Corp. The components of the gain on sale are:

	May 4, 2002
Cash proceeds	$ 411.4
Trade and other receivables	(185.7)
Inventory	(97.6)
Property and equipment	(37.1)
Goodwill	(154.0)
Other assets and liabilities	(11.9)
Selling expenses	(3.6)
Trade and other payables	198.7
Net assets	(291.2)
Gain on sale, before income tax	120.2
Current tax expense	(39.5)
Gain on sale	$ 80.7

Note 3. Mortgages and loans receivable

	May 3, 2003	May 4, 2002
Loans receivable	$ 140.4	$ 120.7
Mortgages receivable	9.0	18.9
Other	0.6	0.6
	150.0	140.2
Less amount due within one year	15.4	23.2
	$ 134.6	$ 117.0

LOANS RECEIVABLE

Loans receivable represent long-term financing to certain retail associates. These loans are primarily secured by inventory, fixtures and equipment, bear interest at rates which fluctuate with prime and have repayment terms up to ten years. The carrying amount of the loans receivable approximates fair value based on the variable interest rates charged on the loans and the operating relationship of the associates with the Company.

Note 4. Property and equipment

May 3, 2003	Cost	Accumulated Depreciation	Net Book Value
Land	$ 83.4	$ –	$ 83.4
Land held for development	81.4	–	81.4
Buildings	451.3	96.3	355.0
Equipment and vehicles	1,320.3	774.7	545.6
Leasehold improvements	263.9	146.7	117.2
Construction in progress	50.9	–	50.9
Assets under capital leases	15.4	5.0	10.4
	$ 2,266.6	$ 1,022.7	$ 1,243.9

May 4, 2002	Cost	Accumulated Depreciation	Net Book Value
Land	$ 75.0	$ –	$ 75.0
Land held for development	78.8	–	78.8
Buildings	412.3	95.1	317.2
Equipment and vehicles	1,194.8	772.9	421.9
Leasehold improvements	247.1	130.3	116.8
Construction in progress	51.5	–	51.5
Assets under capital leases	17.6	6.7	10.9
	$ 2,077.1	$ 1,005.0	$ 1,072.1

NOTES TO CONSOLIDATED FINANCIAL STATEMENTS

Note 5. Deferred costs

	2003 Net Book Value	2002 Net Book Value
Deferred store marketing costs	$ **40.1**	$ 41.8
Deferred financing costs	**7.0**	9.2
Deferred purchase agreements	**16.7**	16.1
Transitional pension asset	**38.1**	25.1
Other	**33.6**	24.8
Total	$ **135.5**	$ 117.0

Deferred costs are amortized as follows:
  Deferred store marketing – 7 years
  Deferred financing – over the term of the debt – 5 years
  Deferred purchase agreements – over the term of the franchise agreement

Note 6. Bank loans and bankers' acceptances

Under the terms of a credit agreement entered into between the Company and a banking syndicate arranged by the Bank of Nova Scotia, a revolving term credit facility of $300.0 was established. This unsecured facility will expire on June 24, 2004, however various provisions of the agreement provide the Company with the ability to extend the facility for a minimum period of two years.
  Interest payable on this facility fluctuates with changes in the prime interest rate.

Note 7. Long-term debt

	May 3, 2003	May 4, 2002
First mortgage loans, average interest rate 9.8%, due 2008 – 2021	$ **25.1**	$ 26.8
Bank loans, average interest rate 6.4%, due September 30, 2004	**60.0**	100.0
Medium term note, interest rate 7.6%, due November 1, 2005	**175.0**	175.0
Medium term note, interest rate 7.0%, due October 2, 2003	**100.0**	100.0
Medium term note, interest rate 7.2%, due February 26, 2018	**100.0**	–
Debentures, average interest rate 10.7%, due 2008 – 2013	**78.3**	83.4
Notes payable and other debt at interest rates fluctuating with the prime rate	**37.6**	27.8
	576.0	513.0
Capital lease obligations, due 2003 – 2011, net of imputed interest	**9.4**	10.6
	585.4	523.6
Less amount due within one year	**150.1**	48.7
	$ **435.3**	$ 474.9

The Company has fixed the interest rate on $45.1 of its long-term debt at 6.4 percent by utilizing interest exchange agreements.
  First mortgage loans are secured by land, buildings, and specific charges on certain assets. Sobeys Group Inc., an indirect subsidiary of Sobeys Inc., has provided the debenture holders with a floating charge over all its assets, subject to permitted encumbrances, a general assignment of book debts, and the assignment of proceeds of insurance policies.
  During fiscal 2001, a short form prospectus was filed providing for the issuance of up to $500.0 in unsecured medium term notes. At the same time the Company negotiated a new unsecured $550.0 credit facility consisting of $250.0 of non-revolving debt to be repaid over five years, plus a $300.0 revolving line of credit. As of May 3, 2003, $190.0 of the non-revolving debt had been retired. The short form prospectus expired on June 22, 2002, in accordance with the terms. On December 20, 2002, (amended on February 17, 2003) the Company filed a final short form prospectus providing for the issuance of up to $500.0 of unsecured medium term notes over the next two years.

Debt retirement payments and capital lease obligations in each of the next five fiscal years are:

	Long-term debt	Capital leases
2004	$ 148.7	$ 1.4
2005	28.5	1.5
2006	183.5	1.5
2007	7.1	1.6
2008	8.4	1.1

OPERATING LEASES

The net aggregate, annual, minimum rent payable under operating leases for fiscal 2004 is approximately $137.1 ($231.9 gross less expected sub-lease income of $94.8). The net commitments over the next five fiscal years are:

	Net Lease Obligation
2004	$ 137.1
2005	132.5
2006	126.1
2007	114.6
2008	108.9

Note 8. Capital stock

AUTHORIZED

	Number of shares
Preferred shares, par value of $25 each, issuable in series as a class	500,000,000
Preferred shares, without par value, issuable in series as a class	500,000,000
Common shares, without par value	499,626,115

ISSUED AND OUTSTANDING

	Number of shares		Capital stock	
	May 3, 2003	May 4, 2002	**May 3, 2003**	May 4, 2002
Common shares, without par value	**65,893,168**	65,876,281	$ **922.7**	$ 918.0
Loans receivable from officers and employees under share purchase plan			**(19.3)**	(16.7)
Total capital stock	**65,893,168**	65,876,281	$ **903.4**	$ 901.3

During the current fiscal year, the Company purchased for cancellation 151,965 (2002 – 221,920) of its common shares, as part of a normal course issuer bid announced on December 13, 2002. The purchase price for the shares was $5.9 (2002 – $8.4) and $3.8 (2002 – $5.3) of the purchase price (representing the excess of the purchase price over the average paid-up value of common shares purchased for cancellation) was charged to retained earnings.

During the current fiscal year 169,387 (2002 – 319,244) common shares of Sobeys Inc. were issued under the Company's share purchase plan to certain officers and employees for $6.7 (2002 – $8.6).

Loans receivable from officers and employees of $19.3 under the Company's share purchase plan are classified as a reduction of capital stock. Loan repayments will result in a corresponding increase in capital stock. The loans are non-interest bearing, non-recourse, and are secured by 705,727 common shares of Sobeys Inc.

NOTES TO CONSOLIDATED FINANCIAL STATEMENTS

Note 9. Capital loss and other items

	May 3, 2003	May 4, 2002
Loss on carrying value of redundant real estate assets	$ –	$ (9.9)
Employee future benefit obligation	–	(9.5)
	$ –	$ (19.4)

LOSS ON CARRYING VALUE OF REDUNDANT REAL ESTATE ASSETS

In the prior year, as a result of a strategic review of the carrying value of redundant property held for resale, the Company determined a write down was appropriate to align the carrying value with the current market value of these redundant properties.

EMPLOYEE FUTURE BENEFIT OBLIGATION

At the time of the implementation of CICA Section 3461, the employee future benefit liability was estimated to be $59.1, based on the information available at that time. In the prior year, the Company requested an updated actuarial valuation of this liability. This valuation using current information, indicated that the previous estimate for former Oshawa employees was understated by $9.5.

Note 10. Income taxes

Income tax expense varies from the amount that would be computed by applying the combined federal and provincial statutory tax rate as a result of the following:

	May 3, 2003	May 4, 2002
Income tax expense according to combined statutory rate of 36.5% (2002 – 39.4%)	$ 103.9	$ 88.6
Increase (reduction) in income taxes resulting from:		
Non-taxable gains	(0.3)	(0.3)
Non-deductible goodwill amortization	–	5.9
Large corporation tax	1.8	1.7
Total income taxes (before capital loss and other items)	105.4	95.9
Capital loss and other items	–	(7.6)
Total	$ 105.4	$ 88.3

May 3, 2003 income tax expense attributable to net income consists of:

	Current	Future	Total
Operations	$ 64.6	$ 40.8	$ 105.4

May 4, 2002 income tax expense attributable to net income consists of:

	Current	Future	Total
Operations	$ 75.8	$ 20.7	$ 96.5
Capital loss and other items	(1.2)	(6.4)	(7.6)
Goodwill	–	(0.6)	(0.6)
	$ 74.6	$ 13.7	$ 88.3

The tax effect of temporary differences that give rise to significant portions of the future tax liability are presented below:

	May 3, 2003	May 4, 2002
Employee future benefit obligation	$ 24.3	$ 26.9
Restructuring provisions	2.7	5.4
Pension contributions	(12.3)	(13.8)
Deferred costs	(14.9)	(10.2)
Deferred credits	(34.9)	–
Goodwill	(4.4)	(9.2)
Fixed assets	(5.5)	–
Other	(2.6)	(5.9)
	$ (47.6)	$ (6.8)
Current future tax assets	$ 2.7	$ 5.4
Non-current future tax assets	28.5	31.2
Current future tax liabilities	(21.1)	–
Non-current future tax liabilities	(57.7)	(43.4)
	$ (47.6)	$ (6.8)

Note 11. Earnings per share

Earnings per share amounts are calculated on the year-to-date weighted average number of shares outstanding (2003 – 65,928,308 and 2002 – 65,877,299).

	May 3, 2003	May 4, 2002
Earnings before discontinued operations	$ 179.0	$ 115.9
Earnings from discontinued operations	–	14.0
Capital loss and other items	–	11.8
Operating earnings (earnings before capital loss and other items, and gain on sale of discontinued operations)	179.0	141.7
Capital loss and other items	–	(11.8)
Gain on sale of discontinued operations	–	80.7
Net earnings	$ 179.0	$ 210.6
EARNINGS PER SHARE IS COMPRISED OF THE FOLLOWING:		
Earnings before discontinued operations	$ 2.72	$ 1.76
Earnings from discontinued operations	–	0.21
Capital loss and other items	–	0.18
Operating earnings (earnings before capital loss and other items, and gain on sale of discontinued operations)	2.72	2.15
Capital loss and other items	–	(0.18)
Gain on sale of discontinued operations	–	1.23
Net earnings	$ 2.72	$ 3.20

NOTES TO CONSOLIDATED FINANCIAL STATEMENTS

Note 12. Supplementary cash flow information

	May 3, 2003		May 4, 2002
A) ITEMS NOT AFFECTING CASH			
Depreciation	$ 124.0	$	101.0
Goodwill amortization	–		16.1
Future tax provision	40.8		70.2
Loss on disposal of assets	0.7		3.1
Amortization of deferred items	17.0		19.0
Employee future benefit obligation	5.1		1.6
	$ 187.6	$	211.0
B) OTHER ITEMS			
Net interest paid	$ 40.7	$	59.4
Net income taxes paid	$ 66.5	$	47.3

Note 13. Related party transactions

The Company leased certain real property from related parties, at fair market value, during the year. The aggregate net payments under these leases amounted to approximately $49.8 (2002 $49.5). The Company was charged expenses of $0.5 (2002 $0.6) by related parties.

In the current fiscal year, the Company received $1.6 from the sale of marketable securities to its parent company. The marketable securities were sold at fair market value, for a gain of $1.4.

At May 3, 2003, mortgage receivables of $2.2 were owing from related parties.

Related party transactions are with the parent company Empire Company Limited and any of its subsidiaries. Empire Company Limited is a majority shareholder of Sobeys Inc., holding 62 percent of Sobeys Inc. common shares.

Note 14. Financial instruments

CREDIT RISK

There is no significant concentration of credit risk. The credit risk exposure is considered normal for the business.

FAIR VALUE OF FINANCIAL INSTRUMENTS

The book value of cash and cash equivalents, temporary investments, receivables, mortgages and loans receivable, and accounts payable and accrued liabilities approximate fair values at May 3, 2003.

The total fair value of long-term debt is estimated to be $622.9. The fair value of variable rate long-term-debt is assumed to approximate its carrying amount. The fair value of other long-term debt has been estimated by discounting future cash flows at a rate offered for debt of similar maturities and credit quality.

INTEREST RATE RISK

The majority of the Company debt is at fixed rates. Accordingly, there is limited exposure to interest rate risk.

Note 15. Contingent liabilities

GUARANTEES AND COMMITMENTS

The Company has undertaken to provide cash to meet any obligations which Sobey Leased Properties Limited (a wholly owned subsidiary of Empire Company Limited) is unable or fails to meet until all of its debentures have been paid in full in accordance with their terms. Any deficiency payment made by the Company will be by purchase of fully-paid non-assessable 5 percent redeemable, non-voting preference shares of that company. The aggregated outstanding principal amounts of these debentures at May 3, 2003, is $40.6. Sobey Leased Properties Limited's principal business relates to leasing real estate locations to Sobeys Capital Incorporated (a subsidiary of Sobeys Inc.) and its subsidiary companies.

At May 3, 2003, the Company was contingently liable for letters of credit issued in the aggregate amount of $27.4.

The Company has guaranteed certain bank loans contracted by franchise affiliates. As at May 3, 2003, these loans amounted to approximately $7.3.

Upon entering into the lease of its new Mississauga distribution centre, in March 2000, Sobeys Capital Incorporated guaranteed to the landlord a performance, by SERCA Foodservice, of all its obligations under the lease. The remaining term of the lease is 17 years with an aggregate obligation of $51.5. At the time of the sale of assets of SERCA Foodservice to SYSCO Corp., the lease of the Mississauga distribution centre was assigned to and assumed by the purchaser and SYSCO Corp. agreed to indemnify and hold Sobeys Capital Incorporated harmless from any liability it may incur pursuant to its guarantee.

Sobeys Capital Incorporated (majority equity investor in IGA Canada Limited) is a member of the IGA Canada Buying Group, and enjoys all the rights, benefits and obligations associated with being a member of this Buying Group. Sobeys Capital Incorporated along with other members of the Buying Group have a performance commitment for any and all vendor payable obligations of the Buying Group. Sobeys Capital Incorporated's commitment is approximately $50.0. After an extensive review it was determined it was not in Sobeys Capital Incorporated's long-term, best interest to remain a member of the Buying Group. On March 26, 2003, the Shareholders of IGA Canada Limited approved a resolution terminating the operations of the IGA Canada Buying Group effective December 31, 2003. On April 14, 2003, the members of the Buying Group were notified of the shareholders intention to terminate the operations of the Buying Group. Accordingly, all Sobeys Capital Incorporated obligations associated with being a member of the Buying Group will cease to exist approximately thirty days after December 31, 2003.

There are various claims and litigation, which the Company is involved with, arising out of the ordinary course of business operations. The Company's management does not consider the exposure to such litigation to be material, although this cannot be predicted with certainty.

Note 16. Employee future benefits

The Company has a number of defined benefit and defined contribution plans providing pension and other retirement benefits to most of its employees.

DEFINED CONTRIBUTION PLANS

The total expense for the Company's defined contribution plans is as follows:

	2003	2002
	11.0	10.1

NOTES TO CONSOLIDATED FINANCIAL STATEMENTS

DEFINED BENEFIT PLANS

Information about the Company's defined benefit plans, in aggregate, is as follows:

	Pension Benefit Plans 2003	Pension Benefit Plans 2002	Other Benefit Plans 2003	Other Benefit Plans 2002
ACCRUED BENEFIT OBLIGATION				
Balance at beginning of year	$ 204.2	$ 206.4	$ 88.0	$ 61.8
Current service cost	2.8	3.7	3.1	1.5
Interest cost	14.8	14.7	6.1	4.2
Employee contributions	0.5	0.4	–	–
Plan amendments	–	–	–	–
Divestitures of SERCA Foodservice	–	–	–	(3.9)
Benefits paid	(17.1)	(23.0)	(4.6)	(4.4)
Curtailment	–	–	–	–
Plan merger	11.8	–	–	–
Actuarial loss	14.6	2.0	(5.3)	28.8
Balance at end of year	$ 231.6	$ 204.2	$ 87.3	$ 88.0
PLAN ASSETS				
Market value at beginning of year	$ 203.5	$ 209.5	$ –	$ –
Actual return on plan assets	(13.3)	9.1	–	–
Employer contributions	15.0	7.5	4.6	4.5
Employee contributions	0.5	0.4	–	–
Plan merger	11.2	–	–	–
Benefits paid	(17.1)	(23.0)	(4.6)	(4.5)
Market value at end of year	$ 199.8	$ 203.5	$ –	$ –
FUNDED STATUS				
Surplus (deficit)	$ (31.8)	$ (0.7)	$ (87.3)	$ (88.0)
Unamortized past service cost	0.3	0.3	–	–
Unamortized actuarial loss	64.7	21.2	11.8	17.6
Accrued benefit asset (liability)	$ 33.2	$ 20.8	$ (75.5)	$ (70.4)
EXPENSE				
Current service cost	$ 2.8	$ 3.7	$ 3.1	$ 1.5
Interest cost	14.8	14.7	6.1	4.2
Amortization	0.2	0.1	0.5	–
Expected return on plan assets	(15.1)	(16.4)	–	–
	$ 2.7	$ 2.1	$ 9.7	$ 5.7

Included in the above accrued benefit obligation at year-end are the following amounts in respect of plans that are not funded.

	Pension Benefit Plans 2003	Pension Benefit Plans 2002	Other Benefit Plans 2003	Other Benefit Plans 2002
Accrued benefit obligation	$ 14.9	$ 14.2	$ 75.5	$ 70.4

The significant actuarial assumptions adopted in measuring the Company's accrued benefit obligations are as follows (weighted-average assumptions as of May 3, 2003):

	Pension Benefit Plans 2003	Pension Benefit Plans 2002	Other Benefit Plans 2003	Other Benefit Plans 2002
Discount rate	6.50%	7.00%	6.50%	7.00%
Expected long-term rate of return on plan assets	7.00%	8.00%		
Rate of compensation increase	4.00%	4.00%		

For measurement purposes, a 10 percent fiscal 2003 annual rate of increase in the per capita cost of covered health care benefits was assumed. The cumulative rate expectation to 2010 is 6%. The average remaining service period of the active employees covered by the pension benefit plans and other benefit plans is 12 and 18 years, respectively.

Note 17. Comparative figures

Comparative figures have been reclassified, where necessary, to reflect the current year's presentation, including required disclosure for discontinued operations.

Company Index

Subject Index

Photo Credits

All images copyright © Photo Disc, Inc./Getty Images, unless otherwise noted.

Logos are registered trademarks of the respective companies and are reprinted with permission.

Chapter 1
OPENER: Loblaw Companies Limited.

Chapter 2
OPENER: The Motley Fool. Page 54: Brand X Pictures. Page 65: Sears Canada Inc. Sears Canada Inc. logo is a registered Trade Mark of Sears licensed for use in Canada. All rights reserved.

Chapter 3
Page 112: Toronto Blue Jays Baseball Club.

Chapter 4
Page 157: Artville. Page 162: Procter & Gamble.

Chapter 5
OPENER: Wal-Mart Stores, Inc. Page 228: Corbis Digital Stock.

Chapter 6
OPENER: Syncrude Canada Limited. Page 262: Brand X Pictures. Page 273: Getty/Digital Vision. Page 276: Corbis Digital Stock. Page 278: Falconbridge Limited. Page 303: Eastman Kodak Company.

Chapter 7
OPENER: Granite Brewery. Page 308: Getty/Digital Vision. Page 314: Artville. Page 317: Bank of Montreal.

Chapter 8
Page 357: Corbis Digital Stock. Page 367: Corbis Digital Stock. Page 369: Brand X Pictures. Page 372: Sears Canada Inc.

Chapter 9
OPENER: Air Canada. Page 402: Artville. Page 418: Artville. Page 419: Getty/Digital Vision. Page 420: eBay.

Chapter 10
OPENER: Quebecor Inc. Page 468: Concordia University.

Chapter 11
Page 534: Microsoft Corporation.

Chapter 12
Page 572: Loblaw Companies Limited. Page 576: Corbis Digital Stock.

Chapter 13
OPENER: Microsoft Corporation.

Chapter 14
OPENER: Molson Inc. Page 671: Corbis Digital Stock. Page 736: Pepsico and Globe Design © 2001.